O'NEILL

1817

NEW YORK, EVANSTON, SAN FRANCISCO, LONDON

O'NEILL

ARTHUR & BARBARA GELB

HARPER & ROW · PUBLISHERS

The first edition of *O'Neill* was originally published by Harper & Row in 1962.

Part of the material on O'Neill as a young man in New London first appeared in *Horizon*, March 1960, under the title "The Start of a Long Day's Journey."

Library of Congress Cataloging in Publication Data

Gelb, Arthur, 1924–
  O'Neill.
    1. O'Neill, Eugene Gladstone, 1888–1953.
I. Gelb, Barbara, joint author.
PS3529.N5Z653 1974   812'.5'2 [B]   73–6760
ISBN 0–06–011487–8

CONTENTS

The illustrations follow pages 264, 552, and 840

ACKNOWLEDGMENTS

A GREAT MANY PERSONS, LIBRARIES, INSTITUTIONS, organizations and publications have given their help and cooperation in the preparation of this book. We will never be able to thank all of them adequately, and can only try to outline the extent of their assistance and indicate the measure of our gratitude.

We acknowledge, first, our debt to Carlotta Monterey O'Neill. With the understanding that we were to have the freedom of complete objectivity, she graciously allowed herself to be interviewed on many occasions, put documents and photographs at our disposal, made us a gift of two privately printed volumes containing O'Neill's writings, cleared our path at the Yale University Library's O'Neill Collection, and facilitated and consented to our quoting from and using the published and unpublished works of her husband. Mrs. O'Neill entrusted us with the details of her life with her husband, forbearing to ask for any power of censorship or to review what use we made of the material.

O'Neill's first wife, Kathleen Pitt-Smith (the mother of Eugene O'Neill, Jr.), and his second wife, Agnes Boulton Kaufman (the mother of Shane O'Neill and Oona O'Neill Chaplin), also furnished us with much valuable information. Mrs. Pitt-Smith granted us extensive interviews and showed us documents relating to her son; Mrs. Kaufman's memoir, *Part of a Long Story* (Doubleday & Company, Inc.), provided a picture of the climate of her marriage to O'Neill between 1918 and 1920. We thank them both.

We are very much indebted to four people whose help, faith and encouragement over five years extended well beyond the bounds of friendship: S. N. Behrman, Brooks Atkinson, Dr. Philip Weissman and Clara Rotter, all of whom allowed themselves to be put upon constantly, and who became integrally involved, in one way or another, in this project.

Our deep gratitude is extended, also, to Oscar Godbout, an ardent O'Neill scholar, and Robert Siegel (who was converted to one)—both spent many hours of their spare time in pursuit of live and documentary information pertaining to O'Neill, which they duly and minutely conveyed to us; to Leonard Harris, who took time out from his professional obligations as a publisher and editor (not ours) to labor over our manuscript; to John Mason Brown, who packed up a suitcaseful of rare books for us and told us to keep them for as long as we wished; to Kenneth Macgowan, who was an invaluable source of information about O'Neill, and who turned over his voluminous correspondence to us; to Frances Steloff, whose Gotham Book Mart was a gold mine of rare volumes and documents, and who spared us many hours of her time; to Irving Hoffman, who put us in touch with people who would otherwise have been inaccessible; to Robert Downing, an encyclopedia of the theatre, who read proofs and kept a sharp eye out for factual errors; to Russel Crouse, Saxe and Dorothy Commins, Angna Enters, Shirlee and Robert Lantz, David and Esther Habin, Mr. and Mrs. Arthur McGinley, Ben and Ann Pinchot, Elliot Norton, James Joseph Martin and Charles O'Brien Kennedy, who, in addition to supplying us with information, extended to us, on more than one occasion, their hospitality; and to Lawrence Langner, who not only talked to us at length and on many occasions about his relationship with O'Neill, but generously allowed us to quote from his comprehensive autobiography, *The Magic Curtain* (E. P. Dutton & Company, Inc.).

Without the help of various libraries, our task would have been an impossible one. We wish first to thank the Yale University Library, whose O'Neill collection is the world's foremost; Dr. Donald C. Gallup and James T. Babb extended us every courtesy in our research there. We are also grateful, at Yale University, to Steve Kezerian.

We are much obligated for the extensive help given us by the New York Public Library's Theatre Collection, and to George Freedley and Paul Myers, who were never too busy to track down that one, last (only it never turned out to be the last) detail; also the library's Berg Collection and John Gordan.

The Princeton University Library, through the good offices of Alexander P. Clark and Alexander D. Wainwright, made its O'Neill collection available to us and granted us many special favors. Dartmouth College was equally gracious in placing the facilities of its library at our command, and we wish to thank Bella C. Landauer, who was responsible for the gift of the O'Neill collection to Dartmouth, and who brought other O'Neill items to our attention. We also thank Donald D. McCuaig, Marcus A. McCorison and Professor Kenneth Robinson for their help at Dartmouth.

At Harvard University, with the assistance of William Van Lennep, we were permitted to examine the O'Neill documents on file at the Houghton Library's Theatre Collection. St. Mary's College furnished us with details of Ella O'Neill's student days, and we thank Marion Mc-

Candless for her exhaustive letters of information and for her book, *Family Portraits*. At St. Mary's, we also appreciate the help of S. Robert Johnson.

Mrs. George Jean Nathan allowed us to see her husband's O'Neill collection, now at Cornell University; we gratefully thank her, also, for allowing us to quote from the published writings of George Jean Nathan.

We owe a debt to the Museum of the City of New York and May Davenport Seymour; the University of Oregon and Horace W. Robinson; Fordham University and Burt Solomon; the Fales Collection of New York University; the University of Washington Library and Jessica Potter; the University of Pennsylvania and Neda M. Westlake; Connecticut College for Women and Hazel Johnson; the University of Notre Dame and James E. Armstrong; the Columbia University Library and Kenneth A. Lohf; the New London Public Library and Frank Edgerton; the Newberry Library and Amy Nyholm; the Boston Public Library and Richard G. Hensley and Mrs. Marjorie Bouquet; the Library of Congress Reference Division and Richard S. McCartney; the Library of Congress Manuscript Division and David C. Mearns.

Our thanks are due, as well, to Actors Equity and Alfred Harding; O'Malley's Book Shop; the American Merchant Marine Institute and Frank Braynard; the Church of St. Ann (New York City) and the Reverend John P. Healy; the Euthanasia Society of America and Dr. Robert L. Dickinson and Mrs. Robertson Jones; the General Service Administration, National Archives (Washington, D.C.), and F. R. Holdcamper; Lawrence Memorial Hospital (New London, Conn.); the Marine Society of the Port of New York; the Mystic Seaport Museum (Mystic, Conn.) and Malcolm D. McGregor; the National Institute of Arts and Letters; the George M. Cohan Music Publishing Company; the Office of the Chief Medical Examiner (New York City); Bellevue Hospital; Norwich (Conn.) State Hospital; Laurel Heights Sanatorium (Shelton, Conn.) and Dr. Kirby S. Howlett, Jr., and Dr. Edward J. Lynch; the New London County Historical Society; The Players and Pat Carroll; the Episcopal Actors Guild and Mrs. Helen Morrison; the Seaman's Institute; Sailors Snug Harbor and Arthur Cochrane and Frederick S. McMurray; St. Joseph's Church and St. Mary's Cemetery (New London, Conn.); the Stamford Historical Society and Miss M. E. Plumb; the United States Lines and Richard Harris; the Office of the Town Clerk and the Office of the City Clerk (New London) and Elizabeth T. Roath; Harkness Memorial State Park (Connecticut State Park and Forest Commission, Waterford, Conn.); Mount St. Vincent-on-Hudson and the Sisters of Charity—most particularly, Mother Mary; the College of Mount St. Vincent and Sister Marie

Jeanette; De La Salle Institute; the Veterans Administration Hospitals in the Bronx and Manhattan and in Bath, N.Y., and the Probate Court, Salem, Mass.

Special thanks are due to the Gaylord Farm Sanitarium, which provided us with background information. We are grateful to members of its staff—Howard Crockett, Mrs. Reba Maisonville and especially to Dr. Sterling B. Brinkley, its director.

We are indebted to the reference libraries and morgues of various magazines and newspapers for their great help, and also for their permission to quote from specific articles. Many of these articles, too numerous to list here, have been acknowledged in the text. First in our gratitude is *The New York Times,* the extent of whose assistance is incalculable, and whose files have been drawn upon more than those of any other publication.

We thank, also, the New York *Herald Tribune;* the New York *Journal American;* the New London *Day* and its managing editor, George E. Clapp; the Oakland (California) *Tribune* and Frank Wootten and Lester Sipes; the Boston *Globe* and Herbert A. Kenny; the Providence (R.I.) *Journal* and the *Evening Bulletin* and I. Talanian; the Lynne (Mass.) *Item* and V. P. O'Brien; the *Oregon Journal;* the Salem *Evening News* and Warren Rockwell; the *Oregonion* and Amanda Marion; the Seattle *Post-Intelligencer;* the Seattle *Times* and Chester Gibbon; *Time* and Content Peckham; and *Variety.*

Among the people connected with O'Neill or members of his family, who gave us their hospitality and in other ways extended themselves to make our job easier, were: Winfield Aronberg, Barbara Burton, Dr. and Mrs. Louis Bisch, E. J. Ballantine, Mrs. Claire Bird, Mrs. Fred Boyden, Louis Bergen, Alfred B. C. Batson, Mrs. Chester A. Beckley, Agnes Casey, Professor Bruce Carpenter, Bennett Cerf, Mrs. Benjamin DeCasseres, Jasper Deeter, Eddie Dowling, Dorothy Day, Eben Given and Phyllis Duganne Given, Charles Ellis and Norma Millay Ellis, Waldo Frank, Mrs. Byron S. Fones, Dr. Shirely C. Fisk, Lillian Gish, Mrs. Samuel S. Greene, Mrs. Pete Gross, Dr. and Mrs. Joseph Ganey, Mrs. Clayton Hamilton, John Hewitt, Joe Heidt, Ralph Horton, Mrs. Smith Ely Jelliffe, Edna Kenton, Alexander King, Joseph Wood Krutch, Louis Kalonyme, Manuel Komroff, Ed Keefe, James and Patty Light, Ruth Lander, Armina Marshall Langner, William L. Laurence, Romany Marie, Mrs. W. E. Maxon, Dr. Frederic B. Mayo, Jo Mielziner, George Middleton, Mrs. Beatrice Maher, Philip Moeller, Ward Morehouse, Frank and Elsie Meyer, Joseph A. McCarthy, Elizabeth Murray, Mrs. Matt Moran,

Nina Moise, Dudley Nichols, George Jean Nathan, Patricia Neal, Sean O'Casey, Dr. Robert Lee Patterson, Florence Reed, Arthur Leonard Ross, Jessica Rippin, Robert Rockmore, Selena Royle Renavent, Paula Strasberg, Mrs. Earl C. Stevens, Lee Simonson, Wilhelmina Stamberger, Bessie Sheridan, Mr. and Mrs. Phil Sheridan, Claire Sherman, Mrs. E. Chappell Sheffield, Mai-mai Sze, Pauline Turkel, Brandon Tynan, Allen and Sarah Ullman, Alice Woods Ullman, Carl Van Vechten and Fania Marinoff Van Vechten, Mary Heaton Vorse, Mrs. Jacob N. Wolodarsky, Charles Webster, Richard Weeks, Francis (Jeff) Wylie, Norman Winston, Mary Welch, Stark Young and William and Marguerite Zorach. We are grateful to them all.

We also thank Elizabeth Shepley Sergeant, whose reminiscences of O'Neill were of great value and who has allowed us to quote from her book, *Fire Under the Andes* (Alfred A. Knopf); Ilka Chase, who granted permission to quote from *Past Imperfect* (Doubleday & Company); Mrs. Dudley Nichols, who consented to our use of letters written by her husband; Mrs. Barrett H. Clark, for permission to quote from *Eugene O'Neill: The Man and His Plays* (Dover Publications); and Mrs. Sherwood Anderson, for her help in locating some of the sources of her husband's writings.

Others who generously furnished us with information and assistance of various kinds are: Jacob Ben-Ami, Walter Abel, Mr. and Mrs. Egmont Arens, Leslie Austin, Margaret Anglin, Dr. Frank L. Babbott, Frank D. Brewer, Charlotte E. Betts, Mary Bicknell, Pincus Berner, Robert C. Brown, Bessie Breuer, Albert Boni, Elizabeth Brennan, Jeanie Begg, Jennie Belardi, Mark Barron, Charles Burns, Chief of Police (Marblehead, Mass.) Samuel H. Bradish, Frederick Brisson, Mark Crane, Dan D. Coyle, Joseph Corky, Holger Cahill, George Canessa, Mrs. Francis Cadenas, Edith Corwin, Ed Kook, Dr. Saul Colin, Melville Cane, Mrs. Albert B. Carey, Carmen Capalbo, Stanley Chase, Harry T. Crowley, Louis Calta, Frank Conroy, Alexander Campbell, Bosley Crowther, Padraic Colum, Aileen Cramer, Cheryl Crawford, Edward Choate, Arthur Cantor, Gloria Cantor, F. V. Chappell, Alexander H. Cohen, Jack Cunningham, Bernard Clark, Joe Cronin, Warren Carberg, Arthur Daley, Harrison Dowd, Jack Dempsey, Olin Downes, Zelda Dorfman, Thomas F. Dorsey, Jr., Barbara Dubivsky, Lawrence E. Davies, Ruth Dutro, John D. Davies, Milton I. D. Einstein, Manny Eisler, Leon Edel, Max Eastman, Donald Friede, Daniel Foley, Mrs. Hall Furber, Lynn Fontanne, John Fenton, Bijou Fernandez, Robert Flanagan, Mrs. Emily Rippin Griswold, Howard Mortimer Green, Paul Green, Max Gordon, Ruth Gilbert, Louis Gruenberg, Dr. Karl Ragnar Gierow, Edward Goodman, Brother Angelus Gabriel, Mrs. Joseph Girsdansky, Carol Grace, Howard Mortimer Green, Jesse Gordon, David Golding, Margalo Gilmore, Marjorie Griesser, Police Lieutenant (Marblehead, Mass.) G. E. Girard, Dr. Gordon Hislop, A. Arthur Halle, Sam Hick, Mrs. Walter Huston, Sol Hurok, Sonia Levine Hovey, James Hammond, Helen Hayes, Theresa Helburn, Dag Hammarskjöld, John Houseman, Mabel Hess, Inez Hogan, Rita Hastings, John Cecil Holm, Granville Hicks, Ann Harding, Robert Hassett, Margaret Heyer, Arthur Hughes, Blanche Hayes, Dr. Daniel Hiebert, Barry Hyams, Don Hartman, Dr. Andrew Harsanyi, Edward Hubler, Catharine Huntington, Louis Isaacs, Dr. Oswald Jones, Bill Johnson, Denis Johnston, Don Janson, Sybil V. Jacobsen, Dr. Robert Klein, Alfred Kreymborg, Leon Kramer, Sadie Koenig, Margaret Kaplan, Gilbert Kahn, Theodore Liebler, Jr., Mrs. William L'Engle, Claire Luce, Alfred Lunt, Frank Leslie, Dr. Sidney Lenke, Scott Lindsley, Louise Larabee, T. H. Latimer, J. Anthony Lewis, Gloria Vanderbilt Lumet, Edward Lazare, David Lawrence, Kyra Markham, Nickolas Muray, Mary Morris, Mrs. Julian Moran, Aline MacMahon, W. Somerset Maugham, Thomas Mitchell, Robert Manning, Marcella Markham, Philip McBride, Mrs. Harold J. McGee, Gilbert Miller, James Meighan, Theodore Mann, Walter Murphy, Mrs. Richard J. Madden, Dr. Merrill Moore, Warren Munsell, Mrs. Mabel Ramage Mix, Bert McCord, Alan D. Mickle, Richard Maney, Sal J. Miraliotta, Edward Morrow, Albert C. Nathanson, Dr. and Mrs. John Norris, Daniel O'Neill, Arnold Newman, Dr. W. Richard Ohler, Clifford Odets, Hal Olver, Henry O'Neill, Dr. B. N. Pennell, Albert J. Perry, Augustus Perry, Joseph Plunkett, Karl Pretshold, Mrs. Percy Palmer, Seymour Peck, Brother Basil Peters, David F. Perkins, Coddington Pendleton, Judge S. V. Prince, Professor Norman Pearson, Arthur Pell, Dorothy Peterson, Sidney Phillips, Stavros Peterson, Frank Payne, Susan Pinchot, C. N. Pollock, Stephen Philbin, James Francis Quigley, José Quintero, George Reynolds, Sawyer Robinson, George Ronkin, George Ross, William Brennan Rogers, Jason Robards, Jr., Jane Rubin, Jay Russell, A. M. Rosenthal, Lennox Robinson, Harold D. Smith, James Shay, Richard Shepard, Mrs. Eunice Saner, Paul Shyre, Mrs. Henry Bill Selden, Dr. Thomas B. Stoltz, Robert Sisk, Arnault G. Schellenberg, Mrs. John Sloan, Louis Sobol, James Shute, Arthur Shields, Bernard Simon, Oliver M. Sayler, Dr. Daniel Sullivan, Wilbur Daniel Steele, Patrolman (Marblehead, Mass.) John Snow, Mrs. George E. Shay, Dr. Kenneth J. Tillotson, John Tucker, Edna Tyler, Clara A. Weiss, Arthur G. Walter, Richard Witkin, Thornton Wilder, Richard Watts, Jr., Mary Williams, Edmund Wilson, Dr. Sophus Keith Winther, Robert Weller, Ted Williams, Mr. and Mrs.

Laurence A. White, Stephen Weissman, Stephen Watts, William Weart, Arthur W. Wisner, Peggy Wood and Sam Zolotow.

In addition to the books previously acknowledged, we are grateful to Random House, Inc., for permission to quote from *The Plays of Eugene O'Neill* (three volumes) and from *The Iceman Cometh* by Eugene O'Neill and *A Moon for the Misbegotten* by Eugene O'Neill. We also thank the Yale University Press for allowing us to quote from *Long Day's Journey Into Night*, by Eugene O'Neill, as well as from *A Touch of the Poet* and *Hughie*, both by Eugene O'Neill.

We are also indebted to the following sources:

Inscriptions: Eugene O'Neill to Carlotta Monterey O'Neill (Yale University Library); *George Pierce Baker and the American Theatre*, by Wisner Payne Kinne (Harvard University Press); *An Anarchist Woman*, by Hutchins Hapgood (Dodd, Mead & Company); *The Complete Plays of Eugene O'Neill: Wilderness Edition* (Charles Scribner's Sons); *History of the San Francisco Theatre*, Volume XX: *James O'Neill*, by Workers of the Writers' Program of the WPA of Northern California (sponsored by the city and county of San Francisco); *The Theatre of George Jean Nathan*, by Isaac Goldberg (Simon and Schuster); *The Intimate Notebooks of George Jean Nathan* (Alfred A. Knopf); *A History of the American Drama from the Civil War to the Present*, by Arthur Hobson Quinn (Harper & Brothers); *Total Recoil*, by Kyle Crichton (Doubleday & Company, Inc.); *The Curse of the Misbegotten*, by Croswell Bowen with the assistance of Shane O'Neill (McGraw-Hill Book Company, Inc.); *A Victorian in the Modern World*, by Hutchins Hapgood (Harcourt, Brace & Company); *Letters of Sherwood Anderson* (Little, Brown & Company); *George Pierce Baker, A Memorial* (Dramatists Play Service); *Conversations on Contemporary Drama*, by Clayton Hamilton (Macmillan); *Anathema!* by Benjamin DeCasseres (Gotham Book Mart); *A Bibliography of the Works of Eugene O'Neill*, by Ralph Sanborn and Barrett H. Clark (Random House, Inc.); *A Wayward Quest*, by Theresa Helburn (Little, Brown & Company); *Time and the Town*, by Mary Heaton Vorse (The Dial Press); *Our American Theatre*, by Oliver M. Sayler (Brentano's); *Movers and Shakers*, by Mabel Dodge Luhan (Harcourt, Brace & Company); *Living My Life*, by Emma Goldman (Garden City Publishing Company, Inc.); *Whatever Goes Up*—by George C. Tyler and J. C. Furnas (The Bobbs-Merrill Company); *John Reed*, by Granville Hicks (The Macmillan Company); *The Road to the Temple*, by Susan Glaspell (Frederick A. Stokes); *The Provincetown*, by Helen Deutsch and Stella Hanau (Farrar & Rinehart, Inc.); *A Research in Marriage*, by G. V. Hamilton, M.D. (Lear Publishers, Inc.); *These Things Are Mine*, by George

Middleton (The Macmillan Company); *The Stage Is Set,* by Lee Simonson (Dover Publications); *Representative One-Act Plays by American Authors,* selected by Margaret Goodner Mayorga (Little, Brown & Company); *Reference Point,* by Arthur Hopkins (Samuel French); *Of Time and the River,* by Thomas Wolfe (Charles Scribner's Sons); *Nine Plays by Eugene O'Neill*—introduction by Joseph Wood Krutch (Random House, Inc.); *The American Drama Since 1918,* by Joseph Wood Krutch (George Braziller, Inc.); *The Gangs of New York,* by Herbert Asbury (Alfred A. Knopf); and *This Is My Best,* edited by Whit Burnett (The Dial Press).

We also acknowledge, with thanks, consent to quote from the following:

"O'Neill Picks America as His Future Workshop," by Richard Watts, Jr., September 27, 1931; "Exile Made Him Appreciate U.S., O'Neill Admits," by Ernest K. Lindley, May 22, 1931; "Nathan Admits O'Neill Flouted Advice He Gave," by Ishbel Ross, March 17, 1931; "Regarding Mr. Eugene O'Neill as a Writer for the Cinema," by Richard Watts, Jr., March 4, 1928; "Eugene O'Neill Talks of His Own and the Plays of Others" (unsigned), November 16, 1924; "Young Boswell Interviews O'Neill" (unsigned), May 24, 1923; "Eugene O'Neill" (unsigned), November 13, 1921; "Eugene O'Neill at Close Range in Maine," by David Karsner, August 8, 1926; Poem ("To Be Sung at the O'Neill Play") in Franklin P. Adams' column, October, 1931. The foregoing are all by permission of the New York *Herald Tribune.*

"The Odyssey of Eugene O'Neill," by Fred Pasley, 1932—by permission of the New York *Daily News;* "A Eugene O'Neill Miscellany" (unsigned), January 12, 1928, and "The Boulevards After Dark," by Ward Morehouse, May 14, 1930—by permission of the New York *Sun;* "O'Neill in Northwest to Get Drama," by Richard L. Neuberger, November 29, 1936—by permission of the *Sunday Oregonian;* "The Ordeal of Eugene O'Neill" (cover story), October 21, 1946—by permission of *Time;* "Softer Tones for Mr. O'Neill's Portrait," by Mary Welch, May, 1957, and "Untold Tales of Eugene O'Neill," by Gladys Hamilton, August, 1956—by permission of *Theatre Arts* magazine, Miss Welch and Mrs. Hamilton; "The Iceman and the Bridegroom," by Cyrus Day, March, 1958—by permission of *Modern Drama* and the author; "The Recluse of Sea Island," by George Jean Nathan, August, 1935—by permission of *Redbook* magazine and Mrs. George Jean Nathan.

Permission to quote from the three-part Profile of Eugene O'Neill by Hamilton Basso, February 28, March 6 and March 13, 1948, has been granted by the author and *The New Yorker;* we thank *The New Yorker,* also, for permission to quote from reviews and "The Talk of the Town," and for a verse by Arthur Guiterman. Permission to quote from "Close-up —Eugene O'Neill," by Tom Prideaux, October 14, 1946, is by courtesy of the author and *Life*, copyright 1946 Time Inc. Permission to quote from "A Weekend with Eugene O'Neill," by Malcolm Cowley, September 5, 1957, has been granted by the author and *The Reporter* magazine.

In addition, we would like to acknowledge our appreciation to the following articles and authors:

"Haunted by the Ghost of Monte Cristo," by Richard H. Little—Chicago *Record Herald*, February 9, 1908; "Personal Reminiscences," by James O'Neill—*Theatre Magazine*, December, 1917; "Nipping the Budding Playwright in the Bud," by Heywood Broun—*Vanity Fair*, October, 1919; "Personality Portraits," by Alta M. Coleman—*The Theatre*, April, 1920; "Playwright Finds His Inspiration on Lonely Sand Dunes by the Sea," by Olin Downes—Boston *Sunday Post*, August 29, 1920; "Enter Eugene O'Neill," by Pierre Loving—*The Bookman*, August, 1921; "The Extraordinary Story of Eugene O'Neill," by Mary B. Mullett—*American Magazine*, November, 1922; "Making Plays with a Tragic End," by Malcolm Mollan—Philadelphia *Public Ledger*, January 22, 1922; "The Real Eugene O'Neill," by Oliver M. Sayler—*The Century Magazine*, July, 1922; "What a Sanatorium Did for Eugene O'Neill," by J. F. O'Neill —*Journal of Outdoor Life*, June, 1923; "Eugene O'Neill," by Charles A. Merrill—Boston *Globe*, July 8, 1923; "Eugene O'Neill—the Inner Man," by Carol Bird—*Theatre Magazine*, June, 1924; "Back to the Source of Plays Written by Eugene O'Neill," by Charles P. Sweeney— New York *World*, November 9, 1924; "Eugene O'Neill Lifts Curtain on His Early Plays," by Louis Kalonyme—*The New York Times*, December 21, 1924; "Fierce Oaths and Blushing Complexes Find No Place in Eugene O'Neill's Talk," by Flora Merrill—New York *World*, July 19, 1925; "Fifteen Year Record of the Class of 1910—Princeton University," 1925; "I Knew Him When—" by John V. A. Weaver—New York *World*, February 21, 1926; "Eugene O'Neill, Writer of Synthetic Drama," by Malcolm Cowley—*Brentano's Book Chat*, Vol. 5, No. 4, July and August, 1926; "Who's Who on Broadway," by Homer H. Metz—New York *Telegraph*, December 25, 1927; "O'Neill Stirs the Gods of the Drama," by H. I. Brock—*The New York Times*, January 15, 1928; "Celebrities and Some Others," by Alfred Batson—*North China Daily News*, February 12, 1929; "Out of Provincetown," by Harry Kemp—*Theatre Magazine*, April, 1930; "The World's Worst Reporter," by Robert A. Woodworth—Providence *Journal*, December 6, 1931; "O'Neill's House Was Shrine for Friends," by Mary Heaton Vorse—New York *World*, January

11, 1931; "O'Neill Is Eager to See Cohan in 'Ah, Wilderness!' " by Richard Watts, Jr.—New York *Herald Tribune,* September 9, 1933; "Eugene O'Neill Undramatic Over Honor of Nobel Prize"—Seattle *Times,* November 12, 1936; "O'Neill Turns West to New Horizons," by Richard L. Neuberger—*The New York Times,* November 22, 1936; "O'Neill Plots a Course for the Drama," by S. J. Woolf—*The New York Times,* October 4, 1941; "Eugene O'Neill Discourses on Dramatic Art," by George Jean Nathan—New York *Journal American,* August 22, 1946; "Eugene O'Neill Returns After Twelve Years," by S. J. Woolf—*The New York Times,* September 15, 1946; "O'Neill on the World and 'The Iceman,' " by John S. Wilson—*PM,* September 3, 1946; "Playwright Eugene O'Neill Back for Play's Première Says He'll Roam No More," by Mark Barron—Associated Press News Feature, October 12, 1946; "Memories of Eugene O'Neill," by Herbert J. Stoeckel—*Hartford Courant Magazine,* December 6, 1953; "Shane O'Neill's Long Journey," by Helen Dudar—New York *Post,* February 7, 1957; "Eugene O'Neill—Notes From a Critic's Diary," by Stark Young—*Harper's Magazine,* June, 1957; "The Bright Face of Tragedy," by George Jean Nathan—*Cosmopolitan,* August, 1957; "A Few Memories of Eugene O'Neill," by Richard Watts, Jr.—New York *Post,* September 8, 1957.

Also, the following stories and articles by Eugene O'Neill:

"Tomorrow"—*The Seven Arts* magazine, June, 1917; "A Letter from Eugene O'Neill"—*The New York Times,* April 11, 1920; "A Letter [from Eugene O'Neill]"—*The New York Times,* December 16, 1921; "Strindberg and Our Theatre"—*Provincetown Playbill,* No. 1, Season 1923-24; "Are the Actors to Blame?"—*Provincetown Playbill,* No. 1, Season 1925-26; "The 'Fountain' Program Note"—*Greenwich Playbill,* No. 3, Season 1925-26; "The Playwright Explains"—*The New York Times,* February 14, 1926; "Memoranda on Masks—A Dramatist's Notebook"—*The American Spectator,* November, 1932; "Second Thoughts"—*The American Spectator,* December, 1932.

Finally, we thank our editors at Harper for their patience and moral support. If we have inadvertently neglected to thank any of the people who gave us their assistance, we ask their pardon, and offer our gratitude.

INTRODUCTION

SINCE MR. GELB AND I ARE ASSOCIATES ON THE NEWS
staff of *The New York Times,* he has told me a good deal about O'Neill
during the five years in which Mrs. Gelb and he have been writing it.
When they undertook the responsibility of writing it they did not foresee
the size it would assume. They had always admired Eugene O'Neill's
plays; they had long regarded him as America's greatest dramatist; they
were fascinated by everything they heard about him from people who
had known him. All they intended originally was a biography of conventional length.

But the more they poked into his bizarre personal life, which they
saw reflected in the dark mirror of his plays, the more engrossed they
became. Everything in his life became significant because everything
affected his plays. He was a highly personal writer who proceeded through
a succession of obsessions from the wistfully romantic sea plays to the
ruthlessness of *Long Day's Journey Into Night.*

Eventually Mr. and Mrs. Gelb had to decide whether they were going
to write a selective biography or a comprehensive life and study. They
decided on the latter. For it became obvious to them that the philosophical
life of the dramatist developed out of the experiences and temperaments
of his mother and father: that the real sources, in fact, were his emotional
and spiritual heritage. The father and mother lived in a spacious theatre
that their son helped to destroy. He retained much of the spacious-
ness of style, but he filled it with bleaker and harsher materials.

Although O'Neill had a charming personality, he was an extremely
complex man. Brooding, restless, distrustful, dramatic, he rejected everything in life that did not bear directly on his writing. Except for his passion for writing, he would probably have drunk himself to an early death,
like his hopeless brother. If the term "beatnik" had existed in his youth, he
would have been recognized as a perfect example of the rootless, rebellious,
dissipated, egotistical, self-pitying renegade. His passion for writing saved
him by imposing on him a certain discipline. He chose between dereliction
and writing. Even after he had made the choice—more or less deliberately,
it appears—he was still "on the lam," like a fugitive from society. He was
forever abandoning what he had in favor of something else he thought he

wanted, but never found. His life was a long day's journey into night.

Those of us who were acquainted with him knew some of this. But his association with the theatre was only a small part of his personal life, and possibly the least significant. The things that mattered most to him and made the deepest impression on him were invisible, at least to most of us—his boyhood, unsettled because his father and mother were frequently on tour; his years at sea and on the beach; his mad gold expedition in Honduras; his aimless days and nights in Greenwich Village; his hand-to-mouth existence in Provincetown. Also, the romantically gloomy books, plays and poems he read from the nineteenth century when the death wish was a literary fetish. These were the things that mattered most.

Although the rootlessness and isolation of much of O'Neill's life have set his biographers many problems, Mr. and Mrs. Gelb have tracked him down with the ingenuity and perseverance of police reporters. They have interviewed more than four hundred people who knew one aspect or another of O'Neill's elusive life. The people who knew him are mortal, like all of us; and people are always the best sources. The printed records confirm only a small part of the facts and impressions that people retain in their memories. Mr. and Mrs. Gelb have been able to relate O'Neill's life directly to his plays. It is not a pretty life. But it is always absorbing; much of it is astonishing. We are fortunate to have it on the record less than a decade after O'Neill's death.

BROOKS ATKINSON

New York, 1961

"MAN IS BORN BROKEN. HE LIVES BY MENDING. THE GRACE OF GOD IS GLUE!"

The Great God Brown, ACT IV, SCENE I

PART ONE
HAUNTING GHOSTS
1846—1912

IN THE EARLY SUMMER OF 1939 EUGENE O'NEILL began work on what he called "a play of old sorrow, written in tears and blood." It was *Long Day's Journey Into Night*—a brutal baring of the forces that had shaped him, an evaluation of his tragic viewpoint, an explanation of his failures as a human being, and a celebration of the fact that he had become, in spite of these failures, the consummate artist that he was.

"I love life," he once said. "But I don't love life because it is pretty. Prettiness is only clothes-deep. I am a truer lover than that. I love it naked. There is beauty to me even in its ugliness. In fact, I deny the ugliness entirely, for its vices are often nobler than its virtues, and nearly always closer to a revelation."

O'Neill, at fifty, felt an urgency to embark on the revelations of *Long Day's Journey Into Night,* for he knew that the mental and physical stamina that had sustained him throughout twenty-five astoundingly productive years was ebbing. Although he no longer cared about having his plays produced—he had not had anything on Broadway since 1934, when *Days Without End* had been coolly received—he did not want to die without leaving a definitive, naked statement of who and what he was.

He was convinced of his own immortality as a dramatist and, while determined to withhold his autobiographical play from the public until twenty-five years after his death, he did want it, ultimately, to take its place in the body of his work. His widow, to whom he left control of all his plays, permitted the script to be published three years after he died; it was immediately recognized as a masterpiece in the United States and abroad.

O'Neill wrote in a dedication of the play that at last he had been able to face his dead. After years of dissecting, analyzing and reconstructing the members of his family and drawing thinly disguised and symbolically heightened portraits of them, he was now prepared to approach them and himself with, as he put it, "deep pity and understanding and forgiveness."

It is true that he pitied and understood. But the fact that he was impelled, years after their deaths, to reveal his father as a miser, his mother as a narcotics addict, his brother as an alcoholic, indicates that he could not entirely forgive. O'Neill, in his fifties, was still torn by alternating hatred and love for his family.

Friends assumed that he wanted to defer publication of *Long Day's Journey Into Night* out of consideration for the feelings of his parents' surviving relatives, who would have been dead when the play finally emerged. Since O'Neill had little affection for his parents' kin, however, it is more likely that the purpose of the delay was to prevent his harsh portraits from being disputed (which, as it turned out, they were—and hotly—by friends of O'Neill's father).

O'Neill was trying to tell an unsuspecting world the truth—if not always the literal truth, at least the artistic truth—about his heritage. He was compelled to go back to his roots, to justify himself, to prove that "the sins of the father are to be laid upon the children."

"I'm always acutely conscious of the Force behind—(Fate, God, our biological past creating our present, whatever one calls it—Mystery, certainly)," O'Neill had written to the theatre historian and critic Arthur Hobson Quinn, fifteen years before beginning *Long Day's Journey Into Night*.

When he started writing the play O'Neill, despite the inroads of a debilitating nervous disorder, was still impressively handsome. His dark hair was streaked with white and there were deeply cut lines about the mouth, at the edges of the eyes, and etched into a lofty forehead. A sparse, gray, triangular mustache roofed a mouth at whose corners lurked the hint of a sardonic smile. The sagging cheeks could not hide high, strong bones, a firm jaw and a chin chiseled from granite. He smiled rarely, but when he did it was like the sudden lifting of a fog; the fog settled again with the same startling rapidity.

His eyes, always an astonishment to those meeting him for the first time, illuminated his face. Large, dark, immeasurably deep, set wide apart under heavy brows, they could stare into depths that existed for no one else. When he turned the O'Neill look on someone, he appeared to gaze into that person's soul. But the appraisal was neither critical nor even disconcerting; it was a look of profound and gentle searching, at once penetrating and reassuring. For nothing shocked him. He was interested only in the motive behind the action.

O'Neill, aged fifty, was regarded as the most distinguished dramatist the United States had ever fostered. Since 1916, when a group of passionate young writers, actors and artists in Provincetown, Massachusetts, presented his one-act play, *Bound East for Cardiff,* he had made a staggering contribution to the American theatre, and had become, except for Shakespeare and possibly Shaw, the world's most widely translated and produced dramatist.

For over a quarter of a century he had battled to lift American drama to the level of art and keep it there, to mold a native, tragic stage literature. The first American to succeed as a writer of theatre tragedy, he had continued shattering Broadway convention and made possible the evolution of an adult theatre in which such playwrights as Thornton Wilder, Tennessee Williams and Arthur Miller could function.

To O'Neill tragedy had the meaning the Greeks gave it, and it was their classic example that he tried to follow. He believed with the Greeks that tragedy always brought exaltation, "an urge toward life and ever more life"; the spectacle of a performed tragedy roused men to "spiritual understandings and released them from the petty greeds of everyday existence." Tragedy ennobled in art what O'Neill often referred to as man's "hopeless hopes." Any victory man might wring from life was an ironic one, O'Neill believed. His viewpoint was that "life in itself was nothing." It was only the dream that kept man "fighting, willing—living."

"To me, the tragic alone has that significant beauty which is truth," O'Neill said in 1921, not long after the premiere of *Beyond the Horizon*, his initial Broadway production and the first of four O'Neill plays to win the Pulitzer Prize. "It is the meaning of life—and the hope. The noblest is eternally the most tragic. The people who succeed and do not push on to a greater failure are the spiritual middle-classers. Their stopping at success is the proof of their compromising insignificance. How petty their dreams must have been!"

In 1939 O'Neill's dream still soared. Despite the fact that he had won the Nobel Prize for literature three years before, he did not think he had yet pushed on to a great enough failure. Although he already had thirty-four published plays to his credit, including the thirteen-act trilogy, *Mourning Becomes Electra*, and had completed the as yet unproduced and unpublished *The Iceman Cometh*, he had set his "hopeless hope" on finishing a Herculean cycle of eleven plays. The cycle, on which he had been working intermittently for about five years, was to span a period of more than 175 years in the history of an American family doomed to what O'Neill characterized as "self-dispossession," or the bartering of their souls for material gain.

But ill-health had forced him to ponder the shelving of his taxing project. Toward the end of 1937 he began to suffer from an illness diagnosed at first as Parkinson's disease and later as a rarer disease, whose nature could not be completely ascertained but which most specialists considered degenerative.

The obscure disorder causes a gradual breakdown of brain cells and results in a lack of co-ordination between nerves and muscles. The sufferer loses the ability to control arms, legs and even tongue and throat, while retaining his mental clarity. He reaches for a sheet of paper and instead of grasping it his hand flies upward; he tries to walk forward, and instead he stumbles backward; he clears his throat to speak and with his tongue cleaving to his palate his voice emerges as a croak, his words unformed.

In O'Neill's case these things did not happen always or all at once. He never knew, though, when or how he was to be frustrated. His symptoms varied in their intensity; some of his doctors believed that psychological causes governed the form of his affliction.

By 1939 palsy was seriously affecting his hands. Even as a young man his hands had trembled slightly, a trait he believed he had inherited from his mother. Now the trembling made it difficult for him to write. To help control the shaking and conserve energy, he formed smaller letters, and his calligraphy became increasingly cramped. Eventually he was squeezing a thousand words onto a sheet of paper the size most people fill with two hundred. Much of his work had to be deciphered under a magnifying glass. He could not set down a creative thought except in his own hand. It was impossible for him to dictate or to use a typewriter.

Thus handicapped, O'Neill turned to work he considered more pressing than the cycle. "I felt a sudden necessity to write plays I'd wanted to write for a long time that *I knew could be finished,*" he wrote to a friend.

On a Tuesday, June 21, 1939, O'Neill's wife, Carlotta, made the following entry in her diary: "Gene talks to me for hours—about a play (in his mind) of his mother, father, his brother and himself. . . . A hot, sleepless night—an ache in our hearts for things we can't escape!" She was referring to the imminence of World War II.

It took O'Neill a little over two years to complete *Long Day's Journey Into Night.* He worked every morning, many afternoons, and sometimes evenings as well. Often he wept as he wrote. He slept badly, and occasionally in the night he rose from the converted Chinese opium couch that served as his bed to go to his wife's room and talk of the play and of his anguish.

"He explained to me that he *had* to write the play," his wife once said.

[6]

"He had to write it because it was a thing that haunted him and he had to forgive his family and himself."

He was living at the time on a 158-acre estate, in a concrete-block house built on the side of a mountain, about thirty-five miles from San Francisco.

The house was staffed, until the war, by efficient servants. O'Neill saw scarcely anyone except his wife, whose job it was to maintain an atmosphere conducive to work.

"Orders were that nobody was to go near him," she later recalled, "not even if the house was on fire. He was never to be disturbed."

O'Neill arose daily at 7:30, dressed, had breakfast on a tray in his bedroom, and then shut himself into his study to work until 1 P.M.

"He would come out of his study looking gaunt, his eyes red from weeping," Mrs. O'Neill continued. "Sometimes he looked ten years older than when he went in in the morning. For a while he tried to have lunch downstairs with me. But it was very bad, because he would sit there and I knew his whole mind was on his play—acts, lines, ideas—and he couldn't talk. I would have to sit there perfectly dumb. I didn't even want to make a sound with the chair that might disturb him. It made me very nervous and it made him nervous seeing me sitting there like that. We decided it would be best for him to have his lunch on a tray, alone."

After lunch O'Neill would lie down for a rest, unless he was at a point in his work where he felt he had to go on a bit longer. But he napped sometime during the afternoon and if the weather was mild he swam in his pool, which, being high over the valley, had an oddly soothing effect on him. Later in the day he and his wife would walk about on their grounds and look in on the chickens O'Neill was keeping as a hobby. He sometimes went back to work until dinner.

In the evenings the O'Neills usually sat before their huge fireplace. O'Neill enjoyed reading Yeats aloud, while his Dalmatian lay at his feet.

"If he felt gay, he would act something out," his wife has said. "He was very charming; he could be the worst ham you ever met. But if he was sick, he would be silent and just sit and think. Sometimes, he wouldn't talk all day long."

When the play was completed in the summer of 1941, O'Neill told his wife, "Well, thank God, that's finished." All but spent from the effort, he was able to write only one more play before his death in 1953—*A Moon for the Misbegotten* (completed in 1943), which is principally about his brother and is in a sense a sequel to *Long Day's Journey Into Night*.

O'Neill presented Carlotta with the original manuscript of *Long Day's Journey Into Night* on July 22, 1941, their twelfth wedding anniversary. In his inscription he declared that it had been her love that had enabled him to face his dead and write about "the four haunted Tyrones."

O'Neill had chosen Tyrone to designate his surname because, steeped as he was in Gaelic history and intensely proud of his undiluted Irish blood, he knew the name was derived from Tir-eoghain, meaning the land of Owen. Owen, who died in A.D. 465, was the ancestor of the O'Neills who for centuries ruled over a section of Ulster, including the part that later became County Tyrone.

O'Neill did not bother to disguise the given names of his father and brother—James and James Jr.—but he called himself Edmund, which was the name of a brother who had died in infancy. And he called his mother, whom everyone had known as Ella Quinlan O'Neill, Mary Cavan Tyrone (Cavan also being the name of a county in Ulster).

Their story was, indeed, born of tears and blood and was the key to O'Neill's tragic outlook in life and art.

II

BOTH JAMES O'NEILL AND ELLA QUINLAN CAME FROM
Irish Catholic families that had immigrated in the frontier days to bustling
cities in Ohio. But that was all they had in common. James, dashing and
handsome, and Ella, shy and pretty, fell in love before realizing that
their outlooks clashed. Though jealously possessive, they were temperamentally unsuited. Like the warring protagonists in the plays their
son was to write, James and Ella became victims of a destructive incom-
patibility.

Ella was the pampered daughter of a middle-class family, which
provided her with a reasonable amount of culture and a higher education.
She leaned toward a mystic view of life, was reserved, a little spoiled,
romantic and innocent. It was difficult for her to make friends; her
shyness was often misconstrued as hauteur and tended to put people off.

James was an actor with no formal schooling, who had fought his
way up from poverty. He was gregarious, adaptable, materialistic, secure
in his Catholicism and, although self-centered, endowed with a charm
that made him universally loved.

Ella could never forgive James for exposing her to his rough-and-
tumble world; and he could not forgive her for the pride with which she
held aloof from that world. Yet each satisfied in the other a perverse
need to torment and pardon. They could express their love only in cycles
of punishment and reconciliation. The untranquil climate of their marriage
is the theme of *Long Day's Journey Into Night*. That play lays open
the wounds of their marriage, hammering at the accusations and guilty
withdrawals and pitiful, abortive attempts at mutual understanding,
insisting with nerve-racking emphasis on the quality and quantity of
their pain.

James and Mary Tyrone, the play's middle-aged couple who stand
for O'Neill's parents, are shown to be at once deeply in love and
irrevocably embattled; Mary still dwells on the fact that she has married
beneath her, out of helpless passion. Her frustration has driven her, long
since, to narcotics addiction. She talks in self-pitying monologues. She has
tried to understand James's ambition and his terror at being unable to

rise to and stay at the top, but she cannot excuse the effect it has had on her.

James, for his part, adores her, but writhes under her withdrawal and contempt. He has had to resign himself to caring for her as one would a child and salvaging the crumbs of their life.

Eugene O'Neill described the same kind of relationship in a much earlier play, in which the protagonists are frankly designated as Ella and Jim. In it Ella and Jim, both in their twenties, marry out of desperation. Each needs and clings to the other, though neither can give the other happiness or even peace. Ella considers herself Jim's superior by birth and background and Jim is forced to concede her superiority. Ella resents Jim's unrelenting fight to overcome his environment; she is furious at being dependent on him; and she is incapable of accepting his self-sacrifice and devotion to her. Jim cannot follow her behind the locked door of her disillusionment.

Jim and Ella literally drive each other insane but they do not let go. In the end Ella is reduced to a childlike state in which she talks to herself madly; Jim's hope of rising above the petty cruelties of life is crushed, and he resigns himself to being Ella's nurse.

"I can't leave her. She can't leave me," says Jim to his sister, who has asked why they don't separate. "And there's a million little reasons combining to make one big reason why we can't. For her sake—if it'd do her any good—I'd go—I'd leave—I'd do anything—because I love her . . . but that'd only make matters worse for her. I'm all she's got in the world! Yes, that isn't bragging or fooling myself. I know that for a fact! Don't you know it's true?"

It was a truth O'Neill understood and could hammer home. He did not bother, in this play, to disguise the true names of his parents for two reasons. The first was that they were both recently dead. The other was that Jim was a Negro and the play, on the surface, seemed to be a study of miscegenation, which no one could dream of relating to O'Neill's own family. The play was *All God's Chillun Got Wings*, written in 1923.

O'Neill never stopped writing of his mother and father. He always portrayed them as lovers communicating in code, neither ever able to find the other's key. Always alive to the intangible gap between his parents, he stated over and over in his plays the theme of man's tragic inability to reach his fellow man. One of the most heartfelt expressions of this theme is voiced by the hero of *The Great God Brown*, also written a few years after the death of his parents. In a scene O'Neill selected to represent the work he considered one of his "most interesting and moving," Dion Anthony, the hero he modeled largely on himself, mourns his parents:

"What aliens we were to each other! When [my father] lay dead, his face looked so familiar that I wondered where I had met that man before. Only at the second of my conception. After that, we grew hostile with concealed shame. And my mother? I remember a sweet, strange girl, with affectionate, bewildered eyes as if God had locked her in a dark closet without any explanation."

Eugene O'Neill's conception of his mother as a girl locked in a dark closet was influenced by *The Spook Sonata*, a play by August Strindberg, one of O'Neill's early literary heroes. In that terrifying drama a woman referred to as the Mummy actually lives in a closet and talks to her family like a parrot. Shortly after his mother's death O'Neill informed a close friend that she had lived in a room from which she had seldom ventured— that, in a way, she was like the Mummy.

Ella revealed herself to no one outside of her immediate family. Among the hundreds of friends and business associates with whom her husband brought her into contact—even among her relatives who spent summer after summer in the harbor resort of New London, Connecticut, where she and James had their only permanent home—there was no one who could say he really knew her. Relatives who survived her did not even know her actual given name; she had been christened Mary Ellen and was called by that name throughout her childhood.

At fifteen, when she went to boarding school, she dropped the Mary and became Ellen, a name she considered more glamorous. She remained Ellen to the time of her marriage (as indicated by her school records and marriage certificate). Some time after her marriage she assumed the name Ella, which she used on all later legal documents, including her will; that is the name engraved on her tombstone in New London.

It appears then that O'Neill used his mother's actual given name in *Long Day's Journey Into Night*, just as he used the real names of his father and brother. But he may not have done so in this case for the sake of biographical accuracy. For if he had wanted to identify Ella as unequivocally as he did his father and brother he would have used her adopted name, by which everyone, including her relatives, knew her. Psychiatrists to whom the point has been raised consider it likely that O'Neill tried to link his mother to the Virgin Mary, to stress symbolically her frustrated desire to have been a nun rather than a wife and mother. He was acutely conscious of his mother's conflict between the pure religious life that half-called her and the worldly one she led with her husband, but with which she could not come to terms.

Ella was born on Grand Avenue in New Haven, Connecticut, on August 13, 1857, at the height of a national financial panic. She was the daughter of Thomas Joseph and Bridget Lundigan Quinlan, who had both come from Ireland.

When Ella was born, her father was in his early thirties and her mother in her late twenties. Quinlan had established himself as a general storekeeper but he found the going difficult. Soon after the birth of his daughter he moved his family, which also included a son, William, to Ohio.

The Quinlans, like many immigrant Irish streaming into Ohio on their way west in pursuit of gold, were attracted by Cleveland. Although it was still reeling from the effects of a state-wide wave of bank failures, Cleveland seemed to offer more immediate opportunities than far-off California, for it was a beautiful lake port city and promised quick financial recovery. It had been joined only a few years before by railroad to Cincinnati, then the biggest city in the Midwest.

In Cleveland, Thomas Quinlan became a news dealer, and with the business boom provided by the Civil War he began to thrive. By 1867, when Ella was ten, Quinlan's business had expanded into a retail shop dealing in books, stationery, "fancy goods," bread, cakes and candies. The Quinlan family had reached respectable middle-class status. Quinlan accumulated a private library; he also bought a grand piano on which Ella, who showed an aptitude for music, was urged to take lessons. By the time Ella was thirteen, he had switched to the retail liquor and tobacco business and moved into a comfortable house in a good neighborhood.

During the next few years, through judicious investment in real estate and increased patronage of his shop, Quinlan became a man of substance. He brought up his children with all the cultural advantages that a prosperous businessman and a devoted father could provide. Holding firm convictions about his children's education, he encouraged his daughter to think she might eventually earn a living through playing and teaching piano. But he let his children know he was going to provide for them in his will, and gave Ella to understand that any independence she might achieve by mastery of the piano was to be a matter of moral satisfaction rather than financial necessity.

His plans for her must have been colored somewhat by wishful thinking, for Ella was not suited temperamentally to making her own way in life. No trace of the rugged adaptability that had brought her parents from Ireland could be found in her pliant personality or in her delicate features. Tall for her generation—about five feet six inches—and slender, she had a pale, smooth skin, large, dark-brown eyes, a wide, tremulous mouth, a high forehead, and long hair that was to change gradually from reddish to dark brown and which she often wore knotted at the back of her head. She had a quick, shy laugh, and a low-pitched voice.

Ella seemed best suited to take her place in Cleveland's well-bred society, probably as the wife of a dependable businessman like her own father. In addition to studying the piano she read the classics from her father's library and, at intervals, was taken by her father to the theatre. Like her friends, she was infatuated with the stock-company actors—and was thrilled by the passionate declamations of the great touring stars.

In September of 1872, when she was fifteen, she was sent to the convent of St. Mary, at Notre Dame in Indiana. Only very well-off families provided their daughters with a higher education, but Quinlan was prepared to give both his children every advantage. To ensure his plans for them he outlined his wishes in an explicit will less than two months after Ella left for the convent.

After bequeathing to his wife all his real and personal property (on condition that she remain unmarried "during the period of her natural life"), he reminded his children of his hopes for them by leaving to William his "Library of Printed Books" and to Mary Ellen his "One Piano Forte." (After her marriage, she moved this heirloom to her house in New London. It figures as an important off-stage prop in *Long Day's Journey Into Night*.)

Quinlan provided for his children in the event of his wife's re-marriage, and took further pains to secure their future in a codicil to his will, which reflected a certain lack of confidence in his wife:

"I devise that my children . . . while they are living with my wife . . . and before either of them shall attain their majority, that they each of them shall receive at the hands of my wife the same opportunities for education and self improvement, and be supported and clothed and treated as my wife knows and believes they would be treated by me and are treated by me now."

Quinlan concluded with a vigorous admonition:

"I also expect of and require from my children . . . that they each of them shall use the talents which they possess and the education which they may acquire to earn for themselves when they arrive at an age proper for them to do so an honest, honorable and independent liveli-hood, not relying upon their mother nor upon such share of the property as may descend to each after her demise nor before then."

Ella, who adored her father and was more attached to him than to her mother, gave every indication of living up to his wishes. She settled down at the convent, situated near the campus of Notre Dame, a boys' school that later became the university. St. Mary's was not at that time an accredited college. It did, however, offer instruction at the college level and since no American university of the period would admit women to its liberal arts courses, St. Mary's was popular not only among Catholics but also among Protestant and Jewish families. For her day and background, Ella was exposed to a cultural cross section.

Her studies, in addition to church history, dogma and catechism, included English, ethics, rhetoric, philosophy, astronomy, French, and courses in the theory and composition of music, as well as piano technique. In *Long Day's Journey Into Night* Mary Tyrone's contention that she could have been a successful pianist is sneered at by her husband: "The piano playing and her dream of becoming a concert pianist. That was put in her head by the nuns flattering her. She was their pet. They loved her for being so devout. They're innocent women . . . when it comes to the world. . . ."

Actually the nun who taught Ella piano was far from being the unworldly woman James imagined her. Her name (mentioned in *Long Day's Journey Into Night*) was Mother Elizabeth. A convert, Mother Elizabeth did not join the Sisters of the Holy Cross until after she became a widow. Born in England, she was descended from Dr. George Arnold, who had been organist at Winchester Cathedral under Queen Elizabeth; she was educated in Europe, was herself a fine pianist and was worldly enough to set the foundation, in 1850, for a music department at St. Mary's that was still adhered to by the college more than a hundred years later.

In Mother Elizabeth's judgment Ella was exceedingly talented. Mother Elizabeth also was astute enough to recognize in Ella a tendency toward self-dramatization. When Ella, who had evinced a strong interest in religion, spoke of wishing to become a nun, Mother Elizabeth knew this was more a romantic daydream than a serious intention and she hurt Ella's feelings by advising her to postpone her decision. Mother Elizabeth's intuition proved sound, for Ella was married just two years after her graduation from St. Mary's.

One of her schoolmates, Ella Nirdlinger, often spoke of her as a beautiful and pious girl to her son, George Jean Nathan, who later became one of the first drama critics to recognize Eugene O'Neill's talent. Another of Ella's classmates was Loretta Ritchie, of Pinckneyville, Illinois, who kept up a casual correspondence with Ella for many years. Ella wrote Loretta of bringing up her children in hotels and sometimes cradling them, as infants, in dresser drawers. Neither Loretta Ritchie nor Ella Nirdlinger snubbed Ella Quinlan when she married, although Ella's literary counterpart, Mary Tyrone, sadly recollects in *Long Day's Journey Into Night*, that after her marriage to an actor "all my old friends either pitied me or cut me dead."

In June, 1875, when Ella was eighteen, she was graduated with honors in music. She received a gold medal engraved with her name and garnered honors for politeness, neatness, order, amiability, and correct observance of the academic rules.

Although *Long Day's Journey Into Night* is biographically accurate in regard to most of the minutiae concerning Ella and James, a mystifying lapse occurs in connection with the description of their first meeting.

Eugene O'Neill has made it appear in the play that Ella was introduced to James by her father during the spring vacation of her senior year at St. Mary's, in 1876. Ella was actually in her senior year in 1875, but this error of a year is less noteworthy than the fact that Ella's father had died before the end of 1874. More interesting is the reference in the play to Quinlan's participation in his daughter's wedding plans, particularly the mention of his purchase of an elaborate wedding dress for her, when, in fact, the wedding took place more than three years after his death. O'Neill deliberately altered the facts to heighten Ella's tragedy. She becomes a more poignant victim when she is thrust into James's harum-scarum theatrical world directly from the sheltering home of her father.

But while O'Neill took license with these details, it is true that Ella's father did become acquainted with James O'Neill in 1871 or 1872. James, at that time, was the leading man at Cleveland's celebrated theatre, the Academy of Music. Quinlan's shop on Superior Avenue was just a block and a half from the theatre, which stood between Superior and St. Clair avenues, in the heart of Cleveland's business district.

Members of the acting troupe visited the shop and it was there that Quinlan and James struck up an acquaintance based on their common Irish ancestry. It was the custom for leading businessmen of the community to befriend actors of prominence; many of the touring stars, who were products of stock companies, could boast of friends in every town on their itinerary; this often made their travels more pleasant, for their local friends could be counted on to wine, dine and even house them during their engagements.

Ella, as a girl of fifteen, met James, who was then twenty-six, in her father's home and developed a schoolgirl's crush on him. But Ella enrolled in the convent in the fall of 1872, about the same time that James left

Cleveland for McVicker's Stock Company in Chicago. While Ella may have dreamed of James and talked to her friends about him, and even imagined herself his wife (when she was not imagining herself a nun), James did not give her a serious thought at that time. During the next three or four years, which he spent in Chicago and San Francisco, James was conducting a fairly hectic love life; it was not until he came to New York in 1876 that he again met Ella—and this time decided he had found his true love.

Their courtship had come about after Ella had spent some months in Cleveland following her graduation and decided that life was pallid there without her father's stimulating presence. She reminded her mother of his wishes, and Bridget agreed to take Ella to New York, where she had relatives, and to let her enroll for advanced studies in music.

Mother and daughter arrived there early in 1876; substantial checks drawn on Quinlan's estate followed them periodically. When James reached New York to fill an acting engagement in the fall of 1876, Ella persuaded a male relative of Bridget's to take her to see him backstage, using James's former acquaintance with her father as an excuse. She had not forgotten her schoolgirl daydreams, and was already half in love with him.

III

JAMES O'NEILL, AT THIRTY, WAS AN IRRESISTIBLY romantic figure. While he was not much taller than Ella—he sometimes wore high-heeled boots on stage to increase his five feet eight inches—he had a compact, well-balanced figure, graceful carriage and nobility of bearing that more than compensated for his lack of physical stature. His hair was black and curled over a high forehead; his eyes were melting and almost as dark as Ella's, but they looked at the world more candidly and could burn with passion. His nose and chin followed classically chiseled lines; his even, white teeth gleamed against a dark complexion, and his lilting voice was a caress. In contrast to Ella's shyness, James's manner was open and sunny. He was a tireless and effective raconteur.

Although James was self-conscious about his lack of formal education, the life he had led made him far more worldly and sophisticated than Ella. He had the easy confidence of a man who knew he could charm the birds out of the trees.

On the stage he added to his natural endowments (aside from high heels) a swashbuckling manner, heroic gestures and a carefully acquired skill with a rapier. These characteristics were perfectly suited to the extravagant melodramas of the era and to the virtuoso recitals of Shakespearean roles for which the public had an endless appetite.

In addition, James had already begun to develop the controlled, melodious voice that could penetrate to the gallery of the huge theatres in which he played. He jokingly referred to his voice as "my organ." He had taught himself the trick of increasing its volume while actually raising it only two or three notes in pitch. In this way he was able to convey fiery emotion without shouting, which set him apart from the stock actors who resorted to ranting.

In 1876 there seemed to be no question that James would rise to the top of his profession. In theatre circles it was predicted that he might succeed Edwin Booth, who was fourteen years his senior. Booth, one of the three American actors who achieved international fame during the nineteenth century (the others were Edwin Forrest and Joseph Jefferson), was considered by many to be the greatest actor of his era.

Beneath the personal warmth that attracted people to James lay a ruthlessness that often characterizes the successful actor. He possessed the slightly inhuman capacity to sweep aside any involvement that might hinder the pursuit of his art. His artistic temperament told him, without his having to analyze it, that if he did not put the advancement of his career before any other consideration he would founder.

As an actor, James belonged first to his profession, and spent himself completely on his audience. But while there was a certain glory in this dedication and an intoxication in the mass worship he inspired, there was also an emptiness. James tried to fill it by drinking. He always kept a bottle in his dressing room and sometimes drained it in a day. He carried his whiskey well, however, and rarely showed signs of its effect, except for a brilliant sparkle in his eyes. Certainly it did not hurt his acting nor did it in any way hinder his career.

The theatre of the day, in which James had been steadily rising for the past seven years, was a national institution that approximated in popularity the motion-picture industry during the 1930's and 1940's. There was scarcely a city that did not support its own resident stock company, with the larger cities supporting two or more. The local companies created their own favorites and in such cities as New York, San Francisco and Chicago it was possible for individual stock company actors to gain enormous local popularity without necessarily attaining national prominence. When famous touring stars visited these cities, the major stock players dropped temporarily into supporting roles.

In an era when leading players in stock companies ruled the public emotions in the same way that movie heroes later would, James O'Neill was sighed over and dreamed about. A Chicago newspaper writer once recalled, in a typical article about him: "Chicago adored James O'Neill. Girls built romances about his private life, some with substantial foundation. . . . One was that the leading lady of McVicker's Stock Company was hopelessly in love with the dashing James and that it grieved him sore not to be able to return her purple passion. Droves of girls went every week just to see the heroine droop and wilt when Jimmy kissed her."

James was a boon to stock company managers, whose prime concern was to elicit waves of emotion from their audiences. Audience response was then a much more tangible quality than it is in today's relatively polite and intimate theatre, and managers went to considerable pains to measure it. Sometimes a manager would sit in an upper box and face the audience during initial performances of a play, to test the potency of the "shock waves" passing from viewer to stage. The play would be doctored on the basis of those waves. If all went well, bursts of applause and cheers would be spontaneously wrung at frequent intervals from the playgoers, who became almost painfully involved in the emotions of the actors and did not wait to applaud politely at the lowering of the curtain. The applause after a scene was occasionally so prolonged that the stars had to acknowledge it by taking bows between acts.

The impact of James's personality and reputation on Ella was devastating. She was hypnotized by the glamour and magic that surrounded him.

Her mother, however, was not overjoyed by the prospect of having James for a son-in-law. The fact that it was Thomas Quinlan who had first introduced James to Ella did not help Bridget feel resigned, even though James seemed to be an upright Irishman and a good Catholic. While it was considered permissible for fashionable families to lionize a prominent actor, a member of the theatrical profession was not held to be a sound matrimonial prospect for a cherished daughter. Even the best of actors led nomadic lives and were subject to financial hazards, and a number of them were known to be philanderers and heavy drinkers. Scandals in their private and professional lives were followed with shivering pleasure in the newspapers. First-class hotels would seldom accommodate actors because of their habit of jumping their rent when, as often happened, their shows closed unexpectedly and left them stranded and unpaid.

Bridget recognized the fact, which Ella ignored, that a sheltered upbringing and refined taste were not adequate equipment for an actor's wife; actors traveled from town to town, often under primitive conditions; and Ella could hardly find herself at home among the rugged troupers who were James's friends and formed almost his whole world. It was not the sort of life that either Bridget or her husband had envisioned for their daughter, and she pointed this out to Ella. But Ella was carried away by the idea of being the wife of James O'Neill and, summoning an uncharacteristic tenacity and resolution, she determined to marry him.

As for James, nothing at this point in his life seemed impossible. He was as determined as Ella to marry and was as confident as she that within a short time he would stand in the front rank of his profession. That he could have deluded himself into believing Ella would make him a suitable wife or a reasonably happy one is even harder to understand than Ella's blind confidence. He was under no romantic illusions about the discomforts of touring and he was certainly aware that Ella could not adapt cheerfully to the wandering life of an actor.

Perhaps the fact that, by the social standards of the day, she was unattainable made the conquest seem sweeter to his ambitious nature. Marrying Ella represented another break with his squalid background. And unquestionably he was captivated by her beauty and innocence, to a point where rational planning became difficult. There was also the incentive of Ella's financial independence; it was not, perhaps, a major factor, but it could help smooth their way.

With the promise of a brilliant future and the conquest of Ella's heart, James had grown a long way from the shabby boy with the thick Kilkenny brogue who had landed with his parents in America early in 1856. His family were what F. Scott Fitzgerald, speaking of his own forebears, once described as "strictly potato-famine Irish," but James would never have acknowledged this fact publicly. In a loquacious and mellow mood, three years before his death in 1920, he gave a lyrical account of his beginnings:

"It was Kilkenny—smiling Kilkenny . . . where I was born one opal-tinted day in October, 1847." (His son Eugene, many years later, pointed out that "like all actors, he cut his age for publication." Actually, he was born October 14, 1846.)

"I beg leave to think," James continued, "that were I permitted to choose a birthplace for any Irishman's child, be he dreamy-eyed son of Erin with star fire in his heart or laughing gossoon with song on his lip and roguery in his eye, 'twould be that same little town in old Leinster."

James was nine, the fourth of six children (three boys and three girls), when his father, Edward, a struggling farmer, and his mother, Mary, arrived at Buffalo in upstate New York. James had outgrown his "skirties," but his younger siblings were still wearing the red flannel garments in which Irish peasant women dressed their children, to prevent them from being abducted by malevolent fairies.

Like the Quinlans, the O'Neills soon left their first landing place and pushed west to Ohio. It was in the same year that the Quinlans arrived in Cleveland—1857—that the O'Neills settled in Cincinnati, about a four-hour train ride away. Unlike the Quinlans, however, the O'Neills did not prosper, although Cincinnati was then the undisputed industrial center of the West. Edward O'Neill was a mystic; soon after his arrival, in response to an ethereal summons from his Celtic ancestors, who warned him of his impending death, he abandoned his family and returned to Ireland, where he died a short time later.

The two older brothers left home (one later joined an Ohio regiment and was killed in the Civil War) and James became the family's mainstay. His life was bleak, but in no instance during the many times he was asked to contribute his reminiscences to various publications did he more than hint at the actual horror of his early existence. By contrast with his son, James was inclined—publicly at least—to imbue life with the gallant optimism and rather conventional pride that had always made him loved and respected outside his family. The views of both father and son were distorted and dramatically heightened by their strangely disparate temperaments.

For example, Eugene O'Neill's impression of his father's boyhood is contained in the lines he wrote for James Tyrone in *Long Day's Journey Into Night*:

"It was at home I first learned . . . the fear of the poorhouse. . . . There was no damned romance in our poverty. Twice we were evicted from the miserable hovel we called home. . . . I cried, though I tried hard not to, because I was the man of the family. At ten years old! There was no more school for me. I worked twelve hours a day in a machine shop. . . . A dirty barn of a place where rain dripped through the roof, where you roasted in summer, and there was no stove in winter, and your hands got numb with cold, where the only light came through two small filthy windows . . . I got . . . fifty cents a week! And my poor mother washed and scrubbed for the Yanks by day and my older sister sewed. . . . We never had clothes enough to wear, nor food enough to eat."

This was true as far as it went, but it was only part of the story. James O'Neill's own romanticized version presents a startling contrast:

"I tried many kinds of work after my father died. I was a newsboy for one day." (He had been hoodwinked into buying a bundle of day-old papers for twenty cents, and barely escaped being turned over to a policeman by his first customer. James thought this was funny.) "Then I was apprenticed to a machinist. Somehow, the clank of iron, the ring of the hammer, the heavy glow of the forge seemed unattuned to the romance of Kilkenny's mossy towers, where walked the shadowy ghosts of Congreve, and Bishop Berkeley, of Dean Swift and Farquhar—Irishmen all, who wore their college gowns in and out of the grassy quadrangle of the venerable seat of learning that is Kilkenny's boast. . . . And so three or four years went along, careless young years, when spare evenings were spent poring over a Shakespeare given me by an elder sister, of losing myself in the land of romance at the theatre where I was an established gallery god."

While the "careless young years" were largely the figment of a mellow imagination, James's lot did improve more than one is led to believe by *Long Day's Journey Into Night*. His sister made a reasonably good marriage when James was fourteen and her husband, who had settled in Norfolk, Virginia, sent for him.

The Civil War had begun. James's brother-in-law did a brisk business in military uniforms. James, who participated, earned a good salary and was rewarded with an instructor provided by his brother-in-law. "For three years I worked in the store all day and studied with my tutor in the evening," James once recalled. "He was a man of liberal tastes, and, liking the theatre, he took me with him twice a week to see the plays. It was then that I formed my taste for the theatre. When the war was over my brother-in-law sold out his business and moved back to Cincinnati, and I went with him. Having saved a little money I tried to go into several small businesses, but was not successful. I found my money going and wondered what I should do."

This account is a relatively sober one for James. In most cases he preferred to embellish. Just three years before his death he was still giving an imaginatively colored story of his beginnings. Describing his introduction to the stage, he wrote:

"I believe I had a subconscious assurance—the promise of a sublime—possibly a ridiculous faith—that I should be an actor one day, although no possibility seemed more remote. However, what's an Irish lad without his dream? And so I carried mine along with me cherishing it."

Many years earlier, however, in writing to A. M. Palmer, a New York theatre manager with whom he had a long association, James prosaically, and no doubt honestly, informed him that he had "drifted to the stage without interest."

"I was fond enough of the playhouse," he added, "and had the curiosity, common among boys, to have a peep behind the scenes so that I took an opportunity to go on as one of the lads in the last act of 'The Colleen Bawn,' which was being played at the National in Cincinnati, Ohio. I began the thing as a lark, but the stage manager prevailed on me to remain."

That was on October 17, 1867, when James was twenty-one. Elaborating on the occasion of his debut, James once recorded: "One evening I was spending the hour before the theatre door should open in a game of billiards with a friend, when there rushed hurriedly into the room a chap named Cooper, who was captain of supers at the old National Theatre. 'What's the matter, Cooper?' asked my friend. . . . 'Confound it,' muttered that functionary, 'my supers have gone on strike and there are no guests for the ball in "The Colleen Bawn." ' 'I'll go if you'll go,' challenged my friend and I in one breath, and Cooper eagerly accepted our offer, directed us how to find the wardrobe man, and fled to find other guests."

The Colleen Bawn, described by critics of the era as a "natural Irish comedy," had been written in 1860 by the prolific and immensely popular Irish playwright-actor, Dion Boucicault, who had completed his first successful play before he was twenty. The Irish in James must have leaped at the chance to participate in this sturdy vehicle. If, before this event, James had been only halfheartedly interested in a theatrical career, there is no doubt that his first brush with grease paint exhilarated him, and from that day on he conceived of no other career for himself than acting.

James stayed on at the National, was paid twenty-five cents nightly and later was promoted to captain of the "supers" and general utility man. His most impressive experience of stage fright occurred during a performance of *Metamora,* in which Edwin Forrest was starring. Forrest, the first of the great actors to cross James's path, had a powerful physique, a voice like a trumpet, a violent temper and a monumental ego that helped to make him one of the most controversial figures of the American stage. He had been for forty years a tremendously popular Shakespearean actor, but he was now nearly sixty and was soon to end his career, a rejected and bitter man.

Suffering from rheumatism, he had emerged from retirement a few years earlier, after a divorce scandal. The play Forrest had chosen to present at the National was written for him in 1829 by a young playwright named John Augustus Stone. Its hero, a bombastic American Indian chief, suited Forrest's acting style. In his repertory for thirty-six years, *Metamora* had brought Forrest a fortune, but, because he had bought the play outright from its author, Stone never received a penny in royalties.

Still imposing despite his years, Forrest was met by enthusiastic audiences at the National.

"When Edwin Forrest came along," James once wrote, "I was entrusted with the part of The Flying Messenger. I rushed on but stuck at the important part." James survived this experience and moved on to bigger, but not always better, things. For the next four years he served his apprenticeship in the theatre, traveling to St. Louis; back to Cincinnati; then to Baltimore, Maryland; Augusta, Georgia; and Washington, D.C.

James soon found himself playing such roles as Hotspur and Macbeth —with the inconsistent brogue that no one had yet thought to bring to his attention.

It was with a stock company in Washington that James supported the second of the trio of great American actors—Joseph Jefferson. Jefferson, who had been acting for thirty-six of his forty years, brought *Rip Van Winkle* to the capital, and James was cast in the substantial role of the young sailor, Heinrich. Dramatized by Boucicault from Washington Irving's story in 1865, the play, with numerous alterations provided by Jefferson, was to be a staple of the road for forty years and was forever to be identified with Jefferson, as he was with it.

James was panic-stricken when Jefferson sent for him at the close of the first performance. He was sure he was about to be picked apart, but Jefferson, smiling genially, waved James to a chair in his dressing room.

"My boy," said Jefferson, "you got six rounds of applause tonight, and that is good. Very good. But there are eight rounds in the part and we must get them."

Then the man James later described as "the kindest and finest of men and of actors" showed him the points where the rounds of applause might be elicited and carefully explained why they had not been forthcoming. "A lesson in acting money could not have bought," James said.

At the next performance he tried to follow Jefferson's advice, but nervousness made him stumble, so that he received only seven rounds of applause.

"Better, my boy, better," was Jefferson's comment. After that, James received the full eight.

At the conclusion of Jefferson's stint with the company, he praised James's acting and encouraged him to study. James was emboldened to ask Jefferson for a list of books that would help improve his technique.

"Shakespeare first, for breadth and depth and height of thought and fancy," said Jefferson, "and for insight into human nature read all the standard old comedies."

Jefferson's advice "unlocked the treasures of the old masters of the stage," James recalled. (He had already devoted considerable time to Shakespeare and knew some of the plays by heart.) "Congreve and Farquhar (Kilkenny bred, both) and along down the line to those other Irishmen Goldsmith and his brilliant young disciple Richard Brinsley Sheridan—I devoured them all—and Dion Boucicault too—together with every French and German comedy I could find."

James's next noteworthy engagement—in 1871—was as leading man at John Ellsler's Academy of Music in Cleveland, where Ellsler and his wife were popular local performers. Ellsler had been a partner of Jefferson and coached him in the dialect for *Rip Van Winkle*. His Academy, at the height of its fame when James arrived, was a three-story brick building, equipped with a vast stage that was hung with red plush curtains. Gas footlights provided the stage lighting, while a huge chandelier illuminated the auditorium; its hundreds of china candles were laboriously lighted every evening from one of the theatre's boxes with a long taper. Many of the top stars made the Academy a regular stop, and the Ellslers did excellent business, charging the customary admission of one dollar for orchestra seats and twenty-five cents for the gallery.

James was now twenty-four. Managers were beginning to acknowledge his magnetic effect on audiences and to cast him in the sort of romantic roles that would hypnotize the ladies into devoted attendance. A Cleveland reporter, recalling James's popularity at the Academy of Music, wrote years later: "He was the patron saint of the matinee girls. He was the ideal of the town—this curly-haired, robust, handsome young Irishman."

James played most of the romantic heroes of the era's melodramas, and as many Shakespearean roles as he could muster. During his first season with the Ellslers he again appeared with Edwin Forrest. This time Forrest was at the end of his career. After a disappointing reception in San Francisco, he had taken to the road again, avoiding most of the bigger cities, where he knew he was no longer welcome. Heretofore jealous of anyone who showed talent, he now realized he was hopelessly out of the running and allowed himself, for once, to take an objective view of another actor's ability. He went so far as to say of James to his own dresser: "If that young man manages to forget his brogue, he is going to make a capital actor." The remark was reported to James, who never forgot it. He immediately set to work on the offending brogue.

Other stars passed through Cleveland, many of them at the top of their success, and James held his own, even when playing the title role of *Macbeth* opposite Charlotte Cushman, whose Lady Macbeth was one of the most formidable interpretations of the era. The deep-voiced Miss Cushman, who preferred to play Hamlet and Romeo and who cordially disliked most men, was so charmed by James that she took the trouble to coach him in the role of Macbeth. She predicted a brilliant future for him, if he would "work, work, work!"

In those days an actor who had less than fifty parts—including the major Shakespearean ones and numerous of the contemporary melodramas and farces—in his repertory was looked upon with scorn. James, by now, had acquired the requisite number. He had also learned, with practice, to suppress the richer part of his brogue, although it still had a tendency to trip him up in impassioned scenes. His reputation had spread as far west as Chicago, where J. H. McVicker ran one of the country's leading theatres. At the time it was outranked only by Wallack's in New York, considered the best theatre in the United States, and Mrs. Drew's Arch Street Theatre in Philadelphia. James accepted McVicker's proposal to star for ten weeks at the head of the stock company, after which he would support a succession of touring stars. Chicago was recovering from the effects of its fire of the year before, and the fever of reconstruction seemed to serve as a stimulus to theatrical activity; McVicker's audiences were loyal.

At McVicker's James met Edwin Booth for the first time. Booth, then thirty-nine, was at the height of his popularity as a Shakespearean actor. He had a superb stage presence enhanced by an artfully modulated voice. He wore his dark hair long, and he had a thin, sensitive face with deep-set eyes. A number of years after Booth's death, James reminisced about his idol: "Booth as a young man was the handsomest actor I have ever seen on the stage. He was the picture of manly beauty. Not only all women, but men, as well, were enthusiastic over Booth's personal charm."

Having weathered a difficult youth, during which he was obliged to act as a guardian and buffer for his eccentric father, the famous actor Junius Brutus Booth, young Edwin had developed as a first-rate performer in his own right. He had overcome a tendency toward alcoholism, recovered from the death of his first wife, for which he blamed himself in part, and emerged from the retirement into which his brother's assassination of Lincoln had plunged him. James was as taken with Booth's personal dignity as with his intellectual, low-key acting style.

A Chicago newspaper, summing up James's development as an actor toward the close of his engagement at McVicker's, said: "Most of all did he become the pattern of Edwin Booth. So keenly did he study Booth that he copied even his defects in mannerisms. He dressed like him, posed like him, and finally came to speak like him." Concluding on a mixed note of flattery and caution, the article declared that "after the study of a year, he is the equal of some stars and the superior of many more," but warned James to develop his own style and not carry imitation too far.

Ironically, James was to come much closer to emulating Booth's tragic personal life than his triumphant professional one. Booth had taken as his second wife Mary McVicker, daughter of J. H. McVicker; like Ella Quinlan, Mary had been a student at St. Mary's Academy (she was about seven years older than Ella). She had attempted to become an actress, but her stage career was no more successful than her marriage. After several years of disillusionment, she became insane. She was to die at thirty-one, leaving Booth with one more unhappy memory to add to his collection of personal disasters.

James admired Booth's fortitude and reticence in the face of tragedy. Perhaps the memory of Booth's courageous resignation helped sustain James later when he was faced with a comparable situation in his own life.

"Booth was not only the greatest actor without a doubt the world has ever seen, but the noblest man the stage has produced," James once said. "It is hard to tell how lovable he was personally, how high minded and lofty was his purpose and how pure his character, but we who knew him intimately will always reverence him above all other men we ever met in life."

Booth gave James an unprecedented professional opportunity, which, in detailed accuracy even as to the date, Eugene O'Neill has recorded in *Long Day's Journey Into Night*. The speaker is James Tyrone:

[26]

"In 1874 when Edwin Booth came to the theatre in Chicago where I was leading man, I played Cassius to his Brutus one night, Brutus to his Cassius the next, Othello to his Iago, and so on. The first night I played Othello, he said to our manager, 'That young man is playing Othello better than I ever did!' That from Booth, the greatest actor of his day or any other! And it was true! And I was only twenty-seven years old! As I look back on it now, that night was the high spot in my career."

The switching of leading roles from night to night was a custom often followed when two stars of equal stature appeared together for a run. But as James was nowhere near Booth in importance, this particular occurrence was extraordinary. Booth had not intended to include *Othello* in his repertory at McVicker's at all, but the Chicago press had challenged him by predicting that he would not dare play the role in the wake of the Italian tragedian, Tommaso Salvini, who had acted *Othello* just a week or two before. *Othello* was Salvini's most famous portrayal and audiences on both sides of the Atlantic had been electrified by the terror with which he could fill a stage. Salvini was a giant of a man who believed in steeping himself so thoroughly in a role that it became almost an inseparable part of his personality; he used to terrify his Desdemonas by the realistic ferocity with which he attacked them during the strangling scene.

Booth could not overlook the challenge. He promptly announced *Othello* for the first week. Rivalry among stars was part of the theatrical tradition, with the public gleefully participating. Animosity between players could reach destructive heights; many people could still recall the Astor Place riot of 1849, which had been the result of a feud between Edwin Forrest and the English tragedian William Charles Macready. Forrest blamed Macready for his having been hissed during a performance of *Macbeth* in England. He retaliated by attending Macready's performance of *Hamlet* and hissing his rival. Theatre patrons in both countries were shocked by the incident, and when Macready visited America, outraged supporters of both stars fought a bloody battle in and around New York's Astor Place Opera House, where Macready was playing *Hamlet*. Forrest was considered by many to be morally responsible for the riot, which resulted in twenty-two deaths and several hundred injured.

Tempers were not so volatile in 1874, and Booth adopted a peaceful means of putting his rival in his place.

"He could not only play the part of Othello as well as Salvini," James later told a Boston journalist, "but he could do something which Salvini would never attempt—he could play Iago." There was more truth in the latter statement than in the former; theatre historians who classify Booth's Hamlet and Iago among the greatest ever seen have described his Othello as overintellectualized and lacking in passion.

But James was loyal to his idol. Continuing his reminiscence, he said: "And so after one performance in the title role, Mr. Booth determined to appear the next night in the latter character, and I was cast for Othello. I was in a quandary. I knew that everyone who would be in the house that night would know me; that nearly all of them would have seen Salvini and Booth, and that they would expect me to fail. To imitate either one or the other of the well-known actors too closely would be bad policy; yet how to introduce something original puzzled me. It came like a flash at the last rehearsal."

James said nothing to the other members of the cast about the innovation he planned for the evening performance. Actors seldom bothered with such formalities, for there was no director to keep them in line; co-ordinated performances of the classics were a rarity.

Productions of Shakespeare were individual tours de force. The star, if he was so inclined, might "direct" other members of the cast, but usually he was too preoccupied with his own strategy for wringing response from the audience to pay attention to his supporting company. Rehearsals were sketchy, the star withholding anything resembling a performance until actually playing before a paid audience. His supporting players followed suit, with the result that each performer took a stance and declaimed his big speeches oblivious to the rest of the cast. How he gestured, how he moved, how he intoned was determined by him alone. Audiences came to see their idols go through their paces—not to see ensembles interpreting a play.

The attention given to scenery and costumes also was negligible by modern standards. If the canvas was richly painted and the decorations lavish and ornate, the scenery drew good notices from the press; it was of minor significance whether the background furthered the mood of the play or whether it was appropriate to its period or place. The costumes were a matter of individual taste; each player provided his own, without regard for authenticity of period or location; it was enough to look elegant.

In the romantic melodramas that alternated in stock repertories with the classics, however, there was often more stress on the mechanics of the scenery than on the ability of the actors. These were the action-packed thrillers that foreshadowed the movies, boasting shipwrecks and near drownings in ocean waves (lumpy canvas groundcloths manipulated from below), raging fires (strips of red and yellow cloth, fanned from the wings), and howling snowstorms (barrels of confetti sprinkled from the flies). The stage manager co-ordinated the action; but just as long as the players drowned, scorched and shivered on cue, they could do the rest of their business as they saw fit.

James was merely following established procedure when he privately decided on the bit of business that was to distinguish his Othello. The cast was going through the third scene of the third act on the afternoon before the performance.

"Of course, this is your scene, O'Neill," Booth said magnanimously. "I will be at the side here whenever you want me. And, by the way, O'Neill, I wouldn't wear the sword in that scene if I were you. You will find that it is in your way and that it hampers your movements, while at the same time you will not need it."

The sword in question was an ornament James had acquired during his early barnstorming days. It was an ancient scimitar, and James had never had occasion to draw it from its decorated scabbard. Going offstage, he now tried to pull it out; it came only halfway and then clanged back, as he had anticipated. He decided it suited his purpose. He wore the sword that evening when he went on for the scene. Sidling across the stage toward Booth, he uttered the lines:

> If thou dost slander her and torture me,
> Never pray more; abandon all remorse;
> On horror's head horrors accumulate;
> Do deeds to make heaven weep, all earth amaz'd;
> For nothing canst thou to damnation add
> Greater than that.

James approached Booth, his sword half drawn. When Booth gave his answering lines, James sprang his surprise.

"Nay, stay:—thou shouldst be honest," he said menacingly, and let go of the sword hilt. The sound reverberated through the theatre. The audience, so knowledgeable it could be enchanted by even such a minute innovation, nearly fell out of its seats in its effort to applaud James. Booth called O'Neill back onstage to take extra bows.

"The scene is yours," said Booth. "You couldn't have done it better." To James's relief, Booth never mentioned the brazen disregard of his advice.

Tricks like these were not, however, the sole basis on which James won the hearts of Chicago audiences. He had a genuine flair for Shakespeare that earned their respect. Reviewing a performance of *Othello* in which Booth again assumed the title role and James played Iago, a local critic wrote: "Mr. O'Neill's Iago is deserving of warm encomium. It has some of the care that has always marked the star he supported."

A letter to a Chicago newspaper, written by a playgoer in the early 1900's and preserved by James in a scrapbook he kept, illustrates the power he wielded over audiences in that city. Recalling one night when James was playing Macduff to Booth's Macbeth, during the star's tenure at McVicker's, the letter writer said:

"The house was packed to the doors and when Macduff announced the foul murder, the curtain went down on a war of applause, which continued until Mr. Booth stepped before the curtain—when, all at once, the applause ceased. Mr. Booth walked across the stage from left to right and disappeared. Then the applause was renewed in tones of thunder. Men and women stood up, waving their handkerchiefs and crying, 'O'Neill, O'Neill!' This applause and shouting were deafening. O'Neill came before the footlights, blushing like a boy. The audience had no desire to say to Mr. Booth by their applause that they did not appreciate his great acting. But they did want Mr. O'Neill to know that his fine acting had highly registered. The writer of this letter has witnessed performances of all the great actors, from Edwin Booth to the present day. But he never has witnessed greater acting than James O'Neill's, on the occasion herein mentioned."

It was at McVicker's also that James played Romeo to the Juliet of Adelaide Nielson, probably the only leading lady of whom Ella ever felt a twinge of jealousy. The English-born Adelaide was the loveliest Juliet on either side of the Atlantic. She was twenty-six when she began her triumphant tour of the United States, and her reputation for beauty and mystery had preceded her across the ocean. She was said to have been born out of wedlock and to have supported herself as a factory worker, a nursemaid and a seamstress. Her personal reticence amounted to myth, but it was believed a prominent Englishman had helped her financially while she studied for the stage.

James was impressed but not overawed by the privilege of supporting the exquisite actress, and even played a flirtatious practical joke on her one night.

Instead of letting his head sink to his chest in the death scene, screening his face from the audience, he held his head back, with his face in full view. He knew that Miss Nielson could not fake her kiss without being obvious. She was obliged to give him, as he put it, "a kiss of the sterling variety."

Flustered by the experience, Miss Nielson reproachfully fixed James with her beautiful eyes when the curtain came down.

"How could you? How could you?" she cried.

"How could I what?" asked James, trying to suppress his glee.

"How, how—how could Romeo throw his head back when he was dead?" Miss Nielson asked lamely.

James always had a chivalrous answer for a pretty girl. "Miss Nielson," he said, "your Juliet was the cause of it. It would make anyone come back to life."

At the close of her engagement she begged James to accompany her on the rest of her tour, which, James recalled laconically, "I did not do." But Miss Nielson, not offended, remembered James's Romeo for a long time. In England some years later she was asked to name her finest Romeo. A list of distinguished actors was rejected. "The greatest Romeo I ever played with," she finally said, "was a little curly-haired Irishman. When I played with other Romeos, I thought they would climb up the trellis to the balcony; but when I played with Jimmy O'Neill, I wanted to climb down the trellis, into his arms."

On the strength of his conquests at McVicker's James had received an offer from a rival Chicago company. He joined Richard Hooley, who had managed to make himself an enormously respected cultural force in that city. Hooley had offered him a larger salary and the promise of playing Hamlet, Othello, Shylock, Romeo and other Shakespearean roles on Saturday nights. In addition, James himself was to form the company. For Hooley he assembled a talented troupe which included an actress named Louise Hawthorne. Louise was beautiful onstage, but without her heavy make-up she could not conceal a scar that ran from her temple to her chin. Though married, she appeared to have more than a platonic affection for James. He respected her acting ability, and needed her in his company, and he did not rebuff her. When, after playing successfully in Chicago for one season, Hooley's troupe moved on to San Francisco in May of 1875, she eagerly accepted James's invitation to go along.

San Francisco flourished as a national theatrical center almost as great as New York. The Comstock Lode, miraculously rich in silver, had been discovered in nearby Nevada some years before. There was scarcely anyone in San Francisco who did not feel a sense of participation, however illusory, in its profitable annual yield; the city's busy theatres reflected the inflationary times and Hooley's company scored a hit. Almost immediately San Franciscans took James to their hearts.

In the late winter of 1875-76 James received an offer to join a top-notch stock company in New York the following season—an invitation he had been waiting for. Louise was not included in the invitation, nor did James tender her a personal one. Hurt by his indifference, she made her last appearance with James in a play called *Ultimo,* in March, 1876.

Two months later a "Grand Farewell Benefit" was given for James in San Francisco. Such affairs were frequently arranged in honor of leading members of a stock company. Salaries were often paid on an irregular basis, determined by the amount of money left in the box office after the star had collected his often piratical guarantee and on how honorable the manager happened to be. The proceeds from a successful benefit, therefore, sometimes represented the only substantial income of a stock actor's entire engagement; without this cash he was hard put to keep up his stage wardrobe, let alone appearances. James, who knew how to be frugal and took every precaution to avoid the impoverishment that was a hazard of his profession, needed the benefit less than most of his fellow actors. But he did not decline the honor or the cash.

Although the other members of James's company participated in the farewell tribute, Louise was conspicuously absent. She had returned to Chicago. James left San Francisco for Chicago late that spring. He was to make his New York debut in October with the A. M. Palmer stock company at its Union Square Theatre, but was to join the company on tour in Chicago.

James was not entirely happy about this arrangement. When he reached Chicago, Louise attempted to resume her affair with him, as he had feared she would. Her unreciprocated love for James caused her, on June 27, to throw herself from a window of the Tremont House and she was instantly killed.

Shaken by the tragedy, James had to cope with yet another threatening entanglement. There was a second woman in Chicago, very much alive and extremely interested in James's activities, whose existence made the city a hazardous place for him to be. The woman, whom James knew as Nettie Walsh, called herself Mrs. James O'Neill and was the mother of a two-year-old boy whose paternity she attributed to James—a charge that James could not, with any degree of confidence, deny.

IV

JAMES WOULD HAVE PREFERRED TO BRUSH ASIDE THE
fact of Nettie Walsh's existence. A singularly insensitive woman, she
showed no inclination to help James tidy up his complicated love life, as
the considerate Louise Hawthorne had done. She continued to demand a
certain amount of attention from James, on the strength of having lived
with him for nearly four years and having, as she claimed, borne him a
child.

She had met James in 1871, when he went to Cleveland to act for
Ellsler, and when, by her account, she was only fifteen (the same age as
Ella) and "wholly inexperienced in the ways of the world." In fact, they
were living together during the time James was cultivating Thomas Quinlan's friendship. None of the Quinlans, however, had an inkling that
James was keeping a fifteen-year-old mistress in Cleveland; James always
knew how to conceal the unsavory aspects of his personal life.

James provided Nettie with worldly experience until he left for San
Francisco in 1875. She had been a willing student during those four years,
despite her knowledge that James was simultaneously enriching the experience of Louise Hawthorne. Nettie also pursued other amatory interests
and James saw no reason for acknowledging paternity of the child, born to
her in 1872. With apparently no twinge of conscience he had left Nettie
in Chicago and taken Louise with him to San Francisco.

When James returned to Chicago after his San Francisco triumph he
made some cautious inquiries about his legal responsibility to Nettie, who
had begun announcing that she was his wife. He was told that Nettie had
no legal claim on him, and he evidently considered the relationship terminated when he left for New York. Nettie, as she was soon to demonstrate,
thought otherwise.

It was at this point that James and Ella met and fell in love. But even
though James kept the affair with Nettie a secret from Ella, he had his
troubles overcoming the opposition of Ella's mother to the marriage. It took
James the better part of a year to win over Bridget and make Ella his bride.

He did not, however, allow his negotiations with the Quinlans to interfere with his work. He had come to New York to triumph and he did not
lose sight of his goal. New York's theatrical atmosphere in the 1870's was

not much different from that of other large cities. It had a denser concentration of playhouses, but most of them were run on the stock company principle.

Stars of genuine national stature were scarce. A contemporary New York newspaper sadly commented that "the list of star peformers who can be depended upon to gather large audiences in this city is growing smaller from day to day." The clamor for their services was, of course, as great in New York as elsewhere. But stars did not tour the country so as to arrive ultimately in New York. Once they had fulfilled their brief engagements, even the most successful of them had to continue on tour. Even a play that scored a hit did not run for more than a few weeks; a run of two months was considered spectacular. There was a demand for variety and novelty, and this was reflected in the low caliber of the new plays, most of which were hastily thrown together to suit the talents of one or another of the reigning stars.

Many of the productions laid not the slightest claim to originality; they were either pirated versions of successful European melodramas or slightly doctored versions of plays brazenly stolen from the stock company across the street. The more enterprising of the stock companies supported "house playwrights," among whom Dion Boucicault was a paragon. "House plays" were frequently turned out by their authors at the rate of a dozen a year and they were liable, with no noticeable detriment to their literary quality, to be rewritten by the actors who played in them.

The plays did not really matter to the audiences; either they were sentimental melodramas like *East Lynne,* the intricacies of whose plot (no matter under what title) the audiences knew by heart, or they were Shakespearean and other classical and semiclassical revivals. Audiences came to see actors, not plays—and sometimes not so much actors as personalities.

But, however catholic their tastes, New Yorkers were ardent theatre fans. They arrived at the theatre early and stayed late. Double bills were common and audiences were gluttons for four- and five-act plays. They thought nothing of entering a theatre at seven or seven-thirty and staying until close to midnight.

The New York to which James O'Neill came in 1876, when compared with such cities as London, Paris and Rome, was almost a small town. The area of fashionable residence was circumscribed by Washington Square on the south and Forty-second Street on the north—that area, for all practical purposes, *was* the city. Farther uptown lived Irish squatters in a wilderness of rocks, vegetable gardens and capering goats. The area that later became the Bronx was open country, dotted by little villages at scattered intervals along the railroad tracks.

New York had nothing resembling a skyline. It was architecturally undistinguished, its squat buildings—most of them brownstones—seldom reaching a height of more than three or four stories; its most original and impressive structure was the Brooklyn Bridge, which was then in the sixth year of its thirteen-year construction period. Horsecars jogged along the dusty, untended cobblestone streets, but businessmen could, to save time, ride in the Pullman cars of the steam-engined Third Avenue elevated railroad.

Stylish shops such as A. T. Stewart's, Macy's, Lord and Taylor, Arnold Constable and James McCreery lined Broadway from Ninth to Twentieth Streets, earning for the area the title of the "Ladies' Mile." Tiffany and Company was at Union Square and Fourteenth Street, a convenient place for James to buy Ella's wedding ring, for the square also marked the beginning of the theatre district, which James seldom left.

There were about twenty theatres in New York, of which the most successful were Lester Wallack's, at Thirteenth Street and Broadway, Augustin Daly's, at Fifth Avenue and Twenty-fourth Street, and A. M. Palmer's, on the south side of Union Square.

Wallack, the son of an English actor-manager, played romantic and light comedy roles in his own company. Daly, who had been a theatre critic, went on to adapt popular plays and create stars in the theatre he managed. Palmer, for whose Union Square Stock Company James had been engaged, had created an artistic reputation by imposing discipline and serious rehearsals upon his actors. The Union Square Theatre, built in 1871 as a variety house and taken over a year later by Palmer, could seat 1,200 people—a small capacity for that era. The theatre occupied the lower stories of a hotel called Morton House, where many actors lived.

Union Square, a center of good living and gaiety, had been established as the city's first theatrical district twenty years before, soon after the completion in 1854 of the Academy of Music on Fourteenth Street. Since then the square had drawn the best restaurants, such as Delmonico's, and become a popular site for torchlight parades.

Palmer, a former librarian and a man of education, became, through the reputation of his stock company, a power in theatrical circles. He helped organize the Actors Fund, which looked after the families of indigent players. In 1874 his production of an adapted French melodrama, *The Two Orphans,* brought him a fortune. It was with a revival of this play that he intended to launch his regular fall and winter season for 1876-77. Palmer was winding up a "preliminary season" with a Bret Harte play called *Two men of Sandy Bar* when James moved his wardrobe trunk into the Union Square Theatre in September and began rehearsing.

James was to play the role of Pierre Frochard, the cripple, in *The Two Orphans.* The romantic part of the Chevalier de Vaudrey, which James had acted in San Francisco, was to be played by the company's leading man, Charles R. Thorne, Jr. A favorite of New York theatregoers, Thorne was seven years older than James. Tall, slim and handsome, he had toured as a child with his actor father. Though not in the first rank of actors from a national standpoint, he was extremely effective in the swaggering roles for which he was generally cast. Under Palmer's tutelage he had learned a quiet, dignified style of acting that was considered refreshing by the critics of the day.

A news item on October 2 informed the public that the revival of *The Two Orphans* would "introduce, as Pierre, Mr. James O'Neill, a fresh candidate for metropolitan honors." The production, in four acts, included scenes of an illuminated garden near Paris, a prison courtyard, and a boathouse on the banks of the Seine; among its climatic effects was a snowstorm. The story, which dealt with two cruelly victimized orphan girls, piled villainy upon villainy, until honor and chivalry finally triumphed. It was undoubtedly this play that Ella attended.

Although a responsive audience greeted James's debut, *The Times,* in its review the next day, was cool. Charles Thorne and the theatre's leading lady, Kate Claxton, were lauded by *The Times'* critic, but James was dismissed with a sentence: "Mr. O'Neill is altogether too robust as Pierre." The *Tribune,* on the other hand, found James entirely satisfactory.

The Two Orphans ran until November 20 and was followed by another melodrama called *Miss Multon,* a French adaptation of the novel *East Lynne,* readapted into English. Palmer sent *The Two Orphans* company to the Brooklyn Theatre, but kept the newly popular James at the Union Square Theatre to support Clara Morris in *Miss Multon,* a move that probably saved James's life. For Harry Murdock, the actor who replaced James in *The Two Orphans,* was one of several hundred people who died when the Brooklyn Theatre was destroyed by fire on December 5.

James was cast as Maurice de Latour, a Parisian advocate. His leading lady, Miss Morris, was a wistful, brown-haired actress who had risen to stardom with Daly. She had achieved a sensational success three years earlier as a scar-faced madwoman in a play called *Article 47,* which Daly had adapted for her, and had since been acclaimed as a reigning emotional actress. Her appearance in the title role of *Miss Multon* marked her first New York engagement in two years. She was welcomed back by an enthusiastic audience and the press was equally pleased with her performance. James was overshadowed. *The Times* still declined to be charmed by him: "Mr. James O'Neill, as Maurice, occasionally appeared more astonished at his presence on the stage than au fait of the proceedings he was supposed to be engaged in."

James had expected gentler treatment at the hands of the New York critics and he was bewildered. He couldn't understand why the critics failed to respond to, or even mention, "his handsome face, his luminous black eyes, his fine stage presence, his picturesque and magnetic personality"—attributes that a San Francisco reviewer had recently enumerated as being responsible for James's "rapid rise to stellar eminence." But New York critics continued to measure James unfavorably against their local standards.

His next role, Count Vladimir, in yet another French melodrama— this one set in Moscow and called *The Danicheffs*—again drew a sour comment from *The Times*: "We do not admire Mr. O'Neill's Vladimir— a hard and artificial portrayal." It is true that the anonymous critic did not care much for Thorne's performance either. His portrayal of the serf, Osip, was dismissed as being "deficient in pathos."

In spite of his failure to win over the critics, however, James was building up an avid public following.

If he was hurt or embarrassed by his inability to draw good notices, he concealed his feelings. The Union Square Theatre, despite hard times in general and a dismal theatre season in particular, was having the best popular success of its career. James continued to present a convivial, unruffled surface to the cronies with whom he dined, drank and exchanged shop talk in the restaurants and saloons of Union Square.

Edwin Booth was in town that season, as well as a number of lesser luminaries with whom James was on easy terms. And he renewed his friendship with Adelaide Nielson when she opened in an engagement of Shakespearean repertory at Daly's on May 8, 1877, three days after *The Danicheffs* ended its successful run. It was obviously Miss Nielson whom Ella had in mind when (as quoted in *Long Day's Journey*) she said: "I thought to myself (looking in the mirror) . . . 'You're just as pretty as any actress he's ever met, and you don't have to use paint.' "

V

JAMES HAD NOT NEGLECTED ELLA WHILE STRUGGLING to make his reputation in New York. With her support he had finally persuaded Bridget to set the wedding date for the following month, when he knew he would be free of acting commitments. Meanwhile, he was touring in and around the city with *The Danicheffs*, which was probably why New York was decided on as the locale of the wedding, in preference to Cleveland. But it is possible that a contributing factor to this choice was Bridget's unwillingness to call the attention of her disapproving Cleveland friends to the event.

Throughout most of May Ella engaged in one of her favorite occupations—shopping. Bridget drew a thousand dollars from her Cleveland bank for her daughter's trousseau; Ella had stylish tastes and often spent as much as a hundred dollars on a dress. She opened charge accounts at the best stores along the "Ladies' Mile" and passed blissful hours outfitting herself. The distinctive simplicity with which she dressed was one of her outstanding characteristics; people who could not remember much about her personality could always recall her wardrobe.

James and Ella chose to be married at St. Ann's Church on East Twelfth Street, a few blocks from the Union Square Theatre. It was the church at which most of New York's fashionable Catholic weddings took place, and the members of its congregation, including the restaurateur Lorenzo Delmonico, were drawn from what had come to be known as the "beau monde parish."

If Eugene O'Neill, with his acute sense of foreboding, had been able to select the weather for the day that his parents were married, he would probably not have deviated from nature's choice. A weather story in *The Times* said the day dawned under a "somber pall of clouds that, every lapsing moment, grew deeper and darker. . . . The whole scene was weird beyond description and silently menacing."

The celebration of the nuptial mass was small and quiet. Bridget Quinlan was her daughter's matron of honor and the only guests were a handful of Quinlan relatives. The ceremony had been arranged in privacy and received no mention in the city's newspapers. James, trying to protect his reputation as a bachelor matinee idol, could not afford to mar the glamour that clung to his off-stage personality. He did not wish to interrupt the sighs of the ladies who watched his debonair passage along Fourteenth Street—and paid hard cash to admire him on the stage. Jauntily wielding his cane, James beamed at a world that worshiped him. If Ella, who was almost twenty and blooming with fresh beauty, had any qualms about holding his attention, she did not betray them.

But Ella soon found that marriage to James held other problems. After a brief honeymoon James resumed the touring that was to last another forty years. Ella had her first taste of the tumultuous life that was to prove alien to her but that she was to endure with her husband until his death.

Being married to a touring star in the 1870's and 1880's required endless resilience, an approachable personality, unaffected interest in and warmth for fellow troupers, and an ability to ignore the hardships of unventilated trains, shabby hotel rooms, and the prevalence of whiskey.

Although Ella could be ingratiating, the managers, agents, actors and actresses who were James's constant companions sensed the effort it cost her. Moreover, Ella was helpless domestically. In later years she was to bemoan her confinement to second-rate hotel rooms in small towns, but this life at least provided a screen for her domestic failings. Even in their home in New London, which she and her husband occupied almost every summer until James's death, Ella could not cope with household arrangements. She was incapable of preparing anything more ambitious than scrambled eggs and the engagement of efficient servants defeated her.

Ella was eased into the horrors of touring gradually, for the first four years of her married life were the least hectic in her husband's career so far as traveling was concerned. A few months after the wedding James went with the Union Square Stock Company to Chicago, where the troupe was to have a brief stay before its regular New York season. The Chicago run was successful, but Ella found backstage life distasteful. She spent much of her time in her hotel room during rehearsals and performances. And for the first time she noticed that James drank heavily.

While Ella was jolted by the discrepancy between the romantic life she had envisioned and the drabness of the reality, a worse shock was in store for her.

Early in September Nettie Walsh, learning that James had been married in New York three months earlier, and aware that he was being well paid as a leading man for the Union Square Theatre, brought suit for divorce. The action drew wide notice in the press, not only in Chicago but in New York, Cleveland and San Francisco—wherever James was known.

Nettie Walsh, in her determination to cash in on James's success, spared none of the details of her relationship with him. She claimed she had married James in Cleveland on August 1, 1871, and lived with him as his wife until 1875. She accused him of having fathered her son, now three years old, and of having committed adultery with Louise Hawthorne. She implied, in noting that James had acquired a bride in New York, that he was a bigamist, although she did not specifically state this in her list of grievances. She did, however, point out that her "husband" was a prominent actor, earning $195 a week and that for the past five years he had been earning between $3,000 and $5,000 a year, so that he was now, "being parsimonious in his habits and disposition," worth at least $15,000. Nettie concluded her recital of grievances by requesting a divorce, the care and custody of her child, and suitable alimony.

Since, according to James, there had been no marriage and he had no interest in acquiring custody of the child, whose paternity he did not admit, the crucial point was the alimony. James was not inclined to provide it. Reporters who questioned James backstage on the day that Nettie filed her suit described him as being "quite loath to talk upon the subject." James did, however, characterize Nettie's statement as "false from first to last" and went so far as to acknowledge that he knew Nettie had a child which she attributed to him, but that "the whole thing is a piece of blackmail and an old story which has been tagging me around ever since I began to acquire prominence in my profession." He added that he saw no reason why he should make any public explanation of the matter.

A week later, with Chicago buzzing about the scandal, James did make a public answer through his lawyer, Frank Crane. Crane filed a paper in which James alleged that he had become acquainted with Nettie in Cleveland on August 1, 1871, but that Nettie, so far as he knew, had adopted his name simply for the purpose of the suit and had no legal right to use it. He denied he had married Nettie in Cleveland or anywhere else, adding that his acquaintance with her after he left Cleveland for Chicago in 1872 had "continued at wide intervals of time up to the present." Between 1872 and 1875, James said, Nettie had visited Chicago only twice, and he professed not to know whether these visits were made "for the purpose of renewing the acquaintance."

James further declared through his lawyer that Nettie was "under the influence of sundry designing persons who sought to ruin" his professional prospects and that they had advised her to "set forth a pretended and bogus marriage with that end in view." At the beginning of their acquaintance, James went on, Nettie Walsh "was not a chaste and virtuous woman." He said he had no way of knowing whether he was the father of her child and challenged her "to make a proof, as she may deem most beneficial to her cause," as to his paternity.

James's countersuit ended with the allegation that he had considered the relationship "extinguished" in 1875, when he went to San Francisco. Since that time, he added, Nettie had been "the recipient of improper attentions from divers men," whose names he could not provide; he claimed she was currently living with one of these men, who was not her husband but who provided her with means of support and enjoyed "the marital relations of a husband."

By way of establishing his own probity and refuting Nettie's charge of his affluence, James pointed out the fact of his marriage to Ella Quinlan, which had been "solemnized according to the forms of law and sealed with the obligations of religion in the church." Ever since his marriage, he said, he had been endeavoring to support himself and his wife "in a just and lawful and honorable way." Moreover, he declared, he was not worth $15,000 and he offered to make an exhibit to the court of all his property. But he maintained that Nettie Walsh had no right whatever to call for such a statement nor had she any claim upon his property.

Begging the question of his relationship with Louise Hawthorne, James denied that he was "addicted to vicious and obscene habits." He said he was "living a laborious life and making provisions for the future." He summed up by rejecting every one of Nettie's "outrageous charges" as being "without substance or in fact."

In spite of James's spirited defense, Ella was mortified and could not forgive him for dragging her into a scandal. Her son Eugene later indicated the depth of her wound in *Long Day's Journey Into Night*. He makes it clear that Ella was never able to dismiss the Nettie Walsh affair by causing Mary Tyrone to say: ". . . right after we were married, there was the scandal of that woman who had been your mistress suing you."

It is true that Ella later learned to take what comfort she could from the fact that James was a meticulously faithful husband. ". . . there has never been a breath of scandal about him. I mean, with any other woman. Never since he met me. That has made me very happy. . . . It has made me forgive so many other things," Mary observes in the play.

On October 23, three weeks before James was due to open in a play in New York, the case labeled "Nettie O'Neill against James O'Neill" was heard in Superior Court in Chicago. Judge Williams listened patiently to depositions of witnesses representing both sides. A man named Alfred Seaman testified that James and Nettie had been "clandestinely" married in Cleveland and a woman named Mrs. James Eyster stated that Nettie had lived with her in 1875 and that she "had often urged Nettie to demand recognition as the wife of O'Neill and support from him as such." Nettie's lawyer stated that his client was "suffering from poverty, while the defendant was in good circumstances," but offered no further argument. All in all, the evidence in support of Nettie's claim was not overwhelming.

James, for his part, simply offered an affidavit denying the marriage, and he was supported by sworn statements from two friends, Henry Pratt and John O'Neill (who later became Eugene O'Neill's godfather). James's lawyer also introduced as witnesses two women—one Sarah Howard and a Mrs. Brockman—who alleged that Nettie had once said she was not the wife of James O'Neill, but intended to "make money out of him."

Judge Williams ruled that the evidence before him was insufficient to prove the marriage, but that, pending a hearing on November 26, he would allow Nettie $100 for attorney's fees, and $50 a month for her support.

By November 13 James was in New York, appearing in Palmer's production of a play called *The Mother's Secret*. The Chicago hearing was conducted on December 6, after a postponement, without James being present, but his lawyers rallied their resources, and the court held that it did "not appear that there had been any marriage from the evidence presented." The bill for divorce was dismissed.

Ella shrank from the well-meant sympathy of James's friends. She was convinced that her own friends had nothing but scorn and pity for her, and she began to wonder how she would support the lonely life in which she was trapped.

Her own world, she believed, had shut the door on her and she could not bring herself to enter James's world. "I've never felt at home in the theatre," Mary Tyrone says broodingly. "Even though Mr. Tyrone has made me go with him on all his tours, I've had little to do with the people in his company, or with anyone on the stage. . . . Their life is not my life."

Little by little Ella was retreating, hurt and bewildered, into her dark closet.

Early that winter she and James, together with the rest of Palmer's company, began a train journey to the Pacific coast. On the way the coach carrying the troupe was coupled to a train filled with soldiers returning from the scene of Indian uprisings. A wildly festive greeting awaited the soldiers and the Palmer company in San Francisco. The soldiers were conquering heroes, and James was no less so, having been sincerely missed by the city that regarded him a favorite son. The city also took a tenacious interest in his personal fortune, and it quickly showed Ella that the "divorce" scandal was not forgotten. Soon after their arrival a local journalist, enhancing the facts, wrote: "Mr. James O'Neill, your black-mustached Adonis, had . . . stood in the foremost rank in New York, been claimed in Chicago by three or four wives, and finally comes back to us as handsome, as talented and as well-mustached as ever."

When the company settled in at the Baldwin Theatre, James occupied the star's dressing room.

After panic and depression, San Francisco was recovering its aplomb in the winter of 1878. Members of the new society were as culture-conscious as any group in the East and they saw to it that their theatres flourished. Castles were going up on Nob Hill, real estate was booming once more, and James expanded in the lush atmosphere.

Ella, although she could not shake off her unhappiness over the scandal, found temporary serenity, for she was anticipating her first child. She even managed an air of amused tolerance over the publicity given to James's realistic love-making in a run of Bronson Howard's *Saratoga*. James's innovation fascinated the young men about town, who attended performances repeatedly to time the kisses he exchanged with his leading lady, Nina Varian. Betting pools were organized on the number of kisses Miss Varian would receive each night.

James at this time became involved in the speculation fever that gripped San Franciscans and began investing in real estate and mining operations. He left Palmer's company and joined a San Francisco group, to stay in California close to his investments. Although he eventually lost money on most of these deals, he never lost faith in his judgment as an investor and continued throughout his life to sink a portion of his earnings from the stage into a variety of schemes and properties. As his son Eugene was later to point out:

"He was an easy mark for anyone with a spare gold mine, zinc mine, coal mine, silver mine, pieces of real estate, etc.—and he rarely guessed right."

James did not invest because he enjoyed gambling, but because he had a terror of poverty and thought he was securing his future. The same instinct that made James invest also caused him to be miserly in his personal expenditures. But his desire to hoard was complicated by a wish to appear generous in the eyes of his friends. In the barroom, for instance, he could be counted on to stand his friends to drinks. He was constantly struggling with this duality. He made Ella gifts of expensive jewelry and clothes, but he wore his own clothes until they were threadbare and often economized needlessly on lodgings that caused him and Ella discomfort. His paradoxical attitude toward money resulted, quite naturally, in creating two distinctly different impressions of him.

Not an actor, manager or agent ever had anything but glowing praise for his character and generosity, which was remarkable in a profession where petty jealousies and vindictive gossip are so prevalent. The esteem in which he was held was accurately summed up by a contemporary San Francisco journalist: "Among his fellow actors [James O'Neill] is much respected. . . . He is noted for his kindness to young actors, and if called on will readily advise them about the business of their parts. Although holding the leading position in the theatre, he . . . is generous in allowing anyone in scenes with himself to make a point when they can, and this is the secret of how he gains so many friends behind the scenes. He is charitable to the deserving, and is always ready to help those who are in need of his assistance."

When James O'Neill, Jr. was born at the home of a friend on September 10, 1878, James and Ella seemed, to their acquaintances, to be happy and secure. Ella now had her baby to fill the empty times when her husband was rehearsing and performing.

James's popularity with San Francisco audiences did not flag. His theatre had recently acquired a self-styled director who was, in fact, a stage manager of dynamic ideas and a house playwright of extraordinary nimbleness. One of his earliest feats was an "adaptation" of a successful Bronson Howard play called *The Banker's Daughter,* which was playing in New York; it took him almost no time at all to change the play's title to *The Millionaire's Daughter,* to delete the name of Bronson Howard and substitute his own, which happened to be David Belasco. Although this play and others equally original kept James profitably occupied until early in 1879, he wanted to distinguish himself in a more artistic vehicle. It was at this time that James received an unorthodox, but to him irresistible, offer.

The role was that of Jesus Christ in an adaptation of the Passion play. So strong was James's vision of the dramatic sensation he could make that he was blind to the tawdriness of the script, prepared by an untalented writer named Salmi Morse. A local editor put it neatly when he wrote of Morse that "he was not nice in his syntax."

Morse, who had flowing gray hair, a drooping mustache, abbreviated beard, mournful eyes, and a fanatically religious approach to the arts and to journalism, was regarded as an eccentric even in San Francisco, where bizarre characters abounded.

His dramatization of the life of Christ was, he claimed, the result of twenty years of research in the Holy Land. He had in his possession yellowed parchment documents to prove the authenticity of his findings. Morse was a Jew, but the fact that he proposed to produce what amounted to a Christian religious service did not disturb James any more than the fact that James, an Irish Catholic, should be called upon to play the Nazarene.

Neither of these details, however, escaped the acid observation of San Francisco journalists. Even before the play was unveiled, a good deal of angry protest was registered by the newspapers, encouraged by a handful of Protestant ministers. The bishop of the Catholic church in California had, according to Morse, expressed his approval of the script; but during the subsequent uproar no official of the Catholic Church would take a public stand either for or against the production.

Amidst protest and criticism, James and his cast rehearsed *The Passion* at the Baldwin Theatre, with the sort of biblical concepts that Hollywood's Cecil B. De Mille was to employ seventy-five years later. The man behind the extravagant preparations was young Belasco, who could be seen running about San Francisco, ecstatic over the opportunity that had come his way. He ransacked the city to find one hundred nursing mothers to appear in the tableau, "The Massacre of the Innocents." He rounded up a flock of sheep and engaged two hundred singers and four hundred supers. He visited the Mechanics Mercantile Library, where he stood lost in scholarly study before two biblical canvases that he aimed to reproduce en tableau.

James decided that to do justice to the role of Christ he must become an ascetic. He gave up drinking, tobacco and other worldly pleasures. He ordered solemn rehearsals, after which he retired to his dressing room for contemplation.

His fellow actors and fans were astonished and impressed by James's new personality. He allowed no rough language backstage and tolerated no frivolity. The other members of the production found James's pious approach contagious and began to walk softly and speak gently. Belasco, who knew when to take a cue, carried a Bible and spoke of plans to enter a monastery.

James was bewildered by the reaction of the press, which criticized him for a misguided attempt to mix religion with commercialism. He considered himself a devout man, and he had persuaded himself that *The*

Passion was both beautiful and elevating. Despite threats by irate citizens to take legal action against the production, *The Passion* opened on the night of March 3, 1879.

The results were disastrous. When James appeared on the stage with a halo about his head (created by Belasco), women in the audience fell on their knees in prayer; and during the scene in which he was crowned with thorns, a number of patrons fainted. Some members of the audience, consisting largely of San Francisco's Irish, were so moved by the portrayal of Christ's suffering that they rushed into the streets at the play's end, assaulted passing Jews, and destroyed pawnshops and other Jewish properties.

The critics were hostile, one of them calling the play "an absurd and irreverent money-making spectacle." The editorial pages of the newspapers rang with protest, the Protestant clergy redoubled its denunciation—and it looked as though *The Passion* would be a resounding financial success. But after a run of only eight days it was closed. The manager of the Baldwin had received letters threatening his life, and he was unwilling to take the risk, even for the fortune that seemed assured.

When business fell sharply at the Baldwin during the hastily substituted run of a play called *The Miner's Daughter,* the manager had second thoughts about the wisdom of his decision. Swallowing his fears, he revived *The Passion* on April 15, even though a city ordinance had been hastily passed, making its presentation illegal and its cast subject to prosecution. The attempt at defiance was short-lived. At the end of the performance two police officers served James and the other members of the cast with warrants, and they were led off to jail, still in costume. (Belasco preferred not to share martyrdom with James, and foiled arrest by hiding in the cellar.) James and his company were released on bail and brought into court for trial several days later. The embarrassing episode was finally closed when James paid a $50 fine, and others in the company paid smaller penalties.

Ella was humiliated both as a wife and as a Catholic, but James stuck to his conviction that *The Passion* was "in the nature of a religious service." Some years later he insisted, to an interviewer, that "there was nothing irreverent or theatrical about the performance," but that "its intense solemnity throughout was most impressive." "To my mind," he added, "there was nothing sacrilegious in *The Passion*. . . . If anything, it was in the line of biblical education."

James resigned himself after *The Passion* to more mundane impersonations and San Francisco forgave him for his lapse. At the same time that San Franciscans re-embraced James they politely ignored Lester Wallack, who had arrived in San Francisco to open an engagement at the rival

California Theatre. Wallack was so indifferently received that he was forced to pack up, but before he left the city he vindictively told a reporter: "Sir, you can judge what I think of average San Franciscans when I state my opinion that if Jesus Christ himself came down from Heaven they would give O'Neill the preference in the character."

Toward the end of October, 1880, James took Ella and their two-year-old son back to New York, where James spent the season at Booth's Theatre. During the season of 1881-82, he toured New York State and New England. Believing the time had now come for him to launch himself as a full-fledged star in the East, he selected a vehicle, but once again his judgment proved faulty. The play he chose, and which he bought outright from its author, was *An American King*. It was written especially for James by a young man named Charles Dazey, who wrote his only really successful piece, *In Old Kentucky*, some years later.

An American King was something less than the tour de force James had thought it would be. This unfortunate venture marked the end of James's possible claim to an immortality such as Edwin Booth's. He was now thirty-five, but had not achieved anything near the stature that had once been predicted for him. He had, in fact, already started downhill without being aware of it.

Easy success in foolish roles had made him forget his original goal of becoming a great Shakespearean actor; when he realized what he had done, it was too late. Eugene O'Neill, brooding about his father's misstep seven years after his death, was contemptuous of a contemporary actress who seemed about to make the same error. He told Brooks Atkinson, the critic, in 1927, that this rising actress planned to secure her reputation by playing tricky modern drama—and then devoting herself to great art; O'Neill, undoubtedly thinking of his father, scornfully pointed out that she would have accumulated so many facile mannerisms by that time that she would be lost to the ways of genius.

In January of 1883 James, struggling to keep *An American King* going, received an unexpected offer from John Stetson, the manager of Booth's Theatre in New York. It was the role of yet another French nobleman— but this particular character became in James's hands the be-all and the end-all of stereotyped French noblemen.

Booth's Theatre, built in 1869 by Edwin Booth as a Shakespearean showcase for himself, had failed under his management five years later and was currently pandering to the public taste for French melodrama. Charles Thorne, Jr. had opened in *The Corsican Brothers* on January 8, but became seriously ill two nights later with rheumatic gout. He was hastily replaced and when it became clear that he would not recover in time to play Edmond Dantes in the next attraction, *The Count of Monte Cristo,* Stetson thought of James O'Neill. It is conceivable that Thorne himself suggested James, recalling his popularity when they played together for Palmer. Although James had no way of knowing that this offer held out overnight stardom, he accepted with alacrity, for he had been on the point of abandoning his *King* venture.

Monte Cristo was a rewritten version of the Alexandre Dumas romance, a story that gave color to the heroic dreams of the young men of the day. The form that Stetson planned to use had been doctored by the popular romantic actor Charles Fechter, who had toured in it successfully for several seasons but had died four years earlier. Stetson had acquired the script.

Monte Cristo was to open on February 12. On the 11th, New Yorkers heard of Thorne's unexpected death. He had died so suddenly, of internal hemorrhages, that his father had been unable to reach his bedside in time. Thorne's funeral was held the next day.

That night the cast of *Monte Cristo,* which was supposed to have supported Thorne, supported James O'Neill. It was a significant night in the history of the American theatre—not so much because it launched James on a new phase of his career but because its effect on the career and personality of the actor colored the life and helped to foster the strange genius of his son Eugene. *The Count of Monte Cristo,* which was to bring James the popularity and wealth for which he had yearned, simultaneously put a strict limitation on his career. It became a trap from which he never escaped and into which Eugene O'Neill was born.

In the beginning it seemed to James that he was still on his way up —that *Monte Cristo* marked one more step in the direction of lasting fame and stature. He was still slender enough to look well in tight velvet breeches and close-fitting doublet. Experience had made him an agile swordsman, and he had no peer in grace.

The role of Edmond Dantes might have been written expressly for him; he was the wronged, avenging, triumphant Count to the last inch. How could success in this romantic role detract from the Shakespearean parts he would play later? New York encouraged him in this illusion. Even though James himself realized he wasn't at his best for the première, the first-nighters, not anticipating any great impact from the warmed-over melodrama, were taken by storm.

Some people had to leave before the end of the performance because the curtain wasn't rung down until midnight. But even they had seen enough to tell each other excitedly that the old play had been infused with new life. More than one member of that audience recalled, years later, the churning ocean waves, created by hard-breathing stage hands manipulating a blue ground cloth from below; the waves assumed a newly menacing wetness when James emerged from them with blazing eyes, his breast heaving in gasps of victory after his escape into the sea from the Château d'If. When the liberated Dantes cried out—in a voice that penetrated to the last row of the gallery—"The world is mine!" the audience gave him an accolade which seemed to prove his statement.

That the play achieved the success it did was largely due to the freshness of James's swashbuckling performance, which also inspired the rest of the cast.

James seemed as little able to earn the disapproval of the public as to earn the approval of the New York critics. But his popular success was such that he could afford to ignore the critical carping. The gossipy and prognostically unreliable *Spirit of the Times,* a theatrical journal, noted that in its opinion "The revival of *Monte Cristo* was a failure, and . . . it deserved to fail. . . . Mr. O'Neill is an actor with an Irish name and an Irish accent but without any Irish sympathy, passion or magnetism."

The Irish accent was inaudible, and the magnetism moderately in evidence to the critic of *The New York Times,* who found other faults with James's interpretation and with the production as a whole: "The performance last night was tedious and awkward. The chief actors in the cast seemed unfamiliar with their parts. The cast was, however, respectable and may become, after a few evenings, effective. Mr. O'Neill failed to make an impression of strength because he applied to broad and dashing romantic acting the restrained method of realism. His intensity at the closing scenes of the play was, nevertheless, dramatic and somewhat magnetic."

Many years later James confessed that he had given a poor performance on opening night.

"When Mr. Stetson had billed the play and myself, I had time only for three rehearsals," he explained. "I begged him to postpone the opening for a week, but he said he couldn't. 'I know all the newspaper boys, and will tell them that you had only three rehearsals,' he promised. 'They will understand and overlook crudities.' But on the opening night he was busy and forgot. The next morning the papers were severe.

"The critics were right that time. I was bad. I knew it. But I got at the play with hammer and tongs. I rehearsed all day in my rooms. By the end of the week the play was going well. The public saved the life of the play." It ran at Booth's for a month, closing on St. Patrick's Day, and then went on tour.

Wherever James toured with *Monte Cristo,* playgoers crowded to see him. One of the most interesting and analytical reviews of the production appeared a year after its New York opening, when San Francisco first saw the Count in James O'Neill's version.

Monte Cristo is a great popular success [the San Francisco *News Letter* informed its readers]. It is exciting and interesting in spite of its many absurdities of detail. . . . Dantes in prison protrudes his head through a hole within a few inches from the top of the parapet, and at the same time he goes on mining for his freedom; an order is given to double the guard for the purpose of shooting Dantes as he escapes, and the guard is then withdrawn. In the ballroom scene Monte Cristo transacts business in the presence of the hostess and guests and bandies vulgar and insulting words with a bystander. Danglars [a character in the play] writes a letter with his left hand at the rate of 199 words a minute. Nortier [another character] shouts good-night from his room in the inn, and ten seconds afterwards, by the watch, his would-be murderess announces that he is asleep.

The waves in the Château d'If scene are simply dreadful. The apotheosis of all this absurdity is the scene where Dantes, standing on a two-by-four rock in the midst of bobbing chunks of wood and canvas, receives a shower of salt. That this play, with all these supremely ridiculous details . . . should still excite and amuse, is a proof of its strong romantic interest and powerful dramatic force. It is bound to draw for some time.

That was a modest prediction. James was to take the Count back and forth across the country for over a quarter of a century; to play him more than six thousand times; and to earn well over $800,000 by the impersonation. He was over sixty and his sons had grown up and taken roles in the vehicle before his public would release him from Edmond Dante's grip —and the grip of $50,000 net profit a year that the play eventually brought him. With all his money and prestige on the road, though, he was, as far as audiences were concerned and as posterity remembers him, a one-character actor. His name became a household word to two generations of playgoers, but always linked with that of Monte Cristo. It happened so gradually that James was not, at first, aware of it.

Stetson, realizing he had a money-maker in the Count, signed James to a contract that guaranteed him $1,000 a week, plus a box-office percentage—more than James had ever commanded before.

Ella joined her husband on tour with young Jim, who was now nearly five, whenever the company settled down long enough to make this feasible. The company played most of the major cities of the East and then proceeded west for a series of one-night stands.

Although Ella's every instinct rebelled against the life she now found herself committed to, she seemed to have no choice; James had no more wish to be separated from her than she from him. But traveling was especially difficult at this point, for she was expecting another baby. Restaurants were not likely to be open when they boarded their coach train at dawn and they often had to travel for hours without even a cup of coffee. When they could breakfast before catching their train, they might have nothing more for eight or ten hours. Trying to force herself to eat heartily against the day's privations, Ella would watch in disgust while James took his customary early morning drink or two to stimulate his appetite.

The baby, another boy, arrived in St. Louis. He was given the name Edmund Burke O'Neill, in honor of the English statesman and orator who, having been Dublin born, was an object of James's admiration. Few of James's friends were aware of Edmund's middle name, and mistakenly thought he had been named for Edmond Dantes.

Since the *Monte Cristo* company was scheduled to continue its transcontinental tour to San Francisco, and then, if business warranted, proceed east again, James and Ella decided they must have a base to which they could periodically take their two children. Touring was difficult enough with one child, but with an infant added, it was more than Ella could manage, particularly with the heat of summer coming on.

Soon after Edmund's birth James and Ella went to New London to find a summer home, where, if James himself could not always spend the hot months, his wife and children could. Ella's mother had already taken up residence in New London to be near her sister, Elizabeth Brennan, who had settled there with her husband some time earlier.

James had no ties with any of his own relatives. His mother had died some years before and he would look in only casually on his sister when he passed through St. Louis. Both he and Ella were convinced that New London would offer the roots they both hoped for.

James had long been attracted to the whaling atmosphere of the harbor town; it had been described to him by a friend, John McGinley, who had been in the white goods business in New York. McGinley, whose father had been a New London whaling captain, had fascinated James with tales of the coast town, which, in 1846, had been the second largest whaling port in the world, surpassed only by New Bedford. The McGinley family had settled in New London in the late eighteenth century when John McGinley's grandfather arrived from Londonderry, Ireland.

Now John McGinley had given up his business in New York and

returned to New London to raise a family and help organize the newspaper called the New London *Day*, and he was so engaged when James and Ella arrived in 1883.

At that time New London was one of the most beautiful towns in the East. Built on a succession of low hills, it held a large, deep-water harbor —the mouth of the Thames River that opens into Long Island Sound. The harbor made a magnificent anchorage for the square-riggers, the colorful Sound steamers, and the windjammers that still sailed the seas.

The town's mainstay was small industry related to shipping, textiles, and the tag end of the whaling business, but its possibilities as a summer resort were already recognized—something that did not escape James's business eye. A sprinkling of the socially prominent from New York, Boston, Philadelphia and New Orleans, acknowledging New London as a yachting and swimming paradise, were beginning to build summer homes along Harbor Road, later to be called Pequot Avenue. The road, which ran alongside the Thames to its mouth, was then about a mile long and was paved with ground oyster shells. It extended from the edge of town to a curve of land on which stood a slender white lighthouse, marking the beginning of the Sound.

About halfway between the town proper and the lighthouse the O'Neills bought a small pink cottage and two lots of land overlooking the water. They probably rented a house during their first summer in New London, for the deed to their property, in Ella's name, was dated August 14, 1884. Two years later the O'Neills purchased some adjoining property, including a barn and two additional cottages, one of which, in the 1850's, had housed the district school. (The family that bought the house in 1937, after it had stood vacant for many years, was puzzled to find metal pedestals, such as served to support old-fashioned school desks, screwed into the floor of an upstairs room.) It was this cottage, still standing in New London as Number 325 Pequot Avenue, that James rebuilt in the late 1890's and expanded into a summer home, and in which Eugene O'Neill set the action of *Long Day's Journey Into Night*.

There is every reason to believe that in the early days of their residence in New London James and Ella were warmly accepted. The snobbery that was to bedevil them developed later, with the influx of aristocratic summer residents.

In the year or so following Edmund's birth, James and Ella left young Jim and the baby in Bridget's charge, both in New London and in New York, while they toured with *Monte Cristo*. Although Ella made the trips protestingly and decried the necessity of having to choose between husband and children, her devotion to James overrode her maternal instinct. She felt guilty about leaving her children, but she was incapable of parting from her husband.

The demand for James's *Monte Cristo* was inexhaustible. Stetson, who had been convinced that one season of touring would see the end of its popularity, and was not willing to finance the company further, sold the play to James outright for only $2,000. For once, James had guessed right ("My good bad luck," he later called it, with bitterness) and he could not stop making money with it. He traveled back and forth across the continent, playing in every city and hamlet that had a theatre.

Ella, a dutiful shadow, had left her two sons with her mother in a small Manhattan hotel and had joined James on the road in February, 1885. Soon after, she had word that Jim was ill with measles. On February 27 the baby, Edmund, not yet a year and a half, caught the disease. He was ill for five days and died in the early morning of March 4.

Ella's dismay at having left Edmund grew into an intolerable guilt, which she spent the rest of her life trying to shift to her husband and children. Young Jim was the first to suffer, for Ella was convinced that he had tried to kill his brother. Eugene O'Neill was aware of how Ella felt, as he demonstrated in *Long Day's Journey Into Night* when he caused Mary Tyrone to say to her husband that she had always believed her son went into the baby's room deliberately, to give him measles. Jim was jealous of the baby—hated him, says Mary Tyrone, adding that he had been warned that measles could kill the infant. The real Jim could not have been insensitive to Ella's feelings.

The following fall, only six months after Edmund's death, Jim was packed off to boarding school at Notre Dame, Indiana, where as a minim (or elementary) and high school student he was to spend most of the next nine years. Jim could hardly have failed to interpret his exile as punishment for a crime.

The effects of his banishment did not appear to embitter him until he reached his late teens, however. Initially he seemed eager to make good. In his nine years at Notre Dame he was an outstanding student and an active and popular participant in school sports and other extracurricular activities. He excelled in geography and reading, received special mention in rhetoric, was a monitor in the literary and dramatic societies, and played shortstop on the baseball team.

With Jim off her hands, Ella was free to spend more time on the road with her husband. Occasionally during the next few years James and Ella visited Notre Dame; James was always fussed over at the school and entertained as though he were visiting royalty, which in a sense he was, being by now nationally identified with and idolized as the Count of Monte Cristo. On one such visit he endeared himself to the staff and students, and enhanced his son's popularity, by trading recitations with a group of youngsters, after which he donated a gold medal to be given at commencement to the student who would distinguish himself above all others for good conduct and proficiency in study. The splash James made at school reflected favorably on Jim, but the boy was already beginning to harbor a resentment toward his overpowering father. He was clever enough to hide this, for the time being, but it was soon to emerge in overt rebellion.

James, for his part, was beginning to rebel against another sort of tyranny. He was growing to resent the success that forced him into endlessly re-creating Edmond Dantes. He lost the spirited freshness that had made Dantes so appealing, and he gave automatic and listless performances. His boredom with the role did not pass unnoticed. A San Francisco critic, in December, 1887, almost five years after James had first appeared in *Monte Cristo,* wrote: "In [James O'Neill's] hands it has degenerated into an extravagant melodrama. The romance that amused and interested the intellectual world has become a bit of coarse theatricalism, that pleases only the more ignorant of theatregoers. . . . He is reaping the pecuniary profit of his business sagacity, but it is at the cost of art. If the actor concerned had no previous claim upon critical consideration the matter would not deserve so much comment, but James O'Neill has done admirable work—artistic work—in the past, and it is a cause of regret that he should have abandoned his better abilities."

Other critics sniped at him too. One pointed out that "The Count's irresistible monetary fascination is fast smothering O'Neill's versatility." James was so firmly identified with the part that his friends called him Monte Cristo outside the theatre. They referred to his house in New London as the Monte Cristo Cottage and James himself put up a sign giving it that official designation.

James tried other plays, but the public was apathetic; he went back to *Monte Cristo* and the public adored him.

It was at this time that Bridget Quinlan died in New London. Ella, still grieving over Edmund's death, had no further tears to shed. Her mother's death was no more than a ripple in the sea of melancholy in which she drifted. And James was beginning to reel from the double burden of his artistic deterioration and his wife's increasing depression. It was under these circumstances that Eugene, their third son, was conceived.

VI

"YOU WERE BORN AFRAID. BECAUSE I WAS SO AFRAID to bring you into the world . . . afraid all the time I carried you, I knew something terrible would happen . . . I should never have borne [you]. It would have been better for [your] sake."

These are the words of Mary Tyrone to her third-born son. Whether or not they are literally the words of his mother, it is clear that O'Neill believed, from early boyhood, that they conveyed his mother's true feeling of despair over the fact of his birth. Eugene was not to escape his share of his mother's guilt any more than his brother or father. The sense of guilt was absorbed by him and shadowed his whole life. For he was convinced that it was his birth that made Ella into a narcotics addict.

In *Long Day's Journey Into Night,* he pitilessly reiterates his mother's accusations. Her speeches throughout four acts of the play stress the fact that she was "so healthy" before he was born, that she never had a gray hair or a nerve in her body before his birth. Bearing her third son was "the last straw," she says, adding, "I was so sick afterwards." O'Neill indicated, long before he wrote *Long Day's Journey Into Night,* the effect his mother's despair had on him. In *The Great God Brown,* written in 1925, less than three years after his mother's death, O'Neill's autobiographical hero, Dion Anthony, says:

"Why am I afraid to live, I who love life and the beauty of flesh and the living colors of earth and sky and sea? Why am I afraid of love? Why am I afraid, I who am not afraid? . . . Why must I live in a cage like a criminal, defying and hating, I who love peace and friendship? Why was I born without a skin, O God, that I must wear armor in order to touch or to be touched? . . . Or rather, Old Graybeard, why the devil was I born at all?"

The self-lamented birth of Eugene O'Neill took place in a Broadway hotel room on a Tuesday afternoon, October 16, 1888, two days after his father had marked his forty-second birthday and a month after his mother had turned thirty-one. Ella was still lovely and James, trim and dapper, still presenting a smiling, unruffled exterior, was hollowly assuring audiences from Boston to San Francisco that the world was his.

Although James's tour during the months of September and October, 1888, followed a New England route, Ella had left New London to await her confinement in New York. Despite her precarious emotional and physical condition, James did not feel he could postpone his lucrative tour to be with her. Depositing Ella in New York at a hotel called the Barrett House, he opened *Monte Cristo* in New Jersey the week of September 3. From there, leaving Ella to brood over the impending arrival of their baby, he took up one- and two-night stands in Massachusetts, Maine and New Hampshire. He played without a break through the Saturday night performance, October 13, in Worcester, Massachusetts, and came to New York on Sunday to spend his birthday with Ella. Since Ella expected to be confined within the next couple of days, James remained at the Barrett House. Evidently he canceled his scheduled appearances for the next four nights, for he did not resume his tour until October 18, two days after his son's birth.

Eugene's birthday was damp and gray, with an intermittent light rain. In the theatrical world Edwin Booth and another great Shakespearean actor, Lawrence Barrett, had recently taken the country by storm, appearing together in their first nation-wide tour. On the Rialto, which by that time had expanded to the area between Union Square and Thirty-fourth Street, E. H. Sothern was playing in *Lord Chumley*. James's old mentor, Joseph Jefferson, was announced to appear with John Gilbert and Mrs. John Drew in *The Rivals* within a few days. Gilbert and Sullivan's *The Yeomen of the Guard* was having its American première.

Although the first electric lights had been installed in a theatre six years before, the street lamps above Twenty-sixth Street were still being lighted by oil-tipped torches. Stanford White had recently completed his architect's blueprint for The Players, the newly organized actors' club that was to be opened on New Year's Eve at a house purchased by Edwin Booth in Gramercy Park (James O'Neill was to become one of the club's first members).

Missing from the theatrical scene was the theatre where James had made his New York debut. The Union Square Theatre had been destroyed by fire eight months before, on February 27; almost every actor and actress then in New York had turned out to watch and lament the destruction of a cherished landmark.

Eugene O'Neill's birthplace, at Broadway and Forty-third Street, was then called Longacre Square. (It was not renamed Times Square until sixteen years later.) Because he never had any real roots, Eugene grew up with a dogged sentimentality for the neighborhood in which he was born, as it was in his boyhood. He was always half-humorously resentful of the rapid changes that took place in the area, recalling the quiet side streets of the West Forties, lined with brownstone residences and interspersed with their owners' livery stables, and the tree-lined lane a little farther uptown known as the Boulevard.

The family hotel called Barrett House, which had been built to the imposing height of eight stories in 1883, occupied the northeast corner of Broadway and Forty-third Street. Its windows looked out on cobblestone streets, where horse-drawn carriages passed at a leisurely pace. The Barrett House clock, set into a gabled tower, was a landmark for uptown residents and visitors.

For many years O'Neill was to point out to friends the third-floor room in which he was born, until, in 1940, the hotel was torn down to make way for a two-story structure housing a group of stores and topped by a towering electric sign advertising Kleenex. By the time O'Neill was old enough to enjoy recalling and revisiting his birthplace, the hotel, which had merged with an adjoining structure in 1900, was called the Cadillac. But this did not detract from O'Neill's nostalgia.

"Every time I go past, I look up," he said in 1925. "Third window from Broadway on the Forty-third Street side. I can remember my father pointing it out to me." In at least one instance, he impetuously hustled a friend up to Room 236, knocked on the door, explained his mission to the startled occupants, and was granted permission to look around. Many years later, returning to New York after having lived some years in California, O'Neill found that the hotel had been razed and he complained that he hardly recognized the area any more.

"There is only empty air now where I came into this world," he said.

In 1948, only five years before his death, O'Neill had been gratified to receive from an old friend a photograph of the original Barrett House. O'Neill told his friend, "I know of no gift which could have pleased me more." He had added facetiously that the figure in the picture leaning against the lamppost outside the hotel obviously "had a bun on."

"I remember seeing him there the day after I was born," added O'Neill. "You forget there were men in those days, and when they decided it was fitting they should go on a drunk, *they went on a drunk*. Not like the weaklings of today, who after two days of much mixed drinks have to have an animal trainer bed them down in Bellevue and gently subdue their menagerie visions! In the old days when I was born, a man—especially one from Kilkenny—went on a five year drunk and finished by licking four cops, and then went home to raise hell because dinner was late."

The reference to Kilkenny applied to his father, who began to instill in his younger son a profound consciousness of and pride in his pure Irish ancestry from the moment of his birth by bestowing on him a traditional Gaelic name. Eugene is the Anglicization of Eaghan and Eaghan Ruadh, or Owen Rae, who was the greatest of the O'Neill soldiers to fight the English Parliamentarians. The middle name, Gladstone, which O'Neill later dropped, was given to him in honor of the Liberal English prime minister, then a champion of home rule for Ireland, who, like Burke, was distinguished for his oratory.

Thirty years after he had been christened, when an early play brought him to the attention of the public, O'Neill was enchanted to receive a congratulatory letter from a seventy-two-year-old woman who signed herself Elizabeth Murray and who wished to remind him that she was the nurse who had been with him at his birth.

"I have thought of you many times in the last thirty years," Mrs. Murray wrote, "and I wondered how you and your dear mother were getting along. I carried you in my arms to the church the day you were christened, a beautiful baby."

O'Neill treasured the letter, as he did the photograph of the Barrett House and pictures of himself as an infant in his mother's arms. A man of violent contradictions, O'Neill spent much of his life protesting against having been born, yet he was sentimentally attached to memorabilia of his birth.

Eugene was, according to medical records, a healthy, breast-fed baby, despite the debilitating effect that his birth apparently had upon his mother; he weighed eleven pounds. (Mary Tyrone says, in *Long Day's Journey Into Night*: ". . . that ignorant quack of a cheap doctor— All he knew was I was in pain. It was easy for him to stop the pain.")

Ella, according to relatives, was attended at her delivery by a doctor with whom James O'Neill had struck up a barroom acquaintance. Eugene came to believe that it was James's eagerness to save on medical costs that caused him to choose a doctor so casually. It seems certain that the doctor ordered morphine to ease Ella's pains.

Morphine, a derivative of opium, was in those days available in various preparations without prescription. Many patent medicines containing morphine, such as cough syrups, were readily obtainable at drugstores, and morphine was even listed in the catalogues of some mail-order houses. It was not until World War I that a federal law was passed (late in 1914) restricting the sale of opium and its derivatives; then codeine, a milder drug, succeeded morphine in many patent remedies.

The effect of morphine, in addition to alleviating physical pain, is to blur the edges of reality, removing fears and worries and relegating the user to what O'Neill once described, when speaking of his mother, as "a kind of twilight zone." According to medical evidence, it is unusual for a person to become addicted to morphine unless he actively wishes to sustain the sense of unreality that it provides.

Thus there is questionable validity in the contention, as advanced in *Long Day's Journey Into Night*, that a "quack doctor" started Ella on a vicious habit that trapped her against her will. It is true that a doctor introduced her to the drug, but she herself seized on its effect as a means of escape. Morphine offered her a never-never land in which she could hide. It was many months before she realized that she no longer could do without the drug.

It was many months, also, before James became aware that Ella was an addict. According to a cousin of the O'Neills, Ella's addiction was not suspected by James until, one day, he overheard his wife sending an elevator boy to the apothecary to replenish the patent medicine she had been taking for "nervousness." James was on the point of going out himself and told the boy that he would pick up the medicine.

The druggist, who happened to be a conscientious man, asked James if he knew that the medicine could become habit forming, and James, after further inquiry, was appalled to discover the truth. The fact of his wife's addiction must have been almost incomprehensible to him, for virtually nothing was known of such matters to people of his class. The cousin, a lively-minded, inquisitive girl, learned these facts years later by eavesdropping on a conversation between her elders; she was among the few surviving relatives and friends of the elder O'Neills who was not unduly surprised by the revelation of the mother's addiction in *Long Day's Journey Into Night*.

The words O'Neill has given James Tyrone to speak in the play seem to bear out the facts. Answering his son, who has accused him of neglect in failing to recognize the seriousness of his wife's narcotics habit, and of miserliness in not getting proficient medical help, James protests: ". . . how was I to know then? What did I know of morphine? It was years before I discovered what was wrong. I thought she'd never got over her [childbirth] sickness, that's all."

Eugene began touring with his father as an infant. James had resumed his travels in *Monte Cristo* a few days after his son was born and Ella, though not in good health, rested in New York for only a month or so after Eugene's birth.

"My mother nursed me in the wings and in dressing rooms," O'Neill often said. He elaborated on this to a friend with whom, during one Greenwich Village dawn, he was watching John Barrymore make his unsteady way down a narrow street.

"Barrymore, like a lot of dizzy actors, boasts about having been born in a trunk. As if that were something wonderful. I was born in a theatrical hotel and my mother had to travel and put me in a bureau drawer on two pillows for my cradle. I was fed and dressed and put to sleep in hotel rooms. I can't see that a theatrical life on the road is such a marvelous thing."

In January of 1889, before he was three months old, Eugene was taken by Ella to be inspected by his ten-year-old brother at Notre Dame. "Master Eugene is a beautiful child," reported the Notre Dame *Scholastic* on January 12. "My first press notice," O'Neill would say, years later, displaying the carefully preserved clipping.

George Tyler, the prominent theatrical producer of the first two decades of the 1900's, who spent his early years of training as an advance publicity man for various touring companies, has said that it was one of his obligations, when he worked for James O'Neill, to "scramble round and do things" for Ella, who, with her baby, would be sent ahead of the company to rest from the grind of one-night stands.

One night in Chicago, where Ella had been established to wait for James and his company, Tyler was summoned by a frantic call to her hotel. He discovered that Eugene, then three months old, was "sort of black in the face and gasping and raising Cain." Ella was convinced he was dying. Tyler finally managed to find a doctor, who, after a look at the baby, decided it was nothing more serious than colic.

The disruptive and grueling routine of travel had its more serious effect on Eugene, though. His mother's own attitude toward the wandering life had frozen into cheerless resignation, alleviated by daily attendance at Mass or, alternately, by escape into drugged daydreams. This did not bolster Eugene's sense of security. Even though Ella was spared the more strenuous aspects of one-night stands—under whose rigors James seemed to thrive—the clattering old day coaches on which she rode with Eugene, the indifferent hotels in which they stayed, and the tasteless food on which they subsisted in their moves from city to city created a drab and wearing environment.

A representative route, got up by one of James O'Neill's managers, has survived to indicate what a sample month's tour was like. In one November James's company played Scranton, Pennsylvania; Albany, New York; North Adams, Northampton, Westfield—all in Massachusetts; Hartford and Middletown in Connecticut; Worcester, Massachusetts;

Woonsocket, Rhode Island; New Bedford, Massachusetts; Newport, Rhode Island; Fall River and Boston, Massachusetts; and Providence, Rhode Island—in that order. All but four of these stops were for one night and only two were for full-week engagements.

This went on throughout the theatrical season, with only the summers in New London providing a breathing spell. Eugene's companions, necessarily restricted during the seven years he traveled with his parents, consisted mainly of railroad conductors and hotel porters, in addition to an English-trained nanny named Sarah Sandy.

Sarah was a goodhearted woman and devoted to Eugene. Her only grudge against the world, whether real or imagined, was that her mother had sent her into service while allowing her sisters and brothers to receive an education. Sarah came to Ella highly recommended by a resident at the Barrett House in whose employ she had been for many years. Sarah did her best to compensate her charge for his lack of family life and play-mates. She sometimes took him to stay with her own relatives and, while on the road, zealously sought out aquariums, zoos and circuses for Eugene to visit. His earliest memory of those days was of feeding squirrels in a park in Memphis, Tennessee. A chubby infant, he was dressed for his outings in Little Lord Fauntleroy suits and lace collars, and he wore his light brown hair long, with bangs.

Sarah also told Eugene the sordid details of contemporary murders and invented horror tales of her own, supplementing this instruction with visits to museums where wax effigies of criminals and malformed dummies were on display. In New York she often took him to the Eden Musee, which featured, for a twenty-five-cent admission, "a world of wax" and Hungarian gypsy music.

She probably channeled her frustrations into this vivid form because she felt as isolated and unbelonging as Eugene; her terrified but attentive listener was a perfect captive audience. The reference in *Long Day's Journey Into Night* to Edmund-Eugene's "continually having nightmares as a child," although not related in the play to his nurse, was obviously factual and just as obviously traceable to the imaginative Sarah. On the other hand, her lurid stories may have begun to stimulate an imagination that was later to hold audiences spellbound with vivid accounts of terror and doom.

Both Sarah and Eugene found themselves picking up a firsthand back-stage education. Sarah used to say that she had seen *The Count of Monte Cristo* so many times she could go on stage and play any part at a moment's notice.

As for Eugene, one of his earliest memories (by his own later account) was of his father "dripping with salt and sawdust, climbing on a stool behind the swinging profile of dashing waves. It was then that the calcium lights in the gallery played on his long beard and tattered clothes, as with arms outstretched he declared that the world was his. This was a signal for the house to burst into deafening applause that drowned out the noise of the mechanical storm being manufactured backstage."

Eugene was so steeped in the ways of the theatre that by the time he was five he considered himself qualified to pronounce a professional opinion that both amused and appalled his father. He was paying a call with James on a Cincinnati relative, when a wizened neighbor happened in. Habitually shy and silent, he could not refrain from turning to his father and confiding, in a stage whisper, "Ugly old woman. Wouldn't do for the stage."

He was no better disposed toward pretty, young women who did very well for the stage. He accompanied his mother to the dressing rooms one day after a matinee and hung back bashfully as Ella greeted Margaret Anglin, at that time still a relatively obscure ingénue. "Come in, boy," said Miss Anglin. "Don't be afraid. I won't kiss you." Eugene did not budge. "You might," he said. By this time, Eugene had outgrown his lace collars and long curls; with his ears sticking out and several front teeth missing, he looked the typical, winsome five-year-old.

It is not surprising that Eugene, between bouts of horror with Sarah, casting efforts on behalf of *Monte Cristo,* and dodging the blandishments of ingénues, found early and pleasurable escape into books. A photograph taken of him in New London at the age of seven—which O'Neill, in his later years, referred to as "amusing and characteristic"—shows him seated alone on a rock, gazing sadly and thoughtfully out to sea. He is fetchingly dressed in a dark jacket, short pants, an Eton cap, long dark stockings and high laced boots. Eugene would sit for hours on the smooth yellow rocks that lined the harbor road, reading, sketching, dreaming and wondering what it was like to be a sea gull.

Even as a child he was detached from his physical background, preferring to escape into an imaginary realm where he could not be hurt by a remote mother or an overwhelming father. He was moody and oversensitive. Though he had no more than his fair share of the usual childhood diseases, including measles and typhoid fever, he was plagued by colds and respiratory infections and was often pale. His relatives regarded him as "delicate."

But there was a robust, tenaciously realistic side to Eugene, just as there was a generous, even an indulgent, side to his father. For example, James bought, and Eugene delighted in, a toy railroad, which ran on a track surrounding his house. It was not a miniature electric train, but a coal-burning model in which he could sit and ride around his yard; but he had to stoke the engine himself, with fuel he fetched and carried. He also had a fling at chicken farming, selling eggs to his father at prices well above those of the contemporary market.

VII

IF THE FIRST SEVEN YEARS OF TOURING WITH HIS father injected the theatre permanently into Eugene's blood, those years also gave him a thorough dislike of its conventions.

"My early experience with the theatre through my father really made me revolt against it," he once recalled. "As a boy I saw so much of the old, ranting, artificial romantic stuff that I always had a sort of contempt for the theatre."

Those wandering years also gave him a permanent sense of rootlessness, of not belonging. The ensuing six years, which he spent mainly at Catholic boarding schools, increased his feeling of isolation.

"O'Neill has acute memories of the outbursts of hysterical loneliness that overtook him on every return to his rigid Christian exile," wrote Elizabeth Shepley Sergeant, the journalist and biographer, who, after interviewing him in 1926, became his friend. "Gazing afar upon a stage where a heroic figure strutted, towards a lovely distant mother to whom he stretched his arms in vain, he conceived the world in which he was at mercy of his affections as disastrous." (He no longer had even his nurse, Sarah, to cling to, and this was perhaps an even crueler blow than being parted from his mother; for, whatever her shortcomings, Sarah had provided him with the protective warmth he craved.)

O'Neill, almost always dismayed by the articles published about him, was so impressed by Miss Sergeant's sensitive grasp of the forces that shaped his character that he soon after confided to her the story of his mother's morphine addiction—something he did, painfully, to only five or six people during his lifetime.

The "rigid Christian exile" began with his entry into a convent school on a hill in the northern Bronx, along the banks of the Hudson River. Established by the Catholic Sisters of Charity in Manhattan in 1847 as the Academy of Mount St. Vincent, it later moved uptown and before the turn of the century became an academy very much like St. Mary's at Notre Dame.

James O'Neill, self-conscious about his own lack of formal education, was a martinet about his children's schooling. A sound education was, to his mind, far more important than any amount of domestic coddling. In September, 1895, Eugene, not quite seven years old, entered the boarding school maintained on the grounds belonging to Mount St. Vincent, and known as St. Aloysius Academy for Boys; it had been set up mainly to accommodate the young brothers of Mount St. Vincent girls, and approximated the curriculum of second through sixth grades.

In that same September Eugene's brother, Jim, now seventeen, entered a boarding school a few miles away in the Bronx on the site of what is now Fordham University, and was then called St. John's College and Preparatory School. (Jim had by this time become "Jamie," because of the elder James's discomfiture over hearing his own nickname called out by Sarah during the summers when the family was together in New London.)

Both boys were registered at their schools from the Barrett House, which was still the O'Neill family headquarters when Ella or James were in New York. Relieved of physical responsibility toward both her children, Ella could now shut her eyes and visualize the two respectable institutions in the Bronx where Jamie and Eugene were presumably secure and well cared for—and at a safe distance from her. She could subdue with morphine any intruding doubts about her children's emotional well-being. Since her sons were away, she no longer had to worry about concealing her narcotics habit from them nor explain about her periodic trips to sanitariums, to which her husband had begun sending her for rehabilitation.

Mount St. Vincent had a romantic association with the world of the theatre and James was pleased to call this to Eugene's attention. The fifty-five acres along the Hudson, complete with a pseudo-Norman-Gothic castle, had been sold to the Sisters of Charity in 1856 by Edwin Forrest for the Forrest-like sum of $100,000. Called Fonthill by the actor, the estate included, in addition to the turreted gray-stone castle, whose foundation was hewn from bedrock, a small, gracefully designed, two-story stone cottage that had been the gatekeeper's lodge, in which Forrest himself had lived briefly and in which Eugene was to spend his next five years. Forrest, who had designed Fonthill for himself and his wife, never lived in the castle because they separated before it was completed. The castle served as a priests' residence in Eugene's day, later becoming the library and archives of the college.

Eugene was not happy at Mount St. Vincent. Its lovely, wooded paths and rolling farmlands in the surrounding wilderness of the Bronx, the insistent cries of sea gulls circling above the Hudson, the solicitous attention of the sisters, only increased his sense of deprivation and loneliness.

[65]

He was remembered by the sisters as a "refined and quiet boy," who preferred to spend his free time with books rather than in active play with his companions. Though usually solemn, he had a heart-melting smile.

The foreman of the farm, who cut the grass and always invited the boys to pile the hay and roll in it, remembered Eugene as the only boy who habitually declined the invitation. Sometimes Eugene would stroll down to the river to watch the boats go by, a look of dreamy yearning on his face. One thing he longed for in the rustic setting of Mount St. Vincent was the companionship of his dog. Eugene and a New London cousin both had acquired large, odoriferous hounds, and both had named their pets Perfumery. But Eugene had had to leave *his* Perfumery behind, in the care of another relative named Josephine Brennan.

Eugene begged his teachers to let him keep the dog at school, and finally a sympathetic priest agreed to have a doghouse built on the grounds. Eugene wrote Josephine to get ready to ship Perfumery to school. But the day before the letter reached her, the dog ran under the wheels of a carriage and was killed. Eugene did not speak to Josephine for two years.

The stone cottage in which Eugene lived, ate and studied housed only fifteen boys, ranging in age from seven to twelve. On the top floor were the students' bedrooms, only six in all, and the ground floor included two classrooms and a dining room. Meals were prepared in the main building, nearly a mile away, and carried to the cottage. Although the majority of students came from wealthy families, they were not over-indulged at Mount St. Vincent, but neither were they deprived. The freezing nocturnal trips through the snow to a privy were counterbalanced by generous morning meals of oatmeal supplemented by farm butter and fresh milk.

Cherry trees abounded on the campus and, in season, the boys could feast on the fruit, when the birds did not beat them to it. In the late spring, a section near the Hudson was fenced off as a swimming pool and the boys paddled about under the supervision of a sister. It was here that Eugene had his first lessons in swimming, which later became the only sport he practiced consistently and in which he excelled. In the pastoral surroundings of the Bronx Eugene also developed an interest in nature, which was later reflected in his plays.

A contemporary glimpse of Eugene's schoolmates has been preserved in a quaint volume called *A Famous Convent School*, written by Marion J. Brunowe and published in 1897. Miss Brunowe's encounter with the academy boys occurred in October, 1896, when Eugene was just eight.

In spite of his reluctance to join in the recreational activities of his companions, he was obliged to take a certain amount of outdoor exercise, so it may be assumed that he was among the youngsters immortalized in Miss Brunowe's treacly prose:

"Shouts of clear, high laughter . . . proceed from a group of lads just issuing from yonder picturesque stone cottage . . ." she wrote. "They are all little fellows, but they make a big noise. Here they come, the jolly little chaps, in ones, in twos, in groups, running, skipping, jumping, laughing in unrestrained glee, a glee which is not so wild, however, that good breeding is forgotten.

"No, with the sight of visitors, off go caps; each, to be sure, in the peculiar method of the wearer, from the tiny lad who clutches his head covering quite in the middle of the top, to the small, punctilious Cuban youth of ten, who removes his cap with a grace worthy of his Spanish ancestors. This duty once performed, however, the small men grow supremely indifferent to any presence save their own, and that of the young religious who superintends their sports, and looks as if she might perhaps not be averse to joining in a game now and then herself."

Although Eugene may have been a part of this group physically, he was certainly detached from it spiritually. His roommate for two years, a boy named Joseph McCarthy, who was three years older than Eugene, recalled, at seventy-two, that Eugene did not have much to do with anyone except him.

"He talked very little," McCarthy has said, "and he didn't have much to say to me, either, although he seemed to be fond of me and considered me a sort of protector. Once, I punched another boy in the nose for calling Gene a sissy."

A shy, frail man, suffering from the aftereffects of tuberculosis and a paralytic stroke, McCarthy could still enjoy talking about his former roommate. His eyes crinkled with humor as he recalled a nun who used to jab with her elbows and rap the students' heads to impress the salient points of a lesson on her young charges. ("Do you ever think of Sister M—— who used to knuckle us on the bean? and Sister G——? They often come back to me," O'Neill wrote McCarthy from France in 1930.)

"Gene had an aura of sophistication that endeared him to the sisters— even to Sister M——, in spite of her jabs and punches," McCarthy said. "Most of the boys liked him, too, though they considered him a little queer. He read Kipling and authors way beyond his years—Anatole France, among others. He used to call me 'Mowgli.'" (France, who was later to turn up on the Catholic Index of forbidden books, had not yet been condemned.) Eugene insisted that Joe read everything he read, but declined to discuss the books with him.

"He was mediocre in his studies, and not really interested in anything except his reading," McCarthy recalled. "He did talk, once in a while, about wanting to go to sea. I don't know if it was his own idea or his mother's but he used to wear a sort of sailor blouse and short pants most of the time. And I remember he wrote to his brother, of whom he was very fond."

McCarthy, who knew that Eugene's father was a famous actor, as did the other boys, was not surprised to find that Eugene was willing to take part in school plays, in preference to other extracurricular activities. Eugene seemed bored, though, with the enthusiasm displayed by the other boys for James O'Neill's fencing prowess. Another student at the school, Stephen Philbin, who was Eugene's age, has recalled that the boys used to discuss James's technique with the sword and sometimes tried to imitate his dueling scenes, using sticks for weapons.

The most heated discussions among the boys concerned the Spanish-American War. As there were a good many Cuban pupils at Mount St. Vincent, much comradely patriotism was inspired by the blowing up of the *Maine*. "Remember the Maine," shouted throughout the land, was echoed at Mount St. Vincent and reinforced by picture-postcard novelties depicting the battleship which, when lit by a match, exploded in a highly satisfactory fashion.

From what both McCarthy and Philbin have remembered about the school routine, it would seem that Eugene had ample time to pursue his reading. The boys arose at six-thirty and received classroom instruction from eight until three-thirty. From then until bedtime, at nine, they were more or less free. On Sundays they attended Mass in the Chapel of the Immaculate Conception, situated in a large, pink-brick building which, at that time, also housed the academy's girl students. The enforced weekly religious services, together with concentrated weekday study of the Catechism, had its inevitable effect on the heart and mind of young Eugene.

The "age of reason," as defined by the Catholic Church, had not yet been lowered to seven, as was decreed in the 1900's. Consequently, Eugene did not receive his first Holy Communion until he was twelve, and by that time he was steeped in the Creed, the Commandments and the Sacraments. And yet, even though Catholicism was an integral part of his daily being, and though he was to feel himself pursued for the rest of his life by the "Hound of Heaven," the seed of rebellion against the rigid demands of the Church was already planted. McCarthy, who had a less questioning mind than Eugene's, was startled by a comment his roommate once made, and never forgot it.

"Religion is so cold," the nine-year-old Eugene said.

In a play O'Neill wrote in 1936, *Days Without End,* the hero, speaking of himself in the third person, describes his boyhood disappointment with the climate of Catholicism: "[His parents'] God was One of Infinite Love—not a stern, self-righteous Being Who condemned sinners to torment, but a very human lovable God Who became man for love of men and gave His life that they might be saved from themselves. And the boy had every reason to believe in such a Divinity of Love as the Creator of Life. . . . Later, at school, he learned of the God of Punishment, and he wondered. . . . Afterward . . . he saw his God as deaf and blind and merciless—a Deity Who returned hate for love and revenged Himself upon those who trusted Him!"

O'Neill's early belief was mystically interwoven with his mother's religious life, which, as a boy, he tenderly venerated. Perhaps he was not conscious at the time of how closely the atmosphere of Mount St. Vincent paralleled that of St. Mary's, where his mother had spent her girlhood; but the impression emerged vividly later. In his teens whenever he listened to his mother's long monologues of her years at St. Mary's he could evoke parallel images of the girls at Mount St. Vincent.

His emotions were so intimately entwined with his mother's that in his mind he transposed her as a schoolgirl to the campus on the Hudson—a trick of imagination illustrated by his reference in *Long Day's Journey Into Night* to the "shrine of Our Lady of Lourdes, on the little island in the lake," to which Mary Tyrone recalls having gone to pray in her senior year at school. No such shrine existed on the campus of St. Mary's Academy when Ella was a student there; the shrine was at Mount St. Vincent. Built as a replica of the grotto in France, where Bernadette reported her visitation from the Virgin Mary, the shrine stood on an island in a tiny lake, spanned by wooden bridges.

Ella went to the Mount St. Vincent grotto during her trips to the school to visit Eugene. The walk from the Mount St. Vincent station—which was a stop of the New York Central Railroad—to Eugene's dormitory led past the lake on which the grotto stood. If anything could have called to Ella's wavering faith at that time, it would have been the sight of her girlish prototypes worshiping at the statue of Mary, on whose mystically healing grace Ella was often to call for redemption in later years.

In addition to visiting Eugene and Jamie from time to time, usually accompanied by one of her New London relatives, Ella also saw her sons during school recesses. Despite her emotional stress during this period, she did not offer any objections when Eugene suggested bringing Joe McCarthy to New London with him during Easter vacation in 1897.

Joe always wondered why Eugene had invited him. During the entire week Eugene did not leave the house, saw no local friends, and made no effort to entertain Joe in any way. He seemed oblivious to the fact that he was being deficient as a host. Ella did not offer any suggestions for the boys' diversion, either. She behaved pleasantly and normally, in the eyes of the older boy, who was an orphan. Eugene spent the week reading in his room or on the porch, and left Joe to do as he pleased, after offering him the choice of his father's library.

Vacation over, the boys returned in friendly but unbroken silence to Mount St. Vincent, which Joe was to leave that summer.

During the three ensuing years that Eugene spent at the school, he grew more aware that something was wrong with his mother. His brother's behavior gave the first clue. Jamie, whom Eugene hero-worshiped, was failing in a spectacular way to live up to his youthful promise. Jamie had found out about his mother's addiction and begun to blame himself for the part he believed he had played in Edmund's death and the deterioration of his mother's health.

But, perhaps even more shattering, he had recently learned that there was another claimant to his birthright. On March 9, 1897, Nettie Walsh's son, who had by this time grown to manhood, revived his mother's claim of twenty years earlier.

Seizing on James's presence in Chicago that spring, he filed a bill alleging that his mother, in 1877, had lost her suit for divorce because she had been "misled by designing people" and that James, "by a series of false and plausible promises and also by and through threats of various sorts" against the good name of his mother and his own future prospects, "so worked upon the mother that, by . . . the most outrageous fraud upon the court, the defendant, James O'Neill, procured a decree to be entered in said court finding that no marriage ever existed between Nettie and the defendant, James O'Neill, and dismissed her said bill of divorce for want of equity."

The son went on to point out that his own legitimacy was in question, and that he intended to remove the blemish from his name and re-establish the good name of his mother. He asked that James be restrained from leaving the state and that a receiver be appointed for James's property.

James put his lawyers to work once more and did his best to keep the matter quiet. But the case dragged on for three years, accompanied by a certain amount of publicity, and Jamie eventually learned all the details. (Although the son's suit was no more successful than the mother's in establishing the fact of the marriage, and was finally dismissed in 1900, it cost James money again.)

Jamie started going to pieces soon after graduating from St. John's Preparatory School. He entered St. John's College with the idea of studying law, and although he continued to do very well scholastically, he began to drink, cutting classes and visiting the more gaudy places of entertainment in Manhattan. In spite of his grades, which averaged consistently in the nineties, even in the subject of religion, Jamie had become, by the time he was twenty, a suffering, cynical alcoholic.

It was at this point that he began to be a formative and destructive influence on his ten-year-old brother, whom he both loved and resented. His letters to Eugene were tinged with sneering comments about life and religion that had a lasting effect on the younger boy. Finally, after a flagrant gesture of defiance at St. John's—he brought a prostitute to the campus and tried to pass her off as his sister, on a bet—he was asked to leave. The request was made early in December of 1899, six months before he was to be graduated. Jamie had got into trouble before that. As manager of the baseball team he had failed to meet his players on time at the railroad station; instead, with the train tickets in his pocket, he had gone off to a saloon, where he was discovered, drunk, by one of the team members.

Eugene remained at Mount St. Vincent until June of 1900. He was upset about Jamie, and increasingly worried about his mother. Longing for a reassuring answer, he sought comfort in his religion. He was able to find it, probably for the last time, in the sacrament of Communion, which he received on May 24. Several years after his death a sweet-faced, elderly nun at Mount St. Vincent pointed out to a visitor the altar at which the twelve-year-old boy, having fasted and confessed and made fervent acts of faith, hope, love and contrition, solemnly accepted the body and blood of Christ.

Eugene believed unwaveringly that he had achieved union with God, that he had been granted an increase of grace, and that he would be preserved from mortal sin. The nun, who had not herself known Eugene, had spoken to sisters who remembered him and she had interested herself in his career.

"Doesn't it break your heart to think of the poor little fellow?" she asked the visitor rhetorically, apropos of Eugene's subsequent loss of faith.

Mount St. Vincent kept its boy students only to the age of twelve. The following fall, therefore, on October 16, 1900, Eugene entered De La Salle Institute in Manhattan. This time he lived at home, now a hotel at Sixty-eighth Street near Central Park West, and attended daily classes at the school. Situated on Sixth Avenue and Fifty-ninth Street, with enormous French windows facing Central Park, De La Salle was a Catholic school operated by the Christian Brothers. Elaborately decorated and furnished, it was attended by the sons of wealthy families. The preponderance of successful actors' sons in the student body inspired one of Eugene's teachers, Brother Basil, to arrange contests in reading and declamation among his pupils, to which he invited the proud professional parents.

Ella's experiment in domesticity was abortive and disastrous. Eugene returned to the hotel one day unexpectedly and stumbled upon her in the act of giving herself a morphine injection. She was far more upset than Eugene and accused him of spying on her. Eugene, who barely comprehended what he had seen, bore the tirade quietly, almost numbly. It took him some time and several anguished sessions with his father and brother before he understood what was, and had been for many years, wrong with his mother. Finally the full force of his discovery gripped him.

At that point it was actually a relief to him to be able to pin down, at last, a sufficiently devastating reason for his inbred, tragic view of life. For the first time, too, the bitter pattern of his brother's and his father's life was illuminated for him.

Eugene had already begun to dramatize himself, much as his mother had done as a girl. His misery was genuine, but he heightened it to torment himself. Ella's addiction now provided the reason for his faltering faith. He prayed for her cure, challenging God to prove himself by restoring his mother to health, and demonstrating thereby that he had already lost his faith.

Thinly disguising the facts of this personal crisis in *Days Without End,* he presented the hero's mother as a widow in a weakened condition from having nursed her husband during a fatal siege of flu, rather than as a woman who could not cope with her marriage and had retreated into narcotics addiction. Speaking of his boyhood self in the third person, the hero says:

"Then his mother . . . was taken ill. And the horrible fear came to him that she might die, too. . . . His God of Love was beginning to show Himself as a God of Vengeance. . . . But he still trusted in His Love.

Surely He would not take his mother from him. . . . So the poor fool prayed and vowed his life to piety and good works! But he began to make a condition now—*if* his mother were spared to him! He abased and humbled himself before the Cross—and, in reward for his sickening humiliation, saw that no miracle would happen. Something snapped in him then. . . . His mother died. And, in a frenzy of insane grief— No! In his awakened pride he cursed his God and denied Him, and, in revenge, promised his soul to the Devil—on his knees, when everyone thought he was praying!"

This fictional session of prayer and revolt had its actual counterpart during Eugene's second year at De La Salle. Ella, who did not want him at home watching her with wounded and accusing eyes, had enrolled him as a boarder. Eugene "prayed and vowed his life to piety and good works," asking God to redeem his mother. He deluded himself into believing that he was still firm in his faith, by applying himself with unprecedented zeal to his studies and by doing particularly well in the subject of religion.

That year, under a stringent grading system, he tied for fifth place with two other students in a class of twenty-two. His average mark in religion for the year was 84. English, in which he averaged 87, was one of his best subjects, but his highest grade was 88, in history; his lowest mark was 57, in geometry and algebra, subjects he consistently resisted.

But in spite of his application to good works, Ella was not spared.

By the end of the year Eugene knew he was through with Catholic schools. However strongly James and Ella may have felt about it, they could not induce Eugene to accept any further religious training. He jeered at their arguments, saying that religion had proved of little use to them; why insist on it for him?

He was to maintain later that this year marked the turning point in his life. He confided as much, at sixty, to one of his doctors when he was gravely ill. He entered Betts Academy, a nonsectarian Connecticut boarding school, at fourteen. At fifteen he decided to stop attending church.

It was on a Sunday morning in New London, during school vacation, that he made up his mind never to go to church again. James saw him descending the stairs and told him to get ready, and Eugene informed him of his decision. James took a few steps down the staircase to confront his son and the two began shouting at each other, James attempting to shake sense into Eugene physically and Eugene twisting and pulling under his grip. Grappling and arguing, they reached the ground floor and glared at each other, James rigid with frustration but Eugene standing his ground. James finally went off to church alone.

◈

Eugene's rejection of Catholicism hounded him for the rest of his life. The anguish of this rejection of faith is clearly revealed in *Days Without End*. In the play, completed by O'Neill when he was forty-five, he expressed his torment at having lost his faith and his desire to confess and receive forgiveness. Many of his admiring non-Catholic followers were upset by the dogmatically Catholic profession of the last act, in which the hero declares: "At last I see! I have always loved! O Lord of Love, forgive Thy poor blind fool! . . . Thou art the Way—the Truth—the Resurrection and the Life, and he that believeth in Thy Love, his love shall never die!"

The very title of the play, in fact, echoes the words of one of the first prayers Eugene learned: "Glory be to the Father, and to the Son, and to the Holy Ghost. As it was in the beginning, is now, and ever shall be, *world without end.*"

Although the play seemed to indicate that O'Neill had re-embraced his faith, it soon became evident that he had not. Not long after the production O'Neill once again resigned himself to damnation.

VIII

IN CONTRAST TO HIS EARLY SCHOOL YEARS, THE FOUR years Eugene spent at Betts Academy, in Stamford, Connecticut, were relatively happy ones. He found that he was accepted on his own terms by his schoolmates, and he began to take a more convivial part in their activities, at the same time reserving his right to withdraw when it suited him. His teachers at Betts, like those at Mount St. Vincent, remembered him as a dreamer who often liked to go off on solitary walks.

At fourteen he had grown into a strikingly attractive youth. Tall, thin, with darkening brown hair and uncannily luminous eyes, Eugene inherited the best features of both his parents. He had his mother's sensitive mouth; his hands, with their long, delicate fingers were both his mother's and his father's. His profile, with its strong jaw and prominent nose, was his father's.

Eugene's entrance into Betts in the fall of 1902 marked for him the beginning of an open revolt against religion and convention, which was to intensify with each year. Under the influence of his voracious reading he began to substitute an active atheism for Catholicism and began to defy his father in other ways. Under Jamie's cynical tutelage he also tried, though never quite successfully, to replace his shattered dream of a pure and queenly mother with Jamie's own substitute, the earthy, sympathetic whore. Like many renegade Catholics, he was impelled to attack every tenet of his rejected faith. It was a long time before he recognized that his revolt was actually a search for a substitute faith. He was gradually to become, as Elizabeth Sergeant later noted with his complete approval, "an agnostic in search of redemption."

The years at Betts provided Eugene with his only formal education of a higher order, except for a much later course in playwriting at Harvard University. (His year as a Princeton freshman was to be academically fruitless.) Betts, as it happened, stood ready to drum into him a thorough, practical and liberal grounding in the classics and sciences.

The nonsectarian school, which was one of the best private preparatory institutions in the East, aimed "to surround the boys with a home atmosphere." Its goals were to "concentrate on the individual needs and abilities of each student, to encourage each to proceed at his own rate, and to cultivate in them sound habits of observation and research." A brochure stated that "in observation work the first task of the student is the inspection of things that are constantly before him, such as plants, animals, the stars, etc. He is thus taught first to *see* and then to *tell* what he *sees* going on around him in nature and in practical life, and is required to record his observations in well-systematized note-books."

It was an admirable approach, particularly well calculated to provide basic training for an incipient dramatist; Eugene's sharp eye and ear for the things that were before him later became a major facet of his talent, and all his life he was to keep the voluminous, well-systematized notebooks, which served as the outlines for his plays and which he was trained to use at Betts. The school kept its classes small—there was a student body of only sixty, and a staff large enough to provide a ratio of one teacher to every six pupils.

James and Ella were at considerable pains to see that Eugene found himself always in physically beautiful, as well as academically stimulating, surroundings. Betts Academy, about an hour's train ride from Manhattan, had been built in 1838 on an elevation called Strawberry Hill, in the finest residential section of Stamford. The grounds included a four-acre lawn with football and baseball fields and a tennis court; in winter a depressed section of lawn was flooded and converted into an ice-skating rink. Two rambling, yellow wooden buildings (which burned to the ground in 1908, ending the school's seventy-year existence) provided comfortable living quarters for students and staff, and included modern classrooms and well-equipped athletic facilities.

Eugene had his own room in the three-story main building, which was furnished in Victorian but not unhomey style, with high dresser, iron-frame bed, desk, chair, and throw rug. From his window he could see on clear days the familiar Long Island Sound at which he also gazed in New London. Here in Stamford, as at Mount St. Vincent on the Hudson, New London, and most of the other places he was to live, water formed part of Eugene's background. The combined cost of atmosphere and academic inspiration was $500 a year.

The man who presided, paternalistically, over the outsize family of boys, was William Betts, known, behind his back, as "Billy." A squat man with a handle-bar mustache, Betts was indulgent in everything but scholarship. He was willing to overlook pranks, but he was strict in his academic demands. As one of Eugene's schoolmates has recalled, "Billy knew Latin and Greek backwards and was a stern taskmaster; anyone who stayed the course at Betts *had* to come out with a thorough education and was, invariably, accepted by a top college."

Eugene was a fair student in Latin and French, a good student in natural history, and an excellent one in English. He also did well in Greek and Roman history, which were stressed as a background for learning classical languages and which helped spark his later fascination with Greek drama.

One of his teachers, Arthur Walter, called "Algie" by the boys, waged a four-year battle with Eugene on the field of mathematics. It was never entirely clear, in the end, who had emerged as victor. Eugene would sulkily ask, "What's the good of studying that stuff?" and his teacher would patiently attempt to supply an answer. Walter told James O'Neill, during one of his visits to Betts, that Eugene had failed in algebra; James, distressed, indicated that the school had his full support in any disciplinary measures it saw fit to impose. Although James was a fairly frequent visitor to the school, Ella never accompanied him. Since her presence during most of this period has not been recalled in New London either, it is probable that she was spending considerable time in a sanitarium.

Algie Walter, in addition to being the mathematics teacher, was in charge of Eugene's dormitory.

"His room was across the hall from mine," Walter recalled. "I often invited Gene to come to my room and have a chat, but he never accepted."

Eugene smoked in his own room, contrary to a school rule which banned all smoking. Walter believed that Eugene's requests to attend Mass in town were really excuses for him to have an undisturbed smoke.

"Permission was always granted whenever he asked," Walter said. "We had a few Roman Catholics in school besides Gene, but he never went to Mass with any of them."

Another way to come by a smoke was to visit the town lunch wagon, which provided the only place within walking distance of Betts where the boys could eat out. The wagon was a horse-drawn affair, which was stationed during the day in an alleyway near the firehouse. At night a horse towed it to the center of town, where it became a dinner wagon. The lunch wagon's bill of fare was inferior to that of the Betts dining room, where second helpings of nutritious food were always provided. But the boys enjoyed the wagon's specialty, which the menu ambiguously called "tenderloin." It sold for fifteen cents, and was actually a chunk of pork pounded into a flat slab and fried brown.

A number of Eugene's classmates have concurred in their recollections of him as a popular, if not gregarious, boy, who took normal pleasure in breaking the rules and flouting authority both as an individual and as a member of the crowd. One evening Eugene and a group of friends gathered all the chamber pots in the dormitory and built a tower of them at the top of the stairs outside their rooms. They tied a rope to the bottom pot, and as soon as they were sure all the teachers were asleep, they pulled the rope. The resultant clatter was as terrifying as any of them could have wished. Betts, who was unable to isolate the ringleader, as all the boys had taken an oath to stand together, was inclined to favor Eugene as one of the chief culprits; in his frustration he predicted that Eugene was destined for the electric chair. Eugene was flattered.

Eugene was also among those who sneaked out of the dormitory and raced for town the night the Town Hall burned down. Many other times, and with a less exciting incentive, he participated in the game of tying sheets together from a dormitory window and escaping into town after lights-out at nine o'clock. At times the boys would find Billy Betts grimly awaiting their return. Then they would be penalized with canceled weekend leaves.

When the boys sneaked into town—it was about a mile's walk on a dirt road—they usually headed for a saloon operated by the champion prize-fighter, Bob Fitzsimmons. Fitzsimmons would occasionally look the other way while the bartender slipped them a beer, or even something stronger. If he was in an expansive mood Fitzsimmons, who kept a lion cub as a pet, would sit with the boys and, to their immeasurable delight, tell them of his bouts in the ring. Fitzsimmons would sometimes turn up on the Betts baseball field in the spring to root for the home team, sporting a tall silk hat and holding his lion on a leash. Eugene was as enraptured as anyone.

Although Betts emphasized athletics, Eugene never took an active part in any sport except, once in a while, to swing a desultory golf club, but he had a boundless enthusiasm for athletes that was to last all his life.

Eugene, as some of his classmates have recalled, was interested in, but not completely at ease with nice girls. He made dates with one or two Stamford girls but was uncertain how to entertain them. He asked a Betts boy named Sawyer Robinson, whom he once introduced to a local girl, how much he ought to spend on her. But other of Eugene's classmates had the impression that off campus he was something of a ladies' man.

Eugene had begun to tag along on New York weekends with Jamie, who was methodically teaching his kid brother the ropes. He was an eager pupil, but not an altogether apt one. Although he followed Jamie's example in going through all the motions ("I made sin easy for him," Jamie often remarked), Eugene never believed in what he was doing.

Jamie was "wised up" to the fact that all women had the souls of whores; Eugene was convinced that all whores had souls of gold. Jamie was chronically cynical; Eugene was incurably naïve and romantic. He was incapable of adopting Jamie's hedonistic attitude.

But Eugene kept up an appearance of savoir-faire. He enjoyed displaying his knowledge of the ropes by taking school friends with him to New York to see the current shows, which, due to his father's profession, he could do free of charge. He and another New York boy named Hans, whose father ran Papst's Café, next door to the Majestic Theatre, became close friends for a time. While Hans's access to free tickets was limited to the Majestic, the Betts boys were just as willing to settle for repeated attendance there as for visits to other theatres. The main reason was that *The Wizard of Oz* was having a long run at the Majestic and the student body of Betts was collectively in love with the blond ingénue, Anna Laughlin.

Eugene could be lofty about this mass, unrequited love, for he was personally acquainted, through Jamie, with the musical's star, Lotta Faust. Lotta made such an impression on him that, about two dozen years later, he could still remember her beautiful legs, and he was fond of discussing Miss Faust with other old fans, among them George Jean Nathan.

"There, my boy, was a love-apple," O'Neill once told Nathan, "and who said anything about acting? You could get an effect just looking at her that you can't get from looking at and listening to any dozen current actresses full of the virtuoso stuff. When Lotta sang 'Sammy,' all the great Shakespearean actresses of the day felt like going into hiding."

When Eugene was ready to leave Betts he was an exceptionally well mannered, but at the same time shy and withdrawn, boy of seventeen. He was still conforming in his dress—possibly in imitation of his brother, who was a Broadway fashion plate. Although he was soon to emphasize his revolt against convention by abandoning all semblance of decent attire, during this period he dressed nattily. On weekends and holidays he wore white flannel trousers and dark jackets and on school days he wore knickers and pull-overs.

His fashion sense beguiled the girl who lived next door to him in New London, and who played croquet with him on his front lawn during summer vacations.

"I'll never forget the time Gene came home in brown knickers and squeaky yellow shoes," she once said. "I remember them squeaking along the road past my house."

In spite of his sartorial conformity, Eugene possessed an instantly recognizable quality of being set apart from the crowd. By this time he had swallowed large doses of Tolstoi and Dostoevski, as well as Kipling and the modern French writers, and he had discovered Oscar Wilde. Joseph

Conrad and Jack London fascinated him, and he dreamed of going to sea, although he did not, for the moment, consider it as a serious possibility. He did not, in fact, have any serious plans for his future, even though his father had a faint hope that he might go on the stage, as Jamie had been persuaded to do.

Chafing at his father's heavyhanded paternalism, Eugene consented to go to college. But he chose Princeton rather than Yale, which was where all his college-bound classmates were going, and for which Betts was an acknowledged preparatory school.

IX

IN THE FALL OF 1932 EUGENE O'NEILL WROTE HIS only full-length comedy. He called it *Ah, Wilderness!*, set it in a "large-small town in Connecticut" in the summer of 1906, and made its central character, Richard Miller, a boy "going on seventeen, just out of high school" and ready to enter Yale in the fall. In the summer of 1906 Eugene was seventeen, just out of high school, and ready to enter Princeton in the fall. He spent his vacation in the large-small town of New London.

When *Ah, Wilderness!* was produced there was considerable speculation as to how autobiographical the characters and events of the play were. At the time O'Neill said that the resemblance between Richard Miller's life and his own was trifling. What he really thought of himself and his family did not emerge until *Long Day's Journey Into Night*, set in the New London of 1912, appeared in print. *Ah, Wilderness!*, said O'Neill, was a nostalgic dream of what he would have *liked* his adolescence to have been. "The truth is, I *had* no youth," he added.

Nevertheless, *Ah, Wilderness!* and *Long Day's Journey Into Night* may be regarded, in a sense, as two sides of the same coin—one a benign glimpse of what the O'Neill family, at its best, aspired to be and the other a balefully heightened picture of what it was at its worst.

But while O'Neill based *Ah, Wilderness!* on his own family to some degree, the family of his best friend, Arthur McGinley, served as his principal model. Arthur was the son of John McGinley, who, in 1883, had urged James and Ella to buy a house in New London.

O'Neill was self-pityingly given to contrasting his own boyhood summers in New London with the sort of summers spent by his New London contemporaries, whose parents devoted themselves uncomplicatedly to each other and their children. The McGinley family was the one he particularly admired and envied. Like Nat Miller in *Ah, Wilderness!* John McGinley was the editor (and part owner) of a newspaper; he had helped found the New London *Day* in the late 1800's. Also like Nat Miller, McGinley was the head of a large family. Not only Eugene, but his father as well, regarded the McGinleys' cheerful domesticity with a kind of awe. Once when visiting the McGinleys and observing the easy, close-knit camaraderie that existed among the parents and their seven sons and daughters, James was moved to confess to his friend, "I may have made some money and achieved some fame, but you're the man I envy."

Whenever James appeared as Monte Cristo in New London, he reserved a box at the Lyceum Theatre for the entire McGinley clan. The children would show up for the event scrubbed, shining and eager. Arthur McGinley saw the play nine times as a result of this family ritual.

In *Ah, Wilderness!* O'Neill characteristically used many actual names —or close approximations—of the people connected with the era and locale of which he was writing. The names Arthur, Tom and "Wint" (a nickname for Winthrop) were given to characters in *Ah, Wilderness!* and a boy named Lawrence is mentioned, but does not appear; all four names belonged to the McGinley boys. John McGinley's wife, Evelyn Essex, became Essie, and the daughter, Mildred, took her name from a girl O'Neill had known and remembered in that period; her nickname, in the play and in life, was "Mid" and her last name was Culver, which O'Neill also managed to use by having Mildred mention a friend named Anne Culver.

O'Neill also threw in a reference to a policeman named Sullivan, who was actually Tim Sullivan, a New London fixture. In the play Nat Miller's spinster sister, Lily, drew her name and much of her character from a spinster cousin of Ella O'Neill's named Lil Brennan. It was Lil who often protested to Ella and James that Eugene's reading should be censored, although, in other matters, she was inclined to take Eugene's part against his father. She recognized, for example, that James had made Jamie (and was making Eugene) overdependent on him, and felt it was unreasonable for James to expect his sons to have a mature sense of responsibility unless he changed his method.

However much the youthful Eugene suffered from a lack of warmth in his own home, the adult Eugene, yielding to an inescapable bond of affection beneath his resentment of his father, endowed the character of Nat Miller with at least two of his father's amusing and rather lovable traits. (Responding to a researcher's query a few years after the production of *Ah, Wilderness!*, O'Neill said that Miller was like his father "in some aspects, but totally unlike him in others.")

One of the traits was James's conviction that "a certain peculiar oil" in bluefish had a poisonous effect on his digestion; it was a family joke that Ella served him bluefish under the guise of weakfish. The other trait was James's tendency to repeat stories of his boyhood and young manhood—illustrated in *Ah, Wilderness!* by what was probably the only nontheatrical reminiscence in his repertory, concerning the way he had once rescued a friend from drowning.

Although O'Neill succeeded in drawing two totally disparate families in *Ah, Wilderness!* and *Long Day's Journey Into Night*, he set them both down in the living room of his own home on Pequot Avenue. (The similarity of the two settings is not readily noticed, for the Pequot Avenue establishment is seen in *Ah, Wilderness!* through rose-colored glasses, while in *Long Day's Journey* it is viewed through a glass darkly. Nevertheless, if executed literally for the stage, the two sets could, with the shifting of only a few minor details, substitute for each other.)

Both the Miller and the Tyrone living rooms are first seen empty, with early-morning sunshine streaming through the windows. Porch, doorways bookcases and windows are almost identically situated. In the center of the Tyrone living room is "a round table with a green-shaded reading lamp, the cord plugged in one of the four sockets in the chandelier above." In the center of the Miller living room is "a big, round table with a green-shaded reading lamp, the cord of the lamp running up to one of five sockets in the chandelier above." In the Millers' room "a medium-priced, inoffensive rug covers most of the floor" and in the Tyrones' room "the hardwood floor is nearly covered by a rug, inoffensive in design and color." Yet the Millers find their home cheerful and pleasant, while the Tyrones (with the exception of James, who is indifferent) regard their home as little better than a hovel.

This contradictory view was actually reflected by contemporary New Londoners, depending upon their social strata. James's Irish friends and in-laws thought the house comfortable, attractive, and more than adequate for the four O'Neills. Members of the town's more pretentious families, however, considered it ordinary. Ella, later supported by Jamie and Eugene, was self-conscious about not having a home as grand as those belonging to the better families in the town, and often complained to James that the house was ill constructed, shabbily furnished, and cheaply maintained. She and her sons often accused James of frugality. But James, who had few pretensions and who believed he had done well to come as far as he had from his Irish peasant beginnings, took their abuse in silence.

While there is evidence to support the *Long Day's Journey* (or gloomy) view of the O'Neill home—especially when it began to be neglected in later years—a newspaper article written in 1900 supports the *Ah, Wilderness!* (or sunny) side. The feature writer for the Boston *Sunday Journal*, who visited the O'Neill home for an interview with James (and who may have been a stage-struck, unsophisticated young man), came away dazzled. He described it as "an elegant two-story structure . . . and an ideal spot for rest and recreation."

Set well back from the road on an embankment, the house was surrounded by open porches (which were then called piazzas), shrubbery, flowers, and a sizable expanse of well-kept, velvety lawn.

The reporter credited Ella with "artistic ideas [which] are manifested in the taste with which the interior of the house is arranged." He added: "It is hard to go into any room in which there is not a cozy nook or a comfortable corner. Paintings of real value and rare etchings adorn the walls, while any number of photographs of Mr. O'Neill's professional friends are scattered over tables and writing desks." Among them was a large photograph of Edwin Booth, inscribed to James, that stood on a small easel in a bamboo frame. The reporter was also impressed by James's library, which, he said, included "rare acting editions of old plays, and prompt books of distinguished value" in addition to the works of Rousseau, Emerson, Kent and Farquhar.

The house could not have been cheaply constructed, for the beautiful old wooden staircase, solid door and window frames, and fine, sturdy hardwood floors survived years of later neglect and abuse; even its white shingle exterior and the Victorian gingerbread trimming of the porch eaves, while not especially fetching by modern standards, were solid enough to withstand years of sea-front weather.

But it is true that the house did not compare favorably with the more luxurious homes of other theatrical figures in the town, and Eugene chose to condemn his father for that. One way in which, as a boy, he revenged himself upon James, was by writing his own name in the front of his father's books. Another thing he did was to scratch a large, disfiguring M.C. (for Monte Cristo) into the base of the handsome, polished balustrade of his house. But the worst thing—from James and Ella's point of view—that Eugene ever did as a child was to pour a can of green paint over a box of shiny, metal statuettes depicting James as Edmond Dantes. The paint had hardened, permanently cloaking the little figures in sickly green, before Eugene's crime was discovered.

Neither Jamie nor Eugene approved of James's practice of doing his own work about the grounds. They accused him of trying to save money on help, while James stoutly maintained that he found relaxation in tending his own lawn and shrubbery and that no "lazy loafer" he could hire would do it half as well. Similarly, James's refusal to avail himself of the city's water supply, on the grounds that it was not pure enough, and his use, instead, of an old-fashioned well sunk in his own property, was attributed by his sons to reluctance to pay the water taxes.

While all of this accumulated resentment is spelled out relentlessly in *Long Day's Journey,* no trace of it appears in *Ah, Wilderness!* But, curiously, another vestige of the O'Neill menage does appear in both the nostalgic comedy and the autobiographical tragedy and in almost the same form in both plays. This is the raw, young, rough-spoken Irish maid, or "second girl." In *Ah, Wilderness!* her name is Norah, but she uses the same brogue-larded phrases and is the same thorn-in-the-side to her mistress as Cathleen in *Long Day's Journey.*

The greatest disparity in characterization between the two plays is the mother. Mrs. Miller is nothing like Ella; she is, however, very much like Evelyn McGinley, who bore a physical resemblance to Queen Victoria and had all the maternal, bustling, good-natured officiousness that Eugene missed in his own mother.

And the older brother, Arthur, in *Ah, Wilderness!* is also far removed from actuality. Two years older than Richard, he is a Yale undergraduate and almost as innocent as Richard himself. Jamie, on the other hand, was ten years older than his brother, and no innocent: an actor, a heavy drinker, a favorite in the New London brothels, and a man who knew all the Broadway gossip and could be amusingly informative about the least savory and most personal aspects of all the reigning soubrettes, a number of whom had lost their heads over him.

As for Richard, there was much of young Eugene in his make-up, though part of his personality was borrowed from a contemporary named Charles ("Hutch") Collins. When *Ah, Wilderness!* was produced, Arthur McGinley wrote to O'Neill to tell him he recognized his own family in the play. O'Neill, fearing that he might have embarrassed his friend, wrote back that none of the characters were taken from life.

"They are general types true for any large-small town," he added. "But the boy does spout the poetry I and Hutch Collins once used to." Hutch shared with Eugene (and Richard) a passion for the works of such scandalous writers as Wilde and Swinburne, and both boys could recite long passages from the *Rubáiyát* of Omar Khayyám (from which work the play's title derives; O'Neill substituted "Ah" for "Oh" because he thought the former conveyed a stronger sense of nostalgia). And, like Richard, the two teen-age boys believed that Oscar Wilde had been imprisoned for the crime of bigamy.

It was Eugene who guided Hutch's early reading, but he did not have to guide his taste in clothes. Hutch dressed like a dandy, wearing white flannels and a hat with a London label that elicited both the envy and the scorn of his friends, whose parents referred to him as "Jerry Collins' damn fool." One of Hutch's sartorially drab friends once nailed the hat to a wall as a joke. Both Eugene and Hutch were often seen leaving the New London library with stacks of books under their arms, eliciting the bewildered respect of their less intellectual friends. One such friend, on being questioned about Eugene by a younger boy, was told, definitively, "That Gene O'Neill—he reads *deep* stuff!"

But the seventeen-year-old O'Neill, like Richard Miller, had his lighter, boyish side, though he was sometimes inclined in later years to deny it. While he expressed contempt for the stuffiness of New London, he did participate with pleasure in the Fourth of July rituals, which he later described in *Ah, Wilderness!* The traditional celebrations, with intricate displays of fireworks, started at midnight on July 3 and lasted until midnight of the Fourth. Eugene marked the holiday with his friends rather than with his family, for neither his mother nor his father was interested in or capable of the cheerful give-and-take that pervaded the McGinley and the Miller clans.

Despite his sense of deprivation and his insistence that he hated New London ("It wasn't a friendly town," he once told an acquaintance), Eugene had no wish to forget it. He kept revisiting, in his mind, its physical and emotional landmarks, just as he later persisted in pointing out the Barrett House to his friends. He set three of his major plays (*Long Day's Journey Into Night, Ah, Wilderness!* and *A Moon for the Misbegotten*) in New London, and there are hints of vividly remembered local events and personalities in several others—notably *Strange Interlude,* in which the frenzied excitement of a college rowing meet is re-created.)

Eugene attended many of the Yale-Harvard boat races that were held every year on the Thames and were among the big social events of New London. Members of the competing crews and their relatives and friends crowded the hotels and inns of the town, and a Mardi Gras spirit prevailed, in which Eugene participated.

Eugene also relished listening to the popular player-piano tunes of the day, some of which turned up in *Ah, Wilderness!*—"Waiting at the Church," for instance, and "Bedelia." His nostalgia for the songs of the early 1900's lasted all his life.

O'Neill attributed his love of music, which included contemporary jazz and an indiscriminate smattering of the classical, to his mother's musicianship. He boasted to several close friends that she had been a talented pianist. But though in later life he acquired a sizable record collection and a fine phonograph, nothing could send him into quite the same transports as the tinny sound of a player piano, rendering the tunes of the early 1900's. He humorously confessed as much in a poem he composed in New London a few years later, of which these lines are typical:

> I have tried to fall for the stuff of Mozart
> Handel, Haydn—a dozen or more
> But I guess my ear isn't framed for "beaux arts"
> For I found them all a terrible bore.
>
> . . . .
>
> The long-haired high-brows call me "vulgarian"
> When the "Great Big Beautiful Doll" I croon
> For I'm strong for the music that's real American
> And the joy of my heart is a rag time tune.
>
> . . . .
>
> High-brows, whom classic music quickeneth,
> Heed well the burden of my vulgar rune,
> Your lofty tumbling wearies me to death,
> The joy of my heart is a rag time tune.

Evidence of the strong pull music had on his emotions appears in many of his plays. Besides the popular songs in *Ah, Wilderness!* he used songs to underline mood, evoke atmosphere or convey character in such plays as *The Hairy Ape, The Great God Brown, Mourning Becomes Electra, All God's Chillun Got Wings,* and *The Iceman Cometh.*

Another phase of his boyhood that Eugene cherished and never outgrew was his use of early 1900 slang and colloquialisms. That was the speech in which he felt most at home, and the further he deviated from it, either in conversation or in the dialogue of his plays, the more stilted and ill at ease he became. "The old bean," "in the pink," "palship," and "the glad mitt" were among his favorite expressions long after they had become archaic; in his correspondence he often emphasized these phrases with an exclamation mark, a punctuation to which he was devoted. A number of people who met him in later life (the critics Brooks Atkinson and John Mason Brown, for example) have commented on the extraordinary flavor of his speech. Brown has remarked that he lacked a knowledge of contemporary speech and Atkinson has pointed out that his outdated slang sounded awkward. But O'Neill loved it, and in addition to the colloquialisms of a bygone era he had a fluent command of the unchanging language of the underworld and the demimonde, which, from his lips, sounded as incongruous as the obsolete slang.

One of the last plays he wrote, a one-acter called *Hughie,* is an amazing compilation of argot. The play, less an acting piece than a short story with dialogue, which O'Neill did not intend for production, is about a petty gambler and a night clerk in a seedy Manhattan hotel. In it O'Neill uses the following terms from his working vocabulary: sap, noggin, sucker, puss, moniker, hooked, bangtail, finn, babe, sawbuck, croaked, bum dope, old bones, raw babies, rubbed out, real jack, old turtle, round-heeled, in my book, the sticks, the Big Stem, run-out powder, fall guy, clam shut, hit the hay, crummy dump, the once-over, het up, beat the racket, poor boob, square shake, lap it up, put the bite on.

He derived none of these terms from books—they were all part of what he liked to think of as his "life-experience."

But in 1906 his ideas—like those of Richard Miller in *Ah, Wilderness!*—came almost exclusively from books. In that year Eugene did a good part of his reading in the apartment-office of a dashing New Londoner named Joseph Ganey, who was ten years Eugene's senior, and a contemporary of Jamie. Ganey had been a butcher and a coal dealer, before deciding to become a doctor. Shortly after settling down to medical practice and acquiring "Doc" as his nickname, Ganey made (to Eugene's admiration) an impetuous trip around the world, during which he collected a number of first editions to add to an already sizable library.

Although Ganey did not return Eugene's admiration—he found him sullen and difficult and considered him something of a poseur—he tolerated the boy and did not discourage his reading. Doc Ganey refused to allow Eugene to take any of his precious volumes home with him, but consented to let him read as much as he pleased in the apartment. Often Ganey would return home at three in the morning from a night on the town and find Eugene poring over Wilde, Schopenhauer, Zola or de Maupassant.

From early adolescence Eugene had been devouring the books in his father's library; every summer he read through the works of Victor Hugo and Alexandre Dumas, in addition to Dickens and Kipling. He also read the Irish romantic, Charles Lever, and the volumes of Irish history with which James's library was studded, as well as the philosophy of Emerson and the poetry of Scott and Byron—he could recite *Childe Harold* interminably; only after he had exhausted the supply of recognized classics in his own home did he approach Doc Ganey's more sophisticated library.

But while Richard Miller is depicted as startling his family with lurid and antisocial quotations from disreputable European authors, he is shown to be basically innocent and pure in heart; his "depravity" is solely intellectual. Eugene, on the other hand, was inclined to practice what he preached and, although he was naïve, he was not innocent.

Doc Ganey's "Second Story Club," an informal, raffish, preponderantly Irish organization that would have stood Richard Miller's hair on end, was a milieu in which Eugene felt at home. The club, which met in Ganey's second-floor rooms on Main Street to talk, drink and play cards, was composed of a kind of avant-garde of New London and was regarded with horror by the respectable citizens of the town. Art McGinley, who was tall and lanky and was called "a left-footed Irishman" by his friends because his family was Episcopalian, said, in recalling Doc Ganey, "We ate his food, drank his liquor, wore out his carpets, read his books and got free medical attention." Eugene did not care for cards, but he could hold his own in the other activities.

Unlike Richard Miller, who is shocked by his encounter with a prostitute in a shady hotel and resists her efforts to entice him to an upstairs room, Eugene by now was boastfully at home with the ladies of Bradley Street, a narrow avenue at the northern end of town that encompassed the flourishing red-light district of New London; Jamie had seen to his indoctrination there, and the members of the Second Story Club saw to it that he continued his visits.

The brothels of Bradley Street, about a dozen in all, were housed in rickety wooden structures that flanked the New London police station. This facilitated periodic police raids and generally abetted the convenient working arrangement between the upholders of the law and the practitioners of vice. The girls would lean out the windows and exchange small talk with the policemen while waiting for customers. When a house was raided and the prostitutes haled into court, the judge would ask "Occupation?" and the customary answer would be "Seamstress."

A description of the interior of a Bradley Street brothel was given by O'Neill in *The Great God Brown* and was recognized with delight by some of his old companions in sin when the play was first published.

"An automatic, nickel-in-the-slot player-piano is at center, rear," he wrote. "On its right is a dirty gilt second-hand sofa. At the left is a bald-spotted crimson plush chair. The backdrop for the rear wall is cheap wallpaper of a dull yellow-brown, resembling a blurred impression of a fallow field in early spring. There is a cheap alarm clock on top of the piano."

"Here comes the kindergarten," the seamstresses would call out when

Eugene and his young friends showed up. They usually arrived en masse, for reasons of economy; a round of beer cost one dollar, regardless of how many were in the group.

Eugene and Richard were dissimilar in other ways. There is nothing in Richard's character that suggests Eugene's profound love of the water and ships; nor does *Ah, Wilderness!* more than hint at the fact that the town in which it is set had a tradition of sea history. Eugene, however, rarely missed watching the arrival or departure of the square-riggers that still, in the early 1900's, sailed with breath-taking beauty into New London harbor. That harbor was all but jammed with the floating palaces of millionaires, Navy craft, and a training vessel for Coast Guard cadets. But Eugene was interested only in the romantic schooners that were already becoming something of a rarity and were soon to vanish completely.

He spent long hours talking to the ships' captains and crews, trying to recognize in them the romance he found in Jack London and Joseph Conrad. Ella snobbishly disapproved of Eugene's acquaintances among the old salts who hung about the harbor, just as she deplored the fact that both Eugene and Jamie—and James too, for that matter—seemed to prefer almost any environment to that of their home. She could not even take pleasure in James's purchase of one of the first Packards in eastern Connecticut in a year when there were less than 80,000 automobiles in the entire country; for the kind of gay, duster-and-goggles outings indulged in by the Millers in *Ah, Wilderness!* were simply beyond the O'Neills. Ella was usually driven out in the car alone, and Eugene and Jamie, feeling very devilish, occasionally appropriated it for themselves. In recalling this a year or so before he completed *Ah, Wilderness!* O'Neill wrote to a friend that he and Jamie "once got the car up to a mite over forty. A great day—from which the car never fully recovered!"

Although Eugene had the use of a car, his own rowboat, and good clothes, he often had to borrow a nickel from one of his friends for trolley fare, because his pocket money was restricted; virtually his only source of income was what he could earn from his father for trimming the hedge that surrounded the house: fifty cents for a good day's work that was supposed to teach him the value of money. Yet, in spite of restrictions, Eugene occasionally managed to pay his way into the Montauk Inn, the prototype for the tavern in *Ah, Wilderness!* as well as for the off-stage inn in his later play, *A Moon for the Misbegotten.*

The Montauk Inn was an inelegant establishment furnished with a player piano and upstairs rooms, located on the fringe of New London's most fashionable residential area. It was patronized by coachmen, farmers and prostitutes, who, like Belle in *Ah, Wilderness!*, were partial to sloe gin. A pair of boxing gloves, said by the inn's proprietor to be those with which John L. Sullivan won his final, seventy-five-round bout with Jake Kilrain in 1889, hung behind the bar. (Sullivan, in point of fact, had used bare knuckles to subdue Kilrain in that bout.)

One of the inn's best customers was a pig farmer named John Dolan, who collected garbage on the side and lived in an unbelievably ramshackle house on a disreputable piece of land that he rented from James O'Neill for $35 a month. Dolan was, by even the most charitable estimate, a sloven. In his house, along with his two daughters and two sons, he kept a pig and some chickens.

Tall, thickset and slightly round-shouldered, Dolan dressed in filthy overalls and a tattered brown hat. He couldn't write his name and he had a powerful fondness for the bottle; he also had a thick brogue and a biting Irish wit that was the joy of his drinking companions. He chose to be followed wherever he went by a St. Bernard that adored him.

Dolan, observed by Jamie and Eugene with relish, became Phil Hogan in *A Moon for the Misbegotten*. His uproarious encounter in that play with a young estate owner O'Neill called T. Stedman Harder was drawn from an account Eugene heard at first hand in the Montauk Inn.

Harder (who was modeled on Edward Stephen Harkness, the scion of an enormously wealthy family that summered in New London) confronts Hogan and complains that his pigs have infringed on the estate's ice pond. (Ice from the pond was chopped in the winter and stored in silos to last through the warm weather, and Harder did not care for the taste of pork in his drinking water.) But Hogan accuses Harder of knocking down his own fences in order to lure the pigs into the pond and give them pneumonia.

The same episode also occurs in *Long Day's Journey Into Night*, but as exposition, and with the names altered to Shaugnessy (for Dolan) and Harker (for Harkness).

The ice pond of the plays actually belonged to Edward C. Hammond, whose summer estate adjoined Dolan's farm at the foot of a hill. But the Standard Oil background attributed to Harder-Harker in the plays belonged, rightfully, to the father of Edward Stephen Harkness, who helped John D. Rockefeller found the Standard Oil Company, against which Eugene had a grudge. The Harkness summer estate, which in 1952 became a state park, was known as "Eolia"; it consisted of 235 acres bordering on the Sound, a forty-two-room mansion, formal gardens, and assorted barns, greenhouses, caretakers' cottages, and stables. It was run by twenty indoor servants, including three butlers, and an additional staff of forty groundkeepers, chauffeurs, dairymen, vegetable keepers, gardeners and watchmen. The thought of grubby old Dolan standing up to and routing the inheritor of all this grandeur was enough to send the moody Eugene into gales of laughter that echoed in his mind for many years.

He was still thinking of Harkness and Dolan and the Montauk Inn when, in the early 1930's, he began writing his cycle of eleven plays about an American family. In the only play of the cycle that he completed to his satisfaction, *A Touch of the Poet,* he gave his rich, Yankee villain yet another variant of the name Harkness; in that play his name is Harford, rather than Harder or Harker. O'Neill drew on his memory of Dolan as well as of his own father to create Cornelius Melody—a proud, ambitious, but defeated man, who drops his mask of pride to reveal himself as the son of a shebeen keeper, whose father grew up in a hovel he shared with pigs.

The incident in *A Touch of the Poet,* wherein one of Melody's Irish cronies kicks Harford's lawyer off his property, is reminiscent of the scene in *A Moon for the Misbegotten* in which Phil Hogan expedites the departure of Harder from his farm. And Melody's tavern, though located near Boston in the year 1828, resembles in atmosphere and clientele the Montauk Inn of New London in the early 1900's. Cornelius Melody's daughter Sara can be regarded, in some respects, as a refined version of Hogan's daughter Josie in *A Moon for the Misbegotten.*

Eugene's predilection for types like Dolan and the seamstresses of Bradley Street, combined with his brother's reputation as a heavy drinker (even though Eugene had not yet started drinking heavily himself), made it difficult for him in 1906 to have any communication with a girl like Muriel in *Ah, Wilderness!* The mothers of nice girls frowned at the mention of his name. One of the young daughters of a family with whom the O'Neills boarded from time to time when they had no cook recalled being warned by a friend, "The O'Neill boys are terrible. They're drunk and dissolute." She added with amusement that any girl who valued her reputation made a point of giving both Eugene and Jamie a wide berth.

Ella was understandably chagrined; yet James himself compounded the difficulty by warning the parents of these girls to keep their daughters away from his sons; he thought it his moral duty to caution any of his friends who had impressionable daughters about his sons' profligate habits. Ella, on the other hand, professed to consider none of the New London girls good enough for her sons.

Ella kept mostly to her house, though she occasionally entertained and visited her relatives, the Brennans, and another old New London family, the Sheridans, with which the Brennans had allied themselves by marriage. When she was on morphine she was not fit for social intercourse, and when she was between cures she was too self-conscious and apprehensive to be sociable on a large scale.

Her addiction was a well-kept secret outside the family circle. A few of Ella's younger relatives, who lived to witness the publication and production of *Long Day's Journey Into Night,* found themselves in the uncomfortable position of having to defend, out of family loyalty and pride, a situation they had barely guessed existed and to defend a woman who, because she had held them at arm's length, they did not really know and rather resented. Most of Ella's relatives, in fact, preferred James to her.

Two granddaughters of Bridget Quinlan's sister, Elizabeth Brennan, who were cousins and contemporaries of Eugene and Jamie, have indignantly recalled, contrary to the picture presented in *Long Day's Journey Into Night,* that Ella would never have allowed her husband or sons to keep a whiskey bottle on her living-room table. Nor, they have insisted, was James ever stingy to his boys.

"The boys wore only tailor-made suits," Bessie Sheridan, one of the cousins, once pointed out. "And the O'Neills had a chauffeur and a coachman." Miss Sheridan added that she "always liked Gene—he was a fine boy, simple and good—until he wrote this disgraceful book [*Long Day's Journey Into Night*]." Her sister, Mrs. Irene Moran, has concurred in this opinion. (In 1914, When Eugene published some one-act plays under the collective title *Thirst,* an aunt of the Sheridan sisters threw the volume into the furnace, remarking, "I like a clean taste in my mouth." This narrow approach on the part of some of his relatives did not go unrecorded by O'Neill. A play he wrote in 1921, called *The First Man,* which he later acknowledged as being "painfully bungled," reflects his feelings about the relatives of a sensitive, idealistic man. They are shown as capable of judging others only by the standards of their own limited experience, and bound by petty pride and stultifying conventionality.)

The recollection of another of Elizabeth Brennan's granddaughters, who was only ten years younger than Ella, is, for a poignant reason, both more candid and more revealing. Lil Brennan, one of the few relatives of whom young Eugene was genuinely fond, became, in her late eighties, a victim of senility psychosis. Confined to a state nursing home near New London and out of touch with the world, she vividly relived in her mind her young womanhood in New London. Believing herself to be in her early thirties during the summer of her ninetieth year, in 1957, she spoke to her doctor and a visitor about what she thought were recent events and of people she believed were still living.

"Mama always says, 'Be nice to Ella, she has a difficult life,'" Miss Brennan told her visitor, recalling the period in the late 1800's when, as a young girl, she first became aware of Ella O'Neill. Lil's mother, Josephine McGlyn Brennan, who lived to be ninety-three, was Bridget's niece (and Ella's first cousin) by marriage.

"Mama never can see any wrong in anyone," Miss Brennan added. "But Ella O'Neill keeps to herself; she passes me in the street and doesn't even notice me." With childlike malice she said, "She's *stuck*-up, that's what she is, *stuck*-up," adding knowingly, "and she touches up her hair."

"When I go back to New York next week," she continued vindictively, "I'm going to tell Agnes what she said to me." (The New York she spoke of was that of 1907, and Agnes was her sister, who had died at eighty; they had lived in the city for a while, Agnes studying the piano and Lil trying to establish herself as a milliner. She thought if she could persuade Ella to become her customer she could use this prestige to attract other fashionable women.)

"Do you know what Ella said when I asked her to buy some hats from me? She said she bought her hats at Bendel, but she'd give me her old ones to make over and sell. I was never so insulted!"

Only a young woman as naïve as Lil would have expected Ella O'Neill to buy homemade hats. Ella's hats, like her dresses, were the last word in expensive good taste. She rarely went outdoors without a veil as well. Her relatives thought she wore veils to protect her smooth, white complexion against sun and wind, but more likely she wore them to hide the unnatural, morphine-induced brightness of her eyes.

Her relatives also thought Ella vain, for she wore $50 French corsets. "Don't ever let yourself weigh over 145 pounds," she cautioned the mother of Bessie and Irene Sheridan, in a day when the buxom Lillian Russell set the style for youngish matrons.

Though considered snobbish by her own kin, Ella was, in turn, snubbed by the elite of New London, who were inclined to regard the O'Neills as something not far above riffraff. Their attitude was due to the unsavory combination of James's shanty Irish background, his career as a "road" actor, and his unpretentious mode of living. Among the families that ignored them were the Chappells, whose position and money derived from coal and lumber.

Eugene resented the Chappells for snubbing his mother, although he was content to mention them in his plays only in passing, instead of giving them the sneering, full-dress treatment he reserved for the Harknesses. In *Long Day's Journey Into Night* he calls the Chappells the Chatfields, and has Mary Tyrone refer to them, after they have driven past the Tyrone house and bowed formally to James Tyrone, as "big frogs in a small puddle."

The reference has been cheerfully acknowledged by one of the younger members of the family, who has expressed regret at the narrow-mindedness of New London society in the early 1900's.

Mrs. E. Chappell Sheffield recalled that her mother, returning in her victoria from a drive which took her past the O'Neill house, once remarked: "My, I certainly had a sweeping bow from James O'Neill." But, Mrs. Sheffield added, her mother would not have dreamed of calling on Ella—and Ella, restricted by protocol from calling first, had to swallow the affront.

"We considered the O'Neills shanty Irish," she said ruefully, "and we associated the Irish, almost automatically, with the servant class. As a matter of fact, I remember being very upset when I first started going to church—my father became a Catholic convert—and I recognized only servants in the church. 'Why do we go to the Irish church?' I remember asking my mother, to her embarrassment. We were among the few Catholic families considered acceptable."

O'Neill, visiting Doc Ganey some years after he had achieved fame as a dramatist, said:

"You know, I always wanted to make money. My motive was to be able, someday, to hire a Tally-Ho and fill it full of painted whores, load each whore with a bushel of dimes, and let them throw the money to the rabble on a Saturday afternoon; we'd ride down State Street [New London's main thoroughfare] and toss money to people like the Chappells. Now that I've made as much as I need, I've lost interest."

But the insult still rankled; otherwise O'Neill could not have written so virulently of—for example—Cornelius Melody's hatred for the Yankees who snubbed him.

The same families that shunned the O'Neills were quite willing to receive and call upon Richard Mansfield and his wife. Mansfield, however, who was younger than James and had arrived at success later than he, was a distinguished Broadway actor. Besides, he was every bit as arrogant as the first families themselves, and proved he knew how to live well by running not one but two elaborate estates—one called "The Grange" and the other "Seven Acres"—diagonally across Ocean Avenue from each other. Mansfield often affected a monocle and a cape, and in his role of country squire he too looked down on the O'Neills, to James's mortification.

With this kind of ostracism, it is surprising that James was accepted as a member of the exclusive Thames Club, founded by a group of New London businessmen. Mansfield was a member of the club, as were most of the wealthy and prominent New Londoners. But aside from James and a Brennan relative of Ella's, only a handful of Irishmen gained admittance. James did not disgrace his nationality. Within the club's dignified chambers he was treated with quiet respect, if not with enthusiasm.

He visited the club two or three times a week during the summer months, sometimes bringing an actor friend. He habitually ordered bourbon and milk, a drink remembered as unusual by the club's bartender, a fellow Irishman named Jim Shay.

Shay has also recalled that James often bought drinks for any other club members who happened to be present. His manner was courtly and genial, and he invariably raised his glass in the same toast. "Sunny days and starry nights," he would say, in his deep, lilting voice, the famous O'Neill smile on his lips. He was careful to have only two or three drinks at the club; he did his serious drinking in the less formal atmosphere of hotel barrooms, where he was loved by one and all. "It is hard to find anyone in New London who doesn't know Mr. O'Neill personally," said the reporter for the Boston *Sunday Journal* in 1900.

A particular favorite with the town's Irish, James had been asked some years earlier to run for mayor. He declined, saying that he did not want the title if he could not be present to discharge his duties. When he was again pressed to run, he declined with a ringing speech that finally squelched his would-be nominators: "Every politician seeking office aspires to the presidency of the United States. If I were to enter politics I should want to make that my goal and I can't be president because I was born in Ireland, God bless it!"

One of the reasons why a segment of New London's citizens considered James an apt choice for mayor was his conviction that New London would one day become a main sea terminal for transatlantic traffic—a port city second only to New York and Boston in wealth and prestige. There were good grounds for this belief; for one thing, its three-mile-long harbor was large and deep enough to accommodate ocean liners. New London seemed, to more level heads than James's, to be destined for a great future. James could not foresee the powerful opposition that would arise from an handful of wealthy estate owners and aristocratic natives who were determined to keep New London a noncommercial, exclusive playground. Although there were several strong attempts made by industrial tycoons—J. P. Morgan was behind one of them—to realize New London's commercial potential, they came to nothing, and James ultimately lost a great deal of money on his investments.

The Boston *Sunday Journal* reported that it was "doubtful if there is another citizen in New London who is more enthusiastic about the city than is Mr. O'Neill." The newspaper added that he had invested "a great deal in real estate about the town and has watched its growth carefully during the last ten years." James always seemed to have ready cash for property and was apt to describe himself to his family, not without pride, as "land poor." Eugene's portrait of his father as a miser in *Long Day's Journey Into Night* has been disputed by many old New London friends; typical of how he was regarded, and of how both Jamie and Eugene *knew* he was regarded, is the exchange in *A Moon for the Misbegotten*, which deals with Jamie at a time when his father had been dead for several years. Jamie (in the guise of Jim Tyrone) speaks of his father (to the New London farmer's daughter named Josie), as "an old bastard."

JOSIE: He wasn't! He was one of the finest, kindest gentlemen ever lived.

TYRONE (*sneeringly*): Outside the family, sure. Inside, he was a lousy, tightwad bastard.

James's favorite retreat was the Crocker House, a large hotel on State Street whose bar was the gayest place in town. During the summer months it was always packed with Coast Guard cadets, the cream of the town's leading businessmen, and visiting millionaires off their yachts; William Randolph Hearst was likely to be there, as were various Morgans off the *Corsair*. The Whitney and Astor yachts were often anchored in the Thames and their passengers showed up from time to time at the Crocker House bar.

James held court there in the afternoons and often on into the evenings. One of his intimates was Captain Nat Keeney, an old Yankee sailor with a weathered face, a spicy vocabulary, and an endless repertory of highly improbable stories. (He, too, turns up in *Long Day's Journey Into Night*—as Captain Turner; his namesake, on the other hand, may be found in the one-act play *Ile*.) James, whose own language was fairly restrained—he would never have dreamed of swearing before a lady— enjoyed listening to Captain Keeney's uninhibited speech. Keeney was such a well-known and tolerantly accepted character in New London that no one minded his language. A fussy spinster who was his neighbor once complained to him, in high indignation, that a shopkeeper had insulted her by shouting, "Keep your shirt on!" Captain Keeney listened sympathetically. "Did that goddam sonofabitch say that to you, Miss

R——?" he asked. "Yes, he did, Captain Keeney," replied the spinster, not turning a hair.

Another of James's boon companions was a white-haired, portly, frock-coated, silk-hatted, cane-carrying Irishman named Thomas Dorsey. Eugene, once observing him devour two steaks at a sitting, told Art McGinley that Dorsey should be between the covers of a book. He later put him there, calling him McGuire, in *Long Day's Journey Into Night*. Dorsey was a lawyer and a real-estate promoter, and had a reputation as a wag.

In spite of his local fame Dorsey could not get into the Thames Club, and James regularly met him at the Crocker House. The relationship between the two men was not purely social. It was Dorsey who sold James the bulk of his real-estate holdings in New London—often plots or buildings on which James later lost money. The consummation of their various deals was necessarily accompanied by the consumption of vast quantities of liquor, for which James usually paid.

Often there remained unfinished business to discuss after 11 P.M., when the bars in town closed, and then James sometimes sought out the night clerk at the Crocker House, a tall, thin young man named Alexander Campbell, who was a friend of Eugene's and a member of the Second Story Club. James would persuade Campbell to set out a bottle for himself and Dorsey in one of the hotel's offices. Dorsey had a wonderful time selling James property and James never held it against his friend that his real-estate holdings seldom showed a profit. Eugene and his brother, however, resented it and Jamie often asked Dorsey, albeit in an offhand, contemptuous way, to stop selling land to his father.

Jamie, like his father, had a coterie at the Crocker House. He did not inspire anything like the devotion shown to his father, but he could make people laugh when he was in the mood. The sensational murder of Stanford White in New York was one of the chief topics of conversation at the Crocker House. Jamie, who had a passing acquaintance with Evelyn Nesbit, the chorus girl whom Harry K. Thaw had married and for whom he had shot White on June 25, 1906, professed to have inside knowledge of the affair.

Private testimony not yet published, said Jamie, revealed that Evelyn Nesbit, while unconscious, had been ravished seven times by Stanford White. His eager listeners asked how, if she had been unconscious, could this explicit count have been established? Jamie, talking out of the side of his mouth, as he often did for effect, replied, dead-pan, that Miss Nesbit had a taxi meter secured to a specific part of her anatomy.

Although James often drank as much as a quart a day at the Crocker

House without showing it, there were one or two times when he misjudged his capacity. Once, having spent a long evening in the town toward summer's end, he started walking home along the railroad tracks, which followed for some distance the banks of the Thames. Crossing a culvert, he missed his footing and fell. A couple of passers-by helped him home. Ella, alarmed at his condition, sent for a doctor and a priest despite James's protests. The doctor treated a sprain and several minor bruises and left. The priest, an old friend of James's named Father Joynt, realized that James had been drinking.

"Well, James," Father Joynt said, good-humoredly, "God was with you this time." James, unchastened, replied, "I wish He'd been with me a minute earlier." A week later James played Monte Cristo on crutches.

Another time James, who boasted truthfully that liquor had never caused him to miss an appearance, turned up in a foggy state for a session of *The Count of Monte Cristo* at New London's Lyceum Theatre. In the scene in which he was supposed to come up from the sea, he got lost in the folds of the ground cloth and delayed his appearance for so long that members of the audience, who knew the play almost as well as they knew their own family scandals, were sure James had dropped dead of heart failure and would never emerge again. He did manage to disentangle himself and gasp his way into view. It was the closest he ever came to letting liquor ruin his performance.

Jamie never learned to stand his liquor as well as his father did. He appeared to need it more, and was constantly battling James on the subject. Although James occasionally drank a cocktail before breakfast, he saw no reason why Jamie should emulate him. He fought a losing battle, though, to limit Jamie's drinking. One New London relative, Phil Sheridan (brother of Bessie and Irene), who was Eugene's age, has remembered passing the O'Neill house one day when James, who was cutting the hedge, asked him in for a drink.

"Jamie eyed the bottle with his tongue hanging out, while the Old Man poured me a drink," Sheridan later recalled.

But Jamie often managed to help himself to the bottle on the sideboard, afterwards watering the depleted whiskey until, finally, James put all his liquor under lock and key in the cellar.

X

DURING THE SUMMER OF 1906 EUGENE WATCHED THE
hostility grow between his father and brother. He had been observing
their mutual antagonism during New London vacations ever since Jamie's
acting debut in 1900, following his dismissal from college. James and
Jamie complained about each other to Eugene, and Eugene found himself sympathizing with first one and then the other. Gradually he came
to side with Jamie, for Jamie was clearly the more defenseless. Hatred of
his father, despair over his mother, and disgust with his own shortcomings
gnawed at Jamie and by the time he was in his late twenties his youthful
drinking habits had hardened into chronic alcoholism.

After leaving college Jamie tried halfheartedly to become a newspaper
reporter. But that turned out to be a poorer paying and less glamorous
occupation than he had anticipated, and he soon found it easier to allow
his father to cast him as an actor. (He had occasionally played a small
role with his father's company as a boy, but not with the idea of making
the stage a career.)

Jamie had no real love for the profession, as his father had. He was
vociferously contemptuous of the theatre in general and of his father's
talents in particular. But there seemed nothing else for which he was
suited.

He had his father's looks, but somewhat coarsened. He also had his
father's Irish wit and fondness for quoting Shakespeare (sometimes inaccurately), a fair echo of his resonant speaking voice, and a native charm
without which he would have been insufferable. Many people, indeed,
found him just short of offensive; but because of his humor and the
peculiar pride he took, even at his most drunken, in being impeccably
dressed, he was sometimes not only tolerated but regarded with affection.
It was difficult to reconcile the raging-drunk, furniture-smashing, ob-
scenity-shouting Jamie with the partially drunk, stiffly polite, grandly
aloof Jamie, but he was both men. The change from one to the other was
just a question of a little more or a little less whiskey.

Like his mother, Jamie had a tendency to hold people off, so that
there were not many who knew him well. But even his casual acquaintances have retained an image of Jamie wearing a derby hat, spotlessly

clean white shirt, brightly shined shoes, and on occasion, spats. When rain threatened he was likely to carry a furled umbrella and a well-pressed coat over his arm.

When he was mildly drunk, the fact could be detected only by a strange redness that spread, like rouge, over his cheekbones. James was as familiar with that sign as he was with the drug-induced brightness of Ella's eyes, and he grew ill when he saw it. For as Jamie progressed with his drinking, it was James on whom he vented his spite; Jamie knew how to torment his father to a nicety; later he would apologize with the excuse that it had been "the booze talking." This was a handy, catchall apology used by all the O'Neills for the cutting things they were always saying to each other; even Ella resorted to it, only in her case it was "the poison" talking. (These and a number of similar phrases occur in several of O'Neill's plays.)

Jamie's penchant for behaving outrageously and getting away with it manifested itself early. During a New York vacation from prep school, when he had been forbidden by his father to attend a circus matinee, he decided to flout the order and raise the price of admission on his own. Wandering about the neighborhood of Madison Square Garden, then situated on the northeast corner of the square, he spotted a "Boy Wanted" sign in a luggage shop window. He approached the proprietor, who was absorbed in his bookkeeping, and brashly announced, "I want that job." The irritated proprietor decided to put him in his place.

"You do, do you?" he growled. "Well, go outside and walk down the block and if I call you back, I'll hire you. If I don't, you just keep walking."

"Thank you, sir," said Jamie, and left. In front of the store was a display of trunks and suitcases with price tags attached. Without slowing his pace, Jamie picked up the most expensive bag he could carry and started down the street. The proprietor, who had been watching to see the effect of his own maneuver, shouted: "Here, you, come back." Jamie came back and the proprietor, outmaneuvered, gave him the job. After working a few hours, Jamie talked his boss into giving him not only a small advance on his salary—enough to pay for a circus ticket—but also the afternoon off.

Jamie and his father carried on a similar, but deadlier, battle of wits. Jamie would taunt, embarrass, disappoint and outrage James—and then, by some brash, engaging trick, would win his forgiveness and another reprieve. It became almost a point of honor with Jamie to see how far he could push the Old Man, as he called James behind his back (to his face, even when angry, he called him "Papa") The game of harassment was kept up relentlessly.

Once, when father and son were playing a New York engagement, Jamie swaggered into the office of the theatrical manager who was working out the details of a tour with James. Jamie was out of funds as usual and knew he could not ask his father for a loan, as one had recently been refused; James had periodic impulses to teach Jamie the value of a dollar, although he knew, in his heart, that Jamie would always depend on him and that he would permit him to.

"I want to make you a little bet," Jamie told his father. "The loser can stand the whole office staff to drinks across the street."

Jamie explained that he'd been exercising to improve his chest expansion and bet that his chest measurement exceeded his father's. James, who prided himself upon his robust condition, took the bait, as he invariably did. Though in his late fifties, he could still boast that he had never been sick a day in his life. A tape measure duly demonstrated that James's chest measured forty-three inches, while Jamie's measured only forty.

Smiling triumphantly, James told his son to lead the way across the street. Jamie, affecting chagrin, complied. He ordered drinks for his guests and thirstily downed his own. When the bill, for $6.90, was handed to him, he told the bartender, indicating his father, and in a voice loud enough to carry to him:

"Give the bill to that elderly, gray-haired gentleman at the other end of the bar; he has a wallet stuffed with greenbacks sewn into the front of his shirt, which gives him a chest expansion five inches above his normal one."

After James paid the bill, Jamie gave him a friendly pat on the back, saying, "Sorry, Papa, but six-ninety is just too steep for a struggling young actor."

James realized that he was himself largely responsible for Jamie's flagrant dependence upon him. Although he often deplored it, he also seemed to derive a bitter-sweet pleasure from it. He had started Jamie on his acting career—and his career of dependence—as an understudy in *The Musketeers*, James's first venture under the management of the hugely successful Liebler and Company.

Like a number of producing concerns during the late 1800's and early 1900's, Liebler and Company had begun on little more than high hopes, nerve, precarious credit, and a few hundred dollars in cash. Theodore Liebler's rapid rise as a theatre manager was typical of that era.

The son of a German artist, he started a lithographic concern specializing in theatrical posters. He grew interested in show business when managers who couldn't pay their bills gave him, instead, a percentage of their productions. This kind of payment proved profitable for Liebler and by 1890 he had a thriving establishment in New York's Park Place. Then one Saturday at 12:30 P.M.—on August 22, 1891—there was an explosion in the basement paint shop. It was described in the newspapers as the Park Place Disaster; sixty-one people lost their lives when the five-story building collapsed.

Liebler, who had no explosion insurance, was forced to abandon his business. He had been able to salvage a little money, and now decided to produce a play. Someone with funds to invest and an interest in the theatre was fair game for any would-be manager, and such a one was George Tyler, James O'Neill's one-time advance man. Tyler was not in especially good repute as he had, not long before, presented an overblown, open-air production of *As You Like It* in Asbury Park, New Jersey; his box-office receipts on opening night had been insufficient to pay the salaries of his all-star cast, and he had only recently dared to come out of hiding. But Tyler had a scheme, and all he needed was backing. Liebler had the backing, or at least the beginning of it.

The scheme, as Tyler presented it to Liebler, was to present Charles Coghlan in a play Coghlan had just written. The once brilliant old actor, a habitual drinker of champagne, was in debt; Tyler was in disgrace and owed a hotel bill of $200, among his more pressing obligations; Liebler had had no experience in theatre management. It was, therefore, inevitable that these three should get together and produce one of the big hits of the time.

It was called *The Royal Box*. Tyler had told Liebler it could be staged for $750. Because no New York theatre was willing to book the play, it was taken to Canada for a tour. Liebler, meanwhile, persuaded the manager of the Fifth Avenue Theatre, who had just been abandoned by the star of his show, to book *The Royal Box* as a temporary bill. But by that time the Liebler company's funds were exhausted. Undaunted, Tyler, in Ottawa, set about raising some more cash.

To his resourceful brain the quickest way to raise it was to get into a poker game with Lillian Russell. This was not quite as farfetched as it sounds. Miss Russell, who was appearing at a competing theatre in Ottawa, was an avid but notoriously poor poker player. Stage hands vied for jobs in her company, for it was Miss Russell's custom to gamble with them at the end of each performance—and she usually lost.

Tyler arranged to get into one of the games, but that night Miss

Russell drew phenomenally lucky cards, and took what was left of Tyler's cash. Then, with a typically Russellian gesture, she offered to lend Tyler the money to get his show to New York.

The Royal Box was a great success from the moment it opened at the Fifth Avenue Theatre. Liebler and Company followed *The Royal Box* with another hit called *The Christians,* and then invited James O'Neill to star in *The Musketeers,* Sidney Grundy's version of the Dumas novel.

James had been serving as his own manager, but he was perfectly willing to throw in with Liebler and Company, if it meant a chance to get away from *The Count of Monte Cristo* without financial risk. Liebler and Tyler offered him $500 a week, 10 per cent of the gross profits, and an all-star cast that included Blanche Bates, Margaret Anglin and Wilton Lackaye.

At the same time Daniel Frohman, who was in his managerial heyday, announced that *he* was going to produce *The King's Musketeers,* an adaptation of the Dumas novel by Henry Hamilton; it was to star E. H. Sothern, who was thirteen years younger than James—and who was soon to demonstrate, by becoming one of the country's leading Shakespearean actors, that he had the courage and integrity James lacked.

Both *Musketeer* productions—Liebler's at the Broadway Theatre (Broadway and Forty-first Street) and Frohman's at the Knickerbocker (Broadway at Thirty-eighth Street)—ran until mid-April. Sothern opened first, at the end of February, 1899, and James opened on March 13. The competition was unusually lively and theatre fans had a good time arguing about which d'Artagnan was the better.

Although James scored a personal triumph, he found that he had not got very far away from *Monte Cristo.* This bothered him but it did not bother Liebler and Company. At the turn of the century managers were not much interested in making departures. Ibsen's *The Master Builder* was put on for one performance in January, 1900, and Richard Mansfield, that same year, courageously put Shaw's *The Devil's Disciple* into his repertory. But for the most part producers were happy to present minor variations on proved formulas. The most eminent theatre critic of the era, William Winter, was doing his influential best to subdue Ibsen and Shaw, along with other major European playwrights. The public, with his blessing, still wanted to see popular stars in the kind of roles they were used to, and managers paid high prices for playwrights who could provide such vehicles.

James toured in *The Musketeers* and eventually added it to his repertory, which soon after 1900 once again featured *Monte Cristo,* this time with

Jamie in his supporting cast. This production of *Monte Cristo* was elaborately mounted by Liebler and Company and had its unveiling at New York's Academy of Music. It boasted nine big sets, the first one representing the port of Marseilles, complete with a ship in full sail gliding into the harbor.

James still had more agility on stage than many actors half his age. One of the actors engaged for *The Musketeers* was David Perkins, whom James chose because of his merits as a swordsman.

"O'Neill enjoyed having actors in his company who could put up a good fight," Perkins explained. "Those dueling scenes weren't faked much —we used real rapiers with only slightly blunted points—and they were genuine displays of fencing skill, except, of course, that the right man had to end up winning."

There was one scene in *The Musketeers* in which, after much leaping about in a bedchamber and on the bed itself, Perkins ended up losing.

"I used to have bruises on my knuckles from O'Neill's sword thrusts," he recalled with satisfaction.

But James was no more immune to danger than Perkins in the scenes involving sword play. During one performance, in a scene where three men attacked him at once, the action became so impassioned that James was stabbed through his leather doublet, inches from the heart, and barely escaped a nasty cut. James took this in stride. "Watch yourself, or you'll have a dead man on your hands," he cautioned his overzealous adversary backstage. But he said it with a smile.

James himself had wounded his son during a performance at the Olympic Theatre in St. Louis in 1903. During a dueling episode, James caught Jamie's wrist with the edge of his sword. The audience gasped as Jamie, with a cry of pain, staggered backward and fainted in his father's arms. Jamie played the rest of the tour with his arm tightly bandaged during performances, and supported by a sling off stage. Although remorseful, James turned the accident into an object lesson. "Think of him being an actor," he would say, "and he never learned how to fence!"

When Jamie first joined his father's company he began in small parts, for which he received $20 a week. Not long after, his father allowed him to make his debut as Albert, Edmond Dantes' son, at more than double that salary. His first appearance in the role—at McVicker's, the old O'Neill stamping ground in Chicago—was a success.

"Last evening's entertainment," wrote a critic for a Chicago newspaper, "was made particularly charming by the debut of James O'Neill, Jr., who by his unusual resemblance to his father promises another generation of

Monte Cristo. . . . He acts extremely well too and the fact that he plays Albert in the play and is Dantes' son makes the instance of his appearance fraught with charm. He had a lot of enthusiastic applause for his civility to dramatic art and his nice temper. . . . I suppose generation after generation will go on watching the O'Neills exterminating villains, one at a time."

James periodically continued trying to shake off the stranglehold of the Count. In 1903, still for Liebler and Tyler, he chose a four-act adaptation of a Conan Doyle story, billed variously as *Brigadier Gerard* and *The Adventures of Gerard,* but it was a flop. He tried several other plays, but kept going back to *Monte Cristo,* for nothing else he did was as financially rewarding—not even an all-star revival of *The Two Orphans,* which played first in New York and then had a nineteen-week tour of one-night stands in the South and Southwest, followed by about a month and a half of longer runs in big cities.

That was Jamie's real introduction to the rigors of the road and he did not stand them well. An actress, Bijou Fernandez, who replaced Margaret Anglin in the cast when the play went on tour, once recalled those nineteen weeks with horror.

"We almost died doing it," she said. "I don't know where they found all those cities." Miss Fernandez, who was a novice at touring, would go to her hotel after the evening's performance and leave word to be called an hour before the train was scheduled to arrive next morning, which was often as early as five o'clock. She was grateful to James for his advice, offered soon after the tour began, to ignore the timetable and ask the hotel clerk to call her when he had the latest word about the train's actual time of arrival. This often saved hours of waiting at the station.

No amount of well-meant advice had any effect on Jamie, however. Drunk after every performance, he was often so late the next morning that the train had to be held for him.

In New Orleans Jamie nearly succeeded in cremating himself when his cigarette set fire to his mattress. An actor in the company named Tom Meighan tried, briefly, to reform Jamie. He would take him out for something to eat after the show and then deposit him at his hotel with instructions to go to bed. But Meighan gave up when he found that Jamie would go out to a bar as soon as his back was turned.

The Two Orphans tour marked the beginning of Jamie's wildest and most public defiance of his father. James reacted with what dignity he could muster, but, as he was himself a perfectionist in his demands on other members of his company, his son's flouting of professional ethics was especially humiliating. Jamie did not try to spare his father's feelings before the rest of the company. He made jokes about his own drinking and his slovenly attitude toward the tour. He abused James, ran down the production, and kept on drinking.

For some time Jamie continued to play the role of Albert in *Monte Cristo* and also doubled in the small part of an old man. As Albert, he wore light, buff-colored buckskin tights, which fitted him like his skin; he did this with his father's tacit approval, to attract the women in the audience. But his father did not approve of the women who usually filled the boxes to ogle Jamie. A number of them were prostitutes, whose acquaintance Jamie had made on earlier tours. Jamie would take every opportunity to strike poses at the stage apron, thereby drawing unfavorable comments from the local critics.

But James liked even less a little game his son had invented to play during a scene in which Jamie had to kneel and receive Monte Cristo's blessing. Jamie would conceal a strip of muslin in his hand and, as he knelt, would surreptitiously tear it, causing a rending noise that sounded as if his tights were splitting. His father would grow so furious that the color of blood showed through his make-up.

"Someday it's really going to happen to you," James would fume at his son the moment they were both off stage.

In his other role as the old man in the first scene, Jamie enjoyed making his entrance wearing a frowsy gray wig, which he never combed, and the youthful black eyebrows that belonged to Albert.

"Horrible, horrible," James would mutter. He knew, and he knew that his cast knew, that he would have dismissed any other actor for such behavior.

One New Year's Eve, when the company arrived in San Francisco, Jamie and a friend rented a furnished room, where they thought they could hide. They drank through the night and ended by smashing the china basin, windows and furniture. On New Year's Day before the matinee Jamie's landlady presented herself at the theatre shouting for James O'Neill and claiming payment for the damage. A young man, John Hewitt, who at one point doubled as stage manager and actor with James's company, took the landlady's message to James.

"Governor," said Hewitt, using the title everyone in the company gave James, "I have some very unpleasant news for you on New Year's Day."

"Well, out with it, lad," said James.

"Your son . . ." began Hewitt.

"Ah, my son of the Golden West?" asked James, with heavy irony.

Hewitt told him what Jamie had been up to, and presented the landlady's bill for $80. James wrote out a check. "Case dismissed," he said, smiling ruefully.

Jamie arrived a few minutes later, barely in time for the curtain. He was pale and numb.

"My son of the Golden West!" James greeted him, and added a jeering noise that resembled a Bronx cheer. Jamie went through his part mechanically. At the end of the performance James asked his son, with genuine solicitude, "How are you feeling, laddie?"

Jamie needed his liquor as badly as his mother needed her morphine. He never traveled without a bottle in his suitcase, and on long trips he always packed two or three. Once the company was about to make the big hop from Denver to Salt Lake City and the train had been held up for him for five minutes. Hewitt was giving him a hand up to the train's platform, when Jamie's suitcase opened and two bottles fell out and smashed on the ground. Jamie was almost in tears over the squandered alcohol.

In the small towns where the company played the actors would often fall asleep to the sound of Jamie's voice, singing in the town's only tavern. Even when Jamie was at his most inebriated he could not be goaded into a barroom brawl; when he saw that a situation was slipping out of his control he would put out his hand, like a policeman halting traffic. "What, ho!" he would say, in a frozen voice, turning his back and lurching away with a pathetic attempt at dignity.

If there was a town prostitute, Jamie would find her. In the larger towns he was frequently called for at the stage door by the leading madam, who would bear him triumphantly away in her carriage. At the end of a run in St. Louis he sent word to the theatre that he was not leaving with the company. He had found a pretty, twenty-year-old brunette in the best bordello and had fallen in love with her. Hewitt had to drag him away by main force.

Ella, who was still making the longer stops on James's itinerary, would come to the theatre from time to time to meet her husband and take a casual look at her son, of whom, at this point, she gravely disapproved. She was distant to Jamie backstage and appeared distressed at her husband's calm acceptance of his behavior. On the other hand, it seemed to members of the company that she made a point of being attentive to Eugene, who sometimes accompanied her during his school vacations. This caused James to favor his elder son over Eugene and fanned the various touchy O'Neill tempers into new flame.

Eugene, when he visited backstage, had the eager curiosity of any youth who gets a chance to look behind the scenes. He would play with the props and question the actors and stage managers. Hewitt, for example, once demonstrated the way coconut shells, tapped on a piece of marble covered with chamois cloth, simulated hoofbeats. Jamie teased him, but in an affectionate, big-brotherly way that made Eugene glow. During performances, which Eugene watched from the wings, he had eyes only for Jamie. Jamie clowned and strutted for him and told him of his exploits, and little by little Eugene was drawn into what James thought was a filial conspiracy to undermine him.

Toward the end of the season in the spring of 1906 James was faced with a new problem. Ella, whose most recent sanitarium treatment had had good results and who seemed to be making a real effort to overcome the drug habit, developed a breast tumor. Her doctors suggested an operation and recommended a French surgeon. James immediately made plans to go to Europe. He told friends that he was going abroad for a vacation, prior to opening a new play in the fall.

Ella's operation was successful and James, for the first time in years, threw himself into the spirit of a real holiday. He visited the Château d'If, the historical castle used by Dumas as the scene of the Count of Monte Cristo's incarceration. The old man who served as superintendent and guide for pilgrims to the ruin near Marseilles had been running through his travelogue, which included a reference to Edmond Dantes' imprisonment and escape, for so many years that he had come to believe Dantes had really existed. A member of James's party whispered to the old man that one of his guests was an actor who had played the Count of Monte Cristo more than three thousand times in the United States. Overcome by emotion, the guide threw his arms around James, exclaiming, "Mon Dieu, j'ai trouvé un Edmond!"

James went to London early in July to attend a benefit for Ellen Terry, and then visited his own Ireland. During his travels he kept up a galloping correspondence (later published in a New York newspaper) with the author of his forthcoming play, a young New Yorker named James Slevin. The play, called *The Voice of the Mighty,* was about John the Baptist, and James was certain it would be a success.

"When in London I attended a revival of Wilde's *Salomé,* and in a way I can say I enjoyed it," James wrote to Slevin from Dublin. But James's perceptivity was not acute, for in the next breath he went on to compare *Salomé* with *The Voice of the Mighty,* which was something like comparing *The Playboy of the Western World* with *Peg o' My Heart.*

"Though you have written your play on the same subject," continued James, "you have taken an entirely different view. Your choice of situations is not the same and your handling is quite the opposite. He tells his story in most picturesque language, delicate figures and subtle conceptions, but very little action. You, on the other hand, have presented your play in a series of strong dramatic actions and incidents, painted your pictures with a broader brush and with a more virile hand. His pleases the student —yours will please the people." James, like many actors, was a pushover for rhetoric.

James and Ella returned to the United States in late July, 1906. James arrived in New London bursting with a new batch of the Irish stories he loved to tell in barrooms and, when he could hold the attention of his family long enough, in his own living room. Eugene absorbed their racy flavor and the earthy ring of their wit. These stories, as much as the grim philosophy of Nietzsche and Strindberg, became an ineradicable part of his literary heritage, as he was later to demonstrate in such plays as *A Moon for the Misbegotten* and *A Touch of the Poet*. Eugene was amused, for instance, by his father's sketch of the Irish railway porter who, said James, "simply can't help being funny."

"On one of my trips through the Emerald Isle," recounted James, who just couldn't help being lyrical, "I got into a third-class car by mistake with a first-class ticket; a zealous porter wrathfully pulled me out of the car and told me 'I was chating the Kumpany.' After I was comfortably seated in the first-class compartment, he put his head in and asked: 'Is there anyone there for here?' But even this genius was eclipsed by the conductor of the train who, before the train departed, fiercely rang a bell and bellowed in gloomy warning: 'This train shtops nowhere at all!'"

James's memory was so good and his gift of mimicry so fluent that both Jamie and Eugene considered it their duty to belittle these abilities. James would frequently talk about how hard he had to work as an actor.

"You call that work?" asked Jamie, who had a pretty good memory himself and sometimes condescended to learn all the subsidiary roles in James's touring repertory, so that he could take over for any actor who defected or was indisposed on tour. James, of course, had meant he had to work hard to be a *good* actor, but, as always, he was both stung and challenged by Jamie's disparagement and accepted Jamie's ten-dollar bet that he could learn Goldsmith's *The Deserted Village* in a week; Jamie even persuaded Eugene to make a similar bet that *he* could learn the role of Macbeth in the same period.

James had played the role himself only a few months earlier at the Metropolitan Opera House in New York, during a testimonial performance for Modjeska, in which the Polish star had played Lady Macbeth.

He had, on that occasion, caused a bit of a backstage sensation when it was discovered, just before the murder scene, that he had somehow forgotten to provide himself with a costume. He went on in an ancient dressing gown of his own, wearing it with such aplomb that no one in the audience dreamed of questioning its suitability.

Since neither Eugene nor Jamie could afford to lose the bet, they both applied themselves to the task of memorizing. At the end of the week Jamie recited *The Deserted Village* for his father and collected his bet—proving nothing except that he could work harder in a petty cause than in a worthy one. Eugene then began *Macbeth,* taking his cues from James; he was letter-perfect, but before he had gone very far James closed the book and fixed Eugene with his penetrating eyes.

"You certainly have a good memory," said James, "and I see you've worked hard, but never go on the stage."

Eugene couldn't help laughing. Nothing was further from his mind.

XI

EUGENE ENTERED PRINCETON ON SEPTEMBER 20, 1906, and left a little less than nine months later, having established beyond a doubt that he was not college material.

Woodrow Wilson was the university's president, and, while Eugene had nothing against Wilson personally, he soon decided that Princeton was excessively tradition-bound, self-consciously superior and clannish. Eugene scowlingly put on the black beanie that was required dress for freshmen, but he conspicuously refrained from any word or deed that might have been mistaken for school spirit. Moreover, he quickly concluded that the university offered little in the way of intellectual challenge or stimulation.

"Why can't our education respond logically to our needs?" he rhetorically asked Olin Downes some years later when Downes interviewed him for the *Boston Sunday Post*. "If it did, we'd grab for these things and hold on to them at the right time—when we've grown to them and know we need them. It was not until I had to shift, mentally as well as physically, for myself that my awakening came. When I was studying Shakespeare in classes, I was afraid of him. I've only recently explored Shakespeare with profit and pleasure."

O'Neill found profit and pleasure during his college year in authors he had discovered on his own.

"Wilde, Conrad and London were much nearer to me than Shakespeare at that time," O'Neill said. "And so, later, was Ibsen. . . . I needed no professor to tell me that Ibsen, as dramatist, knew whereof he spoke. I found him for myself outside of college grounds and hours. If I had met him inside, I might still be a stranger to Ibsen.

"I am perhaps excusing myself for the way I loafed and fooled and got as much fun and as little work as I could out of my one year at Princeton, but I think that I felt there, instinctively, that we were not in touch with life or on the trail of real things, and that was one consideration that drove me out."

Eugene's idea of being in touch with life and going after the real things included private experiments with absinthe and incense in his dormitory and the pursuit of prostitutes in Trenton, New Jersey. A book by the torrid, best-selling novelist Marie Corelli inspired the dormitory experiment.

One night, declining the invitation of a couple of other freshmen to go into town, Eugene shut himself into his room with a bottle of absinthe and a couple of sticks of incense. When his friends returned they found Eugene (or Gene, as they had begun to call him) blazing drunk. The bottle was nearly empty and the room, reeking of incense, was lit by a single, naked bulb, covered with red paper.

He had kicked over the radiator cover and was starting to break the furniture when his friends intervened. Eugene had no more inherited his father's capacity for holding his liquor than had Jamie.

Although the handful of freshmen with whom Eugene condescended to be friendly were flabbergasted by his behavior and opinions, they were also beguiled. He never went out of his way to make friends and wasted no time with anyone who didn't immediately interest him. But to people he found responsive he was instantly, if offhandedly, charming.

Despite the disapproval of many of their classmates, three freshmen remained loyal to Eugene throughout his Princeton year. They were roommates and their names were Ralph Horton, Tom Welsh and Al Zimmerman. Unlike Eugene, they had all led sheltered lives, had attended recognized Princeton prep schools (rather than Betts), and knew how to conform to the undergraduate atmosphere of the university.

"Princeton was a difficult place to get along in with only three or four friends," Horton once pointed out, recalling Eugene's willful isolation. "Gene wasn't popular. He wouldn't put himself out to make friends, and as a result he didn't have many." Horton remembered the difficulty he, Welsh and Zimmerman encountered in trying to get Eugene accepted by their eating club.

At that time freshmen ate in the Commons, on the ground floor of University Hall (which was later torn down and replaced by Holder Hall). Groups of twenty to fifty freshmen would organize themselves into a club, whose members would then regularly dine together in a small room off the Commons. Nonclub members ate in a nonconvivial, community area. Horton, Welsh and Zimmerman belonged to a club that called itself the White Hat and, after making friends with Eugene, proposed him for membership. He was promptly blackballed. His reputation for being a destructive drunk was partly responsible, but his remote attitude contributed equally.

The three tried again on successive Monday nights to get him into the club, with the same result. Finally Welsh, who was president of the club, appointed Horton and Zimmerman as tellers. Eugene's name was re-submitted and the tellers, ignoring the negative votes, announced that Eugene was elected. The club members who had cast the negative votes were puzzled, but since it was already spring they did not make an issue of it, and for the final weeks of the term Eugene dined wearing a white hat.

Eugene's little room upstairs in University Hall was a magnet for Horton and his roommates, and for another freshman named Richard Weeks on whom Eugene had consented to smile darkly. According to Horton, Eugene was "far more advanced, intellectually, than anyone else in our group." He would hold forth by the hour, quoting poetry and philosophy with supreme self-assurance.

When he had had a few drinks he was likely to climb onto a table. Standing with the slight stoop that was characteristic, gesturing eloquently with his long-fingered hands, his cheeks flushed, his eyes blazing, he would expound on religion, literature and politics. His four listeners thought him a rebellious, romantic, Black Irishman, smoldering with wild dreams that they scarcely understood.

Once he concluded a harangue which informed them he was an atheist, with: "If there is a God, let Him strike me dead!" The others could not suppress shudders. "I was eighteen at the time," Weeks later recalled, "and I was afraid that God would heed him."

Another time, however, Eugene took pains to explain that he was not, after all, an atheist, but rather an agnostic. The only reason he was not an atheist, he went on, with more fervor than originality, was because the human mind was incapable of comprehending infinity; he said there was something beyond the human mind—and that something might be God.

Eugene was obliged to make a formal concession to religion at Princeton, for attendance at chapel was compulsory every other Sunday and twice during the week. Each student had to hand a signed card to the clergyman, as a check on his obedience to the rules.

"Sometimes we'd try to slip St. Peter, as we called the clergyman, two cards—one for ourselves and one to cover up for an absent friend," Horton recalled.

But there were times when this ruse did not work, and Eugene had to sit through a number of sermons delivered by Henry Van Dyke, who was usually the speaker. Van Dyke, who had left his Presbyterian pastorate in New York to become professor of English literature at Princeton in 1900, did not impress Eugene favorably. Twenty-five years later he wrote:

"I hold Van Dyke in grudging memory because . . . his sermons were so irritatingly stupid that they prevented me from sleeping."

If Eugene conformed in his religious requirements, he did not bother to do so in his academic ones.

"Gene was lawless, as far as the university was concerned," Weeks once said. "One of the things he would do was take books out of the library and never return them. One time I got a book out for him and after he left Princeton—with the book—the library got after me to return it. I wrote Gene and he sent back the book—to my surprise."

Among his more lawless activities were his reckless cutting of classes and his extended absences from the university. Once he went with a classmate to New York and stayed a week. When they returned, they told Horton and Weeks about their holiday, which included a visit with a couple of whores in a brownstone in the upper Twenties. Another time Eugene went to New York with Horton, and he proudly pointed out a two-dollar house in which lived a woman many years his senior who had recently fallen in love with him. He gloated about his conquests, which, at that time, included a married woman in New London and several loose ladies of Trenton.

Eugene took Horton with him several times to New York's Hotel Lucerne, at Seventy-ninth Street and Amsterdam Avenue, where his parents were staying. Horton, who, years later, did not recall seeing James or Ella, did remember the Lucerne's bar, which had the best free lunch in town; it included lobster salad.

Eugene would often return from weekends in New York with detailed stories of his own and Jamie's escapades. He held his friends spellbound with accounts of how Jamie and another actor carried on a three-day orgy with two popular young actresses.

Eugene tried to pass on to Horton and Weeks some of the worldly knowledge he had gained from Jamie. He took them to Trenton, where he introduced them to hotel barrooms and displayed his prowess as a drinker. Once he told a bartender, "I want something to knock the top of my head off." The bartender obligingly fixed him a libation called a Yale Punch. Horton and Weeks joined him. None of them ever discovered what its ingredients were, but it had the desired effect.

Most of the time, though, Eugene drank Old Fashioneds, which Weeks, who had never heard of them, considered exotic. Another drink (for lean days) to which Eugene introduced his friends was English stone ale. It came in tall stone bottles, and had the effect of four beers.

Many nights Eugene would slip off to Trenton on his own, to visit a girl of whom he was especially fond. She was known, locally, as the

Widow of Nassau Hall. He often talked about her in idyllic terms and grew irate when his friends made ungallant comments about her reputation.

Eugene seldom appeared troubled by lack of funds and was always well dressed. The only commodity he seemed unable to supply for himself was a smoke. One of his friends, from whom he constantly cadged cigarettes, kept a special supply of Sweet Caporals, which he knew Eugene disliked, in order to discourage him. Although he sometimes spoke to his friends of "putting the bite on the old man" for extra funds, he was in no sense deprived. About 40 per cent of his fellow undergraduates were earning part or all of their way through Princeton, but Eugene was not required to lift a finger. His expenses including spending money, amounted to about $1,400 during his freshman year, which James apparently parted with willingly for the sake of his son's education. Eugene must have appreciated James's generosity and felt kindly disposed toward him at the time. Horton has recalled that Eugene went so far as to put in a good word for *Monte Cristo,* which he described as the only non-Shakespearean play that had withstood the test of time.

Between drinking and women, Eugene had little time for classes. At mid-term one of the few exams he passed was French. He took no interest in the extracurricular activities of the college and was unenthusiastic even about attending football and baseball games.

Eugene revealed his mixed feelings about college sports six years after he left Princeton, when he wrote a one-act play called *Abortion.* In this early effort, however lacking in literary merit, there is evidence of his keen eye for his surroundings and there are a number of autobiographical references to his year at Princeton and to the one immediately following.

The setting of the play is "a dormitory in a large eastern university in the United States," and the action takes place during a typical Princetonian celebration of a sports victory. The hero, a youth named Jack Townsend, is a college baseball star. Like many of O'Neill's plays, *Abortion* ends on a note of violence, when Jack, who has got a girl into trouble and then indirectly caused her death, shoots himself.

Eugene's college career ended less dramatically. It did not even end as colorfully as fans of George Jean Nathan have been led to believe. Nathan, after many years of friendship with O'Neill, felt obliged to reveal the lighter side of a nature that was generally regarded as somber, and he did not balk at invention to establish that O'Neill had a rowdy sense of fun. Nathan invented the legend that O'Neill was thrown out of Princeton for an act of vandalism against the university's president. He even made up some phrases in which O'Neill had "told" him the story—"Princeton . . . [kicked] my tail out of the place as an undergraduate because I was too accurate a shot with an Anheuser-Busch beer-bottle and hit a window in Woodrow Wilson's house right where he lived," the critic (in *The Intimate Notebooks*, published in 1932) quoted the dramatist as saying.

O'Neill, who often told several versions of a story himself, did not let Nathan's fiction disturb their friendship, but he did deny the story periodically.

"I liked Woodrow Wilson," he told Hamilton Basso, of *The New Yorker*, after Nathan's story had been widely circulated. "I wouldn't have done a thing like that if I had been swimming around in a lake of vodka."

O'Neill did incur disciplinary action but it was for throwing stones, not beer bottles. He and Weeks and another undergraduate got drunk in Trenton one Monday night during the early part of June. They missed the last trolley to Princeton and took the 1 A.M. train to Princeton Junction, three miles from the university. From there they were obliged to walk. As they were passing the stationmaster's house, a dog barked at them.

"There's a dog barking at us, Gene," said Weeks drunkenly. "I don't think we should tolerate that."

Eugene agreed, and the three picked up stones and hurled them in the general direction of the barking, which was also the direction of the stationmaster's front porch. Exhilarated by the sounds of vandalism, the boys climbed onto the porch and Eugene kicked over pieces of furniture. The stationmaster appeared at his front door and shouted threats at them. The three turned and made for the railroad tracks, which they followed home, satisfied that their evening had been well spent.

The next day the stationmaster lodged a complaint with university authorities, and after a few days of investigation Eugene, Weeks and their companion were questioned. They confessed, and were summoned before the Discipline Committee on Saturday. Eugene did not turn up, but was punished in absentia with a four-week suspension, to be effective at the beginning of the sophomore year. Weeks and the other undergraduate received the same penalty.

The dean wrote of the incident to all three fathers, and Eugene intercepted his letter. Weeks confessed to his father ahead of time, waited out his suspension the following fall in New York, and returned to Princeton.

Eugene had decided on his own to quit college, and had failed to take any of his final examinations. He was dropped in June by the Committee on Examinations and Standings "for poor scholastic standing."

One of his last impressions of Princeton was of a hectic student parade and bonfire, in celebration of Yale's defeat in a baseball game. He recorded the details of this event in *Abortion*.

He also expressed his disdain for the conventional, college-bred, American youth in several later plays, by introducing the type as a counterpoint to the autobiographical, sensitive, burningly idealistic artist-dreamer. Harder, in *A Moon for the Misbegotten*, is one example of the despised species:

"No matter how long he lives, his four undergraduate years will always be for him the most significant in his life, and the moment of his highest achievement the time he was tapped for an exclusive Senior Society at the Ivy university to which his father had given millions. Since that day he has felt no need for further aspiring, no urge to do anything except settle down on his estate and live the life of a country gentleman."

Sam Evans, in *Strange Interlude*, is another example:

"Although he is twenty-five and has been out of college three years, he still wears the latest in collegiate clothes and as he looks younger than he is, he is always mistaken for an undergraduate and likes to be. It keeps him placed in life for himself."

Eugene wanted no Ivy-stamped niche in life. He was convinced he could learn more out of college than in. Like Shaw and O'Casey, he ultimately demonstrated that a college education was not essential to the writing of great plays.

XII

EUGENE'S FIRST STEP IN SELF-EDUCATION WAS INTO Benjamin R. Tucker's "The Unique Book Shop," on New York's Sixth Avenue. Tucker, a New Englander of colonial and Quaker ancestry, had become a philosophical anarchist at eighteen. He was in his early fifties when Eugene met him and had a career of journalism and agitation behind him. He was the founder and editor of an anarchist publication, *Liberty*, whose first issue had declared: "Monopoly and privilege must be destroyed, opportunity afforded, and competition encouraged. This is 'Liberty's' work, and 'Down with Authority' her war cry."

Tucker had published, with his own limited funds and at no profit, many European works that had not previously been translated into English. Among them were books by the French anarchist Proudhon, Zola's *Money* and *Modern Marriage* and Mirabeau's *A Chambermaid's Diary*. He also published Shaw's *The Quintessence of Ibsenism* and Wilde's *The Ballad of Reading Gaol*.

Tucker was perhaps the best-known member of America's individualist-anarchist movement, which advocated that "all the affairs of men should be managed by individuals or voluntary associations, and that the State should be abolished." Individual liberty was for Tucker the only satisfactory way of life; he argued in favor of "the right of the drunkard, the gambler, the rake and the harlot to live their lives until they shall freely abandon them."

He did not submit a plan of how to provide and maintain equal liberty for all, but he did manage to put his theories into practice for himself. He rejected religion, and considered the formalities of marriage and divorce absurd. Anarchists, wrote Tucker, "look forward to a time when every individual, whether man or woman, shall be self-supporting . . . when the love relations between these independent individuals shall be as varied as are individual inclinations and attractions; and when the children born of these relations shall belong exclusively to the mothers until old enough to belong to themselves." Tucker himself lived with a woman he never married and by whom he had a child.

Eugene was introduced to Tucker in the late spring of 1907 by a young radical named Louis Holliday, who, though he had not attended Princeton, knew some of O'Neill's friends there. Sandy-haired, stocky, exuberant, Holliday had taken a liking to Eugene, which Eugene returned, and they met frequently in New York. Years later, when Eugene had isolated himself from all the radical acquaintances of his youth, he often spoke of Holliday, who by then was dead, as having been one of his few "real friends."

Eugene spent many hours at The Unique Book Shop absorbing Tucker's ideas, reading his books, and learning of the other anarchists of the day. Tucker found him an eager, if unsophisticated, pupil. Eugene was outgrowing a tendency to announce, like Richard Miller in *Ah, Wilderness!*, "I'll celebrate the day the people bring out the guillotine again and I see Pierpont Morgan being driven by in a tumbril!" and "After you, the deluge, you think! But look out! Supposing it comes before? Why shouldn't the workers of the world unite and rise? They have nothing to lose but their chains!" He was still apt to sign his letters "Yours for the revolution!" and he enjoyed quoting: "From each according to his ability; to each according to his needs."

From Tucker, Eugene began to get a clearer idea of the divisions and variations within the anarchist ranks. For instance, Tucker explained to him that, unlike the more popular militant anarchist school, individualist-anarchists were content to attack the established authority of government with words rather than bombs. Tucker had defined his own stand in 1892, when as a result of the Homestead Strike Alexander Berkman shot Henry Clay Frick. In 1906 the anarchist world continued to regard the affair with profound interest, for Berkman, who had been in prison for fourteen years, had just been released. Berkman and his champion, Emma Goldman, were at odds with Tucker because he had declined to defend Berkman during his imprisonment. "The hope of humanity," he had written, "lies in the avoidance of that revolution by force which the Berkmans are trying to precipitate. No pity for Frick, no praise for Berkman—such is the attitude of 'Liberty' in the present crisis." Berkman was one of Emma's several lovers, and she writhed under this slight.

Emma Goldman, passionate, tempestuous, long-suffering and humorless, considered Tucker heartless and unrealistic. How could anyone calling himself a believer in anarchy fail to endorse Berkman's noble attempt to remove Frick? In her fervid autobiography Emma has described Berkman's assassination attempt as a "heroic deed," but from her account it is not hard to see why an intellectual like Tucker preferred to steer clear of it. Berkman, although armed with a gun, dynamite capsule and poisoned dagger, had failed to dispatch Frick. Emma was indignant that Berkman, after putting three bullets into Frick and stabbing him in the thigh, had then been "pounded into unconsciousness" by Frick's rescuers. She was even more indignant when her former mentor, Johann Most, a prominent anarchist leader, dismissed Berkman's deed as unnoteworthy and suggested that Berkman had used a toy gun. Frick began to recover from his wounds, and Emma was furious that people blamed Berkman for the fact that Frick was still alive.

Tucker also told Eugene about Max Stirner, whose book, *Ego and His Own*, he had translated some time earlier and which had been a forerunner of the anarchist movement in America. Eugene bought a copy and was impressed with Stirner's philosophy of egoism, which disdained all social and ethical standards.

"As for good and evil!" wrote Stirner. "I am I, and I am neither good nor evil. Neither has any meaning for me. . . . My concern is . . . not the True, the Good, the Right, The Free, etc. . . . but simply my own self, and it is not general, it is individual, as I myself am individual. For me there is nothing above myself."

But Tucker's most significant contribution to Eugene's education was in introducing him to Friedrich Nietzsche's *Thus Spake Zarathustra*. Eugene was enthralled by Nietzsche, and remained so all his life. When nearly forty and solidly established as America's leading dramatist, he wrote to a friend (the critic and poet-essayist, Benjamin de Casseres):

"Zarathustra . . . has influenced me more than any book I've ever read. I ran into it through the bookshop of Benjamin Tucker . . . when I was eighteen and I've always possessed a copy since then and every year or so I re-read it and am never disappointed, which is more than I can say of almost any other book."

Eugene made it a habit to copy passages from Nietzsche and commit them to memory. He always felt kinship with the German philosopher, who had died in 1900. Nietzsche, the son and grandson of Protestant pastors and descended from a line of theologians on his mother's side as well, had undergone a loss of faith comparable to Eugene's and become a devastating critic of Christianity and its ideals. Many aspects of O'Neill's later life strikingly paralleled those of Nietzsche's. The drooping black mustache O'Neill grew in his late twenties, the solitude in which he spent his last years, the tremendous strain he put on his creative spirit, the somber satisfaction he took in being misunderstood, and the final collapse—all are a mirroring of Nietzsche.

Thus Spake Zarathustra, written in the style of an Old Testament prophet, was Eugene's Catechism. At eighteen he swallowed it whole, just as he had, at eight, absorbed the Catholic Catechism. But, unlike the Catechism, which he kept trying to forget, *Zarathustra* was permanently digested, even though, in his later years, he confessed, "Spots of its teaching I no longer concede."

Instead of the Catechism's:

"What is man? Man is a creature made up of a rational soul and an organic body"—Eugene now embraced:

"Man is a rope stretched between the animal and the Superman—a rope over an abyss."

Instead of the Catechism's:

"What is a rational soul? A rational soul is a spiritual substance, endowed with intellect and free will, and immortal . . ."—Eugene seized upon:

" 'Body am I, and soul,'—so saith the child. And why should one not speak like children? . . . the awakened one, the knowing one, saith: 'Body am I entirely, and nothing more; and soul is only the name of something in the body.' "

For the Golden Rule's enjoiner, "Love thy neighbor as thyself," Eugene eagerly substituted Nietzsche's:

"Do I advise you to neighbor-love? Rather do I advise you to neighbor-flight and to furthest love! Higher than love to your neighbor is love to the furthest and future ones; higher still than love to men, is love to things and phantoms. . . . My brethren, I advise you not to neighbor-love —I advise you to furthest love!"

Eugene also tried to emulate Nietzsche's poetic style. Although, in later years, he professed to have had no real literary leanings until he was well into his twenties, he now began to write poetry. It was derivative from Baudelaire as well as from Nietzsche—and it was not good. Baudelaire and Dowson had joined Swinburne and Wilde in his admiration. James considered most of his son's literary heroes degenerates and suspected, not without some justification, that Eugene was attracted to them as much by the sordid details of their personal lives as by the cadence of their language.

James did not hold Eugene's view that he should spend his young manhood loafing. After allowing Eugene a recuperative summer in New London, during which he frequently reminded him that he had thrown away his chance of a proper education, James found him his first job, as secretary to a small New York mail-order firm dealing in cheap costume jewelry. The company, in which James had invested some money, gave prizes of phonograph records to children who could peddle a certain quota of tawdry rings and pins among their neighbors and relatives. James thought Eugene could utilize his literary background in handling the correspondence for the firm, but Eugene decided otherwise. He proved singularly inept at the job and devoted most of his office hours to reading. His evenings were spent on the town.

In the fall of 1907 James and Jamie were on tour again with *Monte Cristo* and Ella kept the apartment at the Lucerne for herself and Eugene. But the opportunity this offered for intimacy between mother and son was not used by either. Like her husband, Ella always seemed less at ease with her own children than with their contemporaries.

Like James, but more quietly, Ella was inclined to befriend and put herself out for youngsters she considered talented and in need of encouragement. She took under her wing, for a time, a second cousin named Agnes Brennan, who was a few years older than Eugene and showed promise as a pianist, and also Agnes' young friend, Sadie Koenig, who was studying in New York with the same music teacher. Sadie's struggle to earn her keep and pay for music lessons reminded Ella of her own brief, though far more comfortable, student days. Ella went out of her way to be kind to Sadie, who, she knew, often had to walk from her rooming house on Seventh Street to the music school on Twenty-third Street because she could not afford the fare for the horsecar. Ella encouraged Sadie and Agnes (who was being financed by a member of her family) to visit her often at the Lucerne, where she would serve them coffee and cake, and inquire about their progress.

"Mrs. O'Neill was a wonderful woman," Miss Koenig later recalled. "She gave me help and advice when I really needed it."

In spite of her gratitude and admiration, however, Sadie could not help noticing that Ella behaved strangely at times—being drowsy, incoherent, repeating herself or trailing off into vague silences. Sadie had no idea what was wrong with Ella, but she did suspect that Eugene pained and disappointed her. He was frequently at the hotel when Sadie and Agnes visited and seemed, to the innocent young woman, to be "a kind of bum."

According to Miss Koenig, Eugene was often drunk and almost always argumentative. He would come in and fling himself onto a bed, and Ella would ask, in front of the two girls, "Are you at it again?" Eugene would yell back at her from the bedroom, "You'd be better off if you'd sleep a little more." The two argued incessantly and Eugene sometimes mocked his mother in what seemed, to Sadie, an outrageous fashion.

Once Ella said to Sadie, as she was leaving, "I hope you'll be a success someday. Study hard so you won't have to struggle later." Eugene then put his arms around Sadie and warned her drunkenly, "Now, you work hard, and don't touch any liquor."

Because of her family connection with the O'Neills, Agnes was somewhat more inured to their unconventional behavior and tried to make light of it. But Sadie was very much upset.

Eugene left both the mail-order company and the Lucerne in the early fall of 1908. (Soon after, the company went bankrupt as an aftermath of the panic of 1907, leaving James with one more bad investment to write off.) Somehow Eugene persuaded his father to give him a few months of grace.

Late that fall Eugene moved into a studio on Broadway and Sixty-sixth Street, in a building then called the Lincoln Arcade. The studio was shared by two young artists named Edward Keefe and George Bellows. Keefe was a tall, dark, good-looking New Londoner who wanted to paint, and who later became an architect in his home town. Bellows, a graduate of Ohio State University, also wanted to paint and eventually became a leader of the "ash can" school of art. Keefe, who had known Eugene in New London as a fishing and swimming companion and a fellow member of Doc Ganey's Second Story Club, was more receptive to Eugene's idea of having a good time than was Bellows. It was Keefe on whom Eugene tried out his radical thinking, dragging him off to Tucker's bookstore for doses of Nietzsche and Stirner.

They adopted a Saturday night ritual, in which they were occasionally joined by Louis Holliday, that included visits to a number of notorious establishments in the area known as the Tenderloin. By the late 1800's New York had achieved an international reputation as a wicked and gaudy city. The Tenderloin, stretching from Madison Square to Forty-eighth Street between Fifth and Ninth Avenues, was its center of vice. It was not only the red-light district but the site of gambling dens, illicitly operated saloons, and the headquarters for the most active criminals.

White slavery flourished, opium dens abounded, and a corrupt Tammany Hall, under the resourceful guidance of Richard Croker, cleared hundreds of thousands of dollars annually in protection fees, bribes, and percentages in the area's enterprises. The Tenderloin, which had been known earlier as Satan's Circus, got its name from a police inspector who, on being transferred there from a quiet area of the city, expressed his satisfaction that after a long time of making do with rump steak, he could now avail himself of some tenderloin.

Eugene and Keefe tried, with severely limited funds, to be a part of this gaily sordid life. They started their Saturday night rites at Mouquin's, a French restaurant on Sixth Avenue and Twenty-eighth Street which was frequented by the high and low life of Broadway. The restaurant, housed in a wooden mansion, had a reputation for excellent French cuisine at moderate prices and it was here, according to Keefe, that they "ate dinner after a fashion."

Properly primed, they wandered over to the Haymarket, a combination restaurant, dance hall and variety stage, where prostitutes gathered and where liquor was served all night long. Diamond Jim Brady could often be found there, entertaining out-of-town visitors. Pickpockets, petty thieves and pimps made it their headquarters.

Located on Sixth Avenue, just south of Thirtieth Street, it was an ugly, yellow, brick and frame building three stories high. Shuttered by day, its windows blazed with light at night and far into the early morning hours. Erected as a variety theatre after the Civil War, the building retained the galleries and boxes which lined three of its walls above the main floor.

While the ground floor was reserved for dancing and drinking, the galleries had been fitted out with cubicles where, for a dollar or two, a customer could watch one of the girls do the kind of dance popular at French peep shows.

It was here that Eugene took several strides forward in his program of education. Although he could not often afford to be more than an onlooker, he absorbed everything. He set down his impressions in a sonnet called "The Haymarket," which was later published in a New London newspaper:

> The music blares into a rag-time tune—
> The dancers whirl around the polished floor;
> Each powdered face a set expression wore
> Of dull satiety, and wan smiles swoon
> On rouged lips at sallies opportune
> Of maudlin youths whose sodden spirits soar
> On drunken wings; while through the opening door
> A chilly blast sweeps like the breath of doom.
>
> In sleek dress suit an old man sits and leers
> With vulture mouth and blood-shot, beady eyes
> At the young girl beside him. Drunken tears
> Fall down her painted face, and choking sighs
> Shake her, as into his familiar ears
> She sobs her sad, sad history—and lies!

O'Neill made a firsthand study of young girls with painted faces and sad histories.

"Those babes gave me some of the best laughs I've ever had," he once confided to George Jean Nathan, "and to the future profit of many a dramatic scene."

The heroine of *Anna Christie* is a prostitute, and a total of fourteen streetwalkers ply their trade in seven other of his published plays; additional prostitutes figure as offstage characters in another five plays.

Although O'Neill acknowledged their function, he continued to be far more interested in their souls. Having rejected Jamie's view that they were fascinating vampires, he conceived of them as children of fate. For the most part, Eugene believed, they were girls of arrested emotional development, capable of a dogged and childlike loyalty to anyone who was kind to them. Eugene accepted the fact that a girl could drift into the profession out of helplessness. He met many who told him their histories of a losing struggle to stay alive by respectable standards.

O'Neill first took up the cause of the prostitute in a one-act play called *The Web,* which he wrote in 1913 and whose heroine was a girl named Rose Thomas. Rose is helplessly bound to a pimp named Steve, with whom she lives and who mistreats her and takes all her money. In a state of advanced tuberculosis, Rose would probably have given up trying to stay alive if it were not for her baby, whom she loves, nourishes and protects in the squalid room where Steve keeps her. An escaped gangster who intercedes for her with the brutal Steve asks her:

"Why d'yuh stand fur him anyway? Why don't yuh take the kid and beat it away from him? . . . why don't yuh cut this life and be on the level . . . git a job some place?"

Rose replies: "D'yuh suppose they'd keep me any place if they knew what I was? And d'yuh suppose he wouldn't tell them or have somebody else tell them? Yuh don't know the game I'm up against. I've tried that job thing. I've looked for decent work and I've starved at it. A year after I first hit this town I quit and tried to be on the level. I got a job at housework—workin' twelve hours a day for twenty-five dollars a month. And I worked like a dog, too, and never left the house, I was so scared of seein' some one who knew me. But what was the use? One night they have a guy to dinner who's seen me some place when I was on the town. He tells the lady—his duty he said it was—and she fires me right off the reel. I tried the same thing a lot of times. But there was always some one who'd drag me back. And then I quit tryin'. There didn't seem to be no use. They—all the good people—they got me where I am and they're going to keep me there. Reform? Take it from me it can't be done. They won't let yuh do it, and that's Gawd's truth."

The same sense of being trapped by circumstances is expressed by

O'Neill's later heroine, Anna Christie. Confessing her past to her father and the man with whom she has fallen in love, Anna says:

"It was one of them cousins . . . the youngest son—Paul—that started me wrong. It wasn't none of my fault. I hated him worse'n hell and he knew it. But he was big and strong. . . . That's what made me get a yob as a nurse girl. . . . And you think that was a nice yob for a girl? . . . With all them nice . . . fellers yust looking for a chance to marry me, I s'pose. . . . What a chance! They wasn't looking for marrying . . . I was caged in . . . yust like in jail . . . lonesome as hell! So I gave up finally. What was the use? . . . men, God damn 'em! I hate 'em. Hate 'em!"

O'Neill's language had become less finicky by 1920, when he wrote *Anna Christie*, but his sentimental sympathy for whores was basically unchanged, and it never did change. At fifty-eight, shortly before *The Iceman Cometh* was produced, he was asked if it was true that the play had a cast of fourteen men and three tarts.

"There are fourteen men and three—uh—*ladies*," he replied.

And at sixty-three he was still defending the honor of prostitutes. He bristled when a mild-mannered friend made a casual remark about an Army experience involving a "two-bit whore." He resented the slight, much in the same way that the "ladies" in *The Iceman Cometh* insist on the distinction between "tarts," a designation they are glad to own up to, and "whores," which they stolidly maintain they are not. Not many of Eugene's friends were interested in making such nice distinctions, and Ed Keefe, for his part, was content to characterize the girls at the Haymarket as "pretty good." As he has remembered it, though, "We were only living *at* the life, trying to be a part of it; we didn't have the money to do it right."

They did have enough money, if they were careful, to end their evening at Jack's, an oyster house at Sixth Avenue and Forty-third Street. A hangout for writers and newspapermen, Jack's was open day and night and was famous for its Irish bacon and sea food and for its efficient staff of waiter-bouncers.

The theatre was another form of entertainment open to Eugene and Ed Keefe. Eugene could still obtain complimentary tickets to almost anything he wanted to see, and there was a great deal of glittering nonsense on display. Show business was continuing its expansion to meet the demands of a growing city. About thirty playhouses dotted the Rialto, roughly from Joe Weber's theatre on Twenty-ninth Street to the Colonial vaudeville house on Sixty-second Street, with the center of activity now established at O'Neill's birthplace—Times Square.

The name of the square had been changed from Longacre to mark the erection of *The New York Times* building in 1904. Two dozen theatres were situated in its vicinity.

One of the biggest hits of the season—it ran for 496 performances—was *The Man from Home,* written by Booth Tarkington in collaboration with Harry Leon Wilson. Somerset Maugham's *Lady Frederick* was a success at the Hudson Theatre; Ethel Barrymore was playing the title role, which had been turned down by the vainer Mrs. Pat Campbell and Viola Allen, among others, because the heroine was a mature woman who had to appear, in one scene, seated at her dressing table devoid of make-up.

The Easiest Way, by Eugene Walter, was being hailed as a radical departure from the tepid native drama of the period. Produced by David Belasco, the play had for its heroine a woman named Laura Murdock, who had a somewhat tarnished reputation. And despite its florid and sentimental language, it further flouted convention by ending unhappily. Laura's curtain line was being quoted all over town: "Dress up my body and paint my face. I'm going to Rector's to make a hit—and to hell with the rest!"

Eugene attended many of the current productions, but he drew the line at *Monte Cristo* when his father brought it to New York for a brief engagement early in the season. He sent Keefe and Bellows, refusing to accompany them.

He still enjoyed musicals and attended a good portion of the twenty or so produced during the 1908-9 season, including two by Victor Herbert and one by George M. Cohan. What he liked most about musicals was the chorus girls, who bore no more resemblance to the dedicated Broadway ballerinas of today than a peacock bears to a sparrow. In an era of famous beauties—Ziegfeld had staged his first *Follies* in 1907—chorus girls reigned over the city's night life. Eugene could not begin to afford them, as they were accustomed to being courted by the wealthiest men about town and expected to be lavishly entertained. But he got to know some of the younger girls through Jamie and would occasionally take them out.

"The girls in those days," he recalled in his later years, "were less ambitious and more fun."

For Eugene at that time there seemed to be no middle ground between chorus girls and whores. He considered himself too worldly for innocent dalliance, and the fact that his rakish behavior irritated his father added spice to his adventures.

Keefe has recalled a time when Eugene, for some reason, was particularly angry with his father. "I'm going to fix the old bastard," Eugene told his friend. He secured the company of a girl from a French bordello (paid for out of the allowance he received from his father). The girl had violently red hair, and neither her presence nor her profession could possibly have been overlooked. Eugene seated her next to him in a box he had reserved at the New York Theatre, where Anna Held was appearing in *Miss Innocence,* a musical produced by her husband, Florenz Ziegfeld. Eugene was reasonably sure that someone among his father's army of acquaintances would recognize him and give James a report. Someone did and James, as often happened when he found himself flouted by one of his children, fell back on Shakespeare, reciting King Lear's "How sharper than a serpent's tooth it is to have a thankless child!"

Tiring suddenly of their gay life, Keefe, Bellows and Eugene abandoned New York in midwinter for Zion, New Jersey, a town not far from Princeton, where James owned a small farmhouse and a bit of land.

Arriving at the station on a frosty afternoon, they hired a buggy to take them to the O'Neill farm. The house, which only someone as young and heedless as Eugene could have regarded as habitable, was situated at the bottom of a snow-covered hill, with a stream running behind it and snowy hills surrounding it. Eugene and his friends found living conditions primitive, for the house, unoccupied for many years, was in a state of decay.

In order to heat the three downstairs rooms they decided to live in, they had to tear out a false front that guarded the fireplace and clean the chimney. The kitchen, located in the middle of the house, contained an oil stove, on which they did their elementary cooking. Keefe, the only one able to cope with the stove, acted as chef; his specialty was dried pea soup, but he varied this occasionally with bacon and eggs, purchased from a nearby general store. Eugene, who was incapable of cooking anything at all, chopped wood for the fireplace. The room with the fireplace served as their sitting room, and another room, in which they discovered a broken-down bed and a sagging spring propped up on wooden boxes, became their bedroom.

Since the only feasible sleeping arrangement was for two of them to share the bed while the other slept on the spring, and since the former arrangement promised to be the warmer one, they tossed a coin to determine who would have to sleep in cold solitude. Bellows lost.

All three throve on camp life. Eugene spent his time walking and chopping wood during the day and writing poetry in the evening. Keefe and Bellows turned out forty paintings between them, a number of which vividly reflected the blue cold of their environment. Since there was nothing in view but hills, they painted hills from morning till night. Since there was no reason to shave, they all grew beards. Shaving would have been difficult in any case. Even washing was a problem. The only water available came from a well pump and sometimes the water in the bucket started freezing while it was being carried into the house. One of the conveniences of the farmhouse that amused them all was the family privy, which had three toilets of graded sizes. The privy was the only spot from which the farmhouse could be painted, and Keefe availed himself of this vantage point.

Eugene's father, in a fit of generosity, sent some liquor and a box of cigars to the farm, and Louis Holliday was invited out for a weekend to share these riches. The three young men spent no money except for basic provisions. The only unforeseen expense was incurred by Keefe, who got his shoes wet and put them by the fire, where they burned to cinders and had to be replaced.

The outing lasted five weeks. Eugene, Bellows and Keefe arrived back in New York bearded, lugging finished canvases, and flushed with frontier spirit, to resume residence in their studio.

XIII

IN THE LATE SPRING OF 1909 EUGENE HAD HIS FIRST significant encounter with a girl who, in the words of a young blade in *Ah, Wilderness!*, was not "a real swift baby." She fell, rather, into the category of "dead Janes," a phrase used by Eugene to describe respectable girls with whom there was not likely to be "something doing."

Eugene was not yet twenty-one when he met Kathleen Jenkins. She was an extremely pretty, vivacious girl of Eugene's age, a little spoiled and a little bored. Her father, Charles Jenkins, whose family came to America before the Revolution, was for a time associated with Tiffany and Company and was commodore of the Larchmont Yacht Club in Westchester. He later moved to Chicago with his wife, Kate Camblas, a volatile woman whose Corsican ancestors claimed kinship with Napoleon Bonaparte. She left her husband in Chicago in 1899, when Kathleen was ten, and moved to New York, where her father, Henry Camblas, had taken a seat on the New York Stock Exchange.

Kathleen was brought up, as were most of her friends, to believe that the best use she could make of her time and her endowments was to give and attend parties and make a good marriage. Her mother often gave Sunday afternoon tea parties, or supper parties, at which Kathleen could shine. Kate Camblas Jenkins was resentful about her own marriage; she had married Charles Jenkins because her parents had thought him a better catch than the man she really loved. But Jenkins had taken to drink.

Kathleen's mother, worried that alcoholism could be inherited, encouraged her daughter to sip cocktails at fifteen, believing that an early acquaintance with liquor would forestall any tendencies toward the Jenkins failing.

At twenty Kathleen resembled the lovely girls Charles Dana Gibson was drawing. She had big blue eyes, her fair hair was piled high on her head, and her carriage was a graceful imitation of the Grecian bend. Bored by eager beaux from her own environment, Kathleen was beguiled by the strange, dark, handsome young man who was presented to her. Eugene had met the beau of one of Kathleen's girl friends, and was taken to the Jenkins home, on Broadway near 113th Street. Eugene, always shy in the presence of a nice girl, was emboldened by Kathleen's obvious interest in him and invited her out.

Even at twenty Eugene revealed a paradoxical nature. Vain and egotistical at times, he could also be touchingly helpless. Throughout his life he remained a puzzle to the people who knew him best, for he was given to swift reversals and conveyed sharply different impressions of himself— often deliberately. He was worldly in experience, yet naïve in its application to his own life; shy and sentimental one instant, hard as nails the next; an incipient artist of uncanny insight and sensitivity, yet a man who often misunderstood and failed those who depended on him; a victim of self-pity, and a hero challenging the fates.

Eugene was subject to black moods of despair, which he sometimes attributed to his Irish ancestry. These moods were intensified when he drank. His drunken violence most often was spent upon women with whom he was romantically involved, but Kathleen and one or two others he knew in his twenties were notable exceptions. Kathleen saw only the gentler side of his nature—or, perhaps, she closed her eyes to his darker side, because she was not equipped to understand it.

Many years later, recalling the youthful romance, she said: "We could never have made a go of it; I'd be foolish to imagine that I could ever have given him the kind of understanding he needed." But at the time she saw only that he was mysteriously different from any other man she had ever met. He wrote poetry for her that was both exotic and tender; he carried with him an aura of strange romance that was enormously appealing; he lived in a world she scarcely knew existed, but which he made sound fascinating and desirable. She fell quickly in love with him.

Eugene, who could never resist being loved, was bewitched by Kathleen. He was less in love with her than with the romantic image of her love for him, but the emotion was strong enough to keep him in New York that summer, courting her. Before he quite realized what was happening he found that Kathleen, assuming he was as earnestly in love as she, expected him to marry her. He did not want to hurt her. But neither did he feel he could marry her—as much for her sake as for his own. He was not working and had neither the prospect nor intention of it. He was entirely dependent on his father for support and, while that arrangement sometimes made for strained family relations, he was, on the whole, satisfied. He did not see how the acquisition of a wife could help his situation, for he knew that James would not tolerate it.

Reverting in panic to his little-boy dependence upon James, he confessed to his father the depth of his involvement with Kathleen, stressing that she was a nice girl who really loved him. James, always suspicious that any girl interested in his son was actually after Monte Cristo gold and ignoring the fact that Kathleen's family was well enough off not to need any O'Neill financing, told Eugene that Kathleen must be a gold-digger; even worse, she was not a Catholic. James would take matters into his own hands and get Eugene out of the country for a while.

Thus reassured, Eugene could present himself to Kathleen as the helpless victim of an unyielding father. But Kathleen was unwilling to let the matter rest there and Eugene eventually subscribed to her point of view.

James, between rehearsals of the new play he was going to do in September, cast about for a way of removing Eugene and came up with a plan to send him on a mining expedition. Ella had invested some of her money in a gold mine in Spanish Honduras and an engineer named Earl Stevens was about to go there with his wife to investigate the holding.

Stevens, a native of Oregon, was eleven years older than Eugene and had graduated in 1905 from Columbia University. James, whose own mining interests were widespread and varied enough to have brought him into contact with numerous engineers, had formed one of his fatherly attachments for Stevens, and he thought the young mining expert would have a stabilizing effect on Eugene. James did not mention to Stevens the real reason for wanting to send Eugene on the trip. Instead, professing a fear he had never felt, James told Stevens that he was sending Eugene away for a while to remove him from "theatrical" influences.

Eugene was interested in his father's plan to make him a miner. Looking for gold in Honduras sounded like an agreeably protracted adventure. Satisfied that there would be no consequences to face, one way or another, he bundled Kathleen onto a ferryboat for Hoboken, New Jersey, on October 2, 1909, about a week before he was scheduled to sail for Honduras. They were secretly married in Hoboken Trinity Church, the Rev. William G. Gilpin, a Protestant minister, officiating. Eugene put his age down as twenty-two on the marriage certificate, although his twenty-first birthday was still nearly two weeks away. He listed his occupation as "engineer," his residence as Zion, New Jersey. He and his bride agreed to keep the marriage secret for the time being. It could not be for long as Kathleen was pregnant.

Eugene was to sail for Honduras from San Francisco and Kathleen saw him off at his train in New York. Eugene considered it rather a good joke on his father that the girl from whom James was separating him was already his wife.

XIV

THE YOUNGER SON OF THE O'NEILLS CAME INTO MAN'S estate aboard a banana ship. His twenty-first birthday found him afloat in the Pacific Ocean, off the coast of Mexico. He celebrated by having his picture taken, first with Stevens and then with Mrs. Stevens, a pretty brunette not much older than he. Both photographs showed Eugene dressed in a neat, dark suit and high white collar, a self-conscious smirk on his clean-shaven face, and a cigarette between the thumb and forefinger of his right hand.

Stevens and his wife had gone ahead to San Francisco to make arrangements for the expedition and Eugene had joined them there. The three sailed down the western coast of Central America and docked at El Salvador. After hiring a native couple as guide and servant, they made their way on muleback to the Honduras capital, Tegucigalpa. Then they continued by mule to the Rio Siale, where they set up a base of operations for the expedition. While looking for mine sites they had to clear trails by machete and on at least one occasion the two men lost each other overnight in the jungle.

"I guess I looked like a Preparedness Day parade," the younger of the explorers later recalled. "I had a cartridge belt around my waist and a Colt revolver at one hip. Then I had a bandolier over one shoulder and a carbine slung over the other and I carried a machete dangling from the other side of my belt. Of course, it was the custom for a man to carry side arms in that country in those days, but I never saw anything to shoot but lizards."

Oddly enough, the reminiscent O'Neill never referred to the presence of Mrs. Stevens on the journey. It is a fair guess that he conceived a romantic notion about her. The first play he ever wrote—in 1913—was *A Wife for a Life,* which has a gold-mining camp background and deals with a young miner named Jack and his partner, an older man with whose beautiful and virtuous wife Jack has fallen in love.

While O'Neill never admitted having dreamed up the idea for this unrewarding effort in Honduras, he did credit his journey with supplying the physical background for a later and considerably more worthwhile project. *The Emperor Jones,* written in 1920, is set largely in a tropical forest, whose primitive state closely resembled the unexplored regions of Honduras through which Eugene and the Stevenses cut their way late in 1909.

Discussing *The Emperor Jones* on one occasion, O'Neill said: "The effect of the tropical forest on the human imagination was honestly come by. It was the result of my own experience while prospecting for gold in Spanish Honduras."

In his stage directions for that play, he wrote:

"The forest is a wall of darkness dividing the world. Only when the eye becomes accustomed to the gloom can the outlines of separate trunks of the nearest trees be made out, enormous pillars of deeper blackness. A somber monotone of wind lost in the leaves moans in the air. Yet this sound serves but to intensify the impression of the forest's relentless immobility, to form a background throwing into relief its brooding, implacable silence."

Describing his own jungle experiences many years after his return from Honduras, O'Neill recalled that a group of Indians from a rubber expedition passed his camp one day and told him and Stevens that another river farther on was choked with gold.

"We started in a mahogany dugout canoe," O'Neill said. "We had to go down the Rio Siale, into a larger stream, to the mouth of a river the Indians had described. Then we started up the stream. It was unexplored territory—nobody had gone in. We didn't get very far. It was a narrow, swift river, and trees had fallen across. At each bank the jungle grew so thickly that it was impossible to move through it. We gave up and came back."

Eugene found the jungle pure hell. In addition to the Little Formless Fears—the superstitious hallucinations he later ascribed to Jones, and which came to haunt him in the black jungle denseness—every variety of flying and crawling insect molested him. He could stomach neither the rations (iguana, wild pig, and monkey fried in grease and, inevitably, the tortilla) nor the natives, whom he described as "lazy, ignorant, human maggots." One evening the man who served as guide absent-mindedly lost his employers, leaving them to spend the night far from their campsite, listening to the yowls of a jaguar.

Eugene was almost joyful when, after about five months of this sort of thing, and no sign of the gold he had come for, he was stricken with malaria.

"I'd get an attack of the fever at two o'clock in the afternoon of every other day," he recalled later, "and, though the climate was hot, I'd sit at the campfire and chatter my teeth out."

Leaving Stevens to dam his unnavigable river, Eugene, led by an Indian guide, made a ten-day return trip by mule to Tegucigalpa. Shivering with fever, he presented himself at the American consulate. The consul put him to bed, summoned a doctor, and nursed him for three weeks. During the nights, which are cold in Tegucigalpa, the consul, who could not supply enough blankets to keep his patient warm, added a cover of some worn American flags.

Before he was well enough to leave Honduras Eugene received word that the dam had burst and that Stevens, too, was calling it quits. O'Neill and Stevens did not meet again until the winter of 1936 in Seattle, Washington. By that time Stevens, without O'Neill's knowledge, had become a trumpet player with the Portland Symphony Orchestra, and O'Neill had won the Nobel Prize. O'Neill, who had gone to Seattle to find background material for a play, instituted a search for Stevens not long after his arrival.

"O'Neill believes that Stevens is now operating a gold mine somewhere in Oregon," reported Richard L. Neuberger, the journalist who was later to become a senator. After interviewing O'Neill for the *Oregonian*, Neuberger wrote: "If Mr. Stevens should by any capricious chance read these words and would communicate his address and whereabouts to the writer of this article, care The Oregonian, Mr. Eugene Gladstone O'Neill would be greatly appreciative."

Stevens did read the words, and was surprised and delighted. He was surprised because fourteen years earlier he had received a very courteous, but explicit, brushoff from O'Neill, in response to a request for financial backing in an Oregon mining venture. O'Neill had written Stevens at that time that it was hard to imagine that the Honduras adventure had really taken place, adding facetiously that the image of himself "loaded down like an arsenal with ammunition, knives and firearms" would make "a first rate comedy hero of romance, especially if my faithful (?) mule could also play a part."

Stevens was delighted that O'Neill did not bear him a grudge for having had to turn him down. He communicated with O'Neill and both Stevens and his wife were promptly invited to dinner and to spend the night. "I look forward to seeing you both," O'Neill informed Stevens, "—although I shall feel a bit embarrassed, because as I remember myself in the Rio Siale days, I was a very obstreperous young Nut, and must have been a great trial to have around!"

[136]

The reunion was successful, but soon after that O'Neill became ill and moved to California. Stevens, who outlived O'Neill by three years, never saw him again. But from time to time he gazed nostalgically at the photographs of the two eager young men and the pretty girl who had gone on a romantic adventure in a romantic world.

The end of Eugene's Honduras expedition marked the beginning of two of the most significant years of his life.

"I was invalided back to New York via the Panama Canal," was the way he later summed it up, somewhat mystifyingly. The canal was not opened until five years later. But he was always conspicuously silent about the melodramatic climax that took place on his return to New York.

Although he had tried hard to believe, in the jungle, that Kathleen was an unfortunate memory that would evaporate, he could not quite convince himself that this was true. He had received a letter from her in Honduras saying she could no longer keep the marriage a secret; her pregnancy was now obvious. Eugene had been obliged to write his father about the marriage and James, of course, was furious, but he still imagined he could suppress the whole affair. James miscalculated the reactions of Kathleen and her mother as blandly and as arrogantly as he had once miscalculated those of Nettie Walsh.

Eugene arrived in New York at the end of April; his gold-mining adventure had lasted six and a half months. James, who had been touring since the end of November in *The White Sister,* the play in which he had opened just before Eugene left, hastened to New York from Washington to scold his son and plan new strategy.

When O'Neill started writing plays he indicated sardonic awareness of the similarity between his entanglement with Kathleen and his father's affair with Nettie Walsh. In the one-acter called *Abortion,* for instance, the hero, Jack Townsend, becomes involved with a girl of whom he is fond but does not love enough to marry. Eugene had solved his own problem by marrying Kathleen but with no thought of assuming any husbandly duties, and the lines he later wrote for Jack Townsend reflect his own sense of guilt and unhappiness. Speaking of the "sweet, lovely girl" he does not love, Jack says to his father:

"Yes, yes, I know it, Dad. I have played the scoundrel all the way through. I realize that now. Why couldn't I have felt that way at the start? Then this would never have happened." (In the play, "this" is an abortion; in fact, Eugene could have been accurately referring to his own irresponsible marriage.)

But, continues the hero, "at that time the whole thing seemed just a pleasant game we were playing; its serious aspects appeared remote, unreal. I never gave them a thought."

The father in *Abortion* is, like most of the fathers in O'Neill's plays, modeled on James O'Neill. He is a "kindly old man of sixty or so . . . erect, well-preserved, energetic, dressed immaculately but soberly" and he has himself been something of a rake in his youth, as a result of which his son expects a certain amount of sympathetic understanding. Thus in response to the father's "if you did not love this girl, why did you,—why, in the first place—?" the son says:

"Why? Why? Who knows why or who, that does know, has the courage to confess it, even to himself. Be frank, Dad! Judging from several anecdotes which your friend . . . has let slip . . . you were no St. Anthony. Turn your mind back to those days and then answer your own question."

As a final indication of Eugene's sense of identification with his father's profligate youth, Eugene called the girl in *Abortion* not quite "Nettie," but "Nellie."

James was on untenable ground. He could not play the stern Victorian with Eugene. He simply had to swallow the situation and sit out the storm—which broke a few days after Eugene's return from Honduras.

Halley's comet, which had appeared early in the year, had by May 4 grown alarmingly bright in the skies over Manhattan; it continued to grow brighter until May 19, at which time the earth was scheduled to pass through its 46-million-mile-long tail. Superstitious throngs spent that day on their knees, praying for deliverance; the arrival of the comet, which since 2616 B.C. had been frightening emperors, kings and popes out of their collective wits, heralded the arrival of Eugene O'Neill, Jr., on May 5. (Like the true son of his father, Eugene Jr. was later to claim the appearance of the comet for his personal omen of disaster.)

On May 6 the *World* took Mrs. Jenkins' word for the details of the marriage. It announced, in bold headlines, "The Birth of a Boy Reveals Marriage of 'Gene' O'Neill." The subhead declared, "Son of Actor Was Wed Secretly Last July to Kathleen Jenkins, Who Was Sweetheart of His Childhood." Mrs. Jenkins had decided to put the O'Neills in their place and to have her moment. The baby, who was born with black eyes, and weighed in at a strapping ten and a half pounds, was, Mrs. Jenkins informed the *World* reporter, "the image of his dad."

"It was at the request of Mr. James O'Neill that my daughter's marriage was kept a secret," Mrs. Jenkins added. "Mrs. O'Neill had been ill all winter and the announcement of her son's marriage, it was feared, would have grave consequences to her. She was told only recently. She seemed pleased when she learned of the baby's birth." (Mrs. O'Neill was so pleased that, when the *World* reporter tried to reach her at the Lucerne, she was unavailable.)

Making a propitiatory gesture toward the O'Neills, Mrs. Jenkins said to the reporter, "My daughter told me that she had begged Eugene to be married by a priest, but he declined. But the child is to be baptized in the Catholic faith, as Kathleen feels it would be a sin not to do so. . . . He will be named Eugene Gladstone O'Neill, 2nd."

James wanted no part of Eugene Gladstone O'Neill, 2nd, baptized or not. His reaction to the announcement was stony silence. His son's reaction was no less stolid. Mrs. Jenkins and Kathleen, in fact, had no idea Eugene had returned to the United States. The same *World* story reported that "young 'Gene,' as he is familiarly known, does not know that he is a father, and will not know it for probably six weeks, as he is mining down in Honduras."

It was this newspaper article that first told Eugene of his fatherhood. Entering a familiar Manhattan bar on May 6, he was greeted jocularly by the bartender and informed that drinks were on the house. Questioning this generosity, Eugene was given a broad wink, and presented with the copy of the *World* that carried the announcement of Eugene Jr.'s birth.

Mrs. Jenkins realized a few days later that in James O'Neill she had met her Waterloo, when her triumphant earlier announcement backfired. Under a two-column picture of Kathleen, looking pensive, the *World,* on May 10, ran the caption, "Mrs. O'Neill, Who Is a Mother, Does Not Know Husband Is in City." The *World* reporter had found Eugene at 123 West Forty-seventh Street, not far from the Green Room Club, a social center for actors. According to a friend of Eugene's at that address, said the *World,* the missing husband had been in residence there "for a week at least." And at the Green Room Club an obliging clerk revealed that Eugene and his father had dined there on May 4. "Gene also had been seen at Broadway restaurants in the last few days," the *World* added helpfully.

"The young mother is still in ignorance of her husband's presence in this city," the newspaper continued. "She believes him to be in a mine in Honduras, working to make a fortune for her and their infant son. Since O'Neill's return to New York he has not called upon his wife, according to her mother, Mrs. Kate C. Jenkins, at whose home Mrs. O'Neill is living. When Mrs. Jenkins was told yesterday that her son-in-law was here, she at first refused to believe it. She was so shocked she could say nothing for several minutes. Then, with tears of mortification filling her eyes, she exclaimed:

" 'It seems impossible that Gene is in town and has remained away from his wife and their baby. There must be some mistake, but if there is not, Eugene's attitude is inexcusable. He knows how we all feel toward him and that he could have come to this house to live any time since his marriage to my daughter. There would have been no "Mother-in-law" about it, either, and he knew that. I felt toward him as if he were my own. If he is living in New York without coming to see his wife and baby, I am pretty certain who is responsible for his behavior. No, I will not say now who that person is.' "

James O'Neill knew whom she had in mind. For the moment he had won his point; now he underlined it by whisking Eugene off with him as the hastily appointed assistant company manager of *The White Sister*. He intended to let the Jenkins family simmer for a while and did not want Eugene within their reach.

Eugene was upset but helpless, for he felt he had no choice but to submit to his father. A friend has recalled that Ella later told her that Eugene had wept when the full implication of his responsibility struck him, soon after the birth of Eugene Jr. There is evidence in his plays that he brooded for some time about the various alternatives possible in a situation such as his and Kathleen's. In addition to *Abortion*, two other early plays, *Servitude* and *Before Breakfast*, deal with men who regarded themselves as having been trapped into marriage. And one of his last plays, *A Touch of the Poet*, introduces the same theme.

Eugene's first professional association with the theatre did nothing to alter his opinion that American drama was chiefly claptrap. *The White Sister* was not much of an improvement over *Monte Cristo* insofar as its high-flown sentiments and improbable dialogue were concerned; it was representative of the mawkish melodramas that were still being complacently produced. Even such innovations as *Paid in Full* and *The Fourth Estate*, while dealing with realistic, contemporary subjects, were cloaked in melodramatic speech and contrived denouement. Edward Sheldon, possibly the most original and daring playwright to enter the field in the 1900's, had contributed *Salvation Nell* in 1908, when he was only twenty-two, and fresh out of Professor George Pierce Baker's playwriting course at Harvard.

The Only Law, by Wilson Mizner and Bronson Howard; *Is Matrimony a Failure?* by Leo Ditrichstein; *The Melting Pot*, by Israel Zangwill; *The Passing of the Third Floor Back*, by Jerome K. Jerome; and

Springtime, by Booth Tarkington were among the shows which, with *The White Sister,* had launched the Broadway season of 1909-10.

Like most of the plays of the time, *The White Sister* had been tailored to the talents of a particular star—in this case Viola Allen, the tall, dark-haired actress who had sprung to prominence in controlled, romantic roles. The play was adapted by William Hackett and F. Marion Crawford from Crawford's successful novel.

James was now sixty-three and had for the time being put the strenuous role of Edmond Dantes on the shelf. But other starring roles were not easy to come by and he had accepted the minor role of a bishop in *The White Sister.* He disappointed most of his out-of-town admirers by dropping his youthful, romantic hero characters to support Miss Allen. At least one feature writer went so far as to inquire "why Liebler and Company [producers of *The White Sister*] paid such a large salary to have James O'Neill in the cast, when the part could be played perhaps not quite so well, but satisfactorily just the same, by some actor at one quarter the allowance." The writer answered his own question: "The reason is very plain. When the firm embarked in the theatrical business . . . their chief asset was Mr. O'Neill in 'Monte Cristo.' He gave the firm an opportunity to book some good routes and helped somewhat to bring the firm into the prominent position which it holds today. There is a certain amount of sentiment attached to the engagement and with George C. Tyler the salary is of no consideration. It is merely having the services of a man highly esteemed who was once the firm's mainstay."

In spite of his critical attitude toward his father at that time, Eugene nevertheless thought it slighting that James was reduced to playing a supporting role in a trivial play. His resentment ripened in retrospect and in 1920, soon after his father's death, he confided to George Tyler, with whom he was then associated in the production of one of his own plays, that his father "suffered as a retribution in his old age (for having confined himself so long to *Monte Cristo*) the humiliation of supporting such actor-yokels" as Viola Allen.

The White Sister was the story of a pure-spirited girl who, believing her soldier-lover dead, renounces the world to become a nun. Five years later the man returns, having escaped from captivity at the hands of his enemy, and tries to persuade her to give up her religious life and return to the world and him. She resists, and he shoots himself. Although New York received the play with tempered enthusiasm, out-of-town audiences loved it. Viola Allen reaped most of the glory, but the critics were kind to James and he still had his fans.

Women who had swooned over him as a young man remained devoted to him as an aging one. The once firm line of his jaw sagged a bit and there was more than a suggestion of a double chin; his hair was gray, his hairline was receding, and there were tired lines under his eyes that make-up could no longer hide, but the eyes themselves could still flash with fire.

"I am told that Mr. O'Neill is annoyed by women who gather at the stage door," wrote a woman reporter who devoted half a newspaper column to James's "rose-petal hands."

Two seasons before appearing in *The White Sister,* James had revived Edwin Forrest's old acting stand-by, Sheridan Knowles's *Virginius,* which he considered a "poetic masterpiece" almost on "a level with the tragedies of Shakespeare." At the end of the third act of *Virginius,* on opening night, he made a wry little speech that went over with the audience better than the play.

"I thank you," he said, "for your generous appreciation. Though for the last thirty years I have occupied a somewhat conspicuous position on the stage, I have seldom visited New York. I am sure I don't know why. I am no worse than other actors.

"Tonight's greeting encourages me to say that I intend to be back among you every year of the few years that are still left to me, playing something of this sort, and when I depart for that bourn from which no traveler returns I trust you may be able to say of me: 'Ah, well, he could do something else than act dear old Monte Cristo.'"

Taking their cue from James, who had by then been on the stage for forty-three years, newspaper and magazine feature writers seized the opportunity to interview him exhaustively and sentimentally. Briefly James's star shone once more in New York. But, despite the flurry of revived interest in him and his gallant curtain speech at *Virginius,* his faith in his own immortality was not justified. Less than a dozen years after his death people had not only forgotten he had ever played anything but Monte Cristo, they had all but forgotten him as anything but the father of Eugene O'Neill.

In 1910 most observers, James among them, thought Eugene would not amount to anything. But James was pleased to have his younger son's company in *The White Sister* because Jamie, who had been with him during most of his recent tours, was making one of his rare excursions on his own. Jamie had appeared with his father in *Virginius* in the role James had once played in support of Forrest; he had drawn from one critic the comment that he "gave good promise." It was eight years since his "promising" debut as Albert in *Monte Cristo.* Now, at thirty-two, Jamie was appearing in a James Forbes comedy, *The Traveling Salesman,* in the featured role of a salesman named Watts.

Eugene functioned less than brilliantly as an assistant company manager for *The White Sister.*

"A courtesy title," he once explained. "I had to sit at the gallery door and see that the local ticket taker didn't let in any of his friends." He added that once he and the ticket taker had become acquainted everything worked out "all right."

Several people who have recalled his presence on the tour expressed doubt that he functioned at all. He seemed to have come along for the ride. According to Theodore Liebler, Jr., son of the producer and an avid observer of his father's theatrical activities, "it didn't cost the company anything to have young O'Neill travel along."

"In those days," he said, "you could get a free baggage car on the railroad if you bought a block of twenty-five passenger tickets. Even with a company numbering around fifteen, it was the economical thing to do. *The White Sister* company was relatively small, so Eugene could travel in one of the paid-for, empty seats. I'm sure his father arranged to have him do something to justify his being there."

Eugene's reaction to his brief term of employment was disgust at having to wear a tuxedo on the nights he helped preside over the box office or hovered over the ticket takers. He soon found a way, however, to change both his environment and his costume.

XV

IN THE LATE SPRING OF 1910, WHEN *The White Sister* was nearing the end of its run in Boston, Eugene abruptly yielded to a longing that had been growing for some time. Drawn to Boston's Mystic wharf, as he had been drawn to the docks of New London, he lingered at the waterfront watching the clipper ships put out to sea, talking with the crews of newly arrived vessels, and thirsting for the romance that lay beyond the horizon. He decided he must go to sea.

Actually, it did not happen quite as fast as O'Neill, looking back, remembered it. Before "signing up" he consulted his father. James thought a sailor's life might have a good effect on Eugene's health and teach him responsibility. A sea voyage would also remove Eugene far from Kathleen and show her and her mother that the O'Neills did not consider the marriage binding. James intended to arrange a divorce when Eugene returned. He was pleased with Eugene's plans. The barque's captain was willing to take Eugene as a passenger for a small fee, provided he lend a hand with the less arduous work on the voyage. James agreed to stake his son.

"It happened quite naturally," Eugene said later, "as a consequence of what was really inside of me—what I really wanted, I suppose. I struck up one day by the wharf in Boston with a bunch of sailors, mostly Norwegians and Swedes. I wanted to ship with somebody and they took me that afternoon to the captain. Signed up and the next thing we were off."

The impulse that sent O'Neill to sea was more than a quest for adventure, more than an urge to be the kind of supertramp he admired in the novels of Jack London—although he did have a desire to model himself on London, who had shipped out at seventeen.

"I wanted to be a he-man; to knock 'em cold and eat 'em alive," he once explained. But that was only part of it. Shipping out was an escape from circumstances that were suffocating him, into an atmosphere he sensed would set him free. The moment he felt the deck roll under his feet he realized he was, at last, in his natural element. For the first time in his life he felt he belonged.

The sea gave him a sense of religious ecstasy, which he tried for the next thirty years to put into words. He made a groping start during his first voyage. Sitting on the deck one day after he had stood his watch, he began writing a poem called "Free" ("Actually written on a deep-sea barque in the days of Real Romance," he said years later):

Weary am I of the tumult, sick of the staring crowd,
Pining for wild sea places where the soul may think aloud.
Fled is the glamour of cities, dead as the ghost of a dream,
While I pine anew for the tint of blue on the breast of the old Gulf Stream.

I have had my dance with Folly, nor do I shirk the blame;
I have sipped the so-called Wine of Life and paid the price of shame;
But I know that I shall find surcease, the rest my spirit craves,
Where the rainbows play in the flying spray,
'Mid the keen salt kiss of the waves.

Then it's ho! for the plunging deck of a bark, the hoarse song of the crew,
With never a thought of those we left or what we are going to do;
Nor heed the old ship's burning, but break the shackles of care
And at last be free, on the open sea, with the trade wind in our hair.

Eleven years after writing "Free," he expressed similar sentiments with more originality and—though the form is prose—more genuine poetry:

"Oh, there was fine, beautiful ships them days," says Paddy, the old Irish sailor, in one of O'Neill's great, early plays, *The Hairy Ape*. "—clippers wid tall masts touching the sky. . . . We'd be sailing out, bound down round the Horn maybe. We'd be making sail in the dawn, with a fair breeze, singing a chanty song wid no care to it. And astern the land would be sinking low and dying out, but we'd give it no heed but a laugh, and never look behind. For the day that was, was enough, for we was free men . . . Oh, to be scudding south again wid the power of the Trade Wind driving her on steady through the nights and the days! Full sail on her! . . . Nights when the foam of the wake would be flaming wid fire, when the sky'd be blazing and winking wid stars. Or the full of the moon maybe. Then you'd see her driving through the gray night, her sails stretching aloft all silver and white, not a sound on the deck, the lot of us dreaming dreams. . . .'Twas them days men belonged to ships, not now. 'Twas them days a ship was part of the sea, and a man was part of a ship, and the sea joined all together and made it one."

He never stopped thinking of his exaltation. As late as 1941 he caused Edmund, the sea-struck young protagonist of *Long Day's Journey Into Night*, to say:

"I lay on the bowsprit, facing astern, with the water foaming into

spume under me, the masts with every sail white in the moonlight, towering high above me. I became drunk with the beauty and singing rhythm
of it, and for a moment I lost myself—actually lost my life. I was
set free! I dissolved in the sea, became white sails and flying spray,
became beauty and rhythm, became moonlight and the ship and the
high dim-starred sky! I belonged, without past or future, within peace
and unity and a wild joy, within something greater than my own life,
or the life of Man, to Life itself!"

The ship on which Eugene signed was a steel barque called the *Charles
Racine,* one of the last of the square-riggers to compete with steamers
at the end of the nineteenth century. She was not in a class with the
slender clipper ships; she was, in the phrase Eugene quickly picked
up from his shipmates, an "old hooker." But she could drive fourteen
knots under full sail and Eugene concluded that sailing was the only
way to meet the sea. The *Charles Racine* became for him, in what was
the most flattering description sailors had for a ship, "a home." And the
sea began to symbolize for him both a source of life and a final, ecstatic
freedom from the burden of life. Many years later he dreamed of incorporating this poetic concept into an autobiographical play to be called
Sea-Mother's Son. For it was only in the vast womb of the sea that
O'Neill felt serene.

Conrad's *The Nigger of the Narcissus* was what sparked Eugene's sea
voyage. He had been reading it during *The White Sister* tour and it
struck a responsive note at a crucial time. In *The Nigger of the Narcissus*
Conrad wrote: "The true peace of God begins at any spot a thousand
miles from the nearest land; and when He sends there the messengers
of His might it is not in terrible wrath against crime, presumption and
folly, but paternally, to chasten the simple hearts—ignorant hearts that
know nothing of life and beat undisturbed by envy or greed."

The true peace of God was what Eugene, the renegade Catholic,
sought. He came as close to finding it among the simplehearted sailors
of the *Charles Racine's* crew as he ever could. (Later he discovered a
basic difference between himself and Conrad. "I have a feeling when
I read Conrad," he explained, "that he himself is detached and safe
in the wheelhouse of the vessel, looking down at his men on the deck
and describing their activities. When I write about the sea, I want to
be on the deck with the men.")

"I look on a sailor man as my particular brother," he said not long
after his first voyage. And after he had written his sea plays, he declared
in an interview with Mary B. Mullett in the *American Magazine:*

"I liked [sailors] better than I did men of my own kind. They were sincere, loyal, generous. You have heard people use the expression: 'He would give away his shirt.' I've known men who actually did give away their shirts. I've seen them give their own clothes to stowaways.

"I hated a life ruled by the conventions and traditions of society. Sailors lives, too, were ruled by conventions and traditions; but they were of a sort I liked and that had a meaning which appealed to me." Another time he described the "simple people" he characterized in his sea plays as "direct in action and utterance."

"They have not been steeped in the evasions and superficialities which come with social life and intercourse." he later said. "Their real selves are exposed. They are crude but honest. They are not handicapped by inhibitions. In many ways they are inarticulate. They cannot write of their own problems. So they must often suffer in silence. I like to interpret for them—dramatize them—and thus bring their hardships into the light. . . . Life on the sea is ideal. The ship for a home, sailors for friends, the sea for surroundings . . . I like the man of the sea. He is free of social hypocrisy."

From childhood Eugene had been bedeviled by the meaningless talk of friends and acquaintances. He was rarely at ease with anyone. It was his agonizing shyness, rooted in egotism, that made him fearful of being misunderstood and unappreciated and that drove him into sullen withdrawals or bouts of drinking. Like Cornelius Melody, the haughty, embittered, self-pitying hero of *A Touch of the Poet*, Eugene enjoyed quoting the lines from Byron's *Childe Harold*:

> I have not loved the World, nor the World me;
> I have not flattered its rank breath, nor bowed
> To its idolatries a patient knee,
> Nor coined my cheek to smiles,—nor cried aloud
> In worship of an echo: in the crowd
> They could not deem me one of such—I stood
> Among them, but not of them.

But with the seamen of the *Charles Racine,* as with the prostitutes of the Haymarket and Bradley Street and, later, with the dockworkers and sailors of New York's waterfront, Eugene could mingle happily. With them, there was no fear of being misunderstood or hurt; relationships were on an elementary level. They helped him achieve a sense of identification with humanity. They wore no masks and among them he needed no mask either. There was never any condescension on his part toward his less educated companions—whom he accepted on their own terms, as they did him. He inspired in them immediate respect and love.

Once, trying to cheer up a small-time speakeasy operator and petty gambler who was devoted to him, he said: "Don't be low in the mind. Be like the sailors; no matter how bad things get, there'll always be another ship; there'll always be another woman."

On the *Charles Racine* Eugene learned to live with men whose aims and aspirations were simple and simply stated: a berth on a good ship, a girl and a drink in port, and back again to the sea; no room for petty social ambition. The men were concerned first with the basic law of a windjammer at sea: One hand for yourself and one for the ship. No one begrudged the hand for the ship.

"Discipline on a sailing vessel was not a thing that was imposed on the crew by superior authority," O'Neill told Miss Mullett, when asked how he had managed not only to put up with but to enjoy the restricted life of an ordinary seaman. "It was essentially voluntary. The motive behind it was loyalty to the ship! Among seamen, at that time, this love of the ship was what really controlled them.

"Suppose, just as an example that one of the yards was loose, hanging by a thread, so to speak. Suppose a gale was blowing and the captain or the mate ordered two men to go aloft to secure this loose spar. This might be a dangerous proceeding. The men could refuse to do it. And they would be entirely within their rights, because if any complaint was made of them or any punishment imposed, they could go before their consul at the next port and justify their refusal to obey.

"Now the motive of the captain, or of the mate, in giving the order, might be simply to save a spar which, if lost, would add an item of expense to the owners of the vessel. But the men who risked injury, or even death, by carrying out the order, would be impelled solely by their love of the ship. They wouldn't care about saving the owners a few dollars, nor about saving the captain's face. They would go simply because of their feeling that they owed the service to the ship itself."

The *Charles Racine* had a crew of thirty-five men. Built in Sunderland, England, in 1892, the ship was 200 feet long, with a 38½-foot beam and a gross weight of a little over sixteen hundred tons. She was a tramp, whose home port was Stavanger, Norway. When Eugene signed on as an ordinary seaman—the Norwegian crew classified him as a günman, just one notch above deck boy—she was bound for Buenos Aires with a cargo of lumber.

Eugene's knowledge of the sea had come exclusively from books and the talk of seamen, but he considered himself a natural sailor.

He had no trouble learning to climb the rigging of the fore-, main- and mizzenmasts, and to furl and reef the six types of sail carried by the barque. (His plays are filled with accurate and detailed descriptions of various types of vessels.)

He discovered the thrill of going aloft to the royal and gallant sails, 150 feet above the deck, with the mast sometimes swaying as much as 45 degrees and pitching at the same time. In addition, he learned to do less exciting work, such as holystoning, or scouring the deck on Sundays with a porous sandstone fitted with a stick. The stone was called the "Bible," because it was about the size and weight of one; a smaller stone, held in the hand to penetrate into corners, was called the "Prayer Book."

Eugene also took his turn sluicing down the rigging with a rag soaked in a mixture of tallow and white lead, to prevent the cables that supported the masts from rotting. And he learned to bring the teak railing to snowy whiteness by scouring it with wet canvas dipped in sand.

While the physical activity, the bracing sea air, and the lack of alcohol had a salutary effect on Eugene, the rations did not. The food was only a slight improvement over the fried monkey and tortillas of Honduras: pea soup and salt pork one day, salt pork and pea soup the next. It is true that at the beginning of the voyage the crew feasted on the pigs, chickens and ducks that were slaughtered en route. But these did not last long. On Sundays the men were treated to salt hash or Argentine canned beef and the weekday menu was occasionally varied by dry, salt fish, called stokfish, and usually supplemented by potatoes cooked in sea water.

Fresh water, even for drinking, was scarce; during a long, rainless period, the men were rationed to a pint a day. The water tank was in the hold, and bucketfuls had to be drawn with a suction pump; the ship's carpenter kept the pump locked in his quarters. The caskets containing the ship's provisions of meat were lashed to a rail abovedeck, where the captain could keep an eye on them. Every morning the cook would come up to cut off a piece of meat for the day's dinner.

"Good morning, Captain," he would say, as he approached the casket with his cleaver. If there was a fair wind, the captain would smile benevolently and allow the cook to cut as much meat as he wanted. If the weather was foul and the ship making little headway, the captain was likely to snap, "Cook, you're taking too much. There's enough in that piece to feed an army." The cook learned to take this philosophically; he knew the captain was fuming over lost time and over the implacable opinion of the shipowners that "The wind is always on the side of a good sailor."

If meat was scarce, hardtack, or sea biscuit, always abounded. Eugene learned to break open a biscuit with a marlin spike, shake the worms out of the air holes and soak it in what he later described as "something called coffee," making it possible to chew.

Aboard the *Charles Racine*, Eugene picked up a love of sea chanties as enduring as his affection for the popular land music of the early 1900's. Long after his voyage he was still singing (and slipping into his plays) the songs he heard at sea, such as "There Was a Maid from Amsterdam" and "No More I'll Go A-Roving" (to which he knew all the ribald words), "Blow the Man Down" (which he wrote into *The Moon of the Caribbees*), "Whiskey Johnny" (sung in *The Hairy Ape*), and "Shenandoah" (which he put into *Mourning Becomes Electra*).

In 1920 he asked Olin Downes, who was later to become music critic of *The New York Times*: "Did you ever hear chanties sung on the sea? You never did? It's not surprising. There are even fewer sailing vessels now than there were ten short years ago when I pulled out for the open. They don't have to sing as they haul the ropes. They don't humor a privileged devil who has a fine voice and hell inside of him, as he chants that wonderful stuff and they pull to the rhythm of the song and the waves. Ah, but I wish you might hear that and feel the roll of the ship, and I wish you might listen to an accordion going in the forecastle, through the soughing of winds and the wash of the sea."

And to a friend, the writer Malcolm Cowley, O'Neill would sing "Blow the Man Down," pausing to tell him that the slow rise and fall of the refrain, "Way-o, blow the man down," was like the movement of a ship on an ocean swell, and illustrating his meaning with a wavelike gesture of his right hand.

Eugene spent hours listening to his sailor brothers spin their yarns, many of which turned up later in his sea plays. One story that did not appear concerned the ingenious captain of a square-rigger whose hand-operated, portable foghorn slid overboard during a storm. The captain hoisted a live pig aloft and tied a line to its tail; a tug on the line, so the story went, brought a squeal louder than the loudest foghorn.

In foul weather, when all hands were required to work not only through their own watch but in unrelieved stretches of as much as twelve or sixteen hours, the captain sometimes rewarded his crew with a custom called "splicing the main brace"—a ration of whiskey for all hands. In a ritual not unlike James O'Neill's custom of doling out liquor to his sons, the captain would pour a ration of whiskey for each man as he filed by on the poop deck with a tin cup.

Eugene's spare-time activities were limited. He could read and write, which he did, or learn to make the intricate sailor's knots that many members of the crew practiced, or patch his clothes. (Like the rest of the crew, Eugene dressed in overalls and knitted cotton shirts and often went barefoot; in tropical weather, he wore only trousers.) Or he could participate in Trunk Pleasure, an activity the Norwegians called Sjiste Faarnölse.

Every sailor had a trunk, wide at the bottom and narrow at the top, that he kept by his bunk in the forecastle. In heavy seas, when the forecastle was awash, the trunks would float. A sailor's most precious possession, the trunk held his letters, photographs, and such souvenirs and gifts as he had collected from or for his family and girl friends. Inside the cover was usually painted a full-rigged ship. It was a point of honor to trust one's fellow sailors and leave the trunk unlocked; if anyone did lock his trunk, it was resented as a terrible insult, and everyone would kick at it as he went by, until finally it opened.

O'Neill drew on his memory of this custom for the incident upon which an early one-act play, *In the Zone,* is based. In the play a seaman arouses the suspicions of his shipmates by concealing a locked metal box; it is wartime and they think he is a German spy. They force open the box and find it is full of old love letters.

Trunk Pleasure consisted of sitting around with the chest lids up, each man in turn picking out an item about which to describe a personal experience, real or imagined.

The *Charles Racine* was sixty-five days on the 5,900-mile voyage from Boston to Buenos Aires. All that time she was out of sight of land; during the 4 to 8 A.M. watch Eugene would climb the ratlines to the highest yardarms—called the top floor—and watch the dawn come up on the Atlantic. Wherever he looked the sea met the sky in a vast circle, of which he and the ship were the center. No experience in his later life ever equaled the exaltation of these hours aloft.

"Gene's pride seemed to be in those years," his widow said several years after his death in trying to explain her husband's exultant memories of his sailing days. "He used to talk about his sea years and his flat down on the waterfront, where he slept on the floor.

"And I said to him once, half-jokingly, 'I have dragged you about Europe. I have worked like anything to show you all the beautiful spots, and I have never heard you say once that you liked this or that or the other.' 'Well,' he said, 'I liked them, but they weren't very exciting.'"

◈

To Eugene it seemed exciting to be for the first time really on his own. Separated by six thousand miles of ocean from his father and his father's dole, he tackled the problem of survival.

He arrived in South America with ten dollars, his wages for the 65-day voyage.

"I landed in Buenos Aires a gentleman, so called, and wound up a bum on the docks," he later said, recalling his ten-month stay in South America. He never explained why he did not ship out again on the bark; possibly, as James Tyrone puts it in *Long Day's Journey Into Night,* it was part of his "game of romance and adventure" to have "a bit of being homeless and penniless in a foreign land."

His wages from the *Charles Racine* were gone in one night—spent at a notorious Buenos Aires waterfront saloon called the Sailor's Opera. O'Neill once described it rather mildly:

"It sure was a madhouse. Pickled sailors, sure-thing race track touts, soused, boiled white shirt, déclassé Englishmen, underlings in the diplomatic service, boys darting around tables leaving pink and yellow cards directing one to red plush paradises, and entangled in the racket was the melody of some ancient turkey trot banged out by a sober pianist."

A few years earlier, he supplied the following description:

"Everyone present was expected to contribute something. If your voice cracked your head usually did, too. Some old sailor might get up and unroll a yarn, another might do a dance, or there would be a heated discussion between, say, Yankee and British sailors as to the respective prowess of their ships. And, if nothing else promised, 'a bit of a harmless fight' usually could be depended upon as the inevitable star feature to round out the evening's entertainment."

He confided the more lurid details to several intimate friends and one of them, an attorney, later recalled the occasion.

"O'Neill spent a couple of hours telling me about his sea experiences one day in 1926, when he visited me for a day on a chartered boat. I've never heard more colorful or fouler stories in my life, including when I was in the Marine Corps during World War I. He spoke of the brothels of Buenos Aires and Liverpool and of resisting homosexual advances aboard ship, among other things." A couple of hours of talk at one stretch was unusual for O'Neill, who generally talked haltingly—when he talked—but who was more often silent. And it was extraordinary to hear profanity from a man who by that time restricted himself to an occasional "damn" or "hell."

"Someday," O'Neill told the attorney, "I'm going to publish my experiences and distribute them privately among fifty friends."

O'Neill did not carry out this scheme. However, he did reveal for publication his distilled impressions of the motion pictures of Barracas, a suburb of Buenos Aires, which he attended with his shipmates:

"Those pictures were mighty rough stuff. Nothing was left to the imagination. Every form of perversity was enacted and, of course, the sailors flocked to them."

"But," he added, "save for the usual exceptions, they were not vicious men. They were in the main honest, good-natured, unheroically courageous men trying to pass the time pleasantly."

At the Sailor's Opera Eugene met a young man who later turned up as Smitty in three of his sea plays. In *Bound East for Cardiff* Smitty is a minor character; in *The Moon of the Caribbees,* he is a sailor haunted by the memory of a shattered love affair; and in *In the Zone* he is the owner of the locked box.

The original Smitty was a handsome, twenty-five-year-old Englishman with a blond mustache. The younger son of a nobleman, he had had a traditional British education and been an officer in the British Army. He was, in O'Neill's words, "almost too beautiful . . . very like Oscar Wilde's description of Dorian Gray. Even his name was flowery." But he began drinking too much and his fiancée dismissed him. Miserable and disgraced, he had come to Buenos Aires, ostensibly to make a new career for himself. Instead of taking advantage of the letters of introduction he had brought from powerful British personages to equally influential South Americans, Smitty decided to go on a protracted drunk.

"Between drinks, he'd drink to sober up," recalled O'Neill, who had done his own best to drink Argentina dry.

Smitty had been in Buenos Aires ten months when Eugene arrived, and his money was running out. He and Eugene roomed together for a time, while the young Englishman tried to pull himself together and Eugene tried his hand at one job after another. First came a stint with the Buenos Aires branch of a United States electrical appliance concern. Eugene presented himself as a draftsman to the firm's American manager, but after he had looked blankly at a T square and triangle for a few hours he was obliged to admit that his claim had been somewhat exaggerated. The manager put Eugene to work tracing plans. Eugene bore with the monotony of this job for about six weeks, and then quit to spend what was left of his salary at the Sailor's Opera.

Broke again, he took a job with Swift and Company, in the meat-packing center at La Plata. He was assigned to the warehouse where raw hides were sorted. He was beginning to think he would never get the stench of the hides out of his hair, let alone his clothes, when the warehouse burned down, saving him the trouble of quitting.

Approaching his twenty-second birthday, Eugene decided to try one more respectable job. He found it with the Singer Sewing Machine Company, back in Buenos Aires. The job lasted only until he discovered that he was expected to learn how to take apart and put together the dozens of different models Singer then had on the market.

For a while he went through the motions of reporting for work but was fired when the boss discovered he was less interested in bobbins and needles than in hanging about the waterfront.

A California engineer and surveyor named Frederick Hettman, who had recently arrived in Buenos Aires, befriended Eugene when he first landed. After being introduced in a hotel, Hettman discovered that Eugene was the son of his stage hero. "From that moment, we became friends," said Hettman, and added:

"O'Neill didn't busy himself too much with work. He lived modestly in a pensión and several times he couldn't pay his rent. Once, before leaving on a surveying trip to the interior, I decided to pay his rent in advance for several months so that he could live in peace. I then went to Córdoba and when I returned to Buenos Aires I didn't find him there."

Out of funds, and feeling he had exhausted the possibilities of working on land, Eugene had signed on a British tramp steamer carrying mules to Durban, South Africa.

Once again he found himself afloat on his birthday. The voyage was not pleasant. In later years Eugene could not even recall the name of the ship, possibly because he preferred not to. (O'Neill enjoyed telling friends about the time, after he had become an established playwright, when he ran into a man who had been on the cattle boat with him and who was then a bus driver for sightseeing tours through Chinatown, a career adopted by a number of old sailors.

"Hello, Jack," O'Neill greeted his former shipmate. "What are you doing?"

"Oh, herding these rubbernecks around," answered Jack. "What's your racket now?"

"Nothing much," said O'Neill. "I'm fooling around the theatre a little."

"Yeah, I thought you'd turn out an actor like your old man sometime," returned Jack. "You were a bum sailor.")

Eugene did remember, though, that his hope of seeing a bit of Africa was quashed; he was not allowed off the ship because he lacked the $100 required to enter the country. He sailed back on the same ship to Argentina, which was less finicky about the financial status of its visitors, and from early December of 1910 to May of 1911 he not only gave up all pretense of working but did his best to hit bottom.

"In the months after his return, O'Neill's health and good looks deteriorated," Hettman later recalled, with considerable restraint.

The sentiments O'Neill later applied to his heroine, Nina Leeds, in *Strange Interlude* were at this point applicable to him. Like Nina, Eugene headed for the gutter for the security of knowing he had reached the depths and there was no farther to go. Or, in the words of yet another self-destructive O'Neill protagonist, Orin Mannon of *Mourning Becomes Electra,* he buried himself "so deep at the bottom of hell there is no lower you can sink and you rest there in peace!"

In later years O'Neill described those derelict months in Buenos Aires as the time he was "on the beach." He recalled them with a certain amount of relish. There was an episode, for instance, involving a two-week job as a stevedore, loading a square-rigger called the *Tia Mandra.*

"That old bucko of a first mate was too tough," O'Neill once said. "He was the kind that would drop a marlin spike on your skull from a yardarm." He went back to beachcombing.

How far he descended is illustrated by something he told Hamilton Basso, who in 1948 was assigned to write O'Neill's "Profile" for *The New Yorker:*

"I was then twenty-two years old and a real down-and-outer—sleeping on park benches, hanging around waterfront dives, and absolutely alone. I knew a fellow who used to work on a railroad down there and who had given up his job. One day, he suggested that we hold up one of those places where foreign money is exchanged. Well, I have to admit I gave the matter serious consideration. I finally decided not to do it, but since you aren't given to taking a very moral view of things when you are sleeping on park benches and haven't a dime to your name, I decided what I did because I felt that we were almost certain to be caught. A few nights later, the fellow who had propositioned me stuck the place up with somebody he'd got to take my place, and he *was* caught. He was sent to prison and, for all I know, he died there."

In 1948 O'Neill could be detached. At that time when he was asked by the playwright Robert Sherwood to autograph a volume of O'Neill plays for a library in Argentina, O'Neill wrote a long inscription in which, according to Sherwood, "he expressed the doubt that there was a single park bench in Buenos Aires that had not, on occasion, served him as a bed."

But in 1910 there was nothing very amusing about his situation. He didn't have the money to pay for a bed in even the cheapest rooming house.

When he was not sleeping on park benches and trying to avoid the brutal plain-clothes police who patrolled the park and were known as the Vigilantes, he slept on the waterfront with other down-and-outers—sailors, mostly—in shacks made of sheets of galvanized metal, which he and his companions scavenged from discarded sections of storage sheds. He picked up a half-starved waif and installed her in one of these hovels as his mistress. He begged for food and for liquor—a cheap white rum called cachaza and a brew called caña.

He got food by following an old sailor custom. When he was hungry he made his way to any ship that happened to be in port; he lowered a greasy rope, at the end of which dangled an even greasier can, to the port-hole of the ship's galley. The bonds that existed among seamen inspired the ships' cooks to feed their destitute brothers, many of whom were fellow members of the Industrial Workers of the World (Wobblies) who had been organized in 1905. Eugene was in sympathy with their aim to overthrow capitalism, although his own contribution to the cause consisted of echoing the patter he had heard in Benjamin Tucker's bookstore. But he was a brother in appearance, and his tin can was always filled with food—the best the ship had to offer—which was often horrible enough.

Although Eugene was indistinguishable from his fellow outcasts and was convinced, at the time, that he belonged to their ranks spiritually as well as physically, some small inner voice urged him not only toward self-preservation but even toward creativity. He wrote at least one poem during that period; it was called "Ashes of Orchids." He also began making notes of what he saw and heard; not long after he returned from sea he told a girl in New London that he had had an idea at the back of his mind that he might want to write some day and that it had occurred to him that shipping away was a means of getting material. While it was certainly not his principal motive, it turned out to be a vital factor in his writing.

"My real start as a dramatist was when I got out of an academy and among men on the sea," O'Neill said in 1920, six years after he had drawn on those days to enrich the dialogue of *Bound East for Cardiff*, his first major one-act play—and the first serious contribution by an American to the field of sea drama.

"D'yuh remember the times we've had in Buenos Aires? The moving pictures in Barracas? Some class to them, d'yuh remember?" asks the dying sailor, Yank, in that play. ". . . And the days we used to sit on the park benches along the Paseo Colón with the Vigilantes lookin' hard at us? And the songs at the Sailor's Opera where the guy played ragtime—d'yuh remember them? . . . And La Plata—phew, the stink of the hides! I always liked Argentine—all except that booze, caña. How drunk we used to git on that, remember?"

Bound East for Cardiff was the first of four O'Neill plays eventually collected under the title, *S.S. Glencairn*. While these are referred to as *the sea plays* and are an accurate and personal record of the two years O'Neill spent among sailors, it is an interesting fact that of the forty-five plays he authorized for publication or production no less than thirteen are set entirely or in part aboard ship, and in six more the sea figures as an integral part of the action. The variety of O'Neill's sea settings during the period of his creative years illustrates his sustained preoccupation with the subject:

A steamer's life raft, adrift in a tropic sea (*Thirst*, 1913)

A section of boat deck of the S.S. *Empress* (*Warnings*, 1914)

The life boat of a passenger steamer adrift off the Grand Banks of Newfoundland (*Fog*, 1914)

The forecastle of the S.S. *Glencairn*, on the North Atlantic (*Bound East for Cardiff*, 1914)

A section of the main deck of the *Glencairn*, at anchor off an island in the West Indies (*The Moon of the Caribbees*, 1916)

The seaman's forecastle on the *Glencairn*, somewhere in the submarine zone (*In the Zone*, 1916)

The captain's cabin on board the steam whaling ship *Atlantic Queen* in the Arctic Ocean (*Ile*, 1916)

The main deck of Columbus' flagship, on a calm sea off the West Indies (*The Fountain*, 1920)

The barge *Simeon Winthrop* at anchor in the harbor of Provincetown and at dock in Boston (*Anna Christie*, 1920)

The fireman's forecastle, a section of the promenade deck, and the stokehold of an ocean liner on the Atlantic (*The Hairy Ape*, 1921)

The poop deck of the royal junk of the Princess Kukachin, at anchor in the harbor of Hormiz, Persia (*Marco Millions*, 1923-1924)

The afterdeck of a cabin cruiser anchored in the Hudson River (*Strange Interlude*, 1926-1927)

The stern of a clipper ship moored at a wharf in Boston (*Mourning Becomes Electra*, 1929-1931)

And the six plays, written between 1916 and 1920, which deal with sailors or the influence of the sea, are: *The Long Voyage Home*, *Where the Cross Is Made* (later expanded into the full-length play *Gold*), *The Rope*, *Diff'rent*, and *Beyond the Horizon*.

Although O'Neill's first sea plays—*Thirst*, *Fog* and *Warnings*,—were based on stories he heard from his shipmates, they were unsuccessful exercises in symbolism; he had his first real artistic success with the *Glencairn* plays, all drawn from firsthand knowledge.

The *Glencairn* was his fictional designation for the S.S. *Ikalis,* which O'Neill—finally responding to that small voice that urged him to live—boarded in Buenos Aires for the voyage home.

XVI

IN THREE OF THE FOUR S.S. *Glencairn* PLAYS O'NEILL
has given an accurate picture of the British tramp *Ikalis* on which he spent
the month of May, 1911. (The fourth play, *The Long Voyage Home*, although using some of the same characters, is set in a London waterfront
dive.)

The *Ikalis* had been built eleven years before in Glasgow, Scotland,
for a British firm, the Leyland Shipping Company; she was one of a dozen
tramps, including two sister ships, owned by the company. Like the *Charles
Racine*, the *Ikalis* had no fixed itinerary; she ran mainly between Atlantic
and Indian Ocean ports, picking up cargoes as she found them. Her crew
of about thirty, including coal passers and firemen, was representative of
the mixture to be found aboard the commercial steam vessels that had all
but replaced the slower but far more beautiful barques. Many of the
crewmen were deep-water sailors who had made the reluctant change
from sail to steam when they found that desirable berths on windjammers were becoming scarcer and scarcer. Most of the *Ikalis* crew were
unmarried; men with family attachments wanted berths on ships with
regular runs.

Although the majority of the sailors were from Liverpool, there was a
sprinkling of other nationalities. The captain of a tramp could not be
choosy about his crew. Living quarters were cramped, the work was hard,
the pay low and the food atrocious. The captain had to be satisfied with a
number of inexperienced men, or "scenery bums," who came along for the
ride and usually jumped ship at the first port that beckoned. In the days
before the maritime unions a sailor's life was both freer of restrictions and
more hazardous.

O'Neill had not yet qualified as an able-bodied seaman when he
signed on the *Ikalis*, which carried six A.B.'s and three ordinary seamen.
Assigned mostly to scrubbing, painting and chipping during the
voyage, he envied the A.B.'s their lighter work load and studied them to
learn what he could about the chores aloft, the handling of lines and
rigging and the art of boxing the compass.

In the *Glencairn* plays O'Neill used composite types based on the *Ikalis*
crew.

"I have used the members of the same crew throughout [the cycle]," he wrote to a magazine editor in 1917 when submitting the one-acters, "because, judging from my own experience as a sailor, I thought I had . . . picked out the typical mixed crew of the average British tramp steamer."

Later, enlightening a friend, he described the *Glencairn* characters as "extreme types and simple types." They were composites of men he had known on the *Charles Racine,* on the Buenos Aires waterfront, on the *Ikalis* itself, and a little later, in a New York waterfront saloon. After writing the *Glencairn* series, he went on to develop some of them further in *The Hairy Ape, Anna Christie, Beyond the Horizon,* and several other plays.

Five members of the "typical mixed crew" aboard the *Glencairn,* in addition to Smitty, are Yank, an American seaman, "dark-haired, hard-featured . . . a rather good-looking rough"; Driscoll, "a powerfully built . . . brawny Irishman with the battered features of a prize fighter"; Olson, "a stocky, middle-aged Swede with round, childish blue eyes"; Cocky, "a wizened runt of a man with a straggling gray mustache"; and Paddy, "a squat, ugly, Liverpool Irishman."

O'Neill knew them all, in somewhat different guises. But only Cocky, Yank and Olson had actual prototypes aboard the *Ikalis.* Smitty, of course, was transplanted from Buenos Aires and projected into the *Glencairn*'s forecastle, and O'Neill was yet to meet the real Driscoll and Paddy.

The original Olson, who was the model for the shanghaied sailor in *The Long Voyage Home,* was a Norwegian A.B. on the *Ikalis,* who had followed the sea since boyhood. He had not been home once in twenty years and used to tell O'Neill and his other shipmates that the great sorrow and mistake of his life was that he had left the farm where he was born, to run away to sea.

"He was a bred-in-the-bone child of the sea if there ever was one," O'Neill once recalled. "With his feet on the plunging deck he was planted like a natural growth in what was 'good clean earth' to him. If ever a man was in perfect harmony with his environment, a real part of it, this Norwegian was.

"Yet he cursed the sea and the life it had led him—affectionately. He loved to hold forth on what a fool he had been to leave the farm. There was the life for you, he used to tell the grumblers all in the forecastle. A man on his own farm was his own boss. He didn't have to eat rotten grub and battle bedbugs and risk his life in storms on a rotten old 'lime-juice' tramp. He didn't have to wait for the end of a long voyage for a payday and a good drunk.

"No, Sir, a man on his own farm could get drunk every Saturday night and stay drunk all day Sunday if he wanted to! (At this point the forecastle to a man became converted to agriculture.) Then, too, a man on a farm could get married and have kids.

"Finally, the Norwegian, having got rid of his farm inhibition for the time being, would grin resignedly and take up his self-appointed burden of making a rope mat for some 'gel' in Barracas he had promised it to the next trip down."

The voyage from Buenos Aires to New York took about a month. The *Ikalis* stopped at Trinidad to refuel and take on a load of cacao; it was this stop—with the ship anchored half a mile out from land in the shallow harbor that would not permit closer navigation to the island—which suggested the background of *The Moon of the Caribbees,* against which Smitty was superimposed.

O'Neill was not sorry to leave the *Ikalis* when she docked in New York early in June. With a couple of his shipmates he made for a waterfront rooming house and saloon on Fulton Street near West Street opposite the West Washington Market. He had about twenty-five dollars—his month's pay from the *Ikalis*—and the first thing he and his thirsty shipmates did was head for the bar.

O'Neill had been gone about a year. As far as his family or anyone else might judge, he returned with nothing more to show than that with which he had left—a lack of purpose, no achievement, and an unquenchable thirst for liquor. Apparently he felt that James would not welcome him— or, perhaps, he really considered himself one with his brother sailors and wanderers and could not cut himself adrift from them. Whatever his reasons, he did not try to get in touch with his father for a month. As for Kathleen, he was content to wait until his father should issue instructions, and it never crossed his mind to see her or his son.

He paid $3 for a month's rent at the Fulton Street rooming house known as Jimmy-the-Priest's. He settled down among the sailors, stevedores, truckers, anarchists, Wobblies, prostitutes, telegraphers, printers, and assorted down-and-outers who inhabited the grisly, vermin-infested three-story establishment and whom, more than thirty years later, O'Neill recalled as the best friends he ever had. The rooming house was one of a dozen or more that flourished on the waterfront before the Seamen's Institute was built in 1913, providing sailors with a decent place to go to.

The proprietor of Jimmy-the-Priest's had earned his name because he looked much more like an ascetic than a saloonkeeper. In *Anna Christie* O'Neill called him Johnny-the-Priest and described him accurately:

"With his pale, thin, clean-shaven face, mild blue eyes and white hair, a cassock would seem more suited to him than the apron he wears.

Neither his voice nor his general manner dispels this illusion which has made him a personage of the waterfront. They are soft and bland. But beneath all his mildness one senses the man behind the mask—cynical, callous, hard as nails."

The saloon had a back room where anyone who could not afford the price of a bed could sleep with his head on the table; all he needed for this privilege was a nickel to buy a schooner of beer or a shot of bad whiskey.

"Gorky's *Night's Lodging* was an ice cream parlor in comparison," O'Neill once said.

Jimmy did not allow fighting on his premises; anyone who wanted to settle an argument was obliged to step outside to a stretch of concrete known as "the Farm." However, Jimmy did not mind if his patrons enticed visiting farmers or other out-of-towners into the bar, got them drunk and robbed them. O'Neill did not participate in this activity, but some of his friends did.

One of them, a broken-down telegrapher known as "the Lunger," who eventually succumbed to tuberculosis at Jimmy's and who occupied the thinly partitioned room next to O'Neill's, tried to teach him the International Code. But his attempts generally took place late at night, when both were drunk, and the next day Eugene could never remember what he had learned. He did remember enough of the Lunger's personality to dramatize him, as James Knapp—his affliction became deafness, rather than consumption—in the one-act play *Warnings* which was written three years later.

O'Neill's room, which he entered as seldom as possible, was dusty, unheated, and lighted by one small kerosene lamp. It had a grimy window leading out to a rickety fire escape. Two narrow beds covered with threadbare spreads and inhabited by bugs took up most of the space. Three dollars was not enough to buy privacy even at Jimmy-the-Priest's and Eugene had a succession of roommates.

By spending no money on food Eugene managed to stretch out his ship's pay for several weeks. Roomers at Jimmy-the-Priest's were entitled to a plate of free soup at noon every day, and O'Neill lived on that and five-cent whiskey. When he was not sleeping off a drunk, swapping stories in the bar or singing sea chanties, he toured the waterfront with his friends or loafed on a bench in Battery Park, which he regarded as one of the pleasantest areas of the city. From there he could watch the ships entering and leaving the harbor, follow the bustle of loading and unloading on the piers along West and South Streets, and observe the cavalcade of groaning trucks on the streets leading into the heart of Manhattan.

The New York waterfront, which has held the attention of countless poets, artists, novelists and essayists, did not fail to stir O'Neill; but at the time he observed its rich life less through the eyes of a writer than through the eyes of his companions, who were an integral part of it. As he sat warming himself in the park he was indistinguishable from the idling sailors and bums who spent their time on its benches.

Once again his female companions were mainly whores. One of them, Maude, who lived on West Forty-seventh Street, professed to be in love with him. From time to time she joined him in waterfront saloons.

O'Neill's money was going. He had already paid $3 to keep his room through July, but he worried about what he would do in August. Rather than ship out again and be cut off from his liquor supply, he decided to try for a handout from his father and he wrote to James in New London. James, happy to learn that his son was back, sent him money, but stipulated that it was for train fare home. O'Neill promptly spent it on liquor. When he sobered up, he decided against asking his father for more.

At Jimmy-the-Priest's Eugene had become acquainted with a burly, red-headed Liverpool Irishman named Driscoll, a fireman who had sailed on tramps like the *Ikalis* and was about to sign on for another voyage. Liverpool Irish was, to sailors all over the world, a synonym for tough customer; the sons and grandsons of the original Irish settlers in Liverpool had traditionally followed the sea. According to O'Neill, Driscoll was "a giant of a man and absurdly strong."

In July Driscoll signed for a berth on a passenger liner, the S.S. *New York,* bound from New York to Southampton and Cherbourg. Eugene went with him to Pier 61, where the bosun was picking his crew for the liner, applied, and was accepted as an able-bodied seaman at the salary of $27.50 per ocean crossing. Proud of his newly acquired rating, he carried his sea bag aboard the *New York* on July 22.

The S.S. *New York* was an American Line ship that had been built in Scotland the year of Eugene's birth; like her new A.B., she was approaching her twenty-third year. A fast ship for her day—she could do twenty knots—the *New York* had seen service during the Spanish-American War as an auxiliary cruiser called the U.S.S. *Harvard.* She had been remodeled after the war and given new boilers and two new raked funnels to replace her three old ones. With her three masts, her clipper bows and her covered promenade deck, the *New York* (together with her sister ship, the *Philadelphia*) was the first twin-screw, de luxe passenger liner between New York and Europe.

From a seaman's point of view, however, the luxury liner was anything but luxurious. Once again, in spite of his elevated rating, O'Neill found himself holystoning during his four-hour watch. He also performed a chore called soogie-moogie, the scrubbing down of outside bulkheads with a piece of hammock cloth soaked in a caustic solution that turned the fingernails black.

O'Neill once said that what he detested about this detail was being patronized by the "aristocratic" passengers strolling on deck. Another chore was helping to maintain the standing rigging. A.B.'s rarely took the wheel, but they took in the lines and made the ship fast at pier and occasionally Eugene stood a two-hour watch in the crow's-nest. Being an A.B. aboard the *New York* was, in Eugene's words, "an ugly, tedious job and no place for a man who wanted to call his soul his own." He added that it was "hard work without any romance."

"There was about as much sea glamour in working aboard a passenger steamship as there would have been in working in a summer hotel," he said on another occasion. "I washed enough deck area to cover a good-sized town." He grew sick of being an A.B. who wielded a mop as the chief implement of his seamanship.

Provisions for the crew were a little better than on the *Ikalis,* but the pay was not much higher and the patronizing by the passengers outweighed the more humane attitude of the ship's officers.

The master of the *New York* was W. J. Roberts, nicknamed "Blackie" by the crew. He was a stout, kindhearted Southampton Englishman, who looked like an Italian. The Shipping Articles he signed before leaving New York included such stipulations as the prohibition of flogging and all other forms of corporal punishment by the master and his officers. Each member of the crew received a navy-blue jersey with "American Line" printed in white across the chest, wool caps and high-waisted blue pants; O'Neill and his fellow seamen wore these when leaving or entering port to make a good impression on the passengers, but during watches they dressed in old dungarees.

O'Neill received his meals in small pots with handles. In addition to his daily rations of lime or lemon juice with sugar, to prevent scurvy, he was entitled, among other items, to four quarts of water a day, one and a quarter pounds of salt beef on Tuesday, Thursday and Saturday (the men called it "salt horse"), one pound of salt pork on Monday, Wednesday and Friday, one pound of fish (dry, preserved, or fresh) on Friday, and one pound of canned meat on Sunday.

On paper, the diet sounded fairly palatable, but when the food was not rotten it was so badly prepared that it was all but inedible. O'Neill, accustomed to worse fare, didn't really care what he ate, but he companionably joined his shipmates in grumbling.

The seamen, who occupied the forecastle and slept in three-tiered steel bunks, were a tough lot, composed mainly of English, Irish and Swedes, with only a scattering of Americans. If a man had a toothbrush in his sea bag he was ridiculed for being a dude; if he came on board with a suitcase he was likely to be laughed off the ship. But, tough as they were, the coal passers and firemen of the stokehole were tougher.

Those men, a breed apart, who were as contemptuous of the sailors as the sailors were of them, seemed endowed with inhuman powers of endurance. One of them combed his hair with a scrubbing brush. Stripped to the waist in the suffocatingly hot and airless pit where the furnaces and boilers were located, the coal passers plunged their heavy shovels into bins piled high with coal, to replenish the mounds behind the firemen; the firemen thrust open the furnace doors with *their* shovels, flung the coal into the flaming mouths and slammed the doors shut.

They worked at a hideous pace to keep the furnaces supplied with the three hundred tons of coal the ship consumed every day. They groaned about sweating "blood for steam," and this was almost literally true. Not infrequently an exhausted stoker would put his head in the coal chute as a load came down from above, so that he could be knocked out and laid up for a rest. Although this procedure might easily have killed an ordinary man, it didn't seem to give the stokers more than a bad headache. They had hard skulls, toughened up by occasional coal-shovel fights. Often the result of such a battering was a permanent, bluish discoloration of the skin.

But even without this disfigurement, and away from the stokehole, firemen and coal passers were an unlovely sight. When Mildred, the jaded society girl in *The Hairy Ape,* is confronted by Yank, the fireman, in the stokehole of the ship that was modeled by O'Neill on the S.S. *New York,* she exclaims, "Oh, the filthy beast!" and faints.

This was not an exaggerated reaction. Even ashore, no amount of scrubbing could obliterate the embedded rings of black dust around the eyes and in the creases of skin of the stokers. In recognition of their superhuman labor, the stokers were doled out a cup of rum following each watch, after which they collapsed into instant sleep on their narrow bunks. Four hours later they were back in their inferno, breathing flame and dust and sweating blood.

Driscoll was such a stoker. "He thought a whole lot of himself, was a determined individualist," O'Neill later said. "He was very proud of his strength, his capacity for grueling work. It seemed to give him mental poise to be able to dominate the stokehole, do more work than any of his mates."

O'Neill's friendship with Driscoll at Jimmy-the-Priest's caused the fireman to overlook the natural animosity of his calling toward the A.B. and enabled Eugene to get an intimate glimpse of the kind of man and environment he later interpreted in *The Hairy Ape*. In that play the fireman, Yank, is described as being "broader, fiercer, more truculent, more powerful, more sure of himself than the rest [of the crew]." Yank, despite the superficial alterations of name and nationality (he is an American), was modeled on Driscoll. Driscoll is also a character (name unaltered) in the *Glencairn* plays, and he is Lyons in O'Neill's only published short story, "Tomorrow."

A sort of offshoot, or mutation, of Driscoll also appears in the *Glencairn* plays in the person of Paddy, a squat, ugly Liverpool Irishman. Paddy, incidentally, turns up again—but this time transformed into an old, wizened Irishman—in *The Hairy Ape* and, with the same characteristics, in "Tomorrow." In both the story and the play, Paddy is given to singing, "in a thin, nasal, doleful tone," the old chanty, "Whiskey Johnny." It is interesting also to note that in *The Moon of the Caribbees*, written four years before *The Hairy Ape,* a crew member says to Paddy: "You ain't no bleedin' beauty prize . . . a 'airy ape, I calls yer."

The first stop of the *New York* was the Irish port of Queenstown (later renamed Cobh) on the south shore of Great Island in Cork Harbor, seventy-five miles from James O'Neill's birthplace in Kilkenny. Queenstown was the closest Eugene had come to the island he had talked and read about since childhood, and to which he felt something in him belonged; but the crew was not allowed ashore. He had to wait until the ship had discharged her passengers at Southampton, England, where she stayed only about five hours, deposited the rest of the passengers across the English Channel at Cherbourg, and returned to dock at the American Line's home port at Liverpool, where she was to remain for a week.

Liverpool for O'Neill was sailor town, its vast docks not much different from the New York waterfront or that of Buenos Aires. There, as in New York, sailors were considered fair game. Just as in New York, the operators of Liverpool waterfront dives had working arrangements with thugs and streetwalkers to extend invitations, sometimes accompanied by a cheap bottle of free booze, to incoming sailors. A sailor who accepted the

invitation was likely to find himself not only relieved of his month's ac-
cumlated wages within a few days, but in debt to the boardinghouse proprietor.

Two methods were used—crimping and shanghaiing. The first of
these practices involved a conscious, if somewhat muddled sailor; he was
obliged to sign over his future pay to the boardinghouse operator before
his gear was released to him. Shanghaiing consisted of putting a thoroughly
drunk—or knocked out—sailor aboard an undermanned vessel, in return
for payment from the ship's master and whatever cash the sailor could be
robbed of.

An American Line sailor named Starbuck Perry enjoyed telling O'Neill
and his friends how he had been a victim of a kind of shanghai-in-reverse,
when a tramp on which he had once completed a voyage in Buenos Aires
put out again, before Perry had collected his wages. Perry, a huge, tough
sailor who lived to be ninety, and who, in the words of another
shipmate of O'Neill's, "took nothing from no one," had a permanently
bashed-in head and wore an incongruous goatee. One of the most
talkative and colorful men who ever put to sea, he greatly supplemented O'Neill's fund of knowledge. He knew Jack London and was not
too modest to admit that he had often held London spellbound by his tales.

It is probable that O'Neill modeled the setting of *The Long Voyage
Home*—which deals with the shanghaiing of the sailor Olson and is set
in "the bar of a low dive on the London waterfront—a squalid, dingy room
dimly lighted by kerosene lamps"—on a notorious saloon in Liverpool.
The proprietress of this dive, which had sawdust on the floor and was
patronized largely by the toughest of the Liverpool-bred firemen, closed
her eyes to the activities of a man called Shanghai Brown, who would
have shipped his own father to China for two pounds and who kept her
supplied with customers. Nick, the crimp, in *The Long Voyage Home*,
could have been patterned on Shanghai Brown— "round shouldered, . . .
his face . . . pasty, his mouth weak, his eyes shifty and cruel . . . dressed
in a shabby suit which must have once been cheaply flashy" and a man
who pronounced Buenos Aires "Bewnezerry."

A fellow A.B. named James Quigley joined O'Neill and Driscoll during
their Liverpool leave. Quigley, who was still putting out to sea as a
bosun forty-five years later, recalled how in Liverpool he and O'Neill
used to flirt with the "Mary Ellens." Aiming to make life pleasant for men
in uniform, Mary Ellens were not hardened professionals, but amenable
amateurs with a soft spot for sailormen. According to Quigley's pithy recollection, "They were good girls, ready to say hello to any friendly sailor
—and they wore no pants."

Quigley and O'Neill made the acquaintance of a couple of Liverpool whores, in addition to the good girls.

"Gene was so handsome," Quigley once said, "that he didn't have to look for women. They'd come over to his table and ask for the privilege of sitting down with him." O'Neill was partial to a wide-hipped, languorous blonde, who wore a red rose in her bosom and drank bitters in her whiskey to keep her sober. He called her Cecilia, though that was not her real name.

One evening O'Neill confused and delighted Cecilia by fixing her with his dark eyes and murmuring:

"My heart has dreamed dreams I might never have known—a beautiful whore!"

A few minutes later, when Quigley bent down to pick up a dropped match, he couldn't resist fondling Cecilia's ankle under the table. She withdrew indignantly and returned to her dreamy contemplation of O'Neill. Grateful for her loyalty, O'Neill kept up a running joke about Quigley's trying to steal his girl. He displayed his characteristic chivalry toward Cecilia. When another seaman said something slurring about her one night in a bar and included Quigley's girl in the insult, O'Neill and Quigley started a free-for-all from which they both emerged with black eyes.

In return for O'Neill's and Quigley's loyalty the whores gave them needed money when their leaves ended. O'Neill told Quigley that no one but a whore would have been so generous.

O'Neill did not make the return trip on the *New York*, which was laid up for repairs. Instead he transferred to her sister ship, the *Philadelphia,* on August 19. Except for her master, Captain A. R. Mills, who weighed over two hundred pounds, drank close to a bottle of whiskey a day, and cultivated an enormous walrus mustache, the *Philadelphia* was just like the *New York.* The *Philadelphia* reached New York on August 26, 1911, and O'Neill collected his wages, less the amount he had spent in the canteen. This came to $14.84. He obtained his "mutual release" from the American Line vessel and headed back to Jimmy-the-Priest's, where he recorded his mixed feelings about his trip in a poem he called "Ballad of the Seamy Side" (later published in a New London newspaper):

> Where is the lure of the life you sing?
> Let us consider the seamy side:
> The fo'c'stle bunks and the bed bugs' sting,
> The food that no stomach could abide,
> The crawling "salt horse" flung overside
> And the biscuits hard as a cannon ball;

What fascination can such things hide?
"They're part of the game and I loved it all."

Think of the dives on the waterfront
And the drunken brutes in dungaree,
Of the low dance halls where the harpies hunt
And the maudlin seaman so carelessly
Squanders the wages of months at sea
And maybe is killed in a bar room brawl;
The spell of these things explain to me—
"They're part of the game and I loved it all."

Tell me the lure of "working mail"
With two hours sleep out of twenty four,
Hefting bags huge as a cotton bale
Weighing a hundred pounds or more,
Till your back is bent and your shoulders sore
And you heed not the bosun's profane call;
Such work, I should think, you must abhor!
"It's part of the game and I loved it all."

"I grant you the food is passing bad,
And the labor great, and the wages small,
That the ways of a sailor on shore are mad
But they're part of the game and I loved it all."

There is no doubt that he did love it and continued to love it all his
life. He never shipped to sea again, but neither did he ever tire of recalling
his sailor days. He kept his discharge certificate, listing him as "E. G.
O'Neill, A.B.," among his most cherished papers.

XVII

JIMMY-THE-PRIEST'S, LIKE NEW LONDON, ATTAINED A permanent significance for O'Neill. He used it in 1920 as the setting for the first act of *Anna Christie* and in 1939 as a background for *The Iceman Cometh*. In addition, much of the firsthand knowledge of whores, gamblers and waterfront characters he displayed in other plays came from the half dozen months he lived at Jimmy's.

One of O'Neill's roommates there during the period between October, 1911, and January, 1912, was a man named Chris Christopherson.

"He had sailed the sea until he was sick of the mention of it," O'Neill recalled later. "But it was the only work he knew. At the time he was my roommate he was out of work, wouldn't go to sea and spent the time guzzling whiskey and razzing the sea. In time, he got a coal barge to captain. One Christmas Eve he got terribly drunk and tottered away about two o'clock in the morning for his barge. The next morning he was found frozen on a cake of ice between the piles and the dock. In trying to board the barge he stumbled on the plank and fell over." (Christopherson's accident actually occurred in October. O'Neill's sense of drama was sometimes superimposed on his recall of facts.)

Chris, his name unchanged, became Anna Christie's father, and his obsessive hatred was immortalized by O'Neill in the phrase, "ole davil sea."

Another of Eugene's acquaintances at Jimmy's was a drunken, ex-British Army officer who went by the name of Major Adams. In his sixties, the major spent much of his time reliving battles of the Boer War. Arbitrarily reduced in rank by O'Neill, the major later became "the captain" in *The Iceman Cometh*. In the play he is "as obviously English as Yorkshire pudding," a man who, when drunk, strips to the waist to display the ragged scar of an old war wound on his left shoulder and clings to the pipe dream of returning one day to England, which he had left in disgrace after gambling and drinking with regiment money. The major himself died of drink not long after O'Neill met him.

O'Neill spent hours, sometimes days, sitting in Jimmy's back room listening to the life stories, the maudlin dreams, the shattered hopes of his friends. He described the feeling of resignation at Jimmy's when he had one of the characters in *The Iceman Cometh* remark, early in the play: "It's the No Chance Saloon. It's Bedrock Bar, The End of the Line

Café, The Bottom of the Sea Rathskeller! Don't you notice the beautiful calm in the atmosphere? That's because it's the last harbor. No one here has to worry about where they're going next, because there is no farther they can go."

The habitués of Jimmy's, O'Neill once said, "were a hard lot, at first glance, every type—sailors on shore leave or stranded; longshoremen, waterfront riffraff, gangsters, down-and-outers, drifters from the ends of the earth." O'Neill, just turned twenty-three, was younger than most of them but he "belonged."

"I lived with them, got to know them," he said. "In some queer way they carried on. I learned at Jimmy-the-Priest's not to sit in judgment on people."

His sense of security at the bottom of the sea was jolted one day when he heard that Driscoll, who to O'Neill represented the acme of belonging-ness, had committed suicide. Quigley had heard the story at sea and brought it back to O'Neill. Driscoll was sailing on a passenger liner when he jumped overboard; a passenger spotted him and shouted and Driscoll was pulled out. But two voyages later, passing through the enshrouding fog banks off Newfoundland, he plunged again. It was hours before his shipmates missed him.

O'Neill brooded a long time about the why of Driscoll's suicide, for he had believed that Driscoll, of all people, "wasn't the type who just gave up." He concluded that Driscoll's sense of belonging had been shaken. Later he supplied a dramatic reason in *The Hairy Ape* by showing Yank's disintegration when his faith in the importance of his superhuman endurance in the stokehole was shattered.

While brooding about Driscoll, O'Neill still clung to the conviction that he was himself a spiritual brother to the gang at Jimmy-the-Priest's and that he had no ambition to change his surroundings. He was like them in his preoccupation with getting and staying drunk and in his method of picking up drinking money when his cash ran out. With his dockworker or seafaring friends he sometimes ambled down to the water-front and earned a few dollars carrying mail sacks on or off the ships. But a less strenuous method of securing liquor was to "lower the boom on the live ones," which meant watching the incoming ships for sailors he knew and putting the touch on them.

Nevertheless, something in O'Neill prodded him to look outside from time to time. Although his excursions seldom amounted to anything more energetic than a hunt for small change, it is difficult to accept his own later affirmation that he considered himself at that time irrevocably a member of the End of the Line Café. It made a more romantic story to remember it that way—his subsequent redemption acquired a dramatic impact that delighted his Irish sense of extremes. But it is highly doubtful, for instance, that any other member of the brotherhood at Jimmy's would have had the interest or the ambition to make several trips uptown to see the newly arrived Irish Players in their first New York appearance.

George Tyler had brought them over from Dublin's Abbey Theatre. Headed by Sara Algood, Maire O'Neill, Cathleen Nesbitt, Arthur Sinclair and J. M. Kerrigan, the company opened its repertory at the Maxine Elliott Theatre on November 20, 1911. To theatre lovers, the program of plays by Yeats, Synge, Lady Gregory, and Lennox Robinson was an exciting event, but to the working-class Irish it was a threat and a challenge.

Tyler knew that the troupe had run into trouble in Dublin with *The Playboy of the Western World*, where the hero's swaggering was taken seriously as an attack on the Irish character. But Tyler hoped things might go smoothly in New York despite rumblings in the Irish press. On opening night fifty plain-clothes policemen mingled with the audience, which, Tyler noticed, included "a suspicious number of square-jawed lads and colleens." When the curtain was raised they threw vegetables and stink bombs at the actors. The police finally rushed them out of the theatre, and the performance was resumed.

"Funny business that was," Tyler later wrote. "The play was written by an Irishman, the company was Irish, the rioters were Irish, the cops were Irish, and it was an Irish judge that fined them all for disorderly conduct."

The Irish Players went through their announced repertory during the next few weeks, but they failed to draw large audiences.

O'Neill was among the minority that attended faithfully, using the entree provided by his father's connections. He found himself particularly responsive to Synge's one-act play, *Riders to the Sea*.

"It was seeing the Irish Players . . . that gave me a glimpse of my opportunity," he later told an interviewer, indicating that his state of mind at the time was not completely hopeless. "I went to see everything they did. I thought then [in 1911] and I still think [in 1923] that they demonstrated the possibilities of naturalistic acting better than any other company." Though he considered himself Irish to the core, he once remarked, apropos of the rioting, "The Irish can't laugh at themselves."

Shortly before Christmas O'Neill received a letter from a lawyer representing his wife, whom he had all but forgotten. The lawyer had learned of his whereabouts from James, who was touring the vaudeville circuit in a condensed version of *Monte Cristo* and had evidently decided to let Eugene take his own time to outgrow the derelict stage. Kathleen was seeking a divorce, the lawyer informed O'Neill when they met. The lawyer had already been in contact with James's attorney and it had been agreed that Kathleen would support the child and would not ask for alimony. What the lawyer wanted from O'Neill was his co-operation in furnishing Kathleen with the grounds for a New York State divorce. The whole thing seemed shabby and ignoble to O'Neill and he felt sorrier for Kathleen than he did for himself. But he agreed to the lawyer's proposal.

On December 29 O'Neill went to a brothel at 148 West Forty-fifth Street with three companions. He selected a girl and took her upstairs while one of his companions, an attorney named James Warren, a friend of Kathleen's mother, waited. After two hours Warren went upstairs where, according to his later court testimony, he "saw this Eugene O'Neill and this woman in bed together; O'Neill at the time was undressed." The woman also was "undressed," according to Warren, who added that Eugene "left there with me about six o'clock in the morning."

The grounds for divorce having been duly established, O'Neill, in disgust, proceeded to drink himself insensible.

A new year dawned but it held no symbol of hope for O'Neill. After a few more days spent in drinking at Jimmy's he went uptown with a friend in search of escape. Finding a five-dollar bill, they decided to try their luck at a gambling den on Forty-fourth Street just east of Sixth Avenue.

Until a few years before, the place had been owned by Dick Canfield, under whose management it had become the most famous gambling house in the United States. Canfield had been forced out of business by District Attorney William Travers Jerome in 1904, partly as a result of public indignation over the reputed fleecing of a member of the Vanderbilt family, who reportedly lost $100,000 to Canfield in a single night's play. Canfield's house was reopened by others and was still actively in business in 1912. (Just a few blocks west of Canfield's was the gambling establishment operated by Herman "Beansy" Rosenthal, in partnership with police Lieutenant Charles Becker. An avid follower of underworld news, O'Neill later enjoyed recalling that he had gambled in a house a block away from where Beansy was murdered six months later.)

Eugene and his friend had a winning streak and within an hour they were $200 ahead. Since the gambling houses of the era served free champagne, Eugene and his friend were also by that time noisily drunk. They were thrown out but allowed to keep their cash. It was a cold night and the last thing Eugene remembered before he drew a blank was being in a Broadway saloon and thinking, "I wish I was south in New Orleans."

This story, with the exception of the detail about his wish to be in New Orleans, was published in newspapers in various inaccurate versions after O'Neill had become a well-known dramatist. Most of the versions ended with O'Neill's affirmation that he remembered nothing until several days later, when he awoke in the upper berth of a train pulling into New Orleans, and to his astonishment saw a poster announcing the imminent arrival of James O'Neill in *Monte Cristo*. This instance of father and son turning up almost at the same time in the same place after their long estrangement is invariably pointed out as "coincidence" and apparently O'Neill himself chose to regard it as such. As late as 1931 he wrote to a friend that his father had "happened" to play New Orleans while he himself was there "broke, on the tail end of a bust . . . just as things were becoming desperate."

But only a month or so before his arrival in Louisiana Eugene had been in touch with George Tyler, one of his father's oldest friends. And it is clear that he was keeping an eye on the theatre in general and on his father's whereabouts in particular. It seems more than likely that he longed to return to paternal authority, but since he had chosen to show his father he could exist on his own his capitulation had to appear coincidental.

XVIII

O'NEILL'S RESUBMISSION TO HIS FATHER WAS NOT effected without a conscious struggle. He was still seething with the childish sense of rebellion James had always inspired in him.

When O'Neill arrived in New Orleans and "discovered" that his father would soon be there he apparently made an effort to get away. He went to the waterfront seeking a berth on a vessel bound for Nova Scotia or some other place that would include a stopoff at New York, where he could jump ship; he failed to find a berth and spent the rest of his small supply of cash in barrooms.

"I had seaman's papers," he later informed a friend, "but no ships seemed to be taking on anyone—at least not ships bound for New York where I wanted to return."

When James arrived O'Neill looked him up and as he put it, "braced him for the fare north." But James, for reasons best known to himself, decided the time had come to give Eugene another chance to become a wage earner. He offered his son a job acting with his company.

"It was a case of work or walk home," O'Neill told his friend, adding, "I acted for the rest of the tour over the Orpheum Circuit." He failed to note that he did not stay with the company quite to the end of its prematurely abandoned tour or that it was partly due to him that the tour *was* prematurely ended.

After greetings of mixed pleasure and dismay had been exchanged between Eugene and his parents and brother, James told his son that he was to assume a role in the play as an assistant jailer.

"You'll go on with Charlie in Utah," he told him, referring to Charles Webster, a nineteen-year-old actor who, in spite of his lack of professional experience—he had played in only one other production before joining James's company—was doubling in the roles of Albert (Monte Cristo's son) and chief jailer. Ogden, Utah, was the next stop after New Orleans.

"But I'm not an actor," Eugene protested feebly.

"Do what I say," ordered James. "You'll have only one line and Charlie will tell you what to do."

On the train to Ogden Eugene worried about his acting debut, although his role consisted of only two words.

On the first night in Ogden young Webster helped the miserable, sweating Eugene into his trappings, which included a bulky black coat with an attached cape and a flowing mustache that was hooked inside the nostrils with wires. Eugene stumbled on stage with Webster in the scene in which the Abbé Faria dies in his cell. Webster went through his business of unlocking the cell door with a monstrous bunch of keys, letting the light from his lantern fall on the body of the abbé, kneeling down and putting his ear to the abbé's chest, and then fixing a dark look on his assistant. That was Eugene's cue. His line was:

"Is he . . . ?" To which Webster replied, "Yes, he's dead." Eugene's nervousness had communicated itself, and Webster found himself delivering the news of the abbé's demise in an overwrought falsetto. The blackout which followed this exchange, instead of being fraught with audience tension, was filled with derisive laughter. Eugene and Webster exchanged stunned looks in the semidarkness and bolted for the wings. As they fled, they could hear James's bewildered voice: "What happened? What happened? I'll kill those boys."

Webster and Eugene climbed up into the flies and hid until James, still calling out, "Where are they? I'll kill them," was obliged to take his place on stage for the next scene. When Eugene finally had to face his father he tried to laugh off his discomfiture by commenting wryly, "A chip off the old block, eh?" Whereupon James returned, "Say, rather, a slice off the old ham." But when some reporters, having heard that James O'Neill's younger son was making his debut with the company, came backstage after the performance, they found James smiling and unruffled. One of the reporters, having been introduced to Eugene, remarked, "He's a very handsome boy, Mr. O'Neill; he takes after his father." James replied, with just the right note of paternal pride, "He's much better looking than I ever was."

Eugene was not his father's equal in gallantry. Years later he remarked of the tour:

"That cut-down version was wonderful. Characters came on that didn't seem to belong there and did things that made no sense and said things that sounded insane. The old man had been playing Cristo so long he had almost forgotten it, so he ad-libbed and improvised and never gave anybody a cue. You knew when your turn came when he stopped talking."

It is true that the vaudeville version of *Monte Cristo*, condensed from four acts to four scenes and reduced to about forty-five minutes' playing time, was a horribly botched affair. But it is doubtful that Eugene would have been any more sympathetic or co-operative if it had been a respectable production. By his own gleeful admission, he preserved his honor "by never drawing a sober breath until the tour had terminated." He wrote to one friend many years later that "the alcoholic content was as high as the acting was low," adding that he was graduated from the Orpheum Circuit with the degree of "Lousy Cum Laude." He further assured his friend that if the tour had lasted just a little longer he would also have won his "D.T." His only regret, he continued, was that he was unable to warn the audience in advance about his performance so they could all get drunk before witnessing it.

"Although I was only on the stage for minutes at a time," he said, "I imagine there are still people in this country who awake screaming in the night at the memory of it." On another occasion he remarked that the "general frightfulness" of the production reached "a high spot in the lousiness of my acting," adding, "I couldn't have been worse if I'd been playing *Hamlet*."

James himself was less than satisfied with the production. Although he never showed it to his colleagues, he was humiliated at having to return at the age of sixty-two to the unbecomingly youthful, and uncomfortably athletic Edmond Dantes, and as the second (if featured) half of a vaudeville bill. The tabloid *Monte Cristo* was presented twice a day—after a trained horse act and a group of flying acrobats.

Not that vaudeville wasn't considered an eminently respectable, if slightly lowbrow medium. Movies were still in their silent infancy and many stars, in order to keep active and earn good money between legitimate stage appearances, took to the vaudeville circuit in one-act plays or condensed versions of longer plays. Even Sarah Bernhardt made a vaudeville tour, stipulating she would not appear with animal acts or blackface comedians. But Sarah played the more powerful and more lucrative Keith Circuit, whose Palace Theatre in New York was the Olympus of vaudeville. The smaller Orpheum chain, which radiated out of Chicago and San Francisco, exerted its influence mainly in the West.

James, however, did not take *Monte Christo* to vaudeville as a novelty or even for the large salary—the whole company received only $1,250 a week, as compared with Bernhardt's $7,000. He did it because he seemed unable to draw audiences playing anything else, and because the time had finally come, after twenty-eight years, when legitimate theatre audiences had tired of his old melodrama. And though James was now a relatively rich man, he wanted to earn more. Fear of the poorhouse had become an obsession.

James's desperation was understandable: his wife needed constant medical care and protection and he was the sole support of the thirty-five-year-old Jamie, who would have been blacklisted by every manager in the country long since if he had had to rely on his own ability. In addition, he knew that Eugene, despite recent efforts to be independent, would continue to turn up with new financial demands; James could not bring himself to abandon him, even though at times he was tempted to do so. And so James continued to squeeze more life from *Monte Cristo*, at the same time feeling misunderstood and unappreciated by the three people for whom he was so pathetically laboring.

James had played *Monte Cristo* five thousand times and even the indignant critics and journalists had given up chiding him. The more perceptive were aware of his tragedy and wrote of him sympathetically.

One such article was written in 1908 for the Chicago *Record Herald* by a clever reporter named Richard H. Little. Chicago had been welcoming, encouraging and analyzing James for over thirty-five years. At this point he was back at McVicker's, where he had first played in 1872; he was giving *Monte Cristo* in repertory with *Virginius*.

"Haunted by the Ghost of Monte Cristo," read the caption over the story, in two-inch-high letters.

"James O'Neill has been the Count of Monte Cristo 5,678 times," Mr. Little began. "I went over to McVicker's last week to ask him why, and fell among press agents.

"I first asked the man in the box office why James O'Neill had played Monte Cristo 5,678 times."

"How the 'ell do I know? Stand back, I'm checking the line," was the answer.

"Then appeared on the scene," Mr. Little went on, "one J. Findlater-Byth." He was James's press agent and when asked the same question he looked pleased and invited the reporter to join him in a drink. After this reinforcement Findlater-Byth, looking even more pleased, disappeared to return a few mintes later with James's general manager and his general representative. Hopefully Mr. Little again voiced his question. But J. Findlater-Byth suggested that "before proceeding to the discussion of the main question, all hands be piped forward to splice the main brace." The main brace was duly spliced. Mr. Little then waited patiently while the press agent, the general manager and the general representative discussed J. Findlater-Byth's activities as a Reuter's correspondent during the Boer War. (He later lent part of his personality to *The Iceman Cometh.*)

Mr. Little put his question again more elaborately and after a while it occurred to all concerned that they should repair to the "governor" himself for an answer. They went backstage.

"I don't know," said the manager, "whether it is because he has played Monte Cristo so many times—next week, you know, will be the twenty-fifth anniversary of his appearance as Edmond Dantes—or whether it is because he so identifies himself with the part that has caused the public to clamor for it when, if he had his way, he would long ago have put it on the shelf.

"But when he is Edmond Dantes on the stage he is Edmond Dantes back in the wings until we shake him and bring him back to himself. I always make it a point to be back of stage myself or have somone else here ready to seize him when he comes off the stage in *Monte Cristo* and take him back to his dressing room. Otherwise he would blunder around here for I don't know how long before he got himself out of the part."

At last Mr. Little confronted James in his dressing room.

"Why have you played *Monte Cristo* 5,678 times?" he asked.

"Why?" mused James, looking dejected. "Well, because I cannot get rid of the cursed thing."

"Oh, you love your art, governor," hastily interposed J. Findlater-Byth. "And the artistic possibilities of Monte Cristo are so great that you feel it would be an imposition on the public to put aside a play that so appealed to the emotions and has such a great influence on so many."

"Do I, Jimmy?" asked the governor. "Thanks. But I would like to bury Edmond Dantes so deep that he would never come to life again. Edmond Dantes is the old man of the sea around my neck. I have carried him twenty-five years but he won't let go. I can't break his hold.

"I want to play *Virginius* and *Julius Caesar* . . . But I can't shake this Nemesis, this nightmare, this spectral shape of Monte Cristo. It haunts me and I can't escape it."

"You're sick, governor," said J. Findlater-Byth.

"No," said James, "I'm not sick. I was never sick in my life. . . . Every year I start out with the fixed determination that I am done with Edmond Dantes forever, and before I know it he has me by the throat and I am climbing the rock once more and shouting: 'Mine the treasure of Monte Cristo; the world is mine.'

"No, when I play Monte Cristo they pack the house. When I play *Virginius*—well, they give me good audiences, but they don't take me as I want them to take me."

James left to go on stage and J. Findlater-Byth called Mr. Little's attention to the fact that it was thirteen minutes past ten, and that it was his invariable custom at thirteen minutes past ten to take a gentle stimulant. After J. Findlater-Byth had had his stimulant, he took Mr. Little back to the box office where, J. Findlater-Byth thought, Mr. Little might find an even better answer to his question.

At the box office Mr. Little observed the large number of people buying tickets who belonged to the older ranks of playgoers; he stopped one of them and got as articulate an answer to his question as any reporter could have hoped for:

"I don't exactly know," began the ticket buyer. "I suppose it's a habit with me. I saw O'Neill play Monte Cristo twenty-five years ago. I've seen him since whenever it was possible. I suppose I've seen that piece forty or fifty times, and I never get tired of it. I suppose it belongs to the old days, but if they only puts plays over nowadays that gripped me like *Monte Cristo* does I'd be for them, but they don't.

"Say, honest, in all this riot over musical comedy and broilers and show girls and vaudeville that they have nowadays do they give you anything that makes the chills shoot up and down your spine like *Monte Cristo?*

"Say, when O'Neill climbs up there out of the sea with the salt water dripping off his clothes and waves his knife and yells, 'The world is mine,' I want to stand up on a chair and holler.

"I don't suppose it affects young people that way. They're spoiled by the class of plays they see nowadays. I took my granddaughter to see O'Neill down in New York a short time ago and she was much disappointed because he only *said* 'The world is mine.' She wanted to know why he didn't stay up there on the rock and *sing* it.

"I told her that it wasn't a song, that it was a line in the piece. 'Oh, no, Grandpa,' she said, 'it's a song, "Love me and the world is mine."'

"Well, maybe it is, but I would just as lief that O'Neill didn't sing it.

"*Monte Cristo* is human. I don't care how impossible they say it is. At least it always seems to make a direct appeal to me and I hope O'Neill goes on playing it for another twenty-five years. He may think that Shakespeare is greater, but what is greater than to feel that you have touched the heart, whether you do it in a classic or in a melodrama? I've bought seats for three nights next week and I'm only sorry I can't come every night."

Mr. Little was impressed. He went backstage to say good-by to James and found him still musing over the question.

"I am as much a prisoner of the Château d'If as Edmond Dantes ever was," said James. "The other day I saw in a Sunday illustrated paper a picture of a California redwood tree with the various events of the world's history pictured around in the order they had occurred since the tree began to grow. When it was a little shoot, just appearing above the ground, Christ was born in Bethlehem. And so pictured out at various heights of the tree are drawings symbolic of the great episodes of the world. And, while these things were happening, away out in the California forests this redwood tree was growing.

"Do you know, I feel like that redwood tree. Twenty-five years, the time I have been playing *Monte Cristo,* is not long, and yet when I think back over that period I feel older than the California redwood.

"In that time I have seen great actors spring from obscurity to fame, flourish and die. I have seen careers built up and torn down. Children have been born and grown into men and women. Little towns where I once played one-night stands, or passed by entirely, have become flourishing cities. Inventions never thought of when I began playing Edmond Dantes have revolutionized everything.

"And all this time I have been climbing up on a rock, waving a knife, and announcing that the world was mine.

"Do you wonder I want to escape from it all? I want them to remember me as Virginius, but they won't. I suppose that I will be Edmond Dantes throughout the play and down to the final curtain."

The final curtain for Edmond Dantes was not far off when James, in October, 1911, began to tour the tabloid version of *Monte Cristo.* When he brought it to Cincinnati near the start of the vaudeville tour, although he and the production were hailed as "most welcome," it was noted sadly that "James O'Neill has passed the meridian of the physical; his hairs are whitened, if his brow is unwrinkled, and there is scarcely that elasticity of tread that marked his graceful posings when he was the foremost romantic actor of our stage." Cincinnati, of course, was bound to evoke memories of the past for James, and he confided to a local reporter:

"I suppose when a man gets to my age he begins looking backward. You see, I am over sixty." (Actually, he had just turned sixty-five).

"I am not so inclined to look backward in other places," said James, "but when I stand before the old National I am carried to the beginning; getting back to the present my life passes in review. I suppose I stood down there an hour. I was wondering where, had I not gone on the stage, I would be now; whether I would have been more, or less, successful; whether I would be here at all; whether I would be more or less happy. You can't help such thoughts, you know, at this time of life."

That was about as much of his personal attitude as he could bring himself to reveal; and even that, with its expression of doubt as to his happiness and success, was more than he usually committed himself to for the record. James's sense of failure and his intimations of mortality were heightened as the tour proceeded. In Chicago and Memphis, where he played in January, 1912, and soon after, in New Orleans, his reception was gentle and loyal—but it was a reception accorded to a relic of the past and James felt this keenly.

Jamie stood ready to trample on his father's wounded feelings. When Jamie was lectured by his father for going to a bar between shows without taking off his costume and make-up, Jamie retaliated: "Why worry about it? You're what I'll be twenty years from now."

Jamie was no longer playing Edmond Dantes' son. He looked too dissolute for the role. He was playing a character called Nortier and had given up any pretense of performing. He had all he could do not to fall down on the stage; on one occasion, in fact, when he was on stage with his brother during a particularly emotional speech of James's, he did fall down and pulled Eugene down with him.

Eugene was not, like Jamie, deliberately bent on torturing his father; his attitude was that if James was going to "sandbag" him, as he put it, into playing with the company, then his father would have to put up with the result—which was one long drunken frolic. Some of Eugene's antics were merely embarrassing to James personally, but others struck at his professional pride and even threatened his career. For Eugene, like Jamie, was never sober when he arrived at the theatre; James watched him warily every night.

Eugene occasionally doubled in the part of a silent messenger. James never knew if Eugene would come on stage with the "prop" message he was required to deliver or if he would search his costume for the paper and finally hand his father empty air, causing snickers in the audience. Even worse, Eugene was sometimes drunk enough to stagger on stage, confront one of the other characters (or even James himself) and say, "So there you are, Tim Sullivan!" (Tim Sullivan was the New London policeman of whom James was fond, but not fond enough to have his name introduced into the dialogue of *Monte Cristo*.)

Jamie's mischief was more malicious. One time he launched a campaign to get young Webster to give an embarrassing reading of one of his lines. The line, spoken by Albert to Monte Cristo, who in the play is about to allow himself to be sacrificed in a duel with his son, was: "Count, I harshly challenged you last night but I thought it my duty to repress calumny." Night after night Jamie would station himself next to Webster as he awaited his cue in the wings and mutter in his ear, "I thought it my duty to repress *calomel*" (a purgative). One night Webster did slip just as Jamie had intended. The audience was delighted; James was mortified. Later that night, when Jamie and a companion were threading their way through the dark alley that led from the theatre to the street, someone threw a bucketful of water down on Jamie from a dressing-room window. Jamie never found out who threw the water, but he always suspected Webster.

James tried for a time to set his sons an example of moderation. After the evening performance, he took them to a bar, bought them one drink apiece, and then said good night pointedly and went to his hotel. Eugene, recalling this ritual, told an Irish Catholic friend that it was like going to daily Mass. But as the boys knew that James was going home to a bottle of good liquor, the routine had little effect on them; the free drink was just a start for the night's celebrating.

By the time the company reached Denver in February Jamie and Eugene's escapades were getting wilder and more resourceful. One Saturday night Jamie sent Eugene to a local madam who esteemed Jamie highly. Eugene arrived and found the madam awaiting him with six of her most attractive girls. But Eugene had an impulse to outdo Jamie and told the madam that *she* was the girl of his choice. She was so flattered that she sent the girls off, shut the house, and spent the weekend in cozy, alcoholic privacy with Eugene. Eugene staggered away at dawn the following Monday. When he entered his hotel lobby the desk clerk gave him a contemptuous look, which seemed to be concentrated on his legs. Eugene followed the direction of the clerk's gaze and saw that several inches of flaming red satin hung beneath the hem of his overcoat; he had put on the madam's kimono and forgotten to return it before leaving. For the rest of the day he and Jamie made his triumphant siege of the bordello an excuse for celebrating and by evening, when they turned up at the theatre, not even the stoical James could persuade himself that they could get through a performance. He had to cancel a show because of his sons' drunkenness and it was probably the blackest day of his professional life.

James, not only humiliated by his sons' efforts to disgrace him, was crestfallen at the lack of excitement his production engendered in towns where he was used to being met with ovations. Added to his burden was Ella's behavior. She had been traveling with him and had been in a trancelike state for several weeks. Although no one in his company, incredible as it seems, suspected Ella of taking narcotics, they were uneasy about her. They thought she was an invalid suffering from arthritis.

James, between his sons' drinking and his wife's morphine stupor, was at the end of his rope. Afraid to leave Ella alone in their hotel room, he often brought her to the theatre with him, where she sat in his dressing room during the performance. She ignored her sons and seemed oblivious to her surroundings—except in one instance. Obeying a strange impulse, she would sometimes leave the dressing room and stand in the wings during the ballroom scene. This was one of the emotionally charged high-lights of the play. It is during this scene that Monte Cristo discovers that Albert, whom he believes to be the son of one of his enemies, Fernand, is really his own son. This is the high-voltage dialogue that unravels the facts:

MONTE CRISTO (*who has forced Albert to his knees*): Fernand, I hold thy heart in my hand.

MERCEDES (*the boy's mother, who had been married to Monte Cristo before his imprisonment and presumed death, and who later married Fernand*): What will you do?

MONTE CRISTO: I will kill him.

MERCEDES: You dare not!

MONTE CRISTO: Why not?

MERCEDES: Because—he is your son!

MONTE CRISTO: My—!

At the point where James forced Webster to his knees, Ella shuddered and began moving like a sleepwalker toward the stage. James was supposed to be glaring down into Webster's face, but if he lifted his eyes an inch or two he could see over Webster's head, into the wings. His startled look always told Webster that Ella was there again.

James was afraid that Ella might reach the stage one day, but some-one always tapped her and brought her out of whatever reverie it was that this scene inspired in her.

James showed the effect of his personal and professional harassment, first, by sudden and unusual irascibility toward some members of his com-pany and, second, by giving up one scene that involved an elaborate change of costume and make-up and which he found he no longer had the strength for. He foisted his part in the scene on young Webster, and then pro-ceeded to question Webster's ability to act it. It was uncharacteristic of James to shirk a job and even more unlike him to taunt an inexperienced actor who was trying his best to juggle three roles. The part James un-loaded on Webster was that of Monte Cristo disguised as a Jewish peddler.

Webster had a bad time with the Jewish dialect. Supposedly stumbling in from a storm drenched, he had to say "Vot vedder, vot vedder," and several other lines in a similar vein. James nagged him about his accent. He would call Webster to his dressing room and say the lines for him over and over.

In frustration—probably James was thinking that the unskilled accent would be attributed to him—he told Webster, "Go to the pawnshops and talk to the Jewish people and learn their accent and mannerisms."

Eugene undertook to defend Webster.

"He's doing fine. I don't know how he does it," he would tell James.

"Of course," Webster admitted, "what Gene admired was the fact that I could memorize and play three roles; he had trouble getting his one line down pat."

James relented, however, toward the end of their stay in Denver. Webster, whose voice was affected by the altitude, played his various roles one night almost gasping for breath.

"Very good tone color, tonight, my boy," said James, "very good tone color." That night he was feeling expansive over a minor victory he had just won from his sons.

"Boys," he had told them the day before, "I've been invited to dinner at Elitch's Gardens and I'm to bring you along. For God's sake, stay sober."

Naturally, they did nothing of the kind. Shortly after their arrival they took out a bottle and had nearly emptied it by the time dinner was announced. James observed their condition and as they sat down opposite him at the crowded table he pinned them with a look of such stern command that neither of them uttered a word throughout the meal. Although his triumph amounted to a demonstration that his sons were taciturn, rather than drunken, he *had* won. It was a small victory, though, in the face of the big defeat that followed.

On February 14 *Variety*, the Bible of the entertainment world, carried the following item, datelined Denver:

"After next week James O'Neill will end his Orpheum Circuit tour. . . . The production and star have been favorably received, but Mr. O'Neill's support brought adverse comment all along the line and the voluntary cancellation has followed. The sketch had still about eighteen weeks of Orpheum time contracted for."

Eugene had the grace to feel ashamed. Before the final week was played out he deserted the company. He soaked up all the alcohol he could absorb and somehow made his way back to New York—and Jimmy-the-Priest's.

XIX

DURING THE NEXT THREE MONTHS, WHENEVER EUGENE was sober—even momentarily, because of lack of funds—things looked so black to him that he would have drunk anything, even varnish diluted with water, to make him forget he was alive. Since he did on one occasion actually try varnish-and-water and went on to sample camphor-flavored wood alcohol, it is astonishing that he didn't succeed in killing himself in the early spring of 1912.

If he needed excuses for drinking at that time, he had them. Pangs of conscience were part of his trouble. (In *Long Day's Journey Into Night*, set six months after the vaudeville episode, Edmund in what is surely a reference to Eugene's behavior on the tour, speaks to his father of "all the rotten stuff I've pulled!" and adds, "I've treated you rottenly, in my way, more than once.")

Another factor in his depression was worry about his mother. James had sent Ella to a sanitarium near Denver. Eugene always suffered over the humiliation he knew she underwent each time her illness was exposed to strangers.

He was filled with helpless rage over what he and his family had done to each other. He drank until he could no longer think or feel—and until even drinking wasn't enough to blot out his misery.

He began to wonder seriously if, after all, it would not be better for him to kill himself, as had Driscoll—his friend from Jimmy-the-Priest's and the S.S. *New York*. O'Neill made an unsuccessful suicide attempt. Later, his roommate succeeded by jumping out a window. O'Neill called this man Jimmy Anderson in his short story entitled "Tomorrow," and James Cameron (nicknamed Jimmy Tomorrow) in *The Iceman Cometh*. Jimmy's background was strikingly similar to that of James O'Neill's erstwhile press agent, J. Findlater-Byth. O'Neill once said that his roommate had been a graduate of Edinburgh University, who, "until the beginning of his social decline, was a highly valued correspondent of one of the greatest European news agencies."

"He covered the South African War, for instance," added O'Neill. "There came an appalling tragedy in his life. The booze got him and he had reached the depths. . . . But always my friend—at least always when he had had several jolts of liquor—saw a turn in the road tomorrow. He was going to get himself together and get back to work. Well, he did get a job and got fired. Then he realized that this tomorrow never would come. He solved everything by jumping to his death from the bedroom at Jimmy's."

The short story, written in the first person by a fictional character called Art, begins, "It was back in my sailor days, in the winter of my great down-and-outness, that all this happened." The setting is "Tommy-the-Priest's," and Jimmy is Art's roommate, a man who keeps a "dyspeptic geranium plant" that never blooms on the window sill of his room. Jimmy, forty-five, has wispy gray hair, a jowly face, faded blue eyes and a craving for affection. To the astonishment of his fellow boarders at Tommy's, he goes on the wagon and lands a job on a newspaper. He returns from his first day's work and starts drinking again. He confesses to Art that he couldn't do the work. "I'm done—burnt out—wasted!" he says. "It's time to dump the garbage. Nothing here."

At his most drunken, Jimmy tells Art a long story he has told many times before, about his brilliant early career; but this time he adds the details of how he found his wife being unfaithful to him, and says that this discovery started him drinking ten years before. Finally he collapses dead drunk on his bed and Art goes downstairs to join his other friends. Not long after, they hear a crash in the courtyard outside; it is Jimmy's geranium plant that has fallen, and soon after they hear another crash; this time it is Jimmy.

The story ends:

"We rushed into the hall and out to the yard. There it was—a motionless, dark huddle of clothes, a splintered, protruding bone or two, a widening pool of blood black against the gray flags—Jimmy!

"The sky was pale with the light of dawn. Tomorrow had come."

For his own suicide attempt, Eugene chose a less violent method.

He made the rounds of neighborhood drugstores, collecting veronal tablets, which at that time could be had in small doses without a doctor's prescription. Returning to Jimmy-the-Priest's, he tossed down what he estimated to be a lethal dose and went to sleep in his room. A couple of his friends found him there, guessed his condition, and began walking him and pouring coffee down his throat. Eugene, coming to his senses, offered no objection. When his friends had put him back on his feet, they decided to have a doctor look him over. They took him to Bellevue

Hospital. At the admitting office Eugene was pronounced fit and dismissed. His companions, however, were detained and thrown into the alcoholic ward.

The story of Eugene's suicide attempt, like that of his departure from Princeton, has many versions. He himself told it to several people, each time embellishing it, like a true Irishman, with different details. In George Jean Nathan's version, published in *The Intimate Notebooks*, an unconscious O'Neill was sped by ambulance to Bellevue, worked over by two interns, and revived three hours later. Nathan ended the story with Eugene's friends rushing to James O'Neill and returning four hours later with part of the $50 they had received from him to pay the hospital fee; they divided what was left of the money with Eugene, who then "rolled over, grinned satisfiedly, and went happily and peacefully to sleep."

O'Neill's writings and his later jocularity in recalling this episode indicate that he was making a macabre gesture rather than a sincere attempt to kill himself. At least one friend (a doctor who attended him when he was in his fifties) has said that O'Neill specifically told him he changed his mind about wanting to die after swallowing the veronal. One thing seems clear. The attempt was a gesture aimed largely at his father. Eugene waited until James had returned from Denver, sometime in May, before going out to buy his veronal.

In 1919 O'Neill wrote *Exorcism*, a one-act play based on his suicide attempt. In it a bedeviled young man of good family descends to the gutter and decides to swallow poison; two drunken friends revive him and his initial despair at having been brought back to face the same dreary world changes to enlightenment and hope. He realizes that he is not the same man, that his devils have left him. The play ends with his awareness that the attempted suicide has actually killed his old self and that he is a new man with new hope in himself and life. The play, though it had a brief production, was never published because O'Neill had second thoughts about it and destroyed all the copies of the script he could obtain.

Exorcism, however, was neither the beginning nor the end of O'Neill's literary preoccupation with death. The subject, like whores and the sea, is one that recurs consistently in his writing, starting as early as the plays he wrote in 1913. A psychiatrist, after analyzing him for six weeks when he was in his early thirties, concluded he had "a death wish." Any layman can draw the same conclusion from an analysis of his work—particularly *Long Day's Journey Into Night*, in which O'Neill gave the character representing himself the name of his dead brother, Edmund, and referred to the dead brother as Eugene. Aside from this wishful exchange of names, other evidence of the death wish may be found in twenty-five of his forty-five published plays in which a total of forty characters suffer violent or unnatural deaths. Of these, nine are suicides. Twenty-one of the poisoned, diseased, mangled, strangled, sliced, drowned, electrocuted, cremated or bullet-riddled men, women and children meet their ends in full view of the audience. For plays not equipped with corpses O'Neill has provided dialogue in which the word "corpse" is used frequently, both in its literal sense and in a symbolic sense. Moreover, there is scarcely a play in which the word "ghost" does not appear—usually in conjunction with the word "haunted"—and in three plays—*The Emperor Jones, The Fountain* and *Gold*—ghosts or spirits materialize on stage. In *Lazarus Laughed* (four acts, four violent deaths, two on-stage corpses) there are seventy-seven references to death in Act I alone.

As was the case with the protagonist of *Exorcism*, Eugene's attempted suicide seemed to have satisfied his inner rage, and for a time he was relatively calm. The attempt also had the desired effect of bringing James to a mood of remorse and forgiveness. James, in fact, had several things to be grateful for that spring.

Ella had left the sanitarium and seemed well enough to encourage James's hope for her complete recovery. Eugene had succeeded in getting his first piece of writing published—it was the poem, "Free," which he had written on the *Charles Racine;* it appeared in the Pleiades Club Year Book in April, and though the publication was limited to five hundred copies and distributed mainly among members of the club, it demonstrated (in James's eyes) that Eugene was good for something. The Pleiades Club, which was composed of actors, artists and writers, who met at such places as the Hotel Brevoort in Greenwich Village, in the interest of what they called "Bohemian good fellowship," had a discriminating membership. People like Mark Twain accepted invitations to address the club. James was proud of Eugene's literary debut.

Not least among James's reasons for satisfaction at this period was the fact that Eugene's worrisome alliance with Kathleen was finally being severed, and on terms that he considered advantageous. James rejected the thought that he was a grandfather, and only recently he had been infuriated by a story Ella told him. She had been walking on Fifth Avenue with a friend, when a nurse, wheeling a beautiful child of about three, had passed them. The friend recognized the nurse and knew her to be employed by Kathleen's mother. Being a woman of little tact, she turned to Ella and said:

"Do you see that little boy? That's your grandson!"

Ella had never seen him before, and she returned to James badly shaken.

As for Kathleen, she appeared to be just as well satisfied as James that her relationship with his family was being ended, although she had been willing to leave all the arrangements in her mother's hands, just as Eugene had submitted meekly to his father.

"My mother thought it was bad for my reputation to be a gay, grass widow," she said, recalling her first marriage. "I was completely free, because my mother had a nurse and a maid, and after I nursed the baby for two weeks there was nothing to tie me down. But my mother felt I should either stop going out with men, or get divorced. When I agreed to the divorce, she said I mustn't ask for a cent of alimony, as she would support me and the baby."

The divorce trial took place before Supreme Court Justice Joseph Morschauser on June 10, 1912, in White Plains, New York, where Kathleen had gone to establish a legal residence. She was represented in her suit by the law firm of Van Schaick and Brice, of New York. The complaint alleged formally: "On the 29th day of December, 1911, at 140 West 45th Street . . . in New York, the defendent [who did not appear in the case] committed adultery with a woman whose name is unknown to the plaintiff," and that "at divers times during the months of June, July, August and September, 1911, the defendant committed adultery with a woman named Maude W———. . . ."

Kathleen, who by law was precluded from giving testimony that would further the proof of adultery, testified only that the marriage was at Trinity Church in Hoboken, New Jersey, on July 26, 1909 (setting the date back two months for the sake of her reputation) that the issue was a son, and that at the time of the trial she was a resident of 17 Church Street, White Plains.

Testimony concerning the adultery was given by James C. Warren, of 34 East Fifty-eighth Street, New York, who explained to the court that he was a friend of Mrs. Kate Jenkins, as well as of Eugene O'Neill, and who described the circumstances of Eugene's dalliance on the night of December 29, 1911. Mrs. Jenkins was called as a witness to identify a picture of O'Neill.

Kathleen was awarded an interlocutory decree of divorce on July 5, giving her the custody of the child. The final judgment was signed on October 11.

Eugene was wistful about Kathleen. To the end of his life he spoke of her with respect, sadly reflecting on one occasion (after several entangle-ments and another marriage): "The woman I gave the most trouble to has given me the least."

By July James and Eugene had had a heart-to-heart talk about Eugene's future, and Eugene had agreed to spend the summer in New London and try to do some writing—possibly for the New London *Telegraph,* where James thought he could arrange a job for him. Jamie would be there too, and James was almost afraid to believe in the prospect he foresaw of a united family enjoying a peaceful, productive summer together.

PART TWO
THE BIRTH OF A SOUL
1912—1920

THE YEAR 1912 WAS THE MOST MEMORABLE IN EUGENE
O'Neill's life, for it was then that he determined to become a dramatist.

He made the significance of the date clear when he set the action of
Long Day's Journey Into Night in 1912 and underlined his dramatic
intent by telescoping the events of several months into a single, supercharged day. For some reason, though, he could not bring himself to reveal,
either in the play or in any of the dozens of public statements he made
about his beginnings as a dramatist, that the idea for his lifework was
already formed in the summer of 1912; he always preferred to give the
impression that the thought of writing plays did not enter his head until
early the following year, when a breakdown in health forced him to take
stock of his life.

But a number of people who knew him well that summer have recalled that he was already making notes for plays, and several people have
remembered the surprise and embarrassment they felt at hearing Eugene
say to James on more than one occasion: "Someday you'll be known as
the father of Eugene O'Neill."

In August, 1912, when Eugene was nearly twenty-four, he became a
reporter on the New London *Telegraph*. Published daily except Sunday,
the morning newspaper had been founded in 1885 and taken over in the
early 1900's by an attorney named Frederick P. Latimer. Latimer was a
man of liberal principles, integrity and warmth; as a friend of James
O'Neill, he acceded to his request that Eugene be taken on.

The staff consisted mainly of editors whose lively and divergent interests in foreign and political news gave the *Telegraph* a far more cosmopolitan flavor than was the case with its more reserved and circumscribed
competitor, the New London *Day*. The *Telegraph* devoted considerable
space to national news, particularly of New York City's underworld, and
local coverage required only a handful of reporters. The newspaper employed a red-faced printer's devil who fetched pitchers of ale for the
reporters. As there were no copy readers on the *Telegraph*, the reporters
wrote their own headlines.

Reporters and editors worked in a musty office and like most newspapermen of the era spent a good deal of time playing poker, gossiping and

making up for lost sleep at their desks. The reporter's desk was his card table, bar and bed—and sometimes the place where he wrote a story. Such local news as was covered ranged from fires and the fainting of fat women in the public square to the "classy scraps" that invariably took place among celebrating sailors on Saturday nights. The reports frequently were colorful. "Brandishing a razor in one hand and a bedpan in the other, John Jones of no certain address ran amuck in the city hospital yesterday" was the lead of one such story.

Staff members took their meals at an all-night hashery that featured a horseshoe bar flanked by mirrors. Jamie O'Neill made the bar a port of call around three in the morning and could be counted on to give the reporters an impromptu performance, highlighted by graphic grimacing before the mirror.

Eugene found himself among friends at the *Telegraph*. He was particularly encouraged by Latimer, with whom he hit it off at once.

"He's the first one," O'Neill once told the drama critic Barrett Clark, "who really thought I had something to say, and believed I could say it." Clark, who was preparing a book about O'Neill in 1925, went to Latimer for confirmation.

"As we used to talk together and argue our different philosophies," said Latimer, who had by that time sold his interest in the *Telegraph*, "I thought Eugene was the most stubborn and irreconcilable social rebel I had ever met. We appreciated each other's sympathies, but to each, in the moralities and religious thought and political notions, the other was 'all wet.'" (1912 was a year of blossoming for the socialist idea; an illustrated socialist monthly called *The Masses* was founded in New York, and the millionaire Harry Payne Whitney bought the *Metropolitan Magazine* and installed the British Fabian socialist, H. J. Wigham, as its editor. Jack London was holding court for young radicals in Greenwich Village; it was the year when O'Neill's political consciousness was at its most acute.)

Latimer, who considered O'Neill the paper's cub reporter, was impressed with his modesty, his native gentlemanliness, his wonderful eyes, and his literary style.

"It was evident at once that this was no ordinary boy," Latimer recalled, "and I watched what he thought, wrote and did with extreme interest. From flashes in the quality of the stuff he gave the paper, and the poems and play-manuscripts he showed me, I was so struck that I told his father Eugene did not have merely talent, but a very high order of genius." Latimer found O'Neill "emphatically different," and admired his wit, his iconoclasm and his sympathy with the victims of man-made distress. He recognized O'Neill's imagination and appreciated the vigor of his writing style, the heat of his spirit, and his scorn for commercial value or conventional fame. "If he could be in only one of two places in a town—the church or the jail—I know where I would find him!" Latimer summed up.

O'Neill's city editor, Malcolm Mollan, was less inclined to be tolerant of the cub reporter's "genius." Mollan wore a silk hat and carried a cane. He cheerfully admitted that he was the sort of city editor who "faithfully lived up to the tradition that such a creature must cut the hearts of his subordinates to ribbons with malignant criticism," and once wrote, recalling O'Neill's five-month stint on the *Telegraph*:

"Time was when . . . I used to bawl out, 'O'Neill!' and O'Neill would come to my desk and say, 'Yes, sir.'"

"This is a lovely story about that Bradley street cutting!" Mollan would say. "The smell of the rooms is made convincing; the amount of blood on the floor is precisely measured; you have drawn a nice picture of the squalor and stupidity and degradation of that household. But would you mind finding out the name of the gentleman who carved the lady and whether the lady is his wife or daughter or who? And phone the hospital for a hint as to whether she is dead or discharged or what. Then put the facts into a hundred and fifty words—and send this literary batik to the picture framer's!"

Mollan remembered O'Neill's abashed, puzzled look as he carried away his story and the way he "pulled his hair about his eyes while he tried to do a conventional, phlegmatic news item in newspaper style."

Mollan was aware that facts, standing by themselves, did not surprise O'Neill and so did not interest him. "It was what they signified, what led to them and what they in turn led to, their proportionate values in the great canvas of life, that intrigued his rapt attention," according to Mollan. "What difference did it make whether this particular brother of the ox, who had graven the proof of his upbringing on a woman's body, was called Stan Pujak or Jo Wojnik? What difference whether the knife found a vital or missed it by a hair? What O'Neill saw in the affair was just one more exhibit in the case of Humanity vs. the State of Things, another dab of evidence of the puzzling perversion of mankind, with its needless conflicts and distorted passions. He saw squalid bestiality usurping normal humanism in human beings. What he saw he wrote, that others might see. He had to."

O'Neill soon realized that he was misplaced as a newsgatherer. "I was a bum reporter," he told friends and interviewers complacently in later years. Some of his fellow reporters on both the *Telegraph* and the *Day* would have amended that statement. One of them later wrote that Eugene was "The World's Worst Reporter." Under that headline, nineteen years later, Robert A. Woodworth, then writing for the Providence (R.I.) *Journal,* recalled that Eugene would sit in a corner of the city room smoking and dreaming while other members of the small staff "ran their legs off."

"Hey, Mal, when is that guy going to get busy and do some work?" Woodworth would ask city editor Mollan in disgust. "As far as any of the crowd [at the *Telegraph*] can remember," Woodworth added, "he never typed a thing in the late lamented *Morning Telegraph* office which savored of genius."

One of the stories O'Neill covered, and for which he did manage to get the facts, concerned the arrival in New London on August 17, 1912, of Theodore Roosevelt. The story is a good example of his newspaper style:

Colonel Theodore Roosevelt, who is jocosely described by various pet names ranging from Bwana Tumbo to Chief Running Bull, passed through here on the east bound limited at 3:38 yesterday afternoon and his presence in a Pullman car at the Union Station drew a crowd of 150 people. The colonel was distinctly visible from the platform and he bowed de-e-e-lightedly to the onlookers. He did not offer to come to the car vestibule at first.

Among the assembled throng was the rotund and genial Attorney Thomas F. Dorsey, who made the acquaintance of Colonel Roosevelt some years ago when his train passed through here. Teddy wasn't going to get away from New London without a handshake from somebody, not if Mr. Dorsey knew it. So the amicable disciple of Blackstone drew an engraved calling card from his pocket, carefully dusted it off and marched in with it to the hero of the jungle. The awestruck crowd without the portals watched the colonel accept the proffered pasteboard and give Mr. Dorsey the glad mit.

Then the engine bell sounded and the colonel accompanied Attorney Dorsey to the door of the car and waved a farewell to the spectators.

If O'Neill did not exactly distinguish himself as a newshound, he did earn a local reputation as a sardonic poet. A column entitled "Laconics" appeared on the editorial page of the *Telegraph,* and consisted of contributions from members of the staff. It varied in form from day to day—sometimes it was a string of topical jokes, sometimes anecdotes, and sometimes caustic editorial comment—and was usually written in a humorous vein. Eugene's entries were invariably in the form of poetry, and his untitled poem ("with apologies to J. W. Riley") which appeared not long after Roosevelt's visit, was one of his first contributions:

Our Teddy opens wide his mouth,
N'runs around n'yells all day,

N'calls some people naughty names
N'says things that he shouldn't say,
N'when he's nothing else to do
He swell up like he'd like to bust,
N'pounds on something with his fist
N'tells us 'bout some wicked trust,
I always wondered why that was—
I guess it's cause
Taft never does.

He tells the farmers how to sow
N'shows the cav'lry how to ride,
N'if you try to say a word
He's angry, n'he says you lied.
N'when it's quiet over here
He goes way far acrost the seas
N'gets a great big gun n'shoots
The elephants n'chimpanzees
I always wondered why that was—
I guess it's cause
Taft never does.

Eugene's hours on the *Telegraph* were from five in the afternoon to one in the morning and he worked on Sundays to help get out Monday's paper. He rode to work on a bicycle, presumably to save trolley fare, although cycling was a popular means of transportation even among local businessmen. (In one of his poems for "Laconics," after enumerating the pangs felt by Caesar, Joan of Arc and Napoleon in their various hours of trial, he noted: "I grant you their sorrows were great and real/ But comparison makes them light/ With the gloom I feel as I ride my wheel/ To work on a Sunday night.")

His salary was $12 a week, and there was an unconfirmed rumor among the *Telegraph* reporters that it was paid by James. One story that made the rounds not long after Eugene had begun to work concerned a night when some inebriated reporters, in the old-fashioned newspaper tradition, showed up for work several hours late. One of them promptly fell asleep at his desk; two others were making noisy attempts to wake him when O'Neill walked in, only slightly drunk, but just in time to be spotted by the exasperated city editor, who promptly fired him.

"Hell, you can't fire him," the *Telegraph*'s manager, Charles Thompson, was reported to have said. "His father pays his salary." Whether this was the fact or whether Mollan relented out of kindness, Eugene stayed on for a while longer, happily contributing his rebellious ideas to a paper that was prepared to embrace and endorse them. The *Telegraph* even printed Eugene's lampoon of its own inner workings:

When my dreams come true—when my dreams come true—
I'll be sitting in the office here with nothing else to do,
But to write a comic story or to spin a little rhyme,
I won't have to do rewriting, I'll have lots of leisure time
For to sit and chatter politics and dream the whole night through,
I will never cover socials when my dreams come true!

When my dreams come true I will never stoop to read
The proof of advertisements telling people what they need.
I will only write the stories that are sure to make a hit,
And the mighty city editor will never cut a bit,
But put them in just as they are and compliment me, too,
I'll be the star reporter when my dreams come true.

When my dreams come true there will not be a mistake
In a single line of copy that the linotypers make
I will never have to count the letters framing up a head
And every night at twelve o'clock will find me home in bed.
I will shun the railroad station and the police station, too,
And only cover prize fights when my dreams come true.

When my dreams come true all my comments wise and sage
Will be featured double column on the editor's own page.
Personals will be no object, I won't have to go and hunt
The history of the tug-boats that infest the water-front.
Fire alarms may go to blazes, suicides and murders too,
I'll be editing Laconics when my dreams come true.

Despite the fact that the mechanics of newsgathering were beyond him, Eugene found the *Telegraph's* policy congenial and its atmosphere stimulating. The paper had guts—so much so that it was doomed to failure in the stuffy climate of New London. (It folded in 1919, leaving the field to its more strait-laced competitor, the New London *Day*.)

An example of the open-mindedness of the *Telegraph* and its refusal to be bullied by its readers into any narrow channel of opinion is an editorial that appeared in its columns on October 5, 1912. Since Eugene, by that time, had contributed several more verses in the same satiric vein as his commentary on the methods of Teddy Roosevelt, including a stab (in the style of Rudyard Kipling) at his pet target, Standard Oil, and a parody of *Hiawatha* dealing snidely with a publicized New London waterways convention, he was probably as much as anybody the cause of the editorial's being written.

Under the heading "Confidential," the *Telegraph* declared:

Some months ago the Editor received a postal from an anonymous person, expressing his appreciation of the usefulness of The Telegraph but inquiring rather pointedly, "When in h—l will your paper make up its mind whether it is a republican or a democrat?"

Happily or unhappily no such decision seems imminent. As long as we keep the words "Independent Newspaper" at the head of the page we shall try as best we can to live up to the profession. If we ever take up a party affiliation we shall announce the fact with the boldest type in our fonts. . . .

The ownership of this newspaper is in the hands of a Democrat and two Republicans, each with different personal bias and political tendencies as between conservatism and progression. Among these three are the editor and the business manager.

The city editor, who runs things while the rest of us are perforce in our beds, is a fierce Bull Moose. He divides his time between doing his work and cussing the owners.

Our genial chief news-gatherer, Joseph Smith, 2nd, is a wildly enthusiastic Democrat. For a long time he said his prayers as often as not to Champ Clark, and his democracy is just as much a part of his religion as his ideas of marriage. There is a faint suspicion in some quarters that Mr. Smith attended the Democratic rally Thursday evening.

Another important staff official may be a mixed "socialist and anarchist." As far as possible we keep him off political assignments. But he writes satirical verse which is so really clever that we feel obliged to print it, albeit with the blue pencil in pretty constant use. [This, obviously, was a reference to O'Neill, and, just as obviously, he was not unappreciated.]

There are others.

Out in the composing room we have every shade of political opinion known since Brutus slew Caesar.

A few weeks later, just before the presidential election that was to decide between Roosevelt, Taft and Wilson, the *Telegraph* carried a tirade by "Eugene Gladstone O'Neill" that began:

There's a speech within the hall, echoes back from wall to wall,
Where the campaign banners swing;
And the voters sit so patient, listening to the tale so ancient,
That the old spell binders sing.
You have heard the story of thieving Trusts
And their lawless lust for gain;

You have heard that song—how long! how long?
'Tis the same old tale again!
We have fallen for that same bull, dear lass,
Many a season through,
Till we're getting fed up with the old tale, the cold tale, thricetold tale,
Yes, we're just about sick of that Long Tale, the tale that is never new . . .

(Soon after, O'Neill cast his vote with the nearly one million others who, that year, supported the Socialist party's candidate, Eugene V. Debs.)

Art McGinley, who was Eugene's best friend in New London, also was a reporter on the *Telegraph*, despite his father's association with the *Day*. (Art, who was to remain a newspaperman, had worked first on the *Day* and later went to the Hartford *Times*, where he became sports editor.) Eugene and his friend often drank together on their days off or after work. Many times Eugene would go home with McGinley in the early morning hours and rudely wake Art's sister, who would obligingly move into a spare room so that Eugene could have her more comfortable bed. Or if there happened to be no one at home in Eugene's house, the two would stay there. Once when they were making a noisy night of it a neighbor telephoned James in New York and complained that Eugene and his friend had a "concubine" in the house. James called his son to find out what was going on and was only partially reassured on hearing from Eugene that the charge was untrue.

"Gene and I wanted to drink America dry," McGinley once said, referring to those days. In the bars of New London, particularly McGarry's and Neagle's, in which the two reporters spent a good part of their salaries, O'Neill enjoyed holding forth on anarchism, Irish kings and Irish independence. To McGinley he also confided his ambition to be a great writer, and he often recited his first attempt at a short story, written in his teens. About a boy on his way to visit his girl, it began, "Jimmy Trevalyan walked up the winding path. . . . It was early May and in the treetops the birds, drunk with the wine of spring, sang their roundelay."

Ed Keefe, O'Neill's erstwhile roommate in New York, used to join them now and then and the three would make their way to Holt's grocery store on Main Street, which, like many groceries of the period, had a barroom in the rear. The chief attraction for O'Neill at Holt's was a bartender named Adam Scott. Scott was a powerfully built Negro of over six feet, with arms that hung below his knees, huge hands and a round, bald pate. Though he tended bar during the week, he was an elder of the Shiloh Baptist Church on Sundays. Before taking a drink himself, he would always rub a drop or two of the liquor into his head; then, raising his glass, he would exclaim: "My best to every human being who breathes the breath of love." His rival for political leadership in New London's Negro community was a man named Jim Lewis, headwaiter at the Crocker House. O'Neill would tease Scott, pretending he had heard that Lewis was becoming a threat to Scott's supremacy.

"I'm a God-fearing man," Scott would say, "but someday I'm going to forget my Holy Ghost and slap the bejeezus out of that baby."

"How do you reconcile yourself, Adam," McGinley or Keefe might ask him, "to being religious and tending bar?"

"I'm a very religious man," Scott would reply, "but after Sunday, I lay my Jesus on the shelf."

Scott, who appointed himself a kind of unofficial bodyguard to Eugene and his friends, would tell them, "I gotta look after you boys. I gotta see nothing happens to you boys."

Scott's impressive personality was employed by O'Neill in one of his major works, *The Emperor Jones*. While part of the play came from other sources, it was Scott's bravado, his superstition, his conviction that he was a religious man, that became the traits of Brutus Jones. O'Neill even reproduced some of his figures of speech, as in this line:

"Doesn't you know dey's got to deal wid a man was member in good standin' o' de Baptist Church? . . . [but] it don't git me nothin' to do missionary work for de Baptist Church. I'se after de coin, an' I lays my Jesus on de shelf for de time bein'."

O'Neill's social life continued to be centered in Doc Ganey's Second Story Club, which convened nearly every night during the summer of 1912. Sometimes, instead of meeting in Doc's office-apartment, the club members would repair to a cottage Ganey had acquired on the Niantic River, on the other side of New London from the Thames. There they would take turns cooking, all except Eugene, who could no more share the amateur chef's enthusiasm for preparing food than for eating it. Doc Ganey, who was subsequently married to and domesticated by a vivacious woman much younger than himself, was at that time interested in a woman named Kate. His relationship with Kate did not enhance his reputation among the respectable citizens of New London. On one occasion the members of the Second Story Club disguised Kate as a man in order to smuggle her into the all-male audience at a cockfight.

O'Neill and Keefe went to considerable trouble in New London to live up to their reputations as young roués, not by smuggling women into cockfights but by flouting the rules in equally outrageous ways. Although O'Neill's relatives and his family's acquaintances knew that he did not behave conventionally, they would have been horrified by some of his escapades. Once he and Keefe talked a doctor they knew into giving them a prescription for a drug containing hashish.

"I've been reading about it," O'Neill told Keefe. "It's not habit forming." Keefe lost his nerve and the experiment was never carried out. Another time O'Neill and Keefe picked up two girls—both from nearby towns—and took them to a seedy hotel near the railroad station.

"We were so polluted," Keefe later recalled, "that we signed our real names on the hotel register. We each took a room. After half an hour Gene came into my room and said, 'Let's get out of here. I'm sick of these pigs.' That was a term he picked up from his brother. We left the two girls in the rooms and walked out without paying the bill."

It had been three years since O'Neill's marriage and the consequences had not inspired him to try respectability again. He endeavored to avoid the respectable girls of New London, but they sought him out. His good looks, shyness and apparent gentleness, his quality of seeming to suffer from some unfathomable wound, were irresistible to many. When compounded by his sinister reputation as a divorced man with a child, his glamour and desirability were magnets for all but the very timorous. And there were a number of distinctly untimorous maidens in New London. Luckily for most of them, Eugene had learned caution since his entanglement with Kathleen.

There was a girl, for example, who was spending the summer at Groton, across the Thames from New London. Apparently she sat glued to her window in the Griswold Hotel, which faced the river, watching for Eugene with field glasses; for every time he ventured into the Thames in his canoe, she sprang into her rented rowboat and met him more than halfway. When James learned of this idyll, he warned his son: "You just tell that young lady there's no money here."

A girl named Mabel Ramage was another with whom O'Neill spent some time that summer; she did not pursue him, but a certain amount of initiative was necessary on her part, as well as on the parts of all the New London girls he took up with, because of the taboo against him.

Mabel was dark-haired, blue-eyed and fair-skinned. She worked in an elegant confectionery on State Street owned by Stavros Peterson, the most affluent member of the Second Story Club. His confectionery, patronized by the elite of New London, charged high prices for his superb concoctions. Like a chemist mixing a formula, Peterson blended his own chocolate and came up with a syrup so thick and rich that it could not be put through the fountain pump; it was poured, instead, from gleaming silver pitchers. His ice-cream sodas were served in precious white goblets. And no Du Pont, Morgan or Rockefeller would have thought of returning to his yacht without a supply of Peterson's marrons glacés.

Mabel was one of fourteen girls who worked as glorified waitresses and were more decorative than utilitarian. Most of them were daughters of conventional New London families who wanted a taste of independence, and their work was light.

O'Neill generally visited Peterson's on payday to cash his salary check and order a chocolate ice cream soda. It was there that his eye fell on Mabel, in whom, as it happened, Peterson also was romantically interested.

Eugene would take Mabel walking.

"My mother was adamantly against my going out with Gene," she has remembered. "He called for me once or twice at my home and my mother was openly hostile. He didn't call there any more after that."

Instead, he met her at the confectionery, to Peterson's irritation. Mabel saw Eugene only about a half dozen times in all, but he left a vivid impression, as he did with every girl toward whom, however briefly, he turned his attention.

"I was fascinated with him," she later said. "He seemed so mature and different from other boys. I was flattered to be getting attention from a man like that."

Mabel could not reconcile what she had heard of Eugene's evil reputation with his behavior to her.

"He never used bad language, and was always polite," she recalled. "He was the perfect gentleman. He never even tried to kiss me. He used to call me 'Queen Mab' and he wrote a couple of poems for me, which I put inside a magazine to hide from my mother." She added ruefully that the magazine was thrown out one day—with the poems.

Toward the end of September O'Neill met the girl who, exactly twenty years later, served as the model for the young heroine, Muriel McComber, in *Ah, Wilderness!* Although in 1912 O'Neill himself was nearly twenty-four, and by this time quite different from the Richard Miller of his play (and the girl was three years older than the play's fifteen-year-old Muriel), their romance had very much of the same breathless, innocent quality with which O'Neill tenderly imbued the relationship between Muriel and Richard. The clandestine meetings, the parental disapproval, the exchange of notes through an intermediary, and the earnest plans for marriage were nostalgically recalled elements in O'Neill's courtship of the girl he fell in love with in the early fall of 1912.

Her name was Maibelle Scott and some of her friends called her

"Scotty." She was tall and slender, with long, light-brown hair, large blue eyes, a peaches-and-cream complexion, enchanting dimples, and a soft, appealing voice. Doc Ganey, who was a connoisseur, and who had watched Maibelle stoop to make a graceful adjustment to her garter one day, regarded her without reservation as "a beauty."

Maibelle was the granddaughter of Captain Thomas A. Scott, who had built Race Rock and Sarah's Ledge, two famous lighthouses in Long Island Sound. Her father was a master diver, who had salvaged wrecks off the coast of Connecticut and later shifted to running a general store on Pequot Avenue. (Muriel McComber's father, in *Ah, Wilderness!* is the proprietor of a dry goods store.) The Scotts, who lived a street away from the O'Neills, were an eminently respectable New London family and had been casually acquainted with the O'Neills for many years.

In the summer of 1912, a year after Maibelle's graduation from high school, her married sister, Arlene, rented one of James O'Neill's houses while awaiting completion of repairs on a permanent home she and her husband planned to occupy. Known as the Pink Cottage, the rented house was next to the one in which the O'Neills lived. Arlene and her husband, Byram Fones, became better acquainted with the O'Neills that summer and Maibelle, who dropped in on her sister frequently, had a glimpse of Eugene now and then, as he did of her.

One Sunday at the end of summer Eugene on his bicycle overtook Arlene as she was walking down Pequot Avenue. He dismounted and walked beside her, mumbling a few awkward pleasantries and then, summoning his courage, said, "I don't know your sister well, but I'd like to."

Arlene asked him smilingly if he would be at the wedding of a mutual friend, Bessie Young. The wedding was to take place on Tuesday at the Young home on Pequot Avenue. Eugene replied he would be there. "Well, then you'll meet my sister," said Arlene. Bessie had been a childhood friend of his. Her father, a deep-sea diver, had died in 1905 and her young, widowed mother took in table boarders. The O'Neills had been patrons there during periods when Ella found herself unable to cope with the problem of domestic help. All the O'Neills had been invited to the wedding, and although Ella declined, she invited Bessie to her house and asked her to accept the loan of table napkins for the reception. As a wedding gift, she gave Bessie two fine pieces of cut glass.

"Mrs. O'Neill was very refined," Bessie recalled. "She always wore a hat, even when she came up the block to have her meals at our house. Often she'd skip a meal, and Mr. O'Neill would explain that she was ill. I always felt there was something strange about her." But Bessie had no inkling that it was narcotics addiction.

As it happened, O'Neill was assigned by the *Telegraph* to cover the wedding—scheduled to take place in the evening. Fearful that he would not be able to impress Maibelle sufficiently in the role of a reporter, he got himself up in a black silk cape and top hat borrowed from his father. He had had the foresight to grow a small mustache—an adornment which periodically appeared and vanished that summer. With the garments he borrowed a bit of his father's technique as well. Learning, when he arrived at the Youngs, that Maibelle was among a group of girls fluttering in last-minute excitement around the bride in an upstairs room, he stationed himself at the foot of the staircase. He could not descend a staircase in the style of Monte Cristo to achieve his effect, but he did the next best thing. As he heard girlish voices taking leave of the bride he majestically ascended the steps and managed to confront Maibelle on the landing. He made her a sweeping bow and murmured, "At last, we meet," fixing his dark eyes on her astonished blue ones.

There was no time to pursue the effect, for O'Neill did have to take a few notes and make himself agreeable to the other guests, among whom was Mabel Ramage. After the ceremony O'Neill bundled up his cape and hat, mounted his bicycle and sped to the *Telegraph* office, where, inspired by thoughts of the delectable Maibelle, he dashed off the following story that appeared in the paper the next day, September 25. (He could not work Maibelle's name into the story until the third paragraph, but it led a list of others):

A very pretty wedding took place last evening at 8 o'clock at the home of Mrs. Frances Young, 267 Pequot Avenue, when her daughter Bessie Eleanor Young was married to Percival Frazer Palmer of Noank. The marriage service was performed by the Rev. J. Romeyn Danforth of the First Congregational church in this city.

The bride wore a charming gown of crepe meteor over white satin trimmed with silk lace and carried a shower bouquet of Killarney roses. The bridesmaid was Miss Jennie Payne, who wore white lace over pink satin and carried a bouquet of pink roses. The best man was Frederick Anderson of Staten Island. Miss Faith Howard and Miss Mildred Howard acted as flower girls and preceded the couple carrying baskets of pink carnations. Miss Angenetta Appledorn was the pianist and played both the Mendelssohn wedding march and the one from Lohengrin.

The young ladies who served were: Miss Maibelle Scott, Miss Mildred Culver, Miss Jennie Strictland, Mrs. Byram Fones, Mrs. Eric Barr. . . .

O'Neill did not trust the effect of the cape to last until the next day. He telephoned Maibelle at ten-thirty that night and asked if he could see her again. He need not have been anxious.

"I was terribly impressed with Eugene," Maibelle said years later. "Aside from his being so handsome, he was vastly sophisticated—and, of course, I knew that he had been married and had a child; as a matter of fact, when I first began seeing him, he was still married." Although an interlocutory decree had been awarded Kathleen in July, the divorce did not become final until October 11. Critics have remarked that O'Neill's omission, in *Long Day's Journey Into Night*, of any reference to his married state in the summer of 1912 was rather extraordinary; here, again, the Freudians are quick to point out that the fact was on his mind, as indicated by his introduction into the play of a servant girl named Cathleen, the only member of the cast of characters who was not a Tyrone (or O'Neill).

It is easy to understand O'Neill's fascination for a sheltered girl like Maibelle; the actress Lillian Gish, who became a friend of O'Neill's years later, once remarked that *she* had found it "very impressive" to learn "how fully he had lived at such an early age!"

Although Maibelle was more than willing to be in Eugene's company, she discovered that her family, with the exception of her sister, was far from happy about the relationship. Maibelle was hurt and bewildered by their attitude. She found Eugene gentle, well-mannered and considerate. He was always sober when she saw him and she couldn't understand why his father thought it necessary to warn her father to keep her away from Eugene.

When she heard that James had told her father she was too good for Eugene, that he was a "no-good, drunken loafer," it simply drew her closer to him, for she was absolutely convinced that there was no truth in James's statements. She was intelligent, sensitive, surprisingly free of small-town prejudices, and self-confident enough to trust her own judgment. Even when James, trying to enlist the help of Maibelle's mother in breaking up the romance, told her that his son "fell for every pretty face he saw," Maibelle refused to believe anything bad of Eugene.

But there was no point in flaunting her defiance of her parents, so Maibelle took to visiting more and more often at her sister's house. Arlene, despite the fact that her husband also disapproved of Maibelle's seeing Eugene, refused to join forces with the rest of her family. She was convinced Maibelle could be trusted to follow her own judgment and that it was nobody's affair but her own and Eugene's.

Maibelle would come to Arlene's house and, soon after, Eugene would amble over from next door. Arlene realized that the meeting had been prearranged.

Their dates consisted mostly of quiet walks on the outskirts of town, as any appearance in a public place was instantly reported as scandal and stirred up Maibelle's family anew.

Once they went together to the Lyceum Theatre to see *The Bohemian Girl*, so incensing Maibelle's family that they subsequently eschewed all public appearances. They had very few friends in common who were willing to flout public opinion by entertaining them together, but Eugene's boss, Frederick Latimer, and his wife were among those willing to take the risk. The Latimers had them to dinner a number of times and a friend who lived up the Thames, near Norwich, risked censure by inviting them to his house occasionally. And once they spent a few hours together on a yacht belonging to a neighbor of the O'Neills.

Maibelle and Eugene saw each other nearly every day for more than a month. They generally met at three in the afternoon in front of Mitchell's Woods, part of a large estate back of the O'Neill house, on Montauk Avenue, a thoroughfare that ran parallel to Pequot. They would walk toward Ocean Beach, a modest boardwalk and bathhouse establishment at the westerly tip of New London, about three miles from the O'Neill house. Or they would sit on the pier of the Pequot House, a casino that fronted on the Thames, and from which, at teatime, the strains of a dance orchestra floated out to them. They usually separated at dusk, since Eugene was supposed to be at the *Telegraph* by five o'clock.

Their relationship, as Maibelle later recalled it, was conducted largely on an intellectual plane, for Eugene could not help proselytizing and Maibelle was an avid pupil. He instructed her what to read and gave her, as his first gift, a copy of *Thus Spake Zarathustra*, which he inscribed with a quotation from the text that he believed was applicable to the atmosphere in which they found themselves:

Almost in the cradle we are given heavy words and values. "Good" and "Evil" such cradle-gift is called.

And we—we carry faithfully what we are given, on hard shoulders over rough mountains! And when perspiring, we are told: "Yea, life is hard to bear."

But man himself only is hard to bear! The reason is that he carrieth too many strange things on his shoulders!

But he hath discovered himself, who saith: "This is *my* good and evil." Thereby he maketh mute the dwarf who saith: "Good for all, evil for all."

Maibelle not only read and labored to understand the book but tried to persuade her friends to read and accept it. This was one of the things that upset her family.

Eugene continued to present her with books. He gave her volumes of Schopenhauer and Wilde and she dutifully read and discussed them with him. They wrote each other several letters a day, even though they were going to meet later. Most of the letters, far from discussing sentimental matters, dealt with the texts of the books Maibelle was reading under Eugene's supervision. In his letters Eugene would ask Maibelle to pay special attention to one or another passage or he would interpret some bit of philosophy he thought she might misunderstand.

There were, however, tenderer messages and poetry mixed in with the lectures, such as the following:

My Sentiments as expressed by Arthur Symons:

> I wandered all these years among
> A world of women, seeking you.
> Ah, when our fingers met and clung,
> The pulses of our bodies knew
> Each other: our hearts leapt and sung
>
> . . . .

Like it?

Have you my Oscar Wilde with you? Just want to know, that's all.

Answer all questions this time like a good Big Girl. [Maibelle had chided him for patronizing her with the endearment "little girl."]

Eugene also sent Maibelle many poems of his own creation, which she kept even after O'Neill had disappeared from her life. In addition to these personal poems, he gave her the poetry subsequently printed in "Laconics," and also the original, penciled version of "Free." All the love poems he wrote for "Laconics" were written with Maibelle in mind. "Only You," which appeared a few days after he met her, is typical:

> We walk down the crowded city street
> Thus, silently side by side
> We loiter where mirth and misery meet
> In an ever refluent tide.
>
> You thrill with the joy of the passing throng
> Or echo its weary sighs
> You gaze at each face as it hurries along
> —But I only see your eyes—

I only see your eyes, my love,
I only see your eyes
For happiness or misery
Are only real when seen by me
Reflected in your eyes.

We walk down the crowded city street
Lingeringly, side by side
You throb with the city's ceaseless beat
While I in a dream abide.

For how can its harsh triumphant din
Make me shudder or rejoice?
When the only sound in the dream I'm in
Is the music of your voice.

The music of your voice, my love
The music of your voice.
The world's vibrating symphony
Seems vague and most unreal to me
I only hear your voice.

Of the poems that were too personal or too serious to submit to the *Telegraph* two are interesting for their preoccupation with "phantoms grim," "dead pleasure's ghosts" and "murdered youth." Eugene also copied for Maibelle an Ernest Dowson prayer, indicative of the struggle he was still waging with his Catholic heritage; it was sprinkled with references to "Thy Terrible Judgment Seat" and "Thy angry glance," and was hopeful of "a choice of graces."

Maibelle and Eugene had an eager ally in Mildred Culver, who was Maibelle's best friend. (It was "Mid" Culver whom Eugene had in mind when he drew Mildred Miller in *Ah, Wilderness!*—the girl who carried Muriel's notes to Richard.) Mildred, who had grown up in New London with Maibelle, was almost as fascinated by Eugene as was her friend and was delighted to act as go-between in the romance. In addition to carrying notes she also helped arrange a number of their secret meetings. Her mother was a schoolteacher, and the Culver house, three blocks away from the O'Neills, was often empty.

Mildred would leave Eugene and Maibelle alone in a room of her house, and keep a lookout for her mother, for Mrs. Culver, too, took a dim view of Eugene's reputation.

Mildred, however, shared Maibelle's opinion that Eugene was maligned by their elders and she was convinced that he had no evil intentions toward Maibelle. "I think he loved her because he knew she loved his true self. He wasn't used to her kind of girl; she was a complete surprise to him," Mildred once observed.

Eugene and Maibelle rarely quarreled and were nearly always happy together. Because he seldom showed Maibelle his brooding, somber side or breathed a hint to her of the painful relationship with his parents and brother, she was startled by the revelations in *Long Day's Journey Into Night.*

"I have no recollection of Gene being disturbed about his family," Maibelle said. "He never gave me the impression that he resented his father, and even took it calmly when James O'Neill warned my parents against him."

Once Eugene told Maibelle, in rebuttal to those who claimed his reputation was unsavory, "I am *not* responsible for filling any of the orphanages or cemeteries in New London." It never occurred to her to doubt him.

"I do remember," Maibelle said, "that he was always short of cash, and didn't dress especially smartly, but he was never sloppy."

Maibelle knew that Ella was ailing but had no chance to observe her at close quarters; James she knew fairly well, and liked except for his— to her inexplicable—attitude toward Eugene. Jamie, although she barely exchanged two words with him, she detested.

"He really was a drunk and a slob," she said. "And he had a nasty way of looking at people."

Maibelle knew that Eugene had tried to commit suicide. He told her about it one day, adding that the way he would like to die was by swimming out into the wake of the moon, so far that he could not return. Apparently that was an effective image, for he evoked it also for Mildred Culver and a number of other girls who never forgot it.

"To this day," Mildred Culver remarked after O'Neill's death, "whenever I look out my front window and see the full moon on the Sound, I think of Gene and wish he might have gone that way."

After they had been seeing each other for a short time, Eugene and Maibelle began to talk of marriage.

His salary had been raised to $18 in October. But Maibelle thought that insufficient, and suggested they wait. She knew he had faith in himself as a writer; he often told her he would be a famous one, and she agreed with him. To prepare herself to be a good wife she enrolled in the local business college and studied shorthand.

"I did it so that if Gene, after we were married, had a profound thought in the middle of the night, I'd be able to leap out of bed, take my pad and pencil, and record it for him." How effectively this would have worked is in doubt, for Maibelle did not show talent as a secretary; on one of her tests, she spelled asparagus "asparroggross."

Somewhere toward the middle of October—not in August, as *Long Day's Journey Into Night* indicates—Eugene developed a bad cold, which he thought he had caught in a downpour while riding to work. He could not shake it off, and eventually was bedridden with a dry cough, fever, chills and night sweats. He couldn't report for work at the *Telegraph* but continued to send poems to the "Laconics" column. One of these contributions, "The Call," published in November, indicated the restless-ness that his prolonged illness inspired:

> I have eaten my share of "stock fish"
> On a steel Norwegian bark;
> With hands gripped hard to the royal yard
> I have swung through the rain and the dark.
> I have hauled upon the braces
> And bawled the chanty song,
> And the clutch of the wheel had a friendly feel,
> And the Trade Wind's kiss was strong.
>
> So it's back to the sea, my brothers,
> Back again to the sea.
> I'm keen to land on a foreign strand
> Back again to the sea.
>
> I have worked with a chipping hammer
> And starved on a lime-juice tramp.
> While she plunged and rolled, I have cleaned the hold
> Or coughed in the bilges damp.
> I have sweated a turn at trimming,
> And faced the stoke-hold's hell,
> And strained my ear in attempt to hear
> The relieving watch's bell.
>
> So it's back to the sea, my brothers,
> Back again to the sea.
> And where I'll go, I don't quite know—
> Just back again to the sea.
>
> For it's grand to lie on the hatches
> In the glowing tropic night
> When the sky is clear and the stars seem near
> And the wake is a trail of light,
> And the old hulk rolls so softly

On the swell of the southern sea
And the engines croon in a drowsy tune
And the world is mystery!

So it's back to the sea, my brothers,
Back again to the sea.
Where regrets are dead and blood runs red,
Back again to the sea.

Then it's ho! for the moonlit beaches,
Where the palm trees dip and sway,
And the noontide heat in the sleeping street
Where the restless burros bray.
I can hear the bands on the plazas
In towns of a far-off land,
And the words come strong of a deep sea song,
"We're bound for the Rio Grande."

So it's back to the sea, my brothers,
Back again to the sea.
Where regrets are dead and blood runs red,
Back again to the sea.

I'm sick of the land and landsmen
And pining once more to roam,
For me there is rest on the long waves crest
Where the Red Gods make their home.
There's a star on the far horizon
And a smell in the air that call,
And I cannot stay for I must obey
So good-bye, good luck to you all!

So it's back to the sea, my brothers,
Back again to the sea.
Hear the seagulls cry as the land lights die!
Back again to the sea.

For a few weeks there was no suspicion that Eugene had tuberculosis, and Ella made frequent references to Eugene's "bad cold" which would soon clear up. But here factual resemblance to *Long Day's Journey Into Night* ceases for the moment. Jamie was not even at home at the time; he had gone to a sanitarium to undergo one of his periodic cures for alcoholism. James was in New York, except for weekends, making the motion-picture version of *The Count of Monte Cristo* for Daniel Frohman, who, with Adolph Zukor, had begun operating the Famous Players Film Company. Eugene was being treated by two doctors, both with excellent reputations, one of whom was the distinguished chief of staff of New London's Lawrence Memorial Hospital. By November 15 his condition had been tentatively diagnosed as pleurisy, and he was devotedly being taken care of by a registered nurse he selected himself. Her name was Olive Evans.

The nurse, who had patience, understanding and a sense of humor, was about the same age as Eugene and had known him casually for many years. She was called on the case by Dr. Harold Heyer, who was assistant to New London's leading surgeon, Dr. Daniel Sullivan. Both doctors were regarded highly and bore no resemblance to the "quack" O'Neill described as having taken care of him in *Long Day's Journey Into Night*. ("I think Gene must have been out of his mind when he wrote that play," Olive Evans once remarked without rancor.)

There *was* a New London doctor who was known as the town quack and to whom O'Neill may have been referring (as "Dr. Hardy") in *Long Day's Journey Into Night*. This doctor's fee was twenty-five cents and stories of how he opened boils with a penknife and allowed children to die of ruptured appendixes were legion in the town, and it is conceivable, though unlikely, that Ella went to him for morphine prescriptions.

It was Dr. Heyer who ordered Eugene to bed when he developed fever, and suggested that a nurse attend him. Eugene asked him to send for Olive, in preference to a stranger.

"At first Gene was very ill with what we thought was a bad cold," Olive later recalled. "He had a high fever and had to stay in bed and have cold bed baths to bring his temperature down. He was very shy and modest, and I had to put him at ease when I bathed him by repeating what I had often heard my nursing superintendent say to patients: 'I think no more of washing a back than of washing that door.'"

Olive tended Eugene constantly, taking off only four hours a day. He coughed a great deal and fluid developed in his right lung. Dr. Heyer, who paid daily visits, called Dr. Sullivan to draw off the fluid with a hollow needle. He had to puncture the lung through the chest to do this.

"It was terribly painful," Olive said, "but Gene was very brave; there was hardly a grunt from him."

Once the liquid had been drained on November 26, Eugene felt much better. His fever went down and he was allowed to get out of bed and sit in a chair facing the sun. But he had to rest a great deal, for he was subject to occasional hemorrhages. Eugene occupied the front bedroom on the second floor, which overlooked the Sound. Olive had a room directly across the hall.

According to Olive, O'Neill's was the best room in the house. He read a great deal in bed, spent considerable time writing, and showed Olive snatches of dialogue and sketches of characters and notations about settings for plays—including a description of a character called Chris. He informed Olive he had gone to sea partly because he thought he might want to write someday, and it was a way of obtaining material. He kept his notes in an old-fashioned bureau that had divided drawers. Olive thought him "a brilliant boy, but a little warped."

Olive told Eugene that in her opinion a lot of his ideas for plays were "immoral."

"You are so naïve," replied Eugene. "If I didn't want to be polite, I'd say stupid." Having discovered Olive's weak spot, he pressed his advantage, and attempted to shock her with stories of his love affairs in New York and Buenos Aires and of the derelicts he had lived with at Jimmy-the-Priest's. Once he told Olive that his parents happened to see him and Jamie with a couple of girls and Mr. O'Neill warned his wife, in earshot of the boys, "Now aren't you proud of your sons. Look at those tarts!" O'Neill recalled the story in criticism of his father. "The old man is always throwing up what we do," he said.

Now and then, O'Neill succeeded in embarassing Olive with his lurid stories.

"Later, other girls told me how he used to try to scandalize them," Olive said. "But he didn't only enjoy shocking women; he loved to shock men, too. A number of men I knew took a strong dislike to him—the man I later married was one of them."

But Olive was not put out enough to consider leaving the case. She had, as a matter of fact, by this time become involved in his romance with Maibelle and was a coolly amused observer.

Ella had found out about the notes passed between Maibelle and Eugene and asked Olive not to act as messenger. Her reason, unlike James's, for discouraging the romance was that Maibelle was not good enough for Eugene.

When Eugene started feeling better and was able to go outdoors occasionally, he found a different way to make use of Olive. On weekends Eugene would persuade her to suggest that James hire a carriage, on the grounds that an outing would expedite his recovery. After riding with her patient a few blocks, Olive accommodatingly left the carriage, and Eugene picked up Maibelle at a prearranged spot. (Somehow, despite Ella's surveillance, he always managed to communicate with Maibelle.) After one such meeting, Eugene came home in a rage. He told Olive he had been riding with Maibelle an hour, and that she refused to remove her veil so that he could kiss her. His anger subsided long enough for him to compose a poem called "Love's Lament." He signed it "Tigean Te Oa'Neill" and sent it off to the *Telegraph*, where it was duly printed:

There ain't no nothing much no more,
And nothin' ain't no use to me;
In vain I pace the lonely shore,
For I have seen the last of thee.

I seen a ship upon the deep
And signalled this here fond lament:
"I haven't did a thing but weep
Since thou hast went."

Alas! fur I ain't one of they
What hasn't got no faith in love.
And them fond words of yesterday
They was spoke true, by heaven above!

Is it all off twixt I and you?
Will you go and wed some other gent?
The things I done, I'd fain undo,
Since thou hast went.

O Love! I done what I have did,
Without no thought of no offense
Return, return, I sadly bid
Before my feelings get intense.

I have gave up all wealth and show
I have gave up all thoughts of fame,
But, oh! what joy 'twould be to know
That thou hadst came!

In a more tender style, and not for publication, Eugene wrote Maibelle:

Have I not known enough of doubt and dearth
O God, great God, that Thou shoulds't sternly place
A wall between my lips and her fair face
And make me taste of Hell while still on earth? . . .

O'Neill told Olive that Maibelle was the only girl he really loved. Soon after the episode in the carriage he left the house again, presumably to meet Maibelle, and with the same unsatisfactory results. This time he failed to come home long after dark. James telephoned the Crocker House and reached somebody who volunteered to find him.

Two men finally brought him home—so drunk he began smashing things.

"I don't think Gene cared at that point whether he lived or died—he was just desperate about Maibelle," Olive said.

"I yearn to see her all the time," Eugene told Olive the next day.

Olive was aware of a strangeness in Ella O'Neill during her stay in the house on Pequot Avenue. Once in a while Ella would come into Gene's room and urge him to sit in the sun in front of his window. He would do so, but with obvious irritation. Ella spent most of her time downstairs. Olive, hearing her sobbing quietly, concluded that she was distressed about Jamie being confined to a sanitarium. For Ella did not seem, to Olive, to be really worried about Eugene's health. Olive would ask Eugene whether he wanted her to go to Ella to see if there was something she could do for her.

"No, leave her alone," he would answer.

Olive found Ella quiet but "sweet." She did little except play the piano and sit, usually with her hands folded, on the veranda or in the parlor.

Olive marveled that Ella was never demonstrative toward her son, but she recognized affection in her voice when she spoke to him. "Not that there was much conversation between them," she observed. Sometimes Eugene would call downstairs, "Mama, will you please play something for me?" There was great tenderness in his voice when he made the request.

Another thing Ella would do to oblige Eugene was prepare eggnogs for him.

The O'Neills were keeping house in a sketchy fashion. Their only servant was a cleaning woman. According to Olive, "the house was clean, but it was not neat." Eugene's meals were brought over in a basket by a young Irish girl from Mrs. Young's house, as were Ella's. James ate out when he was in New London.

At this period Eugene was as hostile toward his father as he was tender toward his mother. The complexity of his conflicting and constantly shifting emotions toward James defy rational interpretation.

"The Old Man and I got to be good friends and understood each other the winter before he died," Eugene wrote to Art McGinley in 1932, just after he had drawn an idealized James in *Ah, Wilderness!* "But in the days [1912] you speak of, I was full of secret bitterness about him—not stopping to consider all he took from me and kept on smiling."

Eugene told Olive he resented his father, and he never said anything nice about him. He complained of the way he had been dragged about as a child. James, however, appeared to be genuinely concerned about Eugene.

"Of course, he was always a little theatrical," Olive observed. "When he arrived home for the weekend, he would step out of his horse-drawn hack and come up the front steps with his arms flung wide, expecting Mrs. O'Neill to rush into them in greeting, which she did. Then he would go straight up to Gene's room."

"How are things going, son?" he would ask.

Eugene would mumble something and turn his back on James. He never invited him into the room. James would hesitate in the doorway, looking worried and uneasy. With his own robust constitution—he still liked to brag that he had never been sick a day in his life—he was always a little contemptuous of the physically weak or broken.

The tension between them was plain to see. One Sunday Olive heard Eugene ask his mother, "Has the Irish peasant gone to Mass?"

"Oh, Genie, please," Ella answered weakly.

James attended Mass every Sunday at St. Joseph's Church, contrary to O'Neill's description of James Tyrone, who is pictured as being negligent about his formal observance of religion. Ella's relatives, in fact, were constantly after James to bring Ella with him to church. (They had long since given up on Eugene.)

But another aspect of James's character, his miserliness, on which his son harped in *Long Day's Journey Into Night,* is more difficult to evaluate. It is clear that James did not try to cut corners on medical expenses for Eugene during the early stage of his illness. As for James's concern, constantly reiterated in the play, with turning off lights to save on electricity, this was a crotchet of many householders in the early 1900's. In an era when a pound of ham cost 17 cents and a pound of best tub butter 32 cents, and when a family of four was used to dining at home very well for under $60 a month, the charge of between $7 and $10 a month for the newfangled commodity electric light seemed out of all proportion. There were few heads of families who did not feel, like James, that they were being duped into making the electric light company rich, and it was customary to burn only those lights which were essential to illuminate a small area.

Theodore J. Liebler, Jr., son of the founder of Liebler and Company, who was devoted to James O'Neill, once recalled, in defense of James's concern with saving on electricity: "In 1912, my family was worth about three quarters of a million dollars—and we always switched off lights.

Like the O'Neills and most of their friends, we had started converting to electricity in the early 1900's, and we all tried to save on lights in those days. When electricity was first installed, the company figured that the users had to pay for the installation of dynamos and other equipment. They had to get some of their money back, so the original charges were high."

The crux of the matter of James's penury, however, seemed to revolve, for Eugene (if his preoccupation with it in *Long Day's Journey Into Night* may be used as a guide), on James's wish to send him to a state farm to be treated for tuberculosis. Edmund Tyrone, in the play, becomes almost inarticulate with rage at the thought that his wealthy father is going to allow him to be a charity patient. In this one instance, paradoxically, Eugene chose to distort the truth in his father's favor. Although *Long Day's Journey Into Night* indicates that James was shamed by his son into sending him to a heavily endowed, semiprivate sanitarium, the fact is that James *did* send Eugene first to the state farm.

James considered his financial condition at this time more precarious than ever. Actually, he was worth somewhere between $100,000 and $200,000 in cash and real estate. But his huge income from *Monte Cristo* was at an end; he knew he would never play Edmond Dantes again. In addition, another film company came out first with a three-reel *Monte Cristo* photoplay. James's five-reel version could not be widely released; there was no market for two *Monte Cristo* movies.

"I remember how bitterly disappointed Mr. O'Neill was when it was decided the picture would not be released," Olive Evans said. Although it was shown in a few theatres that had not taken the competing movie and was advertised as the first feature-length film ever produced in the United States, James's *Monte Cristo* was soon withdrawn.

It is true that James had accepted a role in a projected Broadway play, for which his salary was to be $400 a week, but he had no guarantee that it would be a success; he was convinced that his earning days were over, and since neither of his sons was able to support himself, he saw the poorhouse looming. Perhaps he did feel, as Eugene accused him, that tuberculosis was a fatal disease and that it was useless to spend a lot of money treating it; the thought may have crossed his mind that, since Eugene was going to die anyway, it would be better to save his money for the living members of his family. Tuberculosis in the early 1900's was called "The Great Killer" and was the leading cause of death in the country; the national death rate for the disease was 204 per 100,000 population.

By the end of November Eugene's condition became a little worse and his doctors began making tests for tuberculosis. Ella apparently did not know of the doctors' suspicion or else was too dazed to understand. In any case, she left Eugene alone with Olive on Thanksgiving Day. She may have gone to join James in New York. Eugene was accustomed to his family's habit of ignoring holidays, but on this particular Thanksgiving, a gray day with a promise of snow in the cold air, he longed for company. Friends like Art McGinley had come in to visit him from time to time during his illness, but most of his New London companions were not acceptable to Ella, so that he was left pretty much to his own devices. Since a visit from Maibelle could not be arranged for some reason, Eugene in lonely despair asked Olive to call Mildred Culver.

"I talked my mother into letting me go to visit Gene," Mildred recalled. "I made it a sob story—poor Gene, all alone and ill on Thanksgiving Day." Early in the evening she wrapped herself in her brother-in-law's Navy boat cloak and walked through the softly falling snow to Eugene's house. She sat by his bed and talked to him about Maibelle.

A few days later Eugene learned he had tuberculosis. His case was not severe, the doctors said, but it was advisable for him to go to a sanitarium. He met Maibelle that evening and told her about it.

"It didn't occur to me to be frightened of contagion," Maibelle later said, "and I kept on seeing him for a while, whenever he was well enough to get out of bed." Early in December, however, Maibelle left for a trip to Florida with her family.

Eugene had grown depressed. Late in November he wrote a poem called "The Lay of the Singer's Fall," in which he described a gifted youth whose spirit was plagued by the devil of doubt; first his faith, then his heart, then his soul died. "When Truth and Love and God are dead/ It is time, full time, to die!" says the Singer in the last stanza. The poem ended with these lines:

> And the Devil in triumph chuckled low,
> "There is always suicide,
> It's the only logical thing I know."
> —And the life of the singer died.

James had made his decision to send Eugene to the Fairfield County State Tuberculosis Sanitarium in Shelton, Connecticut, a few miles west of New Haven. The institution charged $4 a week for those who could pay; those who could not were supported by the state. Possibly Eugene even encouraged James's decision, in order to wallow more fully in self-pity; he was often seized by such masochistic impulses. Apparently his destination was an ugly secret between father and son, for neither Maibelle nor Olive

—nor, indeed, any friend or relative of the O'Neills—has recalled hearing anything about it.

James's behavior toward his son before he left for Shelton was incredible. He was sending Eugene off to what he knew was considered a pauper's institution—and now he called in the best tailor in New London to fit Eugene out. The tailor's name was Charles Perkins.

James asked Olive to stay in the living room during the fitting, because Eugene was not sure of his strength.

"Mr. O'Neill wanted me to be around all the time," Olive said. "He sat in a rocker while Mr. Perkins fitted Gene for a beautiful suit and overcoat. Mr. Perkins was a very dignified man, and I was surprised when Mr. O'Neill called him just 'Perkins.' He sat there suggesting alterations and trying to be helpful, but Gene acted as though he didn't hear him; he was very critical about the fit, and would pinch in a place where a pin should go to mark an alteration. He just ignored his father."

On December 9, a Monday, Eugene's signature appeared for the last time in the *Telegraph*, at the end of a poem called "To Winter":

"Blow, blow, thou winter wind,"
Away from here,
And I shall greet thy passing breath
Without a tear.

I do not love thy snow and sleet
Or icy floes;
When I must jump or stamp to warm
My freezing toes.

For why should I be happy or
E'n be merry
In weather only fitted for
Cook or Perry.

My eyes are red, my lips are blue
My ears frost bitt'n;
Thy numbing kiss doth e'n extend
Thro' my mitten.

I am cold, no matter how I warm
Or clothe me;
O Winter, greater bards have sung
I loathe thee!

On that same day the *Telegraph* ran a story that began: "James O'Neill, the noted actor, will close his residence on Pequot Avenue today and will leave for New York, where he will begin rehearsing tomorrow for the wonderful scenic production, 'The Deliverer,' which will be played for the first time at the Century Theatre in about six weeks." (The title was subsequently changed to *Joseph and His Brethren;* it was a biblical spectacle by Louis N. Parker.) There was no mention of Eugene in that story, but a separate item, that no one recalls having read, announced briefly that Eugene was leaving for Shelton for a "rest cure."

Ella went to stay with relatives in New London. In the afternoon Eugene, James and Olive boarded a train for New Haven. Olive had no idea that she was taking Eugene, on December 9, on the first leg of a journey to the state sanitarium at Shelton. She thought he was on his way to a semiprivate institution in Wallingford, Connecticut, called Gaylord Farm. She always assumed that Eugene had gone directly to Gaylord Farm, as did everyone else.

She said good-by to Eugene at the station in New Haven. As Eugene stepped off the train, a baggage truck with three coffins rolled across his path.

"My God, what a reception," she remembered Eugene saying.

XXI

JAMES AND HIS SON ARRIVED FROM THE RAILROAD
station in a hack at the Fairfield County State Tuberculosis Sanitarium
on the evening of December 9, 1912. They found it a crude and dismal
place. It consisted of a farmhouse, converted into a primitive infirmary,
and a row of wooden shacks. What James thought of the sanitarium to
which he was consigning his son can only be conjectured. He left him
there after meeting Dr. Edward Lynch, who was a good friend of Dr.
Sullivan.

Dr. Lynch, who later rose to be superintendent of the sanitarium—
it eventually became a fine, modern institution and its name was changed
to Laurel Heights—never forgot his first meeting with Eugene.

"He was tall and thin," Dr. Lynch recalled. "He was neatly dressed
in a dark-gray, single-breasted suit. He had pleurisy with effusion, a form
of tuberculosis."

Eugene was Fairfield's 547th patient and probably its most ephemeral.
He stayed there for only two days. Although he had lived in hovels
during his seafaring and beachcombing days, he preferred not to die in
one. Dr. Lynch quickly realized that Eugene was miserable and that his
mental condition would not favor his physical recovery. After making
certain that Eugene did have some choice in the matter, which the indigent patients in the sanitarium did not, Dr. Lynch advised him to
apply to Gaylord Farm in Wallingford.

"I told him he'd meet a better class of people at Gaylord," Dr. Lynch
recalled, "and that, since Gaylord took only minimal cases, his chances
for recovery there would be much better."

Dr. Lynch wrote to James O'Neill at the Lambs Club in New York,
explaining that Eugene planned to leave for treatment elsewhere. He
pointed out that his son's condition was emphatically in need of adequate
treatment but that the chances were "very good" for recovery.

Eugene arrived in New York on December 11. After some bitter
wrangling, he persuaded his father to send him to the man regarded by
many as the country's leading chest surgeon and a pioneer in the treatment of tuberculosis—Dr. James Alexander Miller. Eugene gained Dr.
Miller's interest in his case and, on December 17, the surgeon wrote to

the director of Gaylord, Dr. David R. Lyman, describing Eugene as a young man in "excellent general condition" and "a very favorable case." He asked Dr. Lyman to let him know immediately if Gaylord could receive O'Neill.

Dr. Lyman wrote back that he could.

With the dramatic timing that so often characterized the rhythm of his life and with the aid of the elements with which he seemed attuned in some mystical fashion, Eugene contrived to arrive at Gaylord on Christmas Eve during a blizzard. This time James, although he was busy rehearsing for a January opening of *Joseph and His Brethren,* had set out with his son by car on the eighty-mile drive to Wallingford, Connecticut. They had a hazardous trip and Eugene arrived much later than expected by the sanitarium staff. One of the patients has remembered being told that the O'Neill car had broken down on the way.

Eugene's impressions of Gaylord have been accurately recorded in his play, *The Straw,* written in 1918 and 1919. The play, most of whose action is laid in the Hill Farm Tuberculosis Sanitarium, has as its hero a tuberculous young newspaper reporter named Stephen Murray, who closely resembles the Eugene of 1912. Like Eugene, Murray begins writing seriously at the "san" during his enforced period of physical inactivity. In a number of ways O'Neill's description of him is a self-portrait:

". . . a tall, slender, rather unusual-looking fellow with a pale face, sunken under high cheek bones, lined about the eyes and mouth, jaded and worn for one still so young. His intelligent, large hazel eyes have a tired, dispirited expression in repose, but can quicken instantly with a concealment mechanism of mocking, careless humor whenever his inner privacy is threatened. His large mouth aids this process of protection by a quick change from its set apathy to a cheerful grin of cynical good nature. He gives off the impression of being somehow dissatisfied with himself but not yet embittered enough by it to take it out on others. His manner, as revealed by his speech—nervous, inquisitive, alert—seems more an acquired quality than any part of his real nature. He stoops a trifle, giving him a slightly round-shouldered appearance."

In 1924, in dedicating a volume of his plays to a nurse at Gaylord with whom he had kept up a correspondence, O'Neill wrote: "I confess I believe there is a great deal of the 'me' of that period in 'Murray'—intentionally!"

Unlike such private, profit-making institutions as the tuberculosis sanitariums at Saranac Lake in New York and at Asheville in North Carolina, which were large and expensive, Gaylord Farm was small, non-profit and somewhat experimental. Situated in rolling farm and orchard country, its 293 acres had once been the home of three generations of Drs. Gaylord. The sanitarium was still called a farm because its immense barnyard and dairy made it almost self-sustaining. The Blue Hill mountains formed part of its scenic background, of which the most picturesque grouping was the Sleeping Giant—one flat hill representing the head, a broader one the paunch, and a third, flatter and longer, the legs. Viewed from Gaylord the mountains had a smoky blue color.

Gaylord Farm was established in 1904 with one doctor, one nurse and six patients. The Great White Plague was then considered incurable except, possibly, in one of the two well-established sanitariums, or in a high altitude such as Colorado or the Swiss Alps. Financed largely by the Anti-Tuberculosis Society of New Haven and aided by a small, annual state fund, Gaylord Farm dedicated itself to proving that tuberculosis could be checked in any climate where plain good care, with rest as its vital factor, was administered. Patients were charged $7 a week.

Eugene was immediately reassured by the atmosphere of Gaylord and the thoroughness of its procedures. Soon after his arrival he underwent a comprehensive examination and was put to bed. The examination confirmed previous diagnoses that his case was a light one, and noted that he caught cold easily, was subject to severe attacks of tonsillitis, was nervous and, though he could fall asleep easily, was in the habit of waking up six or seven times a night.

Long after he had recovered from tuberculosis he enjoyed telling friends about his stay at the sanitarium, attributing a variety of reasons to the onslaught of the disease. To McGinley he confided that he had probably picked it up in the Argentine when he was a beachcomber; to the critic Kenneth Macgowan, with whom he later became associated in the production of his plays, he said he had contracted tuberculosis at Jimmy-the-Priest's, where, he maintained, he had slept in a bed previously occupied by a man who had died of the disease; to the theatrical press agent Joe Heidt, whom he met somewhat later, he declared that the disease had been brought on by riding his bicycle in the rain in New London. To the writer Benjamin De Casseres he once offered a more elaborate explanation:

"I got such a dose of those germs—at least, this seems to me the reasonable dope—while living at Jimmy-the-Priest's with 'lungers' numerous among the lodgers of its airless rooms—cells, better—that later when I got run down after a long siege of booze, [and a] theatrical tour with its strain of free—not always—love and of pretending I was pretending to be an actor—the little bugs got me. And at that, thanks to a constitution from my father that I had done my damndest to wreck completely, I only contracted a very slight incipient case."

Still later, while traveling in Europe and hearing of some London newspaper reports that he was dying of tuberculosis in Switzerland, he wrote to a friend in New York: "Even my old doc must laugh. I was the most incipient case he ever had—never coughed a cough in six months, and was pronounced entirely cured."

Nevertheless, Eugene was concerned about his health and on one occasion, ten years after he had been pronounced cured at Gaylord, he was fearful the "little bugs" had returned to make an end of him. He was staying with a friend, Eben Given, in Provincetown, Massachusetts.

"Gene came down with tonsillitis," Given later recalled. "He had a slight hemorrhage and he thought it was a recurrence of T.B.; he was convinced he was going to die. My father, who had some medical knowledge, examined him and was able to assure him that there was nothing wrong except a little burst blood vessel in his throat."

There is no doubt that O'Neill grew acutely conscious of the state of his health once he seriously began writing, at twenty-five. He collected doctors the way a sportsman collects game trophies and proudly sustained friendships and correspondences with many of the dozens of physicians of various specialties and qualifications who were called in to attend him during the last forty years of his life. While it is true that during his final twelve years he was gravely ill—so ill that a series of specialists could do little to help him—it is also true that prior to this period he often imagined himself in worse condition than he actually was, and delighted in bagging a fresh doctor for his collection.

In 1912, when O'Neill became a patient at Gaylord, its guiding force was a thirty-six-year-old Buffalo-born doctor named David Russell Lyman, who had been educated in Virginia. He turned up in O'Neill's play, *The Straw*, as Dr. Stanton, described by O'Neill as follows: "A handsome man . . . with a grave, care-lined studious face lightened by a kindly, humorous smile. His gray eyes, saddened by the suffering they have witnessed, have the sympathetic quality of real understanding. The look they give is full of companionship, the courage-renewing, human companionship of a hope which is shared. He speaks with a slight Southern accent, soft and slurring."

A former T.B. patient himself and later a member of the medical staff of Dr. Edward L. Trudeau's Saranac sanitarium, Dr. Lyman had taken charge of Gaylord at its inception, when he was only twenty-eight. With the devoted assistance of a trained nurse named Florence R. Burgess, a widow nine years his senior, Dr. Lyman helped make Gaylord into a model tuberculosis sanitarium, where new methods were tried and proved. (Mrs. Burgess, in *The Straw*, became Mrs. Turner, "a stout, motherly, capable-looking woman with gray hair.")

In 1912 X-ray had not yet been employed for diagnosis nor had any miracle drugs been discovered to fight the disease. Gaylord placed great emphasis on a homelike, benevolent atmosphere. Training in self-care was stressed, much in the same way that an educational institution might instruct its students. Gaylord patients, in fact, regarded themselves upon discharge as graduates of a beloved alma mater.

Some years after leaving Gaylord O'Neill humorously signed a letter to Dr. Lyman: "Your alumnus, Eugene O'Neill." The patients looked on Dr. Lyman, whom they affectionately called "Dr. David," as a heaven-sent benefactor devoted to their struggle to conquer the disease. Each step toward recovery was like the mastery of a difficult lesson, and was rewarded by a specific privilege.

During the first three or four months of a patient's stay at Gaylord he was confined to bed in the main building, called Tuttle Infirmary, which accommodated thirty-one men and women. As he gained in weight and strength he was allowed, first, the privilege of walking unescorted to the bathroom and, second, taking an unassisted tub bath. If he continued to gain during the next two or three weeks, he was permitted to sit for an hour in a reclining chair between bed periods, then to be transferred to one of several cottages on the grounds, and later to leave bed for one meal, then two, and finally three. If no setback occurred during this time, he was allowed to go to the main hall for social activities, such as playing cards or checkers.

After that came sessions of regulated exercises—first, a daily walk of fifteen minutes, which was gradually increased to one hour in the morning and one hour in the afternoon. By the time he reached this point the patient was ready to be discharged.

Because he had only a touch of T.B., O'Neill moved more rapidly from one step to the next than the majority of patients, whose stays averaged about thirteen months. With the regimen of rest and wholesome food—milk was a diet requirement and most of the supply was produced on the farm—O'Neill gained twelve pounds within four weeks. By the end of January, with his weight up to 158, he was ready to move into a cottage.

Hart Cottage, the gift in 1905 of a New Haven businessman, was of the approved type for tuberculosis patients. Because fresh air was considered an important part of the treatment, O'Neill slept on one of the cottage's two open porches—even in the bitterest winter weather. The enclosed middle section of the cottage, which accommodated four patients, consisted of a dressing room with clothes lockers. By the middle of February O'Neill's weight was found to be above normal, and his appetite good. While he had no cough or fatigue and did not complain of pain, he still had a slight "drawing" sensation at "the right base."

The staff and patients were aware that Eugene was the son of James O'Neill; many of them had seen James in *Monte Cristo*. Not long after his arrival, someone called Eugene's attention to a copy of *Vanity Fair*, which contained an article about a wild champagne party and show put on at the Berkeley Theatre by the Friars Club during the first week of January. The show—a mock trial entitled "A Giggle"—listed James as a member of the cast. He played the defendant "charged with putting the bull in Bull Durham." James was an avid clubman—he belonged to the Lambs and to the Knights of Columbus in addition to the Friars and The Players—and it was a part of his attitude never to let any personal sorrow interfere with his being a good fellow in public. Eugene, however, might have construed James's participation in "A Giggle" as callous and it is not inconceivable that Eugene's antagonism all his life toward joining anything was inspired by rebellion against his father's overwhelming tendency to be hail-fellow-well-met.

Once he realized that he was making progress toward recovery Eugene allowed himself to relax mentally and even enjoy his surroundings. He made friends with several staff members, among whom he was especially drawn to a nurse named Mary Clark. She, too, became a character in *The Straw*; O'Neill called her Miss Gilpin.

Miss Clark was as Irish as Eugene and could respond to him with wit and humor. She was thirty-three when Eugene met her at Gaylord—a tall, dark-haired, dark-eyed, strong-minded woman who had come to the sanitarium as a patient in 1910 and stayed on to work after her recovery. Eugene once referred to Miss Clark as the "angel of old pneumo-thorax" and his fondness for her is recorded in a stanza from a birthday poem he wrote to her on May 24, 1913, which he called "Ballad of the Birthday of the Most Gracious of Ladyes":

> Hope's Hebe to the fever-toss'd!
> (Some figure of speech, you'll agree)
> Kindest of bosses that e'er bossed!
> I'm almost glad to have T.B.
> Else I'd never have met you—see?

And real true friendship's none so rife,
With all my heart I shout to thee—
Top of the morning and long life!

Writing to Miss Clark ten years later, after she had published the poem in a hospital magazine at Eagleville, Pennsylvania, O'Neill declared that although seeing the poem again had given him nostalgic pleasure, he realized its literary merits were negligible. "But—whisper!—I think as a poet I'm a very good playwright," he added.

(In fairness to O'Neill it must be pointed out that he did not, as a mature artist, regard any of his early poetic flights as noteworthy. "Everybody writes poetry when he's young," he once said. And while he reluctantly allowed his *Telegraph* poems and a few more that had been printed in other publications to be collected in a limited-edition bibliography published in 1931, he resisted other efforts to bring out collections of his poetry. "It would be a shame to waste good type on such nonsense," he wrote to one would-be editor in 1936.)

Eugene kept in touch with Mary Clark for many years, and sent her several volumes of his published plays. In one of them—a collection containing *The Straw, The Emperor Jones* and a play called *Diff'rent*, written in 1920—he wrote:

"To Miss Mary A. Clark, with affectionate remembrance of our friendship at Gaylord Farm and of her great and continued kindness to me while I was a patient there—the spirit of which kindness I have tried dimly to portray in 'The Straw' without, however, presuming to make any personal sketches out of the characters in that play." (O'Neill had by that time fallen into the almost automatic habit of denying that any character in any play, however obvious the derivation appeared, was based on an actual person; since he knew that nearly all his plays contained characters recognizable to some people, a blanket denial that he ever drew from life was the safest way to guard himself against recrimination.)

Two other nurses of whom Eugene was fond were Wilhelmina Stamberger and Catherine Murray. Miss Stamberger, when Eugene met her, was twenty-seven—a tall, slender, blonde probationer, or nurse in training, on the Cottage side of the sanitarium. She, too, had previously been a patient at Gaylord; Dr. Lyman had not been optimistic about her chances for recovery, but she had a remarkable fighting spirit. After struggling back to health she studied nursing and returned to Gaylord to practice her new career. Miss Howard, in *The Straw*, is a composite of Miss Stamberger and Miss Murray, who died in the 1920's.

"Catherine Murray was the nurse on duty all through O'Neill's stay at Gaylord," Miss Stamberger recalled after O'Neill's death, when she was in her seventies. "I may have been the outward model for Miss Howard, but Catherine Murray was the one who used to have long chats with O'Neill."

O'Neill has indicated that Miss Murray made a strong impression on him, by borrowing her surname for the hero of *The Straw*. And in a letter to Mary Clark in 1923, after he had lost touch with Miss Murray, he wrote: "How and where is she now, do you know? I remember her interest in my writing, her genuine friendship for me."

The people who at this point in his life—and for the next year or two—took an interest in Eugene's writing earned his undying admiration and gratitude. For Eugene had found what was to be more than his life-work—a reason for life itself, or, more precisely, his reason for having suffered and searched and struggled—his justification for having been born.

O'Neill expressed his public attitude about this discovery in 1923 to a reporter of a little magazine called the *Journal of Outdoor Life:*

"It was at Gaylord that my mind got the chance to establish itself, to digest and valuate the impressions of many past years in which one experience had crowded on another with never a second's reflection. At Gaylord I really thought about my life for the first time, about past and future. Undoubtedly the inactivity forced upon me by the life forced me to mental activity, especially as I had always been highstrung and nervous temperamentally."

He added, however: "No, it isn't exactly true that my first urge to write came at the San. Previous to my breakdown I had done quite a lot of newspaper work . . . and this experience started me, although the work itself was junk of a low order."

Three years earlier, just after *Beyond the Horizon* had opened, calling widespread attention for the first time to O'Neill's talents, he was asked, "What was your early ambition?"

"I didn't have any idea," he said. "My ambition, if you call it that, was to keep moving—to do as many things as I could. I just drifted along till I was twenty-four and then I got a jolt and sat up and took notice. Retribution overtook me and I went down with T.B. It gave me time to think about myself and what I was doing—or, rather, wasn't doing. I got busy writing one-act plays."

Since Eugene's stay at Gaylord lasted less than six months, he only had time to make a tentative start on the one-acters; he completed only one play, *A Wife for a Life*, which he later destroyed and which gave no hint of the direction his creative mind was soon to follow. (This was the play with a mining-camp background, drawn from his Honduras experience.) He later said he had "dashed it off in one night," adding that it had been intended as a vaudeville skit.

"But this was not a play," he maintained. "In fact, my friends in vaudeville crudely insisted it was not a vaudeville skit, either! It was nothing."

At the time he wrote it, though, he thought enough of it to apply for a copyright; the New London *Telegraph* caught his enthusiasm and printed the following item, soon after his return from Gaylord:

"Eugene O'Neill, son of James O'Neill the eminent actor, has written a vaudeville sketch. Mr. O'Neill yesterday received the copyright for the act from Washington. He expects to market it this fall. Mr. O'Neill has considerable literary talent, which was evidenced when he was a member of The Telegraph staff. He heretofore has confined himself to poetry and has written much worthy verse; this is his first venture into theatrical writing."

It was not an auspicious venture, but because it was his first, a sampling of the dialogue should be recorded.

The young hero, Jack, has been in love for a year with his mining partner's wife, Yvette. The partner, designated simply as the Older Man, suspects that his wife, who has since left him, had a lover, but does not know it was Jack, nor does Jack realize that his love is the wife of the Older Man. He proceeds to tell the Older Man about his sad affair:

"One rarely speaks of such things. I've never told you but I will now if you care to hear it. . . . She was the wife of a broken-down mining engineer from the States, over twenty years her senior . . . he was a drunken brute who left her alone most of the time. . . . Personally I never saw him. It was probably better that I did not. You see I fell in love with her on the spot and the thought of how he treated her made my blood boil."

The Older Man, beginning to tumble to the truth, asks, "in stifled tones," which Jack does not notice:

"What was the name of the mining town you mention? I've been in that country [Peru] myself—many years ago."

"San Sebastien," says Jack, naïvely. "Do you know it?"

The Older Man replies, "in a hoarse whisper," that he does.

Jack, still unaware that he is addressing Yvette's husband, tells him the rest of the story.

"I went to see her often," he says. "He was always away it seemed. Finally, people began to talk. Then I realized that the time had come and I told her that I loved her. I shall never forget her face. She looked at me with great calm eyes but her lips trembled as she said: 'I know you love me and I—I love you; but you must go away and we must never see each other again. I am his wife and I must keep my pledge.' "

"You lie!" cries the Older Man, half-drawing his pistol.

"Why what do you mean? What is it," asks Jack, still in the dark.

"Nerves I guess," says the Older Man. This satisfies Jack. After a few more similar exchanges the Older Man decides, nobly, to send Jack off to join Yvette, who now believes herself to be a widow.

"What tricks Fate plays with us," soliloquizes the Older Man. "When he told me his name that first day I noticed that it was the same as the man's I was looking for. But . . . I never for an instant harbored the idea that he could be the John Sloan I was after." His curtain line is: "Greater love hath no man than this that he giveth his wife for his friend."

Awful as it was, *A Wife for a Life* established a new pattern of life for O'Neill. After completing the script he went on, while still at Gaylord, to make notes for several other short plays he was to complete within a year. Abruptly O'Neill found himself transformed from a man of action into a man of inaction. For seven years he had been in violent motion—hell-raising at Princeton, getting himself married and divorced, prospecting in Honduras, touring in vaudeville, shipping to sea, beachcombing, drinking, trying suicide. Finding himself no longer able to make a physical response of violence to everything in life that tormented him, he turned his fury inward—and made the miraculous discovery that he could be a creator instead of a destroyer.

At this crucial moment in his life he was tremendously influenced by two works he read: Dostoevski's *The Idiot* and Strindberg's recently translated play, *The Dance of Death.*

He once told Manuel Komroff, one of his editors at Boni and Liveright when that house was publishing his plays, that if it had not been for these two works he might never have begun writing. They were, in his words, tangible evidence that "a powerful emotional ecstasy, approaching a kind of frenzy," could be communicated by a writer. *The Idiot* and *The Dance of Death,* said O'Neill, had "the feeling and sensation" he wished to communicate to an audience.

Strindberg was by far the stronger of the two influences, for he had not only chosen the literary medium to which O'Neill felt drawn but had an outlook on certain aspects of life that came uncannily close to O'Neill's own. *The Dance of Death* struck an overwhelmingly responsive chord. In that powerful and monstrous play Strindberg put into words what other people found incredible and repulsive, but what O'Neill had for a long time recognized as one of the motivating forces of his parents' relationship with each other and the resultant effect upon him. Compare Jim's speech

in *All God's Chillun Got Wings*—"I can't leave her. She can't leave me"
—with Alice's speech about her husband in *The Dance of Death*: "We
have been trying to part every single day—but we are chained together
and cannot break away." And, in reply to the family friend's comment,
"Then he loves you," Alice says, "Probably. But that does not prevent him
from hating me." Strindberg summed up what O'Neill had not before
seen so pungently stated: "It is called love-hatred, and it hails from the
pit!"

Even Strindberg's ideas about the appropriate way to commit suicide
matched O'Neill's. In *The Dance of Death*, Alice's daughter, Judith,
suffering over the threat of separation from her young lover, speaks of
killing herself with him by swimming out into the sea until they drown.
"There would be style in that," she says.

Strindberg was more than a literary kindred spirit to O'Neill; like
O'Neill's other literary hero, Nietzsche, he became in some ways a pattern
for O'Neill's life. The son of incompatible parents—his mother was a
barmaid and his father believed he had married beneath him—Strindberg
was constantly tortured; he was an iconoclast and a mystic, a bold innovator
in the theatre, and often misunderstood and condemned. He too was
driven by furies, unable to cope with marriage, fated to disastrous relationships with his wives, mistresses and children. He died in May, 1912—
the month and year that O'Neill had tried to commit suicide.

In 1936, accepting the Nobel Prize, O'Neill acknowledged his debt
to "that greatest genius of all modern dramatists, your August Strindberg."

"It was reading his plays," O'Neill said, "when I first started to write,
back in the winter of 1913-14, that, above all else, first gave me the vision
of what modern drama could be, and first inspired me with the urge to
write for the theatre myself. If there is anything of lasting worth in my
work, it is due to that original impulse from him, which has continued as
my inspiration down all the years since then—to the ambition I received
then to follow in the footsteps of his genius as worthily as my talent might
permit, and with the same integrity of purpose."

O'Neill found that in writing he could escape from a hostile world. He
could belong. "As long as you have a job on hand that absorbs all your
mental energy you haven't much worry to spare over other things,"
O'Neill informed a young author many years later, adding, "It serves as a
suit of armor." Once this realization took hold, Eugene found that writing
was his life, that without writing as the focal point of his existence he
had no life.

In 1924 O'Neill made a devastatingly revealing comment to Dr.

Lyman, who had sent him a routine medical inquiry for Gaylord's records. In response to the printed query, "How much [working] time have you lost from vacations?" O'Neill wrote: "Writing is my vacation from living—so I don't need vacations."

O'Neill came to regard his recovery from illness at Gaylord and his simultaneous discovery that he was a dramatist as a kind of rebirth. He once described this period at Gaylord as "the time I should have been cast down by my fate—and wasn't." Seven months after he had left the sanitarium he wrote to Dr. Lyman: "I am looking forward to some fine spring day when I shall be able to pay the Farm a visit. . . . If, as they say, it is sweet to visit the place one was born in, then it will be doubly sweet for me to visit the place I was reborn in—for my second birth was the only one which had my full approval."

A few years later—in 1919—he said in a letter to Dr. Lyman:

"In the measure that I love my work, and am proud to have been able to do the little I have, so much the more deep is my gratitude to you and to Gaylord Farm for *saving* me for it. My blessings on the Farm 'spring eternal,' and the recollections of my stay there are, and always will be, among the most pleasant of my memories."

Perhaps only an O'Neill could have counted a bout with tuberculosis among his cherished moments. Certainly those moments, besides revealing his mission, continued to influence his work for many years. The firsthand knowledge of tuberculosis gained at Gaylord was applied in a number of his plays, starting with *The Web,* which he wrote right after leaving the sanitarium. The heroine of his second play is a victim of the disease, as is the hero of *Beyond the Horizon,* and, of course, the autobiographical protagonist of *Long Day's Journey Into Night.* But O'Neill's most vividly and distressingly tuberculous heroine and his most comprehensive discussion of the disease occur in *The Straw.*

Eileen Carmody was the name O'Neill chose for his pathetic heroine, and she, too, had an actual counterpart at Gaylord. Her story did not end as romantically or as sentimentally as Eileen's, however.

Eileen was modeled on Catherine Mackay, a girl from Waterbury, Connecticut, nicknamed Kitty. Like Eileen, she was from a large, Irish, working-class family. A fellow patient at Gaylord described her as "not really pretty, but a girl with depth." O'Neill's description of Eileen in *The Straw* was probably applicable to Kitty Mackay, except for her age, from which he subtracted a few years:

"Her wavy mass of dark hair is parted in the middle and combed low on her forehead, covering her ears, to a knot at the back of her head. The oval of her face is spoiled by a long, rather heavy, Irish jaw contrasting with the delicacy of her other features. Her eyes are large and blue, confident in their compelling candor and sweetness; her lips, full and red, half-open, over strong even teeth, droop at the corners into an expression of wistful sadness; her clear complexion is unnaturally striking in its contrasting colors, rose and white; her figure is slight and undeveloped."

When Eugene met Kitty in March, 1913, she was twenty-three. She had been a patient at Gaylord for five months about a year before, and though not as much improved as Dr. Lyman would have wished her to be, had been discharged in May, 1912, because, as the sanitarium report put it, she was "worrying greatly over home affairs."

Her mother was dead and several young children at home were demanding her attention—a fact her father did not spare her on his visits to the sanitarium. Kitty had an aunt and a grandmother living in New Jersey and it was arranged for her to go there with the two younger children. "Relatives can look after them and patient can sleep out and take cure there," Kitty's report read. "Patient worrying so, the above course seems best under the circumstances."

But by the end of the year Kitty's condition had deteriorated, and after an exchange of letters with Dr. Lyman, she was readmitted to Gaylord, this time as a charity case, so that her father would not have to shoulder the expense. Her chances of arresting the disease were now considered only fair.

Kitty drew Eugene's attention almost at once. Employing his usual technique, he set about educating her. An unworldly girl and an emotional one, she responded to Eugene with more fervor than he had anticipated and with far more than was healthy for her. Gaylord had a strict rule about emotional entanglements among its patients: "Scatter your attention; Do not concentrate."

"The interference of the healthy heart with the cure of the sick lung is . . . a real problem to me," Dr. Lyman once wrote with specific reference to O'Neill and Kitty. There were, technically, two things for which a patient could be asked to leave Gaylord. One was a love affair and the other was drinking. Eugene broke both of these rules. He pursued a romance with Kitty and occasionally slipped into town at night for beer. Dr. Lyman later confided to Doc Ganey, whom he met in New London, that Eugene had been "a problem." That he did not send him away was possibly due to the fact that Eugene was not there long enough for his misbehavior to be fully documented.

For Kitty, the problem was more serious. She was much sicker than Eugene and knew that being sent away from Gaylord would amount to a death warrant; no other institution was inclined to accept a patient who had proved undesirable elsewhere. And without care the patient was liable to die of the disease. Kitty took chances nevertheless—to her ultimate sorrow.

One of Kitty's roommates, Emma Halper, later expressed astonishment that the romance could have flourished as it did, although she was aware that Kitty was emotionally involved and often unhappy. Emma considered herself responsible for the three fellow patients with whom she shared a bungalow. She was the oldest and had had a long bout with tuberculosis.

"It must have been almost impossible for them to meet and be alone," Emma said. "Kitty was always in bed in our cottage at the proper time, and if she sneaked out later to meet Eugene, I certainly didn't know about it. They couldn't have had much time together during the day either. One of the ways Gaylord had of enforcing the nonromance rule was the manner in which the patients' daily walks were scheduled; on one day the men would walk the Cheshire Road and the women would walk the Wallingford Road. Next day they'd switch. Patients of both sexes did congregate in the main hall at designated social hours, and that is where Eugene and Kitty first met."

Emma had her initial inkling of Kitty's interest in Eugene when she came back from Mass one day. Looking pensive, she told Emma, "Gene wasn't there." Emma soon realized that Kitty was falling in love. It began with her borrowing books from Eugene (he had brought so many with him to Gaylord that the porter who cleaned his bungalow used to mutter, "That man and his damned books"). Much as it had been with Maibelle, the relationship between Eugene and Kitty revolved around her being a dutiful student. But Eugene did not treat Kitty as gingerly as he had Maibelle. He mocked her Catholicism and enjoyed shocking and confusing her. It was evident to the other patients that she cared far more for him than he did for her.

As a matter of fact, Eugene still fancied himself in love with Maibelle. He wrote her in Florida of his daily progress, sent her snapshots of himself and his nurses, and described his interest in Kitty. He may, however, have detected a coolness in Maibelle's response, for one day he showed Kitty a picture of Maibelle and remarked, "See her? She's through."

Eugene wrote also to Olive Evans, and sent her a poem he had written about Kitty. For Maibelle, he composed a tender love poem called "To Maibelle from a Recliner."

Having established himself, to his own satisfaction, as something of a rake, and full of assurance about his future, O'Neill found by the end of May that his case was arrested and that he was free to leave Gaylord. He now weighed 162 pounds—a gain of sixteen since his admission—and was considered as fit as anyone could be who had just had tuberculosis. He wrote to tell his father that he was ready to come home, and James responded to the news with an anxious letter to Dr. Lyman indicating his fear that Eugene's condition might still be infectious; was it true, James asked, that no one, not even Eugene's "ailing mother," could become infected with tuberculosis by "living in the same house and eating at the same table" with Eugene? James went on to imply that, rather than jeopardize Ella's health, he would arrange to have Eugene go elsewhere for the summer.

If Dr. Lyman was surprised by this letter, he gave James only the slightest hint of it. He replied that in Eugene's case there was no danger of contagion, adding, "in his present condition he would not be a menace to anyone."

Apparently James was shamed. He wrote to Eugene, asking him to return to New London.

Dr Lyman cautioned Eugene, in parting, to rest for the summer and to avoid all strenuous exertion for the next year, though he could resume work in the fall. He was told he was in "A-1 shape," and the prognosis was excellent.

O'Neill left Gaylord on June 3. He said good-by to Kitty without a qualm. She was discharged six months later and returned to the tedium of her life in Waterbury. She never saw Eugene again.

In *The Straw*, O'Neill has his hero, Stephen, leave the sanitarium knowing that Eileen is in love with him but unable to reciprocate her love. He returns four months later on a visit to find her dying and heroically determines to marry her in an effort to restore her will to live. To his own astonishment he finds that he truly loves her and forces himself to believe that her life can be saved. "We'll win together. We can! We must!" says Stephen to the nurse-superintendent. "Happiness will cure! Love is stronger than—Oh, why did you give me a hopeless hope?" The implication, however, is that they will win through, clutching "the straw" of the title.

But for Kitty there had been no hope at all. A little over a year after leaving Gaylord she was dead.

XXII

EUGENE RETURNED TO NEW LONDON WITH A DAWNING sense of tolerance for his father and a deeper sense of pity and compassion for his mother. Illness seemed to have broadened his capacity for understanding his family, and his newfound determination to write had somewhat increased his ability to be objective about them. "We were a very close family—*too* close," he said later.

Dimly aware that Eugene was taking the first steps that might lead him out of the emotional miasma that bound all the O'Neills, the other members of the family regrouped. Ella and Jamie draw closer to each other, making James feel more an outsider; and James, in turn, attempted to ingratiate himself with Eugene by praising *A Wife for a Life* and offering to appear in the skit in vaudeville—if he could find backing.

Jamie, who had always believed that his mother needed to be protected from his father, considered himself her only mainstay. Sick in mind and soul, and without Eugene's tough-mindedness and spiritual resources, Jamie could persuade himself that his tender devotion to his mother gave his own life some justification. He continued to drink steadily but quietly through the summer, spending most of his time in the house as a self-appointed buffer between Ella and occasional visitors—mostly family or friends of Eugene. On such occasions Jamie would usually find an excuse for his mother to withdraw, citing her poor health and her need for rest.

When Ella was up to it, she would accompany Jamie on short motor trips or visits. Once, out for a walk with Ella, Jamie suggested dropping in on a family in the undertaking business. Scandalized at the idea of visiting the "shanty Irish K——s," Ella said she preferred to call on the S——s, a respectable but dull family. "What's the difference?" asked Jamie. "You go to one you see stiffs; you go to the other you see stiffs."

Ella was amused by Jamie in spite of herself and appreciated his companionship. She found him easier to be with than Eugene, who made her feel guilty over her failure as a mother.

Though Jamie devoted himself to Ella, he sometimes grumbled about his role to friends. He told his cousin Phil Sheridan, "I'm the goat for this family—not only the goat, but the nannygoat."

Jamie, at this time, was suffering from the pangs of unrequited love for a beautiful and popular actress named Pauline Frederick, who was in the cast, with him and his father, of *Joseph and His Brethren.* (The play had been running successfully on Broadway since January, 1913, and was to go on tour in September, after a summer layoff.) Pauline had long, black hair and had been likened by at least one contemporary critic, to Cleopatra. She was fond of Jamie, but refused to marry him unless he gave up drinking. Though Jamie tried several times to meet this requirement, he could never stay on the wagon for more than a few weeks at a time. All during the summer he continued to woo her wistfully by sending her a dozen roses almost daily, with money he begged from his father.

Joseph and His Brethren, a lush biblical spectacle that featured fifty sheep, three camels, several donkeys and an elephant, in addition to a human cast of ninety—not counting supers—had been mounted by George Tyler at Broadway's Century Theatre; it represented the public enthusiasm for Eastern pageantry that had been stirred a bit earlier, also by Tyler, with *Garden of Allah.*

James, who doubled in the roles of the 106-year-old Jacob and Pharaoh, had scored a personal triumph in the play, as had Miss Frederick, who played Zuleika, and the young actor, Brandon Tynan, who starred as Joseph. Jamie played the minor role of Naphtali.

Eugene, heeding Dr. Lyman's advice, spent the summer relaxing and reading and making notes for future work. He began seeing Maibelle again, but less often than before his illness.

"I had matured," Maibelle recalled, "and was less impressed with Gene's worldliness; some of the glamour had worn off for me." Eugene did not importune Maibelle, but saw her when she wished—and began expanding his field of operations among other "nice" girls of New London who, he had discovered, were neither as frightening nor as inaccessible as he had formerly thought.

His continued progress as a rake was made considerably easier for him by the fact that in September, when James and Ella closed the New London house and left with Jamie to rejoin *Joseph and His Brethren,* Eugene moved across Pequot Avenue to live and board with a family named Rippin, which included three attractive, unmarried daughters in their twenties—all, from Eugene's point of view, in urgent need of intellectual enlightenment.

The Rippin family was a matriarchy dominated by Helen Maude Rippin. Tall, motherly, resourceful, she was the youngest of twenty children, who had grown up in the English village of Whitney on the Wye. She married James Rippin in Rutland, England, and they came to New

London one Guy Fawkes Day in the 1880's. A wonderful cook and a lively raconteur, Mrs. Rippin had an endless supply of energy, humor and homely wisdom. With her husband, who was shorter, quieter and more self-effacing, she moved into a brown-shingle house, called "the Packard," in 1907.

The front of the house faced Pequot Avenue and the back looked out on the Thames. In 1913 it was still one of the few houses on the river side of Pequot Avenue. Its high back porch, built over the basement, seemed suspended above the narrow beach and commanded a view of the harbor and the Groton shore line, then a serene expanse of greenery broken only by a few well-spaced, stately homes, set back from the riverbank. When a storm was brewing, and the harbor was crowded with schooners seeking shelter, yachts would tie up at the narrow Rippin dock; while waiting out the storm, their owners accepted the Rippins' invitation to help themselves to water from the big, round well at the side of the house.

Not long after moving into the Packard, Helen Rippin began taking in boarders. The house, built on an incline, was bigger than it looked from the Pequot Avenue side. On the beach side, below the porch, a large dining room had been created, which was entered from a stairway in the upper—or living room—level of the house. The O'Neills occasionally took their midday meals at the Rippins'. One of the daughters, Jessica, who was still living in the Packard many years later, retained vivid memories of those summer days in the early 1900's.

"James O'Neill wasn't the only celebrity who boarded here," she said. "A lot of famous people used to eat with us. People liked to come here. It was like a private home; my mother cooked, and my sisters and I helped serve. We didn't take in strangers."

But the O'Neills did not want to eat in the general dining room with the others, and so were served in a private alcove at one end of the room, at a table near the window that faced the river. When, as often happened, they were late for their meal, the Rippin sisters watched for them, because the sooner the girls could clean up, the sooner they could have time for themselves. James and Ella would walk together with Jamie and Gene following behind. They would poke along, single-file, down the stairs to the dining room. James would sit at the head of the table, his wife at the foot, and the two boys between them. To the Rippin girls, they all seemed taciturn and moody, although not impolite. They struck Jessica as "a funny bunch."

Both Jessica and her sister Emily, who was the family beauty and served as waitress, were aware that there was something not quite right about Ella.

"On several occasions," Emily once said, "Mrs. O'Neill acted as though she didn't know me. She looked pale and strange, and at first I thought she was sick. When she was like that, she'd push the plates away from her, not seeming to notice when food spilled from them onto the table or floor. Mr. O'Neill and the boys ignored her, and went on eating as though nothing were wrong."

Both sisters have remembered being startled once when Ella, after being served, moved her arm in a wooden gesture and swept off the table all the plates and cutlery that were before her. James, beyond making a brief apology to Emily, took no notice of the incident, nor did the boys. Jessica and Emily began to suspect that Ella drank; but their mother assured them that Ella was "not that kind of woman." Mrs. Rippin had no satisfactory explanation for her behavior, however.

Sometimes, as had been the case when the O'Neills boarded at the Youngs', Ella did not turn up at all at mealtime.

"Mamma won't be down today. She doesn't feel well," Eugene would tell one of the Rippins. And a basket would be prepared for her, which the boys would take home. Often the basket would contain cornmeal muffins, of which Ella was fond.

Mrs. Rippin, who did all the cooking herself, was devoted to James, and James, who had an Irishman's deep-rooted prejudice against the English, was willing to overlook Mrs. Rippin's unfortunate origins, partly because she made excellent corned beef and cabbage and Irish stew. He treated her with the utmost gallantry, often bowing before addressing her in the stance of the old romantic actor, his head back, and one shoulder held higher than the other.

"I've traveled all over the world," he once told her, "and have never found anyone who could cook meat the way you do." He fell into the habit of greeting Mrs. Rippin as his "Portia," and amused her by coming into the kitchen after his meal and giving a private recitation. Sometimes he gave her lines to learn and would play a scene with her on the following day, to the delight of her daughters. Mrs. Rippin adored this, but her husband was inclined to be sulky about it, so the scenes were usually played behind his back.

Emily was about as close to being an intimate friend of Ella as anyone in New London. Ella indicated her fondness for Emily by inviting her on automobile rides from time to time. They would be driven five or six miles into the country and, though Ella did not talk much, she seemed to enjoy having Emily sit with her. She once told Emily that she had gone through two fortunes, and that was why her husband would not let her have any money. Another time she told her about Gene's troubles with his first wife.

Ella occasionally visited Mrs. Rippin in the evening. Once she came to call with Jamie, who was always a welcome visitor at the Packard.

"He would keep you laughing," Jessica recalled. "We all loved him; his only fault was liquor." The Rippins, with the exception of the quiet father, were a high-spirited family, who enjoyed their own private jokes and were a trifle ill at ease in Ella's presence. They stood on less ceremony with Jamie and Eugene. Jamie, in fact, took Emily out once on a date. When they returned, Eugene rudely teased Jamie, in front of Emily, by remarking, "What a drop from Pauline Frederick!"

When Eugene went to stay with the Rippins in the fall of 1913, it was understood that the arrangement was to be more in the nature of a personal favor to James O'Neill than a formal business arrangement. James undertook to send Mrs. Rippin a weekly check of $13, of which $12 was to pay for Eugene's room and board and one was to be his personal allowance.

"If Eugene comes to stay with us," Mrs. Rippin told James, "he'll have to live as simply as we do." James agreed to this, and Eugene found himself with no choice but to live a wholesome life.

"With his dollar a week he didn't have much to spend on girls or liquor," Emily later said. "He'd often walk into town because he didn't have trolley fare. And quite often we would buy cigarettes for him because he couldn't afford them. As far as I know, he didn't drink; I certainly never saw him drunk during the nine or ten months he stayed with us." Those months, in addition to proving the most healthful he had ever spent, were also the most productive. Shortly before Mrs. Rippin's death in 1941 Eugene wrote her that living in her home had helped him become the playwright he was.

O'Neill was given a room that opened onto the back porch. He used the porch itself to sleep on, simulating conditions at the sanitarium. The Rippins hung rugs at one end of the porch to shelter him from the wind, and he slept out on the coldest winter nights, with the sound of small breakers washing up on the beach below him and the harsh call of gulls to wake him in the morning. He had a black-and-white cat named Friday to keep him company. Friday, who was put out every night, considered Eugene a fellow outcast. Many years later, in a letter to the Rippins, O'Neill referred nostalgically to "that winter . . . when Friday used to climb to my porch on zero nights and crawl into the bed with me, leaving the rat he had killed thoughtfully on the floor for me to step on in case Nature called me to get up."

O'Neill built up his health by taking midwinter dips from the Rippins' beach. "At the risk of gaining a reputation for eccentricity before my literary fame warrants such an indulgence," O'Neill wrote to Dr. Lyman, "I have gone in swimming in this Long Island Sound at least once a week ever since I left Gaylord last June. I haven't missed a single week. The coldest the water has ever been when I took my plunge was thirty-three degrees. I haven't had a cold (hear me rap wood) nor has the Demon Tonsillitis, formerly a familiar spirit of mine, paid me a single visit. I thought this might interest you as a 'lunger's' experience."

He enclosed a snapshot, taken by one of the Rippin sisters. It showed a well-muscled, scowling young man, dressed in a two-piece bathing suit, standing on a strip of beach with the water and the Groton shore line visible behind him. On the picture, O'Neill wrote, "Taken—(cross my heart)—Jan. 1, 1914, New London, Conn. Water—39°. At his feet, Eugene drew an arrow pointing to a patch of snow, and beneath this, he scribbled the quotation:

> The uniform 'e wore
> Was nothin' much before
> And rather less than 'arf o' that be'ind.

"I was in bed with tonsillitis one cold winter day, and my doctor was visiting," Emily once said, "when Gene happened to walk past my door, wearing his bathing suit. The doctor wanted to know who that was and where he was going in that outfit. I told him Gene was going swimming. The doctor went outside and watched Gene run up and down the beach, which had clumps of ice on it, and then plunge into the icy water. The doctor came back and told me, 'That boy is crazy.'"

Although O'Neill was supposed to have his meals with the family, Mrs. Rippin thought he would be more comfortable eating alone, and considerately served him a tray in his room. He ate ravenously and uncritically, with an appetite that had been trained at Gaylord.

"His coffee cup used to shake in his hands when he first came to stay with us," Jessica observed. "But after about four months, the trembling got better."

O'Neill seemed to relax and blend into his environment more thoroughly at the Rippins' than he had ever done in New London. He grew extremely casual about the way he dressed. He went about in old, dirty, white ducks and the worn American Line jersey he had salvaged from his sea years, and often went barefoot—a habit that probably accounted for a three-month siege of hookworm, from which he was recovering in September.

"He felt fancy dressing was for the capitalists; he had all those anarchist ideas," Jessica recalled tartly. "He would write long, radical poems and read them to us. One of them was published in Emma Goldman's magazine" (*Mother Earth*).

Another poem was published in the New York *Call*, a socialist newspaper, in May, 1914. Called "Fratricide," it was a scathing attack on capitalism, a defense of the labor movement, and a plea for pacifism rolled into one. A nineteen-stanza poem, these verses are typical:

> Ho, ho, my friend, and think you so?
> And have you not ready history?
> This much of war, at least, we know:
> The jingoes are the first to flee.
> The plutocrats who cause the woe
> Are arrogant but cowardly. . . .
>
> The army of the poor must fight,
> New taxes come to crush them down.
> They feel the iron fist of Might
> Press on their brows the thorny crown.
> They see the oily smile of Right.
> They don the sacrificial gown. . . .
>
> What cause could be more asinine
> Than yours, ye slaves of bloody toil?
> Is not your bravery sublime
> Beneath a tropic sun to broil
> And bleed and groan—for Guggenheim!
> And give your lives for—Standard Oil! . . .
>
> Comrades, awaken to new birth!
> New values on the tables write!
> What is your vaunted courage worth
> Unless you rise up in your might
> And cry: "All workers on the earth
> Are brothers and WE WILL NOT FIGHT!"

Although O'Neill knew how to be gravely and charmingly polite, he seldom bothered to produce any polish for the Rippin girls.

"He slouched, shuffled and mumbled," Jessica said, with distaste. (O'Neill's father had been trying for years to correct Eugene's slovenliness. "Get that hump off your back; straighten up and let the words come out," James would say.)

During the time O'Neill was boarding with her family Jessica was working at a school in Philadelphia. She came home only for weekends and holidays. (The third sister, Dolly, who lived at home, was less interested in O'Neill than her sisters. She held a job in a dentist's office in New London, but was at home in the evening.)

Jessica, a year older than O'Neill, who was now twenty-five, was somewhat contemptuous of what she considered his parasitical existence. But she did not dislike him; actually, she found him rather appealing, in spite of her disapproval of his character. A tall brunette with blue eyes and a keen sense of humor, Jessica enjoyed watching O'Neill's maneuvers. ("He was always trying to 'make' us," she said.) He began in his usual way, by attacking what he considered her unenlightened mind; he gave her a copy of Boccaccio's *The Decameron*, and sat and watched her reaction as she read it. Reacting like any properly brought up girl, Jessica was embarrassed—and delighted. Next O'Neill proceeded to tell her in detail of his sundry love affairs.

"He used to talk of girls as 'pigs,'" Jessica said.

One day, when Jessica and O'Neill went for a walk, he told her about his plan for "the perfect marriage." Jessica thought it was disgusting and cynical—precisely what O'Neill wanted her to think.

"My wife and I will live on a barge," he said. "I'll live at one end and she'll live at the other, and we'll never see each other except when the urge strikes us."

Jessica was repelled by O'Neill's ideas but enjoyed his companionship; what made it even more enjoyable was the knowledge that her father disliked the young man and disapproved of his presence in the Packard. Mr. Rippin, with three unmarried daughters in his house, had protested against taking O'Neill as a boarder. It was only because his wife was fond of Eugene and laughed at her husband's fears that he finally accepted the plan.

Even before O'Neill began living at the Packard, Mr. Rippin would station himself in the basement when the O'Neill boys paid a call in the evening; much to the girls' embarrassment, he would bang on the furnace as a signal that the visit had lasted long enough.

Jessica was usually careful not to give her father cause for alarm. But once she was frightened. O'Neill took her in his rowboat to a cove on the Groton side of the Thames. They went blueberry picking on the shore and O'Neill happend to sit down on a ripe blueberry patch. As they were about to row back home, Jessica noticed, not without mirth, that his white ducks had been stained a vivid blue. Fearful that her father would conclude that she had been dallying among the berries with

O'Neill, she persuaded him to sit in the water and try to soak off the circumstantial evidence, but it stayed on. Jessica's heart was in her mouth as she distracted her father's cold eye from O'Neill, who sidled awkwardly into his room to change when they got home.

O'Neill, too, was afraid of Mr. Rippin. Once he was swimming off the Rippin dock and came up and found Jessica standing there. He joined her and started talking to her, but he happened to look toward the house and saw Mr. Rippin watching. "I see your father," he mumbled, and hastily dived back into the water. ("You astound me by what you say of your father's interest in articles about me!" O'Neill wrote to Jessica in 1926. "I had imagined I was forever in his bad graces. But perhaps he is looking for the resounding knocks, what?") But his fear of Mr. Rippin in 1913 did not prevent his trying to kiss Jessica, whose interest in him did not extend along those lines.

"Who would want to kiss that cruel mouth?" Jessica once asked, with a recollective shudder.

Emily was slightly more receptive. She, too, came in for a share of Eugene's educational program, and because she was the only sister who was always at home—it was her job to help her mother with the running of the household—she was more consistently exposed to Eugene's persuasive personality. She also read *The Decameron*.

"My father knew the book," she recalled, "and when he heard we were reading it he was furious; we had to hide it to finish it."

Emily was less harsh than Jessica in her judgment of Eugene.

"He had a beautiful smile—when he smiled," she remembered. "But he could get a mean look on his face at times." Emily, who took after her father, was the shortest member of the Rippin family; a brunette, with hazel eyes, a rosebud mouth and a seductively full figure, she was a matter of some concern to Mr. Rippin, though her mother was not worried about her safety. Mrs. Rippin trusted O'Neill and considered that she had done her maternal duty by warning Emily never to let a man kiss her until she was engaged. Emily's response to this advice was, "I couldn't miss all those kisses," and Mrs. Rippin would tell her jokingly that she was a bad girl, and smile indulgently.

"Gene was not a rapist," Emily remarked. "You were safe with him as long as you wanted to be safe." And Emily concluded, after allowing Eugene to give her an experimental kiss, that she wanted to be safe. But this did not alter the casual, friendly, flirtatious tenor of her relationship with him. This relationship was regarded with suspicion not only by her father but also by a married brother who was often at the house.

"One day my mother and father had to go uptown," Emily recalled, "and Gene told me that he'd like to walk me uptown a little later on, when he had to go to the library to meet Maibelle. My brother, who happened to be visiting and had been about to leave, announced he was staying when he heard what Gene said. He was afraid to let me stay alone in the house with Gene. Later, when we walked uptown together, I told Gene why my brother had stayed home. From then on, he called my brother 'Mr. Platitude.' "

O'Neill treated Emily to the same discourses on women with which he regaled Jessica. He told her, apropos of the girl-on-a-barge relationship, that he would leave the girl there to drift and shift for herself when he'd had enough of her. (Apparently this was an image that appealed strongly to him; he never carried out the plan, but some years later he set Anna Christie's love affair with a sailor on a barge.)

According to Emily, "He was always talking about women. He seemed very lustful; he'd go into details about the nights he'd spent with women, and how long he'd stayed with each of them." He also tried to speak to Emily of his mother but could seldom manage more than a halting reference to her.

"My room was near Gene's, and he'd sometimes walk in and talk to me in the morning," Emily said. "I think he suspected I knew something was wrong with his mother." Once he told Emily that Ella had recently been away to a sanitarium.

"My mother was ill, but she's better now," he added.

O'Neill was treated pretty much as a member of the family, especially by Mrs. Rippin, of whom he grew extremely fond. Having never had her brand of warmth from his own mother, he accepted, almost with awe, the mothering she proffered; he would often stand or sit near her while she attended to domestic chores, listening to her homely advice and basking in the maternal strength she exuded. Mrs. Rippin was white-haired, with hazel eyes like Emily's, a figure that was ample but not stout, and an erect carriage; her most distinguishing feature was a smooth, unwrinkled complexion, which she kept till the day she died.

Once, when O'Neill had been complaining to Emily that most girls grew to look like their mothers, Emily said, "I guess I'll look like mine." O'Neill regarded Emily with new interest. "That's all right," he replied.

Mrs. Rippin, aware that O'Neill lacked a sense of warmth in his own family, drew him as much as she could into the bosom of her own. That Christmas O'Neill had his first experience with a united family holiday. Mrs. Rippin gravely took his suggestion about the color of the winter bathrobes she was sewing as Christmas gifts for her daughters, and she was touched by his surprise and gratitude at finding gifts for himself from all the Rippins on Christmas Day. Later that evening he bought four boxes of candy for the Rippin women. He told Jessica that he had never bought a gift for a girl before.

"If he could get by on a poem," Jessica later observed, "that pleased him no end." O'Neill had presented Emily with a "Ballad to Emmy" three days before Christmas, which touched and flattered her. In it he referred to her "form divine" and her "sparkling eyes."

Although Emily and O'Neill kept up a tender, if lighthearted flirtation, both were simultaneously occupied in other romantic pursuits. Not long after, Emily became engaged to the man she eventually married.

"Eugene always had a photograph of a girl in his room," Emily recalled, "but it was not always the same girl. And he'd moon about whichever was the current one, while playing some popular record like 'Song of Araby' or 'Tango' on the victrola. I guess Maibelle was his strongest interest most of the time, but there were others."

Actually O'Neill's romance with Maibelle was drawing to an end. The truth was, as she confided to him not long after, that she had met and fallen in love with a young Coast Guard officer; this was early in 1914, and soon after she decided to marry him. He was handsome, soft-spoken, gentle-mannered and substantial; to Maibelle he appeared a far more promising matrimonial prospect than Eugene.

XXIII

DURING HIS STAY WITH THE RIPPIN FAMILY, FROM September, 1913, to March, 1914, O'Neill completed at least six one-act plays and a full length one. The exact number is difficult to determine because he destroyed some of his early efforts and gave conflicting accounts of the nature and scope of his work during this period.

He told the Rippin sisters, in 1926, that he had never done as much work in so short a space of time as he had in the winter spent at their home. Adding that he did not like to attract undue attention to the plays he wrote there, he said: "They are pretty bad and the less remembered about them, the better."

In one published account of work accomplished during that period O'Neill listed ten plays. But ten years later, in 1935, he compiled for the critic Richard Dana Skinner a list which included for the same period only six plays; he stated at the time that "nothing of importance" had been written after that until the summer of 1916. Still later, in 1946, he revised the count to ten one-act plays and two full-length ones. "That's the year I thought I was God," he told an interviewer. "I'd finish them and rush down to the post office to ship them off to Washington to be copyrighted before somebody stole them."

In any case, of the plays completed at the Rippins' the only ones that have survived in published form—seven in all—are *The Web, Fog, Thirst, Recklessness, Warnings, Abortion* (the script in which he evoked his Princeton days), and one three-act drama, *Servitude. Abortion* and *Servitude,* together with *A Wife for a Life* (which he completed at the tuberculosis sanitarium) and two plays written shortly after his stay at the Rippins', were published without O'Neill's permission in 1950 as *The Lost Plays of Eugene O'Neill.* A publisher had seized on O'Neill's negligence in allowing the copyrights to expire; O'Neill would have preferred them to remain unknown.

His first attempt at the Rippins' in the early fall of 1913 was *The Web,* originally entitled *The Cough,* about the tuberculous prostitute, the pimp and the gangster. Writing in 1944 to Mark Van Doren, teacher and poet, to whom, at Van Doren's request, O'Neill was sending the original manuscript of *The Web,* O'Neill said, "I love it, but I sure don't like it." (He was parting with the manuscript for the benefit of a War Bond Drive, and it was later presented to Princeton University.)

When writing the play, he labored over the opening speech, delivered by the prostitute, Rose:

"Gawd! What a night! (*laughing bitterly*) What a chance I got!" was the way he finally left it. His first draft also included such overwrought lines as: "and he'll make me go, too (*with sudden hatred*) damn him! If I only had some coin I'd soon tell him what I think of him, him and his kind! But there ain't a sou in the place."

In *The Web,* melodramatic as it is, can be detected the first glimmer of what became one of O'Neill's chief literary preoccupations—the inevitable crushing down of Man by Fate, the "hopeless hope" through which Man, striving for the unattainable, wills his own defeat, and the tragic nobility of this losing battle. The plight of the prostitute, Rose, though she is scarcely a figure of noble proportions, becomes briefly poignant when she seizes on the hopeless hope of a new life offered by the gangster; obviously, her dream has no chance of fulfillment, and when the pimp shoots the gangster, making it seem as though Rose has killed him, fate has her where it wants her. "She seems to be aware of something in the room which none of the others can see," O'Neill wrote in the stage directions, "—perhaps the personification of the ironic life force that has crushed her."

The same theme recurs in three more of the seven plays O'Neill is known to have written with hectic intensity in his little room at the Rippins'. In *Thirst* it is the sun, glaring down "like a great angry eye of God," which symbolizes relentless fate. The play, representing O'Neill's only recorded brush with cannibalism (a subject Tennessee Williams was to explore more thoroughly four decades later), focuses on a Dancer, a Gentleman and a West Indian Mulatto Sailor adrift on the life raft of a wrecked steamer. The Dancer and the Gentleman, driven mad by thirst, suspect the silent Sailor of hoarding water. The Dancer offers herself to him, but he resists her, stolidly insisting he has no water. The Dancer finally dies, and the Sailor takes out his knife, muttering, "We will live now. . . . We shall eat. We shall drink." The horrified Gentleman pushes the Dancer's body from the raft, the Sailor stabs the Gentleman and loses his own balance, and the two fall into the shark-infested water.

Fog, also set on the sea, takes place in a lifeboat and is a murky, symbolic exercise in which "a menacing silence, like the genius of the fog, broods over everything." The play is interesting for two reasons: its fog symbol was to become a frequently employed background effect in

O'Neill's later plays, particularly *Long Day's Journey Into Night*; and its three chief characters are symbolic types which O'Neill went on to develop, in various guises, in many of his mature works—the Business Man, representing materialism; the Poet, representing art and creativity (and O'Neill himself); and a Polish Peasant Woman, representing blind, hopeless faith. There is also a Dead Child, which seems to stand for the spiritual—or mystical—triumph over fate, for it is the crying of the Dead Child, unheard by the Poet or the Businessman, that guides a rescue craft to the lifeboat and results in saving their lives.

Warnings is a realistic play in two scenes about a ship's wireless operator who has lost his hearing but failed to inform his captain; the operator's handicap results in the ship sinking. The play contains several one-dimensional portraits of children, who held no attraction for O'Neill; none of the children in his mature works are much of an improvement over the four in *Warnings*. ("I don't get them," says Stephen Murray, in *The Straw*, tersely reflecting O'Neill's own lifelong attitude.) Mrs. Knapp, the protagonist's wife, is a forerunner of all the faded, irritable, narrow-minded wives who, in later plays, turn up to bedevil their various over-sensitive mates. Knapp himself is the Victim of Fate.

These four plays—*The Web, Thirst, Fog* and *Warnings*—have settings and characters with which O'Neill, at twenty-five, had been on intimate terms, and despite the stiffness of their language and their melodramatic denouements, they were significant for the authentic flavor of their backgrounds and for their concern with a large theme. (John Mason Brown once pointed out that, though O'Neill's earliest one-act plays were "crude and sorry affairs . . . they already betrayed one of the qualities which were to set his work apart from that of all his contemporaries. His characters were not merely in conflict with one another. They were at war with the agents controlling their destiny, and these agents were not indifferent to them. This link between mortals and forces shaping their lives was the mighty concern which gave a kind of majesty to the feeblest and poorest of his plays.")

Another startling thing about these plays is that they were written as though their author lived in a theatrical vacuum. Eugene was by no means oblivious of the sort of thing to which the commercial theatre was dedicated. Yet he turned his back on every concept of that theatre: the subject matter, the language, the unrelieved tragedy were all alien to the Broadway theatre of that period. Only in the plays of the European dramatists was anything like O'Neill's attempted symbolism or realism to be found. O'Neill had already determined to follow his inner vision without regard for what was popular.

The closest he came to aping his contemporaries of the New York stage was in a fifth play, called *Recklessness*. Set in the library of a rich man's summer home in the Catskill Mountains, it was as contrived as a French farce but not at all funny; it was, in fact, exactly the sort of melodrama O'Neill himself considered outrageous.

The heroine, Mildred, young, beautiful, voluptuous, is in love with the young, handsome, earnest chauffeur of her nasty, rich, middle-aged husband. ("You have never loved me," says Mildred to her husband. "I have been just a plaything with which you amused yourself.") The husband, Baldwin, discovers the liaison and sends the chauffeur off to die in a defective automobile. He thoughtfully arranges to have the chauffeur's body brought back for Mildred to see. On viewing the body Mildred shrieks and falls senseless to the floor. Soon after, she shoots herself. "Mrs. Baldwin has just shot herself," says the nasty, rich, middle-aged— and now triumphant—husband to a trembling maid. "You had better phone for the doctor, Mary." Curtain.

It is not surprising that O'Neill preferred to forget that play and another, longer one he called *Bread and Butter,* which was never published. At the time he was writing it, however, he had high hopes for it.

"I am hard at work finishing a four-act play which, by God's grace, may see the footlights next season," he wrote to Dr. Lyman in the winter of 1914.

He seemed impelled to justify himself to Dr. Lyman. He had been embarrassed by the question sheet that had reached him from Gaylord in January. In answer to the form question, "What have you worked at the last year since May 1, 1913," he wrote: "The Art of Playwrighting— also prostitution of the same by Photo-play composition." And in answer to "What have been your average weekly earnings when at work?" he put down "$30." Then he wrote a long-winded accompanying letter, in which he went to childish lengths to impress Dr. Lyman.

"Fearing that the answers on my question sheet may prove misleading in the case of one who is unjustly suspected of being a member of the more-or-less Idle Poor Class," he wrote, "I hasten to take advantage of your charitable offer to read the egotistic spasms of former patients.

"You must acknowledge that to ask a struggling young playwright with the Art for Art's sake credo how much he earns per week in terms of contaminating gold, is nothing short of brutal . . . while my adventures with High Art have been crowned with a sufficient amount of glory, I am bound to admit they have failed to be remunerative."

It is conceivable that O'Neill did try his hand at a photoplay or two, through the good offices of his father, but the work could not have amounted to much. None of the Rippins has any recollection of his working at such a job; nor does the "$30" a week conform to their memories of his dollar-a-week allowance. As a matter of fact, it was Dolly who paid for the postage when O'Neill sent his manuscripts to producers and to the copyright office. When he became famous, he promised, he'd pay her back. He never did.

None of the girls really believed he *would* become famous. Jessica, who considered his plays terrible, was nevertheless awed by his endurance. "He would work in his room, sometimes far into the night, banging away at his typewriter," she recalled.

Although the girls thought the subject matter of his plays was "morbid," they did once participate in a private production of one of them— but what it was they have been unable to remember. James Rippin, their brother, in spite of his suspicion about O'Neill's morals, was more interested than the girls in his scripts; he read them and encouraged him.

Eugene also received encouragement of a sort from his father. Aside from offering to play in *A Wife for a Life*—a project that never materialized— James read and tried his best to admire *Thirst, The Web, Warnings, Fog* and *Recklessness*. He was pleased that Eugene was concentrating on something other than drink and dissipation, but the direction of his son's literary interests bewildered him. Nevertheless, he urged producers he knew to read Eugene's scripts.

"It's funny now to look back and think of the bright way I behaved when James O'Neill used to bring me round the plays that his young son Gene had written and ask me to tell him what I thought of them," George Tyler wrote in 1934. "I didn't see any particular reason to suppose that Gene should be taken seriously. I figured it was just run-of-mine paternal pride that made his father bring me those scripts of his. So I'd take them in and forget about them for a while—maybe read a little, but I wouldn't take an oath I did that often, and I'm certain that I can't remember at all what they were like—and then I'd give them back to his father with the customary polite remarks about how Gene undoubtedly showed signs of talent, and deserved encouragement, but needed more development and had better wait a while."

James also asked Brandon Tynan, his fellow actor in *Joseph and His Brethren* to read the plays. Tynan was one of the young men upon whom James, to the ill-concealed annoyance of both Jamie and Eugene, bestowed fatherly affection. In his early thirties, Tynan, who was Dublin-born and had an attractive, boyish manner, was on his way up in the theatre. He had enough of the actor's temperament and more than enough of all the qualities Jamie and Eugene lacked to endear himself to James from the beginning of their acquaintance in *Joseph*. Tynan returned James's devotion. He respected and responded to him as neither of James's sons was capable of doing. During the run of *Joseph*, for example, the two men attended church together every Sunday.

"I don't think Mr. O'Neill really understood Eugene's plays," Tynan once said. "I thought they were interesting, though, and took them to Holbrook Blinn." Blinn was a prominent actor who, at that time, was presenting what would now be called avant-garde plays, by American and European writers, at the Princess Theatre in New York. But he did not like Eugene's plays, and James began to wonder if the scripts had any merit and if his son had any talent. He continued to encourage his writing, however, as at least a step toward independence. Besides, James welcomed the opportunity of drawing closer to his younger son, for he had been shut out almost completely by Jamie.

Earlier that year Eugene had motored with Art McGinley to Hartford to see *Joseph and His Brethren*. On entering the dining room of the hotel before the performance they found James and Jamie seated at tables at opposite ends of the room. The two were not on speaking terms, and Eugene and McGinley spent fifteen minutes with each of them.

"The camel in the first act is the only regular guy in the company," Jamie confided to Eugene and McGinley. This was a sweeping statement in view of the fact that the camel had recently stepped on Jamie's foot during a performance and spat at him; Jamie was convinced that a camel's saliva was poisonous.

"Look at him—a thirty-five thousand dollar education and a thirty-five dollar a week earning capacity," James jeered, when Eugene and Mc-Ginley shifted to his table.

But at that, Jamie was being overpaid. He maliciously twisted his lines on stage. In Chicago he delivered the line, "Let Reuben tell his own tale," as "Let Reuben smell his own tail." In a last act scene during which members of the company sat around a table loaded with fruit, Jamie chewed on grapes and aimed the pits at the other actors. One night he did something much worse. James had a scene in which he appeared as Pharaoh, seated on a throne at the top of twelve steps. His speech was long, and it was always a trying time for him because his memory was not what it had been. All the supers were simulating rapt attention. Jamie, playing an old wise man dressed in a flowing white robe, also was supposed to be absorbed. But he was drunker than usual and swayed from side to side. James's eye fell on his son and he faltered. Then he began silently to weep.

One of the actors in the company, a young Englishman named Leslie Austin, had learned James's speech so that he could prompt if necessary. But Austin was so overcome by James's anguish that he could barely utter the lines himself.

After this episode, James stopped speaking to his son. But he would not allow him to be dismissed from the company.

Jamie had a better excuse than usual for his behavior. He had lost hope of winning Pauline Frederick, after having made another unsuccessful effort to give up drinking.

"When a member of the *Joseph* company went on the wagon," Brandon Tynan said in recalling that period, "he would join what the stage hands called 'The Order of St. Joe.' This was an informal walking group that I started during the tour. I used to take a five or six-mile hike every afternoon, no matter what the weather, in order to keep in trim. The stagehands would draw satirical sketches of us in action and post them backstage. They thought we were mad as March hares. We always ended our walks at a fountain, drinking chocolate sodas. The day Jamie joined our Order, the stagehands drew him drinking a soda and looking sick. He stayed on the wagon for about two months. Then it got to be too much for him."

Tynan found it necessary to exercise because he had an unusually taxing role as Joseph. In addition to thirteen costume changes, he had to make three complete changes of make-up.

James had no small job of make-up and costuming himself; for a man of sixty-eight he was still surprisingly agile. Day after day he arrived at the theatre two hours before curtain time to make up as the 106-year-old Jacob. For the second act he changed to the swarthy make-up of Pharaoh, and wrapped his loose robe in yards of bandages to conceal them beneath the tight-fitting costume he wore in that role; he didn't have time before his reappearance as Jacob to make a complete costume change, and he could barely manage to switch make-up, remove the Pharaoh costume and loosen the bandages. Once, uncharacteristically, James put on his Jacob costume over his street trousers and prepared to go on that way. He did a little jig backstage just before the curtain went up and the stage manager noticed the trousers. He scolded James for being slipshod and James, not at all offended, apologized.

Leslie Austin, who was present when this happened, was astonished at the lack of temperament with which James took the reprimand. "Most stars of Mr. O'Neill's stature would have exploded at such effrontery," he recalled emotionally. "But James O'Neill was a memorable exception. *There* was a man who breathed truth and sincerity."

One day, as the company was leaving Kansas City by train, Brandon Tynan handed Leslie Austin a telegram from his brother. It said, "Mother died this morning. Don't leave the company."

"I sat in the coach, trying to make up my mind what to do, when Mrs. O'Neill, who had been told the news, slipped into the seat next to mine," Austin recalled. "She was wearing something dark and her face was pale; she reminded me of my own mother. I don't remember what she said, but she sat with me for half an hour and then she kissed me on the cheek and left. I felt better, and must have told her I'd stay with the company, because Mr. O'Neill took her place next to me and told me I was doing the right thing in not leaving."

James assured Austin that he knew how he felt. He said that years ago, when appearing in San Francisco, he had received word of his mother's death but continued playing "for the sake of the company and the theatre."

Ella traveled with the company until the spring of 1914. On April 1, a New London newspaper carried the announcement that James, who had left the *Joseph* company in Indianapolis the week before "because of the serious sickness of his wife," would not rejoin the play that season. It is possible that Jamie's behavior had something to do with his decision.

In spite of his troubles James, when he returned to New London, found time to gratify a wish of Eugene's to have his five completed one-act plays published. Richard C. Badger, head of a Boston publishing company called Gorham Press, which had brought out plays by Augustus Thomas and Rachel Crothers, among others, liked Eugene's scripts and was willing to publish them under his firm's imprint—with the stipulation that the author bear the printing cost. In a spurt of generosity James gave Eugene the $450 Badger wanted for the job, and on March 30, 1914, a contract was signed, guaranteeing Eugene 25 per cent of the gross proceeds from the sale of the book. Badger contracted to print a thousand copies.

The 168-page book, a thin, gray-and-tan volume bearing the title *Thirst And Other One-Act Plays,* came out in August and had an unspectacular sale. Eugene gave copies to most of his friends and relatives. Not long after this Badger offered Eugene the unsold volumes (which included practically the entire edition) at thirty cents a copy.

"With the usual financial acumen of an author," O'Neill informed Mark Van Doren in 1944, "I scorned his offer as a waste of good money on my lousy drama!" (Eventually Badger found a buyer in Frances Steloff, who, in 1920, became the proprietor of a bibliophilic gold mine in New York called the Gotham Book Mart. Miss Steloff bought Badger's stock of *Thirst* plus his contract with O'Neill for $200; she had not read *Thirst* before making the purchase, but her instinct proved sounder than O'Neill's. Less than twenty-five years later *Thirst* became a collector's item, selling for as much as $150 a copy.)

If *Thirst* did not sell at first, it was not the fault of Eugene's earliest and stanchest supporter, Clayton Hamilton. Reviewing the *Thirst* volume in a magazine called *The Bookman,* early in 1915, Hamilton wrote:

"This writer's favorite mood is one of horror. He deals with grim and ghastly situations that would become intolerable if they were protracted beyond the limits of a single sudden act. He seems to be familiar with the sea; for three of these five plays deal with terrors that attend the tragedy of shipwreck. He shows a keen sense of the reactions of characters under stress of violent emotion; and his dialogue is almost brutal in its power. More than one of these plays should be available for such an institution as the Princess Theatre in New York."

(Years later, O'Neill attempted to cheer a friend whose book had received indifferent notices with these words: ". . . to me it is actually a surprise that it got as much comment as it did. This sounds a bit over-cynical perhaps, but I have reason! My first book of one-act plays—*Thirst*—received just *one* review in the whole U.S.A.—a very brief one written by a critic who happened to know me slightly.")

Hamilton's interest in O'Neill caught fire in the spring of 1914, when with his bride of a few months he visited New London to look at a beach cottage he was thinking of renting for the summer. In his early thirties, Hamilton was the drama editor of *The Bookman* and *Vogue* and a lecturer in playwrighting at Columbia University. He was considered something of a boy wonder, and O'Neill knew him by reputation and as an acquaintance of his father's.

Hamilton, who had met James at The Players, had spent his vacations in New London in previous years and was a friend of the Rippin family, who called him "Mr. Ham." Described once as a "snow-capped mountain of a man," Hamilton was rotund, easygoing and prematurely white-haired; he had a Rabelaisian sense of humor and a gusto for life and art.

He and his wife, Gladys, a slender, aristocratic-looking woman, were dining at the Rippins' one afternoon when Eugene entered.

"I didn't pay any special attention when he came in," Mrs. Hamilton later recalled, "but suddenly I was aware of his two eyes and his silence sitting opposite me."

"I looked the lad over," Hamilton said, recalling his own first impression of O'Neill. "He had large and dreamy eyes, a slender, somewhat frail and yet athletic body, a habit of silence and an evident disease of shyness." On another occasion Hamilton remarked that, since O'Neill's speech was "rather hesitant and he never said very much, he was less impressive to listen to than to look at."

O'Neill, instinctively hostile toward anyone who was a friend of his father's, commented to Jessica, when the Hamiltons had left the dining room, that he found Hamilton patronizing. Jessica bristled. She respected Hamilton more than anyone else she knew. He was one of the few people with whom she could talk freely—and from whom she believed she could learn about the theatre and literature; Hamilton was a part of a cultured world, and he fascinated her. Hamilton also could amuse her, as he did most people; his cheerful, sophisticated humor made O'Neill's groping, self-centered morbidity particularly exasperating to Jessica by contrast.

Hamilton referred to the Rippin girls as "The Seventeen Daughters of the House of Rippin." He enjoyed teasing Mrs. Rippin by referring, whenever possible, to his bulldog as his "bitch." Mrs. Rippin considered this ungenteel and retaliated by chiding him for sleeping late in the morning and being lazy. Hamilton and his wife rented a cottage on Alewife Cove, beyond Ocean Beach and about a mile and a half from the Rippin house, and O'Neill decided to give Hamilton the benefit of the doubt; shyly he began making overtures. He would swim from the beach in the cove, and one day he walked into the house uninvited.

"I've been writing some one-act plays," he said to Hamilton. "Would you read them and tell me if I'm any good?"

Hamilton read them. What he thought he recorded later in his review. But, more important than his opinion of the plays, Hamilton gave encouragement and suggestions for future development. He refused O'Neill's request for advice about technique, explaining that the technical problem was less important than the primary problem of what to write about.

Hamilton then advised him to find out what aspect of life, if any, he was familiar with at first hand, what characters in life he had really observed. "It happened that the life he knew best was the life of the sea, because he had so lately been a sailor; and I made the obvious suggestion that this might be a fortunate fact," Hamilton later said. "There had been several novelists of the sea and poets of the sea—Mr. Conrad and Mr. Kipling and Mr. Masefield, for example—but there never yet had been a dramatist of the sea. The average playwright knew nothing whatsoever of the sea; and any one who really knew the sea and who could learn to say something about it in dramatic form would find a new field open to him."

Hamilton had in mind something a little more concrete then the *Thirst* plays, though he assured O'Neill that even those showed "appreciable promise."

O'Neill responded to this advice by writing a one-act play in May, called *Children of the Sea.* This play, with only minor changes, was later produced as *Bound East for Cardiff* and eventually was published as the second of the four S.S. *Glencairn* plays. (One of the changes involved Driscoll's praying when Yank dies at the play's end. In the original *Children of the Sea* Driscoll speaks the line, "Our Father who art in Heaven." In the published version Driscoll does not speak the words; instead, his "lips move in some half-remembered prayer" and he makes the sign of the cross.)

"Very important from my point of view," O'Neill said of *Bound East for Cardiff* when in 1935 he compiled a chronological list of his plays. "In it can be seen, or felt, the germ of the spirit, life-attitude, etc., of all my more important future work."

Bound East for Cardiff is the simple story of the sailor Yank dying in his bunk aboard a tramp steamer.

"It ain't as bad as people think—dyin'," Yank says to his friend Driscoll. "I ain't had religion; but I know whatever it is what comes after it can't be no worser'n this." Yank speaks of the hard life of a sailor and of his regret at never having settled down on a farm—"Just a small one, just enough to live on"—and worries briefly that God might "hold it up against" him for having stabbed a man during a dock fight; he asks Driscoll to buy a box of candy for a barmaid in Cardiff who has been good to him—"She tried to lend me half a crown when I was broke there last trip." Finally, saying "S'long, Drisc!" he dies.

The "spirit" and "life-attitude" revealed by *Bound East for Cardiff* were tragic. No one had dared to write contemporary tragedy for the American stage, but it was the only aspect of life that O'Neill was moved to express; and in the beginning it was often misunderstood.

"I know you're impervious to what they are pleased to call my 'pessimism,'" he wrote to Mary Clark, his Gaylord nurse, in 1923. "I mean, that you can see behind that superficial aspect of my work to the truth. I'm far from being a pessimist. I see life as a gorgeously-ironical, beautifully-indifferent, splendidly-suffering bit of chaos, the tragedy of which gives Man a tremendous significance, while without his losing fight with fate he would be a tepid, silly animal. I say 'losing fight' only symbolically, for the brave individual always wins. Fate can never conquer his—or her—

spirit. So you see I'm no pessimist. On the contrary, in spite of my scars, I'm tickled to death with life!"

Clayton Hamilton, in addition to pointing the way for O'Neill, supplied a bit of essential advice one day when the two happened to meet at the New London railroad station. O'Neill told Hamilton he had just mailed the script of what he described as "really my first long play" to a Broadway manager. He innocently expected the play to be read at once, and thought a reply—possibly an acceptance—would be forthcoming within a week. He asked Hamilton what he thought the chances of acceptance were for an unknown author's play.

"When you send off a play," Hamilton told him, "remember there is not one chance in a thousand it will ever be read; not one chance in a million of its ever being accepted—(and if accepted it will probably never be produced); but if it is accepted and produced, say to yourself it's a miracle which can never happen again."

O'Neill left the railroad station slightly dazed. But, as he later told Hamilton: "I reflected that you knew whereof you spoke, that I was up against a hard game and might as well realize it and hew to the line without thought of commercial stage production. Your advice gradually bred in me a gloomy and soothing fatalism which kismeted many a rebuff and helped me to take my disappointments as all an inevitable part of the game."

O'Neill never forgot Hamilton's counsel. "Yes, of all the help you were in those years, I think that bit [of advice] ranks brightest in memory," he informed Hamilton on still a later date. "It was a bitter dose to swallow that day but it sure proved a vital shock-absorbing tonic in the long run. It taught me to 'take it'—and God knows that's the first thing most apprentice playwrights need to learn if they are not to turn into chronic whiners against fate or quitters before their good break comes."

His new philosophy was that tough breaks for a beginner were, as he put it, "a test you have to pass through to prove yourself to yourself."

If the "first long play"—presumably O'Neill had dismissed *Bread and Butter* as too clumsy an effort to be included even among his forgotten works—had been read by the manager to whom it was addressed, it is doubtful he would have been impressed. It was the three-act *Servitude*, and it had nothing of the firsthand familiarity with a phase of life advocated by Hamilton. It was, in fact, an inane and immature drawing-room melodrama. If it owed its inspiration to Ibsen or to Strindberg, those two authors would not have been proud to acknowledge the debt.

Its plot has to do with a successful and egotistical novelist who does not appreciate his wife. Various intricate complications, including the introduction of a second, unhappily married woman, reunite the novelist and his wife. The play is noteworthy among its author's works for only two reasons: it contains neither violence nor sexual aberration, and it has an unequivocally pat and happy ending. It, too, was later listed by O'Neill as "destroyed," but was included, without his permission, in the volume published in 1950 as *The Lost Plays of Eugene O'Neill.*

Possibly the most interesting item in that volume is a sketch called *The Movie Man* (also listed by O'Neill as destroyed), written in July, 1914, after O'Neill left the Rippin home to rejoin his father in the family house. It is a broad, one-act farce that mocks both the Mexican Revolution and the brash techniques of the American movie makers. Set in the suburb of a large town in northern Mexico, it deals with the efforts of a couple of Americans to persuade a Mexican general to live up to the terms of a contract he signed with a motion-picture company, stipulating that he fight his battles at the movie makers' convenience. The general, Pancho Gomez, was clearly modeled on the formidable Pancho Villa.

More interesting than the play itself is the fact that it was inspired by the enfant terrible of American journalism, John Reed, whom O'Neill had met earlier in the year in Greenwich Village (where O'Neill occasionally strayed when he could muster enough money to leave New London). Reed was covering the Mexican Revolution for the *Metropolitan Maga-zine.* Young, good-looking, quixotic and a passionate rebel, he personified the brilliant, glamorous foreign correspondent of the era. His colorful articles on Pancho Villa for the *Metropolitan* were drawing international attention between the end of 1913 and April, 1914. The *Metropolitan,* editorially socialistic, listed among its contributors at that time Booth Tark-ington, Joseph Conrad, Richard Harding Davis, H. G. Wells, George Bernard Shaw, Havelock Ellis, Rudyard Kipling, Lincoln Steffens and Fannie Hurst—as well as the violently antisocialistic Theodore Roosevelt. Reed was the *Metropolitan's* pet.

At twenty-six he was almost a legend. Members of literary and journalistic circles spread stories of his exploits. Recently he had been arrested in Paterson, New Jersey, and spent four days in jail with other victims of the Paterson silk strike. One anecdote that O'Neill helped circulate concerned Reed and Theodore Roosevelt, who had recently been defeated for the Presidency by Woodrow Wilson. Roosevelt detested Villa and Reed detested Roosevelt. When the two men chanced to meet in the offices of the *Metropolitan,* the air crackled with animosity.

"Villa is a murderer and a rapist," Roosevelt said.

"What's wrong with that?" asked Reed aggressively. "I believe in rape."

Roosevelt grinned. "I'm glad," he said, "to find a young man who believes in something."

Reed, who met O'Neill before leaving for his assignment in Mexico, was enormously taken with him. Himself an idealist, poet and incurable romantic, Reed was enchanted with O'Neill's stories of his wild youth, his adventures at sea, and his moody charm. O'Neill was equally taken with Reed and when Reed suggested that he join him in covering the war O'Neill agreed eagerly.

Sonya Hovey, who later became a screen writer, and whose husband, Carl, was managing editor of the *Metropolitan*, recalled that Reed told her husband he had met "a talented young man who had to get away and had nowhere to go." Reed was held in such esteem that he could not be denied. Mrs. Hovey said that the magazine advanced Reed $300 to cover O'Neill's expenses, and agreed to consider any articles he might submit. Hovey had no hope that the articles would be of value; he was humoring his star reporter and regarded O'Neill as Reed's companion rather than as a correspondent.

Mrs. Hovey said she had a clear recollection of receiving several short pieces from O'Neill, but whether they came from Mexico and whether, in fact, O'Neill ever got to Mexico at all, is a riddle. O'Neill, who loved to tell of his days at sea, who spoke often of his trip to Honduras, who relished recalling all his "he-man" exploits, never said a word for publication about having gone to Mexico. The Rippins have not recalled any prolonged absence of Eugene's during the period Reed was in Mexico, nor have other friends remembered his mentioning such a trip. Either he went for a very short time and kept singularly quiet about it or something happened at the last moment to prevent his leaving. The only indication from O'Neill himself of a fleeting interest in the Mexican Revolution is *The Movie Man*.

With the writing of that play, in July of 1914, Eugene marked the end of one phase of his literary launching. Once again he turned to Clayton Hamilton for help and advice. "My father doesn't think my plays are any good," he said, "and won't think of staking me."

"The problem," as Hamilton once recorded, "was to get around his father. Eugene did not want to be put to work; he wanted to write plays; and he did not relish the idea of another winter in New London. So he asked me if I could not get the old gentleman to . . . send him to Harvard to study with Professor Baker. Eugene allowed me to infer, with all due respect to Professor Baker, that his main idea was to get out of New London and that Harvard might be a good excuse; but his father was rather difficult to get around, because Mr. O'Neill had the ready argument that he had sent Eugene to college once before and that the boy had run away."

Hamilton suggested that, since some of the one-act plays which Eugene had been trying to write were rather promising, it might be a good plan to send one or two to Professor Baker to find out what he thought about them.

George Pierce Baker had been conducting a postgraduate course at Harvard called English 47 since 1905. The course and its teacher had become famous when one of its first pupils, Edward Sheldon, wrote *Salvation Nell* while still a student there.

O'Neill, acting on Hamilton's advice, wrote to Professor Baker on July 16, 1914. His letter was at once cocky and defensive.

"Let me explain my exact position," he stated. "My university training consists of one year (Freshman) at Princeton University, Class of 1910. . . . All my life I have been closely connected with the dramatic profession. My father is James O'Neill, the actor, of whom you may perhaps have heard. . . ."

He went on to inform Professor Baker that, while he had read "all the modern plays I could lay my hands on, and many books on the subject of the Drama," he realized such a system of study was inadequate. "With my present training I might hope to become a mediocre journeyman playwright," he said. "It is just because I do not wish to be one, because I want to be an artist or nothing, that I am writing to you."

O'Neill ended his letter with the hope that Professor Baker would "look favorably upon this earnest desire of mine to become your student . . ."

Baker did look favorably and replied that O'Neill could enter, pending his submission of a sample of his dramatic writing. O'Neill complied and was duly notified that he was accepted.

O'Neill's cousin Lil Brennan added her urging to that of Clayton Hamilton and, according to Hamilton, "Mr. O'Neill was finally persuaded to send Eugene to Harvard, although he still maintained that the boy would never amount to anything." It had probably slipped his mind that nearly twenty years earlier, in an interview for the New York *Mirror,* James had expressed an emphatic conviction that America needed a training school for persons who wished to learn the techniques of playwrighting.

"Now and then," James had said, "a genius may write a play without any great degree of technical knowledge. . . . The average writer for the stage, however, has to serve a dramatic apprenticeship of some sort before he is qualified to write a play of any practical value."

Ella Quinlan O'Neill

*Museum of the
City of New York*

James O'Neill

*From the John H. James Collection,
New York Public Library*

*James O'Neill
as Virginius, 1907;*
below left *in a
benefit appearance;*
below right, *as Christ,
1879.*

Top and below right, *from the
Theatre Collection, New York
Public Library*
Below left, *Brown Brothers.*

James O'Neill in THE COUNT OF MONTE CRISTO *as the prisoner after his escape from the Château D'If and as the avenging count. Below, left, in* MUSKETEERS, *1907.*

Above right, *Culver Pictures, Inc.* Below right, *from the John H. James Collection, New York Public Library*

The Barrett House, a family hotel on the street, later renamed Broadway, where Eugene O'Neill was born on October 16, 1888. Thanking a friend who unearthed this picture and sent it to him years before his death, O'Neill wrote facetiously that the figure leaning against the lamppost obviously "had a bun on."

Muray

James O'Neill, Jr.

Monte Cristo Cottage,
New London.

Commercial Engraving
Company, New London

Eugene, Jamie and Jame
on the porch of Monte
Cristo Cottage.

Yale Collection of
American Literature

Below left, *Kathleen
Jenkins O'Neill,
Eugene's first wife.*

From New York World,
May 10, 1910

Eugene, on his twenty
first birthday, and
Earl Stevens en route
for Honduras.

Mrs. Earl Stevens Collectio

Two sides of the coin: AH, WILDERNESS! *and* LONG DAY'S JOURNEY INTO NIGHT. *Left, Eda Heineman and George M. Cohan as the parents and Elisha Cook, Jr., as Richard Miller; below, Florence Eldridge and Frederic March as the parents, Bradford Dillman as Edmund Tyrone and Jason Robards, Jr., as Jamie.*

Left, *Museum of the City of New York*
Below, *Gion Mili Photograph*

Charles Gilpin, above left, as The Emperor Jones, 1920.
Museum of the City of New York

Eugene with a Spanish priest and Mrs. Earl Stevens, Honduras, 1910.
Mrs. Earl Stevens Collection

Eugene with Kitty Mackay (the model for Eileen Carmody in THE STRAW) *and a nurse at Gaylord Farm, Wallingford, Conn., 1913; before a therapeutic swim, on the Rippins' beach, January 1, 1914; and as a burgeoning writer in New London, 1913.*

Muray

In 1914 James was more interested in investing in real estate and in gadgets than in Eugene's education as a playwright. It was about this time that he put some money into a device he said would be "wonderful for the ladies"; it was the recently invented zipper.

Toward the end of August James went to New York to rehearse with new members of the cast of *Joseph and His Brethren,* which was about to take to the road again. The war in Europe, affecting international trade, was having a corollary effect on the health of the Broadway theatre, and the new tour of *Joseph and His Brethren,* one of Liebler's big money-makers, was almost their last hope of staying in business. Tynan, Pauline Frederick and Jamie were all to rejoin the cast.

On August 29, the New London *Telegraph* deemed it newsworthy to announce:

"Eugene G. O'Neill of Pequot Avenue has been admitted to the class in higher English at Harvard University conducted by Professor Baker. This is a post-graduate course and specializes in playwrighting . . ."

Perhaps O'Neill's only regret at the prospect of leaving New London was a romantic attachment he had lately developed for a spirited brunette named Beatrice Ashe. His romance with Maibelle was tapering off, and he was desultorily pursuing the Rippin girls and various other young ladies of New London. He was so determined not to miss any opportunity that he once slipped a note under the door of a neighbor of Maibelle's sister, who was being visited by a young niece. It was addressed, simply, "To the Beautiful Unknown." Nor had O'Neill neglected, during this period, to leave his mark, with either casually distributed poems or extravagant protestations, on such girls as Maibelle's friend, Mildred Culver, and his former nurse, Olive Evans.

Many girls in that innocent era carried about autograph books in which they invited friends to set down facetious or sentimental remarks. O'Neill, despite his stature as a twenty-five-year-old dramatist and cynical man of the world, wrote in Mildred's book: "I Hereby Confess that I love parsnips, that I once wrote a love letter to Lena Cavalleri [sic] in English, which I afterwards found out she cannot read, that I have read 'Mademoiselle de Maupin' (sh!) and liked it, that I do not think State Street and Broadway have much in common, that politics are my idea of the acme of futility, that I voted for Eugene Debs because I dislike John D. Rockefeller's bald head." This nonsense was followed by the printed line, "For This I Am Prepared To Pay A Penalty." On a second, concealed page, O'Neill declared that his "Idea of Utter Bliss" was "Being the tenor in a Broadway musical comedy and singing a kiss song—with appropriate pantomime"; that for him "The Acme of Discomfort" was "Trying to write a poem in this book with three people bending over my shoulder saying 'how clever' "; and that his conception of "The Supremely Ridiculous" was "Getting into a crowded car with One Girl and her mother (?) and finding coin of the realm is in one's other suit—and Mother pays the fare."

In a companion book, kept by Mildred Culver, O'Neill answered a few questions and signed his entry with an ink drawing of a skull and cross-bones. In Olive Evans' book O'Neill wrote only, "I do not like parsnips."

By contrast with O'Neill's wordy contribution, Maibelle's effort in Mildred Culver's book seems sophisticated. She "confessed" to "having murdered my second husband just before marrying the first" and declared the custom of breakfast in bed to be the height of her ambition.

It was early in August that Maibelle told Eugene of her decision to marry her Coast Guard cadet. She asked Eugene to return all her letters, and she burned all of his—over two hundred of them—saving only the poems. Their final meeting took place at Ocean Beach. As Maibelle later recalled it, Eugene did not seem devastated by the parting. But many years after, just as his second marriage was breaking up, O'Neill wrote to Maibelle's aunt that there had been only two women in his life whom he truly respected; one was his mother, he said, and the other was Maibelle. When he said good-by to Maibelle he presented her with a copy of *Thirst*, which he had inscribed:

"To Scotty—In memory of all those sweet minutes and days and hours which have 'gone glimmering thro' the dream of things that were'

> 'Youth, take hand to the prayer of these!
> Many there be by the dusty way,
> Many that cry to the rocks and seas—
> Give us, ah give us but Yesterday!' "

He signed the inscription with a formal, "Eugene G. O'Neill," indicating a strong sense of his future worth, which overbalanced any inclination to set down a more intimate signature.

It was about this time that O'Neill fell in love, or so he persuaded himself, with Beatrice Ashe. His fondness for Beatrice was later celebrated publicly in a poem called "Speaking, to the Shade of Dante, of Beatrices," and begins:

> "Lo, even I am Beatrice!"
> That line keeps singing in my bean.

I felt the same ecstatic bliss
As did the fluent Florentine
Who heard the well-known hell-flame hiss.

(The poem was printed in July, 1915, in the New York *Tribune* column "The Conning Tower" and undoubtedly made O'Neill feel he had arrived. E. B. White, in an obituary tribute in *The New Yorker* to the "Tower" instigator, F.P.A., has written: "There are still plenty of writers alive today who will testify that the high point in their lives was not the first check in the mail from a publication but the first time at the top of the Tower looking down in the morning at the whole city of New York. Making the Tower was a dizzy experience. No money changed hands, and this made it unique. . . . If you were skilled in French verse forms, you could even make love to your girl in full view of a carload of subway riders who held the right newspaper opened to the right page. . . . Frank Adams gave a young writer three precious gifts: discipline, a sense of gaiety, a brief moment in the sun.")

Beatrice Ashe, although she was younger than Maibelle, moved in the same circle. She was the daughter of Peter Ashe, the superintendent of the trolley-car system for the district of New London and lived with her parents on West Street, in the town proper. She had a pleasant singing voice and was studying music.

"I used to drive my neighbors mad, practicing scales early in the morning," she has said.

Beatrice had a smooth skin and high color and a flair for clothes. Her New London contemporaries were struck by her various flamboyant costumes. Jessica, for instance, recalled years later a Scotch-plaid skirt and jaunty Scotch cap with a feather; another acquaintance recalled a costume of bright purple; Maibelle remembered her in a gold turban and big loop earrings; and a fourth acquaintance—male—wistfully remembered that she was breath-taking in a bathing suit.

According to her own account, Beatrice met O'Neill for the first time not long after his discharge from the sanitarium; he had asked a mutual friend to introduce them. The romance lasted through O'Neill's stay at Harvard. It was, according to Beatrice, marked by a brisk exchange of letters. Unlike Maibelle, Beatrice did not destroy her letters when her romance with Eugene ended. (Like Maibelle, she married a seaman—a naval lieutenant—in April, 1918.)

According to Emily Rippin, Beatrice once told her Eugene had asked her to marry him and come with him to New York. But, continued Emily,

Beatrice's father was strongly opposed to the match. Art McGinley has confirmed this, adding: "Gene had no job at the time. Can you blame her for turning him down?"

The relationship had not yet been severed, however, when, late in September, 1914, O'Neill took a train for Cambridge—and to his goal of becoming "an artist or nothing."

XXIV

WITHIN A FEW HOURS OF O'NEILL'S ARRIVAL AT CAM-
bridge, he headed for a small house on Massachusetts Avenue not far from
Harvard Square. The address, one of several offering rooms to students,
had been posted on a bulletin board near the Harvard admitting office.

On the second floor were two apartments, one occupied by Katherine
and Bartel Ebel and the other by Katherine's brother, Daniel Hiebert, and
Bartel's brother, August. All four had arrived from Hillsboro, Kansas—
Bartel, a teacher at a Mennonite institution in Kansas, to take a post-
graduate course in Greek at Harvard; his brother to study art in Boston;
and Daniel to study medicine at Boston University. Bartel filled the post
of minister at a Baptist church in nearby Jamaica Plains, but to stretch the
combined family resources a bit further, August and Dan advertised for a
paying guest to share the expense of their apartment.

O'Neill liked the arrangement and promptly moved in. His father was
sending him a weekly allowance, which he considered inadequate. O'Neill's
widow, recalling his petulance over his small allowance, once said: "Monte
Cristo gave him the magnificent sum of ten dollars a week. He was to
pay his board, his room, his streetcar fare, his laundry." She added that
he considered himself fortunate that Katherine Ebel was a very good cook,
and that he had plenty to eat.

When O'Neill entered the playwrighting class, George Pierce Baker
was in his late forties. He was conducting two seminars, each limited to
twelve students, one at Radcliffe and one at Harvard, and an advanced
seminar composed of four men and four women from the previous year's
workshop. Professor Baker was a stage-struck New Englander.

John Mason Brown, who had studied with him, once wrote: "This
Professor Baker who dared to teach such an unteachable subject as playwrighting was the least dogmatic of men. He had no Golden Rules of
Dramaturgy. He did not pretend to be able to turn out playwrights in ten
easy lessons. Indeed he did not claim to be able to turn them out at all. He
was among the first to admit that dramatists are born, not made. But he
did hope to be able to shorten the playwright's period of apprenticeship by
granting him the same instruction in the essentials of his craft that the
architect, the painter, the sculptor and the musician enjoyed in theirs."

Baker's methods were effective but unorthodox—he had no precedent at any other college or university. He worked at a large oak table with his students, who were familiarly known as Baker's Dozen. At the beginning of the semester he outlined the year's schedule. First his students were to select three short stories from any source and, with Baker's approval, settle on one of them to be dramatized into a one-act play. Next, they wrote an original one-act play and, toward the end of the term, a full-length play. They could also submit any other work for Baker's comment if they wished.

Thomas Wolfe, who was one of Baker's students, immortalized him in *Of Time and the River*. Wolfe called him Professor James Graves Hatcher and described him as "a man whose professional career had been made difficult by two circumstances: all the professors thought he looked like an actor and all the actors thought he looked like a professor."

Though not uncritical of Professor "Hatcher's" little vanities and crotchets, Wolfe found him imposing: "a well-set-up figure of a man . . . somewhat above the middle height, strongly built and verging toward stockiness, with an air of vital driving energy that was always filled with authority and a sense of sure purpose, and that never degenerated into the cheap exuberance of the professional hustler . . .

"He wore eye-glasses of the pince-nez variety, and they dangled in a fashionable manner from a black silk cord; it was better than going to a show to see him put them on, his manner was so urbane, casual and distinguished when he did so. His humor, although suave, was also quick and rich and gave an engaging warmth and humanity to a personality that sometimes needed them."

O'Neill was attracted by Baker as a person and impatient with him as a teacher. When Barrett Clark once asked him what he had got out of the course in playwriting, O'Neill said, "Not much out of the actual class-work itself. Necessarily, most of what Baker had to teach the beginners about the theatre as a physical medium was old stuff to me."

O'Neill resented the fact that Baker had told him *Bound East for Cardiff* was not a play. He was particularly offended by Baker's methods when Augustus Thomas, then the dean of American playwrights and the personification of all that was successful, admired—and hackneyed—on the Broadway stage, took over the class as guest lecturer for two morning sessions (a total of six hours). Thomas, who was then fifty-eight, had been writing plays since he was fourteen. He had been an actor, news-paperman, and advance agent for a mind reader; this last job had given him the background for his enormously popular play, *The Witching Hour*, produced in 1907, during which occurred the memorable scene in which a man intent on homicide is hypnotized by another: "You can't shoot—that —gun. You can't pull the trigger. (*Pause.*) You can't even hold the gun. (*Pause. The derringer drops . . .*)" His plays dealt mostly with contemporary social themes, such as *Alabama*, his first success, produced in 1891, which concerned the reunited country.

Thomas, with lightning inventiveness and a glibness that revolted O'Neill, proceeded to define the method for writing a sure-fire Broadway success.

"Suggest the name of a star," Thomas invited the class. (It was unthinkable not to write a play for a specific actor's talents.) One of Baker's young men suggested Margaret Anglin and O'Neill scowled and hunched his shoulders in disgust—not because Miss Anglin had threatened to kiss him when he was five but because he did not care for her lurid acting.

Several other names were suggested, a vote was taken, and Miss Anglin won.

"All right," said Thomas, "we'll write a play for Anglin. She's broad at hip, well-developed—so our story will have to fit a woman of that physical type. She's no longer young or beautiful, so it must be a role for an older woman—a woman with deep emotions; we'll make her a mother—and since we have to have drama—a mother threatened with losing her child."

As the students, with the exception of O'Neill, listened in awe, occasionally catching fire from Thomas' swift outline of detail and offering refinements of their own, Thomas wove a full-length, standard melodrama for them. Within an hour the soupy plot was complete.

"The mother lives in a puritan New England community," Thomas said. "Her townspeople find out she's had a lover. They are shocked. They decide she's not a fit mother for the child. There's a great scene with Anglin, abandoned by all, defending her right to keep the child against all the world."

When he had finished, Thomas told the class, "If you write this up as a scenario, I will put in the dialogue, and guarantee a production."

Baker commented mildly that it sounded a little too commercial. O'Neill was furious. He went from the classroom straight to Boston to get drunk. He had not come to Harvard to study how to write carbon copies of the kind of palatable tripe then being consumed on Broadway. He summed up his feeling some years later when he commented that during this era a popular author was one who built up a thesis for three acts and then proceeded in the fourth act to knock over what he had constructed. "The managers," he said, "felt they knew what the public would accept and

[271]

the plays had to conform to their ideas. The very fact that I was brought up in the theatre made me hate this artificiality and this slavish acceptance of these traditions."

O'Neill loftily determined not only to write plays about what *he* chose but also to make the managers and the public accept them. His arrogant conviction that he could do this was the first visible sign of his genius—though Baker failed to see it at the time. Yet it is true that long before anyone else recognized the fact that the vogue of Clyde Fitch and Augustus Thomas was doomed, O'Neill saw through their hollowness and glib, philosophical posturing. He wanted the stage to come to grips with the big themes, the realities of life.

"If a person is to get at the meaning of life," he said, "he must learn to like the facts about himself—ugly as they may seem to his sentimental vanity—before he can lay hold on the truth behind the facts; and the truth is never ugly." O'Neill wanted to reveal the souls of his characters, not with artificial situations into which the contemporary writers wedged their protagonists, and from which they melodramatically extricated them, but through showing them naked, against their natural environment. "Why not give the public a chance to see how the other fellow lives?" he asked. "Give it an insight into the underdog's existence, a momentary glimpse of his burdens, his sufferings, his handicaps."

Though he wrote feverishly during his eight months at Harvard—nearly always in bed, propped up on pillows, in the position he had been obliged to assume at Gaylord—O'Neill did not make much headway with his big plan. His one-act play for Baker was called *The Dear Doctor*. Baker thought it good enough to sell for vaudeville production, but when O'Neill tried to market it he discovered the short story on which he had based it had been pirated from an existing vaudeville sketch. His long play, *The Personal Equation*, first called *The Second Engineer*, involved a seamen's strike and was an attempt to portray the background and atmosphere of the I.W.W.—which he later did more successfully in *The Hairy Ape*. He said on several occasions in later years that the plays he wrote at Harvard were "rotten."

In addition to the required plays, he collaborated with a classmate, Colin Ford, on a biblical drama in six scenes, called *Belshazzar*, which he destroyed. He also completed a one-acter called *The Sniper*, which he listed as destroyed. But a script of the play was unearthed years later in the copyright office and included in the *Lost Plays* volume.

The Sniper is interesting because of its realistic, almost propagandistic treatment of a contemporary social theme—something O'Neill was later to eschew. It is set on the outskirts of a Belgian village during the early days of World War I and concerns an elderly peasant whose son has just been shot by the "Prussians." When the peasant learns that his wife, too, has been killed, he fires from his house on some Prussians and is himself shot down at the order of one of their officers. The play ends when a priest, who has been praying for the peasant, looks down "with infinite compassion at the still bodies of father and son."

"Alas, the laws of men," he says, as the curtain falls.

According to Heywood Broun, columnist and critic, who had been one of Baker's pupils, O'Neill's bad plays were no worse than most of those turned out in the class.

"There is no denying the fact that a certain number of dramatists have come out of Harvard's English 47, but the course also has a splendid record of cures" was the way Broun put it in 1919 in an article for *Vanity Fair* called "Nipping the Budding Playwright in the Bud."

"People who come to English 47 may talk about their plays as much as they choose but they must write them, too," he went on. "Often a cure follows within forty-eight hours after the completion of a play. Sometimes it is enough for the author to read a thing through for himself. But if that does not avail, there is an excellent chance for him. After his play has been read aloud by Professor Baker and criticized by the class, if a pupil still wishes to write plays, there is no question that he belongs in the business."

Broun added that Professor Baker deserved the thanks of the community not only for Edward Sheldon and Eugene O'Neill but also for the number of "excellent young men who have gone straight from his classroom to Wall Street and the ministry and automobile accessories with all the nascent enthusiasm of a man just liberated from a great delusion."

Describing the sort of plays written by Baker's students, Broun said: "Somebody has figured out that there are 2.983 more rapes in the average English 47 plays than in the usual non-collegiate specimen of commercial drama. We feel comparatively certain that there is nothing in the personality of Professor Baker to account for this."

Nowhere in the world, Broun added, was a woman quite so unsafe as in an English 47 play.

"When I was in English 47," he said, "I remember that all our plays dealt with Life. None of us thought much of it, at that. Few respected it and certainly no one was in favor of it. . . . Some of the playwrights in English 47 said that Life was a terrific tragedy. In their plays the hero shot himself or the heroine or both, as the circumstances might warrant, in the last act. The opposing school held that life was a joke, a grim jest to be sure, cosmic rather than comic, but still mirthful. The plays by these authors ended with somebody ordering 'another small bottle of Pommerey' and laughing mockingly like a worldwise cynic. Bolshevism had not been invented at that time, but Capital was severely handled, just the same. All our villains were recruited from the upper classes.

"Yet capitalism had an easy time of it compared to marriage. I do not remember that a single play which I heard all year in 47, whether from Harvard or Radcliffe, had a single word of toleration, let alone praise, for marriage."

Professor Baker, explained Broun, was "wise enough to realize that it is impossible that he should furnish or even attempt to mold in any way the philosophy which his students bring into English 47 each year.

"He can't attempt to tell the fledgling playwright what things to say and of course he doesn't," Broun went on. "When a man is done with Baker he has begun to grasp some of the things that he must not do in writing a play. With that much ground cleared, all he has to do is acquire a knowledge of life, to devise a plot and find a manager."

One of Eugene's classmates at Harvard—who, like Broun, emerged from Baker's training to pursue a calling outside the theatre—was Bruce Carpenter. Carpenter, who had begun earning a living as an actor at fifteen, eventually settled down to an academic career as an English professor at New York University. He has recalled Eugene's English 47 plays as bad and his personality as haughty.

"O'Neill fitted the old definition of a gentleman—'A man who never offends, except intentionally,' " Carpenter once said. "When I first met him I was impressed. I had seen his father play Monte Cristo and Marc Antony—the finest Marc Antony I have ever seen. I pretended to be older than I was and more educated; I had come from New York and had been on the stage. But I had nothing on O'Neill. He let us all know that he had shipped before the mast. He was very much the gentleman when he wanted to be, but he had an indifference almost bordering on contempt."

When Professor Baker read a manuscript aloud, he would ask for everyone's comment, going around the table. Often, when he got to O'Neill, O'Neill's comment would be, "Huh!" According to Carpenter, nobody else would have dared to be so abrupt; but Baker generally pretended to take no notice of O'Neill's reaction. Baker's method was to read the play without revealing its author and often without identifying the characters by name or even by sex.

O'Neill would sit slouched back in his chair, usually with a sneer on his face. Since he sat with his chair pushed back from the table more than the others, Carpenter always had to turn his head back to see him. Although most of the members of the class wore the Harvard costume of unpressed Brooks Brothers suit, white shirt, tie, and a pummeled hat, O'Neill generally attended class in corduroy trousers, a flannel shirt open at the throat, and as often as not, no tie. Carpenter never remembered seeing O'Neill smile or hearing him say a pleasant word.

"He was self-centered and indifferent," Carpenter said. "He seemed to feel the rest of us hadn't lived. I realize now there was something in his heart that he wouldn't let us see; I couldn't reconcile the O'Neill I knew at Harvard with the genius who later wrote such human plays."

According to Carpenter, O'Neill received no special recognition from Baker at the time. And it is a fact that the play Baker selected for production in his Workshop that year was not by O'Neill, but by a since-forgotten playwright named Edward Massey.

Called *Plots and Playwrights,* Massey's effort was a departure, of sorts, from the standard theatre and even presumed to spoof—in a mild way—the Augustus Thomas method of playwrighting. The play, later produced successfully by the Washington Square Players, concerned a successful playwright, at a loss for a plot, who encountered a young short-story writer during an aimless stroll in Greenwich Village. The writer proposed to illustrate to the playwright that material for drama existed in the apartments of the three-story rooming house before which they had chanced to meet. Snatches of life were then acted out in each of the apartments, with no attempt at a unifying thread of plot. The playwright pointed out that such a "play" would never be a success on Broadway, and proceeded to tie up the isolated scenes in a luridly melodramatic fashion.

The play ended, after the brief introduction of a Shavian waiter, with the suggestion that the short-story writer and the jaded playwright must collaborate to arrive at a more stimulating dramatic form. This represented the limits to which Baker was prepared to encourage his students to revolt against conventional theatre. It was not nearly far enough for O'Neill.

Another of O'Neill's classmates—William Laurence, whose seasoning in English 47 ultimately fitted him for the role of science editor of *The New York Times*—was more aware than any one else of the sulky young man's ambitions and frustrations. The only man at Harvard, according to Carpenter, of whom O'Neill stood in awe (certainly he was not the least in awe of Baker) was Laurence. One of the reasons was that Laurence was a Nietzsche worshiper and had read *Thus Spake Zarathustra* in German.

Laurence, who had worked his way through Harvard as an undergraduate, first doing such menial labor as shoveling snow, tending furnaces and reading gas meters, and later tutoring other students, had a background filled with enough color and struggle to command O'Neill's respect. In addition, he was a garrulous intellectual, and had all sorts of arcane literary knowledge O'Neill admired and envied. To top all, Laurence was more than willing to impart his knowledge to O'Neill; Laurence recalled he rarely stopped talking and O'Neill was a good listener.

A Latvian Jew, subject to an education quota in the port city of Libau, where he was brought up, Laurence had been obliged to provide his own education. He read German and Russian and, like O'Neill, had devoured at random all the books he could find. Nietzsche was his private discovery, come upon in the Libau library. He then saved and skimped to buy a copy of *Zarathustra,* which he carried about with him, as had O'Neill, wherever he went. A copy of *Zarathustra* constituted Laurence's total luggage when he arrived in America in 1905. Still in his teens, he was by then a political exile from Russia.

Stimulated by his reading, which had included Ibsen, Dostoevski and Gorky, Laurence had been traveling about Russia trying to educate the peasants and awaken them to a sense of their social responsibility. The failure of the revolution of 1905 put a stop to his activities and he had to flee the country.

On arriving in America Laurence transferred his proselytizing from the Russian peasants to his Yankee contemporaries. "I wanted to make people hate philistinism," he once said. "I thought the state of literature and culture was generally poor in this country. Everything was so vulgarized. Even people who came here from Russia with taste and hopes became corroded. I wanted to instill the love of good literature in my friends."

O'Neill was, of course, already a literary convert. Laurence attacked his politics—not because they were conventional but because, so Laurence believed, they were confused.

"Intellectually," Laurence said, "Eugene was a philosophical anarchist; politically, a philosophical socialist. I tried to give him a sense of consciousness about the value of labor and the struggle between labor and capital. The play he wrote for the course was a violent labor play. I thought it was the best one written. It had the same impact as Hauptmann's *The Weavers.*"

Laurence had discovered O'Neill soon after Baker's class began meeting —"a strange, taciturn fellow," Laurence found him. "I remember thinking he'd make a good Mephistopheles for *Faust.* For some time he didn't talk at all. Then he began talking, and I found out he was the son of James O'Neill and that he had just had a volume of plays published." Laurence, a devoted theatregoer, hit it off with O'Neill from that point.

O'Neill listened to him talk and talk. He seemed to Laurence to have a hunger to fill in the blank spots in his education. He would often visit Laurence's room in Thayer Hall, which overlooked the Yard.

"We talked about Nietzsche, of course," Laurence recalled. "And I talked my head off about Ibsen's *Brand* and about *Peer Gynt*. I told O'Neill *Brand* and *Gynt* were expressions of the Nietzschean idea of the individualist. I also talked about Greek drama and Gorky. These seemed to open new worlds to O'Neill."

Laurence, who had seen Alla Nazimova's troupe perform in New York a few years earlier, told O'Neill about the troupe's background. Nazimova had come to the United States as an exile the same year as Laurence, bringing with her her entire company, none of whose members spoke English. Renting the first floor of a three-story stable on East Third Street, they built a makeshift stage and installed benches. There they presented, in Russian, plays by Gorky, Ibsen, Chekhov, and Dostoevski. Sometimes during performances the stamping of hooves could be heard from upstairs. Admission was ten cents, but Laurence, when he could not pay, was allowed to attend anyway. He went every night.

He told O'Neill about one backstage crisis, when the actors ran out of cigarettes. They could not perform without cigarettes, which cost only five cents a pack, but among them they could not produce a nickel. Laurence, momentarily flush, bought them a pack and they then gave an impassioned performance. They were a dedicated troupe who did not just want to make money, Laurence pointed out; O'Neill remarked that that was the kind of theatre the country needed.

Laurence, like Carpenter, never saw O'Neill smile. "He used to talk in monosyllables, saying a biting, cutting thing every once in a while," Laurence added.

The two young men used to take long walks through Cambridge and Boston. Once, crossing the Charles River Bridge, Laurence told O'Neill about a paper he had written for a course on rational and irrational fear; to prove his points, he had tried to scare himself by walking to a cemetery at night, and before long he had found himself fleeing in fear. O'Neill appeared to be greatly interested and, Laurence later concluded, may have remembered it when he wrote *The Emperor Jones*.

During the course of other nocturnal walks O'Neill and Laurence would get drunk together.

"At times we were like a combination of Joyce's Bloom and Mulligan," Laurence said. "When we were drunk enough, we'd go to the Boston Common and stand under a huge elm and lecture passers-by, who, at that hour, usually consisted of sailors and their girls. We'd argue for universal sterilization, as the best solution for the human race. We maintained that the advantage of sterilization was freedom to fornicate to our hearts' content and put the abortionists out of business. We were loud, but our audiences seemed to be amused, and we somehow managed to escape arrest."

Laurence was not aware that O'Neill, on a solo lecture tour, was once taken by a policeman to the station house. This occurred, typically, at a time when O'Neill knew his father was in Boston, or nearby; James was notified and obtained his son's release.

But O'Neill had the tact to stay away from his room on Massachusetts Avenue during his drunken weekends. Often he would not be seen by Hiebert or the Ebels from Friday to the following Monday. In their soberer moments O'Neill and Laurence. together with Carpenter and some of their other classmates, would congregate at a Boston spaghetti place to encourage each other's work and compare idea on the theatre. According to Carpenter, Baker found out about the meetings and discouraged them; he thought his students would get some wrong ideas without his guidance.

One member of this group was a man named John Weaver, who came from a wealthy Chicago family. Baker once predicted that it would take Weaver eight years to get somewhere in the theatre; it was exactly eight years later that his first successful play, *Love 'Em and Leave 'Em* was produced. Weaver once recalled that O'Neill's classmates found him forbidding and unapproachable until, one day, Professor Baker read aloud a particularly earnest and lugubrious scenario by a student.

"Several of us gave timid suggestions," Weaver said. "It came O'Neill's turn. He waited some moments. Finally he said, without a smile, 'Cut it to twenty minutes, give it a couple of tunes and it's sure-fire burly-cue.' "

Weaver went on to describe a number of wild evenings spent by him, O'Neill and a wealthy classmate named "Pinky" Elkins. The flavor of those drinking, ranting evenings was much like that of the nights O'Neill had spent with his Princeton classmates eight years before. Elkins frequently entertained Weaver and O'Neill for dinner at his Beacon Street mansion.

"I, very callow and greatly impressed," Weaver later wrote, "and Gene, jocularly insolent, in a brown flannel shirt. feasted amidst quiet elegance and flunkies. An incongruous sight, surely. Always, afterwards, we would go to some new show. Elkins would buy up a whole box, and once we were seated, tear up the rest of the tickets. He was a good scout. He knew what he wanted, and he could afford it. Why not?

"Women were forever calling for Gene. There was something apparently irresistible in his strange combination of cruelty (around the mouth), intelligence (in his eyes) and sympathy (in his voice). I would not say that he was good looking. But one girl told me she could not get his face out of her thoughts. He was hard-boiled and whimsical. He was brutal and tender, so I was told. From shop girl to 'sassiety' queen, they all seemed to develop certain tendencies in his presence."

Weaver maintained that Baker "recognized the smoldering genius which was five years later to flame." This was not quite true. According to Carpenter, the year after O'Neill left, Baker, in response to a question about O'Neill, said: "I'm not sure whether he has any promise or not." This may have been partly pique over O'Neill's failure to return for a second year; at the end of the term in June, 1915, Baker selected O'Neill as one of the four members of the class for advanced work the following fall. Later, Baker said:

"By the end of the year [O'Neill] showed that he already knew how to write well in the one-act form, but he could not as yet manage the longer forms. I was very eager that he should return for a second year of work in these longer forms, but did not know until later that, though equally eager, his means at the moment made this impossible."

O'Neill was even more grudging toward Baker. Laurence recalled that he often derided Baker, accusing him of teaching commercial drama. Nevertheless, he accepted Baker's invitation to join the advanced class and when he left Harvard that spring he had every intention of returning—probably because it seemed the most convenient way for him to go on writing without having to support himself.

Both men subsequently did their best to forget the mutual misgivings that had existed in 1915. Once O'Neill had begun to show his mettle Baker not only became O'Neill's ardent supporter but recalled that he always had been. "He was a most delightful man to work with," Baker said, on one occasion, of his sulky ex-pupil. O'Neill became equally gallant, publicly singing Baker's praises on several occasions and admitting privately that Baker had, more than anything else, given him faith in himself.

During his months at Harvard O'Neill kept in contact with his New London friends—especially with Beatrice. He also corresponded sporadically with Mrs. Rippin, to whom he expressed his gratitude for her care during the previous year. Emily, who had taken a job in a New London jewelry store, saw O'Neill drunk for the first time that winter. He entered the shop with a girl, who was carrying a basket filled with Christmas presents.

O'Neill spent the summer uneventfully in New London, living at his father's house and boarding at the Rippins'. He wrote a one-act comedy, *A Knock at the Door*, which he subsequently destroyed, and made notes for several others; among these were a three-act "farce-comedy" called *Now I Ask You*, a one-act "farce-comedy" entitled *The G.A.M.*, and a pantomime called *Atrocity*, all of which he completed before 1918—by which time he had virtually abandoned the comedy form. With the exception of two one-acters written in 1919—one was *Exorcism* and the other was called *The Trumpet* and he labeled them both comedies—he concentrated on tragedy during the rest of his career. *Ah, Wilderness!* was the one major exception.

O'Neill continued seeing Beatrice and flirting with Emily that summer. One day when he and his father were dining at the Rippins' house Eugene said, "We heard something nice about you, Emily—didn't we, Papa?"

"Yes, Miss Emily, we did," James said.

"The bartender at the Crocker House said you have the best figure in town," Eugene elaborated.

"That's right, Miss Emily," echoed James.

A little later, when Emily became engaged, Eugene studied her fiancé and mumbled, "Emily, I wish you'd let me be the father of your second child."

A clipping from a New London paper preserved in one of O'Neill's scrapbooks at Yale University announced that summer:

"Mr. O'Neill is one of the four chosen from the Harvard class this year and plans to return in the fall for the advanced class."

O'Neill must have had his father's promise of continuing support, for in a letter to Hiebert, mailed from New London on September 21, 1915—just a few days before the opening of the term—he asked Hiebert to find him a place to stay, adding that he would arrive in Boston "Monday about 2:15 P.M."

"I am coming back to Harvard to enter Professor Baker's second year course," O'Neill wrote.

"I want to locate in Boston this year," he explained. "Cambridge is too darn dead."

Whether it was a last-minute refusal of James to finance him or some whim of Eugene's that prevented his return to Harvard is not known, but he never got to Cambridge.

To Professor Baker he wrote, four years later: "A word of explanation as to why I failed to come back for your second year. I wanted to. It was none of my choice. I just didn't have the money, couldn't get it, and had to take a job as a New York dramatic critic on a new theatrical magazine which never got beyond the promotion stage, although I was religiously paid a small salary for doing nothing for three months or so. . . . Oh, indeed, I wanted to come back!"

It seems inconceivable that O'Neill could have thought, just a few days before the term started, that he had the money, only to have it withdrawn by his father at the last moment. But there is much unexplained in the relationship between father and son, and in lieu of any other explanation, the one offered Professor Baker will have to serve.

Whatever the reason for his change of plans, O'Neill, in the fall of 1915, headed for New York. The next nine months, unproductive in literary output, marked a period of gestation, from which emerged a distinctly recognizable genius.

XXV

O'NEILL FOUND HIMSELF IN GREENWICH VILLAGE IN
the fall of 1915 with an evaporated job on a nonexistent magazine. Not
since he had attempted suicide nearly three years earlier had he been so
completely on his own—with no father, or fatherly substitute like Latimer,
Dr. Lyman or Professor Baker to dictate a constructive course. O'Neill
knew that his father expected him to look for an "honest" job, perhaps as
a reporter, and that James had no intention of coddling him while he
tried to find his way as a dramatist.

O'Neill also knew he had no immediate hope of earning a living from
playwrighting. All the scripts he had sent to producers had been returned
—even the two mailed to George Tyler from New London. Tyler's firm
(Liebler and Company), which began losing $3,000 a day toward the end
of 1914, became bankrupt early in 1915. Brooding about this experience
twenty-five years later, O'Neill tried to cheer a discouraged author:

"Here's one rejection experience you will never tie: I sent my first
two long plays to a famous Broadway producer. He was an old friend of
my father's. That should have given me an 'in,' one would think. Well, I
waited and waited. Then I wrote letters. Never a reply. Then I wrote
asking for my scripts back. Nothing happened. Finally a year and a half
later, after a season in which he put on lousy plays and they all failed,
he went into bankruptcy. Six months or so later I got my scripts back—
from the Receiver. They were in the same wrapping in which I had sent
them. It had never even been opened!"

O'Neill scorned the idea of taking a humdrum job and trying to
write plays on the side. Since he couldn't have what he wanted, he
plunged into another bout with the bottle.

Greenwich Village was a good place for a drunken spree. In the years
just before the United States entered the war, the Village was aflame with
radical ideas, violent soul-searching and monumental egotism. Its eager,
young and not-so-young artists were investigating their newly discovered
libidos, and many of them were pleased to wear not only their hearts but
their souls on their sleeves. Uninhibitedly pursuing love and art, emancipated women lived alone or in various freewheeling alliances, in sparsely
furnished and cheaply rented rooms, where candles were the sole illumi-

nation and a batik mat the only decorative note. Journalists like John Reed and Lincoln Steffens met in little restaurants and musty saloons, where meals could be put on the cuff, or at the continental Brevoort and Lafayette Hotels, to exchange ideas on stopping the war and saving humanity. Writers like Harry Kemp and Maxwell Bodenheim and anarchists like the long-suffering Emma Goldman pursued their various chimeras. Mabel Dodge, recently separated from a rich husband, collected people such as Big Bill Haywood and Elizabeth Gurley Flynn in her salon on lower Fifth Avenue—where controversy centered on sex, cubism, and Freud, and voices were raised to extol or decry anarchism, socialism and yellow journalism. The only point on which everyone agreed was that "uptowners," representing middle-class conventions and narrow tastes in literature, art and politics, were contemptible. The Greenwich Villagers were all passionately striving to be and to express themselves, and if the result of this individualism sometimes appeared as naïveté, exhibitionism or even borderline lunacy, it was undeniably alive. Some of them had money but none of them worried about it—that would have been bourgeois.

O'Neill, tenuously connected to this milieu through Louis Holliday—who, with his sister, Polly, was among the first of the Greenwich Village bohemians—blended unobtrusively into his new surroundings. Another friend, George Bellows, was in the Village, along with John Sloan and Art Young, helping to stun intellectual New Yorkers with pictorial contributions to *The Masses*. Neither Bellows nor any of the others who drew and wrote for the magazine were paid. Theoretically run as a co-operative venture, *The Masses* was kept supplied with material by such contributors as Carl Sandburg, Sherwood Anderson, Amy Lowell, Babette Deutsch, Bertrand Russell, Maxim Gorky and Vachel Lindsay. Max Eastman, who had let himself be talked into editing the magazine at no salary, only recently had managed to vote himself a small monthly stipend.

In the era before the war, the Village was part New York slum, part Western boom town, part Paris Left Bank. The area had remained a backwater while the rest of Manhattan grew toward the sky and moved north along Broadway and Fifth Avenue. Most of the Village houses were small and shabby, but they had an Old World flavor their occupants found charming and the streets were a narrow, erratic tangle of curvings and crossings. Only the north side of Washington Square, the uptown boundary of the Village, was still fashionable. A few blocks south of Washington Arch, which dominated the square, the area ceased to make any claim to elegance. In the early 1900's a Negro slum appeared a few blocks south of the arch—devaluating nearby real estate and placing rentals within reach of artists escaping from middle-class backgrounds all over the country.

One of the places a few of these artists were just beginning to investigate was a ramshackle saloon-hotel called, euphemistically, the Golden Swan. Its clientele, which, in 1915, included far more truck drivers, teamsters, gamblers and gangsters than artists, had long since bestowed on the Golden Swan a more descriptive name. They called it the Hell Hole, and with this designation it ultimately achieved some fame as the favorite haunt of Eugene O'Neill. John Sloan and Charles Demuth were among a number of artists who made paintings or etchings of the Hell Hole's seedily picturesque interior.

The Hell Hole was a representative Irish saloon. It had a sawdust-covered floor, rude wooden tables, and was filled with the smell of sour beer and mingled sounds of alcoholic woe and laughter. Its barroom was entered from the corner of Sixth Avenue and Fourth Street—the "front room," in which women were not allowed. Above the doorway swung a wooden sign decorated with a tarnished gilt swan. Farther east, on Fourth Street, was the "family entrance," a glass door that gave access to a small, dank, gaslit chamber known as the "backroom." Wooden tables clustered about a smoking potbellied stove, and it was here that respectable Irish widows came to cry into their five-cent mugs of beer.

Between front and back rooms was a stairway leading to the gloomy regions of the flats above, where Tom Wallace, proprietor of the Hell Hole, lived and rented rooms. In the front room O'Neill could join, with morose pleasure, a group of men every bit as down and out as the denizens of Jimmy-the-Priest's. Here Tom Wallace, large, lugubrious, clean-shaven, an ex-prizefighter and friend of the Tammany Hall leader Richard Croker, would occasionally join his customers in a shot of five-cent whiskey, having emerged from his upstairs quarters. He rarely went out of doors.

Members of a ferocious gang, the Hudson Dusters, made the Hell Hole their headquarters, as did ex-politicians, anarchists (recently out of jail or on their way in), gamblers, touts and pimps. Lefty Louie, the bouncer, presided behind the bar. On the clouded mirror hung a portrait of Richard Croker decorated by crossed shillelaghs and a wreath of encircling shamrocks. The mirror reflected shelves lined with plates of free food. Like most saloons of the era, the Hell Hole served free lunch to its customers and sometimes, inadvertently, to the neighborhood children. A man who grew up near the Hell Hole fondly recalled roller-skating through its swinging barroom doors, grabbing a fistful of food, and skating out through the family entrance; Wallace would thrust his head out of of an upstairs window and shout abuses.

Two other decorative features of the Hell Hole were a grandfather clock and a glass case mounted on a wall in the back room, containing a bedraggled, stuffed swan "floating" on gilded, wooden lily pads. There was also a dumbwaiter, which carried supplies between the barroom and some mysterious, interior region, and served as a speaking tube for Lefty Louie, below, and Wallace, above. A large window was set into the Sixth Avenue side of the saloon, but such light as filtered through its dusty panes was dimmed by the massive structure of the Sixth Avenue el, whose thunder provided a steady background to the barroom noises.

O'Neill learned to know and wait for the pattern of sounds made by the el. In his one-act play *Hughie,* written in 1942, he described the thoughts of the night clerk of a cheap West Side hotel located near the el in the Forties. He wrote: "The Clerk's mind remains in the street to greet the noise of a far off El train. Its approach is pleasantly like a memory of hope; then it roars and rocks and rattles past the nearby corner, and the noise pleasantly deafens; then it recedes and dies, and there is something melancholy about that. But there *is* hope. Only so many El trains pass in one night, and each one passing leaves one less to pass, so the night recedes too, until at last it must die and join all the other long nights in Nirvana, the Big Night of Nights. And that's life."

The noise of the el also could be heard and felt in the Hell Hole's backroom, where a smaller window let in only a sinister ray of light.

It was from the Hell Hole that O'Neill, twenty-four years later, drew most of his major characters for *The Iceman Cometh*—notably Hickey, who, though he contains elements of several other people, including O'Neill's brother, was partly inspired by a man known as "Happy." Happy, a collector for a laundry chain, made regular Friday visits to the Hell Hole, and on such occasions would dispense cheer and free drinks. One Friday he failed to appear, and it was learned he had absconded with the laundry funds. Happy headed west and was never heard from again.

Although the physical setting of *The Iceman Cometh* resembles Jimmy-the-Priest's and takes place in 1912, the year O'Neill lived in that water-front saloon, the play's most striking characters are modeled on people he met in 1915 at the Hell Hole. Especially significant is the portrayal of Willie Oban, who fits neatly into the gallery of O'Neill's self-portraits.

Like a number of O'Neill's principal characters, Oban is part Jamie as well as part Eugene. Willie Oban is described as a Harvard Law School alumnus and a roomer at Harry Hope's, the setting for *The Iceman Cometh.* (Harry Hope is Tom Wallace, and his name, aside from the symbolism conveyed by the word "hope," is deliberately suggestive of Hell

Hole, just as Oban, an odd surname, suggests O'Neill.) Oban is given to blurting, from the depths of an alcoholic dream, "Papa! Papa!" He has the same sort of resentful emotional dependence on his father as Jamie and Eugene had and feels overshadowed by him; there are references to his family sending for him in the saloon periodically to "give him the rush to a cure," and Oban's reference to his father as "The King of the Bucket Shops" is suggestive of Eugene's derisive references to James as "My father, The Count of Monte Cristo."

In the winter of 1915, O'Neill was as sodden, self-pitying, hopeless and self-destructive as Willie Oban. Several people who met him that year were convinced he was drinking himself to death.

The Hell Hole habitué who made the most searing impression on O'Neill was an incredible man named Terry Carlin, who in *The Iceman Cometh*, is called Larry Slade. Only a suggestion of this man's personality and background and his impact on O'Neill's thinking emerge from the play. Actually Carlin had a greater effect on O'Neill's philosophy than any other living man. O'Neill's physical description of Larry Slade in *The Iceman Cometh* applied accurately to Carlin: "tall, raw-boned, with coarse straight white hair, worn long and raggedly cut." Larry is sixty, a roomer at Harry Hope's and a one-time syndicalist-anarchist.

"He has a gaunt Irish face with a big nose, high cheekbones, a lantern jaw with a week's stubble of beard, a mystic's meditative pale-blue eyes with a gleam of sharp sardonic humor in them. . . . His clothes are dirty and much slept in. His gray flannel shirt, open at the neck, has the appearance of having never been washed. From the way he methodically scratches himself with his long-fingered, hairy hands, he is lousy and reconciled to being so. . . . His face [has] the quality of a pitying but weary old priest's."

When O'Neill met Terry Carlin that winter in the Hell Hole, Terry was in his fifties. He was thin and his hair was still dark. His blue-gray eyes had flecks in the irises from a gunpowder explosion, and he had long yellow teeth and long bony fingers. He was unkempt and unclean by choice. He had not worked for a living in many years, but he always found someone to keep him in liquor.

Terry lived entirely on his Irish charm. Jack London and Theodore Dreiser liked and admired him. He was a facile, often brilliant talker. A disciple, like O'Neill, of Nietzsche, Terry took the German philosopher more literally than O'Neill and considered himself superhuman, in the image of Nietzsche's spiritual and intellectual superman. By his own standards, he was a compassionate man; to those who could not follow the mystical turn of his mind he appeared cold-blooded, almost inhuman.

There was much in Terry's background that paralleled O'Neill's and drew the two men close. In addition, O'Neill found in Terry another fatherly mentor.

Born Terence O'Carolan, Terry shortened his name for reasons of his own. Like James O'Neill, he sprang from Irish peasant stock and his family, too, migrated to America when Terry was a boy. The O'Carolan family, including mother, father and seven children, settled in New York in the 1860's and tried to subsist on the father's salary of $8 a week. As James had done, Terry went to work at an early age in a sweatshop. And though Terry could be as winning and outgoing as James, he was far more sensitive and imaginative. His thoughts turned on the social injustice he saw around him and, long before he embraced anarchy as a creed, his thinking was socialistic.

Terry worked for ten years—until he was twenty—as a journeyman tanner and currier; he soon excelled at his trade, but his heart was in reading, not work. He spent his spare time with books, giving himself a remarkable, if one-sided, education.

Like the O'Neill family, the O'Carolans were an emotionally inter-dependent clan. "We clung desperately to one another long after the necessity was past," Terry once informed the journalist Hutchins Hapgood, who described Terry at length in a volume called *An Anarchist Woman*. This book, actually the story of a young woman named Marie, who had been Terry's mistress, had been published a few years before O'Neill arrived in Greenwich Village; whatever details of his life and philosophy Terry did not personally impart to O'Neill during the winter of 1915-16, O'Neill found in *An Anarchist Woman*, which he read with fascination.

Terry, like O'Neill, had a dearly loved brother named Jim, whom he once described as "my other ego." It was because of an experience involving Jim that Terry decided, when he was in his early thirties, to become a social exile. His brother, who had a good job with a Pittsburgh tannery and owned $25,000 worth of stock in the company, asked Terry, who by then was regarded as an expert in the leather manufacturing field, to come to Pittsburgh. Jim's firm was losing thousands of dollars a week because of a flaw in the manufacturing process, and Jim thought Terry could find and correct the flaw. Terry had been happily living in a Chicago slum with Marie, whom he had rescued from a career of prostitution; he worked only occasionally to provide the bare necessities for himself and Marie.

"It was with the utmost repugnance that I quit my happy slum life," Terry wrote to Hapgood, "but I loved Jim, and it was the call of the ancient clan in my blood. When I arrived in Pittsburgh, without a trunk, and with other marks of the proletarian on me, Mr. Kirkman, the millionnaire tanner, showered me with every luxury—every luxury except that of thought and true emotion. Never before did I realize so intensely my indifference to what money can buy. My private office in the shop was stocked with wines and imported cigarettes: but I was not so well off as in my happy slum."

Terry toiled for a month and finally found the source of the trouble, in an obscure process. He was able to advise Kirkman how to correct it and was responsible for saving the firm a fortune.

"I had put no price on my services," Terry continued. "For Jim's sake, I had worked like a Trojan, physically and mentally, for a month. With unlimited money at my disposal, I had drawn only twenty dollars altogether, and this I sent to Marie, to keep the wolf away."

Kirkman offered Terry the job of running the shop at a large salary and with the chance to buy $2,000 worth of stock. But Terry said he would not exploit the workers, who earned only $7 or $8 a week and that he would not permit any worker to be discharged for incompetency. He had never met a man he could not teach, he told Kirkman, nor had he ever discharged a man. Not even Jim could persuade Terry to stay, and he departed with nothing but his railroad fare to Chicago, though Jim assured him that Kirkman would send him between $500 and $1,000 for his services. But within a few days Jim found that Kirkman had no intention of sending Terry a penny; he was angry at the spurned offer, and used the excuse that no written or verbal contract had been made for Terry's services. Jim resigned from the firm in protest, in spite of the fact that he had a wife and children to support.

Terry was crushed by the chaos he had brought on Jim and by the lopsidedness of a world in which love of money could play such a vindictive role.

"Mr. Kirkman thought all the world of Jim and could not run the shop without him. Nor could he recover from the blow, for he loved my brother, as everybody did," Terry wrote to Hapgood. "Mr. Kirkman died a few weeks afterward, and after a year or two the firm went into the hands of a receiver. All this happened because of a few paltry dollars, which I did not ask for, for which I did not care a damn—and this is business! I heartily rejoice, if not in Mr. Kirkman's death, at least in the dispersion of his family and their being forced into our ranks, where there is some hope for them."

Regarding his brother, Terry added: "Jim was one of the maimed ones in my family. . . . Years ago, defective machinery and a surgeon's malpractice made one arm useless. The Pittsburgh affair broke up his beautiful home."

Although Jim O'Carolan and Jamie O'Neill had been maimed by life in different ways, the resemblance between the two was startling and provided yet another bond between Terry and Eugene. In his last years Jim O'Carolan withdrew from life, just as Eugene believed Jamie was doing. "I have . . . a desire to be considered a dead one," Jim wrote to Terry, "and am doing all but the one thing that will make my wish a reality. I am long tired of the game.　The chase for dollars I am performing here is very disgusting to me. . . . It is a hell of a life and I wish it were done."

Jim O'Carolan had been dead many years when Terry and O'Neill met, but Terry still held poignant memories of him. "He died of that great loneliness of soul which made of his wasted body a battered barricade against the stupidity which finally engulfed him," Terry said. Some years later, when Jamie O'Neill died, Eugene said almost the same thing about his own brother.

Another area of sympathetic understanding between Terry and Eugene was their lost Catholicism. "Though we were Catholics on the surface," Terry once said, describing his family during their early years in America, "we were pagans at bottom." Terry described his brother's deathbed comment, when it was proposed that a priest be sent for: "I hire no spiritual nurse," said Jim.

"There must be some meaning," Terry wrote, "for all this ancient agony. Oh, that I might expand my written words into an Epic of the Slums, into an Iliad of the Proletaire! If an oyster can turn its pain into a pearl, then, verily, when we have suffered enough, something must arise out of our torture—else the world has no meaning. . . . It cannot be that I came up out of the depths for nothing. If I could pierce my heart and write red lines, I might perhaps tell the truth. But only a High Silence meets me, and I do not understand. . . . I feel like a diver who has nigh strangled himself to bring up a handful of seaweed, and so feels he must go down again—and again—until he attains somewhere the holy meaning of Life."

Terry left it to O'Neill to pierce his heart and write with red lines. O'Neill became, in a way clearly discernible from his plays, Terry's spokesman. "How be a mouthpiece for the poor?" Terry had asked, many years before he met O'Neill. "How can art master the master-problem? They who have nothing much to say, often say it well and in a popular form; they are unhampered by weighty matters. It takes an eagle to soar with a heavy weight in its grasp. The human being, rocking to and fro with his little grief, must give way in depth of meaning to him who is rocked with the grief of generations past, present, and to come. It is then that love might rise, love so close to agony that agony cannot last: the love that will search ceaselessly, in the slums, in the dives, throughout all life, for the inevitable, and will accept no alternative and no compromise."

O'Neill became Terry's eagle. Terry put into words for him many of his own half-formed ideas and gave him insight into others. For example, O'Neill's own early attitude toward prostitutes was strengthened by Terry's more articulate one.

"The kind of prostitution you contemplate is no worse than the kind often called marriage," Terry once told a friend of Marie's who came to him for advice on following a career in the streets. "Selling your body for a lifetime is perhaps worse than selling it for an hour or for a day. But the immediate result of this kind of prostitution which you plan is very terrible practically. It generally leads to frightful diseases which will waste your bodies and perhaps injure your minds. . . . Perhaps you will be better off so than in domestic drudgery. It is a choice of evils, but if you are very brave and courageous you may perhaps get along without either. But if forced to one or the other, I recommend prostitution. It may be worse for you but, as a protest, it is better for society, in the long run."

It was Terry or, rather, his Marie who provided O'Neill with the basis of his characterization of Anna Christie. Marie, like Anna, had tried being a "nurse girl" at one time, before taking to the streets. After being rescued and redeemed by Terry, Marie eventually abandoned him and went off to a mountain retreat. The sense of being washed clean, of being reborn, that Anna found at sea on her father's barge, Marie found in the hills of California. She described her feelings in a letter she wrote to Terry:

"I am intoxicated by all this beauty and love the very air and earth. I feel the ecstasy of the aesthetic fanatic . . . I feel newborn and free. The air is scented with balsam and bay, and a pure crystal stream flows through this valley between two hills covered with giant redwood trees, and rare orchids . . . toss wantonly in the breeze on the tree and hilltops. . . . At night I sleep as I have never slept—a deep dreamless slumber. I awake to a cold plunge in the stream. Oh, it just suits me! I am tired of people, tired of tears and laughter, of men that 'laugh and weep,' and 'of what may come hereafter, for men that sow to reap.' . . . Everything in the past is dead. . . . I have become happy, healthy, and free, free without hardness. . . . I will now lave myself with the pure crystal waters and make myself clean again, and then look on the sun once more."

The speech O'Neill wrote for Anna—the sort of speech he once described as "the native eloquence of us fog people"—echoes the words of Marie's letter:

"I feel old . . . like I'd been living a long, long time—out here in the fog. . . . It's like I'd come home after a long visit away some place. It all seems like I'd been here before lots of times . . . why d'you s'pose I feel so—so—like I'd found something I'd missed and been looking for . . . And I seem to have forgot—everything that's happened—like it didn't matter no more. And I feel clean, somehow—like you feel yust after you've took a bath. And I feel happy for once—yes, honest!—happier than I ever been anywhere before!"

Marie also could have been pointing the way for a Nina Leeds and *Strange Interlude* when she wrote to Hapgood, of a friend: "I am fascinated by Rose. . . . I always like to be near her when there is no one else around. She reveals herself to me then; in fact quite throws off the mask which all women wear. In order to encourage her to do this, I apparently throw down my own mask. Oh, how I gloat over her then, when she shows me a side of her life and betrays secret thoughts and feelings to me half unconsciously! Sometimes I succeed in having her do this when there is a third person present, and the look of hatred which passes across her face when she perceives she has made a mistake, is a most interesting thing to see."

Terry effectively discussed with O'Neill the concept of the mask worn by all men to conceal their souls. "Words only conceal thought and do not express it," he said; O'Neill repeated this remark, as his own, to countless friends in the following years.

Terry eventually gave up everything. He ceased to be interested in the anarchist movement, with which he had been intellectually, if not physically, involved; he refused even to try to earn a living, explaining that he was "driven to be a parasite, for honest living there is none."

"Never have I seen Life more triumphant and rampant, more brimming over with hope and defiant of all conditions, hygienic and otherwise," he wrote to Hapgood, after becoming a hobo. "I am very 'crummy,' badly flea bitten, overrun with bed bugs, but, redemption of it all, I am free and always drunk." He was also, on occasion, drugged. "I had to seek surcease in my old remedy of hashish and chloroform, which was a change from suffering to stupidity," he wrote to Hapgood.

❖

By the time O'Neill met him, Terry had, like Larry Slade, retired totally from life. He stayed drunk, or drugged, content to sleep where he could, eat what little he could beg—and talk to anyone who would listen. Unfortunately for O'Neill, in the process of absorbing Terry's ideas, he also absorbed, for the moment, Terry's nihilism.

Terry's hobo existence was what held the strongest appeal for O'Neill that winter. But long before Terry's creative thinking took a grip on O'Neill's own, many of the destructive aspects of Terry's personality influenced O'Neill.

Once more O'Neill became a derelict. He did no writing except some poetry, though he put on a brave front for Dr. Lyman, whose yearly questionnaire followed him to New York early in 1916. Listing his address as a "hotel" at 38 Washington Square, he declared that he was working as a dramatic critic and receiving $25 a week, and that he spent six or seven hours a day writing. He did, on occasion, occupy a room at 38 Washington Square, a rooming house; but he infrequently went to bed at all, preferring to doze, when he was exhausted, at a table in the back room of the Hell Hole. Occasionally he and Terry slept in empty lofts.

In his long career as a parasite Terry had got to know all the methods of survival. A favorite device was to send a presentable-looking friend to one of the Greenwich Village real estate agents in search of quarters. The friend would be taken to see a flat, and in leaving, would press a lump of clay against the door latch, to prevent it from locking. Then he would tell Terry or O'Neill the address of the empty flat, and the two would move in with a couple of mattresses and some orange crates, on which they arranged their books and bottles of whiskey; if they couldn't find mattresses, they slept on newspapers. Their food was the Hell Hole's free soup, and sometimes oysters which they could buy cheaply by the sack at the Fulton fish market.

In the spring of 1916 O'Neill and Terry were joined by a temporarily affluent newspaper reporter, with whom they rented a spacious unfurnished flat on Fourth Street between Washington Square and Sixth Avenue. Because the three occupants tossed empty oyster shells, cigarette butts and other refuse into a corner and let it accumulate, the premises came to be known as the "Garbage Flat." Writing to a friend many years later, O'Neill said he remembered the flat "fondly and vividly."

"I ought to," he added. "I christened it. . . . it continued to be unfurnished except for piles of sacking as beds, newspapers as bed linen, and packing boxes for chairs and tables. Also, it remained unswept. Toward the end of our tenancy, there was a nice even carpet of cigarette butts, reminding one of the snow scene in an old melodrama. And—well, in short, the name I gave it was by no means in any way a libel."

Like Terry, O'Neill made it a point never to be sober. O'Neill was by this time in an advanced state of alcoholism. It was essential for him to have a shot of whiskey on waking up in the morning, but often it was agony for him to get it down.

Robert Carlton Brown, who was a successful writer of magazine fiction and also a contributor to *The Masses*, once recalled meeting O'Neill during that winter and being appalled by his condition.

"I used to see a lot of Gene at the Hell Hole," Brown said. "I liked him because of his Irish temperament, his wanting to drink, and his love for travel. Often, he had no place to sleep, and sometimes, after a night spent drinking at the Hell Hole, I'd take him with me to the apartment of a friend who was out of town. I'd buy a pint of whiskey before we went to sleep somewhere around dawn, fill an eight-ounce tumbler and put it near Gene's bed. He looked so weak I thought he was going to die. Sometime during the next afternoon I'd be awakened by a low, feeble call from him. He'd want me to help him lift the glass to his lips."

Brown, who also knew Terry, remembered O'Neill's great affection for him and believed it was Terry who saved O'Neill's life that year by forcing him to take food once in a while.

Terry seemed to have a genuine fondness for O'Neill, even if the immediate result of his affection was to help drag O'Neill into the gutter which he himself inhabited so cozily. When they were living together, it was often Terry who ambled over to the Hell Hole with an empty tin container for soup. He would also beg free whiskey, which, as often as not, he got.

One day Terry returned with soup and whiskey to a flat on Third Street, recently discovered by him and O'Neill and furnished with the unexpected luxury of a big brass bed. O'Neill was lying on the bed, awake and trembling, but with determination in his eyes. He told Terry he had made up his mind to quit drinking.

Advising him against quitting cold, Terry suggested tapering off and then sticking to a regimen of moderate drinking. But O'Neill said he had to quit completely and at once. Terry shook his head pityingly, polished off the whiskey he had brought for O'Neill, and vanished, leaving his roommate twitching on the bed.

Within an hour, Terry had rounded up ten of the most unsavory characters he could find, including an aged whore, a drug addict and several thugs. He sent each one, in turn, to stare silently at O'Neill, who was using all his self-control to pull out of his hangover. By the time the last of Terry's little army had gone, O'Neill was begging for a drink—which Terry happily supplied.

Back on his alcoholic routine, O'Neill moved with Terry into an abandoned loft on Fulton Street, probably to be nearer to the supply of oysters. Unfortunately, when O'Neill ran out of cash on Fulton Street, it was harder to come by free whiskey. When Terry was not around to panhandle for a drink, O'Neill would drag himself off his mattress in the morning and walk all the way to the northeast corner of Twenty-seventh Street and Madison Avenue. This was the only place where his credit was always good—the barroom of the Garden Hotel.

Trembling from the effort of his hike, O'Neill would prop himself against the bar and order his shot. The bartender knew him, and would place the glass in front of him, toss a towel across the bar, as though absent-mindedly forgetting it, and move away. Arranging the towel around his neck, O'Neill would grasp the glass of whiskey and an end of the towel in one hand and clutch the other end of the towel with his other hand. Using the towel as a pulley, he would laboriously hoist the glass to his lips. His hands trembled so violently that even with this aid he could scarcely pour the whiskey down his throat, and often spilled part of it. ("Bartenders are the most sympathetic people in the world," O'Neill often told friends years later.)

The Garden Hotel was a place where O'Neill had felt at home for a long time. A four-story, red-brick building without an elevator, it was more rooming house than hotel. James had lived there on and off since 1911 or 1912, when he was in town without Ella. Jamie stayed there with him, and Eugene sometimes joined them between his bouts of wandering. The hotel was across the street from the original Madison Square Garden and was a gathering point for fight promoters, circus people, six-day bicycle racers, gamblers and racketeers, as well as actors.

"The circus men who stayed there I knew very well," O'Neill once said. "Not only the circus men, but the poultry men, the horse breeders and all others who displayed their wares at the old Madison Square Garden. I used to meet them all in the bar."

More recently James had taken a suite at the Prince George Hotel, a luxurious establishment on Twenty-seventh Street and Fifth Avenue, a block and a half from the Garden Hotel. James and Ella now considered the Prince George their permanent New York home. But James continued to drop in for a drink now and then at the Garden Hotel and to take some of his meals there. Jamie preferred the Garden to the Prince George as a place to live.

That winter, the tour of *Joseph and His Brethren* having ended with its producers' bankruptcy, James regarded himself as retired from the stage. Liebler and Tyler had managed to raise just enough money to move the company out of St. Louis, where Brandon Tynan played Joseph for the last time with tears in his eyes. James was now nearly seventy. Without touring or rehearsing to occupy him, he had nothing much to do but watch helplessly as Jamie disintegrated and Eugene drifted, apparently in the same direction as his brother.

James and Ella lived comfortably in an eighth-floor suite at the Prince George, consisting of a bedroom, parlor and bath. According to an Irish porter named Dan Foley, the O'Neills' routine went something like this: Every morning at about 8:30 or 9:00, James would breakfast in the hotel dining room. About 9:30 James left to drink with his cronies at The Players or the Lambs. Soon after his departure Jamie arrived from the Garden Hotel to visit his mother—a daily duty he rarely shirked. He sometimes brought her freshly baked rolls, which she loved with her morning coffee.

"He'd give his mother a couple of kisses and stay there with her for two or three hours," Foley has recalled. "He helped himself to his father's whiskey. I'd see him leave, all smiles."

Jamie safely departed, his father returned to the hotel at about four in the afternoon. At six James and Ella would go down to the dining room. Sometimes Ella would accompany James to the theatre, or else she would return to her room while James joined friends in the Prince George Tap Room, where women were not allowed. If James was reasonably sure he would not run into Jamie or Eugene, he might stroll the short distance to the Garden Hotel bar. But he could not often be sure of missing Jamie.

"I used to go over to the Garden Hotel bar on my way home after work," Foley once recalled. "Jamie was usually there drinking, and sometimes his brother was with him. One night I remember seeing Gene and Jamie on the sidewalk outside the Garden Hotel, with their arms around each other. They were talking and kissing each other, both as high as kites."

Although James found it painful to see his sons, he still could not bring himself to abandon them. He eased his conscience by continuing to keep them both on dole; every day he left a dollar for each of them at the cashier's cage of the Prince George Hotel.

Louis Bergen, who was one of four bartenders at the Garden Hotel, recalled a period when James and his two sons lived in rooms on the first floor. This was during a time Ella was in a sanitarium.

"Every morning James O'Neill and the boys would come into the bar, and Mr. O'Neill would go through a routine of giving each boy his daily allowance," Bergen said. "Usually, there'd be an argument. The old man would tell the boys they'd never amount to anything. The boys drank the bar rye—ten cents a shot, from a bottle I kept on ice; it was the worst thing you could drink. I knew it would kill Jamie eventually. The old man liked old-fashioneds; he'd usually wait until I wasn't busy, so I could take time to fix one the way he liked it. I'd crush the orange in it for him."

When the boys ran out of money, Bergen would ask them, "How are you fixed?" And if they shook their heads ruefully, he would put a bottle on the bar near them and walk away.

"The old man was very generous to me," Bergen added. "He offered to set me up in a café, once. He also wanted me, at one time, to take care of some property he owned in New Jersey. I turned down his offers, because I liked it at the Garden. It was a good bar; good food and no phony liquor."

The Garden bar was one of the busiest in the neighborhood. It, too, had a back room, which served as a restaurant, and it, too, provided O'Neill with a number of acquaintances whose characteristics later turned up in *The Iceman Cometh*. Before *The Iceman Cometh* was produced, O'Neill said that the setting was a combination of "three places I actually lived in." He did not specify the places, but they were obviously Jimmy-the-Priest's, to which he still paid occasional visits in 1915 and 1916, the Hell Hole, and the Garden Hotel.

Among the customers at the Garden Hotel was the policeman who had arrested Harry Thaw for shooting Stanford White on the roof of Madison Square Garden. Another regular was a man nicknamed "the Colonel": months behind in his rent, he solved his financial problems one day by marrying the elderly proprietress of his boardinghouse. There was a doctor, who had been barred from practice for drunkenness, and a young, department store publicity man named Frank, who was married to a beautiful, vacuous blonde. "What do you talk to her about?" O'Neill once asked Frank, to Bergen's amusement.

"Gene spoke so seldom," Bergen recalled, "that a lot of people thought he was a dummy. But when he did say something, it had meaning." Bergen was aware that O'Neill wanted to be a playwright and used to watch him making notes for plays on the margins of a *Bartender's Guide*.

Bergen, who recalled that one of the favorite anecdotes of his customers at the Garden involved James O'Neill, liked to tell it this way:

"One day the old man knocked off early from rehearsals and came into the bar, where everyone was placing bets on the day's big race—the annual Brooklyn handicap. Some of Mr. O'Neill's friends coaxed him to place a bet, but he didn't like to gamble on horses. Finally, though, he asked what horses were running, and when he heard that one of the entries was Irish Lad, he decided to place a ten-dollar bet on him. The odds on Irish Lad were forty to one, and everyone laughed at O'Neill. He asked who was riding Irish Lad, and when he was told it was a jockey called Frankie O'Neill, he bet another ten dollars. Someone called out that his colors were green and white, and O'Neill put down another ten dollars. By this time everyone in the bar was laughing like crazy. Irish Lad won, and then nobody laughed except Mr. O'Neill."

Jamie was an avid horseplayer when he had the cash and would sometimes place Bergen's bets for him, along with his own. Although Eugene was only mildly interested in horse racing, he was devoted to boxing and six-day bicycle racing, and often attended these events at Madison Square Garden. Several friends with whom, in later years, he attended sports events, attributed O'Neill's enthusiasm for sports to the natural admiration of a man not physically robust for men who lived by their physical endurance. All his life O'Neill admired feats of strength, and often sought the acquaintance of outstanding fighters, ballplayers and other athletes.

While O'Neill did not share his brother's passion for gambling, he had an intimate knowledge of gamblers and their argot, most of which he picked up at the Garden Hotel and which he used in his one-acter *Hughie*. Although the play is set in 1928 in a West Side hotel, the two characters in the script, a seedy gambler and a night clerk, were modeled on people he met at the Garden. The hotel's patrons also provided members of the raffish crew portrayed in *The Iceman Cometh*. Ed Mosher in *The Iceman Cometh* was based on a circus man named Bill Clarke, known affectionately as "Clarkey," whom O'Neill met that winter at the Garden Hotel.

Clarke, whom O'Neill later helped support, often paid for the drinks; compared with O'Neill, Clarke was affluent. Like O'Neill, he was willing to drink anything, and when funds for whiskey had been depleted he would sample wood alcohol flavored with Worcestershire sauce. Clarke, using the name Volo, had been the first man to perform a daring bicycle stunt called the loop-the-loop.

"One of my old chums," O'Neill once said, "was Volo the Volitant, a bicycle rider whose specialty was in precipitating himself down a steep incline and turning a loop or so in the air." A good Catholic, Clarke always said a Hail Mary when he began his stunt. Nevertheless, shortly before O'Neill met him, he fell and broke his back. After recovering from his accident he became a guide with a Manhattan sightseeing bus service.

Another man O'Neill met at the Garden Hotel, and who remained a friend for many years, was a Scotsman named William Stuart. Known to everyone as "Scotty," he was a brawny, big-featured man who had fought in the Boer War and later had been apprenticed to a woodcarver who worked on ships. Scotty earned his living by teaching a woodcarving class at a settlement house in Greenwich Village. With Scotty or Robert Brown or one of his other drinking companions O'Neill would thread his way between the Garden Hotel and the Hell Hole and sometimes, when the proprietor did not feel like extending his hospitality beyond the legal closing hour, he would move on to one of the nonalcoholic meeting places of Greenwich Village, such as Romany Marie's or Polly Holliday's. These were dimly lit cafés that stayed open all night, where the proprietors knew all their customers by their first names and were usually willing to stake those who couldn't pay to coffee and food.

Polly Holliday had opened the first café in the Village that became a meeting place for intellectuals. She was living with a man named Hippolyte Havel, whom O'Neill later portrayed as Hugo Kalmar in *The Iceman Cometh*. Hippolyte, a short, stocky, black-haired man, once likened by a friend to a ragged chrysanthemum, was a well-known figure in the Village. When O'Neill met him he was doubling as Polly's lover and cook. Born in Hungary of a gypsy mother, Hippolyte had been released from an insane asylum in Europe after the psychiatrist Krafft-Ebing pronounced him sane—an opinion that was not wholeheartedly shared by all his Village friends. After the asylum had come jail, from which he had escaped to London. In London he met Emma Goldman, became her lover, was helped by her to reach Chicago, and joined her radical circle, editing the anarchist newspaper *Arbeiterzeitung*.

Hippolyte was usually the center of attraction at Polly's, with his extravagant and profane denunciations of the bourgeoisie and his temper tantrums. He and Polly did not live peacefully, for Polly had a roving eye, and though Hippolyte was theoretically committed to a tolerant attitude about sexual freedom, he tended to lose his perspective where Polly was concerned. Polly's grievance against Hippolyte was of a different nature. One night, after Hippolyte had made a particularly noisy scene at the restaurant, she complained to one of her customers that Hippolyte was not acting in good faith, because he hadn't committed suicide. "He promised me over and over again," she said, "but he just won't keep his word."

Theodore Dreiser, while living in the Village and struggling to gain recognition, once told a friend, "Havel is one of those men who ought to be supported by the community; he is a valuable person for life, but can't take care of himself."

Although O'Neill enjoyed Polly's because of Hippolyte and also because he often ran into Louis Holliday there, his favorite place after the Hell Hole closed for the night was Romany Marie's, in Sheridan Square. Marie was Mrs. Damon Marchand, a buxom, flamboyant woman with a heavily accented, throaty voice who, though her family had been conservative Rumanians and she was respectably married, dressed like a gypsy and pretended to be one. She recalled that O'Neill turned up at the restaurant she operated with her husband almost every night during that winter.

"There was never a question of anyone having enough to eat," Marie said, "as long as there was food on my stove." Marie's specialty was Turkish coffee and she served no liquor.

One day, not too long after Marie and her husband had begun operating the little restaurant—as at Polly's, the male member of the partnership presided in the kitchen—half a dozen members of the Hudson Dusters gang paid them a visit. Organized in the late 1890's, when other vicious gangs like the Gophers, the Five Pointers, the Marginals and the Pearl Buttons terrorized Manhattan, the Dusters commandeered an old house below Horatio Street, on Hudson, which paralleled Sixth Avenue. This was their club, and here, to the helpless fury of their law-abiding neighbors, they entertained the waterfront prostitutes at all-night parties, with refreshments supplied by the merchants of the area. No one dared complain, for the Dusters became irritated when they were thwarted. One local saloonkeeper who refused to donate six kegs of beer for a party was subsequently robbed of his entire stock of liquor and his establishment was wrecked. Prominent members of the Dusters bore names like Kid Yorke, Circular Jack, Goo Goo Knox, Rubber Shaw, Honey Stewart and Ding Dong. Many of them were cocaine addicts and their narcotics-inspired courage made them a menace not only to the merchants but to the police.

One of their best-known feats of daring and revenge had taken place shortly before O'Neill came to the Village, and people were still talking about it. A policeman named Dennis Sullivan, who was assigned to the Charles Street Station, declared his intention of singlehandedly smashing the Hudson Dusters gang. He got ten of them arrested and the Dusters, after deliberation, set out to teach Sullivan a lesson. They did so one night when Sullivan was about to arrest another of their members in Greenwich Street. Four of them jumped on him, grabbed his coat, nightstick, shield and revolver, and beat him unconscious with blackjacks and stones. They rolled him on his back and ground their heels in his face to make a lasting impression.

Sullivan was hospitalized for many weeks, and the triumph of the Dusters was joyously celebrated not only locally but by gangdom in general. A member of the Gophers was so impressed by the Dusters' feat that he was moved to congratulate them in a poem (his name was One Lung Curran, and he was the acknowledged poet laureate of the West Side gangs):

> Says Dinny, "Here's me only chance
> To gain meself a name;
> I'll clean up the Hudson Dusters,
> And reach the hall of fame."
> He lost his stick and cannon,
> And his shield they took away,
> It was then that he remembered
> Every dog has got his day.

He went on through half a dozen more stanzas, which described the attack in detail, and the Dusters had the poem printed and distributed among the Village saloons and barbershops.

Naturally, Romany Marie did not welcome the Dusters' patronage.

"They were a fierce-looking gang, and everyone knew them by reputation," Marie said. "It was early in the evening and our place was packed, but when they came in, the customers quietly began to melt away."

Marie watched helplessly as her place emptied out, and regretted that O'Neill was not there, for she knew that they liked and respected him.

"Give us the strongest drink you have in the house," one of the Dusters demanded.

"The strongest drink is Turkish coffee," Marie said nervously.

"Serve it," ordered the tough.

Marie served three rounds of coffee, her husband looking on apprehensively from the kitchen. Then Marie, emboldened by her knowledge that she could call on O'Neill for protection, looked the leader straight in the eye, and told him, "You've had enough coffee." She presented her bill, which came to $4.50. She charged 25 cents a cup for her coffee, and was sure the thugs would consider this exorbitant. To her astonishment, the leader reached into his pocket and brought out the cash, pushed back his chair, and swaggered out, followed by his men. They made straight for the Hell Hole, where they encountered O'Neill.

"That Romany Marie is some dame," the leader told him. "She put us out of her place, and made us pay for our coffee; her husband was scared, but she wasn't." O'Neill, angry, asked the gangsters to keep out of Marie's place in the future, and his request was obeyed.

The Hudson Dusters, who were predominantly Irish, admired O'Neill and considered his friendship a privilege. His appeal to such people was extraordinary. Somehow he evoked and held their respect and admiration, and in many cases a dogged love. They called him "the Kid," and when a fight broke out in a saloon one of them always shouted protectively, "Look out for the Kid!"

Early that winter one of the Hudson Dusters—possibly Ding Dong, whose accomplishments as a thief were highly respected—noticing that O'Neill went about in a threadbare overcoat, or just a jacket lined with newspapers to keep out the cold, told him: "You shouldn't oughta dress like that, Gene. Tell you what. You make a trip up Sixth Avenue right away. Pick out any overcoat you want and tell me the store. I'll hand you over the coat tomorrow."

O'Neill was touched, but declined the offer.

O'Neill's main concern that winter, when he was sober enough to think clearly, was with the revolutionary theories that occupied his anarchist and socialist friends; the handful of poems he scribbled—most of them while sitting in the back room of the Hell Hole—included a ballad called "Revolution" and one called "Dirty Bricks of Buildings." But several others indicated a gloomy interest in the condition of his heart. "What Do You See, Wan One?" "Good Night," and "The White Night" do not have a political ring to their titles.

O'Neill was still exchanging letters with Beatrice, but since he seemed unable to consolidate that relationship he took advantage of more accessible prospects. He did not have to extend himself, for women still gravitated toward him in spite of his ragged condition.

For a while he amused himself with a beautiful, black-haired woman named Becky, who was also the mistress of Big Bill Haywood and various others who lived in or passed through the Village. But it was not until late in the winter that he felt the stirrings of love again. There was, as with most of O'Neill's romances, an obstacle. The new object of O'Neill's affection was an exquisite, twenty-four-year-old, married woman named Louise Bryant Trullinger. The fact that she was married was not what bothered O'Neill, however; what upset him was that his friend John Reed had met her first and that she had recently become his mistress.

Reed, home from covering the European War for the *Metropolitan Magazine* and nursing bruises from a tempestuous affair with Mabel Dodge, had gone to visit his family in Portland, Oregon, and while there had fallen in love with Louise. She had chestnut hair with a blonde sheen, eyes that could deepen from gray to blue, a slender figure, and a provocative, gamine quality. Within a few weeks of the meeting she had left Portland and her husband, Paul, who was a dentist, to follow Reed to New York, where she moved into his Washington Square apartment. Reed, lyrically in love, displayed her proudly. "I think I've found Her at last," he wrote to a friend. "She's wild, brave and straight—and graceful and lovely to look at."

Louise was undeniably wild—and brave, too, in the sense of being recklessly eager to squander herself; she was avid for romance and adventure and determined to make something of herself as a writer. She had attempted journalism with some success; in alliance with Reed, to whom she was genuinely devoted in her own way, she began to advance her writing career in New York. But she was also very much subject to her emotions and found it difficult to resist anyone who seemed to need her. Louise wanted to be all things to all men. She was, by instinct, a vivandière.

In his naïveté O'Neill was slow to recognize this quality in her. For weeks he adored her silently, resigned to the fact that she was Reed's girl and ashamed of himself for hoping that she could ever be his. It was understood by Reed's friends that he and Louise would be married as soon as she could arrange a divorce. Troubled though he was by Louise's relationship with Reed, something made O'Neill hang on to his dream of getting Louise for himself. When, in the spring, he learned that Reed and Louise were planning to spend the summer in Provincetown among a group of writers and artists, many of them from Greenwich Village, he decided he would go too.

His long mood of despair was over. Perhaps he had needed the plunge into the depths to make him aware, once again, of the possibilities of life. Miraculously, he was not only alive but still in fairly good health.

In the spring of 1916 O'Neill headed for Provincetown, where he was finally to find recognition.

XXVI

ONLY RECENTLY DISCOVERED BY A SMALL GROUP OF Greenwich Village artists and writers, the Provincetown to which O'Neill journeyed in 1916 was a quiet fishing settlement, proud of its whaling background, at the tip of Cape Cod. The town's two narrow streets, Commercial and Bradford—connected by a multitude of tiny alleyways— ran parallel to the Provincetown harbor. Along these streets were clustered the cottages and shops of the village. Wharves were strung out from most of the houses lining the bay side of Commercial Street. Behind Bradford Street stretched miles of dunes and scrub grass extending to the Atlantic. Provincetown's population was divided among three groups—families of the early Portuguese settlers, descendants of the first Puritan arrivals, and "outsiders," who included such year-round residents as the town doctor, businessmen and a few artists.

Provincetown had been claimed as a haven for Manhattan's avant-garde by Mary Heaton Vorse. Widowed in 1915 for the second time, Mrs. Vorse supported herself and her children by free-lance writing. She first visited Provincetown during the summer of 1906 to give her children sea air, fell in love with the village, and bought an old house that she later turned into a year-round residence. Hutchins Hapgood, a college friend of Mrs. Vorse's first husband, was the second of the writers to arrive, and after him came other New Yorkers in search of a summer refuge. Two among them were George Cram Cook and his wife, Susan Glaspell.

Cook, called "Jig" by his friends, was the next in the series of older men to cast a notable influence on O'Neill's life. O'Neill's senior by fifteen years, he was a Greek scholar and university professor from Davenport, Iowa. He had left a wife and children to marry Susan Glaspell, a burgeoning writer. Cook loved working with his hands. He was six feet tall, powerfully built and had enormous vitality and a contagious enthusiasm for history and the arts. Although not a first-rate writer himself, he sensed genius in others and had the ability to stimulate other people's talent. Erudite and mystical, Jig regretted not having been born a Greek of the fourth century B.C. He yearned to re-create the Athenian cradle of art and philosophy and spent his life trying to impose his dream on his surroundings.

Cook had a mane of white hair and a habit of twisting a shaggy lock between his fingers when moved or excited. Kind, patient, visionary, he inclined to be pontifical and vain. He could be hurt by any slight of his well-meant guidance. Susan Glaspell, a delicate, sad-eyed, witty woman, worshiped her husband and devoted herself in equal measure to him and to her writing; it was she who provided the backbone of their income.

Cook and Susan Glaspell had participated in the birth of the Washington Square Players in Greenwich Village in the winter of 1914. Although that little group, which became the foundation for the Theatre Guild, was organized in protest against the commercialism of Broadway, it was not experimental enough for Cook. The Washington Square Players were interested in giving American writers a hearing, but were even more attracted to the European experimentalists. Cook dreamed of a theatre that would exist solely for the expression of native talent—that would, in fact, inspire the emergence of such talent—"a threshing floor," he said, "on which a young and growing culture could find its voice." In the summer of 1915 he made a beginning toward the realization of this dream by inviting his friends to write one-act plays as "an experiment."

None of Cook's friends were professional playwrights, but several were short-story writers. Their unfamiliarity with the dramatic form was, in Cook's opinion, precisely what suited them to be pioneers on his threshing floor and to break up some of the old theatre molds. They were not to adhere to any rules or precepts of the Broadway theatre, which, Cook assured them, existed only as a money-making enterprise. They were to stumble and blunder and grope their way toward a native dramatic art. The idea appealed to Cook's friends. All of them—journalists like Hapgood; artists like Charles Demuth, Bror Nordfeldt, and William and Marguerite Zorach; short-story writers like Wilbur Daniel Steele; novelists like Neith Boyce (Hapgood's wife) and Susan Glaspell; magazine writers like Mary Vorse and even a few professional theatre people like the actor Frederic Burt—warmed to the project.

One-acters were then the vogue among young intellectuals who wanted to make a pointed protest against the aridity of Broadway and transform the drama into an art seriously related to life. The one-act form was easier to sustain for both the writer and the experimental producing ensemble. Like the short story, which had developed as a literary form by the end of the nineteenth century, the one-acter was the natural means by which to express a single impression, mood or idea effectively.

It had, of course, become familiar in Europe, and little theatres in various parts of America had started providing an outlet for short plays by amateur dramatists, both gifted and commonplace.

The movement took hold in New York in 1914. A few members of the Liberal Club—an organization of earnest thinkers and tireless talkers that congregated on the ground floor of a MacDougal Street brownstone in Greenwich Village—were inspired to begin their own theatre. Lawrence Langner, a patent lawyer with a fervor for the drama, and Ida Rauh, the stage-struck wife of Max Eastman, proposed renting a playhouse and forming an acting group. Albert Boni, who, with his brother Charles, had recently opened the Washington Square Book Shop next door to the Liberal Club, protested that a stage was an unnecessary appendage to the presentation of plays.

The matter had been resolved when Robert Edmond Jones, one of the few members of the Liberal Club with professional experience in the theatre, wandered into the Boni bookshop. Jones, a reddish-haired, bearded New Englander who had attended Harvard with Albert Boni, was just back from Europe, where he had studied stage design.

"Do you have to have a stage to put on a play, Bobby?" asked Boni.

"Of course not," answered Jones. "You can put on a play right here."

The Washington Square Book Shop was as much a social center as a commercial enterprise—an adjoining wall of the Liberal Club had recently been broken through to allow members easier access to the store—and a number of Boni's friends were on hand during this exchange. One of them suggested staging a production then and there. Since the Boni brothers seldom had a paying customer in the shop, nothing stood in the way of the impromptu performance. The store consisted of two large rooms, each thirty feet square, with ceilings fourteen feet high. The rooms were divided by sliding mahogany doors, and their frames served as the proscenium. The group separated into actors and audience, and selected Lord Dunsany's *The Glittering Gate* as its vehicle—simply because there were several copies of the play on the shop's shelves. Bobby Jones tore off ten feet of wrapping paper and with it improvised two columns. Two tall men stripped to the waist and stationed themselves at the columns to play guards of the glittering gate, and the scene was forthwith acted.

It took a few more months and a good deal of fast talking by the enthusiastic participants in this production before the money was raised to rent a real theatre. Such was the beginning of the Washington Square Players. The Bandbox Theatre, on Fifty-seventh Street near Third Avenue, became their headquarters in February, 1915, and their first bill was a catholic mixture of one-act plays by Maurice Maeterlinck, Lawrence Langner (writing as Basil Lawrence, not to offend his associates in the legal world), and Edward Goodman, who was appointed head of the group because he had had some experience producing one-acters for an organization called the Socialist Press Club. The following month the group presented plays by Leonid Andreyev, John Reed and Philip Moeller, who was a founder of the company. Before the season was out two more plays by Maeterlinck, one by Octave Feuillet and one by Chekhov had been presented.

On the day the group became a corporate body, the writer Hiram Kelly Motherwell interviewed several members in the back room of the bookshop on MacDougal Street.

"We've got to assert the rights of the human soul," Philip Moeller told him. "The American theatre has no place for the subtler nuances of drama. The whole system is wrong. The acting is mechanical, the production lifeless and the scenery damn—no, it is worse, it is positively mid-Victorian. The trouble is that the whole system is commercial. The American theatre is aiming at nothing but the dollar."

In spite of the lofty aims of the Washington Square Players, they rejected a play submitted by Jig Cook and Susan Glaspell, called *Suppressed Desires,* as being *too* much of a departure. Out of pique Cook and his wife decided to stage the play on their own, and it was this decision that initiated the second of America's most famous "little theatre" groups—the Provincetown Players.

The Provincetown Players, however, were not yet thought of when, the following summer, Bobby Jones mounted *Suppressed Desires* on an improvised stage and with makeshift scenery in the Hapgood house on the Cape.

Described by its authors as "a Freudian comedy," the play was a spoof of the prevalent misinterpretations of the theories of Sigmund Freud, and was an amusing example of the advanced ideas held by the Cooks and their friends. They were so modern, as the local Provincetown newspaper pointed out admiringly, "that they not only write about modern things, but satirize them."

On the same program with *Suppressed Desires* in the Hutchins Hapgoods' home was *Constancy,* a one-act play that Tapgood's wife, Neith Boyce, had based on the love affair between John Reed and Mabel Dodge. The casual production of the double bill came to be reverently regarded as the birth of the Provincetown Players (which was officially organized the following year). Jones sat the audience in a room facing Hapgood's wide, seaside veranda to watch *Constancy*. Behind the backs of the audience he set the stage for *Suppressed Desires* and, when *Constancy* was over, the audience turned its chairs to face an alcoved room representing a Greenwich Village apartment.

Stimulated by their successful experiment, the Cooks, Hapgoods and several other friends commandeered an old fishhouse at the end of a tumble-down wharf owned by Mary Vorse and proceeded to turn it into a theatre.

Christened the Wharf Theatre and characterized by Jig Cook as the "shining object" on which artistic native drama could make its long-delayed arrival, the playhouse—twenty-five feet square and fifteen feet high—was little more than a shell. Through the planks of its floor at high tide the bay could be seen and heard and smelled. Under Cook's direction an ingenious stage was built. Only ten by twelve feet, it was sectional and mobile and could be slid backward onto the end of the wharf through the two wide doors at the rear of the theatre, to provide an effect of distance. Those doors, through which fishermen had once hurled their catch, could be flung apart to expose the most realistic sea backdrop any theatre ever had. The vast bay was revealed, dotted by lights of passing vessels and swept by the beacon of a lighthouse.

A five-dollar contribution by each of the members of the company—by then it numbered thirty—provided for the needed tools and equipment. Two days before the opening, after the group had been toiling over arrangements for several weeks, the fishing shack caught fire; though the flames were quickly subdued, two of the interior walls were blackened and the curtain was destroyed. The troupe inventively stained the uncharred walls black to match the burned ones, hung them with old fishing nets for added atmosphere, and replaced the curtain.

As lumber was scarce in Provincetown, nothing could be done about building seats during the summer of 1915. Consequently, in that first season—when *Constancy* and *Suppressed Desires* were revived (along with another satire by Jig Cook called *Change Your Style*, about two rival art schools, and a symbolic political play by Wilbur Daniel Steele called *Contemporaries*)—members of the audience carried their own chairs to and from the theatre.

In New York during the winter of 1915-16—the winter O'Neill drifted about Greenwich Village—the "Provincetowners" made plans for the following summer; they thought longingly and talked ambitiously of their theatre on the wharf and of the native American drama they were trying to fan into existence. And during that time, packed among O'Neill's scanty belongings, lay *Bound East for Cardiff,* a script Professor Baker scorned, and no producer would mount—a script that awaited adoption by a group of idealistic artists.

Though the Provincetowners were not aware of O'Neill when they hastened back to their theatre in the late spring of 1916, O'Neill was aware of them. Years later he acknowledged it was John Reed who first brought him to Provincetown. Reed had not been there the summer of 1915, but by 1916 he had become Jig Cook's most ardent disciple. Eagerly he echoed Cook in his desire to "get back to Greece"—to create an atmosphere in which the American equivalent of the Dionysiac dance could be born. Reed, who had seen native drama in Mexico, agreed with Cook that such theatre could be created out of group spirit and free expression of ideas on an experimental stage.

Although O'Neill had an idea of what was going on in Provincetown, he did not hurry to become a part of the group, because he dreaded groups of any kind. Nor, in spite of Reed's invitation, did he head directly for Provincetown that summer. Instead, he and Terry Carlin, like a pair of stray dogs cautiously sniffing a doubtful bone, made for the adjoining town of Truro. Living was cheap in Provincetown, but it was even cheaper in the hull of the wreck on the Truro beach where O'Neill and Terry established squatters' rights.

Terry read and O'Neill swam, gradually working off the effects of his drunken winter. He kept his eye on Provincetown, warily watching the progress of the new theatre. Having adopted the name Provincetown Players, the group had managed to drum up a subscription audience of eighty-seven, each member paying $2.50 for a pair of tickets to each bill.

With this fund the Players installed lighting and bought enough lumber to build benches. They optimistically announced a season of four bills of three one-act plays each, although not more than six playlets were even partially committed to paper. They got off swimmingly with a revival of *Suppressed Desires* and a satire by Reed, called *Freedom,* about four prisoners with divergent ideas on the meaning of what it is to be free (like *Suppressed Desires,* it had been turned down by the Washington Square Players). The third play was apparently so unremarkable that its plot has been forgotten by all concerned; by Neith Boyce, it was entitled *Winter's Night.*

By the time these plays had been mounted, the group's treasury was all but depleted—even though $13 was the biggest outlay ever made for a production. Jig found it necessary, therefore, to solicit single admissions to supplement the funds from subscribers. The money came in, for

Provincetown's growing summer colony was excited about the theatre.

But that still left the problem of a second bill. Wilbur Steele completed an insignificant play called *Not Smart* and several other members of the group submitted scripts, but nobody could agree on a bill strong enough to carry the next program.

O'Neill had an infallible sense of timing; most of his entrances into and exits from the lives of the people he affected were achieved with a flourish. What drew him to Provincetown at this moment of the theatre's crisis was the fact that he and Terry had exhausted their funds. Terry, who thought of Hapgood as a likely source, took O'Neill with him to Provincetown to borrow $10. Presumably O'Neill returned to Truro with his share of the loan, while Terry strolled about Provincetown greeting people he knew from Greenwich Village. Susan Glaspell, encountering Terry just at the time she was near desperation over the format of the Players' second bill, asked: "Haven't you a play to read to us?"

"No," answered Terry, according to Miss Glaspell's account in her book, *The Road to the Temple*. "I don't write, I just think, and sometimes talk. But Mr. O'Neill has got a whole trunk full of plays."

Hapgood's version, however, set down twelve years after Miss Glaspell's, was that O'Neill showed him and Neith Boyce *Bound East for Cardiff* and that Neith took it to Jig and urged him to stage it.

In any case, it was arranged for O'Neill to go to the Cooks' house the evening the final vote was to be taken on which three plays would comprise the second bill at the Wharf Theatre. *Bound East for Cardiff* was read aloud to the assembled group, which by now included Harry Kemp, the "hobo" poet, his beautiful red-haired wife, Mary Pyne, and Kyra Markham, an attractive young woman from Chicago who wanted to act.

Frederic Burt read the play in the living room, while O'Neill sat moodily in the dining room, afraid to hear, afraid to see the faces of the listeners. As soon as the reading ended, a smile lit the face of John Reed. Louise Bryant, who had joined Reed in Provincetown and was writing one-acters like the rest of the group, regarded O'Neill with new interest. As for Jig Cook, he was all but stunned by the realization that he had found the dramatist who could express his idea of native theatre. The group's response to O'Neill's genius was immediate and wholehearted.

Susan Glaspell later summed up the mass enthusiasm for O'Neill's play:

"He was not left alone in the dining room when the reading had finished. Then we knew what we were for."

The voting became a mere formality. *Bound East for Cardiff* was put into rehearsal and two weeks later led Wilbur Steele's *Not Smart* and a pallid morality play by Louise Bryant called *The Game* on the second bill of the Provincetown Players' 1916 summer season.

Jig Cook played the dying sailor, Yank, on the tiny stage arranged to represent the forecastle. The scenic effects were largely supplied by nature.

"The sea has been good to Eugene O'Neill," Susan Glaspell wrote later. "It was there for his opening. There was a fog, just as the script demanded, fog bell in the harbor. The tide was in, and it washed under us and around, spraying through the holes in the floor, giving us the rhythm and the flavor of the sea while the big dying sailor talked to his friend Drisc of the life he had always wanted deep in the land, where you'd never see a ship or smell the sea. It is not merely figurative language to say the old wharf shook with applause."

O'Neill himself recalled his debut as a dramatist more laconically: "It's rather a curious coincidence that my first production should have been on a wharf in a sea town. . . . *Bound East for Cardiff* . . . was laid on shipboard; and while it was being acted you could hear the waves washing in and out under the wharf."

E. J. ("Teddy") Ballantine, an actor who had come from England with Mrs. Pat Campbell's production of *Pygmalion* and was vacationing in Provincetown, staged the production. John Reed played one of the seamen, Harry Kemp another, and O'Neill, undaunted by his previous acting disaster in *Monte Cristo*, played the Mate, speaking one line: "Isn't this your watch on deck, Driscoll?" He also doubled as prompter, standing behind a board partition and breathing so nervously that he distracted the other performers.

O'Neill was now not only a published but a produced dramatist. Even though his producers were experimental amateurs, they appreciated his work and stimulated him to go on writing—an incentive that had nearly left him the winter before.

He and Terry moved into a shack diagonally across the street from the house occupied by Louise and Reed. They ate out of cans and threw the empty cans out their back door. Occasionally they varied their diet with fish presented to them by the Portuguese fishermen. A sign reading "Go to Hell" was nailed to the front door. In spite of the enthusiasm of the Provincetowners for O'Neill's work and their eagerness to befriend him, he held somewhat aloof; his shyness rendered him incapable of mingling, and he didn't know the meaning of the phrase "small talk."

During the conversations of his peers he habitually maintained a morose silence. It was only with a subject he considered important that he would talk—and then it was sometimes all but impossible to interrupt him; he could carry on a monologue in a low, halting voice until he had exhausted every facet.

Because there were few people with whom he could relax, many of his acquaintances considered him taciturn; and no one—not even those with whom he felt at ease—found him chatty. For companions he preferred the Portuguese fishermen and members of the Coast Guard station who stood lonely watch over Provincetown's treacherous waters. It was partly because of his social malaise that he continued to drink, but he worked, between alcoholic binges, with new vigor.

O'Neill's shack had a long ramp running down to almost the water's edge. Day after day he would stand leaning against the wide door frame gazing out to sea, sometimes for hours. When, at last, he had drunk his fill of gazing, or the sun, or whatever held him so immobile, he moved swiftly, but not running, into the water and began to swim. He swam straight out without swerving to right or left. Kyra Markham, who happened to live next door to O'Neill that summer, used to worry about him. "His head became a tiny dot in the distance," she said, "and sometimes he went so far that I could not see him at all."

Others experienced a similar sense of misgiving while watching O'Neill in the sea. Louise Bryant was spellbound by his marathon swims. She would watch for him from her window and join him on the beach. She and Reed always entertained a houseful of guests, drawn there mainly by the fact that Hippolyte Havel was the cook. Hippolyte's menus were inventive and his after-dinner conversations provocative. Once, after Reed had expounded on some radical cause, Hippolyte furiously accused him of being "a parlor socialist," to which Reed retorted, "And you're a kitchen anarchist!"

Hippolyte's fickle love, Polly Holliday, also was in Provincetown that summer, as was her brother, Louis, and Reed's house resounded to their talk. Although Reed was as gregarious as O'Neill was withdrawn, he found the bustle of his household distracting when he wanted to work. He would often glance enviously at O'Neill's "Go to Hell" sign across the street—and he was grateful to be able to escape from Provincetown from time to time for magazine assignments, even though it meant parting, momentarily, from Louise. Reed was not in the best of health; he was having a recurrence of a chronic kidney ailment, and Louise was restless. Knowledgeable friends watched Louise indulgently and were amused when her glance appeared to focus on O'Neill.

To O'Neill it was not a laughing matter. He was deeply and unhappily in love with her. Because, with him, to fall in love was to idealize, he was convinced that Louise, committed (although not yet married) to Reed, would be offended by his love. He not only concealed his feelings but tried to avoid her; he was the only one to whom it was not plain that Louise was pursuing him. Finally contriving to see O'Neill alone one day, she confided that because of Reed's illness they lived together as brother and sister.

O'Neill and Louise became lovers. What Reed's position was no one could quite understand, but all three seemed to find the arrangement satisfactory and they continued to work amicably together that summer. Mabel Dodge, Reed's recently discarded mistress, familiarized herself with the situation when she arrived in Provincetown and decided Reed might need consolation. "I thought Reed would be glad to see me if things were like that between him and Louise—but he wasn't," Mabel has candidly recorded.

When The Players chose O'Neill's *Thirst* for their fourth bill (plus a revival of *Contemporaries* and *Change Your Style*), Louise portrayed the thirst-crazed Dancer and O'Neill the taciturn West Indian Mulatto Sailor who entertained the notion of dining on her. The production gave O'Neill and Louise a chance to play (with deadly earnestness) a love scene remarkable for the stiffness of its dialogue and the bizarreness of its action:

DANCER (*putting her hand on [the sailor's] shoulder she bends forward with her golden hair almost in his lap and smiles up into his face*): I like you, Sailor. You are big and strong. We are going to be great friends, are we not? (*The Negro is hardly looking at her. He is watching the sharks.*) Surely you will not refuse me a little sip of your water?

SAILOR: I have no water.

DANCER: Oh, why will you keep up this subterfuge? Am I not offering you price enough? (*Putting her arm around his neck and half whispering in his ear.*) Do you not understand? I will love you, Sailor! Noblemen and millionaires . . . have loved me, have fought for me. I have never loved any of them as I will love you. Look in my eyes, Sailor, look in my eyes! (*Compelled in spite of himself by something in her voice, the Negro gazes deep into her eyes. For a second his nostrils dilate—he draws in his breath with a hissing sound—his body grows tense and it seems as if he is about to sweep her into his arms. Then his expression grows apathetic again. He turns to the sharks.*)

DANCER: Oh, will you never understand? Are you so stupid that you do not know what I mean? . . . I have promised to love *you*—a Negro sailor—if you will give me one small drink of water. Is that not humiliation enough that you must keep me waiting so? . . . Will you give me that water?

SAILOR (*without even turning to look at her*): I have no water.

DANCER (*shaking with fury*): Great God, have I abased myself for this? Have I humbled myself before this black animal only to be spurned like a wench of the streets? It is too much! You lie, you dirty slave! You have water. You have stolen my share of the water. (*In a frenzy she clutches the sailor about the throat with both hands.*) Give it to me! Give it to me!

SAILOR (*takes her hands from his neck and pushes her roughly away. She falls face downward in the middle of the raft.*) Let me alone! I have no water.

The play was not very successful and was never produced again, but one member of the group—the writer Edna Kenton—has recalled that it was, at least, realistically mounted. "By some fine trick of lighting and by sliding the stage back through the rear door, the players playing over the sea seemed to be literally floating in it in their perilous raft," she added.

However, William Zorach, the sculptor, who, with his artist wife, Marguerite, designed some of the settings for the Provincetown productions, later remembered irritably that O'Neill insisted on using a sea cloth with someone wriggling around underneath it, much in the style of the Château d'If scene in *Monte Cristo*.

O'Neill did not confine himself to acting in his own plays. He took a small role in a play by Reed, and Wilbur Steele, who also was in the cast, recalled that though the part consisted of only two lines O'Neill used to shake with fright every time he walked on stage.

O'Neill also managed to complete one short play that summer. Entitled *Before Breakfast,* it was probably the first of his scripts that was recognizably Strindbergian. He had been influenced by *The Stronger,* a two-character play in which one does all the talking. Like most of the one-acters he completed during the next year or two, *Before Breakfast* was written in the comfortable knowledge that he would have an experimental stage on which to produce it exactly as he pleased.

It is a monologue by a shrewish, unimaginative wife, who has become embittered by her forced marriage to a sensitive, unsuccessful writer and whose incessant nagging leads to her husband's off-stage suicide. The play evolved from O'Neill's curiosity to test the staying power of an audience subjected to a one-character diatribe, and it paved the way for the expository monologues he wrote into his long plays.

O'Neill also made notes for, but did not write until later, another one-acter called *Ile*, about a whaling captain whose frustration over an unsuccessful voyage develops into monomania. The play was suggested to O'Neill by Mary Vorse, who had known the man on whom O'Neill modeled the central figure of *Ile*. His name was Captain John Cook— O'Neill, in the play, called him Captain Keeney—and he drove his men to the point of mutiny by insisting on staying at sea for two years, in order to harvest his quota of whale oil; his wife, Viola, who accompanied him on the voyage in 1903, went mad from a combination of monotony and witnessing her husband's cruelty to his men. She spent the rest of her deranged life in Provincetown.

O'Neill advised Mary Vorse to write the story, but when she said she couldn't, because she knew the Cook family too well, he told her he would use it. Several years passed before O'Neill met Mrs. Cook. One winter night, as he was walking along a snowy street in Provincetown, he noticed her some ten paces in front of him. Suddenly a black cat crossed her path. She gave it a kick that sent it sailing onto the steps of a barbershop several yards away and called out in a clear voice, "No goddam black cat is going to cross *my* bow!"

On nights when the moon was full she could be heard wailing hymns. She took pains to keep all her kitchen knives sharp and had a habit of greeting her husband, when he came home from a trip, with "There's blood on the deck, John Cook! What do you know about that, John Cook?" It was rumored that Cook barricaded his door at night. But when he was away his wife would be heard talking to herself about her husband with pride. In her yard, while brushing out his shore clothes, including a derby hat, she would chant: "Never better a pair of legs went into any pants than Johnny Cook's legs" and "Never a better head went in any hat than Johnny Cook's head." When she hung up his drawers, she would say, "Takes a big rear to fill these drawers!"

O'Neill discussed his ideas for *Ile* and other plays with Louise in the summer of 1916 and also encouraged her with her own writing—which was more ambitious than inspired. While she had a high opinion of her abilities, she was perceptive enough to appreciate O'Neill's superior talent and took a strong interest in his work. He showed her what he was currently writing, including the usual love poems. The titles of two poems, neither of them ever published, were "Moonlight" and "Silence."

As the summer drew to a close, Jig Cook and John Reed decided they would take their theatre with them to New York that winter. Susan Glaspell has written of her concern over this plan:

"I was afraid for [Jig] . . . I was afraid people would laugh at him, starting a theatre in New York—new playwrights, amateur acting, somewhere in an old house or a stable. . . . I said I did not think we were ready to go to New York; I feared we couldn't make it go. 'Jack Reed thinks we can make it go,' he said. Those two were the first to believe—adventurers both, men of faith."

O'Neill later described Cook as "a really imaginative man, imaginative in every way," adding that "he was against everything that suggested the worn-out conventions and cheap artificialities of the commercial stage." On another occasion he told a friend, "If I hadn't had the Provincetown Theatre, I would have had to write commercial plays like Sam Shipman."

There is no doubt that O'Neill owed a great deal to Cook. He was the first man to have enough faith in O'Neill to devote his full time, talent and energy to seeing that he had a hearing.

"You don't know Gene yet," Cook told Edna Kenton, shortly before he left Provincetown that summer. "You don't know his plays. But you will. All the world will know Gene's plays some day. This year, on the night he first came to Provincetown and read us *Bound East for Cardiff,* we knew we had something to go on with. Some day this little theatre will be famous; some day the little theatre in New York will be famous—this fall the Provincetown Players go into New York with *Cardiff* on their first bill. We've got our group of playwrights and they've got to have their stage. Gene's plays aren't the plays of Broadway; he's got to have the sort of stage we're going to found in New York."

On September 5 The Players met to draw up their manifesto. The setting forth of a credo posed something of a dilemma for such an anarchic group, and it was worded, finally, with such looseness as to make it almost inoperable.

"Organization is death!" cried Hutchins Hapgood with individualistic fervor. The group ended in resolving "that it is the primary object of the Provincetown Players to encourage the writing of American plays of artistic, literary and dramatic—as opposed to Broadway—merit.

"That such plays be considered without reference to their commercial value, since this theatre is not to be run for pecuniary profit. . . .

"That the president shall cooperate with the author in producing the play under the author's direction. The resources of the theatre . . . shall be placed at the disposal of the author. . . . The author shall produce the play without hindrance according to his own ideas."

O'Neill approved of the name, Provincetown Players, but suggested adding "The Playwrights' Theatre." He was very much aware that this little theatre could give him his real opportunity to prove himself. He knew of the experimental Intimate Theatre, opened in 1907 in Stockholm, for which Strindberg had written what he called "Chamber Plays" and which presented only new plays, most of them by Strindberg; O'Neill had a good idea of his own potentialities. No doubt he saw himself as the future Strindberg, and the Playwrights' Theatre as America's Intimate Theatre.

The amended name was unanimously adopted. No one except two officers—the president and the secretary—were to be paid. (Jig Cook, subsequently voted in as president, received $15 a week, as did Mrs. Bror Nordfeldt, secretary.)

Cook was instructed to find a theatre that would fit into The Players' working budget of $320—$80 was left over from the summer's productions and eight contributions of $30 each had been made by the better-heeled members.

Enjoining everyone to "write another play," Jig Cook departed happily for New York, leaving O'Neill inspired by his vision.

A Provincetown newspaper expressed Jig's faith when it stated:

"They [The Players] have put on two plays by Eugene O'Neil [sic], a young dramatist whose work was heretofore unproduced and who, they are confident, is going to be heard from in places less remote than Provincetown."

XXVII

"EVEN KNOWING WE DID IT, I AM DISPOSED TO SAY what we did that first year couldn't be done," Susan Glaspell has written of the Provincetown Players' initial season in New York.

Jig Cook found his "theatre" on the day he arrived in New York from Provincetown in mid-September—the parlor floor of an ancient brownstone at 139 MacDougal Street, a block south of Washington Square. It was owned, as were the adjoining buildings that housed the Liberal Club and the Washington Square Book Shop, by Jenny Belardi, a handsome, amiable Italian woman.

Mrs. Belardi in her early forties was still wistful about a frustrated ambition to be an actress. With her sister, Mary, she had struggled to make a living in the business world to please her mother and by 1904 the two women had managed to save enough to buy the brownstones at 135 and 137 MacDougal Street. Renting these out as apartments, they reserved a flat for themselves at Number 137 and eventually acquired 133 and 139 as well.

Still stage-struck, and numbering the Liberal Club and the Washington Square Book Shop among her tenants, Mrs. Belardi was used to the ways of artists and bohemians; she was delighted to rent the parlor floor of 139 to Jig Cook—for $100 a month—and to add her name to the Provincetown Players' list of subscribing members.

While renovating the three and a half rooms of the parlor floor into auditorium, stage and dressing room, the Provincetowners mailed a circular announcing their aims to a select group of a thousand New Yorkers. Three hundred became subscribers immediately and two hundred followed within two months. The Playwrights' Theatre was obliged to operate as a private club in order to sidestep various city building ordinances. Tickets could, therefore, be sold by subscription only.

A season subscription cost $5, in addition to annual membership dues of $4. Among those chosen to receive the circular were a few theatre critics of whose taste the Provincetown Players approved. These critics were invited to become paying patrons, not reviewers. The Provincetowners wanted no publicity; they were experimenting for the sake of their own artistic growth and sought the sympathetic support of friends, not evaluation by Broadway standards.

Toward the end of October the two front rooms of Number 139 had been converted into an auditorium and the rear room into a stage measuring only 10½ by 14 feet; the theatre itself was 44 feet long by 15 feet wide and held 140 seats. Tiered benches were erected, precariously supported on stilts and having low wooden backs that added élan but little comfort; the walls of the auditorium were painted a soft, dark gray; the proscenium arch was decorated in blues, reds and gold; a limp canvas curtain, neither decorative nor opaque, was hung and a minimum of lighting equipment was installed.

The building was unheated, the seating accommodations were crude, the single dressing room was no bigger than a closet, and the state of scenery, costumes and actors was chaotic, but on October 27 the Playwrights' Theatre was ready to announce its opening bill. Balloting by the members on October 7 at John Reed's Washington Square apartment had determined that the première would consist of O'Neill's *Bound East for Cardiff*, Louise Bryant's *The Game*, and a comedy called *King Arthur's Socks* by Floyd Dell, who was on the staff of *The Masses*.

O'Neill, having followed the others down from Provincetown, reluctantly assumed his share of the labor involved in preparing the first bill. He was assigned to supervise the staging of *Bound East for Cardiff*, which, as no one was more aware than he himself, would be the first production of an O'Neill play in New York. Once again he agreed to play the Mate. Louise was on hand to supervise *The Game*, and Teddy Ballantine took over the direction of *King Arthur's Socks* from its panicky author.

Opening on Friday, November 3, the program did not create the slightest ripple in the world of the commercial theatre. Broadway, pursuing its traditional course, was oblivious of the dynamite fuse lit in the Village, which would glow and sputter and then in a few years explode. Uptown that week the critics had cheerfully reviewed, among other works, *Old Lady 31*, by Rachel Crothers and *Good Gracious, Annabelle*, by Clare Kummer. They were getting ready to welcome, during the coming week, a mixed bag that included a revival of *Ben Hur* at the Manhattan Opera House; a play with music by Victor Herbert and Irving Berlin called *The Century Girl*; and the première of George Bernard Shaw's *Getting Married*.

Although a couple of critics attended the Provincetowners' first bill as paying guests, none of them mentioned the fact in print. But the subscription audiences spread the news that here was a group worth watching. James O'Neill, who saw his son's play, was among many who offered their congratulations. For *Bound East for Cardiff* was the hit of the triple bill, as it had been in Provincetown. With the second program, presented two weeks later, the ranks of subscribers multiplied. This bill included *Suppressed Desires* (finally, to Jig and Susan's satisfaction, making its debut in New York); a dialogue between a husband and wife called *Enemies,* by Hutchins Hapgood and Neith Boyce, and John Reed's *Freedom,* previously produced on the Cape.

The Provincetowners settled into a harum-scarum existence of writing, building, rehearsing and acting. Everything except the writing was accomplished on a scrupulously amateur scale. Practically any young visitor to the Village could affiliate himself with a production if he showed the proper enthusiasm for the troupe's artistic aims and *lacked* professional training. If an actor demonstrated during his audition that he knew too many of the facile Broadway practices, he was rejected. The Province-towners were impatient with all the uptown conventions, including salaries. They were much freer and had more fun, but their lack of professional standards and discipline often caused last-minute scrambles about misplaced costumes, half-painted sets and defecting thespians.

O'Neill, too self-absorbed to concern himself with the theatre's problems except as they directly affected him, did not participate in the productions of his fellow playwrights; nor was he even particularly friendly with more than a few of the members. He attended some of their meetings so that he could vote on selections of plays and on policy, but, as in Provincetown, he did not allow anyone but the Cooks, Reed and Louise, Hutch Collins (O'Neill's New London friend who had joined the group as an actor), and another friend, "Scotty" Stuart, to know him well. O'Neill had persuaded Scotty to take the important role of Yank's friend, Driscoll, in *Bound East for Cardiff.*

There were a few others, on the fringe of the group, with whom O'Neill was on close terms—Louis Holliday, the indestructible Terry Carlin, and one new friend, Frank Shay, who also played a role in *Bound East for Cardiff.*

Shay had inherited the Washington Square Book Shop from the Boni brothers, who had gone on to bigger things. Shay was as Irish as O'Neill in temperament and enjoyed nothing better than a rousing, hypothetical argument with O'Neill as to which of them was descended from the more illustrious Gaelic line. The two Irishmen made a striking picture—Shay, with his blazing, blue eyes, tawny shock of hair and sandy mustache, and O'Neill, dark-eyed, dark-haired, dark-mustached and glowering—as they traded extravagant verbal blows with esoteric Celtic references, all designed to prove that the O'Shays or the O'Neills were really the purest, the strongest and the most anciently established clan.

It was Shay who, that year, published *Bound East for Cardiff* and *Before Breakfast,* as part of a pamphlet series entitled "The Provincetown Plays." *Bound East* was issued in November and included also the two plays that had been presented on the same bill at the Playwrights' Theatre. Although Shay printed 1,200 copies for sale at fifty cents each, most of them were distributed free to writers, actors and others interested in the work of the Provincetown group, and the pamphlet brought O'Neill no more income than had the *Thirst* volume. Since he earned nothing from the theatre either, he was still obliged to live on the dollar a day provided by his father, for he would not, or could not, take a part-time paying job, as did many of the Provincetowners.

He kept up his reports of a mythical income to Dr. Lyman, however, declaring, in the 1919 Gaylord Farm questionnaire, that he had earned an average of $40 a week from the writing of plays during 1917 and 1918. Actually, he was not stretching the truth too much, for by the end of 1917 he began drawing a small weekly income in royalties. But in the fall of 1916, and up until the fall of 1917, he had nothing to depend on except his father's dole. He supplemented this by eating at places like Marie's and Polly's at his hostesses' expense, bunking with friends when he could and sleeping for a while in an abandoned store on Christopher Street. His father wanted him to live at the Prince George with him, O'Neill told Art McGinley later that year. But O'Neill preferred to be alone— so much so that he rented a second-floor room he could not afford in a boardinghouse in Washington Square, operated by Mrs. Adele Marchesini. When he was $46 in arrears he did what any true son of an old touring actor would have done; he melted away, leaving behind a trunkful of manuscripts and clothing. He confessed to this episode in 1924, apropos of an inquiry by a friend as to whether he had read a certain book. O'Neill said he had owned the book once "but a hardhearted landlady on the square requisitioned it, along with my extra clothes and trunk and other works, for a matter of neglected rent." (The trunk was thrown out by Mrs. Marchesini after she had stored it for a time, when a rainstorm flooded her cellar and damaged its contents beyond salvage.)

One manuscript O'Neill had the foresight to take with him was *Before Breakfast,* the one-act monologue he had written in Provincetown. The Provincetown Players presented it as part of their third bill on November 17, along with a play by Neith Boyce called *The Two Sons* and a verse play by Alfred Kreymborg called *Lima Beans. Lima Beans* was so advanced that not even the Provincetowners understood it. Its cast of characters was listed as the Wife, the Husband, the Huckster and the Curtain. In his stage directions Kreymborg had loftily written: "If there must be a prelude of music, let it be nothing more consequential than one of the innocuous parlor rondos of Carl Maria von Weber. As a background color scheme, black and white might not prove amiss." He went on to enjoin the Curtain, which was to be "painted in festoons of vegetables," to rise "gravely."

Kreymborg was the editor of *Others*, a magazine dedicated to the radical movement in poetry; it was printed at cost by a Russian anarchist who lived in the Bronx and called himself Mr. Liberty. O'Neill showed Kreymborg some of his own poems, but Kreymborg found them "rather sketchy." *The Masses*, however, accepted a poem, "Submarine," and printed it in its issue of February, 1917. For some reason, O'Neill did not sign it:

> My soul is a submarine.
> My aspirations are torpedoes.
> I will hide unseen
> Beneath the surface of life
> Watching for ships,
> Dull, heavy-laden merchant ships,
> Rust-eaten, grimy galleons of commerce
> Wallowing with obese assurance,
> Too sluggish to fear or wonder,
> Mocked by the laughter of waves
> And the spit of disdainful spray.
>
> I will destroy them
> Because the sea is beautiful.
>
> That is why I lurk
> Menacingly
> In green depths.

The third bill presented by the Provincetown Players was not successful, but it is noteworthy because it marked O'Neill's final appearance as an actor. In *Before Breakfast*, he played the off-stage role of the husband, Alfred, whose hand is seen reaching for a bowl of shaving water and whose voice is heard in a death gurgle as he slashes his throat.

O'Neill clearly had himself in mind as the model for the suicidal husband, for even his brief stage note about the hand is autobiographical: "It is a sensitive hand with slender fingers. It trembles . . ." He once said that he had cast himself in the production because he wanted to measure from the stage the reaction of the audience to a lengthy monologue. For the role of the nagging wife, Mrs. Rowland, the Provincetowners chose Mary Pyne, who concealed her good looks with the make-up of a drab, pinched virago.

The bill received no reviews in the press, but when *Before Breakfast* was revived at the Provincetown Playhouse a dozen years later as the curtain raiser for a longer play, the critic for the *New York Times,* who was then signing himself J. Brooks Atkinson, called it "a turgid one-act monologue." "If memory serves," he added, "it was never an enthralling piece with its assembly of all the stock gloom of the theatre in the space of one act. . . . Mr. O'Neill was . . . a glutton when he composed this familiar interlude of drink, poverty, infidelity and domestic horrors."

James O'Neill expressed somewhat similar sentiments when he saw *Before Breakfast* in rehearsal for the first time.

"My boy, why don't you write pleasanter plays?" he asked. But he was pleased that his son was getting recognition, even on so circumscribed a plane; and in a burst of love and gratitude he offered to help with the staging of *Before Breakfast.* O'Neill might have received this offer more graciously had he not been smarting over his father's recently expressed espousal of a play written by Brandon Tynan. Called *Melody of Youth,* it was a romantic comedy that had opened in February, 1916, at the Fulton Theatre. In it James had insisted on playing the twenty-line role of a blind beggar.

"I don't care how small the part is," James had written in a publicized letter to Tynan. "As one of the older generation of players I want to make a little offering to one of the most promising representatives of the younger generation." James had played the part for two weeks, waiving his salary as a public tribute to the young man he lovingly referred to as "my son."

Thus the real son was not mollified by his father's offer of interest in the production of *Before Breakfast,* though in later years he denied having resented his father's staging suggestions. Several accounts of a battle between father and son over Mary Pyne's interpretation of her role were subsequently related and O'Neill's recorded comment, on reading one of these accounts, was "Nuts!"

"There was no question of his directing." O'Neill once noted. "I got him down to make suggestions on the acting. He made some I didn't agree with, but also some I thought were fine and which the actors were glad to follow."

According to eyewitnesses, Mary Pyne had the sense to do everything James O'Neill told her—grandiloquent gestures, melodramatic inflections and all. And James, gratified, said to her: "You are a most intelligent young actress. I don't need to give you any further instruction."

As soon as he had gone, his son redirected her from beginning to end and, still according to eyewitnesses, mumbled about his father's "old fogey" approach. It was not easy for Eugene to forgive his father for regarding Brandon Tynan as "one of the most promising representatives of the younger generation."

The fourth bill was no more successful than the third had been. It included a play called *The Obituary,* by a dentist from Rochester, New York, who was a nephew of Emma Goldman's. His name was Saxe Comminsky, but he had abbreviated it for professional purposes to Saxe Commins, and his connection with the Provincetown group was through Teddy Ballantine, who had married Commins' sister, Stella. Commins was unhappy in his adopted profession and longed for a foothold among the artists of Greenwich Village. *The Obituary,* however, did not further his literary ambitions and it was not until some time later that he managed to make a rather spectacular exchange of his dentist's chair for an editor's desk.

Because O'Neill had written no new plays since *Before Breakfast,* the group, for its fifth bill—on January 5—somewhat desperately pulled O'Neill's *Fog* out of the *Thirst* volume. Hutch Collins played the Business Man whose ideology clashes with that of the Poet as they drift in a lifeboat through the fog banks of Newfoundland. The two plays that accompanied *Fog* were not much better, and The Players showed signs of faltering. Jig Cook was unable to elicit the kind of professional discipline that the Provincetowners were beginning to realize was necessary for sustained artistic effort. And he no longer had the support of John Reed, whose flair for organization was somewhat more compelling.

Reed had left New York on November 12 to enter Johns Hopkins Hospital in Baltimore; he went for tests but, as he had anticipated, it was decided he must be operated on for the removal of a kidney. He and Louise Bryant had been married in Poughkeepsie a few days before. Louise went to Baltimore for the operation and stayed until she was assured Reed's condition was satisfactory. Then she returned to New York. The fact that she was now Mrs. Reed did not inhibit her relationship with O'Neill. Reed was not discharged from the hospital until December 13, and then he had to work hard and often far afield to pay his hospital expenses.

Reed's absence was convenient for O'Neill, as he was now able to move into the Reed apartment. Marguerite and Bill Zorach, who lived next door to the Reeds, were among a number of friends who noted the arrangement. As one of these friends later observed, "We all had a rationale about sex—we had discovered Freud—and we considered being libidinous a kind of sacred duty." The tangled personal relationships of that period were conducted with an air of righteous innocence; monogamy, in fact, was practiced somewhat sheepishly. Moral indignation was reserved for the big issues, such as art versus philistinism and pacifism versus participation in the European War.

To Louise, O'Neill's need of her was the justification for her devotion. She told Marguerite Zorach of her faith in O'Neill's writing. Reed needed her too. "You have no idea what it's like living with Jack," she said to Marguerite. "His war images come back to him—he goes through hell."

O'Neill, though he may have had some misgivings as to how it would all end, was painfully happy with Louise and dramatized his great love for her.

"When Louise touches me with her fingernail, it's like a prairie fire," he told Terry Carlin exultantly.

His love throve, but his writing did not. The Provincetown's sixth bill had no play by O'Neill. It had become clear not only to him but to most of the other writing members of the group that personal supervision of their own plays and active participation in the production of other members' plays left little time for creative effort. O'Neill in particular discovered that it was impossible to write amid the distractions of the Village. He needed more than a locked door to insulate him. It was hard to say no to a friend who wanted a drinking companion or a good argument. He needed complete seclusion, a wide, physical barrier between himself and his friends.

The fortuitous arrival of Nina Moise, a young woman who had staged some plays with small stock companies in California and Massachusetts, raised the faltering spirits of The Players. Nina wanted to act and was planning to apply for a role with the Provincetown Players. But a friend told her the company had all the actors it needed and apprised her of its urgent need of a director with professional experience. Nina went to the Samovar, a café on West Fourth Street which provided meals for the Provincetowners under a club arrangement. She presented herself to Jig Cook, who asked her to meet him later at the theatre. When she arrived, she found the sixth bill in rehearsal—Neith Boyce's *Winter's Night*, reconstructed from Provincetown, and two trifles called *Pan* and *The Dollar*.

"I'd never seen anything like it," Nina later recalled. "The actors didn't know enough not to bump into each other."

She lent a hand with the bill and accepted an offer to stay permanently by the all but defeated amateurs. After going uptown to collect her belongings she moved into a three-dollar-a-week garret on Washington Square.

"I wasn't paid anything, and I rarely went north of Fourteenth Street again," she once said.

She received program credit as director of two of the three plays on the next bill, which opened on February 16. The Provincetowners called this "the war bill" and for it they unearthed *The Sniper*, the antiwar play O'Neill had written at Harvard. O'Neill watched Nina take competent control and in mid-February he fled to Provincetown. Although he was interested in hearing how his plays were received, he was not interested in seeing the end product and rarely witnessed a public performance of his plays. But he nearly always attended rehearsals scrupulously, through the final dress rehearsal, helping with background suggestions, making additions or deletions of dialogue when he deemed it absolutely necessary, and suggesting stage business—although he believed he had included all essentials in the script.

"Gene's plays were foolproof and almost directorproof," Nina Moise has said. O'Neill tried his best to make them actorproof, as well, by detailing every nuance he wanted his actors to convey; while his written instructions about characters turning pale or sweating or, as in one instance, chewing gum "like a sacred cow forgetting time with an eternal end," seem pointless and impossible to project, they are actually important road signs for the intelligent actor, and many of O'Neill's actors have expressed gratitude for them. Most good actors who have played O'Neill are also aware that he had the experienced craftsman's knowledge of the number of words an actor can handle comfortably on each intake of breath.

After the opening night of one of his early plays Nina Moise asked O'Neill, "Gene, how did you like it?"

"I didn't see it," he answered, to her amazement. "The theatre on opening night is no place for a nervous man." Later he told Nina, "When I finish writing a play, I'm through with it."

"Gene was concerned with plays, not theatre," she said. And this held true of O'Neill throughout his career. Some years later he explained to a friend why he stayed away from his own plays after they had opened.

"A play may be damn well acted from an acting standpoint," he said, "and still be far from the creator's intention." Many productions of his plays, he added, had featured excellent acting, but there had never been a production he recognized as being "deeply" his play. "That's why I never see them," he said. "A play is written about living and is seen on the stage as acting."

Heywood Broun, who had switched from sports writer to drama critic of the *Tribune* in 1915, found the Provincetowners' work of sufficient worth, in March of that year, to write one of the first reviews the group received. Although The Players still refused to seek recognition or to give free tickets to critics, a few of the more enterprising reviewers continued to pay their way. The bill Broun reviewed was the eighth and, while O'Neill was not represented, it featured an interesting play by Pendleton King called *Cocaine*, about two penniless, dope-addicted lovers who decide to commit suicide by turning on the gas, only to discover that the gas has been shut off because they have not paid their bill.

After the ninth and last bill, which was also O'Neill-less, Burns Mantle expressed his opinion in the *Evening Mail* that the season's achievement was "as sound as it is modest," adding: "We never thought anything could live for a year in New York without a press agent."

Clayton Hamilton also deemed the work of the Provincetowners worthy of comment. He passed over the more professional Washington Square Players, who, having moved from the Bandbox to the Comedy Theatre on West Thirty-eighth Street, continued to mix foreign plays with the native efforts of writers such as Ben Hecht and Edward Massey. Hamilton lauded the Provincetowners for writing, acting and producing plays "merely for the love of doing so."

He pointed out, however, that the Provincetown Players' staging was "for the most part unworthy of serious consideration" and that their acting was "amateurish and uncertain." "But," he concluded, "the plays produced by the Provincetown Players are strangely interesting and strikingly impressive."

Actually, O'Neill's only major contribution that first season, as he himself realized, had been *Bound East for Cardiff*. He preferred to forget *Fog* and *The Sniper*, and allowed *Before Breakfast* to be preserved only because he considered it an interesting experiment.

Once in Provincetown, O'Neill found he could concentrate again on writing. In a short period, before the end of April, 1917, he turned out four plays—*Ile, The Moon of the Caribbees, The Long Voyage Home* and *In the Zone*—all of which have survived the test of time. The last three are today considered classic examples of their form and continue to be revived regularly by both professional and amateur groups throughout the world. O'Neill, while conceiving of the plays as units in a series, did not write them to be played together in any particular order, nor did he regard them as a connected story; he felt that each was complete in itself and independent of the others. But it was *The Moon of the Caribbees* that was his own favorite because, as he later noted, it was his "first real break with theatrical traditions." It was, as he often declared, the only one-act play of which he was "really fond."

The break with tradition lay in the play's disregard for plot or action and its concentration on the creation of pure, poetic mood. A languorous dialogue among a group of lonely seamen afloat under a West Indian moon, it set the tone for such later, fragile mood plays as *The Glass Menagerie* of Tennessee Williams. Brooks Atkinson once described *The Moon of the Caribbees* as "a drama of silences."

O'Neill worked on the play in a small hotel called the Atlantic House, where he had rented a room, and occasionally he wrote on the beach with a blanket wrapped around him. (He believed the cold sea air was good for his lungs.) The proprietor of the Atlantic House, who was also its chef, amused himself by shouting a customer's order to the kitchen, then hurrying to his stove to cook it himself.

That spring Provincetown, like the rest of the country, was swept up in war hysteria. America's participation in the war seemed inevitable. Threats of German U-boat invasions were a daily topic of conversation on the exposed Cape and safety precautions along the coast were tightened. O'Neill was not popular among the patriotic villagers, for he was known as a member of a group of outspoken pacifists—Reed notable among them. He was a natural object of suspicion, somewhat like Smitty, of *In the Zone*, which O'Neill was to write a few weeks later.

One day in late March O'Neill and a friend, Harold De Polo, who was a short-story writer, returned from a walk across the dunes and sat down to a meal in a hotel grandly named the New Central. A local constable, Reuben Kelly, informed them they were under arrest. The charge, he said, was vagrancy, but it soon evolved that the arrest had been made at the instigation of the chief of the United States radio station in North Truro, who had somehow persuaded himself that O'Neill and De Polo were German spies. (A much-embellished later account had Constable Kelly trailing O'Neill across the dunes, hiding while he watched O'Neill take out "a little instrument that flashed in the sun," and leaping to the conclusion that O'Neill was using a "wireless gadget" to signal to an enemy ship. The "gadget" turned out to be a typewriter.)

Actually, as reported the next day (March 29) by the Provincetown *Advocate*, the arrest was made "for the purpose of ascertaining if O'Neill and De Polo were the men who had been seen . . . prowling about the radio grounds." O'Neill preserved this story in a scrapbook that later went to Yale University.

"I was the victim of war hysteria," he once said in recalling the episode. "Somebody over at the wireless station watched us and decided we were German spies. We were having dinner in a hotel in town one evening when some Secret Service men pounced on us at the point of a revolver and carried us to the lockup in the basement of the Town Hall. We were held incommunicado for several hours. They wouldn't even let us see a lawyer."

From the account in the Provincetown *Advocate* it is evident that the incident caused quite a local stir:

"All manner of rumors were rife Wednesday afternoon and evening regarding incidents of the arrest," the *Advocate* reported, in part. "The street statements to the effect that the arrested men drew revolvers upon the arresting officer, that the pair were found armed, that plans of the radio station and grounds and Provincetown Harbor were found in the possession of the pair were all wholly false statements.

"Not only were they not identified as the men who when queried by radio guards some time ago as to their presence near the wireless grounds replied, 'Our doctor has advised us to walk for health,' but they were fully able to explain the reason for their presence here and account for their movements in a manner satisfactory to their inquisitors."

One local policeman, who was not quite convinced of O'Neill's innocence in spite of the *Advocate's* assurances, appointed himself O'Neill's shadow, and took to steaming open O'Neill's mail. If he happened to see O'Neill before his mail had been officially delivered, the policeman would present a brief résumé of what he could expect. "Your Ma's writ, but your girl's let you down," he might say.

His girl, as a matter of fact, had been toiling in his behalf and his mail was professionally productive. Louise knew Waldo Frank, who, with James Oppenheim and Van Wyck Brooks, was running a literary magazine called *The Seven Arts*, and she spoke to him about the possibility of publishing O'Neill. (Among its contributors were Robert Frost, Amy Lowell, Theodore Dreiser and Sherwood Anderson; Reed had recently contributed an essay called "This Unpopular War.")

"Our magazine was very serious, almost religious—we considered ourselves the organ of cultural nationalism," Waldo Frank once said. "We were disciples of Walt Whitman and were creating the voice Whitman wanted. Louise was just around; she was a 'flaming youth' girl, an Irish beauty, thin, with pale skin, very romantic. She was intellectually alive and responsive, although not profound. She told me about O'Neill, and said he had written a story we might want. We laid our main stress on stories, although we used poetry and nonfiction articles, too."

Frank liked the O'Neill story Louise showed him—it was "Tomorrow," the first draft of which he had written in 1916. Frank wrote O'Neill an inquiring and encouraging letter to Provincetown, and O'Neill mailed Frank another copy of the story, promising to send scripts of several one-act plays as soon as they were typed.

Frank sent back the story with suggestions for changes and O'Neill devoted an afternoon and evening to revising and cutting it by a thousand words. He returned the manuscript with its handwritten corrections, having been unwilling or unable to retype it. Conceding that Frank's editorial suggestions had been valid, he explained:

"When I first wrote the story I planned it as the first of a series of Tommy the Priest's yarns in which the story teller was to hog most of the limelight—a sort of Conrad's Marlow—and once I had that idea I couldn't let go, and it rode me into the anti-climax."

The story was accepted for publication. (Twenty-seven years later O'Neill said of "Tomorrow": "I thought it was pretty devastating stuff at the time, and so evidently did Van Wyck Brooks, Waldo Frank, etc., although I doubt if they were as overwhelmed by its hideous beauty as I was.")

About a week later, O'Neill sent Frank, at his request, a neatly typed page of biographical data for the magazine's "Notes on Names" department, and on April 30 O'Neill mailed copies to Frank of In the Zone, The Long Voyage Home and The Moon of the Caribbees. Frank thought the plays good, but The Seven Arts decided against publishing them. The magazine did publish "Tomorrow" that June and sent O'Neill a check for $50—the first respectable sum he had earned from creative writing.

By the end of May, O'Neill was in New London, staying with his family. The United States had entered the war on April 6, and O'Neill's principal concern was to keep himself out of it. He decided to consult with his father, and take up a position of watchful waiting near his draft board, since 325 Pequot Avenue was still his official address.

O'Neill's lack of patriotic fervor, while it ostensibly annoyed his father, was heartily endorsed by his New York and Provincetown friends. Reed, testifying before the House Judiciary Committee on conscription, was declaring that nothing could induce him to serve in the Army.

"You can shoot me if you want," he told the committee. He had no personal objection to fighting, he said, but he was convinced that this particular war was a commercial conflict, that it was unjustified on both sides, that Europe was "mad" and that America should keep out of it. His stand was based on principle, for he was certain he would not be called to serve because of his poor health. In June he leapt to the defense of Emma Goldman and Alexander Berkman when they held an anticonscription meeting in the Bronx.

Louise Bryant echoed Reed's unpopular stand and approved of O'Neill's disinclination to be drafted. But she was restless and unhappy. After quarreling with Reed she went to New London to spend a few days with O'Neill and his family. It is a matter of conjecture how Louise was received by Ella and James or whether they were even aware of her relationship with their son. The Rippin sisters, however, to whom O'Neill introduced Louise, saw at once that he was in love.

"Gene brought Louise Bryant to have dinner at our house," Jessica recalled many years later. "It was obvious that he thought she was pretty terrific." Emily added that O'Neill made no secret of being in love with her.

After dinner O'Neill asked Jessica and Emily what they thought of Louise. The girls were noncommittal, but agreed, privately, that she was "sloppy."

Apparently Louise did not find what she wanted in New London; but neither did she choose to rejoin Reed in New York. Instead, early in June and defying the German submarine menace, she sailed for France.

O'Neill was hurt by Louise's departure, but he was even more worried about his standing with the Army. He had already claimed exemption on the grounds that he was an arrested tubercular case, but, anxious that his motives not be misconstrued as cowardice or lack of patriotism, he now tried to enlist Dr. Lyman's help.

"I am not trying to dodge service but, from what I hear, conditions in the camps and at the front are the very worst possible for one susceptible to T.B.," he wrote Dr. Lyman. "I would be very grateful for your advice. I want to serve my country but it seems silly to commit suicide for it."

Dr. Lyman replied promptly but not, from O'Neill's point of view, reassuringly, that only the examining Army surgeon could decide whether or not an arrested tubercular case should be exempted.

There was nothing to do but wait, brood and drink—and upset his father with anarchist-pacifist jargon and noisy denunciations of his country's military policy.

His gloom reached a peak by mid-August, when Louise—who had returned from France—wrote to tell him that she was going to Russia with

Reed to report on the Revolution. Reed, having been exempted from military service because of his kidney operation, was accredited as a correspondent for *The Masses, The Call,* and *The Seven Arts.* (None of the well-paying newspapers and magazines were now willing to use his material because of his widely publicized antiwar stand, and the money for his passage was raised by friends.) Louise had found the tonic for her depression by becoming a free-lance correspondent. She and Reed sailed from New York on August 17. There had been no formal break with O'Neill. He was still in love with her and she professed to be still in love with him, but her chance for adventure and personal recognition lay with Reed. O'Neill, angry with himself for being unable to offer her any comparably glamorous opportunity, went on a binge.

When he drank excessively, Eugene grew increasingly abusive toward his father. James was on vacation from a play called *The Wanderer,* which had opened February 1, 1917, at the Manhattan Opera House and was to resume its run in the fall. A biblical drama based on a German book about the prodigal son, it featured James, aptly enough, in the role of the father. James thought the play a classic and Eugene thought it was a waste of his father's ability.

One night Eugene came home very drunk and told his father it had dawned on him that James was the worst actor in America. Then he amended his statement. An actor named Corse Payton, he shouted, was the worst.

"You are the second worst," he said.

James had had enough. He called Art McGinley, who was helping Eugene console himself that summer, and urged him to take Eugene to Provincetown.

"Gene needs a change," James told McGinley dryly. "I think it would be a good thing for both of us if there were at least a temporary separation."

McGinley jocularly recalled the incident. "We left New London by popular request," he said. "There was no shedding of tears in the public square when O'Neill and I departed."

The two men, far from sober when they boarded the Provincetown boat at Boston, enjoyed their crossing. They shared their bottle with members of the crew until the captain, getting wind of their activities, threatened to put them in irons. When they arrived at Provincetown Jig Cook was waiting to greet them.

O'Neill and McGinley moved into a small apartment over a general store on Commercial Street owned by John Francis, the most generous and accommodating of landlords. Francis had got the rooms ready for O'Neill earlier that spring, shortly after his arrest as a "German spy."

Francis was one of the most popular residents in Provincetown. In the evenings the sea captains congregated in his store around the cracker barrel, smoking and chewing tobacco and basking in the warmth of his personality. They good-humoredly ignored a sign that read: "Please loaf in the back room." A rotund, baby-faced man with kindly eyes framed by steel-rimmed glasses, Francis was so tenderhearted that people often wondered how he managed to eke out a living. He never collected the rent on his apartments from anyone who seemed hard up and he extended unlimited credit. He subsidized O'Neill for nearly a year.

Francis loved O'Neill, as he loved all strays, and O'Neill loved him. When Francis died in 1937, a friend sent O'Neill a newspaper obituary. "I feel a genuine sorrow," O'Neill wrote in thanking his friend for the clipping. "He was a fine person—and a unique character. I am glad the article speaks of him as my friend. He was all of that, and I know he knew my gratitude, for I often expressed it."

Francis had allowed Terry Carlin to live rent-free in the rooms reserved for O'Neill, pending O'Neill's arrival. In the summer of 1917 O'Neill, Carlin and McGinley shared the apartment. Harry Kemp and his wife lived across the hall, and the rest of the Provincetown Players also had settled down in various houses and apartments.

Sometime during the period O'Neill was living in the Francis apartments the ceiling beams of his room acquired a decorative inscription from Hindu philosophy:

"Before the ear can hear it must have lost its sensitiveness. Before the eyes can see they must be incapable of tears. Before the soul can fly its wings must be washed in the blood of the heart. Before the voice can speak it must have lost its power to wound."

The inscription, burned by a poker deep into the wooden rafters, its letters formed boldly and with uniform precision, has been cited by many Provincetowners as O'Neill's handiwork, though no one can recall having witnessed the job or hearing him say he did it. In fact, it is more likely that Terry Carlin, whose hand was steadier and more skilled, was the artisan.

Jig Cook was delighted to have O'Neill back and even more delighted to be able to discuss the casting of his new plays, which would be presented at the Playwrights' Theatre in the fall and winter. Jig tried to take care of his cherished playwright, encouraging him to eat when O'Neill seemed inclined to neglect himself and urging him to open a bank account with his small fund of cash, to forestall his spending everything on liquor.

"Everyone there admired O'Neill's work," McGinley said, recalling his first exposure to O'Neill's intellectual friends. "I remember a reading of an O'Neill play at Cook's house. The actress reading it interrupted her recitation every few minutes to say 'Here's the great new American playwright in the making.' No one disputed her.

"I was definitely the unlettered member of the aggregation. The conversation was often so far above my level, it might have been in another tongue. The whole colony was preaching internationalism—one world, one flag and so on. They used to call me 'McGinley the Patriot' because I admired Wilson and supported the country's stand in the war."

Bewildered one day by a particulary esoteric conversation about psychoanalysis, McGinley told O'Neill he didn't know what some of the Provincetowners were talking about.

"Don't pay any attention," O'Neill said. "A lot of them are pretenders."

But McGinley was flattered (although it came to nothing) when Jig, trying to line up a cast for the fall production of *The Long Voyage Home,* pointed out McGinley as "a natural for the part of the drunken Russian."

Unwilling to take unlimited advantage of John Francis' generosity, O'Neill and McGinley lived mainly on oatmeal, which they cooked in their room in an ancient double boiler over a hot plate. James had arranged for them to have their meals at a hotel, but the paid-for meals were largely liquid. One day they found the beach littered with squid, and tried to cook them. They quickly went back to oatmeal. Despite an urgent need for cash, O'Neill, according to McGinley, refused an assignment he believed would compromise his literary talents.

"Gene was a man of principle," McGinley said. "He got an offer from a Broadway producer who had seen his work in New York. He wanted Gene to write a play about submarine warfare. There was a substantial advance payment attached to the offer."

"All they want is a story to wrap around a lot of spectacular stage effects," O'Neill told McGinley. "That would be cheap theatre, melodrama, claptrap, and I'll have nothing to do with it."

McGinley has recalled O'Neill's routine that summer as being one of alternate drinking, working and swimming. His swimming had grown even bolder than the year before; he would swim to the fishing boats and often board them, to their occupants' astonishment and dismay. More than once he was warned by the fishermen that he would surely drown.

"Gene would spend a few weeks swimming, boating, fishing and so on," McGinley related. "Then he would decide to go to work, and all else would be off his slate. I have seen him work from sunup all through the long day and into the small hours of the next morning. He would shut himself up and write and then pound away at the typewriter hours on end. He would write something, not like it, and then rewrite it until he was satisfied with the result. He had a tenacity that was amazing."

Sometime during that summer Professor Baker visited Provincetown and one day encountered O'Neill in town. It was their first meeting since O'Neill had been at Harvard. Baker knew about the Playwrights' Theatre and closely questioned O'Neill about his part in it. They discussed the group's production of *Bound East for Cardiff*, and O'Neill reminded Baker he had not considered it a play when it was first submitted to him at Harvard. Baker made it clear to O'Neill that he was interested in his work and asked O'Neill to keep him informed about his future productions.

In O'Neill's official list of work accomplished during the summer of 1917 he has mentioned only two projects—a short story (never published) about stokers, "containing the germ idea of *The Hairy Ape*" (which he finally wrote as a play during three weeks in 1921), and an outline for the idea of *Beyond the Horizon,* which was to be his first full-length play to reach the stage. In both of these works O'Neill expressed for the first time on a large scale his "hopeless hope" philosophy, painting with sweep and grandeur the tragic theme that was soon to distinguish him from all American playwrights who had come before.

The story has been told by several of O'Neill's friends that the title for *Beyond the Horizon* was suggested by a conversation he had with a feeble-minded boy on a Provincetown beach.

"What's out there?" asked the boy, gazing out over the Atlantic.

"The horizon," O'Neill is said to have replied.

"And what's beyond the horizon?" asked the boy.

The story may be true. It is always difficult in the case of an O'Neill play, to evaluate the many sources from which he drew inspiration. *Beyond the Horizon,* like most of his major works, was written on several levels, all of them discernible but so well blended by the undefinable catalyst of his genius that probably even he was unaware where one level began and the other ended.

He drew elements of the physical setting for *Beyond the Horizon* from his immediate surroundings. The farm was one he had seen tucked away in the hills of Truro, beyond Pilgrim Heights. Great poplars lined the approach to the farmhouse and the roar of the sea could be heard, always, in the near-distance. A byway across the dunes, called the Atkins-Mayo Road. lent its name to the two families who are the play's protagonists.

O'Neill's personal situation with regard to Louise inspired some elements (but not literally) of the plot. *Beyond the Horizon* is in one respect a triangle play. Two brothers are in love with the same girl—Ruth Atkins. O'Neill wrote himself into the part of Robert Mayo, the younger, who has "a touch of the poet." Robert makes the mistake of declaring his love for Ruth and staying with her on the farm, instead of following the sea as he had planned. Thus by winning he loses. There is something of Reed in the hardier older brother, Andrew, who, having lost Ruth, takes Robert's place as a sailor. But it was pure art that enabled O'Neill to alter an unresolved personal situation into one in which the poet wins the girl while losing his soul and the adventurer grows materialistic in the face of poetic experience he cannot appreciate. O'Neill believed that Reed had made off with his Louise; Robert, in the play, believes that Andrew has robbed him of his birthright.

On another level O'Neill interpreted the conflict between the two men in terms of the brother rivalry he understood so well from his own relationship with Jamie. He added the ingredient of father-son antagonism, infusing the Mayo family with the passions and conflicts that governed his own family. James O'Neill's disappointment that Jamie had not followed him successfully in the theatre evolved as the farmer Mayo's stony unforgiveness of Andrew, when he abandons the farm. The father's first name, significantly, is James.

On yet another level O'Neill drew on his experiences as a sailor and as a tubercular, fusing literal fact with artistic symbolism. Robert dies of tuberculosis. And if James Mayo is a New England version of James O'Neill, and Andrew is part Reed, part Jamie and part symbol, Robert is not only O'Neill himself in many guises but also part Olsen, the sailor who, a few months earlier, had been the model, in *The Long Voyage Home*, for the Swedish seaman who has run away from the farm and longs to return. This particular source of the characterization of Robert was conceded by O'Neill and is an interesting example of the way inspiration sometimes struck.

"At exactly the right moment, when I was floundering about in the maze of the novel-play [*Beyond the Horizon*] he [Olsen] turned up in my memory," O'Neill once said. "I thought, 'What if he had stayed on the farm, with his instincts. What would have happened?' But I realized at once he never would have stayed, not even if he had saddled himself with the wife and kids. It amused him to pretend he craved the farm. He was too harmonious a creation of the God of Things as They are. As well expect a sea gull to remain in a barnyard—for ethical reasons.

"And from that point I started to think of a more intellectual, civilized type—a weaker type from the standpoint of the above-mentioned God—a man who would have [Olsen's] inborn craving for the sea's unrest, only in him it would be conscious, too conscious, intellectually diluted into a vague, intangible, romantic wanderlust. His powers of resistance, both moral and physical, would also probably be correspondingly watered. He would throw away his instinctive dream and accept the thralldom of the farm for, why for almost any nice little poetical craving—the romance of sex, say.

"And so Robert Mayo was born, and developed from that beginning, and Ruth and the others, and finally the complete play."

Elsewhere O'Neill explained the genesis of the play in more general terms.

"I have never written anything which did not come directly or indirectly from some event or impression of my own, but these things develop very differently from what you expect. For example, I intended at first in *Beyond the Horizon* to portray in a series of disconnected scenes the life of a dreamer who pursues his vision over the world, apparently without success or a completed deed in his life. At the same time, it was my intention to show at last a real accretion from his wandering and dreaming, a thing intangible but real and precious beyond compare, which he had successfully made his own. But the technical difficulty of the task proved enormous and I was led to a grimmer thing: the tragedy of the man who looks over the horizon, who longs with his whole soul to depart on the quest, but whom destiny confines to a place and a task that are not his."

Whatever combination of environment and intuition it was that sparked *Beyond the Horizon,* it marked O'Neill's first coming to grips with his long-held dream of being a writer of tragedy.

"I have an innate feeling of exultance about tragedy," he said, in one of his innumerable attempts to explain and justify the form of expression to which he irrevocably committed himself in the summer of 1917. "The tragedy of Man is perhaps the only significant thing about him. What I am after is to get an audience to leave the theatre with an exultant feeling from seeing somebody on the stage facing life, fighting against the eternal odds, not conquering, but perhaps inevitably being conquered. The individual life is made significant just by the struggle.

"The struggle of man to dominate life, to assert and insist that life has no meaning outside himself where he comes in conflict with life, which he does at every turn; and his attempt to adapt life to his own needs, in which he doesn't succeed, is what I mean when I say that Man is the hero. If one out of ten thousand can grasp what the author means, if that one can formulate within himself his identity with the person in the play, and at the same time get the emotional thrill of being that person in the play, then the theatre will get back to the fundamental meaning of the drama, which contains something of the religious spirit which the Greek theatre had— and something of the exultance which is completely lacking in modern life."

Elaborating on this theme on another occasion, he said:

"The tragedy of life is what makes it worthwhile. I think that any life which merits living lies in the effort to realize some dream, and the higher that dream is the harder it is to realize. Most decidedly we must all have our dreams. If one hasn't them, one might as well be dead. The only success is in failure. Any man who has a big enough dream must be a failure and must accept this as one of the conditions of being alive. If he ever thinks for a moment that he is a success, then he is finished."

XXVIII

LEAVING SOME OF HIS PERSONAL POSSESSIONS IN THE safekeeping of his accommodating landlord, John Francis, O'Neill followed the Provincetown Players back to New York in the fall of 1917. He brought with him his melancholy over Louise's departure, and displayed it with self-conscious martyrdom. His gloom, in fact, was so palpable that some of the Provincetowners feared it would affect his creativity.

James O'Neill was less considerate of his son's feelings and still not entirely convinced of his talents. Although he soon came to regret and even vigorously deny his lack of faith in Eugene, there is no doubt he believed at this time that his son was a parasitical dilettante. He had no intention of allowing Eugene to become his permanent ward, as had Jamie. He kept after Eugene to take a job and threatened to withdraw his allowance.

"If you want to write, why don't you write for a newspaper?" James asked, with what he deemed utter reasonableness. Eugene grumbled to his friends about his father's ultimatum. How could he be a playwright if he had to devote himself to a job? Eugene made halfhearted attempts to find work, but when his father left town he gave up.

The Wanderer reopened in Philadelphia, and on October 11, less than three weeks before Eugene was to receive his first important recognition from the New York critics, James O'Neill celebrated his fiftieth anniversary as an actor. *The Wanderer* was to be his last play; after a half century in the theatre, he had read his final press notices. Nevertheless, he was still making the kind of public pronouncements about the theatre that made Eugene shudder. They seemed, to Eugene, to be oblique slaps at his own efforts.

"There is but one kind of acting for me—that of the classic drama," declared James to a reporter for the Philadelphia *Record*, lumping *The Wanderer* with the plays of Shakespeare. "It has the old heart quality in it, the appeal that the public cannot resist." In Boston, where *The Wanderer* also toured, James befriended an eighteen-year-old student, Harry Crowley, who wanted to go on the stage. "Oh, Harry," James told him, "I wish my boy Gene loved the stage as you do. All Gene wants to do is scribble."

Ella O'Neill, who was more heartened than James by her son's literary progress, had accompanied her husband to Boston. Crowley met them both there in a quiet family hotel where he worked as a desk clerk in order to pay his way at the New England Conservatory of Music. (The hotel was run by a woman named Miss Fritz, and her establishment was called the Fritz-Carlton.) James, remarkably spry for a man of seventy-one, would occasionally cross the hotel lobby to Crowley's desk in a lively hornpipe. Ella walked a little behind her husband. At sixty she was gray-haired but erect and dressed in dark colors. That October, she candidly displayed her pleasure over Eugene's triumph at having a play published in *The Smart Set*.

"Isn't this wonderful?" she said to a young relative, proudly showing the magazine. "Eugene has made seventy-five dollars!"

The Smart Set was a leading literary magazine. It called itself "a magazine of cleverness" and the two men who ran it, George Jean Nathan and H. L. Mencken, had absolute faith in their ability to recognize cleverness when they saw it. They saw it in O'Neill's *The Long Voyage Home,* the first of three one-act plays by him which they published. (*Ile* appeared in the May, 1918, issue and *The Moon of the Caribbees* in August, 1918.)

The Smart Set provoked a good deal of controversy in intellectual circles. Nathan and Mencken were sometimes vulgar, often brilliant, and always irreverent. Their iconoclasm held a vast appeal for O'Neill. One of the leaflets issued from *The Smart Set* offices, for example, announced that "A woman Secretary is in attendance at all interviews between the Editors, or either of them, and lady authors. Hence, it will be unnecessary for such visitors to provide themselves with either duennas or police whistles."

O'Neill did not expect *The Smart Set* to publish his plays. When he submitted them he wrote to Mencken that he knew they were not the sort of thing the magazine used but that he would like an opinion on them. Mencken replied that he liked them, and had turned them over to George Jean Nathan, who served as the magazine's drama critic. O'Neill then received a letter from Nathan praising the plays, and was astonished when all three were subsequently accepted for publication.

This was the beginning of a long friendship between O'Neill and Nathan. Nathan, six years O'Neill's senior, had been a drama critic since 1908—first for the New York *Herald* and later on a contributing basis for various magazines including *Harper's Weekly*. He had been coeditor of *The Smart Set* since 1914.

Having studied in Germany, Nathan was an advocate of the European drama and had long been deploring, in a lone but strident voice, the shoddy state of the American theatre, holding up for his readers such examples of vigorous drama as the plays of Strindberg and Ibsen and ridiculing, often with the wildest abandon, the plays of such sacrosanct Americans as Augustus Thomas, Charles Klein and Eugene Walter. Handsome, vain, sybaritic and didactic, Nathan throve on controversy, loved stepping on toes, and was a gallant fighter in any intellectual cause he believed in. He believed in O'Neill and did not content himself with merely saying so in print. He pushed O'Neill's cause personally and fervently with a number of the younger and more daring Broadway managers. Some years after publishing *The Moon of the Caribbees* in *The Smart Set,* Nathan wrote, in an introduction to the published play:

In O'Neill [the American] theatre has found its first really important dramatist. To it he has brought a sense of splendid color, a sense of vital drama and a sense of throbbing English that no native playwright before him was able to bring. . . .

O'Neill came into the American drama at a propitious moment. His entrance clicked with all the precision and critical timeliness of the entrance of the United States Marines in a piece of popular Whang-doodle. Just as this drama seemed about to be laid low by unremitting stereotyped dullness and preposterous affectation, he jumped upon the scene with a bundle of life and fancy under his arm, hurled it onto the stage, and there let it break open with its hundred smashing hues to confound the drab and desolate boards. Instantly—or so it seemed—the stage began to breathe again; instantly the painted back-drop became real and instantly the canvas rocks became solid, substantial. . . .

The essential difference between O'Neill and the majority of his contemporaries in the field of American drama lies in the circumstance that where the latter think of life (where they think of it at all) in terms of drama, O'Neill thinks of drama in terms of life.

If O'Neill's first important literary recognition came from publication in *The Smart Set,* his first impact in the theatre came with the production of *In the Zone.* Considered not experimental enough for the Playwrights' Theatre (an opinion in which O'Neill concurred), the play was presented on October 31, 1917, by the Washington Square Players, whose production standards were more professional than those of the Provincetown Players. The cast included William Gillette (Olsen), Frederick Roland (Smitty), and Bienzi de Cordova (Cocky). On the bill with *In the Zone* were *The Avenue,* by Fenimore Merrill; *His Widow's Husband* by Jacinto Benavente; and *Blind Alleys* by Grace Latimer Wright, in which Katharine Cornell, who had made her debut with the Washington Square Players the year before, acted a major role. Most of the critics singled out the O'Neill play for their highest praise.

An anonymous critic for *The Times* devoted three quarters of his review of the four-play bill to *In the Zone*, describing it as "heartfelt," "vivid with picturesque character," and "tense with excitement." " 'In the Zone' was of a very high order, both as a thriller and as a document in human character and emotion," he said.

The equally anonymous critic for the *Evening World* declared that the Washington Square Players "fired their best shot with 'In the Zone' by Eugene O'Neill, who, I'm told, is the son of that fine old actor, James O'Neill." The *Herald* reported, also anonymously, that the O'Neill play "registered so realistically that several spectators laughed awkwardly in its tense moments as a result of the nervous strain of the sustained thrill."

In a signed review in the *American*, Alan Dale called *In the Zone* "perhaps the best and most agreeably acted of the playlets," adding: "The idea is well worked up. It is all quite thrillingly suggested. The scene itself is capital. The atmosphere is rife with danger." For the *Globe*, Louis Sherwin reported that "the best of them all is 'In the Zone,' by Eugene O'Neill, whose remarkable talent for drama was first shown by his 'Bound East for Cardiff.' I don't know where this young man got his knowledge of the speech of seafaring men, but this is the second play he has written about them with remarkable power and penetration. He makes the sailors in the forecastle of a tramp steamer passing through the submarine zone live for you with a vividness that is quite astonishing."

In the minority were Ralph Block, of the *Tribune*, who did not even mention *In the Zone* in his review of the bill, and an anonymous critic for the *Sun*, who took O'Neill to task for being repetitious, a charge O'Neill was to hear often during his career.

But the reviews, on the whole, were so good—and the audience reaction so enthusiastic—that O'Neill suspected *In the Zone* was not a very good play.

"When *everybody* likes something, watch out!" he once told an interviewer, recalling his first hit. And to Barrett Clark, who praised *In the Zone* when it was published in 1919, O'Neill wrote:

"I by no means agree with you in your high estimate of *In the Zone*. To me it seems the least significant of all the plays. It is too facile in its conventional technique, too full of clever theatrical tricks . . . this play in no way represents the true me or what I desire to express. It is a situation drama lacking in all spiritual import—there is no big feeling for life inspiring it. Given the plot and a moderate ability to characterize, any industrious playwright could have reeled it off. . . ."

In the Zone was also the first play from whose production O'Neill made any money—further proof, in his opinion, of its artistic worthlessness.

While tasting the beginnings of fame through his popular one-acter O'Neill had not neglected his development with the Provincetown Players, by now claiming a subscription audience of nine hundred. The Players opened *their* season with *The Long Voyage Home,* on November 2, 1917, two days after the Washington Square Players had presented *In the Zone.* Nina Moise directed the production and Jig Cook and Hutch Collins were in the cast.

The Playwrights' Theatre had been refurbished. Though the audience still sat on benches, the backstage accommodations had been greatly enhanced. The troupe rented the floor above the parlor for cloak room, lounging room, business office, dressing rooms and storage of scenery. They also added two salaried workers. One was a property man-cum-carpenter, Lewis Ell, who designed sets, walked on in minor roles, and immortalized himself as the author of a sign on a backstage door: "Cloze the door was you born in a stabel." Nina Moise was the other new salaried member, with the title of general coach.

In addition to *The Long Voyage Home,* the season's first bill included *Close the Book,* a thin comedy by Susan Glaspell about an emancipated girl, and a murky "dramatic poem" by James Oppenheim called *Night.* The program was favorably reviewed, though not on the same scale as that of the Washington Square Players; the Playwrights' Theatre still maintained a policy of no free tickets to critics and an attitude of indifference to fame. However, the success of *In the Zone* impelled several critics to buy tickets for the bill featuring another O'Neill play.

The first public recognition of O'Neill as a figure of growing importance came on November 4, 1917, two days after the première of *The Long Voyage Home.* He was the subject of a feature article in the Sunday drama section of *The Times,* under the provocative two-column headline, "Who Is Eugene O'Neill?" The mystery of Eugene O'Neill's identity was solved in about four hundred words in space surrounded by ads for current Broadway productions: *Tiger Rose,* by William Mack, at the Lyceum, and *Polly with a Past,* by Guy Bolton and George Middleton, at the Belasco; Morris Gest's production of *Chu Chin Chow,* and the Charles Dillingham and Florenz Ziegfeld, Jr., production of *Miss 1917.* There was also an ad for the new Theda Bara movie, *Cleopatra,* playing at the Lyric:

What Anthony paid for Cleo's clothes
Only the Great Sahara knows.
In Thedapatra she wears a rose!

In Greenwich Village that season the Provincetown Players acquired several new members who were to devote themselves to the Playwrights' Theatre. Among them was a slender, handsome intellectual, James Light, who had been studying English literature and philosophy at Ohio State University and had accepted a scholarship at Columbia University in New York. His education began at Pittsburgh's Carnegie Tech, where he majored in architecture and painting. One day he looked critically at his drawings and decided they were not first-rate. He concluded he would never be as good as Michelangelo or El Greco, the two painters he most admired, and he abandoned painting.

When he reached New York in October Light headed for the Village to find a place to live. He ran into Charles Ellis, also a former student at Ohio State, who had arrived in New York to study painting at the Art Students League. They decided to share expenses and rented a big room above the theatre at 139 MacDougal Street. While unpacking, Light listened curiously to the sounds of hammering below and investigated.

"There were four people there—Jig Cook, Hutch Collins, O'Neill and Lewis Ell," Light said in recalling his introduction to the Provincetown Players. "Ell was doing the hammering. He was working on the benches in the auditorium. The other three were on the floor, a half bottle of whiskey near them, shooting craps. They asked me to join them, and since I had a few dollars in my pocket, I did. O'Neill's hands were very big and the others watched him suspiciously when he picked up the dice."

When the game was over, Light and O'Neill fell into conversation. O'Neill mentioned something about swimming—Light's sport at Ohio State—and a bond was quickly established. Light, whose father had been a carpenter and builder, then ventured to criticize the construction of the benches. He pointed out that the job could be more efficiently handled with a ripsaw. Jig Cook promptly turned over the project to him.

"I started sawing immediately," Light said. He was also pressed into service as an actor. Susan Glaspell's *Close the Book* had not been completely cast, and one day when Light, looking professorial, happened to pass with an armload of books an actor suggested him for the role of Peyton Root, an English instructor. Light acquitted himself so well as both carpenter and actor that he became permanently attached to the

Playwrights' Theatre. He attended lecture courses at Columbia, but abandoned his plan for a degree.

Light's second appearance was on the bill which opened November 30 and ended December 4. The troupe, grown a trifle overambitious, staged four one-acters—two of them by the eccentric poet Maxwell Bodenheim, one by Rita Wellman, who had caused a minor flurry the year before with an antiwar play entitled *Barbarians,* and O'Neill's *Ile.* The first Bodenheim play was called *Knot-Holes,* was set on "a road by a graveyard . . . anytime," and its cast consisted of the Sleepy Mayor, the Jaunty Bricklayer and two Ghosts. Opus number two was *The Gentle Furniture Shop,* also set "anytime," and also peopled by symbols. Light appeared in Rita Wellman's play and Hutch Collins portrayed Captain Keeney in *Ile.* Only the O'Neill play, which Nina Moise directed, was considered successful by the Provincetowners; it was responsible for increasing the subscription audience and necessitated the scheduling of extra performances.

Jimmy Light's roommate, Charles Ellis, also had been pressed into service. Starting, like Light, on the physical side of a production, he soon found himself on stage, entrusted with major roles.

It was Jig Cook who discovered his acting ability. Ellis was painting scenery for a three-act play by Cook called *The Athenian Women*— the theatre's fifth bill in March, 1918, and its most ambitious one to date. It had a cast of thirty-three.

"I was painting my heart out on a cutout of the Acropolis," Ellis recalled. "Suddenly I heard Jig's voice call out from the back of the auditorium."

"You are going to play the part of the boy who designed the Acropolis," pronounced Cook, and promptly dismissed the actor who had already been cast for the role.

Two bills earlier, in December, 1917, Cook had discovered another gifted amateur—Edna St. Vincent Millay. Recently out of Vassar and already preceded by a reputation as a poet, she went to see Cook for an acting role and was engaged for Floyd Dell's play, *The Angel Intrudes.* Miss Millay, who was living in the Village with her two sisters, Norma and Kathleen, told them about her new job but did not suggest that they join her. It was Charles Ellis who finally drew Norma into the group, where she became one of its leading actresses.

"Charlie started taking out Vincent and ended up living with me," Norma Millay once recalled with satisfaction, adding casually, "We were married in 1921—my mother thought it was high time."

❖

Though enjoying his success, O'Neill was again finding the strain of the city an impediment to work, and he now added the excuse of his melancholy over Louise to do some intensive drinking. Sometime before the end of 1917 he had managed, however, to write a three-act play called *Now I ask You,* which he described as a farce; a one-acter, about the I.W.W., called *The G.A.M.,* which he described as a "farce-comedy"; and another one-acter called *Atrocity,* which he described as a "panto-mime." None of these was ever produced and he later listed them among his "destroyed" works. He also wrote two poems during this period, neither of them ever published. One was called "Eyes," presumably dedicated to Louise, and the other "Tis of Thee." Both were written in saloons, where he was then spending most of his time.

One of the saloons popular with the Provincetown group was Columbia Gardens, run by Luke O'Connor. It was here that Jig Cook and Susan Glaspell had first made their plans to produce plays in Provincetown. O'Connor, who possessed the Irish charm and temperament O'Neill admired, had a red face, wore stiff high collars that squeezed his neck, and excelled as a bouncer. His greatest pride lay in the fact that the poet John Masefield had once worked for him as bar boy. Masefield remained loyal after he achieved fame and from time to time sent a copy of his latest book to O'Connor, who kept the volumes behind the bar and needed no urging to display them to his customers.

O'Connor was respected for his generosity in cashing checks for his customers. The writer Holger Cahill, for whom O'Connor once cashed a $50 check, told him: "Gee, Luke, that was nice of you. Don't you ever get any rubber checks?"

O'Connor vanished for a moment behind the bar, then reappeared with a stack of checks a foot high. They had all bounced.

O'Connor's saloon, decorated with cut-glass mirrors and tall Chinese vases, was on Eighth Street and Sixth Avenue, four blocks north of the Hell Hole, and across the street from night court. Like the Hell Hole, it was rarely referred to by its formal name. It was known as the Working Girls' Home, a name bestowed one afternoon by Mary Heaton Vorse, after observing a trio of prostitutes push through the swinging door of O'Connor's.

To O'Connor's on occasion came Jamie O'Neill, seeking his brother—not quite able to conceal his resentment of Eugene's success, not quite able to decide whether to praise Gene or disparage him.

"See my brother's play last night?" he once asked Romany Marie. "Isn't he great?"

"Why aren't you?" retorted Marie.

"Someday I'm going to be," answered Jamie, with heavy irony.

He was forty. His face had become flabby with alcohol, his eyes puffed and glazed. But he still kept up a mechanical pretense of being a Broadway playboy and behaved as though he was slumming when he looked in on his brother at the Hell Hole or at Romany Marie's or Polly Holliday's. One friend of O'Neill's has described Jamie coming into the Hell Hole "looking down his long nose." Jamie's attitude was so patronizing that the friend could not refrain from asking Eugene why he stood for it, and offered to punch Jamie for him.

One time Holger Cahill and Jamie were having a discussion at O'Connor's about comedy and tragedy in literature and Jamie said, "People think my life is a comedy, but it's a goddam tragedy."

"Gene and his brother were both soaked in self-pity," Cahill later remarked. "Jamie was jealous of Gene; he once told me Gene was overrated."

Few of O'Neill's Greenwich Village friends liked Jamie. One exception was Art McGinley, who roomed with Jamie briefly that winter, and sometimes joined him in idling before the Film Café on West Forty-ninth Street. Occasionally Eugene would seek them out there.

"All the actors would go by," McGinley recalled. "Sometimes one of them would snub Jamie, and then he'd tell me he had once gotten that actor a job with his old man's company."

So futile was Jamie's present, so dismal his future, that he was willing to take refuge even in his sorry past. The contrast between him and his brother reached its height that year. For both Jamie and Eugene knew that Jamie's life was over—and that Eugene's was on the verge of triumph. If this knowledge made Jamie sullen, it made Eugene gentle. He treated Jamie with tenderness and affection. But he was no longer Jamie's worshipful kid brother.

Eugene went his own way, regretfully leaving Jamie behind. His way often led to the Hell Hole; and by now most of the Provincetown group had learned to follow him there. Maxwell Bodenheim later described an encounter with the young playwright in *The New Yorker*:

"When I first met O'Neill ten years ago he was seated in the back room of the Hell Hole. . . . He was talking to the Hudson Dusters on the subject of a friend of his—Scotty, who had defrauded the gangsters in a furniture deal—and he managed to smother their rage and induce them to forgo their intended vengeance. He did this with a curious mixture of restrained profanity, mild contempt and blunt camaraderie, which showed that he shared the spirit of these roughnecks and yet failed to share it."

What it was that O'Neill shared with a Sioux Indian who one day drifted into the Village, wearing fringed leather pants, a red shirt and a dour expression, no one ever found out; but the two would sit together for hours at a table in the Hell Hole, glumly drinking, in apparently compatible silence.

O'Neill's friendship with a man named Joe Smith was more obvious. Joe was in his forties, a light-skinned Negro with Caucasian features, broad shoulders and a slim waist. He was married to a white woman, known as Miss Viola—a big blonde who blazed with supposedly "hot" diamonds; whenever she and Joe were hard up she would pawn her jewelry. Joe was a watchman for an auction company and, it was rumored, supplemented his income with a pair of loaded dice. On several occasions, when O'Neill had drunk himself insensible, Joe took him home to his sister's house and saw that he was nursed back to health; more than once Joe fed him during a lean period. After his wife died Joe moved into a second-floor flat in an old frame building on Cornelia Street. His friends knew he was at home if they saw a bottle of gin in the window—his signal of welcome.

"You're as welcome as the flowers in May" was his habitual greeting to whoever climbed the stairs to his rooms. In his apartment he had an old player piano. He was fond of music, particularly of "To a Wild Rose," and kept the instrument going while entertaining visitors.

O'Neill loved to go to Joe's place or join Joe in the Hell Hole. He found it amusing to watch Joe tinker with the Hell Hole's player piano untill it disgorged its nickels; these Joe distributed to anyone who couldn't afford the price of a beer. Joe also had a way with pigs. Wallace, the proprietor, had bought a pig and fed it on garbage in the cellar of the Hell Hole. He was planning to cook it for Christmas. As the holiday approached, O'Neill and his friends got into the habit of fetching the pig from the cellar and offering it whiskey. It was a strong pig, and when it was drunk it became unmanageable, rushing about the backroom, upsetting chairs, and behaving as O'Neill was apt to behave when he had exceeded his limit. Because of the pig's eccentricity, the Hell Hole habitués referred to it as "O'Neill's son." Joe Smith, the only one who was able to subdue the pig at such times, would croon into its ear until it grew quiet and could be led back to the cellar.

"You got to reason with him," Joe would explain.

That was the sort of thing O'Neill enjoyed. Not that he laughed or showed his mirth with anything approaching abandonment.

"Gene would try to keep his laughter down, to strangle it," James Light once said. "Sometimes he'd walk into a corner and get it over with. He couldn't abandon himself to laughter; that would have stopped all thought activity. Instead, he was busy seeing the extension of the joke— he was ready to carry the humor of the situation a step further in his mind."

Dudley Nichols, who became a friend of O'Neill's in later years, once expressed a similar opinion:

"The loud laugh was not for him. Very likely because his mind was too humorous for that. Think of the loud laughers you have known. No, I'm sure the really humorous men have never been loud laughers. But I suppose it is nothing either for or against a man. I do know that I have never laughed so delightedly and with my whole being so much as I did on several memorable occasions with O'Neill, for the simple reason that he was making me see something funny through his own rich mind, something that I had not perceived to be side-splitting until he pointed it out. On these occasions he would chuckle until he would become speechless—yet only a soft chuckle.

"Sometimes the wittiest people do not understand the nature of humor, for wit is generally compounded of quick intellect, imagination and—malice, deny it as we may. O'Neill had no trace of malice, but I daresay its manifestation in others amused him at times, as it does all of us.

"I have always remembered a motto of the great art critic, Elie Faure. He said: 'We must take everything tragically, nothing seriously.' That is precisely what O'Neill did. For the tragic view of life embraces all the humor and absurdity of human beings."

Sean O'Casey, with whom O'Neill had a brief but felicitous friendship, recalled that O'Neill made *him* laugh many times. According to O'Casey, O'Neill told him jokes that "only two Irishmen can share." "This man could be gay," O'Casey said. "It was good to have heard his laughter."

Few people with whom O'Neill was on intimate terms, however, whether or not they were Irish, failed to perceive or respond to his peculiar brand of humor. From cultivated and sophisticated men like Nichols and Light, from the poet and wit O'Casey, to a self-educated, rough-hewn ex-sailor like Slim Martin, an Irishman with whom O'Neill spent much time in the Village, they all seemed able to analyze and appreciate it.

"Gene smiled often," Martin once said. "He had smiling eyes, always, among friends. If a thing amused him, he'd tip back his head with a quiet little laugh—rather, a chuckle. He never laughed out loud; who does, but children? He had an excellent sense of humor, but a poor sense of comedy, as he was kindly, and comedy invariably seems based on cruelty."

O'Neill did not often contribute to the lively conversations that went on around him. He regarded the Hell Hole much in the same way that certain pubs in Ireland are regarded: as places in which to listen. His ear was extraordinarily sensitive, as the flavor of his dialogue often attests. Much of that dialogue was absorbed in the saloons of Greenwich Village. But, although O'Neill was reluctant to talk, there was one story— an enormously complex and drawn-out joke—that he never tired of repeating.

Sometimes it took him over half an hour to tell it. Almost everyone O'Neill knew for any length of time heard him tell it at least once and many heard it several times. George Jean Nathan vowed that O'Neill told it to him regularly twice a year, including a time that it lasted the duration of a seven-mile walk. It was the story known as "The Old Bean" and concerned the adventures of an old drunkard who was convinced that he could and did cope with every obstacle that fate placed in his path.

One episode of the Old Bean saga concerns the drunkard's triumph over D.T.'s. This is the way O'Neill would tell it:

"There was a guy in the bar very drunk. He told everyone how he used his old bean. 'Look at me,' he said. 'When I take my ninth I'll use my bean and go home and go to bed—not like you guys.' He drank his ninth and left.

"One night, two weeks later, he turned up at the bar, covered with bandages and walking with a limp. 'Where you been?' everyone asked him.

" 'Yes, boys,' he said, 'If I hadn't used the old bean, I wouldn't be here now. Remember the last time I was here? Well, I went home that night, got undressed and got into bed. Then I heard a knock at the door. I opened it and in came a little guy in uniform with a rifle on his shoulder. He marched up and down near my bed. I wanted to go to sleep, so I grabbed him by the back of his neck like I would a cat and threw him out. I went back to bed and five minutes later I heard a loud bang on the door. I opened it and in marched the same little guy, this time with a squad of little guys. He pulls out a sword and yells to the squad, 'Ready, Aim—' and just before he said 'Fire!' I used the old bean and jumped out the window!' "

XXIX

THERE WERE TWO PATRONS OF THE HELL HOLE WITH whom O'Neill relaxed completely and talked endlessly. One was Terry Carlin and the other was Slim Martin, whose full name was James Joseph Martin. Slim was tall, rangy and rugged, with a strong jaw, beak nose, blue-gray eyes and an engaging grin. An average-sized friend once compared the experience of walking with him to strolling with a giraffe. Slim had the weathered complexion of a sailor, which he had been for several years; the powerful muscles of an ironworker, his trade for the past year, and a strong philosophical bent. He was also Irish and a poet and a member of the I.W.W.

In 1917 Slim's work was sporadic. He might find a job on the construction of a new apartment house, and remain employed for a month or two, earning $30 to $40 a week—good pay in that day. Then he would be out of work until he could find another building project. He would spend his mornings looking for work and, if he failed to find a job by lunchtime, would drift into the Hell Hole. He had no ties, no obligations, except to an aunt in Brooklyn who fed and housed him. In the Hell Hole, he believed he was rounding out his education. He did odd jobs for the Provincetown Players, just to be allowed a niche in their company.

At the Hell Hole in the afternoon he usually encountered Terry Carlin and O'Neill.

The exchanges between Martin, Carlin and O'Neill came close to reproducing the conversations of a Dublin pub. The brogue that renders Irish pub talk lyrical, no matter how mundane the topic, was lacking from the speech of the three American Irishmen, but their range was probably wider and certainly more unconventional. (Their talk has been reconstructed partly from Slim's uncannily accurate memory, partly from correspondence, and partly from the recollections of other contemporaries.) Often they devoted themselves to pulling apart their three "old-country, dumb, Irish fathers"—Slim's phrase.

SLIM: "The comical ideas that they brought from the old country!"

TERRY: "With them, it's obey, or feel a touch of the stick."

O'NEILL: "Always a conflict between the old-country parents and the new-country offspring."

TERRY: "And the Irish ghost stories!"

SLIM: "Always the fog, the bog, the will-o'-the-wisp and the dog or pig turned to the devil before your eyes!"

But always, too, the blazing pride of their Irish ancestry, felt by all three, despite parental despotism, despite rejection of the faith of their Irish parents.

Slim claimed to be agnostic, like O'Neill. But Terry disdained that label; he was a mystic.

SLIM: "You're as pantheistic as Omar, Terry. You're a mystic only when you've been looking too long at the wine when it's red."

TERRY: "Like now?"

SLIM: " 'Scuse me, Terry. I'll buy a drink."

Appreciative grin from O'Neill.

Literature was not neglected by the three philosophers. One day Joseph Conrad was the subject.

SLIM: "Never heard of Conrad."

O'NEILL: "What? You'll have to read *The Nigger of the Narcissus*, Slim."

SLIM: "Oh, I've read that—in Portland, in the Wobbly hall. Talked it over with Jack Reed."

O'NEILL: "But you said you didn't know Conrad."

SLIM: "Hell, I let a book drop open at a page and start reading. If I like it I read it to the end and then go back to the beginning. I never look at who wrote the book."

O'NEILL: "You should."

SLIM: "Ever walk over the Brooklyn Bridge?"

O'NEILL: "Sure."

SLIM: "Who built it?"

Blank look from O'Neill. Equally blank look from Terry.

SLIM: "The authors' names are cast on steel plates and put up at both towers of the bridge to be read from the footway.'"

O'NEILL: "That's not the same. That bridge will last only a few years. A book or a poem may last for thousands."

SLIM: "The author hopes."

O'NEILL: "My plays will, I hope."

SLIM: "I hope for you, too, Gene."

Quiet laughter from Terry.

O'Neill's ideas for future plays were often the subject of discussion.

He was still mulling over his short story, which he was soon to expand into *The Hairy Ape,* and had asked Slim to take him to a meeting of the I.W.W. But there were other ideas for plays, far in the future.

"Some day," said O'Neill, "I'll do a play about Marco Polo"—this, six years before *Marco Millions* was drafted.

And another time:

"I want to write a play about the sons of Mary and the sons of Martha"—this, eight years before writing *Lazarus Laughed.*

Recurrently the theme of Greek tragedy came up, explained and elaborated upon by O'Neill and Terry for the furtherance of Slim's education.

O'NEILL: "In Greek tragedy the characters are inexorably pushed on the road by fate. Once a Greek tragedian started to write a play, his characters never could deviate from that road on which fate was pushing them. Life itself is the same as that. You get on a road and no matter what you do or how you try to change or correct your life, you can't do it, because Fate, or Kismet, or whatever you call it, will push you down the road."

But Slim could enlighten O'Neill, too, on a variety of odd subjects:

"There's no such thing as skid row. It's skid *road*—a lumberjack term—the road you drag the logs along to load them on the skidway. It takes us hoboes to tell you about things like that, Gene."

And sometimes their knowledge blended with and supplemented each other's.

SLIM: "What do you mean by 'symbolism,' Gene?"

O'NEILL: *"The Cherry Orchard* is a symbol, and *The Sea Gull* and—in *Hamlet*—take the phrase 'When we have shuffled off this mortal coil' —the coil is a symbol for life. The coil would be a line like a ship's hawser."

Slim (*the ex-sailor, grasping the idea*): "Yes, the hawser is coiled up, and as you throw it to the dock it goes shuffling off—and if the other end isn't secure, the line will go." (*Thoughtful pause.*) "And what do you think Shakespeare meant by 'I know a hawk from a handsaw'? What sort of hawk do you think he meant, Gene?"

O'NEILL: "Why, a bird, Slim."

SLIM: "No, you're wrong there. A hawk is also a tool. A handsaw is one of the main tools of the carpenter, but a hawk is a plasterer's tool—a little square with a round handle in the bottom, to hold mortar."

O'NEILL: "I never understood that. I thought it was a hawk flying in the air."

They went on to discuss the fact that Shakespeare had lifted his plots from other writers.

TERRY: "True, he plagiarized. But he said it better."

O'NEILL: "Everything has been said before. There's nothing new to write about—always the same old things, the same old lies and the same old loves and the same old tragedy and joy. But you can write about them in a new way, in your own way."

On philosophy:

SLIM: "Terry, your Schopenhauer and Nietzsche and Marx, and your Plato and Spinoza—I've read them. They're all nuts. They contradict themselves from chapter to chapter, book to book.

TERRY: "Of course. That's what philosophers are for."

On women:

TERRY: "If you go fishing and a woman comes along, you're not going to pay attention to the fish. She can't get a worm on the hook—you've got to do it. They're insatiable in their demands. If you want to buy an automobile, you go and look at the engine and braking and other mechanical features. But she opens the door to look at the seats, the color, the upholstery. They're forever demanding. Nothing is good enough for them."

SLIM: "That's terrible, Terry. After all, the demanding women are the ones that are pushing you up the road and are causing you to progress and bring on innovations, new inventions. We'd be satisfied to get along with an old pick and shovel. But they say maybe they'd like a steam shovel. So we find a steam shovel."

TERRY: "You can't trust them. You can't depend on them. You're a sap to idealize them, Slim. I know. I know. I'm a lot older than you."

SLIM: "Well, that's right. Go back to Kipling's ladies and 'learn about women from me' (*singing mockingly*):

> "I've taken my fun where I've found it,
> An' now I must pay for my fun,
> For the more you 'ave known o' the others
> The less you will settle to one . . ."

(Twenty-five years later in *Ah, Wilderness!* O'Neill slightly misquoted two other lines from the same poem. Richard Miller drunkenly declaims to the tart, Belle: "But I wouldn't do such, 'cause I loved her too much/ But I learned about women from her.")

O'NEILL (*after a long, barely audible seizure of chuckling*): "Don't you do it, Slim. Learn about women on your own. The hell with what Terry tells you."

TERRY: "Slim, you believe women are wonderful and that you'll fall in love and be happily married someday; and Gene believes he's going to be a great playwright. That's only to keep you going. That's your pipe dream. Everyone needs a pipe dream to keep him going. You're both kidding yourselves. It won't work out. But you have to have pipe dreams to live in this dizzy world."

O'Neill and Slim often talked about the sea and when they did Terry fell silent.

GENE: "One of the greatest kicks I ever got was when I became an A.B. The sea calls to the blood of all the Irish."

SLIM: "Yes, there isn't a square foot of Ireland more than sixty-five miles from the sea. In the pre-Christian days the Irish fared to North America in curraghs. Who built the Druid worship places in Massachusetts, if not the Druid-Irish?"

Terry accused Slim of romanticizing.

On the subject of masks:

O'NEILL: "If people would take off their masks, we'd know more about them. The truth is always concealed."

TERRY: "That's what Pilate said when he sentenced Jesus. What is the truth?"

O'NEILL: "If I could only find a way to let people's inner thoughts be known on the stage—if I could use masks—if I could take off the mask to let the inner thoughts be known to the audience, and put on the mask to show the outer thoughts—I'm planning to write a play using masks."

On health (Slim, like O'Neill, was something of a hypochondriac):

SLIM: "I'll probably wind up with T.B., working out in the rain and cold all the time."

O'NEILL: "T.B.! You give me a pain in the neck. You and Terry, both with chests like barrels, and you're both worried about T.B. They wouldn't be able to kill either of you with an axe."

Slim, who outlived O'Neill, did finally contract tuberculosis. When O'Neill died in 1953, Slim reflected from his hospital bed:

"Gene's life was tragic. He never achieved what he really wanted, artistically. The gap between his achievements and his frustrations was so great, they didn't at all balance.

"Gene was a thoroughgoing, loyal, kindly, warmhearted, generous and lovable gentleman from his heart out and to all people. The downtrodden, especially if they were courageous, were heroes and friends, and when he had success and adulation he would leave a group of befurred and jeweled and tophatted socialites and those he dubbed 'the sons of Mary' to walk over and say hello and chat with one of those he called 'the sons of Martha.'

"And you could be in shirt sleeves with the soil of labor black in the sweat of your face. He was truly a man and a friend."

XXX

THE WINTER OF 1917-18 WAS ONE OF THE COLDEST IN memory. It was also a year of high tensions and fast-vanishing romantic visions. It was the final year of the war, the dawn of the Russian Revolution. The aging children of Greenwich Village burned brighter than ever with idealism—and waited breathlessly for the millennium. Some believed it would dawn in Bolshevist Russia, others that it would emerge in a renaissance of Art.

It was the end of an era of innocence and pure romance, the prelude to Prohibition and the roaring twenties. Two of the voices of radical idealism were already being smothered; *The Seven Arts* and *The Masses* could not survive the antiwar policy they had espoused. Max Eastman, Floyd Dell and Jack Reed were under indictment for articles said to have sought obstruction of recruiting and enlistment. It was becoming more difficult, even in the freedom of Greenwich Village, to be a radical, unfettered, freewheeling, individualist. Labels were beginning to be applied —communist, pacifist, immoralist, coward.

The artists and writers of Greenwich Village clung together in a sort of valedictory frenzy, sensing the end of their golden era. They huddled in saloons, in each other's apartments, in the club rooms above the Playwrights' Theatre, seeking shelter around the punch bowl and the whiskey bottle and the schooner of beer, trying to ward off the cold winds and the even colder climate of antipathy in which they would all have to shoulder the responsibilities of a postwar world. The winter of 1917-18 marked the end of a way of life.

For many of the Provincetowners the last-ditch battle against the violation of their glorious adolescence was fought in the Hell Hole. O'Neill lived there, almost literally. If he was late to a meeting or a rehearsal, someone would be sent to fetch him from the Hell Hole—not from his home, for no one really knew where he lived; as one of his friends has recalled, "Gene would just show up and vanish." Soon someone would have to be sent to find whoever had gone to find O'Neill and before long the whole group would be at the Hell Hole, drinking, talking, singing. No one wanted to go to sleep and often they would stay up all night, warming themselves on Wallace's liquor, his potbellied stove, and their dreams.

In the early part of that winter O'Neill conscientiously fanned the flame of the torch he carried for the still-absent Louise. At times it seemed to some of his friends that his suffering was less acute than his sense of drama. They believed he was playing the role of the heartbroken lover rather than feeling it. In any case there were at least four other women ready to console him. (Two of them he later used as characters in his plays and from the others he borrowed suggestions of character, and possibly their names.)

One was Nina Moise. (Although Nina lent nothing discernible of her personality to the heroine of one of his later plays, *Strange Interlude*, the first part of the drama is set in the period during which O'Neill knew her, and he had a trick of mind that caused him to incorporate in his scripts the names of people who influenced or impressed him during a time in his life that paralleled the one he was writing about; the name, therefore, may have sprung to his mind when he was creating Nina Leeds.)

"I didn't like Gene when I first met him during the production of *The Sniper*," Nina said. "He was morose, sullen, uncommunicative." It wasn't long, however, before she fell under the spell of his "moody, tormented eyes" and felt the power of the man, "terribly potent, terribly lonely." He told her of his love for Louise—"She's the only woman I love or ever will love"—and Nina was moved, even though she thought he was exaggerating.

Nina was wary of O'Neill's group and rarely joined them in the Hell Hole. She did go to Luke O'Connor's, though, and to some of the private parties, and sat by rather timorously, watching the others drink.

One night, at a birthday party, she was sitting by O'Neill, holding an untouched glass of punch—a blend of wine and gin. O'Neill taunted her about her abstinence and she impulsively drained the glass.

"You're a god-damned fool," said O'Neill, with a mocking grin. "I wouldn't drink that trash." And he took a deep draught from the bottle he carried with him.

One time O'Neill sat in Nina's room until five in the morning, telling her the story of his life—with a few deletions. He never mentioned his mother or discussed his childhood, nor did he dwell on his bout with T.B. He did refer to his former illness once, however, when Nina asked him how he stood in the draft.

"They wouldn't have me any more than they would a rattlesnake," he told her. His fears on that score had been put to rest; the Army had told him it did not want him.

"I got married before I left for South America," O'Neill interposed casually, at one point in his narrative. "You know, Nina, somewhere in the world I have a son."

Nina gasped, as he had intended her to do.

"Don't be so god-damned sentimental," said O'Neill. "I've never seen him."

O'Neill enjoyed playing on her emotions.

"Nina," he murmured once, "I make the poet's plea in *Candida*."

Nina was caught off her guard and stammered an inadequate answer. Later she recalled that the poet's name was Eugene; and when she studied the Shaw comedy she found that the poet had many of O'Neill's characteristics, such as shyness, awkwardness and a "haunted, tormented expression." She read the scene in the last act to which O'Neill had referred and grew even more distressed. It was the scene in which Candida, confronted by the husband who needs her and the poet who worships her, asks each what inducement he has to offer for her love. The poet's plea is: "My weakness. My desolation. My heart's need." If Nina had only remembered Candida's answer ("That's a good bid, Eugene") it would have had the virtue of being both graceful and noncommittal, for Candida, of course, rejects the poet.

"Gene took his women and left them," she later observed. "He ran with a crowd of people I then considered supreme sophisticates, and I certainly was not sophisticated. Maybe that interested him."

What probably attracted O'Neill most was Nina's sympathetic understanding of his work. He approved her handling of the plays she had already directed for the Provincetowners, and that winter he showed her a script of *The Moon of the Caribbees*. Although O'Neill knew it would not be produced until the following season, he carried the script about with him lovingly and allowed friends to read it as a mark of trust and as a test of their sensitivity. Nina passed the test; she understood how much of himself he had put into the play.

The second of the women to whom O'Neill found himself attracted that winter was Dorothy Day. Dorothy, the daughter of a newspaperman, was tall, slender and attractive. She chose her father's profession, working first as a reporter on the *Call*, then as assistant to Max Eastman and Floyd Dell on *The Masses*, and finally on *The Liberator* when *The Masses* was suppressed by the government. Although caught up in the bohemianism of the Village, she had a hidden side to her personality, a side as unfathomable and untouchable, in its way, as O'Neill's dark reserve. Her family was Protestant, but there was in her, even during her most thoughtless moments, a half-submerged, mystic urge toward Catholicism. She played and drank and sang with the crowd; yet, after a night spent joyously in the Hell Hole, she would find herself drawn to St. Joseph's Church, on Sixth Avenue. There in the icy dawn, knowing nothing of the tenets of Catholicism, she would kneel during early morning Mass.

It was Michael Gold who introduced Dorothy to O'Neill. Gold, who, like John Reed, later became a Communist, was then an unlabeled radical. O'Neill liked him but disagreed with his idea that art should express a political point of view.

"Art and politics don't mix," O'Neill once told Gold, when urged by him to dramatize the "class struggle."

"When a playwright starts writing propaganda he ceases to be an artist and becomes, instead, a politician," said O'Neill.

Gold was one of Jig Cook's discoveries. He was an assistant truck driver when he brought Cook a one-act play he had written. Wasn't Cook urging *everyone* to write a play—to express something native on the threshing floor of the Playwrights' Theatre? Gold found Cook strangely impressive, even at first sight, and overwhelming when he began to talk "like a character in a Dostoevski novel." Cook studied Gold's play—it was staged later that year—and interpreted it for the young truck driver.

"He talked as though he had known me for years," Gold has written. "He made me feel like a god! It was what he did for everyone, great, small, dumb or literate."

Gold knew Dorothy from *The Masses*, to which he had been a contributor, and brought her to the Playwrights' Theatre, where she would occasionally fill in for an actor who had failed to show up for rehearsal. After rehearsals Dorothy mingled with the others at the Hell Hole.

"We'd sit around and talk," she recalled. "In the back room of the Hell Hole you couldn't talk without the others hearing you. Everyone table-hopped. We were very happy and very young. There was such joy in the discovery of people and ideas. Mike Gold discussed art and revolution. Hippolyte Havel talked about his past and drank. Gene recited 'The Hound of Heaven,' which was my first real link to Catholicism."

The Francis Thompson poem had replaced Baudelaire and Swinburne in O'Neill's repertory. The farther he withdrew, personally and artistically, from his Catholic roots the more keenly he felt the terror of his flight. "The Hound of Heaven" by the ardently Catholic poet, exemplified for O'Neill the exhilarating terror of the flight.

> I fled Him, down the nights and down the days;
> I fled Him, down the arches of the years;

I fled Him, down the labyrinthine ways
Of my own mind . . .

O'Neill could recite the 183 lines of the poem. He had been studying it since 1913, when a nurse from Gaylord Farm sent it to him in New London. Hearing O'Neill recite "The Hound of Heaven" had a lasting effect on Dorothy Day. The idea of the pursuit by God's love fascinated her, stirred in her a feeling that someday she would have to pause in her own flight.

"I used to ask Gene to recite it over again," she said. "He didn't need any urging. He recited it with his head down, in a monotonous voice." He would also recite Thompson's "To the Dead Cardinal of Westminster," lingering over the lines:

> Life is coquetry
> Of death, which wearies me,
> Too sure
> Of the amour;
>
> A tiring-room where I
> Death's divers garments try,
> Till fit
> Some fashions sit.
>
> It seemeth me too much
> I do rehearse for such
> A mean
> And single scene.

"Gene would recite over and over again, 'It seemeth me too much/I do rehearse for such/A mean/And single scene,'" Miss Day said. "I had the feeling he considered drinking his rehearsal for death. He drank his whiskey straight, and not to get drunk, but to keep going."

When the Hell Hole closed, O'Neill and Dorothy would often walk down to the waterfront, stopping at taverns on the way. One of O'Neill's favorite saloons was in the fish-market section.

"We went there to get away from the Village," Dorothy Day said. "Many times we'd stay up all night. Gene seemed to have a great deal of physical strength."

Sometimes Mike Gold would walk with them and when they arrived at South Street they would sit on a pier and Gold would sing melancholy Jewish songs. Once in a while, they rode down to the piers with a truck driver who had come into the Hell Hole. Then they would walk—perhaps to Hiram Motherwell's apartment on Lexington Avenue in the Thirties. O'Neill would ring Motherwell's bell and wake him up at two or three in the morning, and Motherwell would serve them coffee. Other nights they would go to Romany Marie's and stay there till the Hell Hole opened again at six.

"We'd clean up in the wash room, send out for more coffee, and sit around some more," Dorothy said. "After a while, I'd get into a cab and go to *The Liberator*." Often O'Neill would telephone Dorothy there and ask her to return to the Hell Hole, she was wasting her time working, he said. She would spend three or four hours at *The Liberator* and go to her apartment for a nap.

"Then I'd meet Gene for dinner—and start all over again," she said.

Dorothy, too, knew that O'Neill was suffering over Louise. She considered O'Neill "a one-woman man" and was convinced Louise was the great love of his life. She, too, gave him sympathy and was entrusted with a copy of *The Moon of the Caribbees*. She sat by him in the Hell Hole while he wrote poetry and on one occasion she, Bodenheim and O'Neill collaborated on a poem to which each contributed a verse. And she listened while he talked about Strindberg and Ibsen and recited from *Peer Gynt* or while he tried to explain Hippolyte Havel to her.

Dorothy and some of her young friends considered Hippolyte a decrepit old man, a character out of the past. From time to time he would leap up from his chair and do a little dance or raise a sodden head to cry out, to whoever had violated one or another of his cherished concepts, "Bourgeois pig!"

That year, having given up trying to conquer his jealousy of Polly Holliday, Hippolyte had attached himself to a visiting suffragette. He turned his room over to her and slept on the floor outside the door. "I am her little doggie," he would announce dolefully in the Hell Hole. When the others laughed at Hippolyte, O'Neill came to his defense.

"He's been in every jail in Europe. He's suffered," O'Neill would say quietly. Echoing some of Hippolyte's phrases, O'Neill once told Dorothy: "The bourgeois concept of marriage is baby carriages, rubber pants and a conventional apartment."

Dorothy felt that O'Neill was haunted by the fear of death. When she later joined the Catholic Church she came to believe that O'Neill, like many other people she subsequently encountered, suffered from rejection of the love of God.

"People don't want that love," she once said. "Man fights against the Light." Miss Day, who eventually became a founder and editor of *The Catholic Worker* and head of a Catholic mission house in lower Manhattan, often reflected about the man she had known as a groping young genius. In her mission, where outcasts and derelicts waited to be fed and clothed and to try to kiss her hand with the reverence tendered a saint, she thought many times of that cold, wild, happy winter in Greenwich Village, and of O'Neill.

"Gene was single-minded in his objective," she once said after his death. "Nothing could distract him. Nothing could devour him. In that sense, there was a kind of purity in him. He was not attracted to evil, but to darkness. He was absorbed by death and darkness."

"One day recently, when I was saying the rosary, I noticed a candle dripping, and I was suddenly reminded of a line from 'The Hound of Heaven'—'Life's dripping taper.' It made me think of Gene.

"I pray for him even now. There is no time with God. All the prayers said for him after his death would be of avail at the moment of his death. I pray that Gene turns to the Light."

The third woman in whom O'Neill was compassionately interested that winter was Christine Ell. Christine undoubtedly served as the model for the purehearted Irish giantess, Josie Hogan, in *A Moon for the Misbegotten*. There are elements of her personality and history also in *Anna Christie*, and she was probably in O'Neill's mind when he drew the Mother Earth prostitute, Cybel, in *The Great God Brown*.

Like Josie Hogan, Christine Ell was a large woman, five feet nine inches tall, wide-hipped and big-breasted. Charles Demuth, Bror Nordfeldt and other artists painted her green-eyed, leonine face and thick, shining, untidy, tawny hair. Some of them captured the quality of pain and love that lay under the surface of her bawdy smile. She was self-conscious of her bulk and made fun of herself. Also like Josie, she was convinced that she was basically unattractive to men. The illegitimate child of a Danish peasant woman and a Danish Army captain, she had been brought to America by her mother and stepfather and forced into domestic service and then into factory work. At fourteen her stepfather seduced her, and soon after that she broke away from her family and began to have casual love affairs. She considered herself an outcast until, one day, she chanced to hear Emma Goldman speak in Denver on the subject of society's blame for, and abandonment of, woman of her class. Christine discovered that in espousing the concept of anarchy she could feel the sense of self-respect and dignity that had eluded her. At Emma's urging she went to New York and opened a small restaurant. She married Lewis Ell and together they moved back and forth between Greenwich Village and Provincetown.

Christine was joylessly unfaithful to Lewis, and he alternated between moods of murderous jealousy and abject forgiveness. To Hutchins Hapgood, who first met her in Provincetown, Christine confided that she was miserably unhappy. She hated herself for the way she treated Lewis, she said.

"Why is it that I must act as I do?" she asked Hapgood, weeping. "I long to have a perfect lover, one that satisfies me. Lewis doesn't know how to express himself to me. If all goes well he is quiet, never says anything, and doesn't go out with me to the theatres or our parties. It is only when he is jealous that he can express himself, and I want him to be near me all the time and he cannot be. When I see how far away he is I cannot stand it. I try to console myself with other men, but Lewis is always there in my thought, standing between me and them and making it impossible for me to realize the dream of my life, of an utter sympathy with some man. So I hurt him all the time, yet I know too that I help and stimulate him, that through me life is richer and more interesting to him."

That winter the Provincetowners had installed Christine and her stove on the second floor of the playhouse, so that a club dining room would be available to The Players during rehearsals and after performances. The Players, including O'Neill, paid a minimum fee for their meals and held many of their opening night, closing night, and unclassified celebrations there.

"In the afternoons," according to Edna Kenton, "Christine would bring in pots of tea, several packages of biscuit, salt and sweet, a jar of jam or a wedge of cheese, and then sit down again to the peeling of potatoes or the stringing of beans for dinner while she talked with us on aesthetics or free will versus determinism, or the latest upset in our always creaking machinery of 'organization.' She made milk toast for the half sick or wholly weary, let us choose between cherry cobbler and lemon pie, gave us corn bread or Boston brown on demand, treated us not only to 'home cooking' of the very best, but to home privilege of choice, as well."

Christine was more than a good cook and conversationalist; she took small roles in the productions and was ready to be helpful or entertaining in any capacity required of her. She was a gifted mimic and often provided the chief amusement at parties with an imitation of Mary Vorse growing drunk in her ladylike way in the Hell Hole, or of Ida Rauh, who had earned the sobriquet "Duse of MacDougal Street," practicing dramatic grimaces before a mirror. But the pathos of her personality was always close to the surface. To O'Neill, who became one of her casual lovers, she personified what he once called "a female Christ."

Although he was as much amused by her wit and her escapades as anyone, O'Neill was acutely aware of her inner agony. Several of her lovers have recalled the strangely virginal quality that belied the affected coarseness of her manner. There was a paradoxical delicacy of spirit concealed in her hulking body, of which she was both proud and ashamed, a quality keenly felt by O'Neill and later reproduced by him in the character of Josie Hogan.

In October of 1917 a friend of Christine's turned up in the Village, seeking to support herself and assorted members of her family.

Her name was Agnes Boulton and within six months she would be O'Neill's wife. She was twenty-four years old, pretty in a way that superficially resembled Louise's Irish loveliness (although she was of English descent), and clever enough to have gained a modest reputation as a writer of novelettes and short stories that appeared, for the most part, in pulp magazines. Agnes had a pale, bony face and large, gray-blue eyes. Her hair was light brown and fell to her waist when she did not confine it, as she usually did, in a conch-shaped bun at the back of her neck. Unsure of herself and rather shy, she often seemed even younger and more ingenuous than she was. Uncertain about where she was going, she assumed an air of breezy bohemianism.

Agnes was one of four sisters, and the daughter of a gentle, blue-eyed, white-mustached portrait painter from Philadelphia, Edward William Boulton.

Born on September 19, 1893, while her parents were visiting London, she had been brought up in the New Jersey seaside town of West Point Pleasant. She arrived in Greenwich Village that fall from a farm she owned near Cornwall Bridge, Connecticut; she had left behind her mother, father and two-year-old daughter, Barbara, whose father—a man named Burton—had been dead for some time.

Agnes had met Christine on a previous trip to New York. She was also acquainted with Harry Kemp and Mary Pyne, who spent the summer of 1917 at her farm.

Recalling her arrival in New York the fall of 1917, Agnes has written in her memoir, *Part of a Long Story:* "Well, I hoped doubtfully that my family would be happy on the farm . . . I was going back in the spring . . . I had to go to New York for their sake and mine, to make more money, and I would return!"

Agnes arrived with $100, an order for a novelette, and the hope of finding a part-time job to round out her income. She took a room at the Brevoort, recommended by Mary Pyne as a "very cheap" hotel. She then went in search of Christine, who had told her about a factory where it was possible to work short shifts and where she thought she might apply for a job. After finally reaching Christine by telephone at her restaurant above the Playwrights' Theatre, she accepted an invitation to meet her at the Hell Hole at ten-thirty that night.

Entering the saloon a few minutes early, Agnes settled herself nervously at a table in the back room where, before long, she felt herself being scrutinized by a dark man wearing a seaman's sweater under his jacket and a suit that looked to her as though it had been slept in. She found his look disturbing—"both sad and cruel," as she has described it. The man was O'Neill, and he was, as a matter of fact, brooding about her resemblance to Louise.

Agnes had almost made up her mind to leave the Hell Hole when Christine swept in, embraced her, greeted the somber, staring man and introduced him as "Gene O'Neill."

After several hours in the Hell Hole, during the course of which Jamie joined them, O'Neill walked Agnes across Washington Square to the Brevoort. Standing in front of the hotel, O'Neill, who had been silent in the Hell Hole, began to talk.

"I wish I could remember what he said," Agnes later wrote in her memoir. "I don't think I quite knew, even then."

But he conveyed an impression of sadness and his eyes were dramatic as he told her, finally, something she did remember:

"I want to spend every night of my life from now on with *you*. I mean this. Every night of my life."

Agnes parted from O'Neill in bewilderment. She heard nothing from him for several days and saw him next at a party to which Christine had invited her. O'Neill treated her with polite indifference, although to her it appeared obvious that he was very much aware of her presence and way trying to arouse her jealousy. He was attentive to Nina Moise and made a dramatic gesture that was designed to startle everyone present with his suffering over Louise. Climbing onto a chair in front of the mantelpiece, he opened the glass face of a large clock and pushed back the hands, chanting: "Turn back the universe and give me yesterday!"

Agnes, preparing to leave the party, encountered Mary Pyne and Susan Glaspell. From them she learned that she resembled Louise Bryant, who, she was told, had broken O'Neill's heart.

It was not long before Agnes realized she was in love with O'Neill and she was convinced that sooner or later he would fall in love with her. She discovered he was a playwright, but this did not particularly impress her, as she was uninterested in the theatre. Her main concern was with disentangling O'Neill from the various women who appeared to have a prior claim. This she managed to do, and it was soon generally conceded in O'Neill's circle that Agnes was his girl, although no one regarded the relationship as permanent.

Aware that Louise would not stay in Russia forever, O'Neill's friends were convinced she would reclaim O'Neill on her return. But not all of them approved of his new temporary arrangement. Scotty, for example, detested Agnes, and she detested him in return. And Dorothy, with whom Agnes had become friendly—on several occasions, Dorothy took Agnes along to Mass at St. Joseph's—also felt uneasy about the relationship. Like a number of others, Dorothy was waiting for O'Neill to make good his promise to leave the Village and go to Provincetown, where he could work. The Provincetowners were in need of plays; they had, in fact, found it necessary to resort to advertising for new playwrights in drama publications. Some of them were vaguely worried that Agnes, with her unconcealed lack of interest in the theatre, might not have a stimulating effect upon their prize playwright.

"During this time Gene was going to the Provincetown Theatre . . . almost every afternoon and evening and often I was with him," Agnes has written, adding casually, " 'Ile' was produced and 'The Long Voyage Home,' and there was much happening that may be of importance to those interested in the theatre."

By mid-January a malaise had settled on the Provincetowners; they all seemed to be waiting for O'Neill to come to some sort of decision. He had told Dorothy and Agnes and many others that he planned to go to Provincetown soon to work, but he kept postponing his departure. Meanwhile he continued to visit his favorite haunts, usually accompanied by Agnes.

There were frequent tiffs and lovers' quarrels, some of them remarked upon by O'Neill's friends. Holger Cahill, for example, recalled one night in the Hell Hole when Agnes suddenly pushed back her chair and ran from the saloon. O'Neill pursued her, and neither of them was seen for several hours.

Cahill thought O'Neill was ridiculous with women, wasting his energy chasing girls who were only too willing to capitulate. Once, for example, he and O'Neill met a couple of pathetically willing young nurses in a barroom, and O'Neill insisted on lengthily wooing, with poetry, the one who was earmarked for him—as though deliberately putting off the moment of too-easy conquest. "The trouble was that O'Neill was nearly always the seduced, instead of the seducer," said Cahill. "Sometimes he resented it, though there seemed to be nothing he could do about it."

❖

One of the things that was keeping O'Neill in New York that winter was the impending arrival of Louis Holliday, who had been in the West for several months establishing himself as a fruit grower. Very much in love, Holliday had left the city at his girl's request that he cure himself of drinking and find dependable work that would enable them to marry. Holliday had abstained from drinking, had grown fit and happy at his labor, and saved enough money to keep himself and a wife. As soon as he returned to New York in January he telephoned his girl and asked his friends to stand by for a celebration. Everyone was in high spirits, for Holliday, in his newly found strength, was particularly endearing.

On January 22 they gathered at the Hell Hole—O'Neill, Agnes, Dorothy, Christine and other old friends, including Charles Demuth and Terry Carlin. No one realized, at first, what had gone wrong. Holliday was drinking. When he got drunk enough he announced that his girl had fallen in love with someone else.

Holliday was a quiet man, and he did what he had to do quietly. Sometime during the evening he induced Terry Carlin to give him a large dose of heroin. Terry took narcotics from time to time, and it was entirely within his code of ethics to provide a friend with what he could not help but know was a lethal dose; if someone wanted to kill himself, Terry could summon no moral reason for trying to prevent him.

The party moved from the Hell Hole to Romany Marie's. It was not until Holliday began to look ill that O'Neill found out about the heroin. Ill with shock himself, O'Neill left. Dorothy, who also knew what Holliday had done, stayed on at Marie's, thinking she could help him.

A little before six-thirty in the morning Holliday, foaming at the mouth, collapsed at a table. Marie called for an ambulance, but before it arrived Holliday was dead. His sister, Polly, who had been summoned, informed the doctor that Holliday had suffered from a weak heart, and the doctor diagnosed the cause of death as heart trouble. Arriving a few minutes later, the police accepted the diagnosis. No one ever quite understood why, since at least a dozen people knew about the heroin, no mention of narcotics was entered into the official records of Holliday's death; for a time many of Holliday's friends were haunted by the possibility of a police investigation.

The episode had an appalling effect on Holliday's friends. The abrupt, senseless, vicious end of a life that had been filled with vitality and hope became an omen of disaster. They suddenly felt mortal and threatened. Christine wept hysterically. Charles Demuth went about like a man in a trance. Dorothy fled from the Village and threw herself into a nursing career at a municipal hospital, probably inspiring the manner in which O'Neill later caused his Nina Leeds in *Strange Interlude* to expiate her sense of guilt over her fiancé's death. O'Neill plunged into drunkenness.

Holliday's death was a painful memory O'Neill carried with him always. Years later he spoke of it to his closest friends, and of his great fondness for Holliday, indicating that he had partly based the character of Don Parritt, in *The Iceman Cometh,* on Holliday. Parritt is a youth who has betrayed his anarchist mother to the police and comes to be judged for his treachery by Larry Slade, his mother's former lover. While these details were O'Neill's invention, the relationship between Larry (based on Terry Carlin) and Parritt symbolized the one between Terry and Holliday. In the play Larry falls into the role of Parritt's executioner, in the sense that he endorses Parritt's decision to commit suicide. O'Neill considered Terry to have been Holliday's executioner in the same sense. He held no rancor for Terry, but he pondered on the "why" of his action.

When O'Neill finally roused himself from his drinking spell he had come to a decision. No one was surprised when he packed his things and left for Provincetown. What did startle some of his friends was that he took Agnes with him.

o'neill's selection of agnes boulton was made with characteristic lack of insight about what he wanted or could reason ably expect from a woman. He had married one woman he did not love and had been in love with three women who would not marry him. Now he was about to marry a woman he did love, but who did not fulfill his stringent requirements for a wife. He demanded an all but impossible ideal of wife-mistress-mother-secretary; a foil for his self-dramatization; a woman who could understand and appreciate him and devote herself entirely to his artistic aims. He was not prepared to compromise and few women could have lived up to this ideal.

O'Neill may not have been able to put it into words at that time, but in letters he wrote years later to friends he clearly indicated that what he wanted—and needed—was a woman who had the force of character and the zeal to meet and match him on a matrimonial battleground. He craved a Strindbergian, love-hate relationship.

Two months after he rushed off with Agnes and three days before he married her O'Neill hinted to Nina Moise about his confused feelings and tried to apologize for and justify his seemingly inconsistent behavior.

"I'm sorry I didn't get a chance to have a long talk with you before I left—or, rather, I'm not sorry," he wrote. "What use for Mr. Hyde to discuss Dr. Jekyll. . . .

"One part of me fiddles betimes while Rome burneth, while the other part perishes in the flames—a martyr giving birth to the soul of an idea. One part of me is the author of my life—tearing his hair in a piteous frenzy as he watches his 'worser' half playing the lead in distorting the theme by many strange grimaces. Believe me, from line to line, the poor wretch can never tell whether the play is farce or tragedy— so perverse a spirit is his star."

Agnes respected O'Neill's work but considered her own career to be of almost equal importance. Although she was frightened of his Irish temper, she did not appear to be in awe of him as an artist, nor willing to coddle his moody artistic temperament. Being basically uninterested in the theatre, she sometimes felt left out of O'Neill's friendships with members of the Provincetown group. (Susan Glaspell, for instance, made her feel inadequate.)

She had not given much thought to housekeeping as an art and was casual in her domestic arrangements. O'Neill lived haphazardly and Agnes drifted with him.

Though initially shy, she enjoyed being with people she knew— enjoyed society for its own sake and found it painless, and even fun, to exchange the pleasantries and banter from which O'Neill shrank. She was instinctively generous and easygoing and found it difficult to understand O'Neill's miserliness of self, his hoarding of energy and resources, in order to pour everything into his work.

But most of all, from O'Neill's egotistically demanding point of view, she failed to rise to the challenge of his possessive love. Lacking his requisite sense of drama, she apparently found it difficult to sustain the high-voltage pitch of agony-ecstasy that O'Neill was bent on attaining— an emotional pitch that was, conceivably, a substitute for the violent physical passion he did not seem capable of achieving.

Agnes and O'Neill were, however, in accord on a relationship that excluded children. When Agnes accompanied O'Neill to Provincetown she had not seen her daughter in three months nor did she make an effort to see her for many more. ("I . . . wrote my family," she has recorded, "but as I recall it, everything was all right everywhere and there was nothing to take us out of this co-operation of work and living.") She was shocked, however, when O'Neill told her casually, several months after their marriage, that *he* had a child he had never seen.

O'Neill and Agnes moved into two rooms provided by John Francis, one of them furnished with a primitive stove, and there settled down to writing. It took O'Neill only a few days to taper off his drinking, and soon he was happily continuing his work on *Beyond the Horizon* and toying with ideas for a couple of short plays. Agnes devoted herself to turning out novelettes.

Not long after they arrived O'Neill and Agnes made the acquaintance of Alice Woods, a charming, sophisticated, forty-seven-year-old writer who had come to Provincetown from Europe when the war started. Born in Goshen, Indiana, where she included Booth Tarkington among her friends, she went to Paris early in the century to study art, and lived on the Left Bank. Miss Woods, who divorced her husband, an Impressionist artist named Eugene P. Ullman, in 1903, was the author of several books, a contributor of short stories to *The Smart Set* and other literary magazines, and the mother of two schoolboys whom she had brought up in France.

She discussed writing with O'Neill and received his encouragement to turn one of her published short stories into a one-act play called *The Devil's Glow,* which was presented by the Provincetown Players that March. She also entertained him with stories of the life she had led in Europe, where she had moved in a circle that included Gertrude Stein and Henri Matisse.

In recalling her acquaintance with O'Neill and Agnes in Provincetown Miss Woods said that Agnes, whom she rather liked, appeared to be "out of place."

"I thought it was shocking for a woman to live under those conditions," she added. "Agnes looked like a typical young American girl. She wasn't subtle enough to play the game that Gene seemed to be playing."

One day O'Neill and Agnes arrived at Miss Woods's house for tea. Agnes was in tears. She told Miss Woods that O'Neill wanted to marry her but that she would not agree.

"Why not?" asked Miss Woods. Sobbing, Agnes said that O'Neill was still in love with "that girl."

O'Neill looked haggard, said nothing, and stared out the window at Miss Woods's orchard, brown and bare under melting snow.

The girl about whom Agnes was concerned was Louise. Recently returned from Russia, Louise had written to O'Neill saying she must see him, and O'Neill believed he was obligated to meet her and explain his new attachment. Louise, in Agnes' mind, was "invested with all the wiles of the serpent."

Louise had left Russia on January 20—perhaps, as Agnes assumed in her memoir, because rumors of O'Neill's new love had reached her, but more likely because she was eager to break into print with a firsthand account of what was happening in Russia. She left ahead of Reed, who had decided to stay abroad and attend the third All-Russian Congress of Soviets. Louise arrived in New York February 18 on a neutral ship, the Norwegian *Bergensfjord,* and began preparing a series describing her experiences in Russia for the New York *American.* Published early in the spring, the articles caused quite a splash. Louise wrote of the bloody events in Russia, managing to imbue her reports with a personal flavor of daring and risk. Her stories were colorful and colored, filled with idealism about the revolution, but often moving. She became a kind of martyr —undoubtedly she saw herself as a combination of St. Joan and Mata Hari—when she later appeared before a Congressional committee to testify about bolshevist activities, and goaded some senators into denouncing her as a menace.

With her beauty, daring and journalistic flair, Louise quickly established herself as a heroine. It is small wonder that Agnes was uneasy. Letters from Louise continued to arrive. Agnes could "see" O'Neill remembering the "dark, passionate travail of their love."

O'Neill was in a dilemma, and Alice Woods took it upon herself to help smooth the way for him and Agnes. She consulted with a local druggist, John Adams, who was fond of O'Neill and had once got him out of the Provincetown jail, where he had been held for drunkenness. In a long talk with O'Neill, Adams evidently convinced him that he must reassure Agnes by breaking off with Louise unequivocally. O'Neill finally decided to write a letter of explanation to Louise and, on April 12, 1918, he and Agnes were married.

Miss Woods helped arrange the details of the wedding, but was called away to Boston on business on April 12 and could not accept O'Neill's and Agnes' invitation to be a witness at the ceremony. They were married by a Methodist minister because there was no justice of the peace available.

Two days later O'Neill described the wedding to Nina Moise, who was working in New York on the production of his recently finished one-act play, *The Rope:*

"We were married two evenings ago—in the best parlor of a parsonage by the most delightful . . . Godhelpus, mincing Methodist minister that ever prayed through his nose. I don't mean to sneer, really. The worthy divine is an utterly lovable old idiot and the ceremony gained a strange, unique simplicity from his sweet, childlike sincerity. I caught myself wishing I could believe in the same gentle God he seemed so sure of. This sounds like sentimentality but it isn't. It's hard to describe—the wedding of two serious children he made out of it; but it was startlingly impressive. The meaning behind the lines 'got across with a punch' to both of us. . . ."

Soon after the wedding Agnes and Alice Woods were invited to dinner by an architect, whose first name happened to be Starling, and his Bostonian wife, who disapproved of O'Neill. They did not invite Miss Woods's sons either, and the two women made a pretense of hauteur as they went off unescorted. O'Neill and the two boys spent the following morning with an encyclopedia and the Book of Knowledge, compiling a list of all the nastier characteristics of starlings, whose ornithological name, they gleefully discovered, was *Sturnus vulgaris.*

The younger of Alice Woods's two sons—Allen Ullman, in later years an artist—was eleven that spring. O'Neill and Agnes had a significant effect on him, which grew even more potent as he entered adolescence.

He dwelt on Agnes' beauty, the soulful looks she and O'Neill exchanged, and the jealousy they displayed toward each other. He worried about their fights and about O'Neill's violent drinking bouts and thought them the most tempestuously romantic couple outside the pages of a book.

O'Neill's prospects at this time were looking up a little. He had recently stumbled on a source of income that could keep him in modest comfort (it was this that had helped persuade him he could support a wife). His windfall came from the unexpected success of *In the Zone* as a vaudeville vehicle.

The team responsible for the project consisted of an advance publicity man recently out of high school and a nineteen-year-old actor. The ex-actor, Albert Lewis, and the ex-advance man, Max Gordon, had recently formed a flourishing producing partnership.

Gordon was in charge of booking and Lewis presided over production. They produced only one-act plays for vaudeville, sending out the whole package with the star, and averaged fifteen shows on the circuit at the same time—usually the Keith or the Orpheum.

Lewis would read or go to see anything that promised to be a twenty-five- or thirty-minute vehicle for vaudeville, and had at one point considered *Bound East for Cardiff*, but reluctantly rejected it on the advice of a co-worker in his office, who thought it "too highbrow for vaudeville."

But the following year, after seeing *In the Zone* at the Comedy Theatre, he was convinced it would be a hit in vaudeville.

Lewis spent several days trying to track down O'Neill, and was finally put in touch with him by Edward Goodman, the head of the Washington Square Players. Lewis made his offer, but O'Neill rejected it. "He thought the vaudeville proposition was degrading," Lewis said.

O'Neill changed his mind, however, after Lewis persuaded Martin Beck, then in charge of the Orpheum Circuit, to see *In the Zone*. Beck told Lewis that if he could stage the one-acter as well as the Washington Square Players had done, he would book it, guaranteeing a 25 to 40 week run.

"This was a terrific proposition," Lewis added, "and O'Neill finally decided that he just couldn't turn it down; he really needed the money." (This was the point at which he had decided to get married.)

O'Neill received a $200 advance, and $70 a week in royalties, which was split fifty-fifty between him and the Washington Square Players. Lewis staged the play with Horace Brahan, a well-known actor, in the leading role of Smitty. He sent it first to Proctor's Theatre in Newark, then to the Palace in Chicago, and then, for a week each, to the various towns on the Orpheum Circuit. It was an immediate success and toured for thirty-four weeks.

Even James O'Neill was amazed at the play's success and held his temper when Eugene wrote to announce his marriage to Agnes. James had not met Agnes and could neither approve nor disapprove of her as a wife for Eugene. The fact that she was English born did not predispose him to think well of her, but at least he would not be called upon to support her as he had once assumed the case would be with Kathleen.

James actually began changing his tune about his "scribbler" son in June, 1918. Still playing in *The Wanderer*, he was interviewed in New York by a reporter for *Town Talk* who was a Eugene O'Neill fan. James included Jamie in his paternal pronouncement, although he had to stretch his imagination to find something about his middle-aged first-born of which he could brag.

"James O'Neill Jr. . . . is an actor and has had success on the stage and in films," the *Town Talk* man reported from facts supplied by James. "He was bitterly disappointed recently when the Army doctors rejected him, for the O'Neills are fighters. The other son is Eugene O'Neill who has several one-act plays to his credit, all of them successfully. We saw one of them lately at the Orpheum and all of us liked it immensely. It was called 'In the Zone.'"

The royalties from *In the Zone* were the first "big" money O'Neill ever made—it proved to be the most popular of all his one-acters, both in the United States and abroad—and he followed its fortunes zealously. (In later years he often pointed out to friends what he considered the incongruity of the play's success: "a large cast, all men, no love interest, no star.")

Much more impressive than the financial success of *In the Zone* though, was the fact that an important Broadway producer had taken an option on his three-act tragedy, *Beyond the Horizon*. Soon after completing the play, in early April, O'Neill sent it to Nathan at *The Smart Set*. Nathan read it immediately and took it to John D. Williams.

Williams had produced John Galsworthy's *Justice* two years earlier and, together with Arthur Hopkins, Winthrop Ames and Brock Pemberton, was leading a revolt against the tingle-and-tinsel tradition of David Belasco and Charles Frohman. Although *Beyond the Horizon* was a departure far beyond anything that Williams had yet dared, Nathan thought he had the courage and imagination to take it on.

An oddity in the managerial ranks, Williams was a soundly educated college man. He had attended Harvard, where he had been a member of one of Professor Baker's early classes. He had received his theatrical training as Charles Frohman's business manager. He produced plays he liked (along with those he knew were commercial) even though he often lost money on them. With rueful self-mockery he once declared:

"Intelligence and good taste, both or either, is fatal to successful play producing anywhere in America, because, handicapped by either of these, you are apt to produce the kind of play you think other college graduates will go to see. I found that out when I put Mrs. Fiske in *Erstwhile Susan*, John Barrymore in Galsworthy's *Justice* and his brother, Lionel Barrymore, in *The Copperhead* and Richard Bennett in a comedy of Manchester life called *Zack* by the author of *Hobson's Choice;* and again the same truth smote me amidships when I produced *Our Betters, Three for Diana*, etc., plays of substance, some taste, real acting and containing some interesting angles on life. And what happened?

"Every college graduate ran as fast as he could past the theatres containing these handstitched college graduate plays, put on by a college graduate. And they didn't stop running until they landed in the front row of the *Follies;* failing that, they ran over to see *Girls, Girls, and Nothing but Girls, Oh, You Girls,* or *The Skidding of Tottie Coughdrop.* In fact, if it hadn't been for what I used to call hoi polloi, unfortunate illiterates, poorly bred people, lowbrows, in short, the vast majority who never have and never will get nearer to a college than the Germans will to honesty, this brief chronicle of an eye-opening, exciting but perilous career would be dated either from Mills Hotel, a dairy lunch, or the Poorhouse."

Putting his faith once more in substance and taste, Williams, in one of the most rapid transactions in the history of show business, at once sent O'Neill a check for $500 as an option for six months. O'Neill, believing the time had come when he would make Broadway accept him on his own terms, was elated. He did not dream it would be nearly two years before *Beyond the Horizon* finally reached the stage.

In addition to writing the long play, *Beyond the Horizon,* and the one-acter, *The Rope,* between the beginning of February and the end of April, 1918, O'Neill also wrote a short play called *Till We Meet* (which he tore up). His working life out of town was as austere as his social life in New York was hectic. He never took a drink during a working period, even when it extended over several months, and early in his career he dispelled the legend that had begun to circulate about his writing while drunk.

"Altogether too much damn nonsense has been written since the beginning of time about the dissipation of artists," he said, in a statement to Barrett Clark that was widely quoted during the twenties. "Why, there are fifty times more real drunkards among Bohemians who only play at art, and probably more than that among the people who never think about art at all. The artist drinks, when he drinks at all, for relaxation, forgetfulness, excitement, for any purpose except his art. You've got to have all your critical and creative faculties about you when you're working. I never try to write a line when I'm not strictly on the wagon. I don't think anything worth reading was ever written by anyone who was drunk or even half-drunk when he wrote it. This is not morality, it's plain physiology."

While he was deep in a project, he worked with iron-willed concentration. When he was finishing the last act of *Beyond the Horizon* he kept at it for as much as seven hours a day. He was ruthless in his editing, as witness the unhesitant destruction of whole scripts he considered unworthy. By the time he had completed *Beyond the Horizon*— less than five years after he began to write plays—he had decided to disown or had actually torn up eight of his twenty one-act plays (all but one of them—*The Sniper*—before production) and five long plays. *Beyond the Horizon* was the first long play he did not destroy. All the plays he kept were rewritten, occasionally as many as a dozen times. In addition, and contrary to legend, he made cuts—and big ones—when he believed, or could be persuaded to believe, that they were warranted.

But he often disagreed with a producer or director on the nature of cuts, and in these instances it was difficult, sometimes impossible, to shake him. He was usually convinced, while he was writing a play, that it was going to be his best, or most interesting, or most startling, or most original; when he finished, he continued to live in this state of euphoria— until he was seized with an even better or more startling idea. Then *that* became his biggest, or finest, or most original.

Most of the time he seethed with ideas and could barely get his thoughts down on paper as fast as they came. Characters, themes, situations, crowded unbidden into his mind. Plots came to him even in his dreams. Often he wrote a play in mosaic-like segments; although he usually began with a scenario, he did not necessarily proceed from there to the first act. Sometimes he wrote a complete scene for the second or third act before he wrote a line of dialogue for the first. He said he wrote scenarios to get rid of mistakes before tackling the actual play.

Sometimes his ideas would develop fully and clearly before he had set down a word, and sometimes not. But even in the cases where he wrote a detailed scenario, he rarely referred to it when he tackled the actual writing of the play.

In addition to a scenario, O'Neill frequently made sketches of his stage settings and outlined the genealogy, history, habits and other important facts regarding his characters.

While his conception was always grand and boundless, his work habits were prim. He had to have twelve sharpened pencils neatly laid out on a table before him at the beginning of his workday. His papers and reference books were always in organized piles and bundles. Often he penciled his notes and scenarios in small notebooks. His handwriting was precise and minute, and a number of theories have been advanced by his friends for this peculiarity—among them a thrifty desire to conserve paper, a need to conserve physical energy, and the control that small writing gave him over the slight tremor of his hand. O'Neill himself once offered an explanation when he was asked about the relatively large handwriting he used in his early correspondence with George Tyler (later presented to Princeton University).

Writing to the Princeton Library, in 1943, O'Neill said:

"I made myself write larger in letters so they could be read easily. And my handwriting was naturally a bit larger, anyway, when I wasn't absorbed in creative work. The more concentrated and lost to myself my mind became, the smaller the handwriting. At least, this seemed to be the general rule then. If you ever look over the early one-act sea play scripts . . . you will find the handwriting large by comparison with later work. The minute style grew on me. I did not wish it on myself, God knows, because it made it so hard to get my scripts typed—forced me to type a lot of them, which was a damn nuisance."

O'Neill's power of concentration, in those early months in Province-town, was so complete that he could write in a kind of open balcony above the room he and Agnes shared, undisturbed by her moving about to cook or work below.

The Rope, which O'Neill wrote on that balcony while also working on *Beyond,* is one of his most interesting plays for several reasons. Set in a barn, it contains the germ of a plot and character for the important long play *Desire Under the Elms,* completed five years later. One of its chief characters is Abraham Bentley, who is a grotesque version of Ephraim Cabot, of *Desire.* Bentley is a "tall, lean, stoop-shouldered old man of sixty-five. . . . His face is gaunt. . . . His eyes peer weakly from beneath bushy black brows . . ." (Ephraim Cabot is "seventy-five, tall and gaunt . . . but stoop-shouldered from toil. . . . His eyes are small . . . and extremely near-sighted . . .")

Bentley, like Cabot, is given to enhancing his bitter denunciations of his family with quotations from the Bible. He is, also like Cabot, held responsible by one of his children (in this case a daughter) for having driven his first wife to her death with overwork, and he is resented by his child, as is Cabot, for having married a flamboyant young woman after his wife's death. The second wife is not a character in *The Rope*, as she is in *Desire*, but it develops, through exposition, that she has had a son who was probably not Bentley's.

This son, unlike the one in *Desire*, lives to grow up and is a young man when *The Rope* opens. He has run away from the farm, having stolen some of his father's money. Here the intricacies of family relationships and plot differ from *Desire*, but the similarity of theme is still obvious. Both plays, of course, were rooted in O'Neill's own submerged feelings toward his father and mother. A psychiatrist, who has made a study of the longer play, has described it as "unconscious autobiography."

The rope of the title refers to a noose that Bentley has rigged up to a rafter in the barn, which, he has indicated with hideous cheerfulness, is there to await his young son's return. The son, a ruffian almost as unpleasant as Bentley, does return. He sneers at, but superstitiously avoids touching, the rope, which his father invites him to hang himself on, and goes off to plot with his half-sister's husband to steal the rest of Bentley's money, hidden somewhere on the farm. The ironic twist comes when Bentley's granddaughter, a slightly imbecilic child of ten, enters the barn alone, climbs on a chair and grabs at the suspended noose, preparatory to having a swing. The rope separates from the beam at her touch, and a bag of twenty-dollar gold pieces drops to the floor. Bentley's little joke turns out even better than he had planned, for the child, an infant spendthrift, sends each coin in turn spinning over the edge of the cliff, below which lies the ocean. The curtain comes down as she is flinging handfuls of money into the sea, gleefully calling out, "Skip! Skip!"

The child's name, as it happens, is Mary, which was often O'Neill's symbolic designation for his mother. There is also a little girl named Mary in *Beyond the Horizon*, and another little girl named Mary in *The Straw*, written a few months later.

The two Marys in *The Rope* and *Beyond* are sickly, either in mind or in body; the Mary in *Beyond* actually goes to the extreme of dying, and the Mary in *The Straw*, to stretch the symbolism just a bit further, is the sister of a tubercular who is on the point of death.

None of the Marys, incidentally, is a recognizable human child. The Mary in *Beyond* is just one of a series of children whom O'Neill killed off in his plays by one device or another. He did not understand or like children. He did not want to have any with Agnes; he thought they would threaten the perfection of his love and violate the sanctity of his artistic life. When he and his wife made a brief trip to New London that spring, Mrs. Rippin asked Agnes if she and Gene expected to have children and Agnes, according to the Rippins, replied that probably all they would have was a book.

O'Neill did not think too highly of *The Rope* by the time it was in production because by then he was engrossed in the much more exciting project of *Beyond the Horizon*. He was content to leave casting and direction of *The Rope* to Nina Moise, though he did take the time to discuss some aspects of the production with her by mail. *The Rope* presents what is probably the first well-documented instance of O'Neill's attitude toward a play in production and, though it is a one-acter and one of his earlier efforts, it is representative of his attitude toward the production of all the later, longer plays. He often asked for comment or criticism, but rarely paid any heed to it—unless it coincided with ideas of his own. He always hoped for and asked for a superb cast of actors and was almost always disappointed. The fact was that only two or three actors ever lived up to O'Neill's conception of what their performances should have been. (It is true that in this respect he resembled many of his fellow dramatists, but since O'Neill never wrote vehicles for specific actors, in his case the disparity between a written role and its embodiment was always more intense.)

"I know you will let me know of any cuts which may appear advisable," O'Neill wrote to Nina Moise on April 9. "You know I'm no stickler when it comes to cuts when I can *see* them."

When Nina ventured suggestions for cutting, however, as in the case of old Bentley's biblical quotations, O'Neill did not altogether "*see* them," and, in fact, he reinstated a number of them on the ground that the rhythm of the dialogue would otherwise be spoiled. And when Nina complained about Luke's and his brother-in-law's plan to use physical torture on Bentley if necessary to make him reveal the hiding place of his money, O'Neill expostulated: ". . . isn't it exactly what a drunken Luke would immediately think of, feeling the grudge he does—and with his sweet mother's influence squirming in his heredity?"

O'Neill also objected to Nina's cuts in the expository dialogue. If the cast were bad, he explained, the play would drag and the extensive cuts were justified, but if the play were "acted naturally, all that exposition will come right out of the characters themselves."

"*Make them act!*" he enjoined Nina. "Don't let them recite the lines."

O'Neill did, however, make some cuts himself in an attempt to speed up the ending—convinced, all the while, that in a topflight acting company none of the cuts would be necessary.

The Rope opened for a week's run at the Playwrights' Theatre on April 26, with Charles Ellis giving a highly praised performance as the ruffian son, Luke. Also on the bill were a play by Susan Glaspell called *Woman's Honor* and a two-character play called *The Hermit and His Messiah,* in which Jig Cook played the Hermit. Heywood Broun, still journeying downtown on behalf of the *Tribune,* gave *The Rope* a glowing review, assaying it as "in the best vein of Eugene O'Neill."

O'Neill arrived from Provincetown with Agnes to inspect *The Rope* and discuss with Williams production plans for *Beyond the Horizon.* But Williams was vague and O'Neill, disappointed, indulged in a week's drinking spree with Jamie. O'Neill, accompanied by Agnes, ran up a sizable bill at the Garden Hotel, where Jamie was still living. To pay the bill and get himself, Agnes and Jamie (who had decided to visit Provincetown) comfortably back to the Cape, O'Neill applied to Albert Lewis for an advance on royalties. He took Agnes with him to Lewis' office, to render his plea more poignant.

"O'Neill asked me for three weeks' advance," Lewis recalled. "I'd never done such a thing before, but I finally agreed to it."

When Agnes and O'Neill returned to Provincetown, Jamie joined them in their room in the Francis Flats, sleeping on a cot behind a thin partition. Jamie's presence was apparently oppressive. One morning, Agnes has written, Jamie greeted her and O'Neill with: "What ho, kids! For a newly married couple you rattle the bedsprings not at all! I can hear every time you turn over in bed, but that's all!"

According to Agnes, neither she nor O'Neill had given the matter of privacy much thought when they invited Jamie to share their room with them, even though they had agreed earlier that no one was ever to intrude on their relationship. "It must be *he and I,* in a world of our own," Agnes later wrote, adding, "As for my little girl . . . so preposterous would have been the idea of poet-genius with a child around that I don't think the idea even occurred to me." But, she added, this did not mean she didn't think of her daughter now and then; by way of illustration, she cited a sonnet she had composed for the child the previous winter.

Jamie was finally transferred to another room, offered at a cut rate by John Francis, who feared that O'Neill could not concentrate in such crowded quarters. O'Neill did, at last, start working again, but though he and Agnes stayed in Provincetown until November of 1918, those half-dozen months were not very fruitful. He completed only three one-acters.

One was entitled *Shell-Shock*, a script he destroyed without having submitted it for production. Another, *The Dreamy Kid*, produced the following year, was the story of a Negro gangster who visits his dying mother and is captured at her bedside. Based on characters O'Neill had met through his Negro friend Joe Smith, the play was melodramatic and sentimental, more in the vein of *The Web* than in his later style, and was not notably successful when it was presented by the Provincetowners.

"Of course, I by no means rate it among my best one-act plays for genuine merit," he later told a friend who congratulated him on the production, "but I did think it would prove theatrically effective and go over with a bang to an audience."

The third one-acter was *Where the Cross is Made*, written because the Provincetowners wanted a "strong" O'Neill drama with which to inaugurate their third season, as they had their first and second. They did not want to begin with the as yet unproduced *The Moon of the Caribbees*, because they considered their stage too shallow to create the necessary illusion of tropical island, sky and sea. *Where the Cross is Made*, however, proved even more demanding in stage technique. It was as experimental, in its way, as *Before Breakfast* (and not much better). In the case of *Cross*, O'Neill's expressed purpose was to try to find out not how long an audience could endure listening to a monologue but whether or not an audience could be made to believe itself insane. To this end he introduced three ghosts.

It was the first time O'Neill employed such a device (he was to to do so again in *The Emperor Jones* and *The Fountain*), and though he never said so, he undoubtedly believed that what was good enough stagecraft for Shakespeare was good enough for O'Neill. The work of any serious dramatist, of course, is "influenced" by Shakespeare, but in O'Neill's case the influence was literal. What other contemporary writer would have attempted to use such inimical Shakespearean effects as ghosts and apparitions, not to mention soliloquies and asides, on the New York stage, and in a realistic, native setting? O'Neill borrowed as liberally and literally from Shakespeare as he did from the Greeks. His use of masks in such plays as *The Great God Brown* and of the chorus in *Lazarus Laughed* is no less traceable to the Greeks than are the ghosts and asides to Shakespeare.

But if the ghosts in *Where the Cross is Made* were Shakespeare's, the fanciful and at the same time oddly pedantic stage directions for the play were strictly O'Neill's and pointed to the sort of instructions he would continue to write—enjoinders to trees to weep, houses to brood, and actors to turn all sorts of unlikely colors. The stage directions for *Where the Cross is Made* also contain a sample of the genuinely poetic style that O'Neill occasionally achieved during this period:

"Moonlight, winnowed by the wind which moans in the stubborn angles of the old house, creeps wearily in through the portholes and rests like tired dust in circular patches upon the floor and table. An insistent monotone of thundering surf, muffled and far-off, is borne upward from the beach below."

The play as a whole is not elevating, being concerned with an aging sea captain whose deranged mind is fixed on the day his lost ship, commanded by a drowned crew, will return with a nonexistent treasure, marked by a cross on a map. In the end the doddering captain succeeds in transferring his insane vision to his son, who "sees" the crewmen bring their treasure-laden chests to the waiting captain. O'Neill saw *Where the Cross is Made* as a *folie à deux* that might possibly be potent enough, when played, to inspire the audience to a kind of *folie en masse*. (Some critics have read into it a religious symbolism; the cross, they claim, stands for the Crucifix, and the treasure for the spiritual harvest men seek and cannot find.)

According to Agnes Boulton, the idea for *Where the Cross is Made* came to O'Neill, in part, from a short story she conceived but could not carry out. O'Neill later told George Jean Nathan that he originally planned it as a long play, but telescoped the last act into a one-acter because of his eagerness to be represented on the Provincetown Players' opening bill. (This was by way of defending himself against the charge that he had expanded *Where the Cross is Made* into a long play he later completed, called *Gold*. "The reverse is the real truth," he explained to Nathan.) He sent the one-acter to Nathan, who liked it and told O'Neill he would be pleased to publish it in *The Smart Set*, if not for its impending production.

O'Neill did not think much of the play as art. "It was great fun to write, theatrically very thrilling, an amusing experiment in treating the audience as insane—that is all it means or ever meant to me," he assured Nathan.

By fall of 1918 O'Neill was at work on the first draft of *The Straw*, the play based on his stay at the Gaylord Farm tuberculosis sanitarium. He settled on the title after first trying *The Miracle, Eileen Carmody,* and *The Cough* (which he had previously rejected in favor of *The Web.*) Later he described the play as "a tragedy of human hope."

Anticipating the objections that would be raised against a play about tuberculosis patients, he told an interviewer: "My whole idea is to show the power of spiritual help even when a case is hopeless. Human hope is the greatest power in life and the only thing that defeats death. I saw it at close quarters for I was myself an inmate of a tuberculosis sanitarium and through hope and spiritual help beat it."

But he was unable to work on *The Straw* with his wonted concentration, for he expected momentarily to hear from John Williams, who had indicated that *Beyond* would soon be produced; there was talk of casting John and Lionel Barrymore in the roles of the two brothers, and this was a prospect exciting enough to turn the head of even the saturnine O'Neill. He kept taking out his copy of *Beyond* and tinkering with the dialogue.

Early in November of 1918 O'Neill reluctantly left Provincetown for New York. He had not planned his departure until *Beyond* was set for production, and it was still not scheduled. John Barrymore had signed for Arthur Hopkins' production of Tolstoi's *Redemption* on October 3, and O'Neill could not persuade Williams to commit himself on casting, much less on a production date. Under the circumstances O'Neill would have preferred to stay in Provincetown to sulk about Williams' "dilatory tactics," as he described them, but Jig Cook insisted that he come to New York for the production of *Where the Cross is Made*. Cook foresaw trouble, and he was right.

The Provincetowners had moved into new quarters that season, at 133 MacDougal Street, a few doors down the street from their former theatre. Although they had found a benefactor in the Philadelphia art collector Dr. A. C. Barnes, who donated $1,000 to the new playhouse, the move cut so badly into their treasury that Jig contributed a month's room rent to help out and used the stage as his bedroom.

Number 133, owned by Mrs. Belardi, had once been a stable and later a bottling works. Much bigger than the first theatre, it could seat two hundred, had a spacious basement for workshop, dressing rooms and storage, and ample space for clubrooms and restaurant on the second floor. Downstairs on an auditorium wall was an old hitching ring, around which one of the Provincetown artists painted the legend: "Here Pegasus was hitched."

The rent was $400 a month, but Mrs. Belardi was never in a hurry to collect it. Once, when the Provincetown treasurer apologized profusely for being able to pay only part of the rent, Mrs. Belardi told her, "Sit down, have a glass of wine. Your debt is *your* worry, not mine."

In addition to a new stage, a graded auditorium floor, and benches that were a little more comfortable than those at 139, the Provincetowners also acquired a part-time secretary, Mary Eleanor Fitzgerald. Called Fitzi by everyone, she was a tall, blue-eyed, auburn-haired woman of Irish and pioneer American stock, with depths of vitality and warmth. A friend of Emma Goldman, with whom she had worked on the anarchist publication *Mother Earth,* and of Alexander Berkman, with whom she had worked on another radical pamphlet, *The Blast,* Fitzi had been an ardent spokesman and worker for anarchist, labor and pacifist causes. In her early forties when she joined the Provincetowners late in 1918, Fitzi knew her political career was nearing an end; the following year, when Emma Goldman and Berkman were deported from the United States, Fitzi abandoned politics and concentrated her organizational ability on the Provincetown Players. She and O'Neill were attracted to each other almost from their first meeting, and soon became close friends. Prodigiously generous, tender and fearless, Fitzi had the mother-earth quality O'Neill always sought in women; she made it easy for him to confide in her.

With Fitzi as secretary and Jig Cook now elevated to the position of director, the Provincetowners began their third season in a somewhat less anarchic spirit. They had begun to enjoy reading favorable reviews in the newspapers and were a bit more self-conscious about their experimental work; they could not help worrying just a little about what the critics might say. Whereas they would have presented a play like *Where the Cross is Made* the season before without any thought beyond the one that its author had something to prove or something to learn, now they balked at the flagrant implausibility, at the technical difficulties involved in making O'Neill's ghosts look ghostlike (rather than ludicrous), at the author's insistence on being allowed to "produce the play without hindrance, according to his own ideas." Nina Moise had left the Provincetown to work in California, and Ida Rauh was chosen to direct *Cross.*

Although O'Neill did not care much for the arrangement, he tried not to be too disagreeable at first. He was even willing to admit that his director was right—about at least one trivial inconsistency he had allowed to creep into the play. Lounging with O'Neill on a couch before rehearsal one day, Ida Rauh studied the script and murmured to O'Neill:

"You playwrights are nothing if not unreasonable."

"How so?" asked O'Neill.

"This part calls for a one-armed seaman," she said, indicating the role of the captain's son, who had been crippled at sea.

"Easy!" said O'Neill, thinking Ida was concerned about how an actor could fake the loss of an arm. "He just keeps his arm inside his—"

"But," interrupted Ida, "the stage directions read: 'He places both elbows on the table in a gesture of despair.'"

[384]

The forgetful author grinned, and hastily changed the direction to read "he . . . sits down, resting his elbow . . ."

O'Neill was adamant however, about the ghosts, even when Ida and other members of the group demanded to know how, when the first row of seats was only four feet from the 12-foot-deep, 26-foot-wide stage, an illusion such as O'Neill called for could be created:

"The forms of Silas Horne, Cates and Jimmy Kanaka [three drowned seamen] rise noiselessly into the room from the stairs . . . Water drips from their soaked and rotten clothes. Their hair is matted, intertwined with slimy strands of seaweed. Their eyes, as they glide silently into the room, stare frightfully wide at nothing. Their flesh in the green light has the suggestion of decomposition."

"With all the will in the world to see ghosts," Edna Kenton once recalled, "we saw nothing but Lewis and Foster and Ward [the three men portraying the ghosts] panting over the treasure chest. . . . We begged Gene at the dress rehearsal, as if it were a favor to the dying, to cut out the ghosts."

"They're rotten," O'Neill admitted. "But they won't be so bad tomorrow night—beyond the first twenty rows, anyway. This play presumes that everybody is mad but the girl [the captain's daughter], that everybody sees the ghosts but the girl. Everybody but the girl means everybody in the house but the girl. I want to see whether it's possible to make an audience go mad too. Perhaps the first rows will snicker—perhaps they won't. We'll see."

But he did not wait to see in person. After the final dress rehearsal he and Agnes left town.

The play opened on November 22, with Hutch Collins playing the demented captain, Jimmy Light his equally demented son, and Ida Rauh portraying the daughter. On the same bill were Edna Millay's *The Princess Marries the Page* and *Gee-Rusalem!* a farce by Florence Kiper Frank. The bill did not evoke an enthusiastic response from the critics. Typical of the comments was the review in the *Morning Telegraph* on November 23: "If you want to enjoy the sensation of going mad, you will find the want supplied . . . [at] 133 MacDougal Street." The critic implied that the sensation was not worth the trip.

"The Provincetowners make the critics pay," complained the New York *Review* on November 30, adding not quite accurately, "Only one critic, however, loved his art enough to put up the price of a seat at the opening of the Provincetowners. This reckless spendthrift was Heywood Broun of The Tribune." (A little later O'Neill wrote to Nina Moise complaining that the Provincetowners missed her guidance, and that Ida Rauh had been ill-advised to take on the double task of directing and acting in *Where the Cross Is Made.*)

The Provincetowners writhed under the attack, held a policy meeting, searched their souls—and decided thenceforth to send free tickets to the critics.

O'Neill had gone with Agnes to New Jersey, to live in a house Agnes owned in West Point Pleasant, a seaside colony about a two-hour train ride from New York. Agnes had been obliged to turn out her mother, father, daughter and sisters, who had moved into the house earlier that fall, not knowing that Agnes and her husband intended to occupy it.

The whole thing was typical of the sort of scatterbrained arrangements O'Neill and Agnes were inclined to make. Agnes had been out of touch with her mother and didn't know she had left the Connecticut farm; O'Neill was up in the air about the *Beyond* production, but he and Agnes couldn't afford to wait in New York. Provincetown was too far, in view of the fact that O'Neill would have to be in town again in a few weeks for the production of *The Moon of the Caribbees,* which the Provincetowners had finally decided to schedule for their second bill that season.

When O'Neill and Agnes seemed to have no alternative but the New Jersey house, which Agnes owned by virtue of having paid off its mortgage some time earlier, Agnes explained the situation to her family in some embarrassment. They, in equal embarrassment, packed up and moved into a rented cottage not far away. Because of Agnes' pledge to O'Neill, the Boulton family—none of whose members O'Neill had met—was not to make its presence in the neighborhood known to him.

O'Neill, therefore, lived for several months within a short drive of Agnes' family, without having any idea of their proximity. Agnes did not see them either, except for a brief visit with her daughter at Christmastime, and a few stealthy meetings with her father at the local hardware store, where he had taken a job to help pay for the rented cottage.

Agnes, however, had met O'Neill's parents. Before leaving for New Jersey, O'Neill had taken her to see them at the Prince George Hotel. According to Agnes, both James and Ella received her cordially and seemed pleased to have her for a daughter-in-law.

O'Neill found Agnes' house, surrounded by pine trees, "a fine quiet place" in which to work.

For Agnes, however, life was neither fine nor quiet the first weeks in New Jersey. Her tenure was fraught with hazards other than those of keeping her family out of sight of O'Neill. She guessed he was not comfortable, partly because the house was old and cold and rather primitive, with numerous coal stoves to be constantly attended, and a noisy windmill —somehow responsible for the water supply—creaking outside the window. Also she knew O'Neill was edgy about Williams and *Beyond the Horizon,* nervous at the prospect of having to go back to New York for rehearsals of *The Moon of the Caribbees,* unable to settle down to work on *The Straw,* and worried about money.

The end of the war in November had cut off O'Neill's one steady source of income—the royalties from his one-acter with a war theme, *In the Zone.* Audiences were losing interest and the vaudeville tour began petering out. The war's end had as little significance for O'Neill as its beginning; just as his concern with World War I had been confined largely to his own efforts to stay out of it, its termination was now a personal inconvenience.

"My luck after touching only the high spots last spring has become a mole," he wrote to Nina Moise. "*In the Zone* staggered through the influenza, with a six-weeks layoff, only to fall a victim to the premature hand of Peace-on-Earth-goodnight-to-war-plays. . . . Sherman got the wrong pig by the ear. *Peace* is hell!"

Although he was perhaps exaggerating when he bemoaned the peace, O'Neill had taken a decided turn in his political thinking. He had, in fact, in his own words, become "indifferent toward political and social movements of all kinds."

"Time was when I was an active socialist, and after that, a philosophical anarchist," he said, not long after the war's end. "But today I can't feel that anything like that really matters. It is rather amusing to me to see how seriously people take politics and social questions and how much they expect of them. Life as a whole is changed very little, if at all, as a result of their course. It seems to me that, as far as we can judge, man is much the same creature, with the same powers and the same weaknesses, as in the time when the Aryan race started toward Europe from the slopes of the Himalayas. He has become better acquainted with those powers and those weaknesses, and he is learning ever so slowly how to control them. The birth-cry of the higher men is almost audible, but they will not come by tinkering with externals or by legislative or social fiat. They will come at the command of the imagination and the will."

O'Neill stopped glowering long enough to write a one-act play before he went to New York in December. Agnes Boulton has described the sordid local characters who, she has said, inspired the play. They were, she has written, a family consisting of father, mother and three beautiful, blonde, unmarried and mysteriously pregnant daughters: ". . . each girl in

[387]

turn became pregnant. No one knew how this happened, for they talked to no one. . . . As to what happened to the girls after their babies joined the little group of other unidentified babies, I hadn't been able to learn, but it seemed to me I had heard that they just vanished, and nobody knew where." O'Neill entitled the play *Honor Among the Bradleys*. He tore up the script soon after writing it, on the advice of George Jean Nathan, to whom he showed it, and who was amused by its characters but contemptuous of its style. "A very false and feeble piece of work, which you 'bawled me out' for writing," O'Neill reminded Nathan soon after.

O'Neill arrived in New York for rehearsals of *The Moon of the Caribbees*, leaving Agnes in New Jersey to look after the stoves. Hutch Collins appeared as Driscoll, Charles Ellis as Smitty, Scotty Stuart as Old Tom, the Donkeyman, and Lewis Ell as the First Mate. Teddy Ballantine, who was playing uptown in *Redemption*, the show O'Neill was praying against, in the hope that if it closed John Barrymore would do *Beyond*, suggested a member of his cast to direct *Moon*. He was Thomas Mitchell, who later achieved fame as a movie star.

The play opened on December 20. "They put *The Moon* on the second bill," O'Neill wrote to Nina Moise, "and what with the small stage, the large cast—(which was never large at rehearsals, as you can guess), and the different sets, well—just use your imagination! The director—I forget his name—couldn't do anything under such conditions and didn't have personality enough to overcome them."

Although Mitchell made no impression on O'Neill at the time, the two men met again some years later when O'Neill suggested Mitchell for a role in the movie version of *The Long Voyage Home*.

"I knew little or nothing of directing," Mitchell has confessed, "but they were all amateurs at the Provincetown, so it didn't matter. I wasn't on in *Redemption* until about 10:30, so I was able to direct rehearsals downtown and still make my own show. I only saw O'Neill a few times during the production and he struck me, then and subsequently, as a moody, withdrawn man, but very gentle."

On the bill with *The Moon of the Caribbees* were a comedy by Susan Glaspell and Jig Cook called *Tickless Time* and a play called *The Rescue* by Rita Creighton Smith. *Moon* barely got on, opening night; the Caribbean Island, off which the S.S. *Glencairn* is anchored in that play, was a beaverboard cutout about four feet long, and a few hours before the opening it was discovered in the back yard of the theatre, where someone had left it lying all day in the rain. A new island was cut out, painted and shoved into place minutes before the curtain was raised.

Although *The Moon of the Caribbees* has since earned a place of respect among the literature of one-acters, Heywood Broun, for one, found it disappointing. "It spins a rather pointless tale about an uninteresting young man," he wrote.

The bill that included *The Moon of the Caribbees* was the last one in which Hutch Collins played. Not long after, he caught a severe chill during a rainstorm and was taken to St. Vincent's Hospital in serious condition. The influenza epidemic was at its peak, and Hutch came down with pneumonia and died in the hospital. He was in his early thirties, one of the most gifted actors the Provincetowners had known and the second of O'Neill's old friends to die within a year. Louis Holliday's death had shocked and hurt O'Neill, but with Hutch Collins much of O'Neill's New London youth died.

During the period from January, 1919, to early May, O'Neill nearly completed *The Straw* and worked hard on a new play, *Chris Christopherson* —which he first called *Tides* and was later to rewrite as *The Old Davil* and then as *Anna Christie*. The play gave him trouble from the beginnig, and O'Neill never felt he had brought it off. Its central character was, at first, the coal barge captain O'Neill had known at Jimmy-the-Priest's, who had got drunk and frozen to death on a cake of ice near his barge one Christmas Eve. In this early version Chris's daughter was a nice girl who had grown up away from her father in Leeds, England; the conflict revolved around Chris's opposition to the daughter's marriage to a first mate named Anderson. Chris was convinced that the "old davil sea" would end in breaking his daughter's heart, as it had her mother's.

But O'Neill's chief concern at this time was the delay over *Beyond the Horizon*. The day of production was still indefinite, for Williams had been having trouble with other productions that season, and had not had time to think about casting O'Neill's play.

O'Neill decided to put his problem to Professor Baker, who, he knew, kept in touch with Williams, an erstwhile Baker pupil. As a matter of fact Williams had already informed Baker that he had *Beyond* under option. O'Neill wrote to Baker on May 9:

"Not once but a dozen times since our chance meeting in Provincetown two years ago have I determined to write to you, but each time I hesitated, reflecting: Better wait until you have something real to relate."

O'Neill then outlined his plight. He explained that Williams had intended to produce *Beyond* with the Barrymores as soon as *Redemption* concluded its run, but that *Redemption* refused to conclude. Williams had renewed his contract, he added, and now promised a production before December.

"But my system has absorbed so much hope in the past six months that I am now immune," he wrote. "I turn a callous, cauliflower ear to all managerial fair promises. I have ceded my winter home in Spain for a permanent residence in Missouri."

O'Neill went on to inform Baker that since he had last seen him he had finished two long plays in addition to *Beyond*—*Chris Christopherson* and *The Straw* (which was still untyped). He asked Baker if he would allow him to send the plays so that he could read them, and ended the letter on a note of apology for not previously offering his appreciation to Baker for the year he had spent under his tutelage:

"I realize I must have seemed woefully lacking in gratitude because, seemingly, I have never had the decency to write—and I know the interest you take in the work of your former students. But I'm really not as bad as that. In all honesty, I have waited more out of small-boy ambition than anything else. I was confident that the night would come when I could approach you with the digesting-canary grin, and, pointing to the fiery writing on the wall of some New York theatre, chortle triumphantly: 'Look, Teacher! See what I done!' "

When acknowledging O'Neill's letter Baker asked for a copy of *Beyond*. O'Neill dispatched a script in haste and word came back from Baker that he was delighted with it. From that point on, admiration between teacher and pupil steadily grew and O'Neill's early comments about the little he had got out of Baker's Workshop were gradually erased from memory.

Although John Williams was still silent about his plans for producing *Beyond*, other Broadway producers were showing interest in O'Neill. One of them was James O'Neill's old friend George Tyler, who was beginning to wonder how he could have misjudged young Eugene's abilities so badly a few years before. Tyler had rallied after the bankruptcy of Liebler and Company and had become a successful manager on his own. He was producing plays for Laurette Taylor and Jeanne Eagels, and had recently discovered a young actress named Helen Hayes.

That April Tyler asked O'Neill, much to the latter's amusement, to doctor a play. The invitation was courteously declined, despite the fact that O'Neill could have used the money—for it seemed, somewhat to the bewilderment of both Agnes and O'Neill, that Agnes was pregnant. O'Neill had already arranged with John Francis to find him an inexpensive—and isolated—cottage near Truro for the spring and summer; how they were going to manage in October, when the baby was due, they had no idea. Their often-discussed desire was to own the remote lifesaving station on the edge of the Atlantic; it had been abandoned by the Coast Guard and jointly bought and remodeled some years earlier by Mabel Dodge and Sam Lewisohn, the millionaire philanthropist. Lewisohn and Mabel had each used the house for one month during the summer, and it was now on the market for $5,000.

Shortly before they were to leave New Jersey permanently O'Neill went to New York for his long-postponed encounter with George Jean Nathan.

Nathan and O'Neill met for the first time at the Beaux Arts restaurant and recognized each other from photographs.

The approximate date can be gauged from one of O'Neill's letters to Nathan. Written from West Point Pleasant and dated May 1, 1919, it ended with a promise to come to New York "about the middle of the month—when I shall bring [a copy of *Chris*] around to your office personally in the hope of finally meeting you."

But O'Neill had forgotten this when he later told Isaac Goldberg, Nathan's biographer, that he could not remember when his first meeting with Nathan took place.

"It was . . . at some restaurant, I believe, and I was three-fourths 'blotto.' I remember thinking how much he looked like an old friend of mine who wrote animal stories of that era for Street and Smith."

At this point O'Neill had placed himself in the hands of a literary agent. ("Yes, Williams' dilatory tactics drove me to an agent—the American Play Company," he informed Nathan in the letter announcing his impending visit.) The American Play Company had been founded by Elisabeth Marbury, who in the late 1800's had carved a career for herself as the American representative for European playwrights such as Victorien Sardou. An enormously fat woman who loved good food and good conversation, she divided her time between elegant establishments in New York and France and knew everyone worth knowing in society and the arts on two continents; she established herself as an extremely successful agent with offices in New York, London and Paris. In 1914, wishing to lighten the burden of personal responsibility she carried for her clients, Miss Marbury formed the American Play Company in partnership with two men, John Rumsey and Richard Madden. It was Madden who took on O'Neill as the agency's client. Madden did not like to handle anyone whose work he did not wholeheartedly admire. He met O'Neill for the first time during the production of *The Moon of the Caribbees*. With an emotionalism characteristic of a number of men who became O'Neill's friends, he later told his wife:

"I saw this gentle, clear-eyed man and I fell in love with him."

He and O'Neill went to Christine's to eat and talk. Madden told O'Neill how much he liked his sea plays. O'Neill asked him to be his agent, and they shook hands on it. There was never a written contract between them, but Madden continued as O'Neill's agent to the time of his death. Madden always gave his authors devoted personal service. "You don't know how much that means to a writer, Dick," O'Neill once told him.

O'Neill and Agnes left for Provincetown at the end of May, 1919, expecting to move into the little cottage in Truro which John Francis was supposed to have rented for them. To their astonishment they were informed by Francis that James O'Neill had bought from Mabel Dodge and Samuel Lewisohn the converted Coast Guard station, and that it was a gift to the younger O'Neills in anticipation of what James referred to as his "first" grandchild. He had deliberately forgotten Eugene's son with Kathleen, considering him no more kin than his own forgotten child with Nettie Walsh.

XXXII

IT WAS SEVERAL WEEKS BEFORE O'NEILL AND HIS wife could move into their ocean-front house, for it was half buried in sand from the winter's storms.

Facing north at the edge of the Atlantic on a treacherous stretch of coast called Peaked Hill Bar, the house was the closest thing to living on a ship that O'Neill could find without actually heaving anchor. His front lawn was the Atlantic and his back yard a desolate three-mile stretch of scrubwood and dunes. Known as the outer shore, this section of beach was uninhabited except by the Coast Guardsmen who lived in a new life-saving station, a large, boxlike structure half a mile away from their former home. The Coast Guard had abandoned the old house because of the sea's steady encroachment, and its promise to sweep the house away. But this was no deterrent to O'Neill; on him the sound of the crashing surf had a soothing effect.

Like the new Coast Guard station, O'Neill's house was accessible only by foot or horse-drawn wagon. Such was the feeling of wilderness and isolation that the three miles separating the house from the village might have been fifty. The ever-shifting dunes were huge, some of them towering fifteen feet, and one could spend hours clambering around them without seeing anything but sand and sky and clumps of wind-swept beach grass. There was a sense of endless space comparable to being on a ship in mid-ocean.

The coast was so hazardous that boats were pounded to matchsticks on the bars within a matter of hours; wrecks, especially during the winter, were frequent, and corpses often had been laid out in what was now O'Neill's living room. On the other hand, nothing could equal the serenity of a midsummer evening, with its purity of light and air, the sun reddening the sea, and a ceaseless, hissing wind that had no sting.

O'Neill's new home was a constant reminder of the frailty of man and the triumph of sea and wind.

The house had been made cozy and livable by Mabel Dodge, who, despite a predilection for white, had exquisite taste. She applied white paint to the walls of practically every house she ever occupied, and Peaked Hill was no exception. On the walls she hung large china plates with blue and green fish designs, and she covered the white-painted furniture with blue cloth. She left the floors bare, but waxed and polished their hardwood surface.

There was a gasoline pump for water, but no electricity; kerosene provided light and fuel for cooking and an immense open brick fireplace provided warmth. During the winter's storms the sand would drift against the house like snow, burying two-thirds of the front door. Each year the windowpanes were ground frosty by flying sand and had to be replaced. Each year, too, the path across the dunes, called Snail Road, shifted slightly with the changing contours of the beach. And each year the house leaned closer to the sea.

But the magnificent sense of space and timelessness never changed. It was an ideally dramatic background for O'Neill, and the house was a perfect studio. The second floor, reached by a narrow iron stairway, contained the lookout room, surrounded by windows, in which O'Neill worked at a rude desk built for him by his neighborly Coast Guardsmen.

Friends did come to see him, but it required an effort, and he was reasonably safe from intrusion. "No need to wear clothes—no vesture of the unrefined refinements of civilization," O'Neill said of his new retreat. He added that the house still preserved "its old sea flavor."

Not long after moving in O'Neill described the house and its effect on him to an interviewer for *The Bookman*:

"The stairs are like companionways of a ship. There are lockers everywhere. . . . The big boat room, now our living room, still has the steel fixtures in the ceiling from which one of the boats was slung. The look-out station on the roof is the same as when the coast guards spent their eternal two-hour vigils there. The exteriors of the buildings [there were a couple of little shacks nearby] are as weather-beaten as the bulwarks of a derelict. . . .

"The place has come to mean a tremendous lot to me. I feel a true kinship and harmony with life out here. Sand and sun and sea and wind —you merge into them, and become as meaningless and as full of meaning as they are. There is always the monotone of the surf on the bar—a background for silence—and you *know* that you are alone—so alone you wouldn't be ashamed to do any good action. You can walk or swim along the beach for miles and meet only the dunes—Sphinxes muffled in their yellow robes with paws deep in the sea."

O'Neill and Agnes got their supplies and mail either by walking into the village and carrying them back over the dunes or having them delivered by the Coast Guard's wagon. The wagon was drawn by a splayfooted horse called Daisy, who, like the men of the Coast Guard, developed a fondness for O'Neill.

At Peaked Hill O'Neill rose early, breakfasted at eight and then, still conscientiously trying to keep himself at the peak of physical fitness, swam, took long, solitary walks, or exercised with a punching bag. One of his favorite forms of relaxation was paddling his kayak far out in the dangerous waters. He worked until one, lunched, napped and sometimes swam again. Usually he spent several hours in the afternoon reviewing his morning's work. After dinner he and Agnes read until nearly midnight. It was a peaceful, productive life for O'Neill, with few interruptions, and that summer Agnes shared it with him contentedly.

In June (1919) Boni and Liveright brought out a volume of O'Neill's plays entitled *The Moon of the Caribbees and Six Other Plays of the Sea*—the six others being the three additional S.S. *Glencairn* one-acters plus *Ile*, *Where the Cross is Made* and *Rope*, a sea play only by virtue of its setting on a seaside farm. He received an advance royalty of $125 and it was agreed he would get 10 per cent of the proceeds from the sale of the book.

The firm, which was to publish O'Neill until it became bankrupt in 1933, had been founded somewhat casually in 1917. Albert Boni, from whom Frank Shay inherited the Washington Square Book Shop, had gone to work for an advertising agency owned by Alfred Wallerstein. Boni's office contained two desks, one of which, Wallerstein informed him, was reserved for a businessman named Horace Liveright, who used it sporadically as his New York headquarters.

One day, Boni told Wallerstein of his idea for publishing a "Modern Library" of inexpensive editions of the classics. Wallerstein was enthusiastic, and asked if he could be a partner. The two men shook hands on the deal.

The next morning, Boni was startled to see a man walk into his office and sit down. Boni had been working at the agency for six months and this was his first glimpse of the occupant of the empty desk. The man introduced himself as Liveright, spread an assortment of gadgets on the desk and explained he was examining them as possible manufacturing investments. He asked Boni's advice on the likeliest prospect, and Boni selected a jar with a metal cap. Then, carried away by Liveright's friendliness, Boni disclosed *his* projected venture in the publishing field. Liveright nodded approvingly, and the two men parted for lunch. When Boni returned, Wallerstein greeted him reproachfully.

"Albert," he said, "I thought you and I were going to publish the Modern Library together. Horace tells me *he's* going in with you."

Boni looked bewildered. "He neglected to tell me that," he said.

Wallerstein grew thoughtful. Then he told Boni to go ahead with

Liveright. Horace needed a chance to make good, he said. He had never been able to succeed in business, his last failure having been a chain of mills whose principal product was toilet paper. Financed by his father-in-law, Liveright had had the inspired idea of selling the product under the name "Pick-Quick Papers" and cornering the toilet paper market, but his business sense proved unequal to his imagination. The mills soon found themselves encumbered by unmarketable paper. His father-in-law offered to stake him once more, and then wash his hands of him.

Boni decided to let Liveright join him. Liveright invested $12,500, Boni put up $4,000, and the firm of Boni and Liveright was born. (It became Horace Liveright, Inc., several years later when, after constant quarrels over Liveright's mismanagement, the partners tossed a coin to decide who would buy out whom, and Boni lost.) The Modern Library was only a part of the Boni and Liveright enterprise. In the twenties the company gained tremendous importance as the publishers of such previously unheralded writers as Hemingway, Faulkner, T. S. Eliot and Robinson Jeffers. Horace Liveright picked up eccentrics like Bodenheim and Kemp and was the first publisher to promote the writings of Freud in America. The company not only went in for art on a high level (at one point Horace Liveright, Inc., boasted five Nobel Prize winners among its authors) but it made money—much of it dissipated by Liveright on wine, women and gambling.

With an enterprising publisher, an alert agent, and the completed scripts of three long plays, O'Neill, at thirty-one, still lacked a Broadway producer who would produce. He continued to rely on the Provincetown Players for experimentation but had lost faith in John Williams' plans for a Broadway production of *Beyond the Horizon.*

Impatiently seeking Broadway recognition, O'Neill began bargaining with George Tyler, to whom Richard Madden, his agent, had submitted *Chris Christopherson*—the script about the coal barge captain and his daughter. Tyler was less evasive than Williams, but, from O'Neill's point of view, not much more satisfactory. That summer O'Neill embarked on the sort of negotiations typical of the drawn-out, frustrating, contradictory, hopeful, naïve, defensive dealings he was often to have with theatrical managers.

He informed Tyler on June 8, 1919, that he was now ready to begin revising *Chris;* that the work should not take long, as it was all mapped out in his head; and that he was pleased to hear that William Farnum—a successful movie star—was considering the play. He expressed doubt, however, that Farnum would accept "such an unheroic, character part."

Five days later he mailed the new material to his agent, Madden. He had tried to strengthen the character of Chris by making his reaction to his daughter's willful acceptance of the first mate's offer of marriage more violent. (The struggle, in this early version of *Anna Christie,* lay primarily in Chris's desire to prevent his daughter from marrying a man of the sea; Anna was a tepid girl, and the first mate was nothing like the tempestuous stoker, Matt Burke, whom O'Neill later developed.)

"I feel sure you will find that the revision I have made fills the bill and strengthens the ending greatly," O'Neill optimistically advised Tyler. But his confidence was short-lived. Tyler thought the revised ending was still weak, and O'Neill retorted: "To be out and out candid, so that you will clearly understand how I feel about it, I don't believe I agree with you." He went on to say that Chris, Anna and the second mate had to react the way they did, and that Chris's attempted suicide—apparently a device Tyler found excessive—was "exactly what the Scandinavian Chris would do."

"I'll promise to think hard and keep thinking hard and preserve an open mind for improvement which the God of playwrights may deign to whisper," he added. "But for me to deliberately rack my inventive powers to strengthen the scene would be a false move. . . . But I'll try hard to *feel* what you do—and pray for light." O'Neill ended with a suppressed sneer for Farnum, who had not yet agreed to take the role of Chris.

Six days later, after much thought, he had cut some of the scene in question; but he still could not see his way clear to making any basic change.

Three days after that he succumbed entirely. "After careful consideration and re-reading I have come to the conclusion that you are right and that the last scene can be much improved by an extensive revision," he conceded to Tyler. "This new construction seems to me a hundred per cent improvement."

By September 25 matters had progressed to the point where Emmett Corrigan had replaced Farnum as a candidate for the role of Chris. Corrigan pleased O'Neill as much as Farnum now displeased him. "Years of the crass characterization of movie work must have left their mark on Farnum," he observed.

Tyler was anxious for O'Neill to come to New York, but O'Neill resisted, on the ground that he was expecting his child to be born any day (Agnes had been told the beginning of October, which proved almost a month too early).

A few days later O'Neill instructed Madden to send Tyler *The Straw,* the play with the tuberculosis sanitarium background. Williams, in whose hands it had been, had released his option (while still holding on to the rights of *Beyond the Horizon*).

"*I earnestly request you to read this play!*" O'Neill implored Tyler. "It is far and away and best and truest thing I have done, ten times more dramatic and heart-searching than *Chris.* . . . I believe you'll agree with me that it's a big thing. Whether you can see your way clear to producing it makes no never-mind—but please give it a hearing."

Tyler was in no hurry to read O'Neill's truest and best. He told O'Neill he was busy producing two other plays.

O'Neill allowed almost a month to go by before inquiring again about *The Straw,* and Tyler answered with disappointing news about *Chris Christopherson.* Corrigan was no longer available, Tyler said, and the production of *Chris* had to be postponed until after the first of the year.

Attempting to cheer himself up, O'Neill rationalized that he was now, at least, free to go on writing without worrying about impending interruptions; and, having forgotten his recent judgment of Farnum as an actor grown crass with movie work, he confided to Tyler that the first of his new projects, *Gold,* would "prove a perfectly corking play for Farnum." *Gold* was the long play about the insane sea captain who saw the ghosts of his drowned shipmates, that O'Neill had in mind when writing the shorter version, *Where the Cross is Made.* O'Neill also made some elaborately jocular references to the state of his finances, which Tyler interpreted as a plea for help, and which O'Neill hastily disavowed:

"Happily, things do not threaten to reach any such dire straits where an S.O.S. would be warranted," he declared, thanking Tyler for offering a loan.

If Tyler was recalcitrant about reading *The Straw,* his press agent, John Toohey, was not. Toohey, who was a founding member of the Algonquin circle and a frequent contributor to the *Saturday Evening Post,* took the trouble to congratulate O'Neill warmly on the play, and O'Neill, responding to this praise, declared that he was "willing to stand or fall" by *The Straw.* He added that he believed American managers underestimated the intelligence of postwar audiences and that they were now ready to accept "something more than just a couple of hours' amusement."

"I take it the principal objection to *The Straw* on popular grounds would be the T.B. element," he said, adding it was his belief that the idea of tuberculosis "is now too familiar to the people at large to be fraught with the old ignorant horror."

Tyler finally read *The Straw* and informed O'Neill that he liked it but said nothing about producing it. O'Neill, having forgotten his insistence that it made "no never-mind" whether or not Tyler wanted to produce *The Straw,* now piteously complained that Tyler's letter had put him "into that torturing state popularly known as 'up in the air.'"

This brought a hasty assurance from Tyler that he would, indeed, produce the play and would pay O'Neill an immediate advance. "A million rousing cheers!" declared O'Neill on November 13. "Your note confirming my hopes reached me today and I feel in the pink of good spirits. . . ." And there the matter rested for several months.

In the meantime, however, Tyler's press agent was trying to stimulate the public's interest in O'Neill. He asked O'Neill if he could send a photographer to Peaked Hill to prepare a publicity layout. He particularly wanted some pictures of O'Neill at work on a play, he said. O'Neill reacted negatively to the suggestion and, although he was to submit many times in the future to both interviewers and cameramen, it was almost always after a struggle. Eventually he grew vain enough to enjoy posing for portraits but he always objected to arranged scenes purporting to show him at work, and, like most public figures, he constantly complained that interviewers misquoted him.

"Come now, Mr. Toohey, that's a bit thick, isn't it?" O'Neill chided the publicity man. "Have a heart and allow me to remain natural. . . . There are so many others just watering at the mouth for that weapon-in-mit close-up that I won't be missed."

He then suggested that a picture of the author *not* at work would be far more effective: "to catch him penless, deskless, his chin unaccountably kept in place without the prop of a sensitive hand, his hair looking like hair and not like a backdrop to accentuate his troubled-by-my-last-act brow, his eyes temporarily soulless but betraying a keen interest in dinner—such a photo ought to establish forever his rep. as a 'sad bad glad mad' eccentric Nut, a defier of all our cherished traditions—and make him A One copy!"

O'Neill and Agnes had reluctantly closed the house at Peaked Hill Bar early in October and moved into the village to await the birth of their child.

In the meantime O'Neill kept in touch by mail with the Provincetown Players, who were getting ready to open their fourth season in New York with *The Dreamy Kid,* O'Neill's one-acter about the Negro gangster and his dying mother. Directed by Ida Rauh, the play—when it opened October 31—was greeted with interest, if not with enthusiasm; it was one of the first plays to be cast with Negro actors in serious roles by a "white" producing company. When *The Moon of the Caribbees* was produced the year before, the roles of the Negro prostitutes had been filled by actresses in blackface, as was then the custom in the New York theatre; outside of their own stock companies, Negro actors were employed only for comic-darky roles or vaudeville acts. Ida Rauh had been enterprising enough to recruit her cast from a Harlem stock company, and the production paved the way for two later O'Neill plays—*The Emperor Jones* and *All God's Chillun Got Wings*—both dealing seriously with Negroes and both cast with Negro actors.

In Provincetown that October O'Neill and his wife occupied, for a reason Agnes has not been able to recall, two tiny cottages across the street from each other. They stored baby clothes in one and lived in the other. The one called Happy Home was heated, and was arranged to accommodate the lying-in, while the other cottage was where O'Neill worked and where he and Agnes slept. Agnes' doctor was the same Daniel Hiebert with whose sister O'Neill had boarded while attending Baker's class at Harvard; Dr. Hiebert, who had by this time delivered scores of babies, had set up practice in Provincetown that year.

In the early morning of October 30, Agnes recognized the onset of labor and O'Neill telephoned Dr. Hiebert. According to Dr. Hiebert, she had an easy birth. He said he had no clear memory of O'Neill's presence on the scene—he had, in fact, a vague impression that O'Neill was off somewhere, drunk, when his heir made an appearance.

The boy was named Shane Rudraighe O'Neill, in honor of the Irish king known as Shane the Proud. (Legend had it that Shane the Proud, on being asked if he had made peace with Queen Elizabeth, replied: "The only peace I made with the queen was in bed.")

"John's a lovely name in any language," Alice Woods told Agnes and O'Neill, with a touch of malice; she was annoyed by what she considered their snobbish fuss over Irish nomenclature.

O'Neill telegraphed his parents and wrote to Tyler, who, as James O'Neill's close friend, had been anxiously awaiting the birth of the Governor's grandchild.

"The Event transpired yesterday, and most successfully," he informed Tyler. "A ten and a half pound boy who looks able to play football right now. His voice already carries further than the Old Man's."

And to Toohey, a few days later, he wrote:

"Yes, it's a boy. If you've got a mob scene rehearsing, I'd like to place him. His Grandpa's voice!"

Pasted as the first item into the scrapbook O'Neill began keeping soon afterward was this paragraph from the *Morning Telegraph*:

"It's a Boy: Eugene O'Neill, novelist and playwright and the son of James O'Neill, is the father of a baby boy that came to his home this week at Provincetown, Mass. This youngster gives the elder O'Neill his first grandson."

PART THREE

THE MAKINGS OF A POET

1920—1926

XXXIII

"I'M STILL AT THE NERVE-RACKING JOB OF WAITING for a [Broadway] production," O'Neill wrote to the critic Barrett Clark from Provincetown on December 13, 1919. "No suitable theatres to be had. . . . It's a great season!" He would not come to New York, he said, "until rehearsals start . . . but when will that be?"

Broadway was suffering from an acute theatre shortage. The Actors' Strike of the summer before had been settled with Actors Equity Association emerging as a strengthened union, and a vigorous season had got under way by October. John and Lionel Barrymore, Helen Hayes, Alfred Lunt, Laurette Taylor, Ina Claire and Ethel Barrymore were appearing in various vehicles and a lachrymose melodrama by Langdon McCormick called *The Storm*, with Edward Arnold and Helen MacKellar, was one of the big hits of the season.

Still fuming over John Williams' unwillingness to schedule *Beyond the Horizon*, O'Neill watched the Broadway scene from Provincetown with dismay. And, unaware of what it would mean to his future, he read with sour anger about a new play called *For the Defense*, produced by Williams on December 19. O'Neill did not dream that this overwrought courtroom drama by a young playwright named Elmer Rice was to serve as the indirect means of getting *Beyond the Horizon* into production.

In the cast of *For the Defense* was the handsome, popular leading man Richard Bennett, two of whose daughters, Joan and Constance, eventually became movie stars. Bennett, then forty-seven, was beginning to be dissatisfied with matinee-idol roles. Not long after the opening of the Rice play, he visited Williams' office, pulled the dusty manuscript of *Beyond the Horizon* out of a cubbyhole and began to read it. He was greatly moved by the play and urged Williams to let him star as the twenty-three-year-old Robert Mayo. He also offered a solution both for the theatre shortage and for the financial risk of presenting a contemporary American tragedy. He suggested that the play be mounted at the Morosco, where *For the Defense* was already established, that as much of the cast as possible be recruited from his own play, and that the new production be presented in a series of special matinees. Williams, who was genuinely interested in giving *Beyond* a hearing, and realizing he would not have to risk more than an investment in some sketchy scenery, agreed to Bennett's plan.

Bennett persuaded three members of *For the Defense*—Louise Closser Hale, Mary Jeffery and George Riddell—to accept roles in the O'Neill play. (Miss Hale had been lauded for her portrayal of Prossy in *Candida* in 1903.) He rounded up Edward Arnold (not yet a movie star) and Helen MacKellar, a successful leading lady, from the cast of *The Storm*, to play the older brother, Andrew, and the girl, Ruth, whom both brothers loved. For the only major role not filled from either company, that of the father, James Mayo, Williams cast Erville Alderson. To most of the actors, appearing in *Beyond the Horizon* was an act of faith and love; it meant rehearsing a second role in addition to performing daily in their established vehicles, and then giving twelve performances a week, instead of eight. But Bennett's enthusiasm was contagious, and soon they had a creditable production.

O'Neill, having waited so long, was caught off guard by the suddenness of the venture and had little chance to object to the makeshift arrangements. Having set his heart on the still youthful John Barrymore, he was not readily reconciled to the middle-aged Bennett in the role of young Robert Mayo; nor did he think the rest of the cast ideal. Moreover, he resented Williams' suggested cuts in the script and was outraged by the unimaginative scenery Williams furnished.

O'Neill wanted the scenes to alternate between indoor and outdoor settings, to illustrate the hero's conflict between his wanderlust and his confinement. What he got was a stock interior and a picture-postcard exterior, thrown together by Williams' assistant, Homer S. Saint-Gaudens —son of Augustus Saint-Gaudens, who had designed the statue of Diana atop Madison Square Garden.

But O'Neill had a choice of the makeshift matinee production or none at all. He settled sulkily for the matinee.

On February 1, 1920, an item on the drama page of *The Times* announced that *Beyond the Horizon* would be performed the following afternoon at the Morosco Theatre, where it would continue to run for "a series of matinees on Mondays, Tuesdays, Wednesdays and Fridays" and be "installed regularly in a theatre when one is available."

At 2:15 on Tuesday, February 3, 1920, the first production of a Eugene O'Neill play opened on Broadway.

The author, hovering at the back of the theatre, hiding behind a pillar to avoid recognition, watched the audience file into the Morosco on West Forty-fifth Street. Most of the first-string critics came, despite the unorthodox hour and the fact that an adaptation of a Georges Feydeau farce, *Breakfast in Bed,* was scheduled to open that night. The critics were tired, having already reviewed roughly one hundred productions since the season's start in late June. (The season began early in those days; ten plays had opened during July and August.) There had been thirty musicals and revues, sixty comedies and melodramas, and six farces. Only a few were productions beyond routine interest—a Shakespearean repertory, a couple of short-lived tragedies adapted from European classics, and an abortive fantasy or two. Certainly nothing like an American tragedy, which was how *Beyond the Horizon* was billed, had challenged the critics' languid spirits.

The two principal critics, Alexander Woollcott and Heywood Broun, took their aisle seats. Both, of course, knew O'Neill's one-acters from the Playwrights' Theatre.

Many of the Provincetowners were in the audience to see their faith in their young genius justified; several remembered Jig Cook's words, repeated on many occasions, "All the world will know Gene's plays someday."

James and Ella O'Neill arrived at the theatre early. Both had undergone transformations. James, at seventy-four, now depended on the support of the cane he once carried purely for effect. He had been struck by an automobile a year before, as he and Ella had stepped from a Broadway trolley at Twenty-seventh Street. Although the injuries had at first been regarded as superficial, his right leg had never completely healed, and his magnificent constitution was beginning to give way.

Ella, who was sixty-three, had recently recovered from the removal of another breast tumor. But more miraculously, she had cured herself of narcotics addiction. With an inexplicable surge of strength, she had told her husband that she was going to stay a few months at a convent— not a sanitarium—and that her family should not worry about her. She had got to know some cloistered nuns, who believed they could help her. After spending the allotted time in the convent, praying and talking with the nuns, she came back completely free of the habit. She began attending church again with something of the lost fervor of her youth.

James and Ella took their seats in a box at the Morosco; to their friends they seemed nervous about what their strange, difficult son was going to show them.

The curtain rose on a badly painted, awkwardly lighted set that was supposed to represent O'Neill's poetically conceived section of country highway, "the horizon hills . . . rimmed by a faint line of flame, and the sky above them [aglow] with the crimson flush of the sunset . . ." But as the grim tale of the two brothers unfolded, their chaotic story told with uncompromising realism, the shabby sets were forgotten and the audience sat in tense, respectful silence, even through the unconscionably long waits between the scenes of each act.

James O'Neill was rigidly erect in his seat, but tears streamed down his cheeks. When the final curtain fell he walked, damp-eyed and beaming, to the back of the theatre and patted his son.

"Are you trying to send the audience home to commit suicide?" he asked huskily.

He then invited Eugene to the Prince George early the following morning so that they might read the reviews together.

Eugene, watching the audience file glumly from the theatre, interpreted the silence as disapproval.

The next morning at the Prince George the O'Neills devoured the reviews. The astonishing fact was that the critics had enjoyed the tragedy.

"I felt sure when I saw the woebegone faces on the audience on opening day that it was a rank failure," O'Neill said a few weeks later. "No one was more surprised than I when I saw the morning papers and came to the conclusion that the sad expressions on the playgoers' faces were caused by their feeling the tragedy I had written."

A number of the critics recognized not only the play's individual merits but the fact that something of broader significance had occurred on Broadway. The theatrical season, wrote Alexander Woollcott, in *The Times,* was "immeasurably richer and more substantial" because of *Beyond the Horizon,* which he described as "an absorbing, significant, and memorable tragedy, so full of meat that it makes most of the remaining fare seem like the merest meringue."

"The only reason for not calling 'Beyond the Horizon' a great play," he added, "is the natural gingerliness with which a reviewer uses that word —particularly in the flush of the first hour after the fall of the final curtain."

Woollcott praised the performers for "rising gratefully and spontaneously to the opportunities afforded by a playwright of real power and imagination," and continued, "the play has greatness in it and marks O'Neill as one of our foremost playwrights [and] one of the most spacious men to be both gifted and tempted to write for the theatre in America."

Reviewing the play for the *Tribune,* Heywood Broun, a little more restrained, called it a "significant and interesting play by a young author who does not as yet know all the tricks." Like Woollcott, who complained that the last act was weakened by being broken into two scenes, Broun took exception to the final act, which he found overlong and a "letdown."

The anonymous critic for the *World* declared that "the deep and acute understanding of human nature and its impulses of which there have been many substantial traces in Eugene G. O'Neill's short plays . . . asserted itself unmistakably yesterday afternoon in the first work of full length from his pen to reach the stage. . . . [It] may be set down at once as this season's most notable play of a serious theme and purpose by an American author."

The critic for the *Herald,* also anonymous, was sterner, characterizing *Beyond the Horizon* as "a formless, unnecessarily long picture of a failure in life—the tragedy of the square peg in the round hole." Nevertheless, he found it "profoundly moving and human in most of its scenes."

Robert Gilbert Welsh, of the *Evening Telegram,* hailed *Beyond* as a great play: "Only once or twice in the course of the dramatic season does a play of such terrific force and such simple directness award the patient theatrical chroniclers . . ."

The *Evening Post's* J. Ranken Towse wrote:

"There can be no question that [*Beyond*] is a work of uncommon merit and definite ability, distinguished by a general superiority from the great bulk of contemporaneous productions."

Though aware that a noteworthy event had taken place in the American theatre, few of the critics evaluated it accurately. It was not that they had never seen contemporary tragedy well performed on Broadway; a number of the Europeans had been adapted skillfully to the commercial stage. Nor had they failed to be impressed on other occasions by the imaginative works of such Americans as Percy MacKaye, William Vaughn Moody and others. But *Beyond the Horizon* was unclassifiable because it combined naturalism and tragedy with native character and contemporary expression. It employed no melodramatic tricks and did not rely on coincidence; it was built upon the development of character alone, and eschewed plot for plot's sake.

It was, in short, something never before attempted by an American for the Broadway theatre: dramatic literature. It was written rather than contrived, and it introduced the possibility, which had long before been realized in Europe, that the commercial theatre could express dramatic literature rather than serve merely as an amusement arena. The critics had trouble finding a niche into which they could put the play and its author.

Woollcott tried, by comparing it with, among other works, *John Ferguson,* by the English writer St. John Ervine, which had been produced the season before. "It is a play of larger aspect and greater force," he wrote, "a play as vital and as undiluted a product of our own soil as any that has come this way since the unforgotten première of 'The Great

Divide.' In its strength, its fidelity, its color, its irony, and its pitilessness, it recalls nothing quite so much as one of the Wessex tales of Thomas Hardy."

But most of the critics, while thrilled by the play and its acting and excited by its innovation, were almost apologetic about endorsing it. They quickly warned that *Beyond* could not be a popular success.

The play's "almost impenetrable gloom," noted the *World* critic, might "deny it the popular attention that it richly deserves, for it is purely tragic in its mood, cruel in its story, and consequently oppressive in the heavy atmosphere of woe in which it is enveloped."

Even Woollcott, its stanchest supporter, cautioned: "As to whether it will be, or could be popular—well, that lies not within the province of this reviewer (nor the wisdom of anybody) to say."

Almost to a man the reviewers found fault with the play's ending, with the awkward scene shifts—and, of course, with the length. (Like Shaw, O'Neill was always to suffer from accusations of long-windedness.) Broun led the attack:

"O'Neill has [by the last act] become so carried away with his theme that he has not been able to hold it away at arm's length and slash and cut in the light of the fact that audiences are human and fallible and demand a brevity in the relation of all happenings which will not keep them in the theatre after 5 in the afternoon or 11 at night."

And Woollcott chided O'Neill for being "a bit intractable in the matter of structure, a bit unyielding both to the habits of the average audience and the physical limitations of the average playhouse. The breaking of his final act into two scenes, a mark of a chronic looseness of construction, is distinctly dissipative in its effect . . ."

O'Neill was both elated and dismayed by the reviews. He realized he had finally done what he had set out to do—force Broadway to accept him on his own terms. And he was not displeased with certain aspects of the production.

"Richard Bennett is just fine as Robert," he told several friends, and he called Helen MacKellar's Ruth "the best thing" in the play, "a perfect portrayal if there ever was one."

But he was distressed at the lack of critical acumen that could blame him for awkwardness in dividing each act into two scenes. Even Woollcott, who devoted his theatre column, "Second Thoughts," to the play on the two following Sundays and who probably did more than any other critic to ensure the play's success, could not refrain from harping on O'Neill's inepitude in that respect.

"Certainly it was a quite impractical playwright who split each of his three acts into two scenes, one outside and one inside the Mayo farmhouse," he wrote in his Sunday column after again lauding the play for its truth and strength. But he indicated that he had entirely missed O'Neill's point. "No essential purpose is served by these exteriors which could not have been served had they been unfolded within the farmhouse without a break of any kind," he said. "Some of a novelist's luxuries must be foregone by a writer when he goes into the theatre, and one of the lessons he must learn is that the ever illusion-dispelling process of dropping a curtain (more than three times) works havoc with the spell."

Woollcott was hitting at the heart of O'Neill's technique; he did write plays like a novelist, and he insisted on the novelist's luxuries. The trouble was that American stagecraft had not yet caught up with him.

On February 15, the following Sunday, Woollcott had an afterthought which he delivered in the form of a left-handed compliment: "The decaying farm, the beckoning road, the imprisoning hills and the sea beyond the horizon could have been conjured up far more illusively by the players in their speech within the farmhouse than by any scenic painter who ever lived . . . a playwright with O'Neill's imagination and dramatic gift can dispense with even such suggestive aids (as the horizon and distant hills), can create with spoken words such effects as make him independent of all the domes, cycloramas and elaborate switchboards in the world."

O'Neill wrote plaintively to Barrett Clark, one of the few people who had understood the reason for the interior-exterior changes:

"Why is it, I wonder, that not one other critic has given me credit for a deliberate departure in form in search of a greater flexibility? They have all accused me of bungling through ignorance—whereas, if I had wanted to, I could have laid the whole play in the farm interior, and made it tight as a drum à la Pinero. Then, too, I should imagine the symbolism I intended to convey by the alternating scenes would be apparent even from a glance at the program. It rather irks my professional pride, you see, to be accused of ignorance of conventional, everyday technique. . . . I've been longing to protest about this to someone ever since I read the criticisms by really good critics who blamed my youthful inexperience—even for poor scenery and the interminable waits between the scenes!"

Later, discussing the scene variations within each act with an interviewer, O'Neill said: "One scene is out of doors, showing the horizon, suggesting the man's desire and dream. The other is indoors, the horizon gone, suggesting what has come between him and his dream. In that way I tried to get rhythm, the alternation of longing and of loss. Probably very few people who saw the play knew that this was definitely planned to produce the effect. But I am sure they all unconsciously *get* the effect. It is often easier to express an idea through such means than through words or mere copies of real actions."

O'Neill was even more upset by the fact that Williams acceded to the critical carping and, after the first performance, cut out the brief final scene to avoid another scenery shift. This was the scene in which Robert, dying, sums up an essential bit of O'Neill philosophy:

"You mustn't feel sorry for me. Don't you see I'm happy at last— free—free!—freed from the farm—free to wander on and on—eternally! . . . It isn't the end. It's a free beginning—the start of my voyage! I've won my trip—the right of release—beyond the horizon!" (Modestly, O'Neill later explained, "The tragedy of Robert Mayo brought an exultation and an urge on the part of the audience toward more life." But it was difficult for the audience to respond hopefully, with this last speech of hope cut out of the play. The scene was restored for the published version which Boni and Liveright brought out in March.)

The review that probably pleased O'Neill the most was written by Ludwig Lewisohn at the end of February for *The Nation*. Lewisohn did not merely praise *Beyond the Horizon* and point out that it "produces in us, as every good tragedy does, the impression—to use the words of a great critic—'that our consciousness of what it means to be human has grown riper' "; to O'Neill's satisfaction Lewisohn also took the trouble to dismiss the two current hits from which the cast of *Beyond* was recruited as "absurd melodrama" (*For the Defense*) and "even shabbier melodrama" (*The Storm*).

To O'Neill's mind, however, the highest praise came six years later, when *Beyond the Horizon* was revived. It was offered by Joseph Wood Krutch, who became drama critic of *The Nation* in 1924 and always remained O'Neill's favorite and most respected reviewer. In a thoughtful essay on tragedy, Krutch stressed that O'Neill's greatness lay in the fact that he had "come nearer than any other American to writing Tragedy," in the sense of the Greeks and Shakespeare. Illustrating his point with *Beyond,* Krutch noted that in that play was "clearly to be seen an instinctive discernment of the laws of such writing."

This play [wrote Krutch] is marked by a sense of tragic fitness which is by no means the inevitable accompaniment of vigor or honesty and which lifts the play, as art, to a higher level than those two qualities alone can ever reach. In the hands of another his story might have become a vehicle for mere pathos or sentiment. If this boy who gives up his dream of a full life of adventure in strange lands for a marriage which chains him to the farm he hates had found in his marriage even the peace of gradual extinction, the play would be essentially a play of sentiment; if his wife had turned out to be merely not the woman he thought her, then his story would be only the story of an unfortunate mistake; but actually it is neither of these things. Divesting himself of every trace of faith in the permanent value of love and presenting it as merely one of the subtlest of those traps by which Nature snares Man, O'Neill turns a play which might have been merely ironic into an indictment not only of chance or fate but of that whole universe which sets itself up against man's desires and conquers them.

As a matinee series *Beyond the Horizon* proved a success with New York audiences in spite of all foreboding. When business at *For the Defense* began to falter, Williams decided not to nurse it. Instead, he closed it, leaving Richard Bennett free to continue in *Beyond,* which Williams moved to the Criterion on February 23 for regular evening performances. But since *The Storm* showed no sign of abating, Edward Arnold and Helen MacKellar had to be replaced. On March 9 *Beyond* was moved again—to the Little Theatre—and Alexander Woollcott, who had tucked the play under an avuncular wing, went once more to review it. He found he liked it even better than before.

No one was more surprised than Williams when *Beyond the Horizon* turned out to be a hit. After attending a performance Professor Baker wrote O'Neill that he was proud of him and offered his explanation for the play's popular success:

"A public which heartily welcomes *Beyond the Horizon* is not the old public. It seems now as if there really were in New York an audience large enough to make successful any kind of drama worthy of attention. With that newer public created out of the War, with the probable greater effectiveness of the dramatists who have been writing successfully for us, with the promise shown by the newer writers, this is no time for pessimism . . . surely we have the right to hope that the next decade will give us an American drama which, in its mirroring of American life, will be more varied in form, even richer in content."

O'Neill himself was inclined to credit the Washington Square Players and the Provincetown Players for creating a receptive atmosphere for *Beyond the Horizon.*

"These groups helped make it possible to present serious dramas," he said in 1936, reviewing his career. He emphasized that they had introduced "culture into the pattern of the stage."

Beyond the Horizon attracted audiences until June 26, when it closed after 111 performances. The play grossed $117,071, but O'Neill's share was only $6,264 because he had accepted a low royalty rate in his eagerness to sign a contract. It was more money, however, than he had ever earned before. (By 1921 he was able to inform Dr. Lyman, without exaggeration, that his average weekly income had risen to "about $300" and that he would "probably double that figure" in 1922.)

O'Neill was more exultant over his artistic triumph than his financial one. "A simon pure, uncompromising American tragedy, which a Broadway manager dared to produce on Broadway, was surely an epoch-making event," he gloated, "and that it actually kept going from February to the end of the season was another tremendous upset." (The play was taken to Chicago in the fall, but was not a success there. "I have the very faintest faith or interest in the road at any time for my stuff," he wrote to Tyler a few months later. "*Beyond the Horizon* was a lesson in that respect. There is not enough of a public to keep my plays going outside of New York.")

Not least among O'Neill's triumphs was his sense of having vindicated himself with his father. Established as a success on his own terms, he was now released from the struggle to come out from behind his father's shadow. He had proved himself right and his father wrong and he could afford to be generous at last. James managed to meet Eugene halfway.

With the air cleared of open hostility, James and Eugene found an opportunity, almost immediately after the première of *Beyond,* to spend several weeks in each other's company. Eugene came down with a mild case of influenza and was obliged to stay in bed at his father's hotel. Ella, who had recently recovered from the illness herself, nursed him. It was the first time that not only James and Eugene but Ella as well had enjoyed a sense of identity as a family.

Jamie continued to be the only unredeemed member. His brother's success and his mother's conquest of narcotics addiction seemed to plunge him into deeper despair. On a protracted drunk when *Beyond the Horizon* opened, Jamie did not reappear until a week or two later. Charles Webster, the actor who had traveled with the O'Neills in the vaudeville version of *Monte Cristo,* met Jamie on Broadway one day toward the end of February.

"I'm going to see my brother's play," Jamie told Webster offhandedly. Webster was astonished that he was just getting around to seeing it. Jamie's feeling for his father was not enhanced by the rapport between James and Eugene, and he seemed determined never to draw another sober breath. One night Jamie ran into another actor-friend, John Hewitt, in Times Square. Although he seemed scarcely to recognize Hewitt, he told him woefully that he had fallen in love with a chambermaid in a

Broadway hotel, but that his father was opposing his marriage to her. He complained to another friend that a night clerk of a seedy West Side hotel had refused to give him a room because of drunkenness. "I know why you're a night clerk," Jamie said he had told him. "It's because you're too dumb to be a day clerk."

James himself had finally faced the fact that Jamie was a total loss. Deciding to settle for what happiness he could find in his younger son, he chose to forget the bitterness he once expressed to friends about Eugene and the lack of encouragement he had provided.

Meeting Clayton Hamilton at the bar of The Players a few days after *Beyond* had opened, James declared, to Hamilton's carefully concealed amusement: "My boy, Eugene—I always knew he had it in him! Remember how I always used to say he would do something big someday? People told me he was wild and good for nothing, but I always knew he had it in him, didn't I?"

And to Harry Crowley, who remembered James's recent remark about Eugene's irritating preoccupation with "scribbling," James showed the same beaming smile, spoke the same words of paternal triumph.

David Perkins, his fencing adversary in *The Three Musketeers,* was one of the few people to whom James mentioned his true feelings about Eugene, Jamie and himself. Perkins caught him at a moment when he was feeling low.

"I never thought Eugene had much ability," he said, "but he surprised me. He's good!" After a pause he added, "I suppose you know about Jamie—" Perkins nodded sympathetically. James was silent for a moment, and then began to talk about his own career.

"I made a big mistake in sticking to *Monte Cristo,*" he said. "And then it was too late. Toward the end I couldn't tour it any more—everything got so expensive—I had to play second-rate theatres . . ." His voice trailed off and he fell into brooding silence. It was the last time Perkins saw him.

On February 10 James suffered a stroke. He was taken to St. Vincent's Hospital in downtown Manhattan, where he stayed for some time, undergoing tests that eventually revealed he had cancer of the intestines.

Eugene was distraught over his father's illness and spent as much time as he could at his bedside. But he had become embroiled in the production of *Chris Christopherson,* which George Tyler, encouraged by the success of *Beyond the Horizon* had decided to present as quickly as possible. Tyler's idea was to try out the play in Atlantic City early in March, perhaps take it to a few other eastern cities, and open it in New York in the late spring while *Beyond* was still drawing enthusiastic

O'Neill audiences. O'Neill was not averse to having two plays on Broadway at the same time and threw himself energetically into rehearsals—but with the usual grumbling about casting and cuts. Although he was for the most part polite and considerate in his contacts with the members of the *Chris* company, he held many private reservations about them. He aired his grievances in long letters to his wife, whom he had left in Provincetown, and to whom, during their frequent separations, he always wrote ardently.

Emmett Corrigan finally accepted the role of Chris Christopherson; as Anna, Tyler cast Lynn Fontanne, who had recently been brought from England by Laurette Taylor. "A startlingly capable beginner," Tyler wrote of Miss Fontanne in his autobiography, "shy and awkward enough— always turned her toes in, and a time she had breaking herself of the habit—but through all her shyness you could see she was blessed with the grand manner even then." O'Neill found the manner a little *too* grand for Anna, but he was overruled.

O'Neill was about to accompany the play's cast to Atlantic City for its première at the Apollo Theatre on March 8 when he received a telegram from Provincetown informing him that Agnes was seriously ill. He rushed to Peaked Hill, finding Agnes not dangerously ill, after all, but sick enough to require his presence.

O'Neill wrote to several friends that he was more distressed at being so far away from his father, who he knew did not have long to live, than he was at having to miss the opening of his play. But he was glad of the chance to unwind from the strain of rehearsals and felt no inclination to return to New York. Although Agnes improved rapidly, he decided to make her illness an excuse for staying in Provincetown.

And he needed an excuse, for fame had begun making demands on him in the form of requests for interviews, luncheons, portrait sittings and even speeches. Typical of his attitude about lecturing was his polite refusal of an invitation from William Lyon Phelps, Lampson professor at Yale. O'Neill declared that he had a prejudice against lecturing "both from the standpoint of personal discretion and of Christian charity toward the audience."

People who had recognized O'Neill's power and talent in his early days of experiment and error were now proud to point out that they always had had faith in him and fond of recalling that they "knew him when." He was beginning to be good copy for magazines and newspapers, and Clayton Hamilton drew an admiring sketch of him in April for *Vogue*:

[416]

[O'Neill] knows nothing, hears nothing and cares nothing about the theatre market that is centered in Times Square. He does not spend his days upon the doormats of the magnates of Forty-second Street, hoping that they will ultimately pay him $500 to get rid of him. He does not spend his leisure hours lunching at the Knickerbocker, hoping to pick up an easy job of adapting a French farce to an American setting or turning a forgotten American farce into a musical comedy. He neither needs nor desires money, because he has never been accustomed to its uses. Like Strickland, in 'The Moon and Sixpence,' he can tell the world to go to hell. He can think his thoughts and dream his dreams, in loneliness, beside the surging and suggestive sea, and he can write great dramas which the silly little world that is centered in Times Square can subsequently look upon with wonder.

There were also those who, unlike Hamilton, formerly had sneered at O'Neill's talent but who now claimed him as their own discovery. One such, a former colleague on the New London *Telegraph,* met Arthur Mc-Ginley on Broadway two days after the opening of *Beyond.* "What did I tell you?" said this man. "I could see the spark of genius way back in his newspaper days." McGinley smiled, recalling the man's words to him one night in New London: "That phony playwright—a writer? Why, he couldn't write home for money."

New friends, most of them genuinely moved by *Beyond* and anxious to encourage a young talent, began coming forward. One of them was the successful playwright George Middleton, a stanch and early O'Neill admirer. Another was St. John Ervine, flushed with his own recent stage successes. Both writers sent O'Neill congratulatory letters soon after the opening of *Beyond,* and O'Neill quickly acknowledged them. To Middleton he wrote (with that little touch of self-pity that he could seldom suppress):

"Your letter is one of the most gratifying things the production . . . has brought to me and I am very deeply grateful for your thoughtfulness in writing it. . . .

"You and St. John Ervine are the only playwrights who have given me a brotherly word of encouragement. . . . And your letters have taught me, I hope—if ever I get the authority for it—to do likewise and write to the first author, whose play I respect—especially if I don't know him— to tell him so; for, through you, I have learned the things that count most of all."

O'Neill kept this promise. He was always generous and thoughtful of young writers who came to him for advice and encouragement. It was one of the paradoxical streaks in his nature that he could be sensitive to the needs of relative strangers and respond to them with both counsel and financial assistance, while he could at the same time be blind, petty and selfish to the people who were closest to him and had the most claim on his understanding. He was growing to be very much like his father.

O'Neill, not yet completely at ease in the role of recognized genius, was having difficulty following his first success with a second. He had completed several scripts and was anxious to press on to other work, but once again he was being delayed by the technical problems of production.

George Tyler was not happy with *Chris,* and wanted O'Neill to join him in Atlantic City to work on the script. O'Neill, who also was dissatisfied with the play for different reasons, was willing to make the changes he thought necessary but preferred to do the rewriting in Provincetown. It was one of his conceits that he did not really need to see his scripts acted to know how they would play; he believed—and surprisingly often he was right—that he could "see" a production perfectly in his mind, and could tell exactly how and where work must be done. (Whenever he was proved wrong he blamed the actors for throwing the picture he had visualized out of focus; he resented the fact that actors were people, rather than puppets; he was affronted when they displayed mannerisms, attitudes, and sometimes even opinions that he had not himself evoked. He always wrote his characters as if he were a novelist, allowing no leeway for deviation. Casting was inevitably a horror to him, for he felt he was yielding, inch by inch, the characters he had created, and losing them to flesh-and-blood aliens, with lives of their own.)

Despite Tyler's misgivings about *Chris,* the Atlantic City reviews were not bad. "The play is full of red-blooded life . . . [and Emmett Corrigan has] . . . one of the finest parts he has ever had in his fine career" read an Atlantic City newspaper on March 10. The critic did not care for Lynn Fontanne's Anna, which, he said, "missed in many ways the heights of emotion and soulful spirit that could have been hers." The remainder of the cast, he added, "offers character parts well played but of no particular dramatic note." The review ended on a note of high praise:

"For the most part the unusual and oftimes crude stagecraft of Mr. O'Neill's construction succumbs to the power of his inborn dramatic gifts. Atlantic City may well consider it the finest piece of drama that has visited this shore this year if not in many more. It is a marvelously dramatic play, a sterling piece of craftsmanship."

But the play was not popular with audiences.

O'Neill, in Provincetown, decided to go over the script. On March 14, he came to the conclusion that the last scene was "weak and all wrong."

He wrote to Tyler that the play must be radically rewritten before it had a New York showing.

"With *Beyond the Horizon* serving as a standard of comparison in their minds you know with what eagerness the critics will seize upon any weak spot in *Chris* and shout it to the skies," he explained.

He proposed to rewrite the love scene between Anna and the first mate to indicate that the mate would not reform and that Anna, in marrying him, would be heading for the same fate of a lonely sailor's wife her mother had endured. This, O'Neill believed, would save the play from conventionality.

"The reason why I haven't seen this before and why I didn't see it that way in the beginning is that when writing the play I was concentrated on a character study of *Chris,* and the love subplot was done any old way as being unimportant except in its reaction on him. I now see that a play is no stronger than its weakest spot and that the artificiality and fakiness of that last scene will ruin *Chris* as a whole, and even spoil my characterization of him."

O'Neill said he would await "with the keenest anxiety" Tyler's word on how the play was received in Philadelphia, where it was headed next. He informed Tyler that Agnes was "still very weak and unable to be out of bed yet." (But in a letter of the same date to a friend at the Playwrights' Theatre, to whom he did not need to justify his continued stay on Cape Cod, he wrote that Agnes was "quite herself again now.")

To Tyler he added: "I hear from home that the specialists have had a consultation over my father's case and have had X-rays taken to decide whether an operation will be imperative or not. If it is, I will have to come to New York, as an operation in my father's present condition will be a matter of life and death. This sickness of the Governor's is really hell to me. The thought that there is a chance of losing him just at the time when he and I, after many years of misunderstanding, have begun to be real pals—well, you can imagine."

On March 17 O'Neill received the reviews from the Philadelphia papers, where *Chris* had opened two days before. They were mixed.

"I had been led to expect . . . that the play would come in for an unmerciful panning, neck and crop, from all the critics," O'Neill wrote to Tyler, "so the notices, though they were hardly what you'd call hysterically enthusiastic, were nevertheless favorable enough to furnish me with a pleasant surprise."

Tyler had written that he could not take the play to New York in its present form and urged O'Neill to come at once to Philadelphia to rewrite it. But O'Neill had decided that the play was not salvageable.

Always ruthless about work he considered to be below his ideal, he was ready to tear up *Chris* and start all over.

"Throw the present play in the ash barrel" was the way he put it to Tyler. "Candidly, that is the idea which strikes me as promising the most chance of future success, both artistic and financial." He already had an inkling of how to reapproach the subject and theme, but could not yet define this for Tyler.

"Suffice it to say," he noted, "that of the present play I would keep without change only the character of Chris—I'd give you a real daughter and lover, flesh-and-blood people—and the big underlying idea of the sea."

What had come to his mind was one of those odd juxtapositions of apparently unrelated characters and events to which he was frequently subject. The real Chris—the Chris of Jimmy-the-Priest's—had had no daughter, as far as O'Neill knew. But he now remembered a blonde girl who worked in a cigarette factory and whom he had met at Luke O'Connor's saloon. The girl had spoken to O'Neill of her father, a barge captain in Boston, and one day she had had a reunion with him at O'Connor's while O'Neill was there. O'Neill's memory of this meeting suddenly clicked into place, and along with the image came a ready-made character and background for the girl, about whom he knew very little; the character and background would be borrowed from Terry Carlin's long-vanished mistress, Marie. (Since O'Neill had never met Marie, he found himself filling in her personality with bits of Christine Ell, the tawny-haired proprietor of the Provincetowners' eating club.)

The new Anna's lover was still to be invented in detail, but clearly he would have to be more virile and elemental than the first mate, Anderson—probably a younger, less intellectual Terry Carlin, but with Terry's bighearted idealism and with, inevitably, some of O'Neill's own early Catholicism woven into the character—in short, the stoker, Matt Burke.

O'Neill said nothing of this to Tyler, adding only that he did not know when he could get to work on the new play. "It would all depend on the back of my head, which works independently of urgings and won't be forced to turn out ideas. So you see this scheme would require a great deal of faith on your part. However I feel enough confidence in my nut when it once gets started on a thing to say that I think I should be able to work out the new play and have the final script to you by next fall . . . this scheme . . . is the very best I have to offer."

He told Tyler that Agnes was still ill and that he could not possibly go to Philadelphia, and it would be of no use anyway.

"Up here I see the real faults inherent in the play itself—my faults. But the only thing I ever get out of seeing a presentation is the actors' faults, which never fail to set me in a rage. I'd rather keep a pleasant memory of the *Chris* cast than have to hate at least fifty percent of them for the rest of my life."

He went on to say that he was perfectly willing to rewrite—in Provincetown, in "the work atmosphere"—if Tyler still wished him to do so, pointing out that he knew Tyler had spent money and energy on the play; he suggested, however, that the play could have been successful if it had not been brutally cut during production.

Tyler decided to abandon the play and sent O'Neill a scolding letter, in which he took him to task for his lack of interest in saving the production. O'Neill retaliated by turning the blame on Tyler. Tyler had erred, wrote O'Neill, in attempting to mount *Chris* as "a general popular success possibility."

O'Neill ended by telling Tyler, who had already begun plans for producing *The Straw*, that he was now going to start work on *Gold*, which was promised to John Williams, because it was "a play that has been very much on my mind . . . demanding to be written." He would finish it in two months, he thought, and then he would "start the new *Chris*."

Simultaneously with the closing of *Chris*, O'Neill's one-acter *Exorcism* was done at the Playwrights' Theatre. (He had written this interpretation of his own suicide attempt in 1919, his least productive year since he had first begun writing.) *Exorcism* was significant for two reasons. First, because it expressed his retrospective view that in failing to kill himself he had actually been reborn to a more hopeful life; and second, because it marked the end of his interest in one-acters.

". . . the one-act play is an unsatisfactory form—cannot go far enough," he later declared, adding, however, that it could be "a fine vehicle for something poetical, for something spiritual in feeling that cannot be carried through a long play."

In two scenes, with a lapse of twenty-four hours between the action of the first and second, *Exorcism* was made part of the Provincetown Players' fifth bill of the season, presented on March 26, 1920. The group was violating its previous policy with that bill by producing a foreign play—*Last Masks*, by Arthur Schnitzler; they did not have enough native material to make up a strong bill. *Exorcism* was directed by Edward Goodman, former head of the Washington Square Players, which group had passed out of existence. The central role of Ned Malloy (O'Neill) was portrayed by Jasper Deeter, who had recently joined the Provincetown group and who later headed a flourishing little theatre called the Hedgerow, near Philadelphia, where O'Neill permitted him to present many of his early plays, royalty-free. Deeter, who owned one of the few typed manuscripts of *Exorcism* that O'Neill did not get around to tearing up after the production, forfeited it when, some time later, he was obliged to jump his rent in Greenwich Village.

In addition to the character of Ned Malloy, the cast included Ned's father and three Jimmy-the-Priestlike characters: Jimmy, Ned's room-mate; Major Andrews and Nordstrom. The play was not widely reviewed, despite O'Neill's new fame, but Alexander Woollcott looked it over before it closed and found it "uncommonly good," an opinion with which its author disagreed.

Woollcott said that it was common enough in the theatre to find a single vivid character stalking amid puppets but that it was "decidedly uncommon to find the secondary roles alive and real and individual." With O'Neill, he added, "the smallest roles have a certain sovereignty." This compliment, O'Neill told a friend, made him uncomfortable, in view of his failure in that precise area with *Chris,* and the back of his mind seethed harder than ever with plans to rectify it, as his work schedule for March, 1920, testifies.

There were a few days in that month when O'Neill was in the hectic position of having (1) an established success on Broadway (*Beyond the Horizon*), (2) an established failure out of town (*Chris Christopherson*), (3) an experimental play in Greenwich Village (*Exorcism*); and was (4) at work on an already-optioned new play (*Gold*), (5) planning the revision of the play that was to emerge as *Anna Christie,* and (6) actively involved in production plans for *The Straw*. Periods like this of multiple activity were to be the rule rather than the exception of O'Neill's life.

In March Tyler had hit on the scheme of doing *The Straw* as a special matinee in Boston; like Williams, Tyler wanted to give an O'Neill play a hearing but—particularly in the light of the *Chris* fiasco—was nervous about it.

Tyler decided to cast the feminine lead for *The Straw* with the ingénue of *Bab,* a comedy he was about to produce in Boston. In the title role of *Bab,* adapted by Edward Childs from a novel by Mary Roberts Rinehart, Tyler intended to display the talents of Helen Hayes, who had recently scored a striking success in *Clarence*. His idea was to ask Miss Hayes to play Eileen Carmody at matinees during the Boston tryout of *Bab*.

O'Neill was indignant.

Helen Hayes, he felt, lacked the maturity and experience for the role of Eileen Carmody. (She was eighteen, as was the heroine of *The Straw*.)

What distressed O'Neill even more was Tyler's plan to put into the role of Stephen Murray (the O'Neill-like hero) a farce actor named John Westley, and to have Westley, who was without directing experience, stage *The Straw*.

O'Neill complained to Tyler that this was "unjust" to what he considered "the best play I have ever written—better even than *Beyond the Horizon*."

The reason he did not want the Boston matinee was that it would constitute an unfair test of the play's merit, and also because it would call for his presence at rehearsals sooner than he could conveniently get away.

"*The Straw* can't go on without me . . ." he told Tyler. "I'm the only one who can tell the cast of the play what, how, and why they ought to behave. And there's another thing: Wouldn't it be unfair to have to give up a month's hard work at creative writing for one experimental matinee?"

But when Tyler replied that he was convinced both of the necessity for the Boston trial and of the appropriateness of Miss Hayes and Westley, O'Neill capitulated—albeit conditionally. The special matinee, he said, should be a test of the actors, and not of the play. If the actors did not "fill the bill" the play should be recast before being brought to New York.

"I refuse to consider Boston's verdict on the play itself to be worth a damn as far as its New York chances are concerned," he went on, "any more than I believe that the judgment on *Chris* in A.C. and Philly gave any indication of what it would have been in New York."

Beyond the Horizon, he suggested, would not have paid its way either in Atlantic City or in Philadelphia.

"I think to produce a play so drastic in its subject matter as 'The Straw' in a town as conventional and hide-bound as Boston is to reduce the play's chances to a minimum," he said. "Without the sanction of New York first applied, they will never stand for it."

Within a few days, O'Neill had withdrawn his reservations about Westley, at least. The actor came to Provincetown during the first week in April to have a long talk about the play. O'Neill found him sympathetic and informed Tyler he would be fine as Murray and that his direction would be "an asset to the piece."

But he still did not like the idea of the Boston matinee. For one thing, Boston had a child labor law which would prevent child actors from appearing in the roles of the Carmody children. Not without justification, O'Neill felt that to use midgets "would simply turn the whole thing into a farce of the most absurd description." For another, O'Neill did not think that the makeshift scenery Tyler intended to provide could authentically simulate a T.B. sanitarium. Then there was the problem of casting the minor characters. O'Neill did not want Tyler to throw in the *Bab* characters simply because they were already there. He said it was equally important that the smallest part in *The Straw* be cast with as much care as Eileen and Murray.

"I sweated too much blood in the writing of the play and I love it too much to permit it to run the slightest avoidable risk even in a special matinee performance," O'Neill advised Tyler. "Either it should be done *right,* down to the smallest detail, or it should not be attempted at all. I have set my heart on this play and I must be convinced that it is receiving the best there is, and is being played as it was written."

He signed his letter, as he had grown accustomed to doing, "With very kindest regards," but he was clearly beginning to feel himself wronged by his father's old friend. Not long after, he got word from Tyler that the Boston matinee idea was being abandoned, largely because the strain of learning two big roles was considered too much for Helen Hayes.

On April 20, trying to be conciliatory, O'Neill wrote to Tyler explaining why he had mistrusted the Boston tryout. "Perhaps my attitude is the result of an abiding aversion and distrust for Boston itself. I sure loathe that town tremendous!" He meekly asked Tyler where he now planned to try out *The Straw,* assured him that he would soon provide a satisfactory new version of *Chris,* and devoted the rest of the letter to personal comment about his father.

"I'm coming down to New York in the near future to see the Governor," he said. "Mrs. O'Neill and I are bringing down his grandson for him to have a first look at, hoping it will cheer him up. . . . Jamie wrote me about Doctor Erdmann's verdict. It seems so damned awful that nothing can be done." Once again O'Neill sent Tyler his "very kindest."

He did take his wife and son to New York and spent some time with his father, who had been released from the hospital but was confined to a bed in the hotel. O'Neill next looked in on *Beyond the Horizon* at the Little Theatre and found a new source of irritation there. He had finished a bottle of liquor with his friend Teddy Ballantine when the two of them decided to see the last act of the play. They slipped into a couple of empty orchestra seats and watched Bennett go through the motions of dying. Ballantine realized at once, as did O'Neill, that Bennett's performance had deteriorated.

O'Neill muttered to Ballantine about "goddam hams" and said he was going backstage to "bawl out" Bennett as soon as the curtain rang down.

Suddenly, drunkenly, changing his mind, O'Neill leaped from his seat and rushed up the aisle, Ballantine stumbling after him.

"What's the matter, sir, are you sick?" asked an usher, as O'Neill shoved his way through the door at the back of the auditorium.

"No," snarled O'Neill, "I'm only the author."

O'Neill was back in Provincetown by the beginning of June and resumed his wrangling with Tyler. He no longer made any effort to conceal his irritation.

His agent, Madden, had informed him that Tyler's new scheme was to try out *The Straw* in Atlantic City. In view of the recent Atlantic City fiasco with *Chris*, O'Neill thought Tyler had lost his wits, and all but told him so. Further, O'Neill had been advised by Jamie that Tyler had discussed *The Straw* with his father as a "Romeo and Juliet" play, and was planning to delete all the "coughing and spitting" and the weighing scene in Act Two.

"I will never consent to change or cut one word of the play on the verdict of Atlantic City, which I regard as worse than ruthless," declared O'Neill. "I only wish my judgment counted for something with you in this matter of my play. . . . *The Straw* is *not* a Romeo and Juliet play, and was never so intended by me, and cannot be produced as such." Besides, he noted, implying that Tyler had not read the play carefully, there were "only about three coughs" in it and "not one spit."

"As I took great care to impress upon Mr. Westley," he added, "I regard the weighing scene as one of the very best, technically and artistically, that I have ever written and . . . I will not consent to any change in it."

If Tyler was unwilling to produce the play as written, he said, he would be glad to return his advance and withdraw the play; he added he would rather have the play published in book form and "have it judged in that way than have my whole meaning misrepresented."

The letter bore no wishes of kindness, but was signed with a curt "Sincerely, Eugene."

Tyler returned an angry answer, accusing O'Neill of calling him an "idiot manager" bent only on financial success and of jumping to "perfectly stupid conclusions," throwing in a gratuitous sneer at *Chris*; O'Neill retaliated by accusing Tyler of trying to turn *The Straw* into a starring vehicle for Helen Hayes.

"You are a manager who, when a playwright rises up in protest against what he believes is to be an injustice to his work, loses his temper and resorts to abuse," said O'Neill.

By now he was so irate, he decided *not* to buy the play back from Tyler. "You will have to keep the play the allotted time, produce it or not just as you see fit," he wrote. "For me it is now deader than John Brown's body, and all that I ask is that I never hear of it again for years, except as a book. No play is worth all this unpleasantness, and *The Straw* is no such great matter that I shall allow my summer isolation to be poisoned by any further thought about its production, or give an actor's damn whether it is produced at all or not. . . . For me to fret and fume and quarrel and argue is silly and untrue to my real nature which is that of an interested but distant spectator." Again he was "Sincerely, Eugene."

Oddly enough, Tyler seemed not at all impressed by a public honor that had come to O'Neill just a few days earlier, nor, for that matter, was O'Neill himself. Neither of them made any reference to the fact that on June 3 the Pulitzer Prize had been awarded to *Beyond the Horizon.*

The prize had been established only three years before by Joseph Pulitzer, editor and publisher of the St. Louis *Post-Dispatch.* As administered through Columbia University, it had been withheld in the category of the drama in its first and third years, 1917 and 1919, and been given only once, in 1918, to the play, *Why Marry?* by Jesse Lynch Williams. In the field of the novel it had been won twice—in 1918 by Ernest Poole, for *His Family,* and in 1919 by Booth Tarkington, for *The Magnificent Ambersons;* no award was made to a novel in 1920.

To O'Neill the prize meant chiefly a financial windfall, for a cash award of $1,000 went with the honor. He received a telegram in Provincetown informing him that Columbia University had selected *Beyond the Horizon* as being "the original American play, produced in New York, which shall best represent the educational value and power of the stage in raising the standard of good morals, good taste and good manners."

"Can you imagine me at the point where Columbia University actually confers one of its biggest blue ribbons on me?" he asked a friend two months later. "And the funniest part of it is that I never knew that such a prize existed until I received a wire this June saying I had won it!"

Much later, in publicly recalling the honor, he said:

"In 1920 I had honestly never heard of the Pulitzer Prize, or if I had, hadn't listened. So when a wire reached me . . . saying I had won it, my reaction was a disdainful raspberry—'Oh, a damned medal! And one of those presentation ceremonies! I won't accept it!' (I have never been fond of medals or ceremonies.)

"Then a wire from my agent arrived which spoke of a thousand dollars and no medal and no ceremony. Well, I practically went delirious! I was broke or nearly. A thousand dollars was sure a thousand dollars! It was the most astoundingly pleasant surprise I've ever had in my life, I think."

The identities of the three-man jury making the recommendations to the Advisory Board of Columbia University were guarded by secrecy and not known to O'Neill. They were Hamlin Garland, Richard Burton and Walter Pritchard Eaton. (It is amusing to note that Augustus Thomas, who detested O'Neill's work, had been a member of the panel during the first two years of the prize's existence.)

Writing of the award some months later (without, of course, revealing that he had been on the jury) Eaton remarked:

Prizes of this sort do not always have great significance; they may, for instance, merely mean that all the other plays were pretty poor. However, it is well remembered that all the other plays were not pretty poor during the year of the contest, and "Beyond the Horizon" was not victor without competition. [The Advisory Board had publicly regretted that Drinkwater's *Abraham Lincoln* was not eligible for the prize by reason of its foreign authorship; the board's appreciation of the play was officially recorded.]

That the judges, though, could have hesitated long over their decision is difficult to imagine, for Mr. O'Neill's drama possesses so conspicuously one merit over all competitors, the merit of a tense, driving emotional sincerity, imparting to the spectator—when he withdraws a little from the spell of the tragedy—the sense that the dramatist has been imaginatively at the mercy of his people; not manipulating them so much as being manipulated by them.

But O'Neill had already forgotten *Beyond the Horizon* and was actually resigned, as he had assured Tyler he was, to forgetting about *The Straw*. *Gold* was his chief preoccupation that June—*Gold* and a plan for something else, something bigger and better than he had yet attempted or that had ever been attempted for the American theatre. His mission being that of an innovator, he could never stand still and was always receptive to anyone who recognized the symptoms of his growth.

George Jean Nathan was one of the recipients, that spring, of O'Neill's confidences about his growing power. O'Neill had sent him the completed script of *Gold* and been heartened to learn that Nathan regarded it as a step forward in O'Neill's development.

Actually the play, which was O'Neill's elaborated version of the theme he had condensed into *Where the Cross is Made,* was one of his less effective efforts. In *Gold* he began with Captain Bartlett's shipwreck on a desert island and his discovery, while crazed with thirst, of a chestful of trinkets that he believes to be genuine treasure. The play follows the captain's rescue and his return home, his plan to go back for the treasure, and the ill-fated journey of the ship to the island without him. The last act is virtually the same as *Where the Cross is Made,* except that the ghosts of the crew are seen only in the captain's mind, instead of materializing on the stage.

Urging Nathan to pay him a visit in Provincetown, O'Neill confided that he had something important to discuss with him "—a scheme quite on a grand scale, and as far as my knowledge goes, an original plan in play writing. I do not mean by this that there is any heavy blank verse, soggy symbolism or bizarre innovation connected with it; but it is an idea which is so large in outline that, even having the temerity to grant one's ability for it, it will take some years of intensive and difficult labor to fill in."

He added that the question in his mind still was: "Is this thing as big as I think; is it worth the labor involved, and from a purely practicable standpoint, can it be done?"

The project he had in mind might have been *Marco Millions,* which he outlined in 1923 and wrote the following year as two plays; or it might have been the nine-act *Strange Interlude,* written during 1926 and 1927; O'Neill's plays were often forming themselves in the back of his mind as much as five years before he began to put them down on paper. Whatever the specific work, it is clear that he had begun toying with the big idea of the multiple-play, to be performed on two or more consecutive nights—an idea that persisted, growing more and more grandiloquent as the years passed.

It is in a way singular that at just about this time Shaw was working on his staggering *Back to Methuselah,* a project that he modestly told Lawrence Langner was "the longest and best play ever written," and that he wanted Langner to produce, with the recently formed Theatre Guild, on five consecutive nights. Although O'Neill knew Shaw's work well, he could not at that time have known of *Back to Methuselah,* nor could he have been aware of the similarity between his own and Shaw's aims to broaden the scope of the theatre audience's endurance.

But O'Neill was intimately acquainted with Shaw's ideas, as set forth in *The Quintessence of Ibsenism.* He had first read it in his senior year at Betts Academy, and continued to dip into it periodically. Although O'Neill was having an uphill fight with his producers in America, he could take comfort from knowing that Shaw had already laid the groundwork for him in Europe. In *The Quintessence of Ibsenism* Shaw wrote:

An interesting play cannot in the nature of things mean anything but a play in which problems of conduct and character of personal importance to the audience are raised and discussed. People have a thrifty sense of taking away something from such plays; they not only have had something for their money, but they retain that something as a permanent possession. Consequently none of the commonplaces of the box-office hold good of such plays. In vain does the experienced acting manager declare that people want to be amused at the theatre; that they will not stand long speeches; that a play must not contain more than 18,000 words; that it must not begin before nine nor last beyond eleven; that there must be no politics and no religion in it.

O'Neill had long since taken these words to heart. He never stopped believing in them, and so great was his faith that he finally succeeded in making American audiences believe in them, too.

As he vowed to Nathan that summer:

"I will not 'stay put' in any comfortable niche and play the leave-well-enough-alone game. God stiffen it, I am young yet and I mean to grow! And in this faith I live: That if I have the 'guts' to ignore the megaphone men and what goes with them, to follow the dream and live for that alone, then my real significant bit of truth, and the ability to express it, will be conquered in time—not tomorrow nor the next day nor any near, easily-attained period, but after the struggle has been long enough and hard enough to merit victory."

XXXIV

IN THE MIDDLE OF JUNE, 1920, JAMES O'NEILL WENT
home to New London to die. He had suffered a relapse in New York;
and, knowing that it was the end, he asked Ella to take him to the only
place for which he had any nostalgia. He knew that staying in Monte
Cristo Cottage was out of the question, but he wanted to be in New
London, even if it meant only a hospital room there.

Ella sent a wire to Dr. Sullivan, who had treated Eugene for pleurisy
in New London, informing him that her husband had cancer. She asked
him to take James as a patient, and Dr. Sullivan arranged to have the
seventy-three-year-old actor admitted to Lawrence Memorial Hospital. Expected by his family to die momentarily, James lingered in the hospital
for two agonizing months.

"He suffered . . . incredible tortures. . . . You can imagine what he
went through," Eugene wrote to Nina Moise. "It was terrible for my
brother, mother and me to have to stand by and watch him suffer and not
be able to help in any way . . . his grand old constitution kept him going
and forced him to drain the cup of agony to the last bitter drop."

For several weeks, James was semiconscious, with moments of clarity
when he was able to talk with visitors. Eugene and his success were uppermost in his mind. He kept the telegram announcing Eugene's Pulitzer
Prize by his bedside and showed it to all of Ella's relatives. To one of them
he said, "Oh, Josie, I can die happy, because I think Gene is going to be
all right." With a feeble return of his Irish spirit he whispered, "Between
us, I didn't think he'd amount to anything." ("It was the greatest satisfaction to him that I had made good," Eugene later revealed to a number of
his Provincetown friends. "I thank whatever gods may be that *Beyond*
came into its own just in time for him.")

One day James said to Eugene, "Well, lad, I tried to drag you in by
the back door of the theatre and now you're on the stage." But he could
not help brooding about his own wasted career.

Monte Cristo, he kept telling Eugene, had been his curse. "How
keenly he felt this in his last years, I think I am the only one who knows,
the only one he confided in," O'Neill later told Tyler.

[430]

In mid-July, his speech failing, James uttered his last words to his son:

"Eugene—I'm going to a better sort of life—this sort of life—here—all froth—no good—rottenness!"

Soon after, he lapsed into a coma from which he never rallied. Eugene continued to visit him daily, sitting in silence at his bedside and dwelling on his father's transformation into a living corpse—a recurring image in the plays he later wrote.

On August 7 a priest was summoned to perform the last rites. Three days later, a few hours past midnight, the hospital informed Ella, Jamie and Eugene that James was dying. Jamie, who asked a friend to drive him to the hospital, muttered: "Helluva time the Old Man picked to die." Jamie was, of course, drunk.

James died at 4:15 on the morning of August 10. His wife and sons were at his bedside when he went to his "better sort of life."

Newspapers all over the country took note of James' death, which in a way symbolized the end of a theatrical era—particularly of the old school of acting. Most of the long and laudatory obituaries failed to mention that James O'Neill had been the father of a Pulitzer Prize-winning playwright.

"There is something about the passing of James O'Neill that touches the heart," said the New York *Clipper*. "For he was the type of popular actor beloved by audiences. His excessive dramatic emotionalism always left an indelible impression on the minds and hearts of those who witnessed his performances . . . he loved the stage as none but one born to it can.

"Whether James O'Neill was a great actor or not will perhaps be best answered by posterity. To the multitudes that went to see him perform in 'The Count of Monte Cristo' he was undoubtedly a great actor. To the more critical, perhaps, he appeared a distinctive player of certain roles. But, in the main, he was a great dramatic personality, a lovable player who gripped his audience and made them feel that he was always giving the best that was in him."

Eugene knew that James had taken a more realistic self-evaluation to his grave. "My father died broken, unhappy, intensely bitter, feeling that life was 'a damned hard billet to chew,'" he told Tyler. "This after seventy-six years of what the mob undoubtedly regard as a highly successful career! It furnishes food for thought, what? . . . his [dying] words . . . are written indelibly—seared on my brain—a warning from the Beyond to remain true to the best that is in me though the heavens fall."

Eugene's initial reaction to his father's death was to get drunk. He had been joined by Agnes at the home of Ella's relatives, the Sheridans, with whom Ella had lived during James's hospitalization. Jamie had been living at the Mohican Hotel in town. To Agnes' discomfiture, Eugene vanished to drown his sorrow, leaving her with his relatives.

Prohibition had theoretically made of New London a dry town, as it had most of the country. Yet it was possible for Eugene, with Jamie's help, to come by bootleg liquor. To the surprise of his relatives, however, he managed to turn up—with Jamie in tow, and only a little late—for his father's funeral on August 12.

James was buried from the Sheridan home and a solemn High Mass, celebrated at St. Joseph's Church, was attended by dozens of his friends, including Edward D. White, Chief Justice of the Supreme Court.

After the coffin was closed, a woman bustled into the church and identified herself as James's sister, Mrs. Platt. She demanded that the coffin be reopened, explaining she had just arrived from St. Louis. Ella, aware that there had been little affection between James and his sister, refused, and after a few moments of embarrassment Mrs. Platt swept out of the church.

James's body was borne to St. Mary's Cemetery, where his infant son, Edmund, and Ella's mother were buried. His pallbearers were members of the Knights of Columbus, under whose auspices James had been dressed for burial in the regalia of the order. Because no representative of The Players was present, Eugene harbored a grudge against the club for many years. On being offered membership in 1933, he declined, saying he could not forgive the club for having ignored his father's death. "My mother was deeply hurt and my brother and I were furious. As well we might be! For my father had been a friend of Booth's, had played with him, and was one of the club's oldest members! You must admit it was a pretty snide, lousy thing to do. Perhaps this will strike you as petty— but it's the way I feel."

(He did, later, accept honorary membership in The Players, after it had been apologetically explained to him that the club's management, responsible for matters of etiquette, had been in transition at the time of his father's death.)

After the funeral Eugene and Jamie went off to continue their drinking. Later that day Eugene showed Art McGinley a royalty check for $1,700 that had just arrived from the Williams office, and offered his friend some of the money.

Ella retired to a room at the Mohican Hotel to be alone, but was soon interrupted by the arrival of the determined Mrs. Platt. This time James's sister inquired after her share of the estate. Ella quickly disposed of her, declaring that James had left everything to his widow.

As a matter of fact James had drawn his will in New London in the summer of 1917, bequeathing to Ella "all of my property, both real and personal . . . to be owned by her absolutely and her heirs forever." There was considerable speculation among Ella's relatives as to why neither Jamie nor Eugene had received a specific bequest; the feeling was that James knew his older son would dissipate any inheritance, and that he wanted to forestall any possibility of Eugene's first wife making a claim on behalf of her son.

James's estate was potentially worth something over $100,000, but nothing like that sum was available in cash and Ella was obliged to set to work liquidating enough property to provide her with an income.

"The treasures of Monte Cristo," O'Neill told a friend, "are buried deep again—in prairie gold mines, in unlubricated oil wells, in fuelless coal lands—in modern Castles in Spain of pure romance."

But Ella approached the job of sorting out James's chaotic affairs with astonishing efficiency and energy. The complicated negotiations in which she found herself involved proved to be a merciful distraction. She had no time for brooding and Eugene observed, with amazement, that she took a keen interest in her business negotiations, accepting her new responsibility with relief and pleasure. Eugene began to think that she might ultimately make James's holdings yield profits that James himself had regarded as lost.

Ella seemed actually to bloom as a widow. Mourning became her—spiritually, as well as physically. (Many years later the image of his mother as a widow came back to O'Neill. "By the title *Mourning Becomes Electra*," he wrote, soon after completing the trilogy in 1931, "I sought to convey that mourning befits Electra; it becomes Electra to mourn; it is her fate; black is becoming to her and it is the color that becomes her destiny.")

Ella had had the aplomb to provide herself, several months before James's death, with an ample wardrobe of widow's weeds, ordered from a Fifth Avenue shop. Her New London relatives, cozily reconciled with her since she had returned to the Church, were now somewhat awed by her. She was more stylish and self-possessed than ever during James's lifetime.

Although she had stopped touching up her hair, and let it go gray where it would, she began using make-up—so subtly that no one could say for sure that she rouged her lips or whitened her skin or shadowed her eyes. She wore a black velvet band around her throat, delicate lace at her bosom, and always chose an appropriate jewel to accentuate the black chic of her gown. Her cousins whispered among themselves that she seemed likely to remarry; Frank Connor, an old friend and brother of James's former manager, was rumored to have proposed.

But Ella did not remarry. She appeared content in her role of widow and executrix of James's estate. She was in and out of litigation with people who tried to sue the estate, busy contacting the far-flung representatives of James's real estate holdings, and liquidating many of his New London investments. Among the first properties she sold—to a bank—was the Monte Cristo cottage.

Ella remained in New London with the Sheridans, and Eugene returned to Provincetown to work, grateful that his mother was being made comfortable. He was so appreciative that she was not to become his problem that he was moved to write the Sheridans, to whom he had never felt close, the sort of letter he knew they would enjoy receiving. He addressed it to Bessie, the unmarried sister. Thanking her for her kindness to him and Agnes, he added, with calculated pathos, that he had never known a home in the sense that the Sheridans had a home. He wished them to "adopt" him, he said, as they had adopted his mother. They would receive a telegram from him one of these days announcing that a couple of cousins were arriving for a visit and asking them to put two more portions of water in the soup. "Now that we've found you again," he concluded, "we don't want to lose you."

In sharp contrast to her demeanor of earlier years, Ella was animated. She laughed a great deal, mostly at Jamie's antics; she spoke with pleasure about the theatre and with affection of the actors who had been James's contemporaries. She talked of Eugene with pride and followed his work with intelligent interest. She seemed, in some ways, to have taken on James's gregarious personality; she even resorted, not flagrantly but not surreptitiously either, to a daily drink or two from a bottle she kept in her room. She regarded this as a healthy stimulant, much as James had done.

Jamie, who stayed at the Mohican Hotel, visited his mother daily. He was overwhelmed by her tansformation into a person of strength and character. Now totally dependent upon her for his every material need, he decided to do what he would never have done for his father. He swore to her and to himself that he would not take another drop of liquor as long as she lived.

XXXV

HIS FATHER'S DEATH DID NOT INTERRUPT THE VIGOR of Eugene O'Neill's creative flow. Within the next three years he completed seven long plays and took a hand in the production of five of these, in addition to the two—*Gold* and *The Straw*—that had been completed earlier.

He wrote three of the seven in Provincetown during less than three months. The first was the completely revised *Chris Christopherson*, now entitled *Anna Christie*; he had promised the play to Tyler and had written it within a few weeks following James O'Neill's funeral. (He decided to keep the new script a secret from Tyler for a while because he didn't want it to interfere with Tyler's production plans for *The Straw*.) The second and third, on which he worked simultaneously in the late summer and early fall of 1920, were *The Emperor Jones* (first called *The Silver Bullet*) and *Diff'rent* (first called *Thirty Years*).

As if in proof of his statement to George Jean Nathan that he would not "stay put in any comfortable niche" the three plays were as disparate in subject matter and treatment as if three different dramatists had written them.

Anna Christie was on the surface a romantic play of the sea, written in a naturalistic style with readily identifiable protagonists, a touching, almost conventional love story, and an almost happy ending. (In four acts, it was the first long play in which O'Neill wrote effective comedy scenes— typically, the comedy was of the barroom variety.)

As O'Neill had rewritten the script, Chris Christopherson was no longer the central character, nor was the principal dramatic conflict Chris's opposition to his daughter's marriage. Rather, O'Neill now focused on the daughter, Anna, as a heroine; he gave her a background of prostitution and brought her into conflict with a stoker named Matt Burke (a substitute for the first mate, Anderson, of *Chris Christopherson*.) Chris was still opposed to his daughter's marriage and his fury at the "old davil sea" was still part of his character—and so was O'Neill's irresolvable problem of how to end the play. Could Matt Burke forgive Anna her past and marry her, and could Anna, though genuinely in love with Matt, really reform? O'Neill believed the play should end in apparent happiness for Anna and

Matt, but he did not want to give the impression that they would really live happily ever after. He could not get this feeling across, though, either to his own satisfaction or to that of George Jean Nathan, to whom he sent the script.

"The devil of it is, I don't see my way out," O'Neill confessed to Nathan. "Anna forced herself on me, middle of third act, at her most theatric. In real life I felt she would unconsciously be compelled, through sheer inarticulateness, to the usual 'big scene,' and wait hopefully for her happy ending. And as she is the only one of the three who knows exactly what she wants, she would get it.

"And the sea outside—life—waits. The happy ending is merely the comma at the end of a gaudy introductory clause, with the body of the sentence still unwritten."

As a matter of fact, he had once thought of calling the play *Comma*. But now he realized he had not made his "comma" clear, and he was going to try a rewrite of the last act which would convey more of a sense of foreboding.

In the meantime he completed *Diff'rent*, a cruel, dry tale of sex repression in New England, also naturalistic in style but unorthodox in subject, and ending somewhat melodramatically. The two-act play had been inspired by his enforced stay in New London during James's illness. Eugene had been brought back into contact with one of his favorites among Ella's relatives, Lil Brennan, and her character and personality provided the point of departure for *Diff'rent*. At that time Lil was in her fifties and unmarried. Other factors, of course, sprang into focus to round out the story, which concerns a pretty girl of twenty in a whaling town in 1890, who conceives the neurotic notion that she and her whaling-captain fiancé are "diff'rent"—set apart from others by an idealistic, sexual purity. The girl, Emma Crosby, discovers that her young man, Caleb, has allowed himself to be seduced by a native girl on his most recent voyage, and she considers this a violation of the ideal and refuses to marry him. The second act takes place thirty years later—in 1920—with Emma a repressed spinster of fifty, encouraging the advances of Caleb's coarse, rascally young nephew, Benny Rogers, while Caleb remains a still-unmarried, hopeful suitor. (The name Rogers crept into the play inadvertently; Lil, herself, had a nephew named *Billy* Rogers.) Caleb hangs himself when he discovers what Emma has become and soon after she follows his example.

O'Neill, who was to draw a gentler picture of Lil in *Ah, Wilderness!* was ahead of his time with Emma Crosby. She was a literary forerunner of Tennessee Williams' nymphomaniac heroine, Blanche Du Bois, and even more closely resembles Alma Winemiller, the sex-starved heroine of Williams' *Summer and Smoke*. Emma reveals her creator's uncanny grasp of the psyche of the neurotic female and its brutal violation.

O'Neill was fond of the play and chose to regard Emma as a universal symbol, although he was emphatic about her having been grounded in fact.

"*Diff'rent*, as I see it, is merely a tale of the eternal, romantic idealist who is in all of us—the eternally defeated one," he wrote soon after finishing the play. "In our innermost hearts we all wish ourselves and others to be 'diff'rent.' We are all more or less 'Emmas' the more or less depending on our talent for compromise. Either we try in desperation to clutch our dream at the last by deluding ourselves with some tawdry substitute; or, having waited the best part of our lives, we find the substitute that time mocks us with too shabby to accept. In either case we are tragic figures, and also fit subjects for the highest comedy, were one sufficiently detached to write it."

O'Neill added that the play was "the truth, the inevitable truth, of the lives of the people in it as I see and know them" and that Emma was "universal only in the sense that she reacts definitely to a definite sex-suppression, as every woman might."

The end was clearly inevitable, he continued. Having refused to accept a compromise, Emma lived on dreams; when the dreams were abruptly shattered, she had nothing more to live for.

"As for Caleb," said O'Neill, "he dies because it is not in him to compromise. He belongs to the old iron school of Nantucket-New Bedford whalemen whose slogan was 'A dead whale or a stove boat.' The whale in this case is transformed suddenly into a malignant Moby Dick who has sounded to depths forever out of reach. Caleb's boat is stove, his quest is ended. He goes with his ship."

While *Diff'rent* has never been considered one of O'Neill's major plays, it is interesting as a forerunner of another study of sex repression in a certain type of New England woman—his much more fully realized Lavinia, in *Mourning Becomes Electra*. O'Neill's interest in this type of woman was heightened and influenced by the Lizzie Borden case. The year in which the first act of *Diff'rent* is set—1890—is only two years earlier than the year that Miss Borden, an allegedly extreme example of the repressed New England spinster, was charged with the hatchet murder of her father and stepmother. Another instance of the Lizzie Borden influence on O'Neill was his use, perhaps unconsciously, of the name, Emma Borden, for one of the townswomen in *Mourning Becomes Electra*.

O'Neill was frequently in contact with the Borden mise en scène during the period when he wrote *Diff'rent*, for his journeys to and from Provincetown were often made via Fall River. Passengers would board the Fall River Line steamer in Manhattan before dinner and arrive at Fall River in the morning. Since the train from there to Provincetown was usually late, O'Neill occasionally had to spend an hour or two in Fall River, where Lizzie Borden still lived. O'Neill and his Provincetown friends sometimes discussed the events that had occurred there in 1892 and pondered whether a woman from a respectable New England family was capable of committing such a cold-blooded crime.

Totally dissimilar to *Diff'rent* in feeling and form was *The Emperor Jones*, which did not reflect O'Neill's absorption either with his own family or with the sea. Written in eight scenes, *The Emperor Jones* was a highly experimental mood play about primitive terror and superstition. A Negro Pullman porter is its unorthodox hero, there is no love story, and the ending is vicious and powerful. Brutus Jones has fled to a tropical island after killing a man in the States. The natives over whom he has set up a despotic rule believe they can kill their "Emperor" only with a silver bullet. They finally revolt and Jones attempts to escape through the jungle, but his own superstitious fears trap him and eventually he is murdered. (In the play O'Neill used two devices with which he had experimented in one-acters—the sustained monologue and the physical presence, on stage, of ghosts that exist only in the fevered imagination of the protagonist.)

"The idea for *Emperor Jones* came from an old circus man I knew," O'Neill said once. "This man, who later was a sparring partner for Jess Willard, had been traveling with a tent show through the West Indies. He told me a story current in Haiti concerning the late President Sam. This was to the effect that Sam had said they'd never get him with a lead bullet; that he would get himself first with a silver one. My friend, by the way, gave me a coin with Sam's features on it, and I still keep it as a pocket piece. This notion about the silver bullet struck me, and I made a note of the story.

"About six months later I got the idea of the woods, but I couldn't see how it could be done on the stage, and I passed it up again. A year elapsed. One day I was reading of the religious feasts in the Congo and the uses to which the drum is put there; how it starts at a normal pulse-beat and is slowly intensified until the heart-beat of every one present corresponds to the frenzied beat of the drum. There was an idea and an experiment. How would this sort of thing work on an audience in a theatre?

"The effect of the tropical forest on the human imagination was honestly come by. It was the result of my own experience while prospecting for gold in Spanish Honduras."

Here, again, is evidence of a blending of the personal past (not only his experience in the jungles of Honduras, but the memory of Adam Scott, the Negro deacon-cum-bartender in New London, supplemented by the personality of O'Neill's Greenwich Village friend Joe Smith, one of whose phrases—"Dey's some tings I ain't got to be tole. I kin see 'em in folks' eyes"—appeared intact in the play), the external present (a casual story told in a bar, fortified by purposeful reading), and the intuitive daring which could translate the pulselike, Congo drumbeat into a theatrical device that would fuse all these elements into a statement of artistic truth.

"I never try to force an idea," O'Neill once told an interviewer, re-affirming what he had told Tyler appropos of *Anna Christie*. "I think about it, off and on. If nothing seems to come of it, I put it away and forget it. But apparently my subconscious mind keeps working on it; for, all of a sudden, some day, it comes back to my mind as a pretty well-formed scheme."

The "old circus man" who had related the story of President Sam was Jack Croak, a friend of Bill Clarke, O'Neill's drinking companion at the Garden Hotel. O'Neill made notes in the memorandum section of the *Bartender's Guide,* which was distributed to favored patrons of the saloon and contained data on how to mix drinks and on major sporting events.

Actually Sam was not the only historical precedent for O'Neill's crea-tion of Emperor Brutus Jones. Another was Henri Christophe, the Negro slave who made himself king of a section of Haiti in 1811 and ruled despotically until he became ill and shot himself in the head. When Guillaume Sam took over the presidency of Haiti in 1915, he too ruled with a bloody hand. Sam was finally hacked to pieces by a voodoo-maddened mob.

Examining his *Bartender's Guide* notes, O'Neill began elaborating on the story. At this point he visited William Zorach and his wife in Province-town to study a rare book they had recently acquired, which contained photographs of African woodcarvings and masks. In developing Brutus Jones, O'Neill conceived of him as an American Pullman porter who mur-dered a companion in a dice game, went to jail, and killed a white guard who taunted him. To find out how Jones would manage to free himself of the leg fetters he wore as a member of a chain gang, O'Neill did not need to consult books or penal authorities; among his mixed circle of friends there happened to be a former member of a chain gang.

"I thought we lived in a free country, and a seventeen-year-old kid

[439]

could go from state to state looking for work," Slim Martin had told O'Neill early in their acquaintance. "Well, I got arrested for vagrancy—carrying concealed ideas, I guess—and I found work, all right. Sixty-eight days on a chain gang in the South, using a pick and shovel from sunup to sundown."

Slim knew exactly how a convict went about ridding himself of leg fetters.

"You can saw through the chain with a hack-saw blade," Slim explained to O'Neill. "But you can also slip the fetter off if you file off the head of the toggle on which the oval-shaped metal cuff is hinged. After filing, you put the fetter solidly against a big stone and hit it with something heavy; this springs the cuff into a more circular shape, and then you can ease it over ankles and feet." O'Neill did not find it necessary to use such detail in the play; it was sufficient to know that Brutus Jones could have freed himself of his fetters and chains.

When O'Neill finally got down to writing his drama, he wrote in minuscule penciled script, cramming the entire play onto both sides of three sheets of typewriting paper.

"This sounds impossible," he later wrote to a representative of the American Academy of Arts and Letters, to whom he was about to send the original manuscript for exhibit, "but it's all there on those few pages, and when you see the handwriting you will believe it."

The Emperor Jones was not quite a full-length play. Because of its brevity and experimental nature, it was earmarked not for Broadway but for the Provincetown Players. Carp as he might about the physical inadequacies of the downtown productions, O'Neill could count on one thing from the Provincetown group that he failed to receive from his Broadway managers: immediate and wholeheartedly enthusiastic production. And for once there was to be a production of an O'Neill play that was close to artistic perfection. *The Emperor Jones* brought Jig Cook out of temporary retirement on Cape Cod and back to MacDougal Street.

"One day . . . Jig and I walked across the dunes to the O'Neills'," Susan Glaspell once wrote. "We were having the big storm with which we often close August on the Cape, and it was a thrilling struggle getting from the town . . . to the abandoned life-saving station on the outside shore . . .

"We had come because Gene had a play to read to us. . . . He used to speak of it as 'The Silver Bullet,' but at dinner that night he told us he wanted to call it 'The Emperor Jones.' Before the cheerful logs in a room where life-boats had swung Gene read us his new play."

Even in O'Neill's halting, low, unmusical voice the monologue of terror mounted with almost unbearable tension. The Cooks sat enthralled, visualizing Brutus Jones, his self-reliance and pride peeling bit by bit, his splendid uniform being torn from his body as he stumbled and clawed his way through the primeval forest; the ever-quickening beat of the voodoo drum, as his crazed subjects crouched and danced in the hills, waiting for their victim to lose his way so they could entrap him; his waste of ammunition on the apparitions that loomed out of the forest; his firing of his final bullet—the silver one—at a nonexistent monster; and his death at the hands of the superstitious natives, who had molded silver bullets with which to kill him.

Jig Cook tackled the script with a frenzy he had never before displayed.

"This marks the success of the Provincetown Players," he told his wife, prophetically. "Gene knew there was a place where such a play would be produced. He wrote it to *compel* us to the untried, to the 'impossible.' "

Deciding that *The Emperor Jones* would open the Provincetown Players' new season, Cook left immediately for New York. The production could only be mounted, Cook believed, against a sky dome to imbue the jungle scenes with a sense of depth and space; the play began with thick forest, gradually thinning out to what Cook thought of as a "pure space."

The dome envisaged by Cook to give the stage a sense of infinity had already been experimented with in Europe but would be the first of its kind in a New York theatre. Unlike a cloth cyclorama, Cook's dome—to be fashioned from iron and concrete—would not wrinkle, would not move when accidentally touched, and would radiate light in all directions instead of absorbing it. Cook realized that such a dome would cost a minimum of $500—nearly the total resources of the treasury—but he was determined to have it. The play would be done properly, Cook promised. Moreover, he would also produce *Diff'rent* that season.

At this point there were five completed plays by O'Neill awaiting production. He was sure of seeing *The Emperor Jones* and *Diff'rent* on a stage within a few months. As for *Anna Christie, The Straw* and *Gold*—there was still no definite word. O'Neill, in Provincetown, decided to get back in touch with Tyler, toward whom he was beginning to feel guilty.

On October 4, 1920, he sent the producer an apologetic letter, pleading worry and nervous tension during the previous spring and asking Tyler to forgive his peevishness over *The Straw* and *Chris*. His comments of last spring, wrote O'Neill, had been "merely childish outbursts" of which he was now ashamed. He asked Tyler for "another chance."

A week later, having been assured that Tyler still wanted to produce

The Straw, O'Neill tried his best to be agreeable.

". . . please don't think I am prejudiced against Miss Hayes for the lead," he wrote, doing an astonishing turnabout. "I know too little of her work to dare take any such stand—and what I do know is very favorable to her."

And on October 24, a few days after reading the good notices Helen Hayes had received in *Bab* on Broadway, he congratulated Tyler on the play's success and said that he was "not glad to lose Miss Hayes for 'The Straw,'" which, he gathered, was what was going to happen as a result of her success in *Bab.* He then suggested, very politely, that either Helen MacKellar or Laurette Taylor might do for the role of Eileen, but implied that it was all in Tyler's hands. To prove that he thought highly of Tyler's taste and judgment, he took him into his confidence about his new work for the Provincetown Players.

"[They] are promising to bloom forth this year with a renewal of their old spirit of adventure into new fields," he wrote. "I have what I consider a very unique piece of drama going on their opening bill—*The Emperor Jones.*"

He urged Tyler to "drop down and see it," and ended his letter with renewed assurance of "all kindest regards." For the moment, at least, though plans for the future were still vague, Tyler and O'Neill had reestablished a potentially harmonious working relationship.

During the latter part of October O'Neill was stunned to learn of the sudden death of John Reed. Only thirty-three years old, Reed died of typhus in Russia on October 17. Though O'Neill had been out of touch with him for a time he had closely followed Reed's activities.

Reed had returned to the United States a few months after Louise, in April, 1918, and been tried—with Max Eastman, Floyd Dell and others—for "subversive activities" on behalf of *The Masses.* The case was finally dismissed, but Reed, still agitating for the radical cause, had become persona non grata. In March of 1919 the Provincetown Players presented his sketch, *The Peace that Passeth Understanding.* A satire on the Paris peace conference, it was played by actors concealed behind masks of Woodrow Wilson, Lloyd George and Clemenceau; the names of the masked actors were withheld.

By now a fanatically committed bolshevik, Reed outspokenly was rooting for revolution in America. When he moved to a house in Croton, New York, and tried to write a report of the Russian Revolution, he was frustrated by federal agents, who had seized his papers and notes and were reluctant to release them. Through the intervention of influential friends, he finally obtained his notes and wrote his book, *Ten Days that Shook the World.*

Published in 1919 by Boni and Liveright, the book was warmly endorsed by Lenin. The endorsement did not help Reed's reputation at home, and when he determined to attend the Communist International in Russia he was unable to obtain a passport and had to smuggle himself out of the country as a ship's stoker, leaving Louise behind. When he was later indicted in the United States for his radical activities he tried to leave Russia to stand trial boldly—and dispense some bolshevik propaganda—but now he found it as difficult to return home as it had been to leave. He was arrested in Finland on some sort of technicality and languished in jail for more than three months until friends secured his release and helped him get back to Moscow.

Louise, also denied a passport, left America illegally, as Reed had done, and managed to join him in Russia. When she met him in Moscow she found him looking older and sadder, with a gentleness she had never seen in him before. He was dressed in rags, was undernourished, and so painfully conscious of the suffering around him that he had lost all interest in his own well-being. When he became ill of typhus he did not have the stamina to get well and, although Lenin himself ordered Reed placed in the best hospital in Moscow, he died after two weeks, with Louise at his bedside.

Reed's body lay in state in the Labor Temple for a week. In a letter to Reed's mother, Louise wrote: "He will be buried in the most honored spot in Russia, beside all the great heroes in the Kremlin. . . . The Russians have been very kind to me. They have spared no effort to make things easier for me. And they loved Jack greatly."

Yet at the funeral no such kindness was manifest, and both Reed and Louise were pitiful, rather than heroic, figures in the eyes of their friends in America. O'Neill, though he had lost interest in politics and could not sympathize with Reed's fanaticism, brooded when he read about the funeral in a clipping from *The New York Times* which a friend mailed to him in Provincetown:

"A large crowd assembled, and the occasion was one for speeches. There were speeches in English, French and Russian. A mixture of rain and snow was falling. Although the poor widow fainted, her friends did not take her away. It was extremely painful to see this white-faced, unconscious woman lying back on the supporting arm of an official who was more interested in speeches than in human agony. The faces of the crowd around betrayed neither sympathy nor interest. They looked on unmoved."

◈

Before the end of October O'Neill was drawn into hectic preparation for *The Emperor Jones,* on which Jig Cook had already been working several weeks.

"Again Jig slept in the theatre for a month to save for the dome," Edna Kenton later noted. "We listened to Jig, truly a madman, telling us over and over again that we must risk our all and put in the dome for *The Emperor.* None of us had read the script yet; we took it on faith as Gene's best play. But we said, all of us, that the dome couldn't go in—not yet. We suggested putting off *The Emperor* to the second bill or the third; whenever we said that Jig never failed to pick up his hat and walk out."

After a while he would return, pleading, "We *have* to do this." And then he would go away again.

When Edna Kenton had not heard from Cook for a day following the last such departure, she began to worry. She went to the theatre to ask Fitzi if O'Neill's script had arrived from Provincetown, and was told it had not. She asked if subscriptions were coming in, and was told they were not. Then Fitzi groaned, "What Jig hasn't done!" and told Edna Kenton to go into the theatre and see for herself what was going on.

"Jig was there alone, at the back of the stage, in a clutter of steel netting, iron bars and bags of cement," she recalled. "He was making plaster, in workman's clothes. In spite of all, the dome was going in. Jig's 'must' had found its only way."

"There's to be no argument about this," said Cook, as Edna Kenton watched him silently. "I've had enough from everybody. The Emperor has *got* to have a dome to play against." And he explained and outlined the play that Edna had not yet read.

"And as he went on," she related, "it began to happen—one of his hours of creative talk of the rarest and finest. Many, many times I was to see that play that made Gene O'Neill famous, played against the dome downtown, against wrinkled cycloramas uptown, in theatres large and small, with different casts and under all sorts of direction. But I was never to see it so clearly as it played itself that morning in the dim little theatre, with no voice but one, no audience but one. From the little Formless Fears to the Crocodile god, the figures emerged and moved in relation to all their scenic values, and against the rough unfinished plaster dome the experimental eight-scene play that was all but monologue acted itself out."

The Players, who had thought Cook madly extravagant in his conception of the dome, began to congratulate him. The dome, it developed, could be put to spectacular use. Viewers seated three feet from the stage had the illusion of vast distance; an actor could stretch his hand to within inches of its plaster surface and still seem to be far away from it. As a result, the sets for *The Emperor Jones* had to be scrapped or redesigned and simpler ones substituted. Cleon Throckmorton arrived at Cook's request to help remodel the sets and remained as designer for the theatre.

Cook, who took charge of the direction, found no casting problems except for the title role. The part of the Cockney trader, Smithers, with the longest speeches among the minor characters, was filled by Jasper Deeter. The roles of various natives, spirits and ghost-prisoners were played by such members of the group as Charles Ellis, Christine Ell and Slim Martin, who blacked their bodies as required. (Slim tripled as a native soldier, a prison guard and a slave.)

But Brutus Jones was a problem, and there is some dispute as to how it was resolved. There are people who recall that Cook was determined from the beginning to cast a Negro in the role—a decision that, as little as five years later, would probably have been an automatic one. But in 1920 no Negro had ever played a major role in an American tragedy, and Jasper Deeter has maintained that Cook at first thought Charles Ellis should undertake the part, playing it in black face. O'Neill, Deeter said, raised no objection to this.

"I was the one who insisted that a Negro play Jones," Deeter added, "and Jimmy Light agreed with me."

Interest focused on Charles S. Gilpin, a Negro who had recently earned some notice on Broadway in a small role in John Drinkwater's *Abraham Lincoln*. Gilpin worked at odd jobs when he could not find an acting role, and the Provincetowners had no idea where he could be located. According to some, Cook found him running an elevator; others are convinced that Cook found him clipping tickets on the Sixth Avenue el. In any case, he was hustled down to the Playwrights' Theatre and a script was thrust into his hands. He read the part superbly.

Gilpin, at forty-one, was handsome, broad-chested, muscular and sad-eyed. The youngest of fourteen children, he was raised in Richmond, Virginia, where he had felt the sting of race prejudice and become embittered by it. His mother was a trained nurse in a Richmond hospital, his father an employee of a steel rolling mill. Articulate, charming, hypersensitive and unstable, Gilpin had worked as an elevator operator, compositor, barbershop porter and, like Brutus Jones, as a Pullman porter. He had acted in vaudeville and with Negro stock companies until 1919, when he won the part of William Curtis, an elderly servant, in *Abraham Lincoln*.

Into the flurry of rehearsals and set building one day came an admirer of the Provincetown Players, Charlie Chaplin. who had already achieved international fame. According to James Light, Chaplin attended a rehearsal of *Jones* and told Cook he would like to play one of the ghost-convicts under an assumed name. The Players thought this was fine, until someone raised the point—more than likely it was O'Neill—that if the news ever leaked about Chaplin's being in the cast, audiences would look for him and disregard the play. Chaplin ruefully bowed out.

O'Neill paid a couple of flying visits to the theatre, watched a rehearsal or two—one whole day was devoted to getting the drumbeat right—expressed his approval of the production, and hurried nervously back to Provincetown. He did not attend the opening night.

Since *Jones* was not full-length, the Provincetowners needed a curtain raiser, and they chose a slight comedy written by Lawrence Langner, called *Matinata*.

In explanation of the oblivion to which his play was relegated after opening night, Langner once observed that it "went off well," but that "all remembrance of my fragile curtain raiser was buried in the avalanche of applause for O'Neill's masterpiece."

An avalanche of applause accurately describes the reaction to *The Emperor Jones* on opening night. The Provincetown Players soon found themselves all but smothered with praise and requests for tickets. With their subscription list rising to 1,500 within a few days, they were no longer in financial difficulties.

The play was not reviewed by the major critics on opening night—which was November 1.

Kenneth Macgowan, then reviewing for the *Globe* and soon to become one of O'Neill's closest friends, said that he, himself, "instinctively" remembered the production as "a tumultuously exciting first night—yet, as a matter of cold fact, the New York critics didn't discover it till the third night." Two plays—*Just Suppose*, with Leslie Howard and Patricia Collinge, and *The Prince and the Pauper*, with Claire Eames and William Faversham—and a musical called *The Half Moon* opened on Broadway the evening of November 1, and the first-string critics were busy uptown.

When they finally got down to MacDougal Street they were stunned. (They might have been even more so had they known that the entire production cost about $600 and that the highest weekly salary—which went to Gilpin—was $50.)

"Eugene O'Neill's 'The Emperor Jones' seems to us just about the most interesting play which has yet come from the most promising playwright in America," wrote Heywood Broun for the *Tribune*. " 'The Emperor Jones' is so unusual in its technique that it might wait in vain for a production anywhere except in so adventurous a playhouse as the Provincetown Theatre. As a matter of fact, the setting of the play on the little stage is fine and imaginative and the lighting effects uncommonly beautiful. . . . The Emperor is played by a Negro actor named Charles S. Gilpin, who gives the most thrilling performance we have seen any place this season. . . . It is a performance of heroic stature."

Alexander Woollcott, whose review did not appear in *The Times* until November 7, hailed the play as "an extraordinarily striking and dramatic study of panic fear."

"It reinforces the impression that for strength and originality [O'Neill] has no rival among the American writers for the stage," Woollcott continued, though he immediately began snarling about the production, which he found clumsy because it consisted "largely of long, unventilated intermissions interspersed with fragmentary scenes." Woollcott, too, had high praise for Gilpin.

Kenneth Macgowan, expanding his newspaper review for the magazine *Theatre Arts,* which in January of 1921 published the full script of *The Emperor Jones,* wrote: "These eight short scenes shake free from the traditional forms of our drama; they carry forward easily and honestly upon the track of discovery. We follow a path that gathers bit by bit the progressive steps in a study of personal and racial psychology of real imaginative truth."

The Emperor Jones brought the Provincetown Players their first real recognition from Broadway audiences and managers. It also thrust them into national prominence—and, soon after, it destroyed them. They were to last only one more season, finished by success. Dedicated to experiment and the freedom of amateurism, they could not survive fame and professionalism.

There were many offers from managers to present a version of *Jones* uptown. A number of the Provincetown Players endorsed the idea but thought the casting should be done with Broadway actors. The majority, however, believed that The Players should actively participate in the Broadway production and share in the box-office receipts. It was an opportunity to make money for the first time. In the end The Players, as participating producers, allowed Adolph Klauber to move the original production uptown, depleting their supply of actors for the next bill downtown, dispersing their concentration on the Playwrights' Theatre, and courting all the headaches and problems of the amateur-turned-professional-too-soon.

Jig Cook went back to the Cape, distressed over the decision, his pride in the production of *Jones* tempered by uneasiness, even by a stirring of jealousy. He felt that O'Neill, whom he had launched and nourished, was getting too big for The Players, and he began to blame O'Neill for tearing down the painfully laid foundation of his experimental theatre.

The Emperor Jones opened on Broadway with special matinees at the Selwyn Theatre on December 27—the same day that the Playwrights' Theatre presented *Diff'rent*. The popularity of *Jones* later led to a regular run at the Princess Theatre, where it arrived on January 29, 1921. The engagement lasted for 204 performances, a spectacularly long run for those days, and then the production began a road tour that was to continue for two years.

Gilpin stayed with the play and continued to be praised and interviewed. And O'Neill, as late as 1946, voiced his admiration of Gilpin's performance:

"As I look back now on all my work," he said, "I can honestly say there was only one actor who carried out every notion of a character I had in mind. That actor was Charles Gilpin as the Pullman porter in *The Emperor Jones.*"

Gilpin was grateful to O'Neill, but aware that his newly acquired stature might be short-lived.

"I am pleased," he said, "especially with the generous praise of the critics. But I don't fool myself about the stone walls that are in my way. Mr. O'Neill made a breach in those walls by writing a play that had in it a serious role for a Negro. The Provincetown Players gave me the chance to do the part. But—what next? If I were white, a dozen opportunities would come to me as a result of a success like this. But I'm black. It is no joke when I ask myself, 'Where do I go from here?'

"Whatever happens, I shall have some evidence to prove that I was not a fool in thinking that a Negro can act. . . . It has been demonstrated that a play can be written that will give a colored actor a chance. Perhaps someone will write another such play. Anyway, if I can't get anything else to play, I suppose I can at least 'play the game.' After all, that's what everyone has to do, one way or another."

Gilpin bumped into one of the stone walls he had mentioned soon after *The Emperor Jones* moved uptown. He was invited, along with several other actors, to be an "honored guest" of the Drama League's annual dinner. A number of the League's members protested at being asked to dine with a Negro, and the League, in some embarrassment, withdrew the invitation to Gilpin.

O'Neill was furious. In spite of his painful shyness, he paid calls, accompanied by Kenneth Macgowan, on most of the other actors who had been invited to the dinner, and asked them to decline their invitations.

One of the actors on whom he called was Jacob Ben-Ami, a Yiddish Art Theatre star, who made his debut on the English-speaking stage a few weeks after *Jones* opened. His performance in Sven Lange's *Samson and Delilah* had been hailed by the critics, and he was invited to be one of the Drama League's guests of honor. But he was not aware of the League's action against Gilpin until O'Neill and Macgowan visited him backstage.

"It was the first time I met O'Neill," Ben-Ami later recalled. "Macgowan did most of the talking, but it was easy to see that O'Neill was terribly intense and hurt by the situation. They explained what had happened, and asked me to decline my own invitation. I said that I would, of course, and I believe that all the other actors they visited did the same."

The result was that Gilpin was reinvited, and the Drama League dinner was a great success—with a thousand guests attending, compared with the previous year's three hundred.

But, though he fought for Gilpin's rights, O'Neill could not help being petty toward him personally at times. As the run of *Jones* continued through 1921, Gilpin began to show himself less and less willing to "play the game"; his behavior became erratic, and O'Neill was incensed.

O'Neill complained that Gilpin, who had grown suddenly finicky about using the word "nigger" (called for by the script), was rewriting the role. Aware that Gilpin was substituting "black baby" and other terms he considered less pejorative, O'Neill was also annoyed by the fact that Gilpin was doing too much drinking to give an effective performance. He went backstage one night and warned his star:

"If I ever catch you rewriting my lines again, you black bastard, I'm going to beat you up."

As a result of Gilpin's behavior, he was not asked to play Brutus Jones in the English production, nor to appear in the New York revival in 1925.

"Yes, Gilpin is all 'Ham' and a yard wide!" O'Neill informed Mike Gold. "Honestly, I've stood for more from him than from all the white actors I've ever known—simply because he was colored! He played Emperor with author, play and everyone concerned. There is humor in the situation but I confess mine has worn out. I'm 'off' him and the result is he will get no chance to do it in London. He was drunk all of last season. . . . So I've corralled a young fellow with considerable experience, wonderful presence and voice, full of ambition and a damn fine man personally with real brains—not a 'ham.' This guy deserves his chance and I don't believe he'll lose his head if he makes a hit—as he surely will, for he's read the play for me and I'm sure he'll be bigger than Gilpin was even at the start."

O'Neill's find was Paul Robeson, a brilliant Columbia Law School graduate who had abandoned a legal career for the stage. O'Neill was right about Robeson personally but he failed to realize that the less intelligent "ham" is quite often the superior actor; his vindictiveness toward actors was so intense that he couldn't be detached. "[Gilpin] is just a regular actor-brain, that's all," he wrote to Gold petulantly. "Most white actors, under the same circumstances, would have gone the same route. The point is, none of them would have *dared* go so far. Gilpin lived under the assumption that no one could be got to play his part and took advantage accordingly."

Robeson, though he gave an excellent performance, was not up to Gilpin in the role of Brutus Jones. Gilpin himself realized this, and was heartbroken. According to Slim Martin, Gilpin visited New York in 1925 from his farm in Trenton, New Jersey, where he was living in semiretirement, to see Robeson in the role. Slim caught up with Gilpin as he was leaving the theatre.

"How's tricks, Charlie?" asked Slim, putting an arm around his shoulder. "Come and have a drink."

"No, Slim," answered Gilpin. "I feel kind of low. I created the role of the Emperor. That role belongs to me. That Irishman, he just wrote the play." He paused to brood, then went on, "I'm used to money, now. I need money. I can't go on living on that farm."

Gilpin never played another major role in New York. He died on his farm five years later, at the age of fifty-one.

XXXVI

PRODUCTION CHORES FOR THE DOWNTOWN OPENINGS
of *The Emperor Jones* and *Diff'rent* kept O'Neill running in and out of
New York between November 1 and December 27, 1920. The anticipated
uptown productions of *The Straw* and *Gold* had still failed to materialize.
Tyler would not be pinned down about the former and Williams avoided
discussion of the latter. And as late as December 9, O'Neill had still not
heard whether Tyler liked *Anna Christie*, the rewritten script O'Neill
had mailed to him several weeks before. O'Neill had, however, heard
from Tyler's publicity man, Jack Toohey, who wrote that *he* liked the
new script, particularly the new character, Matt Burke. "I'm quite stuck
on him myself," O'Neill replied.

Tyler, apparently stalling for time, had suggested that O'Neill write
him a new version of *The Count of Monte Cristo*. O'Neill did not greet
this proposal with enthusiasm.

"I have a sort of grudge against that play—perhaps because I once had
to act in the tabloid vaudeville version," O'Neill informed Tyler.

That December, however, the idea of a new *Monte Cristo* began to
have some strange fascination for him and he seriously weighed the possibilities of modernizing and humanizing the count. He dropped the plan,
however, and did not consider it again until four years later, when another Broadway producer, Arthur Hopkins, asked him to turn *Monte
Cristo* into a vehicle for William Farnum. At that time he badly needed
money.

But it was probably less the money than the possibility of laying
to rest the ghost of James O'Neill that beguiled him. Even after the
Hopkins plan had come to nothing, O'Neill was still haunted by the
idea of bringing back *Monte Cristo*. In answer to an interviewer who
wondered what influence his early travels with his father had on his
writing career, O'Neill said:

"I suppose if one accepts the song and dance complete of the psychoanalysts, it is perfectly natural that having been brought up around the
old conventional theatre, and having identified it with my father, I should
rebel and go in a new direction.

"I think it would be quite amusing, however, to revive *Monte Cristo* sometime because, as I look back upon all the old romantic melodramas, that was the best, and I should say that Bill Farnum is probably the present-day actor most fitted to play my father's part." (O'Neill did not mention that he possessed a print of the film version his father had made of *Monte Cristo*, which, though he never looked at it, seemed to give him satisfaction to own.)

But late in 1920 O'Neill had more pressing problems. Tyler still had no definite plans to produce *The Straw*, Williams was still being evasive about *Gold*—and now Tyler informed him that while *Anna Christie* was an improvement over *Chris*, it was still overwritten. O'Neill grumbled that if one of his plays was not produced soon, he would "have to give up writing for the time and go in for plumbing or some other more lucrative trade." He had been reduced, he said, to having to ask the Provincetown Players for "a mite of royalty per week on *Jones*—something I have never done before—in order to keep going." He added that if *Jones* caught on uptown, things would be easier for him.

Jones did begin to make money for him soon, and O'Neill felt able to underwrite a fairly protracted visit to New York. He looked in on rehearsals of *Diff'rent*, but not until a couple of days before the opening.

The director was Charles O'Brien Kennedy, a professional actor imported from uptown. A quiet, gentle Irishman ten years O'Neill's senior, who had played with John Barrymore in *Redemption* and with both John and Lionel Barrymore in *The Jest*, Kennedy was then appearing in the Sam Harris production of *Little Old New York*. Teddy Ballantine, who had acted with him, had invited him to direct *Diff'rent*.

In accepting the offer, Kennedy told Ballantine he had met O'Neill several times and had been a friend of O'Neill's father.

"The first time I met Gene," Kennedy said, "was in 1909, shortly before he went to Honduras. It was in the old Green Room Club. He was sitting at a table with his father, and I was struck by his dark eyes."

Kennedy was with Aubrey Boucicault, the actor-brother of Dion. Boucicault asked James, "Is this your elder son?" "No," said James, "he's my younger, and I'm sending him on a long trip, to get him away from the theatre."

Kennedy had no idea, at the time, that Eugene was married and was being removed by his father not from the theatre but from a wife. The next time Kennedy saw Eugene was shortly before James's death. They met accidentally at a speakeasy called Geneva Hall, situated across the street from The Lambs, the actors' club of which Kennedy was a member. As they were quietly having a drink, the place was raided.

"Don't you people move!" ordered the police lieutenant, in the best tradition of the twenties. Kennedy happened to know the lieutenant.

"This boy I have with me is the son of James O'Neill," Kennedy whispered to him conspiratorially. "Do you mind if we sneak out?"

"Monte Cristo's boy?" murmured the policeman, and obligingly turned his back. Kennedy hustled Eugene across the street to The Lambs, where they found a bottle and finished their party.

When Kennedy took over the direction of *Diff'rent*, he brought with him the rigid standards of Broadway. He had been given to understand that O'Neill wanted a professional hand and at his first rehearsal he laid down the law.

"Anyone who hasn't reported by ten o'clock in the morning needn't show up at all," he warned his cast. They responded by being on time and working hard. When O'Neill finally appeared, at a dress rehearsal, he was amazed by the professional aspect of the production. He sat silent at the back of the theatre until the rehearsal was over, and as Kennedy walked up the aisle, he put out a hand to stop him.

"Where can we go for a drink?" O'Neill asked. They went to Paterno's, at Third and MacDougal Streets and talked about the play over a couple of beers.

O'Neill had only one suggestion to make about the direction and Kennedy overruled him. The suggestion was that the line, "But you're diff'rent," repeated, with variations throughout the first act ("I look on you as diff'rent," "Promise me to stay diff'rent," "I'm diff'rent," "He'd ought to have acted diff'rent," "Her and me just looks at things diff'rent," "You git to feel diff'rent," "They're diff'rent," "It's all diff'rent," "I ain't diff'rent," etc.) should always be read in the same uninflected tone, regardless of who was delivering the line or what its context. There are at least twenty variants of this phrase in the first act, and O'Neill was, conceivably, trying to achieve an effect comparable to that of the hypnotic drumbeat of *The Emperor Jones*.

Kennedy told O'Neill it wouldn't do. By the time the third "diff'rent" had been delivered in the same tone of voice, he explained, the audience would be tittering.

"Gene understood, and didn't insist," Kennedy said. "That was the beginning of a friendship."

Later the friendship was solidified by their common affection for a remarkable woman. She was Lena Comminsky, Emma Goldman's sister and Teddy Ballantine's mother-in-law. On separate occasions both O'Neill and Kennedy had stayed at her house while her son, Saxe Commins, then practicing dentistry, attended to their teeth.

O'Neill, whose former subsistence on a sailor's diet had permanently impaired his teeth, went to Rochester, New York, where the Comminskys lived and where Commins maintained his office. Commins treated O'Neill free of charge and put him up in his home.

"Saxe once filled a tooth for me," Kennedy later recalled. "He did a very good job, but his heart wasn't in his work. He had the art bug. He used to go to New York whenever a new play of Gene's was put on.

"I never stayed overnight at the house in Rochester, but Saxe would invite me to have dinner there whenever I came through with a show."

Mrs. Comminsky was then in her fifties, tiny and energetic. She and her husband, a tinsmith, were free-thinking Jews. One of Mrs. Comminsky's passions was feeding people, and she was determined to fatten up both Kennedy and O'Neill.

"Mrs. Comminsky would hover over me and say, 'You must eat, you must eat. I tell Gene O'Neill to eat, too. You don't eat enough,'" Kennedy continued. "She was a warm Jewish mother. I used to tell Saxe and his sister, Stella Ballantine, that their mother made me feel as though I was seven years old."

O'Neill once told Stella: "If I had a wife like your mother everything would be fine."

Lena Comminsky and her husband made their own wine.

"When Mrs. Comminsky asked me to taste her wine, I always asked Mr. Comminsky if I could taste his, too," Kennedy said. "They were jealous of each other's product and would have been terribly insulted if I hadn't taken some from each. Gene felt as warm toward them as I did. When he stayed there, he would make his own bed in the morning, so as not to burden Saxe's mother."

The opening of *Diff'rent* on December 27, like that of *Jones*, introduced an exciting new acting talent. She was Mary Blair, one of the first graduates of the Carnegie Institute of Technology Drama School, whom Kennedy cast in the difficult role of Emma Crosby. (Caleb was played by James Light and Benny by Charles Ellis; Cleon Throckmorton designed the set.)

Edmund Wilson, whom she later married, said that Mary Blair "really made the success" of *Diff'rent*. He saw her for the first time in that play and remembered her as "extraordinary." Alexander Woollcott described her acting in *Diff'rent* as excellent, and other critics marveled at the versatility she demonstrated in transforming herself from the sedate, twenty-year-old maiden in the first act to the frumpy spinster of fifty in the second.

There was some dispute as to the merit of the play itself. But Woollcott thought it illustrated "as well as any [O'Neill play] why each as it comes along stands out as an event in the dramatic year."

Kennedy received no credit from the critics, despite his professional standing. The day of recognition for the director as a specific and major factor in a production had not yet arrived; although the status of the man who "staged" the play had risen somewhat above that of stage manager (as in the days when Belasco threw together *The Passion* in San Francisco), plays were still being reviewed as though they were the product of a kind of spontaneous collaboration between author and actors—with an occasional pat on the head for the producer. Reviews that listed the cast of the play in detail and acknowledged the author and producer, rarely, if ever, carried the phrase, "Directed by————." Even scenic designers had begun to come into their own by this time, largely because of the imaginative pioneer work of Robert Edmond Jones. But there was no one remotely comparable in prestige or artistic recognition to the directors of later decades. As a rule, the general public was unaware that any such person as a director was even necessary to a production, and for the most part author, actors and managers were inclined to agree. The man who directed the play was usually either the producer, the leading actor, or less frequently, the author; quite often the play was directed by a combination of all three.

But if Kennedy did not share in the praise of *Diff'rent*, he was also spared the disparagement of those critics who believed it presented a distorted and untrue picture of life. O'Neill was moved to anwer his critics publicly, in a newspaper statement:

"There are objections to the play as pathological, but I protest that is putting the accent where none was intended, where only contributing circumstances were meant. And someone has said to me that all the people in the play were either degenerates or roughs—at which I was properly stunned, because I consider all of the characters, with the exception of Benny, to be perfectly regular human beings even as you and I. Dividing folks into moral castes has never been one of my favorite occupations.

"And then there was someone, I have heard, who attributed to the author Caleb's remark that 'folks be all crazy and rotten to the core.' Upon which I . . . inquire pipingly whether it was [Shakespeare] or Macbeth who said 'It is a tale told by an idiot, full of sound and fury, signifying nothing.' "

To a friend O'Neill added privately, "I honestly believe *Diff'rent* to be, in a great many ways, the best thing I have done." (It was at least the sixth play on which he had bestowed this appraisal.) And to Nathan he confided, apropos of the attacks on the play, "Well, this is rather reassuring. I had begun to think I was too popular to be honest; but this sort of spanking convinces me that, right or wrong, I am right." To another friend, he spoke of his appreciation of Kennedy's service to the play, pointing out that it was all due to Kennedy that the acting and production had been well above the Provincetown Players average.

Diff'rent was moved uptown on February 4, where it played matinees at the Princess Theatre while *The Emperor Jones* continued to play there in the evening.

When O'Neill visited New York for rehearsals he often left Agnes behind in Provincetown, mainly to save on expenses. But he always wrote to her lovingly, telling of his loneliness. He was uneasy in New York and clung gratefully to anyone who showed him sympathy. During rehearsals of *Diff'rent* he struck up a shy friendship with a petite, attractive actress who was understudy to Mary Blair and appeared in the curtain raiser for *Diff'rent*—a play called *What D'You Want,* by Lawrence Vail. She was Jeanie Begg, who had played a small role in *The Emperor Jones* and was to act with The Players in several other O'Neill productions, including a revival of *The Moon of the Caribbees.*

"I used to sit in the theatre watching rehearsals," she later recalled, "and several times Gene moved over next to me, and even took my hand and held it as we sat there. We were both shy, and I never got to know him well. We didn't talk much, as I recall. What could I, a stupid little girl just out of college, have to say to him!"

Many years later Charles Kennedy, who had kept in touch with Jeanie Begg, asked O'Neill to autograph a copy of *The Iceman Cometh* to her; he thought she would be pleased to have the inscribed book. O'Neill was delighted to oblige. He said to Kennedy, "You know, I had a crush on Jeanie once." On the flyleaf of *The Iceman Commeth* he wrote:

"To Jeanie: With many fond memories of the past and the gal who did so much to make 'The Moon of the Caribbees' beautiful! (By the way, I have some photos of you and Teddy B. in that old production.) Good luck, Jeanie, and always my affectionate good wishes.

"As ever, Gene."

When *Diff'rent* opened, Prohibition had been in effect in New York for over a year; January, 1920, was the year of jazz, the speakeasy and the lost generation; it was the heyday of gangsterism, and the renaissance of Negro art and entertainment as suddenly "discovered" in Harlem by white New Yorkers.

But O'Neill was as remote from the upheaval taking place around him as he once had been from the clamor of the war; he became a symbol and a representative of the era, but not in the same way as other contemporary writers. His work did not reflect the times but continued to be a supremely individual expression of his inner preoccupation with timeless themes. And he remained socially detached, as well.

Not the least of O'Neill's frustrations was the fact that the practice of his art required periodic emergence from the cloistered existence he preferred. He always felt that had he been able to express himself as a novelist rather than as a dramatist he would have been spared the continuous contacts with a world that unsettled him. He would have liked to write in a vacuum, without the inconvenient mechanical necessities of stage production.

Fighting and running, he spent his resented time in New York with those of his friends who had the least contact with the established world of art. He avoided the uptown speakeasies and rarely attended parties— though he did go to one where he met Scott Fitzgerald, who enchanted him. As a rule, O'Neill saw only those people willing to join him in the Hell Hole or at two or three other seamy establishments in the Village, where, if he got drunk enough, he could relax.

The Hell Hole still served liquor to a favored clientele, and continued to provide O'Neill with the impressions on which he later drew for *The Iceman Cometh.* The proprietor, Tom Wallace, had made his concession to the Eighteenth Amendment by blocking off his windows with beaverboard and setting a few dusty bottles of patent medicines before the glass, in the fond hope that his saloon would be mistaken for a drugstore. The police pretended to be fooled.

The first time O'Neill entered the Hell Hole after he began to be successful Wallace paid him the signal honor of inviting him into his private upstairs sanctuary.

Wallace surveyed the rumpled, unshaved O'Neill with mock distaste.

"Look how you look," he scolded. "A famous playwright; you're a disgrace to the boys. You got to look like a gentleman now, not a bum. I'm going to fix you up."

O'Neill meekly allowed himself to be pushed into a chair. Wallace whipped out a razor and strop and proceeded to shave the newly famous playwright with all the barbershop flourishes of nose-lifting and ear-pulling.

Stupefied into immobility, O'Neill felt the blood trickling down his face under Wallace's inexpert passes; he wondered whether to risk having his throat slashed in an attempt to escape or to allow Wallace to finish, suffering what he prayed would be only minor injuries.

At last Wallace stepped back to admire his handiwork.

"Bejeez, you look worse than before!" he howled. "You wouldn't bleed like that if there wasn't so much liquor in your blood!" O'Neill said nothing. He was glad to be alive.

Wallace assured him he'd fix him up. He looked about for some bay rum and, finding none, shouted down to Lefty, his bartender, for some gin. He slapped the gin liberally on O'Neill's face, but was still not entirely satisfied with the result.

"Ask one of those whores for her compact," Wallace yelled to Lefty. The compact arrived, and most of its contents were patted onto O'Neill's cheeks and chin.

"How that?" asked Wallace, delighted with himself.

"I don't know whether I've been in a slaughterhouse or a Fourteenth Street whorehouse," said O'Neill haltingly, "but I feel and smell like a combination of both."

O'Neill's loyalty to Wallace and to his way of life were unshaken by his artistic success—which was why all of his old friends remained loyal to *him* long after he had physically removed himself from them. Many of those friends remembered, with admiration, the night David Belasco's secretary, after a frustrating attempt to locate O'Neill, telephoned to the Hell Hole.

Getting Lefty on the phone, the secretary explained that someone at the Provincetown Theatre had suggested that Mr. Belasco might be able to reach O'Neill here. Yes, he was here, said Lefty. The secretary said that Mr. Belasco was very anxious to meet with Mr. O'Neill at his office and would like to talk to him to arrange an appointment. Lefty said to hold on.

"Belasco's on the phone," he told O'Neill. "He wants you to come to his office to see him."

"Tell the sonofabitch if he wants to see me, he'll have to come down here, to *my* office," O'Neill said. A modified version of the message was delivered, and Lefty solemnly poured O'Neill a drink on the house.

O'Neill was more gracious but no more acquiescent about an offer from Harry Minsky, the burlesque impresario. Minsky had taken James Light to lunch. "Would you ask Mr. O'Neill to write something to do with art for me?" said Minsky. "Anything he writes, I'll produce. Tell him that."

"That's the most flattering offer I've ever had," O'Neill told Light, but asked Light to decline it for him on the ground that he was committed to other projects.

When he was not in the Hell Hole O'Neill could sometimes be found at "Pop" Paterno's, now a crude speakeasy disguised as an Italian doll-making establishment. Terry Carlin often joined him there, as did Slim Martin and James Light. O'Neill was now supporting Terry, who was having a wonderful time proving he could stay alive on a Prohibition diet consisting, in part, of canned heat strained through a bandanna.

Hippolyte Havel also was doing his best to stay drunk; and sometimes, when he tired of Paterno's or the Hell Hole, he bought cheap red wine from a bootlegger and carried it into Christine's, where he would spend hours drinking and sleeping. If O'Neill, or Light, or another old friend came in, he would stiffen into momentary alertness and call out, "Hey, bebbie, don't be a fool. Lend me a dollar."

The first time he greeted Jimmy Light in this fashion, Light reached into his pocket and brought out seventy-five cents—all he happened to have on him at the moment.

Havel regarded him owlishly. "Oh, bebbie," he said, "if you don't have a dollar, keep the seventy-five cents." And he reached into his own pocket, took out a roll of bills, and peeled one off for Light.

Although affectionate to his friends, Havel would not tolerate outsiders. Once three slummers gained admission to Christine's and sat looking at Havel with obvious disgust. As O'Neill later characterized him (as Hugo Kalmar) in *The Iceman Cometh,* he was slouched in his chair, his hair hanging over his eyes.

"Isn't it terrible, these foreign anarchists in here," said one of the slummers, a woman. Her words carried to Havel's table. He picked up a silver-topped cane—his one claim to elegance.

"Foreign anarchists?" he shouted at her. "Don't you know America has poisoned the whole world with anarchy? Thoreau! The Oneida Community!" As the woman stared, speechless, Havel screamed: "You are a constipated school teacher!" The woman and her companions quickly departed.

One day O'Neill and Slim were on their way to Sam Schwartz's, another popular Village drinking place, when a cloudburst sent them scurrying back to the Provincetown for shelter. They stood in the basement entrance, waiting for the rain to subside. Slim scanned the sky for an indication of how the weather was going to behave. He heard O'Neill chuckle.

"What do you see to laugh about?" asked Slim.

"You, looking at the sky," said O'Neill.

[459]

"What the hell, Gene," said Slim. "If a sailor or an ironworker doesn't look aloft once in a while to see how the riggin' or the weather is, he isn't going to live long. You know that."

"That's what I was laughing about," said O'Neill. "The sailor sticking out."

Always sensitive to the weather and its effect on people, O'Neill once brooded aloud on the subject to the impresario Sol Hurok, who at that time was a part of what Hurok has called "the Provincetown gang."

"Sol, how do you study people?" he asked. Not waiting for an answer, he continued, "Try to walk at night, a dark night, in a drizzling rain. Get as close to a person as you can and look in his eyes. You don't see real people when the sun is shining or the stars are out. Look at people when it's dark. The weather brings out their true natures."

When the Hell Hole, Schwartz's and Paterno's palled, O'Neill had other sources to tap for liquor. One of them was Luke O'Connor, who had sadly closed his Columbia Gardens and removed himself and his entire stock of liquor to a second-floor flat on Perry Street. Another source of supply was his friend Scotty Stuart, who had turned rumrunner. Scotty had hit on the ingenious device of fitting his boat with two powerful motors, so that he could speed backward as fast as forward. He managed to confuse and elude the revenue agents, and whenever he was in town he saw to it that O'Neill and other friends had all the liquor they needed.

But O'Neill's favorite bootlegger was William Fernandez, known as Spanish Willie. He had been a Hudson Duster, and when Prohibition came he ran what was called a "blind pig." Situated on Third Street, it was ostensibly a secondhand shop. Although it had a windowful of junk bought from the Sanitation Department, the shop was never open; only people Willie knew could gain access to his private chambers, where the "hootch" was served. Willie's quarters, at the end of a long corridor where a gas jet whined, consisted of two rooms and a bathroom, scantily furnished. There was a bed and a hot plate in one room and a wooden table and chairs in the other. Dingy lace curtains fluttered at the window. There were concealed revolvers planted in both rooms, so that Willie could reach one no matter where he was sitting; this was necessary, for Willie had as many enemies as he had friends.

Willie, who was short, heavy-set, polite, ungrammatical, and usually drunk, adored O'Neill. Malcolm Cowley, the writer, has recorded: "Willie worshiped several gods. Haig and Haig were two of these. The others were Man 'o War, Al Smith and Eugene O'Neill."

Whenever Cowley visited him, Willie would say: "Gee, that guy

O'Neill is a regular prince." Cowley has described one visit he made to Willie in the mid-twenties, reporting their conversation as follows:

"Tell you, Malcolm, I feel blue today. The Brooklyn boys is after me. I losted two grand on the ponies. But yesterday my nag comes in and I win about 1,500 smackers. So I guess we stands about even on the series. I want you should taste some of my sacramental wine. Did you hear that Gene was in town?"

"Gene who?"

"Why, Gene O'Neill, of course. You know Gene, don't you? . . . The boys tell me he's coming around to see me tonight. Sure, take another glass. I maybe wouldn't have it, only the police captain is a square shooter. You see, I was rolling a barrel in, yesterday evening it was, and three bulls sees me and holds me up for 150 bucks. When I went round to see the captain he says to the bulls, he says, 'What sort of crooks is youse guys anyway? I want you to play straight,' he says. And he made them give the money back. All but thirty dollars, that he lets them keep for theirselves. Ten bucks apiece. That's square enough. Listen, there's some bloke at the door. Why, Gene, good evening, it's a treat to see you."

After brushing off some cockroaches, O'Neill sat down at Spanish Willie's table.

"I'm glad to hear that you're feeling better, Will," O'Neill said.

"Aw, Gene, that cough wasn't so much. I oughta know better than to sleep in the gutter all night. Say, I just got some fine Scotch off the boat. Won't you have a drink with me?"

Cowley noticed that O'Neill made no effort to talk down to his host. "He was just as grammatical, just as considerate as if he were holding a conversation with Shakespeare or the Prince of Wales," Cowley recalled. "Perhaps this was the reason why all the West Side gorillas worshiped him, and even attended his plays."

"I wish I could report their conversation," Cowley continued. "Every time I try, the words seem to lose their magic. They were speaking of ships and docks and crimes and politics, of gangsters, sailors, stevedores, ward politicians and square-shooting black gamblers—all the figures of that life which seethed between wharves and crimping houses, between dance halls and saloons, all the glamor of a Manhattan which is almost totally unknown. I sat in silence listening. The Elevated went rumbling past while the empty glasses shivered on the table. Finally it was time for him to go. 'Well, you saw him again. Ain't he a regular prince?' asked Spanish Willie."

Eben Given, who saw a lot of O'Neill both in New York and in Provincetown, where he had his artist's studio, used to visit Spanish Willie with O'Neill.

"We knocked, and the door opened a crack, held by a chain," Given recalled. "Eyes peered out. 'Gene!' said a voice. 'Come in!' There was nothing to drink, Willie told us, he was all sold out. But he had some muscatel, which he poured for us. It was horribly sweet and sticky." (O'Neill once told a friend that Willie's muscatel was "obviously extracted from an elephant with a giant syringe.")

While they were drinking and talking, there was a knock at the door. After cautiously looking out, Willie let in a hulking hoodlum, who announced, "Big Andy is back." Willie explained to O'Neill and Given that Big Andy was out to get him. They lingered over the muscatel for two hours, and left.

The next time they visited they found that Willie had been shot in the arm—but not by Big Andy. It was "a pal" who had done it. Willie told them he'd had an argument with his pal. He showed them the bullet hole in his shirt sleeve. But he didn't hold it against his pal, he said. It had just been a friendly misunderstanding.

"It was plain that Willie loved Gene and would have done anything for him," Given said. Willie loved him enough to hide him out once in his house in Brooklyn, where he kept a wife and three children. O'Neill had gone on a bender—it was a time when Agnes was with him in New York—and when he vanished, Agnes asked Eben Given to accompany her to Willie's where she thought she might find her husband.

"When we got there," Given said, "Willie was soused. He tried to paw Agnes, and we got out. We didn't find out until later that Willie had Gene locked up in his house in Brooklyn."

Outside of drinking, the only thing that seemed to give O'Neill any pleasure or release during his visits to New York was attending sports events.

Passionately devoted to the six-day bicycle races, he was willing to pay his way into Madison Square Garden an hour before a race was scheduled in order to secure a good seat. His friends who accompanied him were amused as they watched the soft-spoken O'Neill cheer wildly for his favorites.

"Equipped with enough peanuts to stock a circus, tossing them several feet into the air and catching them in his mouth, [Gene] would sit raptly at the ringside, sometimes until three in the morning," Nathan has written. "He could supply a raft of intimate details about each bicyclist."

O'Neill was almost as devoted to baseball, and knew the batting averages of a number of players. Several times he went out of his way to meet a player, and once in the 1940's he arranged to have someone introduce him to Ted Williams, who had recently wound up a season for the Boston Red Sox with a .406 batting average.

His most fervent admiration, however, was reserved for prizefighters, a passion he shared with George Bernard Shaw. He began keeping an eye on Jack Dempsey when he become heavyweight champion in 1919 and was delighted to find his name linked with Dempsey's by Heywood Broun in *The Bookman* two years later. Broun described the bout between Dempsey and Georges Carpentier in Jersey City on July 2, 1921. Carpentier, the idol of the Paris boulevards, had caught the fancy of the American public; he was a built-up light heavyweight, officially weighed in at 172 pounds, while Dempsey weighed 188. (Shaw had favored Carpentier while O'Neill chose Dempsey.) Dempsey won by a knockout in the fourth round.

"We wish every young American playwright who is about to write a tragedy had seen the fight," Broun wrote. "They would realize then that the school founded by Eugene O'Neill is based on a misconception of the spirit of tragedy. It does not lie in the fact that man is small and helpless in the hands of fate which outclasses him in reach and weight. The tragic fact is that man is almost good enough to win in his inspired moments. He can rock fate but he cannot down it. That is the pity of his struggle. But come to think of it, there is nothing so terribly sorrowful in tragedy after all. Fate like Jack Dempsey wins the title, but the gesture remains with man, the light heavyweight. As he goes down he hears no slow toll of numbers. All that is drowned out by the cheering." O'Neill clipped the paragraph and mounted it in his scrapbook.

O'Neill was present at the Polo Grounds on the night of September 14, 1923, when Dempsey successfully defended his title for the last time. The fight, probably the most exciting heavyweight bout in boxing history, lasted only three minutes and fifty-seven seconds. During its course the challenger, Luis Angel Firpo, "The Wild Bull of the Pampas," was knocked down nine times, and the champion himself was belted out of the ring and into the laps of the sports writers, who promptly threw him back. Dempsey was then twenty-eight, at the top of his form, and a three to one favorite over the twenty-nine-year-old, brawny, but inexperienced Firpo.

O'Neill had invited Harry Kemp to the fight, telling him that the actress Helen MacKellar had arranged to have him meet Dempsey after it was over. Kemp had to decline, and O'Neill provided him with a detailed account of the event when he returned to Provincetown, of how he found himself "behaving like any other real American," standing up on his seat and yelling ferociously.

"When he came to," Kemp once recorded, "he saw he'd snatched a derby from one man's head and broken it over the head of another—neither man noticing the action—'nearly a million people were crazy—literally—for about five minutes!' "

"How about seeing Dempsey after the fight, Gene?" Kemp asked him.

"Oh, yes," said O'Neill. "When Jack came in at the door, the first thing we noticed was his black eye. 'How'd you get the black eye, Jack?' Helen MacKellar asked. 'Aw, Helen,' sheepishly answered the champion, 'I forgot to duck!'

"As he stood framed in the doorway," O'Neill went on, "I thought I was seeing my Hairy Ape in real life. But after we got to talking, apart in a corner, I found him a fine, good-natured gentleman. Dempsey didn't know me from Adam."

"So you like Dempsey?" asked Kemp.

"A splendid chap!" answered O'Neill. "He taught me his peculiar weave and that short jolt to the chin of his—like this!" And O'Neill illustrated on Kemp.

Dempsey seems, indeed, not to have known O'Neill from Adam. Questioned about the meeting, after O'Neill's death, Dempsey vaguely recalled talking to O'Neill "several times."

"I think it was after the Firpo fight that someone brought him to meet me, and that he congratulated me," Dempsey said.

O'Neill made a deeper impression on Gene Tunney, who was to beat Dempsey three years later in Philadelphia. Although Tunney and O'Neill never met, the fighter declared publicly in the late twenties that he had "secretly cherished the thought that Eugene O'Neill is a greater writer even than Shakespeare," a tribute that enchanted O'Neill.

XXXVII

EARLY IN 1921, O'NEILL TOOK STOCK OF HIS CAREER
and prospects in Provincetown. He found the outlook gloomy. Tyler,
having tried and failed to interest Alice Brady in *The Straw,* was again
without a candidate for the role of Eileen Carmody; John Williams was
still dodging O'Neill about *Gold;* the burgeoning Theatre Guild, after
expressing interest in co-producing *Anna Christie* with Tyler, had dropped
the project on the grounds that Tyler's terms were too steep.

O'Neill read articles about himself in the theatrical columns which
speculated politely about when the talented author of *Beyond the Horizon*
and *The Emperor Jones* would have a new, full-length play on Broadway,
and glowered with frustration.

He wanted to move on to other work—was, in fact, already writing,
a new play he called *The First Man*—but was tense with the anticipation
of being interrupted to go into production, and plagued by lack of income.

"Apart from the very deplorable financial aspects of the case," he wrote
to Tyler, "these delays affect the playwright's whole career, not only because his past work is held up, but more importantly because his future
work is held up. I have a lot of work planned out that I ought to get busy
on but it is impossible for me to concentrate properly on anything new
as long as I live in constant expectation of being called down for rehearsals of the old. It is a rotten game all around."

He added that, although current newspaper and magazine articles referred to him as "the White Hope of playwrighting," he might just as
well be the "scurviest typewriter-puncher of the lot." These scurvy hacks,
he said, were having their plays produced with no difficulty while his
plays had to "wait upon every fortuitous wind that blows."

O'Neill did take one step in the hope of increasing his income and
reputation—it was to set a precedent for him—that of allowing a play
to be published before it was produced. On February 11 he informed
Tyler that he had told his publisher to include *The Straw* in a new
collection of his plays to be released in a month or so. "I cannot ask
the publisher to wait any longer," O'Neill explained. "He has already
held the play for a year, waiting for production. And I must get a hearing

for it one way or another." (It was published in April, 1921, by Boni and Liveright, in a volume including *The Emperor Jones* and *Diff'rent*.)

In March O'Neill announced his new play to Kenneth Macgowan, with whom he had established a friendship after Macgowan had favorably reviewed *The Emperor Jones* for the *Globe*. With the acquisition of Macgowan, O'Neill now had a growing group of correspondents—among them Barrett Clark and George Jean Nathan, to whom he gave regular and minutely detailed reports of works in progress. O'Neill's long, explicit accounts over the next twenty years to these men and to others who took their place as recipients of his literary confidences, form a kind of diary of his artistic life—a fascinating documentary of the creative process.

"I have finished the first draft of . . . *The First Man,* and am now going to put it aside to smolder for a while in the subconscious and perhaps to gather to itself a little more flame therefrom," O'Neill confided to Macgowan. "It looks so good now, I'm afraid of it. At this stage of the development, they all look fine, I've found."

His misgivings, as it happened, were well grounded. This was one case in which no amount of smoldering could help.

The First Man turned out to be one of O'Neill's most dismal misses—a pronounced retrogression in his artistic development. In four acts, with a contemporary setting, its form is conventional and it is closely allied in style to some of the long plays he tore up in 1914. Its characters are middle class, its dialogue is intended to be realistic, and its point of view, while iconoclastic, is hardly radical. More surprising, though, is its mechanical awkwardness. (In the first act O'Neill shuffled his two protagonists on and off stage in an amateurishly inept fashion, to allow the rest of the characters an opportunity to talk about them.)

The play's only interest, in fact, lies in the revelation of O'Neill's feelings about his marriage and his parenthood at the time he was writing it.

His hero, who does not at first glance have much in common with O'Neill, is a thirty-seven-year-old anthropologist named Curtis Jayson; he is described, however, as a romantic idealist who has wandered over the globe in search of romance. He has come back to his home town (designated as Bridgetown, Connecticut) to write a scientific book. At this time O'Neill was not yet thirty-three, but he had, of course, recently revisited *his* home town in Connecticut. Curtis' wife, Martha, is thirty-eight, and though considerably older than Agnes, was an idealized Agnes—self-sacrificing, completely absorbed in her husband and his work; Martha has devoted the last ten years to traveling all over the world with Curtis, acting as his secretary, confidante, mistress, mother. It develops that their ideal life of dedication to each other and to Curtis' work had its beginning in the sudden death of their two young children ten years before (undoubtedly symbolic of the two children O'Neill and Agnes had virtually put out of their lives when they married). The ludicrously perfunctory way that O'Neill, in his expository dialogue, kills off these two children is indicative of the panic he felt at the responsibility of parenthood. Martha describes their death to a friend:

"It was a Sunday in winter when Curt and I had gone visiting some friends. The nurse girl fell asleep—or something—and the children sneaked out in their underclothes and played in the snow. Pneumonia set in—and a week later they were both dead."

Throughout the rest of the play Martha keeps saying what a horrible blow the children's death had been to her and Curtis, but it is impossible to believe (after that casual "or something") that either she or her husband ever gave the accident much thought. Later on in the play, perhaps further indulging O'Neill's wishful thinking, another character comments, apropos of the lost children, "They died . . . as children have a bad habit of doing."

O'Neill was not unconscious of his own feelings and apparently made a feeble attempt to argue himself out of them in the rest of the play. The plot of *The First Man* unfolds with Curtis' sense of betrayal when he learns that Martha has deliberately become pregnant again, after all the years of having forsworn children; and the time she has picked to be incapacitated is on the eve, more or less, of his leaving on a five-year field trip into Asia, to search for traces of the first man—a trip on which he had planned to take her.

O'Neill wrote some speeches for Curtis that clearly reflected his own attitude on hearing that Agnes was pregnant. "How can I pretend gladness when—(*vehemently*) why, it would spoil all our plans! . . . It seems like treachery to me . . . Oh, Martha, why do you have to bring this new element into our lives . . . Haven't we been sufficient, you and I together? Isn't that a more difficult, beautiful happiness to achieve than—children? Everyone has children . . . Can you expect me to be glad when you propose to introduce a stranger who will steal away your love, your interest—who will separate us and deprive me of you!" Significantly, Curtis suggests that she have an abortion, a "solution" that O'Neill introduced into a number of plays.

Trying halfheartedly to understand the wife's point of view, O'Neill wrote some speeches for Martha which defended her right to bear a child. But he took his revenge in the end by killing off the wife; Martha dies, after an agonizing labor (gruesome off-stage screams are heard throughout the third act) while Curtis is grimly praying that the child will be still-born. He has no such luck. The child is a strapping, eleven-pound boy.

The play ends when Curtis, who has sworn never to look upon Martha's "murderer," finally does see his infant and immediately vows to bring him up to take Martha's place. Here, again, O'Neill revealed his naïve and unrealistic attitude toward parenthood by having Curtis go off on his long trip, as planned, but promising to come back to the child, "And when he's old enough, I'll teach him to know and love a big, free life."

Having completed *The First Man,* O'Neill again turned his attention briefly to *The Straw,* but he was no longer very enthusiastic about the play.

Tyler had tentatively cast the role of Eileen—with Margalo Gilmore —and was planning to open the play in October. That settled, O'Neill began outlining yet another script—an ambitious project—which he had already discussed with Kenneth Macgowan as "the Fountain of Youth play." He decided to write it in blank verse but to disguise the meter by having the manuscript typed in prose form. Although dissimilar in theme and treatment to *The First Man,* it, too, was rooted in O'Neill's intense preoccupation with his family—notably his father.

The play is about a Spanish explorer (loosely modeled on Juan Ponce de León) who leaves his country for a dream of glory and romance in new worlds; he finds neither glory nor romance, and dies a broken old man—but clutching at a new-found religious belief that "death is no more," that "all things dissolve, flow on eternally!" This is evidently a symbolic interpretation of James O'Neill's journey from the Old World to the New, of his pursuit of glory and romance, and his final realization that it had been "all froth"; James, too, died believing he was going to "a better sort of life," and it was probably his son's need to believe this with him that led him on the mystical search for the Fountain of Youth.

The idea of writing the play, O'Neill later said, "came from my interest in the recurrence in folklore of the beautiful legend of a healing spring of eternal youth." In his fantasies he undoubtedly wished that James O'Neill could have discovered this healing spring and lived long enough to develop the friendship that he and his son had begun too late. The play (it emerged as *The Fountain*) gets bogged down in murky mysticism toward the end and defeats the genuine poetic quality and dramatic tension of the earlier scenes; it is one of O'Neill's artistic failures, but interesting because it illustrates his religious state of mind at the time he wrote it.

In the play O'Neill tried, for the first time on a large scale, to dramatize his private and never-ending struggle with his Catholic conscience.

Strangely, although this religious struggle was the most dramatic factor in O'Neill's dramatic make-up, he could never make it seem vital or moving on the stage when he tackled it head on. None of the plays in which he dealt directly and literally with this theme (rather than obliquely and symbolically) were convincing as drama.

O'Neill kept Macgowan busy that spring and summer furnishing him with suggestions for background reading. (O'Neill had already gone through Frazer's *The Golden Bough* and John Fiske's *The Discovery of America.*)

"Of course," O'Neill explained to Macgowan, "I'll have to combine and relate a lot of scattered facts and then give history a slight rumpling up but it will be necessary to do that to bring out the full truth, the spirit of it, and behind the mere dates, etc. It's in a way lucky that so little real information has come down to us about Juan Ponce. One can re-create him."

Later, in response to Macgowan's somewhat awed query as to how he outlined a play such as *The Fountain*, O'Neill said: "I always let the subject matter mould itself into its own particular form and I find it does this without my ever wasting thought upon it. I start out with the idea that there are no rules or precedent in the game except what the play chooses to make for itself—but not forgetting that it is to be played in a theatre— ('theatre' meaning my notion of what a modern theatre should be capable of instead of merely what it is). I usually feel instinctively a sort of rhythm of acts or scenes and obey it hit or miss."

In his program note for the play, he wrote: "I have simply filled in the bare outlines of [Ponce de León's] career, as briefly reported in the Who's Who of the histories, with a conception of what could have been the truth behind his 'life-sketch' if he had been the man it was romantically —and religiously—moving to me to believe he might have been. Therefore, I wish to take solemn oath right here and now that *The Fountain* is not morbid realism." Privately, he hoped that *The Fountain* would be recognized as dealing with the same theme of "belonging" as *The Hairy Ape,* though the two plays were totally dissimilar in style.

O'Neill's conception of Ponce de León turned out to be a man who, in his youth, is blind to the beauty of love and deaf to the spiritual uplift of poetry; it is not until, at the age of fifty, he receives into his household as a ward the beautiful young daughter of a rejected mistress that his soul awakens. But the girl regards him as a second father, and he goes off on a frantic search for the fountain of youth, to resume his own youth and appeal to her as a lover. This final section of the play evokes echoes of the last act of *Gold*; here, too, a man is driven by an idée fixe to pursue a phantom treasure. And the last scene but one, in which Juan, betrayed and dying at the edge of a forest spring he had believed to be the fountain of youth, is a pseudo-inspirational harking back to some of the phantom scenes from *The Emperor Jones*. Mystical figures rise before him—religious symbols, symbols of death, birth, youth and poetry—and he and they chant about the "meaning of life."

O'Neill spent scene after scene developing the hypocrisy and avarice of the Christian Spaniards and their priests, indicating that their religion was a sham, that they worshiped only gold, that they were blind to the original principles of Christianity—that God, in fact, was dead.

What troubled O'Neill most in writing *The Fountain* was the blank verse style. Some of the friends to whom he showed parts of the script frankly criticized the verse. "I used it," O'Neill explained defensively to George Jean Nathan, "to gain a naturalistic effect of the quality of the people and speech of those times . . . with little care for original poetic beauty save in the few instances where that is called for."

In the late spring of 1921, while he was still at work on the scenario of *The Fountain* and still waiting for production plans to jell on *The Straw*, O'Neill received word that the elusive John Williams was now ready to stage *Gold*. Perversely, O'Neill was not overjoyed by this long-awaited news. In the first place, it meant a summer production, which was inauspicious; in the second place, the play no longer seemed terribly good to him and he was much more interested in staying in Provincetown and completing *The Fountain*.

"To be candid," he later explained to Macgowan on the day *Gold* opened in New York, "I had to wait so long for the production and there were so many disagreeable incidents connected with that wait, that by the time rehearsals started [in early May] I was 'fed up' and rather apathetic about its fate."

O'Neill was particularly distressed because Williams had tried to sell his rights in *Gold* to the Theatre Guild for a large cash sum without letting him know anything about it. Also, Williams had, without O'Neill's consent, offered *Gold* to numerous film companies in an effort to find backing for it. Williams, O'Neill complained, had committed "a breach of all the ethics of friendly association."

It was an irascible and querulous O'Neill who reported for rehearsals in New York in May of 1921. From the beginning he liked nothing about the production. His first annoyance was that Homer Saint-Gaudens, who had helped stage *Beyond the Horizon*, had been engaged to direct the play; O'Neill had not forgiven him for the appalling scenery he had provided for *Beyond the Horizon.* Secondly, he deplored the choice of Willard Mack for the central role of Captain Isaiah Bartlett (he had wanted Lionel Barrymore). Thirdly, he disapproved of the remainder of the cast, with the exception of Teddy Ballantine, who was to play Captain Bartlett's son, Nat (the role Jimmy Light had played in the short version of the play, *Where the Cross is Made.*)

The play opened at the Frazee Theatre on Forty-second Street on June 1. " 'Gold' . . . Shows O'Neill Below His Best"; "O'Neill's 'Gold' Not Glittering," and " 'Gold' Tells a Weird Tale" were some of the headlines over the following day's notices. Several critics complained of its length; it ran over three hours.

Broun in the *Tribune* found the first three acts unrewarding, but he praised the fourth (which he remembered having seen as *Where the Cross is Made*). He chided Williams for a "cheap and tasteless setting."

The Times, abandoned momentarily by Woollcott, who always left town for the summer, was being served by an anonymous critic who found the play "always interesting, occasionally compelling, and yet, for much of its length, curiously unconvincing."

The *Post's* J. Ranken Towse, well into his seventies by this time, summed up his feelings rather pettishly: "A pretentious, extravagant, conventional and youthful romantic melodrama" with performances "not of the kind calculated to brace and stiffen a feeble play."

O'Neill, irate over Mack's dreadful performance (the actor had failed to memorize his lines, and took to extemporizing), got drunk and fled New York, leaving Agnes behind to tidy up his dangling social obligations.

Gold was the last O'Neill play ever presented by John Williams.

On July 1, still smarting from the embarrassment of the production (*Gold* had closed abruptly on June 11, after a ten-day run), O'Neill wrote to Macgowan that he would have written parts of it differently if he had it to do over. But, he said, the play's failure on Broadway "hardly even peeved" him—it was "already such a failure in my mind." (Some years later he lumped *Gold* with *The First Man* and *The Fountain* among several plays he did not like. "I would dismiss [them] as being too painfully bungled in their present form to be worth producing at all," he declared.)

O'Neill spent a tense and nervous summer in Provincetown. For one thing, a number of his New York friends were beginning to arrive for the vacation season, and life was becoming too social. For another, he finally had the prospect of two important productions in the fall; not only was Tyler definitely set, at last, to begin rehearsals of *The Straw* in October but Arthur Hopkins had agreed to take over the production of *Anna Christie.*

"I'm full of future hopes," O'Neill told Macgowan. It gave him "a tremendous urge that more than compensates for the *Gold* fiasco" to know he was with Hopkins.

Work on *The Fountain* proceeded somewhat fitfully in the charged summer atmosphere of Provincetown. The town was beginning to change. Like the rest of the country, it was caught up in the postwar frenzy of jazz, automobiles and bathtub gin. Most of O'Neill's friends were drinking more, now that there was an element of romantic illegality attached to the process.

While it was not easy to go on a protracted drunk in Provincetown—always a "dry" town—it was possible. Liquor had been privately imported before Prohibition without difficulty, but now considerable ingenuity had to be exercised. An agreeable doctor could be persuaded to write a "prescription" for whiskey; there were bootleggers who would sell at cut prices to their old pals, and even though the easiest drink to come by was a horrible brew made from raisins and called tiger piss, it was possible to get a certain amount of it down without becoming ill—at least, for a while. Parties grew wilder and O'Neill had plenty of company in his carousing.

One day he satisfied a longing to spend a hundred dollars on one big drunk. He was not affluent, but he believed the time had come when he could afford to indulge this whim. After tapping various sources, he managed to buy a case of good whiskey and ordered it sent to the home of his friend Frank Shay. Someone brought a phonograph—O'Neill was willing, on occasion, to essay a fox-trot—and a dozen Provincetowners settled down to their party. It went on for two days, with emptied bottles tossed into the fireplace. Finally, there was no one left at the party but Shay and O'Neill. The sound of breaking glass in the fireplace was so entertaining to the two Irishmen that they threw in the household china, plate by plate and cup by cup. As they began on lamps and furniture they passed out.

O'Neill was not apt to treat Agnes chivalrously during his drinking sprees. On more than one occasion he handled her with almost the same fine abandon he had displayed toward the Shays' household effects. He had nearly knocked her off her feet once in the Hell Hole, when he thought she was flirting with Teddy Ballantine. It was all part of his conception of the violence of true love, and he was always pleased when he thought Agnes had goaded him to this sort of response.

Eben Given recalled one occasion when O'Neill tried to drag Agnes by the hair across the dunes. The evening had begun ominously. Agnes and several others had gathered in the house of a friend, preparatory to attending a costume ball at the Town Hall. Agnes was wearing a black lace mantilla, which had belonged to Ella O'Neill. O'Neill arrived, already half drunk, surveyed his wife and tore the mantilla from her head.

Momentarily reconciled, O'Neill and Agnes went on to the ball. O'Neill had got himself up in a sarong and a wild orange wig. He was a grotesque but commanding figure, his skin deeply tanned, the whites of his eyes and his teeth glittering below the flaming headdress. At four in the morning Eben Given, Agnes and a few others left the party and went to a friend's house, but O'Neill had vanished.

"We walked down the street to my car," Given related. "Suddenly, from the depths of the car, something with insane, blazing eyes, a mad leer and an orange wig popped up. We recoiled. It was Gene, of course, very drunk. He and Agnes had rented a room in town for the evening, but Gene now decided he wanted to go back to Peaked Hill. That was when he grabbed Agnes by the hair and tried to drag her off. She yelled, but no one interfered."

(One member of the Coast Guard, Augustus Perry, who spent years of lonely duty in the lookout station at Peaked Hill Bar, once recalled that he and his colleagues would occasionally see Agnes and O'Neill coming home in the early morning hours—sometimes separately.)

Liquor went rapidly to O'Neill's head. It was Given's opinion that O'Neill did not need to go on a protracted drunk to reach a state of ferocity. "He had too much motor for the chassis," Given explained. "Too much horsepower. He was highly sensitive and nervous. Although he was sometimes gay, when he was drinking he was black Irish. When that mood was on him, you could sense the potentialities in the man for destruction and trouble."

O'Neill often entrusted a pint of white mule to Louis Kalonyme, a new friend, who concealed it under his shirt and would follow O'Neill about during the evening, proffering the bottle when requested.

Kalonyme, who sometimes used the byline Louis Kantor, was a young feature writer and art critic for the *Tribune* and had covered the Emma Goldman-Alexander Berkman trial for his newspaper. O'Neill had met him at a party at Mary Vorse's house and asked him if he knew who had written a flattering, unsigned article in the *Tribune* about *Beyond the Horizon*. Kalonyme admitted authorship and O'Neill immediately adopted him as a friend; soon after that he constructed a shack for him on the dunes near his own house. O'Neill enjoyed trading newspaper experiences with Kalonyme, but confessed that when he was working for the New London *Telegraph* he was unable to report a story that didn't interest him.

Kalonyme, who spent a good deal of time with O'Neill that summer, was surprised to discover that O'Neill was terrified of thunderstorms. One evening the two men were walking along the water's edge when a storm suddenly came on.

"I was carrying a small metal flashlight in my hand," Kalonyme recalled. "Gene was panicky. He kept telling me to get rid of the flashlight. I never saw him so agitated, and I was astonished, because I knew he was fearless when it came to swimming or paddling in the greatest waves. Fog made him uneasy, too."

O'Neill also held a number of superstitious fears and beliefs. He once sat in solemnly at a séance arranged by Eben Given at Peaked Hill and appeared as shaken as the other participants when the "spirit" of a drowned sailor manifested its presence by a series of raps on the table. And that summer he adopted a female black cat that had strayed out to Peaked Hill, named it Anna Christie, and regarded it as an omen of hope for his play.

Kalonyme began drinking that summer for the first time—in order to keep up with O'Neill. "Though I started drinking because of Gene, I became a better drinker than he, because I had a stronger stomach," he said years later.

One day O'Neill was locked into a room at the Atlantic House by sympathetic friends who wanted him to sleep off a drunk after a party. The proprietor, Ira Iris, checked on his prisoner twelve hours later and found O'Neill still drunk. He searched the room, uncovered no liquor, and, bewildered, warned O'Neill to behave and sober up. But O'Neill was still drunk three days later. On one of his check ups, Iris finally spotted Kalonyme gliding up the fire escape and handing O'Neill a bottle through the window. O'Neill felt like staying drunk, and Kalonyme accommodated him.

"But when he worked, he worked hard," Kalonyme said, by way of excuse and explanation. "He went about things slowly and deliberately. Many people thought that because he didn't say much he was not an intellectual. What they failed to realize was that Gene, like most creative geniuses, wasn't much interested in what anyone else was doing. He was interested in discussing things only in relation to what *he* was doing."

Kalonyme, who knew Shaw, was fascinated by the contrast in character between the two dramatists. He once gave O'Neill a photograph of Shaw, and O'Neill remarked, "Looking at him makes me a little uneasy." But O'Neill was eager to know what Shaw thought of him.

"I asked Shaw once," Kalonyme said, "and Shaw told me O'Neill was 'a fantee Shakespeare.' What he meant was that O'Neill was a great natural talent, but did not have the literary equipment to control this talent."

The best illustration of the two writers' diverse outlooks, according to Kalonyme, was their reaction to *Ulysses*. Kalonyme discussed the saloon sequences from Joyce's book with both Shaw and O'Neill.

Shaw's comment was: "If what Joyce says about Dublin is true, it should be burned to the ground."

O'Neill commented: "I know all that."

Lawrence Langner, who also knew both Shaw and O'Neill, was, like Kalonyme, the recipient of their comments about each other. According to Langner, O'Neill admitted having been influenced by Shaw—but more "as a man and a writer than as a playwright." As for Shaw, he "greatly admired O'Neill's work as a dramatist, but with his old-maidish temperance attitude, could never get over being shocked at Gene's early drinking."

When Langner reported to Shaw some years later that O'Neill had sworn off drinking, Shaw's comment was: "He'll probably never write a good play again."

In addition to providing a shack for Louis Kalonyme on the dunes, O'Neill also furnished Terry Carlin with living quarters in Provincetown. Carlin slept in a shed near the O'Neill house and functioned as a combination distiller, father confessor to O'Neill, and playmate to Shane. He would make blueberry wine on the beach by filling jars with crushed berries and a bit of yeast and partially burying them in the sand to ferment. Then he would check on his distillery by crawling along the beach, his ear to the bottles, listening for the fermenting process to stop. When a jar was silent, he knew the wine was ripe, and he would dig it up and drink it.

For variety, he once tried shellac. He found a couple of cans that had been washed ashore, and recalled Jack London's advice on how to isolate the alcohol from the shellac: you stirred the shellac in a large can with a stick until you got it whirring fast enough to create a hollow cone in the center. Theoretically, the alcohol would separate from the shellac and collect in the cone. Following this procedure, Terry was thrilled to see a cone forming and greedily tested it with his tongue. The alcohol was there —190 proof wood alcohol—but the shellac closed in, hardening and encasing his tongue. Terry could not get his tongue back into his mouth until O'Neill provided him with enough gin to soak off the shellac.

When Terry was not in pursuit of liquor he was busy collecting edible herbs and roots, performing arcane exercises or working on bizarre inventions. He once built himself a huge wheel of barrel slats and steel, with a chair slung from the center, on which he thought he would roll effortlessly down the sloping beach. He abandoned his invention when his first ride in it cost him a broken rib.

Between drinking sprees and watching the antics of his friends, O'Neill managed to give some time and thought to the subject uppermost in his mind that summer—the impending production of *Anna Christie*.

Robert Edmond Jones had been engaged by Arthur Hopkins to design the settings for the play, three of whose four acts take place aboard a battered coal barge, and O'Neill invited him to Peaked Hill, where the sea had obligingly cast ashore just such a barge. Stranded less than a hundred yards from his house, the barge had been one of a heavily laden procession being towed by a steamer. Encountering rough waters, the captain of the steamer had misunderstood orders from shore, and cut the tow line, resulting in three of the barges being hurled by waves onto the beach; when the storm subsided the owners were able to salvage two of them but only the cargo and fittings of the third. Its huge hulk was so deeply embedded in sand that it could not be budged.

Jones spent a few days sketching it, and no sooner had he finished, when, mysteriously, it began to burn. For two nights and a day firemen and volunteers drenched the O'Neill home to prevent it from catching fire.

Early in October of 1921 O'Neill began attending rehearsals of *Anna Christie* in New York. He took his family with him this time and in an effort to remove himself somewhat from the convivial demands of his Greenwich Village friends moved into an apartment at 36 West Thirty-fifth Street, not far from the Garrick Theatre.

If ever conditions for the production of an O'Neill play were right, this was the time. The man he considered the best manager in the business was mounting his play. The best designer in America was providing the scenery. A respectable Broadway theatre, the Vanderbilt, was where the play was scheduled to open. The publicity was being handled by Hopkins' press agent, Oliver Sayler, a man with whom O'Neill saw eye to eye. And to play his heroine O'Neill had an actress of extraordinary ability and appeal, who needed only one more important role to establish her as an undisputed star. She was Pauline Lord, whose career was being guided by Hopkins and whose most recent success had been in the previous season's *Samson and Delilah*.

Miss Lord did not physically resemble O'Neill's twenty-year-old Anna —"tall, blonde, fully-developed . . . handsome after a large, Viking-daughter fashion." She was thirty-one, delicate, almost fragile, with a tiny waist, small hands and feet, a pale, oval face, and tragic brown eyes. She had been acting since she was sixteen—rarely in the conventional ingénue parts, more often as tragic victims. A superb actress, her technique consisted, in the apt phrase of Elizabeth Sergeant of "betrayal, rather than portrayal."

Like O'Neill, she was shy and withdrawn in company; she admitted to friends that she could act well only when she was unhappy or nervous. O'Neill was delighted with her.

O'Neill was equally delighted with Hopkins, and immediately began comparing him favorably with Williams and Tyler. Their rapport was in no small measure due to the fact that Hopkins, like O'Neill, appreciated silence. Since neither Hopkins nor O'Neill spoke to each other except under stress, it was almost impossible for them to quarrel. Hopkins, who was small, round and apple-cheeked, returned O'Neill's respect and admiration. Charles O'Brien Kennedy, who also enjoyed protracted silences, occasionally dined with O'Neill and Hopkins. During their first meal together they didn't exchange more than a dozen words; three of these issued from O'Neill. "Pass the spaghetti," he said.

Before taking on *Anna Christie* Hopkins, the most experimental and visionary of the commercial producers, had successfully staged such plays as *Redemption* and *The Jest* and failed with a revival of *Macbeth*. He had encouraged Robert Edmond Jones to experiment with new dimensions in stage design and costuming. As idealistic, in his own way, as O'Neill, he believed that Broadway had become "a ceaseless repetition of a familiar and timeworn formula, a bag of tricks which anyone with skill can play and assure himself a certain amount of success" and that there was "no longer any excitement in the experience of playgoing."

"I want people to leave my theatre actually quarreling about what they have seen," he once wrote, in deploring the glibness of Broadway. "There is nothing more tragic to me than the complacent, unmoved faces that pour out of our Broadway theatres after the play."

Born in Cleveland in 1878, Hopkins had been a newspaper reporter, vaudeville press agent and producer of special acts for the Orpheum Circuit until he visited Europe in 1913 and saw what theatre could be in terms of art.

It is hardly surprising that O'Neill considered Hopkins the ideal manager. Hopkins chose plays because he liked and believed in them, not because he thought they would go; he respected his choices as individual works of art, not to be exploited as vehicles. His system had drawbacks. If the play was truly fine, his method worked splendidly. But if the play was not as good as his instinct had told him it was, his reverential treatment made the production seem doubly bad.

But Hopkins' attitude suited O'Neill perfectly, for neither Tyler nor Williams had offered anything approaching his passion. "I become [a play's] suitor," Hopkins had once said. "I lay myself at its feet. I swear everlasting devotion. I promise my all, and like all daft suitors I know no regret."

Inevitably, however, O'Neill's ardor for his producer—even though it was the devoted Hopkins—cooled as opening night approached. By the time of the final run-through he thought the production fell somewhat short of perfection and had misgivings about its reception.

As was his custom, O'Neill did not attend the play's opening on November 2, 1921. Having reluctantly agreed to let Agnes give an opening-night party in their new apartment, he waited there for her to bring him news of audience reaction.

While waiting, he was jolted by a telegram from a friend in Province-town, reporting that his black cat, Anna Christie, was seriously ill. Sending an immediate reply, O'Neill begged his friend to see to it that the cat received every possible medical attention; convinced that the fate of the play was welded to that of the cat, O'Neill grew even more worried about the play's reception and started drinking.

When Agnes returned with a report that the play had gone very well, O'Neill was only half convinced. He panicked as his guests began arriving —among them Pauline Lord and other members of the cast, in addition to his Provincetown friends. With the help of Charles O'Brien Kennedy, he found a temporary refuge.

"When I arrived at the party," Kennedy recalled, "I saw Gene in a corner, besieged by a number of verbose admirers. The appeal in his eyes will never be forgotten by me, but it was impossible to get him away unnoticed. He was unfamiliar with the layout of the new apartment but, after some exploration, I discovered an abandoned bathroom, dark and dusty. The drab wallpaper was peeling and a consumptive bulb shed the only light. Some drinkables were smuggled in and I gave the welcome relief signal. Behind the locked door we sat on the edge of the tub, where he told me the plot of a play called *The Hairy Ape*."

The reviews of *Anna Christie* were uniformly favorable, although several critics complained about the "contrived" fourth act and the "talkiness" of the second. The acting of Miss Lord was praised by all, as was that of George Marion, who played Chris, and the production, as a whole, was enthusiastically applauded.

Woollcott called it "a rich and salty play that grips the attention with the rise of the first curtain and holds it fiercely to the end." He did not, however, rank it among O'Neill's best.

"'Anna Christie,'" he said, "might be described as a work which towers above most of the plays in town, but which falls short of the stature and perfection reached by . . . O'Neill in some of his earlier work . . . [which] had established him as the nearest thing to a genius America has yet produced in the way of a playwright, and, though this 'Anna Christie' of his has less directness and more dross and more moments of weak violence than any of its forerunners, it is, nevertheless, a play written with that abundant imagination, that fresh and venturesome mind and that sure instinct for the theatre which set this young author apart . . . from a lot of funny little holiday workers in cardboard and tinsel."

Heywood Broun, feeling restricted in drama criticism, had left the *Tribune* for the *World* (where he became a combination critic and columnist) and been replaced by Percy Hammond, the pride of the Chicago *Tribune*. Hammond, who eventually achieved the distinction of being O'Neill's pet hate among the major critics, was regarded as a stimulating and controversial stylist, but O'Neill considered him a bigoted egomaniac "suffering from ulcers." Hammond's approach was often negative or halfhearted when it came to O'Neill, and O'Neill deemed him a classic example of the critic who much preferred revealing his own personality to analyzing the play in question.

Hammond seemed to like *Anna Christie* but, according to O'Neill, was incapable of conveying his approval more than halfheartedly.

"If the gloomy trademark of Eugene O'Neill's depressing product has kept you hitherto away from his plays, disregard it for an hour or two and go to see 'Anna Christie,'" Hammond heavily enjoined his readers. "The promise thus suggested is not that you will have a gay time in the observation of that drama, but that its veracious picture of some interesting circumstances will appeal to your intelligence, while its 'meaning' will not in the least irritate you."

The *Post*'s J. Ranken Towse found the play "a remarkable work for a young man, but something that falls a good way short of a masterpiece." He sounded the first note of criticism that was subsequently to throw O'Neill and some of his critics into a minor uproar when he remarked that the fourth act employed "most violent expedients to bring about a happy ending."

Louis De Foe, in the *World*, also felt that the story had been "tampered with in order to give it at least a hopeful if not quite happy ending"; concurring were the anonymous critics for the *Herald* ("the sudden love

. . . brings the happy ending"), and for the *Evening Telegram* ("even if it is arrived at slowly and laboriously, Mr. O'Neill reaches a happy ending"). Even Kenneth Macgowan, writing for the *Globe,* unwittingly stabbed his friend in the back when he wrote: "You may call it the happy ending if you like. It is the acceptance of suffering and happiness lived out into a new life."

Newspapers all over the country began publishing articles about the controversial new play, which caught on quickly with the public. John Mason Brown, in an article for the Louisville (Ky.) *Courier-Journal,* wrote that it was the "happy ending" that worried him most. After praising *Anna Christie* as a notable work, he pointed out: "Here is a young author for the first time giving in to the demands of the professional theatre and giving in at the cost of probability and reality. . . . His artistic concession to popular tastes at the final curtain is a curiously hybrid thing."

O'Neill was furious with the critics. Neither his alliance with Hopkins, nor the commercial success of the play, nor even the really splendid production it had received could console him. It is hard to say whether he was more irate over the fact that his ending had been construed as happy or the fact that he was accused of compromise and contrivance to bring the ending about. "Either I am crazy, or they all are," he wrote to Oliver Sayler.

Alexander Woollcott, in a Sunday article, following the opening, seemed to have understood O'Neill's intention but even he complained of the "bogusness" of the last act.

"The two lovers are interlocked as the final curtain falls," he wrote on November 13, 1921, in *The Times.* "O'Neill seems to be suggesting to the departing playgoers that they can regard this as a happy ending if they are shortsighted enough to believe it and weak-minded enough to crave it. He, at least, has the satisfaction of intimating in his final words that, whereas everything seems cheerful enough at the moment, there is probably no end of misery for everybody hidden just ahead in the enfolding mists of the sea. It is a happy ending with the author's fingers crossed."

O'Neill decided to refute the critics and composed a lengthy defense, which he sent to Oliver Sayler with instructions to pass it on to the presumably sympathetic Woollcott. He said that his "return barrage over the ending" might "arouse some sort of come-back from the other side, and perhaps a general discussion"—provided, of course, Woollcott decided to print it. "At any rate," he wrote to Sayler, "I have got it off my chest and I consider it a fair statement of what I really was aiming at in that fourth act, so much maligned."

But even then it was clear that his heart was less in defending his play than in defending his integrity as a playwright. Actually he didn't like *Anna Christie* any more and was inclined to disown it. The fact that his new baby, born with every advantage, lovingly presented to the public, had proved popular and successful made him wary.

"I hereby set down *Anna Christie* as the very worst failure I have experienced, and the most ironical joke ever played on me—for probably its success depends on the audience believing just what I did not want them to," he said to Sayler. "If it were not for the others concerned in its production, I assure you I would pray for its closing next Saturday."

On December 18 *The Times* ran O'Neill's "explanation" in behalf of his already rejected child in which he said, in part:

"I wanted to have the audience leave with a deep feeling of life flowing on, of the past which is never the past—but always the birth of the future—of a problem solved for the moment but by the very nature of its solution involving new problems.

"I must have failed in this attempt. And I was afraid I would, for I knew what I was up against. A kiss in the last act, a word about marriage, and the audience grow blind and deaf to what follows. No one hears old Chris when he makes his gloomy, foreboding comment on the new set of coincidences, which to him reveal the old devil sea—(fate)—up to her old tricks again. More importantly, no one hears Burke, when for the *first* time in the play, overcome by a superstitious dread himself, he *agrees* with the old man. And more importantly still, no one listens to Anna when she shows how significant she feels this to be by her alarmed protest: 'Aw, you ain't agreeing with him, are you, Matt?'

"Three characters have been revealed in all their intrinsic verity, under the acid test of a fateful crisis in their lives. They have solved this crisis for the moment as best they may, in accordance with the will that is in each of them. The curtain falls. Behind it their lives go on. . . .

"Lastly, to those who think I deliberately distorted my last act because a 'happy ending' would be calculated to make the play more of a popular success I have only this to say: The sad truth is that you have precedents enough and to spare in the history of our drama for such a suspicion. But, on the other hand, you have every reason not to believe it of me."

A week later (on Sunday, December 25) Woollcott scolded O'Neill for his indignation:

"The disposition on the part of many playgoers to regard the final scene of 'Anna Christie' as 'a happy ending' has caused the author of that dramatic and agonizing play a good deal of pain and surprise . . . He is entitled to his pain. But he has no right to be surprised. . . .

". . . He must have foreseen the cruel charge that he had written a happy ending, just as he must have foreseen that that shiny revolver, which he keeps pointing at the agitated audience throughout the final act, would make the playgoers nervous. He can insist until he is black in the face that it is silly of them to be nervous and that he did not want them to be, but the world-weary will smile if he also says he did not expect them to be."

That was enough to sour O'Neill permanently. In one of the swift reversals of which he was capable he began to speak slightingly of the play in public, forgetting that he had once considered it among the "finest." Far from continuing to be hurt by the charge of "trickery," he now claimed that the trickery had been deliberate.

"I never liked it so well as some of my other plays," he disclosed to Malcolm Cowley a few years later. "In telling the story I deliberately employed all the Broadway tricks which I had learned in my stage training." He added scornfully that it had all been "too easy" and that he would never write such a play again, although he could turn out a dozen *Anna Christies* if he wanted to. And when Joseph Wood Krutch asked him in the late twenties if he might edit a volume of his "representative plays," O'Neill answered, "Sure, use your own judgment, with one proviso: *Anna Christie* must not be among them."

By that time *Anna Christie* had successfully completed a road tour, having run for 177 performances on Broadway; had earned him his second Pulitzer Prize; had been made into a silent movie (1924) with Blanche Sweet; and was being filmed as a talkie (1929) with Greta Garbo. It had not earned him a great deal of money (in comparison with the profits earned by writers like Augustus Thomas and J. M. Barrie), having sold for a small price to the movies and having never grossed more than $7,500 a week on Broadway. But it had made his name popularly known, as *Beyond the Horizon* had not.

His name, in fact, was so well known after the run of *Anna Christie* that he decided he no longer needed the distinguishing initial "G" in his signature. He dropped it for the first time in the published version of *Anna Christie,* which Boni and Liveright issued, together with *The Hairy Ape* and *The First Man,* in July, 1922.

But not all theatregoers liked *Anna Christie.* Some found it in bad taste and wrote letters to newspapers and magazines, taking a moralistic view of the play's subject matter. William Griffith, representing a publication called *Current Opinion,* sent a batch of these letters to O'Neill, asking if he wanted to reply to them.

"Such folk," O'Neill answered Mr. Griffith, "are fine, expressive examples of our great, mean-minded, bigot-ridden booboisie—(as Mr.

Mencken calls them)—that is rapidly and surely making this supermoral land the stupid laughing-stock of the ages. . . . Silence is the only answer possible to the yapping of morons. . . . It would take Doctors Freud and Jung combined to state clearly the case against them."

For reasons O'Neill could not control, his tuberculosis sanitarium play, *The Straw*, was in rehearsal at the same time as *Anna Christie* and was scheduled to open in New York only five days after *Anna*. Tyler had finally put it into production with Miss Gilmore in the role of Eileen. John Westley, for whose ideas on the play's staging O'Neill had earlier expressed so much sympathy, was cast as Stephen Murray.

The Straw was to open at the Greenwich Village Theatre, rather than on Broadway, because Tyler considered its subject matter too grim for uptown audiences. Although O'Neill was more interested in the *Anna Christie* production, he did not neglect *The Straw*. He drew carefully detailed sketches of the sanitarium interiors, as he remembered them from Gaylord Farm and he arranged to have Westley visit Gaylord and talk with Dr. Lyman and the head nurse, Mrs. Burgess.

Though Westley returned from Gaylord feeling more cheerful about the play's subject matter, O'Neill was not cheerful about Westley's development in the role of Stephen.

"I remember Mr. O'Neill sitting out front during rehearsals," Margalo Gilmore said in recalling the production. "I don't think he ever spoke to any members of the cast, but I do recall his dramatic, brooding face."

By the time the play was ready for its out-of-town tryout, Tyler was in agreement with O'Neill about Westley's unsuitability and tried to replace him. He was unable to find another actor, though, for the play's initial showing in New London. If Tyler thought that sentiment for James O'Neill would favorably predispose New Londoners towards James's son, he was wrong. The reception of *The Straw* at the Lyceum, where James had once drawn standing ovations for his *Monte Cristo*, was not enthusiastic. The manager of the Lyceum, Walter Murphy, later declared he was not surprised that the play was a flop. "It was disgusting," he said, "everyone walking around holding sputum cups."

O'Neill's boyhood friend, Ed Keefe, went to see the play and liked it. He wrote to O'Neill in New York to tell him so, and O'Neill answered, thanking him and explaining that he had meant to be there for the opening but had been "tied up in New York" on *Anna Christie*. He also informed Keefe that the play had stirred up his New London relatives, the Brennans, because they had taken the "old harridan stepmother"

(Maggie Brennan, wife of Eileen Carmody's father) "as an insult directly aimed at their mother."

"Can you beat it!" said O'Neill. "I've tried to explain that every city directory is pretty full of Brennans, but it's no use."

"It was funny," he added, "*The Straw* opening in New London, when there is so much autobiographical stuff in it connected with that town. When I wrote it three years ago, of course, I never dreamed of that coincidence—or I would never have lazily picked up actual names."

On Monday, November 7, 1921, an ad in the New York newspapers announced the postponement of *The Straw* from that night to Thursday, November 10. Tyler had engaged Otto Kruger as a replacement for Westley and wanted to give him time to rehearse. O'Neill watched a few run-throughs, approved of Kruger, and left New York for Provincetown without waiting for the opening.

The critics, looking forward with interest to another play by the author of *Anna Christie*, attended the Greenwich Village Theatre en masse on November 10. Most of them were a little disappointed, but all in all they gave the play a rather encouraging reception. No one was more surprised than O'Neill.

According to Woollcott, *The Straw* was an "interesting and moving play . . . below the level of the best work [O'Neill] has done for the theatre," but decidedly worth seeing. Macgowan thought it uneven but ultimately powerful. Towse found it inferior to *Beyond the Horizon* but "able, sympathetic and interesting." Hammond wrote that "it does not depress," and told his readers: "If . . . you . . . long for new dejections with which to purge your soul, you may find recreation in the story of 'The Straw.'" Louis De Foe told readers of the *World* that it was "the most depressing play that could possibly be encountered within theatre walls" but conceded that "as a work of imagination it is unquestionably vivid."

Toward the end of November O'Neill wrote to a friend: "I don't think [*The Straw*] will go financially—but I never nourished that feeble hope anyway."

The Straw closed after twenty performances. O'Neill had not bothered going to New York to see it.

In a spirit of remarkable magnanimity, O'Neill told Tyler that he knew the production had given him every possible chance and that, though he had not seen it, friends had reported to him on its artistic merits. The fault, he agreed, must have been in the subject matter. He hoped, said O'Neill, to bring Tyler a play someday that would make up for *Chris* and *The Straw*. But Tyler never produced another O'Neill play.

◈

It was now, at the end of 1921, less than two years since O'Neill had first been greeted as the new hope of the American theatre. In that short span six of his long plays had been staged. Three of them—*Beyond the Horizon*, *Anna Christie* and *The Emperor Jones*—had proved to be financial as well as artistic successes. *Anna Christie* was still running on Broadway and *The Emperor Jones* was beginning a promising road tour. *Gold*, *Diff'rent* and *Straw* had not done well—but three out of six was not a discreditable average in the theatre.

O'Neill had strained the resources of two of Broadway's most successful managers. He had formed what seemed to be a felicitous and enduring partnership with Hopkins. He had an unproduced backlog of one complete play (*The First Man*), one half-finished play (*The Fountain*) and the fully formed idea for yet another (*The Hairy Ape*). His scripts were being published in book form as fast as they were produced (or faster, as in the case of *The Straw*). He had been responsible for the development of a new talent—Charles Gilpin—and the consolidation of a rising one— Pauline Lord. He had quarreled publicly with the critics, castigated at least half a dozen prominent actors, scorned offers from Belasco and Minsky, and declared over and over again his intention to "hew to the line." Without compromising his artistic ideals, without lightening his tragic outlook, he had forced Broadway to reckon with him as a power; and he had finally made his art pay.

At thirty-three Eugene (no longer Gladstone) O'Neill was a celebrity —successful, unyielding and relentlessly in pursuit of new vistas. His greatest successes and his most ambitious failures still lay before him. He knew, better than anyone, that he was just beginning.

XXXVIII

NOT LONG AFTER THE OPENING OF *Anna Christie* AND *The Straw*, O'Neill received a visit in Provincetown from his former city editor on the New London *Telegraph*, Malcolm Mollan. Now working for the Philadelphia *Public Ledger*, Mollan was assigned to interview his one-time cub reporter—the theme of the article to be "Why does a man write plays with tragic endings?" (He apparently had not heard that *Anna Christie* had a "happy" ending.)

Remembering only too well his frequently articulated opinion of the young reporter's "literary batiks," Mollan was dubious about the reception he would receive at Peaked Hill. But O'Neill, now secure enough of his standing to indulge in a bit of noblesse oblige, welcomed Mollan cordially and talked to him more freely than he had to most other interviewers. Mollan's report is noteworthy because it recorded O'Neill's scorn, at a moment of material achievement, for all things materialistic.

"I came down here," Mollan said, "principally to ask you one question —the thing everybody wants to know. Have you any present purpose, or expectation, of writing a play with an out-and-out happy ending?"

"Sure," said O'Neill. "I'll write about happiness if I ever happen to meet up with that luxury, and find it sufficiently dramatic and in harmony with any deep rhythm of life. But happiness is a word. What does it mean? Exaltation; an intensified feeling of the significant worth of man's being and becoming? Well, if it means that—and not a mere smirking contentment with one's lot—I know there is more of it in one real tragedy than in all the happy-ending plays ever written.

"It's sheer present-day judgment to think of tragedy as unhappy. The Greeks and the Elizabethans knew better. They felt the tremendous lift to it. It roused them spiritually to a deeper understanding of life. Through it they found release from the petty considerations of everyday existence. They saw their lives ennobled by it. A work of art is always happy. All else is unhappy."

O'Neill added that an eminent critic recently had observed that tragedy was not native to the American soil and had no place in the American drama. If this were true, O'Neill said, it would be "the most damning commentary on our spiritual barrenness." America was now "in the throes of a spiritual awakening" and the signs were there "for even the maddest joy rider to read."

"A soul is being born," he continued, "and when a soul enters, tragedy enters with it. Suppose some day we should suddenly see with the clear eye of a soul the true valuation of all our triumphant brass band materialism; should see the cost—and the result in terms of eternal verities. What a colossal, ironic, 100 per cent American tragedy that would be—what?

"Tragedy not native to our soil? Why, we are tragedy—the most appalling yet written or unwritten."

Mollan was a little staggered, but recovered his aplomb sufficiently to ask O'Neill if his attitude toward life had grown more cordial with the coming of success.

"I love life," O'Neill answered. "I always have. If, to the superficial, I have appeared not to, it is only because they cannot understand diffident folk who do not wear their hearts on their sleeves. . . . I love human beings as individuals (as any kind of a crowd from a club to a nation they are detestable), but whether I like them or not, I can always understand and not judge them. I have tried to keep my work free from all moral attitudinizing. To me there are no good people or bad people, just people. The same with deeds. 'Good' and 'evil' are stupidities, as misleading and outworn fetishes as Brutus Jones' silver bullet. . . .

"I am a dramatist, that is the answer. What I see everywhere in life is drama—human beings in conflict with other human beings, with themselves, with fate. All else is a side issue. I just set down what I feel in terms of life and let the facts speak whatever language they may to my audience. It is just life that interests me as a thing in itself. The why and wherefore I haven't attempted to touch on yet."

O'Neill had been in Provincetown more than a month when Mollan visited him. After the distractions of New York he found it difficult at first to settle down to work. He and Agnes closed their house at Peaked Hill, as they customarily did for the winter, and moved into rooms in town. During the winter of 1921-22, they lived at the Monroe House, on Bradford Street.

O'Neill's restlessness that winter was partly due to the fact that *The First Man* was still unproduced. He had tried to interest Hopkins in the script (tentatively entitled *The Oldest Man*) but Hopkins had been, in O'Neill's words, "nothing if not enigmatic." Lawrence Langner, upset at his Theatre Guild's having lost *Anna Christie* and eager to add O'Neill to the Guild's roster, asked to see a script of the new play.

"I believe you will find it a strong piece of work," O'Neill told

Langner on November 30. "I like it much myself." But the Guild turned it down, "scoring another black mark" against itself, as Langner later observed.

O'Neill was going through a phase of what he called "uncreative doldrums." He spent his time taking long walks, reading the *Saturday Evening Post* and hating the world.

Like all truly creative people, O'Neill was never happy except when he was working and even then his emotion was less happiness than passionate preoccupation. He seemed to derive little pleasure or consolation from his young son, who, at two, was enchantingly beautiful. While many of his letters in the months immediately following Shane's birth had been full of proud references to his son, there was barely a mention of him any more in his correspondence—though he often inquired politely about the children of his friends.

By the second week in December, however, O'Neill's depression had lifted; he began work on what was to be one of his best plays.

"I have recovered my creative élan and started *The Hairy Ape* with a mad rush," he informed Oliver Sayler on December 10. "Think I have got the swing of what I want to catch and, if I have, I ought to tear through it like a dose of salts. It is one of those plays where the word 'inspiration' has some point—that is, you either have the rhythm or you haven't and if you have you can ride it, and if not, you're dead."

The play he was writing, and which he had outlined in New York to Sayler, Kennedy, Macgowan and Langner, among others, was a dramatic extension of the unpublished short story about ship's stokers written in the summer of 1917—the same summer he had outlined the idea for *Beyond the Horizon*. After smoldering in the back of his mind four and a half years, the "why" of the suicide at sea of his sailing companion, Driscoll, had begun to nag at him again—illuminated now by his own increasing sense of unbelonging in a hostile, materialistic world. Possibly Jack Reed's recent death had revived his interest in the theme of "not belonging," as well as in the psychology of the radical movement, which figures as a background for *The Hairy Ape*. And some of the atmosphere and dialogue for the play was suggested by Slim Martin, who, like O'Neill's Yank, tried to believe that it was the worker who "counted."

"The search for an explanation of why Driscoll, proud of his animal superiority and in complete harmony with his limited conception of the universe, should kill himself," O'Neill later wrote in an introduction to the play, "provided the germ idea for 'The Hairy Ape.'" Some time earlier he had told Elizabeth Sergeant that the play was "unconscious autobiography."

"He chose to write about the hairy stoker, victim of modern industry, a man far removed in circumstance," Miss Sergeant later recorded, "in order to voice through Yank that social rebellion and sense of buffeted frustration which was his philosophic message at the time."

The play, in eight scenes, evolved as a stark and pitiless description of what happens to the stoker, Yank Smith, when his animal superiority is shattered by a chance encounter with an aristocratic young woman who calls him a "filthy beast," translated by Yank's shipmates as "hairy ape." Scene by scene it follows Yank's futile attempt to "show" the girl that he is as good as, if not better than, she and her kind; when this attempt fails, he tries to regain his poise among the I.W.W.'s, who want no part of him either; he finally dies in the arms of a gorilla in the zoo, whom he greets as "brother."

"Even him didn't tink I belonged," says the dying Yank. "Where do I fit in?"

"He slips in a heap on the floor and dies," read O'Neill's final stage directions. "The monkeys [in the adjoining cages at the zoo] set up a chattering, whimpering wail. And, perhaps, the Hairy Ape at last belongs."

In his first conception of the play O'Neill did not plan this ending for Yank. Instead, in a less imaginative climax, he outlined a scene in which Yank returns to his ship and the hell of the stokehole, without his original faith in himself as "the muscle in the steel" but knowing no other place where he belongs any better. O'Neill discussed this projected ending with Oliver Sayler, who later observed:

"Just as so often happens in an artist's work, Yank Smith wouldn't behave as his creator at first thought he ought. The character took the reins in his hand and compelled the playwright to obey orders."

O'Neill had been working on the play for about a week when he gave a progress report to Charles Kennedy:

"I've got the swing of it now, I think. Believe me, it is going to be strong stuff with a kick in each mit—and stuff done in a new way, along the lines of *Emperor Jones* in construction but even more so. . . . You must direct it, of course—that is if you want to—and I know damn well you'll want to when you've read it."

Kennedy did want to direct it, but believed himself obligated to tour with the Hopkins production of *The Claw*, starring Lionel Barrymore. Kennedy had, however, already performed an important service for O'Neill in connection with *The Hairy Ape*. During their conversation in the bathroom on the opening night of *Anna Christie*, O'Neill disclosed his idea for the play and asked Kennedy if he thought a burly, ex-college football star named Louis Wolheim, who had recently acted in *The Jest*, would be a good choice for the role of Yank. Kennedy, a friend of Wolheim's, assured O'Neill that this was very astute casting.

"He hasn't had much experience, though," O'Neill mused. (Wolheim, who had been a discovery of Lionel Barrymore's, had been in silent films since 1916 and on the stage for about three years, but never in a major role.)

"He doesn't need experience; he's got equipment," Kennedy insisted.

Still hesitating, O'Neill confessed that he did not have the nerve to ask Wolheim to play Yank. Wolheim might be insulted, he said, at an offer to portray an ugly brute. Would Kennedy mind talking to him about it in a tactful way? asked O'Neill.

Kennedy made an appointment with Wolheim after hitting on what he considered "a diplomatic approach."

"Wollie," said Kennedy, "would you play the homeliest so-and-so in the world if Gene O'Neill wrote him?"

According to Kennedy, "Wollie roared his profane affirmative." And so, although *The Hairy Ape* was not written to order for Wolheim, the actor was already an established image in O'Neill's mind when he began putting dialogue on paper.

"You can tell Wolheim for me that the lead will be a bigger part than Brutus Jones," O'Neill now instructed Kennedy.

The first draft of *The Hairy Ape* was completed on December 23. Working with intense concentration, O'Neill had been able to finish the draft in less than three weeks. "It was one of those times when the numbers seemed to come," O'Neill informed Macgowan on Christmas Eve. "I was so full of it it just oozed out of every pore. And the result, I think, is at least astonishing, whether for good or evil. It has changed and developed immensely in the doing. . . ."

O'Neill added that the play could not be categorized as any sort of "ism," but, rather, seemed to "run the whole gamut from extreme naturalism to extreme expressionism—with more of the latter than the former." He had tried to dig deep in it, he said, to "probe in the shadows of the soul of man bewildered by the disharmony of his primitive pride and individualism at war with the mechanistic development of society."

His protagonist, he appended, had been changed from an Irishman, as he had first seen him, to, "more fittingly," an American, a New York waterfront tough, "a type of mind, if you could call it that, which I know extremely well."

O'Neill was forced to put aside the manuscript during the Christmas holidays in order to spend some time with his mother and brother, who were planning a six-month stay in California.

The purpose of their proposed trip was to liquidate James's West Coast real estate holdings, valued at about $15,000. Ella also believed a change of climate might do her good. She had been suffering from severe headaches, for which Dr. Thomas Armstrong King, a prominent New York specialist, had been treating her.

Ella and Jamie, completely dependent upon each other since James's death, always dined together at restaurants and attended the theatre together—including the premières of *The Emperor Jones, Diff'rent, Anna Christie, Gold* and *The Straw*. Jamie had not touched any liquor since making his vow and, to friends who saw him during that period he seemed relaxed, gentle and happy, perhaps for the first time in his life. Brandon Tynan, who had not seen Jamie since they had acted together in *The Wanderer,* encountered him in Times Square. Jamie told him that he wasn't drinking any more. "He said he was sorry about the Old Man, and sorry about the way he had behaved on the road," recalled Tynan. "He seemed almost shy about it, but I could see he meant it."

Ella also appeared contented and calm. She still dressed in black, but she wore more jewelry—including a large diamond brooch that had been an anniversary gift from her husband but that she previously had been reluctant to wear because she considered it "too gaudy." When she traveled she carried her other jewels in a chamois bag pinned inside the ample bosom of her dress.

In late December Ella and Jamie boarded a train to make the same trip she had made as a bride forty-four years earlier. Their destination was San Francisco, the city where Jamie had been born.

Ella told Eugene that she was sorry she was not going to be at the opening of *The Hairy Ape* but hoped it would still be running when she returned. If she postponed her trip until a time when Eugene did *not* have a play scheduled for production, she jokingly said to her son, she would never be able to leave.

O'Neill saw them off and returned to Provincetown to complete the script of *The Hairy Ape,* which he now subtitled, "A Comedy of Ancient and Modern Life."

On January 2, 1922, O'Neill wrote to George Jean Nathan that the typing and revising of *The Hairy Ape* were still to be done, but that Nathan would soon have a chance to read the finished script.

"I believe you are going to be very much interested in this play," he added, "whatever your verdict may be on the complete result." (Nathan was always amused by O'Neill's apparent interest in his opinion; O'Neill never paid the least attention to it—unless it was favorable.)

He also informed Nathan that the play was promised to the Provincetown Players, but that he hoped Hopkins would take it uptown after its scheduled three-week run in Greenwich Village. The production would be pretty much out of the hands of the Provincetowners anyway, he added with satisfaction.

"Kennedy, a Hopkins man, will direct," he explained, not having yet heard that Kennedy was going out of town. "Wolheim, a Hopkins actor, will play the lead, I hope. He is the only actor I know who can look it, who has by nature the right manner. Whether he can act it or not, I doubt; but I also doubt if any actor can act it. It is a tremendous part. Finally, Bobby Jones will do the eight sets, which must be in the Expressionistic method. So you see it will not be an amateur affair but can be relied on to achieve results. I doubt if any commercial manager . . . including even Hopkins, would be daring enough to give it a thought."

O'Neill had a typed and revised manuscript of *The Hairy Ape* ready by the third week in January—just a little over six weeks from the time he had set down the first line. Triumphantly, he read it aloud to Eben Given and a handful of other friends at the Monroe House in Provincetown on the morning it was completed.

On January 22 he wrote to Kenneth Macgowan that Hopkins had offered "to help in the directing, gratis, although he has not seen the play—proving him a sport."

"I am quite satisfied with my 'Ape,'" he added. "He seems to me to have realized more in the doing than any other of my plays. He is new, American, and a bit astounding, I think. He will be either a riot—or a complete fizzle—when produced. He is no middle course animal."

Once again, as had been the case with *Anna Christie* and *The Straw*, O'Neill was about to have what he called "the ghastly joy" of simultaneously attending two sets of rehearsals. For he had finally arranged a production of *The First Man*. Augustin Duncan, brother of Isadora, agreed to be the play's producer and star.

When O'Neill moved into his New York apartment early in February, 1922, to attend rehearsals of his two plays he found the Provincetown Theatre very much changed in spirit.

Jig and Susan Cook were still smarting from a disastrous production of Cook's full-length play, *The Spring*, a year earlier. Heavily mystical and encumbered with a large cast, *The Spring*, despite bad reviews at the Playwright's Theatre, had been moved by Cook to the uptown Princess Theatre, where, on its third night, it had sold a total of four tickets.

At that point Cook's friendship with O'Neill had become strained, and the Provincetowners divided into factions. Susan Glaspell, of course, was outspokenly on her husband's side and Edna Kenton openly joined their camp. The idealistic artists of only a few years before were now reduced to childish bickering, and even Cook and O'Neill could not resist the temptation to jeer at each other.

Striking at O'Neill's vanity, Cook once taunted him with: "You can't pass a mirror without looking into it."

"I want to make sure I'm alive," retorted O'Neill.

Later that day O'Neill told Charles Kennedy, "I'm afraid there's too much O'Neill around this place to suit Jig."

In recalling O'Neill's remark, Kennedy said: "Gene and I felt the same way about Cook at that particular time. We thought he was a poseur, that he pontificated too much." Some of the Provincetowners considered this a harsh judgment in view of Cook's great service to O'Neill, but a number of them were in private agreement that Cook, despite his many admirable qualities, could be overbearing. (It was not until several years later that O'Neill was able to evaluate Cook objectively.)

"Jig was not really jealous of Gene," Charles Ellis said, in attempting to analyze Cook's problem, "but he felt rivaled by him; he was afraid of being overwhelmed by youth." Cook's position was genuinely pitiable. He had gone on a protracted drunk soon after the opening of *The Spring*. One day Fitzi and Pauline Turkel, a recent recruit to the Provincetown Players, on leaving the renovated mansion on Grove Street where they lived, found Cook studiously trying to remove a brick from the corner of the house.

The two women watched him for a moment and then Fitzi asked, "What on earth are you doing, Jig?"

"I'm just trying to loosen things up," Cook explained solemnly. "Things need loosening up around here."

O'Neill, not really sensitive to the depth of Cook's wound and convinced that he had outgrown the Provincetown Players and their amateurism, turned his back on their problems—which included an unpropitious beginning of The Players' sixth season. They opened with Susan Glaspell's new long play, *The Verge*, about an egocentric woman who goes mad, and followed this with Theodore Dreiser's four-act study of degeneracy, *The Hand of the Potter*. Neither play was an unqualified success. The third bill consisted of three trifling one-acters, while The Players marked time, waiting for *The Hairy Ape*, scheduled for the fifth bill. For lack of any product of their own to fill the fourth bill, they were obliged to turn their theatre over to a guest company—Ellen Van Volkenburg's and Maurice Browne's Chicago repertory production of *Mr. Faust*.

By this time rehearsals of *The Hairy Ape* had started, the opening announced for early March. Jig Cook, offended that O'Neill had asked Hopkins to help with the staging, took no part in the production. He decided he would go with his wife to Greece for at least a year.

On February 23 the Cooks, Fitzi and Cleon Throckmorton met at O'Neill's apartment to determine what was to happen to the Province-town Players following Jig's departure. After agreeing to incorporate the group and retain the names of the Provincetown Players and the Play-wrights' Theatre, they decided to end the season—following the run of *The Hairy Ape*—with a comedy by Susan Glaspell, called *Chains of Dew*. Then a year's interim would be declared, during which the theatre would be leased to an outside group. On March 1, a day before they sailed for Greece, the Cooks entrusted their proxy votes in the new corporation to Edna Kenton. They did not wait to see *The Hairy Ape*.

The production was taking shape under the combined guidance of Hopkins and James Light, who was O'Neill's choice for director when Kennedy proved to be unavailable. In spite of O'Neill's misgivings, Wol-heim was developing the role of Yank almost as it had been envisioned by its creator. Moreover, O'Neill found Wolheim personally engaging. Wolheim had been a mining engineer, had fought in Mexico with Pancho Villa, and had taught mathematics at Cornell University. As an undergraduate he played fullback on the Cornell team. He spoke French, German and Spanish and could swear fluently in all three languages. He could drink O'Neill under the table, and he liked nothing better than a fight. His physical strength was tremendous. Once he got into a drunken brawl in front of the Astor Hotel and it took four club-wielding policemen to subdue him.

Another time—this was shortly after *The Hairy Ape* had opened—Wolheim was in the Golden Eagle, a restaurant next door to the Province-town theatre. Talking to O'Neill, Agnes, Fitzi and Pauline Turkel with great excitement about the play, he kept repeating how grateful he was to be playing Yank, "the most magnificent part ever written by a con-temporary playwright." The restaurant was nearly empty, and Wolheim paid no attention to the couple staring at him from a nearby table. Carried away by his intensity, he began playing the scene in which Yank is thrown out of the I.W.W. hall. Hurling himself onto the floor, he recited: "So dem boids don't tink I belong, neider. Aw, to hell wit 'em! . . . I don't tick, see? . . . Steel was me and I owned de woild. Now I ain't steel and de woild owns me. Ah, hell. I can't see—it's all dark, get me? . . . Say, youse up dere, Man in de Moon, yuh look so wise, gimme de answer, huh?—"

This was too much for the couple at the other table, and they snickered.

Wolheim stopped dead, but he stayed in character. He leaped to his feet and lunged at the man. It took all of O'Neill's strength to hold him back as the owner of the restaurant quickly got the couple out the door.

Wolheim didn't always start swinging when provoked. One time, in a bar with O'Neill and Light, he was explaining, with elaborate pantomime, the way a certain prizefighter could "roll with a punch." A tall, burly man, quite drunk, took offense to Wolheim's noisy demonstration.

"I'm going to punch your nose right into your forehead," growled the drunk.

Wolheim glared at him and said, carefully emphasizing each syllable: "If you do, and I find out about it, look out." Then he turned his back. The drunk was so nonplused by the warning that he left immediately.

The production of *The Hairy Ape* was cast and designed with great care, even in the minor parts. Mary Blair, the frustrated heroine of *Diff'rent,* played Mildred Douglas, the rich, snobbish young woman who faints at the sight of Yank in the stokehole. She was outfitted with a snowy white crepe de Chine gown, white cloak and white hat with flowing veil, to point up the contrast with the grimy, coal-blackened stokers in their glowing inferno. Just as the settings were the combined efforts of Cleon Throckmorton and Robert Edmond Jones, the costumes also were a collaborative affair. Blanche Hays labored over the problems posed by the gorilla; she and her assistants finally made a suit from dyed goatskins (which became overwhelmingly odoriferous after a while). The head was formed of papier-maché, copied by Miss Hays from a gorilla in the Museum of Natural History.

Miss Hays also worked out O'Neill's idea for masks. The Congo witch doctor had worn the traditional tribal mask in *The Emperor Jones,* but it was in *The Hairy Ape* that O'Neill first introduced masks in the symbolic sense of the Greek theatre. The masks were used in the scene in which a group of society people emerge from church to stroll down the city street on which Yank is wandering, searching for Mildred. In his stage directions O'Neill did not specify masks, although he described the society people as "a procession of gaudy marionettes . . . with something of the relentless horror of Frankensteins in their detached, mechanical unawareness." O'Neill wanted them all dressed alike—the men in Prince Alberts, the women overdressed in gaudy gowns and furs—and he wanted their faces to be identically haughty and vacant.

"The costume part of this was simple," Blanche Hays said, "but the faces stumped me. I suggested using masks, and Gene was delighted." She made the masks of two layers of fine cheesecloth laid over a plaster cast of a face, and painted with several coats of collodion, a liquid which hardens into a skinlike substance; this produced a featherlight mask on which the required features could be painted. (During a dress rehearsal, two actresses fainted from the fumes of the not-quite-dry collodion.) The effectiveness of the finished device led O'Neill to his larger experiments with masks in plays like *The Great God Brown,* and some years later he wrote that he would have used more masks in both *The Hairy Ape* and *The Emperor Jones* had he realized how potent they could be.

"All the figures in Jones' flight through the forest should be masked," he noted. "Masks would dramatically stress their phantasmal quality, as contrasted with the unmasked Jones, intensify the supernatural menace of the tom-tom, give the play a more complete and vivid expression. In *The Hairy Ape* a much more extensive use of masks would be of the greatest value in emphasizing the theme of the play. From the opening of the fourth scene, where Yank begins to think, he enters into a masked world; even the familiar faces of his mates in the forecastle have become strange and alien. They should be masked, and the faces of everyone he encounters thereafter, including the symbolic gorilla's."

O'Neill spent much more time at rehearsals of *The Hairy Ape* than he did at those of *The First Man.* After a couple of weeks he could see that *The First Man* had some glaring weaknesses and that the production was not going to overcome them. Mentally abandoning *The First Man,* as he had *Gold,* he devoted himself entirely to *The Hairy Ape.* *The First Man* was scheduled to open at the Neighborhood Playhouse on March 4 and *The Hairy Ape* at the Provincetown on March 9.

On February 16 O'Neill received a telegram from Jamie in Los Angeles informing him that Ella was seriously ill. The doctors believed she had a brain tumor.

On that same day, before four witnesses, Ella made her will. Unable to write, she dictated her bequests. To Jamie she bequeathed the property in California which they had come to sell, and left the remainder of her estate to "my beloved sons . . . share and share alike." Ella died on the morning of February 28 and O'Neill was informed of her death a day later.

The ensuing week was ghastly. Communications from Jamie about arranging to send Ella's body east were erratic and inconclusive, and O'Neill realized that Jamie had started drinking again. The tension of attending final rehearsals of two plays and anticipating the arrival of his dead mother and drunken brother was almost too much for him.

The First Man opened on March 4 to uniformly bad notices, but O'Neill couldn't bring himself to care. Woollcott's verdict was "prolix, circuitously reiterative and clumsy of gait . . . at times . . . rubbishy," and the rest of the critics more or less echoed Woollcott's opinion, a couple of them taking particular offense to the scene in which Martha screams in prolonged labor.

George Jean Nathan later called *The First Man* "one of O'Neill's worst full-length performances," attributing its failures to the author's "aping the technic of Strindberg," and O'Neill himself, in 1925, decided that *The First Man* was the play with which he was least satisfied to date. It ran for only twenty-seven performances.

On March 9—five days after the première of *The First Man—The Hairy Ape* opened. That same evening the train carrying Ella's body was due to arrive at Grand Central Terminal—an opening night Ella had been obliged to eschew for the sake of business. O'Neill was acutely aware of this irony, as he sent Agnes to the theatre with his friend Saxe Commins while he went to meet Jamie at the station.

The train carried not only his mother and brother, but also the elements of a play he would write twenty years later. *A Moon for the Misbegotten,* written in 1943, discloses the appalling details of Ella's death and Jamie's journey from California to New York with her body. In this play, as in *Long Day's Journey Into Night,* O'Neill called his brother James Tyrone, Jr. The play is set in the fall of 1923, two months before the real Jamie's death, and Jamie Tyrone reveals the story to the girl, Josie Hogan (much as Jamie told it to Eugene shortly before his own death):

"When Mama died, I'd been on the wagon for nearly two years. . . . And I know I would have stayed on. For her sake. . . . She'd always hated my drinking. So I quit. It made me happy to do it. For her. Because she was all I had, all I cared about. Because I loved her. . . . We went out to the Coast to see about selling a piece of property the Old Man had bought there years ago. And—one day she suddenly became ill. Got rapidly worse. Went into a coma. Brain tumor. The docs said, no hope. Might never come out of coma. I went crazy. Couldn't face losing her. The old booze yen got me. I got drunk and stayed drunk. And I began hoping she'd never come out of the coma, and see I was drinking again. That was my excuse, too—that she'd never know. . . . I know damned well just before she died she recognized me. She saw I was drunk. Then she closed her eyes so she couldn't see, and was glad to die! . . . After that, I kept so drunk I did draw a blank most of the time, but I went through the necessary motions and no one guessed how drunk . . ."

No one guessed except his brother. When O'Neill met the train he realized Jamie was in a deplorable state—barely coherent and incapable of locating Ella's casket; O'Neill unassisted, had to make the arrangements for transferring the casket from the baggage car to an undertaker's parlor.

Then he took Jamie to a hotel and tried to put him to bed, while awaiting Agnes and Commins.

While O'Neill was coping with his grim chores, the curtain fell on *The Hairy Ape* at the Provincetown and the theatre resounded to the applause of first-nighters. Dressed in evening clothes, carrying gold-headed walking sticks, borne by chauffeur-driven limousines, the cream of the theatregoing aristocracy had sat on the rude wooden benches of the little theatre, stunned by the elemental force of the play. Also in attendance was the full complement of Broadway critics.

Agnes and Saxe Commins watched the audience rise to shout its approval, then hurried from the theatre to report to O'Neill. Excited about the play and worried about O'Neill, both of them forgot a new, $60 portable typewriter Agnes had just bought for her husband. Entering the hotel Agnes suddenly realized the typewriter had been left in the taxi. She was terrified of O'Neill's reaction; he had inherited more than a little of his father's frugality. But she found O'Neill haggard with despair and too distraught to notice that she hadn't brought the typewriter. O'Neill asked her to stay with Jamie and take care of him; he wanted to walk, and he asked Commins to accompany him.

O'Neill and Commins walked in Central Park until dawn, Commins listening in awed silence as O'Neill unburdened himself. He told Commins of his mother's years as a narcotics addict, of the pain her suffering had caused him and Jamie and their father, of the guilt and love and torment that had shaped and driven the family. Finally he returned to the hotel, exhausted. Commins, still worried about O'Neill's reaction to the forgotten typewriter, borrowed $60 from Fitzi and bought a new one, so that O'Neill would never know of the loss.

O'Neill read the surprisingly tepid reviews of *The Hairy Ape* with considerably more interest than he had read the bad ones of *The First Man*. There were many passages in the reviews that irritated him—passages indicating that the critics had misinterpreted or completely failed to grasp the significance of his message. Towse, for instance, wrote: ". . . in its crude realism and lack of reticence, its misrepresentation, and its unreflecting and imitative radicalism—it is an exceedingly juvenile performance. Apparently designed, primarily as a tract in favor of the I.W.W., it becomes, by its puerile insistence upon details, at once extravagant and conventional . . . it has no real significance and . . . will not help Mr. O'Neill's reputation." (Heywood Broun, in his column in the *World* a few weeks later, wrote that O'Neill had "found a cause" and "become a propagandist.")

Percy Hammond gave O'Neill what the author felt was faint praise when he called the play "the best . . . after 'Anna Christie' "; O'Neill, of course, thought it infinitely superior. Alexander Woollcott supplied some vigorous praise along with several kicks. He called it "a bitter, brutal, wildly fantastic play of nightmare hue and nightmare distortion," but found it "a monstrously uneven piece, now flamingly eloquent, now choked and thwarted and inarticulate." He said it needed "a fierce, unintimidated blue pencil," but he conceded that it had "a little greatness in it."

"It seems rather absurd to fret overmuch about the undisciplined imagination of a young playwright towering so conspicuously above the milling, mumbling crowd of playwrights who have no imagination at all," he concluded.

O'Neill was impelled to answer the critics who did not understand the play and to explain to the public what it was all about.

"Whether *The Hairy Ape* . . . is to be classified as an Expressionistic play or not is of little consequence," he wrote, in one of his many comments on what was to remain one of his favorite works. "Its manner is inseparable from its matter."

But in an interview he remarked that the key to an understanding of the play was the fact that it *was* expressionistic: "People think I am giving an exact picture of the reality. They don't understand that the whole play is expressionistic. Yank is really yourself, and myself. He is *every* human being. But, apparently, very few people seem to get this. They have written, picking out one thing or another in the play and saying 'how true' it is. But no one has said: 'I am Yank! Yank is my own self!' "

O'Neill stressed, however, that, although the play was expressionistic, its characters were not symbols.

"I personally do not believe that an idea can be readily put over to an audience except through [flesh-and-blood] characters," he explained later. "When it sees 'A Man' and 'A Woman'—just abstractions, it loses the human contact by which it identifies itself with the protagonist of the play. . . . I do not believe that the character gets between the author's idea and the audience . . . the character of Yank remains a man and everyone recognizes him as such."

By way of illustrating that his characters were not mere symbols, O'Neill said:

"Many of the characters in my plays were suggested to me by people in real life, especially the sea characters. In special pleading, I do not believe. Gorki's 'A Night's Lodging,' the great proletarian revolutionary play, is really more wonderful propaganda for the submerged than any other play ever written, simply because it contains no propaganda, but rather shows humanity as it is—truth, in terms of human life. As soon as an author slips propaganda into a play everyone feels it and the play becomes simply an argument."

O'Neill elaborated on this point a short time later in a letter to his radical friend, Mike Gold, who had sent him a playscript in which the propaganda showed through:

"You've got the makings of a darned fine, new, amusing play. For Pete's sake don't let it slide. If you want my most candid dope, I think you ought to keep the artist, Mike Gold, and the equally O.K. human being, the Radical editor, rigidly segregated during their respective working hours. I advise this in the name of flesh and blood propaganda!"

The Hairy Ape, O'Neill pointed out on another occasion, was propaganda only in the sense that it was "a symbol of man, who has lost his old harmony with nature. . . . The struggle used to be with the gods, but is now with himself, his own past, his attempt to 'belong.'"

O'Neill had a heightened personal sense of not belonging when he went to look at his mother in her casket.

What he saw bewildered him and filled him with self-pity. The undertaker in California had made up Ella to look doll-like and artificial. O'Neill, who could not reconcile this face with his mother's, later attributed to James Tyrone, Jr., in *A Moon for the Misbegotten* his own reaction: "I can never forget—the undertakers, and her body in a coffin with her face made up. . . . She looked young and pretty like someone I remembered meeting long ago. Practically a stranger. To whom I was a stranger. Cold and indifferent . . ."

O'Neill arranged to have his mother's funeral service conducted from the Catholic church on East Twenty-eighth Street, which Ella had attended after returning to her faith. She was to be buried in New London beside her husband, her infant son, and her mother, but O'Neill decided against a service in New London because he didn't want to face his relatives. He particularly wanted to avoid hearing their remarks about Jamie, who was obviously going to be too drunk to attend the funeral.

The priest with whom O'Neill made the arrangements for the service turned out to be a former classmate of his at Mount St. Vincent. He saw to the placing of the body before the altar of the church, where Ella's friends, the Carmelite nuns who had helped her conquer the narcotics habit, prayed over her through the night.

At least two of Ella's New London relatives, O'Neill's own favorites, attended the funeral—Lil Brennan and her sister Agnes. O'Neill decided to accompany his mother's body to New London, but Jamie did not go. In New London one of his Sheridan cousins gave O'Neill a photograph of his mother holding him as an infant, which he always cherished.

As though to bear him out in his impatience with certain of his relatives, murmurs were already being heard in some quarters about the "disappearance" of Ella's jewelry. It was thought that Ella had left no will, and a few relatives claimed that her jewels had been "promised" to them at her death. O'Neill heard that he and Jamie were suspected of having sold the jewels. Jamie later said they had been lost in California, but whether they had or not was moot as far as any claim on them was concerned, since Ella had made a will, in which she left everything to her sons.

"I was just beginning to enjoy her," O'Neill told Agnes Brennan after the funeral. But in truth Ella's death had sprung one more bond in his creative life—added to the sense of release that had come with James's death. Very soon he would begin writing about both his parents in a personal way, not possible while they were alive.

When *The Hairy Ape* concluded its run in Greenwich Village, Hopkins prepared to move it into the Plymouth Theatre on Broadway. But he insisted on replacing Mary Blair in the role of Mildred Douglas with a beautiful actress whom he admired. She was Carlotta Monterey and she had recently appeared as a sultry siren in a Russian-Turkish melodrama called *Bavu*. (It was produced by Arthur Hopkins and written by Earl Carroll, who had not yet invented his *Vanities*.) Earlier in the season *Vanity Fair* had published a picture layout, featuring the heroines of current "tragedies with happy endings"; among them was Pauline Lord in *Anna Christie*, and O'Neill had pasted it into his scrapbook. Into the scrapbook, along with Miss Lord, had gone the rest of the unhappy-happy heroines included in the display: Helen Mencken, in a play called *The Mad Dog*, Irene Fenwick in *The Claw*, Elsie Ferguson in a play by Zoë Atkins called *The Varying Shore*—and Carlotta Monterey, appearing as "a lady of unhappy morals" in a short-lived melodrama called *Danger*.

Miss Monterey's reluctant acceptance of the role in *The Hairy Ape* brought her into contact for the first time with the man on whose life she was to have a profound effect. The meeting was casual in the extreme, if not actually hostile, and unmarked by any portent of future significance.

"The first time I met O'Neill," she later recalled, "I thought him the rudest man I'd ever seen. And he had no use for me."

Hopkins had been insistent about her taking over the role of Mildred Douglas.

"You're going to replace the girl who's in it now," Hopkins told her. "I told them at the Provincetown that I wouldn't bring it uptown unless they agreed to let me put in a new Mildred."

"That's lovely," replied Miss Monterey. "That'll be a nice atmosphere to do the play in."

Hopkins then asked her if she was familiar with O'Neill's plays. She said she had seen only *Beyond the Horizon* and liked it.

According to her recollection, she did not want to do *The Hairy Ape.* "I didn't want to do *any* play at that time," she said. "I'd recently been in two things—one ran for six weeks and the other ran for twelve [*Danger* and *Bavu*]. I hated the theatre anyway—and I wanted to get back to California—just get away from New York. I wanted to see my mother and my youngster."

(Miss Monterey, then thirty-two, the same age as O'Neill, had been born in San Francisco on December 28, 1888. She had had a daughter by her second husband, a West Coast lawyer named M. C. Chapman, who, within a year, was to obtain an interlocutory divorce decree charging his wife with desertion.)

"I finally decided I would take the part," she recalled. "Actually, it appealed to me because it was a symbol. It was a small part, but also a big one, because of what it stood for in the play.

"One day I was in the theatre talking to someone and a dark young man came over. I'd always heard that O'Neill was dirty, unshaven, messy. This man was clean, neatly dressed, wearing a black tie. We exchanged a few words and he left. 'Who's that?' I asked. 'O'Neill,' I was told. I said, 'You mean the author of this play?'

"I was terribly surprised at his appearance. I was also angry at his rudeness. He hadn't even had the courtesy to thank me for taking over the part on a minute's notice. I could see he didn't think much of me, either. 'Mildew Douglas,' he later used to call the girl I played. And he would tease me by calling me that when he fancied I was putting on airs."

While some critics liked Carlotta Monterey's performance, most of them were unenthusiastic. Alan Dale, in the *American,* for example, wrote that her "small role was played stiltedly and too deliberately."

"Carlotta had the style and refinement Hopkins wanted for Mildred," Charles Kennedy once recalled.

And according to Kenneth Macgowan, "Carlotta got the part because Mary was not enough of a personality for uptown—not luxurious enough."

For some reason O'Neill decided to break his rule and attend the first performance of *The Hairy Ape* on Broadway, on April 17, 1922. Eben Given, who was there, said it was the first time he saw O'Neill in a dinner jacket. O'Neill had begun to dress better since his success; he could afford to, for his income had been averaging $850 a week.

"He looked like a dark prince—with his tan, and his flashing white teeth—as he stood at the back of the theatre," Given said.

"Here they come," called one of the Provincetowners who stood near O'Neill.

"They" were O'Neill's gangster and bootlegger friends from the Village, who hadn't seen him for a while.

One man, who wore a loud check suit and a blazing red tie, said to O'Neill, "Glad to see you, pal. You look great in the fish and chips." O'Neill had sent them free tickets.

"He didn't forget his friends—and they saw him in his finest hour," said Given.

O'Neill did not go back to the theatre during the rest of the *Ape* run—it played at the Plymouth until July 1—and he and Carlotta Monterey did not meet again until four years later; by that time she had married and divorced her third husband, had had a fling as a movie actress, consolidated her reputation as a beauty, come into a substantial sum of money, and more or less given up acting. A number of O'Neill's friends got to know her fairly well during the run of *The Hairy Ape* and from time to time would talk about her to O'Neill, who was not unimpressed with her glamorous, not to say notorious reputation.

Her dramatic flair, like O'Neill's, was even more pronounced off stage than on. Her voice was throaty and her speech cultivated and theatrical. She generally apprised new acquaintances that she was a convent-bred, continent-educated woman, with a heritage of aristocratic European blood —Danish (on her father's side) and French-Dutch (on her mother's). Her appearance—thick, lustrous black hair caught smoothly over her ears; big, dark, smoldering eyes set wide apart, white skin and long, slender neck—suggested the Spanish. It was probably to heighten the Spanish effect that she chose the stage name Monterey, borrowed from Monterey County, near where she was raised. Her real name was Hazel Neilson Taasinge and she had grown up in Oakland, dreaming, according to one contemporary California newspaper account, "of the time when she could be an actress."

Her beauty was of the type that caused both men and women to turn and stare. She was sometimes referred to as "The Swan," because of her lovely neck, and she was several times likened by admirers to an Egyptian queen; one of her husbands, more specifically, compared her with Cleopatra. She made the most of her attributes and camouflaged a figure that tended to be slightly plump with well-cut black dresses. She was always immaculately groomed.

Ilka Chase, the actress and writer, who played with Carlotta Monterey in a melodrama called *The Red Falcon* in 1924, once wrote of her as being "short, with capable hands and feet, and always dressed rather dowdily." But, Miss Chase added, "everything was expensive and of the finest material, and her shoes were made to order of special leathers at great cost. She was the most immaculate creature I have ever known. . . . I never saw her use anything but the sheerest, whitest linen [handkerchief]. From the neck up Carlotta looked Javanese or Russian or something mysteriously exotic, but her sturdy little body proclaimed her Dutch and Danish ancestry. . . . Even at the time when she was sweeping New York as the town's most sultry glamour queen, her apartment shone like a fresh-minted coin. Her bills were paid on the dot, she wore no jewels, and she dressed like a Dutch burgher's wife from the provinces. She was kind and funny, remarkably ribald, and she hated the theatre."

Despite her hatred of the theatre, Carlotta had adhered to it since enrolling in Sir Herbert Beerbohm Tree's Academy of Dramatic Arts in London. Teddy Ballantine recalled that she had been in the class ahead of him when he studied there around 1909. She returned to the United States a year or so later, having married, in England, a wealthy Scotsman, John Moffat. She and Moffat traveled abroad until shortly before World War I ("I had the best things in Europe as a young bride"). She subsequently divorced Moffat, but the two remained on friendly terms. ("He forgave me," she later said. And Moffat once told a friend of hers, many years after the divorce, "I love Carlotta. I'll always love Carlotta.")

She began her professional acting career in a play called *Taking Chances,* with Lou Tellegen, and in 1915 she appeared in the San Francisco company of *The Bird of Paradise,* playing Luana, a Hawaiian girl. She married Chapman, then a twenty-year-old law student, in October of 1916 in Oakland, when she was twenty-five. A year later they had a daughter, whom they named Cynthia.

By the time she took the role of Mildred in *The Hairy Ape* it was clear that Carlotta was never going to be an actress of the first rank; but it was equally clear that she would have an impact as a personality.

Her colleagues enjoyed her company and found her, as did Ilka Chase, kind, funny and ribald. James Light, who was serving as stage manager at the Plymouth, recalled that she enjoyed playing jokes on Wolheim and on Henry O'Neill, who was acting the role of Yank's fellow stoker, Paddy, and who later had a Hollywood career. One day, before a matinee, Carlotta and Light concocted a scheme to "get the boys riled up," in Light's phrase.

"Carlotta was dressed for her entrance in her white gown," Light said. "We left the door of her dressing room ajar and she sat down in one corner and I sat in another. Then we began improvising some impassioned, and largely inarticulate dialogue. It wasn't long before heads began popping in at the door. There we were, at opposite ends of the room, Carlotta sedately reading a book, and my face buried in a newspaper."

O'Neill did not linger long in New York after *The Hairy Ape* had moved uptown. But before he left for Provincetown in mid-May he finally made the acquaintance of his twelve-year-old son, Eugene Jr.

O'Neill's rise to prominence prompted young Eugene's mother, Kathleen, to get in touch with him, suggesting he might like to know his son and help guide his education. Kathleen was motivated by the fact that she was not in affluent circumstances and believed that her son, who seemed exceptional in every way, should have a chance to go to a fine school and college.

When young Gene was five years old Kathleen had married George Pitt-Smith, an office manager, who was divorced and had a son of his own. Pitt-Smith's son, a few months younger than Eugene Jr., spent half his time with his mother and half with his father and stepmother. Kathleen once said that her son loved his stepfather and regarded Pitt-Smith's son as a brother, but she spoke to him often of his real father and taught the boy to think well of him. His childhood, however, was not a happy one. His closest companion was Kathleen's mother, whom he worshiped (and who at sixty-six, had married the man her own parents had forbidden her to wed as a girl).

Kathleen and her new husband moved to a house in Douglaston, Long Island, and soon after that Gene was sent away to boarding school in Peekskill, New York. At six he was already being pushed along the insecure path that his father had followed as a child. There were episodes of running away from school and being sent back. Eventually he learned that home was a place where he spent vacations—and school was the place where he lived. He seemed to adjust to his circumstances and to grow genuinely fond of his mother's second husband. "I was lucky in having a wonderful guy for a stepfather," he once told an interviewer, who wanted to know in what way the divorce of his parents had affected his life.

O'Neill hesitated when the suggestion from Kathleen arrived. He told Louis Kalonyme about it and confessed that he was afraid to meet his son because he might have been brought up to be a conventional and unattractive boy with whom he could have nothing in common.

Kalonyme told O'Neill he had to see his son. Perhaps O'Neill decided to take his friend's advice as a gesture of defiance toward his dead father; he could never, in James O'Neill's lifetime, have brought himself to acknowledge the grandson James had disowned.

The meeting occurred at O'Neill's apartment. Kathleen dressed her son in his best clothes and sent him with her mother to the apartment house where the O'Neills lived. Eugene was instructed to go in and ring the bell.

Gene entered the apartment and found his father waiting shakily. The boy was by far the more at ease of the two and was able to engage his father in a discussion of baseball. To the intense relief of both, they discovered they liked each other.

Later O'Neill told several friends that Eugene was bright and had been brought up carefully, and that he was going to undertake his education.

"Gene came back glowing from the meeting," Kathleen recalled. "Soon after, his father wrote me, thanking me for having raised a son we could both be proud of."

Before O'Neill left for Provincetown he invited Eugene to spend a few weeks with him and Agnes at Peaked Hill during the summer.

XXXIX

WHEN O'NEILL RETURNED TO PROVINCETOWN IN THE spring of 1922 he was not only spent from the strenuous activity of recent months but was beginning to be plagued by increasing financial and emotional problems.

Although the royalties from his plays were now substantial, his expenses were mounting: he was paying for an apartment in New York and maintaining the house at Peaked Hill, which required frequent repairs; he had assumed the cost of his older son's education, and was also helping support Agnes' family. Though he could count on eventually receiving about $75,000 as his share in his mother's will, the estate was still far from being settled.

"Neither Gene nor Agnes seemed to know how to hold onto money," Eben Given once observed. "Gene, for example, really loved good clothes, and when he came into the chips, he bought things like a dozen pairs of white knickers, which were a fad at the time. I remember once when Agnes went to Abercrombie and Fitch and came back with a dozen pairs of golf socks for the knickers."

One cause of O'Neill's emotional stress was the effort required to be even a part-time father to Eugene Jr.; another was his worry over Jamie, who was clearly trying to commit suicide by consuming large quantities of cheap bootleg whiskey. An additional irritant—trivial but nagging—was trouble with his teeth; he was obliged then (as he was to be at intervals throughout the rest of his life) to undergo many long and painful sessions in the dentist's chair.

"I really feel all tired out," he complained to Oliver Sayler in May.

His creative efforts were bent on finishing *The Fountain*, which Arthur Hopkins had finally agreed to produce. (Hopkins was supposedly negotiating with John Barrymore to play the lead, and Jacob Ben-Ami also was under consideration for the role, but plans were still as vague as they had once been for *Beyond the Horizon* and *The Straw*.)

Inadequately barricaded against fame, O'Neill was finding it difficult to work. Even at remote Peaked Hill the outside world was beginning to intrude. In mid-May, for instance, he learned to his profound annoyance that *The Hairy Ape* had run into censorship trouble.

"Charges that Eugene O'Neill's play, 'The Hairy Ape,' is 'obscene, indecent and impure,' have been made by the Police Department, and a copy of O'Neill's manuscript has been forwarded to Chief City Magistrate William MacAdoo," announced a New York newspaper on May 19. The accusations evoked a storm of editorial protest in the press, and reporters clamored for a statement from the author. The author wired one to the *World:*

"Such an idiotic attempt at suppression will bring only ridicule on the poor dolts who started it. Further than that I have nothing to say at present."

The flurry died down within a few days, but it had interrupted O'Neill's work rhythm. He was interrupted again a few days later, but more pleasantly.

On May 21, 1922, the Pulitzer prize was announced for *Anna Christie.* This time, unlike the case of *Beyond the Horizon,* the announcement of the prize had an impact.

In the seven years since the Pulitzer prize had been established, only four plays had earned the award—two of them O'Neill's. On the jury that guided the prize to *Anna Christie* were Hamlin Garland, (who had served in 1920, when the award went to *Beyond the Horizon*), William Lyon Phelps, and Jesse Lynch Williams, who had won the Pulitzer Prize in 1918 for his play, *Why Marry?* (In 1921 the prize for drama went to Zona Gale for *Miss Lulu Bett.*)

"Yes, I seem to be becoming the Prize Pup of Playwriting—the Hot Dog of the Drama," O'Neill jocularly commented to Oliver Sayler on May 25. "When the Police Dept. isn't pinning the Obscenity Medal on my Hairy Ape chest, why, then it's Columbia adorning the brazen bosom of Anna with the Cross of Purity. I begin to feel that there is either something all wrong with me or something all right. . . . 'It's a mad world, my masters!' "

Early in the summer O'Neill nervously welcomed his older son to Peaked Hill for a two-week stay.

"I drove Gene and Agnes to Yarmouth, where they were to pick up young Eugene," Eben Given later recalled. "The boy got off the train alone. He was reticent, just like his father. Agnes sat in front with me on the way back to Provincetown, and Gene sat in back with his son. They didn't speak to each other all the way home. I could see them in the rear-view mirror. They just sat there, sizing each other up, out of the corners of their eyes. Gene would sneak a view of the boy and tug at one end of his mustache, which was a habit of his."

James Light was at Peaked Hill when they arrived. He observed the malaise between father and son; it lasted until Agnes invited them into the house, and suggested a swim.

"The boy hadn't brought swimming trunks," Light said. "Gene got very busy looking for something for him to wear, and finally fixed him up with a pair of his own trunks; once they got into the ocean, the awkwardness between them disappeared."

By the end of two weeks O'Neill had grown fond of his son, but he was not sorry to see him leave, for he did not have the time to devote himself to him. He even begrudged the time that Agnes, not unreasonably, felt he should bestow on Shane, who was now nearly three. O'Neill took an occasional interest in Shane's activities, but he was far from absorbed in him. According to his friends, O'Neill rarely fondled or held Shane in public unless a newspaper or magazine photographer requested him to do so.

"I hardly ever saw Gene play with Shane," Eben Given said, reflecting the impression of most of O'Neill's friends. "I sometimes roughhoused with Shane and carried him around on my shoulders, and Gene might look on in amusement, but didn't join in. He seemed detached from the boy."

Not that Agnes spent much time with Shane either. She was writing sporadically, although she did not pursue her career with anything like the intensity of her husband. One of the Coast Guard men stationed at the nearby lifesaving station, Augustus Perry, recalled: "The maid seemed to play an important role in the care of Shane. I seldom saw his mother on the beach."

The maid to whose care Shane was entrusted was Mrs. George Clarke, who gradually became an indispensable part of the O'Neill household. Mrs. Clarke, called "Gaga" by Shane, was also housekeeper and cook. Born Fifi D'Orsay in Rouen, France, she had married a Provincetown captain whose ship had lain over in Le Havre long enough for him to woo and win her. She had spent most of her adult life in Provincetown and by the time she went to work for the O'Neills she was a staid Cape Cod widow who blended perfectly into the Yankee background.

A big woman with black hair and a kindly face, Mrs. Clarke was a good manager and cook—her fried chicken was famous—and, best of all from O'Neill's point of view, she knew how to be silent. Understanding his need for privacy when he was working, she would turn visitors away from the house while her employer glowered in his tower room. O'Neill grew so dependent on her that he finally capitulated when she demanded that Terry Carlin be barred from the house.

"Terry spat in the kitchen sink this morning," she told O'Neill balefully. "Either he goes or I must go." Despite his devotion to Terry, O'Neill forbade him to enter the house from that day on.

But Terry continued to live in a shack near the house, and he was Shane's frequent companion. To Shane, this seemed natural, and though O'Neill also regarded Terry as a suitable playmate for his son, many of O'Neill's friends marveled at what they considered a rather unwholesome arrangement.

Nevertheless, Terry spent more and more time with Shane as the boy grew older. They would take long walks on the beach and into the woods. Once they went to gather mushrooms, Terry having explained that mushrooms would come to Shane if he whistled. Another time, when Shane refused to return home for dinner, Terry climbed a telephone pole and pretended to talk to the O'Neill house on the wire; "learning" that apple pie was being served, he was able to persuade Shane to go home.

While content to leave Shane largely in the hands of Terry and Gaga, O'Neill did spend some time trying to teach his son to love the water. His somewhat unorthodox method was to wrap an inflated rubber tube around Shane and tie the tube with a short length of rope to a floating log; he then fastened the log by a 100-foot rope to a stake, which he buried on the shore. In this way Shane could stay afloat 100 feet from shore while his father swam nearby. If waves broke over him, he was simply to learn to ride under or over them; if he got water in his mouth, he was to learn to spit it out.

Shane seemed not to mind his rough introduction to the sea and appeared to enjoy his summers at Peaked Hill. He called his home "the house where the wind blows" and accepted his life unquestioningly.

Shane's half sister, Barbara (Agnes' daughter), who was about six years older, was occasionally a part of the O'Neill ménage at Provincetown. Like Shane, she retained only happy memories of the time spent there.

"I hardly remember Mother or Gene there," she once said. "Shane and Gaga stand out most clearly. Shane was the most beautiful, golden-haired little boy you can imagine. His head was a mass of golden ringlets. He was happy and ebullient and I loved him. Gaga absolutely adored him; he was a child marked for special love. He and I used to take our baths together sometimes, with Gaga presiding.

"Once a week Gaga used to go to town to buy groceries and later in the day she would return by horse-drawn wagon piled high with goodies and staples for the week. Always she brought a little present for Shane and me. She always brought us each the same thing—once, little flowers which when dropped in water, open. Once, a little pipe with a wire cup holding a plastic ball—you would blow and make it dance up and down.

"Mother gave me an allowance of a dollar a week. She would especially get silver dollars for this occasion and it was a weekly ritual, receiving this great, big, round silver dollar. And when I had five of them, she took them to the bank and exchanged them for a gold piece.

"Shane and I lived in the ocean and were constant companions. Once we wandered off over the dunes and a couple of hours later found ourselves being pursued by a frantic Coast Guard. Poor Gaga had missed us and feared we might have wandered off into the quicksands.

"Sometimes Mother and Gene would have wonderful evening picnics and invite their friends from town. I remember once when such an event was scheduled and then no one seemed to be getting there and I started to cry—and then Harry Kemp arrived—the first guest. Harry lifted me up in his great arms and hugged me and calmed my fears and said not to worry that there'd be lots of people.

"My mother gave me a typewriter. I'm sure it must have been some old typewriter that didn't work very well—one replaced with a newer. But I loved that typewriter. I don't think I ever even wrote on it—I just looked at it and said to myself, 'It's mine!'

"I think I met Eugene Jr. the same time his father did. We used to race through the grass and leap over the edge of the dunes. He'd race with me and shout, 'Last one is a rotten egg!' I'd usually be the rotten egg, but if he saw I was going to beat him, he'd change it to 'First one to get there is a rotten egg!' He was fun, and full of zest. He taught me pig latin. He used to sleep in one of the smaller outbuildings. He was the bane of Gaga's existence because he had a sweet tooth and was always taking the box of brown sugar from the cupboard and hiding it under his pillow.

"I remember nothing but happiness at Provincetown—except for that dreadful moment when I thought perhaps no one was coming to our picnic.

"I always remember Gene as a gentle, shy man, with a soft light flickering in his eyes."

A reporter from the Boston *Sunday Herald* visited the O'Neills that July and recorded his impressions:

". . . Hungry mosquitos on the dunes . . . O'Neill in a one-piece bathing suit of white duck. He is always in his bathing suit. His body is almost swarthy from the sun's rays. . . . Shane, too, is always in his bathing suit, green in color.

". . . O'Neill has a fifteen-foot kayak. . . . He paddles sometimes three or four miles off shore. . . . 'It's perfectly safe when you know how to handle it,' O'Neill says. 'It was built for me by a man in New London who has a hobby of making such things.' It is made of cedar. Perfectly tight and rides the waves like a cork. 'I use a double-ended paddle and very little exertion is required to propel the boat.'

". . . Shane plays on the beach and O'Neill's wife writes her stories in the room where they used to lay out corpses after a wreck. . . . O'Neill's study is broad, simply furnished, lined with books and decorated with many theatrical photographs. His desk faces the great seaward windows, overlooking the ocean."

O'Neill and his kayak were a symbol of romance to a number of the young women of Provincetown, much as O'Neill and his rowboat had been, ten years earlier, to the girls of New London. Everyone heard of his daring exploits in the kayak, and of his long, lonely, dangerous swims. All of Provincetown was amused over one of his adventures. He and Jimmy Light were practicing surface dives one day, far out from shore. After one dive Light came up and found himself staring, through water-blurred eyes, into a pair of large brown eyes he at first thought were O'Neill's. But he suddenly realized that the eyes were set in a flat brown face decorated with a flowing mustache that did not resemble O'Neill's. He was face to face with a seal, which was regarding him with friendly curiosity. Light shouted to O'Neill, and they both dove. The seal dove with them.

"It stayed there for four days, and played with us whenever we swam out," Light recalled. "It put our diving to shame."

In the evenings O'Neill sometimes attended parties in town. His social life in Provincetown, as a matter of fact, reached a peak that summer. He had somehow allowed his privacy to slip away from him, a situation that led to friction between him and Agnes. He was pursued by women, and though he made only grave and passive responses to such advances, Agnes could not help being annoyed; O'Neill thought Agnes occasionally encouraged a bit of pursuit for herself, and this evoked the inevitable intensification of the jealous scenes that had marked the relationship from the beginning.

By September O'Neill was very much on edge. He had recently responded to the annual Gaylord Farm questionnaire (Do you feel as well as when you left the sanitarium?): "Yes—except for increasing trouble with nerves, diagnosed as from psychological sources."

And in late September, after completing *The Fountain*, he confided to Kenneth Macgowan:

"I've been in such a fit of the psychological 'willies' that writing even a letter has been a hair-raising ordeal. The aftermath of my battle with

[*The Fountain*] I guess. Added to which, long forgotten progeny and other relatives, each with their own problems, made a congregation out here which scrambled the mental ego."

Not the least of his worries was what attitude to take toward the future of the Provincetown Players. After following *The Hairy Ape* with Susan Glaspell's *Chains of Dew* on April 27, 1922, The Players had announced a year's vacation. The Glaspell play, a weak one, had been produced out of desperation to round out the season when *The Hairy Ape* moved uptown. That spring The Players had printed a brave little pamphlet disclosing their plans to subscribers (it was signed by O'Neill, the Cooks, Edna Kenton and Eleanor Fitzgerald):

"At the end of our eighth consecutive and sixth New York season we announce to our playwrights, subscribers and friends an interim of one year. Our ninth season will open in our MacDougal Street playhouse, not next fall, but on Monday, October 31, 1923. . . .

"We dare to believe that the spirit of [our stage] will keep alive the interest in it during the "impracticable' interim of a silent year. . . ."

In spite of this optimistic statement, it was clear that the Provincetown was dead, the reason for its existence gone. The atmosphere in which the Provincetown Players was founded—an atmosphere of hostility toward creative development on the part of Broadway—had been largely erased by the troupe itself. As the critic Joseph Wood Krutch pointed out years later, in a discussion of the "off-Broadway" theatre as it had existed during four decades: " 'Little theatres' are usually, by their very nature, rather short-term projects, and . . . if they are permanently important, it is because they either grow up into big theatres or, having done their job, cease to have any place simply because the big theatres have learned from them what they have to teach. The Washington Square Players grew up [to become the Theatre Guild]. The Provincetown did its job."

Having fostered the development of America's first dramatist of stature, the job it did was unique in the history of the theatre. "No other American playwright has ever had such prolonged preliminary freedom with stage and audience alike," Edna Kenton once observed.

With the fruits of this freedom realized, with O'Neill accepted on Broadway, the Provincetown had truly done its job—a job that no other "little theatre" has since duplicated.

O'Neill was convinced that the Provincetown's original conception—Jig Cook's conception—was no longer a practical one on which to proceed. He wanted the theatre to go on functioning after its year's interim, but on a different basis than before, and he regarded the vague and conflicting plans of its various members as "a mess."

Cautioning Eleanor Fitzgerald to keep his views "under her hat," he wrote to her:

"Primarily, as you will undoubtedly agree, it is all Jig's fault. As I look back on it now I can see where he drove all our best talent that we had developed away from the theatre for daring to disagree with him. This in a supposed group democracy! Then beat it to Greece, leaving a hollow shell as a monument to his egotism. . . ."

O'Neill went on to suggest that a meeting be held in which everyone who had ever been important to the Provincetown should be present, and that everything in the past and for the future should be "threshed out openly."

After the air had been cleared, he said, everyone with "talent, ambitions, ideas"—such as Robert Edmond Jones and Kenneth Macgowan (whose interest in the theatre extended beyond that of a critic)—should be invited to join the Provincetowners in a "fine experimental theatre" where they could express themselves.

"New blood, lots of it, or death, that's the alternative as I see it," he told Fitzi. Jig Cook would probably construe this as an attempt to unseat him, O'Neill predicted, but, unless the Provincetowners were completely reorganized, he would resign.

"There is no good sitting up with a corpse and I will be making the plea not on my own behalf, for through Hopkins I now have an outlet, where he has assured me I can shoot at the moon, demand changes in the theatre, etc., but because I think it for the best of all concerned. . . ."

Explaining to friends that he did not even want to hear of the Provincetown Players for a year, O'Neill turned to more pressing problems, of which the most urgent was where to spend the winter. Evidently he felt that the town of Provincetown was now too cramped for him and that New York was too distracting, even away from Greenwich Village. He and Agnes talked of going abroad, but they had still not decided by the end of September.

"We will probably, in a fit of desperation, wind up in China," O'Neill advised Macgowan. "I'd like that, too, while Europe somehow means nothing to me. Either the South Seas or China, say I. I'm willing to omit the sophisticated stage. . . . But until *The Fountain* is definite, all plans are useless."

Barrymore was definitely not going to do the play, O'Neill added, and asked Macgowan if he could suggest someone for the role of Ponce de León. He also dropped a hint to Macgowan of a new play that had been brewing for some time. It was called *Welded,* but he had formulated it only vaguely, as yet. "Little subconscious mind, say I each night, bring home the bacon!"

A few days later O'Neill grew more cheerful about prospects for *The Fountain*. Hopkins informed him that he hoped to put it into production within a month. Partly because of this and partly because the settlement of Ella's estate seemed to be coming to a head, O'Neill abruptly abandoned his plans to travel abroad and, instead, bought a home in Ridgefield, a lovely Connecticut town fifty-five miles from New York and ninety from New London. The house was to be his year-round home, while Peaked Hill was to remain his summer retreat. Ridgefield was an exclusive estate area and the house O'Neill chose was almost manorial; his acquisition of it was, in a way, the fulfillment of his wish to "belong" in an atmosphere that had been denied his father. In addition, it met his need to escape from the too-congenial atmosphere of Provincetown and New York, while at the same time being within easy reach of Broadway (so he could attend rehearsals) and New London (so he could keep an eye on his property and on Jamie). His choice of an inland residence, far from the sight and sound of the sea, has been explained by James Light, who was told by O'Neill that the country climate might be better for his lungs. (In his 1922 Gaylord Farm questionnaire O'Neill noted that a recent X ray showed "extreme upper part right lung smoky" and that his doctor had advised him to be "careful.") Perhaps O'Neill did try to persuade himself, for the moment, that his lungs, rather than his nerves, were in need of attention.

O'Neill and Agnes, accompanied by Wilbur and Margaret Steele, began looking at houses in Connecticut early in October. According to Eben Given, O'Neill was tempted to buy Stormfield, in Redding, the Florentine-style villa in which Mark Twain had died in 1910.

"Margaret Steele told Gene she thought it would cost about $5,000 to repair the house, and he gave up the idea," Given said. "Not long after, I bought it myself, from the Mark Twain estate, and fixed it up. Although Gene had bought the house in Ridgefield by then, I had the feeling he regretted not having bought Stormfield; he felt it would have been fitting for him to live in a house Mark Twain had lived in."

The house O'Neill bought was set on thirty-one acres of wide lawns, pasture and woodland, called Brook Farm. It included a spring-fed swimming pond, a fish pond, vegetable and flower gardens, a four-car garage, a stable and a barn. The house itself was a traditional, white clapboard, New England colonial, with a paneled center hall extending to a rear terrace. It had a paneled library with a beamed ceiling and a fireplace, and a sun room, both of which opened onto the terrace, a wainscoted dining room with a fireplace, and a thirty-foot living room with French doors leading to a covered patio. Upstairs there were four master bedrooms, two with fireplaces, and servants' quarters. The house was surrounded by huge elms, oaks and pines.

To complete his conception of himself as a country squire, O'Neill bought an Irish wolfhound, the fabled breed of Irish kings. The dog, called Finn, had ruby eyes, was the size of a small pony, and had a tail that swung with the impact of a broom. Finn had a passion for killing the neighbors' chickens, and suffered from the delusion that he was a lap dog.

"Dogs liked O'Neill," Louis Kalonyme recalled. "And O'Neill liked this wolfhound, even though wolfhounds aren't very bright. One night, when O'Neill and I were pretty drunk, he gave me a long explanation of why Irish wolfhounds go mad; as I recall, it didn't make very much sense."

The house and its trappings cost O'Neill more than he could afford (several servants were required to run the estate) and he became harder pressed for cash than ever. He paid $40,000 for the property—a steep price in 1922.

"All of the available money from my plays has gone—and is going—into payment for a home I have recently bought near New York," he told a friend in late October. To help him along, he induced the administrator of Ella's estate, a New London lawyer named Julian Moran, to liquidate various bits of New London real estate and advance him the cash. But the cash never lasted long. He was so short of funds that at one point he was unable to pay the fee of his own lawyer, Harry Weinberger.

"Have a heart!" he implored Weinberger in the late fall of 1922. "That coin from Moran is already spent. I haven't paid a bill hardly since the middle of summer." He added that he owed money for household expenses in Provincetown and Ridgefield, that a bill for $500 for his son's next half year at school was due, and that he had to pay the interest on his mortgage.

"You'll have to wait until the going is a bit fatter. I'm sorry," he told Weinberger. He was trying to sell some of his plays to the movies, and urged Weinberger to work on the sale of *Gold*—"if you can sell that we'll be in clover." But O'Neill was never lucky with movie sales; those properties he did sell, he usually sold on the wrong basis—either he took a percentage, and the movie made no money, or he took a modest cash payment, when he could have made a great deal on a percentage basis.

◈

[516]

Still running away from himself, O'Neill did not find peace in Ridgefield. The thing that gnawed at him most was his increasing antagonism toward Agnes and what he imagined, whether rightly or wrongly, to be her antagonism toward him. They were in love, but their love brought only turbulence. The friction could not be concealed from their friends, a number of whom have reported on it.

"Gene was doing a lot of drinking around that time," Macgowan recalled. "He telephoned me one day in New York from Ridgefield and asked me to bring him a bottle of whiskey on the way to my home in Brewster. When I got to Ridgefield, Gene met me at the door. All he said was: 'I don't like Agnes.'"

Teddy Ballantine, who visited the O'Neills at Ridgefield, was also aware of the jealous tension between them. "Once Agnes tried to sit in my lap as a joke, and O'Neill flared up," Ballantine said. "It was as childish as that—but the fights were bad ones."

Pauline Turkel recalled that Jimmy Light's first wife, Sue Jenkins, once took Agnes away from Ridgefield to keep her from being beaten by O'Neill.

Eben Given conjectured that one of the sources of friction stemmed from too much social life, invited by Agnes. "Gene was roaring ahead, artistically, and he had to be kept free from social demands."

Agnes' daughter said that "lots of people were always coming for weekends from New York," and, confirming this, Louis Kalonyme recalled:

"Agnes liked people; O'Neill liked seclusion. This was one of the obvious causes of friction. But I think another was the question of equality."

What the equality question really amounted to was that Agnes thought she was as much entitled to live her sort of life as O'Neill was to live his; O'Neill considered this outrageous. He wanted to be coddled, waited upon, and obeyed; he believed the importance of his work entitled him to such deference. More than anything else, he wanted Agnes to find her exclusive reason for existence in him and his work. He was shattered at each new indication that Agnes was not as single-minded as he wished her to be.

"Sometimes O'Neill would tell me, in his dramatic way, 'Life isn't worth living. I'm going to put an end to it,'" Kalonyme said. "I'd quote the line from an old vaudeville song—'I'm going crazy—don't you want to come along?' He'd smile and calm down."

Seeking the means of relief most natural to him, O'Neill (using a set of fictional circumstances) began to dissect his relationship with Agnes in the play he had decided to call *Welded*. It was an extreme case of the vicious circle: First, his Strindberg-influenced need for a dramatic marriage relationship; then the torment over this self-induced situation; then the necessity to chronicle, in Strindbergian terms, the havoc he had wrought.

Probably because he was writing about an intensely personal situation at the same time as he was living it, *Welded* did not come off. One of the most transparently autobiographical of his plays (and one of the worst), its theme is O'Neill's favorite one of love-hate. It is about a man and wife, both egoists, who are welded together in a passionate, jealous, possessive love that makes their lives alternately a heaven and a hell. Its point of view is unoriginal, its dialogue trite, when it is not mystically highflown, and its conception of the ideal marriage reflects O'Neill's appalling naïveté in that area of human relations.

The husband and wife have a soul-shattering fight and the wife tries to spend an adulterous night with a former admirer, while the husband attempts to go to bed with a prostitute. Neither can go through with it and both realize that their love welds them to each other; there is no solution for them but to stay together, fighting, reconciling, hating and loving.

There are only four characters in the play. Michael Cape (whose surname O'Neill borrowed from his recently acquired English publisher, Jonathan Cape) is a successful playwright, thirty-five years old. (O'Neill had just turned thirty-four when he began writing *Welded*.) "His unusual face," wrote O'Neill self-descriptively, "is a harrowed battlefield of super-sensitiveness, the features at war with one another—the forehead of a thinker, the eyes of a dreamer, the nose and mouth of a sensualist. One feels a powerful imagination tinged with somber sadness—a driving force which can be sympathetic and cruel at the same time. There is something tortured about him—a passionate tension, a self-protecting, arrogant defiance of life and his own weakness, a deep need for love as a faith in which to relax."

Eleanor, his wife, called Nelly, is a woman of thirty. (Agnes had recently turned twenty-nine.) "Her figure is tall," wrote O'Neill, describing his heroine. "Her face, with its high, prominent cheekbones, lacks harmony. It is dominated by passionate, blue-gray eyes, restrained by a high forehead from which the mass of her dark brown hair is combed straight back. The first impression of her whole personality is one of charm . . ."

The Capes have been married five years (O'Neill and Agnes were approaching their fifth wedding anniversary at the beginning of 1923, when O'Neill was finishing the play). With dramatic license O'Neill made Eleanor an actress; but when Michael scathingly calls Eleanor "You actress!" and compares her lack of creativity to his own genius, it is possible to imagine O'Neill sneering at Agnes for her literary aspirations, so dwarfed by his own achievements.

One of the two remaining characters in the play, a Broadway manager named, simply, John, is the symbol of the intruding world which diverts Eleanor's attention from her husband. Thus, in an early scene, when Michael and Eleanor are discussing their ideal marriage—"Our marriage must be a consummation . . . kept sacred as the outward form of our inner harmony"—and vowing not to fight any more, their love is intruded upon by John's unexpected visit. As they are clasped in each other's arms in an ecstasy of love, a knock comes on the door, to which Michael is oblivious, but which Eleanor feels impelled to answer. It is John, diverting Eleanor's attention from the Capes' sanctified love. After John has been received and then dismissed, Cape jealously accuses Eleanor of being less devoted to their love than he is.

CAPE: . . . You feel the need of what is outside. I'm not enough for you.

ELEANOR: . . . (*Pleadingly*) Haven't I a right to myself as you have to yourself?

CAPE: You fight against me as if I were your enemy. . . . At every turn you feel your individuality invaded—while at the same time, you're jealous of any separateness in me. You demand more and more while you give less and less. And I have to acquiesce. Have to? Yes, because I can't live without you! You realize that! You take advantage of it while you despise me for my helplessness! . . .

ELEANOR: You insist that I have no life at all outside you. Even my work must exist only as an echo of yours. You hate my need of easy, casual associations. You think that weakness. You hate my friends. You're jealous of everything and everybody. (*Resentfully*) I have to fight. You're too severe. Your ideal is too inhuman. Why can't you understand and be generous—be just!

After more bitter argument Cape attempts to throttle his wife and then storms out of the house, swearing that he will kill his unbearable love; Eleanor follows suit. Then come the scenes in which each tries to destroy his love for the other—Eleanor with John and Michael with the prostitute, who is the play's fourth character. In spite of his earlier protestations that audiences reacted unsympathetically to such symbolic designations as "A Woman," O'Neill listed the prostitute as just that; and though she was not an abstraction she was a symbol—one of O'Neill's favorites —the solacing, mother-earth-whore. Reflecting his comments to Louis

Kalonyme on the uselessness of living, O'Neill expressed in this scene his rationalization of suicide. O'Neill spoke through Cape and the lines were his "To be or not to be" speech.

In the scene Cape, at first, is trying to kill not himself but his love; then it occurs to him that he might go a step further:

"I can't! I can't!" begins O'Neill's Hamlet ("with dull, impotent rage"). "Our love must live on in me. There's no death for it. There's no freedom—while I live. . . . Then, why—? (*A pause*) An end of loathing—no wounds, no memories—sleep! . . . (*He shakes his head as if to drive some thought from his mind . . .*) That's over. The great temptation, isn't it? I suppose you've known it. But also the great evasion. Too simple for the complicated—too weak for the strong, too strong for the weak. One must go on, eh?—even wounded, on one's knees—if only out of curiosity to see what will happen—to oneself. . . . Well, good-by, and forgive me. It isn't you, you know. You're the perfect death—but I'm too strong, or weak—and I can't, you understand—can't!"

In style the play embodied what O'Neill thought of as a sort of super-realism; that is, he intended it to be realistic in the sense of symbolic universality and truth, but not realistic in presentation. For example, he called for a stage effect that consisted of two circles of light "like auras of egoism" to pick out and follow Michael and Eleanor throughout the action of the play.

"There is no other lighting," wrote O'Neill in his stage directions. "The two other people and the rooms are distinguishable only by the light of Eleanor and Michael." An interesting idea but, unfortunately, one which served only to emphasize the drabness of the protagonists.

Indicative of O'Neill's frame of mind—both creative and personal—is a statement he made while he was finishing *Welded*. It expressed his increasing preoccupation with getting down to the bare bone of artistic truth.

"I want to write a play that is truly realistic," he said. "That term is used loosely on the stage, where most of the so-called realistic plays deal only with the appearance of things, while a truly realistic play deals with what might be called the soul of the character. It deals with a thing which makes the character that person and no other. Strindberg's *Dance of Death* is an example of that real realism. In the last two plays—*The Fountain* and the one I am working on now—I feel that I'm getting back, as far as it is possible in modern times to get back, to the religious in the theatre. The only way we can get religion back is through an exultance over the truth, through an exultant acceptance of life."

Modern man, he said, had no religion to evade life with. "So we must face life as it is, within ourselves, and do it with joy, and get enthusiasm from it," he added. "And it is a difficult thing to get exultance from modern life."

What he really wanted to communicate to his audience, he declared, was the sense of exultance to be derived "from seeing somebody on the stage facing life, fighting against the eternal odds, not conquering, but perhaps inevitably being conquered."

After finishing the play in the spring of 1923, O'Neill told a friend that *Welded* was "an attempt at the last word in intensity in truth about love and marriage."

A little later he showed the script to George Jean Nathan. Nathan bluntly told O'Neill it was little more than "some very third-rate Strindberg." O'Neill replied heatedly that Nathan (then still a bachelor) couldn't possibly understand the play since he had never been married. He urged Nathan to show it to Mencken, and Nathan subsequently wrote O'Neill, enclosing Mencken's comments, which were not much more flattering than his own.

On May 7, O'Neill replied, scolding Mencken for pointing out that the play was poor realism.

Mencken's criticism of the scene in which Cape harangues the streetwalker, said O'Neill, was "irrelevant as criticism of the play." Mencken had said that Cape was "surely not a man who ever actually lived."

"Well, he surely is to me," said O'Neill. "And, what is more to my point, he is also much more than that. He is Man dimly aware of recurring experience, groping for the truth behind the realistic appearances of himself, and of love and life. For the moment his agony gives him vision of the true behind the real."

Mencken had found the dialogue in this scene banal and the ideas "rubber stamp."

"I'm positive," O'Neill wrote to Nathan, "it's the deepest and truest, as well as the best written scene I've ever done."

O'Neill ended by telling Nathan, "Reason has no business in the theatre anyway, any more than it has in church. They are both either below—or above it."

Clearly O'Neill believed that he had at last discovered in the marriage relationship the substitute for religion he had been seeking. But his newfound faith, like all the others he subsequently embraced, did not last long.

XL

O'NEILL COMPLETED *Welded* IN FEBRUARY OF 1923, but had no idea of when or by whom it would be produced. Although he had demonstrated four times that Art could be popular even in the Broadway showshop, managers did not line up to bid for his new scripts.

Even Hopkins, whose daring O'Neill had overestimated, was now being noncommittal about producing *The Fountain*. O'Neill's stature was still not sufficient to ensure him immediate Broadway production.

The theatres of Europe, on the other hand, were ready to stage practically anything O'Neill's agent would release to them. Hailing O'Neill as the first major American playwright, European critics and theatregoers acknowledged his right to a place among their own prominent writers and accorded him greater eminence by far than did his own country.

By 1923 productions of O'Neill plays were planned for or already running in London, Berlin, Paris, Stockholm, Dublin and Moscow. Not all the plays were greeted with equal enthusiasm in each of these cities, however.

While most of these capitals were ready to rank O'Neill with Shaw, Chekhov and Ibsen, London audiences responded only tepidly to his works. The English public did not care much for *Anna Christie*, for instance, even though one of the most illustrious English critics, William Archer, thought it was "brilliant." Archer, whose judgment was not always discriminating, had become enthusiastic about O'Neill when he read some of the published plays. He wrote from Devonshire to an American relative on October 12, 1922, that he had formed a high opinion of O'Neill from *Beyond the Horizon* and *The Emperor Jones*. *The Hairy Ape*, he said, was "a striking piece of work, but a little too much in the latter-day German style to be quite to my taste." He bewilderingly listed *The First Man* as "brilliant," grouping that play and *Anna Christie* as "great dramas, not mere sketches . . . quite the best plays yet written in America." He went even further than that (and it was pretty far, indeed, considering the active presence of Shaw) when he wrote: "I am inclined to . . . call O'Neill the greatest dramatist now writing in the English language."

Some of O'Neill's plays were given bizarre interpretations in their foreign incarnations. O'Neill was by turns amused and irate over such liberties as Anna's suicide in the Berlin production of *Anna Christie* and the doctored production of *The Emperor Jones* at the Odéon in Paris, in which the régisseur, Firmin Gémier, had bands of Negroes intermittently racing across the stage in pursuit of Brutus Jones. Subsequent publication of these and other O'Neill plays in Europe, however, helped restore the proper focus.

Rudolf Kommer, a German journalist, who translated *The Hairy Ape* into his native tongue, eloquently summed up O'Neill's stature in Europe in 1924:

In journalese, he is being called the representative of American drama. He is nothing of the sort. He does not represent any group, any movement, any current or tendency. He does not announce aesthetic formulae or dogmas, he does not stand for any particular political or religious creed. He is just a major personality, humane and creative, sincere and isolated. (In spite of the alleged leveling influence of American democracy, all great Americans appear as solitary mountains.)

. . . He was not dropped from the skies. His European critics have detected in his plays traces of Strindberg, Wedekind and Freud. But his technique, his atmosphere and the unexplainable essence of his dramatic genius are enthusiastically hailed as something entirely new, as American. No matter . . .—the heir of the European drama has appeared . . . Edgar Allan Poe and Walt Whitman had, and still have, an overwhelming influence on European literature. Eugene O'Neill, although just started, bids fair promise to become the third great gift of America to Europe.

The publication of O'Neill's plays in book form was helping to enhance, if not quite consolidate, his reputation in America as well as in Europe; he was among those rare dramatists whose plays have always had a large and devoted reading audience. By the end of 1923 Boni and Liveright had brought out five volumes of his plays—a collection of the one-act sea plays, *Beyond the Horizon, Gold,* a collection including *The Emperor Jones, Diff'rent* and *The Straw,* and a volume containing *The Hairy Ape, Anna Christie* and *The First Man.*

The publishing firm held O'Neill in greater affection than most of its other authors because the editors hardly ever saw him or heard from him. His own editor, Manuel Komroff, who joined the company in 1922, had been a reporter for the *Call* and the *World* and had met O'Neill earlier in Greenwich Village.

"At Liveright, they liked dead authors, or those who seldom came to the office—and O'Neill rarely came to the office," Komroff said. "Most authors would pester us; they wanted to know why their books weren't selling as well as Dreiser's, or why we didn't advertise them. As far as I can remember, O'Neill never asked us to advertise, or demanded anything special. He'd call up Horace Liveright to ask if a book was ready, and Horace would invite him to come over. O'Neill would say he was too busy. Once in a while, if the matter was urgent, O'Neill would consent to meet Liveright for lunch."

"Why doesn't O'Neill ever come in?" Liveright often asked Komroff petulantly.

Komroff's function with regard to O'Neill was less a job of editing than of liaison. "No one ever touched a word of his plays while I was there," Komroff said.

O'Neill would have been pleased had the same been true of his producers. Disappointed by Arthur Hopkins' less than avid espousal of *The Fountain,* O'Neill began searching, in 1923, for an instrument of production which he could control. He was, as he confided to George Jean Nathan, "desperate for a production." He no longer believed in Hopkins, he told Nathan, adding, "When it comes right down to bedrock he's just . . . a bit brainier and more courageous than most, perhaps— but also a lot lazier and less efficient. There's no hope for me with him. . . . So, as there is no one else, I'll have to help create a new outlet—or remain gagged."

The new outlet soon presented itself in the form of a reorganized Provincetown Players. The Provincetowners' year of inactivity was coming to an end in the summer of 1923 and Jig Cook still lingered in Greece. The founding members wondered whether they should resume operating their theatre without him or discontinue permanently. They cabled to Cook in Athens, asking him to cast his vote for or against the continued functioning of the Provincetown Players and Cook cabled back from Athens on June 19, 1923: "For termination." He elaborated, in a letter from Delphi, to Edna Kenton:

"I am forced to confess that our attempt to build up, by our own life and death, in an alien sea, a coral island of our own, has failed." With obvious reference to O'Neill, he added, "Our richest, like our poorest, have desired most not to give life but to have it given them. We have valued creative energy less than its rewards—our sin against our Holy Ghost. Since we have failed spiritually in the elemental things, and the result is mediocrity, what one who has loved it wishes for it now is euthanasia—a swift and painless death."

Delighted that Cook had relinquished his grip, O'Neill agreed that the Provincetown, as it had functioned in its last few years, should die. But he thought a reorganized Provincetown Players could serve both his own needs and those of the theatre in general. He discussed this idea with Kenneth Macgowan, who had shown an increasing interest in the Provincetown's activities during its last two or three years and with whose ideas on production O'Neill found himself in sympathy.

"Gene had always disliked the idea of a committee running the Provincetown," Macgowan said. "He felt there were too many arguments, and thought the theatre should be run by a firm, dictating hand. He wanted an experimental theatre which would be not only an outlet for himself, but would produce experimental plays or do experimental productions of established classics. He wanted Bobby Jones, for whom he had great admiration, to be given a free hand in design and direction. He thought we should do some of the modern European plays, along with new plays by interesting American writers.

"He suggested that I be the dictator, but I said no, let's have a triumvirate of you, Bobby and myself, and if there's a disagreement, I'll settle it."

O'Neill concurred in this plan and asked Macgowan to outline a program of plays for the Provincetown's 1923-24 season. Macgowan responded with a list that included a production of *The Brothers Karamazov*, *The Taming of the Shrew*—"with Roland Young playing a mild-mannered, little Petruchio"—and a script by Sidney Howard, a new dramatist who had studied with Professor Baker and had recently written an unsuccessful but imaginative play in blank verse called *Swords*. In addition, Macgowan suggested that O'Neill adapt something himself for the coming season.

"Your scheme for the P.P. sounds fine to me," O'Neill advised Macgowan from Provincetown, where he had again gone for the summer. "You can rely on my being all for it and co-operating as actively as possible in every way. It seems to me the only way to save the P.P. theatre and stimulus—(it's real contribution, a thing well worth saving)."

O'Neill hoped to participate actively in the work of the new Provincetown Players, and believed that his spending the winter in Ridgefield would make it easy for him to stay in close contact with the group. "Physically and every other way, I feel up to more in a co-operative sense than I believe I ever have before—constructively speaking," he told Macgowan.

As for actual writing, he would give some thought to adapting *The Ancient Mariner* which he believed might evolve "as a novel form of recitative, pantomime, Expressionist drama."

But primarily, his interest in the venture would be less as a writer than as "a person with ideas about the how and what of production." There were so many things outside of his own plays, he explained, about which he believed he could be theatrically creative and he was willing to work with whoever was interested in his ideas.

"You see," he said, "all these ideas of mine are being incorporated into my own plays bit by bit as they fit in, but I can't write plays fast enough to keep up with the production-imagination section of my 'bean.' It would be suicidal to attempt it, particularly at this time when I am reaching toward the artistic wisdom that in order to keep absorbing I've got to treat each play with more and more concentration of mind and effort over a longer period of time. In other words, if I wish my work to grow steadily more comprehensive and deeper in quality, I've got to give it more and more of my possible sum-total."

Later O'Neill spared a bit of his sum-total to outline in detail for Macgowan a series of plays he wanted to see the Provincetown do. These included the works of Andreyev, Wedekind, Hasenclever and, not surprisingly, Strindberg, whose *The Spook Sonata* he thought should be played in masks. He did not mention, at this point, two other European playwrights he admired—Pirandello and Lenormand—possibly because he foresaw difficulties in getting adequate translations of their works.

He envisioned a sweeping policy that would encompass "radical productions of old plays, revolutionary adaptations of classics, new forms of all kinds—in brief, to give the emphasis to the actor and director for a time and to quicken some of the fine old stuff into modern life." He was sure that such a theatre was an immediate need, and that it could widen the scope of American drama and prove an incentive to new playwrights.

O'Neill's enthusiasm for the new theatre and his pleasure at finding himself once again at Peaked Hill seemed, for the moment, to banish the gloom of the past winter in Ridgefield.

"It's wonderful—same old sea and all," he exulted to Eleanor Fitzgerald, soon after settling in at Peaked Hill. He said he was full of the joy of just being alive. "Haven't known it—except in spare moments— in years. Seem to be ten years younger—all pep! It's a grand and glorious feeling—a regular rebirth from the vale of despair, which about reached its worst when you were out at Ridgefield in December."

O'Neill's state of euphoria lasted through most of the summer, abetted by the fact that he'd got a start on a new play, that Hopkins had come out of hiding long enough to discuss, again, a fall production of *The Fountain*, and that he anticipated making a trip to Ireland. Lennox Robinson, the Irish playwright and manager of the Abbey Theatre, was planning to produce *Diff'rent* in Dublin, and it was to see this production that O'Neill proposed to make the journey.

"I'm all Irish," he told Charles Merrill of the Boston *Globe* that July. "I have always wanted to go to Ireland. My father, of course, knew the old Irish legends and folklore. I started to study Gaelic, but it was too difficult and I had to give it up." (The trip to Ireland did not materialize but, not long after, O'Neill became a founding member of the Irish Academy of Letters, proposed by no less a fellow Irishman than William Butler Yeats; when, some years later, an appeal was made by the Academy for a small, annual subscription to pay postage and other office expenses, O'Neill sent a money order on his bankers, which was cashed annually until his death.)

Gloating a little to the reporter from the *Globe*, O'Neill told him that, having never expected to make much money from playwriting, he had simply written as he pleased, without an eye on the box office. The fact that, even so, his plays had achieved financial success, he said, "ought to be encouraging to those who are trying to write something besides commercial plays."

"As a matter of fact," he added, "there are a great many persons who are trying to write for money, people who have no other motive, and very few who are getting the money. There are fewer writers who are following their own creative instincts, and their chances of making money are much better for that very reason."

At that moment O'Neill was following his own creative instincts by writing a two-play opus he was subsequently to condense into one long, three-act play called *Marco Millions*. The title, which to his intense annoyance was often erroneously construed as *Marco's Millions*, was O'Neill's rather clumsy stab at an American equivalent for the Italian "Il Milione"—"tacked on mockingly to Marco Polo's name by the scoffing rabble in Venice, who thought his stories about the East such awful lies," O'Neill once explained.

O'Neill's aim was "to render poetic justice to a man unjustly world-renowned as a liar"; his point of view was that Marco Polo was no liar—that he did, in fact, see and amass vast riches in the service of the Great Khan—but that he was an arid-souled materialist, immune to and blindly destructive of the beauty and poetry in life.

O'Neill had become fascinated by the character of Marco Polo earlier, while doing research for *The Fountain*. The thirteenth-century Venetian merchant, Marco, fitted perfectly O'Neill's conception of the twentieth-century American businessman, and symbolized American materialism in general. Like all the other abstractions that held his interest, the victory of materialism over idealism had grown out of O'Neill's painful observation of his father.

James O'Neill's self-confessed defeat as an artist and his bitterly regretted acceptance of money and fame served as the goad for O'Neill's portrait of Marco. It also happened that at about this time O'Neill had conceived a strong distaste for one of the early benefactors of the Provincetown Players, Otto Kahn, the New York financier who epitomized for O'Neill the despicable Great American Businessman (soon after, still pursuing the same theme, O'Neill was to call a similar symbol *The Great God Brown*). Kahn was a man of taste, with a genuine interest in art, but O'Neill could not forgive him for having devoted his life primarily to making money. Kahn had often urged O'Neill to write a play about the American businessman, portraying him as a hero and a man of genius, and O'Neill took a wicked, if subsidiary, delight in presenting Kahn with a rather different conception of the hero-genius, Marco.

" 'M. Polo' is proving grand pleasure," O'Neill informed Kenneth Macgowan that summer. "I have tentative plans drawn—floor plans—for all of it, almost. Am reading and taking millions of notes, etc. A lot of what the actual writing must be is now clear—and a lot isn't, but will be, God willing! I'll soon start a lengthy scenario of the whole to find out just how and where I stand—then get right after the writing, I hope. There's a lot of reading still to be done. I feel satisfied with the development—elated, even! The child will be either a surpassing, satiric Beauty— or a most Gawdawful monster. Beauty, I fondly opine. Satiric or not remains to be seen."

Marco Millions got no further than the outline stage that summer; a series of new personal problems and two other plays intervened, and it was not until the winter of 1925 that *Marco* was completed.

XLI

THE GRAVEST PROBLEM FACING O'NEILL IN THE FALL
of 1923 was his brother. After Ella's death Jamie, in O'Neill's own words
to a friend, "gave up all hold on life and simply wanted to die as soon
as possible."

O'Neill was torn between the feeling that Jamie *should* die and a
desire to save and absolve him. Jamie had told O'Neill the story of how
he had spent his time on the train that bore Ella's body from California
to New York: he had picked up a woman and "every night—for fifty
bucks a night" had tried to forget "what was in the baggage car ahead."

Jamie could not live with his guilt and O'Neill, who prided himself
on his tolerance, was so repelled by Jamie's story that it took all his will
power to refrain from judging him. The shock of Jamie's behavior was
something O'Neill had still not got over when, in 1943, he wrote *A Moon
for the Misbegotten.*

That play was Jamie's epitaph, and though it was a brutal exposure
of his brother, it was far more forgiving than O'Neill could reason himself
into being in 1923. The play was, in fact, an imaginative rearrangement of
Jamie's last days, arising as much out of penitence on O'Neill's part as
out of a desire to vindicate his brother. It was typical of the sort of wish
fulfillment to which O'Neill was often addicted in his autobiographical
writings.

The play is set in New London in early September, 1923, two months
before Jamie's actual death. But far from spending his last weeks in New
London—in the play, he was wistfully wooing and being absolved by a
woman who genuinely loved him and might possibly have saved him—
Jamie was actually in a sanitarium in Paterson, New Jersey. He had
been carried there in a strait jacket the previous May.

O'Neill had seen little of his brother since the summer of 1922, when
Jamie visited him in Provincetown; after that O'Neill had encountered
him only on brief visits to New London, where Jamie was living on a
$100 a month allowance from Ella's estate and methodically drinking
himself to death.

One of the few people who spent time with Jamie in the summer
before his final illness was Louis Kalonyme. At sea in New York now

that his mother was no longer there to be attended to, Jamie divided his time between New London, and its ghosts, and Provincetown and his brother. When O'Neill was absorbed in his work, Kalonyme kept Jamie company.

Jamie detested all of O'Neill's friends except Kalonyme.

"You and I are the only ones who can drink Gene under the table," Jamie would tell Kalonyme, with the closest approach to affection that he could then muster. Kalonyme found him an engaging drunk and enjoyed his company; he had no suspicion how close to death Jamie was, even then, or how eagerly Jamie was trying to hasten his own end, but he did see that Jamie was consuming a suicidal amount of poisonous liquor.

"He drank more than anyone I ever knew," Kalonyme later recalled, "—except Terry Carlin, who, incidentally, disapproved of Jamie. People called Jamie cynical, but that was silly. Cynicism presupposes a belief in something, and Jamie believed in nothing. Once, when I met James Joyce in Paris and we talked about the O'Neills, I told him that Jamie should have been a character in *Ulysses*. His profanity was so bad, it's hard to describe. Joyce understood about Jamie; he would have been able to draw a true picture of him."

Jamie did a good deal of bragging and lying to Kalonyme that summer, merely from force of habit. Though he no longer had any interest in Broadway or anything else, he continued to give Kalonyme exaggerated gossip.

"But he didn't exaggerate about his success with women," Kalonyme said. "He used to get mail all the time from women. Of course, some of them were interested in helping him spend his inheritance, but there were evidently quite a few who just found him irresistible, and one of the few things that infuriated him was being doubted about this."

"You lousy bastard, when am I going to catch *you* with a broad?" he would ask Kalonyme, in a restrained moment.

What also angered Jamie was being told he had misquoted Shakespeare.

"If Gene or I corrected him, he'd fly into a rage," Kalonyme said. "He struck me as being both jealous and proud of his brother. He'd tell Gene: 'You may be smart, but I've got the Old Man's voice.' He didn't admire Gene's plays, but he was proud of their success. He was always telling me about how he had protected Gene, and Gene would tell me how he had protected Jamie, and ask me, 'What's the latest thing that bastard has said to run me down?'"

O'Neill felt injured by Jamie on other occasions. Several times

Kalonyme and Jamie went off to fetch a bottle of white mule. On their way back to Peaked Hill they would finish most of it, sheepishly presenting O'Neill with the almost empty bottle.

Though O'Neill made some halfhearted attempts to stop Jamie from drinking, he saw it was a lost cause and usually ended in getting drunk with him. Not infrequently both brothers were ill enough to require medical treatment, which was provided by Dr. Hiebert.

"It was too easy to get liquor up in Provincetown," Dr. Hiebert recalled. "There were always big barns full of white mule in the area."

But Jamie managed to find various sources of liquor in New London, too, and there were more women available there. One of them was a middle-aged milliner, a widow, who helped him spend his money. Although the amounts he was permitted to draw were limited by the administrator of Ella's estate, Jamie contrived to borrow against his inheritance, and when such loans were not forthcoming, he pawned his watch and other personal items. He lived at the Mohican Hotel, a huge, bleak edifice in the center of town, and avoided most of his cronies. He spent his time in small bars, often stumbling back to the hotel in a state of insensibility. The hotel's desk clerk, Coddington Pendleton, who had spent many evenings in earlier years drinking with James O'Neill at the Crocker House, found Jamie lying drunk outside his fourth-floor room early one morning.

In May, 1923, Jamie, only forty-five, looked closer to sixty. His face was a haggard mask, his hair had turned white, and he was losing his eyesight. Various doctors were called to attend him, and increasingly larger amounts for medical fees and drugs—listed as expenses against Ella's estate—indicated that Jamie was making rapid headway in his circuitous plan for self-destruction.

On May 20, in an advanced state of delirium tremens, he was taken by taxi to the sanitarium in Paterson, where he had presumably stayed on other occasions. At the sanitarium he came under the care of a Dr. Millspaugh, who, during the next five months, sent bills totaling close to $2,000 to the administrator of Ella's estate.

A delegate from the administrator's office visited Jamie during July, charging Ella's estate with a $100 taxi fare between Paterson and New London, and O'Neill was kept advised of Jamie's condition during the spring and summer through telephone calls to the sanitarium and telegrams from New London.

One or two of O'Neill's relatives and old friends visited Jamie regularly during the five months he spent at the sanitarium, among them the sister of O'Neill's circus-performer friend, Bill Clarke. Clarke's sister, Mrs.

Frances Cadenas, made a trip to Paterson that summer, after Jamie had been there about a month.

"I used to bring him cigarettes and delicacies," Mrs. Cadenas said. "The first time I visited I found him sitting on a bench on the hospital grounds. He was expecting me, and came toward me hesitantly. He told me he had only five per cent vision. During other visits he would talk to me about Gene—about how much he loved him. Sometimes he'd tell me about dreams he'd had. Once he told me he'd dreamed that Pauline Frederick walked into his room. He described how beautiful she looked."

Jamie's New London cousin, Phil Sheridan, also visited him. He found Jamie subdued, but perfectly coherent, and believed he had a good chance for recovery. On one visit Phil Sheridan was accompanied by a New London friend, Alec Campbell, who recalled many years later that Bill Clarke's brother, Fred, was with Jamie in his room when they arrived.

"Jamie seemed in good spirits," Campbell said. "At one point, he brought out a bottle hidden under his bed, and we all had a shot."

Phil Sheridan wrote to his fiancée on September 21: "Alec and I went over to Paterson, N.J., to see a cousin of mine who is in a private hospital. . . . I doubt if he will ever be the same. His eyes have gone back on him and he is nearly blind."

Sheridan was not prepared, though, for the word that came on November 8 of Jamie's death. Apparently no one had seen him during the previous week, and the news was jolting, even to O'Neill, who was probably the only person who knew that Jamie had no wish to recover.

"The final verdict was pneumonia," wrote Sheridan to his fiancée on November 16, "but I have my doubts. [It struck him that Jamie might have committed suicide.] I thought that he was on the road to recovery and was quite surprised to hear from home that he was in a bad way. Called up the sanitarium a few days before he died and they told me he was out of his mind and getting weaker every day. A couple of days later his brother called and told me he was dead. I will miss him a lot."

O'Neill was ill with flu at the time of Jamie's death, and Agnes arranged to have the sanitarium ship the body to New York. O'Neill was too sick—emotionally and physically—to attend his brother's funeral, which was announced by the newspapers for the morning of November 10.

"I understood . . . that the services would be held at St. Stephen's Church on East 28th Street at half past nine," Sheridan wrote to his fiancée, "so went there a little earlier and sat in the church for about a half hour and nothing like a funeral showed up . . . so went to the undertaker's parlor . . . and found out that the funeral had been postponed to half after ten. Never had such trouble getting to a funeral in my life."

Mrs. Cadenas, who also attended the funeral, later recalled that although O'Neill did not go to the church, he went alone to the funeral parlor to see Jamie in his casket. "I remember Agnes at the church; she cried," Mrs. Cadenas added.

Jamie was buried in New London beside his mother and father, and O'Neill had fresh reasons—albeit legitimate ones—for self-pity.

"I have lost my Father, Mother and only brother within the past four years," he mourned, in a letter to his former Gaylord Farm nurse, Mary Clark, in 1924: "Now I'm the only O'Neill of our branch left. But I've two sons to 'carry on.' However, neither of them will be pure Irish, so I must consider myself the real last one. It makes me feel old and a bit weary sometimes."

And to his Mount St. Vincent school friend, Joseph McCarthy, he wrote, seven years later: "My family were wiped out within three years. . . . There were only the four of us. Booze got [Jamie] in the end. It was a shame. He and I were terribly close to each other . . . he had never found his place. He had never belonged. I hope like my 'Hairy Ape' he does now."

Jamie's death left O'Neill some $73,000 richer, even after all debts and funeral expenses had been settled. One unexpected legacy was a dusty trunk of Jamie's which O'Neill found and opened after his death. It was stuffed with love letters, each packet from a different girl, and each tied with a ribbon and neatly identified with a photograph of the sender.

XLII

JAMIE'S DEATH RELEASED O'NEILL FROM ALL LINGER-
ing restraint of writing about his family. He began to do so unconsciously,
probably not dreaming that he would one day write anything as calcu-
latedly revealing as *Long Day's Journey Into Night* or *A Moon for the
Misbegotten.*

Setting aside *Marco Millions* and forgetting, for the moment, his
stockpile of two unproduced plays (*Welded* and *The Fountain*), he began
working in the fall of 1923 on *All God's Chillun Got Wings.* Originally
conceived as a one-acter, the play was written at the request of George
Jean Nathan for the first issue of *The American Mercury,* the new magazine Nathan was co-founding with Mencken. The first issue was to appear
in January, 1924, and O'Neill was confident that he could meet the
deadline.

As he proceeded to work on the play, though, it grew longer and he
could neither confine it to one act nor complete it in time for the January
issue. O'Neill's longhand first draft was not finished until December of
1923, and though he was immensely pleased with it, he had to notify Nathan that it was probably going to be too long to run in a single issue of the
Mercury; he suggested that the magazine print it in two installments.

"I couldn't keep it shorter, the idea crowded right out of a one-act
form," he confessed. "I've had a great splurge of writing it—8-10 hours
a day—and, whate'er befall, it's been great sport."

Adding that he hoped Mencken would like it, he said he felt "the
result has a real beauty which gives it a blessing."

As it turned out, Mencken did not like the play at all and considered
it unsuitable for the *Mercury.* Nathan insisted on publishing it in the
February issue. For several years—since Mencken had introduced politics
into *The Smart Set*—the two had been at loggerheads. Politics had no
place in a literary magazine, Nathan said—and *All God's Chillun* belonged in the *Mercury.* Nathan won his point, but not long after that
the spectacular editorial partnership was dissolved.

The similarities between *All God's Chillun Got Wings* and *Long Day's
Journey Into Night* are striking.

Although the former is, on the surface, a study of miscegenation, the fact that its hero is a Negro and its heroine a white woman was merely O'Neill's symbolism for the mismated James and Ella O'Neill (whose first names O'Neill used for his principals). In *All God's Chillun* Ella Downey, like Mary Tyrone of *Long Day's Journey,* finds herself the prisoner of a marriage she had at first welcomed as a refuge; and Ella Downey, again like Mary Tyrone, feels herself cut off from her former friends and family because of her marriage. The only difference is that Ella is an outcast because her husband, Jim, is a Negro, while Mary's isolation is due to what she considers her husband's socially unacceptable profession. Also like Mary Tyrone, Ella Downey is unable to feel at home with her husband's friends—in this case, the Europeans among whom she first tries to live because they are free from the race prejudice of her own country.

"Ella didn't want to see nobody," says Jim Harris, explaining to his sister why they have left Europe and come home. Mary Tyrone echoes these sentiments in her speeches lamenting her isolation from her own kind and her inability to feel at home with her husband's theatrical friends.

Apart from its shattering portrait of a man and woman trapped in a bitter love, *All God's Chillun* was a remarkably advanced piece of play-writing for its time. Treating a marriage between a Negro and a white in stage terms, without giving a thought to the incendiary reaction this was bound to evoke, was something only O'Neill would have dared attempt in 1923.

The stage historian and critic Arthur Hobson Quinn, who admired O'Neill, summed up the intellectual attitude of the era when he commented, in 1927, that "upon first reading *All God's Chillun* the reaction is unfavorable."

"The subject is forbidding," he explained. "Literature has usually been content to represent the result of the mating of the white and the Negro race as a tragic consequence to the next generation, but it has spared us the actual miscegenation." O'Neill, he added, had "boldly set precedence at naught."

O'Neill further broke precedent in his idea for abstract stage settings, which were years ahead of their time. The flat in which Jim and Ella live in New York, and in which they gradually smother each other, grows smaller before the eyes of the audience. In the second scene of Act II "the walls of the room appear shrunken in, the ceiling lowered." In the following scene, "the walls appear sunken in still more, the ceiling now seems barely to clear the people's heads."

"The real tragedy," O'Neill once explained in discussing the play, "is that the woman could not see their 'togetherness'—the Oneness of Mankind. She was hemmed in by inhibitions. Ella of the play loved her husband, but could not love him as a woman would a man, though she wanted to, because of her background and her inherited racial prejudice. . . . But the Negro question, which, it must be remembered, is not an issue in the play, isn't the only one which can arouse prejudice. We are divided by prejudices. Prejudices racial, social, religious. Tracing it, it all goes back, of course, to economic causes."

O'Neill added that Jim Harris could just as well have been a Japanese in San Francisco, an Armenian in Turkey, or a Jew. What he did not mention, though obviously it was in his mind, was that Jim Harris could also have been a shanty Irish actor, up against the background and "inherited racial prejudice" of a sheltered bourgeoise.

"These prejudices will exist," O'Neill continued, "until we understand the Oneness of Mankind. Life is hard and bitter enough without, in addition, burdening ourselves with prejudices."

O'Neill drew his title for the play from an old Negro spiritual:

> I got wings
> You got wings
> All God's chillun' got wings.
>
> When I get to Heav'n
> Gonna put on my wings
> Gonna fly all over God's Heav'n . . .

After completing *All God's Chillun Got Wings*, O'Neill directed his attention to production plans for the reorganized Provincetown Players—scheduled to open their season in January. (They had decided to change the name of the theatre itself to Provincetown Playhouse, now that it was no longer strictly a "Playwrights' Theatre.") Over the objections of some of the founding members, Kenneth Macgowan was officially voted into power. On November 8, 1923, the members recorded their approval of Macgowan as "director of production" with "full and final power both in production and business management."

Even with three minds in such apparent artistic harmony as those comprising the new triumvirate—O'Neill, Macgowan and Robert Edmond Jones—friction was bound to arise. Jones, though as much of a pioneer and innovator in his own medium as O'Neill was in his, was too fastidious to approve the choice of *The Spook Sonata* as the initial production. He considered it "a horrible play about horrible people." When his opinion was overruled, he reluctantly agreed to co-direct and co-design the production, but he continued to chafe at it. He did his best to sabotage all of O'Neill's more lurid plans for the presentation and at times seemed physically ill over some of Strindberg's dialogue.

"Gene's idea had been to emphasize every Strindberg cliché with an offstage trumpet blare," Kyra Markham, who was making the costumes, recalled. "I sat in at one of the final rehearsals and found that Bobby had been cutting the most poignant lines, and that we had no trumpet at all. During the rehearsal, Bobby announced that he wanted to cut another line—from the Student's speech in the final scene—'It is always in the servants' quarters that the seed leaves of the children are nipped, if it has not already happened in the bedroom.'

"I charged Bobby with having lost Gene's whole concept. There was an awful row, with Bobby turning white, grabbing his hat and coat and leaving—to be brought back a few minutes later by Kenneth to assure me that he still loved me."

The Spook Sonata opened on January 3 and closed three weeks later, having failed to draw much enthusiasm from the critics. O'Neill, Macgowan and Jones each contributed articles to the *Provincetown Playbill,* and a quotation from Strindberg, expressing a bit of philosophy which O'Neill had long since seized upon as his own, was printed beneath the cast of characters:

"People talk of the Joy of Life as if it consisted in dancing and farcical idiocy. For me, the Joy of Life consists in the mighty and terrible struggles of existence, in the capability of experiencing something, of learning something."

In his own article for the program, entitled "Strindberg and Our Theatre," O'Neill wrote that Strindberg was "the precursor of all modernity in our present theatre" and "still remains among the most modern of moderns, the greatest interpreter in the theatre of the characteristic spiritual conflicts which constitute the drama—the blood!—of our lives today."

"Hence, 'The Spook Sonata' at our Playhouse," O'Neill continued. "One of the most difficult of Strindberg's 'behind-life' (if I may coin the term) plays to interpret with insight and distinction—but the difficulty is properly our special task, or we have no good reason for existing. Truth, in the theatre as in life, is eternally difficult, just as the easy is the everlasting lie."

Two days after the opening of *The Spook Sonata* word came from Greece that Jig Cook was dead.

His death, like his life, had been bizarre. He and Susan owned a dog named TòPuppy, which contracted glanders, an animal disease nearly always fatal. In rare instances the disease can be communicated to people, and Cook became one of the rare cases. He was buried at Delphi, with the rites of the Greek peasants among whom he had lived and who had grown to love and respect him with apostolic devotion. A fugitive, like John Reed, from his native element, he had found a sense of belonging in Greece, as Reed had found in Russia. And, like Reed, who lay buried by the Kremlin wall, Cook was paid a signal honor by his adopted country: the Greek government ordered a great stone from the Temple of Apollo to be placed as a headstone over his grave.

Despite the recent hostility between himself and Cook, O'Neill was grieved and, in retrospect, acknowledged Cook's contribution to the experimental drama in America.

When he learned about Cook's death O'Neill was in Ridgefield, hard at work on another intensely personal tragedy, a play most critics consider one of his greatest. It was *Desire Under the Elms.*

The play was a tremendous advance over his previous full-length works —far surpassing the power of either *Beyond the Horizon* or *Anna Christie,* to which it was linked by its naturalistic style. It combined all the elements most typical of O'Neill at his creative best: the crude, elemental passions of people who harbor the seeds of their own destruction; the brilliant psychological insight into the love-hate relationship of father and son, husband and wife, brother and brother; the cosmic loneliness of man; the hardness of God; and the final acceptance of an inescapable fate.

In *Desire Under the Elms* O'Neill pushed beyond the beginning he had made in *All God's Chillun Got Wings;* preoccupied, as always, with the conflicts of his own family, he allowed full rein to his tortured unconscious. The play has been analyzed at length, in psychoanalytic terms, by Dr. Philip Weissman, a specialist in the psychiatric aspects of the creative process. Dr. Weissman, who never met O'Neill and knew only some of the more superficial facts of his life, concluded, in a study published in 1957, that *Desire Under the Elms* was *the* "unconscious autobiography," just as *Long Day's Journey Into Night* was indubitably the "conscious" one.

Without having access at the time of his study to the dates of the death of O'Neill's parents, Dr. Weissman nevertheless maintained that *Desire* could have been written only "by someone who was recently in the midst of the most intense personal mourning for his mother." What Dr. Weissman's trained instinct told him was, of course, correct.

Although Ella had been dead two years when O'Neill began writing the play, he had been considering its theme for some time; Jamie's death, just before he began the actual writing, had revived O'Neill's sense of loss for his mother and turned his thoughts with renewed intensity to what he considered Ella's outrageous suffering at the hands of both Jamie and James.

These feelings are clearly expressed by Eben Cabot, the twenty-five-year-old son, when he speaks of his dead mother in *Desire Under the Elms*. Eben is convinced that his father worked his mother beyond her endurance, tried to rob her of property which was rightfully hers, and—what is psychologically even more interesting—robbed him, Eben, of a mother. He also accuses his two older brothers, who are in spiritual conflict with him (like the older brother in *Beyond the Horizon*, though on a somewhat more elementary level), of having failed to come to their mother's defense when she needed their protection. The two brothers, in addition to representing Jamie, are, as Dr. Weissman has concluded, also representative of "another aspect of [O'Neill's] own self."

"In their brief appearance, aspects of their histories are more parts of O'Neill's life than his brother's," Dr. Weissman pointed out. "Thus, Simeon, 39, tells us how at the age of 21 he lost his wife Jenn. Jenkins is the maiden name of O'Neill's first wife when he was 21."

The hard-bitten, virile, domineering, stingy, seventy-five-year-old Ephraim Cabot, who attempts to subjugate his young son, is, as previously noted, an extension of the old man in *The Rope*—an unconscious image of James O'Neill, long held by his son, and now fully developed in *Desire*. In addition, as Dr. Weissman pointed out, young Eben's desire for his father's new wife, Abbie, and the subsequent love affair between them represented O'Neill's "usually unallowable unconscious wish [to attain] a maternal and sexual object rightfully belonging to the father." Dr. Weissman further observed the interesting psychological parallel between O'Neill's own undesired fatherhood plus the rejection of his son, Eugene Jr., and the murder of the son born to Abbie and Eben.

(It is probably superfluous to note that Dr. Weissman is a Freudian. When he made his study he was unaware of a fact which might have added significance to his "unconscious autobiography" theory—namely, that O'Neill claimed he had dreamed the whole play one night. He confided this to the actor Walter Huston, among others.)

Fascinating and valid as is the psychiatric insight into the genesis of *Desire*, a number of other aspects of the play are equally significant. *Desire* is the first of O'Neill's works in which the influence of Greek tragedy is clearly manifest. In O'Neill's case, the influence was an extremely literal one. As he did with Shakespeare, O'Neill seized upon the dramatic devices utilized by the Greeks, and thrust them into his own, contemporary dramatic mold. He had not hesitated to use ghosts and soliloquies and did not, now, balk at the fearsome Greek themes of incest and infanticide. He was conversant with the *Hippolytus* and *Medea* of Euripides (a woman falling in love with her stepson; a mother murdering her two young sons for revenge) and saw no reason why such themes could not be translated undiluted to the American stage.

The opportunity for such artistic plagiarism was so obvious that no other American dramatist had dared to try it; it took O'Neill with his single-minded, direct approach to his art to make the attempt.

While the theme and characters of *Desire* were unconscious expressions of O'Neill's own biography and the play's form was inspired by Euripides, its physical setting and some elements of its atmosphere, as in the case of his earlier plays, stemmed from his immediate surroundings and personal relationships. The farm on which the action of the play takes place—identified as being in New England—was actually a combination of the Connecticut farmland amid which he lived at the time of the writing and the grim, lonely New Hampshire farm on which Robert Edmond Jones had grown up.

Jones's impression of New England—"violent, passionate, sensual, sadistic, lifted, heated, frozen, transcendental, Poesque"—was perfectly suited to O'Neill's theme, and O'Neill utilized it, farm and all, as the natural background for his violent, passionate, sensual, sadistic Cabot family. But O'Neill's own extreme sensitivity to nature inspired his conception. Studying the ancient and majestic trees that dominated his Ridgefield estate, O'Neill created twin elms to guard the Cabot farmhouse.

"They bend their trailing branches down over the roof," wrote O'Neill. "They appear to protect and at the same time subdue. There is a sinister maternity in their aspect, a crushing, jealous absorption. . . . They brood oppressively over the house. They are like exhausted women resting their sagging breasts and hands and hair on its roof, and when it rains their tears trickle down monotonously and rot on the shingles."

O'Neill was equally imbued with the stark poetry of the stony land, symbolized by' miles of stone fences. He imparted some of his feelings that spring to Bernard Simon, a young Provincetown Players recruit. Simon, who had been brought to Ridgefield by O'Neill to type the manuscript of *Desire Under the Elms*, accompanied the dramatist on a walk through the woods. O'Neill paused before a stone wall and made what for him amounted to a speech. This was the kind of wall, he told Simon, that he was writing about in the play. Though it now ran through a weedy, uncultivated area, it had once marked a boundary of tilled soil. These walls, he said, were symbols of the old New England farmer's roots—reproachful monuments to the farmers who left their fields to go out west, where there were no stones and where farming was easier. He quoted some of Ephraim Cabot's lines:

"When I come here fifty odd year ago . . . this place was nothin' but fields o' stones . . . I give in t' weakness once . . . arter I'd been here two year . . . they was so many stones. They was a party leavin', goin' West. I jined 'em. We . . . come t' broad medders, plains, whar the soil was black an' rich as gold. Nary a stone. Easy. Ye'd on'y to plow an' sow an' then set an' smoke yer pipe an' watch thin's grow. I could o' been a rich man—but somethin' in me fit me an' fit me—the voice o' God sayin': 'This hain't wuth nothin' t' Me. Get ye back t' hum!' I got afeerd o' that voice an' I lit out back t' hum here, leavin' my claim an' crops t' whoever'd a mind t' take 'em . . . God's hard, not easy! God's in the stones! . . . I picked 'em up an' piled 'em into walls. Ye kin read the years o' my life in them walls."

O'Neill was uneasy on his Ridgefield estate; the house was too big and too grand for him and it oppressed him. He expressed this malaise in *Desire,* not through the son, Eben, but through Ephraim, with whom he alternately identified himself. For example, Ephraim complains of a mysterious "somethin' " in the atmosphere of the farmhouse. "Ye kin feel it droppin' off the elums, climbin' up the roof, sneakin' down the chimney, pokin' in the corners!" Ephraim says. "They's no peace in houses, they's no rest livin' with folks. Somethin's always livin' with ye." During this time, O'Neill told Stark Young, the writer and critic, that he had been hearing (as Young later recorded) "footsteps outside during the night going round the house, and during the day when he was writing he would feel someone looking over his shoulder."

Ephraim, to escape from that indefinable "somethin'," takes to sleeping in the barn—which was a habit O'Neill himself had fallen into. He told Bernard Simon that to escape the company with which Agnes filled the house on weekends he would often flee to the barn. With a bottle of whiskey, he retired to the haystack, sometimes inviting the gardener to join him.

"I have always loved Ephraim so much!" O'Neill later wrote to Kenneth Macgowan, with rare candor. "He's so autobiographical!" (This particular autobiographical quirk reappeared years later in *A Touch of the Poet,* wherein Cornelius Melody, another variant of James O'Neill, leaves his house to sleep in the barn.)

O'Neill's domestic situation had not changed much from the supercharged atmosphere that had nurtured *Welded.* He was still alternating between long periods of work and frenzied periods of drinking, and vacillating between moods of impassioned love for Agnes and black periods of antagonism toward her.

Malcolm Cowley, who, with his wife, visited the O'Neills in November of 1923, later wrote in *The Reporter* about the atmosphere of Brook Farm during the time O'Neill was working on *Desire*. The poet Hart Crane, whom O'Neill admired, also was a house guest at the time.

After lunch on Saturday, O'Neill showed Cowley a copy of a Wilhelm Stekel treatise on sexual aberrations, telling him there were enough case histories in the book "to furnish plots to all the playwrights who ever lived." He indicated, as an example, the clinical record of a mother who seduced her only son and drove him insane.

Taking Cowley upstairs to the room he used for work, "a big bedroom so meagerly furnished that it looks like an abbot's cell," O'Neill opened the doors of a cabinet and showed Cowley the bound ledgers in which he did his writing.

(On the wall of this cell-like bedroom O'Neill later hung an eight-inch crucifix sent from Italy by Stark Young. "Gene always was a Catholic," Young later observed. "You never really give it up." While this was true, in a way, O'Neill did not cherish the crucifix out of any sense of formal piety; like other renegade Catholics, particularly those who have transferred their religious feelings from the church to the theatre, he valued the crucifix for the sense of dramatic ritual it evoked. "The crucifix is a beauty," he wrote to Young.)

Later in the evening, O'Neill took Hart Crane and Cowley down to the cellar, "the only part of the house that seems to arouse his pride of ownership." There he pointed out three fifty-gallon casks of homemade cider.

"Let's broach a cask," suggested Hart. And while O'Neill went for a pitcher and three glasses, Cowley tapped a barrel. "We stand with our full glasses under the bare electric light," Cowley wrote. " 'I can see the beaded bubbles winking at the brim,' Hart says. Gene takes a sip of cider, holds it in his mouth apprehensively, gives his glass a gloomy look, then empties the glass in two deep nervous swallows. After a while we fill the pitcher again. When I go upstairs to bed, long after midnight, Gene is on his knees drawing another pitcher of cider, and Hart stands over him gesturing with a dead cigar as he declaims some lines composed that afternoon."

The next day, according to Cowley, O'Neill continued drawing pitchers of cider instead of working. Then, without Agnes being aware of it, he telephoned for a taxi and was driven to the nearby hamlet of Purdy's, where he vanished.

"Agnes went to New York and spent a frantic week in search of him,"

Cowley recalled. "Afraid of what the newspapers might say, she avoided the Bureau of Missing Persons; instead she made telephone calls to his friends and kept visiting his old haunts, including the Hell Hole. On the last of her visits there, the proprietor confessed to her that Gene had sat in the back room and drunk himself into a coma."

O'Neill had subsequently taken refuge in an upstairs room. Agnes retrieved him and drove him back to Ridgefield, where, a couple of days later, he soberly plunged into work again.

When *Desire Under the Elms* was finished, sometime in March 1924, it became O'Neill's fourth completed play awaiting a hearing. The others were *The Fountain, Welded* and *All God's Chillun Got Wings*—but the last two were now scheduled for production. Kenneth Macgowan and Robert Edmond Jones, with O'Neill himself, were to co-produce *Welded*, though not at their Provincetown Playhouse, where Anna Cora Mowatt's nineteenth-century comedy, *Fashion,* had begun an astonishingly successful revival in early February.

As a conciliatory gesture, O'Neill and Macgowan had accepted Jones's suggestion to revive Mrs. Mowatt's 1845 play about New York society. Jones, who had always been interested in the Victorian period, wanted to do the play according to its original conception as "a soft kind of regret for a fascinating epoch that is gone."

The asides were kept intact and just one line was changed—at O'Neill's recommendation. In the printed version of 1845 Colonel Howard asks Gertrude if she does not miss her friends in Geneva. Obviously this meant Geneva, New York, but O'Neill felt the audience would think of Geneva, Switzerland. Jones suggested that Nyack be substituted, but at the last dress rehearsal O'Neill thought Perth Amboy would be funnier. The mention of Perth Amboy drew the heartiest laugh at each performance and O'Neill liked to say that this was the best line he had ever written.

Because of the success of *Fashion* at their home base, the triumvirate arranged to present *Welded* at the Thirty-ninth Street Theatre. Stark Young, then drama critic for *The New Republic,* was to direct it, at O'Neill's urgent request.

Doris Keane, the toast of London, was to play Eleanor to Jacob Ben-Ami's Michael. But after a week of rehearsals everyone concerned with the production was unhappy. Miss Keane confided to Stark Young that she had thought the manuscript she had read was just a scenario for the completed play, and that she now found she could not act it. She called it "a vulgar, stupid, dogfight play" and begged Young to let her withdraw from the cast. Young, though he had come to agree with her and was embarrassed to let her do the role, considered that his first loyalty was to O'Neill. He appealed to her gallantry, finally persuading her to stay.

"I felt sorry for Gene about the play," Young later said. "I couldn't turn him down when he asked me to direct it. But I'm still ashamed of myself for having let Doris Keane do the role."

Ben-Ami, too, had grave misgivings, although he had loved the script after a first reading. He told Jones and Macgowan that the play would be better off without him, but, according to his recollection, "they begged me to say nothing to O'Neill, because he was in a bad way emotionally; they said they had been breaking their necks to keep him sober and it would be a terrible blow to him if I lost faith in the play." Ben-Ami was no more able to resist this sort of persuasion than was Miss Keane, though neither actor was subsequently thanked for altruism by the author. After the production, O'Neill complained to Oliver Sayler that if the play had been done without the cast, it might have "shone through."

"I knew," Stark Young once wrote, "that Gene's personal life in the period that 'Welded' came out of had not been all smoothness, not between two such vivid temperaments as he and Agnes, for all the love between them, and I felt that [Welded] was in the nature of a confession and a benediction. I can see them now at some of the rehearsals sitting side by side there in the third row and listening to every speech, good or bad, and taking it all as bona fide and their own."

Young's unpublished recollection is a bit more candid. "Gene and Agnes would sit there, like two little birds," he said. "They believed every word of the play. Those vulgar speeches. God!"

Welded opened on March 17, 1924, two years, almost to the day, after O'Neill's previous production, The Hairy Ape, had startled the theatre world.

There had been some shifting about among the newspaper critics since that time. Alexander Woollcott had exchanged his $100-a-week job on The Times for $15,000 a year on the Herald and by 1924 had moved on to the Sun. (The Herald had just been merged with the Tribune, where Percy Hammond still reigned supreme.) John Corbin was reviewing for The Times, Burns Mantle for the News, and Heywood Broun, though still reviewing for the World, was giving more time to a column of commentary; within a year he was to resign his critic's post to Woollcott and confine his writing on the World to his column, "It Seems to Me."

None of the critics liked Welded. (On the same day a comedy called Sweet Seventeen opened at the Lyceum. It was about an adolescent girl named Peeks Farnum and, bad as it was, it outran Welded by forty-eight performances; Welded had stayed for only twenty-four.)

"Eugene O'Neill's 'Welded' is Rather a Lugubrious Conversazione About Love Among the Artists," was the way Percy Hammond's review was headlined.

"Mr. O'Neill is even gloomier than usual in his new play," he went on. "The trouble . . . with the play is that neither character is of the type in which you can become much interested. Mr. Ben-Ami represents a dramatist of the most disagreeable sort. . . .

"Miss Keane is a less unpleasant person. . . . Yet she, too, is a trifle difficult. . . . So far as I could see the only recognizable character in the play is [the prostitute] as she endeavors courageously to entertain her obnoxious visitor in her lowly chambers."

Woollcott remarked that "the milieu of the man and wife was occasionally left to shift for itself so vaguely that there were times when the wrangling two seemed as silhouetted and alone as two back fence cats in debate."

John Corbin, who rarely committed himself during his brief tenure on *The Times*, cautiously described *Welded* as "the work of a highly original and distinguished playwright" but "scarcely a highly original or distinguished play." Burns Mantle mildly advised his readers in the *News* that "for most of our set [*Welded*] must prove ineffective drama, uninspiringly repetitious and not particularly well done," while the reviewer pinchhitting for Broun on the *World* found the first two acts "as true and bold and well-written as anything now to be seen on the New York stage," but the third act "prosy" and "dull."

O'Neill, in spite of being one of the co-producers and having personally selected the director and approved the actors, nevertheless chose to blame the production for the play's failure. "The actors did about as well as they could," he told Barrett Clark soon after *Welded* closed, "but the whole point of the play was lost in the production. The most significant thing in the last act was the silences between the speeches. What was actually spoken should have served to a great extent just to punctuate the meaningful pauses. The actors didn't get that." (Several years later O'Neill classed *Welded* among the several plays that were "too painfully bungled . . . to be worth producing at all.")

O'Neill now turned to *All God's Chillun Got Wings*, which had caused something of a stir in the literary world upon its appearance in the February issue of *The American Mercury*. It had been scheduled for the Provincetown Playhouse at the end of March, when *Fashion* was to be transferred to another theatre. But when March 31 came, and the Provincetown was left empty, a series of difficulties and complications arose, necessitating the postponement of *All God's Chillun*. To fill the gap a twin bill consisting of Molière's *George Dandin* and O'Neill's dramatic arrangement of Coleridge's *The Ancient Mariner*, which had been promised by him as one of several proposed "adaptations," went on at the Provincetown on April 6.

Actually O'Neill contributed very little to the poem except stage directions, less than a dozen words of dialogue, and the concept of playing it in masks. (Later he planned to adapt the Book of Revelation from John, and got as far as marking up a copy of it with notes for staging and sound effects; the project was dropped, and he never again attempted to adapt anything but his own work for the movies.) Neither *George Dandin* nor *The Ancient Mariner* was applauded—"base metal from a cracked test tube in the Provincetown lab," Heywood Broun called it—and the twin bill played for only three weeks. (*Fashion*, on the other hand, was still playing at the Cort Theatre, to which it had been transferred, and did not end its run until the end of August.)

While O'Neill was distressed that his alliance with Macgowan and Jones had got off to a less than brilliant start, he brooded almost as much about a conspiratorial campaign Edna Kenton had been conducting against the triumvirate.

Miss Kenton had convinced Susan Glaspell, who was back from Greece and still grieving for Jig, that O'Neill, Macgowan and Jones had no right to the name "Provincetown Playhouse." Since the playhouse had abandoned the principles set down by Jig Cook, the two women maintained that the name also should be abandoned.

After an exchange of angry letters with Edna Kenton, O'Neill managed to persuade Susan Glaspell that the name was a memorial to Jig, not an insult. In fact, O'Neill went so far as to suggest that a plaque be erected at the playhouse in tribute to his one-time mentor. In a repentant mood, he also suggested the inscription:

"To the memory of George Cram ('Jig') Cook, poet of life, priest of the ideal, lovable human being, to whose imagination and unselfish devotion this Playhouse owes its original inspiration and development as a home for free creative expression."

XLIII

WITHIN THE NEXT SIX MONTHS O'NEILL WAS ABLE TO console himself for the failure of *Welded* with the highly controversial and eminently successful productions of *All God's Chillun Got Wings* and *Desire Under the Elms*.

Even people who were willing to appraise *All God's Chillun* calmly as printed literature were startled by the notion of its being presented on a stage and appalled at the Provincetown's plan to cast a Negro actor as the husband of a white woman.

The impending event was regarded by the newspapers not as a mere theatre item but as significant civic copy. "Mr. Macgowan confirmed the fact that a negro would be used in the male part, and a white actress would play opposite," the *Herald* announced on January 31, and went on: "Those who read the printed version yesterday [in the just-published February issue of *The American Mercury*] considered that the play dealt primarily with ideas and that there was little of the personal element or personal contact in it."

But this did not placate everyone. The Brooklyn *Eagle* published a story, founded on rumor, that the actress, Helen MacKellar (who had played in *Beyond the Horizon*), had been offered the role of the woman and indignantly declined it. The Provincetown formally refuted this, explaining that the role had been offered to and accepted by Mary Blair, but this served only to inspire the following newspaper caption under a photograph of Miss Blair: "White Actress to kiss Negro's hand."

Paul Robeson, who, at the age of twenty-six, was beginning to make his mark as an actor, was signed for the role of Jim Harris, and this fact also was quietly announced by the Provincetown. But any announcement in connection with the play added fuel to the fire, and the Brooklyn *Eagle* was soon pursuing its campaign with the support of, among others, Augustus Thomas, the playwright who had once annoyed O'Neill by his glib lecture at Professor Baker's Harvard Workshop. On February 25 the *Eagle* appealed to Mr. Thomas, who happened to be in Brooklyn making a speech at the Academy of Music, for his comment on the outrage that was to be perpetrated at the Provincetown Playhouse. Thomas obligingly stated that the proposed casting was "unnecessary concession to realism."

"When asked how he would feel about the casting of the play, had it been his," continued the *Eagle*, "Mr. Thomas said: 'In the first place, I should never have written such a play, and in the second place, I should have been willing to do what is usually done in such cases, to permit a white man to play the part of the negro. The present arrangement, I think, has a tendency to break down social barriers which are better left untouched.'"

The *Herald* re-entered the fray in March by publishing a cable from its London bureau that quoted the following comment from an official of England's Actors Association: "We draw no color line."

Although the end of March would have been none too early to get *All God's Chillun* into production, from O'Neill's point of view, it soon appeared that this was not to be. Just as rehearsals were about to start, Mary Blair fell ill with pleurisy and her doctor estimated that she would not be able to work for four or five weeks. The Provincetown was forced to announce a postponement of the production, and the newspapers now had several more weeks to dwell on the evils of the coming event. The *American*, which led the crusade during March, ran a story almost daily about the play.

There was at this period a self-constituted "play jury," which took upon itself the task of passing judgment on what was and was not fit to be seen on the stages of New York City; on March 12, the *American* elicited a statement from one of its members, Brigadier Edward Underwood of the Salvation Army.

"Judging only by what I have seen in the newspapers and what I have heard from members of the play jury," Underwood was quoted as saying, "my opinion is that the production of this play should be prevented, if the charges of its being objectionable are sustained.

"In such a case it is better . . . to forestall production, rather than to permit the play to be given and then attempt to close it up. We naturally are opposed to any play that may be construed as immoral in any way."

The *American* followed this statement with one by John S. Sumner, secretary of the Society for the Suppression of Vice:

"From my information the play is at least a tactless thing, and if it does nothing more than lead to race antagonisms the police powers of the city should be used to prevent its presentation. Such a play might easily lead to racial riots or disorder, and if there is any such possibility, police powers can be exercised."

The *American* was forced to conclude its story somewhat lamely. Having appealed to the license commissioner to take a firm stand, the newspaper was rewarded with his opinion that the Provincetown was "without the jurisdiction of his department."

"No one may legally gain admission to a performance of the Provincetown Players unless a subscriber," said the chagrined commissioner, "because theirs is not a licensed house. Both representatives of the police and of our office have endeavored without success to get into Provincetown performances."

On March 14 the *American* reported triumphantly:

"As a result of the many complaints received at City Hall, it was learned yesterday that Mayor Hylan has ordered an investigation of Eugene O'Neill's play, 'All God's Chillun Got Wings.'. . .

"The protests against the play are based on the fact that in it a white woman kisses the hand of her negro husband. . . . The protests come from both whites and negroes, in about equal numbers.

"In addition to the protests received at City Hall, many white and negro clergymen have expressed themselves publicly in opposition to the play, and many organizations have gone on record similarly.

"The Mayor has no power in law to close a theatre arbitrarily. . . .

"While the question of the theatre's right to operate under a city license, therefore, is removed, it is believed the Mayor could take action to prevent opening of the play if it were shown the presentation might incite riots."

"The danger of race riots," the *American* hopefully concluded, "has been pointed out in many protests."

"There has been discussion," the *American* notified its readers on March 16, without revealing by whom, "of the advisability of substituting an octoroon for Miss Blair." The newspaper added that "if the play actually is produced there will be enough policemen at the theatre to prevent any breach of the peace."

By March 18 the *American* had turned up several more sympathizers: "a leading member of the New York Bar," a member of the staff of the Board of Education, and a founder of the United Daughters of the Confederacy. All of them agreed that the play should not be produced.

On that same day O'Neill was persuaded by his colleagues to prepare a statement for the press, defending the production. Retiring to a room in the Hotel Lafayette on University Place, he labored over the following comments, which, with many corrections and crossings-out, covered two and a half sheets of the hotel's generous-sized stationery:

In answering the criticisms which have been levelled at the forthcoming production of "All God's Chillun Got Wings," it is well to make one point clear at the very start: that I do not admit that they honestly deserve any comment whatever. Almost without exception they very obviously come from people who have not read a line of the play. Prejudice born of an entire ignorance of the subject is the last word in injustice and absurdity. The Provincetown Playhouse has ignored all criticism not founded on knowledge of the play and will continue to ignore it.

Another point whose significance has either been omitted from all the sustained gossip, or else misrepresented: We are not a public theatre. Our playhouse is essentially a laboratory for artistic experiment. Our aims are special. We are not seeking to rival the theatre uptown, we make no attempt to cater to the taste of a general public. Our audience is intentionally a restricted one. Admitting, which we do not, that we are responsible to anyone outside our own organization, it is by our subscribers alone we can with any reason be held to account. Now, have our subscribers protested against the production of "God's Chillun"? Not one. On the contrary, many have written in letters of approval and encouragement, urging us not to "back down" in the slightest. And we shall not.

As for the much discussed casting of Mr. Robeson in the leading part, I have only this to say, that I believe he can portray the character better than any other actor could. That's all there is to it. A fine actor is a fine actor. The question of race prejudice cannot enter here. And it is ridiculous in the extreme that objection should be made to Mr. Robeson. Right in this city two years ago, at a public theatre, he played opposite a distinguished white actress, Margaret Wycherly, in a play called "Voodoo." In one of the scenes he was cast as the king and she the queen. A king and queen are, I believe, usually married. Mr. Robeson afterwards continued in the same role in England with Mrs. Patrick Campbell. There were no race riots here or there. There was no newspaper rioting, either.

Miss Blair is cast for "Ella" because I have always had her in mind. Her performance in the very difficult role of my "Diff'rent" three seasons ago convinced me that she is one of the most talented actresses on our stage. She is playing "Ella" in "God's Chillun" because she likes the play and the part. As a true artist, she does not recognize any considerations but these as having any bearing.

The play itself, as anyone who has read it with intelligence knows, is never a "race problem" play. Its intention is confined to portraying the special lives of individual human beings. It is primarily a study of the two principal characters, and their tragic struggle for happiness. To deduce any general application from "God's Chillun" except in a deep, spiritual sense, is to read a meaning into my play which is not there, and I feel confident that even the most prejudiced could not fail to acknowledge this if they should see the play. Nothing could be farther from my wish than to stir up racial feeling. I hate it. It is because I am certain "God's Chillun" does not do this but, on the contrary, will help toward a more sympathetic understanding between the races, through the sense of mutual tragedy involved, that I will stand by it to the end. I know I am right. I know that all the irresponsible gabble of the sensation-mongers and notoriety hounds is wrong. They are the ones who are trying to rouse ill feeling and they should be held responsible. The silly rumors distorting the play give them an excuse. My play itself has nothing to do with it. These folk don't know it, they don't want to know it, they're afraid if they did there would be no pretext left for frothing at the mouth and otherwise having a delightful time. They peek at a headline about "Ella" kissing "Jim's" hand and their indignation grows stupendous. If they would only take the trouble to look up this passage in the printed play, they would see how entirely innocent of all the inferred suggestion this action is. But they don't. Indignation, right or wrong, that's the good old stuff!

Finally, and plainly, all we ask is a square deal. A play is written to be experienced through the theatre, and only on its merits in a theatre can a final judgment be passed on it with justice. We demand this hearing. We shall play it before our subscribers only, and abide by their verdict in the fullest confidence that the play, produced as it should be, can give no offense to any rational American of whatever creed or race.

Many newspapers printed extracts from the statement on the following day, but the controversy continued.

Mary Blair was well enough to begin rehearsing for *All God's Chillun* in April, and the production was scheduled for mid-May, to follow the twin bill of *George Dandin* and *The Ancient Mariner*. When it became evident that the twin bill would not last until the middle of May, the Provincetown thought it advisable to throw something into the breach—something which would distract the attention of the "sensation-mongers." Accordingly, they got up a revival of *The Emperor Jones,* with Paul Robeson in the leading role. The revival was an immediate success and played to full houses for a week.

Meanwhile, however, the company rehearsing *All God's Chillun,* under James Light's direction, was being harassed by poison-pen letters, threats of reprisal from the Ku Klux Klan, and renewed warnings of legal action.

"I wish I knew how many clippings we paid for," Kenneth Macgowan later recalled. "At the wholesale rate of fifty dollars a thousand, I shouldn't be at all surprised to find that they cost us more than the scenery of *All God's Chillun.* . . . It is no risk at all to say that *All God's Chillun* received more publicity before production than any play in the history of the theatre, possibly of the world."

O'Neill, writing to a friend some months later, said:

"It seemed for a time there as if all the feeble-witted both in and out of the K.K.K. were hurling newspaper bricks in my direction—not to speak of the anonymous letters which ranged from those of infuriated Irish Catholics who threatened to pull my ears off as a disgrace to their race and religion, to those of equally infuriated Nordic Kluxers who knew that I had Negro blood, or else was a Jewish pervert masquerading under a Christian name in order to do subversive propaganda for the Pope! This sounds like burlesque, but the letters were more so."

Not only O'Neill but Paul Robeson, Mary Blair and Jimmy Light were recipients of vicious letters from the Ku Klux Klan.

"We had to intercept Mary's mail, some of the letters were so foul," Light said. "One of the letters Gene got, on official Klan stationery, came from Augusta, Georgia. It started out in language that was reasonable enough, giving the Klan's viewpoint on the production. But it got worse and worse. I was accused of being a Jew hiding under an English Christian name, and O'Neill was called a dirty Irish mick. The writer ended by saying that he knew O'Neill had two sons, and that the boys should be regarded as hostages. 'You will never see either of them again if the play goes on,' he wrote. Gene read the letter to me and then asked me for a pen. In big letters—gigantic, for him—he printed a three-word Anglo-Saxon phrase across the face of the letter and mailed it back to Klan headquarters.

"We also got a bomb warning from someone, stating that if we opened the play we would have a theatre full of dead people on our hands. We didn't let any of this interfere with our plans, but there was a lot of tension all around."

In the midst of rehearsals the mother of one of the white children who appeared in the play's brief opening scene—a sort of prologue, showing Jim and Ella as children—withdrew her child because her husband had telegraphed her from Georgia, refusing to allow the boy to appear on the stage with Negro children.

Four days before the scheduled opening of the play O'Neill was interviewed by the press.

"I admit that there is prejudice against the intermarriage of whites and blacks," he said, in part, "but what has that to do with my play? I don't advocate intermarriage in it. I am never the advocate of anything in any play—except humanity toward humanity."

"But," persisted a reporter, "don't you think . . . the white race superior to the black?"

"Spiritually speaking, there is no superiority between races," O'Neill answered patiently. "We're just a little ahead mentally as a race, though not as individuals. But I've no desire to play the exhorter in any

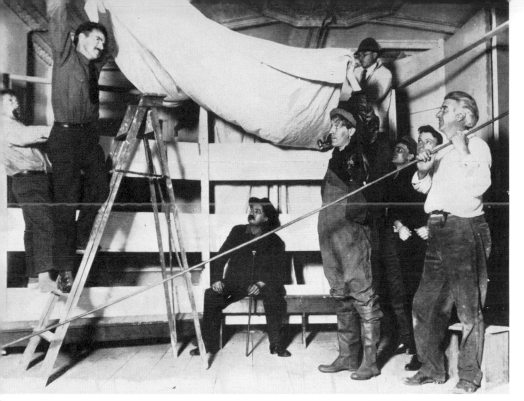

Setting the scene for BOUND EAST FOR CARDIFF at the Playwrights' Theatre, 1916. O'Neill on ladder; Hippolyte Havel, seated; William (Scotty) Stuart, in overalls; Jig Cook, holding pole.

Paul Thompson Photo

A sketch made of O'Neill in Provincetown, 1921, by Leo Mielziner, father of stage designer Jo Mielziner, and right, Louise Bryant.

Muray

Eugene O'Neill and Agnes Boulton in Provincetown.

Muray

Shane O'Neill with his parents in their "back yard" at Peaked Hill Bar, Provincetown, 1922.

A beach party at Peaked Hill Bar, Provincetown, 1921. From left, Henrietta Metcalf, a family friend, holding Shane, Eugene, Edith Shay, an unidentified man, Agnes, Frank Shay and an unidentified woman.   Muray

The house at Peaked Hill Bar being washed into the sea, January 10, 1931.

Photograph, Walter Stiff

Spithead, Bermuda, and bel
left, *the guest house.*

Oona and Mrs. Clark
("Gaga") at Spithead, 1927

Shane and O'Neill,
Spithead, 1926.

Robert Edmund Jones,
O'Neill, Kenneth
Macgowan at Spithead,
1926.

Clara Alexander Weiss
Collection

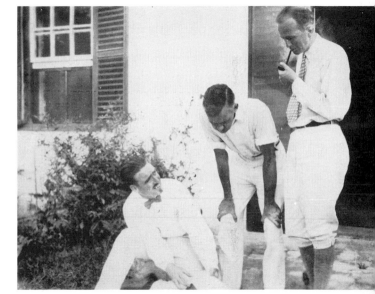

"Sea Mother's Son" at
Hamilton Beach, Bermuda,
1927.

Lawrence Langner Collection

Louis Wolheim as Yank in THE HAIRY APE *and a scene from the play, Provincetown Players' production, 1922.* Left, Muray. Right, *Museum of the City of New York.*

DESIRE UNDER THE ELMS, *Greenwich Village Theatre, 1924.*

Museum of the City of New York

Three Pulitzer Prize plays: top, BEYOND THE HORIZON, 1920 (*Richard Bennett at extreme right*); center, *Pauline Lord as Anna Christie;* bottom, *Lynn Fontanne as Nina in* STRANGE INTERLUDE.

Photographs, Museum of the City of New York

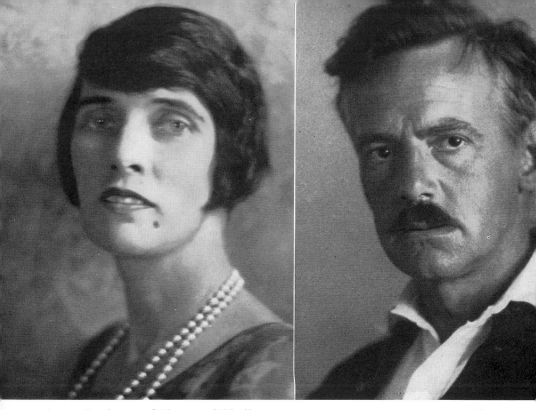

Agnes Boulton and Eugene O'Neill, 1927.　　　　　　　　*Muray*

Oona and Shane with their parents in Bermuda, 1927.

racial no man's land. I am a dramatist. To me every human being is a special case, with his or her own special set of values. True, often those values are just a variant of values shared in common by a great group of people. But it is the manner in which those values have acted on the individual and his reactions to them which makes of him a special case."

Shortly before opening night, Mayor Hylan's office discovered a technicality by which it hoped to stop the production. One aspect of even a non-public theatre's activities over which the mayor's office had jurisdiction was in the issuing of licenses to child actors. The Provincetown had applied for such licenses in the usual way, but it was not until late afternoon of the day of the scheduled opening that the mayor's office would give a definite answer. The mayor's chief clerk telephoned the theatre and said the licenses had been refused. No grounds were given.

The quandary into which this threw the company did not last long. They had ignored the foulest insults, declined to be intimidated by threats of violence, and now they quickly determined that the mayor's action was not going to stop them. James Light would tell the audience what had happened and, if the audience concurred, he would read the opening scene.

The Provincetown's subscribers filed apprehensively into the tiny theatre on the evening of May 15. All the first-string critics came, most of them beguiled by the promise of an incendiary evening. Several policemen were stationed at the theatre to stop the show in case the unlicensed children should attempt to play their scene—and to step in if anyone tried to throw a bomb.

The Provincetowners, not completely trusting the police to be impartial, had made their own arrangements for preserving the peace. The chief feature of these arrangements was a friend of Slim Martin's; Slim himself had a small role in the play.

"Jimmy Light had told me there was a bit part in the play for me as a pug," Slim recalled. "I'd only be on for a few minutes at the beginning, and then I'd walk off for the night—but it was a good bit." (The role was that of the prizefighter, Mickey, who ruins and then deserts Ella, and Slim's two dozen speeches consisted mainly of such lines as "Sure, I knocked his block off," "Cut it out, see! I'm runnin' dis corner," and "I don't have to be perlite wit' her. She's me goil!")

Light asked Slim to hire one of his steelworker friends to stand by as a guard every night, for $25 a week.

"I got Slim Nugent, raised on San Francisco's Barbary Coast, and a man who, in those days, would box anybody on earth six rounds for a twenty-five dollar purse," Slim remarked. "He could really fight, and he loved to, but the first time he saw Paul Robeson he said to me, 'Is that the big ape I'm supposed to guard? Well, listen, if anything starts, you and me just get out of his way and pile up the ones he knocks down.'

"On dress rehearsal night, Jimmy loaded us both up on that Prohibition Johnny-Jump-Up—three fourths fusel oil and one fourth spirits of camphor, with a few drops of creosote to give the stuff that peat-smoke, Scotch taste. My, was I a nervous wreck from it on opening night!"

With police outside and Slim Nugent inside, a keyed-up audience awaited the rise of the curtain. But when the houselights dimmed, the curtain did not go up. Instead, Jimmy Light stepped onto the stage apron and made the following speech:

"The management of the Provincetown Playhouse wishes to announce that the first scene of Eugene O'Neill's play, *All God's Chillun Got Wings,* cannot be given tonight.

"In this scene only children appear. Application for the usual license, which must be issued before child actors can play in New York, was made to the Children's Society on Tuesday. The society officials assured our representatives that the application was legitimate and would be granted by the official who acts upon the society's recommendations to the mayor of New York.

"The application was thereupon filed with the mayor's office. Action was delayed until late this afternoon, when the chief clerk of the mayor's office announced by telephone that the licenses had been refused. . . .

"We will take the matter up with the mayor's office tomorrow morning, and we welcome any aid which you in the audience may feel inclined to give us in securing proper action from the mayor.

"We do not know whether the audience is familiar with the play. The opening scene shows the friendship of the Negro boy, Jim Harris, and a white girl, Ella Downey, and establishes the fact that the color line does not cross childhood.

"The scene takes only a few minutes, and if the audience so desires I will read it to them."

There were cries of "Read!" from the audience, and Light recited the scene. The rest of the play proceeded smoothly.

The audience was, on the whole, sympathetic and neither the police nor Slim Nugent were called on to take any action.

O'Neill did not enter the theatre during the performance, preferring to wait it out at Sam Schwartz's. When Slim Martin finished his brief scene, he joined him there.

"Gene wasn't drinking anything but ginger ale, because he wanted to be sober in case a rhubarb started over at the theatre," Slim said. "If anything started, someone was to come out on the street and give the circus call, 'Hey Rube!' Then Gene and I were to pile out."

"If there's going to be a row over one of my plays," O'Neill told Slim, "I'm too Irish to miss the fun."

Jimmy Light came into Schwartz's after the performance to report that it had gone well, and then he and O'Neill went out to celebrate. They began their drinking at Barney Gallant's, and after a while they returned to the Provincetown Playhouse, requisitioned the tom-tom that was used in *The Emperor Jones* and carried it back to the saloon, where they took turns beating it far into the night.

O'Neill was, perhaps, a little disappointed that none of the dire warnings of riot and strife had amounted to anything. But he was much more disappointed by the reviews.

"When the play opened," he later wrote to a friend, "nothing at all happened, not even a senile egg. It was a dreadful anticlimax for all concerned, particularly the critics, who seemed to feel cheated that there hadn't been at least one murder that first night. . . . The whole affair was really a most ludicrous episode—not so ludicrous for me, however, since it put the whole theme of the play on a false basis and thereby threw our whole intent in the production into the discard."

Some years later, O'Neill, in one of the published collections of his works, enlarged on this remark:

"The preliminary furor over the suggestion that miscegenation would be treated in the theatre obscured the real intention of the play. In the eyes of those who had not yet seen it, or even read the manuscript, it became an incendiary drama threatening to stir up race riots. The actual production must have disappointed the howlers. Nothing happened."

It was evident from the reviews that most of the critics had taken the trouble to read the published version of *All God's Chillun* and had followed with interest the controversy leading up to the production. Several of them even included the complete text of Light's speech to the audience in their columns. But most of them did not like the play.

Percy Hammond called it "mildly dull and audacious," described Paul Robeson as "a dignified and handsome negro of the earnest type," overlooked Mary Blair, and ended his review as follows: "A bit overdone and breathless, it is a vehement exposition of a marriage between a stupid negro and a stupid white woman. If it is possible for you to get an emotion out of that situation, here is your opportunity."

"To me," began Heywood Broun, " 'All God's Chillun Got Wings' is a very tiresome play." After discussing some of the objections which had been voiced in the press, he went on to say, "Caucasian superiority does suffer a little, because Paul Robeson is a far finer actor than any white member of the cast. . . . Mary Blair, as Ella Downey, interested me very little, but this may be set down to the fact that the role which she plays is quite thankless. In the uneven career of Eugene O'Neill I think that 'All God's Chillun' will rank as one of the down strokes."

Woollcott said that "those who attended its first performance in the hope of seeing a few ructions, or possibly even a bloody riot to put in their diaries, were doomed to disappointment" and "those who attended in the hope of seeing a great play or even a good one were also disappointed."

"There is a perceptible chill in the air of the theatre of Eugene O'Neill at present," Woollcott added. "It is the chill of compromise—the compromise with the old realism which results in a kind of half-hearted sublimation of the material world through which his figures move."

Robert Gilbert Welsh of the *Telegram and Evening Mail* was one of the few who admired the play almost without reservation. " 'All God's Chillun' is likely to take a permanent place in the American theatre," he wrote. And John Corbin, as usual, was noncommittal. In the final line of his review in *The Times* he declared that if the play's enemies had been less diligent, there would be scant likelihood that it would have attracted attention beyond "the small circle of those interested in dramatic literature." He did not make it clear whether or not he was a member of that eccentric group.

O'Neill did not often allow himself to brood about adverse criticism. "Yes, the critics on *All God's Chillun* were dumb," he wrote to an acquaintance. "But I always count on their being just that and it would be rather a shock if they ever disappointed me by writing intelligently. The critics in the world to whom I pay any attention I can count on my fingers—well, I'll be charitable and throw in my toes by way of an optimistic gesture! Generally speaking the critic of any kind of art is simply a defeated, envious, inferior type who knows nothing whatever about his subject. He is cheap and the only sane attitude is to take him cheaply."

This was only one of many occasions on which O'Neill privately expressed his disgust for what the critics had to say about his work—"I hate every bone in their heads" was one of his favorite epithets—and he made a number of public pronouncements about them, as well. For example, when asked by one newspaper reporter whether he believed his plays had been "the subject of much stupid criticism," he answered: "What do you mean by critics? They can be divided into three classes: Play Reporters, Professional Funny Men, and the men with the proper background or real knowledge of the theatre of all time to enable them to be critics. The play reporters just happen to be people who have the job of reporting what happens during the evening, the story of the play and who played the parts. I have always found that these people reported the stories of my plays fairly accurately.

"The Professional Funny Men are beneath contempt. What they say is only of importance to their own strutting vanities. From the real critics I have always had a feeling that they saw what I was trying to do and whether they praised or blamed, they caught the point."

On another occasion he had this to say:

"I expect denunciation. It's generally sure to come. But I'm getting awfully callous to the braying, for and against. When they knock me, what the devil, they're really boosting me with their wholesale condemnations, for the reaction against such nonsense will come soon enough. These tea-pot turmoils at least keep me shaken up and convinced I'm on my way to something. I know enough history to realize that no one worth a damn ever escaped them—so it gives me hope. When I'm generally approved of, I begin to look in the mirror very skeptically and contemplate taking up some other career I might succeed at. So it's all tonic."

In spite of the braying against *All God's Chillun,* the play proved to be a good draw at the Provincetown. Continuing efforts to obtain the licenses for the children gave the play sustained publicity, which did not hurt it at all, and it played at the Provincetown in repertory with *The Emperor Jones* until July 5, when it closed briefly, and then reopened at the Greenwich Village Theatre, where it ran until October 10.

O'Neill continued to believe that the play had been undervalued. He stuck by his original estimate of it, making only one reservation about its conception. "All save the seven leading characters," he said years later, "should be masked; for all the secondary figures are part and parcel of the Expressionistic background of the play, a world at first indifferent, then cruelly hostile, against which the tragedy of Jim Harris is outlined."

Toward the end of May, with *All God's Chillun* apparently set for a good run, O'Neill returned to Ridgefield to make final revisions on *Desire Under the Elms.*

In June he arranged for Bernard Simon to spend a few days in Ridgefield typing the revised manuscript.

"I was one of the few people at the Provincetown who could run a typewriter and also read O'Neill's handwriting," Simon said. "Before I went out to Ridgefield to type *Desire,* I had already typed *All God's Chillun* and *The Ancient Mariner.* O'Neill had offered to meet me at the Lafayette and drive me out to his house.

"He was waiting for me in his car, an open car with a cloth top. It was a two-and-a-half hour drive to Ridgefield in those days, through beautiful country. He hardly said a word all the way out. If I commented on the weather or a news event, he'd simply grunt or say 'Yeah.' When we got to the house that evening, he unlocked the door and something jumped on my shoulders and licked my face. I almost fainted. O'Neill switched on the lights, and I saw it was his Irish wolfhound, whose paws reached my shoulders. O'Neill chuckled. 'I should have warned you,' he said.

"O'Neill would sit in front of the fireplace in the evening with his dog. He showed me a large bookcase that included a whole shelf of his own published plays, many of them in the foreign editions."

The morning after his arrival Simon began typing *Desire,* a job which ordinarily would have taken him two days. But O'Neill told him to take it easy, and Simon obligingly spent ten days on the job.

The first morning he had been typing for an hour when O'Neill invited Simon out for a walk. They hiked three miles over hilly country and through woods.

At one point in their conversation Simon ventured to tell O'Neill that he was puzzled by the spelling of the word "Ay-eh" in the manuscript. Simon said he thought this was an odd way to write "Yeah."

"No," said O'Neill. "I don't mean 'Yeah.' I mean 'Ay-eh'! That's the way they talk here. You listen."

Simon listened and, of course, discovered that O'Neill was right.

"One day O'Neill, Agnes and I were having lunch," Simon said. "The table was always beautifully set, and the food very good, but the meals tended to lapse into embarrassing silence. Agnes would try to make conversation, for my sake, I guess, and O'Neill didn't always seem to care for the topic she chose. For instance, she made some comment—this was during an election year, and the conventions were in full swing—about how it might possibly be better for the theatre if the Republicans won. She meant, I suppose, that a Republican victory might safeguard the interests of the rich, who were the principal theatregoers. O'Neill gave her a look of contempt, and muttered something. They almost came to an open quarrel.

"On one of our walks, soon after, O'Neill told me that he felt Agnes was 'capitalizing' on his reputation. He complained that she invited 'social' people from New York to spend weekends at Brook Farm. 'What in Christ have I got in common with them?' he asked me. 'Sometimes I come back from a walk on Friday afternoon and find guests all over the house. Agnes tells them she wants them to meet her husband.' "

It was on these occasions, O'Neill told Simon, that he took to the barn with a bottle.

"O'Neill didn't seem to pay much attention to Shane while I was there," Simon said. "Once I was horsing around with Shane and I pointed to a tree and told him it was almost as high as a skyscraper in New York. Shane told me he didn't go to New York, that the only city he really knew was Danbury.

"Once I asked O'Neill if he'd seen a certain play. He said he hadn't. I asked him about another play, and he said he hadn't seen that, either. 'I don't go to the theatre much,' he told me. 'I don't like it. It's phony.'" ("I hardly ever go to the theatre, although I read all the plays I can get," he once explained. "I don't go to the theatre because I can always do a better production in my mind than the one on the stage. I have a better time and I am not bothered by the audience. No one sneezes during the scenes that interest me. Nor do I ever go to see one of my own plays—have seen only three of them since they started coming.")

On June 1, 1924, at Brook Farm, O'Neill was formally presented with the 1923 gold medal for drama by the National Institute of Arts and Letters. (He had become a member of the Institute in February of 1923; ten years later he was elected to the American Academy of Arts and Letters.) It had taken the awards committee nearly a year and a half to pin him down to a time and place for the ceremony. O'Neill was a hard man to give a medal to.

On May 31, having finally cornered his quarry, Dr. John Finley, a member of the Institute's council, turned the medal over to Edmond T. Quinn, the sculptor, and the next day Quinn drove to Ridgefield and gave it to O'Neill.

"Mr. Quinn made a glorious presentation on our front lawn," O'Neill wrote to Dr. Finley on June 2. "Nothing could have been more impressive. I made a humble speech of two words: 'Thank you,' and the whole affair was noted by all a stunning success."

News of the presentation ceremony reached the ears of George Jean Nathan and H. L. Mencken, who, momentarily united by their common regard for O'Neill and their zest for iconoclastic gestures, summoned the recipient of the medal to the offices of *The American Mercury*. O'Neill, who suspected their motives, asked Jimmy Light to accompany him for moral support.

When the two entered the office they found Nathan and Mencken seated side by side. On the wall of the office, according to Light, hung a huge poster written in French and satirizing Prohibition. "One Drinks Because:—" proclaimed the poster, and there followed a long list of reasons: "Somebody is born; somebody has died; somebody is married; somebody is divorced; the Express from Lyons is late; the Express from Lyons is early—" and so forth.

Nathan and Mencken rose ceremoniously.

"Mr. O'Neill," said Mencken, "we understand that you have received an insult. We shall try to erase it."

Nathan then proceeded to read, by way of citation, some of the more impossible stage directions out of O'Neill's published plays. Light found it difficult to suppress a grin, but O'Neill kept a straight face.

Mencken then declared that he and Nathan would now present O'Neill with a more suitable medal. Nathan whipped out a medal consisting of a horse-blanket pin, to which was attached a large pretzel, from which was suspended a piece of Westphalian ham (whose color Nathan greatly admired), and from which dangled a piece of bologna. O'Neill, still silent and unsmiling, his eyes fixed on the French poster, allowed Nathan to pin the collection of delicatessen to his lapel.

"Now, have a drink," said Nathan, waving genially toward a bottle of Napoleon brandy and four glasses which had been standing on one of the desks when O'Neill and Light entered. Assuming that the joke was over and pleased with himself for having kept a straight face, O'Neill permitted himself a grin and reached for the bottle. He found that it was cemented to the desk, as were all four glasses.

"Something seems to be stuck, Jimmy," said O'Neill, instantly recovering his solemnity. "You try."

Nathan and Mencken, happy as two schoolboys over their little joke, invited O'Neill and Light out for a real drink.

As soon as O'Neill closed the Ridgefield house at the end of June and arrived at Peaked Hill he took up *Marco Millions* again—in addition to working on a detailed outline for another new play that he intended to write the following fall. He even had its title—*The Great God Brown*. O'Neill's energy and output were as prodigious and unflagging as ever. *All God's Chillun Got Wings* was running in New York; *Desire Under the Elms* was scheduled for production in the fall; he was still negotiating for production of *The Fountain;* he was in process of writing the double-length *Marco Millions* and had mapped out the experimental *Great God Brown*. He was also actively participating in the planning of the Province-town Players' coming season.

"Am working hard as hell on *Marco*," he wrote to Macgowan from

Provincetown in July. "It is coming along in great shape and I'm tickled silly with it. It's going to be humorous as the devil if the way it makes me guffaw as I write is any criticism—and not bitter humor, either, although it's all satirical. I actually grow to love my American pillars of society, Polo Brothers & Son. It's going to be very long in first draft, I imagine, but I'm letting the sky be the limit and putting every fancy in. I imagine it's pretty nearly one half done now, but it's hard to estimate. One thing is sure, it's going quicker and is much more full of fun than I had conceived it at first."

He added a postscript to the effect that he was going to write to Oliver Sayler about the possibility of interesting Max Reinhardt and Morris Gest in producing the play in collaboration with himself, Macgowan and Jones; it was too elaborate, he felt (even more elaborate than *The Fountain*), to be done by the trio in Greenwich Village.

"It's a tremendous big thing to stage with lots of crowds, silent and otherwise, to be trained perfectly—or they'll fall flat," he wrote to Sayler. "In fact, it involves everything a theatre can be made (let us hope) to give, and it will take *some* directing! . . . as you probably know, I'm rather 'off of' Hopkins. His dilatory course with *The Fountain* . . . his running out on everything generally, have convinced me that he's not the right sort of Santa Claus for me to believe in."

By the end of August O'Neill had temporarily changed the title of his play to *Mr. Mark Millions*. He was satisfied with the progress he was making on the script and expected to have his first draft completed by the beginning of September. He had also had an idea for another play, on which he was already making notes; he called it *Dynamo* and described it as "queer and intriguing."

But once again, he was in financial difficulties. The income from *Welded* had been insufficient to pay his taxes on the previous year's prosperity; young Eugene's school bill would soon be due for payment; household expenses were accumulating; and Ella's estate was still in a tangled state of probate. Apologetically, O'Neill asked Macgowan for an advance against royalties on the forthcoming production of *Desire Under the Elms*.

His plight was such that he wrote to Eleanor Fitzgerald as well, asking her "by all means" to forward any royalties due him from *All God's Chillun* promptly. "I am very hard up for cash," he said.

In the midst of his own creative work that summer O'Neill read scripts for the coming season's Provincetown Playhouse productions. He also worked on a program of plays for the Greenwich Village Theatre, which he, Macgowan and Jones had decided to take over on a seasonal basis, along with the Provincetown.

The trio of producers had put out a leaflet announcing an expanded program to their subscribers and potential patrons.

The expansion was to consist of a program of "experimental" plays at the Provincetown Playhouse and a program of "repertory" at the Greenwich Village Theatre. Although the trio seemed to know what it was about, it was difficult for the uninitiated subscriber to distinguish the "experimental" from the "repertory" merely by studying the two lists of promised productions.

At the Provincetown the "experimental" list for the 1924-25 season included the as yet unwritten *The Great God Brown* and O'Neill's "adaptation" of the Book of Revelation. (*Brown* was not produced until 1926, and then it was done, not at the Provincetown, but at the Greenwich Village, and the Book of Revelation was never done anywhere); new plays by Edmund Wilson and Stark Young; a translation of Walter Hasenclever's *Jenseits* (translated as *Beyond*) and Congreve's *Love for Love*.

In the Greenwich Village Theatre's "repertory" there was to be *Desire Under the Elms,* a new play by Stark Young, plays by Rostand and Shakespeare, *The Brothers Karamazov,* and "A Gilbert and Sullivan Revival in the spirit of the '70s." (As it turned out, only the Wilson and Hasenclever plays materialized at the Provincetown as promised. *Desire,* one of the Stark Young plays, and *Patience* were presented as promised at the Greenwich Village, and *Love for Love* was done there, too, instead of at the Provincetown—all of which demonstrated that the trio had about as much control over its theatrical future as most visionary producers.)

At the beginning of September, with *Marco* three quarters finished, O'Neill decided he needed a change of atmosphere, and he and Agnes accepted an invitation from Wilbur Daniel Steele to visit in Nantucket. The visit refreshed him, but he backslid as to his resolve to give up smoking—although he did manage to resist all drinking during his stay on the island.

Despite all his financial worries O'Neill, by the end of September, was making plans for the winter that were not calculated to reduce his expenses. Agnes was pregnant again, expecting her baby in April, and O'Neill, restless as ever, decided to close his house in Ridgefield and spend the winter in a rented house in Bermuda. Bermuda was recommended by Dr. Alexander Miller, the tuberculosis specialist to whom O'Neill still went for occasional checkups; O'Neill usually looked for a physical cause when he was feeling nervous, and though his doctors seldom found a valid one in those days, he was always pleased when they recommended a change of climate. O'Neill planned to sail in mid-November and was only awaiting word on when *Desire* would be put into production to settle on a definite date.

"I must know approximately," he warned Macgowan. "I've been counting on its going on four weeks after *Saint* [the play by Stark Young which was to open the season at the Greenwich Village] and making plans accordingly—iron-bound plans this time. . . . I won't be in Ridgefield where I can get to town anytime—not after the middle of November."

It was apparent that any spiritual refreshment O'Neill had derived from his trip to Nantucket had worn off. He was again feeling gloomy about life.

"No, I haven't a thought for the program," he answered Macgowan, in response to a request that he contribute an article to the playbill of the Provincetown or the Greenwich Village. "What thoughts I have, save those which are still going into *Marco* as I go over it, are too pessimistic for publication and my only message to the world is that it can go f—— itself!"

He was very anxious to see Macgowan and talk over his winter's plans, he added. "I've made a discovery about myself in analyzing the work done, etc., in the past six winters which has led me to resolve about what I must do in future."

O'Neill had decided to leave Provincetown about October 21, stopping in New London en route to New York. He had finished the first draft of *Marco Millions*—somewhat to his own surprise it had evolved as "two good long plays of 2½ hours each—at least"—and he was anxious to set forth for Bermuda.

When O'Neill arrived in New York his close friends could see that he was in low spirits. He was unusually tense and nervous, and looked haggard even under the deep coat of Provincetown tan.

One of the things that was undoubtedly worrying him was the impending arrival of another child. His attempts to quit drinking and smoking (sometimes he went on a diet of denicotinized cigarettes), and his restlessness and compulsion to get away (first, on a small scale, from Provincetown and now, on a much grander one, from Ridgefield) were symptomatic of the state that had been growing on him steadily for the past year or two. He told himself that all his future efforts must be poured exclusively into his work, that his development as an artist was his primary, if not his exclusive, object and that everything extraneous must be ruthlessly swept aside. Drinking, he knew—even without his brother's tragic example—could ruin him, and he was struggling to give it up entirely. The demands of friends, even of family, drained him, and he was trying to subjugate these demands to his work. He told Macgowan that he craved a "neat life with a pattern," adding: "I'd like ten walled acres in Siberia with a flock of Siberian wolfhounds to guard them, and layers of broken glass on the walls."

He began to run—subtly at first, from himself, from Agnes, from his children, from all his old associations—when he made his first trip to Bermuda. Still treasuring his worn copy of *Thus Spake Zarathustra,* he had recently underlined:

"Ah, whither shall I ascend with my longing! From all mountains do I look out for fatherlands and motherlands. But a home have I found nowhere: unsettled am I in all cities, and decamping at all gates."

O'Neill did not stop running for the next twenty-five years.

XLIV

BEFORE LEAVING FOR BERMUDA, O'NEILL VISITED DR. Smith Ely Jelliffe, a prominent New York City psychiatrist. Dr. Jelliffe, who was very successful and very social, included many theatre people in his circle of friends and patients. Robert Edmond Jones, Arthur Hopkins and John Barrymore were among those who, at one time or another, paid him professional as well as social visits.

It was Jones who introduced O'Neill to Jelliffe. Wary of psychoanalysis for himself but always eager to accept sympathetic medical advice, O'Neill saw Jelliffe sporadically between 1923 and 1925—not to be analyzed but simply to "talk things over." According to Dr. Jelliffe's widow, Belinda, O'Neill was not "deeply psychoanalyzed" but, rather, received therapeutic help for a variety of specific problems.

Whatever Dr. Jelliffe's merits as an analyst, he was undoubtedly a man of commanding personality and culture.

"He had a particular affinity for the arts and for artists," Mrs. Jelliffe said, "and was able to hold the interest and sympathy of people like Jones and O'Neill."

One of Dr. Jelliffe's patients was Mabel Dodge. An egoist of staggering proportions, Mrs. Dodge had no reticence in discussing her psychoanalysis (or, indeed, any other phase of her personal life).

"I enjoyed my visits three times a week to Jelliffe's office," Mrs. Dodge wrote in her autobiography. "He had a speculative mind with an amusing intuition. . . . The first time I had seen Dr. Jelliffe I remember him coming towards me . . . in his office: Tall, in a black suit of smooth cloth, a little paunchy, his small, green eyes set rather close together, were speculative upon one. 'A Roman Catholic priest,' I had thought at once, for there was something all over him that was like that: in his glance, in the smooth, fine texture of his pale skin, and in his bearing. He was commanding, quizzical, sure of himself, and not to be moved. His features were small and fine, and there was a kind of impudence playing over them."

If Mrs. Dodge's impression of Dr. Jelliffe as a priest was also conveyed to O'Neill, it must have held an additional attraction; as he had always submitted in his youth to the overpowering domination of his father, so was he still inclined to be awed by a symbolically paternalistic figure.

Dr. Jelliffe was in his late fifties when O'Neill knew him. Belinda, who was his second wife and considerably younger than he, admired O'Neill's plays and was somewhat awed by meeting him in the flesh.

Dr. Jelliffe's offices were on the second floor of a brownstone on Fifty-sixth Street. The ground floor held kitchen and dining room and the floors above the offices were Dr. Jelliffe's living quarters.

"One day as I was coming into the house after shopping," Mrs. Jelliffe said, "I saw O'Neill descending the stairs, and, on an impulse, waited to speak to him. He hesitated at the foot of the stairs, looking confused and troubled, and I asked if there was anything I could do for him— call him a taxi, or give him a cup of coffee. He said he was waiting for Bobby Jones to come by and pick him up, and accepted the invitation to have coffee. He followed me to the dining room and while we waited for the maid, he stared silently out at the garden, and I waited silently— and nervously—at the dining room table.

"When the coffee came and I offered him cream and sugar he said 'Black'—and that was all he said until he'd finished his coffee."

"Your husband is a brilliant man, isn't he?" O'Neill finally ventured, as though waking from a trance. Mrs. Jelliffe modestly protested that she was not clever enough to know.

"He *is*," said O'Neill emphatically. "He has a most extraordinary, brilliant mind—with a kindness, too." That seemed to be the end of his conversation, for he lapsed again into brooding silence.

Mrs. Jelliffe felt she must engage him in conversation and made a casual remark about some current topic, adding that she "hated" something or other.

O'Neill's face suddenly came alive. His eyes looked fierce and he said, almost explosively, "Treat that word with more respect!"

Mrs. Jelliffe was momentarily stunned, but recovered herself to say, "Yes, you're right, Mr. O'Neill, it's an abused word."

Then, carried away by her own daring and her feeling that O'Neill was really interested in what she was saying, she told him she had always thought the word "hate" misused and the emotion of hatred misdirected. One should not be taught to suppress hatred, she told O'Neill, but, rather, be instructed *what* to hate. As she warmed to her topic she suddenly felt foolish and stopped, convinced that O'Neill didn't know what she was talking about and had regretted the outburst he had inspired. But he was both interested and amused. Smiling for the first time, he told her he agreed with her and, at her urging, tried to give her his own definitions of hate and love. His definition of love rather surprised her.

"I'm afraid it will sound pedestrian to you," he said. "Love is service."

Mrs. Jelliffe, enthralled at having achieved this degree of rapport with the taciturn O'Neill, was disappointed when the doorbell rang and the maid announced that Robert Edmond Jones was waiting.

A proof of O'Neill's respect for and interest in Dr. Jelliffe was his attendance at a large cocktail party given by the doctor and his wife.

"I had asked Bobby Jones to bring him, though I had heard O'Neill loathed big parties, and I didn't think he'd come," Mrs. Jelliffe said. "I was very surprised when he turned up with Bobby, and worried about how he'd get along." Her fears were allayed when she saw O'Neill seat himself in a corner with Arthur Hopkins—this was before O'Neill had lost faith in the producer.

"Hours later they were still seated together," Mrs. Jelliffe said. "I asked them what they had been talking about and Hopkins told me they had been discussing the lost talent of our land. 'Did you argue?' I asked O'Neill, and he answered, 'Oh, no, unfortunately we agree.'"

It was late October, and O'Neill was straining to be off for Bermuda, when production finally began on *Desire Under the Elms*. Edmund Wilson's *The Crime in the Whistler Room* had ended a brief run at the Provincetown and Stark Young's *The Saint* an equally brief stay at the Greenwich Village Theatre. Both houses were to be filled by O'Neill in November— at the Greenwich Village *Desire* and at the Provincetown a bill composed of his early sea plays (*Bound East for Cardiff*, *The Long Voyage Home*, *In the Zone* and *The Moon of the Caribbees*) collectively produced for the first time in New York under the title, *S. S. Glencairn*. All but one, *In the Zone*, had been presented as a single bill in Provincetown, Massachusettes, the summer before by Frank Shay, who was sponsoring a troupe called the Barnstormers. O'Neill had been delighted to see that the *Glencairn* cycle played well as a unit.

"The individual plays are complete in themselves, yet the identity of the crew goes through the series and welds the four one-acters into a long play," he once observed. "I do not claim any originality, though, for this idea, as Schnitzler has already done the same thing in *Anatol*. And doubtless others." O'Neill thought the cycle would make "a good paying bet" for the Provincetown Playhouse, and Macgowan, who agreed, asked O'Neill for a collective title.

"I don't like *Crew of the Glencairn*," mused O'Neill. "Doesn't sound like anything. *Blow the Man Down* is a good title or some other chanty phrase. *S. S. Glencairn* isn't so awfully wrong. *The Sea Tramp* is another suggestion."

When plans for the *Glencairn* production were completed, O'Neill submitted his sketches for the set of *Desire*. He left less than most authors to the ingenuity of the designer, who, in this case, was Robert Edmond Jones. Always aware of the technical problems inherent in the physical action of his plays—he knew exactly what would and would not work from the purely mechanical point of view—O'Neill continued to draw ground plans for his plays, usually when they were still only in scenario form. The intimate knowledge of stagecraft and actorcraft he had acquired from association with his father's companies made him acutely conscious of everything from the proper placing of doors to the timing of costume changes.

"I know more about a trap door than any son of a bitch in the theatre," he once told a friend. In the case of *Desire* he went even further than a floor plan, for he envisioned a set that would encompass kitchen and parlor downstairs and two bedrooms upstairs of the Cabot farmhouse, and a strip of farm outside. He drew four sketches, each of them showing the pitched-roof farmhouse nestled between two giant elms; in the first sketch, the wall of the house is closed; in the second a panel has been removed, showing the interior of the kitchen; in the third the parlor is revealed, and in the fourth, the two bedrooms, separated by the thin wall through which Eben and Abbie were to stare lustfully at each other.

Jones was delighted with O'Neill's conception and executed it faithfully—too faithfully, perhaps, for the removable panels proved cumbersome and time consuming in production and the elm trees disappointed O'Neill. ("Has *Desire* ever been produced as I wrote it?" O'Neill asked Kenneth Macgowan, some time after its original showing. "Never! There have never been the elm trees of my play, characters almost, and . . . through lack of time to get the changes perfected, . . . the flow of life from room to room of the house, the house as character, the acts as smooth developing wholes have never existed.")

In addition to designing the production (which cost $6,000), Jones also directed it and found the actor to fill the difficult role of seventy-five-year-old Ephraim Cabot. He was forty-year-old Walter Huston, known chiefly as a vaudeville performer. A fairly recent arrival on Broadway, Huston had played only a few light roles. Jones had met him through the actor's sister, Margaret, a dramatic coach whom Jones later married; and he had convinced O'Neill that Huston was right for Ephraim.

In spite of his antipathy to actors, O'Neill grew fond of Huston. He even went so far (forgetting for the moment his earlier, unqualified praise of Charles Gilpin) as to praise Huston as "the only actor" who had brought one of his characters completely to life. He expressed this opinion to Lillian Gish, who shared his admiration for Huston, having toured with him, as a child of five, in a play called *Convict Stripes*. (She had taken her first curtain call seated on his shoulders.) O'Neill later presented Huston with a copy of *Desire* inscribed thus:

" 'God's hard, not easy!' (and so was the part of 'Ephraim'). Yet you made that character live in a way that an author usually sees only in hopeful dreams. So all gratitude from my heart, Walter, and may we collaborate in making many plays live in the future. With deep respect and friendship, always, Eugene O'Neill."

Cast for the role of Abbie was Mary Morris, who had scored a hit in the long-run revival of *Fashion*. O'Neill was as ambivalent about her qualifications as he had been about Helen Hayes, Lynn Fontanne and others.

"Did Mary Morris give you anything in talking over play and part that gives you any line on her understanding of work cut out for her?" he had anxiously inquired of Macgowan in the spring when she was first under consideration for the role. "I mean, did she seem to 'get' it and be gotten by it?" After interviewing her, he felt she was right for the role. He did not even ask her to read the part for him, deciding to take Jones's and Light's word that she was a good actress. "The important thing is her whole attitude and conception and there she's O.K." said O'Neill. "I'll be at rehearsals from the first gun, anyway."

According to Miss Morris, who was married to the actor James Meighan in Provincetown on the day the interview took place, O'Neill did not mention the play at all until just before the end of her visit.

"He knew why I came over, but didn't say anything to me about the part," Miss Morris said. "We swam and ate and then it was getting late and I had to get back to New York for my performance the next day in *Fashion*. Before my husband and I left, I finally asked O'Neill about the part in *Desire*. He said, 'You're going to play Abbie. I knew that from the moment you came in.' That's all that was said."

She opened in the play at the Greenwich Village and received good notices. The play was eventually moved uptown, and during the summer, when Miss Morris left for a vacation, she was replaced by Mary Blair. Miss Morris later rejoined the cast for its road tour.

The role of Eben was filled by one of the old Provincetowners, Charles Ellis, and Norma Millay played a bit part in the scene in which Ephraim gives a party to celebrate the birth of his supposed son; another member of the crowd was Donald Oenslager, who later became a leading Broadway stage designer, and the part of the sheriff in the final scene was played by Walter Abel, who demonstrated both his acting talent and his sprinting ability by doubling in the role of Olson in *S. S. Glencairn;* he would speak his last line (in Swedish dialect) in *Bound East for Cardiff* from the stage of the Provincetown—"Nothin' but yust dirty weather all dis voyage. I yust can't sleep when wheestle blow"—then sprint over to the Greenwich Village Theatre, make a few slight changes in his costume, pick up the rifle he carried as his prop, assume the hard-bitten visage of a New Englander and utter three lines, including the curtain speech: "It's a jim-dandy farm, no denyin'. Wished I owned it!"

Abel later recalled that on November 11, the opening night of *Desire* (*S. S. Glencairn* had opened eight days before), O'Neill visited him in his dressing room at the Provincetown. "He stayed during most of the performance," Abel said, "and when I asked him if he wasn't going to look in on the opening of *Desire,* he told me that opening nights were exaggerated, that the whole idea was false on all sides."

In view of the fact that *Desire Under the Elms* came to be regarded as one of the great American tragedies, its première evoked a rather tepid welcome in the daily press. Percy Hammond, more concerned with his own crotchets than with an objective evaluation of the play, wrote that "O'Neill again eats his heart out in the bitter torments of despair" and went on to say: "Mr. O'Neill's dramas always make me glad that I am not one of the characters involved. My tire troubles; my battles with . . . the composing room after the plays, my loss of appetite and other discomforts, vanish as I observe Mr. O'Neill's people writhing and wailing in difficulties much more incorrigible." The most that Hammond could bring himself to say in praise of the play was that he had "seen few pictures in a theatre so stark" as the scene "when old Ephraim in his bedroom tells Abbie the story of his life . . . [and] his young wife is looking through the wall into the chamber of Eben."

Heywood Broun commented sourly that O'Neill "laid his hand last night upon the shoulder of his finest play and then passed by on the other side." The gist of his commentary was that the play descended into "theatricality" and that O'Neill was "still the true son of the man who played 'The Count of Monte Cristo' more than a thousand times." O'Neill must have read with fury Broun's remark that "it would have been possible last night to count 'one, two, three' as this new tale of vengeance clicked into certain old and well worn grooves."

Alan Dale, writing for the *American,* hit hardest at the play: "The theatrical miasma arising from . . . 'Desire Under the Elms' made even the subway station directly beneath the cantankerous, cancerous proceedings in the playhouse seem delicious."

On *The Times* the ambiguous John Corbin had faded away to be replaced by Stark Young, who had switched from *The New Republic*. Young compared *Desire* to *Beyond the Horizon* and cautiously concluded that it represented progress on O'Neill's part. He described the party scene as being written "with such poetry and terrible beauty as we rarely see in the theatre."

It was evident to O'Neill, however, that none of the daily reviewers had really "gotten" the play and few had even been capable of making the attempt. It remained for the reviewer of *The Nation*, thirty-one-year-old Joseph Wood Krutch, to give *Desire Under the Elms* its first intelligent appreciation. Krutch, who recognized the play's greatness, began his review (on November 26) by indicating that he had a clear grasp of O'Neill's artistic aims and a sound knowledge of O'Neill's significance to the American theatre:

In this age of intellectualized art there is an inevitable but unfortunate tendency to assume of Eugene O'Neill . . . that his greatness must lie somehow in the greatness or the clarity of his thought; to seek in "All God's Chillun" some solution of the problem of race or in "The Hairy Ape" some attitude toward society; and then not finding them, to fail in the fullest appreciation of the greatness which is his. It was not thought which drove him, as a young man, to seek adventure among the roughest men he could find, and it was not thought which he brought back from this and other experiments in life. Something tempestuous in his nature made him a brother of tempests, and he has sought wherever he could find them the fiercest passions, less anxious to clarify their causes for the benefit of those who love peace than eager to share them, and happy if he could only be exultantly a part of their destructive fury. . . . The meaning and unity of his work lies not in any controlling intellectual idea and certainly not in a "message," but merely in the fact that each play is an experience of extraordinary intensity.

Sidney Howard, who had recently made an impact of his own with *They Knew What They Wanted*—it was produced on November 24 by the Theatre Guild—felt so strongly about *Desire* that he wrote a letter to *The New York Times*, which was carried in its drama columns on December 14:

"Desire Under the Elms" is a tragedy, a real tragedy, with the power, starkness and nobility which only real tragedy can assume. If it strikes snags, they are heroic snags of the same stature and quality as those which stagger the closing scenes of "Macbeth." I don't see any criticism of "Desire Under the Elms" which does not as aptly apply to "Macbeth." And I can't, for the moment at least, see much praise for "Macbeth" which might not be applied to "Desire Under the Elms." This will not seem extravagant, in view of New York's recent discovery that Shakespeare was an inferior playwright. If it seem extravagant to our backward respect for Shakespeare's plays, I only ask to be shown anything produced by the English-speaking theatre of recent generations which is half so fine or true or brave as "Desire Under the Elms."

Despite the newspaper critics' lack of enthusiasm, *Desire* filled the Greenwich Village Theatre for two months and was then transferred to Broadway, where, first at the Earl Carroll Theatre and later at the George M. Cohan, it continued to run until October 17, 1925.

Unlike *All God's Chillun,* which had received widespread publicity before it opened, *Desire* did not become the subject of public outcry until after it had moved uptown. The storm broke in January, 1925, but O'Neill was not in New York to observe it. He and Agnes had sailed for Bermuda at the end of November.

Belinda Jelliffe preserved a slightly blurred impression of the day they left, when, apparently, O'Neill used the Jelliffe house as a meeting place.

"There was O'Neill, Agnes and, I think, two children [evidently Shane and Agnes' daughter, who was now ten years old]," she later recalled. "They were all with my husband in his secretary's office and I had the feeling when I went in that I had stumbled into a suspended tableau. Agnes looked vague and distracted, O'Neill looked worried and the children were pale and woebegone. Dr. Jelliffe was speaking of tickets—steamship tickets to Bermuda—which had apparently been lost or misplaced. Since the O'Neills seemed uncertain about what to do, I offered to go back to their hotel and look for the tickets. I vaguely remember getting into a cab with O'Neill and driving to the Lafayette.

"At the hotel, we scratched around in bureau drawers and I guess we found the tickets, because I remember later saying good-by to them all as they left for the pier."

One of the last things O'Neill did before sailing was to instruct his agent, Richard Madden, to send a copy of *Marco Millions* to David Belasco. Having had no encouraging word from Reinhardt or Gest, O'Neill had turned to the spectacular Bishop of Broadway; he had managed to convince himself that everything he had previously despised in Belasco's showmanship was actually just what was needed to put *Marco* across.

"I now have a play to submit to you," O'Neill had written Belasco on November 22. "It has these defects from a production standpoint: it is costly to put on, involving a forestage, music, many scenes, large crowds, etc.—and also *it seems to last two nights*—to be *two* plays, in fact!" O'Neill hastened to add that it had compensating merits, among which were *"real* poetic beauty and philosophy" and the fact that it was *"comedy satire by an American* of our life and ideals." He asked Belasco to write him in Bermuda after reading it.

O'Neill moved into a rented cottage in Paget West, called Campsea, and began to unwind under the mellowing influence of his new environment. "The climate is grand," he informed George Jean Nathan. "There's absolutely nothing interesting to do, and the German bottled beer and English bottled ale are both excellent. And the swimming is wonderful, if you like such, which I do above everything."

Before the end of December he re-wrote *Marco Millions* and mailed the revised version to Belasco. He also began writing *The Great God Brown*.

On January 1, 1925, O'Neill took a step he had been contemplating for some time: he swore off drinking and smoking. He had been advised to do this by, among others, a New York physician, Dr. Maloney, to whom he reported in February that he was "happier and in better shape physically" than he had been in many years.

The only thing he still drank was ale—limited to one glass with his dinner—and he found that this did not create "the slightest yen after more." Not smoking, he found, increased his endurance as a swimmer and abolished his insomnia.

O'Neill, who had made up his mind to live for his work, was convinced that continued drinking would destroy him as surely as it had killed Jamie. Though he had always been intensely concerned with the state of his own health and had taken all sorts of measures to safeguard it, this was the first time he attempted to cope with his alcoholism. Like any newly converted abstainer, he became preoccupied with the subject of his abstinence and talked of it to his friends. He told one close friend that his mother's triumph over drug addiction helped him in his resolve.

He also discussed his abstinence with his next-door neighbor, Dr. Louis Bisch, a psychoanalyst. Dr. Bisch and his wife had two children who played with Shane, and the two families visited each other frequently.

"O'Neill never drank in Bermuda," Dr. Bisch recalled. "But he was very moody. He told me he was subject to moods and explained that he would become greatly depressed after finishing a play, because it never turned out to be what he really wanted—it was then, he said, that he'd go on a bender.

"He seemed to be suffering from both overwork and worry—particularly about financial matters. Once he showed me a cable bill that came to $100; he was very concerned about it. Another thing that worried him was time. He told me it took him hours to answer his fan mail, and that he couldn't afford to employ a secretary. I asked him why he didn't just ig-nore most of the letters and he said he couldn't, that he just had to answer his mail.

"One time when he was complaining to me how broke he was, he sighed and said, if only he could write box-office plays. I asked him why he didn't try to slant his plays a little toward the box office, and he an-swered that he couldn't possibly write any differently.

"He talked a great deal about his health, and one day he asked me to listen to his heart, explaining that it was 'out of place,' located in the middle of his chest. Apparently some doctor had told him that his heart was median, and he seemed very concerned about it. I didn't have a stethoscope with me, but I put my ear to his chest and assured him that it wouldn't affect his longevity or health in general."

Although *Desire Under the Elms* was having a successful run, its profits at the little Greenwich Village Theatre were meager and the proceeds from its uptown engagement were only just beginning to accrue in Feb-ruary. Belasco had not yet committed himself on *Marco Millions*, and *The Fountain*, now two and a half years old, was still not scheduled for pro-duction, even though the Theatre Guild had picked up the option when it lapsed with Hopkins.

On February 6 O'Neill wrote a letter to Madden, which covered a number of things that were currently preying on his mind. The letter is typical of the kind of swift transition from the petty to the sublime of which O'Neill was capable. It began with the discussion of a proposed English production of *Desire* and moved on to a tirade against Horace Live-right, whom O'Neill suspected of trying to practice some sort of fraud. Liveright had sent him, for his autograph, the title sheets of a limited edition of O'Neill's works which was soon to be published; O'Neill had been told the edition would comprise 1,250 copies, but believed that Liveright secretly intended to print and sell several hundred additional copies without paying O'Neill his royalties.

"I wrote Liveright a pretty stiff one last week and from a cable I have, evidently dispatched after four or ten of those cocktails, I judge he is hurt because I refuse to let him bluff me into taking his word for it there were 1,250 sheets sent me to autograph when *I know* there were between 1,700 and 1,800 of them. I got suspicious at the size of the packages and Agnes and I *both counted them!* . . ." (In his letter to Liveright he had said, among other things, "I always thought you were a crook and now I know it." As it turned out, Liveright was blameless in the matter; the printer had made the extra sheets as a margin for spoilage and had mailed them to O'Neill himself. Liveright knew nothing of this. Komroff wrote O'Neill an explanatory letter, and O'Neill apologized.)

Having dispatched Liveright, O'Neill (in his catchall letter to Madden) turned next to his hope that Belasco would soon give an answer on *Marco*. (Belasco, a few weeks later, sent word he would produce the play the following year.) O'Neill then inquired naïvely of Madden, "Do you have to send in script of 'Desire' to committee to make it eligible for Pulitzer Prize? If so, do so. Of course, I know there's no chance for it, but *I do*, for the sake of principle, want to *make* them pass it up." (The committee did pass it up; the prize went, that year, to Sidney Howard's *They Knew What They Wanted*; though O'Neill admired that play, he would have preferred the prize to go, if not to *Desire*, to Maxwell Anderson's *What Price Glory?* "I believe," he said publicly, "that *What Price Glory* is one of the most significant events in the history of our theatre. It is a splendid thing that the first fine, true war play should come from the most reactionary country in the world. It is still more wonderful and encouraging to all who love the theatre that there should be such a great public for it, because even two years ago it would have been possible only at special matinees or for invited audiences.")

O'Neill then asked Madden not to have any more of his royalty money deposited at the rural Connecticut bank where he maintained an account. "I don't want too much [there], as it's a small bank and maybe the cashier is betting on the races—and my money will hoodoo him. . . ." He ended by ordering Madden to "keep after" Theresa Helburn, a co-director of the Guild, for definite word as to when *The Fountain* would be produced. (Word came within a few days: production was postponed until the following fall.)

With no promise of an imminent production, O'Neill decided to stay put in Bermuda until June, and then move directly to Provincetown, thus avoiding the bother and expense of opening Brook Farm for a short season. Agnes, who expected her baby in April, also preferred to stay in Bermuda for the event. "I'm hoping it will be a girl for a change," said O'Neill, apprising a friend of his plans.

Toward the end of February O'Neill heard from Macgowan in New York that *Desire Under the Elms* had become something of a cause célèbre. District Attorney Joab H. Banton, a Southerner who was hell-bent on cleaning up the Broadway stage, had demanded that the play be closed. *Desire* was only one of his targets, however; two David Belasco productions, *Ladies of the Evening* and *The Harem* were also, according to Banton, improper fare for theatregoers, as was the William Brady production of *A*

Good Bad Woman. On February 20 Belasco told reporters that he would rewrite both his plays and have them "moral by Tuesday."

"If," said Brady the next day, "District Attorney Banton has granted David Belasco and others who are producing filthy plays the right to rewrite them, I claim the same privilege. I shall rewrite *A Good Bad Woman* between now and Monday and withdraw my promise to the district attorney to take the play off. I do not propose to be a goat."

Banton had not suggested that *Desire Under the Elms* be rewritten. It was, he said (not having seen the play), "too thoroughly bad to be purified by a blue pencil," and if it was not closed by the following Wednesday, he threatened to put the matter before a grand jury.

"We do not intend to accede to any peremptory demand to take the show off the stage by Wednesday," Macgowan announced to the press. "If we are indicted we will defend the play in the courts. We are gathering many opinions from persons of eminence, who consider this play a fine, strong work."

For a week or more the controversy raged, ending finally in Banton's authorization of a citizen play jury to pass on the morality of any Broadway offering in question. Meantime, Macgowan put out a pamphlet quoting his collection of "persons of eminence" about *Desire.* Among them were William Allen White, Percy MacKaye, Don Marquis, Rachel Crothers and (surprisingly) Augustus Thomas—all of whom said jointly that "the forced withdrawal of Eugene O'Neill's 'Desire Under the Elms' by repressive actions of any kind would be against the best interests not only of artists but of good citizenship." Others represented in the pamphlet were Sidney Howard ("Heroic tragedy does not grow on every bush. We ought to make O'Neill's play the cause for national and racial rejoicing. It is certainly the most noble and elevated work yet written for the theatre by any American"); the Rev. John Haynes Holmes ("No one but a half-wit could attack *Desire Under the Elms* as indecent"); and Dr. Smith Ely Jelliffe ("See the Epistle of Paul to the Romans, Chapter VI, and finally Verse 23 ['The wages of sin is Death'] for the authority of the Bible concerning the morality lesson driven home by O'Neill's *Desire Under the Elms*").

O'Neill received all the newspaper clippings and a copy of the pamphlet, thoughtfully dispatched by Macgowan to Bermuda. He was amused. For a moment or two he toyed with the idea of sending one or another of "several wicked cables" to "friend Banton," but he thought better of it. He was so deeply involved in the writing of *The Great God Brown* that he had no worry to spare over *Desire.*

The play jury did, at length, go to see *Desire* and voted that it should neither be suppressed nor corrected, and Macgowan promptly cabled O'Neill the news. O'Neill professed to have been sure of the outcome all along—although earlier he had remarked to a friend that it had been a surprise to him that the play had "fought its way to the top in New York."

"Fancy that, with infanticide!" he said.

While *Desire* profited from the publicity, O'Neill came to feel eventually that it had suffered artistically.

"We got a large audience, but of the wrong kind of people," O'Neill later told an interviewer. "They came for dirt and found it in everything. It ruined the actors because they never knew how a line was going to be taken."

What bothered him almost as much as the attacks of the "purifiers" were comments of theatregoers who "discovered" profound Freudian influences in the play. Regarding himself as an "intuitively keen analytical psychologist," he felt injured by the suggestion that he consciously drew on Freud's theories to help him convey "truths of the emotional past of mankind."

"I respect Freud's work tremendously—but I'm not an addict!" he snapped to an acquaintance who brought up the subject. "Whatever of Freudianism is in *Desire* must have walked right in 'through my unconscious.' "

And to a friend he wrote: ". . . The Freudian brethren and sistern seem quite set up about *Desire* and, after reading quite astonishing complexes between the lines of my simplicities, claim it for their own. Well, so some of them did with *Emperor Jones*. They are hard to shake!"

Desire continued to be the subject of much analysis in newspapers and magazines both in the United States and abroad. The English critic St. John Ervine, who had written to O'Neill to praise and encourage him when *Beyond the Horizon* was produced, launched an attack on his work in *Theatre Magazine,* in which he called *Desire* "a lamentable piece" and maintained that O'Neill's power was in decline.

The play was subsequently banned in Boston by the mayor and in England by the Lord Chamberlain, in spite of O'Neill's willingness to make some minor revisions in the dialogue, such as the substitution of the word "harlot" for "whore" and "sluttin' " for "whorin'." And when the road company opened in Los Angeles the following year the entire cast was arrested on the charge of giving an obscene play and tried in Municipal Court, awaking memories for O'Neill of the West Coast arrest and trial, nearly half a century earlier, of James O'Neill's company of *The Passion*. The trial, held in April, offered testimony by a police officer who had gone to see the play on behalf of the Board of Education.

"I was painfully shocked," said the policeman. "I blushed. I sat there so embarrassed that I feared for the time when the act would end and the lights would again be turned on. After I left that place I couldn't look the world in the face for hours."

O'Neill, in Bermuda, was content to follow *Desire's* notorious progress with ironic detatchment; he was satisfied that he had attempted to give an "epic tinge to New England's inhibited life" and, through a broad, poetical vision, to illuminate "even the most sordid and mean blind alleys of life"—his "concern and justification as a dramatist."

By the end of March, 1925, he had completed *The Great God Brown,* which he exultantly described to George Jean Nathan as "a devastating, crucifying new one," and which he confidently believed marked the high point of his achievement to date.

"I think it's grand stuff, much deeper and more poetical than anything I've ever done before," he assured Macgowan.

O'Neill's evaluation was largely accurate. *Brown* was devastating, "crucifying" (a significant word) and, in concept and many of its passages, profoundly poetic. It was also "deep"—so deep, in fact, that in parts, particularly the last act, even someone attuned to O'Neill's brand of mysticism could be left foundering. It was also flawed in spots by an incredible awkwardness of language. He could, in the same play, issue the deft line:

"This is Daddy's bedtime secret for today: Man is born broken. He lives by mending. The grace of God is glue!" and the turgid speech:

"The laughter of Heaven sows earth with a rain of tears, and out of earth's transfigured birthpain the laughter of Man returns to bless and play again in innumerable dancing gales of flame upon the knees of God!"

Both passages are from *The Great God Brown* and typify its best and its worst.

When O'Neill began writing *The Great God Brown* in the early winter of 1925 he was still in private mourning for his family. The same mood that had governed the unconsciously autobiographical *Desire* was still upon him—it was, in fact, to extend to *Mourning Becomes Electra,* begun in 1929. (Although neither time nor locale are specified for *Brown,* both recall the New London of O'Neill's youth.) In *Brown* O'Neill wrote about his parents in relationship to himself even more revealingly than he had in *Desire.* Distance had given him greater insight, deepened his sensitivity, and released more of his power to examine his relationship not only with James and Ella but with Jamie as well. Like *All God's Chillun Got Wings,* in its way *Brown* was yet another prelude to the crucifixion of *Long Day's Journey Into Night*.

In *Brown* the four characters who stand for James, Ella, Jamie and O'Neill himself, all die before the play has ended; unconsciously O'Neill was writing the family epitaph. The play depicts O'Neill (in the person of Dion Anthony) as "a stranger, walking alone . . . dark, spiritual, poetic, passionately supersensitive, helplessly unprotected, [with a] childlike, religious faith in life"—an artist, a creator, set apart from his fellow man, unable to make contact with family or friends, locked in a lonely struggle to find God and the meaning of life's mystery, and eventually knuckling under to the callousness of an unheeding and materialistic society.

Dion's parents understand neither their son nor each other, nor can Dion find the means to reach them. One of the most significantly autobiographical speeches written by O'Neill is the one in which Dion mourns his father:

"What aliens we were to each other! When he lay dead, his face looked so familiar that I wondered where I had met that man before. Only at the second of my conception. After that, we grew hostile with concealed shame."

Dion's friend, William Brown (whom he calls "brother"), represents, as does Jamie Tyrone in *Long Day's Journey Into Night*—and Andy Mayo in *Beyond the Horizon*—an antagonist both loved and hated, a symbol of the potentially fine soul grown stunted and envious and destructive, a symbol not only of Jamie but of what O'Neill himself might have become.

In *The Great God Brown*, more than in any other play, O'Neill revealed his unconscious confusion about his own identity; he often seemed to slip into the delusion that he was Jamie—that Jamie was but a harsher, more cynical extension of himself. It was probably this personal confusion that inspired his wholesale—and at times bewildering—use of masks.

Though O'Neill had toyed with masks before, he introduced them as a major dramatic device for the first time in *Brown*. All the leading characters—Brown, Cybel (a whore with a pure and beautiful soul, a solacer of Man), Dion and Dion's wife, Margaret—use masks to cover their faces when they do not want their souls' secrets revealed, and doff them before those they trust. Thus Dion is obliged to wear his mask before Margaret because Margaret cannot understand or cope with the anguish of his naked soul. With the prostitute, Cybel, Dion goes unmasked. Margaret wears no mask before Dion, but goes masked before the world. This much of O'Neill's symbolism is not only lucid but moving; the mystique of the mask of Dion passing, after his death, to Brown is more obscure—and O'Neill himself did little to shed light on it, though he made numerous attempts to do so. For example, in a letter to several New York newspapers in February, 1926, he wrote in part:

I realize that when a playwright takes to explaining he thereby automatically places himself "in the dock." But where an open-faced avowal by the play itself of the abstract theme underlying it is made impossible by the very nature of that hidden theme, then perhaps it is justifiable for the author to confess the mystical pattern which manifests itself as an overtone in "The Great God Brown," dimly behind and beyond the words and actions of the characters.

I had hoped the names chosen for my people would give a strong hint of this. (An old scheme, admitted—Shakespeare and multitudes since.) "Dion Anthony"—Dionysus and St. Anthony—the creative pagan acceptance of life, fighting eternal war with the masochistic, life-denying spirit of Christianity as represented by St. Anthony—the whole struggle resulting in this modern day in mutual exhaustion—creative joy in life for life's sake frustrated, rendered abortive, distorted by morality from Pan into Satan, into a Mephistopheles mocking himself in order to feel alive. . . .

"Margaret" is my image of the modern direct descendant of the "Marguerite" of "Faust"—the eternal girl-woman with a virtuous simplicity of instinct, properly oblivious to everything but the means to her end of maintaining the race.

"Cybel" is an incarnation of Cybele, the Earth Mother doomed to segregation as a pariah in a world of unnatural laws but patronized by her segregators who are thus themselves the first victims of their laws.

"Brown" is the visionless demi-god of our new materialistic myth—a Success—building his life of exterior things, inwardly empty and resourceless, an uncreative creature of superficial preordained social grooves, a by-product forced aside into slack waters by the deep main current of life-desire.

Dion's mask of Pan which he puts on as a boy is not only a defense against the world for the supersensitive painter-poet underneath it but also an integral part of his character as an artist. . . .

Brown has always envied the creative life force in Dion—what he himself lacks. When he steals Dion's mask . . . he thinks he is gaining the power to live creatively, while in reality he is only stealing that creative power made self-destructive by complete frustration. This devil of mocking doubt makes short work of him. It enters him, rending him apart, torturing and transfiguring him until he is even forced to wear a mask of his Success, William A. Brown, before all the world, as well as Dion's mask toward wife and children. Thus Billy Brown becomes not himself to anyone. And thus he partakes of Dion's anguish—more poignantly, for Dion had the Mother, Cybele . . .

. . . in the end out of this anguish [Brown's] soul is born, a tortured

Christian soul such as the dying Dion's, begging for belief, and at the last finding it on the lips of Cybele.

The play's chief obscurity lies in the fact that in the latter scenes Brown impersonates both himself (as he no longer exists) and Dion, in a series of episodes that come perilously close to burlesque. Brown's death scene is written to be played part realistically and part phantasy-pantomime, with Brown himself evaporating and being represented, in the end, by nothing more tangible than Dion's mask.

The demands on the audience in this instance are too great, and O'Neill himself guessed that they would be. "The audience won't know if it's walking backwards or forwards by the time it's ready to leave," he told Dr. Bisch with satisfaction soon after completing the play.

That O'Neill was aware of the inadequacy of his own printed explanation is obvious from another comment he made in his letter to the press:

And now for an explanation regarding this explanation. It was far from my idea in writing "Brown" that this background pattern of conflicting tides in the soul of Man should ever overshadow and thus throw out of proportion the living drama of the recognizable human beings, Dion, Brown, Margaret and Cybel. I meant it always to be mystically within and behind them, giving them a significance beyond themselves, forcing itself through them to expression in mysterious words, symbols, actions that they do not themselves comprehend.

And that is as clearly as I wish an audience to comprehend it. It is Mystery —the mystery any one man or woman can feel but not understand as the meaning of any event—or accident—in any life on earth. And it is this mystery I want to realize in the theatre.

The solution, if there is ever to be any, will probably have to be produced in a test tube and turn out to be discouragingly undramatic.

Much later, looking at *Brown* in retrospect, O'Neill wrote that it had been an attempt "to foreshadow the mystical patterns created by the duality of human character and the search for what lies hidden and beyond the words and actions of men and women."

"More by the use of overtones than by explicit speech," he added, "I sought to convey the dramatic conflicts in the lives and within the souls of the characters. The use of masks enabled me to dramatize the transfer of personality and express symbolically the mystery inherent in all human lives."

XLV

FOR ALL OF O'NEILL'S PROLONGED DISMAY OVER HIS
disastrous relationship with his parents—a dismay he could convey so
forcefully in a play like *The Great God Brown,*—he seemed unaware that
he was imposing the same pattern on his own children. It was as though
the very intensity of his preoccupation with his parents' failure toward him,
the constant attempt to exorcise the hurt that had been inflicted, blinded
him to the fact that he was inflicting the same hurt on his sons. He was
as stonily incapable of understanding them as James had been of understanding him.

The three sons with whom O'Neill furnished Dion Anthony had no
more dramatic validity, bore no more importance to their father, than any
of the children O'Neill created for dramatic effect in his other plays. In
their abortive appearances in *The Great God Brown,* the three sons are
mechanical prigs, mere window dressing—something to illustrate that
Margaret is a mother—and their father is scarcely aware of them. This
was a quite accurate, if perhaps unconscious, representation of O'Neill's
attitude toward his own two sons at the time he finished the play—which
was also a time when he was anticipating the birth of a third child. O'Neill,
like a number of other profoundly creative men, felt no need to be
perpetuated by children. When he was writing, he often described his
efforts to friends as "birth pangs." His plays were his children and he was
both father and mother to them. His claim to immortality rested upon his
plays; flesh-and-blood children were to him at best the necessary appendages
of domesticity and at worst irritating hindrances to his work.

Agnes expected her baby in April and she and O'Neill rented a more
substantial house for the final three months of their stay in Bermuda,
while keeping the seaside bungalow as a place to swim from. In mid-
March O'Neill wrote to Macgowan inviting him, Jones and Light to
visit Paget in April and offering them the bungalow as a guest house.

James Light was the only one of the three who managed the trip to
Bermuda in April, although the others visited later. Light spent a tranquil
time there, discussing *The Great God Brown* with O'Neill and helping
him plan the production. (O'Neill wanted John Barrymore to play Dion.)
They also discussed *The Fountain,* about which O'Neill was growing

increasingly discouraged. "Maybe I'll decide to produce and publish it myself—in a good hot stove," he told Light.

As for O'Neill's domestic life, Light found it fairly serene.

"I remember that Shane tried to get into the spirit of his mother's mysterious condition one day by bringing her a plate of worms and shellfish and other slimy objects and saying, 'Here, this will make you sick.' "

When Light left, O'Neill asked him to tell Macgowan that his and Agnes's "twin girls" were expected momentarily, but that "ladies always make you wait, don't they?"

By May 1, when the "twin girls" had not yet made an appearance, O'Neill complained to a friend that the waiting was getting on his nerves, "while Agnes is as calm as calm—couvade, is that what they call it?"

O'Neill had to endure the discomforts of couvade for two more weeks. It was not until May 14 that Agnes produced her child.

"It's a goil. Allah be merciful," O'Neill cabled Macgowan. "According to indications will be first lady announcer at Polo Grounds. Predict great future grand opera. Agnes and baby all serene."

Both Agnes and O'Neill had been certain of having a girl, and Agnes had written to Mrs. Padraic Colum, wife of the Irish poet, asking if she and her husband could suggest a feminine Irish name that would go well with O'Neill.

"We suggested Oona, the Irish translation of Agnes," Colum later recalled.

O'Neill kept up a semblance of serenity for another month in the midst of his newly enlarged household, principally because he had managed to time things so that he was not writing a new play. For that brief period he grew domestically expansive, claiming to be unaffected by all the commotion of his household. He even encouraged a visit from Eugene Jr., now a handsome boy of fourteen.

Eugene Jr., made the trip to Bermuda by himself. He was still living with his mother and being supported in part by O'Neill, who was paying his way through Horace Mann in New York. Although O'Neill was proud of the boy and, in a semi-detached way, fond of him, his interest never approached genuine fatherly devotion. A year earlier Eugene had fallen from his bicycle near his house and fractured his skull. Kathleen had rushed her son to a nearby Long Island hospital and then telephoned to O'Neill, who was in New York on his way to Provincetown.

O'Neill told Kathleen that his bank account was at her disposal; he arranged for a specialist to visit Eugene and asked Kathleen to keep him informed of Eugene's condition by sending him a night letter, collect, every day. But O'Neill did not postpone his trip to Provincetown. Eugene was in the hospital for five weeks, part of that time in critical condition, and O'Neill never visited him.

By the end of June O'Neill was glad to exchange the domestic hubbub of Bermuda for what he hoped would be the calm of Nantucket. Remote Peaked Hill seemed an impractical summer place for an infant and living in the center of Provincetown promised to be hectic. After a brief stopover in New York, therefore, O'Neill moved into a rented house on a hill in Nantucket, near an old windmill and about half a mile from the wharf.

But in Nantucket he felt neither secure nor happy. He began drinking again.

He left his family on the island and went to New York during July to meet with Macgowan and Jones to discuss the future of the Provincetown Playhouse and Greenwich Village Theatre. The triumvirate's enterprise was becoming shaky and plans for the coming season were up in the air; O'Neill was beginning to be less interested in the programs for the two theatres, and more concerned with the production of his own plays.

While in New York he allowed himself to be interviewed by Flora Merrill, a reporter for the *World*, who questioned him about his views of the contemporary theatre and his own plans for the future.

"I should say," O'Neill answered the question as to whether the American theatre had made any strides in playwriting, acting or production, "that it had progressed furthest in production, but also tremendously in playwriting, and in acting not at all, if you leave out one man who is the exception to all rules because he has real genius, and that is John Barrymore. I feel very strongly about the matter of acting in this country, and in my opinion it is impossible to carry on much further until the actors catch up. Under present conditions, there is no very bright prospect of their succeeding."

(O'Neill's view of Lionel Barrymore summed up how he felt about actors. A few years earlier, after seeing Lionel Barrymore play *Macbeth*, O'Neill criticized his acting in a letter to Macgowan: "My principal reaction was a rage at Barrymore that warn't fit to print. He got between the production and me, darn him. It was only when he was off stage that I could become aware of anything else. That is my main trouble in theatre-going and the real reason why I avoid the show-shops. I can't help seeing with the relentless eye of heredity, upbringing and personal experience every little trick they pull as actors. Thus the actor is ever present to me and the character is lost. Thus in the most tense moment of a play I am struck—with amusement or disgust as the case may be—by the sly, insidious intent—plain to me—of a gesture, a fillip, a change in tempo, a body wriggle.")

Questioned by the *World* about whether he planned to broaden his own scope of activity, particularly whether he might attempt to write a novel, O'Neill answered:

"I have no ambition to go out of my field and become a novelist. I feel that a carpenter should stick to his trade. I don't hold with these novelists who suddenly decide they will write a play. I think it takes years of intensive, hard work to learn your medium if you want to be any good in it. In my opinion, the drama is a darn sight harder medium than the novel because it is concentrated. The only way I would want to write a novel would be if I had seven or eight years to devote to doing ten, all of which I would throw away before I should think I could possibly write one decent book. That is what I did with plays. I must have thrown away a dozen when I first started. Yet I knew the theatre, having been born in it."

Asked who were the great American playwrights of the day, he replied:

"There are none. What's more, I don't believe there is any great playwright in the world, with the possible exception of Hauptmann. The last great one died with Strindberg in 1912—that is, the last undeniably great playwright, because some think Hauptmann is, and some think he isn't."

He added that he was interested in "any sort of play that I hear is good," but that he seldom attended the theatre. "I know that all the worthwhile plays will be published," he said, "so I wait and read them." Musical comedies, he explained, were the exception: "I go to them to get a laugh."

Before returning to Nantucket O'Neill went on the kind of binge he had not indulged in for many months. He ended it at the Macgowan home in Brewster, where Macgowan and his wife nursed him through a severe hangover, involving, as always, a slow tapering off of carefully timed drinks and judicious infusions of soup and milk shakes, interspersed with periods of sleep and exercise.

"I've meant to . . . tell you both how very grateful I am for all you did for me out at your place," he apologized to the Macgowans from Nantucket, where he had once again vowed to stay sober. "I must have been a pretty sorry sight to have about the house and by no means a welcome addition to any family retaining their sanity. . . . Let me know what I owe you for the car, beer, booze, etc. and I'll send you check pronto." He added that he also wanted to send money for a gift for the Macgowan children "from their old alcoholic pal."

Within a few weeks he was off the wagon once again. The arrival in Nantucket of Ed Keefe, one of his New London drinking companions, set him off in August.

Keefe and two friends sailed to Nantucket in a schooner and, hearing O'Neill was there, looked him up.

"Gene was glad to see me and joined my friends and me for dinner," Keefe said later. "Then the four of us rowed to the schooner, which was anchored quite a way out in the harbor, and drank and drank and drank. After a while the two other guys went to sleep. Gene and I kept on drinking. At one point Gene stood up in the hatchway and let his wristwatch fly against the hatch—he was being dramatic about something. Finally we went to our bunks and I fell asleep."

Keefe was awakened by the steward. "I think your friend is overboard," he said. Keefe followed the steward out on deck and saw O'Neill in the water, fully dressed and still roaring drunk. Keefe and the steward pulled O'Neill back on board, stripped him, and put him into a bunk. Soon after, the steward woke Keefe again. Dawn was breaking.

"There's a lady alongside in a rowboat," the steward told Keefe. It was Agnes.

"She had rowed out to collect Gene," Keefe said. "We got him into a raincoat and some slippers and eased him over the side into the rowboat. I watched Gene and Agnes draw away, Gene trying to sit up straight in the boat, Agnes rowing. The sun was coming up as they headed in to shore."

Manuel Komroff, O'Neill's editor, also visited him in Nantucket that summer. The household now seemed peaceful, and Komroff's wife, a painter, started work on a water-color portrait of Shane. O'Neill managed to stay sober and he worked hard—trying to make a few revisions on *The Fountain,* outlining new projects, and doing some research on a subject that appeared to fascinate him, though he never used it for a play. In the early days after the Revolution when Nantucket was a whaling port of great wealth, O'Neill explained to Komroff one morning, some of the captains made trips to China. They returned with exotic gifts for their wives—embroidered silks, teakwood furniture, carved ivory, and opium. It seemed, said O'Neill, that Nantucket women acquired "a nice little taste for opium" and sometimes, while waiting for their husbands to return, they could be seen, dressed in their embroidered silks, staggering through the streets drunk on opium. O'Neill was struck by this picture, so far removed from the traditional one of the stoical New England woman pacing the widow's walk.

O'Neill was much preoccupied during the summer of 1925 with his commitment to the Greenwich Village Theatre. He had recently withdrawn from active participation in the Provincetown Playhouse; for the coming season, it was decided, the Provincetown would be operated by Jimmy Light, with O'Neill serving merely in an advisory capacity, and Macgowan and Jones participating as members of the board of directors. Eleanor Fitzgerald, who was to be manager only of the Provincetown (while also remaining a member of the board of the Greenwich Village Theatre) had asked O'Neill to write something for the program of the Provincetown's opening bill. O'Neill sent a discouraging answer.

"I cannot [write anything] because, temporarily, at least . . . my faith in theatre, Provincetown or otherwise, has bogged down. I'm miscast among the true believers. The future appears to me completely sterilized against the conception of miracles and a miracle, as present day miracles go, is needed. A kick-in-the-false-bloomers-of-Thespis miracle. But even the god in the wind machine and the thunder sheet seems to have given in his Equity notice . . . and left the theatre for the show shop. I don't belong, get me?—because I don't believe. And programs are . . . not the proper medium for painful skepticism."

He went on to outline his pet grievance, the inadequacy of actors; Fitzi, disregarding O'Neill's warning, printed his diatribe (with a few judicious deletions) in the program for the Provincetown's opening bill, probably reasoning that skeptical O'Neill was better than no O'Neill at all.

She entitled the piece, "Are the Actors to Blame?":

I believe that there is no possibility of real progress in the creative interpretation of plays of arresting imagination and insight until we develop a new quality of depth of feeling and comprehensive scope of technique in actors and actresses. For only when a play is self-expressed through sensitive, truthful, trickless acting is "the play the thing."

In the acting lies the acted play. Great acting has frequently made bad plays seem good, but a good play cannot penetrate bad acting without emerging distorted—an uneven, bumpy, ugly duckling of an offspring at whom any playwright father must gaze with a shudder. [Deleted was O'Neill's parenthetical comment: "And Mama Theatre says you are mine? I think she must have spent some dark moments in the alley with an actor!"]

And this in spite of the finest and most intelligent and inspiring direction. Directors can only direct. They cannot give their actors the right developing experience unless they can plan over a long period of years with the same people. This plainly isn't possible under any present system. For actors are conceived by and born of the parts they have been permitted to play.

Are the actors to blame for the present conditions in *all* theatres which urge them toward the easy goals of type casting rather than the long, pain-staking self-training in the acquiring of an art? Well, if actors are partly to blame, then we others of the theatre, including the audience, who accept them, are equally at fault. Do we give them parts other than the apparent one God cast them in as persons? Do we take a chance on them? Not often. [In his letter to Fitzi, O'Neill had written an unqualified "We do not!"]

We cannot afford to in an era when the theatre is primarily a realtor's speculation. One mistake and there comes the landlord with notice of eviction. He is usually not an artist in the theatre, this landlord! He could see Shakespeare boiled alive in Socony gasoline and have qualms only as to our diminishing national Standard Oil reserves. The answer? Repertoire. Genuine repertoire. We all know it—it's as simple as truth—and perhaps that is why we make no attempt to live and work accordingly.

What is the Provincetown going to do about acting? [Deleted was the line "Is it going to attempt to correct its great weak spot, the source of its failure in times past?"] Does it plan to lay emphasis on building up a medium for achievement in acting that will make young actors want to grow up with it as part of a whole, giving their acting a new clear fakeless group excellence and group eloquence that will be our unique acting, our own thing, born in our American theatre as not so long ago Irish acting was born in the Irish Players, modern Russian acting in the Moscow Art Theatre, or modern German acting in the Reinhardt group? All these had humble beginnings as we have had. If we do intend to work with the future of our acting at least equally in view with the artistic production of good plays and great plays, then I am high with hope.

O'Neill had ended his letter to Fitzi thus: "The present theatre of the future is in the actor. Until he goes on we others—I speak as a playwright —can't, except by the inadequate written word. My motto just now is 'write 'em and leave 'em!' And my intuition is that it is better not to do things at all, especially the most beautiful things, than to run the slightest risk of doing them badly. Beauty is in poor enough repute already."

That was too skeptical, even for Fitzi, and she altered it—somewhat ungrammatically—to:

"The immediate theatre of the future is in the actor. Until he gets his real opportunity we others—I speak as a playwright—this applies equally to all artists in the theatre—but wait for ours, or try to be contented with what we know must be an unrealizable dream."

To Macgowan O'Neill recently had voiced the fear that there were not only no good actors but no good, new plays. "I wish we had more definite proof," he said, "that there *are* experiments all written for the doing at the P.P. We had no reason to believe so up to the time I left. That's our main trouble, as it is everyone else's. Where's the stuff? And if there ain't none, what's the good of hanging on to the P.P.?"

By summer he was wondering if there was much good in hanging on to the Greenwich Village Theatre either. It did not seem to be living up to its promise and he questioned its usefulness to him. And it was not, he thought, providing the theatre in general with the stimulus once foreseen nor devoting its best efforts to his own work.

Following the fortunes of both playhouses from Nantucket that September, he deplored the choice of a Maxwell Anderson play called *Outside Looking In,* with which Macgowan had opened the new season at the Greenwich Village Theatre. O'Neill had read it and deemed it "totally without significance" and "depth." But what rankled even more was that Macgowan and Jones had not yet been able to cast *The Great God Brown* —presumably because they were devoting their attention to other, inferior plays.

"I somehow feel we're going bad and have become a young organization with a brilliant past," O'Neill grumbled to Macgowan, just before leaving Nantucket.

Although both the Provincetown Playhouse and the Greenwich Village Theatre were to struggle for existence several more years, O'Neill was to detach himself from them completely after early 1926. *The Fountain* and *The Great God Brown* were produced at the Greenwich Village Theatre in December, 1925, and January, 1926, respectively. They were the last new O'Neill plays presented by the old group. Soon after that O'Neill made a change in his personal as well as his professional life, marking an absolute cleavage from almost all of his former associates.

The Ridgefield house was reopened in October after O'Neill visited New London to look after his still-unsettled estate—and to have a final, spectacular, reminiscent binge with Ed Keefe, Doc Ganey and a brother of Arthur McGinley. ("They are much too swift for me in New London these days," he told McGinley later, when he had gone back on the wagon.)

While in Ridgefield awaiting the triumvirate's productions of *The Fountain* and *The Great God Brown* and Belasco's production of *Marco Millions,* O'Neill began writing a new play, *Lazarus Laughed,* which he had "elaborately and wonderfully scenarioed" in Nantucket. (He had also completed a scenario for what he called "my woman play." Under the title *Strange Interlude* he was to continue working on it during 1926 and 1927; he was also still toying with the idea for the play called *Dynamo,* but had put aside the actual writing of it; if the results of O'Neill's fantastic creative energy were almost equally divided between great plays and bungled efforts, at least he was never content just to mark time.)

As he had to be in New York early in November for rehearsals of *The Fountain* and was too distracted to concentrate on any single project,

O'Neill invited his older son to spend a few days with him. It turned out to be a profitable visit on both sides. In addition to his handsome, foolish Irish wolfhound, O'Neill owned an aggressive, conceited Irish terrier named Matt Burke, in honor of the hero of *Anna Christie*. Matt Burke terrorized the area by chasing chickens and challenging any and all local pets and children to combat, from which he invariably emerged victorious. O'Neill's neighbors were not happy about Matt Burke, but young Eugene fell in love with him, and O'Neill conceived a plan to pacify his neighbors and please his son.

A few days after Eugene Jr. returned to his home in Long Island, a huge crate arrived for him. Kathleen, to whom Eugene had said nothing about the anticipated gift, opened the crate with some misgivings, and tethered its contents to a tree in the yard. When Eugene came home from school Matt Burke was gone. He returned later that evening, bruised and bloody, having established himself as the boss of the neighborhood. The Pitt-Smiths kept him until his death from old age several years later.

During the period he was attending rehearsals of *The Fountain* in New York, O'Neill stayed in a hotel Mondays through Thursdays, returning for the weekends to Ridgefield. Getting *The Fountain* on, after three and a half years of waiting, was an anticlimax for O'Neill, and he was half-hearted about its production. He agreed to the casting of Walter Huston as Ponce de León even though he thought Lionel Barrymore better suited to the role. Ideally, O'Neill would have liked to cast James O'Neill as Ponce de León and he could not reconcile this image with the reality of Huston's characterization. Discussing Huston's technique with Stark Young, and comparing it with that of James O'Neill (who, with distance, appeared to his son to have far greater stature than he had been willing to allow him during his lifetime), O'Neill said: "Here's just the difference: the actors in those days would not have understood my play, but they could act it; now they understand it, but can't act it."

O'Neill grew steadily more impatient with the limitations of his actors. Even when he was able to cast the actor or actress he thought just right for a role he was usually disappointed with the result. A year earlier he had spoken to Macgowan of "the difference there must be always between the author's idea as he sees what he writes and the horrible puppet show the actors transform it into, willy-nilly, good or bad." It never failed to infuriate him that despite his knowledge of actor craft and the pains he always took to forestall an actor's personal interpretation of a role by spelling out every important gesture, look and vocal nuance, he could still not get the effect he wanted.

Referring, in a more jocular mood, to a particular actress who had failed to live up to his expectations, O'Neill once commented: "She is so thick in spots, it hurts you. Not that I wish an intelligence test for actresses. (None of them would get a job then.) Or that I don't like the lady. I do. She is a nice girl—the kind your own mother would approve of you 'keeping,' so to speak."

It is impossible not to suspect that O'Neill's predilection for masks was inspired, in part, by a hopeless desire to obliterate the actor from his plays. He once wrote that he anticipated the actors' objection to masks: "that they would extinguish their personalities and deprive them of their greatest asset in conveying emotion by facial expression." He went on to refute this objection, claiming that masked actors would be obliged, all to the good, to make "their bodies become alive and expressive and participate in drama." His point was valid enough; he was calling on actors to learn and develop the art of mime. But, more urgently, he was willing them to "extinguish their personalities" and stop getting between him and his audience—a hopeless hope, indeed.

The Fountain opened on December 10, 1925, to lukewarm reviews. Woollcott, now happily closeted at the *World,* praised the lavish production Robert Edmond Jones had designed and directed, and found "certain scenes which glow with the eventfulness of history," but observed that "the spark of life was missing a good half the time." His criticism was representative of that of his colleagues.

O'Neill took his defeat mildly. He was relieved that the production was over with—and anxious to get started on the production of *The Great God Brown.*

"A couple of nights after *The Fountain* opened," Slim Martin later said, "I overtook Gene going east on Fourth Street and he asked me if I'd seen the play. I said I had. He told me he thought the critics were right, that the play had no action."

Slim asked O'Neill, "Can't an author tell, while he's writing a play, if it has action?"

"You can't tell how a play will work out till it's produced," O'Neill explained patiently. "If you could, all authors would write hits and turn out as many plays as Lope de Vega."

XLVI

WHEN *The Great God Brown* FINALLY REACHED THE STAGE it became the fifth new O'Neill play to be produced within a period of less than two years. Since March, 1924, *Welded, All God's Chillun Got Wings, Desire Under the Elms* and *The Fountain* had been mounted; not since the two-year period between February, 1920, and March, 1922, which saw the production of *eight* O'Neill plays, had New York been so thoroughly inundated by O'Neill.

Perhaps because of his strong attachment to *Brown* as autobiography O'Neill was willing to devote more energy to its presentation than was usual for him, and he suffered more acutely over the inevitable production snags. He and the other two members of the triumvirate, unable to interest John Barrymore in the role of Dion Anthony, finally selected Robert Keith, and cast William Harrigan, son of the famous comic, Ned, as William Brown. Albert Lewis, who had sent O'Neill's *In the Zone* on its vaudeville tour eight years before, attended an early run-through at the request of Kenneth Macgowan, who hoped Lewis would invest in the production.

"The rehearsal was played without masks," Lewis recalled, "and the actors pantomimed the masks. It all looked very awkward. It was impossible to judge the play's power without the masks. After the run-through I told Kenneth I didn't think the play had a chance. There was a burst of derisive laughter from the balcony, and I looked up and saw O'Neill, who had heard what I'd said. He said he didn't blame me—that it certainly wasn't vaudeville. I was terribly embarrassed, and he tried to assure me he could understand my not being bowled over by the play, that there was no illusion without the masks."

Although *The Great God Brown* was a much more difficult play to evaluate than *Desire Under the Elms,* the critics welcomed it, on January 23, 1926, with more warmth and understanding on the whole than they had accorded *Desire.*

Brooks Atkinson, who, at thirty, had recently replaced Stark Young as *The Times* critic (after editing its *Book Review*), began his appraisal: "What Mr. O'Neill has succeeded in doing in 'The Great God Brown' . . .

is obviously more important than what he has not succeeded in doing. He has not made himself clear. But he has placed within the reach of the stage finer shades of beauty, more delicate nuances of truth and more passionate qualities of emotion than we can discover in any other single modern play."

Richard Watts, Jr., who was pinchhitting for Percy Hammond, wrote: "In 'The Great God Brown' Eugene O'Neill has written a play that for at least half of the time is as eloquent and stirring and richly imaginative as anything that has come from the pen of this foremost of our dramatists. Then, as though the mad ghost of Strindberg had entered into him, he plunges into a veritable orgy of expression until the last scenes of his drama approach chaos . . . but 'The Great God Brown' remains in the end a fascinating, half-mad enigma."

Alexander Woollcott was not inclined to weigh the balance in favor of O'Neill and, though he credited the play with being "now and again poetic in its divination and almost always sturdy with the characteristic fibre of a playwright who has a lonesome, hardy, pathfinding mind," he found "the mask trick" tiresome and overdone and the play, as a whole, uneven to the point of being "precipitous."

Gilbert Gabriel, who had replaced Woollcott on the *Sun*, found the play "a deep-minded and compassionate fantasy, often thrilling in the brightness of its words, sometimes perplexing in the shadows of its meaning."

Joseph Wood Krutch, with more time than the daily reviewers to digest the play, declared in *The Nation*:

"At no time during the course of his career has Mr. O'Neill given us a play more powerful or more confused than this. Never before has he dealt with a passion so nakedly personal, and never before has he allowed the chaos within to shatter so completely the form of the drama. . . . If the effect remains more powerful than clear, more intense than illuminating, that is the result of the immediacy of the material with which the author is dealing. He is himself too close to the passions with which he is dealing to objectify them completely, and they master him quite as often as he is able to master them. Here, in a word, are passions as authentic and as burning as any that ever went into literature, but no one could say that they had been 'recollected in tranquillity.' "

Despite the play's critical and popular success (it was moved uptown to the Garrick Theatre on March 1 and transferred to the Klaw in May, where it continued until September 28, an eight month's run), O'Neill took his habitually dim view of the production, focusing his discontent on the masks. He decided they had confused the audience in the back rows because they were made to look too realistic. They should have been twice as large, he now believed.

"Do the masks in 'Brown' do what the script requires of them?" he asked Macgowan rhetorically. "They do not. They only get across personal resemblance of a blurry meaninglessness. . . . Perhaps the result the script calls for is impossible to attain by the method of combination masks the script describes. I think I see this now."

Still concerned about this a year later, he declared that the masks in the production had not been right, because the triumvirate had had "neither the time nor the money to experiment and get them right before we opened —the old story that prevents anything really fine from ever being done in the American theatre!" What he had really "wanted those masks to get across," he said, was "the abstract drama of the forces behind the people"; instead, he went on, the masks had suggested "only the bromidic, hypocritical and defensive double personality of people in their personal relationships—a thing I never would have needed masks to convey."

"They became an unnecessary trick," he added. "Perhaps I was demanding too much, and it can't be done—but I'm sure with the right masks my meaning would get across, that the play would be mystic instead of confusing—and I'm sure, given the money and time, the right masks could have been made."

As late as 1932, writing for *The American Spectator,* O'Neill was still having afterthoughts about his *Brown* masks. "I would now make the masks symbolize more definitely the abstract theme of the play instead of, as in the old production, stressing the more superficial meaning that people wear masks before other people and are mistaken by them for their masks."

In 1952, by which time O'Neill had completed *Mourning Becomes Electra, The Iceman Cometh* and *Long Day's Journey Into Night*—three plays generally held to be among his masterpieces—he chose a scene from *The Great God Brown* to represent him in an anthology called *This Is My Best.* He picked the third scene from Act I, between Dion, Cybel and Brown, which includes Dion's mourning speech about his parents, explaining that it was "one of the best, and the most self-sufficient when taken out of its context." In an introductory note he wrote:

"Rereading *The Great God Brown* . . . which I haven't looked at for ten years or more, I still consider this play one of the most interesting and moving I have written. It has its faults, of course, but for me, at least, it does succeed in conveying a sense of the tragic mystery drama of *Life* revealed through the *lives* in the play. And this, I think, is the real test of whether any play, however excellent its structure, characterization, dialogue, plot, social significance, or what not—is true drama or just another play."

With the production of *Brown* out of the way O'Neill was anxious to return to Bermuda but was obliged to postpone his trip until late February. He had finally, on the advice of a number of friends and physicians, decided to undergo a brief psychoanalysis. Its chief purpose was to cure him, permanently, of drinking.

O'Neill selected neither of the two psychoanalysts with whom he was already acquainted, although Dr. Bisch did figure indirectly in the decision.

"O'Neill never asked me to analyze him," Dr. Bisch later said, "but we discussed analysis in general on several occasions. He wanted to know if I really thought it helped people. Apparently he talked to some of his friends about my ideas, too. One day, in New York, he invited me to have lunch with him and two friends, whose names I've forgotten. A few days later one of them telephoned me and asked if they could consult me about O'Neill, but not to mention this to him. I invited them to my office. They said they thought analysis might be good for O'Neill but were afraid it could harm him as a dramatist. They were worried that it might destroy his genius, inhibit his artistic freedom. I told them I didn't think it would, that, on the contrary, it might make him even freer. But I warned them that O'Neill would be a difficult man to analyze because he had such a strong ego. Most people who are very shy, I told them, have strong egos; they are certain of their own powers but afraid others won't recognize those powers. I felt analysis of this would help him; I said it would probably enhance, rather than repress, his genius.

"I didn't tell O'Neill's two friends of my privately held deduction that O'Neill was emotionally starved. I had studied his plays carefully and felt they all showed an antagonism toward women, which indicated to me that he had a deep antagonism toward his mother. I believed that O'Neill hated his mother and loved his father. He duplicated his father's profession, the theatre, which is one indication. His father was an actor-escapist; writing is, in a way, also an escape. He also imitated his father in his alcoholism. I felt O'Neill had an unconscious homosexual attraction toward his father, which he carried over to some of his friendships for men. His antagonism toward his mother was carried over to his relationships with women; because his mother had failed him, all women would fail him, and he had to take revenge on them. All women had to be punished."

Dr. Bisch would have enjoyed psychoanalyzing O'Neill to see whether the theories he held as an observant friend could be supported, but the man O'Neill selected as his analyst was Dr. Gilbert V. Hamilton. It is not inconceivable that one of the reasons for this choice was that Dr. Hamilton could analyze him under the terms of a special grant, and that consequently there would be no fee. With a grant set up for him in 1924 Dr. Hamilton had begun a research program into the problems of sexual adjustment in the marital relationship. Published in 1929 under the title, *A Research in Marriage,* Dr. Hamilton's findings were a kind of precursor of the Kinsey Report, and, as such, were acknowledged by Dr. Alfred C. Kinsey in his own work. Dr. Hamilton had selected the very small sample of one hundred married men and one hundred married women (not all of them married to each other) to whom he had presented more than three hundred questions designed to elicit information about their premarital, marital and extramarital sex lives.

According to Dr. Hamilton, he had little difficulty in obtaining his subjects, who were drawn mostly from professional and literary backgrounds. Macgowan and his wife were among them, and so were O'Neill and Agnes. None of the subjects, of course, are identifiable from Dr. Hamilton's charts, but it is easy to guess who the sole male respondent was in one instance at least.

Card Number 15, Question 7, asked if the subject's parents had got along well together, and twenty men answered "No"; Question 8 asked these twenty for "the chief source of friction between them" and of eighteen who blamed their mothers for the trouble, listing such causes as "Mother's nagging," "Mother's sexual inadequacy," "Mother's interest in other men," etc., only one listed "Mother's drug habit."

"In our circle," Macgowan recalled, "the interviews were the table topic of the day."

After completing this survey Dr. Hamilton received additional funds to psychoanalyze six people, and it was under this second grant that he analyzed O'Neill. (Although O'Neill's friends and Dr. Hamilton referred to O'Neill's therapeutic sessions as a psychoanalysis, it lasted only six weeks and fell considerably short of what most qualified practitioners regard as a thorough analysis.)

"Gene agreed to the psychoanalysis to get him on the wagon," Macgowan said. "He told me he was scared, that he couldn't continue the way he was. Agnes was no help to him in that respect. She drank along with him. During the analysis Hamilton had Gene lie on a black leather couch, in traditional Freudian style. When it was over, Gene told me he had no trouble understanding that he hated and loved his father, and that he was suffering from an Oedipus complex. Later, when I was working with Hamilton on a popular version of his book, called *What Is Wrong with Marriage?* Hamilton told me, 'There's a death wish in O'Neill.'"

Though many psychoanalysts agree that they can seldom make lasting headway with alcoholics, in O'Neill's case the cure was essentially effective. Except for a couple of lapses, O'Neill spent the rest of his life as a teetotaler.

With his analysis completed and his passage booked for Bermuda, O'Neill took time out shortly before sailing to attend a dinner party given by Donald Friede, a newly appointed vice-president of Horace Liveright, Inc., which had recently issued a four-volume edition of O'Neill's collected works. Friede had also invited Manuel Komroff and two other Liveright authors, Theodore Dreiser and Sherwood Anderson; there were to be no women present except Mrs. Friede, for some reason that Friede has been unable to recall.

When he received the invitation, Komroff was somewhat taken aback; he pointed out to Friede that Dreiser and Anderson were feuding and that the affair might be uncomfortable.

"Friede said he didn't care," Komroff recalled, "and the dinner was held as scheduled. It was one of the strangest dinners I ever attended. I remember that Dreiser kept folding and unfolding his handkerchief, and there was nothing that could be described as conversation among the three writers. They all seemed to regard each other as freaks and to be wondering what they were doing there. When one of the three did speak, he spoke to Friede or to me, not to the others.

"After dinner, Anderson told a ghost story and then there was a long silence. Finally Dreiser, who was interested in the supernatural and communication with the dead, told, in a harrowing voice and with terrible intensity, the story of how his mother had died in his arms.

"O'Neill just sat there, watching him. I don't think he spoke ten words the whole evening. We had arrived at seven, and we all left about eleven."

Friede's recollection is that O'Neill's conversation was a trifle more expansive—perhaps a matter of half a dozen full sentences.

"Dreiser, who was usually arrogant, seemed to me like a small boy at O'Neill's feet. He asked him questions about his writing technique, all of which O'Neill answered politely."

The party was not a stunning success, and only Anderson appeared to salvage anything from it. About a year later he wrote down the ghost story he had told that night, and it was published in *Vanity Fair*.

"I once told the story to Mr. Theodore Dreiser and Mr. Eugene O'Neill as I sat with them in a room and now have a fancy to put it in print," the piece begins. The story concerns a widowed schoolteacher who moves into a haunted house and strikes up an acquaintance with a ghost. It is embellished with satiric comments on contemporary cultural pretensions and with references to both Dreiser and O'Neill, which Anderson had omitted on the night of the dinner party.

O'Neill's opinion of the story, in either its printed or its recounted version, is not recorded, but he and Anderson later established a cordial friendship.

In Bermuda—from the end of February to the middle of June—O'Neill completed *Lazarus Laughed*, got a good start on *Strange Interlude*, made notes for half a dozen future plays, and purchased an early eighteenth-century house.

"Just a shell," he reported to a friend in describing the house, "but a very fine shell." He added that he and Agnes planned to decorate it gradually and use it as a permanent winter and spring residence. In the meantime they occupied a rented house called Bellevue in Paget East— "a real peach of a house," O'Neill said, "lots of room—beautiful grounds— private beach—all at a big bargain of $150 per." He boasted that it "used to be one of the show places of the island."

During this stay in Bermuda he thought he had finally found the ideal combination of beauty and peace. He swam every day, gained weight (six pounds in less than two weeks), was inaccessible to most of his Greenwich Village and Provincetown drinking companions and felt, once again, "reborn."

"Next to Peaked Hill in the old days," he confided to Louis Kalonyme, "I believe this the most satisfying habitat I've struck. It really has the feeling of home to me who usually feel in most houses like a Samoan in an igloo."

His work was going so well that he was not even perturbed by a series of minor domestic mishaps: Agnes' sister, who was to do O'Neill's typing and had sailed to Bermuda with them, was quarantined in a wing of the house with measles; O'Neill stepped on a coral reef and "tore out the keel" of his foot, necessitating the use of crutches for several days, and their housekeeper-nursemaid, Gaga, "fell down and nearly broke where she was broadest." But he was, he assured all the friends to whom he wrote, "in the pink."

Aside from his work, he let very little except the habitual financial problems occupy his mind; he was concerned over the box-office returns of *The Great God Brown.* "Come on, you 'Brown'! Daddy needs a yacht!" he wrote to Macgowan early in March. And three days later: "I beg to remind the Directors of the Greenwich Village Theatre that they are taking a longer time to pay royalties on *Brown* than any management I have ever known, and having dealt with Arthur Hopkins, this is some statement. . . . I am not Otto Kahn. I have a larger family to support, for one thing. Do you want me to begin selling the investments I made before I left New York, in order to pay my bills down here? It is damn close to that now."

He was also a little worried about the future of *Marco Millions;* Belasco had dropped his option on the play in April, and both Hopkins and another prominent producer, Gilbert Miller, had turned it down. Horace Liveright was now trying to raise the money to produce it, but his prospect of doing so was not very hopeful.

O'Neill, however, was determined not to be ruffled by anything, and he constantly reiterated his satisfaction with his new-found, peaceful way of life.

"I feel sick of all past connotations and think it behooves me to shake them—even Peaked Hill—for the next few years, anyway," he told Macgowan early in April. The thought of going back to Provincetown, he said, rather wearied him and made him sad.

"The old truth is no longer true," he explained. "Too many 'somethin's' hide in the corners. What I need for my new voyage is fresh fair winds and new ports of call. I might welcome a new scheme for the summer months that did not involve too much travel and presented an opportunity for interesting associations with new people, combined with enough water sports and outdoors."

He and Agnes had decided to rent Brook Farm and were going to make Bermuda their home for at least nine months out of the year; they had taken a long lease on the house at Paget East, "at a thousand per—an enormous bargain" and they were going to supervise the gradual restoration of their eighteenth-century "shell."

O'Neill had finished the final draft of *Lazarus Laughed* by the end of April. It was an ambitious and (though he did not think so) a virtually unproduceable epic. It was also, despite the grandeur of its conception, something of a bore. An imaginary reconstruction of the biblical Lazarus' second life on earth, it derived its title (he once told Elizabeth Sergeant) from the "Jesus wept" of the gospel story of the miracle. Before setting to work in early March he had asked Komroff to supply some books he needed "as spiritual background." Among them were Frazer's *Golden*

Bough, Ben Jonson's *The Alchemist,* a "decent history of Imperial Rome," Henri Bergson's *Laughter,* and "anything else about the spirit of laughter among the Greeks or ancients of any sort."

("We discussed the foundations of laughter sometime later," Komroff recalled. "We agreed that we weren't satisfied with the ideas in Freud's *Wit and the Unconscious* or Bergson's *Laughter.* Gene and I talked about the salty underneath part of laughter, which neither of these theories covered; Freud's theories were erotic, related to sex, and Bergson's were based on laughter as mainly mechanistic. Gene and I agreed that laughter was a kind of uncontrollable emotional overflow that we were unable to explain.")

Boiled down to its essence, *Lazarus,* though filled with the exultant laughter of its hero, is a grim attempt on O'Neill's part to deny the finality of death. It conveys the impression that, however impassionedly O'Neill was trying to evoke a sense of joyousness in life and fearlessness of death, he did not convince himself.

Lazarus was foreshadowed by *The Great God Brown.* "It's an age of miracles. The streets are full of Lazaruses," says William Brown, preparing to impersonate the dead Dion—and it echoes the theme of *Brown:*

"Always spring comes again bearing life! Always again! Always, always forever again!—Spring again!—life again! summer and fall and death and peace again!—but always, love and conception and birth and pain again—spring bearing the intolerable chalice of life again!—bearing the glorious, blazing crown of life again!"

The monotony of this speech from *Brown* has nothing on the speeches in *Lazarus.* The line "There is no death," spoken by Lazarus and his followers, is reiterated so often that it loses all meaning long before the play ends.

In his final revision of the manuscript, O'Neill went over all of Lazarus' speeches with the intention of cutting and sharpening them, so that there would be "a building up and progression in his ideas from scene to scene and no repetition except where it is intended for dramatic emphasis on the recurrent 'There is no death,' etc., which the Chorus and the mob take up in their chanting." His idea of "no repetition" and "dramatic emphasis" consisted of using the line or a minor variant of it ("Death is dead") ad nauseam in the course of the play's four acts.

As in *The Great God Brown,* the characters of *Lazarus Laughed* are masked, all except the hero; Lazarus, "freed now from the fear of death," is unmasked, and his face grows progressively younger.

"In masking the crowds in [*Lazarus*]," O'Neill once wrote, "I was visualizing an effect that, intensified by dramatic lighting, would give an audience visually the sense of the Crowd, not as a random collection of individuals, but as a collective whole, an entity. When the Crowd speaks, I wanted an audience to hear the voice of Crowd mind, Crowd emotion, as one voice of a body composed of, but quite distinct from, its parts."

In justice to O'Neill, the play, though unactable, does contain some fine, if isolated passages of poetry, and it was probably these passages that overwhelmed their author. O'Neill often maintained that his best writing was contained in *Lazarus Laughed*.

" 'Lazarus' coming bigger and bigger!" O'Neill reported to Macgowan toward the end of March. "Slower though. Have almost entirely reconstructed and rewritten first two scenes. Ten times better!" By mid-May he was overcome with admiration for the play, though cautiously aware that he might be too close to it for objective analysis.

"I feel as if it were pressed against my eyes and I couldn't see it. . . . Certainly it contains the highest writing I have done. Certainly it *composes* for the theatre more than anything else I have done. . . . Certainly it uses masks as they have never been used before and with an intensely dramatic meaning that really should establish them as a sound and true medium in the modern theatre. Certainly, I know of no play like *Lazarus* at all, and I know of no one who can play *Lazarus* at all—the lead, I mean. Who can we get to laugh as one would laugh who had completely lost, even from the depths of the unconscious, all traces of the Fear of Death? . . . In short, *Lazarus* is damned far from any category. It has no plot of any sort as one knows plot. . . . I had better stop getting more involved in explaining what I can't, for the present, explain to myself."

O'Neill regarded the play as finished in the late spring of 1926 (although he did what he called "some cutting and condensation" in 1927) and sent a copy of it to Nathan, who told him candidly that he did not like it. According to Nathan, O'Neill replied that Nathan's judgment of it couldn't be taken seriously because he was "lacking in all religious feeling and was therefore prejudiced against any such play."

More broadly, O'Neill had voiced to Nathan his own religious feeling about what he called "the death of the old God and the failure of science and materialism to give any satisfying new one for the surviving primitive religious instinct to find a meaning for life in, and to comfort its fears of death with. . . . It seems to me," he said, "that anyone trying to do big work nowadays must have this big subject behind all the little subjects of his plays or novels, or he is simply scribbling around the surface of things and has no more real status than a parlor entertainer."

And to Joseph Wood Krutch, also on the same theme, O'Neill said:

"Most modern plays are concerned with the relation between man and man, but that does not interest me at all. I am interested only in the relation between man and God."

One of the few people who thoroughly liked *Lazarus* was Arthur Hobson Quinn. "I believe it to be the most truly poetic and the most highly imaginative of O'Neill's plays," Quinn wrote, soon after O'Neill had sent him the manuscript and asked for his opinion. "*Lazarus Laughed* marks a new step in O'Neill's interpretation of man's origin and destiny."

O'Neill's subtitle for *Lazarus* was "A Play for an Imaginative Theatre." What O'Neill meant, as he later took the trouble to point out, was "the one true theatre, the age-old theatre of the Greeks and Elizabethans, a theatre that could dare to boast—without committing a farcical sacrilege—that it is a legitimate descendant of the first theatre that sprang, by virtue of man's imaginative interpretation of life, out of his worship of Dionysus. I mean a theatre returned to its highest and sole significant function as a Temple where the religion of a poetical interpretation and symbolical celebration of life is communicated to human beings, starved in spirit by their soul-stifling daily struggle to exist as masks among the masks of living!"

O'Neill was occupied with this subject for some time. Paul Green, whose Pulitzer prize play, *In Abraham's Bosom,* was produced at the Provincetown Playhouse in December and who met O'Neill in New York soon after, later recalled a night when O'Neill "talked freely of his hopes and dreams for a new kind of American theatre—a theatre of the imagination unbounded and one in which the audience especially might participate more vitally and fully."

"He hoped," Green added, "someday to write plays in which the audience could share as a congregation shares in the music and ritual of a church service. 'There must be some way that this can be brought about,' he said. 'As it is now there is a too cold and cut division between the stage and the auditorium. The whole environment of the piece—stage and auditorium, actors and spectators—should be emotionally charged. This can only happen,' he went on, 'when the audience actively participates in what is being said, seen and done. But how, that is the problem. Still, there must be a way.'

"Then he told about his recent efforts somewhat in that direction, the play *Lazarus Laughed.* He seemed to set a lot of store by that play—more, I think, than it deserved—but it was wonderful to see his enthusiasm for it and to catch something of his visioning of a new kind of theatre he felt it portended. 'What I would like to see in the production of *Lazarus,*' he said, 'is for the audience to be caught up enough to join in the responses

—the laughter and chorus statements even, much as Negroes do in one of their revival meetings.' "

No one wanted to present *Lazarus* in New York, and O'Neill, desperate for a production, at one time thought of Chaliapin for the leading role. "Why not have the part of Laz translated into fine Russian," he suggested wildly to Macgowan, "and let Chaliapin do it in his own tongue, rest of the cast in English? It would be a wonderful, strange effect. And as far as most of an average audience understanding what Lazarus means, why it would probably be a lot clearer to them in Russian!"

The play was produced by the Pasadena Community Players in California in 1927—"successfully and imaginatively," according to O'Neill —and some years later by New York's Fordham University Players. ("Mr. O'Neill's ponderous script is something that no one could act with much inspiration," wrote Brooks Atkinson in *The Times* on this occasion.)

It was never done on Broadway. "The cost of mounting such an elaborate play has deterred the New York commercial theatre from risking the gamble," O'Neill wrote in 1934; this deterrent, if it is the only one, has continued to apply.

The O'Neills sailed from Bermuda on June 14. In spite of financial worries and his two unoccupied houses in Ridgefield and Provincetown, O'Neill had undertaken the rental of yet another house in order to ensure a cool and quiet summer vacation; on the recommendation of his agent's partner, Elisabeth Marbury, who had a house on the Maine lakes, O'Neill had decided to rent a nearby cabin, feeling he would enjoy the change of climate and the opportunity to fish and canoe, while keeping up his swimming and tennis. Above all, he wanted to avoid the Provincetown atmosphere—"not that I'm afraid any more but it's no use making it harder for oneself," he told Macgowan, shortly before sailing.

To their shipboard companions on the two-day voyage from Bermuda, the O'Neills presented the appearance of an attractive, prosperous family— Agnes slim, tan and pretty; O'Neill handsome, lean, distinguished, his dark hair edged with silver; and their two children, Shane, now an attractive, delicate boy of five and a half and Oona a shy, pudgy one-year-old with enormous eyes.

They stopped briefly in Ridgefield so that O'Neill could be within easy distance of New Haven, for he was to receive an honorary degree from Yale at the end of June. The impetus for the bestowal of the degree (Doctor of Letters) had originated with George Pierce Baker, who had moved his "47 Workshop" from Harvard to Yale in 1924. Harvard's reluctance to build a theatre and Yale's willingness to do so were responsible for Professor Baker's move. Heywood Broun quipped at the time: "The score is Yale: 47; Harvard: o." O'Neill had derived a quietly ironic enjoyment from the manner in which it had been made possible for Professor Baker to become head of Yale's Department of Dramatic Art—a gift to Yale of $1,000,000 for a theatre, from Edward S. Harkness, of the same New London family O'Neill was later to deride in *Long Day's Journey Into Night* and *A Moon for the Misbegotten*.

In March of 1926 Baker, who had long since forgiven O'Neill for his sulkiness in 1914, said, in the course of a public lecture in New York: "[O'Neill] was a most delightful man to work with, for he brought me maturity and wide experience. I asked him once whether his preference for grim and depressing subjects was not something of a pose. He replied in the negative, declaring that 'life looked that way' to him following his experiences before the mast and as a wanderer in all parts of the world. You watch him, for there's a great deal of poetry in his soul, although he's only just beginning to show you it's there."

Two months later (on May 5, 1926) Baker had written O'Neill in Bermuda, strongly urging him to come to Yale and accept the degree. "When it is given to you next June," said Baker, "it means to me, not only the honor to you but the establishment of this fact: hereafter a man writing on the subject of his choice as his mind urges him to write, will still meet with misunderstanding and doubt but there will be the precedent established that institutions of learning in this country should recognize him if his honesty of purpose results in genuinely significant accomplishment. . . . It is another mile post."

O'Neill replied on May 21, expressing his gratitude. "Coming from Yale," he declared, "I appreciate that this is a *true* honor (in a country so bepestered with false and shoddy varieties!) and that this recognition of my work really should have a genuine significance for all those who are trying, as I am, to do original, imaginative work for the theatre. In addition I feel that, although Yale may have had the matter under consideration before you came there, still it should now, in all justice, be part of their interest to honor you through one of your students, and I would be as ungrateful for the fine encouragement and helpful criticisms received during my year in 47 as some of the malicious darned fools who write articles make me out to be, if this aspect of the honor did not also please me exceedingly." (Baker had tentatively suggested that O'Neill might like one of his own plays to open the new Yale University Theatre and O'Neill offered him *Lazarus Laughed*, an offer that was subsequently declined for various reasons.)

O'Neill and Agnes went to New Haven as guests of Professor Baker, leaving their children in Ridgefield.

"When he received an honorary degree at Yale, an ordeal that he had desperately dreaded in advance," Elizabeth Sergeant wrote, having interviewed him soon after the event, "his wife was amused to discover that he became so interested in the spectacle that he did finally enjoy his own part in it, and instead of dying of stage fright 'took a bow' on the applause."

The degree was bestowed on O'Neill "as a creative contributor of new and moving forms to one of the oldest of the arts and as the first American playwright to receive both wide and serious recognition upon the stage of Europe."

To the eventual chagrin of both Harvard and Princeton, both of which believed they had a more valid claim on O'Neill's loyalty than Yale, O'Neill transferred his total academic zeal to Yale. He sent Eugene Jr. to school there shortly after receiving the degree.

"The Yale honorary degree meant a great deal to O'Neill," according to Norman Pearson, who was an undergraduate with Eugene Jr. and later became a Yale professor. "It was the only such degree he ever accepted." The honor led to the establishment of the O'Neill Collection at Yale, begun during O'Neill's lifetime and supplemented and supported after his death by his widow.

PART FOUR
WILDERNESS REGAINED
1926—1936

XLVII

THE NEWLY ELEVATED DOCTOR OF LETTERS ARRIVED at his rented cabin at the edge of one of the Belgrade Lakes in Maine on July 1, 1926. He unpacked himself and his family—for the first part of the summer it included Eugene Jr. and Agnes' older daughter, Barbara Burton—and promptly came down with a severe cold. Confined to bed, he took up his correspondence with Kenneth Macgowan, whom he had seen in Brewster just before leaving for Maine. He carefully wrote his new address in the upper right-hand corner of his letter—"Loon Lodge"— then drew a long arrow pointing to it from the left-hand corner, where he had scribbled, "This, after living in 'Bellevue' all winter, makes me suspect God is becoming a symbolist or something!"

He complained of his cold—"have been feeling peevish enough to bite nails," he said, adding that he found it difficult to concentrate on *Strange Interlude* and was frustrated about not being able to swim.

"Still," he went on, "it's the first bad cold I've had since around the opening of *Desire* so I suppose I shouldn't beef too much." He liked the lakes and his house, had found a good rowboat and canoe awaiting him, and plenty of fish. With Eugene Jr. and Barbara there, he told Macgowan, "we're a fat family."

Barbara was eleven years old and, in her own words, "madly in love" with sixteen-year-old Eugene.

"Eugene was so dashing and handsome and full of exuberance that he was all I had on my mind," she said. "I remember that he seemed very interested in a girl nearer his own age and this piqued me rather, but I rolled my eyes all the harder and made believe she didn't exist. I think I stayed in love with Eugene all summer and I think he loved it, for he was constantly playing jokes on me which served both to inflate and deflate my ego.

"We children would play quietly down by the water's edge. Absolute quiet was the rule, as regarded Eugene Sr.'s work. A little shack had been built near the cottage and he went there every morning. In all my stays with the O'Neill family there was never a time when Eugene Sr. was not on this schedule of morning work.

"Oona was little more than a baby. She had a rubber bathtub on legs which used to be set in the lake, so no one ever knew whether she was taking a bath or going swimming. I remember that we had wonderful lunches that summer. They would be prepared in the house and brought to the lake.

"Now and then, in my stays with Mother and O'Neill, Mother would give me special jobs to do. At Belgrade Lakes it was to get breakfast and I did it right down to making muffins, I think. I felt pretty important getting a complete breakfast for an entire family every day.

"I remember that we children had some kind of a competition among ourselves as to who could catch the most fish over the summer. It turned out that Shane got the most. He was always a wonderful fisherman and seemed to have some affinity for the silent sitting and waiting involved in fishing. I got second prize and Eugene Jr. came in last."

Eugene Jr. had other interests besides fishing and romping with his step-sister and half-brother. He was now a tall, lanky, open-faced boy, who got on well with his father. An honor student, about to start his final year at Horace Mann, Eugene was already discussing plans with his father to enter Yale in the fall of 1927. Eugene Jr. spent a lot of time that summer with Frank Meyer, a fifteen-year-old boy whose family lived about a mile and a half up the lake from the O'Neills.

"I was in a store in town one day," Meyer recalled years later, "talking to some friends. One of them was a Horace Mann boy, who recognized Gene Jr. when he came in, and introduced us." Meyer, who was to remain a lifelong friend of Eugene's, added:

"Gene and I both read a great deal that summer, and his father took an interest in our reading; in fact he lent me several books, among them *Tristram Shandy*. O'Neill worked in his cabin every day until about three in the afternoon, and sometimes I spent the late afternoon hours there with young Gene, O'Neill and Agnes. At one point during the summer Gene and I were both reading *The Great Pacific War* by Hector C. Bywater, a projection of a naval war between the United States and Japan. I remember we invented a game based on the book, which we played with O'Neill and Agnes. There was a strong intellectual warmth between Gene and his father."

Once he had shaken off his cold, O'Neill tried to persuade himself that he could work efficiently, even though surrounded by domesticity; but *Strange Interlude* was coming along with difficulty. On August 7 he lamented to Macgowan:

"I did most of a second scene two separate times and tore them up before I got started on the really *right* one! . . . there's going to be more work on [*Interlude*] than on any previous one—much more—with no end to the going over and over it, before I'll be willing to call it done. If I get it—and the first draft of some new one—by next June I'll think it a good year. The point is my stuff is much deeper and more complicated now and I'm also not so easily satisfied with what I've dashed off as I used to be."

He was also concerned about what he now realized was a less than enthusiastic reception of the *Lazarus* script, which had been going from producer to producer.

To Fitzi, who *did* like the play, he wistfully confided:

"Jimmy [Light] also wrote me a corking letter about his feeling for *Lazarus* and his feeling for the 'me' in it. It is a lonely road at times, or at least in moments of self-indulgence in self-pity one likes to feel it is! And such letters are worth a gallon of 'licker' in making you stick out your chest and step out again. Also your own, dear Fitzi."

O'Neill took time out from writing and playing father that summer to play the benign artist bestowing an interview—or rather two interviews. The first was for a New York *Herald Tribune* reporter named David Karsner, who sought him out in Maine early in August.

O'Neill, Karsner reported, was optimistic about the future of the American theatre; new managers were beginning to demonstrate that they were interested in producing plays of quality and were willing to settle for modest profits. It was impossible, in any case, to regard the theatre as a rational business enterprise, he observed.

"If the United States Steel Corporation were run on the basis of a theatre for one week Judge Gary would be out in front of Trinity with a tin cup," he told Karsner. "All about my cradle and throughout my boyhood I was hearing the dogma of the theatre as a business proposition from every conceivable standpoint."

The second interviewer was Elizabeth Sergeant, who met O'Neill that summer for the first time. She had been assigned to do a series of articles for *The New Republic;* among her other subjects were Robert Edmond Jones, Elinor Wylie, Pauline Lord, Paul Robeson, H. L. Mencken, Willa Cather, Robert Frost and Oliver Wendell Holmes. Miss Sergeant's studies were subjective, literary impressions, rather than objective, journalistic biographies; she looked for and interpreted essences rather than facts. In O'Neill's case she was particularly successful, and her sensitive, intuitive rendering of him—she called the essay "Man with a Mask"—pleased him greatly and won her his devoted friendship.

Miss Sergeant spent a week at Belgrade Lakes, seeing O'Neill every day. (When she left, she looked up a number of O'Neill's friends, among them Dr. Hamilton, to whom O'Neill himself directed her.)

"You cannot be near O'Neill without recognizing in him a unique temperament with a unique power of concentration," she later wrote. "No Pope was ever more vowed to his cult than this man of thirty-eight to his task as an artist." She went on to observe that, though O'Neill was "quite Irish enough to enjoy, in his secret heart," his reputation as foremost American playwright, there was "nothing crystallized about him." He was a man in a state of growth, she said.

"The range of his imagination knows no limits," Miss Sergeant reported. "He gives the impression of being still at the very beginning of a career which is incalculable, except that it will be precipitate, fertile, concentrated, and solitary.

"When O'Neill steps lightly along some pagan shore with Shane, he walks a little behind, a tall figure, in a bathing-suit, with limbs burnt to a pagan blackness: and on his face the look, not of a 'father,' but of some trusting elder child who has grown up into a strange world."

O'Neill's enthusiasm for the domestic life waned after about five weeks. ("Domesticated? Indeed, Yes," he declared, with somewhat forced cheerfulness, to an old acquaintance with whom he had been out of contact some time. "With four children . . . it is hard to avoid it. And Eugene is sixteen now and taller than I! And I am thirty-nine [actually his thirty-ninth birthday was still two months off] and my hair is graying behind the ears . . . and my face is so wrinkled from the storm and stress of being a dramatist that it looks like a map of Mars showing the canals!")

By mid-August, O'Neill was beginning to feel that he "could do with less progeny about." He was, seemingly, not cut out "for a pater familias," as he grumbled to Macgowan, and, he said, "children in squads, even when indubitably my own, tend to 'get my goat.'" He added that children had "their recompensing order too," but that he felt he and Agnes could do with more real friends to talk with. "Especially I feel that I could," he said, "for, my days of rum living, I am quite confident, being over forever in this world, I rather feel the void left by those companionable or (even when most horrible) intensely dramatic phantoms and obsessions, which, with caressing claws in my heart and brain, used to lead me for weeks at a time, otherwise lonely, down the ever-changing vistas of that No-Man's-Land lying between the D.T.'s and Reality as we suppose it. But I reckon that, having now been 'on the wagon' for a longer time— a good deal—than ever before since I started drinking at fifteen, I have a vague feeling of maladjustment to this 'cleaner, greener land' somewhere inside me. It is not that I feel any desire to drink whatever. Quite the contrary, I rather wonder that I ever had sought such a high-priced release, and the idea of it is (what must be fatal to any temptation!) dull and stupid to my mind now. But it is just like getting over leprosy, I opine. One feels so normal with so little to be normal about. One misses playing solitaire with one's scales."

His last remark was a truer indication of his real state of mind than even he himself perhaps suspected. He *wanted* to play "solitaire with his scales," had a need to take headlong chances with his life, was possessed by a desire to shatter personal tranquillity, was as intoxicated with what Edgar Allan Poe called "the Imp of the Perverse" as he had ever been by alcohol. Poe, in a short story (one of O'Neill's favorites), illustrated this particular form of intoxication with diabolical brillianee:

We stand upon the brink of a precipice. We peer into the abyss—we grow sick and dizzy. Our first impulse is to shrink from the danger. Unaccountably we remain. By slow degrees our sickness and dizziness and horror become merged in a cloud of unnamable feeling. . . . It is merely the idea of what would be our sensations during the sweeping precipitancy of a fall from such a height. And this fall—this rushing annihilation—for the very reason that it involves that one most ghastly and loathsome of all the most ghastly and loathsome images of death and suffering which have ever presented themselves to our imagination—for this very cause do we the most impetuously approach it.

Since O'Neill had been deterred from plunging into the abyss of alcoholism, he unconsciously sought some other emotional chasm—one that would destroy the carefully cluttered pattern of his life. He was not long in finding it.

On August 18, in a letter to his New London friends, the Rippins, from whom he had recently heard after a long silence, O'Neill dropped a phrase that sounded casual, but portended upheaval:

"I like these Maine lakes for a change," he wrote. "I've never been here before. Quite a few theatre people—Florence Reed just a quarter mile away and Carlotta Monterey, the famous beauty (she played in my *Hairy Ape* in New York at the Plymouth Theatre), visiting not far away."

Carlotta Monterey was the house guest of Elisabeth Marbury that summer. She and O'Neill had not met since their uncordial encounter at the Plymouth Theatre in the spring of 1922. Since that time Carlotta had married and divorced her third husband, Ralph Barton. Barton, an artist and caricaturist for *The New Yorker*, was a handsome bon vivant, black-haired, blue-eyed, with charming manners. Friends of the Bartons were distressed by their separation, for, though aware of Barton's philandering, they believed that the couple had been passionately in love. "Carlotta was mad about Barton," Carl Van Vechten, the novelist, once said. Van Vechten and his wife, the actress Fania Marinoff, were friends of the Bartons and, later, of O'Neill. Another of the Bartons' friends, the portrait photographer Nickolas Muray, once recalled the gay life the Bartons led together.

"Ralph and Carlotta used to give very lavish parties," he said. "I remember one party when Jimmy Walker was present. Another time they had a professional wrestling match staged in their living room. And at one party Charlie Chaplin, who was an intimate friend of Ralph's—I photographed them together once in a Greek coin pose—arrived and took over. He did double-talk in half a dozen languages, I remember. He played a number of instruments—violin, trombone, clarinet, piano, among others. There was an apparently inexhaustible supply of food and liquor, always elegantly served. Carlotta was a marvelous hostess. Although the guests were numerous, they were all carefully selected; everyone wore dinner jackets, of course."

Another aspect of the Bartons' married life has been described by Ilka Chase:

"Ralph and Carlotta's life together was stormy and passionate, and she would arrive at the theatre [during the run of *The Red Falcon*, in which Miss Chase had a small role and Miss Monterey a large one] in a seething, emotional turmoil and pour her misfortunes into my willing ears. As she was very beautiful, Ralph was not the first man who had made her unhappy. . . .

"She and Ralph lived in a studio apartment, and I used to love to go there, because they had wonderful books and pictures and delicious little dinners; but they dined at half past six even when Carlotta wasn't playing, and I never could understand why. It had something to do with their temperaments, I imagine; their temperaments were prominent, and everybody relaxed when they got a divorce. Just before the upheaval Mrs. Barton had given Mr. Barton a fur-lined overcoat, and she was furious when she thought of the expense, but she had to laugh when, in going around the apartment gathering up his personal lares and penates preparatory to Moving to My Club, Ralph had asked sheepishly if he might take his fur-lined overcoat with him. Not that he cared about the coat, he said, but it would be something to remember her by. Carlotta always thought he had hocked it."

The party ended abruptly, early in 1926. In March of that year Carlotta brought a divorce action against Barton, charging him with "misconduct at the Hotel des Artistes, 1 West Sixty-seventh Street," on the preceding January 2. Like Carlotta, Barton had been married twice before,

[614]

but, unlike her, he had no interest in practicing monogamy; her choice of locale and date for the grounds of divorce were practically limitless.

No one expected Carlotta Monterery Barton to stay single for long.

Carlotta once gave an acquaintance this account of her meeting with O'Neill in Maine:

"I was living there very quietly. I walked and swam. One day my hostess [Miss Marbury], who was an old lady, said, 'The O'Neills are coming to tea, would you please stay in this afternoon?' 'What O'Neills?' I asked her. She told me Eugene O'Neill, the playwright. Well, I didn't see why I had to stay and meet that awful man again, but I *was* a house guest, and out of politeness I *had* to stay. The O'Neills drove up in a car.

"Agnes O'Neill got out of the car, and O'Neill followed her. The first thing she said to me was, 'Oh, *you* are Carlotta Monterery. I've been wanting to meet you!' At another point she said, 'Tell me about your sex life!' 'Well!' said I. 'I *have* no sex life. I've just been divorced.' 'Oh,' Agnes squeaked, 'but you must have a lover! Don't you have a lover?' 'No,' I said, 'no lover.'

"O'Neill remembered me and he tried to be friendly, but I was cold to him. All through tea, Agnes kept chattering about all the writers and theatre people she knew. She kept turning to me and saying, '*You* know him—or her—don't you, Miss Monterey?' 'No,' I said, 'I'm afraid I don't. I don't know anyone. I live very quietly.' It was an awful tea."

It is hard to believe that Agnes was quite as idiotic, or Carlotta quite as self-possessed, as Carlotta's account conveys. She had a tendency to "remember" events in a light that flattered her.

"After tea," Carlotta continued, "my hostess asked me to take O'Neill down to the bathhouse so he could swim. I didn't want to, but I did it—not very graciously.

" 'You don't like me, do you?' O'Neill said as we were walking down to the lake.

" 'Why, Mr. O'Neill, I don't know you. How can I like or dislike you?' I answered. But then I did bring up his rudeness to me that day in the theatre, and he explained that he'd just come from seeing his mother's body in the undertaking parlor, where it had arrived from California." (Either O'Neill's memory had tricked him or else he was deliberately playing on Carlotta's sympathy; Ella's body had arrived in New York on March 9 and had been laid to rest in New London several weeks before O'Neill and Carlotta had met.) "He told me they'd painted up the face so—the way they do in San Francisco—that she looked like a painted doll. He couldn't relate that face to his mother, and he'd been terribly upset when he met me.

"O'Neill went into the bathhouse and appeared a few minutes later wearing a woman's bathing suit. It must have belonged to my hostess—it was huge, and hung on him perfectly ridiculously. I guess there just weren't any men's suits in there, but he didn't care. He wanted a swim, and he just paid no attention to how he looked. I decided then that he couldn't be so bad, after all. He dived in and swam—he swam magnificently—and the suit kept billowing up. It was *most* indecent."

Florence Reed, who, with her husband, Malcolm Williams, owned a large house with a beach not far from the O'Neill camp, inadvertently provided O'Neill and Carlotta with a meeting place. Miss Reed was fond of O'Neill and kept a sisterly eye on him.

"He was extremely shy, dear, sweet and gentle," she said. "We always found interesting things to talk about. Gene would paddle over in his canoe to our beach almost every afternoon, and very often I'd take out one of our canoes and paddle across the lake, which was about half a mile wide, with Gene swimming alongside. He'd use the side stroke and talk to me all the while he was swimming. On the other shore he'd rest about twenty minutes and then swim back, using the backstroke. Once he told me about *Lazarus Laughed* while he was swimming, and another time he described the plot and characters of *Strange Interlude*. I had a hard time concentrating on keeping the canoe headed in the right direction.

"When we'd get back to my house, there'd be a tray with drinks waiting; Gene always took tea. One afternoon when we'd just gotten back from a canoe-swim trip, and Gene was sitting on the porch drying off in his bathing suit, we heard a station wagon drive up. It was Bess Marbury and Carlotta and some other people, come over for a visit. Gene pussy-footed away when I went to receive them, but I saw that Carlotta spotted him as he walked through the garden toward his canoe, and that she talked with him.

"When Bess and her guests left, I noticed a scarf on the porch and I asked my husband if he had any idea whose it was. He said he thought it was Carlotta's.

"The next afternoon, after Gene had arrived as usual, a station wagon drove up and Carlotta got out, asking about her scarf. She and Gene talked awhile."

Miss Reed was not surprised that O'Neill found Carlotta attractive.

"She was miraculously immaculate, and a wonderful housekeeper," Miss Reed said. "There was nobody like her. Agnes' house, on the other hand, always seemed to smell of diapers and lamb stew, and there was

[616]

always a lot of noise from the kids. It drove O'Neill almost out of his mind. He finally built himself a plywood shack near the water, about a hundred yards from the house, to get away from the noise and the smells.

"Agnes seemed to live in mortal fear of O'Neill. She tried very hard to please him. Once she drove over to my place alone, and when she started to leave, her car wheel got caught in a sapling and it took fifteen minutes to free it. She was in a terrible state because she thought she wouldn't get back in time to fix Gene's supper. Bess Marbury, by the way, was very fond of Agnes and though she liked Carlotta, too, she was distressed when she realized that Gene seemed to be interested in Carlotta."

Why the O'Neills, who lived on the lavish scale they did, could not manage to provide themselves with an efficient housekeeping staff and comfortable quarters for O'Neill to work in is a mystery none of their friends has been able to explain. Most of the friends assumed that both the O'Neills were simply incapable of organizing their domestic life.

Barbara Burton once said that, while the atmosphere in the O'Neill household had seemed to her, on most of her visits, to be "happy," she supposed that the last years were not.

"Perhaps the first few years were a happy disorder and the last few years a not-so-happy disorder," she added.

"I recall that at the end of the summer in Maine my mother gave me a five-dollar gold piece and a box of candy and that I felt something sad about our parting which was beyond the sadness of saying good-by. Looking back now I can realize that that summer was probably the beginning of the end, so far as my mother's marriage to O'Neill was concerned. I recall a handsome, dark-haired woman coming to swim there once and that she wore a boyish, white, wool-knit, bathing suit, with no overskirt, such as bathing suits usually had at the time. I felt there was something very glamorous about this woman, who, in retrospect, I know was Carlotta Monterey."

According to Carlotta, O'Neill asked Elisabeth Marbury for Carlotta's New York address after she left Maine, and Miss Marbury countered by asking O'Neill to address Carlotta in her care, which he did. "Of course," recalled Carlotta, "he finally did get my address, and when he came to New York he visited me."

O'Neill stayed in Maine until well into October. He did not want to leave until he had completed the first part of *Strange Interlude*.

But he was willing to interrupt his work briefly to go on a number of pre-dawn fishing trips with Agnes and his old Greenwich Village and Provincetown friend, Harold De Polo, who was a dedicated angler. (De

Polo later managed to spin a five-page yarn about O'Neill's prowess as a fisherman for a magazine called *Outdoor America*; he called it "Meet Eugene O'Neill—Fisherman," and it was illustrated with a photograph of O'Neill, grinning over a five-pound pickerel he had plucked from the inky waters of a lake in the foothills of the White Mountains.)

Although O'Neill stayed on in Maine beyond the summer, he spent less time working on *Strange Interlude* than he did in worrying about the productions of his completed plays—and in fretting over the deterioration of the Greenwich Village Theatre. Early that spring the Greenwich Village had been merged with the Actors' Theatre, which was backed by Otto Kahn. In O'Neill's opinion, the Greenwich Village had been engulfed. The new Actors' Theatre planned to lease an uptown playhouse for the production of experimental plays, but no house had been found by as late as August.

"I feel very discouraged about the Actors Combine," O'Neill wrote to Macgowan. "Combine? As far as I can see the G.V. has been simply swallowed up by a vastly inferior, quite brainless organization! . . . What have we gained, for Christ sake? We have no money to do any real work with, and we've lost our absolute control." (Macgowan was the nominal head of the new group, but O'Neill believed he would be seriously hampered in his operations by the Board of Directors, which included such actors as Ethel Barrymore, Katharine Cornell and Alfred Lunt, and the Founders, who included Jules S. Bache, Howard S. Cullman, Marshall Field, John D. Rockefeller, Jr., and, of course, Otto Kahn. Most of them, O'Neill thought, would be opposed to any really experimental and vigorous production Macgowan might propose—particularly a production of *Lazarus Laughed*, which was on their agenda but for which no money was forthcoming. Robert Edmond Jones had already withdrawn from the group and gone abroad.

"Who has gained by this?" O'Neill asked Macgowan. "Certainly not Bobby—if he had elected to stay in, for he would be more cramped than before. Certainly not I! On the contrary, I feel deeply humiliated by being swallowed by an organization for which I have no respect and which gives me nothing in return in the way of advantages for production of my plays!"

Were it not for his friendship with Macgowan, he said, he would instantly withdraw from the new group, and added angrily that he was sick of Macgowan's having to "beg money from these tin-horn bastards, Catholic or Jew, for my plays." Their opinion was worthless in any case, he said.

Macgowan, for his part, was trying to make the best of a dubious bargain. *Lazarus* required a lot of money, he pointed out to O'Neill. "A huge production with 120 people doesn't slip onto the stage easily," he answered. "Money has got to be found outside, which is just what would have happened at the G.V. or would happen with any theatre of ours. . . . There's something terribly deadening in the way time and troubles . . . can eat into patience and courage and people that have worked together with so much in common as Bobby and you and I.")

O'Neill complained about the situation to Nathan. The Actors Theatre, he said, was still attempting to raise the money for *Lazarus Laughed* "from the ranks of their million-talking, jitney-giving Lorenzoes." He was afraid, he added, that he would "soon have to go on a search for an insane—therefore truly generous—millionaire and start my own theatre. . . ." O'Neill was getting "fed up with the eternal show-shop from which nothing ever seems to emerge except more show-shop. It's a most humiliating game for an artist. Novelists have all the best of it."

Then, to Macgowan, O'Neill proposed an alternative plan that would solve the problem of his permanent relationship to the theatre. He proposed an O'Neill repertory theatre.

He suggested Jimmy Light as the director of this theatre, which would open October 1 with a revival of *Anna Christie* with Pauline Lord "if possible" and perhaps "with last act revised, or playing alternate last acts for novelty"; this would run from three to five weeks, to be followed by a revival of *The Straw* for a two-week run and *The Emperor Jones* for a three-week run, bringing the season to the last week of November. "Then opening of my new play each year, whatever it was, this to run four weeks or less, if only half-liked, and, if a big success, not more than eight weeks (to first of February) at our theatre before being moved."

That would be followed by "an experimental new production of a classic with the emphasis on the acting" for four weeks, and then four weeks of "either an original modern play or a revival of a modern play with the emphasis on originality of production." This, he explained, would take the season to either March 1 or April 1, depending on how long O'Neill's new play had run. After this would come two to three weeks of *All God's Chillun* being played "on alternate nights by an all-white and all-colored cast, or some such touch like that," followed by four or five weeks of *The Hairy Ape* with "a chance of getting Wolly that late in season."

For the following season, O'Neill's outline was:

Beyond the Horizon, three to four weeks; *Gold*, two to three weeks; *The Great God Brown*, three to four weeks; a new O'Neill play, four weeks, a classic revival, four weeks; *Welded*, one week; the *Glencairn* cycle, two weeks; and *Desire Under the Elms*, four or five weeks.

O'Neill would work with the director of this theatre all during the summer, he said, "for certain hours, outside my writing, daily," and he would attend all rehearsals from the beginning of the season to the first of the year, "by which time everything would be planned to last detail for remainder of season." O'Neill cockily believed such a theatre would pay for itself, and that gradually it would develop into "a true repertory theatre."

"You see," O'Neill concluded, "I've got to have a chance to grow in the theatre and make it grow. I've got something I ought to contribute beyond plays. This Actors' Theatre promises no such opportunity—much less than I have enjoyed hitherto—and I can't help being convinced that, for me, it is a backward step. I also feel you are going to find that your absolute dictatorship will be double-crossed the moment you step on their prejudices." Macgowan submitted O'Neill's repertory plan to Otto Kahn, but nothing ever came of it.

On October 10, 1926, O'Neill informed Macgowan that he was leaving Maine and would be in New York on the following Thursday. He proposed that Macgowan accompany him to the Yale-Dartmouth football game in New Haven on October 16, which, he noted, was his birthday. "Ought to be one of high spots of year," he said. "Perhaps I won't get tickets, but guess I will, all right. Old Doc O'Neill, the Yale grad, has his rights!"

Old Doc O'Neill evidently overestimated his influence at Yale or else he changed his mind at the last minute, for he did not attend the game. He celebrated his birthday in a more spectacular and less characteristic fashion.

Some months earlier he had met a pretty, young, blonde actress and dancer who was appearing in a Ziegfeld revue called *No Foolin'*. Her name was Claire Luce (she was later to create the role of Curley's wife in *Of Mice and Men*) and she was at that time in love with one of O'Neill's close friends, who was proving somewhat elusive. Gregarious and popular herself, Claire Luce had been struck by O'Neill's aura of brooding loneliness. Partly because she had an impulse, as she has put it, "to bring him down to earth" and partly because she enjoyed talking to him about his friend, she persuaded him to celebrate his birthday with her at a Fifty-second Street night club.

"I wanted him to mingle with people, see some gay life," she recalled. "We had champagne, and O'Neill enjoyed every minute of it; his eyes sparkled and he laughed—until the birthday cake I'd ordered was brought to our table, and everyone in the club sang 'Happy Birthday' to him. Then he began sinking lower and lower in his chair. But he insisted he was having fun.

"That was all I'd planned, but the celebration suddenly developed a spontaneous life of its own. The waiters began marching around our table,

[620]

singing, and finally the guests got up and joined the march."

A newspaper columnist later reported a climax to the evening which Miss Luce could not remember, but allowed might have occurred. The columnist, Sidney Skolsky, claimed to have this story from O'Neill himself: "Went to a nightclub only once in his life," the columnist reported. "He said it would be the last time. That evening, during a lull in the entertainment, the owner of the club made an announcement to the effect that America's greatest playwright was among those present. The spotlight soon found O'Neill and he was forced to stand and take a bow. Later, when ready to leave, he was presented with a bill for sixty dollars. He looked at the check for a moment, took out a pencil, and wrote across it: 'One bow—sixty dollars.' He walked out."

XLVIII

O'NEILL SPENT A LITTLE OVER A MONTH IN NEW YORK during the fall of 1926, staying mostly at the Harvard Club and living like a bachelor. He had sent Agnes and the children ahead to Bermuda, for the Ridgefield house was now up for sale. Whether or not he had deliberately planned it that way, he had created a perfect atmosphere in which to pay court to Carlotta and to luxuriate in the sense of being an extraordinarily attractive, successful, distinguished man-on-the-loose. He was "playing solitaire with his scales" and, for the moment at least, enjoying it immensely.

Carlotta was a beautiful, poised, independently rich, knowledgeable woman whose attention would have flattered any man. During the few weeks O'Neill spent in New York in her company, his retrospective discontent with the domestic atmosphere in Bermuda grew stronger. He and Carlotta agreed that his life had not been ideally arranged for the dedicated pursuit of his work—and they ultimately concluded that an alternative was at hand and should be seized.

"What Gene craved more than anything else was order," Carlotta later said. "He reached a point where he couldn't work any more in his surroundings."

Though she later made it a point to deny there was anything in the nature of romantic love in their relationship—"After all, we were both nearly forty when we met and we'd each been married a few times," she said, "and what Gene needed was someone to manage his life for him, not romance"—their liaison eventually assumed the proportions of an epic love affair.

"When Gene came to New York after Maine, he called me and asked if he could come to tea," Carlotta once told an acquaintance. "When he arrived he began to talk about his boyhood. He talked and talked as though he'd known me all his life, but he paid no more attention to *me* than if I had been a chair. He talked about how he'd had no home, no mother in the real sense, no father in the real sense, and how deprived his childhood had been. I sat and listened, and at first I was a little worried and then I was deeply unhappy. I thought it was terrible that of all people to be so stricken, it should be this man, who had talent and had

[622]

worked hard. And his face would become sadder and sadder, and he would talk and talk, and then, suddenly, he would look at the clock and say he had to go and would rush out—and come back the next day and go on. Well, that's what got me into trouble with O'Neill; my maternal instinct came out—this man must be looked after, I thought. He broke my heart. I couldn't bear that this child I had adopted should have suffered these things.

"One day when he came to tea he had a cold—he always had a cold— and he looked at me with those tragic eyes and said, 'I need you.' He kept saying, 'I need you, I need you'—never 'I love you, I think you are wonderful'—just 'I need you, I need you.' Sometimes it was a bit frightening. Nobody had ever gritted their teeth at me that way and said they needed me. And he did need me, I discovered. He never was in good health, he always had a cold, he wasn't properly fed or anything."

O'Neill tried at first to reconcile his need for Carlotta with his sense of loyalty to Agnes. The struggle was unpleasant, for he did have a strong belief in the marriage sacrament—a literal, Catholic conviction of its sanctity (despite the seeming contradiction of his early divorce) and a firm belief in monogamy. He also believed, however, that intense, unvarying, mutual love was not only possible but vital to the sanctity of marriage; he had, therefore, to persuade himself that he no longer loved Agnes and, even more important to his philosophy (or rationalization), that she did not love him. He may have believed it when he told Belinda Jelliffe that love was service, but he indicated more accurately how he felt on the subject, in relation to Carlotta, when he wrote a speech for the Irish Nora Melody in *A Touch of the Poet*. Nora tells her daughter:

"It's little you know of love, and you never will, for there's the . . . divil of pride in you . . . and it'll kape you from iver givin' all of yourself, and that's what love is. It's when, if all the fires of hell was between you, you'd walk in them gladly to be with him, and sing with joy at your own burnin', if only his kiss was on your mouth!"

Certainly O'Neill, if not Carlotta, had to feel a love as intense as Nora Melody's before he could consider sweeping aside the eight years of his marriage to Agnes. He spent the next months talking himself into the proper state of mind and some friends who were sympathetic to both him and his wife had the impression that Agnes, whether from willfulness or overconfidence, abetted him.

O'Neill sailed for Bermuda on November 27, and though he did not see Carlotta again for several months, she was rarely out of his mind during that time.

"I'm not what you could call perfectly at peace with God," O'Neill wrote to Macgowan, who was in his confidence, a day or two after his arrival in Bermuda. ". . . I envy those simple souls to whom life is always either this *or* that. It's the this *and* that desire—more than desire, need!—that slowly poisons the soul with complicated contradictions. . . . Do not mistake my rebellious cries for whinings. Beauty, either here or there, is worth whatever price one has to pay for it, here or there. . . . Oh very much so!"

O'Neill was genuinely happy for a while to be "home" again with Agnes and his children. "But—oh Christ," he sighed, "there are also other things—'on the other side of the hills'—the curse of being an extremist is that every ideal remains single and alone, demanding all-or-nothing or destruction. . . . 'What haunted, haunting ghosts we are.' . . ." O'Neill was concerned about "the gossips," and asked Macgowan if they were on his trail.

A few days later he again wrote to Macgowan: "Any little errand? Yes, while I remember it—and much obliged. Enclosed is a card and a check. Have the same roses sent to Carlotta . . . to get to her on Christmas a.m. Don't forget this now, old top!"

The check was for $25, which, in 1926, could buy a lot of roses.

"I encouraged Gene's relationship with Carlotta," Macgowan admitted years later, "because I thought she would keep him sober, which I didn't think Agnes could do."

"Emotionally I'm still up in the air," O'Neill confessed to Macgowan at the end of December. ". . . it hain't purty."

It was nearly a year before O'Neill was able to manipulate matters in such a way that seemed to him self-justifiable but, whether he could acknowledge it himself or not, he was already irrevocably committed to Carlotta before he left New York.

Nevertheless, he proceeded full tilt with his elaborate and expensive plans to remodel the Bermuda "shell" he had bought. All of O'Neill's houses had names—he was drawn to the manorial, his only snobbery, because he wanted to do what his father had failed to do, to carry on the proud tradition of his Irish ancestors and show the pretentious Yankees what noblesse oblige really meant. His new Bermuda home was called "Spithead."

It was a large, solid, pink-sandstone house, set in spacious grounds, surrounded by gardens, guarded by a wrought-iron gate, and it over-looked the water from a point on Hamilton harbor. O'Neill remodeled the interior, had all the walls painted pumpkin yellow, and built a large concrete dock. He also kept an eye out for the ghost of Hezekiah Frith, a privateer who had owned the house in the 1700's and who, reputedly, had been haunting Spithead at intervals since his death. There was a smaller house on the grounds into which the O'Neills moved in December while the slow work of reconstruction was going on.

"We're still sort of living in trunks," he informed Macgowan on December 7. "Our smaller house is ready but our furniture isn't. But we'll be in soon." By mid-December O'Neill's kayak had arrived and he was enjoying the water, but by the end of the month he was fretting over the inconveniences of living in their overcrowded little house. "I am working in a bedroom with children, carpenters, plumbers, masons . . . doing all sorts of chorus work in the near vicinity," he complained, but added: "The place will be a wonder when it's fixed up—absolutely ideal for me and will surely pay me big dividends in the work I shall do here. I love it."

He continued to send Macgowan regular reports on Agnes and the children; they were all physically well, he said, but Agnes was troubled about her father, who was very ill of tuberculosis.

The four months between December and May were not domestically tranquil ones.

O'Neill indicated he was concerned that Agnes' suspicions had been aroused when he cautioned Macgowan, in mid-December, "Don't 'understand' in your letters. They are read not only by me!" And one visitor to Spithead, who was a friend of Carlotta's, felt that Agnes' welcome was chilly. He was Ben Pinchot, a photographer who was a partner of Nickolas Muray. Pinchot was planning a trip to Bermuda in January or February of 1927 and mentioned this to Carlotta, whose sultry beauty was much in vogue at the time and who frequently posed for him. Like the other celebrities who sat for Pinchot and Muray, Carlotta was sent by such fashionable magazines as *Harper's Bazaar* and *Vanity Fair,* with which the Pinchot-Muray studio had contracts.

"Carlotta asked me if, when I went to Bermuda, I would be seeing Gene, whom I had also photographed, and when I said I would, she gave me a script of one of his plays, I think it was *Lazarus Laughed,* and asked me to return it to him," Pinchot said. "When I got to Bermuda I called Gene and he invited me to lunch. I arrived at the house with gifts for Shane and Oona, but I thought Agnes was cool to me. At lunch hardly a word was spoken. You could feel the tension. After lunch, when I was alone with Gene, I gave him the script. 'What do you think of Carlotta?' Gene asked me. 'I think she's a very lovely woman,' I said. Gene was all smiles."

The O'Neills had a number of other visitors between January and

May, most of whom recalled that the household appeared to be at sixes and sevens. Elizabeth Sergeant spent six weeks with the O'Neills during March and April.

"When my book, *Fire Under the Andes* [which contained the magazine essays on O'Neill, Jones, *et al.*] was published, I went for my first copy to Knopf," Miss Sergeant said, "and took it away with me in a taxi. The taxi was hit by a truck, I was injured, and the book was spattered with blood. When O'Neill heard about my accident he asked me to come to Bermuda to recuperate after I got out of the hospital."

At Spithead, according to Miss Sergeant, Agnes privately told her that O'Neill wouldn't allow liquor in the house because he wasn't drinking, but that Miss Sergeant might have a bottle of brandy to keep in her closet if she wished.

"One day, Agnes told me that she had fallen in love with O'Neill and married him because he was drunk all the time and needed her help. She said she had thought she was marrying a bohemian, and that she enjoyed going to parties, but that Gene seldom wanted to; she sometimes went by herself to cocktail parties. Gene told me he didn't like going out because he was so shy that he needed a woman to take over for him. I didn't know about Carlotta at the time, but later, when he introduced me to her, I gathered that he had been referring to her. Carlotta was at home everywhere."

One reason that O'Neill avoided cocktail parties—aside from his shyness—was that he really had no use for the Bermuda social crowd and resented Agnes' attempts to become a part of it. It was *Welded* all over again—but this time there was a magnet that was exerting a stronger and stronger pull on O'Neill.

A couple—Mr. and Mrs. Joel Huber—who owned a house not far from Spithead (and who, much later, bought the O'Neill house) gave a party one day which O'Neill did attend. The Hubers were people for whom O'Neill had some affection.

"I was very surprised when O'Neill turned up," Huber said, "and I began to understand why he usually preferred to stay away from parties, after the incident that took place in my house."

O'Neill told Huber he had just finished a strenuous piece of work and that he felt as though the world had been lifted from his shoulders. Another guest, who overheard O'Neill's remark, brightly observed that he understood exactly how O'Neill felt.

"I feel the same way every time I finish writing an advertisement," he said.

O'Neill gave him a long look, then turned to Huber and said, "I'm not a conceited man, Joe, but I think that's funny."

Elizabeth Sergeant observed that Agnes seemed to feel O'Neill was thoroughly dependent upon her. "Whenever Gene or she had to leave each other even for a short time, Gene would cable or write her constantly. I had the impression, though, that Gene was getting less dependent on her since he had given up drinking, and that she was foolishly overconfident of him.

"It seemed to me that Shane was neglected by both Gene and Agnes. Once I found Shane walking and shivering by himself near the water in the late afternoon. I took him into the house and asked him if he wanted me to read to him. He was delighted.

"On the other hand, Agnes was always gracious and kind to any of Gene's old down-and-out cronies who would turn up from time to time. She was always glad to put them up."

Another visitor, the writer Bessie Breuer, considered O'Neill a devoted parent.

"Gene was in a dream most of the time," she said, "and that gave people the impression he may not have been paying attention to his children, but actually he was terribly attached to them." Miss Breuer, who was as fond of Agnes as she was of O'Neill, was aware that things were not serene between them.

"At the time I was in Bermuda, Agnes seemed sick," she said. "She didn't seem able to cope with anything. She would have trouble even in finding a shoe."

James Light and his bride, Patty—he had been divorced from his first wife—spent seven weeks with the O'Neills in the late winter; the visit was O'Neill's belated wedding present to them. According to Mrs. Light, there was a good deal of domestic tension throughout their visit. Agnes, Mrs. Light later recalled, was not even on hand to greet them when they arrived; O'Neill, she said, told them he and Agnes had quarreled and that Agnes had "gone off somewhere."

Despite domestic friction, O'Neill worked at a feverish pace. He spent four weeks revising *Lazarus Laughed*. He then reread *Marco Millions*, which he decided to have published, since a production was still not in sight. And, finally, he went back to work on *Strange Interlude*.

"I am intending to start work on *Strange Interlude* tomorrow," he wrote to Macgowan on December 30. 1926. "—the 31st—hunch—one year on the wagon, my boy! I am going to drink fifty lime squashes watching the new year in."

Earlier he had told Macgowan, "With all that's inside me now

I ought to be able to explode in that play in a regular blood-letting by the time I get to it." Although there is less of O'Neill's relationship to his family in *Strange Interlude* than in most of his other major plays, there are recognizable traces of all that was "inside" him at the time of its writing.

In evidence are several echoes of mourning, such as the speech by a character (Charles Marsden) who recalls the death of his father, saying: "how dim his face has grown! . . . he wanted to speak to me just before he died . . . I bent down . . . his voice had withdrawn so far away . . . I couldn't understand him . . . what son can ever understand? . . . always too near, too soon, too distant or too late!"

The play is chiefly noteworthy for its "asides"—herein employed to reveal the concealed thoughts of the protagonists. Like the stage use of masks, the device was so old that it seemed new and daring. In spite of the asides, however, the play was neither new nor daring in the epic sense of some of O'Neill's true masterpieces. Barrett Clark, to whom O'Neill outlined *Strange Interlude* in 1926, ventured to question whether an audience would sit through nine acts listening to characters speaking their thoughts aloud "with no regard for the ordinary conventions of the theatre or of normal social intercourse."

"And why not?" asked O'Neill. "Everything is a matter of convention. If we accept one, why not another, so long as it does what it's intended to do? My people speak aloud what they think and what the others aren't supposed to hear. They talk in prose, realistic or otherwise—blank verse or hexameter or rhymed couplets."

The trouble was that a good deal of what the characters had to say was mundane and did not lay open any of the profound soul's secrets O'Neill imagined they did.

The play's principal character, Nina Leeds, though weighted by O'Neill with heavy literary symbolism, is in some ways a classic example of the soap-opera heroine. She is made up of bits of all the women O'Neill had ever known and incorporates aspects of all the female characters he had thus far depicted. Endowed by the sum of O'Neill's own fantasy-idealism and love-hate, she is a fitfully fascinating monster, embodying what O'Neill regarded as all that is both purest and blackest in Woman.

She is, by turns, an innocent lover of a noble boy (Gordon Shaw, a college paragon whom she sends off to World War I without having gone to bed with him); a guiltily mourning fiancée (Gordon is killed in the war); an embittered daughter (she blames her father for having prevented the consummation of her love, out of his own possessive jealousy);

a wanton (her subsequent guilt compels her to give herself to as many wounded war veterans as will have her); an unbelievably self-sacrificing wife (she marries a boy, Sam Evans, she does not love, because he worshiped Gordon Shaw and because he needs her); a criminal (she submits to an illegal abortion, when she discovers there is insanity in her husband's family); an ardent mistress (she takes a lover, Edmund Darrell, in order to present Sam with the child they both crave, and then finds she cannot give Darrell up even after her purpose has been achieved); a pseudo daughter (after her father's death she pursues a platonic relationship with an old family friend, Charles Marsden, who loves her asexually); a mother (first a happy one, then a jealously possessive one); a mean mother-in-law (she loses her son to a girl she loathes on sight); and, finally, a widow, longing to "rot away in peace" (her husband dies of a surfeit of high spirits).

Nina's battle cry is one of O'Neill's own favorites—"Life is a lie."

"Say lie," Nina at one point commands another character, repeating the word herself: "L-i-i-e! Now say life. L-i-i-f-e! You see! Life is just a long drawn out lie with a sniffling sigh at the end!"

"I made notes for *Strange Interlude* in 1923 [after hearing in Provincetown] from an aviator, formerly of the Lafayette Escadrille, the story of a girl whose aviator fiancé was shot down just before the Armistice," O'Neill once said. "The girl had gone to pieces from the shock. She had married, not because she loved the man, but because she wanted to have a child. She hoped through motherhood to win back a measure of contentment from life."

Elizabeth Sergeant had predicted accurately when she wrote, of O'Neill, that "soon we shall see a play that will have the length, breadth, and thickness of a novel." *Strange Interlude* is a novel in everything but form. A nine-act play covering more than twenty-five years, it was originally written to be performed on two consecutive evenings. But O'Neill later cut it, though retaining nine acts, to the point where it could be done at one sitting, albeit a sitting that began at 5:30 in the afternoon, paused for an eighty-minute dinner intermission, and ended after eleven at night.

"I had the idea for three years, and I worked harder on it than on any other play I've written," O'Neill said not long after its completion.

For a time O'Neill toyed with the title *The Haunted* (which he later used as the title for Part Two of *Mourning Becomes Electra*). The title he finally settled on is used twice in the text of the play: "Our lives are merely strange dark interludes in the electrical display of God the Father!"

Nina remarks at one point. And, again: ". . . the only living life is in the past and future . . . the present is an interlude . . . strange interlude in which we call on past and future to bear witness we are living!"

The play's most transparently autobiographical character is significantly named Edmund (like the later Edmund in *Long Day's Journey Into Night*). Here given the surname Darrell—the name of a family living near the O'Neills in Bermuda—Edmund is described thus: "dark, wiry, his . . . dark eyes analytical. His head is handsome and intelligent. There is a quality about him, provoking and disturbing to women, of intense passion." O'Neill's indifference to children was transmitted to Edmund Darrell, as was, even more interestingly, O'Neill's fictionalized conflict about Carlotta. Darrell, illicitly in love with Nina, struggles against his passion. "Sometimes I almost hate her!" he says. ". . . if it wasn't for her, I'd have kept my peace of mind . . . no good for anything lately, damn it! . . . but it's idiotic to feel guilty." And, later, he muses: "By God, I won't! . . . got me where she wants me! . . . I'm caught . . . she touches my hand, her eyes get in mine, I lose my will . . . I'll go away . . . forget her in work!" (O'Neill prophesied the outcome of his own conflict; in the end, Darrell succumbs to Nina.)

O'Neill also attributed facets of his own personality to Charles Marsden, a novelist who is afraid to write about life and afraid to live it. To him fall many of the lines that expressed O'Neill's own bitterness toward women, as well as O'Neill's attitude toward contemporary novelists.

"Even the best of modern novels," he wrote to Joseph Wood Krutch three months after completing *Strange Interlude*, "strike me as a dire failure. . . . They are all . . . so padded with the unimportant and insignificant, so obsessed with the trivial meaning of trivialities that the authors appear to me as mere timid recorders of life, dodging the responsibility of that ruthless selection and deletion and concentration on the emotional which is the test of an artist—the forcing of significant form upon experience."

Yet O'Neill was in sympathy with Marsden. "I like [him] very much —next to Nina," he wrote to Krutch. "I've known many Marsdens on many different levels of life and it has always seemed to me that they've never been done in literature with any sympathy or real insight."

Today *Strange Interlude* seems almost as melodramatic as *Anna Christie*—the play O'Neill despised. The asides in *Strange Interlude*, for instance, are often embarrassingly glib slivers of psychoanalytical jargon and the charge of Freudian influences on O'Neill can be convincingly supported in the case of this play. Some of the obvious and self-conscious psychoanalytical passages are plainly traceable to O'Neill's session with Dr. Hamilton. For example, Darrell's prescription for a sound life for Nina: "She needs normal love-objects for the emotional life Gordon's death blocked up in her." Or, again, Darrell's textbook comment on an Oedipal situation: "Perhaps he [Nina and Darrell's son] realizes subconsciously that I am his father, his rival in your love; but I'm not his father ostensibly, there are no taboos, so he can come right out and hate me to his heart's content!"

Even the boy in question, aged eleven, is given to precocious Freudian observations: "That's why Darrell hates me being called Gordon," he mutters to himself, ". . . he knows Mother loved Gordon better'n she does him. . . . Now I know how to get back at him . . . I'll be just like Gordon was and Mother'll love me better'n him!"

Another instance of Freudianism has been pointed out by Cyrus Day, professor of English at the University of Delaware. According to Professor Day, the nine acts of *Interlude* and the name Nina symbolize the nine months of a woman's pregnancy.

Yet O'Neill stood ready to defend himself just as vigorously from the justified charge of conscious psychoanalytical writing in this play as he had from the unjustified charge brought against *Desire Under the Elms*. Responding to a friend who had commented (not adversely) on the "complexes" of the characters, O'Neill declared:

". . . I feel that, although [*Interlude*] is full of psychoanalytical ideas, still these same ideas are age-old to the artist and that any artist who was a good psychologist . . . could have written 'S.I.' without ever having heard of Freud, Jung, Adler & Co. . . ."

Strange Interlude ultimately served its purpose by demonstrating for O'Neill that an American public was willing to accept a play as long as a novel, thereby paving the way for the even longer and greatly superior *Mourning Becomes Electra*. But unlike *Mourning Becomes Electra*, *Strange Interlude* is dated.

In 1927, by virtue of its length and the novelty of its asides, the play appeared to be a typically untypical O'Neillian innovation and seemed to many theatre people to be startlingly powerful, even in the manuscript stage. One of these people was Lawrence Langner, of the Theatre Guild, with whom O'Neill's relationship had been no more and no less cordial than it was with other contemporary Broadway producers, whether they had displeased him by producing his plays or infuriated him by rejecting them. Langner and the Guild had declined several of O'Neill's earlier efforts—*Anna Christie* was the one they regretted most—and more recently had been negotiating with him for *Marco Millions.*

Langner, advised by his doctor early in March to spend a couple of weeks in a warm climate, shrewdly decided to combine his vacation with business. He sailed for Bermuda, where, he had heard, O'Neill was at work on a new play.

O'Neill and Langner discussed the possibility of the Guild's producing *Marco Millions* and then O'Neill, full of his new play, told Langner about *Strange Interlude* and its characters who spoke their thoughts aloud.

"The idea fascinated me," Langner later wrote, "and I asked him if I might read the play. He also told me that it would take six hours to play it. In view of our experience with 'Back to Methuselah,' this did not daunt me."

A few days later Langner spent an evening at O'Neill's home discussing *Strange Interlude.* According to Langner, O'Neill had already promised the script to a well-known American actress, but if she did not like the play, he said, the Guild could have it. Meanwhile, Langner could read it.

O'Neill gave Langner the first six acts of the manuscript, which, he has recalled, were "half again as thick as any ordinary play—so long that nearly forty pages were subsequently cut out of it." Langner went to bed intending to read at least part of the play before he fell asleep. "All night long I read and read," he said, "and at four o'clock in the morning, my eyes strained and throbbing, I finished the sixth act . . . I judged it one of the greatest plays of all time."

Elizabeth Sergeant, who was present during some of Langner's talks with O'Neill, recalled that Langner told O'Neill that, though he wanted very much to do the play, he was sure it wouldn't run for more than a few weeks. "There was a good deal of shop talk," Miss Sergeant said, "and at one point Agnes walked out; later she told me that she simply couldn't stand any more talk about the theatre."

Langner left Bermuda at the end of March, promising O'Neill that he would try to obtain a quick decision from his fellow board members about *Marco Millions.* O'Neill, on his part, promised to send Langner a completed script of *Strange Interlude* as soon as he had edited it.

He changed his mind about editing the script, however, and entrusted it to Elizabeth Sergeant on April 4 for delivery to the Guild. He had decided he was "too close to the play" to do a good job of editing, and told Langner: "You and the committee will have to make allowances for rough spots . . . I would have liked to let this play rest for a couple of months more at least and then go over it before submitting it to anyone, but as you told me you are now in the midst of plans for next season, I am taking a chance on its present form."

The actress to whom O'Neill had promised to submit the play and to whom he also sent a script by Miss Sergeant, was Katharine Cornell, who had achieved her first big success in 1921 in *A Bill of Divorcement*. By 1925, with her performance in *The Green Hat*, she had become an established star and O'Neill thought she "would be ideal for the lead."

On April 13, O'Neill received a long letter from Langner, explaining that the Guild's committee were willing to produce *Marco Millions* if O'Neill would do some substantial cutting. Lee Simonson, one of the committee members and the Guild's scenic designer, estimated that the play, as written, would cost $30,000, which was considered exorbitant.

"I do not want you to interpret the Guild's objection to the spectacular aspects of the play as being based entirely upon the expense involved," Langner hastened to assure O'Neill. "They feel that a delightfully human and ironic comic situation is now overweighted by mass scenes of a spectacular character, and that the play would be considerably improved from the acting standpoint if the production could be scaled down."

O'Neill talked himself around to seeing the production the Guild's way. He wrote to assure Langner that he was always willing to cut and would co-operate fully on *Marco Millions*.

Regarding *Strange Interlude*, Langner reported to O'Neill that everyone was reading it "at high speed" and that the first reactions were "highly favorable." (Langner later recalled, however, that not all of his fellow directors shared his enthusiasm. One of them even went so far as to say that if all the asides were taken out the play would be greatly improved.)

By the end of April Katharine Cornell had let O'Neill know she did not want to do the play; she had rejected it in favor of Somerset Maugham's *The Letter,* earning herself a permanent niche in O'Neill's gallery of unfavorite actresses. Langner now felt the time had come to push with all the vigor at his command his campaign to get O'Neill on the list of Guild writers.

"Aided by Theresa Helburn and Maurice Wertheim [two members of the committee]," Langner later wrote, "I conducted a frenzied campaign to secure the production of 'Strange Interlude.' On April 21st, I wrote the Board a stinging letter."

"We now have an opportunity of making a connection with Eugene O'Neill, who is considered throughout the world as the greatest dramatist

America has ever produced," the letter said. "Let us . . . admit that a man whose plays are being given in London, Paris, Berlin, Prague, Vienna and Moscow is unique among American dramatists, and that by doing his plays we not only honor him, but we honor ourselves . . .

". . . Indeed, the theatre being what it is today, it almost devolves upon the Guild to produce this play, as the only surviving art theatre in America . . . even if it be accompanied by financial loss. . . .

"I was right about the psychological moment for starting the Theatre Guild; I was right about the psychological moment for building the Guild Theatre; I was right about the psychological moment for starting the repertory; AND I KNOW I AM RIGHT ABOUT THE PSYCHOLOGICAL MOMENT FOR COUPLING UP WITH O'NEILL."

The Guild committee responded with a tentative acceptance that annoyed O'Neill. Apprised by his agent of the Guild's conditions, O'Neill wrote to Langner, on May 1:

"The way Madden outlines it your position about the play remains vague to me—a half-acceptance that must be as unsatisfactory to you as to me. Surely now that you have all read it and know the dramatic guts of it and its new method you ought to be able to make a definite decision. All it needs is an intensive cutting of words, phrases, sentences, speeches, from first act to last, such as I always do on all my plays—but certainly no drastic reconstruction is called for. And I don't feel that I should be called on, as Madden says you suggest, to submit this cut script to you in order to get a decision."

O'Neill refused to do any more work on the script until he had the Guild's unequivocal promise of a production.

"What I mean is that you should have enough confidence in my ability to trim this play down to be able to predict for yourselves what the final product will be," he said. "After all, you are not dealing with any novice in the theatre. . . . And the legend that I don't attend rehearsals is all rot. I didn't in the old P.P. days because I was never in New York and when I was I was never 'on the wagon.' But of late years it has been different."

He said he intended to be "very much on the job," attending rehearsals "from the first day to the last."

Adding that, though he did not want Langner to force the Guild's hand, he had to take this position because of "imperative financial circumstances." He would leave for New York on May 14 on the next steamer, he said, if Langner felt there was a basis on which they could talk.

Langner replied that was fine with him and invited O'Neill to stay with him and his wife, Armina, in their New York home on Eleventh Street.

O'Neill was doubly anxious to be in New York, because rumors had been circulating of a romance between Carlotta and the banker James Speyer. (On April 14 the *American* had published a gossipy item under the heading, "Speyer's Friends Doubt Betrothal."

"Close friends of James Speyer, New York banker and philanthropist, expressed surprise yesterday at reports hinting a tentative engagement between him and the beautiful actress, Carlotta Monterey," the item read. "Said one: 'I am sure Mr. Speyer, in New York, and Miss Monterey, in California, will be more surprised at the story than we are. Of course, there isn't a thing to it.' " (Carlotta said years later that a friendly affection existed between her and Speyer, who was many years her senior, and that Speyer had, in fact, asked her to marry him. But when she told him she was in love with O'Neill, Speyer graciously surrendered the field. Later, after Carlotta had introduced Speyer to O'Neill, Speyer declared that O'Neill needed her and that she would be good for him.)

O'Neill stayed with the Langners for a week in May, discussing all phases of *Marco Millions* and *Strange Interlude,* both finally taken by the Guild unconditionally.

"We gave him a front room," Langner recalled, "and he used to go out every night and call on Carlotta. He told me he had fallen in love with her. He said one reason he got on so well with her was that she was such a good manager; she was able to organize the material side of his life —arranging for railroad tickets, and so forth. Agnes, he said, could seldom plan ahead; she was easy-going and helpless, and needed to be looked after by *him*. But it wasn't until later that year, in November or December, during rehearsals of 'Marco' and 'Strange Interlude,' that he talked to me about divorcing Agnes."

During his week's stay at the Langners' O'Neill spent an evening becoming better acquainted with another Guild director, Theresa Helburn.

"I remember the first time Eugene O'Neill came to dinner with me," Miss Helburn later wrote. "It was the evening of the day Lindbergh flew the Atlantic. We had meant to talk of plays and production problems, but we were, of course, like everyone else, under the spell of that adventure and we talked instead of what lay behind the apparent simplicity of that amazing flight, behind its clean-cut success, its almost poetic precision. I can imagine no one more sensitive to all its implications than O'Neill, with his sense of the romantic and the dramatic, with his memories of lonely nights at sea and his knowledge of stark realities."

On another evening, the Langners gave a party for O'Neill, but he seemed unhappy about being the guest of honor.

"I avoid parties," O'Neill told Langner. "In my younger days I used to drink to get up nerve to meet people. Since I've quit drinking it's gotten worse."

After the party, which had included several Negroes, Langner said to O'Neill, "You seem to have stood it pretty well."

"I suppose so," said O'Neill. "But it's like those Negro people who were here. They were putting up a good front, but underneath it they were nervous as hell."

O'Neill returned to Bermuda at the end of May, secure of two Broadway productions for the coming season.

"It was a delightful week at your place," he wrote to Langner, expansively, on May 31. "I had grown rather stale and depressed down here, but now I feel refreshed and keen."

O'Neill remained in Bermuda—with one interruption for a trip to New York in mid-September—until late November of 1927. This gave him another six months to wrestle with his conscience about Carlotta. He spent the first part of this period wrestling, also, with a five-week siege of what he called "Bermuda summer flu." And, since he had not yet begun work on a new play, he caught up with his correspondence.

He had lately taken some additional theatre critics into his confidence. Already on cozy terms with Arthur Hobson Quinn (whose *A History of the American Drama*, containing correspondence to Quinn from O'Neill, was to be published in October), Isaac Goldberg (whose article for the Boston *Transcript* in October, 1925, called "Playwright and Critic," had included a series of letters exchanged between O'Neill and Nathan, later reprinted in his book, *The Theatre of George Jean Nathan*) and Barrett Clark (whose book on O'Neill had been published the previous August), he now began consolidating his more recent acquaintance with Joseph Wood Krutch and with Benjamin De Casseres. To both Krutch and De Casseres he sent copies of *Strange Interlude*, and to all of his critic friends he wrote with disarming candor and intimacy of his aims and ambitions in the theatre, apologizing, at times, for the "roughness" of drafts of plays he was sending them, analyzing their comments on his work, and "appreciating" their "appreciations."

"It was fine meeting Mrs. Krutch and you," he appended, in a letter to Krutch on June 10, in which he wrote of arrangements he had made to send a *Strange Interlude* script to him. "Let us get together again when

I get back to town." In discussing the new techniques he had employed in *Strange Interlude* and *Lazarus Laughed,* he told Krutch he felt there was "no theme too comprehensive or difficult to handle in the theatre."

And to De Casseres, who had written him an appreciation of *Lazarus Laughed,* he confided on June 22:

"Your long letter was a treat. Here in Bermuda one rarely gets the chance, especially now in the slack season, to say a word to a human being above the intellectual and spiritual level of a landcrab and this solitude gets damned oppressive at times."

And again to Krutch, on July 15:

"I'm almost finished with the cutting and minor rewriting of [*Interlude*] . . . My fear in writing a first draft is always of omitting something, so there are bound to be many repetitions. I usually have a first draft at least one fourth too long—almost intentionally, for I've gotten so cutting is a labor of love with me and I get a keen satisfaction out of it second only to the actual creating. . . . All best to Mrs. Krutch and you! I'll hope to see you soon. There is so much I would like to discuss with you."

O'Neill did not, of course, neglect his oldest supporter and sounding board, George Jean Nathan, who had recently written an article in praise of *Strange Interlude* (in which he took something of a slap at Otto Kahn for failing to provide funds at the right time and in the right place).

"Poor Otto!" O'Neill wrote to Nathan on July 15. "I already hear his protest that he *did* contribute to the Provincetown Players and Greenwich Village fund to start their seasons—but they had always lost all that before they came to my plays."

To Goldberg, on August 7, he promised a script of *Strange Interlude* as soon as he should arrive in New York "the last week of this month. . . . How's that?"

And to De Casseres on August 11 (after receiving a copy of *Theatre Magazine* containing a piece he had written about O'Neill, in which De Casseres had spoken of O'Neill's having "shoved away the vultures":

"My vultures are still flapping around, thank God, hungry and un-dismayed; and I am very proud of them for they are my test and my self-justification. I should feel a success and a total loss if they should ever desert me to gorge themselves fat and comforted on what the newspaper boys naïvely call fame. But luckily they are birds that fly from the great dark behind and inside and not from the bright lights without. . . . I look forward to some last visit when their wings will blot out the sky and they'll wrench the last of my liver out; and then, I predict, they'll turn out to be angels of some God or other who have given me, in exchange, the germ of a soul."

And, finally, to Nathan, shortly before sailing for New York at the end of August:

"It has been, physically speaking, a bad luck summer for me . . . but it has been very fertile for my work. In addition to the long intensive jobs on *Interlude* and *Laz* [which he had again revised] I've got my next, *Dynamo,* ready to start the dialogue and I've had four ideas for new plays that I think are the real stuff."

In New York O'Neill added one more critic to his collection—Brooks Atkinson, who was introduced to him by Manuel Komroff and subsequently became another of his friends and correspondents, and another recipient of news about works-in-progress and of unproduced playscripts. Atkinson, who kept a diary, set down this engaging picture of O'Neill after meeting him on September 22, 1927:

". . . I had never met O'Neill before except in passing. I have long admired him from afar as one of the heroes, living in the far-off realm of poetry but firmly rooted in human existence. . . .

"O'Neill's face is marked with experience. It is not tired. It is vivid; there is something immediately magnetic about his personality. He has the physical strength of one who understands the strength of nature. Although he is generally unconscionably shy, even awkward, he was at ease today and talked on many themes. About his own work he is neither modest nor presumptuous. He talked of art—of 'Lazarus Laughed' and 'Strange Interlude,' both unproduced—frankly, and smiles agreeably over his practical difficulties. With the arrogance of the true artist he is contemptuous of directors and actors who are not capable of producing him; he is charmingly frank in despising rich men who do not put huge sums of their private fortunes at his disposal for producing his work in proper style. I like him immensely for his ability to see all these minor forces in true perspective. Although he is gentle and sympathetic I am sure he would trample down anything in his path. He is not to be denied.

"We talked of human character, Maugham, Galsworthy, the current stage, the Dempsey-Tunney fight last night, and other natural subjects. O'Neill is naturally a recluse. I was delighted to get on so swiftly with him. But he is the kind of man whose seclusion one instinctively respects, and, on his side, he never takes the initiative. He left me with a glow all afternoon. I felt that I had been in contact with the genuine article."

O'Neill returned to Bermuda for October and part of November, recovering from the New York tempo, which, he had complained to a friend, "sure rattles the old bean of one grown used to Bermuda bicycles and hacks." The Guild had finally decided to open *Marco* at the beginning of January and *Interlude* at the end of January. O'Neill planned to be in New York for about two months, seeing both plays through their final rehearsals. Shortly before leaving Bermuda, in mid-November, he wrote of his plans to De Casseres, urging him and his wife, Bio, to come back with him to Spithead at the end of January for a visit.

O'Neill arrived in New York toward the end of November, as scheduled. He never returned to Bermuda to live.

XLIX

ONE EVENING IN MID-DECEMBER OF 1927 O'NEILL, accompaned by his vultures, arrived at the New York apartment of Benjamin and Bio De Casseres. Mrs. De Casseres had never met her husband's new friend, but from her husband she had heard something about O'Neill's life in Bermuda with Agnes and the children. In view of O'Neill's invitation to them to go back with him to Bermuda and his enthusiasm over the new house, De Casseres and his wife had no reason to suspect that there was any rift in his domestic life. Neither of them had ever met Carlotta nor did they know anything about O'Neill's interest in her.

Mrs. De Casseres sat silent that evening while her husband and O'Neill talked theatre and art. She had an affinity for the occult, being an amateur practitioner of palmistry, and from what she knew of O'Neill's work and personality she thought he might be interested in her gift. During a lull in the conversation, she turned to O'Neill and, with no other prelude, said, "I am interested in palmistry. I would like to look at your palm. May I?"

With a ghost of a smile, O'Neill held out his hand; his eyes seemed to challenge her.

Mrs. De Casseres was instantly seized with what she later described as "an inner illumination." She began to read his palm excitedly, convinced that every word she uttered was irrefutable truth but totally unable to fathom the source of her information.

"You are not a poet, you are a psychologist," she began slowly. "You explore. You uncover the roots of things." Then more rapidly, in a trance-like voice, she continued: "You are never going back to Bermuda. You will live in Europe and San Francisco. You have a long journey before you. You are leaving your wife. Another woman is in your life now. Most people will think you met her recently, but you met her five years ago. There will be a great deal of publicity and you will have a struggle for a divorce before you are able to marry her. Your plays will be successful. You will live for twenty-five years."

Suddenly the strangeness of her own words sounded loudly in her ears and she broke off. Everything she knew about O'Neill with her reasoning mind denied their meaning, and she felt a sense of panic. O'Neill said nothing, indicating by neither word nor gesture that what Mrs. De Casseres had told him had made any impression on him. The conversation between De Casseres and O'Neill was resumed, haltingly, and soon after, O'Neill left.

Mrs. De Casseres was miserable. She was sure she had offended O'Neill and embarrassed her husband. De Casseres tried to comfort her, but she could not forgive herself. She spent an anguished, sleepless night.

The next morning at ten o'clock, the telephone rang in the De Casseres apartment. Mrs. De Casseres answered and O'Neill asked for "Ben." De Casseres accepted his invitation to lunch. At lunch O'Neill, in considerable agitation, told De Casseres that he had been stunned by his wife's performance the evening before. Only a few close friends knew he and Carlotta were in love, he said, and no one but he and Carlotta knew they had decided to marry; even they themselves did not know yet when and how it would be arranged. He had not even disclosed his decision to Agnes, he said, and didn't know how to tell her. He asked De Casseres if his remarkable wife would read his palm again, and if he could put some questions to her. De Casseres said he would ask her.

"I didn't want anything more to do with it," Mrs. De Casseres said, "but Ben finally persuaded me. He telephoned O'Neill to come over, and when he arrived, we clasped hands and were both completely at ease. I chided him for not having given me some sign the evening before, and he said he had been too overcome to speak. For an hour or more he asked me every conceivable question about the future."

This extraordinary incident, which was to have an equally extraordinary sequel some months later when O'Neill wrote to Mrs. De Casseres for guidance, has been confirmed by a number of O'Neill's friends, to whom he later confided it; but its real significance is that O'Neill himself believed implicitly in Mrs. De Casseres' ability to foretell the future.

O'Neill's appreciation of Mrs. De Casseres' gifts extended to her husband, for whom he now developed an even stronger interest and affection. In fact, when De Casseres asked O'Neill to write a foreword to his new book, *Anathema! Litanies of Negation,* which was to be published in a few months, O'Neill, out of gratitude, broke a long-standing rule and complied. He had always refused to write introductions even for his own published plays on the ground that he "wasted more labor on them than on half a play because that form of writing comes desperately hard to me." A few years earlier he had turned down a request for an introduction to a book by a Provincetown Players acquaintance, Em Jo Basshe, explaining that he had twice refused to write them on the ground that they were "needless." "I am not fitted for doing an introduction, anyway," he added. "Now if I were to write yours I'd be most surely making two enemies out of friends whose works I also respect."

But O'Neill was willing to risk making three enemies for De Casseres. His foreward to *Anathema* was the only such contribution he ever made to the work of another writer.

"To me, 'Anathema!' is a unique and inspiring poem," O'Neill wrote, in part. "It is the torment and ecstasy of a mystic's questioning of life. . . . Benjamin De Casseres is the poet who affirms the chaos in the soul of man. His *no* is a *yes!*"

O'Neill, who had seldom spent an inactive week in his life, plunged into a whirlwind of activity between the end of November, 1927, and the beginning of February, 1928. He had moved into a two-room suite at the Hotel Wentworth, at 59 West 46th Street, and began simultaneously pursuing his romance with Carlotta, attending rehearsals of both *Marco Millions* and *Strange Interlude* and wrestling with his conscience about his family in Bermuda.

He had recently acquired two new friends with whom he was on intimate terms during this brief period—and who abruptly dropped out of his life soon after.

One of them was Norman Winston, a successful builder and planner who had made financial contributions to the Provincetown Playhouse, and who had met O'Neill through Jimmy Light. The other was Robert Rockmore, a New York lawyer and a friend of Winston's.

"Gene would stay with me sometimes at my Seventy-second Street apartment, and he would telephone Carlotta," Winston said in recalling that period. "They'd talk for a long time. Most of his meetings with her were at her place, but once or twice she called for him at my apartment house, downstairs.

"We had long talks about Carlotta, and about his situation with Agnes. When he wanted to talk, we'd often go for a ride in my car. Gene told me he thought that women were jealous of Carlotta because she was so beautiful and that they said malicious things about her out of jealousy.

"Once I invited him to stay with me at my house in Stamford, on Long Island Sound. There was a walk that led down to the water and we stood there one night looking at the moon reflected on the water, and Gene told me, 'If I were thinking of suicide, I'd swim along that reflection until I was exhausted and couldn't swim any more.' I asked him if he was thinking of suicide at the moment, and he said no, but that if he ever wanted to do it, that would be a good way.

"Gene was interested in hearing about other people's suffering—not for the personal anecdote, but because the individual's story represented suffering in general. I once told him about how my mother died when I was twelve. She died of cancer, and I had to leave school to nurse her. The day she died I wanted to kill myself. Gene kept coming back to the story. Sometimes he would tell me a little about *his* family, as though exchanging confidences, in order not to expose me. But he seemed incapable of finishing his thoughts about them. He'd say, 'Our family . . . there was a great deal of tragedy . . . we drifted apart . . . my mother . . .' Several times he attempted to tell me about his mother, but he could never finish the sentence. He seemed to be bearing a cross, quietly. But he did say, several times, that one day he would write the story of his family. I told Gene about my mother's funeral, about how, when my mother's casket was put on the hearse, a horse-drawn one, the funeral parlor man told the driver to hurry up; I thought he was telling the driver to hurry the burial, and I threw myself on the driver and tried to pull him down. Gene was very much affected by this. He'd ask for more details; he seemed to enjoy having me work up his own emotions.

"I felt Gene was struggling to fight his alcoholism, that it wasn't an easy thing for him, even after all the time he had been on the wagon. Once I visited him at the Wentworth, and took a bottle with me. I had a few drinks, and forgot to take the bottle away with me when I left. When I got home I remembered the bottle, and was afraid it would be too much of a temptation for Gene, so I sped back to the Wentworth to pick it up. Gene hadn't touched a drop, though."

Rockmore also paid occasional calls on O'Neill at the Wentworth.

"One of the first things Gene told me after we had become friends," Rockmore said, "was that he had always felt there was a strange affinity between the Irish and the Jews. 'There's something that draws me toward Jewish people,' he said. 'It must be something we have in common from way back.'

"One of Gene's major weaknesses, I felt, was women. He didn't understand them, and there were few he respected. I do remember his telling me he had a lot of respect for Lillian Gish. 'There's a girl who has one of the smartest beans,' he once told me.

"He was a mass of contradictions. He had moods when he was absolutely silent, and others when he was so garrulous you couldn't get a word in edgewise. Once I invited him and another friend out on a boat I used to charter on Sundays. Gene told us for four hours about his sea experiences. Usually, he sweated when he was with strangers, he'd always be wiping his hands. There were times when his speech would be that of a man of culture, and other times when he could lapse into the vulgarity and profanity you would expect of an ex-sailor. He hated the Broadway practice of calling people by their first names; he didn't ask me to call him Gene until I'd known him for two months.

"He rarely spoke to me of his family, and when he did it was limited to his brother, Jim. One day he asked me if I'd take him to the races at Belmont Park, and as we drove out he told me that horse racing was one of the contributing factors in his brother's downfall, and that while he had been tempted many times to visit the track, the unhappy memory of his brother's experiences had deterred him.

"When we got to the track, I tried to give him some advice on how to bet, but he took a long sheet of paper from his pocket and said he wanted to play his own choices; he had stayed up late the night before and handicapped his selections. I asked him where he'd learned to do this, and he answered seriously, 'I didn't use the usual method of picking horses by past performance, weight, distance, and comparative time; I did it by the use of numerology.' He played his way and I played mine—and we both succeeded in losing all six races that day."

Rockmore was surprised to learn that one of O'Neill's chief diversions was reading detective stories, several of which he recommended to his friend. He also liked to read the sports pages of newspapers and Damon Runyon, whose slang was a source of enjoyment to him.

"At the time I first knew Gene he told me he had never been to a concert. He knew little, really, of classical music or of painting or any of the arts except dramaturgy. One day I invited a young violinist to my home to play especially for Gene. He played some Bach. Gene liked him and was very touched that he had played just for him. The violinist was about to make his debut at Carnegie Hall, and I invited Gene to share my box for the performance. He was so appreciative, he decided to introduce me to the six-day bicycle races. He showed me a series of tickets he had bought to the Garden. We arrived at ten at night, and I left at two, bored to tears. Gene stayed on, probably right through the night. He told me he was waiting for a jam.

"Some time later I met Gene at Carnegie Hall with Carlotta. I gathered she was trying to give him a little culture. During intermission, I went up to him, and he started to talk to me about music. He said that Koussevitsky was the world's greatest conductor, and I told him that was nonsense, that there was no one in the same class with Toscanini. I felt he was just trying to show off for Carlotta.

"Sometimes Gene tried to live up to an image of himself as a public figure, but he could never keep it up for long. I remember once I managed to persuade him to go with me to a fund-raising dinner for the

Provincetown Playhouse, even though I knew he hated that sort of thing. I convinced him that his attendance would help the cause. At the end of dinner one of the Provincetown directors got up and, after a few words about the need for money, unexpectedly called on Gene to speak; he thought some comment from O'Neill might help start the flow of funds.

"Startled at being called on, Gene sat there scowling for an embarrassing moment, then slowly drew himself from his chair, looked unsmilingly around the room, and in a quiet, emotionless voice, said: 'The Provincetown did its best work when it didn't have a quarter.' Then, before the significance of his carefully chosen words had a chance to sink in, he muttered, in a low voice that only those of us seated at his table could hear, 'Sit down, you son of a bitch, sit down.' He thereupon obeyed his own admonition; he had expressed his gratitude to the Provincetown in his own highly individualistic manner."

One day during rehearsals for *Marco Millions,* which had begun on November 22, Rockmore picked up O'Neill at the theatre for a lunch appointment. O'Neill was silent as he and Rockmore walked away from the theatre and Rockmore, knowing his moods, did not try to make conversation. At length O'Neill said, "You know what I just did? I just agreed to cut a whole scene that was written with my blood."

Although O'Neill had consented to make cuts in *Marco* in order to pare expenses and conform to the inadequate stage equipment of the Guild Theatre, he was not happy about it—no happier than he ever was with the production of any of his plays. In order to be done as O'Neill had originally conceived it, *Marco* would have required mechanical apparatus that was out of range of the Theatre Guild's resources.

The scenic scheme devised by Lee Simonson, one of the era's prominent designers, was ingenious and beautiful, within its limitation; but, even simplified, the scene shifts were distracting, for the action, instead of flowing smoothly and rhythmically, was chopped up by a lowered curtain and overlong waits. Even more disturbing, however, to the unity and meaning of the play was the Guild's elimination of some human scenery which O'Neill's script had called for.

In three of the six scenes of Act I, showing, respectively, exteriors in Persia, India and Mongolia, O'Neill had asked for a symbolic group consisting of a nursing mother, two children at play, a young man and girl embracing, a middle-aged couple, an aged couple, and a coffin; all remained motionless throughout the scene, unaffected by the remarks addressed to them by Marco, "only their eyes . . . staring fixedly but indifferently at the Polos." In each scene these figures were dressed and made up to represent their particular racial backgrounds. The repetitiveness of this symbolic group and its cumulative effect—or lack of effect—on Marco was significant to the play, and the Guild's decision to drop it as costly and unnecessary window dressing was an artistic mistake. What with this and similar deletions, *Marco Millions*, as produced, was not the play O'Neill had written Like *All God's Children Got Wings*, which was ahead of its time socially, *Marco Millions* was ahead of its time mechanically.

Alfred Lunt was cast as Marco—he later jokingly referred to the role as the only "juvenile" of his career—and Margalo Gilmore, who had played Eileen Carmody in *The Straw*, was signed for the role of Princess Kukachin. A number of other well-known or soon-to-be-known actors appeared in the large cast, some of them doubling or tripling in roles. Among them were Morris Carnovsky, in two roles, Albert Dekker, in three, and Henry Travers, Mary Blair, Dudley Digges and Sanford Meisner.

Lunt, one of the few actors whom O'Neill did not later single out for attack, found O'Neill pleasant but remote. "O'Neill was there during rehearsals, seated at the back of the theatre, but I did not get to know him; he was not an easy man to know," Lunt later said.

Rouben Mamoulian was assigned to direct the play. Not yet thirty, he had completed his first important directorial job for the Guild a few months earlier—the Du Bose and Dorothy Heyward play, *Porgy*. The Guild then felt he was ready to tackle *Marco Millions*. Commenting editorially on this choice, a *New York Times* drama columnist observed: "After O'Neill saw the first act of 'Porgy,' he was quite willing to allow young Mamoulian to handle his play. It seems a rather remarkable thing that a recognized playwright should be willing to entrust a most-cherished work to the hands of a comparative youngster, whose direction of 'Porgy' was his first big job in this country."

When *Strange Interlude* started rehearsals, O'Neill found himself favoring one play over the other, as had been the case when *Anna Christie* and *The Straw* had been simultaneously in rehearsal and when *The Hairy Ape* and *The First Man* had been in preparation at the same time. He apparently knew how to pick a winner when it came to the production of his plays, for he had been right in both cases—and he was right again when he pinned his faith on *Strange Interlude* rather than *Marco Millions*.

Because of the play's length, an unusually long rehearsal period of seven weeks had been allotted. The Guild, then operating as a repertory company, did not try out its plays on the road, which suited O'Neill exactly. Although circumstances later obliged him, occasionally, to submit to the pre-Broadway tryout routine, he always objected at first on the ground that the customary hotel-room tinkering with the script was unnecessary in his case, since he had done all the revising and rewriting there was to be done by the time the play was ready for rehearsal and that the obligatory cutting and trimming could be achieved *during* rehearsal. Unlike the majority of American playwrights, O'Neill declined to consider audience reaction on the road as a gauge by which to alter his plays, particularly since in the instances in which plays of his *had* undergone out-of-town tryouts the result had been failure, anyway.

Since he never, to begin with, wrote a play with the box office in mind, he was not likely to be influenced by the box-office receipts of a pre-Broadway tour. To him, commercial success was always secondary, and nothing could induce him to make major structural changes in a play once he had grappled with his characters and resolved, to his own satisfaction, all their problems. O'Neill's adamant self-confidence, like Shaw's, was irritating to his producers, directors and stars, who, as a matter of course, were given to demanding—and getting—rewritten "motivations" or more "sympathetic" dialogue, or even a change from an "unhappy" to a "happy" ending.

For weeks before *Strange Interlude* went into rehearsal O'Neill, complying with his promise to the Guild, worked on cutting the play. He had long script sessions in a little office atop the Guild Theatre with the play's director, Philip Moeller. Then in his late forties, Moeller was the first to raise the role of director to prominent artistic status in the American theatre. A founding member of the Washington Square Players and a member of the Guild's board of directors, he had staged Shaw's *Saint Joan,* Molnar's *The Guardsman* and Sidney Howard's *They Knew What They Wanted.* He and O'Neill got on well together once O'Neill's initial reserve had melted.

"Gene was hard to warm up to," Moeller said. "He seemed so lonely, always looking for happiness. He was an outsider; everything was bitter and wrong for him. But there was no small meanness about Gene. He had tremendous integrity, was one of the most honest human beings I've ever known. And of all the people I've known, he possessed the most intense dramatic sense. He lifted his early, melodramatic background into tragedy and great theatre. He did not, like Shakespeare, have both the dramatic and the theatre sense—that is, he lacked the sense of when to end scenes; but the dramatic sense is the more important."

When it came to cutting *Strange Interlude,* which Moeller knew he must insist on, he exerted the utmost tact, and O'Neill, who came to respect Moeller's own artistic dedication, generally submitted to the proposed cuts, although sometimes after intensive argument.

At one point during the production O'Neill wrote to Moeller saying that the play might have to be performed on two successive nights. Moeller persuaded him that this was not a good idea. O'Neill was also willing to yield to Moeller's solution for presenting the play's asides, a problem the director had wrestled with a long time before beginning his discussions with O'Neill.

"Very early in my study of the script," Moeller said, "I realized that I should have by some means or other to create a new technique. Here was a play which was, in the presentation of its dialogue, a curious triple mixture of methods, old and new. There was the ordinary dialogue. There was a special use of a variant of the old-fashioned soliloquy—and then, to add to the difficulty, there was also a startlingly new sort of dialogue, a species of spoken commentary which is a kind of autobiographical criticism and analysis, by the person speaking, of thoughts which either intensify or contradict or comment upon the speech or speeches which are being heard."

He discussed several schemes: one was to have a particular zone of the stage where these "mental asides" would be spoken—a sort of lonely island of introspection to which, somehow or other, he would have to get his players and then get them back again for the ordinary dialogue; a second idea was to have a distinct differentiation of the quality of voice used between the spoken dialogue and the thoughts overheard; a third was a system of change of lighting either of the characters speaking the "silent" thoughts or of those on the stage who were not supposed to hear them. Moeller soon scrapped all three ideas because he felt that the members of the audience would quickly become tired of the trick and be so concerned with watching it work that they would miss the play.

"I finally evolved the idea of arrested motion," Moeller said. "The actual physical action and usual dialogue of the play was to be momentarily arrested. There was to be a space of physical quiet in which the unheard thoughts could, so to speak, be heard."

The idea came to Moeller during a train trip, on which he had taken along a copy of the *Interlude* script.

He was deep in the script and its problems when, suddenly, the train stopped. Glancing out the window, Moeller watched the activity on the station platform. It was activity without sound, for no noise could penetrate the sealed windows of the compartment. Activity-without-sound suggested the alternative of sound-without-activity.

"Unconsciously, this may have been the hint; this may or may not have been the way my mind got it," Moeller recalled. "'Why not, for a moment,' I thought, 'stop the physical action of the play and allow the mental commentary to tell us its hidden secret simply, directly and without any obviously elaborate and intricate preparations?' "

Moeller then drew up and presented to O'Neill a scheme whereby when an actor had to deliver an aside everyone on stage would freeze into the position and attitude of the moment and remain so until after the mental comment had been made. O'Neill approved of the idea, and Moeller then attempted to solve his next headache.

The casting of Nina, though the role provided an actress' field day, was something of a problem. After Katharine Cornell had rejected it, O'Neill suggested Ann Harding, who, he felt, "really looked the part." But he agreed to go along with Langner and Moeller, who offered it to Alice Brady; O'Neill had sought Alice Brady for previous plays but she had eluded him as persistently as the Barrymore brothers. She turned out to be as resistant as ever to appearing in an O'Neill play, and the Guild's next choice was Lynn Fontanne, the wife of their leading man in *Marco Millions* and a candidate for the role of Princess Kukachin in that play. Although O'Neill did not cherish the memory of her appearance in *Chris,* he nevertheless accepted her.

"When I went into *Strange Interlude,*" she recalled, "O'Neill asked me if I remembered a conversation we'd once had during the production of *Chris,* when I told him that I wished someone would write a play exposing possessive mothers, showing how some of them ruin their children's lives. 'This is it!' O'Neill said, pointing to a script of *Interlude.*"

Although O'Neill grudgingly acknowledged, after seeing Lynn Fontanne rehearse Nina, that she suited the role, he was impervious to her personal charm. She has attributed his resistance to shyness; like her husband, she found O'Neill "difficult to get close to." But O'Neill had different reasons. He had heard that Lunt was currently referring to *Strange Interlude* as "a six-day bisexual race," and Miss Fontanne's attitude toward the script was no better calculated to endear her to O'Neill.

"There were a good many lines intended by O'Neill to be taken seriously, that I thought would get belly laughs from the audience," she said. "It would have hurt the play. For instance, I would have to say in an aside something like, 'Ned has the bluest eyes I ever saw; I must tell him so.' Then I would go to Ned and tell him he had the bluest eyes I ever saw. I felt it was unnecessary to say this twice. I told O'Neill I thought it would be better if I looked at Ned's eyes with admiration the first time, silently, instead of saying the line as an aside. I asked him if I could cut the line. He said, 'No, you can't. Play it as I wrote it.' But the play was so long that I felt O'Neill wouldn't realize if I cut a line

[649]

here and there, so, with fear and trembling, I cut a few of those horse-laugh lines. O'Neill never knew about this sly business of mine."

During rehearsals O'Neill told Langner, "If the actors weren't so dumb, they wouldn't need asides; they'd be able to express the meaning without them."

"My plays make stars," he told Langner on several occasions, implying that the reverse was never true; indeed, he was inclined to believe that when he had a successful production, it was in spite of, rather than because of, such stars as appeared in it.

"As to casting," George Jean Nathan once wrote, "[O'Neill] is generally opposed to so-called name actors. 'They distract attention from the play to themselves,' he argues. 'My plays are not for stars but for simply good actors. Besides, you can never count on the idiosyncrasies of stars; they may not stick to a play and may so damage its chances on the road. I'm afraid of them. . . . Also, they sometimes want you to change certain things in your play. Not for me!' "

"Gene never liked anyone to make a success in one of his plays," said Carl Van Vechten, who got to know O'Neill well during this period. "He was jealous of good actors in his plays. One of the few actors he liked—because he wasn't a star—was Earle Larimore."

Larimore was cast as Nina's husband, Sam Evans; Glenn Anders played Edmund Darrell and Tom Powers played Charles Marsden, all of them, according to Langner, excellent choices. Langner recalled that the rehearsals of *Strange Interlude* were "marked by considerable argument." Oddly enough, the arguments were not about O'Neill's opposition to making cuts, but the reverse.

"Time after time," Langner later wrote, "Gene insisted on cutting out comedy lines or 'laughs' when, in his opinion, they interfered with the emotional build of a scene. Philip Moeller . . . adored the comedy and every time Gene solemnly cut out an amusing line, Phil would plead vociferously for its return. 'I hope he doesn't realize that line is funny,' Phil once remarked to me, 'for if he does, out it'll go.' "

George Jean Nathan was at a rehearsal one day when Moeller called on O'Neill to insert a line of comedy. "I'll tell you what to do," Nathan later quoted O'Neill as saying. "Just turn slowly around after the character has spoken, drop your pants, and disclose to the audience your backside painted an Alice blue. That should do it."

According to Langner, O'Neill would occasionally lose all patience with his cast and, beckoning Langner out of earshot of the stage, would "give vent to his feelings about some of the acting in language he certainly did not learn in school in Stamford." Theresa Helburn, however, once recorded that O'Neill sat "quiet and impassive in the front row, hour after hour," and responded quickly and confidently to all questions from cast and director.

"To suggestions of changes he usually answers 'no,'" continued Miss Helburn. "But not arbitrarily, nor is that the end. He evidently considers them all for some time seriously and frequently returns the next day having found a way to meet a suggested change that has dramatic value without damaging the fabric of his play. It is the same about cuts. He almost never makes them on the spur of the moment. He listens to the director's ideas but he takes his script home and brings it back the next day cut or not cut, as the case may be, according to his leisured judgment. People have called O'Neill stubborn in rehearsal but it is the stubbornness of inner conviction, a most valuable quality in a medium so easily the prey of contrived effects and emotional tricks as the theatre. And it is not impractical conviction; it is founded on long experience and an expert sense of 'theatre'—the rightful heritage perhaps of an actor's son. But O'Neill doesn't like compromise. Often we have said to him, 'Gene, the audience won't stand for that.' To which he has replied, 'The audience will stand for anything provided we do it well enough.'"

In mid-November, even before *Marco* went into rehearsal, attention was focused on O'Neill with the publication of *Lazarus Laughed*. *Marco* had been published the previous April, the third major play that O'Neill had allowed to be issued in book form before stage production. The published versions of his plays were selling very well, both in America and abroad, and late in 1927 Liveright decided to put out a $10 illustrated edition of one of its best sellers, *The Emperor Jones*. Limited to 775 copies, this was to be followed by a limited, illustrated edition of *The Hairy Ape*. O'Neill paid meticulous attention to the published versions of his plays. Often he restored cuts that had been made during production, and a number of his published plays are greatly rewritten versions of the produced ones.

According to Saxe Commins, who was soon to replace Manuel Komroff as O'Neill's editor at Liveright, O'Neill was acutely conscious that the published version of his work was the thing that would live.

"The book has to be right," O'Neill would often tell Commins, after they had spent days correcting and editing manuscripts and galley proofs. In the case of *Strange Interlude*, O'Neill made so many corrections on the proofs that Liveright found it cheaper to reset the whole thing than to correct each sheet individually.

Alexander King was selected to illustrate *The Emperor Jones*. Much later, after years of obscurity and ill health, he became a popular author and television personality.

King, then a twenty-five-year-old artist, had been traveling and sketching in Europe and Africa on a private grant of $5,000 from Otto Kahn, and when he returned to the United States in the fall of 1927 he brought some of his drawings of African Negroes to the young Liveright vice-president, Donald Friede. Friede, who thought the drawings qualified King to illustrate *The Emperor Jones,* asked him to leave them in the office, explaining that O'Neill would be coming in soon and could look them over.

"The night before O'Neill was expected at Liveright, I couldn't sleep," King said. "Donald was supposed to meet me at his office at two o'clock, and I was there at one. Donald was to introduce me to O'Neill, and this was my big chance. Two o'clock came, and Donald hadn't shown up. I sat in the waiting room, sweating blood. O'Neill arrived a minute or so after two. Still no Donald. I was so desperate, I went over to O'Neill and introduced myself to him and told him about my pictures. 'Where are the pictures?' he asked. I said they were in Donald's office, and he asked me to show them to him."

The two were about to enter Friede's office, when Liveright popped out of *his* office and, ignoring King, took O'Neill by the arm and began guiding him in the opposite direction. O'Neill resisted, saying, "I'm going to have a look at some pictures." Reluctantly Liveright joined him while King displayed his work. One picture, that of a slave being auctioned off, with a man's fingers in the slave's thigh, drew O'Neill's first comment: "That's a pretty extreme picture." "It's an extreme situation," replied King.

"I could see, and so could Horace, that O'Neill liked the pictures," King said. "Horace jumped on the bandwagon and began shouting about how great the drawings were. Donald entered at this point, perspiring and grinning. He joined Horace in his praise, and the two of them began slapping each other on the back triumphantly."

On January 8, 1928, the day before *Marco Millions* was to open at the Guild Theatre, *The New York Times* Sunday drama section ran a long article, surveying O'Neill's career, and quoting, from various sources, the opinions of leading European writers about O'Neill's stature. Shaw, Franz Werfel, Thomas Mann, Maxim Gorky, Hugo von Hofmannsthal and Gerhardt Hauptmann were among those who believed it was considerable.

The Times article failed, however, to include the opinions of John Galsworthy and Arnold Bennett. Galsworthy, in the course of a recent

London theatre season, had picked *Beggar on Horseback,* by George Kaufman and Marc Connelly, over *Anna Christie* as an impressive example of American drama. And Bennett had declared:

"As for Eugene O'Neill, I respect him, just as much as I can respect any sentimentalist, but I hold George Cohan to be a vastly superior playwright."

To accompany the many articles being devoted to him, photographs of O'Neill were much in demand, and he found himself obliged to sit frequently for portraits. Perfectly conscious of his somber good looks and of the heightened value his photograph gave to stories about him, O'Neill did not mind posing. Nickolas Muray, whose studio was now on East Fiftieth Street, was the man who photographed him most often during this period.

"I kept O'Neill in continuous conversation," Muray said, "so he wouldn't know when the picture was being taken. I had a silent shutter on the camera, so my subject wouldn't be aware of the moment I was snapping it." Once, out of gratitude, O'Neill gave Muray a snapshot of himself as a little boy in high-laced shoes, sitting on a rock in New London, a picture that has since been widely reproduced.

"One day I had a sitting with Carlotta," Muray recalled, "and I forgot that O'Neill was coming in. Their sittings overlapped, and I asked O'Neill if he'd mind my keeping Carlotta in the studio until we were all finished and could go out to lunch together. I didn't know, at the time, about their interest in each other. O'Neill, of course, did not mind at all, and we went to lunch at the Crillon; I had to return to my studio for another sitting and I left them there together."

Later Muray photographed O'Neill and Carlotta together several times, but these pictures were for their private use; one of them was the then-popular, Greek coin pose—two profiles, cheek on cheek.

It was just two years after the production of O'Neill's previous play, *The Great God Brown,* that *Marco Millions* opened on January 9, 1928; actually, the strange fact was that nearly *four* years had elapsed since an O'Neill play—*Welded*—had opened on Broadway. *All God's Chillun Got Wings, Desire Under the Elms, The Fountain* and *The Great God Brown* had all had their initial showings at either the Provincetown Playhouse or the Greenwich Village Theatre.

Several playwrights of distinction had lived up to earlier promise or emerged in that period. Sidney Howard's *Ned McCobb's Daughter* and *The Silver Cord* had both had successful runs in the 1926–27 season. George Kelly had won the Pulitzer prize in 1926 for *Craig's Wife* and

Paul Green for *In Abraham's Bosom* in 1927. Maxwell Anderson's *Saturday's Children* had had a successful run in 1927, as had Robert Sherwood's *The Road to Rome*. Philip Barry's *Paris Bound* had just opened. Two first plays by new playwrights, both promptly hailed as gifted young men, had opened at the end of 1926 and the middle of 1927; they were *The Trumpet Shall Sound* by Thornton Wilder and *The Second Man* by S. N. Behrman. The Theatre Guild had produced all of Howard's plays and the Behrman play, filling in their seasons mainly with the works of Shaw, Werfel and Molnar.

Marco Millions was greeted with only moderate enthusiasm by the critics. Percy Hammond thought it "too long and contemplative" to suit every taste, but said that the initiated would find it "a splendid and thoughtful burlesque in which Mr. O'Neill's less morbid ironies are exposed rather than hidden in an ambush of laughing sarcasm."

Brooks Atkinson, in *The Times*, characterized both play and production as "lavish." "Mr. O'Neill's sauve yet cool-headed lampoon of the American Babbitt has not been lost," he said, even "through all the cloth of gold, rococo investiture of the play. . . . With consummate artistry the Guild production keeps all the elements of Mr. O'Neill's imaginative play in true proportion."

In his review for the *World* Alexander Woollcott declared that the production provided "much to rejoice the eye and a little something to please the ear, even . . . something here and there to stir and tickle the mind." But he thought the play, on the whole, "almost grotesquely elaborate and solemnly pretentious."

Gilbert Gabriel, writing for the *Sun*, was overjoyed to find O'Neill finally being produced by the Theatre Guild. "Here was proof positive and decorative," he wrote, "of the best known American dramatist's new coming to the Guild. A coming which will soon release his 'Strange Interlude,' too, for the benefit of artists and experimenters." As for *Marco*, he liked it, but warned that it was not O'Neill's best play.

Some time before the opening of *Strange Interlude* on January 30, O'Neill had made up his mind to marry Carlotta. Norman Winston was the first person to whom he confided his decision. O'Neill said that he and Carlotta had talked over everything and decided to go away together. He did not speak of marrying Carlotta as an immediate possibility for, he explained, he had not yet arrived at an understanding with Agnes.

But while he now felt himself committed to Carlotta, O'Neill was still struggling with his bond to Agnes. He had written to her warmly several times, urging her to leave Bermuda and join him in New York, presumably hoping that she might, by her presence, loosen his tie to Carlotta. He assured her that, whatever she might feel, he was devoted to the children and did not want to hurt them. If Agnes had not by this time discovered her own "imp of the perverse," she might have realized that O'Neill was imploring her to put up a fight for him and, if she had been willing to use the weapons in her possession, she might ultimately have won. But Agnes, her pride wounded, would not fight. ("Gene told me once that he had cabled Agnes to come to New York," Bessie Breuer said, "and that Agnes had flatly refused.")

O'Neill asked Winston what he thought about his plan to go away with Carlotta. Winston told O'Neill it was a good idea. "If you find it doesn't work out," Winston said, "then you can break up for good." Privately, Winston did not think it *would* work. "I couldn't see them as a couple," he later remarked.

O'Neill told Winston he was going to Bermuda for a few days to talk to Agnes and would call him when he got back. "Then we can map out a plan," O'Neill said.

On O'Neill's return, he and Winston lunched together at the Wentworth.

"I hadn't seen Carlotta or heard from her," Winston later said, "I had a feeling she was deliberately avoiding O'Neill's friends. O'Neill told me at lunch that he'd talked with Agnes and that she had seemed 'surprised' at his wanting to marry Carlotta and had cautioned him to wait. She agreed that it would be a good idea for him to take a trip before starting divorce proceedings. Gene began discussing plans for his trip with me, and asked me to try to work out some way for him and Carlotta to slip away quietly, without attracting attention, as soon as possible after *Strange Interlude* opened."

O'Neill also took Elizabeth Sergeant into his confidence.

"He came to see me toward the end of rehearsals of *Strange Interlude,*" she said. "He told me he was going to marry Carlotta and that he felt bad about Agnes and the children. 'I didn't want this to happen,' he said. He wanted me to meet Carlotta, and we made a date. Carlotta was charming, but I felt, somehow, that she was more in love with the Great Dramatist than with Gene. She was enormously poised, a woman with the grand manner, completely in command. She had her own income, was a woman of the world; this gave her standing in Gene's eyes."

A different impression was retained by Robert Sisk, then publicity man for the Theatre Guild. Unlike Miss Sergeant, Sisk, who continued on terms of friendship with Carlotta even after O'Neill's death, believed that Carlotta was "deeply in love" with O'Neill. "I think she had her problems with him," Sisk said. "I don't think anyone would deny that Gene was a difficult man at times. The difficulty comes out of the agony you go through when you try to create something."

"Gene told me he was disappointed that he wouldn't be able to get a divorce before he left with Carlotta," Elizabeth Sergeant added. "He said that Agnes refused to regard the situation as anything more than a passing affair, that she expected him to come back to her, and that he had had to agree to postpone the divorce."

Carlotta herself, in recalling the events leading up to her marriage to O'Neill, once said, "I didn't want to marry him at first. But I appreciated him as an artist. There was no mad love affair between us. O'Neill was a tough mick, and never loved a woman who walked. He loved only his work. But he had respect for me. I had an independent income, and I told him I'd marry him if he would let me pay one half of all the household expenses. He went to Bermuda, and when he came back, he said he needed a home. 'I want a home properly run,' he told me. And that is what I did for him. I saw to it that he was able to work."

O'Neill belied Carlotta's temperate evaluation of their relationship by presenting her, that Christmas, with a three-volume edition of the writings of William Blake, addressing her, on the fly leaf, as "Dearest One," wishing her a "Loving Christmas," and signing himself "Your Gene."

In his new role as escort of a fabled beauty O'Neill became something of a dandy. Carlotta expected him to live up to her own standard of well-ordered elegance, and he seemed rather pleased to comply. He spent hours being fitted for suits by a tailor to whom Winston introduced him. He appeared before Langner one day carrying a malacca cane and told Langner that the cane was symbolic of the new and superior life he was going to begin living. He also began wearing, somewhat sheepishly, a mink-lined, black overcoat which Carlotta, probably recalling the impact of a similar gift on Ralph Barton, had bought for him. He displayed this item of sartorial splendor to a number of friends.

"Gene telephoned me at my office one day and asked me, very solemnly, if I would drop in at his hotel on my way home from work," Rockmore recalled. "I assumed he had something important to communicate. When I got there, I knocked at his door and he called to me to come in. He was standing in the middle of the living room looking portentous, and didn't say hello, just asked if I'd wait a minute, and then he vanished into the bedroom. He appeared a minute later wearing an overcoat with a mink collar, looked quizzically at me for a moment, and then opened the coat, to show me the fur lining."

"How do you like it?" O'Neill asked.

"Very nice," said Rockmore, who happened to detest fur-trimmed coats for men.

Later O'Neill dropped in on Jimmy Light and his wife, unannounced. Patty Light opened the door to him and stared at the richly enveloped figure.

"Gene stood there with a shy, boyish look on his face, saying nothing, waiting for me to comment on the coat. Of course, I told him it was lovely. His eyes seemed to say, 'I've won my bet on life.' The coat, I think, typified for him worldly success, a thing he had never run after but which had found him in spite of himself."

The set designer for *Strange Interlude*, Jo Mielziner, then at the beginning of his career as one of the theatre's most successful scenic artists, also was singled out by O'Neill for a showing.

"Philip Moeller told me one day at rehearsals that O'Neill was going to call me the next morning at home to talk over some aspect of the set," Mielziner said. "O'Neill was always extremely interested in the technical problems of design and lighting and often made perceptive comments about them. But this time he had an ulterior motive in coming to talk to me. He phoned very early in the morning and said he'd be over right away. Would I lean out of my window—I was living on the top floor of a brownstone in the East Sixties—and watch for him as he got out of the taxi?"

Puzzled but accommodating, Mielziner did as he was asked, and was treated to the sight of O'Neill's fur coat emerging from the taxi.

"He climbed up the stairs and came in, with the coat open to reveal the lining," Mielziner said. "He was beaming. He showed off the coat, frankly vain about it, and then took it off and dropped it on the floor."

O'Neill made a similar gesture, a mock repudiation of grandeur, more genuinely a few days later when he went, with Winston, to call on Joe Smith, his old friend of the Hell Hole days.

"At the last minute, Gene didn't have the nerve to appear before Joe in the coat," Winston recalled. "He was truly too embarrassed to display it. He stopped in the dark passageway leading to Joe's apartment, which was in an old house in Greenwich Village, and found a hook near the basement door. He hung his coat there before knocking on Joe's door and retrieved it after the visit."

O'Neill had for some time been supplementing Joe Smith's income— a small pension from the company that had once employed him as a night watchman—and Joe referred to O'Neill's checks as "my royalties."

O'Neill's new, mink-coated existence did not prevent him from remembering other of his former cronies, to whom he had always been generous. He asked Winston to look after Terry Carlin and left money to be doled out to Terry during O'Neill's impending trip abroad. In addition, though he rarely saw Terry any more, he maintained a charge account for him at a general store in Provincetown.

"I would meet Terry in Greenwich Village once a week after Gene left for Europe, to give him the money," Winston said. "We'd drink, and he'd reminisce about the old days."

Shortly before the opening of *Strange Interlude*, Alexander Woollcott, who had been taking a dimmer and dimmer view of O'Neill since his early championship of *Beyond the Horizon*, got hold of a script of the new play and wrote, for *Vanity Fair*, a withering article, predicting it would be a spectacular failure. (To friends, he described the play as "the Abie's Irish Rose of the intelligentsia.") Many of Woollcott's acquaintances believed that the article was prompted less by Woollcott's objective evaluation of the play than by his personal dislike of George Jean Nathan, who had written his praise of *Strange Interlude* earlier. Woollcott's bosses on the *World*, Herbert Bayard Swope and Ralph Pulitzer, agreed that their critic had behaved unethically in writing, for another publication, an advance condemnation of an important play and made plans both to chastise him and to obtain an unprejudiced critique for the *World*. O'Neill, somehow, got word of what was up.

He did not attend the final dress rehearsal on Saturday, January 28. (He had attended a rehearsal the day before and made a speech of gratitude to the cast. "I'll never forget that 'thank you' speech," Lynn Fontanne said. "It was very short, but I suffered for O'Neill. I never saw a man who found it so difficult to express his thoughts.") The play was to open Monday at the John Golden Theatre, after the cast rested on Sunday.

"I remember that dress rehearsal very well," Robert Sisk said. "Gene had given me a number where I could reach him after it was over. The rehearsal was hysterically successful and I telephoned him in some excitement. He was completely calm. 'I'm not surprised,' he said."

But by Sunday O'Neill's calm had crumbled.

"Gene telephoned me to ask me to go for a ride with him in a chauffeur-driven car he'd rented for the afternoon," Rockmore said. "He told me he felt edgy about the opening. He was silent during most of the drive—we cruised through the park for about an hour—but just before he dropped me off at my apartment he told me, 'You know, Woollcott is going to have his wagon fixed. Right before the performance tomorrow he's going to be lifted from the assignment of reviewing my play and a reporter will cover it instead.' He didn't tell me how he'd found out about this."

At four o'clock on Monday afternoon Theresa Helburn telephoned O'Neill to ask him if he wouldn't change his mind about attending the opening. He said he would not.

At 5:15 he was mentally, if not physically, with the first-nighters, as they began filing into the 900-seat John Golden Theatre. No member of the Broadway audience was more conscious than O'Neill that, once again, theatre history was being made. O'Neill had shaken the theatre world with *Beyond the Horizon, The Emperor Jones, The Hairy Ape, Desire Under the Elms,* and *The Great God Brown.* He had progressed (always as an innovator) in a dozen years from a naturalistic-poetic one-act sea play through longer dramas of masked symbolism and expressionism to a nine-act play-novel that needed an unprecedented five hours plus dinner-break to unfold. (Curiously, during the next quarter century no one but O'Neill himself challenged this record—with his equally long *Mourning Becomes Electra* and *The Iceman Cometh* in 1931 and 1946.)

O'Neill had chosen to spend the evening with one of the friends of his bumming days, Bill Clarke, the ex-circus man who used to drink with him and Jamie at the Garden Hotel. Clarke and O'Neill dined together in O'Neill's suite at the Wentworth. At 7:30 the telephone rang, and O'Neill listened to a report from the theatre.

"Well, everything seems to be going all right," he told Clarke. Then he gave him a look of profound sadness. "It would be nice to have Jamie here now," he said. After a pause he added, "You were good to me in the old days, Clarkey. I've never forgotten it."

The man who was selected to replace Woollcott was Dudley Nichols, a twenty-seven-year-old star reporter, who had come to the *World* from the *Evening Post.* Nichols, who soon after distinguished himself as a Hollywood writer (notably as the author of *The Informer*), had met O'Neill sometime earlier, during the writing of *Strange Interlude.* Nichols had inquired how his work was coming and O'Neill replied that he was writing "the life of a woman without the padding of a novel."

"About four in the afternoon on January 30, I was told to go uptown and cover *Strange Interlude*," Nichols later recalled. "I was profoundly moved and wrote, as I remember, almost two columns. O'Neill, who didn't really care about reviews, though he quite naturally hoped they would be favorable, told me later that he owed much to my review for the immediate success of the play—though that was very likely more generous kindness than fact. He told me in later years—with a grin—that he should 'have had that review framed.' "

Nichols did indeed outdo himself in praising the play.

"The Theatre Guild produced Eugene O'Neill's 'Strange Interlude' last night and it needs all the restraint a reporter can muster not to stamp the occasion, without a second thought, the most important event in the present era of the American theatre," he began. Focusing on the audience, which, he pointed out, had sat in the theatre from a quarter past five until after eleven, with an hour's intermission for dinner, he went on: "The most that can be said for the play is that when the 900 persons went with illuminated faces out of the small John Golden Theatre at the later hour their faces registered tiredness but not boredom, weariness but not ennui. It was the honest fatigue of people who have shared profound emotional experiences." (Otto Kahn, horrified at the idea of appearing at the theatre in evening dress at 5:30 when the curtain rose, sacrificed most of his evening's meal by going home to change during the dinner intermission at eight o'clock.)

" 'Strange Interlude,' " Nichols added, was "not only . . . a great American play but the great American novel as well." Remembering O'Neill's phrase, he said, "It is a great novel without any of the novelist's padding." As for the asides, he commented that "the amazing thing is that this convention is quickly accepted by an auditor after the first shock of its novelty wears off."

By contrast with Nichols' effusion, Brooks Atkinson's evaluation in *The Times* was restrained.

"Fresh from the five hours of Eugene O'Neill's 'Strange Interlude,' he began, ". . . one can soberly report that this nine-act drama at least maintains the interest to the end. . . . Written by our foremost dramatist, acted intelligently by a notable troupe of actors, directed intelligently by Philip Moeller and sponsored by the Theatre Guild, 'Strange Interlude' commands the respectful interest of the enthusiastic playgoer to whom experiment is never dull. All this one can earnestly report, without believing that 'Strange Interlude' is distinguished as a play or that Mr. O'Neill's combination of the novel and drama techniques is a permanent addition to the theatre." Atkinson went on to describe the play as a "psychopathic melodrama" and characterized the asides as being, often, "fortuitous" or, worse, "nickel-weekly jargon . . . [offered] as thinking."

"In the fable of 'Strange Interlude,' " Atkinson continued, "Mr. O'Neill has returned to the morbidness of his middle-period, a preoccupation with dark and devious human impulses, twisted and macabre. Nor does his point of view sweeten the unsavoriness of his material . . . Mr. O'Neill does not illuminate his theme with pity or interpret its significance." The asides, Atkinson thought, contributed little in the way of substance. "What fresh light do they reflect upon character? What do they express which cannot be conveyed vividly through the silent instrument of acting? What, in fine, distinguishes 'Strange Interlude' from the old three-decker novel?" he asked.

Gilbert Gabriel, in Nichols' camp, wrote, in part:

" 'Strange Interlude' stands firm and giant-sized as a giver of new scopes, as a hewer of ways for such truths as the usual drama can scarce imply, as a method to meet the need, today's immense need, for plays that can ably cope with Freud. If only for that reason—and I guarantee to find you others—it is the most significant contribution any American has made to the stage."

Percy Hammond ended up a little more positive than negative if this summary of his opinion may be used as a clue:

"Although Mr. O'Neill has done everything he can to spare us the task of thinking, 'Strange Interlude' is not a play for lazy drama lovers. His unlimited employment of 'asides' to describe the unspoken thoughts of his characters is more of a whip than a cushion to our imagination, and it keeps us busy. . . . If you are a semi-serious patron of the theatre, here is an opportunity for you to invest time, trouble, money and faith in a long, complete and agitating study of life as it is seen through Mr. O'Neill's brooding and acid eyes."

The New Yorker, which had recently begun making itself felt as an arbiter of sophisticated opinion in the theatre through Robert Benchley's reviews, described *Strange Interlude* as "an interesting stunt carried about four acts too far; not much more important than that."

"In purporting to give voice to the thoughts of his characters," *The New Yorker* said, "Mr. O'Neill lays himself open to comparison with James Joyce, Virginia Woolf, and the other stream of consciousness novelists. It is a comparison he can ill support. The turbulent stream of consciousness Joyce photographs so perfectly finds itself, in 'Strange Interlude', confined to neat concrete containers which are far more like summaries of the momentary situation as Mr. O'Neill wishes one to understand it than like what the characters are actually thinking at the time. They create the impression that Mr. O'Neill has done the groundwork which every dramatist must do, so much to his own satisfaction that he hasn't been able to rub any of it out, or that, unwilling to trust anything to his actors, he is trying to do their work for them too."

Faced with such a variance of opinion, the New York theatregoing public made up its own mind. It decided *Strange Interlude* was something to see, and the play became O'Neill's biggest hit. It ran in New York for seventeen months (414 performances) and later two touring companies canvassed the country, playing to capacity audiences. It won O'Neill his third Pulitzer Prize and was made into a motion picture starring Norma Shearer. It was, naturally, banned in Boston (it was produced instead in nearby Quincy in 1929) and was prodigiously written about in newspapers and magazines throughout the country. Alexander Woollcott, for instance, did not take his opening night defeat lying down, in spite of the humiliation.

"The real joke came afterwards," Nichols recalled. "Theatre reviews in the *World* were published under a stock head, with Woollcott's name in smaller type beneath it. Evidently old John Corbin had read my review without noticing that my name had replaced Alec's, and he wrote a warm note of congratulation to Alec for his fine notice of *Strange Interlude*. It was Alec himself who revealed it, stalking into the City Room to tell it with a burst of mocking laughter. I daresay one side of Alec's mind couldn't resist telling a joke while the other side didn't, to say the least, enjoy it. A complex fellow, Woollcott. It was shortly after this that he left the *World*."

Woollcott did manage to have the last word, as far as the *World* was concerned, for he was not barred from expressing his opinion of *Strange Interlude* in his column, "Second Thoughts on First Nights," and this he did a week after the opening. He didn't like the play all over again.

Strange Interlude eventually netted O'Neill $275,000, a small fortune in that era of low taxes; it was far more than he had ever made from a play before (and he invested a good share of his royalties in the stock market). Although he had always maintained that he had known the play would succeed, he did have one or two retrospectively derogatory remarks to make about it. In 1932 he commented, in print: "As for *Strange Interlude*, that is an attempt at the new masked psychological drama . . . without masks—a successful attempt, perhaps, in so far as it concerns only surfaces and their immediate subsurfaces, but not where, occasionally, it tries to probe deeper."

A day or two after the opening of *Strange Interlude*, O'Neill visited Alexander King and his wife.

"My wife asked O'Neill to autograph a book for her, and she asked him which was his favorite play," King recalled. "He told her it was *Lazarus Laughed*, and he signed our copy of it for her. I told O'Neill I would soon have a few drawings for him to look at for a projected illustrated edition of *The Hairy Ape,* and he said he wouldn't be able to see them, as he was going abroad."

O'Neill had made elaborate plans to leave the country quietly. He did not want Agnes to know where he was going, when he was leaving, or how long he intended to stay away; indeed, he himself did not realize then how long it would be before his return to the United States, although the manner of his departure indicated that he intended to return within a few months, for he left files of manuscripts, notes, letters and books behind at Spithead. He also left his still unsettled New London estate (though he had managed by this time to liquidate some of it and negotiations on the rest were pending), and his still unsold house in Ridgefield. The house in Provincetown he had given to Eugene Jr. There were a lawyer and an agent to deal with any problems that might arise from his real estate negotiations and his two Broadway plays, but, all in all, it was a fairly intricate artistic, financial and domestic situation on which he was walking out, with nothing much more than the notes for his new play, *Dynamo,* in his pocket, his hat in his hand—and his mink coat on his back.

He did take leave of Eugene Jr., of whom he was growing increasingly proud. Eugene, now a freshman at Yale, had recently contributed a poem to his class publication, *The Helicon,* and the "entrance into the field of literature by Eugene O'Neill, Jr.," had been duly noted by *The New York Times* that December. In saying good-by to Eugene, O'Neill enjoined him to secrecy about his plans.

As for Carlotta, she was leaving behind her eleven-year-old daughter, Cynthia. Like Agnes, who had not allowed herself to feel encumbered by a daughter when she had gone off with O'Neill to Provincetown ten years earlier, Carlotta had a convenient mother (Mrs. Nellie Taasinge) with whom to leave her child; also like Agnes, Carlotta knew she must arrange things so that the possessive O'Neill would not be inconvenienced by a stepdaughter. Cynthia had not been an integral part of Carlotta's daily life, any more than Barbara had been of Agnes', in the early days of her friendship with and marriage to O'Neill.

O'Neill and Carlotta were going to sail for England, but O'Neill wanted none but his closest friends to know this. Typical of the sort of subterfuge to which he resorted to cover his tracks was a letter he wrote on February 9, from the Hotel Wentworth, to someone who wanted him to sit for a portrait.

"I am afraid that I will have to postpone the date until I get back from California, for I am leaving in a couple of days. . . . But I will be back in three months." To others whom he wanted to throw off the scent he also named his destination as California—the professed reason being that he wished to attend rehearsals of *Lazarus Laughed,* which was being readied for April production by the Pasadena Community Playhouse.

He even wrote a farewell letter to eight-year-old Shane, in Bermuda (to whom he had given no inkling of his imminent departure when he had last seen him), saying he had to "travel way across America to California to watch them putting on another play of mine, *Lazarus Laughed,* in the city of Pasadena." (O'Neill did not go near Pasadena or the production of *Lazarus.*)

"Write me a long letter sometime soon and tell me everything you and Oona are doing because it will probably be a long time before I will be able to see you both again. . . .

"Always remember that I love you and Oona an awful lot—and please don't ever forget your Daddy. . . .

"All my love to you, dear son!" (Shane later published this letter in *The Curse of the Misbegotten,* a book about his family written in collaboration with Croswell Bowen.)

Kenneth Macgowan was one of the people to whom O'Neill confided his real plans. "I thought Carlotta would help Gene, and I encouraged him to go away with her," Macgowan later said.

O'Neill spent his last evening before sailing at Norman Winston's apartment in the company of Winston and Robert Rockmore.

"Gene was terribly nervous about leaving the next morning," Rockmore said. "He told me, 'This is the worst struggle I've ever had against taking a drink, but if I have *one,* I'm off.' He didn't take one."

"The last time I saw Gene was just before he sailed," Winston said. "He was afraid the newspapers might find out about his leaving, so everything was hush-hush. I was to take him through steerage to his cabin the following morning, so that he would avoid the ship news reporters. Carlotta would go directly to her own cabin.

"We spent a few hours at my house, and then Gene guided me along the waterfront, pointing out some old haunts of his. Later, we hired a car and drove for the rest of the night. We went up to Westchester and came back close to dawn. After we had coffee in a restaurant, I took him to the ship and got him through steerage. Then I went up on deck to see if the coast was clear. It was, so I rejoined Gene, settled him in his cabin, and then we both went to Carlotta's cabin. Carlotta was being very theatrical. She said she was going to introduce Gene to the sophistication of Europe. She told me that she wanted him to be as familiar with the crowned heads of Europe as he was with the people in this country."

"Gene had never seen England," Carlotta told an interviewer some years later, having forgotten, or perhaps dismissed, O'Neill's earlier sojourn in Liverpool, as a seaman. "I was brought up in England and France, and it was a great pleasure taking him there and showing him all the things I had loved so."

L

THE SEA WAS CHOPPY, AND THERE WERE SEVERAL
passengers aboard ship who might have recognized O'Neill, so both he
and Carlotta kept mostly to their cabins.

One of the first people to hear from O'Neill when he reached London,
a city with which he promptly fell in love, was Kenneth Macgowan. On
February 22, 1928, O'Neill wrote to him from the Berkeley Hotel, describing his new-found joy. He was traveling incognito, he told Macgowan,
so that nothing and no one could intrude on his bliss.

"God, I wish I could tell you how happy I am!" he exclaimed. "I'm
simply transformed and transfigured inside! A dream I had given up even
the hope of ever dreaming again has come true! I wander about foolish
and goggle-eyed with joy in a honeymoon that is a thousand times more
poignant and sweet and ecstatic because it comes at an age when one's
past—particularly a past such as mine—gives one the power to appreciate
what happiness means and how rare it is and how humbly grateful one
should be for it. And dreaming it all over in these days when the dream
has become flesh and the flesh dream, it really seems to my mystic side
as if some compassionate God, looking back at Carlotta's unhappy life
and mine, had said to himself, well, they deserve each other if they have
the guts to take the gift. And we did have—and here we are!"

Dispelling any doubt about the ardor of their relationship, he went on:

"To say that Carlotta and I are in love in the sense of any love I
have ever experienced before is weak and inadequate. . . . I could beat my
brains out on the threshold of any old temple of Aphrodite out of pure
gratitude for the revelation! It is so damn right in every way! We 'belong'
to each other! We fulfill each other!"

O'Neill told Macgowan that his future plans were vague and depended in large part on "what Agnes does or doesn't do—or whether she
has the honor to keep the pledge we have always made to each other."
The "pledge," he explained, had been made in the days of their first romantic attachment, binding either to give the other his freedom if ever
one of them should fall in love.

"I love someone else deeply," O'Neill had written Agnes, soon after
leaving, in a letter that was later made public in a newspaper account of

the estrangement. "There is no possible doubt of this. And the someone loves me. Of that I am deeply certain. We have often promised each other that if ever one came to the other and said they loved someone else that we would understand—that we would know that love is something which cannot be denied or argued with."

O'Neill assumed that Agnes would keep her "pledge." In mid-February several New York newspapers published stories announcing that Agnes was arranging a legal separation from O'Neill, through the offices of O'Neill's lawyer, Harry Weinberger. The stories hinted at "a packet of letters" from Carlotta Monterey to O'Neill as being the cause of the separation.

Agnes, O'Neill believed, would ultimately agree to divorce him. "She is fine and sound at bottom," he said. But he added that he feared she might be influenced in her actions by "that Philadelphia Social Register bunch of futile women with money" who were her friends in Bermuda. One way or the other, though, O'Neill continued, it didn't really matter, as long as he could live and write where people minded their own business and approved of love without moral didoes. He and Carlotta might stay away a long time, he said; they were thinking of going to Greece and Egypt and the Far East and South Africa and the South Seas.

"There's a good bit of the old Gene O'Neill: A.B.—his spirit refined and minus the spirits that kept it going—reborn in me," he added. "I *feel* life again—without fear this time."

O'Neill and Carlotta planned to rent a villa on the coast of France, Italy or Spain, where he could get to work on *Dynamo*—something not too isolated or too near, not "too farmy and not too swank," where they could have a car and a boat, and be close enough to a town "to mingle when we need a change."

He thanked Macgowan for having been a friend to both him and Carlotta "when friends to *both* were almost nil" and told him to spread the word among his "pseudo friends" in New York that O'Neill had been heard from and that for the first time in his life he was really happy.

Having crossed from England to France, O'Neill and Carlotta motored from Calais through the French countryside, arriving in Paris on February 26, to negotiate with real estate agents. Then they were off again by car, passing through the château country in Touraine—"the most beautiful and dramatic places I have ever seen," O'Neill said of the great estates he visited—and on to the south, to look at villas in the neighborhood of Biarritz ("Not Biarritz itself, of course; that is too resorty," he said). Stopping briefly at a hotel in Biarritz, O'Neill went out and bought Carlotta a gift—a stuffed, scrawny, hairy, grotesquely funny monkey ("He had long arms, like Gene," Carlotta later said). O'Neill christened it Esteban in honor of a young Spanish nobleman, ruined by narcotics, whom he had known in Buenos Aires. His full name, which O'Neill enjoyed rattling off, was the Marquis Esteban de Gonzales, Grandee of Spain. The monkey, leering wickedly through its whiskers, occupied a sofa or chair or bed of every home Carlotta lived in until her death in 1970.

By early March O'Neill and Carlotta had moved into a rented villa in the little village of Guéthary, in the Pyrenees. Called Villa Marguerite, it was a charming old house with stone balconies, set in the woods and boasting a tennis court and private beach with a rowboat. Their lease was for six months. They were not far from the Spanish frontier, and hoped to take several trips into Spain.

"Altogether the prospects are bright and we are both very happy," O'Neill reported to Macgowan. "Carlotta has so far done all the talking in French for the firm but I find that a lot of my five years of it in prep school and college comes back to me and I can usually understand all that is said—if they go slow—although when I come to reply I find myself automatically stumbling into Spanish! A queer combination of having once learned to read one language and to have picked up a jabbering knowledge of another [in Argentina] . . . what with Carlotta's English accent and Spanish appearance and my own God-knows-what-but-not-typically-Yank mug and my inability not to say 'sí' when I ought to say 'oui' and the general supposition that we are both Montereys—well, we puzzle the folks a bit, but agreeably, because they see we are in love and so it must be all right, whatever it is."

O'Neill said he had received no mail from New York since leaving and wondered what had been happening there and in Bermuda. He hoped all was "fair weather both in the commercial and domestic fields of drama, but I must say I haven't lost any sleep over the dearth of news."

Again his boyish rapture could not be contained:

"Carlotta has been marvelous to and for me! . . . And she is so deeply in love it fills me with a humble awe and gratitude. Well—! I am a bit in love myself, what?"

No small part of O'Neill's happiness was based on the fact that it was not costing him a great deal of money, for he and Carlotta were splitting fifty-fifty on all expenses.

"We are quite uneventfully happy and more in love than ever," O'Neill reported to Macgowan in a self-congratulatory letter almost two months later. "That this happiness has stood the test of an absolutely secluded life in which we see no one but each other, in which no one even speaks English, in which for six weeks it did practically nothing but rain day after day, in which the strain of uncertainty about what Agnes would do has been—and still is—particularly trying, in which the fear of being recognized and landed in the tabloids is ever present—that our love has waxed under a trial that would have turned a great many into a series of destroying brawls is something we are mighty proud of, and in years to come I'm sure we'll look back on it with a feeling of gratitude. It is a good thing to face all possible music at the start. It gives you a good measure of the living-with worth of the other. Carlotta is a brick!"

O'Neill went on to tell Macgowan that Agnes appeared to be going ahead with her divorce plans, but that she was making what he felt were unreasonable demands about the financial settlement.

However, on the same day (April 27) that O'Neill was relaying this optimistic news to Macgowan, (and unknown to O'Neill), the *World* carried what it called an "authorized interview" with Agnes, in which Agnes said that she was not seeking a divorce or separation and that she was, in fact, planning to rejoin her husband in London "soon." (Two good friends of Agnes', Allen Ullman and his wife, Sarah, later said that Agnes delayed the divorce because she did not feel O'Neill was offering her a fair alimony arrangement.)

"Mr. O'Neill's name became coupled in published reports with that of Carlotta Monterey, actress and former wife of Ralph Barton," said the *World*: ". . . It was because of these published reports that Mrs. O'Neill saw fit to clarify the situation yesterday. . . .

"Where Miss Monterey is she said she did not know. But her husband, she explained, is touring with friends in France, preparing to start work on 'Dynamo,' an unheralded O'Neill drama. He went abroad primarily, she said, because repairs were in progress at Spithead. . . .There was nothing strange about a trip to Europe by her husband, she added. She has always wanted Mr. O'Neill to do this, but his dreams in the past had been centered on 'going to China.'

"Mrs. O'Neill said she hopes her husband is enjoying himself. She refused to say that her failure to leave for Europe with him had constituted what other celebrities have referred to as a 'marital vacation.' Nevertheless she believes in an occasional change of air—'for the man'—she added quickly. There could be no misunderstanding.

"If Miss Monterey were one of the friends who had been with her husband, Mrs. O'Neill continued, he had never informed her of it. She had a letter received but three days before if proof were needed. It began 'Dearest Agnes.' . . .

"Harry Weinberger, for many years Mr. O'Neill's lawyer, paid a recent visit to Mrs. O'Neill in Bermuda, strengthening the old reports of marital disagreement. But the wife explained that this was a business visit purely, in connection with a mortgage on a house or something of that kind. . . ." (Weinberger, O'Neill wrote to a friend, had attempted while in Bermuda, to remove O'Neill's personal papers and manuscripts—an attempt in which he was only partly successful. "The files I left in my Bermuda house when I went to Europe in 1928 [were] never recovered," O'Neill informed the Princeton University Library fifteen years later, when an O'Neill exhibit was being set up. "They were either destroyed or stolen.")

"It became apparent that whatever the domestic nature of the interlude she failed to regard this as a strange or unusual one. . . ." the *World* continued. "The fact that her husband 'for so long a time led such a quiet, secluded life' was another reason given by the wife for recent 'gossip.' If Mr. O'Neill is 'even seen once at the theatre with a good-looking person, rumor starts,' she added."

Even though he was unaware of Agnes' statements, O'Neill had long since changed his mind about her being "fine and sound at bottom." He had concluded, with the sort of emotionalism that frequently accompanies a divorce action, that Agnes was being obstinate and highhanded—two of the more flattering adjectives he applied in letters to various friends. He seemed stunned and wounded that Agnes had not meekly accepted his terms and that she was not being rational and agreeable in accepting his own highly irrational and disagreeable behavior toward her. To Macgowan, he hinted darkly at the influence her Bermuda acquaintances were exerting over her, calling them, this time, "worthy society drunken-neighbor friends" who had evidently advised her to "take me for all I've got."

"I am too old to start in being a sucker, and Carlotta has agreed with me that I should put up a battle," he continued, "so I've written Harry [Weinberger] to tell her to go to hell if she won't take what I offered." (The offer amounted to an income—based on his earnings—that might fluctuate between $6,000 and $10,000 a year and which, he had said earlier, was "an agreement more generous than Sinclair Lewis' wife got from him, considering he must have been making three times my income!")

"She'll never get as much out of any court," O'Neill said, "and if she refuses to get a divorce I can eventually starve her into it. It would, of course, entail sacrifices." What he had in mind was restricting his own income by withholding productions of any of his plays for a few years, and living abroad on Carlotta's income.

"But," he exploded, in a burst of self-pity, "what a rotten mess to have

[670]

wished on one by a person who is really bound in honor by a pledge made repeatedly during our years together that if either fell in love the other would divorce at once! There was even a no-alimony clause to the pledge! It's sickening to one's opinions of human nature!" He went on to point out, self-righteously, how he had supported members of Agnes' family for years and had always "let her run bills regardless." (What O'Neill appeared to have lost sight of was that the "no-alimony" agreement—if, indeed, such an agreement existed—had been made when Agnes was earning her own money and had only one child—not O'Neill's—to support. She complained to friends that she felt O'Neill's financial offer was ungenerous, in view of his potentially high earning power and the fact that he planned to marry a woman of independent means.)

"Agnes is dead for me now and that's her epitaph in my memory!" he said, adding, "I had hoped to remain her friend and help her—but I don't want yellow friends!"

In the midst of distracting news about Agnes, which was affecting his peace of mind even more than he was willing to admit, O'Neill was working on his new play, *Dynamo*. He had half finished it by the end of April and was very pleased with it. In addition, he was contemplating a series of plays for which he had previously jotted down a note or two and which he never wrote; it is interesting because it foreshadowed some of the consciously autobiographical plays of his later years, including *Long Day's Journey Into Night*:

"The grand opus of my life—the autobiographical *Sea-Mother's Son*—has been much in my dreams of late," he informed Macgowan. "If I can write that up to what the dreams call for, it will make a work that I flatter myself will be one of those timeless Big Things. It has got me all 'het up.' It should be a piece of writing not like any that has ever been done before, the way I plan it. My subtitle is to be 'The Story of the Birth of a Soul'—and it will be just that!"

O'Neill was taking elaborate precautions to safeguard his and Carlotta's privacy. He enlisted the help of Macgowan—and, soon after, of Louis Kalonyme—in spreading a false trail; he appeared to derive a childish and somewhat vindictive pleasure in confusing his acquaintances in the United States. He asked Macgowan to circulate the report that he was in Prague, and would soon be traveling to Russia and Italy—when, in fact, he had quite a different itinerary planned. He wanted to stay with Carlotta in France until summer's end, and if, by then, Agnes had gone through with the divorce, marry Carlotta in Germany. He and Carlotta would then spend a short time in England, from where they would set sail for South Africa. They would take a house in Natal for the winter, where O'Neill would write one of the plays for which he had been making notes, and in the spring they would visit Suez and Greece, where he would write another play.

From there they would journey to India, Hong Kong, Peking and Honolulu—returning, in 1930, to the United States. He and Carlotta expected to find a house in California and settle down there permanently.

O'Neill never did get to South Africa, Greece, India or Honolulu, and he and Carlotta did not settle down in California until ten years later. But he was right in one prediction: "divorce or no divorce, productions in New York or no productions, the States probably won't see me again for two years. . . ."

He told Macgowan to conceal his letters from everyone, and asked him to write him, in future, care of the Guaranty Trust Company in London, since he might be obliged to leave the Villa Marguerite abruptly.

Two days later—on April 29—he confirmed his apprehension about having to leave Guéthary to Benjamin De Casseres.

"The scent after me here in France has been getting pretty hot and I'm afraid every day of being smoked out—which would be fatal, under the circumstances, and playing right into my wife's hands, to say nothing of the scandal which would injure the last person in the world I want to hurt—so I'm beating it away from here very soon and seeking remoter distant pastures, just where I haven't decided yet. . . .

"It's the lousiest situation I was ever placed in—like being out in an open field with the enemy sniping at you and you can't run (for reasons connected with others) and you can't fight back (for other reasons connected with others). Not that I'm complaining. It's worth it and inside I'm deeply at peace and happy and confident of the future. But it's hell on the nerves. . . . For the first few weeks here everything looked rosy but since then fresh alarms and complications about which I have to make complicated decisions have been pounded at me in every mail. To use a ring expression, 'it's raining boxing gloves!' "

Early in May, Louis Kalonyme was invited for a week's stay at Guéthary. He had gone abroad before O'Neill and Carlotta left New York in February, and O'Neill had been trying to reach him for two months.

Kalonyme found O'Neill in a state of nervous tension.

"He was going through a bad time about Agnes and the children; he really loved the children," Kalonyme said. (But in O'Neill's many long and intimate letters to friends during that period, though he went into minute detail about his feelings regarding Agnes, there is scarcely a mention of how he felt about being separated from his children.)

Kalonyme also found O'Neill distressed about the attention he was receiving from the press. "While I was there," he said, "a reporter tried to get in touch with Gene, and I saw the reporter for him. He told me that Eugene Jr. had been interviewed at Yale for a New York newspaper; he had been asked who he thought was the world's greatest playwright and he'd answered 'Shakespeare and O'Neill.' I told Gene about this and he smiled and said, 'Why did he bring up Shakespeare?' He was very pleased."

O'Neill became so edgy that he broke his prolonged abstinence. He and Kalonyme drove to a village, bought a bottle and drank themselves literally insensible. Carlotta discovered them piled on beds in a guest room of the Villa Marguerite and was furious. However, she forgave them both. Kalonyme left a day or two later and, soon after, O'Neill became seriously ill with what Carlotta described as "a bad nervous breakdown."

O'Neill, penitently referring to the episode several weeks later, wrote to Kalonyme: "My nervous outfit after the disastrous upset when you were here (about which remember to be forever silent!) has been all shot. . . . I'm sorry your trip here got involved in such stupidity. Better luck next time! At least, I'm sure now of what *won't* happen again in my life. I was getting overconfident and doing too much playing around and testing myself and experimenting, and I needed to take a good one on the chin and a long count to show me I have retired from the ring! So it may have been all for the best. In fact, I know it was, when I stop to consider."

Kalonyme later recalled that O'Neill continued to refer guiltily to his lapse from sobriety.

"Gene kept writing me to 'forget that incident in May,'" Kalonyme said. "And Carlotta wrote me regularly, too, giving me reports about Gene's health and saying she thought the best way to keep him in good health in the future was to prevent all gossip about Agnes' activities from reaching his ears. Carlotta said Gene would forget all about the unpleasantness with Agnes until someone brought up the subject. She was wrathful about what she called O'Neill's 'false friends' in New York, who insisted on writing him about Agnes and upsetting him; she was particularly incensed by Norman Winston, who, she thought, was being disloyal to O'Neill by listening to and passing on Agnes' grievances. Once, I remember, she wrote me: 'I feel we should keep all disloyalties from Gene.'"

In mid-June O'Neill and Carlotta left for a brief motor trip through the South of France and Spain. O'Neill, triumphantly having passed his driver's test the week before in Bayonne, planned to do the driving.

"The Renault is all I hoped for it," he told Kalonyme the day before leaving, "a peach of a car—everything about it perfect. It has sure proved a Godsend to me in my present scrambled mental state."

That June the reporters renewed their efforts to corner O'Neill, for his name was again in the news. He had recently won the Pulitzer Prize—his third—for *Strange Interlude*, and now Agnes announced she would go to Reno "shortly" to institute divorce proceedings against her celebrated husband.

In a statement to the press Agnes said: "We have decided to give legal form to the separation of our lives which has existed in fact for over two years. I had attempted the experiment of giving an artist-husband the freedom he said was necessary for his dramatic success. Perhaps, from the standpoint of dramatic art and the American theatre, my decision may be a success; matrimonially it has already proved a failure.

"This illusion of freedom—so long maintained by the male sex, particularly by the artistic male—is very much an illusion. Now I know that the only way to give a man the freedom he wants is to open a door to captivity." (As it turned out, however, she did not leave for Reno until the following March.)

Among the places O'Neill and Carlotta visited during their motor trip was San Sebastián, Spain, where they attended the Grand Prix auto races. At a hotel in San Sebastián they encountered Lee Shubert and his attorney, William Klein. Shubert and Klein, piqued that a Shubert booking called *Maya* had been closed down earlier in the year by that guardian of Manhattan morality, District Attorney Banton, had, soon after, suggested that *Strange Interlude* be closed also. "Why should the district attorney close *Maya* and allow *Strange Interlude* to continue?" Klein had asked plaintively in the columns of the New York press. He had not seen it, he said, but had heard it was immoral. And Shubert, in a publication he owned called *The New York Revue*, had also asserted that *Strange Interlude* was "of a low moral tone." Banton had thereupon ordered an official censor to see *Strange Interlude* but had been stymied by the fact that the censor could not obtain a seat, since the play was solidly sold out for weeks in advance. In the San Sebastián hotel, Shubert and Klein shook hands with O'Neill cordially "as though neither had ever heard of a play called *Strange Interlude*," O'Neill later reported to a friend. "It was a funny scene."

O'Neill and Carlotta were back in Guéthary by June 21. In order to keep up his subterfuge for the benefit of reporters and acquaintances, O'Neill asked Kalonyme, who was traveling in Germany, to pick up local postcards and send them to Guéthary; O'Neill then filled in messages to friends in New York and returned the cards to Kalonyme for posting in Germany.

Kalonyme continued to be the recipient of frequent and affectionate communications from Carlotta.

"Saxe Commins visited O'Neill and Carlotta in July," Kalonyme said, "and Carlotta wrote me about what a dear person he was. She said she had discussed with Commins the difficulties of her and Gene's situation, and Commins sympathized about their problem with Agnes. Carlotta was madly in love with Gene, and seemed really to suffer over what they both felt was a betrayal of trust."

By the end of July O'Neill had grown so mistrustful that he even tried to mislead his good friend De Casseres as to his whereabouts.

"Right now I am in Paris for a few days," he wrote to De Casseres. "By the time this reaches you, I will be off again for a place still unknown even to me. . . . All's well with me and, in spite of constantly moving about Europe, the work goes on as well as ever." (Actually, he returned to Guéthary.)

O'Neill completed *Dynamo* early in September. The play did not promise well for future work in the new life he was forging. It seemed, indeed, to contain all the splenetic resentment against Woman that he was trying so hard to assure himself he did not feel—that he claimed had been utterly superseded by the love and inner tranquillity of his relationship with Carlotta. It was not the work of a man who had resolved his emotional conflicts or was "deeply at peace and happy and confident"; it was a diatribe of hatred and self-pity—an angry play by an angry man. It was also a bad play.

"[*Dynamo*] is a symbolical and factual biography of what is happening in a large section of the American (and not only American) soul right now," O'Neill told Nathan soon after it was finished. "It is really the first play of a trilogy that will dig at the roots of the sickness of today as I feel it. . . . The other two plays will be *Without Ending of Days* and *It Cannot Be Mad.*" (O'Neill subsequently abandoned the trilogy, as he did *Sea-Mother's Son,* but he later wrote a play he called *Days Without End;* he hated to throw away a title much more than he minded throwing away a play.)

The idea for *Dynamo* had come to O'Neill several years earlier, when he chanced to pass a hydroelectric plant in Stevenson, Connecticut, near his Ridgefield home. He had stopped to visit the plant and had retained a vivid image of the dynamo, "huge and black, with something of the massive female idol about it, the exciter set on the main structure like a head with blank, oblong eyes above a gross, rounded torso," which he used in the setting of the last part of the play.

As the play took shape it became the story of a boy in his late teens, the son of a didactic, overbearing minister, who revolts against the religious teachings of his childhood to embrace the religion of Electricity. Driven mad by the conflict between his lust for a girl and his desire to attain a pure, idealistic oneness with the God Electricity or, as it gradually becomes transmuted for him, the Mother-God Dynamo, the boy, Reuben Light, murders the girl and flings himself upon the dynamo, electrocuting himself. If Reuben typified the American soul, then America was a nation of dangerous schizophrenics—but quite possibly O'Neill believed that to be true.

Through the character of Reuben, O'Neill revealed his own search for the ideal love—a combination of mistress and mother, which he believed he had finally found in Carlotta. In *Dynamo* these two aspects of woman are separate and irreconcilable and their symbolism is confused. The slightly sluttish young girl, Ada Fife, represents lust, which, O'Neill seems to be saying, must be sacrificed to the Mother-God Dynamo in order for Man to find peace. At the same time Ada's mother, to whom Reuben transfers his feelings for Ada (when he is not busy worshiping Dynamo) represents a sort of maternal handmaiden of the Mother-God, being big, placid, cowlike and undemanding. She apparently represented for O'Neill also a fantasy aspect of his own mother; her dreamy trances are referred to by her husband and daughter as "dope-dreams." (In a significant comment to a friend soon after completing the play, O'Neill wrote that *Dynamo* was about "the psychological mess a boy got into because he suddenly felt that the whole world had turned against him and betrayed him into cowardice: Most of all his mother whose betrayal really smashes him.")

Of Mama Dynamo herself Reuben says, in one of the speeches O'Neill referred to as "Interludian asides": "It's like a great dark idol with eyes that see you without seeing you—and below it is like a body . . . round like a woman's—as if it had breasts—but not like a girl—not like Ada—no, like a woman—like her mother—or mine—a great, dark mother!—that's what a dynamo is!—that's what life is!"

There is also an indication in *Dynamo*, of O'Neill's preoccupation with his sea-mother theme (which he had foreshadowed long before in *The Hairy Ape*—"men that was sons of the sea as if 'twas the mother that bore them"); "You're like her—Dynamo—the Great Mother—big and warm—" Reuben tells Ada's mother. "But I've got to finish telling you all I've come to know about her—how all things end up in her! Did I tell you that our blood plasm is the same right now as the sea was when life came out of it? We've got the sea in our blood still! It's what makes our hearts live! And it's the sea . . . made that river that drives the turbines that drive Dynamo! The sea makes her heart beat, too!"

All the characters in *Dynamo* are unlovely and unlovable; none evokes the slightest pity from the reader, though each in turn (with the exception of Mrs. Fife) articulates at great length his or her self-pitying story. Each feels, as O'Neill himself was feeling, outrageously betrayed in one way or another. O'Neill's fury at Agnes ("I don't want yellow friends!") is petulantly echoed in the play's dialogue. "Oh, if you'd only make a prize jackass of that yellow Nancy son of his!" says Ramsay Fife, speaking of Reuben to his daughter. "He's yellow!" says Reuben of his father. "You're a yellow rat!" says Ada to Reuben—and so forth.

"I was going through a lot of trouble in family matters when I was writing [*Dynamo*]," O'Neill later conceded to George Jean Nathan. But he did not concur in Nathan's opinion that the play was "close to caricature."

"I thoroughly disagree with you about the play," he said. "It is *not* far, far below me, I'm sure of that! Wait and see! It will come into its own some day."

O'Neill sent copies of *Dynamo* off to the Theatre Guild the first week in September, along with sketches of the sets and elaborate instructions and explanations for the production, in case the Guild wanted to do it, of which O'Neill was not at all certain. (He asked for quick decision by cable.) The instructions to the stage designer (a job that was to fall to Lee Simonson) were particularly detailed and incorporated a good deal of his general creative philosophy.

He wanted to stress the importance, he said, of starting early in rehearsals to get the sound effects of thunder, water flowing over the dam, and the hum of the generator "exactly right." These were not incidental noises but significant dramatic overtones, he went on, and his preoccupation with sound effects had a valid reason. A critic had once observed, he said, that the difference between O'Neill's plays and other contemporary work was that O'Neill always wrote "primarily by ear for the ear," that most of his plays, "even down to the rhythm of the dialogue," were constructed along the lines of a musical composition.

"This hits the nail on the head," said O'Neill. "It is not that I consciously strive after this but that, willy-nilly, my stuff takes that form. (. . . Certainly I believe it to be a great virtue, although it is the principal reason why I have been blamed for useless repetitions, which to me were significant recurrences of theme.) But the point here is that I have always used sound in plays as a structural part of them. Tried to use, I mean—for I've never got what the script called for (even in *Jones*), not because what

I specified couldn't be done, but because I was never able to overcome the slip-shod, old-fashioned disregard of our modern theatre for what ought to be one of its superior opportunities (contrasted with the medium of the novel, for example) in expressing the essential rhythm of our lives today."

Explaining the script to Langner, O'Neill said the dialogue was "Interludian" but that the play "deals with more direct, less cerebral people."

O'Neill had no intention of returning to America for the production of *Dynamo*, in the event the Guild accepted it. He and Carlotta had decided in August that the time had come for their big trip.

From Paris on September 14 he sent Richard Madden, his agent, a long list of final instructions:

"This will probably be my last word to you for some time, as I'm sailing for the Far East—India and way stations on to China—the first week in October." He told Madden he had sent two scripts of *Dynamo* to the Guild and was mailing one to him.

"I've also sent the Guild all the instructions, warnings, advice, etc., regarding the production I thought necessary. . . . It only remains now for them to accept it. Perhaps they won't. I don't know. It's a drastic type of play and you never can tell what reactions you're going to get from a committee of six people. However, I'm hoping."

"I can't tell you how much this trip to the East means to me," he added. "It's been the dream of my life to live there for a while and absorb a bit of background. It's going to be infinitely valuable to me in its bearing upon my future work. So I really feel grateful to my domestic upset for dragging on so miserably and making it impossible for me to return to New York, for otherwise my author's conscience would force me to come back for rehearsals." Half of the time that he would be gone, he continued, would be devoted to hard work in "some sort of semi-permanent place."

His "domestic broil," he said, was dragging on. Agnes had finally realized that she and O'Neill should not be represented by the same lawyer, and she had engaged her own. O'Neill believed that Agnes' lawyer was "stirring up every antagonism we'd agreed to forget."

"You know I'm no tightwad, especially where my children are concerned," O'Neill wrote, "but I'll be damned if I'll be 'taken.' . . . So I have to battle, willy-nilly. These guys [the lawyers] treat me as if I'd had an *Interlude* back of me every year in the past and would have every year in the future. The success of that opus has certainly given me an opulent rep!"

A day later O'Neill wrote a parting letter to De Casseres in which he reiterated his conviction that *Dynamo* was one of his best plays, and that it would be the first of a trilogy whose overall title might be *God is Dead! Long Live—What?*

He went on to describe what he called his "grand major opus" (*Sea-Mother's Son*), about which, he said, he was doing much thinking, and which would take years to complete—"years with probably a play or two sandwiched in to change the subject a bit. . . . It's growing and growing in me and it fills me with a grand enthusiasm. It will have scope enough to contain all of life I have the guts to grasp and make my own. And it will not be like anything ever written before in its form and intensity. . . . It will have ten or more 'Interludes' in it, each deeper and more powerful than 'S.I.' and yet it will all be a unity. Believe me, Ben, I'm going to bullseye a star with that job or go mad in the attempt. . . ."

He felt himself supported by love and peace, he added. "I won't have to do the whole thing of living, dreaming and working all by my own effort all the time any longer. I'll have more strength to give to my job. It's grand! I'm very happy!"

But he indicated that his happiness was marred by hostility toward Agnes a week later when, from Guéthary, where he had gone to pack for his trip, he wrote a venomous five-page letter to Kenneth Macgowan. He sounded quite a lot like his father, as he protested the financial inroads Agnes was trying to make in order to ensure adequate support for O'Neill's own children. She was asking for double the amount of money for Shane and Oona, each, as he had given Eugene's mother for Eugene's support, he told Macgowan, and he had set detectives to work digging up clues about Agnes' past, in order to have something to hold over her head and "get her off her revengeful high horse." He went into detail for two pages about what he thought the detectives might find. "By God, you know, it is funny!" he wound up. "I grin—when I'm not boiling with rage!"

Forgetfully discounting the periods of ardent love he had spent with Agnes, and the impassioned love letters he had written to her over the years, O'Neill added that he "wouldn't have stayed married to her a year" if he had not "had alcohol to close my eyes . . . alcohol and work, which would account for 95% of the time."

The hatred he formed for Agnes was to have a scarring effect on his relationship with Shane and Oona. His subsequent neglect of them—a thing that even his closest and most worshipful friends have found it difficult to understand or pardon—sprang from this hatred. He regarded himself as duped and cheated, and he planned, quite deliberately, to be revenged.

"Believe me, Kenneth," he wrote, "once I'm free of that baby I'm going to arrange my life and affairs so I'll make her pay for this!" Obviously he meant he would "make her pay" through the children.

But, again, he tried to convince himself—and Macgowan—that the violence of his anger was negligible.

". . . while I'm worried and enraged by this, it doesn't touch me inside and I'm not hurt by it," he said. ". . . she's too dead, and I've too much real love inside me to protect me. . . . But I did hope she'd get started on a divorce before I embarked so I could sail with an entirely free mind. . . ."

"I'll send you cards and things from the East and let you know how we are—and where. I'm in the pink physically—but tired of nerve and a bit spiritually nauseated . . ."

On October 4 Langner cabled O'Neill: "Dynamo accepted with enthusiasm." A day later O'Neill and Carlotta sailed from Marseilles. Aboard ship O'Neill acknowledged Langner's cable with a postcard:

"This is written three days out from Marseilles on a balmy Mediterranean. Your cable was delivered just as I sailed and did much by way of a cheery bon voyage. I feel safe about Dynamo now and am already starting preliminary work on the next one. This voyage is going to mean a lot to me. I'll write a letter as soon as I'm settled in Hong Kong or wherever it is to be."

Despite his high hopes, O'Neill ultimately found no peace or satisfaction in the East. And his contemplated journey of a year lasted only four months. During the early part of the voyage, however, he was in jubilant spirits. "Grand trip!" he exclaimed to Madden in a card he wrote on the Indian Ocean, enroute to Ceylon. And when he landed in Saigon at the end of October, after stopping in Singapore, he sent a card to De Casseres showing an opium-smoking native: "I've never fallen for this brand of Nirvana, but this guy looks as if he couldn't be altogether wrong! I'm staying in Saigon awhile—most interesting place so far." Early in November he reached Hong Kong, which he found dull. He wrote from there to Langner, still full of big plans for future travel:

"Have decided not to stay here. Not very interesting and climate hot now and damp and enervating. No place to work. So, on to Shanghai, Kobe and Yokohama. Will probably settle in Japan."

By mid-November he was in Shanghai; it was as far east as he got. O'Neill had with him his copy of *Thus Spake Zarathustra*; during the trip he copied into a notebook the following Nietzsche quotation:

"I am a wanderer and a mountain climber," said he unto his heart. "I like not the plains, and it seemeth I cannot long sit still.

"And whatever may become my fate and experience—a wandering and a mountain climbing will be part of it. In the end one experienceth nothing but one's self."

O'Neill was experiencing himself and not enjoying it; he was suffering from a bad case of guilt. The first glow of his rapturous love for Carlotta had worn off, he was not writing, and he had too much time to think about the way in which he had walked out on his children. As always when he was not releasing the pent-up storms of his nature in creative work he had to explode into physical action. Unchastened, after all, by his disastrous fall off the wagon in Guéthary, O'Neill began drinking again in Shanghai. This time he quarreled with Carlotta. And to O'Neill, when drunk, a quarrel did not mean merely angry words; it meant violent accusations, followed by maudlin remorse and, eventually, physical and mental collapse.

A day or two after reaching Shanghai, and getting settled in his hotel, O'Neill was recognized by an acquaintance of the early Province-town Players days, who had become a reporter on a British morning newspaper. He was a twenty-eight-year-old Canadian named Alfred Batson. Batson, not connected with the Provincetown in any official capacity, had, like other aspiring intellectuals of the day, hung around the theatre and occasionally exchanged a few words with O'Neill.

"I was walking past the Palace Hotel one morning at the corner of Nanking Road and the Bund," Batson recalled, "when I saw a tall man in front of me. I was sure it was O'Neill, and with him was a beautiful woman. Shanghai was like a small town as far as the foreign population went in those days—less than two thousand—and any foreigner stuck out like a sore thumb. I walked up to the man, looked at him, and said, 'It is!'"

"What are you doing here, Red?" asked O'Neill. "How are you?"

Batson explained that he was working for the *North China Daily News*, which had 7,500 readers from Yokohama to Singapore.

"Does the paper amount to anything?" asked O'Neill, immediately sensing danger.

"It's been here since 1860, and it's British, and if we say today is Sunday, our readers believe us, even if it's really Monday," replied Batson.

O'Neill implored him to keep his name out of the paper. Batson willingly agreed, explaining that as far as his editor was concerned, O'Neill's presence in Shanghai would mean very little. O'Neill, reassured, introduced Batson to Carlotta, told him where he was staying, and asked him to keep in touch.

During the next couple of days Batson accompanied O'Neill on sightseeing tours. "He loved to spend time at the Police Museum," Batson said, "where they had an exotic display of torture items confiscated from the Chinese. I introduced Gene to the chief of detectives, an Englishman named George Gilbert, who took us on a tour of the exhibits. Several of them particularly fascinated him—one called 'Death of the 1,000 Cuts,' which illustrated the way the police, in the old days, would wrap a victim in wire, and slice off bits of flesh from between the wires to get him to confess; another involved the victim's being fastened to a wall, which had a hollowed-out niche backed by chicken wire; the victim's stomach would be placed over the niche, a rat would be placed *in* the niche, and then sticks of fire would be poked at the rat through the chicken wire, leaving only one way for the rat to go."

One morning O'Neill called Batson and asked him to come over to his hotel for breakfast.

"When I got there," Batson said, "he was already drunk. He said Carlotta was packing her trunk."

Batson had to go to work, but later in the day O'Neill telephoned him again. As soon as he was able Batson returned to the hotel, and O'Neill announced that Carlotta had left him.

"He was very drunk by this time and told me a rambling story about her departure. They had argued, he explained, because he had refused to leave his room, where he was quietly and happily getting plastered. O'Neill said he had become jealous—he added he now realized there had been no basis for his jealousy—because Carlotta, requiring an escort, had asked the respectable, married, assistant hotel manager, a Swiss, to be her guide on a sightseeing expedition. 'I hit her when she got back,' he told me, morosely."

"Let's go out and see some Chinese people," O'Neill suddenly suggested to Batson. "You go get dressed, and call for me at ten o'clock."

Batson led him to a taxi dance hall operated by an American named Jimmy James. The girls were Chinese, and O'Neill was greatly taken by their delicate beauty. O'Neill and Batson ordered champagne and watched the proceedings from a table. After a while O'Neill began feeling sorry for the girls who weren't chosen to dance and bought each of them a bottle of champagne.

A little later O'Neill was astonished and delighted to find that the men's room attendant was a boy with a gold ring in his ear.

"Why do you work?" he mumbled to the uncomprehending attendant, who mumbled something back in Chinese dialect.

"That's right," said O'Neill. "To hell with Capitalists!" He took out a roll of bills, and shoved it into the boy's hand. Batson quickly retrieved it, peeled off one bill for the boy, and stuffed the rest back into O'Neill's pocket. They stayed in the dance hall, drinking, until two in the morning. When they left O'Neill got no farther than a few feet, when he sat down on the curb and began to weep.

"D'you know," he told Batson maudlinly, "I'll make Carlotta a helluva husband."

"Why?" inquired Batson, who had begun his drinking at least twenty-four hours later than O'Neill and was soberer. O'Neill informed Batson he had been "a son of a bitch" to Agnes, and a terrible father, and a long string of other self-recriminatory things.

"Across the street from where we were sitting," Batson recalled, "was the police station. There was a change of shift going on, and the traffic police, who were generally Indians—tall, bearded, turbaned men in dark-blue coats with silver buttons, came over and listened to Gene. They started beating their chests and laughing.

"I finally managed to get Gene back to his hotel. He was in terrible shape by this time, and I was scared. Carlotta was gone, of course, and I didn't know what to do with him. He was shaking and sweating. It was almost four in the morning. I called for a doctor—a Dr. Alexander Renner —and he came up and gave Gene something to quiet him. He said Gene would need care and rest and that he'd arrange to get him a room in the British hospital. As soon as I saw that Gene would be taken care of, I left.

"The next day I went to visit him at the Country Hospital on Great Western Road. He had a nice room, overlooking some greenery. He seemed better. After we'd talked for a while, he asked me to go out and get him a pint of liquor, which I refused to do.

"A couple of days later I went again. I was told, at the reception desk, that Gene had another visitor, and I was asked to wait. After waiting a while, I left. The next day the same thing happened, and I asked the girl at the reception desk if Gene's visitor was a beautiful woman. I was told yes, and figured it was Carlotta. I didn't go back, and didn't see Gene again, ever." (Soon after, however, he received a gift from O'Neill; it was a cigarette case, engraved: "To Alfred Batson, from 133 Macdougal Street to Shanghai. Gene O'Neill, 1928.")

Carlotta had, indeed, located her penitent O'Neill, and was visiting him and sending him messages. O'Neill answered one of her notes (which he dispatched from the hospital by coolie) asking God to bless her, and assuring her of his love, and begging her forgiveness.

"I'll be a good 'un in future—do my damndest best to!" he added.

"A million kisses, Blessed!"

While O'Neill's presence in Shanghai as a sober tourist held no interest for Batson's editor, his presence as a sick man in a hospital did. Arriving at what seemed to him a satisfactory compromise between his friendship for O'Neill and his loyalty to his paper, Batson wrote a quiet story announcing O'Neill's arrival in Shanghai, and saying that he was "recuperating . . . from a severe indisposition contracted recently in Singapore by under-estimating the force of the sun's rays while bathing. . . . While in Shanghai he is anxious to live quietly and to regain his health."

"I'll never forget my experience in the hospital [at Shanghai]," O'Neill later wrote Joseph Wood Krutch, "teetering on the verge of a nervous breakdown and lying awake nights listening to the night target practice of a Welsh regiment whose garrison was two blocks away, and to the beating of Chinese gongs keeping the devils away from a birth or a bride or a corpse or something devils like! It nearly had me climbing the walls of my room and gibbering a bit."

Within a week representatives of American newspapers were scouring Shanghai in force. For two weeks—from December 10 through December 24—reporters played the game of "Who's Seen O'Neill?"

On December 10 *The New York Times* (via the Associated Press) reported that O'Neill was confined to his bed in Shanghai and quoted Dr. Renner as saying his illness was "a slight nervous breakdown and bronchitis . . . the result of overwork and the strain of travel." On December 11 *The Times* reported that O'Neill's attorney, Harry Weinberger, had received a cable informing him that O'Neill "was in perfect health; that, while he had a little touch of influenza requiring a few days in a hospital, he was now out and there was nothing serious." On December 13 *The Times* (via special cable from its correspondent in Shanghai) revealed that O'Neill was planning to sail for Honolulu shortly and spend the winter there. *The Times* added that the dramatist was "extremely reticent and inclined to view the public's interest in his health with disfavor."

On December 14, this time in a full-column story, *The Times* reported O'Neill as having "vanished."

"The strange case of Eugene O'Neill took another angle today," the story ran, "when it became known that the American playwright, who has been convalescing in a hospital and hotels here for the last fortnight, arose from his sick bed yesterday and departed from the Astor House." O'Neill's disappearance had become known after Dr. Renner made public the contents of a letter he had received from O'Neill.

"I came to China seeking peace and quiet," O'Neill had written, "but I have found more snoops and gossips per square inch than in any New England town of 1,000 inhabitants. This does not apply to American newspaper correspondents, who have been most decent, carrying out their duties in a most gentlemanly manner.

"I am going to Honolulu and then, perhaps, to Tahiti, if Honolulu adopts the attitude that I am a politician whose life must be public. At any rate, I will find peace and solitude if I have to go to the North Pole.

"My bronchitis cough is gone, and my nerves are returning to normal and I expect to be in the pink of condition in the shortest time."

"The hotels throughout the city deny knowledge of Mr. O'Neill's whereabouts," continued *The Times*. "The steamship companies say they know of no such person sailing on their liners or having made reservations. Dr. Renner . . . professes complete ignorance of the playwright's movements."

The *Times* man had picked up the misinformation that O'Neill was traveling with "his secretary, Mrs. Tuwe Drew, a Swedish masseuse, who described herself as also a graduate physician." (Actually, Mrs. Drew was Carlotta's maid and her name got into the newspaper stories when, at O'Neill's request, she assumed the role of his representative and tried to throw reporters off O'Neill's and Carlotta's track. As O'Neill later explained to Kalonyme, "in spite of the fact that Mrs. Drew was shocked to death, she presented a stolid front and lied like a major and a good scout.") O'Neill's efforts to travel "virtually incognito," added *The Times,* had gained him "far more publicity than ordinarily is accorded here to anyone, even of his prominence." The Associated Press speculated that O'Neill might have boarded an obscure Japanese steamer for Japan and quoted Dr. Renner as scoffing at the idea "that the playwright possibly was remaining in hiding in Shanghai." Other papers carried rumors that O'Neill might have been done in by bandits.

O'Neill and Carlotta had slipped out of Shanghai on the steamer *Coblenz* and docked at Manila on December 18. O'Neill was disguised as a minister and he was entered upon the steamer's passenger list as the Rev. William O'Brien. When he was confronted by a Filipino newspaperman who had his picture, however, O'Neill admitted he was the playwright.

On the following day, the Associated Press sent out word that O'Neill had chosen to remain aboard the ship, and had spent "a sleepless night, due to the heat and noise of loading cargo," adding, "he looked haggard today." On the same day the *Times* Manila man cornered him also and stamped him as, irrefutably, O'Neill. He was "nervous and trembly," reported *The Times* and quoted O'Neill as saying that since the tropics were no good for him he was proceeding to Europe for complete rest.

The New York *Herald Tribune* was moved, on December 22, to include an editorial about the shenanigans in Shanghai and Manila:

"One sympathized with Eugene O'Neill the other day when reports came that he had fled all the way to Shanghai to find solitude and had not found it. He has fled now to parts unknown in the hope still of finding it. . . .

"Everyone knows . . . how the integrity of one's own spirit is corrupted by an environment in which gossip and rumor confuse one's own being or entangle it needlessly with the confusions of other people. . . ."

Lawrence Langner, anxious about O'Neill's health and about tabloid speculations over his "death" and "kidnaping," had cabled him at Shanghai, and the cable caught up with O'Neill when the *Coblenz* touched at Hong Kong. O'Neill answered on December 24 from Singapore: ". . . Feel well now. Much idiotic publicity Shanghai, Manila. My discovery, disappearance, kidnaped, bandits, death, etc. Merry Christmas to all."

Arthur McGinley, too, had sent an anxious cable and received the following reply: "News of my death premature. Now I'm in a class with Mark Twain."

O'Neill and Carlotta were back in France by late January, 1929. They rented another house, the Villa Les Mimosas in Cap d'Ail. At last O'Neill could settle down to write again. Despite the unpleasantness of the final weeks of his voyage and the curtailment of his round-the-world trip, he seemed determined to count the journey a success—or at least to convey the impression to his friends that it had been a success; he tried to suppress the drinking episode, discussing his illness with all his friends but omitting to mention his lapse from sobriety. (The Chinese writer and artist, Mai-mai Sze, who later became a friend of the O'Neills, and often talked about China with them, observed with amusement, "Gene and Carlotta traveled to the East like a pair of tourists." Saxe Commins, who visited them in France soon after their return, carried snapshots home with him showing O'Neill and Carlotta posing in Chinese costumes they had bought in Shanghai.)

"Had a wonderful trip East and got a lot out of it in spite of snooping reporters and severe illness," O'Neill informed Horace Liveright on January 29. In a later letter to Liveright—and in almost identical letters to Nathan, De Casseres and Komroff—he was more expansive: "I feel as if a million impressions had been jammed into my brain, and that they weren't half digested yet and it would be some time before they would be. . . . But I couldn't work out there."

At Cap d'Ail O'Neill tried to begin work on a play but he had difficulty deciding which of several projects to go ahead with—*Sea-Mother's Son,* or the second play in the *Dynamo* trilogy, or a new play on the Electra theme (for which he had been making notes since 1924). His precise reasons for dropping *Sea-Mother's Son* as he then conceived it may never be known, but it was the reaction to the production of *Dynamo* in New York that finally helped him decide to abandon the other two plays of the projected trilogy.

Dynamo opened at the Martin Beck on February 11. "Wish I could be with you," O'Neill cabled the Guild's Theresa Helburn, "but domestic deadlock unchanged and will never return States until Carlotta and I are married."

Philip Moeller directed, and Dudley Digges, Helen Westley and Glenn Anders were among the members of the cast. According to Lawrence Langner, "It was diffused in effect, and the meaning was difficult for the audience to understand. We greatly missed Gene at rehearsals for clarification and cutting, and had to do the best we could."

Lee Simonson had taken great pains to follow O'Neill's suggestions for the physical production, and after the play failed, he wrote in his book *The Stage Is Set:*

"A designer is more truly creative when he fails with the poet, as I did with O'Neill in *Dynamo,* than when he succeeds with the playwright who is nothing more than an observer. I have never shared more directly the excitement, the adventure, and the power of the modern theatre than in following the trail of O'Neill's mind from a power-house on a Connecticut river to the play that it inspired."

As for the critics, at least one of them voiced a positive opinion.

"Writing on the most essential theme of modern life, Mr. O'Neill has strength and breadth, and a lashing, poetic fury," said Brooks Atkinson.

Percy Hammond was several degrees less favorable: "Mr. O'Neill makes 'Dynamo' an astonishing play. It is sometimes ludicrous, frequently raving, often encumbered with laborious 'interludisms,' and generally an entertainment for the rarer playgoer."

On the *Sun,* replacing Gilbert Gabriel, Richard Lockridge took an even less charitable view when he wrote that the play "mirrors not only the obscurities of its theme, but further and perhaps more lamentably, the uncertainty with which its author has formulated his own thoughts in regard to it."

St. John Ervine, who had been summoned to the *World* from London to replace Alexander Woollcott after the latter's resignation (much to the disgust of Dudley Nichols, who had thought *he* would get the job, and who resigned from the *World* shortly thereafter), was the hardest of all on the play:

"Each new piece that Mr. O'Neill produces leaves the poet in him more attenuated than before. In a little while, unless a miracle is performed, the poet will perish . . . mainly he prefers to be sour and incoherent and extraordinarily dismal . . .

"Must Mr. O'Neill forget that he was once a poet? Is he obliged to go on with this Greenwich Village sentimental cynicism? . . . His pathetic efforts to be an intellectual and to think deeply about man's destiny have so far landed him only in a bog in which he flounders helplessly and oftentimes ludicrously."

Robert Benchley, on *The New Yorker,* disliked *Dynamo* very much indeed, and one of the magazine's contributors, Arthur Guiterman, was inspired to submit a four-line poem: "Eeny, meeny Mynamo/ I have been to 'Dynamo'/ All except the girl in red/ it was worse'n what you said!"

The "girl in red" was Claudette Colbert, who played the role of the seductive flapper, Ada Fife, and whose legs attracted considerable attention. The critics were in almost unanimous agreement about her charms and talent, but O'Neill believed that her legs had distracted audiences from concentrating on the deeper meaning of the play.

"Henceforth," O'Neill later told Nathan, "I myself cast not only actresses, but legs!"

It was obvious, within a week or two after its opening, that *Dynamo* was doomed to failure. (After seing it Noël Coward called it "A womb with a view.")

O'Neill continued to defend it for a while, but his defense (painstakingly documented in letters to friends) grew weaker and weaker.

"Perhaps when you saw *Dynamo* on the stage," he wrote to Nathan a few days after the opening, "you got a new light on it. I hope so. In rereading it lately it seemed so essentially a thing that must be seen and heard in a theatre in order to appreciate its true value. It also seemed badly in need of cutting."

And a week after the opening he wrote to Liveright:

"I know that the majority of the notices were antagonistic but this is what I have always expected—about the same break in the press that I got on *Brown* and *Desire.* Everyone seems to think now that these two plays got a very good press but the facts are that the majority vote was against them, very much so. And I knew what to expect—or rather I didn't give enough of a damn even to give it a thought—when tackling a subject that was bound to rub so many folk the wrong way. We'll wait and see what the thirty thousand Guild subscribers will have to say about it. Theirs is the verdict of on or off, at least." (The verdict was off; the play closed after fifty performances.)

To Madden, on February 28, he confided:

"The notices of *Dynamo* did not seem so disappointing to me, considering the nature of the play. . . . As you know from experience, there has always been this division of opinion about my plays—and always will be, I hope, for it is a sign of real life and guts. *Strange Interlude* was a miraculous exception which won't happen again. . . ."

To De Casseres, on March 12, O'Neill confessed that he felt "very guilty toward the play" because he had let it out of his hands much too soon—before he had a chance to get the right perspective on it.

"Also . . . . I had no right to let it go without being there, no matter how good the Guild performance seemed. No one knows what I see in my stuff during rehearsals, or the changes I suggest or veto, because I have never been given any credit for it, but believe me no play of mine ever failed to gain immeasurably from my being around. Without handing myself any bouquets, I think I've a better theatrical eye and ear than most in the game. . . .

"I have your letter written after you read the play and you call it 'a masterpiece' up to the third act. . . . And you know as well as I do that every play that reads well ought to act well, unless it's a purely literary play and therefore not really a play. This is a truism as axiomatic as the stupidity of Heywood Broun." (Broun, who disliked O'Neill's more recent plays, had commented some time before: "The truth of the matter is that O'Neill has no message. His philosophy of life is that of a saturnine sophomore. With the aid of an extraordinary mastery of dramatic technique he has managed to make a wholly immature point of view seem profundity itself to a vast camp of followers.")

A little later O'Neill backed down somewhat.

"Well, I guess you're right!" he admitted to De Casseres. "I've been sweating over the proofs of *Dynamo* and getting more and more dissatisfied."

After the play had closed, O'Neill told Langner he was resigned to its failure.

"I blundered horribly in shooting off my mouth about a trilogy and the meaning of it," he said. "I didn't mean what is usually meant by trilogy, of course, and I didn't mean 'message,' 'solution' or anything definite. But it gave them all a clue as to how they should misinterpret—and, as they were gunning for my next play, they seized on it eagerly. My own fault, though! . . .

"When I read it over—after settling here—too late—I was appalled by its raggedness and, in the third part, vagueness and complicatedness. It was in no shape for production."

As late as May, 1929, O'Neill told a friend:

"*Dynamo* doesn't count. . . . It was written at a time when I shouldn't have written anything. The whole [Agnes situation] was hounding me by every mail. I had to drive it out of my head each day before I could write. I was in a continual inward state of bitter fury and resentment. I drove myself to write because I felt it was time I turned out another play. Of course, I was blind to this at the time . . . I made every fool mistake possible in the *Dynamo* affair. My brains were woolly with hatred."

By July he had turned almost full circle and he informed Krutch:

"I wish I'd never written it, really—and yet I feel it has its justified place in my work's development. A puzzle. What disappoints me in it is that it marks a standing still, if not a backward move. It wasn't worth my writing and so it never called forth my best. But a good lesson for me! Henceforth unless I've got a theme that demands I step a rung higher to do it, I'm going to mark time and play the country gent until such a theme comes."

And, finally, to Moeller he declared: "I've had plenty of flops before without it bothering me a whit. This time I flopped in my own eyes and I still kick myself now and then at the thought. Maybe it's good medicine at that. Here's to the next."

Still unsettled about a new project and the state of his domestic future, O'Neill continued to complain to his friends about Agnes and her "delaying tactics" until well into the spring of 1929.

The nasty weather that greeted his return to the South of France did not help his frame of mind. It was cold and snowy during February and O'Neill looked longingly at the Mediterranean under his window, praying for bathing weather. At length he received word that Agnes had met with his lawyer, consented to sign a formal separation agreement, and planned to leave for Reno.

"When that is gone through we'll be able to have a little peace," O'Neill wrote to Nathan on February 14. "We've sure earned it."

The waiting, he now revealed, was no longer caused by financial quarrels—the money end of it had already been settled. The delay, he told Nathan, was based on Agnes' initial reluctance to accept a proviso, stipulating that she should write no articles about O'Neill or about their married life.

If he and Carlotta, he added, did not have to worry about protecting children from scandal, it would be easy to come out into the open and "tell everyone to learn to like it or go to hell!" The whole thing, he said, had been a hard test of his and Carlotta's relationship and had done a lot for them, for which they were both "grateful."

Two days later New York newspapers carried the announcement that the Eugene O'Neills had "agreed to separate." The *American* gave prominent space to the story; some of the "facts" were slightly awry:

"Mrs. Agnes Boulton O'Neill," the story said, "has accepted the terms of a separation agreement with her husband, by which each agrees 'to live as though unmarried.' Under a separate 'gentleman's agreement,' not included in the formal contract, she will sue for divorce in Reno, Italy or Mexico. . . .

"Simultaneously with Mrs. O'Neill's acceptance of the agreement . . . there came word from the Orient, where O'Neill was last reported, that the friendship of the playwright and Carlotta Monterey, actress, was near an end.

"The brunette stage beauty is planning to return to this country soon, according to a friend of Mrs. O'Neill. . . ." (A few days earlier the *Herald Tribune* had quoted a letter from O'Neill to a friend announcing that he planned to marry Carlotta.)

"It was learned yesterday that efforts by O'Neill and his lawyer, Harry Weinberger . . . to compel her to continue the use of Agnes Boulton as her pen name were unsuccessful. Mrs. O'Neill covenants, however, not to exploit her marital relations with O'Neill either in interviews, memoirs or autobiography. . . ." (Another newspaper quoted Agnes as saying: "It was unnecessary even to include that provision. Mr. O'Neill must think he has a corner on fame.")

The *American* also reported that in a letter O'Neill wrote "he advised his wife she never would 'amount to a damn so long as you depend on me.' He closed with the admonition: 'Get to work!'"

The newspaper added that the agreement would be sent by Weinberger to O'Neill for his signature within a day or two.

The document duly reached O'Neill in France, and he signed and returned it. But Agnes had still not left for Reno as late as March 12.

"When will I return [to America]?" O'Neill asked De Casseres on that date. "Ask my wife! As soon as she deigns to grant me my liberty and I can marry again. . . . Ask Bio to try concentrating on my hand. I will hold it out and imagine her looking at it at eleven-thirty P.M. on April 1st (I pick that date because it's easy to remember). That will be six-thirty P.M. in New York. Are you set? I want to know when that peace is coming she promised me! Believe me, I can do with it!"

The tension of their situation had caused an argument between O'Neill and Carlotta, almost as bitter as the one in Shanghai. Again filled with remorse, O'Neill wrote her a long and anguished apology:

"I am drowned in despair that dissension should have again sprung up between us. And I am so bewildered by this ugly and mad thing, so appalled by its utter insanity, that I feel lost, defeated and done for. Why? Why? Why, in God's name! I love you! With all my soul and body I love you—with all the strength of my spirit! There is nothing I would not do to make you happy; and I have tried so hard to do so. . . .

"I love you! I love you! You are my life and everything! And you love me! And everything else is a lie! And we are such God damned fools to torture each other so over the other things that have no meaning!"

O'Neill had been in deadly earnest about his petition to Bio De Casseres. A few days after patching up his quarrel with Carlotta he wrote to De Casseres again:

"Tell Bio I yearn to know her reactions on April 1st. I'll be terribly interested to hear about it."

On April 1, at the specified hour, Mrs. De Casseres concentrated. It came to her that July was the month when O'Neill's problems would be solved and he would find peace. She wrote O'Neill at once, telling him what she had learned and advising him to curb his impatience. (Agnes had left for Reno by the end of March, to begin the required period of residence, a fact of which Mrs. De Casseres may or may not have been aware.) For the next three months she waited eagerly for news from O'Neill and watched the papers for word of the divorce proceedings.

O'Neill answered Mrs. De Casseres on May 10:

"Your letter with its benign prophecy was most welcome and helped much to encourage me, and it seems to me, in the light of the gradual clearing up of my domestic embroilment, and the plans I have made for my future, that you will just about hit the facts on the head as to time and the relief and peace that will then be mine. . . . You will remember you said that last night [in New York] that not until I was 41 would the new era begin." (O'Neill was five months away from his forty-first birthday.)

He added that he thought it would be at least then before all his affairs were "smoothed out 'for keeps' and my inner self freed from the dead, consciously alive in the new, liberated and reborn."

O'Neill had been so much encouraged by Bio De Casseres' prediction (and by Agnes' departure for Reno) that he began looking, with Carlotta, for a permanent residence. They had decided to stay in Europe for the next few years instead of going, as they had once planned, to California. During April they house-hunted in Touraine ("In the beautiful valley of the Loire," as O'Neill put it, "the land of Rabelais and Balzac"), and by May they had found what they wanted—nothing less than a forty-five-room château, called Le Plessis, at Saint-Antoine-du-Rocher. In every way it was about as far as O'Neill could get from Monte Cristo Cottage on Pequot Avenue; neither Brook Farm nor Spithead had come anywhere near this Continental grandeur. Carlotta set about making their new quarters comfortable and engaging a corps of servants to run the castle.

"Gene had never lived in a château," Carlotta later reminisced (loftily relegating her husband-to-be to the ranks of some odd minority group). "He thought the idea of living in a château very chichi and putting on airs. But I said, No, I will show you how simple châteaux are. I wanted him to see that people could live graciously and comfortably without all sorts of modern conveniences. And we rented one for three years. It was a lovely old place with beautiful towers and marble floors. No electric lights, no heat, everything simple. No bathroom. We had forty-five rooms, so I took one bedroom and made it into a bath. And Gene saw, even though he was a rather tough Irishman, that you could really be polite and live in a charming place and you didn't have to be ridiculous. I made him very comfortable. I bought him a long bed, and it was the first time in his life he was able to sleep stretched out; I thought it was disgraceful that he'd never had a proper bed before."

O'Neill blended into the château as graciously as Carlotta could have wished him to. He was delighted with the surrounding woods and farmland, with the livestock (supervised by the proprietors), and with the elegant furniture and tapestries of the rooms. He was almost equally delighted with the proprietors themselves—three sisters, one of whom was a vicomtesse and one a marquise. O'Neill confided to a friend that he thought the sisters were "really quite pleased" to have a writer for a tenant. They had all gone out and bought copies of *Strange Interlude* and, as O'Neill liked to remark, had "survived it without turning a hair, although confessing they had their own opinion of a woman like Nina."

"We have a really beautiful place," O'Neill wrote to Joseph Wood Krutch on June 11, inviting him to visit, "out of the track of tourists in real French Touraine country, with a home with all sorts of room, grand old furniture, acres and acres of farmlands and woods, privacy and nature and peace to the Nth degree! I hope you are tempted by these glowing details! I admit I am extravagantly enthusiastic about it. I feel as if I'd at last come home—the sort of home I've always craved for and couldn't have achieved in our U.S.—and I expect to be happy here as

[693]

never before and to accomplish real work. All my turmoils are at last seeping down to bedrock and definite peace is in sight."

Already an ardent Francophile, he added that his new home was about ten "kilometers" from Tours. (His Francophilia, however, did not extend to his spelling; not long after, he wrote, the plural of château as "châteaus.") He thought he would not return to the United States "for years." And, as another signpost on the new road he was traveling, he cautioned Krutch to keep his address confidential, because "there are so many people I don't want to see and they are always the ones who drop in without ceremony."

In New York, Bio De Casseres was still anxiously watching the newspapers every day, hoping that her prediction of happiness for O'Neill in July would come true. On July 2 she was rewarded with newspaper stories from Reno announcing that Agnes O'Neill had filed suit for divorce the day before. The formal charge was desertion. According to several New York newspapers, Agnes, in her complaint, alleged that her husband had deserted her and had "continued to remain away from her against her wishes and without her consent." The agreement reached between O'Neill and Agnes stipulated that she was to receive one-third of his net income unless it exceeded $10,000 a year and that O'Neill would pay $2,400 a year for the support of Shane and Oona until they became of age or married. The Ridgefield house had finally been sold and Spithead was given outright to Agnes. Control and custody of the children was to be shared equally by both parents.

A clause in the agreement provided that Agnes should endeavor to keep out of the press and refrain from discussing her former married life for publication.

("Mrs. O'Neill," said one New York newspaper account, "has kept this part of the agreement while in Reno and has refused to see any newspaper correspondents and even insisted that her divorce complaint and copy of the agreement be sealed. She has made her home at an isolated ranch near Pyramid Lake, thirty miles from Reno.")

The divorce was granted the next day, after a fifteen-minute hearing behind the closed doors of the judge's chamber. Mrs. De Casseres breathed a partial sigh of relief and continued to await word that O'Neill and Carlotta were married.

Agnes returned to her home in West Point Pleasant, where she had left four-year-old Oona in charge of an aunt (Agnes' sister, Cecil) and Gaga. Despite her distress at the callous way in which O'Neill had walked out on Shane and her worry over his emotional state at being abandoned by his father, Agnes had sent Shane to a boarding school in Lenox, Massachusetts, in the fall of 1928, six months before she left for Reno. Not yet nine, with a shy, almost morbidly sensitive nature, Shane had apparently been given no explanation of the actual state of affairs that existed between his parents. He was learning some harsh facts of life in much the same way that O'Neill himself had learned them, and just as O'Neill's older son Eugene had learned them.

Returning "home" to West Point Pleasant for the summer vacation, Shane found little to reassure him. Gaga, who had raised him from infancy and whom he adored, had died in his absence and Agnes was still in Reno. Soon after Agnes returned she incurred some unpleasant publicity that may have added to Shane's bewilderment and uneasiness.

An Albany newspaperman she had met recently, named James Delaney, was arrested in nearby Toms River, for drunken driving. The story was reported in the New York newspapers.

"Mrs. O'Neill Intercedes: Saves Man From Going to Jail After Crash in Her Car," read the headline over *The Times* account: "J. J. Delaney of Albany, a newspaperman, escaped serving a thirty-day sentence in jail following his conviction for reckless driving and driving while intoxicated when Mrs. Agnes O'Neill, divorced wife of Eugene O'Neill, playwright, yesterday paid his fine.

"Delaney was arrested by State troopers after he had struck three autos in Point Pleasant while driving Mrs. O'Neill's car. Arraigned before Justice of the Peace Bennett, he was fined $451 on the two charges and, not having the money, was sentenced to jail.

"His release was obtained by Mrs. O'Neill, who paid the fine and promised to pay for the damages to the three cars.

"Since her divorce Mrs. O'Neill has been living in Point Pleasant. She said Delaney was on his way to get ginger ale for a party."

Agnes continued to be loyal to Delaney for some years, and a number of her friends, who respected her devotion to him, have sympathetically recalled the difficulties inherent in her situation.

"She couldn't marry him, although they loved each other," Sarah Ullman has said. "She had to have the alimony. Her kids loved him. He would pal around with Shane and take him fishing. He was a very charming man."

That Delaney returned Agnes' devotion has been attested to by another friend, Elizabeth Murray, herself a resident of West Point Pleasant.

"Jimmy told me once that Agnes was the most beautiful woman he had ever seen," Mrs. Murray said. "I remember once, when I was visiting

[695]

Agnes in the evening, Oona, who was then about seven, called down from upstairs, 'Jimmy, kiss Mother good night for me.' "

Two days after the announcement of Agnes' divorce, the New York tabloids began speculating (along with Bio De Casseres) about when O'Neill would marry Carlotta. One of the newspapers announced, with an air of significance, that Carlotta's former husband, Ralph Barton, was seeking a divorce from his fourth wife, whom he had married shortly after Carlotta divorced him. (Carlotta's imminent marriage to O'Neill had apparently unnerved Barton; he had always been jealous of Carlotta and couldn't stand the thought of her remarriage.) The tangled matrimonial arrangements involving O'Neill, Carlotta and Barton continued to provide the tabloids with a source of gossip.

"Between the pair of intellectuals [O'Neill and Barton]," said one newspaper, "there are already five divorces." It proceeded to list Barton's three ex-wives and O'Neill's two—but somehow overlooked Carlotta's three ex-husbands. Another newspaper soon amended this oversight, throwing in the thrice-divorced Hendrik Van Loon (who was on the verge of remarrying his divorced second wife), and making a full-page, illustrated story out of what it called the "Dizzy Matrimonial Merry-Go-Round of the Literary Lions." "If these people—philosophers, seers, men apart—cannot manage their domestic affairs on a sound and permanent basis, what hope is there for the ordinary bewildered citizen?" asked the article plaintively.

O'Neill and Carlotta were married on Monday afternoon, July 22, 1929, in Paris. It was nearly a year and a half since they had left New York together. They exchanged wedding rings—thin gold bands—both bearing engraved quotations from *Lazarus Laughed*. The ring O'Neill gave Carlotta was inscribed: "I am Your laughter." The one Carlotta gave O'Neill was inscribed "—and You are mine!"

It was a little over eleven years since O'Neill had written to a friend, of his marriage to Agnes: "It's hard to describe—the wedding of two serious children [the minister] made out of it; but it was startlingly impressive. The meaning behind the lines 'got across with a punch' to both of us. . . ."

This time there was no minister, but O'Neill was equally ready to be stirred.

"The French civil ceremony proved to be quite impressive—we liked it, felt it meant something—not like our buy-a-dog-license variety in the U.S.," he wrote to Langner. He had already cabled Langner the day after the wedding to announce the "grand news." He also cabled Saxe Commins, who, with his wife, Dorothy, had recently visited him and Carlotta. It was

Commins who brought the news to Bio De Casseres. She was enormously relieved that her deadline had been met.

"Saxe," she said, "who did not much care for climbing the four flights up to our apartment, felt it important enough to deliver the news in person on the morning of July 23."

"I think the peace that Bio promised me is due to set in," O'Neill wrote to De Casseres four days after the wedding. And Carlotta, soon after, wrote to Theresa Helburn: "We feel we have earned our happiness!"

O'Neill authorized Weinberger to release the story of the marriage to the press (being careful to add the misleading information that he and Carlotta were going to the Tyrol for a honeymoon) and the New York newspapers carried it on July 24. O'Neill also cabled Ben Pinchot permission to release a portrait for which he and Carlotta had sat before leaving for Europe. It was used in the next issue of *Vanity Fair* and subsequently reprinted in newspapers throughout the world. In this photograph O'Neill looks handsome and distinguished. He wears a meticulously fitted dark suit, white shirt, and wide, striped tie. He gazes directly at the camera, with a suggestion of a smile at the corners of his mouth, his eyes speculative, his hair, touched with silver, in a thick wave over his right temple, his dark mustache immaculately trimmed. Carlotta, stunningly beautiful, looks at O'Neill rather than at the camera; her thick, dark hair is brushed sleekly back, her neck is arched and her chin tilted upward, as she regards her husband with serene adoration.

Between them Carlotta and O'Neill had begun creating a legend about the handsome, romantic, remote, château-dwelling O'Neill, secluded in work and in love. For the next twenty-six years of O'Neill's life Carlotta devoted herself to protecting her husband's seclusion and perpetuating the legend.

LI

"OH, FOR A LANGUAGE TO WRITE DRAMA IN! FOR A speech that is dramatic and isn't just conversation! I'm so strait-jacketed by writing in terms of talk! I'm so fed up with the dodge-question of dialect! But where to find that language?"

O'Neill uttered this cry in a letter to Joseph Wood Krutch when he began outlining his trilogy, *Mourning Becomes Electra*. His words conveyed his artistic frustration and sense of inadequacy in tackling the most ambitious project of his career.

He had started work on *Mourning Becomes Electra* soon after his marriage, and referred to it, always, as "Carlotta's play." "I gave him a lovely home to write it in," Carlotta later explained, "where things were always right. I lived to make a home for him where he could work. He had never had that before."

The play became Carlotta's favorite of all her husband's works. "I feel so strongly personally about it," she said. "We went through such a horrible time with it. Gene used to want to tear it up. When he finally finished it he felt he never wanted to write another play."

O'Neill once said it was the play from which he "received the most personal satisfaction." Certainly it was the highest expression of his art, with the possible exception of *Desire Under the Elms,* since he had begun writing.

The idea for *Electra* had been brewing in his mind for several years, but a combination of factors influenced his decision to shelve other half-formed projects in favor of *Electra* at this particular time.

First of all, his conception of the Electra theme fitted in with the current trends of his emotional life: passion, frustration, guilt, mourning and retribution were themes he felt he could handle on the grand scale, having recently elevated himself to the heights of a grand passion.

His decision was also prompted by his newly professed indifference to speedy Broadway production. He knew he was tackling something very big and very difficult, a job that might take several years to complete. He determined to take all the time he needed and let the Broadway show shop fend without him.

In addition, the fact that Eugene Jr. was now distinguishing himself as a Greek scholar at Yale helped in a minor way to influence O'Neill's decision to attempt a classical trilogy. At this point O'Neill was almost pathetically anxious to solidify his relationship with his older son, whose scholarship he admired. *Electra*, O'Neill vaguely believed, would give them a strong bond of intellectual interest.

Although O'Neill made numerous preliminary notes for the trilogy during the summer following his marriage, he postponed the real spade work until fall. The summer tourist season, he knew, would bring many of his friends abroad—he had, in fact, issued a number of invitations—and would prevent his getting down to serious writing.

O'Neill had been beguiled by the possibility of a modern conception of the Electra legend since the spring of 1926, when he had tried to persuade Macgowan to produce the Hugo von Hofmannsthal version. He thought it the only modern verse play that was both truly poetic and truly dramatic. During this period O'Neill had done some research into Greek language and history.

"I'm going in very heavily these days for the study of religion along certain definite lines I have mapped out as a sort of large background for certain work in the future I have in mind," he had informed Komroff at the time. "Am also starting to study ancient Greek which I never 'took' at college or prep. If in three or four years I'm able to read Greek tragedy in the original and enjoy it—the sound as well as the meaning— I'll have made a grand refuge for my soul to dive deeply and coolly into at moments when modern life—and drama—become too damn humid and shallow to be borne."

That same spring he began making entries in an exhaustive work diary that was to record, over a period of five years, the fascinating progression of *Mourning Becomes Electra*.

In an entry dated "Spring, 1926," he indicated his interest in creating a modern psychological drama rooted in Greek legend; he weighed the relative advantages of up-dating the Electra or the Medea tragedy, but wondered if it was possible "to get modern psychological approximation of the Greek sense of fate into such a play, which an intelligent audience of today, possessed of no belief in gods or supernatural retribution, could accept and be moved by?"

Aboard ship bound for Shanghai in October, 1928, he decided that the Electra legend best suited his purpose. A month later, his artistic intuition told him to discard the legendary ending of the Electra saga ("she peters out into unmarried banality," he noted) and to substitute a "tragic ending worthy of [her] character." Why should the Furies have allowed Electra to escape unpunished, he asked himself rhetorically.

Returned to France, O'Neill began making more frequent and longer entries in his diary.

He decided to set his modern "Greek tragedy" in a small New England coastal town at the close of the Civil War; his "Agamemnon" would be a brigadier general in Grant's army and the play would begin on the day of Lee's surrender. The play's family would live in a neo-Greek house of the type popular in the early part of the nineteenth century—"this fits in well and absolutely justifiable, (not forced Greek similarity)—" O'Neill noted, adding that a New England background was "best possible dramatically for Greek plot of crime and retribution chain of fate—Puritan conviction of man born to sin and punishment . . ."

He would use only Orestes and Electra among his New England Agamemnon's children, not bothering to invent modern equivalents for Iphigenia and Chrysothemis, and he would further depart from the Greek legend by explaining Clytemnestra's hatred of her husband in terms of sexual frustration—"[Agamemnon's] Puritan sense of guilt turning love to lust," wrote O'Neill.

The modern Electra was fated always to be her mother's rival in love, and always to be defeated. As O'Neill carefully went on to note:

"Electra adores father, devoted to brother (who resembles father), hates mother—Orestes adores mother, devoted to sister (whose face resembles mother's), hates his father—Agamemnon, frustrated in love for Clytemnestra, adores daughter, Electra, who resembles her, hates and is jealous of his son, Orestes—etc—work out this symbol of family resemblances and identification (as visible sign of family fate) still further— use masks (?)"

In May of 1929 O'Neill began searching for suitable New England names for his characters; he wanted to retain the suggestion of the Greek names if he could manage it without being obvious. For Agamemnon he thought of Asa, or Ezra Mannon; for Clytemnestra, Christine; for Orestes, Orin; for Electra, he hesitated over Eleanor, Ellen and Elsa and finally settled on an approximation of Homer's Laodicea—Lavinia. He then selected and explained his title: "'Mourning Becomes Electra'—that is, in old sense of the word—it befits—it becomes Electra to mourn—(it is her fate)—also, in usual sense (made ironical here), mourning (black) is becoming to her—it is the only color that becomes her destiny—."

He also decided to follow the Greek form structurally and write his play as a trilogy; the first play would deal with Agamemnon's homecoming and murder, the second with Electra's revenge, and the third with the retribution that would overtake Electra and Orestes.

When O'Neill had reached this point in his preliminary outline, he paused to take stock of his artistic philosophy, past and future. He made up his mind that he was not going to let anything but his own creative tempo determine his output. Reflecting that he had written eighteen long plays during the past eleven years, he concluded it was "too much"— that he had often forced the plays just to keep himself occupied. He felt that now he would be content to rest and relax in the periods between creation. "America has had a bellyful of my stuff for a while," he told friends.

He elaborated on some of these ideas to Eleanor Fitzgerald that May:

"My interest in the productions steadily decreases as my interest in plays as written increases. They always, with the exceptions you know, fall so far below or beside my intent that I am a bit weary and disillusioned with scenery and actors and the whole uninspired works of the Show Shop. . . . Believe me, as far as production is concerned, I sigh for the old Provincetown days, the old crowd and zest. As it is, I think I will wind up writing plays to be published with 'no productions allowed' in red letters on the first page. For when I think of that dreary ordeal of disillusionment and compromise called rehearsals, with the best end in sight a 'competent' production, I sure turn sick."

Too much "travail of blood and spirit" went into the writing of his plays for him to expose them to what he knew was an unfair test, he said. He added that he was deadly ill with being a public personage and that he was planning his life ahead so that he could go back to his old private life of "unpestered artist," even if it meant holding back plays from production and publication until he was forgotten.

"I've learned a lesson," he said. "Forty is the right age to begin to learn and I think my new work is going to show more poise, more patience with itself to reach at perfection, more critical analysis of itself and contemplation, more time given it for gestation and genuine birth, more pains. . . . It's time I achieved a more mature outlook as an artist, and now I know I have."

Perhaps, O'Neill speculated, it had required a complete upheaval of his life for him to attain this new attitude.

"I've everything to back me up now—love of the kind I've always wanted, security and peace," he said, adding that he was looking forward to years of undisturbed, difficult work and a joy of living he had never known before, to give him strength and patience for his work. He had, at last, found a sustained plan of life in which living would collaborate with writing instead of always being an obstacle to be overcome and beaten under by writing.

On June 20, at Le Plessis, O'Neill noted in his diary that he had finished the scenario of the first play of the trilogy, *Homecoming*.

On July 11 his diary entry indicated that he had finished the scenario of the second play in the trilogy; he had entitled it *The Hunted*.

He wistfully recorded the difficulty he had had (a difficulty unknown to the Greek tragedians) in plotting his crimes so that his criminals could escape detection. ". . . still," he wrote, "even history of comparatively recent crimes (where they happen among people supposedly respectable) shows rural authorities easily hoodwinked—poisoning of Mannon in 'Homecoming' would probably never be suspected (under same circumstances) even in New England town of today, let alone 1865."

Toward the end of July, overwhelmed by the scope and grandeur of the job he was attempting, and convinced that he alone among contemporary dramatists had "the guts to shoot at something big and risk failure," O'Neill advised Krutch that his new play was "an idea and dramatic conception that has the possibilities of being the biggest thing modern drama has attempted—by far the biggest!" One would have to go back to the Greeks and Elizabethans to find anything comparable, he said, but added, "I don't promise by a long shot that after it gets ground down by my inadequacies it will prove any such lofty stature; but at least this time I'll have the satisfaction of knowing I failed at something big, and thus be a success in my own spiritual eyes. If I fail! I have hopes, damn it!"

In August O'Neill completed the scenario for the third play of the trilogy, *The Haunted*. "Have given Yankee Electra tragic [fate] worthy of her—and Orestes, too," he noted. He then set aside the project for a month and allowed it to simmer in his unconscious.

There was much he wanted to think about before he began on the actual dialogue. "It is going to be difficult, this!" he confessed to Nathan on August 31. "It would be so easy to do *well*. The story would see to that—and that's the danger I want to avoid. It has got to have an exceptional quality to lift it above its easy possibilities and make it worthy in some sense of its classic antecedents—or it will be a rank flop in my eyes no matter what others may think of it. So I'm going to do a lot more of tentative feeling out and testing before I start."

He was waiting, he said, until he saw many uninterrupted months ahead of him; there had been visitors, trips to Paris to the dentist, and other distractions breaking in, and he would have to return to Paris for a long session with the dentist in September.

"So won't be on my way until October," he said. "But I grow more and more enthused by this idea. . . . It keeps growing richer and I don't grudge the delay because I know it is moving."

No matter how hard he tried to isolate himself, O'Neill seemed unable to avoid being a storm center. If he was not the subject of a domestic scandal or the object of an international search, his work was incurring the wrath of censors on Broadway or being banned in Boston. Now, in the midst of his splendid European seclusion, he became the victim of a widely publicized lawsuit. Fresh from battles with lawyers over the separation and divorce, he was plunged into an aggravating court case involving an alleged plagiarism.

Strange Interlude was in the second year of its run at the John Golden Theatre, and road companies had already been launched on successful tours, when, on May 27, 1929, a woman using the pen name of Georges Lewys, instituted a suit in federal court charging O'Neill with having stolen his play from her 1924 novel, *The Temple of Pallas-Athenae*. Miss Lewys wanted $1,250,000 in damages and an injunction against the play as both acted and published. Claiming that she had submitted her book to the Theatre Guild and to Horace Liveright, Inc., prior to the production of *Strange Interlude,* she brought her charges against the Guild and Liveright, as well as O'Neill.

Copies of *Strange Interlude* and *The Temple of Pallas-Athenae* were filed with the complaint. Many points of alleged similarity were marked by Miss Lewys, who prepared a page-by-page comparison in which she pointed out similar lines, ideas, situations and characters:

"The heroines marry young men from insane families, sacrifice themselves and remain married to their husbands. Boys are born in each case and the heroines fall in love with the fathers. The boys grow up handsome, tall and athletic, and fall in love with beautiful young women. The mothers show jealousy of their prospective daughters-in-law. . . . In both stories the name of the doctor . . . ends in 'ell' [Cramwell and Darrell].

"The plots each cover twenty-five years. In both stories the husbands of the heroines suffer strokes which end in death on the eve of the marriages of their wives' sons. In each story when the husband suffers a stroke a doctor and a layman pick him up. In both stories the husbands are pictured as weaklings.

"In both books on page 155 the doctors discuss the moral phases of selective paternity. In both books the lovers and heroines fall in love with each other; the heroines furnish their husbands with money. The mothers, in both stories, are dead before the stories start."

O'Neill was at first dumfounded, then furious—mainly because it was going to cost him money to defend himself from charges that he knew were absurd.

"Some blackmail! Some gal!" O'Neill exploded to Liveright on June 14. "I cabled Harry [Weinberger] she's crazy, but she's crazy like a fox! A million dollars worth of publicity for nothing! And I lose no matter how I win! It's a grand law that permits such stunts to get by! By God, I'd like to get the hussy somewhere and make an example out of her! This plagiarism stuff, where playwrights are concerned, has ceased to be a jest!"

And to Stark Young, on June 20, he fumed:

"I've had about as much of a certain kind of success in *Interlude* as could be hoped for. You might add, as much as my stomach can stand! What a success! This plagiarism suit is the fitting final note of cheapness to wind up the whole affair! Still, I'd be a liar if I said the money wasn't welcome, even though I feel the play earned it under the false pretences of a ballyhooed freak."

But money was threatening to become something of a problem. Because of the pending lawsuit a movie company which had been on the point of buying *Strange Interlude* temporarily withdrew its offer. O'Neill asked Komroff to look for books utilizing similar themes, to prove that it was a theme in the public domain. And during July and August he tried to raise some cash—quite a lot of cash, in fact—by offering a set of his original manuscripts for sale to an avid collector. O'Neill did not undervalue himself. The price he put on this potential collectors' item was $100,000. The collector did not want to pay more than $50,000, and the deal fell through.

In early August, T. R. Smith, one of the officers of the Liveright firm, forwarded to O'Neill an agent's inquiry about the possibility of acquiring the original manuscript of *Strange Interlude*.

O'Neill advised Smith that he did not want to break up his set of original manuscripts unless the price offered for *Strange Interlude* were "particularly tempting." He was holding on to the lot "pending a gigantic offer from some frenzied collector which hasn't materialized!" he said, adding that he was anxious to sell the collection while he was still "young enough to appreciate the value of money" and that his price was as high as the traffic would stand. O'Neill was not, ultimately, able to dispose of his scripts en masse. Within a couple of months such collectors as once might have been willing to pay the price were busy trying to collect what funds they could salvage from a collapsed stock market; the autumn of 1929 was not the ideal time to offer luxury items for sale.

Despite his financial worries, it never occurred to O'Neill to curb his style of living. He clung to his château and began entertaining a series of guests, quietly but luxuriously. Among the first to receive the hospitality of the castle were George Jean Nathan and Lillian Gish.

"I had been with many married people," Miss Gish later said, "but I had never seen a man and woman so passionately in love. They didn't seem to need anything outside of each other; they didn't need anyone except each other. Carlotta gave Gene everything she could think of to bring a smile to his face. She wanted everything that touched him to look beautiful, everything around him, including herself. She was his wife, mother, housekeeper, secretary, nurse, mistress, companion—and almost his tailor. If there was a tray to be brought to him, Carlotta brought it. She had a great sense of beauty. We often used to dress for dinner at Le Plessis. There was never anything casual."

Nathan's report on the O'Neills, which he later published in *Cosmopolitan,* revolved about one of his friend's hobbies, reflecting happy New London memories of John Dolan and his democratic pigs.

"When Gene was living in a French château," Nathan wrote, "a neighboring château was occupied by the recently married Duke of Windsor. To maintain, as he said, the aristocratic atmosphere of the neighborhood, O'Neill raised a litter of pigs in his back yard and bestowed upon them such names as the Duc de Haut Sauterne, Jean Louis Hohenzollern, and Fifi d'Arc. His wife wasn't greatly fetched by the general idea, but—always eager to please her husband—she refrained from offering any open criticism, particularly at table when pork chops were being served."

Nathan was also amused by O'Neill's work habits. At Le Plessis, he sat in a huge chair that had been ordered from England. It resembled a barber's chair, with built-in shelves for reference books and a board on which O'Neill could rest his pad.

Nathan's visit commemorated a milestone in his friendship with O'Neill. For O'Neill, finally, began addressing him as George, instead of Nathan.

"O'Neill is very slow in making friends," Nathan wrote. "He tests a potential friendship much after the technique of a fisherman, trying out various personal and metaphysical lines, flies and worms to determine what kind of fish the stranger is . . . Once he has made a friend for himself, that man remains a friend, in his eyes, until Hell freezes."

In August, not long after Nathan's departure, O'Neill welcomed Eugene Jr. to Le Plessis. Eugene was now nineteen and, as his father remarked with pride, had grown to a strapping six feet two inches and weighed 180 pounds. O'Neill had recently financed a tour of Germany for his son.

"He isn't the usual college youth from Yale and yet he has enough of that about him to be no intellectual young prig," O'Neill reported to Nathan. "A fine youth, truly! I am proud of him—and I think he is of me—and our relationship is naturally brotherish with none of the forced 'pal-father-son' bunk in it. When I survey his merits and think of the rotten mess of a life I was at his age, I have no fatherly superiority assumptions, believe me! . . . Carlotta likes him and he likes her, and I'm sure he feels more at home with us than he ever did when with me in the past."

Eugene Jr. gave as glowing an account of his visit as his father could have wished. He reported to his friend Frank Meyer that Carlotta had accepted him warmly and that he was having a wonderful time at Le Plessis. To his mother he sent two charming snapshots of himself and his father, whom he strongly resembled; both photographs showed father and son seated near the front entrance of the château, clad in bathrobes and swim suits. O'Neill's robe was a gaudy, flowered one and Eugene's a conservative, striped one. In one photograph they were both scowling into the sun. Eugene, the classical scholar, scribbled on the back: "I and paterfamilias. We are really not as mad as we look." (Carlotta arranged for Eugene Jr. to be properly photographed by Ben Pinchot on his return to the United States. "We sent her the proofs," Pinchot's wife, Ann, recalled, "and she ordered some pictures and paid for them herself. I suppose they were a gift for O'Neill's birthday, or some other special occasion.")

Carl Van Vechten and his wife, Fania Marinoff, also were visitors at Le Plessis. Miss Marinoff, who was an actress, had known Carlotta before her marriage to Ralph Barton.

"At times," she later said, "Carlotta and I were as close as two sisters. Then, for unknown reasons, Carlotta would not write or see me for long periods. But eventually we would take up our friendship again where we had left off.

"Carlotta was an extraordinary woman. She went beyond the wifely duties for O'Neill. She did everything for him, was even his typist. She did nothing by halves. She was the most generous human being I've ever known. I always felt Ralph Barton had made a big mistake in letting her divorce him. Carlotta was a one-man woman."

Barton himself evidently came to feel he had made a mistake. "Ralph was very egotistical," Van Vechten said. "He was upset when Carlotta married Gene, partly because he couldn't stand the idea of her marrying someone more celebrated than he was. He knew my wife and I were friends of the O'Neills, and whenever he saw us he would say, 'Give Carlotta my love.'"

Barton attempted to make even more overt advances to Carlotta through Lillian Gish. Miss Gish saw Barton in Paris before visiting the O'Neills, and Barton asked her to take a letter from him to Carlotta. She refused.

"I told him I couldn't go to a man's house as a guest and hand his wife a love letter from another man," Miss Gish said. "Ralph dramatized himself. When he was married to the French composer, for instance, he had two bedrooms in his house, one painted white and one painted black. The black one, he told me, was for sleeping during the daytime, because he liked to sleep in a dark room."

Fania Marinoff has used the same words as Miss Gish in describing Carlotta's devotion to O'Neill—'She was a wife, mistress, secretary, friend and nurse."

Carlotta herself has affirmed this view of her role. "I had to work like a dog," she said many years later in recalling her life in the château. "I was Gene's secretary, I was his nurse. His health was always bad. I did everything. He wrote the plays, but I did everything else. I loved it. It was a privilege to live with him, because he was mentally stimulating. My God, how many women have husbands who are very stimulating?" (Shortly before her marriage to O'Neill, Carlotta had said to Louis Kalonyme: "He gives me so much—and I am so humbly grateful for his love. . . . There are times when his love gives me an ecstatic religious feeling! . . . I am so desperately desirous of giving him back some little bit of all the great beauty and happiness he gives to me! . . . Think what a blessed woman I am!")

"Gene and Carlotta were both very possessive and jealous," Miss Marinoff once observed (and her husband added that O'Neill was the more possessive of the two). "Neither of them needed anyone else. At Le Plessis, Carlotta would always dress up for Gene in the evening, even when they were alone. She had bought dozens of evening gowns, just for Gene. I often went shopping with her and helped her choose her clothes, because our tastes were very similar."

Van Vechten had a taste for detective fiction and jazz records, two forms of relaxation in which O'Neill indulged at Le Plessis. Prior to his visit Van Vechten had sent O'Neill a new detective story, which O'Neill enthusiastically acknowledged, and some records, which O'Neill referred to as "some camellias!"

" 'The St. James Infirmary' is right in my alley!" O'Neill wrote to Van Vechten in September, 1929. "I am now memorizing the words. Do you know Mr. [Louis] Armstrong? If so give him my fraternal benediction. He is a darl." O'Neill also thanked Van Vechten for some Bessie Smith recordings, adding that it was good to have Bessie around "wahooing in the peaceful French evenings."

O'Neill, who worked in the mornings and spent the rest of the day relaxing—and giving his unconscious a chance to operate on the problems ahead—spent many of his leisure hours walking in the woods surrounding his property and driving a fast new car that had replaced his Renault. It was a Bugatti, and he would drive it at breakneck speed up and down the countryside, where no speed limits were imposed.

"Gene had a marvelous time with that racer," Carlotta said. "When he was very nervous and tired he would go out in it and drive ninety-five, even ninety-eight miles an hour. He would come back looking nineteen years old—not a wrinkle in his face, and perfectly relaxed. He took me out in it one day and they almost had to pry me out of the car when we got back. I was gone, I was so terrified.

"But I had encouraged him to buy the car. I encouraged him to have everything on earth he could have that he'd never had, because it was the only time he had really made money. I thought it was good for him. And it did help him.

"Of course, there were quarrels about, for instance, his having shoes made to order. We had an awful row about that because he said I was making him into a gigolo or something, but finally I got him there, and he ended up by having seventy-five pairs of shoes before we got back to America. Then I introduced him to tailors, and he got a complete wardrobe. By the time he was finished getting things, the Depression came, and he was ever so pleased that he had everything he needed. He didn't have to buy a thing for years, except maybe a sports jacket."

Theresa Helburn, who, with her husband, dined at Le Plessis one evening, remembered being called for at her hotel in Tours by O'Neill. "Gene, how swank you look!" was Miss Helburn's greeting. O'Neill, she recalled, blushed. "All my life I've wanted this," he told her.

Elizabeth Sergeant held a less sanguine view of O'Neill's delight with his new role. "Although Gene seemed pleased to have seventy-five pairs of shoes and a racing car," she said, "and a printed menu on the table for dinner every night, I don't feel it was the best in Gene that appreciated all this. He really was an extremely simple person and, on his own, he would never have striven for those things. I don't think he was really happy in Touraine—partly because he never could be really happy except when living by the sea."

Miss Sergeant's view was not calculated to endear her to Carlotta, and eventually she was dropped by the O'Neills. She was one of many friends who, over the next fifteen years, were gradually cut off; nearly all of them blamed the amputative process on Carlotta.

This was a natural conclusion, since before his marriage to Carlotta O'Neill had seldom refused to see anyone who took the trouble to seek him out in whatever fastness he had chosen to seclude himself, and Agnes had been too gregarious to wish to shun visitors. Carlotta, aware of O'Neill's inability to resist the importunities of friends, took upon herself the role of guardian. She saw that O'Neill needed the intervention of a kind of supersecretary, who would protect him not only from all needless interruptions to his work but also from his own inability to say no. One of the first requests O'Neill made of Carlotta after their marriage was that he never be required to answer the telephone; she complied, even though she was often accused—and knew she was accused—of "intercepting" calls to her husband.

When O'Neill placed himself, with a certain sense of relief, under Carlotta's protection, she went at her job seriously and perhaps a trifle overdramatically, for she had a dramatic nature. The urbane Dag Hammarskjöld, who held the post of Secretary General of the United Nations from 1953 until his death in 1961, and who became a friend of Carlotta some time after her husband's death, analyzed her relationship with O'Neill in these terms:

"Carlotta was like an overprotective mother to a son about whom she suspects weakness."

Carlotta was O'Neill's buffer. It devolved upon her to write or speak the dismissive or severing phrase, and she did not always perform her function gently. She undertook on O'Neill's behalf what Strindberg has graphically described as "the labor of keeping the filth of life at a distance"—a labor, many of O'Neill's friends felt, that she pursued with too much relish. Nevertheless, she did so, in almost every case, because O'Neill desired it, either actively or passively; in those cases where the cutting off was not actually instigated by O'Neill it was usually done with his tacit consent, for both were united in the effort to preserve to the utmost O'Neill's privacy and peace of mind for work.

Some of O'Neill's friends concluded that people were cut off entirely against his will. But no one who knew him well during the early years of his marriage to Carlotta would have ventured to describe him as henpecked. If he deferred, in some cases, to Carlotta's dislikes and prejudices (and she had many), it was the natural deference of a husband in love.

O'Neill realized that he lacked the tenacity and will to resist the time-wasting, unrewarding demands made by trivial social intercourse. He also realized that, encouraged and protected by Carlotta, he *could* resist. Though it was doubtless humiliating to those who were resisted, O'Neill and Carlotta declined to see people who, they believed, would waste their time, either by becoming a source of contention between them or merely by boring them.

A certain amount of shifting and shaking up of old friendships was inevitable, as it usually is in the case of a couple marrying after divorce. And to this shake-up may be attributed the first wave of amputations, which included most members of the Provincetown group who had been common friends of O'Neill and Agnes. Among these were such intimate friends of O'Neill as Eleanor Fitzgerald and James Light. Several of his Greenwich Village friends, including Mary Vorse, Susan Glaspell and Frank Shay, were told by Harry Weinberger that O'Neill had been angry because none of them had written to congratulate him on his marriage to Carlotta. Mrs. Vorse, on hearing this, promptly sent him a letter.

"I wrote twice," she said, "but got no answer. I asked Susan and Frank and several others if they'd written. They all had, and none had received answers." Bessie Breuer, who also wrote to O'Neill, was answered by Carlotta. "I wrote to Gene again, and again was answered by Carlotta," Miss Breuer said. "I just gave up writing."

There were also certain friends of the transitional period who, perhaps because of their too intimate knowledge of the love-affair between O'Neill and Carlotta before their marriage, were dismissed after the marriage. Among these was Robert Rockmore. Norman Winston was dropped because Carlotta regarded his friendship with Agnes as disloyal. Kenneth Macgowan, who had been O'Neill's closest friend over the longest period of time, was now removed from intimacy, though he still continued to see the O'Neills occasionally.

Oddly enough, and even in spite of the Depression, O'Neill (who had been careful in his investments and lost only about 50 per cent of his holdings) continued to support, though rarely to see, such friends as Terry Carlin, Joe Smith and Bill Clarke. And he was still a soft touch for other old friends who found themselves temporarily down on their luck, such as Charles O'Brien Kennedy. "Enclosed is a bit to help a bit," he wrote to

Kennedy, sending a check in October, 1929. "Don't ever give it a thought until you are on easy street and then some again."

Benjamin and Bio De Casseres and friends who were also business associates of O'Neill's, such as the Langners, Manuel Komroff, Richard Madden and Robert Sisk, continued on cordial terms with both the O'Neills, as did Nathan, Louis Kalonyme and the Van Vechtens. And Saxe Commins, though he had known O'Neill since his early Greenwich Village days and throughout his marriage to Agnes, became a much closer friend after O'Neill's marriage to Carlotta. O'Neill kept up a steady correspondence with Commins and both he and his wife, Dorothy, were visitors at Le Plessis. O'Neill worried about Commins being out of a job in November, 1929, rejoiced when a son was born to him and Dorothy in the summer of 1930 (the baby was named Eugene, and O'Neill became his godfather); and cheered when, in January of 1931, Commins landed a job with Horace Liveright. When Komroff left the firm to devote himself to writing, Commins became O'Neill's editor.

Several people dropped out of O'Neill's life because they themselves simply did not make the effort to continue the friendship. Robert Edmond Jones, for instance, though he remained a friend in spirit, rarely saw O'Neill after his marriage. This also applied in the case of some of his old New London friends, such as Arthur McGinley.

It is true that a number of people whose friendships were later terminated seemed to fall into no category except that of Carlotta's dislike, but O'Neill did not fight to keep these friends and was not devastated, as some of them believed, by losing them. In cases where O'Neill did feel a strong sense of attachment, he would not permit Carlotta's whim to govern him; but such cases were rare. For the most part O'Neill did not care enough to oppose his wife and make her unhappy. Carlotta came first, and when O'Neill yielded to her, though it may have cost him a pang, he knew he was gaining more than he gave up, in terms of peace.

James Light was one of the first of the old friends to fall under the ax. Light, who held the theory that O'Neill was miserable with Carlotta and that she was forcing him to abandon his friends, visited Le Plessis in 1930. One of the things Light wanted to talk—or rather commiserate—with O'Neill about was the final collapse of the Provincetown Playhouse toward the end of 1929, soon after the Wall Street crash; the Provincetown, dependent for so long upon the contributions of such financiers as Otto Kahn, no longer had any funds to support it. Light, out of a job, wanted O'Neill's permission (it was granted) to present *The Emperor Jones* in Germany.

Light had a hint of what was in store for him even before he traveled from Paris to Touraine to see O'Neill, for he had been given a somewhat grudging invitation, which did not include his wife.

"Gene and Carlotta and I sat down together, and Carlotta asked me, in a frigid voice, if I was in Paris to start a new branch of the Provincetown Players. She called me 'Mr. Light,' which surprised me, considering that we'd worked together and been so friendly during the run of *The Hairy Ape*. I said, 'No, Carlotta,' and she told me to call her Mrs. O'Neill. I was stunned."

Light stayed at the château for several days. He felt that O'Neill was withdrawn.

"I couldn't get to him," Light said. "He didn't talk very much, and when he did talk he didn't look at me. When we walked on the grounds at Le Plessis, Carlotta always seemed to turn up. She never left Gene and me alone together the whole time I was there."

Light interpreted this as "spying" on Carlotta's part; he thought she wanted to prevent O'Neill from confiding to him that he was unhappy.

He was not asked for a second visit, and O'Neill gradually broke off the relationship, later, by dodging Light's proposals to meet when he was in New York, pleading illness, overwork, or an imminent departure from town.

Walter Huston, to whom Carlotta evidently had no objection, also was among O'Neill's guests at Le Plessis. His visit took place on a winter's day, and O'Neill, bundled in a heavy overcoat, and accompanied by a liveried chauffeur driving a limousine, met Huston at the Tours station.

"Let's go for a ride," O'Neill suggested to Huston later that afternoon, after he had shown him the grounds of the château and the swimming pool he had built on the estate the previous spring.

"O'Neill took the wheel of his car and promptly shot off at ninety miles an hour," Huston later reported. "He said, 'This is how I amuse myself.'"

Robert Sisk, another visitor at Le Plessis, arranged in the spring of 1930 to bring a trio of newspapermen out to see O'Neill. They were John Byram, then drama editor of *The New York Times*; Richard Watts, Jr., then movie critic and second-string play reviewer for the *Herald Tribune*, and Don Skene, the sports writer, who was a journalistic legend. O'Neill already knew and liked Watts, but Skene was the man he was most anxious to see, for Sisk, in arranging the date, had told O'Neill that Skene was a friend of "Sparrow" Robertson, the idolized sports writer of the Paris *Herald*. Robertson, who wrote with a happy disregard for syntax, was a Runyonesque character for whom O'Neill had great admiration; he read his column regularly and with relish. "Why, he's the greatest writer in the world," O'Neill had once said publicly.

Watts later wrote that with Skene, O'Neill "positively blossomed."

"He loved sports and old popular songs and stories about colorful characters, and these were Don's special fields," Watts continued. "The result was an evening of gay conviviality, with songs, that was sheer delight, with O'Neill the most enchanting of hosts."

Ward Morehouse was another New York journalist who visited Le Plessis. After a late-evening session with O'Neill, before an open fire in the living room, Morehouse reported (in the New York *Sun*) that O'Neill was "a happy man."

O'Neill told Morehouse he did not intend to live permanently in France. "Nothing like that," he said. "No nonsense such as renouncing America. There's such a thing as being sensibly patriotic. But living away from America has been a good way to get to know it—to see things that you couldn't see before."

Morehouse described his departure from Le Plessis:

"The O'Neills . . . were standing at the doorway, he was clad in a heavy sweater and she was trim and smart in Parisian sport clothes, when the chauffeur whirled through the driveway in Carlotta's magnificent French car. Eugene O'Neill extended his hand and grinned. 'Yes,' he said, 'tell them we're coming back.' "

(Unlike the case of Richard Watts, whose visit to Le Plessis deepened a friendship, Morehouse's visit marked the end of one. "When I went to Biarritz later that spring," Morehouse said, "I wrote to O'Neill telling him that I would be passing through the Touraine country with a couple of friends soon, and asking if he'd mind if we came over to the château for a swim in his pool. O'Neill wrote back that he *would* mind. As I recall, he said, 'It would greatly disturb me.' We never spoke to each other again. When he got back to New York, we saw each other one day in the lobby of the Madison Hotel, and we each pretended we hadn't recognized the other.")

In spite of the low wages of French servants and the style in which the O'Neills kept house, they were both irritated with what they regarded as the sharp practices of the local French with whom they had to deal. Carlotta later told Ilka Chase that she had hated keeping house in France because the tradespeople fleeced them. "The day came," according to Miss Chase, "when Carlotta could stand no more." And O'Neill, when he returned to America, told an acquaintance that his bills in France had always been higher than they should have been; at one point he had had to hire a French lawyer to make sure he wasn't being bilked.

One of the O'Neills' most precious acquisitions in France, of which they never regretted the price nor questioned the value, was a beautiful Dalmatian called Silverdeen Emblem, and nicknamed Blemie by the O'Neills. O'Neill and Carlotta, who never had a child together, regarded Blemie as their son, and, though they kept other pets from time to time, Blemie was accorded a unique position in their hearts and lives.

Blemie was everything a dog should be—a comfort to his master and mistress "in time of sorrow," as O'Neill later recorded, "and a reason for added joy in their happiness." No dog, he said, was "as well bred or as well mannered or as distinguished and handsome," and no dog could ever wear, with equal distinction, the collar, leash, overcoat and raincoat the O'Neills had made to order for him at Hermes in Paris.

"Blemie acted as host at Le Plessis," Lillian Gish recalled. "He would receive you at the door, go with you on a walk, follow the servant who brought in your breakfast tray. When a guest left, Blemie would throw himself on the floor with a sigh of relief, as though saying, 'Thank heavens, they're gone.' He behaved exactly as though he were worn out with having performed the duties of a good host."

Blemie was also trained to respect his master's need for quiet. "Like the servants, he went around on tiptoe when Gene was working," Carlotta said.

LII

DURING HIS TWO YEARS ABROAD, WHILE DEVOTING
grueling months of uninterrupted labor to *Mourning Becomes Electra* and
keeping an eye on the progress of the *Strange Interlude* plagiarism suit at
home, O'Neill also followed with keen interest the fate of various European productions of his plays. He had a good opportunity to observe at
close quarters what the Europeans really thought of him as a dramatist,
for his plays were being produced in London, Stockholm, Budapest, Berlin,
Vienna and Moscow. Only one major European country neglected him.

"Nothing happens about my stuff in France, for which I am sorry
because I love France," he told a friend in May, 1929. "But considering the present-day rot of the French theatre, how could it?"

The following September, however, the Franco-Russian actor-producer
Georges Pitoëff presented *The Hairy Ape* at the Théâtres des Arts. O'Neill
did not see the production but, soon after, he met Pittoëff and liked him;
and through Pittoëff he met the French dramatist Henri René Lenormand,
who, with his actress-wife, was invited to visit at Le Plessis.

"I like . . . Lenormand immensely," O'Neill wrote to Nathan,"—a fine
sensitive artist."

Some of O'Neill's plays were critically condemned—notably the Berlin
production of *Strange Interlude*, which starred Elisabeth Bergner.

"The thing that makes me especially sick about the discussion of this
production and that of the *Hairy Ape* in Paris," O'Neill observed at the
time, "is the evident fierce animosity to Americans as artists. They
are forced to see our industrialism swamping them and forcing them to
bad imitation on every hand and it poisons them. They are bound they'll
die at the post rather than acknowledge an American has anything to show
them in any line of culture. It's amusing—and disgusting!—this clinging
to their last superiority out of the past."

But by May, 1930, O'Neill had forgotten about the adverse reaction
to some of his plays in his excitement over the Moscow Kamerny Theatre's
impending visit to Paris. The Kamerny was scheduled to exhibit, among
its repertory productions in Russian, two plays by O'Neill—an event their
author did not want to miss. He and Carlotta made plans to go to Paris
to attend the performances. He wrote with boyish pleasure to a friend in

New York of his "satisfaction" that "one of the world's most famous modern theatres, touring the capitals of Europe, selects for two out of the three straight dramas of its repertoire the works of an uncultured Yank!

"I feel as if I wasn't a total loss as an American delegate at large of the arts," he added.

The two O'Neill plays presented for two weeks at the Pigalle by the Kamerny, under the direction of Alexander Tairov (who had seceded from the Moscow Art Theatre in 1914 to head the Kamerny with his Swedish actress-wife, Alice Koonen) were *Desire Under the Elms* and *All God's Chillun Got Wings*. O'Neill was especially struck by the production of *All God's Chillun*, whose title had been translated, *Negro*.

Negro had already scored a success in Moscow, and Tairov was one of O'Neill's most ardent fans. "If you were to ask me who is the most brilliant, the most important among contemporary playwrights," Tairov said, "I would answer without hesitation: O'Neill."

O'Neill returned the compliment. After seeing the Kamerny productions he visited the actors backstage and then sent them a note, dated June 2, 1930:

"Having witnessed your productions of *Desire Under the Elms* and *All God's Chillun Got Wings,* my feeling is one of amazement—and most profound gratitude!

"Let me humbly confess that I came to the theatre with secret misgivings. Not that I doubted that your presentation would be a splendid thing in itself, artistically conceived and executed. I knew the reputation of the Kamerny as one of the finest theatres of Europe too well for that. But I did have an author's fear that in the difficult process of translation and transformation into another language and milieu, the inner spirit— that indefinable essential quality so dear to the creator as being for him the soul of his work—might be excusably, considering the obstacles, distorted or lost."

O'Neill added that the productions rang true to the spirit of his work and were interpreted by "that rarest of all gifts in actors and actresses— creative imagination." With an effusiveness he rarely displayed toward actors, he declared himself in "kinship" with them, assuring them that, despite the barrier of language, he felt that "we had known one another a long time and were united in old and tried friendship—comradeship!— by the love of the true theatre."

George Jean Nathan later twitted O'Neill about his enthusiasm for the Tairov productions. "But you don't know a word of Russian," said Nathan, "how could *you* tell?"

O'Neill regarded him pityingly and answered:

"You should have seen the way Tairov's wife, in the role of the girl [in *All God's Chillun*] brushed those books off the table in that scene in the last act!"

Nathan once wrote that O'Neill had attended the performances as Baron Rothschild's guest.

"Arriving in the box that had been set aside for him," Nathan reported, "[O'Neill] was cordially received by two gentlemen, both of them charming in the warmth of their manner and reception. To one of them he took, as he subsequently expressed it, an instant 'shine.' . . . To this one, he devoted his whole attention for the evening, listening with close and genial interest to everything he had to say, and periodically shushing aside the other, who from time to time would seek, timidly and politely, to edge in with a suggestion or passing word. As he was leaving the theatre, he addressed a sotto voce query to his companion of the evening. 'Who *is* that fellow?' he demanded. 'That—why that's your host, Baron Rothschild!' replied the other. A look of grieved concern seized O'Neill's countenance. 'Good God, then who are you?' 'I?' returned the other, 'I'm Jack Campbell, a reporter on the Paris *Herald*.' It took O'Neill a week to recover his equanimity. 'That's what happens,' he subsequently said to me, 'when I go to the theatre!' "

Along with his interest in the foreign productions of his plays O'Neill developed an enthusiasm, while in Europe, for the recently developed "talkies." For some time he had held the belief that motion pictures, even in their silent stage, promised artistic possibilities. Years earlier he had toyed with a scheme to adapt *The Emperor Jones* into a silent film (it had come to nothing) and he had been impressed by the 1925 silent version of *Anna Christie*, with Blanche Sweet starred (and for which O'Neill had received only $7,000). Soon after its release O'Neill told an interviewer that *Anna Christie*, his only play that had been put on film to date, was "a delightful surprise."

"I consider it remarkably well acted and directed, and in spirit an absolutely faithful transcript," he added. "I would certainly welcome any like treatment of my work either in the films or on the stage."

A year later O'Neill again thought about preparing something specifically for the screen and discussed with Nathan his plan to write a film play for Lillian Gish. "Although there is nothing very definite in my mind," O'Neill had informed Nathan in the summer of 1926, "I would certainly like to meet her and have a chat so that I could get started thinking definitely about some of the vague film ideas in my mind."

In April of 1927, in Bermuda, O'Neill actually went to work on an original movie story, entitled *Ollie Oleson's Saga*. "Although this is a comedy of sorts," he had told Nathan, "my past experiences with the film folk does not lead me to expect that they will ever find it suitable. The one I had in mind for Miss Gish is still in my mind but it doesn't seem to develop into any sort of connected whole."

Undaunted—and, for that matter, unsolicited—he made another stab at writing for films in 1927; he rewrote two of his plays, *The Hairy Ape* and *Desire Under the Elms,* and sent both scripts to Richard Watts, Jr., giving him permission to discuss them in print if he so chose. Watts, of course, did choose, and devoted his *Herald Tribune* column of March 4, 1928, to the interesting news.

Discussing O'Neill's attitude toward "the new medium," Watts pointed out that the playwright, "instead of regarding it as a field for his patronage, has seriously considered its problems, its potentialities, its requirements and its limitations. And having considered them carefully he has re-written, not as photographed stage plays, but rather as creative works in a new field of expression, two of his finest works. . . .

"Mr. O'Neill . . . is by no means a constant picturegoer. Though interested by pictures, he sees but few of them, yet these have caused him to grow enthusiastic over the potentialities of this new medium. 'The Last Laugh' seems to him the finest of films, because it was a complete artistic work in itself, without dependence on any other manner of expression."

Watts wrote that it was seeing Emil Jannings in *Variety* that first inspired O'Neill with the desire to write for the screen.

" 'The Hairy Ape' seemed to O'Neill an excellent vehicle for the First Actor of the Cinema," continued Watts, "but the affinity between role and player did not blind him to the requirements of the cinema. So, with a magnanimity hitherto unknown among playwrights slumming in the films, he rewrote the play as a scenario by the simple means of casting aside the stage version and regarding the work as a motion picture."

O'Neill altered both plays considerably. In the case of *Desire*, he trans-formed Abbie Putnam, the New England woman who is the play's pivotal character, into Stephanie, a Hungarian immigrant girl. O'Neill also altered the woman's status—from the role of the new wife of old Ephraim Cabot, the patriarchal farmer, to that of his housekeeper.

Stephanie sets Ephraim and his three sons against each other, hoping they will destroy one another, leaving her in possession of the farm. The two older brothers go to California to seek gold, and then kill each other over its possession. In a fight over Stephanie, Eben kills his father. Stephanie summons the sheriff, and, in the end, confesses her complicity in the crime. The screenplay was never bought; when, after O'Neill's death, a film version of *Desire Under the Elms* was finally made, it retained the alteration of the New England Abbie to an immigrant girl, but in most respects it stuck closely to the original play. Even so, it was not a success.

In *The Hairy Ape* screenplay, which was not bought either, O'Neill strengthened the role of Mildred Douglas, whom Yank pursued and carried off after the stokehold episode. The film adapted from *The Hairy Ape* in 1944 departed much more radically from the original play than O'Neill's scenario and was an artistic and financial failure.

O'Neill always felt that motion-picture directors lacked the imagination and daring to transpose his works to the screen, but believed that one day they might. He confided to Watts at Le Plessis that the motion-picture medium had somewhere within it great possibilities for an entirely new school of playwriting. And when Walter Huston visited him in 1930, O'Neill suggested that Huston act in his film versions of *The Hairy Ape* and *Desire Under the Elms*. Huston reported, on his return to America, that while O'Neill had not yet seen a talkie, he had "tremendous respect for its limitless possibilities."

Regardless of what he told Huston, O'Neill had in fact seen a talking picture—his first—in Paris, some months earlier. It was *The Broadway Melody*.

". . . and, think what you will of me," he had written Nathan in November, 1929, "I was most enthusiastic! Not especially at the exhibit itself, naturally, but at a vision I had of what the 'talky' could be in time when it is perfected. Looked at from the personal angle, I saw how its technique could set me free in so many ways I feel still bound down—free to realize a real Elizabethan treatment and get the whole meat out of a theme. Not that the 'talky' folk are ever liable to let me realize any of these dreams but I think the day may come when there will develop a sort of Theatre Guild 'talky' organization that will be able to rely only on the big cities for its audiences."

O'Neill then revealed what had probably been all along at the bottom of his attraction to motion pictures: "As for the objection to the 'talkies' that they do away with the charm of the living, breathing actor, that leaves me completely cold. 'The play's the thing,' and I think in time plays will get across for what their authors intended much better in this medium than in the old."

Another aspect of the "talkies" that beguiled O'Neill was the possibility of combining an acted play with a filmed background which would reveal (as a sort of substitute for asides) the thoughts and memories of the characters. Although he never attempted to carry out this scheme, he continued to give it some thought during the following years.

As for the sound version of *Anna Christie*, released in 1930 with Greta Garbo starred in her first talking role, O'Neill informed Watts that he was anxious to see it because he admired Garbo. But a year later he told Watts he had not seen it and was not going to, because friends had warned him it was bad. He was, however, still hopeful about the future possibilities of motion pictures. He was contemplating a version of *Lazarus Laughed*, he said, in which only the actor playing Lazarus would appear on the stage, while the rest of the production would be filmed.

"He believes," Watts reported, "that this would make the difficult production feasible and that, in addition, it would be helpful to the mood of the play, in showing its protagonist as the one live person in a world of marionettes."

O'Neill was far less sympathetic to the medium of radio as an art form. In response to a fellow American who had written to ask him about certain aspects of radio broadcasting in France, O'Neill replied that he knew nothing whatever about the radio situation "over here."

He himself did not own a radio, and did not intend to. "Life is quite noisy enough," he said, but added that he might be "crabbed" from having heard one of his one-acters "cast upon the air in England!"

A few years later the actor Harrison Dowd wrote to O'Neill requesting permission to do *The Moon of the Caribbees* over a Hartford, Connecticut, radio station. O'Neill granted permission, but expressed doubt that Dowd would succeed in circumventing the radio censors, and felt that a censored version of the play would "fall flat." (Excerpts from *The Emperor Jones* with Charles Gilpin had done just that, in 1920, when transmitted "through the huge horn," as one newspaper put it, as the first serious drama to be broadcast "in the history of the radio wireless.")

Years later, in 1948, O'Neill softened his attitude somewhat about the air waves in a statement that included a prediction about the effect of television on the theatre: "It is possible to write well for the radio. Norman Corwin has shown that to be true. But I feel that radio should stick to its own medium and not try to act as a substitute for the theatre. It has a field all its own. When television becomes more prevalent, still another method will be used. But no matter what happens, neither films nor ether waves will ever take the place of reality."

LIII

"AFTER SEVERAL FALSE STARTS, ALL ROTTEN, THINK
I have hit right line for first draft now," O'Neill recorded in his *Mourning
Becomes Electra* work diary in October, 1929.

His basic conception of the main characters was at this point well established and clearly indicated that, despite its classical derivation, this
play was to be yet another examination of the emotional fabric of the
O'Neill family.

As he had conceived it, the legend now fitted into his own specific
frame of reference. Lavinia (here a symbolic representation of O'Neill
himself) loses, in rapid succession (and in the same order as O'Neill)
first her father, then her mother, then her brother.

Her father, Ezra Mannon (Agamemnon) returns from the Civil War
to his unfaithful wife, Christine (Clytemnestra); Christine poisons Ezra
because she wants to marry her lover, Adam Brant (Aegisthus), and
Lavinia (Electra) and Orin (Orestes) murder Adam in revenge; Christine
commits suicide and Orin, guilt-ridden by her death and by his incestuous
involvement with Lavinia, follows her example.

Finally Lavinia condemns herself to a life locked away from the
world—bound, as she declares, "to the Mannon dead"—as O'Neill felt
himself bound to and haunted by his own dead. "I'm the last Mannon,"
says Lavinia at the end of the play, echoing O'Neill's mournful cry to a
friend, soon after Jamie's death, "I'm the last of the O'Neills!"

Although Lavinia is a woman, she is, in many ways, one of the most
personally revealing characters O'Neill ever created, and her final speech
is one of the most soul-baring O'Neill ever wrote; it incorporates both his
consuming preoccupation with the act of suicide and his mordant belief
in the inevitability of an even crueler self-punishment:

"I'm not going the way Mother and Orin went," Lavinia declares.
"That's escaping punishment. And there's no one left to punish me. I'm
the last Mannon. I've got to punish myself! Living alone . . . with the dead
is a worse act of justice than death or prison."

And then O'Neill, with uncanny insight and foresight, proceeded,
through Lavinia (at a time when he was ostensibly at the height of per-

sonal peace and happiness), to forecast his own fate in the last years of his life:

"I'll never go out to see anyone! I'll have the shutters nailed closed so no sunlight can ever get in. I'll live alone with the dead, and keep their secrets, and let them hound me, until the curse is paid out and the last Mannon is let die! (*With a strange cruel smile of gloating over the years of self-torture*) I know they will see to it I live for a long time! It takes the Mannons to punish themselves for being born!"

In early November of 1929, O'Neill resumed work on the play, after a long interruption in Paris at the dentist's. He believed he was finally on the right track, after having, as he put it, got himself "terribly messed up searching for new ways and means and styles." He now planned to do the job with "the utmost simplicity and naturalness," and felt it would "come with a rush from now on."

"I'm going ahead and let it write itself. The result will probably be a modified, simplified 'Interlude' technique," he told Nathan.

His plan was to work furiously, holding himself rigidly to an act a week, and get the first draft of the twelve acts in the three plays done by February 1. He would then set the play aside for six months, take a trip somewhere, and write the first draft of another play already developing in his mind (*Days Without End,* which he did not finally get down to writing until 1932).

O'Neill worked with rapt concentration for three months—he advanced his private deadline for the completion of the first draft from February 1 to March 1—allowing himself no interruptions. (He would not even take time off to read Manuel Komroff's new book, sent to him by the author; he explained, apologetically, "I may be foolish, but I have never been able to read anything but trash when I was hard on the job. It throws me off. Either I lose some of the desired concentration for my work or else I can't concentrate on the book because I'm obsessed with work.")

By January 7, O'Neill was more than halfway through with the draft, having reached his seventh act (third act of the second play.)

"I am working longer hours than I ever have before as a day after day stint," he reported to Nathan. "Sometimes I think it's grand and other times that it's rotten—as usual." He added that the dialogue was not, after all, to be "Interludian," and that everything else he had tried by way of experiment had been unworkable.

"There are plays," he said, "of direct passion and intensity, and involved, inhibited cerebrations don't belong in them. I monkeyed around with schemes for dialogue and ideas for production until my head ached— but the story I had to tell made all such stuff seem futile and I finally settled down to the direct and least noticeable way, and I find I can get everything said about these characters' souls, hearts and loins that can be said."

On January 15 O'Neill presented Carlotta with the notebook containing his entries about the characters and plot of the first two plays of the trilogy. He scribbled the following inscription: "To Carlotta—my wife—these first fruits (very unripe!) of my work in Our New Year—with all my deepest love and gratitude for all you have meant to me!—and all your help!"

On February 19 O'Neill informed Liveright that he was nearly finished with his first draft and described it as "a large affair," but declined to reveal any details until the play was finished. He said this would probably not be for a long time, for to him the end of a first draft meant about two-fifths finished with the total work on the play.

"I am feeling more than a little washed up, I have worked so damned hard and steadily," he added, "and as soon as I write curtain on the first draft I am going to Italy for a month's vacation."

He wrote "curtain" two days later—February 21, 1930. Exhausted but exhilarated, he made preparations for his holiday, planning, upon his return from Italy, to copy and revise the entire manuscript from beginning to end in longhand. He would then set the manuscript aside while he made a first draft of a new play, after which he would copy and revise *Mourning Becomes Electra* for the third and—he hoped—final time.

"When you consider," he told Nathan just before leaving for Italy, "that there are twelve full-sized acts—four to a play—in this opus you can see I am a glutton for punishment! But I think the results will justify the pains taken. By this method, which I think I will adopt hereafter with all my stuff, I think I should get all out of my material it is possible for me to get."

Never before, he added, had anything ridden him so hard. "Carlotta has been a brick," he went on. "She has collaborated by keeping the old château running with uncanny efficiency so that nary an outside worry has touched me or bogged my stride even for a moment. A most marvelous wife and friend! I am steeped to the ears in gratitude—and more than gratitude! And though it has been lonely for us collectively and individually at times, nevertheless we've been happy and made quite a pleasant life of it alone together here."

The O'Neills returned, refreshed, from their vacation in Italy and by the end of March O'Neill was again immersed in *Electra,* having abandoned his plan to set it aside for six months; he found that it was still riding him to the exclusion of any other idea. On March 27 he recorded some of the pain of his creative birth pangs:

"Read over first draft 'M.B.E.' Scrawny stuff but serves purpose as first draft—parts damned thrilling but lots more lousy—not enough meat . . ."

He would write a second draft, he told himself, incorporating the use of masks and asides. He was most dissatisfied with the way in which he had conveyed the "sense of fate" and wanted to indicate more vividly what he called "the unrealistic truth wearing the mask of lying reality."

He would also strive, in his second draft, for a more formalized structure of the trilogy, using a shipboard scene at the center of the work to symbolize the sense of escape and release conveyed by the sea to the Mannons. In addition he would use as an underlying theme repeated references to an idyllic South Sea island, whose appeal of peace was to illustrate the Mannons' "longing for the primitive and mother symbol—yearning for prenatal, noncompetitive freedom from fear . . ."

The sea chanty "Shenandoah," O'Neill went on to note, should be used "as a sort of theme song—its simple sad rhythm of hopeless sea longing peculiarly significant—even the stupid words have striking meaning when considered in relation to tragic events in play." He also determined to use the townsfolk as a stylized chorus at the beginning of each play.

Four days later O'Neill began on the second draft.

He had been at it for about a month when he advised Benjamin De Casseres that "there's a hell of a lot to be done yet before it's what it ought to be—and then it won't be!"

The second draft was completed in four months. By mid-July, 1930, O'Neill was feeling "drained out." He had never worked so intensively over such a long period before, and almost regretted that he had ever begun such an ambitious project. He tried to cheer himself up with the reminder that a mental let-down was normal at this point. "After all," he wrote in his diary, "do know I was deeply moved by each play as I wrote it—that test has always proved valid heretofore . . ." He would set the play aside while he went to Paris for dental work—"best anodyne for pernicious brooding over one's inadequacies!—anything else seems like best of all possible worlds when your nerves are prancing to sweet and low down of dentist's drill."

To amuse himself in Paris between sessions with the dentist, and perhaps to help take his mind off the agonizing business of writing *Electra*, O'Neill made a midnight appointment with Louis Gruenberg, the composer, who was preparing an operatic version of *The Emperor Jones*. The meeting lasted until four in the morning, during most of which time

Gruenberg tried to persuade O'Neill to write the libretto. O'Neill was less enthusiastic about opera than about movies, and Gruenberg was compelled to resort to his own literary talents. (Upon receiving the libretto from Gruenberg some months later O'Neill declared that he was pleased with the results. The work was performed in January, 1933, at the Metropolitan Opera House in New York, with Lawrence Tibbett playing the title role in black face.)

On July 18 O'Neill, having returned to his castle, reread the second draft of his trilogy and found it better than he had expected, but still in need of considerable work. Chiefly, he thought, the asides seemed unnecessary—"don't reveal anything about the characters I can't bring out quite naturally in their talk or their soliloquies when alone"—and he decided to delete them.

He began rewriting on July 20. ". . . think I have hit on right rhythm of prose—monotonous, simple words driving insistence—tom-tom from 'Jones' in thought repetition," he said in his diary.

On August 23, having tabulated the time spent thus far on *Electra*, O'Neill wrote to Komroff that he had "put in over 225 working days on this new job since the middle of last November, which is harder than I've ever worked at a stretch before." He added that he was left "sick with writing at the end of each day," and pointed out that the two long-hand drafts he had completed constituted, in effect, six full-length plays since the previous November. This was work, "even as handwriting," he said. He was now going over his second draft, he continued, and would then lay it aside for a few months, after which he would rewrite it for the final version.

"How is it going?" he asked rhetorically. "Well, some days I think it's grand and others I want to burn it. . . . It's like an old man of the sea on my back. I think if I'd known what a job it would be I'd have quit before I started. (But of course that's a lie!)."

He added that he and Carlotta were planning to go to Egypt that winter.

"Egypt has always called me," he said. "I've a greater intuitive hunch for their feeling about life and death than for that of any other culture—and I think the aspects of the country will confirm this. I expect in a queer way to feel spiritually and psychologically at home there."

By September 16 O'Neill had completed his rewritten draft. He had eliminated the asides, but kept the technique of what he called "stylized soliloquies" and also the use of masks.

A few days later he was in Paris—again for a session with the dentist, who was gradually replacing all his teeth with false ones—and in his hotel room he read through his new "stylized-soliloquies version" twice. This time he had fresh misgivings. The soliloquies, he felt, retarded, rather than advanced the plays' rhythmic flow. He decided to take them out, along with the masks.

On September 21, still in Paris, O'Neill consoled himself for the grueling labor he had put into his stylized soliloquies version, and outlined a scheme for what he hoped would be his final draft of the trilogy. The previous draft had not really been wasted effort, he mused, because it had given him new insight into his characters. But he now had to tackle the difficult job of translating the essence of the soliloquies into straightforward dialogue—"as simple and direct and dynamic as possible . . . let [the characters] reveal themselves—in spite of (or because of!) their long locked-up passions, I feel them burning to do just this!"

He thought he could retain the effect of masks, without actually using masks, through skillful make-up. ". . . in repose," he wrote, "the Mannon faces are like lifelike death-masks . . . this can be gotten very effectively by make-up, as can also the family resemblances—(make-up isn't a lost art in European theatre, why should it be in ours?—only our shiftless inefficiency)—I can visualize the death-mask-like expression of characters' faces in repose suddenly being torn open by passion as extraordinarily effective . . ."

O'Neill worked on this new version at Le Plessis until October 15, then left for a month's trip to Spain and Morocco. He had decided to put off his trip to Egypt, as he believed his final draft of *Electra* would occupy him most of the coming winter. From Seville, at the end of November, he wrote to Komroff that Spain was "very interesting to an old Catholic!"

Back at Le Plessis, he reviewed the work he had done before taking his vacation and found himself "fairly well satisfied," but wrote in his diary that he had several new ideas he urgently wanted to try out.

By early December his "big Opus," as he described it to De Casseres, was in its last stages. He could not tell yet how good or bad it was, he said, because he had no more perspective on it now than "a fly has on the flypaper to which he's stuck."

Weakened by his unremitting exertion on the play, O'Neill fell ill of flu around Christmas time. Carlotta caught the malady, recovered, then had a relapse and was obliged to enter the American Hospital in Paris for treatment. The new year found O'Neill in the Hôtel du Rhin, Place Vendôme, in Paris; here, though still not fully recovered himself, O'Neill worked on final revisions, sending the manuscript to a typist in sections, while waiting for Carlotta to recover and visiting her every day. Her hospital stay lasted three weeks.

The thought of returning to Le Plessis depressed O'Neill. His romantic castle had been a disappointment to him that winter, and he was about ready to scrap his beloved French countryside.

"Just now," he reported to Komroff on January 20, 1931, "the fair land of Touraine resembles the dismal swamp. . . . You may gather from this that I am a bit fed up with the smiling country of la belle France in the wintertime. And by God, I am! I would not spend another winter here for anything. Their climate is too much for me."

At the beginning of February, things began to look a little brighter to O'Neill. On February 2 the typing of the play was finished and the next day Carlotta was able to leave the hospital. He and Carlotta made plans to vacation in a sunny climate, but first they had to return to their gloomy chateau—and there, once again, O'Neill read over the *Electra* manuscript and found it wanting.

"[I] don't like most of new stuff—" he wrote in his diary on February 7, "—all right, but introduces too many added complications—trying to get added values has blurred those I had—too much of muchness—would need another play added to do it right—and would be wrong even then!—can't crowd intuitions all hidden aspects of life forms into one work! . . ." The revision occupied him for nearly two weeks.

It had rained almost steadily since his return to Le Plessis, and what O'Neill now craved was a change to warm weather and a chance to swim. Accordingly, he and Carlotta booked passage on a ship sailing from Lisbon for the Canary Islands on February 25. Notifying Nathan of his impending trip, O'Neill brought him up to date on the status of *Electra*.

"It has been one hell of a job!" he said. "Let's hope the result in some measure justifies the labor I've put in."

Adding that, despite his closeness to the play, it left him "moved and disturbed spiritually," he went on:

"I have a feeling of there being real size in it, quite apart from its length; a sense of having had a valid dramatic experience with intense tortured passions beyond the ambition or scope of other modern plays. As for the separate parts, each play, each act, seem better than I hoped."

O'Neill took the *Electra* manuscript with him to the Canary Islands and read it again—this time with only minor reservations.

"[It] looks damned good to me," he wrote in his diary at Las Palmas on March 8 "—funny how typed pages bring out clearly values that too-long familiarity with long-hand had rendered vague and undynamic . . ."

But the play needed cutting and condensing, and O'Neill had little rest during his "vacation."

He and Carlotta returned to Paris by way of Casablanca and Tangier, and by April 9 O'Neill was able to write triumphantly in his diary: "All work finished—script off to Guild."

O'Neill had abandoned his plan of putting the play aside for a long gestation period. In a characteristic turnabout, he was now eager for a Broadway production, more than willing to leave the serenity of his château, and anxious to return to America and the despised show shop.

It is interesting that just about the time O'Neill began work on *Mourning Becomes Electra,* which was instrumental later in earning him the Nobel Prize, his name was being mentioned as a contender for that honor. In November, 1929, an article in the Paris *Herald* had listed him, along with Sinclair Lewis and Theodore Dreiser, as a possible recipient of the honor, "which mention," O'Neill said to a friend at the time, "is at least a step forward for us Yanks!" O'Neill observed, however, that the award was much more likely to go to Thomas Mann. "I hope so," said O'Neill. "He deserves it. I think his work, with a few exceptions, is great stuff." (Mann, of course, did receive the award that year.)

The following summer O'Neill had told Nathan in Paris that he valued his new-found happiness with Carlotta far more than the Nobel Prize.

"On careful consideration—and no sour grapes about it because I have had no hopes—I think the Nobel Prize, until you become very old and childlike, costs more than it's worth," O'Neill said. "It's an anchor around one's neck that one would never be able to shake off. . . .

"I'll tell you what I want and it's the God's truth. I want just what I've now at last and for the first time in my life got! . . . The last time I saw you I told you I was happy. A rash statement, but I now make it again with a tenfold emphasis . . . you don't know into what a bog of tedium and life-sickness I was sinking. I was living on my work as a fellow does on his nerves sometimes, and sooner or later my work would certainly have been sapped of its life because you can't keep on that way forever, even if you put up the strongest of bluffs to yourself and the world in general. Now I feel as if I'd tapped a new life and could rush up all the reserves of energy in the world to back up my work. Honestly, it's a sort of miracle to me, I'd become so resigned to the worst."

Despite O'Neill's estimate of European chauvinism, the Nobel Prize was bestowed on Sinclair Lewis the following year. In his speech before the Swedish Academy in Stockholm on December 12, 1930, Lewis took the opportunity to pay O'Neill a compliment, while at the same time taking a slap at his fellow countrymen who were not overjoyed by the Academy's choice. On his way across the Atlantic to accept the prize, Lewis said, he had amused himself by fancying what the reaction of his countrymen would have been if some American writer other than himself had been singled out for the honor—Dreiser, for instance, or O'Neill. He explained that, although Dreiser had cleared the trail for honesty and boldness in American fiction, if he had won the prize "you would have heard that his style . . . is cumbersome, his choice of words insensitive. . . ."

"And," Lewis said, " had you chosen Eugene O'Neill, who has done nothing much in the American drama save to transform it utterly in ten or twelve years from a false world of neat and competent trickery to a world of splendor, fear and greatness, you would have been reminded that he had done something far worse than scoffing, that he had seen life as something not to be neatly arranged in a study, but as terrifying, magnificent and often quite horrible, a thing akin to a tornado, an earthquake or a devastating fire."

O'Neill read Lewis' address to the Swedish Academy and was both grateful for his praise and amused by his invective. "I was tickled to death with the whole address," he later told Nathan.

An announcement of less world-shaking significance than Lewis' speech in Stockholm, but one whose symbolic impact was felt by O'Neill, had taken place a few weeks earlier. On January 10 his old house at Peaked Hill Bar—the first home he had owned, the place where he had written all or parts of such plays as *Beyond the Horizon, Anna Christie* and *The Emperor Jones*—was claimed by the sea that now separated him by 3,000 miles and an immeasurable spiritual distance from his once beloved Provincetown.

For Eugene Jr., to whom his father had given the house as a gift, just as James had given it to O'Neill, it meant the loss of a pleasant summer retreat. But for the man who thought of himself as the Sea-Mother's Son, it meant one more exclamation point in the ironic drama of his life. The Sea-Mother had claimed a tangible chunk of O'Neill's past—the accumulated and nearly forgotten clutter of half a dozen years.

Susan Glaspell cabled O'Neill the news, and received a cable of thanks, in which O'Neill asked that anything that had been salvaged be kept for Eugene Jr., including the sturdy old desk on which he had written his plays.

The New York *World* carried a long, intimate story about the house and its celebrated former occupant by Mary Heaton Vorse. Mrs. Vorse described the leave-taking visits to the house, shortly before it was engulfed by the waves, of such former friends of O'Neill as Edmund Wilson, Hutchins Hapgood, Edna St. Vincent Millay, Frank Shay and Sinclair Lewis.

"The old house has come to its tragic end—an end which seemed fitting," Mrs. Vorse ended her article. "The Provincetown Players are no more. My wharf, upon which their theatre stood, was demolished in a storm years ago. The falling of Peaked Hill Bar closes a chapter."

In March, while he was in Las Palmas, O'Neill again became the subject of news in his own country. Early that month the *Strange Interlude* plagiarism trial finally took place, and for about a week O'Neill's name appeared regularly in the headlines of the New York newspapers. The case was tried in the Woolworth Building in the chambers of Federal Judge John M. Woolsey, who, two years later, rendered the historical decision lifting the ban on James Joyce's *Ulysses*.

The first session, on March 11, ended when the defense counsel made a motion to dismiss the suit on the ground that even if the ideas of Miss Lewys' book and O'Neill's play were alike, there had been no plagiarism, because ideas could not be copyrighted. The motion was denied, and the trial continued the next day, with Miss Lewys emerging as a rather foolish woman under Harry Weinberger's caustic cross-examination.

On the following day O'Neill's denial, by proxy, was read from the witness stand. Weinberger placed one of the defense counsels, Alan Hays, on the stand, and asked him to answer questions that had been put to O'Neill earlier at the direction of Federal Judge William Bondy. Hays thereupon read O'Neill's statement to the effect that he had not read *The Temple of Pallas-Athenae* prior to writing his play, and that neither the Theatre Guild nor Liveright had suggested that he use the book as a basis for a play.

Weinberger then introduced in evidence photostatic copies of pages from O'Neill's work diaries, which contained a synopsis, written in 1923— a year before Miss Lewys' book had been published—of *Strange Interlude*, together with notes on thirty-two unwritten plays.

In his statement, as read by Hays, O'Neill also said that he had discussed the play during its writing with George Pierce Baker, Kenneth Macgowan and George Jean Nathan, among others. He had never heard of Miss Lewys or her book, he said, until he read in 1929 in a Paris newspaper that she had filed suit against him and then he had read her novel at the suggestion of Harry Weinberger.

Weinberger then took the witness stand himself, with a view toward asking himself some questions regarding an interview he had had with O'Neill the previous summer.

Judge Woolsey, reflecting the general jocularity of the proceedings, smilingly remarked, "It would be terrible, wouldn't it, if you asked yourself a question you couldn't answer."

Fortunately, Weinberger found himself able to answer all the questions he put to himself, and he was replaced on the stand by Lawrence Langner, and then by Liveright's editorial manager, T. R. Smith, both of whom denied that they had read *The Temple of Pallas-Athenae* and both of whom presented to the court their copies of the book with uncut pages.

The trial was resumed on the following Monday. On that day the high spot was the testimony of no less a figure than George Jean Nathan, and the newspapers made the most of it. "Nathan in Court Tilt Aids O'Neill Defense" read the prominent headline in *The Times,* over a story which ran a column and a half. "Nathan Admits O'Neill Flouted Advice He Gave," read the headline over an even longer story by Ishbel Ross in the *Herald Tribune.*

The courtroom on that day was so crowded by curious onlookers that the doors and aisles were blocked. The session lasted until after seven o'clock at night, with the courtroom still filled to capacity. Judge Woolsey, who later declared that the trial had been "most interesting," took advantage of Nathan's presence on the witness stand to fill in some gaps in his own literary background, as, for instance, when Nathan mentioned in passing that he did not like all of O'Neill's plays, notably *Welded,* which he declared "seemed a ridiculous exaggeration of the Strindberg method."

"What is that method?" inquired the judge.

"It is," Nathan obligingly responded, "the intensification of the dramatic action, of which O'Neill is so fond. If he stems from anyone, he stems from Strindberg. He carries his emotions to levels that become unnatural."

Miss Lewys' attorney, Daniel F. Cohalan, attempted to establish that Nathan and O'Neill had discussed *The Temple of Pallas-Athenae* one night in New York. Cohalan had convinced himself that such a conversation had occurred, and he tried to demonstrate that Nathan had been too drunk at the time it took place to be able to remember it.

"You say that you walked with O'Neill from his hotel, the Lafayette, to Sill's Oyster Restaurant on Sixth Avenue and that during that long walk you and he did not discuss my client's book at all?"

"The principal topic of conversation during that walk was the legs of Lotta Faust [the musical comedy star who had entranced O'Neill during his Betts Academy days]."

"Did O'Neill do much drinking that night at dinner?"

"He didn't touch a drop."

Cohalan tried to rattle Nathan by inquiring into his own drinking that evening.

"By careful count," said Nathan, "I had two Martinis, two small glasses of Chianti, three small glasses of beer, and a green mint frappé."

"And you insist, nevertheless, that you still remember accurately what you and O'Neill talked about during your walk to the restaurant?"

"If I can accurately remember the number and nature of the drinks I had, it is naturally easy for me to remember such a simple thing as Lotta Faust's legs."

Arthur Garfield Hays, attorney for Boni and Liveright, brought Nathan's testimony to an end, falling into the same vein of bantering ridicule that had characterized the whole trial.

"Do you wear your handkerchief in the upper right-hand pocket of your jacket," he demanded, "because Duke Louis, a character in Miss Lewys' book, did likewise?"

Nathan denied the allegation, and explained to Judge Woolsey that he wore his handkerchief in a right-hand pocket so that he would not crush the cigars which he carried in the left-hand pocket of his vest. Judge Woolsey pronounced this very sensible.

Summing up his case, Cohalan declared that O'Neill was "too cowardly" to come to America to defend his own suit and asked the court to take this into consideration. Weinberger replied by describing Miss Lewys as a "hysterical woman."

"One of the rackets in America is the plagiarism racket," he added, "and any successful author is likely to be its victim."

Judge Woolsey thereupon interrupted to offer a bit of literary criticism of his own, pointing out that he had read both *The Temple of Pallas-Athenae* and *Strange Interlude* twice, and that O'Neill's characters lived before him while Miss Lewys' characters were not so vivid.

Defense counsel Alan Hays asked the court not only to render a decision favorable to the defense but to discourage baseless suits by making the plaintiff pay the court costs. Judge Woolsey was interested in this proposal, and asked Hays to furnish him with a precedent.

Cohalan declared that this stand was "audacious" and asked it to be noted on the record that the "time has not yet come in this free land when a wronged person shall be prevented from hiring reputable counsel."

Judge Woolsey, smiling, said, "Gentlemen, I've taken all these fine points into consideration. There's no need to expand on the matter any further."

After due deliberation Judge Woolsey, on April 22, handed down his decision, and O'Neill, reading of it in France, may have had the grace to blush a little for his low opinion of his country's legal processes. Judge Woolsey not only dismissed Miss Lewys' complaint but penalized her by directing her to pay $17,500 in counsel fees to the attorneys who had opposed her suit. (Of this, $7,500 was to go for O'Neill's expenses, $5,000 for the Theatre Guild's, and $5,000 for Liveright's.)

Judge Woolsey's opinion covered forty-two printed pages. In it he said:

"Neither the evidence of the plaintiff nor the argument and brief of her counsel, nor a careful analysis of the two books since the trial, has in any way tended to decrease my first impression that there is not any possible ground for the contention that 'Strange Interlude' is an infringement on the plaintiff's book.

"On the contrary, my reflection in regard to the case and a reading of relative authorities and text books has ripened my first impression into a conviction that the plaintiff herein has made a wholly preposterous claim. . . .

"I find that the plaintiff has utterly failed to make out by any direct evidence that Mr. O'Neill had any access to her book before he wrote or while he was writing 'Strange Interlude.' "

O'Neill's moral victory was complete; but financially he did not fare so well, nor did the other defendants, for Miss Lewys was unable to pay the penalty ordered by Judge Woolsey. After considerable stalling she filed a petition of bankruptcy in the summer of 1933, explaining that she had total assets of $100 in household goods. But she did not, at least, ever sue anyone again, and it was believed that her example became something of a deterrent to others.

O'Neill had been so irked by the charges brought against him that, despite his aversion to joining anything, he gave his support to a committee headed by Channing Pollock that was to work for a change in the plagiarism law, a change enabling the courts to dispose of baseless suits immediately. Around the same time he joined another committee that proposed fighting the Mastic censorship bill, a measure calling for state censorship of the New York stage. O'Neill, aligning himself with his fellow Pulitzer Prize winners who had also been asked to voice their opposition, cabled from Europe that he was "absolutely opposed to any compromise with any form of censorship." Several years earlier, protesting against a similar censorship bill, O'Neill had made a clear statement of his feelings:

"The history of theatre censorship proves that it never has much effect on the evils it ostensibly aims to eliminate, while it always ends by becoming a stupid tyranny used by reactionary bigotry and intolerance to suppress all freedom of expression. The censorship which begins by banning a strip tease show always finishes by deleting Shakespeare, condemning as treason a play which hints George Washington might not have chopped that tree, or forbidding as blasphemy a drama doubting the Jonah whale legend. In the light of what has happened in censor-loving Europe and Asia I think any American should reject with disgust any attempt at censorship in any form whatsoever."

O'Neill was back in the news a few days following the trial. *The New York Times* devoted half a column to the announcement that his new play, which was "three in one," was on its way from France to the offices of the Theatre Guild. And on April 29 the Guild reported that the play had arrived.

"I could not put it down, once I started reading, and had to go on and read the three plays, one after the other," Langner wrote to O'Neill. "The effect was to knock me silly for the rest of the day."

The Guild's board accepted the play joyfully and O'Neill was asked to come home as soon as possible to help with its production.

He and Carlotta left Le Plessis early in May and boarded the Holland-America liner *Statendam*. Their lease on the château still had a year to run, and they planned to return to France after the production of *Electra*, which they estimated would be within six months.

But, like Peaked Hill Bar, Brook Farm and Spithead, Le Plessis became one more abandoned home for O'Neill. He had the remarkable capacity of being able to walk away from a country estate as casually as he had once moved his orange crates out of an unpaid-for Greenwich Village flat. He seemed unable to regard any house as a home, however much he had craved it at first and however elaborately it was appointed for him.

Shortly before sailing for the United States O'Neill had sat in his tower workroom and written an inscription to his copy of the final long-hand version of *Mourning Becomes Electra*. He dated it April 26, and gave it to his wife:

"To Carlotta:
"In memory of the interminable days of rain in which you bravely

suffered in silence that this trilogy might be born—days when I had my work but you had nothing but household frets, and a blank vista through the salon windows of the gray land of Le Plessis, with the wet black trees still and dripping, and the mist wraiths mourning over the drowned fields —days when you had the self-forgetting love to greet my lunchtime, depressing such preoccupations with a courageous, charming banter— days which for you were bitterly lonely, when I seemed far away and lost to you in a grim, savage, gloomy country of my own—days which were for you like hateful, boring, miserable enemies nagging at nerves and spirit until an intolerable ennui and life sickness poisoned your spirit!

"In short, days in which you collaborated, as only deep love can, in the writing of this trilogy of the damned! These scripts are rightly yours and my presenting them is a gift of what is half yours already. Let us hope what the trilogy may have in it will repay the travail we have gone through for its sake! I want these scripts to remind you that I have known your love with my love even when I have seemed not to know; that I have seen it even when I have appeared most blind; that I have felt it warmly around me always—(when in my study in the closing pages of an act!)—sustaining and comforting, as warm, secure sanctuary for the man after the author's despairing solitude and inevitable defeats, a victory of love-in-life—mother and wife and mistress and friend! And collaborator!

"Collaborator, I love you!"

LIV

THE RETURN OF O'NEILL AND CARLOTTA TO THE United States in 1931 was even more melodramatic than their departure had been two and a half years earlier. Again, their efforts to achieve privacy were unavailing; but this time it was Carlotta's discarded husband, not O'Neill's rejected wife, who thrust them into the limelight.

They slipped into the country quietly enough on Sunday, May 17.

"When we docked in New York," Carlotta recalled, "I arranged with an official of the steamship company to let us escape without notice by the ship news reporters. Gene, Blemie and I remained down below until we were summoned. We were then speeded through customs and into a taxi. I was relieved that we'd been able to avoid publicity."

The O'Neills went to their suite at the Madison Hotel, reserved for them by Carl Van Vechten. As soon as the Theatre Guild was informed of O'Neill's arrival, it made plans for a press conference to be held the following Thursday morning. To avoid the strain of individual interviews, O'Neill was to discuss his new play with the full contingent of New York's theatre reporters.

Fatigued by their trip, the O'Neills secluded themselves in their suite for the next two days, had all their meals sent to their rooms, and rested.

On Wednesday in the early hours of the morning Ralph Barton decided to make Carlotta a grim, belated wedding present. In his penthouse, just a few blocks away from the Madison Hotel, he sat down at his typewriter and wrote a long note, which he headed, "Obit." He put on his pajamas, got into bed, lit a cigarette, thumbed through a worn copy of Gray's *Anatomy* until he came to a section dealing with the heart, set the book aside—still open to that section—smoked another cigarette and then shot himself through the head.

"Everyone who has known me and who hears of [my suicide]," he had written in his farewell note, "will have a different hypothesis to offer to explain why I did it. Practically all of these hypotheses will be dramatic and completely wrong. Any sane doctor knows that the reasons for suicide are invariably psychopathological and the true suicide type manufactures his own difficulties. I have had few real difficulties. I have had, on the contrary, an exceptionally glamorous life, as life goes; and I have had more than my share of affection and appreciation.

"The most charming, intelligent and important people I have known have liked me, and the list of my enemies is very flattering to me. I have always had excellent health, but since my early childhood I have suffered from a melancholia, which in the last five years [the period since his divorce from Carlotta] has begun to show definite symptoms of manic-depressive insanity.

"It has prevented my getting anything like the full value out of my talent, and the past three years has made work a torture to do at all. It has made it impossible for me to enjoy the simple pleasures of life. I have run from wife to wife, from house to house and from country to country in a ridiculous effort to escape from myself. In doing so, I am very much afraid that I have brought a great deal of unhappiness to those who loved me.

"In particular, my remorse is bitter over my failure to appreciate my beautiful lost angel, Carlotta, the only woman I ever loved and whom I respect and admire above all the rest of the human race. She is the one person who could have saved me had I been savable. She did her best. No one ever had a more devoted or more understanding wife. I do hope she will understand what my malady was and forgive me a little.

"No one thing is responsible for this and no one person—except myself. If the gossips insist on something more definite and thrilling as a reason, let them choose my pending appointment with the dentist or the fact that I happened to be painfully short of cash at the moment.

"No other single reason is more important or less temporary. After all, one has to choose a moment; and the air is always full of reasons at any given moment. I did it because I am fed up with inventing devices for getting through twenty-four hours of a day and with bridging over a few months periodically with some beautiful interest, such as a new gal who annoyed me to the point where I forgot my own troubles. . . .

"I kiss my dear children—and Carlotta."

Barton's body was discovered at ten o'clock on Wednesday morning by his maid. The police were called, and it wasn't long before most of Barton's friends in New York had heard of his suicide. Carl Van Vechten lunched with O'Neill and Carlotta at the Madison that day and found that they had already been informed of Barton's death and of the contents of the suicide note. Harold Ross, editor of *The New Yorker* and a close friend of Barton's, had called Carlotta to cushion the shock.

"Gene was very quiet during the lunch," Van Vechten later said.

"He had evidently discussed the suicide with Carlotta before I got there. But Carlotta talked about it. She said she couldn't understand this horrible thing—that Barton wasn't in love with her."

Benjamin and Bio De Casseres had been invited to dine with the O'Neills that evening and when they learned of Barton's suicide they expected that O'Neill would cancel the dinner, but he did not. When they arrived, O'Neill said, "Well, Ralph Barton blew his top." That was the only reference to the subject during the evening.

The following morning the newspapers featured stories about the suicide, and the O'Neills figured prominently in the headlines. "Ralph Barton Ends His Life With Pistol; Artist in Note Mourns Loss of Third Wife, Carlotta Monterey, Now Wed to Eugene O'Neill," read the front-page headline in *The New York Times*. That was bad enough, but O'Neill and Carlotta were even more distressed to read that Barton's brother, Homer, an actor, had declared that Ralph had paid the O'Neills "a friendly visit" upon their arrival in New York. "My brother was still in love with his third wife, Carlotta Monterey, and the realization that he had lost her broke his heart," Homer added.

O'Neill was not happy at the prospect of his scheduled press interview at the Theatre Guild; he was certain that the reporters would question him about Barton, and he was tempted to cancel the whole thing. Finally he hit on a way to forestall such questions. He had his attorney, Harry Weinberger, issue a statement to the press regarding Homer Barton's comments, and he asked the Guild press agent to stipulate to the reporters that their questions must be confined to the subject of *Mourning Becomes Electra*.

"Mr. and Mrs. Eugene O'Neill," Weinberger told the newspapers, "have asked me to state that, contrary to newspaper reports or statements by Homer Barton, brother of Ralph Barton, they have not seen Mr. Ralph Barton since their return to the United States, and Mrs. O'Neill, the former Carlotta Monterey, desires to state definitely that she never saw or heard from Mr. Barton since her divorce from him more than five years ago."

Meanwhile, one of the Guild's press agents, Joe Heidt (who, in Robert Sisk's absence from town, was arranging the O'Neill interview), had telephoned all the drama desks and city desks of the New York newspapers, requesting them to instruct their reporters not to ask questions about Barton or Carlotta.

"They all promised," Heidt recalled. "Later that morning the reporters and photographers turned up and were jammed into the Guild's board room."

John Chapman, critic for the New York *Daily News,* was one of those present.

"O'Neill went through with the interview, but he stipulated that he would be questioned by only one of the twenty or thirty reporters present," Chapman noted years later. "He was pallid and shaking and sweating when he faced his lone inquisitor—and so was I, for I had been chosen to do the questioning."

In spite of O'Neill's plea, a reporter managed to put a question about Barton, and O'Neill felt obliged to answer, elaborating on the Weinberger statement. He said he and Carlotta had not seen Barton "since our arrival here on Sunday.

"As far as I know I never met Ralph Barton," he continued. "He did not call on us. I do not question his brother's sincerity, for Mr. Barton might have told him that he had called. He was in a very peculiar mental state. I know that he had made no effort to see Mrs. O'Neill."

According to Heidt, the press "behaved beautifully" during the interview, which lasted for an hour and a half.

O'Neill declared, among other things, that living abroad had enabled him "to see America more clearly" and "to appreciate it more." He answered questions about the relative merits of the European and American theatre—Europeans, he said, would "soon be coming over here to learn from us" and added that "the American stage has a dynamic quality and freshness theirs lacks." He discussed his plans for the future—he and Carlotta would go to California soon to visit Carlotta's relatives, but he would do no work for the motion pictures, not because he had "a snooty attitude toward the pictures" but because he had work of his own planned for the next five years.

He would go back to France after the production of *Electra,* he said, and live there until his lease on the château expired and then would settle down in America, perhaps on a plantation in Virginia—somewhere where there was sun.

Explaining his scheme for the production of *Electra,* he said there would be a preliminary week for the critics, during which *Homecoming* would be presented on Monday and Tuesday, *The Hunted* on Wednesday and Thursday, and *The Haunted* on Friday and Saturday; after that, the plays would be given in rotation, one play each week.

"I don't know," he admitted, "whether the Guild is going to agree to that." He said that rehearsals would begin in mid-August and that the director and leading actors would be selected within a few days.

"There are no asides in the play," he said, in answer to a question, adding that he did not think the soliloquy technique would work except in rare instances. Asked what direction his new work would take, he replied:

"One of my principal obsessions is the reintroduction of masks as a medium in the theatre. One of my next plays is to be a play of masks. My idea about masks is that they can be made acceptable to the modern audience—as they were in ancient times—but in a new sense. People do recognize, from their knowledge of the new psychology, that everyone wears a mask—I don't mean only one, but thousands of them. I believe people will come to accept them in the theatre. I don't think *The Great God Brown* had a long run merely because it was a novelty."

After the reporters left, Heidt and O'Neill congratulated each other on how well things had gone. A woman reporter lingered to ask more questions about Barton but O'Neill refused to answer them, feeling he had more than met his obligation. He was now presumably safe from further inquisition, for his address in Manhattan was a secret and he had safeguarded the privacy of his immediate future by announcing that he was going to California.

But O'Neill's tranquillity was shaken when Heidt happened to look out the window.

There were several taxicabs lined up at the curb, all with reporters in them, presumably waiting for O'Neill to leave so they could trail him to his hotel.

O'Neill was anxious to leave, and Heidt thought he could get him out of the Guild building without being followed, by taking him over the roof of an adjacent building and out a side street exit; but Heidt was afraid, at first, to suggest this to O'Neill. Finally he did suggest it, and O'Neill immediately agreed.

The building adjoining the Guild housed a skating rink, and Heidt called the rink and asked for permission to cross their roof, "so they wouldn't think we were a couple of burglars and take a shot at us." Then Heidt guided O'Neill to Room 64, the Guild rehearsal room on the top floor. There was a fire ladder leading from there to the roof, and the two men climbed it, crossed to the adjoining building, and went down the rear fire escape. Heidt put O'Neill into a cab. O'Neill had a smile on his face as he left.

Then Heidt walked around the block to the front of the Guild building and told the reporters that there was no use their waiting, because O'Neill had left. They refused to believe him. They said they knew there was an apartment in the building and that O'Neill obviously intended to spend the night there. They were so preoccupied with tracking O'Neill, that it did not occur to them to wonder how Heidt had managed to get out of the building. He went home himself and when he returned the next morning at ten, there were still three cabs in front of the Guild. "They'd been there all night long," Heidt said. "They never did find out where O'Neill was staying, and after a while the Barton thing died down."

When he returned to the hotel O'Neill told Carlotta that the male reporters were fine. "It was the women reporters whom he despised," Carlotta later said. "He told me they had asked personal, prying questions."

The O'Neills changed their minds about going to California and rented instead a comfortable house in Northport, Long Island, set on seven acres of private beachfront overlooking Long Island Sound. They moved in on June 10, having signed a four-month lease at a cost of $3,500. The house was on a slight elevation, its windows commanding a sweeping view of the Sound and, on clear days, of the Connecticut coast. Flashes of light from the lighthouse tower at night and the sound of the lighthouse horn on foggy days reminded O'Neill of New London, and he was seized with a desire to revisit his old home. Carlotta thought it unwise, but O'Neill insisted, and they made the trip.

"I said, 'Don't do it, darling, don't do it,' " Carlotta recalled. " 'Don't ever try to go back; keep your ideas, but don't go back.' No, he must go. So we took the car and went. We drove along Pequot Avenue, and he said, 'I can't find it, I can't even see it.' In the time that Gene had been away several little houses had been built along the water, and everything was so changed that he couldn't find his house at first. I was thunderstruck when I saw it, this quaint little birdcage of a house, sitting there. Somebody had bought it, and we didn't go in. Gene said, 'I shouldn't have come.' And I said, 'Well, never mind, you have come, now let's get out of here.' And he said, 'Yes, let's go away, I don't want to look at it,' and that was that."

O'Neill and Carlotta, unknown to them, were observed on Pequot Avenue by the sister of the girl whom O'Neill was to idealize in *Ah, Wilderness!* a little over a year later. Maibelle Scott's sister, Arlene, happened to be looking out her window when O'Neill and Carlotta (whom she had never met, but recognized from photographs) stepped out of their car for a moment to stare at Monte Cristo Cottage.

In spite of his disappointment over the nostalgic journey, O'Neill was connected by more than memory with New London. A number of Ella's relatives were still living there, among them Agnes and Lil Brennan; O'Neill was fond enough of Agnes Brennan to send her a needed $300 when he learned she could not meet a mortgage payment on her house.

In Northport, across the sound from New London, O'Neill rocked on his porch and dwelt on the scenes of his youth. Late in July he jotted down a few notes for a play he was thinking of calling *Nostalgia*. He did not write a play with that title, but no doubt his nostalgic comedy, *Ah, Wilderness!* was slowly taking shape in his mind.

Since his return from Europe O'Neill had been trying also to establish some sort of contact with his more immediate and less palatable past. Through Harry Weinberger he negotiated for a meeting with Shane and Oona, from whom he had now been separated for more than two years. He seemed to find it inconvenient to exercise the "visitation rights" granted him under the divorce decree. But a meeting finally was arranged that summer. O'Neill and Carlotta called for Shane, who was ten, and Oona, who was six, in a chauffeur-driven car and took them for a ride. The reunion was not a notable success. Neither O'Neill nor Carlotta was at ease with the children and Shane, about to enter the preparatory school, Lawrenceville, in the fall, was even more shy and withdrawn than his father had been as a child. Though Carlotta later declared that she had found Shane "a sweet, charming child," the meeting was not repeated for many months; O'Neill was determined to avoid all contact with Shane's and Oona's mother, and his stubborn hatred of her overwhelmed whatever affection he might have held for his two younger children.

As for Eugene Jr., O'Neill continued to be fond and proud of him— though not to the extent of attending his wedding. Eugene Jr. married a Forest Hills girl, Elizabeth Green, on June 15. Though the ceremony took place in Long Island, not far from Northport, only Eugene's mother and Elizabeth's father attended. Young Eugene, whose life, in many ways, was to mirror that of his father, had been granted special faculty permission, while still a junior at Yale, to marry and return in the fall to complete his senior year. He was just twenty-one, only a little older than his father and mother had been at the time of their marriage. Tragedy had already touched his life; his young stepbrother, to whom he had been close, had recently died in a fall from the nineteenth floor of an office building in New York.

Eugene visited his father in Northport after his honeymoon, and O'Neill was newly impressed with him. A top-ranking honor scholar, Eugene had won, in May, the Winthrop prize, one of the chief awards of the scholastic year.

O'Neill told his son he was still making revisions on *Mourning Becomes Electra*, editing the script both for production and for publication. Liveright was anxious to bring it out in book form as soon as possible after its Broadway premiere, for O'Neill had demonstrated with *Strange Interlude* that a published play could be a national best seller.

In discussing the sources of *Electra* with his son O'Neill found that Eugene Jr. far outshone him in his knowledge of Greek tragedy.

Lillian Gish visited the O'Neills at Northport one weekend when Eugene Jr. also was present. Encountering her after a session with his son, O'Neill remarked with a smile, "I can't talk to him. He's too erudite for me."

Before moving to Northport for the summer, O'Neill lunched with Brooks Atkinson, and Atkinson politely asked what background reading he ought to do to help him understand the trilogy when he went to review it for *The Times* in the fall. O'Neill replied that he need not do any research, that the play was self-contained and not at all esoteric. Would Atkinson like to read it? O'Neill asked. Atkinson said he would, and took the bulky manuscript with him to his summer home in Durham, New York.

"I had a lot of things to do around my place during the day," Atkinson later recalled, "and I read the three plays during the evenings. I was not overwhelmed, and I decided I'd read them again before communicating with O'Neill. Apparently he was nervous about my reaction and impatient at not hearing from me quickly. He telephoned me from Northport. When O'Neill's call came through on my crank phone, I could hardly hear his voice; it was impossible to discuss anything, and I said I'd write him."

Atkinson did write, saying he thought the public would be overwhelmed by the first play, disappointed by the second, and would find the third better than the second. His letter crossed one from O'Neill, in which the dramatist asked for his opinion on the best method of presenting the trilogy. O'Neill still believed that each play must be allotted an evening to itself, and was concerned primarily with whether the evenings should be consecutive or staggered. The Guild, he wrote Atkinson, did not see eye to eye with him on his plan to open all three plays the same week, allowing two days' performances to each. O'Neill said the Guild wanted to "start week by week—on account of the difficulty of swinging the whole thing in one week."

"My answer," O'Neill went on, "is that it *is* a difficult thing, obviously, and should be done in a strikingly unorthodox manner to emphasize the unusualness of the job and get the full impact of its dramatic quality concentrated—also that my carefully planned suspense from play to play would be frittered away over an opening of weekly intervals—that that is not my trilogy as I wrote it! Of course, after an opening week in which the whole work is revealed, I think a week by week basis afterwards would be justified and not harmful to my intent since the three plays would already have been shown as a closely-knit whole."

Atkinson wrote back that he would like to see the three plays presented one right after the other, within a three-day span.

"It is gratifying that you agree with me and even go me one better in advocating a straight three performance scheme," O'Neill replied. "Of course, you are right, that is *the* right way. My day's interval between plays is really a compromise with the difficulty of straight production and the strain on whoever plays Lavinia."

Then O'Neill took up some of Atkinson's criticisms of the trilogy, expressing a willingness to discuss them further but not conceding their validity. (Atkinson, for example, found Orin's speeches of self-analysis undramatic, and O'Neill flatly disagreed, but promised to listen analytically to these speeches during rehearsals.)

He asked Atkinson to choose a time when he could come to stay for a day or more at Northport. By mid-August the visit had not yet been arranged, and O'Neill wrote Atkinson that it didn't matter where they got together, "the important point is, let's get together somehow."

"I agree that a good deal may be accomplished by a revival of our discussion—from my selfish point of view, at least!" he said. "The more of the inner workings and background of the writing of the trilogy I can set before you—and of my work in general—the better for me in the sense of my getting more value out of your criticism, for or against."

A fresh point of view would give rise to self-critical questionings of great value, he went on, adding that most criticism of real value did not come until after the opening, when it was too late.

"That's *one of many* reasons," he explained, "why I'm always glad to have any critic (whose opinion I respect, and whose right to criticize the drama I admit) read my scripts before the openings."

He said it was unfortunate that most producers violently objected to this, adding that producers wanted a "surprise value at all costs" and that they believed the acting and directing would be judged better when the critic knew nothing of the play he was supposed to interpret.

In preparation for his forthcoming discussion with Atkinson, O'Neill reread—in galley proofs—the entire trilogy. He found he liked it and in a lengthy and self-congratulatory entry in his work diary, he noted that the plays had "power and drive and the strange quality of unreal reality that I wanted." He was elated that he had achieved his primary goal of approximating the sense of fate conveyed by Greek tragedy purely in modern psychological terms, and without having to resort to the Greek convention of supernatural forces.

He felt that technically he had achieved a "unique thing in dramaturgy

—each play complete episode completely realized but at same time, which is important point, not complete in that its end begins following play and demands that play as an inevitable sequel—few trilogies in existence in drama of all time and none of them has this quality . . ."

Despite his satisfaction with the trilogy as a whole, O'Neill did extensive cutting and editing, particularly on the first and third plays, and new galley proofs had to be made. Early in September he studied them and then noted, in his final entry in the work diary, that Act Two of *The Haunted* was "weak spot still—needs rearranging—but will postpone final decision on this until I hear cast read plays—then it will hit my ear."

The problem, however, would not leave his mind, and George Jean Nathan, during a visit to Northport, found O'Neill brooding about it.

"One night," Nathan later wrote in *Cosmopolitan,* "after a particularly trying day and the mopish gloom it had imposed upon him, O'Neill burst into my bedroom at three A.M., gleefully shouting that he had at last seen what was wrong with the play; what it needed was simply the transposition of a first act scene into the third act.

" 'Maybe,' he proclaimed, 'if I were a drinking man, I would have seen it more clearly at the start. There are times in the writing of drama when a bit of cloudiness can bring a sudden gleam of light more effectively than too-long studious analysis.' "

Toward the end of summer O'Neill and Atkinson finally set a date to suit them both, and Atkinson went to Northport.

"It was a pleasant place," Atkinson recalled. "Carlotta was invisible for the most part, and Blemie was present at all meals. Gene drank a lot of Moxie. He swam in the afternoon. We were both enchanted when a Boston steamer, headed for New York, passed by.

"We discussed *Electra* some more. I felt it was overwritten and that the public might resent three nights. Gene, of course, disagreed."

Atkinson expressed his admiration for the handsome, chauffeur-driven Cadillac O'Neill had acquired, and about which O'Neill had previously—and apologetically—written him. ("Yes, it's a Cadillac 12!" O'Neill had said. "But lest this sound too pretentious for a serious-minded Dramatist, let me hasten to explain I snared it second-hand. Only used 2,000 miles, ironclad guarantee attached, looking brand new, over one thousand dollars off, who could resist this splendid gift of world depression? Not I, who have always been an A One snob when it came to cars and boats, which must have speed and line and class or 'we are not amused.' This snootiness dates back to early boyhood days. My father, the Count of Monte Cristo, always got me the classiest rowboat to be had, and we sported the first Packard car in our section of Connecticut.")

As for the chauffeur, Carlotta explained that O'Neill detested driving in traffic. When her husband returned to this country, he never drove a car himself, she said.

O'Neill and his wife continued to live in Northport during the first weeks of September, though they had signed, in July, a long-term lease on an eight-room duplex apartment in a new building at 1095 Park Avenue. During the first part of September O'Neill was, as he wrote to a friend, "half in, half out of town—half moved into apartment, half moved out of here."

Since 1095 Park Avenue was to be their permanent home—or so they thought, with their habitual optimism—Carlotta lavished on its decoration all her considerable talent as a homemaker. O'Neill's study, in particular, was designed to give him the utmost comfort, with a nautical atmosphere provided by brass ship's lanterns and pictures and models of clipper ships.

Rehearsals for *Electra* began in the second week of September. Like *Strange Interlude*, it was to forego an out-of-town tryout, and, because of its unusual length, seven weeks instead of the customary four were allotted for rehearsals.

Robert Edmond Jones, who had not worked on an O'Neill play since *The Great God Brown,* nearly six years earlier, was to design the sets and Philip Moeller was to direct. There was little or no disagreement about the casting of two of the major parts—Christine and Orin Mannon; Alla Nazimova, the Russian actress famous in the United States for her Ibsen roles, was chosen to play Christine, and Earle Larimore, who had endeared himself to O'Neill as Sam Evans in *Strange Interlude,* was cast as Orin. The role of Lavinia finally went to Alice Brady (who had turned down Nina in *Strange Interlude),* but not before O'Neill had offered it first to Ann Harding.

Ann Harding had met O'Neill in the later days of the Provincetown Players but did not know him well and, as she later said, "had no idea that he was particularly aware of my existence."

"I was quite overwhelmed with the signal honor of receiving from O'Neill the galley proofs of *Mourning Becomes Electra* and a most gracious letter indicating that I was his first choice for the title role," she added.

"At the time, I was under contract to Pathé Studio and did everything but blow up the entire lot to convince the obtuse gentlemen in command of my fate that it would greatly enhance my value to them to release me for *Electra*. Unable to make them see the light, I tried to break my contract—but that proved hopeless, as well. It is the major tragedy of my professional life that I was deprived of that great opportunity."

O'Neill, discouraged over losing Ann Harding, complained to friends that the "damned talkies" made the always difficult casting problem almost an impossible one. "Everyone you think of is tied up out there," he said.

"We felt," Lawrence Langner later wrote, "that Alice Brady was the finest actress available for the part of Lavinia, but we were afraid of losing her because of her peculiar reaction to *Strange Interlude*. Theresa Helburn and I did our best to woo her into accepting the role. We were helped in this by her father, William A. Brady. . . . We signed Alice to her contract, the details of which we negotiated over the telephone with her father."

"This cast may work out well—after a fashion," O'Neill glumly informed a friend on September 20. "Don't know. Hope so."

O'Neill attended rehearsals scrupulously from the beginning, and Carlotta nearly always accompanied him. Unlike Agnes, she took an active role in the productions of all her husband's plays. ("It was bad enough," Moeller once remarked, half jokingly, "to have to direct a show with the author present—here was his wife, too! But there was never any ill feeling.")

"I used to sit by Gene and take notes and things," Carlotta said. "With *Mourning Becomes Electra* we sat seven weeks. I never was bored a minute; it was wonderful."

O'Neill did a good deal of cutting during the first two weeks—mostly cutting that he, himself, felt would heighten the trilogy's impact—and it was soon discovered that the over-all playing length was not so great as had originally been supposed. All schemes for separate productions on different nights for the three plays were, accordingly, abandoned, and it was decided to present the trilogy in one chunk, like *Strange Interlude,* but beginning a little earlier in the afternoon, ending a little later at night, and shortening the dinner intermission, to make up the approximately hour and a half longer that *Electra* would run. The Theatre Guild issued an announcement to this effect, explaining that the first complete rehearsal had disclosed that "the unity and suspensive action of *Mourning Becomes Electra* would be aided if the plays were presented in a single day."

O'Neill was more expansive and more in contact with this cast than he had been with others. He was especially affable to Alice Brady, who was a friend of Carlotta's. One day during rehearsals Miss Brady's dog, Sammy, got into a fight outside the theatre with Blemie, and O'Neill had to separate them. He picked up Sammy and carried him into Miss Brady's dressing room.

"Sammy met my dog outside," O'Neill told her. "Sammy sniffed and said, 'My mother's appearing in your father's rotten play,' and my dog naturally leaped on him. Sammy should know better."

O'Neill had a great deal to say to Miss Brady, in a more serious vein, about her interpretation of Lavinia. In an interview shortly after the opening, Miss Brady told about it. O'Neill, she said, hammered in the fact constantly at rehearsals that no sentimentality must creep into the characterization of Lavinia and that "no one should feel sorry for her" at the final moment when she boards herself up in the Mannon house with her memories of the dead.

"Personally I feel that Mr. O'Neill meant Lavinia to be a symbol, rather than a living, breathing human being who buys hats and gloves and eats lamb chops," she added. "I may be wrong, but I'm quite sure that Lavinia could never eat a lamb chop. I simply couldn't imagine it. I think that's why Mr. O'Neill insisted that I wear a deathlike mask in my make-up.

"The part is not 'me' at all. I had to create a character totally foreign to my nature and to anything I had ever done before. Then, the play is not like any ordinary play where if you drop a word you can substitute another. You must say every word exactly as it is written. Otherwise you throw the whole rhythm of the play out. . . .

"But I love the part. It has a tremendous sort of abstract excitement for me. In the last few days of rehearsals and at the opening I became so wrapped up in it that I lost all sense of time."

As rehearsals progressed, according to Carlotta, "Gene became fascinated by the characterizations of Nazimova and Alice Brady—and of Earle Larimore—but particularly of the two women."

"But he also became aware that they were less and less what he had written," Carlotta added. "They were so wonderful, from their point of view, that they did no harm to the play—but they were not what Gene had fancied. For instance, Alice, who was Irish and French, was playing a New England woman—a thing like that disturbed him." (Much later O'Neill told an interviewer: "Alice Brady and Alla Nazimova gave wonderful performances in *Mourning Becomes Electra*, but they did not carry out my conception at all. I saw a different play from the one I thought I had written." And to the playwright S. N. Behrman he once remarked that *Electra* had every nationality represented in its cast *except* New England.)

One of the smaller roles, that of Seth, the seventy-five-year-old

Mannon gardener and man-of-all-work, was filled by the thirty-eight-year-old Arthur Hughes. After having been interviewed and approved by O'Neill and Moeller, Hughes was turned over to Cheryl Crawford, the Guild's casting director. Miss Crawford informed Hughes that he would have to sing the song "Shenandoah" in the play, and Hughes was appalled.

"I loved music," he said, "but I couldn't carry a tune, and I told Cheryl Crawford I couldn't sing. She said, 'Oh yes, you can. You just work at it.'

"I wanted to be in the play so badly that I did work at it. I bought a copy of the song at Schirmer's, and started practicing it, with my wife's help. I kept singing it to myself everywhere I went, on the street, in the subway, everywhere. Often I'd forget the tune, and I'd call my wife in a panic and she'd sing it to me over the telephone.

"Then came the day of the first run-through, and I had to sing it in front of O'Neill and Moeller. I sang it, wavering back and forth, and at the end Moeller, who was a connoisseur of music, turned to O'Neill and said, 'Well, Gene, what do you think?' 'Fine, fine!' O'Neill answered. 'This man *can't* sing!'

"O'Neill liked the idea of the singing being a little off key," Hughes explained. ("The voice," O'Neill had written in his stage directions, "is thin and aged, the wraith of what must once have been a good baritone.")

During rehearsals O'Neill rarely left the theatre for lunch. Carlotta packed sandwiches for him to eat in his seat. "We never ate in restaurants," Carlotta once explained, "because Gene would get so nervous in a public dining room. His hands would begin to shake and his face would sort of sink and he would get circles under his eyes and he would begin to sweat."

At the end of a run-through one day, O'Neill climbed on stage and was timidly accosted by a fragile old woman who played one of the villagers. O'Neill listened courteously while she asked him something about one of the scenes, then started to answer her question. Some Guild officials, gathered in discussion with Nazimova on the other side of the stage, called to O'Neill to join them.

With a curt, "Wait a minute, I'm talking to this lady," he turned back to his interrogator and spent another five minutes patiently answering her questions.

Several weeks before the scheduled opening of *Mourning Becomes Electra,* the writer and artist S. J. Woolf interviewed and sketched O'Neill in one of the Theatre Guild offices; the interview subsequently appeared, with a large portrait, in *The New York Times Magazine.*

"It is well to travel occasionally," O'Neill told Woolf, "but if a man wants to write about his country he must live in it. The tempo, the attitude, the psychology of Europe are different, and one unconsciously absorbs these things. An author is of necessity influenced by his surroundings. To write of Americans, one must live in America, breathe its atmosphere, experience its reactions, live its kind of life, and feel the pulse of the people."

O'Neill, Woolf reported, was very different from what one expected him to be, "more fragile, more tenuous, more apart. Behind his quiet manner there is a tenseness of nerves, which his long, thin fingers emphasized as they beat a tattoo on his thigh or dug themselves into the palms of his hands."

"One of the things I regret," O'Neill said, "is the passing of the experimental group theatre." He complained about the fact that there were "commercial managers who are doing the same things they were doing ten years ago," because they failed to credit their public with "as much sense or taste as it has."

"I believe," he also said, "that we have the best directors, the best writers, the best actors and the best scenic artists in the world right in this country, but all of them are going along each in his own way. If all this talent could be collected and made to work together I am certain that productions could be given here that would be unequaled."

(O'Neill was prepared to back this conviction with cash. Cheryl Crawford, together with two other Guild workers, Harold Clurman and Lee Strasberg, was at that time helping to organize the Group Theatre. She told O'Neill about the Group, explaining that they wanted to produce Paul Green's *House of Connelly*. She then asked O'Neill if he would help them get started. "Right then and there he gave us a check for a thousand dollars," Miss Crawford said.)

Woolf, concluding his interview with O'Neill, wrote:

"Suddenly O'Neill looked up and smiled. It was a boyish smile and an awkward one—as if he had just become aware of his long lapse into silence. Then, pointing to a drawing of Shaw that was hanging on the opposite wall, he remarked: 'I wish they would take that down; the old gentleman seems to be laughing at me.'"

On October 26, the day before the opening of *Electra*, O'Neill made his usual, painful speech of farewell to an exhausted cast. Carlotta, who was by his side, jocularly remarked that O'Neill's next project, when he was rested, would be a twenty-minute vaudeville sketch—an announcement loudly cheered by all. Carlotta then bestowed a sprig of Scotch heather upon each member of the cast for luck, and she and O'Neill went home to compose opening-night telegrams—Carlotta sending a wire of her own to Philip Moeller, thanking and blessing him.

O'Neill, carrying on his joke with Alice Brady, sent flowers, in Blemie's name, to her dog, with a note saying that he (Blemie) hoped Sammy's "mother" would do a good job in his (Blemie's) "father's" play.

The first-nighters began arriving at the Guild Theatre a little before four in the afternoon of October 27. (The early hour was for the benefit of the critics; subsequent performances began at five and ran until nearly midnight.)

Among the early arrivals were Herbert Bayard Swope, Dorothy Parker, Edna Ferber, Elmer Rice and Otto Kahn. Kahn went home as he had at the intermission of *Strange Interlude*, during the dinner hour following *Homecoming*, to change into evening clothes. For those who did not wish to dine in neighboring restaurants, or go home to dress, sandwiches and coffee were served in the lobby of the theatre. *The Hunted* and *The Haunted* were separated by a fifteen-minute intermission, and the trilogy came to a close, on opening night, shortly before eleven.

Though the marathon performance proceeded smoothly, Alice Brady, for one, later confessed that she had never before been so nervous on an opening night.

"When I made my first entrance and started to talk," she said, "I could hardly hear my own voice. I was nearly crying from fright and was absolutely sure that I'd forget my lines. You see, Mr. O'Neill kept changing and changing the lines at every rehearsal. He even made some minor changes on the day of the opening performance. So that every time I'd think of a line, I'd wonder with horror whether that was the line which had been cut or changed in the script.

"After the first two scenes, however, I was all right. But I wouldn't go through it again for anything in the world."

"During the first intermission," Langner later recorded, "I saw Papa Brady, then in his seventies, bounding up the aisle like a schoolboy, his eyes bright with joy. I congratulated him on Alice's performance. 'She should have done *Strange Interlude* but she didn't ask my advice on that,' he said."

The reviews were extraordinarily enthusiastic. Even Robert Garland, who had now become the critic for the recently amalgamated *World-Telegram*, hailed the play, though he seemed to choke over several qualifying phrases before he could get the words out: "The good news from Fifty-second Street is to the effect that, to put it baldly, Mr. Eugene O'Neill has at last turned out a masterpiece." Percy Hammond also voiced approval: "From four o'clock in the afternoon yesterday until eleven at night, Eugene O'Neill heckled Life in one of the bitterest and lengthiest of his attacks upon that popular institution . . . even if you prefer your plays short, as I do, you will arise from your chair, as I did, and join the others in earnest salvos of appreciation. . . . All that is needed to enjoy it is endurance and the spirit of an intelligent fanatic. . . . I congratulate Mr. O'Neill and the Theatre Guild for . . . a thoughtful, earnest, theatrical and sanely delirious stunt."

Richard Lockridge, on the *Sun,* ventured the opinion that *Electra* was O'Neill's "first play of lasting importance" and declared that O'Neill had finally emerged as "an artist in the theatre—as perhaps the outstanding artist in the theatre of today."

John Mason Brown, who was already established as a lecturer on the theatre and was in addition serving as the drama critic of the New York *Evening Post,* wrote:

"It is a play which towers above the scrubby output of our present-day theatre as the Empire State Building soars above the skyline of Manhattan. Most of its fourteen acts, and particularly its earlier and middle sections, are possessed of a strength and majesty which are equal to its scale. It boasts, too, the kind of radiant austerity which was part of the glory that was Greece.

"It is one of the most distinguished, if not the most distinguished, achievements of Mr. O'Neill's career. It is . . . uneven, but so . . . are the Himalayas. . . . It is an experiment in sheer, shuddering, straight-forward story-telling which widens the theatre's limited horizons at the same time that it is exalting and horrifying its patrons."

Brooks Atkinson, elated with the revised script, evaluated the play as "a universal tragedy of tremendous stature—deep, dark, solid, uncompromising and grim . . . heroically thought out and magnificently wrought in style and structure. . . . Mr. O'Neill . . . has never before fulfilled himself so completely; he has never commanded his theme in all its variety and adumbrations with such superb strength, coolness and coherence. To this department, which ordinarily reserves its praise for the dead, 'Mourning Becomes Electra' is Mr. O'Neill's masterpiece."

Gilbert Gabriel was equally enthusiastic:

"Leaping groggily over the several corpses strewn on the Guild Theatre's boards when 'Mourning Becomes Electra' has ended, I rush— with the rush of a last-minute report—to bear witness that here is a grand scheme grandly fulfilled. And that the Guild has again to thank Eugene O'Neill for a success of extraordinary size and import and ennobling prestige. And that no play in years has won so stirring an ovation at its close."

The New Yorker's Robert Benchley, though he enjoyed the play, attempted to reduce it to size. *Mourning Becomes Electra,* he maintained, was less Greek tragedy than "good, old-fashioned, spine-curling melodrama."

". . . are we not forgetting one very important source of [O'Neill's] inspiration, without which he might perhaps have been just a builder of word-mountains?" wrote Benchley. "Was there not standing in the wings of the Guild Theatre, on that momentous opening night, the ghost of an old actor in a white wig, with drawn sword, who looked on proudly as the titanic drama unfolded itself, scene by scene, and who murmured, with perhaps just the suggestion of a chuckle: 'That's good, son! Give 'em the old Theatre!'? The actor I refer to needs no introduction to the older boys and girls here tonight—Mr. James O'Neill, "The Count of Monte Cristo" and the father of our present hero. . . .

"It is his precious inheritance from his trouper-father, his father who counted 'One,' 'Two,' 'Three' as he destroyed his respective victims, one at the curtain to each act; it is his supreme sense of the Theatre in its most elementary appeal, which allows Eugene O'Neill to stand us on our heads (perhaps our heads would have been more comfortable) and keep us there from five in the afternoon until almost midnight. In this tremendous play he gives us not one thing that is new, and he gives us nothing to think about (unless we are just beginning to think), but he does thrill the bejeezus out of us, just as his father used to, and that is what we go to the theatre for. . . .

"While we are on our feet, let us drink once again to the Count of Monte Cristo."

There was unanimous praise for the direction and the acting and, as in the case of *Strange Interlude,* articles of appraisal and analysis continued to be written about *Electra* for many months after its opening—not all of them favorable. St. John Ervine, for example, back in England after the collapse of the *World* in April, 1931, wrote a two-part criticism of the published version of *Electra,* in which he took umbrage at the claim of O'Neill's publisher that O'Neill was "generally regarded as the world's greatest dramatist."

"*Generally?*" cried Mr. Ervine. "There happen to be alive simultaneously with Mr. O'Neill the following American dramatists: Marc Connelly, Susan Glaspell, Paul Green, Sidney Howard and Elmer Rice, in addition to two authors of light comedies, Mr. Philip Barry and Mr.

S. N. Behrman. . . . The following British dramatists are also contemporaneous with Mr. O'Neill: Sir J. M. Barrie, John Galsworthy, Harley Granville-Barker, Somerset Maugham, Sean O'Casey, Sir Arthur Wing Pinero and Bernard Shaw. . . . Clearly, if Mr. Eugene O'Neill is superior to all of these authors, he is a most remarkable man, and his plays, therefore, must be tested, not by local and contemporary standards, but by standards that are universal. Mr. O'Neill, in brief, is to be placed in comparison with the great Greeks, with Shakespeare, with Molière and Racine, with Ibsen and Strindberg and Chekhov. Can he bear to be compared with them?"

It took Mr. Ervine the better part of his two long articles to answer his own question in the negative.

Joseph Wood Krutch, on the other hand, felt that O'Neill not only could bear comparison with Ibsen, the Greeks and Shakespeare but that Ibsen, for one, suffered by the comparison. In an introduction to a collection of O'Neill's plays in 1932, Krutch wrote:

"By common consent, Eugene O'Neill is acknowledged to be the most distinguished of the group which created the serious American drama . . . the best of [his] work is also the best of our contemporary dramatic literature. His is the first name to be mentioned in any discussion of the American theatre of today, and he is the only one of our playwrights who has a wide international fame. . . ."

Mr. Krutch said that *Mourning Becomes Electra,* "like all supremely great pieces of literature," was "primarily about the passions and primarily addressed to our interest in them."

"Once more we have a great play which does not 'mean' anything in the sense that the plays of Ibsen or Shaw or Galsworthy usually mean something," he continued, "but one which does, on the contrary, mean the same thing that 'Oedipus' and 'Hamlet' and 'Macbeth' mean—namely, that human beings are great and terrible creatures when they are in the grip of great passions, and that the spectacle of them is not only absorbing but also and at once horrible and cleansing. . . .

"To find in the play any lack at all one must compare it with the very greatest works of dramatic literature, but when one does compare it with 'Hamlet' or 'Macbeth' one realizes that it does lack just one thing and that that thing is language—words as thrilling as the action which accompanies them. . . . But no modern is capable of language really worthy of O'Neill's play, and the lack of that one thing is the penalty we must pay for living in an age which is not equal to more than prose. Nor is it to be supposed that I make this reservation merely for the purpose of saying that Mr. O'Neill's play is not so good as the best of Shakespeare; I make it, on the contrary, in order to indicate where one must go in order to find a worthy comparison."

Electra continued to be more than merely theatre news. *The Times* was moved to comment on it editorially on October 31:

"Poor New England! She appears to be fated to chronic depression . . . hush, hark, crash, bang! what is that?

"It is another cheerful little Eugene O'Neill bulletin about New England. This time it is a couple of murders, a suicide and the regular assortment of repressions, explosions, seductions, lusts and incests. Critical opinion seems to be unanimous that Mr. O'Neill's restatement of the complicated family troubles of the Atreus family has resulted in a dramatic masterpiece. But it does seem a bit hard on New England, coming after the same author's celebrated 'Elms' of a few years ago. Surely there are enough trunk murders in Los Angeles, enough love-nest slayings in New Jersey, enough axe murders in Seattle, to suggest a respite for the country east of the Hudson. . . . New England has been accused of so many things that there's danger of people coming to regard Horror as peculiarly a New England product."

And someone composed a jingle, parodying an old song, which appeared in F.P.A.'s "Conning Tower":

"My sister was Electra, / Like yours, you will allow; / And you may have a mother / That needs a bullet now. / I've come to this great drama, / Destruction for to deal; / And if you dare insult me, sir, / I'll tell Eugene O'Neill."

To enlighten the public about the creative torment that had gone into the making of *Mourning Becomes Electra*, O'Neill permitted Joe Heidt to distribute mimeographed copies of his work-diary entries to newspapers and magazines. (The *Herald Tribune*, among other publications, published the diary in its Sunday edition of November 8, 1931.)

O'Neill, bewailing once again his own lack of poetry, had the following afterthought about his play:

"With *Mourning Becomes Electra,* masks were called for in one draft of the three plays. But the Classical connection was too insistent. Masks in that connection demand great language to speak—which let me out of it with a sickening bump! So I had to discard them. There was a realistic New England insistence in my mind, too, which would have barred great language even in a dramatist capable of writing it, an insistence on the clotted and clogged and inarticulate. So it evolved ultimately in the 'mask-like faces,' which expressed my intention tempered by the circumstances. However, I should like to see *Mourning Becomes*

Electra done entirely with masks, now that I can view it solely as a psychological play, quite removed from the confusing preoccupations the Classical derivation of its plot once caused me. Masks would emphasize the drama of the life and death impulses that drive the characters on to their fates and put more in its proper secondary place, as a frame, the story of the New England family."

Although the play received high praise and ran for 150 performances in New York, it did not capture the Pulitzer Prize. The winner was a musical—*Of Thee I Sing*—by George Kaufman, Morrie Ryskind, and George and Ira Gershwin.

The production of *Electra* was, in a sense, the climax of O'Neill's career. He was to complete six more plays, but only three of them were produced on Broadway in his lifetime. And of the three, only the light-hearted and atypical *Ah, Wilderness!* was an unqualified critical and popular success.

O'Neill and Carlotta did not, of course, attend the opening night of *Electra*. Instead, they drove to Northport for their first rest after seven solid weeks of rehearsal.

In mid-November O'Neill decided he needed a vacation far from New York, and he and Carlotta left for a three-week visit to Georgia.

It was during this trip that they decided Georgia was the place where they wanted to live, and they began building an expensive home there very soon after. They returned to New York in early December, but it was for a stay of only a few months; O'Neill found himself unable to settle down to any serious work in the distracting atmosphere of the city.

Among the people O'Neill entertained before he left for Georgia were George Tyler, who had got in touch with him after a long silence, and Joseph McCarthy, his roommate from Mount St. Vincent.

McCarthy did not find the reunion particularly exhilarating. "Gene was mostly silent," he said. "I'm afraid I stole a look at the sideboard before dinner. Gene said, 'I don't drink any more,' and he didn't offer me a drink, either."

The O'Neills invited Nathan to their apartment to celebrate the critic's fiftieth birthday on February 14, 1932. They asked Nathan to bring a friend, and he selected Atkinson.

"We got tight at a speakeasy before we arrived," Atkinson recalled. "Carlotta took a dim view of this."

Another guest during this period was George Pierce Baker, with whom

Carlotta was charmed. It was Baker's visit that inaugurated her O'Neill collection at Yale.

"Gene had given me all the manuscripts—five or six drafts of *Electra* —and I didn't know what on earth to do with them," she explained. "I told Baker about them, and said I didn't know whether to put them in a bank vault, or what. He suggested that I start an O'Neill collection, and he discussed this with the Yale Library, which, of course, was delighted."

On March 15 O'Neill's social life reached a high point when he made an appearance at a formal dinner.

The dinner, sponsored by the Theatre Guild at a midtown hotel between the first and second plays of the *Electra* trilogy that evening, honored Gerhart Hauptmann. In addition to Hauptmann, who was also the Guild's guest at the play, those present included Carlotta, Frau Hauptmann, and Hauptmann's secretary, Elisabeth Jungemann, later to become Lady Beerbohm. There was also an interpreter to translate the compliments exchanged by Hauptmann and O'Neill; neither spoke the other's language.

Not long before leaving Le Plessis, O'Neill had been gratified to read of Hauptmann's high opinion of him. In a conversation in Berlin with a *Herald Tribune* correspondent, Hauptmann had declared:

"Yes, a few of your playwrights have interested me considerably. There is Eugene O'Neill, for example, whose work I admire profoundly; he is one of the really great figures in modern drama. O'Neill is an example of what I mean when I say America is producing, and will produce in ever greater quantities, an art I feel is indigenous; it belongs to the American soil. No European dramatist could possibly have written those plays. The drama, under him, has found a new type of artistic expression. In some plays O'Neill is a really vital social force. I esteem his *Hairy Ape* as one of the really great social plays of our time. In other plays O'Neill is a sensitive poet; a really fine poet. His Negro play, *All God's Chillun Got Wings*, made a marked impression on me. It treats a very important problem intelligently, and above all, beautifully."

At the dinner O'Neill could now return the compliment, and he assured Hauptmann that he, along with Ibsen and Strindberg, had greatly influenced his own work. Hauptmann replied that he had easily followed the first part of *Electra* despite the language barrier, and that it was a beautiful play.

Upon his departure from the United States a few days later, Hauptmann told ship news reporters that *Electra* was the only play he had seen during his three-week visit and that "the two outstanding things in my visit, the whole of which has been delightful and interesting, were meeting O'Neill and attending *Mourning Becomes Electra*." (About a dozen years later, when he was in his eighties, Hauptmann wrote his own *Elektra* —part of a Greek tetralogy, which he completed two years before his death, in 1946.)

It was not more than a few weeks later that O'Neill left for Georgia, in another effort to seek isolation far from Broadway.

LV

IT WAS ILKA CHASE WHO HAD RECOMMENDED SEA ISLAND as a new home for the O'Neills. In the copy of *Mourning Becomes Electra* that O'Neill presented to Miss Chase not long after he moved to Georgia, he wrote: "To Ilka, who found our Blessed Isles for us, with the profoundest gratitude." The allusion was to the South Sea Islands of *Mourning Becomes Electra*, repetitively mentioned by various of the play's characters as symbolic of a longed-for peace.

Carlotta, interviewed by a reporter for a Boston newspaper in March, 1932, said that Sea Island seemed "a sort of fulfilment of the 'Blessed Isles,'" about which her husband had written. And in January of the following year, commemorating the date of his reconciliation with Carlotta in Shanghai, O'Neill echoed her sentiments more intimately. He inscribed a volume of his plays to her, quoting a speech made by his Americanized Aegisthus, Adam Brant, to Clytemnestra-Christine (". . . the sun drowsing in your blood, and always the surf . . . singing a croon in your ears like a lullaby! The Blessed Isles, I'd call them! You can forget there all men's dirty dreams of greed and power!") and adding:

"Blessed and Beautiful One, whose love and tenderness have made in my life a Blessed Isle of Peace and Beauty, I, the Blest, who love you, again as ever give thanks to God for you! . . ."

The "Blessed Isle" discovered by the O'Neills in Georgia was one of a group famous for its cotton and its traditional gentility, rather than for tropical glamour, and the $100,000 residence that Carlotta designed for her husband to live in was substantial rather than romantic. Described by Carlotta as "bastard Spanish peasant style," it was built of greenish-white stone (to cut down the hot southern sun's glare), contained twenty-two rooms, and boasted a courtyard and formal garden in front and a stretch of beach leading to the Atlantic at the back. (Eventually an eight-foot wall was constructed around the house to ensure privacy from staring passers-by.)

O'Neill's study, on the second floor, jutted out over the ground-floor dining room, and its curved wall, suggesting that of a galleon's prow, had windows facing out to sea. Inside, the study was fitted as a ship's cabin, with exposed wooden planking on ceiling and walls, a built-in bunk-sofa beneath the curved windows, and other nautical accouterments. A circular iron stairway led from the study to the "crow's-nest" on the roof; the whole effect was not unlike that achieved by O'Neill's own Isaiah Bartlett, the demented captain in *Gold*.

Mrs. Ben Pinchot, wife of the photographer, who interviewed Carlotta at some length during this period, kept the sheaf of notes she made for a projected magazine article (which did not materialize) and which shed a contemporaneous light on life in Georgia with the O'Neills. Carlotta told Mrs. Pinchot she had had a mental image of what she wanted to build, "down to the last towel rack," before one brick of the Sea Island house was put into place.

"After her experiences at the château," Mrs. Pinchot noted, "Carlotta was very decisive in her admiration of American plumbing, and she made certain that kitchen and bathrooms had the best—including, she told me, a bidet. The house was both comfortable and practical—no waste or extravagance, for display purpose; only a clean and precise and beautiful compactness."

Another feature of the house, recalled by several visitors, was high washstands in the bathrooms, making it unnecessary to stoop to brush one's teeth.

The huge living room, rising the full height of the house, was painted the same greenish white as the outer walls, and was furnished with somewhat austere comfort; on the walls hung old icons and the masks from *The Great God Brown*.

Before moving into their house, and while supervising the final stages of construction, O'Neill and Carlotta stayed at the nearby Sea Island Inn. While Carlotta attended to the details of decoration, O'Neill worked in his room at the inn, and one night he took time out from thinking about the new play he was outlining to write Carlotta an impassioned letter:

". . . Mistress, I desire you, you are my passion, and my life-drunkenness, and my ecstasy, and the wine of joy to me! Wife, you are my love, and my happiness, and the word behind my word, and the half of my heart! Mother, you are my lost way refound, my end and my beginning, the hand I reach out for in my lonely night, from my ghost-haunted inner dark, and on your soft breasts there is a peace for me that is beyond death! . . ."

The O'Neills named their new home Casa Genotta, romantically combining their two first names; the Italianate designation was a rather fanciful one to apply to a modern Spanish mansion set in the deep

American South and occupied by an Irishman and his Dutch-Danish-French wife.

During the hot summer months O'Neill labored over his new play, *Days Without End,* which was proving to be a particularly troublesome project and was to undergo many metamorphoses. Money problems also were plaguing him again—but in this, as he acknowledged, he was not alone. The Depression was in full sway. Refusing a loan to George Tyler in September, O'Neill explained, apologetically:

"I am up a tree with everybody else . . . all the *Electra* money has gone into the house I've built down here, with a balance still owing, and I'm cash broke and borrowing myself to keep me over until *Electra* opens up again on the road—praying it will stay out when it does open! . . . I feel damned badly about having to return a negative reply to your letter, and I want you to know it's the flesh and not the spirit that is weak. . . . I don't expect to be on my feet again for a year and a half—even if I get all the breaks and 'Prosperity' shows some signs of revival."

He added that there was "just one chance" he might be able to assist Tyler—if the "talkie" of *Strange Interlude* proved successful enough to encourage Hollywood to buy another O'Neill play.

But such a chance, O'Neill felt, was slim, in view of the fact that he had been able to sell only two plays to Hollywood in all his years of writing.

The movie version of *Strange Interlude,* bought by Metro-Goldwyn-Mayer soon after the settlement of the plagiarism suit, was released in the late summer of 1932. Even with Norma Shearer playing Nina and Clark Gable playing Edmund Darrell, the movie was not the overwhelming financial success that had been hoped for, although it was given a tremendous Hollywood build-up and was the film sensation of the year.

O'Neill, in spite of his pessimism, did make an effort in the fall of 1932 to stir up some movie interest in his old plays and United Artists, soon after, bought *The Emperor Jones,* which was released in 1933 with Paul Robeson as the emperor and Dudley Digges as Smithers.

Setting aside a third, and still unsatisfactory, draft of *Days Without End,* O'Neill allowed a very different sort of play to write itself during the month of September, 1932. He awakened early one morning, having dreamed a full-length play with every scene vividly etched in his mind. (Unlike William Archer, who once had a similar experience, O'Neill did not, upon further analysis, discover that the dreamed play was one Ibsen had already written; O'Neill's dream-play proved to be uniquely his own.)

He sat down at his desk at seven in the morning and worked steadily until late afternoon, by which time he had written a detailed scenario of *Ah, Wilderness!* Within six weeks he had completed the play in its final version.

"Only once before, in the case of *Desire Under the Elms,* has a plot idea come to me so easily," he later said. "I wrote it more easily than I have written any other of my works and then went back to *Days Without End.*" (He had apparently forgotten that eleven years earlier he had written *The Hairy Ape* in three weeks.)

Just before O'Neill began work on his reminiscent comedy, he was thinking with fond amusement about one of his father's crotchets. His agent, Richard Madden, had asked him if he wanted to release *Electra* to a certain English producer, and O'Neill had advised him to release the play only if the producer was willing to pay a substantial advance.

"I've sworn off giving plays to the English for nothing," said O'Neill. "If James O'Neill of Monte Cristo fame heard that I ever gave the cursed Sassenachs the slightest break he'd come back from the grave and bean me with a blackthorn! My, but didn't he love them!"

O'Neill referred to *Ah, Wilderness!* as a "Comedy of Recollection."

"My purpose," he later explained, "was to write a play true to the spirit of the American large small-town at the turn of the century. Its quality depended upon atmosphere, sentiment, an exact evocation of the mood of a dead past. To me, the America which was (and is) the real America found its unique expression in such middle-class families as the Millers, among whom so many of my own generation passed from adolescence into manhood."

Temporarily consigning the completed script of *Ah, Wilderness!* to a desk drawer, O'Neill took up *Days Without End* again in October and continued to wrestle with it for the next five or six months. Although this was the play originally conceived as the second in the series of three plays concerned with the "soul's sickness" theme, of which *Dynamo* had been the first, it actually bears more resemblance (both in the quality of its writing and in its description of an idealized marriage relationship) to *Welded.* It is justly regarded by many critics as one of O'Neill's worst plays. Like *Welded,* it was too close to its subject—which in this case was O'Neill's struggle to believe, through a return to Catholicism, in the eternity of his and Carlotta's love. O'Neill himself described *Days Without End* as a "modern miracle play" which "reveals a man's search for truth amid the conflicting doctrines of the modern world and his return to his old religious faith."

Days Without End was the last play in which O'Neill used masks. In view of his philosophy about masks, expressed during this period with renewed vigor, it is somewhat surprising that he should have abandoned them so completely. For, far from giving any hint that he was through with the mask concept, he expressed, at this time, a far-reaching interest in the use of masks in the contemporary theatre.

"Why not give all future classical revivals entirely in masks?" he had asked, rhetorically, in a recent newspaper article. "*Hamlet,* for example. Masks would liberate this play from its present confining status as a 'star vehicle.' We would be able to see the great drama we are now only privileged to read, and to identify ourselves with the figure of Hamlet as a symbolic projection of a fate that is in each of us, instead of merely watching a star give us his version of a great acting role."

O'Neill, like John Loving, the split-personality hero of *Days Without End,* was at the time of the play's writing engaged in a personal struggle over religion. The Hound of Heaven, having sporadically pursued him over the past thirty years, came as close to overtaking him, in 1932, as He ever would. Several lines from the Francis Thompson poem are, in fact, quoted in the text of the play. The symbolic ending he had used in *Welded* (the hero's outstretched arms, forming a cross, as he accepts the religion of love) became a specifically stated religious ending in *Days Without End.*

A friend of the O'Neills had recently introduced them to some Jesuit priests, and O'Neill had a number of talks with them.

"They were intellectuals," Carlotta said, "and Gene had respect for them. He discussed aspects of *Days Without End* with them. I was prepared to join the Catholic Church myself, if Gene wanted to go back; I would have done whatever was necessary to make him happy. But he did not go back. That was his last flirtation with Catholicism."

Days Without End is, like *Welded,* essentially the story of a passionately idealistic marriage between two insistently possessive people. But, whereas the hero and heroine of *Welded* are fated perpetually to act out their "love-hate" at a feverish pitch, and both are equally the victims and the victimized, in *Days Without End* the heroine is the victim and the hero's two selves fight a battle over her soul; in the end the cynical, destructive, doubting self (designated as Loving) is vanquished by the newly inspired John, and the now-harmonious personality of John Loving, standing in church with his arms upstretched to a life-size crucifix, closes the play with a line echoing the religious fervor of *Lazarus Laughed:*

"Love lives forever! Death is dead! . . . Life laughs with God's love again! Life laughs with love!"

O'Neill's personal religious conflict, always associated by him to some extent with his father, was dramatized in the play by means of a James

O'Neillian character, in the guise of a Catholic priest; he is John Loving's uncle and former guardian, Father Baird. Father Baird's physical characteristics, his relationship with John Loving, and his manner of speech persistently evoke James O'Neill, and the hero's final submission to Catholic belief was probably, in O'Neill's mind, a symbolic gesture of submission to his dead father—a gesture he repudiated, however, soon after he had made it.

He ultimately came to deplore the ending of *Days Without End*. Indeed, in his early outline for the play (which he was uncertain whether to call *Without End of Days* or *On to Hercules*), he planned to have the hero commit suicide rather than be redeemed by a return to his old religious faith. O'Neill's irresolution over his hero's end drove him frantic at times, since it was his own, as well as John Loving's, dilemma.

"Gene would walk up and down the beach, painfully wrestling with the problem," Carlotta recalled. "He couldn't make up his mind whether or not to have the man go back to the Church. At one point he thought of having him shoot himself at the church altar, and he discussed this idea with the Jesuit priests and they persuaded him not to use it. He finally ended with the man going back to the Church. Later he was furious with himself for having done this. He felt he had ruined the play and that he was a traitor to himself as a writer. He always said the last act was a phony and he never forgave himself for it."

"To my Carlotta," O'Neill wrote on the first longhand script (which was the fourth draft of the play, then called *Without End of Days*). "The first throes—and who better than you knows what throes they were!" And later, on the second longhand script, now called *An End of Days* he wrote, "To Carlotta—This, our Pangs Without End offspring!"

George Jean Nathan, who detested the play, largely because of its religious ending (but who, shortly before his death, did a remarkable about-face and joined the Catholic Church), took some comfort from the fact that O'Neill later admitted the ending was wrong. The hero's final gesture, O'Neill told Nathan, called for alteration—a reversion to the dramatic scheme as he had first conceived it, and O'Neill said he would rewrite the last scene of the play for the definitive edition of his works. (But O'Neill never got around to making this revision; presumably, he was willing—perhaps even anxious—to leave for the record that one bit of testimony to his struggle and near return to the religion of his parents.)

O'Neill finally settled on the title, *Days Without End*, partly because of its derivation from the prayer book phrase, "world without end," and partly, as he once explained, because of the two meanings the word "end" could have—that is, the title could mean days without goal, as well as having the meaning of eternity, as in the prayer.

While *Welded,* in many respects, suggested O'Neill's relationship with Agnes, *Days Without End* is transparently based on his relationship with Carlotta. And, to judge by two parallel speeches from the plays, the climates of the two marriages, at least in their early stages, were not totally dissimilar.

Here is Michael Cape, speaking to his wife, in *Welded;*

"But haven't we realized the ideal of our marriage. . . . We swore to have a true sacrament—or nothing! Our marriage must be a consummation demanding and combining the best in each of us! Hard, difficult, guarded from the commonplace, kept sacred as the outward form of our inner harmony! . . . God, what I feel of the truth of this—the beauty!"

And here is Elsa Loving, speaking of her husband, in *Days Without End*:

"He said no matter if every other marriage on earth were rotten and a lie, our love could make ours into a true sacrament—sacrament was the word he used—a sacrament of faith in which each of us would find the completest self-expression in making our union a beautiful thing. . . . And our marriage has meant for us . . . freedom and harmony within ourselves—and happiness."

(Inscribing a set of bound, uncorrected proofs of the final play to Carlotta, O'Neill quoted the first twenty-four words of this speech, adding: "And ours has, hasn't it, Darling One!")

There are many other indications that *Days Without End* was very much Carlotta's play: it is set in 1932 in the Lovings' New York duplex apartment; (the O'Neills were still living in a New York duplex apartment when preliminary work on the play was being done and when O'Neill's meetings with the Jesuit priests took place); the wife, Elsa, has been married before to a man who, like Ralph Barton, was flagrantly unfaithful to her; and John Loving has restored her faith in love, as O'Neill (or, at least, so he was convinced) had restored Carlotta's. "Daughter, you are my secret, shy, shrinking one, my pure and unsoiled one, whom the world has wounded . . ." O'Neill wrote to Carlotta, while working on the play, "but . . . I swear my oath at life, that my life shall be between you and all wounds and hurt hereafter!"

As in the early months of their life together in the château, the O'Neills found in Casa Genotta all they desired in a home. The few carefully selected friends who were asked to visit were struck by the well-ordered serenity of their lives.

According to Ilka Chase, who spent a few days with them, the house was "quiet and exquisitely clean, with special boxes and bags to keep the mildew out of things and with little colored maids polishing like Dutchmen."

At mealtimes, she added, the food was "put on side tables, the maids withdrew, and we helped ourselves. Not being spied on was a kind of fetish with them."

The isolation at Casa Genotta was as complete as the O'Neills could wish and only the most tenuous threads linked them to New York and the rest of the world. One such thread was the new literary magazine, *The American Spectator,* to which O'Neill had agreed, in a rare departure from habit, to contribute some non-dramatic writing. George Jean Nathan, Ernest Boyd, Theodore Dreiser, James Branch Cabell and O'Neill were the joint editors of the magazine, which made its first monthly appearance at the end of October, 1932, and became one of the notably short-lived and undistinguished ventures in American publishing annals. In addition to the editors, all of whom were represented in the first issue—O'Neill by the brief "Memoranda on Masks"—such people as Clarence Darrow, Joseph Wood Krutch, Havelock Ellis and Lincoln Steffens contributed articles; promised for future issues was a wildly incongrous group including Virginia Woolf, Gerhart Hauptmann, Mussolini, Stalin, Thomas Mann, Sean O'Casey and Sherwood Anderson.

The magazine sold for ten cents a copy, it carried no advertising, and the editors served without pay. An editorial in its first issue (undoubtedly written by Nathan) declared: "The moment the editors feel that *The American Spectator* is becoming a routine job, is getting dull and is similarly continuing merely as a matter of habit, they will call it a day and will retire to their estates."

The moment came less than two and a half years later.

"Well, we are tired of the job, although it has been a lot of fun," read a *Spectator* editorial in March, 1935. ". . . So we are merrily concluding our performance."

Sherwood Anderson, who had become a *Spectator* editor at the end of 1933 at Dreiser's urging, wrote a succinct obituary of the magazine in a letter to a friend:

"I went in after Dreiser pleaded with me, and a very short time later Dreiser got sore at the others and resigned. . . . In answer to your question . . . I don't think there was ever any crying need for the magazine. It was a short time after this that the magazine folded up and I lost any connection with it. I felt that it had accomplished little or nothing."

❖

Lawrence Langner and his wife, Armina, visited the O'Neills at Sea Island in the spring of 1933, along with Fania Marinoff.

"In Casa Genotta," Langner recalled, "the household revolved around Gene's writing. In the morning he worked in his study until noon. Then, attired in his dressing gown, he came down to the beach where Carlotta, Armina, Fania and I were sunning. After a while we went swimming in the sandy colored water which is, to me, one of the most unattractive features of Sea Island. Gene was the best swimmer and swam far out to sea, followed by Armina; the rest of us hugged the beach."

Although Sea Island was at its best during the time of the Langners' visit, it grew humid and hot in the summer and according to Langner, was "by no means the paradise the O'Neills expected it would be."

"Indeed," he later recalled, "so damp was the atmosphere that special bronze had to be used for all the window hardware, for ordinary metal would rust away."

Langner discovered another "unpleasant feature of the island" when he asked Carlotta why all the bushes in the patio were clipped up a foot from the ground. "That's so we can see if there are any snakes under them," she told him, explaining that the island abounded in rattlesnakes.

"Gene added smilingly that these were relatively harmless compared to the pretty little pink coral snakes which also disported themselves in this paradise," Langner reported. "Fania, who hated snakes even more than I did, trod very gingerly around the countryside after this, and I was never quite at ease either."

Another visitor—one who came strictly to talk business in the spring of 1933—was Bennett Cerf. Then in his thirties, Cerf had inherited money while still in his teens and had become one of Horace Liveright's C.O.D. vice-presidents in the early 1920's (practically anyone who would put up cash could exchange it for a vice-presidency at the chronically cash-poor Liveright offices). In 1925 Cerf had bought, for $235,000, Liveright's most lucrative adjunct, the Modern Library, which issued inexpensive editions of the classics. The transaction elevating Cerf, at the age of twenty-seven, to the presidency of the Modern Library, had taken place on an afternoon in May, 1925; as Cerf later recalled, the occasion was made even more memorable by the presence in the waiting room of a man armed with a gun and bent on assassinating Liveright.

Would-be assassins were more or less a routine of Liveright's existence; there is at least one recorded instance of a woman who got close enough to take a shot at him. What with dodging bullets, gambling, and general high living, Liveright did not have much time to devote to his firm's financial affairs—and the supply of rich vice-presidents not being inexhaustible, particularly during the Depression, Liveright's firm finally began to totter.

"Horace managed the firm very badly," Manuel Komroff said. "There was never a year that we made less than a million dollars, but there seldom seemed to be a day that we had a nickel in the bank."

Saxe Commins, still O'Neill's editor at Liveright, had got an inkling of the firm's shaky position early in 1932, and old ties of friendship impelled him to advise O'Neill to safeguard his stake in the company. At O'Neill's request, the company's treasurer, Arthur Pell, signed a statement on March 24, 1932, to the effect that the contracts between Liveright and O'Neill "shall cease and be void . . . and all rights owned by us thereunder shall revert to you, if our corporation shall . . . be declared bankrupt, whether voluntarily or involuntarily, or if we suspend business or have a receivership appointed for our business."

A little over a year later, in May, the firm went bankrupt. Commins' warning had saved O'Neill a good deal of money, and O'Neill was grateful. When the news of the bankruptcy was announced, at least a dozen publishers approached Richard Madden in the hope of acquiring O'Neill. Cerf, under whom the Modern Library was flourishing, had by this time set up a subsidiary company called Random House, which put out expensive, limited editions of classics; Random House had published no contemporary books to date, and Cerf decided now was the time to begin.

"While everyone else was converging on Madden," Cerf later recalled, "I took a plane to Sea Island. Getting O'Neill meant prestige, but it also meant getting a playwright whose works sold like novels. I knew Gene slightly from the time I had worked for Liveright, and I wired him that I was coming, and asked him to reserve a room for me at the inn. He met me at the airport and said I must stay at his house, which I did. He agreed to come with our firm on condition that we engage Saxe Commins; I said all right, we shook hands on it, and I went back to New York and told Madden to disperse his forces." (Random House also picked up Robinson Jeffers that year and was brilliantly launched on a new phase of publishing.)

The fifth draft of *Days Without End* was typed by Carlotta in the spring of 1933, and O'Neill spent the early part of the summer revising it. It had grown unpleasantly hot in Georgia by July, even with the Atlantic breeze, and O'Neill and Carlotta decided to exchange their increasingly less blessed isles for the Adirondack Mountains for a few weeks. They stopped in Manhattan en route and O'Neill gave Lawrence Langner the scripts of both *Days Without End* and *Ah, Wilderness!* The Guild executives unanimously liked *Ah, Wilderness!* but, as Langner later observed, "There were some differences of opinion about *Days Without End* . . . and Gene sensed the controversial nature of the play and was greatly worried as to which of these plays should be produced first."

O'Neill pondered on the problem in the Adirondacks. From Faust, New York, on August 7, he wrote to Langner:

"*Days Without End* is nothing if not controversial, especially in its Catholic aspect. It is sure, fail or succeed, to arouse much bitter argument. It will be well hated by the prejudiced who won't see the psychological study end of it but only the general aspect. And, technically too, there will be much argument pro and con. Now I feel strongly that such a post-production atmosphere, if *Days Without End* were done first, would be fatal for *Ah, Wilderness!*

"Give all this careful thought, all of you, and I know you'll agree."

A day later he elaborated on the subject to Langner:

"There is a lot to be said on both sides, and I've been saying it all to myself until I'm quite gaga and confused and my opinion is worthless. All I know is that any play of mine that immediately follows *Electra* is in a bad spot—no matter how good it is; and I'm so close to both these two plays that I really don't know just how good or bad either of them is. This is particularly true in the case of *Ah, Wilderness!* which is so out of my previous line. Has it got something finer to it then its obvious surface value —a depth of mood and atmosphere, so to speak, that would distinguish it from another play of the same genre, the usual type? I felt it had when I wrote it. (Nathan, for example, says most emphatically yes.) But now, frankly, I'll be damned if I can trust myself to judge. I simply don't know. It's up to you Guilders to decide. Has it charm and humor and tender reminiscence enough to disarm the people who will feel that dramatically it is a terrible letdown after *Electra*?"

The Guild officials thought it had. They decided to open their 1933-34 season with it, and they immediately put it into production.

George M. Cohan, who had turned down the leading role in *Marco Millions* and who had never appeared in a play written by anyone but himself, was invited to portray the father, Nat Miller. Both Langner and O'Neill were correct in their belief that the play's setting, July 4, would strongly appeal to the self-styled Yankee Doodle Dandy and might help persuade him to accept the assignment.

In taking the role, Cohan said that he did not regard this departure in his career seriously and that the Guild just needed "a good song and dance man" for the play. There was always a chance, he added facetiously, that O'Neill might decide to appear the following season in a Cohan play.

"O'Neill's regular," Cohan said a few days after the play opened.

"I've known a lot about him since he's been coming along, but I never met him before. His father and my father were pretty good friends. They practically started the Catholic Actors Guild. O'Neill knows a lot of stories. He knows all the old circus jokes. I picked him for a winner in that first play he had, *Beyond the Horizon.* I knew right away he had the goods. Jeez, he's written a pile of them, hasn't he? Well, if this play doesn't make a hit, I'll take the kid into vaudeville with me. But I come first. It's got to be Cohan and O'Neill. That's *my* game."

O'Neill returned the compliment by inscribing a copy of *Ah, Wilderness!* to Cohan: "With deep gratitude and appreciation for all your grand portrayal of Nat Miller has meant to this play—and with the real friendship of one (I hope) regular guy for another! Cheers, and then again cheers, to and for you always!"

With rehearsals launched in September, O'Neill allowed Richard Watts, Jr., to interview him about Cohan, *Ah, Wilderness!* and his future work.

"I cannot overemphasize," O'Neill told Watts, "how delighted I am at having Mr. Cohan in a play of mine at last. I think he likes the comedy, too. But he did tell me that one of the things that first attracted him to it was the fact that the first act takes place on July 4. I really didn't mean the setting as a shrewd device to lure Mr. Cohan to a part I wanted him for, but I realize now that he was amused at the connection the date has with his own career."

Discussing the play, O'Neill said, "I call the work a comedy because it is on the whole more gay than grave, but as Mr. Cohan says, it is and it isn't a comedy in the usual sense." He added that he did not intend the play as a satiric treatment of life in the first decade of the twentieth century but, rather, as a nostalgic picture of the America of its day. "Perhaps," he said, "it is because I am growing old that I begin to look back fondly on my youthful days in a part of the country that was my one real home in those times."

Answering Watt's questions about *Days Without End* by briefly describing its plot and technique, O'Neill somewhat prematurely mentioned that he was already working on a new play to be called *The Life of Bessie Bowen,* in which the protagonist would speak her thoughts aloud, as in *Strange Interlude,* but in which the other characters would not.

"I do not plan to confine myself to any one type of technique," he added. "Rather, I plan to use the method, whether it be naturalism or symbolism, that happens to fit in with the sort of drama I am writing."

Rehearsals for *Ah, Wilderness!* proceeded according to form—that is, according to O'Neill's form, which was to cut and pare where he saw fit and decline to cut for mere length, which was where the Guild often saw fit. O'Neill was comfortable working with Philip Moeller, who directed, and Robert Edmond Jones, who designed the setting. Cohan was agreeable, and Carlotta's presence at all rehearsals and her obvious influence on O'Neill's decisions were taken in good part by the members of the production.

Ruth Gilbert, a young actress without much previous experience, was selected for the part of Muriel Macomber. Her round, ingenuous, baby face and engagingly childlike voice vividly evoked Maibelle Scott for O'Neill. But Ruth herself felt that her natural qualities were not precisely right for the part. After being signed for the play, she was formally introduced to O'Neill and Carlotta, and told them her plan to subdue her own personality in favor of her conception of Muriel. "For heaven's sake, child, *don't* change!" Carlotta expostulated.

Miss Gilbert, who conceived a warm regard for O'Neill that was apparently reciprocated (he loyally insisted on having her in *The Iceman Cometh* twelve years later), recalled with amusement the time when O'Neill sang "Bedelia" to the assembled cast.

"No one seemed to know the tune, and Philip Moeller kept saying, Oh, yes, we'll have to get a copy, but nobody did," Miss Gilbert said. "Finally, after three weeks, when we came to that scene, O'Neill called Moeller to the footlights and whispered something to him. Moeller announced that Mr. O'Neill would hum the tune. He'd been sitting there for three weeks, too shy to volunteer, but that day he finally did sing it for us."

Mrs. Ben Pinchot, who saw both the O'Neills occasionally during the rehearsal period—her husband made several photographs of O'Neill in connection with the play, working in a studio that was a few doors away from the Guild Theatre—would see Carlotta hurrying along West Fifty-second Street in the September heat, on her way to rehearsals.

"While O'Neill was casting," Mrs. Pinchot recalled, "Carlotta did all the routine chores, running errands, saving him time and energy. She used to pass the studio, carrying a paper bag with Gene's lunch: a pint bottle of milk and rye bread and butter sandwiches. For when O'Neill was in the midst of rehearsals, he did not leave the theatre even for meals. Carlotta evidently never suffered from a slavish regard for fashion, for that summer, when skirts were a good thirteen inches from the ground, she wore hers longer. I remember seeing her pass one day, looking striking in a white silk dress, a black jacket with short sleeves and a black straw toque that sat squarely across her white forehead above the dark, thick brows. Her favorite shoes were low-heeled slippers with buckles."

As for O'Neill, Mrs. Pinchot thought him "in good shape, and not too nervous," though she recalled that his hands sometimes shook badly. She was struck by his insistence that none of her husband's photographs of him should be retouched. O'Neill was the only man who ever made that request of Pinchot—and whose request Pinchot could respect; O'Neill did, literally, want every line, every gray hair, even the faint pouches under his eyes to appear.

"Oddly enough," Mrs. Pinchot recalled, "Carlotta preferred profile pictures of herself. Although Ben considered her a great beauty, she admitted that full-face pictures disturbed her, for she felt her eyes were too close together, which wasn't true at all. I liked her. I remember her speaking about the cruel treatment she had received at the hands of Gene's friends, who, she said, disliked her and gossiped about her. This seemed to hurt her very much."

Because *Ah, Wilderness!* was a comedy and the actors needed a chance to time their laughs before a paying audience, the Theatre Guild decided in favor of a pre-Broadway tryout of at least a week. O'Neill at first protested when Langner asked him to join the company in Pittsburgh for the week, but he finally agreed to go.

"I had the greatest difficulty in getting him to come to the theatre at all after the dress rehearsal," Langner has written, "and even then he would come in only for certain scenes. I asked him why he had this phobia against attending performances of his own plays, and he told me that it did not relate to his own plays, but to being present in a crowded theatre, which made it very difficult for him to sit still and watch the play."

Langner could not reconcile this attitude with the fact that O'Neill was able to sit in crowded arenas such as Madison Square Garden "where he did not appear to have the slightest discomfort in mixing with crowds of thousands."

This inconsistency may be explained by O'Neill's feeling that at a bicycle race or a prize fight he could lose himself in a setting where he was anonymously absorbed; in a theatre he was among a masked intelligentsia, a group that always unnerved him.

"A preliminary week out of town is no help to me and never will be," O'Neill wrote to Langner, shortly after the Pittsburgh experience. "I can't see or react with an audience around. The Pittsburgh week of *Ah, W* and my attendance at that performance taught me nothing whatsoever I didn't already know, except to transpose *one speech* on account of a laugh— which I could just as easily have done from my hotel in N.Y. on information from Phil [Moeller]. The cuts I made were made in N.Y. before I left for Pittsburgh . . . and my seeing the show in Pittsburgh did not affect my judgment in that respect. After all, you know where a script can be cut, if absolutely imperative, and where it can't be cut, time or no time, without watching a sticky audience react!"

O'Neill did, however, make one "cut" in Pittsburgh. The Guild thought the play was running about ten minutes too long and commissioned Russel Crouse, who was handling publicity for *Ah, Wilderness!*, to ask O'Neill to reduce the script's playing time by ten minutes. Crouse dutifully delivered the message but told O'Neill he anticipated his reaction and added that, as a matter of fact, he agreed with him.

"Right," said ONeill. "To hell with them."

The next day Crouse was on his way out of his room at the Hotel Schenley, where O'Neill also was staying, when the telephone rang. It was O'Neill.

"Come down to my room right away," O'Neill commanded. Crouse said he couldn't, he was on his way to the theatre to supervise a press interview he had arranged for Cohan.

"I have to see you right now," O'Neill insisted.

Crouse explained he would be back in an hour or so and would see O'Neill then.

"I have that ten-minute cut for you," said O'Neill.

Crouse was in O'Neill's room within seconds.

"Sit down," said O'Neill genially.

"I'm late," answered Crouse. "Just give me the script with the cuts marked."

"There isn't any script. Sit down," repeated O'Neill, with a self-satisfied grin.

Crouse threw O'Neill a trapped and pleading look, and O'Neill finally relented. He explained that he had decided simply to telescope the first two acts into one, eliminating a ten-minute intermission.

Amused by O'Neill's tactic, Crouse submitted the "cut" to the Guild, which did not accept it. The play continued to be presented in the original four acts, *with* its extra ten minutes of over-all running time.

Ah, Wilderness! was to open at the Guild Theatre on October 2. The only play of note that had already arrived that season—on September 26—was Sidney Kingsley's *Men in White* (it outran *Ah, Wilderness!* by a small margin of performances and won the Pulitzer Prize).

O'Neill looked forward cheerfully to the opening of his comedy. Fit and vigorous at forty-five, he was full of grandiose plans for future work, which (as outlined on paper and in his mind) called for a quarter century of concentrated writing.

The reviews of *Ah, Wilderness!* were generally good, and with the popular George M. Cohan to bolster them, it was apparent from the start that the play would be a hit.

"As a writer of comedy," wrote Brooks Atkinson, "Mr. O'Neill has a capacity for tenderness that most of us never suspected. 'Ah, Wilderness!' . . . may not be his most tremendous play, but it is certainly his most attractive. . . . Mr. O'Neill's point of view is full of compassionate understanding. . . . And in spite of its dreadful title, 'Ah, Wilderness!' is a true and congenial comedy."

Percy Hammond was less enthusiastic. "The play is all right," he wrote, "but it doesn't rank with its acting."

Few of the critics could suppress passing comments—some gentle, some rather snide—about O'Neill's strange about-face from direst tragedy to sentimental comedy, but most of them forgave him and recommended the play to their readers. All lavished praise on Cohan and most had a kind word for Philip Moeller and Robert Edmond Jones as well. The play ran for 289 performances in New York, and eventually a company was formed in California with the role of Nat Miller played by Will Rogers. *Ah, Wilderness!* was one O'Neill play that Hollywood quickly appreciated and Metro-Goldwyn-Mayer released a film version in 1935, padding the part of Uncle Sid for Wallace Beery and with Lionel Barrymore in the role of Nat Miller.

"I have a deep personal affection for that play—a feeling towards it that is quite apart from any consideration of it as a piece of dramatic writing by me as a playwright," O'Neill wrote to a friend who had sent him a congratulatory letter.

He asked Brooks Atkinson to interview him, so that he could explain the play's background—probably to clear up any doubt in the public mind that the play was strictly autobiographical; he did not want anyone to have the idea that his youth had been a happy one. Atkinson enjoyed the interview.

"With 'Ah, Wilderness!' off his chest and the notices enthusiastic and the prospects cheerful," Atkinson wrote in *The Times* on October 8, "Mr. O'Neill felt like talking about anything. He was even willing to listen; and from the point of view of the interviewer that was bad. Mrs. O'Neill efficiently intercepted the telephone calls, the messengers and the waiters, thus isolating a corner of New York where an amiable dramatist could call his soul his own. And at high noon on the day after the première his soul was in excellent condition. Until December, when his next play, 'Days Without End,' goes into rehearsal, he was to be scot free. His enthusiasm spread the conversation alarmingly. Sea Island Beach, the Adirondacks, Medan in Sumatra, swimming, climates, Cecil Rhodes, George M. Cohan —it hardly mattered what he talked about. After all, he did not have to write the interview. And so he could genially waste time by observing that the whippoorwill family (suborder Caprimulgi) has four branches in North America—chuck-will's widow, Eastern whippoorwill, Eastern night-hawk and Florida nighthawk—as though it mattered on Broadway."

Atkinson went on to report that there were fragments of autobiography in *Ah, Wilderness!* but that O'Neill disclaimed anything but a superficial kinship with Richard Miller or his family. "Now that [the play] is on the stage," Atkinson continued, "and acted very much to his taste . . . Mr. O'Neill is his own best audience. He is ashamed to admit how much the comedy amuses him. Some things have to be confidential. . . .

"To judge by his plans and projects there is a great deal more to come. At the age of forty-five, Mr. O'Neill is a little grayer around the temples and the lines are a little more firmly drawn on his face, but his eyes have the luster of a man who is in good health and spirits and who is eager to go on vigorously with the job. It is this interviewer's private opinion that the tension has relaxed a good deal. Mr. O'Neill seems to be having a pretty good time; like a good many of the rest of us, he can laugh without brilliant provocation. Unless he disciplines himself to be less genial on the occasion of a formal interview it will soon be impossible to remember exactly what he said. What the interviewer said is always easier to recall."

O'Neill's geniality with respect to at least one aspect of the *Ah, Wilderness!* production did not last very long. Cohan's personal triumph in the play went to his head and soon he was embellishing his performance with bits of extra business. The curtain was coming down later and later each night. Finally, when the play was running twenty-five minutes overtime, the Guild management sent a note to Cohan asking him to please see to it that the curtain came down at eleven. Cohan retaliated by sending his valet to the Guild office with a warning that if any member of the management entered the theatre while the play was in progress, he would walk off stage. Then he went right on ad libbing until 11:25 every night.

O'Neill was less concerned about the late curtain than about the values of his play; he thought they were being distorted by Cohan's private performance and did not hesitate to go backstage and have it out with the actor. Evidently Cohan took O'Neill's reprimand in good part, for their relations continued cordial. O'Neill later presented Cohan with an autographed, leather-bound edition of *Days Without End,* inscribed with the profession of "All friendship!"

O'Neill returned to Casa Genotta a few days after the opening of *Ah, Wilderness!* to rest until the end of November, when he would have to be back in New York for rehearsals of *Days Without End.*

At Casa Genotta his birthday gift from Carlotta awaited him. It was an ancient player piano, complete with rolls of the old songs he loved. It resembled the barroom-scene piano of *Ah, Wilderness!* and had been located for Carlotta by a music bureau. Originally having ornamented a New Orleans bagnio, the piano was decorated appropriately with paintings of naked women. O'Neill christened it Rosie and showed it off to visitors with childlike delight.

"Gene adored that piano," Carl Van Vechten recalled. To record O'Neill's pleasure with his new toy, Van Vechten photographed him sitting at it, his hands on the keyboard, a rare grin of complete happiness on his face. Van Vechten, who took up portrait photography as a hobby in the early thirties, said that O'Neill enjoyed posing for him. "I could have photographed Gene all day if I'd wanted to," he added. "I took hundreds of pictures of him in every kind of pose, and he never asked me to destroy any of them."

Robert Sisk was another witness to the romance between O'Neill and Rosie.

"The piano was green with age, and Gene kept a box of nickels on top of it," Sisk said. "He'd drop a nickel in the piano and listen blissfully to the damn thing tinkle."

"Gene loved to sing," Lillian Gish, another visitor to Casa Genotta, recalled. "He'd sing along with the player piano, sometimes with Nathan. They were no Ezio Pinzas, but it was amusing to listen to them."

"With a derby hat full of nickels at his side," Nathan once wrote, "he used to sit with me for hours . . . purring in blissful contentment as he dropped nickels in the slot, watched its front light up, and kept time with his foot to 'Alexander's Ragtime Band.' . . . Rosie was soon the talk of the neighborhood."

It was a good thing O'Neill had Rosie to cheer him, for during October and November he struggled some more over *Days Without End,* still unsure of his hero's (and his own) resolution of the religious problem. He wrote to Langner of his worry about how the play, with its clearly stated Catholic viewpoint, would be accepted and pleaded for a painstakingly careful production.

"I'm especially anxious to have your sympathetic backing on this particular play, not only because it's a tough one to get over and is bound to arouse a lot of antagonism, but because I want to lean over backwards in being fair to it and getting it the best breaks," he wrote on October 29. "For, after all, this play, like *Ah, Wilderness!* but in a much deeper sense, is the paying of an old debt on my part—a gesture toward more comprehensive, unembittered understanding and inner freedom—the breaking away from an old formula that I had enslaved myself with, and the appreciation that there is their own truth in other formulas, too, and that any life-giving formula is as fit a subject for drama as any other."

What O'Neill was saying, in effect, was that this play, like *Ah, Wilderness!* was in part an attempt to understand and sympathize with his father, as he had not been able to do during most of James O'Neill's lifetime. His struggle to re-embrace Catholicism probably sprang less from an inner conviction on his own part than from a need, long dormant, to earn his father's approval and acceptance. But, as had always been the case during his father's lifetime, the moment O'Neill began to submit to his father he felt the opposing need to rebel against him; this was obviously at the root of O'Neill's conflict over *Days Without End.*

Whatever his private problems over the play, he was determined that it should have a proper hearing, and he discussed with Carlotta, whose interest was possibly even greater than his, who should play the role of Elsa Loving. They had agreed that Earle Larimore was right for the part of John, and that Ilka Chase should play Elsa's friend, Lucy Hillman, the woman with whom John commits adultery. But their uncertainty about the actress suitable for the role of Elsa, who, being modeled on Carlotta, was naturally a matter of deep personal concern to them both, was less easily resolved. O'Neill rejected the Guild's suggestion of Jane Cowl for the role, calling her "a starry ham, if there ever was one," and Carlotta discussed with Langner the possibilities of both Alice Brady and Nazimova for the role, but in the end, the actress selected was Earle Larimore's wife, Selena Royle.

Both the O'Neills arrived in New York at the end of November for rehearsals, and O'Neill continued to suffer over the play. According to Langner, he had a new problem: he could not make up his mind whether John's uncle should be a Catholic priest or a Protestant minister. "He shifted back and forth in rehearsals," Langner said. O'Neill took an unequivocal interest in the crucifix that Lee Simonson was having made for the final scene of the play; it was about one and a half times life size, and Simonson had it carved by artisans out of real wood.

Selena Royle's impression of O'Neill, whom she met for the first time at rehearsal, was of "a tired man with great depths of long-fought-for peace." Because of O'Neill's and Carlotta's affection for her husband, Miss Royle was greeted with more than the usual cordiality extended by the O'Neills to a leading lady.

Larimore had impressed on his wife that she could not call Eugene O'Neill "Gene" on the first, or even second meeting, and she was greatly relieved that after the second or third day of rehearsals he called her Selena and she was able to say Gene.

"When we met over tea in the afternoons before and during the play, it was Carlotta who carried the conversational ball. There was much amused talk, one day, about the size of Gene's bed, in which he did a great deal of his writing; and I recall Carlotta once commenting on the length of Gene's arms, which she laughingly and lovingly compared to a monkey's.

"I never remember his saying anything about Larry to me, but I believe that Larry was his favorite actor. I know he realized that Larry had much the same problem about alcohol that he himself had conquered, but it was not his way to advise or caution. Gene gave Larry several books and bound proofs of his plays, some of which had his corrections written down in longhand, and all of which had affectionate dedications.

"Carlotta was very beautiful, and I was amused at her little-girl enjoyment of all the massages, hair dressings and facials she was indulging in in New York, that apparently she couldn't get at her country place." ("Carlotta and I are both very fond of Earle and Selena," O'Neill declared to a friend, eight years later.)

O'Neill had begged Langner to obtain permission from Equity for an extended rehearsal period, so that *Days Without End* would not have to go out of town before opening on Broadway. An extra week was granted, but it was ultimately decided to take the play to Boston for a week anyway, beginning January 1. There, despite O'Neill's protests that he could not work on a play out of town, he voluntarily eliminated three and a half pages from the script.

O'Neill and Carlotta dined with Philip Moeller on the evening before the play opened in Boston, and Moeller's sense of the significance of the play in O'Neill's life impelled him, the following morning, to sum up his impressions of the meeting. In his Boston hotel room on January 1, 1934, Moeller sat down at his desk and wrote, in his almost illegible longhand:

"A few notes of a conversation with Gene and Carlotta, after dining last night, which may be of interest to some one writing G's definitive biography fifty years hence.

"The evening was less difficult than I had anticipated. During dinner

I switched the talk in the direction of the musical structure of G's plays and then to persecution of the Jews. [Moeller later explained that he brought up the topic of Hitler's persecution of the Jews to encourage O'Neill to discuss religion in general.]

"After dinner inevitably the talk took on the direction of religion. It is obvious from what was said that [*Days Without End*] is more *her* play than *his*. They both, definitely, acknowledge this.

"She says G. was and is still a Catholic and that she hopes he will return definitely to the faith and that she would gladly go with him, whenever he is ready, but he must not be forced.

"There were long disquisitions over the mystic beauty of Catholic faith. He said the end of the play was undoubtedly a wish fulfillment on his part.

"He told me about the simple trusting happiness of some of his Catholic relatives. He wants to go that way and find a happiness which apparently he hasn't got and which obviously this perfect marriage doesn't seem to bring him? He acknowledged that the beginning of the 'study scene' was his autobiographical projection of a life theory. This I had sensed from the beginning.

"I told him [the play] was difficult to do because of the closeness to himself in it and his personal sentiments. [It was then] they both agreed it was more her play than his.

"Much of the strange religious hatred of the alter ego, G. said, came from his acquaintance with a lunatic boy who came to see him in Bermuda, a boy obsessed with a religious hatred complex and a persecution mania.

"All the evening G. was very direct and appealing, now that his resentment to the way things were going has lifted. When he's in this mood he is deeply likable.

"Madame was, again, amply rich in banalities—but her striving to hold it all together is somehow appealing and irritating at the same time.

"The five weeks have been a difficult experience, particularly controlling myself in the face of G's hurt vanity. For an important person and surely a 'theatre-genius' he has some very human crevasses in his make-up. But this making spiritual peace may be his end as an important creator. I told him I believed in the creator having the church's gesture of quest and seeking. He didn't think that was necessarily contradictory to the mind's spiritual peace he craves. Well, I wonder.

"And the tragedy of the situation is that [Carlotta] doesn't realize that he hasn't really got what she wants to bring him. Psychologically, the relationship is tremendously fraught with possibilities. Will supernal ease and superficial comfort win out and will his writing, with the important element of it, survive?"

O'Neill's unhappiness over the production of *Days Without End* stemmed partly from his own mixed feelings about how he wanted the play accepted. On one hand, he wanted official Catholic endorsement and, on the other, he wanted his public to discount such endorsement and to evaluate the play on its literary merits alone. He had made concessions to Catholic dogma, which he believed entitled him to official Catholic acceptance, yet he was not happy about having made these concessions and furious when they were regarded as insufficient in some Catholic quarters.

He was particularly enraged, for example, when Russel Crouse, having been asked to lunch by a priest in behalf of the Catholic Writers Guild, was informed by the priest that he personally would endorse the play if O'Neill would make clear in the script that the heroine's first husband had died, rather than leaving a suspicion that there might have been a divorce. When Crouse reported the conversation to O'Neill, he muttered, "To hell with them! I don't *say* she's divorced, in so many words—and I *won't* say the husband died; let them draw their own conclusions."

At least one Jesuit priest, the Rev. Gerard B. Donnelly, was moved, however, to write a staunch endorsement of the play in a Catholic publication. Father Donnelly called *Days Without End* a "magnificently Catholic play, a play Catholic in its characters, its story and its moral."

Actually, the play was well received in the predominantly Catholic city of Boston. Elinor Hughes, critic for the Boston *Herald,* lauded it and H. T. Parker, dean of American critics, rendered a highly favorable opinion in the Boston *Transcript.*

Days Without End opened in New York at Henry Miller's Theatre on January 8, 1934. On the day of the première, O'Neill invited Art McGinley, who was visiting New York, to his suite at the Madison Hotel and showed him letters from various Catholic officials, who liked the script. O'Neill did not attend the opening, and waited in his hotel room for reports on the play.

The majority of the New York critics disliked it.

"One of the most amazing things about Mr. O'Neill is his capacity for seasoning his valiant career with bad plays," wrote Atkinson. "His 'Days Without End' . . . belongs in that doleful category. . . . As a piece of dramatic craftsmanship it represents another one of Mr. O'Neill's experiments. Here he has employed a mask to distinguish between the outer and inner consciousness of his hero; and with the assistance of the Theatre Guild, he has succeeded brilliantly. His use of the mask is cogent and discerning. But in this column's opinion, 'Days Without End' lacks size, imagination, vitality, beauty and knowledge of human character. Sometimes Mr. O'Neill tells his story as though he had never written a play before. In view of his acknowledged mastery of the theatre it is astonishing that his career can be so uneven. . . ."

Percy Hammond confined himself largely to an outline of the plot, committing himself to only two scraps of opinion—one that a good deal of the play was "apt to be as boresome as the telling of a nightmare" and the other that "in spite of Mr. O'Neill's rambling surgeries in 'Days Without End' he comes through every now and then as the sensational showman he was born and bred to be."

John Mason Brown declared that "the sorry fact remains that, in spite of the Guild's first-aid treatment and the script's obvious sincerity of purpose, this latest drama of Mr. O'Neill's must take its place along with 'Dynamo' and 'Welded' among the feeblest of his works. It is as heavy-handed and pretentious as only its author can be in his less fortunate efforts. Indeed so static is most of its tricky writing and so trite is the conclusion toward which it labors that one hates to think of what a first-night audience would have done to it if the program had not carried Mr. O'Neill's name."

Robert Garland, with characteristic grace, described the play as "an inept and shoddy specimen of sectarian makebelieve. Holy hokum, you might almost call it." Gilbert Gabriel expressed his disappointment only a trifle more gently. He found it "a miracle play without simplicity, without eloquence, without dignity . . . a religious tract clumsily tied to unpicturesque claptrap and most threadbare wording."

Though much of the tone of the press was indignant, Burns Mantle of the *Daily News* and Richard Lockridge of the New York *Sun* liked the play. "A forcefully written argument worked into an interesting physical pattern the play seemed to me," wrote Mantle. "Not an entertainment for those who frankly have little or no use for the drama of souls. But a fascinating study for students and the secretly mystified of all faiths. A thrill for the true religionist." And Lockridge found it "a strange and moving play of the struggle in a man's soul; a play so conceived as to amount to a profession of faith. Its last two acts, and particularly its climactic scene, are so rich in poetic naïveté as to seem unbelievably foreign to Broadway."

Most of the critics admired Earle Larimore's performance, and had high praise for Moeller's direction and Simonson's semi-abstract settings, but it was clear from the start that the play was neither a critical nor an artistic success.

The matter, however, did not rest there. *Days Without End* was by

America's leading dramatist, and it was an apparently pious play by a man whose point of view had heretofore been anything but pious. Like *All God's Chillun Got Wings, Days Without End* became the subject of much heated and biased controversy—less on its artistic merit than on its religious content.

Richard Dana Skinner, critic for the Catholic *Commonweal* and a man whom O'Neill had consulted during the writing of the play, did his best to drum up support for it. In a long article called "The Critics and 'Days Without End,'" published in the *Commonweal* on January 26, he wrote:

"The critical comments on this play in the New York daily newspapers have been no less astonishing than the play itself. . . . The trouble, as I see it, is this—that the reality of the struggle toward faith is exceedingly remote from the Broadway consciousness. It is accepted as something which obviously does not go on in the world but with which most people are familiar only in terms of poetry or in terms of psychological dissection. . . .

"Faith cannot be made objective in material terms. The inherent dramatic values in "Days Without End" are therefore lost to those who either have no faith or who have never experienced it.

"In fairness, then, both to Mr. O'Neill's extraordinary play and to the critics who do not see its inner beauty and dramatic strength, we can only accept the fact that when two groups of people do not speak the same language of the soul, it is very hard for them to discover a plane of mutual understanding. . . .

"Mr. H. T. Parker, who viewed the play without the mental hazards of the New York firstnighters, considers it to be one of O'Neill's most important plays. If I am not greatly mistaken, the verdict of New York theatregoers will be the same. . . ."

As it happened, Skinner *was* greatly mistaken; the play ran only long enough to fulfill the Guild subscription list.

While *Days Without End* made a firm friend of Richard Skinner, it cost O'Neill the friendship of Benjamin De Casseres, who seemed to regard the play as a personal insult.

"When Ben saw the play," Bio De Casseres said, "he blazed. He thought O'Neill had betrayed his Demon. He equated O'Neill's 'fall' with the fall of Lucifer."

De Casseres went home and, in a white heat of fury, wrote a vicious and not particularly skillful parody of *Days Without End*. Entitled "Drivel Without End," the article paraphrased the dialogue of some of O'Neill's earlier characters, as for instance: "The Emperor Jones: Pussonally, pop,

I prefers the crocodiles of the Nile to the hyenas of Rome if I must be et," and: "Anna Christie: Father, I would rather see you dead drunk under a table at Jimmy-the-Priest's than see you one of the Pope's clean little choir-boys. Here's a slug of brandy—empty the bottle: it'll snap you out of your salvation fantods," and: "Chris Christopherson: So that Ol' Davil See— the Holy See—got you, did it!" and so on, in the same vein.

De Casseres sent the article to Isaac Goldberg, who was then associated with the literary magazine *Panorama*. Goldberg was always happy to receive material from De Casseres and frequently published his contributions; this time, though, he set the piece in type with many misgivings. In the end he decided not to run it, and mailed a proof of the article to De Casseres with a letter, explaining that he simply could not bring himself to publish it, as he had too much respect for O'Neill. De Casseres thereupon had the article privately printed as a pamphlet and sent copies of it to a number of his literary acquaintances. After reading it, Nathan said he was glad De Casseres had had the courage to write it. He harbored similar sentiments about the play, Nathan added, but could not bring himself to say so publicly because of his intimacy with O'Neill.

De Casseres did not neglect to send a copy of the pamphlet to O'Neill. Some time later O'Neill wrote to De Casseres, making no reference to the article and expressing no animosity. There were, however, no further letters exchanged between the two men and they never saw each other again. (Two weeks before De Casseres died, in 1945, according to his wife, he said, "I'm sorry I wrote that about O'Neill.")

O'Neill's reaction to the newspaper reviews was to send a telegram to the cast of his play, thanking them for their "splendid" work and telling them to ignore the bad reviews. "This is a play we can carry over the critics' heads," he predicted inaccurately, "So carry on with confidence in the final result and make them like it. Are we downhearted? No. We will get them in the end . . . Again my gratitude to you all."

Selena Royle saw O'Neill for the last time shortly after the opening of *Days Without End*. "I think," she said, "that it was his poem to Carlotta, and he was very badly shaken by the reception."

O'Neill indicated how he felt about it to several other people, in his subsequent letters and inscriptions. To Moeller, he inscribed a copy of the script: "A difficult one, this—but, whatever the profound wisecracks contra may be, we know we have made it live!"

And to Langner, he inscribed a special edition of uncorrected proofs: "Again, thanks for your fine co-operation in helping this opus to a fine production! Whatever its fate in the Amusement Racket which New York vaingloriously calls The Theatre, it will have been heard by a few of them it was written for, thanks to the Guild, and will live for them. So what the hell!"

In Sea Island, where he retreated not long after the opening, O'Neill was notified by the Guild's business manager, Warren Munsell, of the play's imminent closing.

O'Neill answered that he had half-expected the bad news, but had been "hoping against hope."

"The public for that play—and by public I mean all those (believers or unbelievers) who are sensitive enough to feel some spiritual significance in life and love—are not easy to lure into the theatre," he said. "They simply are not interested in the modern theatre."

He added that he had never had any illusions when writing the play that, "except by a 'modern miracle,' it could be a popular success."

"If ever there was an art for art's sake labor, it was mine in *Days Without End!*" he declared. "And for me it is a success."

He was certain, he said, that the play would be more readily accepted "in other countries where the Catholic foreground will be taken matter-of-factly and not give the critics the self-consciously modern, blind jitters."

William Butler Yeats, "no Catholic," O'Neill pointed out, had cabled him to say the Abbey Theatre wanted to produce it immediately.

"If a poet like Yeats sees what is in it," said O'Neill, "all my hard work on it is more than justified." (Two years earlier Yeats had publicly stated that O'Neill was "very much like Milton in some ways.")

A few days later, O'Neill commiserated with Russel Crouse:

"Well, at any rate, *Days Without End*—(an ironical title, what, in view of its run—but then I always was an ironical cuss!)—is now off you and that should be a relief. As it honestly is to me—for hoping against hope is a wearying game, and the handwriting on the wall was always plainly to be read—in red ink."

O'Neill told Crouse he was not going to begin work on a new play for some time. He was intent, he said, "on doing a little serious loafing and for-getting of 'Ye Olde Show Shoppe,'" as he was "stale as hell on the drama." And when he did start writing again, he added, he was not at all sure he would take up the previously mentioned *The Life of Bessie Bowen.*

Days Without End was subsequently produced not only in Ireland, with considerable success, but also in Holland and Sweden, and O'Neill took pleasure in pointing this out to a South American critic who sent him an essay about his plays in December of 1934.

"In New York it was entirely misunderstood by the critics, as I expected it would be, for a play that even mentions any religion these days is doomed in advance—especially doomed if the religion happens

[784]

to be Catholicism," he advised his correspondent. "They took the easy line of attack that I must have gone back to Catholicism and the play was Catholic propaganda—and then let their pseudo-sophisticated prejudices shriek anathemas. . . . Of course, the simple fact is I chose Catholicism because it is the only Western religion which has the stature of a real Faith, because it *is* the religion of the old miracle plays and the Faustian legend which were the sources of my theme—and last and most simply because it happens to be the religion of my early training and therefore the one I know most about."

Twelve years later, in one of those total reversals of which O'Neill was capable, he tried to explain to the writer Kyle Crichton why *Days Without End* had failed: "The critics didn't understand it and also it wasn't very good. That may account for it."

The production of *Days Without End* marked the beginning of a period of public decline for O'Neill in the United States (and this despite the fact that he won the Nobel Prize two years later). It was also a turning point in his life in other respects—a turning point that had actually begun, almost imperceptibly, with the production of *Mourning Becomes Electra*.

Still ahead of him was the writing of two undisputed masterpieces, *The Iceman Cometh* and *Long Day's Journey Into Night,* and still ahead, also, were twenty years of personal turbulence and tragedy. In these years he would see fewer and fewer people and have less and less direct contact with the theatre and with his times.

Robert Sherwood, himself vigorously in contact with the contemporary social, political and economic scene, once observed of O'Neill with wonder and, possibly, awe: "Spiritually he seemed to contract rather than expand in the climate of success. More and more, he withdrew himself from the world, living in one retreat after another."

By the end of 1934 O'Neill had determinedly retreated into the past.

LVI

THE INTERLUDE OF REST SOUGHT BY THE O'NEILLS
at Sea Island was interrupted in April, 1934, when they were compelled
to be in New York to defend themselves in a lawsuit. A Bronx elevator
operator had charged that the O'Neills' chaffeur-driven car had injured
him two years earlier in a traffic accident near White Plains, New York.

As in the case of the *Strange Interlude* plagiarism trial, O'Neill
managed to avoid an appearance in court. Taking the stand in his stead,
Carlotta declared that her husband was "unfit to work at the present
time," was "very nervous," was unable to leave his hotel room, and saw
no one but herself and his physician. O'Neill's attorney informed the
court that his client was, in fact, suffering from a "nervous breakdown,"
a claim that was made for and by O'Neill with rather startling frequency.

Testifying that her chaffeur had been proceeding slowly at the time
of the accident because she was "much too nervous" to allow him to drive
fast, Carlotta maintained that the claimant, Louis Gans, could not have
been badly hurt; he had been able to walk from his car and argue with
her chauffeur, she said. Nevertheless, Gans was awarded $3,000 (he
had asked for $25,000).

Whether or not O'Neill was actually incapacitated at the time of the
trial, he was at least consistent in his claim, calling off, among other
engagements, a projected meeting in New York with Sherwood Anderson.
On May 12, 1934, Anderson wrote to him of his regret at having missed
him in New York, and sympathized with his illness. "The more I see of
the theatre," Anderson said, "the more I realize what you have done for
it and you may be sure that everyone who cares about the theatre wants
to see you well and at work again."

O'Neill had recovered sufficiently a few days later to lend his
presence to an exhibit at the Museum of the City of New York honoring
his own and his father's careers.

"We were terrified that he wouldn't like it," May Davenport Seymour,
curator of the museum's theatre collection, later recalled. "There were
two mask caricatures of him that someone had loaned us. He inspected
them, and walked around examining every other item in the collection,

while I stood there, shaking. He then said, 'Miss Seymour, you've made us look wonderful.' "

O'Neill returned gratefully to Sea Island, happy in the knowledge that his new, long-range program of work would make it unnecessary, for many months, to be in New York. He did not anticipate a production for another two years or perhaps longer. He was beginning to regret that he had mentioned working on a new play, for his public (as represented by the newspapers' drama reporters) was insistent on hearing some word from him about the play's progress.

"For a long while now," said the *The New York Times* drama section that June, "rumors and reports have had Eugene O'Neill hard at work on 'The Life of Bessie Bowen.' They have painted him as bending over his typewriter night and day, rushing the play through for next season's use. Unfortunately, the whole thing seems to have been a mad whimsy. In reply to a pathetic query comes the following from Mr. O'Neill:

" 'No plans. Am determinedly resting. Don't even know now if Bessie Bowen will be the next one I write when I do start work again. No new production next season.' "

"Gene's one dream," Carlotta later said, in partial explanation of her husband's protracted absence from Broadway, "was *never* to have to go to New York for production. The only thing he cared about was his writing. He used to say, 'Oh, God, if only some Good Fairy would give me some money, so I'd never have to produce a play, and I could just write, write, write and never go near a theatre!' "

Even though he managed, for the next dozen years, to fulfill this dream, he did find it necessary to make occasional trips to New York. The same tiresome chore that had periodically taken him from the seclusion of Le Plessis to the bustle of Paris continued to interrupt his artistic isolation at Casa Genotta—sessions with his dentist. To compensate him for these frustrating and painful interruptions, he sometimes contrived to make his visits to New York coincide with the advent of the six-day bicycle races; and in the fall of 1934 he found he could arrange a double amelioration. Sean O'Casey, whom he was anxious to meet, was to be in New York for the production of his play, *Within the Gates*, and George Jean Nathan offered to introduce them.

O'Casey, in his first (and only) trip to the United States, arrived in a brown suit and a cap, bringing with him nothing but an extra set of underwear, a single shirt, a pair of socks and a sweater. He registered at the Royalton Hotel, where Nathan lived, and spent the first hours after his arrival testing all the electrical gadgets in his room and carefully distributing his few items of wardrobe among the drawers of his bureau.

During his first meeting with O'Neill on October 16, O'Casey told him that he thought of New York as a series of little villages and that he loved to talk to the newsboys at Forty-second Street and Sixth Avenue. *Within the Gates* opened on October 22, and a few days later O'Casey confided to O'Neill that he had been in the audience on opening night and every night since. He spent the intermissions in the dressing room of Lillian Gish, who was playing the role of the young whore.

"I can't stay in the lobby," he told O'Neill. "People come up to me and ask what the play is about. I can't tell them. I don't know."

The first meeting between O'Casey and O'Neill had made them fast friends.

Nathan had brought O'Casey to the Madison Hotel, where O'Neill usually stayed during his visits to New York. O'Casey, who did not make friends quickly, found O'Neill to be "a warmhearted man one couldn't help liking."

O'Neill reciprocated the affection.

"When O'Casey told my husband, 'You write like an Irishman, not like an American,'" Carlotta once said, "Gene was so pleased he didn't know what to do."

"He and I fell for each other at once—at least I know I fell for him, and I believe he fell for me," O'Casey later said. "The first visit was on O'Neill's birthday. George Jean bought some toys for him as a little joke, for O'Neill would take anything from G.J.N., and it was plain to me that these two men loved each other. Of course, I knew O'Neill well by the great work he did for American and International Drama; but everyone knows this—or should know it, anyhow. My social alliance with this great man, while I was in America, told me that as well as being a great playwright, he was a great and lovable man; deeply thoughtful of the world's woes, but holding fast within him the delightful qualities of a child—reminding me of: 'Except ye become like little children, ye are in no wise fit for the Kingdom of Heaven.' Well, if there be a heaven, certainly Eugene was fit to live there. English critics didn't care for his work; but then they are, I fear, nearsighted, looking at the playfulness of the magpies, but with eyes too weak to watch the soar of an eagle in the upper skies."

O'Casey especially admired *The Great God Brown, Strange Interlude* and *Mourning Becomes Electra* and was impressed by the fact that O'Neill went successfully "back to the Greeks." "But you have to remember that he's Irish, particularly in his humor," O'Casey once said, adding that O'Neill made him laugh often, telling him jokes that "only two Irishmen can share."

During the birthday meeting, Carlotta presented O'Neill with a pair of slacks, and O'Neill modeled them for O'Casey and Nathan, causing them both to roar with laughter.

"I'm not a very good dresser, you know," O'Casey later said, "but O'Neill was a dandy of a dresser."

One day O'Neill, O'Casey and Nathan lunched together in O'Neill's suite at the Madison.

"O'Casey and I, before joining him," Nathan later reported in an article entitled *The Recluse of Sea Island,* published in *Redbook* magazine, "had coached ourselves in a plot to take him to task, with a great show of indignation on our part, for his burial of himself from all contact with the world and his fellow-men. Slowly and, we thought, with a pretty histrionic skill, we edged against his self-defense with lush arguments as to the necessity of an artist's—and particularly a dramatist's—mingling with the stream of life if he is to comprehend it and interpret its depths and mutations. As the hours passed, O'Neill began to indicate, first a mild restlessness, then a growing mood of irritation, and finally an open hot rebellion. Jumping out of his chair . . . he confronted both of us and, his face flushed, made what is the longest speech that he has made in all the years I have known him.

"'What you fellows have been saying,' he exploded, 'is damned rot! That mingling with people and life that you talk about, far from giving anything to an artist, simply takes things away from him, damned valuable things. If he hasn't everything in himself, he is no good. The life outside him can steal from him, but it can't contribute a thing to him, unless he is a rank second-rater. You talk of the thrill of cities, as against the so-called loneliness and stagnation of the country. What is the thrill? A lot of meaningless noise, a lot of crowding bores, a lot of awful smells, a swirl of excited nothingness! You talk of the thrill of a city's beauty. Well,' (pointing out of the window) 'look at those skyscrapers! What are they, what do they stand for? Nothing but a lot of children's blocks! Do you mean to say that they've got anything to do with the great soul of humanity, with humanity's deep underlying essence, and hopes, and fate? You're both bughouse!'"

O'Neill, according to Nathan, gave both of them "a black and completely disgusted look" and abruptly left the room—but returned ten minutes later in a better mood.

O'Neill admired O'Casey enough to venture into the meaningless noises and crowds of Broadway to attend a performance of *Within the*

Gates. And before departing for Sea Island he accompanied O'Casey and Nathan on a ride through Central Park in a hansom cab. O'Neill and O'Casey never met again but they continued to exchange letters, O'Neill writing from his various elegant retreats in the United States and O'Casey from his modest flat in Devon, England.

Some years after O'Neill's death, on the occasion of naming a Broadway theatre in his honor, O'Casey was asked to send a few words of tribute. He responded with alacrity and enthusiasm:

You do well to honor a theatre-building with the great name of Eugene O'Neill; for what finer memorial could a great Dramatist have than that of a temple dedicated to the Art he loved, and to which he added many a wide and deep honor, and, more than once, a glory.

The soul of O'Neill was a restless one, always seeking out the storm, crying out from the midst of tumbling waves, loudly enough to be heard above the tumult of the strongest winds, till the dark lull of death brought silence and a well-earned peace.

Yet this man could be gay. Yes, indeed, for I saw him so: I was with him a number of times in the company of his dear friend, George Jean Nathan, and then we talked and talked merrily in the surge of a gay time together; and then often I saw the somber face of the Dramatist break into the sunniness of deep and generous laughter. It was good to have met this remarkable man; to have looked into his deep, wine-dark eyes; to have pressed his hand as the hand of a friend in joyful and lasting affection; and to have heard his laughter.

I am glad that in his American soul there was, not only the touch of a poet, but also the touch of an Irishman, for the O'Neills had their origin in Ireland. This great Dramatist of America and the world tells me again that our Shamrock twines a leaf or two around every flower symbolizing each State of O'Neill's great and urgent Country. The Shamrock is an unassuming and humble plant, but it is always there.

Settling down to serious work again at Sea Island in the late fall of 1934, O'Neill outlined a project of work even more ambitious than the *Electra* trilogy. *The Life of Bessie Bowen* was a part of this plan, initially conceived as a three-play cycle, with the first set during the American Revolution, the second in 1840, and the third (*Bessie Bowen*) in the present. He now decided to condense the span of time—1857 to the present—but to expand the cycle to four, or possibly five, plays, tracing the fortunes of an American family named Harford; the cycle was to have the over-all title *The Calms of Capricorn.*

O'Neill envisioned the cycle as the crowning achievement of his career and was ready to devote years of work—even the rest of his life—to it, if necessary. He had already begun making detailed charts of the Harford family's genealogy, and now he sketched a vast program of research, requiring extensive reading on the social, economic and political history of the nineteenth century.

Aside from being ambitious in scope, O'Neill's new project indicated the continuation of a literary trend evinced with the writing of *Ah, Wilderness!* He had turned inward and backward, driven to examining and evaluating the past. The present no longer held much significance for him, and the future held none at all. Of the plays he was still to write, or attempt to write, only the one about Bessie Bowen (and this only in part) was set in the present.

The action of the rest of the cycle plays took place before 1900, and the three major plays he completed outside the cycle were set in 1912 (*Long Day's Journey Into Night* and *The Iceman Cometh*) and in 1923 (*A Moon for the Misbegotten*). O'Neill was beginning, more and more, to live with and brood about the ghosts of his past and to search in that past for an answer to the meaning of his own life. He became almost compulsively fascinated with the study of one generation's effect on the next—"The Harford curse," one of his cycle characters calls it.

If his time had not run out, O'Neill's search for an answer in the past would very likely have carried him, as it did Shaw, back to Methuselah. ("If you keep on going back," Carlotta chided him at one point during his work on the cycle, "you'll get to Adam and Eve.") But it is interesting to note, in comparing the outlooks of O'Neill and Shaw, that Shaw, who was childless, had enormous interest in and curiosity about the future; if he went back to Methuselah, he also propelled his vision far forward into a future which no child of his would ever inhabit. O'Neill, the father of three children, had no interest in the world his progeny would inhabit. He was preoccupied excusively with the world that had shaped his forebears and himself. In his view the O'Neills ended with him.

As O'Neill built up the background and themes of the separate stories of his cycle, he was convinced that five plays were definitely needed to round out his concept; and he decided to find a new over-all title for the cycle and to use *The Calms of Capricorn* as the title of the first play. He put down the titles and settings of all five:

The Calms of Capricorn, set during 1857, in a New England farmhouse, aboard a clipper ship at a Boston dock and on the South Atlantic, and outside San Francisco's Golden Gate; *The Earth's the Limit*, set during 1858-1860, in a San Francisco hotel and atop a pass in the Sierras;

Nothing is Lost Save Honor, set during 1862-1870, in San Francisco, New York and Washington; *The Man on Iron Horseback,* set during 1876-1893, in New York, Paris, Shanghai and the Midwest; and, finally, *The Life of Bessie Bowen,* which he had also thought of calling *The Career of Bessie Bolan* (or Bowlan), but which title he now abandoned in favor of *A Hair of the Dog,* set during 1900-1932, in a mansion in the Midwest.

Before writing his detailed scenarios of the five plays he indicated which of the characters would be carried over from one play to the next, whom they married, when they died, and which of their children perpetuated the family name. Since many of these notes were subsequently destroyed by O'Neill, it is possible to reconstruct his scheme only fragmentarily.

The cycle's central figure was to be a woman called Sara Harford (born Melody), daughter of an Irish immigrant, who becomes a powerful matriarch through her marriage to Simon Harford, scion of a wealthy Yankee family. Sara (a widow at thirty-eight) and her children were to be characters in *The Calms of Capricorn,* and were also to appear in *The Earth's the Limit* and *Nothing is Lost Save Honor,* by the end of which play, if, indeed, she was destined to survive to the end, she would have attained the age of sixty-two. It is possible that Bessie Bowen (or Bowlan) of the final play, *A Hair of the Dog,* was to make an appearance in an earlier play and that she was to become the wife of one of Sara's sons.

According to Carlotta, who typed the manuscript of *A Hair of the Dog,* Bessie was a completely fictional character; she epitomized the twentieth century, feminist, business tycoon. During the final play's span of thirty-two years, she was to become the head of a huge automobile manufacturing company.

"Gene wanted to write about different phases in the history of America," Carlotta explained. "How women entered the field of industry, how the great automobile empires evolved, about banking and shipping and the decline of the clippers.

"He was always working on several of the plays at once. He would work on one until he felt he was stuck, get a thought about another one, and work on that."

By early spring of 1935 O'Neill was toying with the notion of pushing his story further back in time. He wanted to examine the character of Sara Melody Harford in greater detail, to introduce her parents as characters, and also to go into more of the early history of Simon's family;

he now thought there might be as many as eight plays in the cycle, and he selected the over-all title, *A Touch of the Poet,* to indicate the touch of Irish blood brought by the Melodys to the Harford family.

There were few interruptions to work at Casa Genotta during the winter and spring of 1935. Carlotta efficiently supervised the running of the household, answered those of her husband's letters that he did not care to answer himself, snubbed such acquaintances as might have had a distracting effect on their routine, and acted the gracious hostess to a chosen few who were welcome in the sanctified atmosphere of the Blessed Isles. O'Neill wrote fewer and fewer letters during this period but he did take time out, in January of 1935, to telegraph to Mrs. George Pierce Baker. Professor Baker died on January 6, and O'Neill sent his wire on January 8:

"Words are stupid and futile at such a time but I want you to know how profoundly I sympathize and that I feel deep personal grief at the loss of one of the truest friends my work has ever known."

Then he composed a letter to *The New York Times* about Baker, which appeared on January 13:

Only those of us who had the privilege in the drama class of George Pierce Baker back in the dark age when the American theatre was still, for playwrights, the closed shop, star system, amusement racket, can know what a profound influence Professor Baker, who died last Sunday, exerted toward the encouragement and birth of modern American drama.

It is difficult in these days, when the native playwright can function in comparative freedom, to realize that in that benighted period a play of any imagination, originality or integrity by an American was almost automatically barred from a hearing in our theatre. To write plays of life as one saw and felt it, instead of concocting the conventional theatrical drivel of the time, seemed utterly hopeless.

In the face of this blank wall, the biggest need of the young playwright was for intelligent encouragement, to be helped to believe in the dawn of a new era in our theatre where he would have a chance, at least, to be heard. And of the rare few who had the unselfish faith and vision and love of the theatre to devote their life to this encouragement, Professor Baker's work stands pre-eminent. It is that encouragement which I—and I am sure all the playwrights who knew and studied under him—will always remember with the deepest appreciation.

Not that the technical points, the analysis of the practice of playmaking taught in his class, were not of inestimable value to us in learning our trade. But the most vital thing for us, as possible future artists and creators, to learn at that time (Good God! For anyone to learn anywhere at any time!) was to believe in our work and to keep on believing. And to hope. He helped us to hope—and for that we owe him all the finest we have in memory of gratitude and friendship.

O'Neill finally managed, a few months later, to arrange his long-postponed meeting with Sherwood Anderson, who was now in the South himself, at his home in Marion, Virginia. Anderson lunched at Casa Genotta on April 16, 1935, and a few days later wrote to O'Neill of his pleasure at having seen him.

"It was only too short for me," Anderson assured him. "I had a thousand things I wanted to talk with you about but knew it would take me a long time to get started. I was delighted to find you at work again and in good spirits. I know you are always after something not too easily comprehended and that you continually have to go through your own little hells. You have always been a man I have looked up to as one of the few great figures of the time and I am sorry that I cannot see more of you."

But Anderson expressed a more candid opinion of the visit on April 24. Writing to a friend (in a letter subsequently published in a volume called *Letters of Sherwood Anderson*), he said:

"We went . . . to spend a few hours with [Eugene O'Neill] on our way North. You know he married the actress Monterey—reputed to be one of the really beautiful women of America. I thought her cold, calculating. Certainly she is not one of the women who make a house warm.

"Gene is a sick man. He says he is better than he has been for a long time and told me of a vast scheme, a series of eight plays in sequence. I take it they are to be all connected and played night after night, the same characters coming and going through the various plays. God knows it is [an] ambitious enough scheme, but will he ever pull it off? He is a very very sweet fine man but I did feel death in his big expensive house. He has drawn himself away, lives in that solitary place, seeing practically no one. He needs his fellow men. I felt him clinging to me rather pitifully."

On the same day that Anderson was expressing his misgivings about O'Neill to his friend, O'Neill was writing to Anderson, in words that seemed to justify the novelist's sense of O'Neill's melancholy isolation.

O'Neill declared that he, too, had found the visit "all too brief."

"I felt as you did that there was a devil of a lot I wanted to say but that it was too long a story to start then," he said, adding that he hoped another visit could be arranged soon. Returning Anderson's compliment,

O'Neill declared that he had long felt a spiritual kinship with him, "and so, the foundation of lasting friendship."

Not long after, Anderson wrote to Theodore Dreiser:

"Say, Ted, write a nice note to Gene O'Neill. I've a hunch he is just now a down pin."

A number of friends and acquaintances during this period shared Anderson's impression, but others held quite a different view. Mrs. Ben Pinchot, for example, described the O'Neill's life as one of "placid though monotonous routine."

"O'Neill gets up at seven and is at work by eight," she wrote in notes to herself at the time. "Under no circumstancves is he disturbed until one-thirty, when the gong chimes for lunch. Unless he is in the midst of a troublesome bit of writing, he does not return to work after lunch.

"In the summer, lunch is served on the veranda facing the ocean. O'Neill eats sparingly, is fond of cold meats, salad and fresh fruits.

"After lunch, he reads the mail that Carlotta has sorted out for him— reports from his agent on royalties, personal notes from friends, letters from embryo playwrights, letters asking for aid, encouragement or autographs.

"Weather permitting, he swims daily, then lies on the beach and lets the sun bake him a deep brown. He likes to fish, as much for the opportunity it affords him to sit in a boat and ruminate on future plays, as for the sport. He also takes lonely walks along the beach.

"He spends many afternoons trimming the palm trees, pruning bushes, coaxing the magnolias and gardenias to richer bloom, planting trailing vines that will eventually cover the garden walls. These walls are a necessity. During their first years at Sea Island, the O'Neills were overrun with sightseers and curiosity seekers who prowled around the grounds.

"They drive to the mainland occasionally, or go on a shopping trip to Brunswick, the nearest town, and sometimes to a movie.

"Late in the afternoon the O'Neills meet in the patio for tea—which, for them, means a tall, cool drink of fruit juices, made by Carlotta. She tries various combinations—carrot and orange juice, grapefruit and beet juice, and so forth. She says that, besides being marvelous thirst quenchers, they have the quality of a tonic. The O'Neills seldom entertain, although occasionally they receive visitors from New York.

"In the country O'Neill usually wears corduroy slacks, a sweater-shirt of which he is particularly fond, and a loose tweed jacket.

"In the quiet hours of dusk, O'Neill relaxes. He plays with Blemie, wanders through his garden, prodding Baltimore and Ohio, his pet turtles, and tends the big pool that is filled with countless, unnamed goldfish.

"Dinner, at seven, is a substantial meal, always finished with fresh fruit for dessert. After dinner, the O'Neills retire to their living room, to read or play gin rummy, or just to talk. They go to bed at an hour that sounds ridiculous to a city dweller."

The routine described by Mrs. Pinchot was a Spartan one, and O'Neill himself had wistfully confirmed this view of his life soon after moving to Casa Genotta, when he wrote to his cousin, Phil Sheridan, contrasting his wild days in New London with his present asceticism.

"I haven't even sipped a glass of beer in seven years now," he said, forgetting, as he always did, his binges in Guéthary and in Shanghai. "I hear you tie or better that mark. Well, well, who would have thought it, what? And Art McGinley gone good, too! No Crocker House barkeep would ever have imagined marvels like that! There's something almost corrupt about it!"

But in December of 1935 the atmosphere at Casa Genotta became emphatically, if briefly, bacchanalian. George Jean Nathan, after a visit, sent the O'Neills a keg of Edelbrau beer. It was several hours before O'Neill, Carlotta and their servants discovered that the secret of starting the beer lay in opening the bung hole; it was several additional hours before they managed to pry the bung hole open. But, once opened, the beer flowed and flowed.

Carlotta gave Nathan a humorous report of the effect his gift had on the household. She and O'Neill had drunk beer with lunch, beer instead of tea, beer for dinner and beer for a nightcap. "Rosie plays and the Edelbrau flows," she said.

Another visitor to Casa Genotta was Saxe Commins. He brought a football with him, because he thought it would amuse O'Neill to kick it along the beach. After Commins left, the chauffeur, Herbert Freeman, took over as O'Neill's opponent in the kicking game.

"The chauffeur, who was also the butler, had been a college football player," Commins said. "Carlotta adopted the English style of addressing servants, and called him Freeman. He was a great, big, nice guy, who helped around the house and grounds."

Russel Crouse also was pressed into service as a football player when he visited the O'Neills. Crouse was among the group of friends who had the impression that O'Neill was more isolated at Sea Island than he wanted to be, but in retrospect he acknowledged that he may have misjudged the situation. Many years later he told Hamilton Basso of *The*

New Yorker, "O'Neill is one of the most charming men I know, and I've known him for twenty-five years, but I can't say I understand him. His face is a mask. I don't know what goes on behind it and I don't think anyone else does."

On another occasion Crouse explained that he never presumed to ask O'Neill about his personal motives. "When you were with him," he said, "you felt you were in a presence. You waited for him to reveal himself." If you waited, you apparently got results. During one visit, Crouse recalled, O'Neill told him in detail the plots of fifteen plays he had outlined for the future.

"Carlotta, in a way, walled Gene in," Crouse, a notably gregarious man, observed. "I think there were people he might have enjoyed seeing, if left to himself. For instance, I remember that once Joseph Hergesheimer was in Sea Island and telephoned to ask if he could see Gene. Carlotta said no, Gene was too busy working. She reported this to me indignantly. 'I told Hergesheimer, certainly not!' she said. I felt Gene would have liked to see Hergesheimer, but he never argued with Carlotta about these things. Another time I ran into Bobby Jones and I said I hoped he would visit Gene. He told me, 'Carlotta won't let me near him!' " (On later occasions, however, Jones was welcomed by both Carlotta and O'Neill.)

Fania Marinoff, who was aware that the company at Sea Island was exclusive in the extreme, once observed that "visitors made both Gene and Carlotta very nervous."

"I know that the preparations they had to make for Sherwood Anderson's visit threw them both into a state of distress," she added. "They did cut off people who had been close friends, on what seemed to be slight provocation. It was my understanding that Ilka Chase, for example, had telephoned them very late one evening and that this upset them so much they stopped seeing her. But the people they continued to see were treated with extraordinary generosity. After one visit to Casa Genotta, Carlotta insisted on giving me a pair of old, Spanish earrings I had admired when she wore them. She handed them to me just as I was leaving."

The Langners, who paid one of several visits in March of 1935, found everything serene and running "like clockwork."

"The first morning I was there," Langner later reported, "after doing his morning's work, Gene came out and sat on the beach where I was taking a sun bath and as we both looked out over the ocean, the waves breaking at our feet a few yards away, he told me about his plan for his new plays. They would literally take years to write. We were not to expect to receive the first of them until the last was completed because he would be making changes in them until the very last one was done. Each play would be complete in itself, yet each of the plays would be part of a whole."

The plays, O'Neill told Langner, would deal with several generations of a family, an admixture of old Puritan New England stock and Irish-American blood.

"Galsworthy's 'The Forsyte Saga' seemed like child's play in comparison, as Gene traced the effect of the grandparents on the children and their grandchildren, reminding me of the Biblical prophecies as to the sins of the parents being visited upon their children unto the third and fourth generations," Langner added. "I marveled at the scope of the work he was attempting, and wondered whether, in the hot, damp climate of Sea Island, he would have the strength to last out the ordeal he had set for himself. . . . I was troubled about the climate at Sea Island and its effect on Gene. No matter how hard Carlotta tried, she fought a losing battle against the dampness coming from the warm sea air laden with salt moisture, and the continuous heat of summer."

Langner was struck, that summer, by what he described as "Gene's consciousness of his own immortality."

"I've never known anyone else but Shaw to have this," he said.

"Gene was obviously not working just to garner the success of the day; he was always measuring himself. And he kept everything meticulously, as though fully aware that all of his notes and manuscript material would some day end up as valuable items in a library."

One of the most succinct descriptions of O'Neill in his splendid island isolation has been furnished by Somerset Maugham, who shared with the O'Neills an interest in the Orient. Maugham, himself not a gregarious man, was startled by the extremes to which O'Neill went to safeguard his privacy. Maugham once wrote that when, on shipboard, he listened to his fellow passengers carol, "Should auld acquaintance be forgot," his instinct was to murmur, "Please, yes." But he felt that O'Neill was carrying things too far.

"When he was living on an island off the coast of Georgia," Maugham said, "I spent two or three days with him and Carlotta. The house he lived in was by the sea, and far from any other habitation. I didn't see another soul while I was there, but he constantly complained and said he must leave the island because it was so thronged with people."

Carlotta and O'Neill talked with Maugham about the possibility of their making another trip to China and Maugham recommended a book about Peking, which Carlotta ordered after his departure.

Perhaps the best clue to whether it was O'Neill or Carlotta who insisted on total privacy was furnished by a couple of inscriptions O'Neill wrote during this time on the manuscripts he was constantly presenting to his wife. It seems evident, from these inscriptions, that whatever mask O'Neill wore before his friends, he required no society but that of his wife and no home but that of her love.

On their sixth wedding anniversary, that July, he wrote:

"Six years of it and I *love* it! Your Gene, Darling!"

And later that year, on her birthday:

"To Carlotta . . . my heart's and soul's gratitude for her love, which is this Stranger's only home on this earth!"

By late spring of 1935, O'Neill had nearly completed the scenarios of three of the cycle plays. Carlotta was concerned about the effect of the Georgia heat on her husband's health, and considered a trip to a cooler climate, but finally decided, with him, to try to bear the southern summer, rather than interrupt his trend of thought. He was deep in books about the political, financial, spiritual and cultural history of the United States.

Carlotta thought she could keep the house cool enough for O'Neill to work in. "What my Irishman wants, he shall have," she remarked to Russel Crouse.

In O'Neill's mind the cycle now definitely included seven plays, and he had not rejected the possibility of adding an eighth. His interest in the Melody family and the early Harford history had already taken him back to 1828. The title, *A Touch of the Poet,* no longer designated the whole cycle but was to be used for the first play, set in a village outside Boston, before Sara Melody's marriage to Simon Harford. The next play in the sequence was to be set during 1837-1846 (ten years before *The Calms of Capricorn*) in various houses near Boston occupied by Simon and Sara after their marriage. This play O'Neill called *More Stately Mansions,* deriving the title from the poem by Oliver Wendell Holmes: "Build thee more stately mansions, O my soul!"

On September 17, 1935, O'Neill described his struggles with the cycle to his former mentor, Clayton Hamilton, who had sent him a copy of his new book, *So You're Writing a Play!* (Hamilton had dedicated it to O'Neill.)

O'Neill told Hamilton he would have to postpone reading the book for a time. He was so preoccupied, he said, "by the thousand and one technical and psychological problems involved in rounding out the detailed outline of the interrelationship between the seven plays of this Cycle" that by the time he completed his daily stint he loathed "the very mention of the word play!"

"No time in which to read a book on play-writing, you'll agree!" he explained.

Soon after writing this letter, O'Neill began on the actual dialogue of his first cycle play, *A Touch of the Poet*. Despite its period setting and historical context, the play was, like so many of his others, emotionally and psychologically the story of his own family.

The hero, Cornelius Melody, son of an Irish shebeen (or saloon) keeper who bought his way up the social scale in Ireland, is a disgraced officer who fought in the Napoleonic Wars on the English side and then immigrated to the United States with his wife and child.

Though he is an ex-soldier turned saloonkeeper in a small town outside Boston (rather than an actor touring the hinterlands), he has many characteristics in common with James O'Neill. He is a handsome ladies' man, he is addicted to the bottle but knows how to carry his liquor, "his heavy-boned body has a bull-like, impervious strength, a tough, peasant vitality," he is looked down upon by his "aristocratic" Yankee neighbors, and he is as theatrical in his manner as a matinee idol. He poses before mirrors, gesticulates flamboyantly, recites grandiloquently, tells highly colored anecdotes of his past, and lapses into Irish brogue in moments of extreme emotion.

His relationship with his wife and child—in this case a daughter—is the characteristic O'Neillian one of love-hate. Their quarrels are frequent and bitter and guiltily regretted, with phrases like "it's the poison talking" or "it was the drink talking." But the bitterness and frustration always return, and the ghosts of old dreams are never shaken off. Like Mary Tyrone, who, in *Long Day's Journey Into Night* drags her wedding dress from an attic trunk, Cornelius Melody exhumes his resplendent major's uniform from the attic to symbolize his proud, vanished youth and help him relive his past.

In the Melody marriage, as in the Tyrone marriage, one partner lives on "dope dreams" and is protected and coddled by the other; in *A Touch of the Poet* this particular phase of the relationship is reversed, however, with the wife, Nora, being the protector. But the daughter, Sara, bears the same taunting, scornful relationship to her father that Jamie Tyrone bears to James, and her mother, like Mary Tyrone, tries to make peace between them. Sara is a typical O'Neill heroine, a blood sister to both Abbie Putnam in *Desire Under the Elms* and Josie Hogan in *A Moon for the Misbegotten*. Like both Abbie and Josie, she deliberately sets out, for materialistic reasons, to seduce the man she wants. And like Abbie and Josie, she finds herself trapped by her own emotions. Like Josie, too, she seduces her man with her father's knowledge and tacit consent.

[800]

A Touch of the Poet introduced the first member of the cycle dynasty, in the person of Simon Harford, who, when the play ends, is about to marry Sara. (He became an off-stage character in O'Neill's final version of the play, and he materialized as one of the central characters in the unfinished *More Stately Mansions.*) Melody foreshadows the next play of the cycle, *More Stately Mansions*, in a last-act speech which refers to his daughter: ". . . and she'll live in a Yankee mansion, as big as a castle, on a grand estate of stately woodland."

O'Neill finished his first draft of *A Touch of the Poet* in the spring of 1936 and immediately began writing the dialogue for *More Stately Mansions.*

Working like a man possessed, he would often write straight through the night.

"I would find him exhausted in the morning when I brought in his breakfast," Carlotta later recalled.

O'Neill was plunged so deep into work and into the past that he now excluded almost everything and everyone in the contemporary world —except his wife. He scarcely acknowledged the existence of his two younger children. Shane had been to Sea Island for a brief and unsatisfactory visit, and O'Neill's contact with him and Oona was now largely confined to a desultory postcard correspondence, with the task of any longer communications being delegated to Carlotta. His only contact with Agnes was through his lawyer over such matters as the children's schooling. But while he was withdrawn from Shane and Oona, he spared time to keep in touch with Eugene Jr., who made few emotional demands on him. O'Neill saw him from time to time, and continued to finance his studies, which now included trips abroad.

Although he was completely out of touch with almost everyone from the old Provincetown group, he was stunned when he read, in January of 1936, of Louise Bryant's death. Louise was forty-nine when she died in Paris under circumstances as bleak as any O'Neill could have created for one of his heroines. Louise's life, after Reed's death, had followed the classic lines of the romantic heroine doomed to live too fully, too soon.

In 1923 she had married William C. Bullitt (later United States ambassador to Russia and France). They had a daughter, and for a while Louise seemed to enjoy her transformation from stormy petrel to diplomatic hostess and mother. She could not play her new role for long, however. In 1930 Bullitt divorced her, and she drifted back to Greenwich Village, moving into an apartment in Patchin Place which she had once shared with Reed. She drank excessively and became involved in a series of sordid, petty scandals, at least one of which resulted in a court case. Several of the old Provincetown Playhouse people saw her occasionally, and one of them, Mary Ellen Boyden, was with her a few weeks before she died.

"I met her in a Greenwich Village speakeasy," Mrs. Boyden said. "She was sitting at a table with another woman. She was drunk and had a black eye. I took her to her apartment, and she told me this was where she had lived with Reed. She talked on and on about Reed, and how much she had loved him."

It was soon after this that Louise vanished from the Village, to turn up in Paris. On January 6, while climbing the stairs of a shabby little hotel on the Left Bank, she collapsed and was taken to a hospital. Newspaper accounts said she had been stricken with a cerebral hemorrhage, but rumors were carried back to New York that she had been taking drugs.

That April, during a particularly arduous session with the cycle, O'Neill was invited to New York to speak at a dinner launching the first Critics Circle Award. Established by the New York drama critics in protest against the Pulitzer Prizes in drama, the award went to Maxwell Anderson for *Winterset*. Presumably the drama critics had been fuming ever since the Pulitzer Prize had gone to *Of Thee I Sing* instead of to *Mourning Becomes Electra*. O'Neill declined to interrupt his work to make a personal appearance, but he did take time to write a long letter (which was read in part at the dinner by Brooks Atkinson). The letter contains a rare utterance—public or private—in favor of critics:

". . . in honoring Mr. Anderson's work you do honor to yourselves and the American theatre and start the Critics Circle award with genuine distinction. May all your future awards have a like distinction, and may your future be a long one! If that isn't wishing you the best of good wishes then I don't know what is!

"And it seems to me that the Critics Circle award deserves the very best in the way of good wishes from all those who have the future of our drama at heart. I confess I admit this with considerable reluctance. It is a terrible, harrowing experience for a playwright to be forced by his conscience to praise critics for anything. It isn't done. It never has been done. There is something morbid and abnormal about it, something destructive to the noble tradition of what is correct conduct for dramatists. In short, it gripes. Nevertheless, conscience drives me to reiterate that I think the Critics Circle award is a damned fine idea."

Two months later O'Neill voluntarily interrupted his work again to write an unsolicited tribute to someone whose work he admired more than Anderson's. Maxim Gorki had died on June 18. On Casa Genotta stationery O'Neill penciled the brief note he later mailed to a Russian publication in New York.

"Gorki is not dead," he wrote in part. "His genius and his spirit of tragic understanding and pity for humanity which characterized his work will live as long as true literature is read."

O'Neill found himself haunted, that spring and summer, by one of the characters he had introduced in *A Touch of the Poet* and who also appeared in *More Stately Mansions*. The character was Simon Harford's mother, Deborah, a beautiful aristocrat, whose mysticism and remoteness suggest Ella O'Neill. Deborah (originally called Abigail) makes only a brief appearance in *A Touch of the Poet*, but the appearance is a poignant and disturbing one. In *More Stately Mansions* she was to be a more dominant character, fighting Sara for Simon's love—"with charm and subtlety," according to Carlotta, "while Sara fights with her body."

O'Neill paused in the writing of *More Stately Mansions* to brood about Deborah's background, and decided he had not given it enough scope. He determined to begin the cycle even earlier and to add an eighth play after all. Entitling it *And Give Me Death,* he set it during 1783-1805, when Deborah was seventeen, and laid its action in Rhode Island and Paris, one scene taking place in 1804 on the day of Napoleon's coronation.

He was not yet satisfied, however, and decided to go back still further, to 1755. He outlined one more play, *The Greed of the Meek,* and set it during 1755-1775 on a farm in Rhode Island. The scope and nature of *And Give Me Death* and *The Greed of the Meek* are suggested in a speech delivered by Deborah to Sara in *A Touch of the Poet*—a speech which, out of the cycle's context, reads more like a long note O'Neill made to himself about the earlier cycle characters than like an integrated part of the individual play:

Simon is an inveterate dreamer—a weakness he inherited from me, I'm afraid, although I must admit the Harfords have been great dreamers, too, in their way. . . . Simon's great-grandfather, Jonathan Harford, had it. He was killed at Bunker Hill, but I suspect the War for Independence was merely a symbolic opportunity for him. . . . Simon's grandfather, Evan Harford, had the quality too. A fanatic in the cause of pure freedom, he became scornful of our Revolution. It made too many compromises with the ideal to free him. He went to France and became a rabid Jacobin, a worshiper of Robespierre. He would have liked to have gone to the guillotine with his incorruptible Redeemer, but he was too unimportant. They simply forgot to kill him. He came home and lived in a little temple of Liberty he had built in a corner of what is now my garden. A dry, gentle, cruel, indomitable, futile old idealist who used frequently to wear his old uniform of the French Republican National Guard. He died wearing it. But the point is, you can have no idea what revengeful hate the Harford pursuit of freedom imposed upon the women who shared their lives. The three daughters-in-law of Jonathan, Evan's half-sisters, had to make a large, greedy fortune out of privateering and the Northwest trade, and finally were even driven to embrace the profits of the slave trade—a triumphant climax, you understand, of their long battle to escape the enslavement of freedom by enslaving it. Evan's wife, of course, was drawn into this conflict and became their tool and accomplice. . . . I am sorry they are dead and cannot know you. They would approve of you, I think. They would see that you are strong and ambitious and determined to take what you want. They would have smiled like senile, hungry serpents and welcomed you into their coils. Evil old witches! Detestable, but I could not help admiring them—pitying them, too—in the end. We had a bond in common. They idolized Napoleon. . . . The Sisters, as everyone called them, and all of the family accompanied my husband and me on our honeymoon—to Paris to witness the Emperor's coronation.

O'Neill now had a projected nine-play cycle, and he chose a new, over-all title for his mammoth work: *A Tale of Possessors, Self-Dispossessed*. He returned to the writing of *More Stately Mansions*, now chronologically the fourth play in the sequence.

During July, while New York sweltered in a heat wave, Sea Island remained relatively comfortable with the eighty to eighty-five degree weather tempered by a cooling sea breeze. But a month later the heat had descended. O'Neill wrote to Langner on August 12, 1936, that it was "a hell of a hot, oppressive summer" at Sea Island. "We just continually drop and drip," he said.

Reporting on the progress of the cycle, he cautioned Langner not to expect "an American life" in the accepted sense.

"I mean," he explained, "I'm not giving a damn whether the dramatic event of each play has any significance in the growth of the country or not, as long as it is significant in the spiritual and psychological history of the American family in the plays. The Cycle is primarily just that, the history of a family. What larger significance I can give my people as extraordinary examples and symbols in the drama of American possessiveness and materialism is something else again. But I don't want anyone to get the idea that this Cycle is much concerned with what is usually understood by American history, for it isn't. As for economic history—which so many seem to mistake for the *only* history just now—I am not much interested in economic determinism, but only in the self-determinism of which the economic is one phase, and by no means the most revealing—at least, not to me."

Plaintively bewailing the difficulties of his task, he added:

"Try a Cycle sometime, I advise you—that is, I would advise you to, if I hated you! A lady bearing quintuplets is having a debonair, carefree time of it by comparison."

The heat became unbearable by the end of August and O'Neill and Carlotta decided that their Blessed Isles would not do.

Once more O'Neill turned his back on a home that had failed to live up to his expectations. Provincetown had been too crowded, Ridgefield too close to New York, Bermuda too social, Tours too rainy, Manhattan too noisy—and Sea Island was too hot. O'Neill and Carlotta headed for the northwest.

LVII

PART CONSCIOUSLY AND PART UNCONSCIOUSLY, O'Neill in his own life was tracing the path of his cycle family. As he had finally outlined the saga of his self-dispossessing family, it had its roots in New England, as O'Neill did—in his case, Connecticut, in the case of the Harfords, Rhode Island. (Part of the action of the second play was, in fact, to take place in Newport, a harbor and resort town comparable to New London in the 1800's.) Like O'Neill himself, members of the Harford family were to move back and forth across the United States, with excursions to Paris and Shanghai.

Though as far as can be determined no scenes of any of the plays were to be set as far north as the state of Washington, some of the Harfords, as indicated in *A Touch of the Poet,* were to have been involved in the trade of the Northwest. This was one of the reasons why O'Neill decided to stay for a while in Seattle. Another was the change of climate that he and Carlotta craved. The writer and teacher Sophus Keith Winther, a resident of Seattle, had visited Sea Island not long after publishing a critical study of O'Neill's plays, and urged O'Neill and Carlotta to come north.

The O'Neills rented a house outside the city, on the slopes of Magnolia Bluff, overlooking Puget Sound. They planned to stay for several months, but circumstances cut short their visit within six weeks.

It was an eventful six weeks, however, beginning and ending with a good deal of attention from the local press.

On November 3, the Seattle *Times* reported:

"The dramatist, an erect, trim figure with graying hair and his beautiful brunette wife, both of whom had come across the continent without being identified, [today] stepped from the Empire Builder at the King Street Station, to be greeted by Dr. Sophus Keith Winther of the University of Washington English Department.

"O'Neill, who will spend a year in the West gathering material for new plays, chatted later before the fireplace of his new Seattle home about the things he hopes to do during his stay here.

" 'I'm doing a play which is dated in the period around 1860 and 1870 —about the time the railroads came across the country,' he said, 'and I'm going to make Seattle my headquarters for at least three months while I am in the Northwest. I'll be going into Oregon and, perhaps, as far east as Butte, to get the material I need.' "

O'Neill then confided some of the problems confronting a playwright.

"Women's clubs and writers' clubs and other organizations want me to talk," he said, "and I can't make a speech. They never quite believe that, and so I have to write letters about it."

Nine days later O'Neill was obliged to cope with just such a problem again. An organization in Sweden wanted him to make a speech, and he had to write a letter declining to do so, but it was probably the least painful letter he ever wrote in his life. On November 12, 1936, O'Neill was awarded the Nobel Prize in literature and was requested to come to Stockholm on December 10 to accept the award from King Gustaf. O'Neill was the second American to win the literature prize, and the first American dramatist. Because no prize had been made in literature the year before, he received an accrued cash award of $40,000, along with the honor.

It was Carlotta who brought him the news on the morning of the 12th, after she had received a telephone call. When Seattle newspapermen descended upon him, O'Neill admitted that the report had not come as a complete surprise.

"There were rumors I'd be named," he told reporters, "I couldn't help but know that—but I was sure it would be like two years ago, when the same sort of rumors were current. And I didn't really think the award would go to an American so soon after Sinclair Lewis received it in 1930 —and I felt that if it did go to an American, it might be Dreiser. He deserves it."

Later in the day, when O'Neill received official notification of the award from the Swedish consul, he said he would not be able to arrange his affairs in time to be in Stockholm for the presentation.

To a feature writer for one of the press services O'Neill confided that he would use the $40,000 to pay taxes. While he accepted with good grace the inevitable, daylong onslaught of the press, he drew the line at being interviewed before the newsreel cameras. A newsreel representative came up with the bright idea of having O'Neill and Carlotta re-enact their reception of the news and even went to the trouble of writing them a script: the telephone would ring, Carlotta would answer and register astonishment and joy, she would hurry to her husband and say, "Gene, you've won!" and O'Neill would make a suitable response—all while the cameramen were grinding away. O'Neill was amused when Sophus Winther told him of this scheme, but he was disinclined to co-operate.

"The movie representatives could not get to see O'Neill without working through me," Winther later said, "and since I would do nothing to promote their aims, they finally left Seattle without seeing him."

A reporter for the Seattle *Times,* who had evidently heard about the movie script, decided to turn it to his own use, and he wrote his interview in the form of a play—without, however, outlining any dialogue in advance; he permitted O'Neill to ad-lib. He called his playlet *One Thursday Morning,* and listed the cast as Eugene O'Neill, Carlotta Monterey O'Neill, Dr. Sophus Keith Winther and a Reporter:

"(The scene is set in a well-furnished living room. A cheerful fire blazes in the hearth and outside, the fog curtains the view of the Sound. The playwright is found seated on a large green velvet davenport. He is wearing a gray sweater and flannels. Beside him is his wife, dressed in a red sweater, suit, and wearing a pair of gray suede shoes she received this morning from London. Dr. Winther stands before the fireplace and a reporter is perched on a chair.)

"REPORTER: How did you hear about the award, Mr. O'Neill?

"O'NEILL (with a smile at his wife): My wife told me. She woke me up this morning to tell me.

"MRS. O'NEILL: Dr. Winther woke me up to tell me about it.

"DR. WINTHER: The Associated Press woke me up to tell me.

"REPORTER: Were you surprised, Mr. O'Neill?

"O'NEILL (who is in a good humor): Well, not exactly. I've had telegrams of congratulation from New York this week—just on rumor. But I didn't know for sure . . .

"REPORTER: Do you know what particular play it was awarded for?

"O'NEILL: No. I don't know. I don't know how they fix that.

"MRS. O'NEILL: I hope it was for *Electra.* . . ."

The reporter inquired about O'Neill's current project and on being told it was "a tremendous thing" set in the East, the West, and the Midwest, the reporter asked if O'Neill was getting "atmosphere" in Seattle.

"Something like that," he answered. "I have to live in a place before I can write about it. I have to have the feeling of living there. Of course, the western part of the play takes place in 1870, but I'm going to travel all around the West. Just looking and talking to tradespeople—that's the way I get the feel."

Asked if it was "a very long play," O'Neill replied:

"Oh, yes. It goes on forever. I feel as though I've been writing it forever. I started out with four plays and now it's eight plays and it might be nine plays—that's a luckier number, anyway." He added that he hoped the first play would be produced the following October.

"With one play a season," he remarked, "people can go on seeing it forever. And when all eight plays are produced I hope they will run them all off on successive nights—that ought to knock the audiences cold. They'll never want to see another play."

O'Neill told his interviewer, in conclusion, that he never wrote about a place unless he had lived in it, but that he did not always write about places he had lived in.

"I'll never write a play about the South," he declared. "In Georgia you sweat half the year—and there aren't any union hours for sweating. I wrote part of this play half naked with bookkeeper's black sleeves on my arms, blotters under my hands, and I sat on a bath towel."

O'Neill did very little work during the next few weeks. He spent long hours just sitting before the windows of his rented house, resting and thinking.

"The view across the sound with the Olympics in the background (when it is clear!) is beautiful," Carlotta wrote to Lawrence Langner. "Gene loves to watch the boats go by and hear the seagulls and the foghorns."

But neither she nor O'Neill thought Seattle suitable as a permanent residence.

"In the winter there is much fog and rain," she wrote to Langner a week later. "We must find a place to live if we ever sell our present home [in Georgia]. And northern California seems best in many ways. But, we'll just look everywhere and be very sure."

Answering the letters and telegrams of congratulation that poured in took up much of O'Neill's time between November 12 and the second week of December, the date set for leaving on a house-hunting expedition. Some of the letters were from friends of the past with whom he had lost touch, and his answers were tinged with melancholy. To Mary Clark, the Gaylord Farm nurse, for instance, he wrote:

"You are one of the very, very few of my old friends I have heard from. Most of them are dead, the rest estranged for one reason or another, the principal reason being just the wear and tear of time."

And acknowledging a telegram from Kenneth Macgowan at greater length, he said warmly and perhaps a trifle guiltily that the Nobel award made him think back and remember the days when Macgowan's friendship was "such a constant encouragement" and when he "worked so hard and unselfishly" to help put O'Neill's work across.

"You are one the finest guys and one of the best friends I have ever known, Kenneth," he went on, "and I rate it a damned shame and loss that circumstances in the past few years have placed us so far apart in these

U.S. that we never get a chance even to say howdy to each other . . . I often dream of what a grand break it would be if you and Bobby and I could get together again, and start again in New York on our own with a resurge of the old spirit to prompt us. . . . Maybe I'm getting aged and crabbed but there seems nothing left—outside of the Radical propaganda on 14th Street—which has any definite ambitions toward any goal. . . . I don't know of one producing group that has the guts to hew to the line as we did. And so, outside of my job of writing plays, I've just about lost all interest in the theatre."

He indicated the source of his melancholia when he revealed that he was physically worn out from the past seven months' work on his "damned cycle." Instead of finding rest in Seattle, he said, the Nobel Prize had thrown him into turmoil.

"So it is not an unmixed blessing. In fact, so far, I'm like an ancient cab horse that has had a blue ribbon pinned on his tail—too physically weary to turn round and find out if it's good to eat, or what."

Though he might, half mockingly, disparage the award to an old friend, he believed he was entitled to the unreserved congratulations of his fellow writers in America. Many of them did, indeed, hurry to proffer their good wishes, among them Sinclair Lewis and Sherwood Anderson. (In his letter of thanks to Lewis, O'Neill agreed with him that Gorki should have won a Nobel Prize.) But a number of people from whom O'Neill had expected to hear remained silent. In a letter to S.N. Behrman, who *did* wire his congratulations, O'Neill said he had heard from no other American playwright. This is difficult to believe, but possibly he exaggerated because he was furious at not having heard from Maxwell Anderson, in whose praise O'Neill had written so eloquently just a few months earlier. (Nathan later reported that Anderson had been the only important American playwright from whom O'Neill had *not* heard, which seems more reasonable; Nathan quoted O'Neill as telling him, "It just didn't seem polite—that's all.")

The award evoked considerable praise both in the United States and abroad, in addition to the expected adverse comments.

"An excellent decision," George Bernard Shaw said from his home at Ayot St. Lawrence. "I always thought that this year's prize should go either to Upton Sinclair or O'Neill, so America would have received it in any case. Of course, I am very pleased."

"I cannot count myself a great admirer or close student of O'Neill's work," commented J. B. Priestley in London, "but I am sincerely glad to learn that a man who has devoted himself with such deep seriousness to our English-speaking theatre has been awarded the prize. I think such an award may increase the seriousness and responsibility of our theatre."

A couple of days later William Butler Yeats and Lennox Robinson sent word from Dublin to *The New York Times* of their much greater enthusiasm:

"I am delighted that Eugene O'Neill has received the Nobel Prize, because I have the greatest admiration for his work," commented Yeats.

"I think O'Neill is one of the most distinguished dramatists of today," said Robinson. "I am proud the award has come to him, not only in recognition of his great art but also because he is of Irish parentage. I am especially happy to recall that I was personally responsible for putting on the first O'Neill play in Ireland at the Drama League season in Dublin.

"Those of us associated with the Abbey Theatre are very pleased that this European recognition has come to such a worthy recipient. O'Neill's contribution to the drama is very valuable indeed, particularly his later work in which he experiments with new forms."

The Times, in its own editorial comment, declared unequivocally, "He deserves it."

"Although American playgoers have had to bear with him during two or three periods of transition, and have had to suffer two or three disastrous plays from his pen," the annoymous editorial writer continued, "he has long dominated our theatre on the basis of vigorous work performed. His successive days of wrath have yielded a stout library of malevolent tragedies that include several masterpieces. . . .

"For years he has been the boldest influence in our drama, grimly reaching out after big themes and, in his best work, dominating them by the power of his imagination and the depth of his feeling. None of the practical considerations of journeyman playwrighting has ever drawn a compromise from him. He has repeatedly cracked the old molds by the largeness of his dramatic vision. When the good news comes to him from Stockholm it finds him immersed in his most ambitious work, and that would have been true of him at almost any point in his career. The award of the Nobel Prize to Mr. O'Neill confirms a general respect and admiration for his stature among men of letters."

An opposing opinion, however, was voiced by Bernard De Voto, in the *Saturday Review of Literature* on November 21.

"You will find the majority opinion in nearly any paper you may pick up," De Voto began. "Unquestionably most of the critics and most of the public who think about literature at all will regard the award of a Nobel Prize to Eugene O'Neill as a gratifying recognition of great talent. A minority will not, however, and because what may be a signal weakness rather than a great strength of our literature is involved, The Saturday Review cannot let the occasion pass without expressing that minority opinion. For the Nobel Prize . . . is supposed to recognize only the highest distinction in literature, and Mr. O'Neill falls short of that. He falls short of it both absolutely and relatively. Whatever his international importance, he can hardly be called an artist of the first rank; he is hardly even one of the first-rate figures of his generation in America."

De Voto went on to develop the astonishing theory that it had been the Theatre Guild that had foisted O'Neill on the public as a figure of literary importance, and that the award of the Nobel Prize was largely due to O'Neill's "prestige and publicity," which neither the critics nor the public dared to dispute. (O'Neill, in response to an anxious inquiry from Theresa Helburn, calmly replied that he had never heard of De Voto.)

By way of relaxation from granting interviews and answering his mail, O'Neill went fishing in Puget Sound, skimming over the choppy waters in the motorboat of a friend. He planned, later, to tackle the chinook salmon of the Columbia River. Combining rest with research, he made motor trips through Oregon, once driving over the winding road to the foot of Mount Ranier and questioning the people he encountered about their work and their backgrounds.

Toward the end of November he consented to be interviewed by Richard L. Neuberger, then a reporter for the *Oregonian*, later the Democratic senator from Oregon.

O'Neill told Neuberger of his concern over the decline of the theatre as a widespread, living art. Far too few people in America, he explained, had the opportunity to see "actual living actors" perform a play. He said the theatre projects of the Works Progress Administration, set up by the government to help combat the Depression, might ultimately be the answer to this problem.

"Take one of my own plays, for example," he added. "It will be presented in New York; then the Theatre Guild will take it on a road trip. After that it's dead. If you want to see a revival, you have to go to Europe. I think other playwrights will tell you the same thing.

"The WPA theatre projects can change this. They have the opportunity to bring legitimate stage productions to every community in America, whether that community be rural or urban. The WPA can present important plays before audiences that never before have seen an actual stage production. The possibilities in this respect are thrilling."

He added that the WPA should "try to find young talent, both on the footboards and at the typewriter," and should encourage and help such talent.

[812]

The art theatre, he told Neuberger, could not exist without subsidy and assistance.

"Heretofore the American idea of the theatre has been dictated by business considerations," he said. "Millionaires gave money for art museums, grand opera and archaeological expeditions, but the theatre budget had to balance. Relatively little of their money went to the theatre."

He added that the paying of union wages to stage hands, the high cost of traveling units, and similar expenses made it almost impossible for the art theatre to exist without financial aid.

For a time, he emphasized, the American theatre was only a place of amusement.

"Amusement is important," he continued. "Do not underrate it. But culture is also significant."

"O'Neill hopes the WPA project will help to revive some of the culture and the color of the period of his father and Booth," wrote Neuberger. "He believes the government program should include a resurrection of the classics—Shakespeare, the Restoration comedy, the Elizabethan drama."

Shifting his questioning from the theatre to politics, Neuberger found O'Neill enthusiastic over President Roosevelt's overwhelming re-election. (It was an enthusiasm not shared by Carlotta.)

"The results of the recent election indicate that the people intend to preserve their freedom," O'Neill told his interviewer.

Having already decided that he was not physically up to attending the Nobel awards ceremony, O'Neill, by this time feeling really ill, struggled during the latter part of November to write a speech that could be read for him on December 10 in Stockholm. Reporters began asking for copies of it before the month was out. Russel Crouse, to whom some of the requests were directed, wrote O'Neill asking if he could have a copy, and O'Neill replied:

"I wish you'd make plain to the Press boys, if they want the speech . . . that it's a banquet stunt and limited to a few minutes. They are liable to confuse it with the long Sinclair Lewis speech they quoted in '30, but his was a discourse to the Swedish Academy. This discourse affair—so I am informed by a letter from the Secretary of the Academy—is a thing you can wish on the Academy, if you are heartless enough, and the members are duty bound to stay awake, and grin, and bear it. But, the Secretary's letter adds, few literary Nobel winners have delivered such a discourse. As for me, well, I'll give you one guess how I am going to win the grateful regard of the Academicians for my sensitive consideration of them."

[813]

O'Neill, after apologizing for not being in Sweden to receive the award, declared in his "speech":

It is difficult to put into anything like adequate words the profound gratitude I feel for the greatest honor that my work could ever hope to attain—the award of the Nobel Prize. This highest of distinctions is all the more grateful to me because I feel so deeply that it is not only my work which is being honored but the work of all my colleagues in America—that the Nobel Prize is a symbol of the coming of age of the American theatre.

For my plays are merely, through luck of time and circumstance, the most widely known examples of the work done by American playwrights in the years since the World War—work that has finally made modern American drama, in its finest aspects, an achievement of which Americans can be justly proud, worthy at last to claim kinship with the modern drama of Europe, from which our original inspiration so surely derives.

This thought of original inspiration brings me to what is, for me, the greatest happiness this occasion affords, and that is the opportunity it gives me to acknowledge, with gratitude and pride, to you and to the people of Sweden, the debt my work owes to that greatest genius of all modern dramatists, your August Strindberg. . . .

Of course, it will be no news to you in Sweden, that my work owes much to the influence of Strindberg. That influence runs clearly through more than a few of my plays and is plain for everyone to see. Neither will it be news for anyone who has ever known me, for I have always stressed it myself. I have never been one of those who are so timidly uncertain of their own contribution that they feel they cannot afford to admit ever having been influenced, lest they be discovered as lacking all originality.

No, I am only too proud of my debt to Strindberg, only too happy to have this opportunity of proclaiming it to his people. For me, he remains, as Nietzsche remains, in his sphere, the master, still to this day more modern than any of us, still our leader.

And it is my pride to imagine that perhaps his spirit, musing over this year's Nobel award for literature, may smile with a little satisfaction, and find the follower not too unworthy of his master.

The New York Times was pleased with O'Neill's speech, and took the occasion to comment editorially on its straightforwardness, modesty and warmth, comparing it favorably (by implication) with Sinclair Lewis' "war dance over the prostrate body" of his native land.

A week or so before sending off his speech O'Neill, growing more absorbed with his past, had instituted the search that soon after reunited him with Earl Stevens, who had guided him through the Honduras jungles twenty-seven years earlier. On locating Stevens in Portland, in the brass section of the Portland symphony orchestra, O'Neill urged him to come for a visit as soon as possible, explaining that he had to leave on a trip in a few days and would not be back in Seattle "for four or five weeks." The reunion took place on December 9. A week later O'Neill and Carlotta left for California by train. They did not return to Seattle in five weeks or, in fact, ever. The house on Magnolia Bluffs became one more gate at which O'Neill, the stranger, was destined to decamp.

PART FIVE
HOPELESS HOPE
1936—1953

LVIII

THE O'NEILLS ARRIVED IN SAN FRANCISCO SHORTLY
before Christmas of 1936, planning to make the city their headquarters
while canvassing northern California for a place to live. But they had
another reason for stopping there. Carlotta wanted O'Neill to consult a
doctor who had attended her many years earlier, when she was living in
her native California. O'Neill's health had been steadily worsening during
the past weeks, and after seeing Dr. Charles A. Dukes, an Oakland
surgeon, he was advised to enter Oakland's Merritt Hospital. Carlotta, at
the end of her own strength and suffering from a severe cold, also was
ordered to bed by Dr. Dukes, and both the O'Neills became patients at
Merritt Hospital on December 28, the date of Carlotta's forty-eighth
birthday.

At four in the morning of the following day O'Neill underwent an
operation for acute appendicitis; Dr. Dukes, who had removed Carlotta's
appendix in the same hospital years before, performed the surgery. By
this time Carlotta was so ill herself that she could not be at O'Neill's
bedside.

Dr. Dukes and hospital officials had been sworn to secrecy by the
O'Neills and it was not until four days later that they permitted an announcement of their whereabouts. The announcement was carried on
January 4 by most of the New York newspapers and was embellished upon
by the local papers, which were delighted to discover that they had the
recent Nobel Prize winner in their community. Dr. Dukes' bulletin stated
that O'Neill was "still too ill to receive visitors, but is progressing nicely
and should be able to leave the hospital within the next ten days." Carlotta,
still suffering from the effects of "fatigue, a near breakdown and a heavy
cold that had just missed turning into pneumonia," was reported to be
"convalescing as satisfactorily as possible under the circumstances." The
O'Neills had adjoining rooms and both their doors bore the sign, "No
Visitors." Dr. Dukes added this statement to the press:

"Mr. O'Neill is an inordinately shy man despite the fact that his talents
have made him a world figure. He is still a sick man. Both he and his wife,

seeking peace and quiet in the North, were much disturbed when their privacy was invaded following the announcement of the Nobel Prize."

The year 1937 had not begun auspiciously for O'Neill. Though he was not yet forty-nine and was again at a turning point in his life, with the prospect of a new home and a mammoth literary project, he was beginning to show signs of physical deterioration and premature old age.

After recovering from his appendectomy he was beset by other distressing physical symptoms. He developed kidney trouble, a prostate condition, neuritis, and an intensification of the tremor that had plagued him, on and off, for many years and that soon after was diagnosed (erroneously, as it turned out) as Parkinson's disease. While he was still to enjoy periods of relative euphoria, they were few.

From the beginning of 1937 to the end of his life he was more or less regularly in the hands of doctors and at the mercy of drugs and medical regimens. At times, aware that his illness was considered progressively degenerative, he felt himself to be a slowly dying man. He was sustained almost solely by his consuming drive to give the world a few more masterpieces.

O'Neill spent over ten weeks in Merritt Hospital. Carlotta was released sooner, but she was still confined to bed on January 6, when she wrote to Earl Stevens, thanking him for a letter of sympathy and inquiry to her husband.

She informed Stevens that although O'Neill was making a good recovery, he was still too weak to answer his mail. The recuperative period, she had been warned by her doctor, promised to be a trying time and for the moment, she said, she and O'Neill were both "prisoners."

On January 11, with his doctor's consent, O'Neill allowed reporters to interview him in his hospital room. He talked mainly about his cycle, which he still referred to as consisting of eight plays and characterized as dealing with "a far from model American family." He said the first play and drafts of two others were completed, but that he wanted to finish five of them before releasing the first for production.

O'Neill then announced his intention of buying a permanent residence in northern California. "I've thought perhaps we could get a sheep ranch in the Napa valley—and evict the sheep," he said. "But that's not definite. It's only a hope and a dream thus far. The Napa valley is the loveliest spot I have ever seen."

In answer to questions about the state of the contemporary theatre, he reiterated his enthusiasm for the Federal theatre project, adding: "The Continent seems pretty dead. I don't know of any Scandinavians. The only two Englishmen writing plays are two Irishmen [Shaw and O'Casey]."

Commenting on Carlotta's absence from the interview, a reporter asked if she was still in the hospital. O'Neill said she was, but had a cold "and she looks it."

The reporters remarked on the pile of mystery and detective stories by his bedside, and O'Neill cheerfully volunteered that he was "one of the greatest fiends around on that score."

"There'll be no work for me for a while," he concluded ruefully. "My doctor won't allow it."

On January 29 the local newspapers announced that O'Neill's Georgia house had been sold and that O'Neill would be well enough to leave the hospital soon, to find a new home in California. But actually the picture was not quite so rosy.

While O'Neill's appendectomy had been routine, an ensuing prostate and kidney condition had created new problems and O'Neill would be obliged to remain in the hospital for a month or more. Carlotta, therefore, hurried to Sea Island to dismantle her house, planning to rent a place in California for the summer preparartory to finding a permanent home.

O'Neill pined for Carlotta during her absence. "I am beginning to feel as old as the Nile," he wrote to Theresa Helburn, "waiting for Carlotta to return, so very long does this first real separation of ours seem. . . . Such are the pangs of love and how lucky I feel to be panged!"

Carlotta was still away when, on February 17, Carl E. Wallerstedt, the Swedish consul in San Francisco, visited Merritt Hospital to present O'Neill with the gold medal and embossed diploma that represented the Nobel Prize. In a ceremony that lasted (by Dr. Dukes' order) only five minutes, Mr. Wallerstedt told O'Neill:

"It is customary for Nobel Prize winners to go to Sweden to receive their awards, and only on rare occasions is the order reversed.

"This is one time when custom must give way to emergency, as my nation no longer seeks to defer honor to a man who has won the highest award which can be made in his chosen field of endeavor."

He added that he hoped O'Neill would soon be well enough to make his promised trip to Sweden.

"Thank you. I will go as soon as I am able," murmured O'Neill, unaware that a world war and, later, his own invalidism would prevent his ever making the trip.

No one attended the ceremony except Dr. Dukes and O'Neill's nurse. O'Neill was so weak his knees shook as he rose from his chair to receive the medal and scroll, and his hands trembled as he accepted them. The scroll, embossed with characters symbolizing O'Neill's work, had been designed especially for him and the gold medal was the same as all the others awarded in the field of literature. The diploma stated in Swedish that O'Neill was chosen from all playwrights in the world for 1936 literature honors by the Swedish Academy "for his creative drama, for characters marked by virility, honesty and strong emotions as well as for depth of interpretation."

On March 11 Carlotta, having disposed of the contents of Casa Genotta, collected her husband at the hospital and carried him off to San Francisco. Having found no house to suit them in the Napa valley, the O'Neills bought land, instead, in the San Ramon valley, deciding to have a house built for them. In the meanwhile, they rented a twenty-two-acre estate in the San Francisco Bay area near Lafayette.

At the end of May, in response to an inquiry from a *New York Times* drama reporter, O'Neill wired back: "Consider me for the nonce as one retired from the racket." He added that no part of his eight-play cycle would be produced the following season, that his illness had suspended all work on the project, and that he did not know how soon he would be able to get back to it.

Being the guardian of an ailing as well as a celebrated man, Carlotta now devoted herself full time to the job of protecting her husband's privacy. It was a battle fought vigorously and with decreasing patience and tact as the years wore on. Few people knew how ill O'Neill really was and how vital to him it was to have serenity during his periods of creative power. Carlotta's unremitting efforts on his behalf fostered the legend of the great man isolated from the world, guarded by a jealous, possessive wife. Only a handful of O'Neill's friends understood the relationship between Carlotta and O'Neill, whose tendency to indulge in melodramatic self-pity now reached a peak. Occasionally, in moments of despair, he implied to a sympathetic friend—particularly to one who was not overly fond of Carlotta—that his seclusion was not entirely voluntary. Frustrated by his ill-health and inability to work at the rate he wanted to, he found a certain sadistic relief, from time to time, in turning his rage on Carlotta and in the subterfuge that it was she, rather than he, who was antisocial. At bottom, however, he continued to adore and depend upon her. Not long after moving into their rented home he inscribed the Nobel Prize edition of his plays, recently published by Random House, to Carlotta, "the Noblest Prize of all!" with, "as always," all his love.

That August he wrote to George Jean Nathan about his health, his hopes and his plans:

"Carlotta is in a frenzy of creative activity over the new house. I needn't tell you, who know her capability in this regard, that this means it is going to be some house! And the site has the most beautiful view I have ever come across. Wait and see if you don't agree when you visit us next year—as you certainly must. We expect to be able to move in by the first of the year—barring delay thro' strikes."

In one of his periodic surges of optimism about his health O'Neill added that, though he had "low spells still now and again," he was beginning to feel "pretty fit" and had been "flirting" with the cycle; but he would not risk hard work on it for a while to come—"perhaps not until we are settled in our new home."

The end of September found O'Neill's health still further improved and he confided to Barrett Clark that his mind was full of fresh ideas about the cycle, which, he said, "goes back to my old vein of ironic tragedy— with, I hope, added psychological depth and insight."

To Clark he revealed both his soaring plans for the cycle and the shadow of a doubt that he could sustain the physical effort to complete it. "The whole work will be a unique something, all right, believe me," he said, "if I can ever finish it."

The technical problem alone was overpowering, he added. "I have to think in terms of nine plays, and a continuity of family lives over a space of 150 years, while I am writing each play. But given time and health I can do it."

He must still guard his health and work cautiously, he said, but he hoped by the first of the year to be ready to "really drive ahead."

O'Neill had again changed his mind about the production of the cycle plays, having decided to withhold them all until the last one was completed. At that point the cycle's status was one play (*A Touch of the Poet*), completed except for final polishing; another (*And Give Me Death*), in a long first draft requiring drastic revision; and intricately detailed scenarios of all the others, plus voluminous notes.

Later that fall, O'Neill acknowledged receipt of an essay Clark had sent him, in which Clark had drawn parallels "between the situation in contemporary Russia and the period in France when the Robespierres and his kind were 'liquidating' the earlier leaders."

"A true play about the French Revolution ought to make a grand satire on the Russian one," O'Neill answered. "Or . . . a play or novel depicting the history of any religion would apply rationally in the same way."

Summing up the essence of his "ironic insight," O'Neill added:

"God with a change of whiskers becomes the State—and there's always a Holy Book—dogmas—heresy trials—an infallible Pope—etc., etc., until you become sick. It appears we apes always climb trees—and fall out of them—with a boringly identical behavior pattern. . . . The last . . . sounds pessimistic . . . whereas I feel full of hope these days. For, noting the way the world wags, I am sure that Man has definitely decided to destroy himself, and this seems to me the only truly wise decision he has ever made!"

O'Neill continued to take a reasonable interest in his own immediate future, however, despite his cheerful forecast for the future of man. He observed with pleasure the building progress of his new house, anxiously followed the fluctuations of the stock market, tested his still improving health by keeping regular, if curtailed working hours each day, and attended an occasional football game with Carlotta at the University of California in Berkeley.

Replying to a message from Nathan on his forty-ninth birthday that October, O'Neill declared:

"The day passed without undue repining about Time's relentless chiseling. In fact, I can say candidly that I felt younger in health on this birthday than I have for two or three years. So what ho!"

The O'Neills moved into their new house in late October, 1937, while the carpenters and painters were still at work. Designed by Carlotta, who, a friend once remarked, had an "edifice complex," it was smaller than Casa Genotta but in its way just as elegant.

"I wanted to build a Chinese house," Carlotta explained. "But I didn't have the money, so I built a sort of pseudo-Chinese house." The cost of even a pseudo-Chinese house was considerable; it was built of white concrete blocks, designed to resemble adobe. The roof was black tile, the doors and shutters were painted Chinese red, and the ceilings were of deep blue. Carlotta collected most of the furniture, some of which was authentic Chinese and some of it copies, through Gump's in San Francisco.

"I left the white blocks rough and unpainted on the inside," Carlotta said, "and I put all my beautiful, very delicate and graceful Chinese furniture against these rough stones, which made a very beautiful effect."

Part of the effect was created with mirrors—dark green or blue in the living and dining rooms, and a black one in O'Neill's bedroom, which, some of his friends recalled, returned a gratifyingly ghastly image when he stared into it. His bedroom was also furnished with a huge, ebony opium couch, converted into a bed.

The house was in Danville, about thirty-five miles from San Francisco, but there was no hint of its proximity to the city. It was built into the side of a mountain, about 2,800 feet up.

"There was nothing there, nothing at all," Carlotta said. The view across the valley from their 158 acres of wooded hillside was breathtaking. Their large patio faced a mountain range, whose highest peak, Mount Diablo, was often wrapped in mist.

"We really have an ideal home," O'Neill informed a friend some time after getting settled, "with one of the most beautiful views I have ever seen—pure country with no taint of suburbia, and yet we are only fifty minutes' drive from the heart of San Francisco—my favorite American city, although I don't like any city much."

Access to the grounds was by a private road guarded by electrically operated gates that opened at the push of a button from the house.

The O'Neills christened their new home Tao House, meaning, in Chinese, "the right way of life." Their Chinese friend, Mai-mai Sze, listened tolerantly when Carlotta consulted her about the name.

"I didn't think it was particularly apt," she once told an acquaintance, "but I thought, what does it matter, if it amuses them. The O'Neills had a naïve, romantic idea of China—the wisdom, the pageantry and so forth were superficially conceived and romanticized by them."

After moving in, the O'Neills began planning a garden and building a swimming pool.

"Gene was always looking for the perfect place where he could swim in the sea for twelve months of the year," Carlotta said. "Well, we had traveled all over the world and couldn't find such a place so, finally, we decided on a swimming pool. He didn't really think so much of the idea, but it was better than nothing, so we built a pool on the side of our mountain. It overlooked the whole valley. Gene told me he had a strange feeling swimming in this pool, looking down from it on the valley, because, of course, most pools are flat and you look up at the hills from them."

Among the earliest visitors to Tao House were Lawrence Langner and his wife, who, at O'Neill's request, brought along S. N. Behrman.

Behrman, whose only contact with O'Neill had been the exchange of correspondence over the Nobel Prize, was struck by his host's exquisite manners.

"O'Neill had the kind of manners you find in Europe, but rarely in this country," said Behrman, whose reputation rested upon urbane comedies. "Carlotta talked a blue streak while we were in the house, and after a while O'Neill took me out into the garden. He said, 'I thought it would be nice to have a word with you.' We talked about vaudeville. I told him I used to go to Keith's in Boston every Monday afternoon when I was at Harvard, and later to the Palace in New York. I knew a lot about vaudeville, but he knew more.

"He then described, in a very dramatic way, how the newsreel photographers had wanted him to act out a little play in Seattle when he won the Nobel Prize. We had a good laugh about it. We also discussed our common enthusiasm for San Francisco.

"Later, he showed me the Nobel Prize. It was very impressive. We became quick friends that day."

Langner, recalling the same occasion, said that O'Neill displayed the prize "with almost childlike pleasure" and without "the slightest suggestion either of undue pride or modesty on his part."

O'Neill found it difficult to settle into a work pattern in his new house; carpenters and painters were still coming and going and, in addition, a spell of rainy weather had brought on an attack of neuritis. He had managed to finish an initial draft of one more cycle play, *The Greed of the Meek,* by the end of February, 1938; but like the first draft of *And Give Me Death,* it still required considerable work.

"I feel so utterly lousy at present writing—after a wisdom tooth extraction which made my neuritis worse than ever, as they claim it always does for a while—that I'd hate to prophesy when I'll begin to take interest in the Drama again," O'Neill wrote to Nathan on February 28.

That spring the O'Neills, after some deliberation, decided to invite Shane to visit Tao House during his school vacation. O'Neill had not seen his son in more than a year. Shane was their first overnight guest.

At eighteen Shane was thin, handsome and shy, bewildered about his relationship with his father and confused about his future. He was now a high school senior—attending his third boarding school within a period of seven years. After leaving Lawrenceville, in New Jersey, he had been sent by Agnes to the Florida Military Academy and, finally, in the middle of his senior year, he was transferred to a preparatory school in Colorado. Though Shane was popular with his fellow students, his grades and his conduct had been, in all his schools, erratic; he had sporadically displayed an interest in a writing career, and was now considering becoming a newspaper reporter after graduation.

Shane returned to school after his stay at Tao House feeling as much a stranger as his father had been at the same age and, like his father, acutely conscious of being overshadowed by a celebrated parent. Shane, however, lacked his father's tough-mindedness—the saving quality inherited by his sister, Oona.

O'Neill casually mentioned Shane's visit in a letter to Nathan late that May, in which he urged his friend to pay a visit to Tao House so that he might discuss the cycle with him.

"I'm hard at it again and the old bean is functioning better than it has in years," he added. "I'm encouraged to hope that my particular allotment of the fatal-forties period of physical bog-down and mental meandering is about over and I can take up where I left off when I finished *Mourning Becomes Electra*."

While passing over Shane's visit, O'Neill made much of an illness contracted by his dog, Blemie, to whom he and Carlotta were becoming increasingly attached.

"We came near losing Blemie last week," he related, "and there was much sadness in the Hacienda O'Neill. An intestinal complaint due, I fear, to his lack of will power regarding horse turds, the old rake! Teams have been up here cutting the hay. Enough said. A good vet pulled him through and he's fairly fit again. He says he can't understand it, that something he drank must have disagreed with him."

Carlotta was sufficiently concerned to write Nathan a letter of her own on the same day, humorously denying her husband's allegation about Blemie's ingestion of what she referred to as "muffins," and explaining that Blemie's malady had been an infected intestine. She bewailed the fact that she and O'Neill were so devoted to the dog, but added that Blemie had, after all, been "the most pleasant and amusing child" she and O'Neill had had, and also the "most grateful."

Speaking of Blemie to an acquaintance many years later Carlotta described the way he spent the evenings with her and O'Neill before the fire at Tao House: "Blemie would sit first by me and then by Gene, not to hurt anybody's feelings."

O'Neill decided one day that in addition to Blemie he also had to have a prize Irish setter. He wrote to Ireland to inquire about buying one and finally, after elaborate arrangements, an Irish setter arrived at Tao House. The dog was named Ben. Having been locked in a crate for two days, Ben was overwrought when he arrived, and when Blemie bounded out to greet him, Ben bit him on the nose. This was too direct an insult for even the gentlemanly Blemie to overlook, and the two dogs became sworn enemies.

"They had to be kept in separate rooms when they were in the house," Carlotta recalled with amusement, "but they made a truce out of doors. I would take one of them on a leash and Gene would take the other when we went for walks. When we reached the woods, we'd release them, and they'd have a wonderful time stalking rabbits together. But the minute they got back to the house, they became hostile and had to be separated again."

The relationship between Ben and Blemie was further complicated when, one day, a small mongrel bitch from a neighboring farm wandered onto O'Neill land. "The bitch was in heat," Carlotta said, "and Blemie kissed her politely and followed her off into the woods. I assumed they were married. Some time later one of our French maids told me she'd heard the bitch had had puppies, and didn't we want to take Blemie over to the farm to see his children. I asked Gene, and he grinned and said yes. So we all trooped over to the farm, Gene, I, Blemie and several of the French servants."

O'Neill's grin grew wider when he saw the puppies; they all looked like Irish setters.

"The servants were simply convulsed," Carlotta said. "They made the sign of horns. They thought it so terribly funny that poor Blemie had been cuckolded. Blemie walked back home with his head down. After that he was through with women."

In addition to amusing himself with Blemie and Ben, O'Neill took a flyer in poultry.

"He had to have chickens, of all things," Carlotta said. "He wanted to have what he'd liked as a little boy and could never have enough of, because his parents were always on the road and he had no permanent home. He kept ordering different kinds of chickens, and I was kept busy typing up data about them and sending orders."

Charles O'Brien Kennedy recalled that the only time he ever heard O'Neill brag about anything was when he described a rooster raised at Tao House, and named Sugar Ray Robinson.

"Sugar Ray," Kennedy said, "fought everything, animal or human, that came near him, but by tact and perseverance the master soon had the battler eating corn out of his hand."

Discussing farm animals with O'Neill on another occasion, Thomas Mitchell, the actor, remarked that he had become greatly attached to the animals he had once raised in Oregon and hated to see them marketed.

"I know what you mean," O'Neill said sympathetically. "I had a rooster once that I became terribly fond of."

In the fall of 1938 the pastoral tranquillity of Tao House was threatened by the gradual defection of the French servants. On October 5 O'Neill reported to Nathan that "the Family O'Neill is mediumly in the pink, thank you kindly, convalescent not so much from the Hitler jitters as from a rash of servant trouble." He said it was difficult "to get anyone to work in the country here" and that they had recently hired a Japanese couple.

O'Neill had been working on the cycle daily for the past seven months and he told Nathan that, "like Ol' Man River" it rolled on.

"I finished the first draft of the fourth play [*More Stately Mansions*] about a month ago," he said, "and since then have been going over it, doing considerable revision. When I have that done, I'll rewrite one scene in the third play. Then I'll have these two plays pretty well set and finished, and shall give myself a brief rest before starting the fifth play [*The Calms of Capricorn*]."

Two weeks later O'Neill was ill again—this time with rheumatism. Answering the Van Vechtens, who sent him greetings on his fiftieth birthday, he wrote: "Blemie remarked to the cat: 'The Old Man doesn't look a day over 183.' And he was right. I didn't feel a bit older than that, either."

The O'Neills celebrated Christmas, 1939, quietly and in the English manner Carlotta had adopted. On Christmas Eve Carlotta and ONeill wrapped gifts for each other, the servants and Blemie. Carlotta decorated a big tree, with O'Neill lending a hand. The servants were called in, lined up, and given their presents, and then Carlotta and O'Neill dined in lonely splendor. After serving their master and mistress, the servants were dismissed to their own dinner—a festive one, with wine. On Christmas Day the servants were let go to visit their families, and Carlotta prepared a cold meal of leftover turkey.

With his Christmas gift to Carlotta that year O'Neill enclosed a note in an envelope bearing her name and embellished in the corners by four silhouette drawings; the drawings were crudely, but unmistakably, representative of four plump, bewhiskered cats—a recurrent symbol in O'Neill's written messages to his wife. The note conveyed all his love and gratitude for "the beauty and peace" Carlotta's love had brought him, and asked her to accept the "million poems," he was not poet enough to write to "your eyebrows and your eyes and your lips—and your etcetera!"

The new year, which, before it was out, would see the beginning of World War II, found O'Neill still deep in concentration on his cycle. In response to Sam Zolotow, drama reporter for *The New York Times*, O'Neill telegraphed on February 3, 1939:

"Nothing new to report except recently finished fourth play [*More Stately Mansions*]. Five still to go which means five years at present rate. According present plan no production until whole cycle finished and don't think it advisable make public until then. Possible I may write play outside of cycle in meantime if I can keep elephant opus out of my mind long enough but no definite idea on this and it isn't probable."

A little later that month O'Neill heard from Stark Young, after having been out of touch with him for a while, and brought him up to date on the cycle. "It's a tough job, much tougher than I had expected," he explained. "In fact, if I had foreseen the time and labor involved, I would have tried to forget the idea in favor of something less soul-grinding. But as Al Capone said of the rackets, once you're in, you're in, and there's no out."

From winter through spring O'Neill labored without taking the rest he had promised himself. He revised *A Touch of the Poet* to relate it more closely to its sequel, *More Stately Mansions*.

"That's the devil of this job, the amount of time spent on such revision," he complained to Nathan in May. "Sometimes, I feel sick about it —the constant driving on while seeming, in the light of final completion, to be making no progress."

To Nathan he also expressed his disappointment at learning that Sean O'Casey's latest play had turned out to be a political tract.

"I suppose," he said, "these lousy times make it inevitable that many authors get caught in the sociological propaganda mill. . . . But O'Casey is an artist and the soap box is no place for his great talent. The hell of it seems to be, when an artist starts saving the world, he starts losing himself." O'Neill added that he, himself, had on occasion been tempted to preach salvation, but had always managed to resist the impulse; for his true conviction was that "the one reform worth cheering for is the Second Flood, and that the interesting thing about people is the obvious fact that they don't really want to be saved—the tragic idiotic ambition for self-destruction in them."

Robert Sisk, who had abandoned his publicity post with the Theatre Guild to write movie scripts in Hollywood, discussed some of the broader aspects of American politics during this period with O'Neill.

"He hated statism, and felt that it was the great evil of the world," said Sisk. "He was horrified at Hitler, of course, and not always impressed by some of the American statesmen, either; he was, in fact, skeptical of politics in general. He even went so far as to outline a play, dramatizing his hatred of statism [and demonstrating, thereby, that the soap box did, after all, hold a certain allure]. He sent me the outline with a jocular letter, asking me to show it to Louis B. Mayer and Sam Goldwyn and get him a million dollars for it."

◆

In June, 1939, O'Neill put aside the cycle and started writing a play he had been thinking about for five months. The play, begun on June 8 and completed on November 26, was *The Iceman Cometh*. In preparation for its writing he asked Saxe Commins, his Random House editor, to dig up some old anarchist literature. One of the items Commins found for him was a copy of *The Flame*, published in 1914 by Hippolyte Havel (who became Hugo Kalmar in *The Iceman*).

Regarding the future as a blank, O'Neill became more and more immersed in his own past. He set the play in 1912, the year of his attempted suicide—an act whose non-consummation he still occasionally regretted. His early, unanalytical sense of identification with the pipe dreamers of Jimmy-the-Priest's and the Hell Hole, was now—as O'Neill saw the end of his own life approaching—transmuted into a final and explicit expression of his philosophy of "hopeless hope."

Harry Hope's saloon was the play's setting, where the derelicts who drank themselves insensible every night became symbols of O'Neill's own unattainable dreams—dreams whose bitter frustration he need never have known had he succeeded in killing himself with sleeping pills and whiskey twenty-five years earlier.

The play's surface story concerns a traveling salesman, Theodore Hickman (Hickey), who murders the long-suffering wife to whom he has been consistently unfaithful, in the belief that he is thus giving her peace. The play, however, has subsurfaces and sub-subsurfaces, and is perhaps the most intricately and symbolically coded of all O'Neill's plays; it is also probably his greatest. *The Iceman Cometh* has been lengthily analyzed in print from psychiatric, religious and metaphysical viewpoints, and it may ultimately accumulate as large a body of scholarly discourse as *Hamlet*. One of the more perceptive and illuminating analyses was made to a friend by Dudley Nichols, with whom O'Neill discussed his play intimately during the time he was writing it. (Nichols was working on the screenplay of *S.S. Glencairn*, which was released in the fall of 1940 under the title *The Long Voyage Home* and became the most successful of all the movie adaptations of O'Neill's plays.)

"The iceman of the title is, of course, death," Nichols observed. "I don't think O'Neill ever explained, publicly, what he meant by the use of the archaic word, 'cometh,' but he told me at the time he was writing the play that he meant a combination of the poetic and biblical 'Death cometh'—that is, cometh to all living—and the old bawdy story, a typical Hickey [and Jamie O'Neill] story, of the man who calls upstairs, 'Has the iceman come yet?' and his wife calls back, 'No, but he's breathin' hard.' Even the bawdy story is transformed by the poetic intention of the title, for it is really Death which Hickey's wife, Evelyn, has taken to her breast when she marries Hickey, and her insistence on her great love for Hickey and his undying love for her and her deathlike grip on his conscience—her insistence that he *can* change and not get drunk and sleep with whores—is making Death breathe hard on her breast as he approaches ever nearer—as he is about 'to come' in the vernacular sense. It is a strange and poetic intermingling of the exalted and the vulgar, that title."

The truth of the play, as O'Neill explained to Nichols and to two or three other close friends, was that Hickey had long ago begun to harbor a murderous hatred for his wife; she represented his own, punishing conscience.

"God, how Hickey had begun to hate his wife!" said Nichols. "When he gave her a venereal disease, and she forgave him—he wanted to kill her then, deep down in his unconscious. But of course the idea couldn't enter his conscious mind—because he 'loved' her, as she 'loved' him. He'd been on that hop for years. So, when he finally had to kill her, knowing he had to be true to his own nature and go off to Harry's saloon for a shot of Hope, a big drunk and a week with the tarts and bums, he first had to cook another pill of opium and grab the beautiful pipe dream that he was killing her for love—so she wouldn't suffer any longer from his incurable debauchery."

Hickey's delusion vanishes when he discovers that with Evelyn's death he no longer has the desire to go off on a drunk; he is forced to grasp at a new pipe dream—that his release from a guilt-ridden marriage has cleansed him and removed the need for debauchery.

"How fiendishly clever the human mind is!" said Nichols. "When one dream is punctured, when we are finally brought face to face with ourselves or with 'reality,' the mind jumps to another pipe dream and calls it truth—calls it facing reality!"

But Hickey's new pipe dream also vanishes when he discovers that his friends in Harry Hope's saloon will not buy it; they are appalled when they discover he has murdered his wife and regard it as the act of an insane man. Hickey, forced to seize still another illusion, convinces himself that his friends are right—that he is insane.

"I don't see the play as pessimistic," Nichols observed. "It's surely not a gloomy play. O'Neill himself delighted in its laughter. He'd chuckle over the tarts and the others—he loved them all. He didn't feel that the fact that we live largely by illusion is sad. The important thing is to see that we do. The quality of a man is merely the quality of his illusions. We like illusioned people. No happy person lives on good terms with reality. No one has even penetrated what reality is."

A fascinating interpretation of the religious symbolism in *The Iceman Cometh* has been published in *Modern Drama* by Professor Cyrus Day, who has pointed out what he calls "several tantalizing resemblances" between the play and the New Testament:

Hickey as savior has twelve disciples. They drink wine at Hope's supper party, and their grouping on the stage, according to O'Neill's directions, is reminiscent of Leonardo da Vinci's painting of the Last Supper. Hickey leaves the party, as Christ does, aware that he is about to be executed. The three whores correspond in number to the three Marys, and sympathize with Hickey as the three Marys sympathize with Christ. (The implications of this resemblance are not without precedent: Christopher Marlowe, it will be recalled, was accused of saying that the women of Samaria were whores.)

One of the derelicts, Parritt, resembles Judas Iscariot in several ways. He is the twelfth in the list of the dramatis personae; Judas is twelfth in the New Testament of the Disciples. He has betrayed his anarchist mother for a paltry $200; Judas betrayed Christ for thirty pieces of silver. He is from the far-away Pacific Coast; Judas was from far-away Judaea. Hickey reads his mind and motives; Christ reads Judas's. Parritt compares himself to Iscariot when he says that his mother would regard anyone who quit the "Movement" as a Judas who ought to be boiled in oil. He commits suicide by jumping off a fire escape; Judas fell from a high place (Acts 1:18) or "hanged himself" (Matthew 27:5).

. . . these resemblances can hardly be coincidental. They are no more than an undertone, to be sure—one of many undertones or subordinate layers of meaning—but they are consistent with the main theme of the play, and they account for some of its otherwise unaccountable features; for example, the emphasis on midnight (see Matthew 25:5-6) as the hour appointed for Hope's party, and the unnecessarily large number of derelicts in Hope's saloon.

Don Parritt may well have been O'Neill's symbol for Judas. But, more factually, he was based on a man named Don Vose, whose mother was a friend of Emma Goldman. Vose, through his mother, had entree into inner anarchist circles. He was the stool pigeon whose information enabled William J. Burns to pin the bombing of the Los Angeles *Times*, in 1910, on the McNamara brothers. Through Vose's betrayal, Burns picked up two anarchists who had collaborated with the McNamaras. It was Saxe Commins, who, being Emma Goldman's nephew, had a special interest in the Don Vose story, and who told it to O'Neill. Commins was surprised to see "his" character turn up in *The Iceman Cometh*.

"In writing *The Iceman Cometh*," O'Neill later told Croswell Bowen, who interviewed him for the newspaper *PM*, "I felt I had locked myself in with my memories."

This was literally true, and it applied to the next three plays he wrote as well. Circumstances seemed to conspire to throw O'Neill back on his past, even if he had not been inclined to go back himself. In 1939 the Writers Program of the WPA in northern California sent O'Neill the manuscript of a monograph on James O'Neill, which was to be a volume in a history of the San Francisco theatre. The writer in charge of this segment of theatre history was Patrick O'Neill, a coincidence of nomenclature that immediately put O'Neill in sympathy with the project. "I'm glad to know an O'Neill wrote the monograph, and I want to congratulate you on it," he said to his namesake.

In complying with Patrick O'Neill's request to check certain facts in James O'Neill's career, O'Neill was obliged to search through ancient documents which, inevitably, stirred up old memories. He found yellowed theatre programs, his parents' wedding certificate, photographs of James, Ella and Jamie—and he went to the bother of composing a long letter, in January of 1940, correcting errors and adding bits of detail; it was subsequently incorporated into the monograph. A little later that year, when he was already at work on his own version of James O'Neill's life in *Long Day's Journey,* he advised Patrick O'Neill, with what may have been unconscious irony: "No one appreciates better than I do how difficult it must have been to dig up reliable material."

When O'Neill finished *The Iceman Cometh* at the end of 1939, he found he could not go back to the cycle. He told Lawrence Langner, who was, naturally, eager to present a new O'Neill play, that production of any part of the cycle would be out of the question for some time to come.

"Go on as if you never heard of it," he said. "I've made myself put it aside for the past seven months. Had gone terribly stale, as I told you when we talked over the phone, and did not start the fifth play beyond getting it all ready to start. Since then I have been working on other things. But forget all that, too, until further notice, because it does not mean I will have anything for you to consider in making your plans for next year."

O'Neill's poor health and his crowding memories of the past had brought him to a low point by the spring of 1940. The European war depressed him still further. But in spite of his melancholy he took the trouble to befriend and encourage Patrick O'Neill, who, as a struggling young writer, had caught his sympathy and imagination. Responding to a letter in which the younger O'Neill had enclosed a rejected magazine article, O'Neill quixotically offered to "buy" it himself.

"I'll pay you fifty dollars for it—" he said—"hardly a munificent offer, but I can't afford any munificence just now." He added that the young writer had his "full permission" to continue peddling the article to magazines, and if he succeeded in selling it, to consider the money "velvet."

A little over a month later—when the fall of France had plunged O'Neill even deeper into gloom—he could still find time to commiserate with the young writer.

"This is a tough time to place an article of this kind," he sympathized. "From all I hear the war has had a much greater unbalancing effect on everyone in the East than here on the Coast." He added that he, himself, was as unbalanced as anyone could be by the tragedy of France, as he had lived there for four years.

A few months later, when Patrick O'Neill had still not succeeded in selling his article, O'Neill advised him to adopt the long-range philosophy that sooner or later he would come through. "And when you do," said O'Neill, "it will make everything you have to bear now worth while. And keep on writing, no matter what! That's the most important thing."

And toward the end of the year, when Patrick O'Neill had had a near miss in getting a book accepted by a leading publisher, O'Neill consoled him in words that came from the heart:

". . . such discouraging incidents have happened to every writer who ever amounted to a damn. . . . go on with your work . . . no matter what it cost you. . . . Publication is important but it can wait because it is outside you. What's inside you can't wait on the whim or luck of externals."

O'Neill was reiterating his own feelings. Earlier that year—in July—he had written Lawrence Langner, explaining why he had kept the existence of *The Iceman Cometh* a secret and indicating how strongly he believed, as far as his own work was concerned, that publication—or, in this case, production—could wait, because it was "outside" him. It had been six years since the last Broadway production of a new O'Neill play.

"I was afraid you would want to produce [*The Iceman Cometh*] right away and I don't want the strain of any production now," he told Langner. "There are other good reasons against it, too. . . . To tell the truth, like anyone else with any imagination, I have been absolutely sunk by this damned world debacle. The Cycle is on the shelf, and God knows if I can ever take it up again because I cannot foresee any future in this country or anywhere else to which it could spiritually belong. . . .

"I'm working again on something—not the Cycle—after a lapse of several months spent with an ear glued to the radio for war news. You can't keep a hop head off his dope for long!"

The reference to "dope" and "hop head" was significant, for the "something" O'Neill was working on was *Long Day's Journey Into Night*. He had begun writing it in the summer of 1939.

Like Lavinia Mannon in *Mourning Becomes Electra*, O'Neill had at last brought himself to face his dead. Dropping all guises in which he had cloaked the members of his family in such plays as *All God's Chillun Got Wings, Desire Under the Elms, The Great God Brown* and *Mourning Becomes Electra*, he now faced them head on, not bothering to alter any autobiographical details, except for the sake of dramatic intensity. *Long Day's Journey Into Night* was also the final play into which O'Neill wrote himself as a leading character (this time undisguised except for the name); Edmund Tyrone became the last in O'Neill's long gallery of conscious and unconscious self-portraits—ranging from the land-locked dreamer, Robert Mayo, in *Beyond the Horizon,* through the tubercular newspaper reporter, Stephen Murray, in *The Straw,* the semi-incestuous Eben Cabot, in *Desire Under the Elms,* the possessive Michael Cape in *Welded,* the defeated idealist, Dion Anthony, in *The Great God Brown,* the suicidal Reuben Light in *Dynamo,* the rebellious adolescent, Richard Miller, in *Ah, Wilderness!* to the religion-seeking John Loving in *Days Without End.*

O'Neill was a spiritually, mentally and physically tormented man during the two years it took him to write *Long Day's Journey Into Night.* He was as much tortured because it was agony to relive his painful past as because he was guilty at laying bare the secrets of that past.

"At times I thought he'd go mad," Carlotta recalled. "It was terrifying to watch his suffering."

In July of 1940, when he was about halfway through the writing of the play, he paused to convey a fervent anniversary greeting to Carlotta:

"Darling Wife: Here's congratulating myself for the blessing of you these eleven years!

"Time falters, civilization disintegrates, values perish, the old beauty becomes a gutter slut, the world explodes, the income tax rises, the years grow heavy on us and Blemie—

"But still! There is love that does not die . . . so what the hell!"

With O'Neill's permission, Lawrence Langner obtained a script of *The Iceman Cometh* from Bennett Cerf at Random House and then wrote its author that he considered it one of his major works. O'Neill answered on August 11, 1940 that he was "damned pleased" Langner liked the play.

"Personally I love it!" said O'Neill. "And I'm sure my affection is not wholly inspired by nostalgia for the dear dead days 'on the bottom of the sea,' either! I have a confident hunch that this play, as drama, is one of the best things I've ever done. In some ways, perhaps *the* best. What I mean is, there are moments in it that suddenly strip the secret soul of man stark naked, not in cruelty or moral superiority, but with an understanding compassion which sees him as a victim of the ironics of life and of himself. Those moments are for me the depth of tragedy, with nothing more that can possibly be said."

On his fifty-second birthday O'Neill found himself working with a new surge of strength. "I'm feeling fine and working my head off these days, crisis or no crisis," he wrote to the Van Vechtens, thanking them for their birthday wire on October 20, 1940. In December, on Carlotta's fifty-second birthday, he wrote her a poem called "Quiet Song in Time of Chaos," reflecting his appreciation of her love as a haven of peace.

O'Neill also wrote a little prose essay that month for Carlotta that was far more affecting than his poem. Blemie was growing old and infirm and both Carlotta and O'Neill knew his time was running out. O'Neill feared that Carlotta would take his death very hard and tried to console her by writing "The Last Will and Testament of Silverdeen Emblem O'Neill." The testament was a tender expression of O'Neill's philosophy and might have served, in part, for his own epitaph, as well as Blemie's.

"I, Silverdeen Emblem O'Neill (familiarly known to my family, friends and acquaintances as Blemie) . . . do hereby bury my last will and testament in the mind of my Master . . ," the essay began.

"I have little in the way of material things to leave. Dogs are wiser than men. They do not set great store upon things. They do not waste their days hoarding property. They do not ruin their sleep worrying about how to keep the objects they have, and to obtain the objects they have not. . . .

"I ask my Master and Mistress to remember me always, but not to grieve for me too long. . . . It is painful for me to think that even in death I should cause them pain. Let them remember that while no dog has ever had a happier life (and this I owe to their love and care for me), now that I have grown blind and deaf and lame, and even my sense of smell fails me so that a rabbit could be right under my nose and I might not know, my pride has sunk to a sick, bewildered humiliation. I feel life is taunting me with having overlingered my welcome. It is time I said good-by, before I become too sick a burden on myself and on those who love me. It will be a sorrow to leave them, but not a sorrow to die. . . . What may come after death, who knows? I would like to believe with those of my fellow Dalmatians who are devout Mohammedans, that there is a Paradise where one is always young and full-bladdered; where all the day one dillies and dallies with an amorous multitude of houris, beautifully spotted . . .

"I am afraid this is too much for even such a dog as I am to expect. But peace, at least, is certain. Peace and long rest for weary old heart and head and limbs, and eternal sleep in the earth I have loved so well. Perhaps, after all, this is best."

By the end of 1940 O'Neill had finished *Long Day's Journey Into Night* except for some final polishing, to be completed the following spring and summer.

"I typed this play twice," Carlotta said, "because he went over it a lot. I wept most of the time, it upset me so."

Since O'Neill did not intend *Long Day's Journey* to be published until long after his death, and did not want anything about its contents made public, he left scarcely any recorded comments on it, referring to it only obliquely on the few public occasions that he mentioned it at all. But he did allow a few close friends to read the manuscript, telling them that it would not be published until twenty-five years after his death. One of these friends was Russel Crouse, by this time the celebrated co-author of *Life With Father*. O'Neill described *Long Day's Journey Into Night* as "very different from *The Iceman* but just as good."

"Much more so than *The Iceman*," he told Crouse, "it is not a play which should be published or produced now. If you ever come out here for a visit . . . I'll let you read it. When you do, you will see why I have good reason to withhold it."

The year 1940 ended for O'Neill with another of his periodic illnesses —this time a long siege of bronchitis, through which Carlotta devotedly nursed him. Even after he had recovered physically, he found himself once more in a depression that unfitted him for work.

". . . the world chaos is always on one's mind no matter what one does, and the nearer spring comes with its invasion of England threat, the greater the tension will grow," O'Neill brooded to Langner early in 1941. "I doubt if I will be able to find any escape in writing, although I shall try. When there is too much tension, something in you goes on strike. Of course, I've done little since I've been sick except fiddle around with a few notes.

"Regarding *The Iceman Cometh*, it is no time for that. And no time for me, believe me, to bet my health against the strain of producing it."

At the end of March O'Neill had another reminder of his past. Clayton Hamilton sent him a clipping announcing the death of Mrs. Rippin, his landlady in New London.

"Although I haven't seen or heard from any of the family in many years," he wrote to Hamilton, "it brought the old days on Pequot Avenue back and made me feel damned sad. She was a fine woman and I had a deep affection for her."

O'Neill told Hamilton, as he had been telling other friends, that his cycle was "on the shelf." But, in truth, he had been tinkering with it on and off all during the writing of *The Iceman Cometh* and *Long Day's Journey Into Night*. And it had grown, if not on paper, at least in his mind. On May 21 he wrote in his work diary: "I have not told anyone yet of expansion of idea to eleven plays. Seems ridiculous—idea was first five plays, then seven, then eight, then nine, now eleven—will never live to do it—but what price anything but a dream!"

That spring Carlotta had one of her periodic brushes with an invader from the outside world which, electrically operated gates notwithstanding, constantly threatened to jar the right way of life at Tao House. Lester Sipes, a reporter for the Oakland *Tribune*, was sent by his city desk to question O'Neill about his alleged refusal to allow a local college group to present *Mourning Becomes Electra*.

Sipes managed to get inside the gate and prevailed on a servant to take a note into the house. An answering note came out from Mrs. O'Neill confirming the report and explaining that *Electra* was not for amateurs because it was "too difficult." Mrs. O'Neill did not appear in person, and Sipes was told that O'Neill was not at home. Later, Sipes's city editor again asked him to check with the O'Neills, this time on an Associated Press story, and it was decided that the story should be mailed to O'Neill, asking for comments.

"Mrs. O'Neill blew her top," Sipes later said. "She telephoned my house, and gave both me and my wife a royal chewing down. Her call was rather rambling, but the gist of it was that she and her husband didn't want to be bothered all the time, and why didn't I move out of the country. Being somewhat new on the job at the time, the only retort I could think of was to suggest that since I was there first, why didn't she move out. Apparently she simmered down, because she wrote me a letter a few days later, which I took as a sort of apology.

"It said that she was very sorry about the personal unpleasantness that had developed as a result of her husband's refusal to discuss his work or his private life, and went on to say that she did not think it essential for the press to know what one lone writer was doing, in a time of war and crisis.

"She also said that the only thing of any importance to her household was that her husband be left in peace to work, and that she intended to continue her job as his wife, nurse, housekeeper and secretary regardless of any unpopular criticism such protection of her husband might bring.

"In fairness, the O'Neill's probably wanted privacy intensely and had a hard time achieving it. Some of their neighbors in Danville were rather resentful of their attitude, but I can't say that I really blamed the O'Neills. A friend of mine in the meat business thought rather highly of them. Mrs. O'Neill even sent his wife and children some candy."

Early that summer O'Neill had a visit from his daughter.

"Oona is here," he informed Charles O'Brien Kennedy in July. "I, too, find her a most delightful and charming young lady."

Kennedy was one of O'Neill's few friends who took an interest in the O'Neill children and went to the trouble of sending him word about them. An interest in the O'Neill children, which necessarily meant being in contact with Agnes, would probably not have commended itself to O'Neill in anyone else; but Kennedy was such a gentle, discreet man and a friend of such long standing that O'Neill was willing to accept his interest in Shane and Oona, and even encouraged it in a mild way.

He told Kennedy, for example, that he was "extremely grateful" for his kindness to Shane and Oona.

"I particularly appreciate your helping Shane toward a conception of his Grandpa as the old timers remember him," O'Neill said. "He is more likely to be impressed that way than hearing about him from me.

"Shane will be all right once he finds a definite line for his life. Just now, he doesn't know what he is or where he wants to go. Considering the beautiful bloody mess the world is in, who can blame him? For all of us, the one certainty is uncertainty, and the only answer is a question."

Oona was sixteen in the summer of 1941, but looked considerably more mature. Physically she combined the best features of her father and mother. She had long, black hair, a pert nose, a generous mouth, and a well-developed figure. Unlike Shane, she was self-confident and seemed to know exactly where she was going. Although the menage in which she had grown up was somewhat irregular, she had been sent to one of the best private schools in New York and been given access to what Agnes considered the best social circles. One of her close friends, a schoolmate at Brearley, was Gloria Vanderbilt, who was impressed with what she once described as "Oona's wonderful quality of Oriental objectivity about

Formal portraits of the
dramatist and
Carlotta Monterey, 1926.

Muray

O'Neill and Carlotta
shortly before their
departure for Europe.

Ben Pinchot

Le Plessis.

Honeymoon in Europe.   *Angna Enters Collection*

Eugene, Jr., with his father at Le Plessis and, right, on his election to Phi Beta Kappa at Yale, 1931.

Blemie and his master, Northport, L. I., 1931.

Alla Nazimova (standing) *and Alice Brady in* MOURNING BECOMES
ELECTRA.   *Museum of the City of New York*

Casa Genotta.

Top left, *Mr. and Mrs. Eugene O'Neill in France;* top right, *in Seattle, 1936, after hearing of the Nobel award;* left, *O'Neill with "Rosie" the player piano at Casa Genotta, 1934;* above, *at Tao House, 1940.*

Top left and right, *Associated Press Photos*
Above, *Rose Covarrubias*

Charles Chaplin and Oona O'Neill shortly after their marriage.

Associated Press Photo

O'Neill's handwriting had shrunk drastically over thirty years. (*The writing from both letters has been proportionately reduced in these facsimiles.*)

Left, *Frank Leslie Collection*
Below, *University of Pennsylvania*

O'Neill and Carlotta at a rehearsal of THE ICEMAN COMETH.

George Karger–Pix

A scene from THE ICEMAN COMETH, *the last O'Neill play produced in the author's lifetime.*

George Karger–Pix

A preliminary reading of THE ICEMAN COMETH.

George Karger–Pix

O'Neill's grave in Forest Hills Cemetery, Boston, shortly after his burial.

life." Another close friend, Carol Grace, echoed this opinion: "She was able to stand off and see things. She had enormous understanding."

Carlotta did not quite concur in this laudatory opinion. In fact, she found Oona "a snippy little girl."

Recalling Oona's visit to Tao House, Carlotta said:

"She saw me darning a pair of her father's socks one day and asked me 'what on earth' I was doing. I said, 'What do you think I'm doing? I'm darning your father's socks, of course!' Oona curled her lip and said, 'You'd never catch me dead doing a thing like that. I'm going to marry a rich man.' "

O'Neill's health continued to be bad during the summer and fall, but he managed to put the final touches on *Long Day's Journey*. He presented the manuscript to Carlotta that July, on their twelfth wedding anniversary.

"Dearest: I give you the original script of this play of old sorrow, written in tears and blood," he wrote. "A sadly inappropriate gift, it would seem, for a day celebrating happiness. But you will understand. I mean it as a tribute to your love and tenderness which gave me the faith in love that enabled me to face my dead at last and write this play—write it with deep pity and understanding and forgiveness for *all* the four haunted Tyrones.

"These twelve years, Beloved One, have been a Journey into Light—into love. You know my gratitude. And my love!"

O'Neill's health continued unsteady during the next few months. In October, he complained to Russel Crouse of "recurrent spells when suddenly, at the least strain, I fold up and have to go to bed and am no good for anything—even out here where I live the simplest kind of life."

Sustained work was difficult, he said. "The mad tragedy of world catastrophe is too much on my neck. My mind is distracted—as whose isn't who isn't an idiot."

It was two months later that the Japanese attacked Pearl Harbor. O'Neill's initial reaction to the long-anticipated reality of total war was relatively mild. By this time he was feeling better and working again, and he took comfort from the fact that the blackouts now mandatory on the West Coast were "not half as disrupting as I thought they would be."

O'Neill ended the year 1941, as always, with a Christmas-birthday message to Carlotta:

"Sweetheart: In this time of chaos, when all old dreams and hopes are blown to dust, there remains for me—as ever, but now so much more than ever!—only you! I love you, Darling."

◆

During 1942 O'Neill began work on a new script that he failed to complete. Entitled *The Last Conquest,* it was evidently something he had been asked to write on behalf of the war effort, for he referred to it as "a propaganda play."

"I love the idea," he wrote to Crouse in March. "It's a very different thing from any of the obvious stuff, both in theme and technique. But every time I think I'm on the way, I get laid up again with some ill or other. This winter has been hell. I haven't written a line, hardly. It isn't war jitters, either, although I suppose subconsciously they helped to make bad physical matters worse, along with personal stuff that got my goat."

The tremor in O'Neill's hands had become severer and seizures more frequent; his doctors had prescribed a belt arrangement with a piece of steel about fourteen inches long and five inches wide that ran along his spine and that seemed to help him, although it was very uncomfortable.

Carlotta herself was suffering from arthritis and overwork; her staff had shrunk from six to two, and she was obliged to assume a number of unaccustomed household chores, in addition to nursing O'Neill and doing his secretarial work.

Freeman, the mainstay of their staff, had enlisted in the Marines, but was stationed in San Francisco and came to visit them whenever he could. According to Carlotta, she and O'Neill had come to regard Freeman as "really the only child we have," and both the O'Neills were greatly distressed by his absence.

O'Neill was also irritated and upset about his daughter. Nathan reported some current gossip-column news about her and O'Neill endorsed Carlotta's opinion of her as "the glamour girl." Oona had been attracting the kind of notoriety O'Neill abhorred. That April, while in her final semester at Brearley, she had been voted "New York's Number One Debutante," and had been interviewed at the Stork Club, where she pertly insisted that she was "shanty Irish." An interview with Earl Wilson, the New York *Post* columnist, had found its way to O'Neill in California, and he was furious when he read his daughter's flippant remarks. Wilson asked Oona how her father would feel about her "triumph" and she replied, "I don't think he's going to be wild about it. I won't write; I'll just let him find out about it himself." She also confided that, though she had just finished taking college board entrance examinations, she was planning to study art in New York the following year and was "also going to find out whether I'm any good at acting."

Oona was not yet seventeen and her ideas of glamour and fun were not much different from those of other girls similarly situated. But O'Neill bridled at what he considered her pursuit of frivolity. So, for that matter, did one of Oona's admirers, the then unknown young writer, J. D. Salinger. Salinger had been introduced to Oona at her home in West Point Pleasant in the fall of 1941, soon after her visit to Tao House, by a friend of her mother's, Elizabeth Murray. He began seeing her in New York and, though he confessed to Mrs. Murray that he was "crazy about her," the romance did not run smoothly. "Little Oona's hopelessly in love with little Oona," Salinger told Mrs. Murray after a date he'd had with her in New York the following December. But he continued to see Oona and write to her.

In spite of his distress about his two younger children, O'Neill managed to take some pleasure in another project he had begun that year. It was a series of half a dozen one-act plays—the first one-acters he had attempted since abandoning the form in 1920—to be called *By Way of Obit*. The most lighthearted of his projects during this period, it was destined, like the Gargantuan cycle, to remain unrealized.

"Gene started writing these plays as a diversion," Carlotta said. "He was writing so many serious things at the time that this was something to play with. It required no responsibility and it amused him."

One of the playlets dealt with an old Irish chambermaid O'Neill had known when he and Jamie lived at the Garden Hotel.

"They would wake up in the morning with hangovers," Carlotta said, "and the chambermaid would be scrubbing the bathroom. She would tell Gene stories and gossip, and Gene would encourage her to talk."

O'Neill wrote scenarios for three or four of the plays, but completed only one, which he called *Hughie*. Like *The Iceman Cometh*, it illustrated O'Neill's thesis that man cannot live without illusions, that he must cling to his pipe dreams, even knowing they are pipe dreams, in order to survive. *Hughie* is more short story than play and consists largely of a monologue on the part of a small-time gambler and horse-player named Erie Smith, who is down on his luck. Although the playlet is set in a West Side hotel and the time is 1928, its two characters (Erie's foil is the night clerk of the hotel) would be at home in Harry Hope's waterfront saloon of 1912. Erie is a less astringent Hickey, a Hickey not burdened with O'Neill's symbolic message of despair, a coarser, more elementary type—but a blood brother nonetheless. O'Neill described Erie and Hickey in almost the same words. Both are short, stout, balding, with boyish faces, blue eyes, button noses and pursed mouths. Both have the shrewd glance and breezy, familiar manner of the wised-up sales-man confident he can always find a sucker. Underneath the façade both are on the verge of crumbling.

O'Neill did not intend *Hughie* or any of the other plays in the series to be given conventional stage productions. He told Carlotta that he was thinking of some new technique, possibly utilizing a filmed background and sound track. But he did not pursue the idea. He shrugged off the problem, saying: "It would require tremendous imagination. Let whoever does it figure it out. I wouldn't want to be around to see it." He had his wish, for the play was not produced in his lifetime.

Not long after finishing it, in July of 1942, he sent *Hughie* to Nathan, who liked it.

"It has its own quality, I think," said O'Neill, "which makes it a bit different from anything else of that kind—at least, as far as my knowledge goes. And it gives you an idea of how the others in the series will be done."

Also during that summer and fall O'Neill revised his third cycle play, *A Touch of the Poet,* probably because it was the one play in the series that bore the closest relationship to his present creative state of mind. In its final version it was of a piece with *The Iceman Cometh, Hughie* and another new play he was thinking of writing, which turned out to be *A Moon for the Misbegotten.*

A Touch of the Poet goes back to the alcoholic pipe dreams; the "kick" goes out of the liquor for Cornelius Melody when he comes face to face with his illusions, much as it does for the bums in Harry Hope's saloon when Hickey confronts them with reality; Melody, like Hickey and like Jamie Tyrone, who is the hero of *A Moon for the Misbegotten,* commits spiritual suicide when he finds he can no longer believe in his pipe dream.

It is also a fair guess that O'Neill sharpened the hostile relationship between Melody and his daughter when he rewrote *A Touch of the Poet,* in the light of his own violent feelings toward Oona. ". . . things have happened in the past week which upset me and kept me on the nervous jump," O'Neill confided to Nathan that October, referring to news he had just had of Oona's latest adventure. (She had arrived in California with her mother and tried to break into the movies, despite the fact that she had been accepted at Vassar. A bit part with a summer stock company the previous July had banished all thought of a higher education, and she was now openly defying her father's wishes, to the accompaniment of considerable publicity.)

" 'Nervous jump' is no mere expression these days," O'Neill went on, referring to his physical condition for the first time as Parkinson's disease and adding that it had grown "progressively worse" in the past few years.

". . . now there are days when it is physically impossible to write at all," he said. "This infuriates me, as you can imagine, and that doesn't help." He told Nathan there was no cure, and that "the remedies to counteract it have such a bad effect on me, I prefer the Parkinson's."

When he stopped to think about "the world drama," he went on pessimistically, it seemed ridiculous to be bothering about his own writings, in any case. What, ultimately, was the war being fought for? he asked rhetorically. "My own prediction is, for the same kind of peace treaty which has followed all wars, because the same kind of greedy politicians and money diplomats will make it. Those boys' trade is never to learn anything. . . . I cannot understand how anyone who has read history can waste time in sentimental wishful thinking about the next peace. I have no doubt of our final victory in the war, but I have nothing but doubt about our even wanting to force a just peace on Europe—even if that were possible. People have one attitude now, 'it must never happen again,' but the minute an armistice is signed they will change and be fed up and say 'for Christ's sake let's forget the war. We won, didn't we? To hell with it.'. . ."

In November Nathan invited Carlotta to visit him for a rest and a holiday. She was touched and grateful, but she declined, explaining that she could not possibly leave her husband alone in his condition of nervous depression and poor health. It was taking all her energy and resourcefulness to bolster his spirits, and part of her effort was spent in keeping away from him newspaper accounts of Oona's doings.

By the year's end the O'Neills were all but marooned in their big house in the valley. Because of his tremor, O'Neill could no longer drive a car, and Carlotta had never learned to drive; it was impossible to find a chauffeur to replace Freeman, and the O'Neills had thought, at first, that they would have to leave Tao House; after some soul-searching, they decided to stay.

"We've succeeded in finding someone—the hardware man in Danville—to drive me to the doctor's in Oakland every two weeks for the imperative treatments," O'Neill reported to Russel Crouse in December of 1942." Now that gas rationing is with us it will take tough figuring to do this on an 'A' Book, but what the hell! We do have good tires and will continue to get by some way and remain reasonably cheery. Compared to the farmers around here, who face an impossible situation in so many respects, we are on velvet and suffer no hardships."

As for his work, he said, it was progressing almost imperceptibly. Either "something or other" would intrude on his concentration or he would be physically incapacitated every time he made an effort to get started. "A case of one damned thing or another," he complained.

Around the same time O'Neill wrote to Theresa Helburn: "My health has been bad. . . . Some days I can't write—I mean physically can't write longhand—and couldn't type even if the old dog could change tricks and compose on a typewriter. . . . I've had to give up the physical work around the grounds—I used to take care of quite a lot—because it brings on spells of complete exhaustion when I feel like a wet anaemic fly crawling up a cold windowpane."

That Christmas—1942—O'Neill wrote Carlotta another "Song in Chaos," which seems to have been influenced less by the lyric poets he admired than by Irving Berlin. The first of three stanzas is typical:

> What if the world be mad?
> You are near.
> What if the mind be sad?
> You are here
> In my heart,
> My dear.

LIX

O'NEILL, WHO REACHED HIS FIFTY-FIFTH BIRTHDAY
in 1943, had been writing steadily for thirty years. At this point in his
life he was hoarding an unproduced backlog of four plays, as well as drafts
of eight cycle plays. *The Iceman Cometh, A Touch of the Poet* (the only
completed cycle play), *Long Day's Journey Into Night,* and *Hughie* were
finished to his satisfaction; by the middle of the year he would complete
A Moon for the Misbegotten, the last play he would ever write.

In addition, he had notebooks filled with play ideas and outlines,
destined never to be written. Among them were a projected play about
Aeschylus, for which he prepared a four-page outline of the Greek
dramatist's life and work; a draft of part of Act One and additional notes
for a play he intended to call *Gag's End;* five pages of notes for a play
about Don Juan of Austria and Philip II; two pages of notes for a work
he labeled *Negro Play;* three pages of notes for a play about Robespierre;
and nineteen pages of notes for a play about China.

Suspecting that his writing days were nearly at an end, yet trying to
believe they were not, O'Neill wrote to a former Provincetown Players
colleague, Jasper Deeter, of the work he had accomplished in recent years,
observing ruefully, "Not so bad, I suppose, considering sickness, but I
would be a liar if I said I found the record satisfying—so much work
and so little finished."

As he labored over *A Moon for the Misbegotten* in the early part of
1943, O'Neill found it increasingly difficult to control the purely mechanical process of writing. There were many days when the tremor in his
hands was slight and when, by steeling himself for the effort and forming minute letters with his pencil, he could cover page after page. But
there were days when his fingers could not hold a pencil at all and no
effort of will could produce anything but a tremulous, illegible scrawl.
His desperation on such days terrified Carlotta.

"I nearly went mad, and so did he," Carlotta said. "It was terrible to
see him come out of his study, shaken and miserable."

Carlotta confided to Theresa Helburn that the situation was becoming more difficult every day. "There is nothing to do for Parkinson's, it
just gets worse and worse," she explained. "And now that I have fallen

apart I am not so brave in facing it! There are days when my heart aches so I can hardly face him—which, of course, is the worst possible thing for him. . . . I am really stuck, for the first time in my life, as to what is the best thing to do regarding a future home for Gene. He should have warmth, ocean and sand (!), doctors and good nourishment."

O'Neill attempted to dictate his thoughts to Carlotta but found it impossible. Thinking that perhaps the mere presence of another person— even someone as close to him as his wife—was the stumbling block, Carlotta bought him a recording machine. They experimented painstakingly together, O'Neill reading passages from *Long Day's Journey Into Night* and *The Iceman Cometh* into the machine from different distances, and playing back the results; but, though he mastered the technique of the machine, his mind could not function creatively when he was left alone with it. An electric typewriter was tried but that, too, proved useless. His thoughts, he told Carlotta, flowed from his brain, through his arm and into his pencil; there was no other process by which he could write. O'Neill continued to wrestle doggedly with his pencil.

"As he got more and more ill," Carlotta said, "his writing not only grew smaller, but it was all crooked and shaky. No one could read it but me. And I would type his manuscripts over and over for him. He would change a few words, and make me type the whole page over. I nearly went blind."

In a letter he sent in January of that year to the librarian of Princeton University, who was preparing an exhibit of his manuscripts, O'Neill remarked, apropos of some of the handwritten documents under discussion:

"I always hated typewriting and was very bad at it. Of late years, I can't write anything but minute, but there is a physical reason for that— the curse of Parkinson's disease—it's easier to control the tremor in minute writing." In a later letter he added, with a jocularity that belied his distress: "I've always had [the tremor] more or less, but it was not bad in the period in which the Princeton scripts were written. Now, Mrs. O'Neill, who has typed all my plays for years, has to operate with a magnifying glass and a book on Egyptology. These are the times when she wonders if, after all, our marriage was not a grave mistake."

A Moon for the Misbegotten was written as much in "tears and blood" as *Long Day's Journey Into Night*. Like *Long Day's Journey*, to which it is a sequel, it was a play of "old sorrow," carrying the story of Jamie O'Neill to its bitter conclusion. Carlotta believed that O'Neill was writing it to give Jamie "his final due." She did not like the play, feeling, she once said, that it was "unnecessary to rub it in." O'Neill relived the last years of Jamie's life with demoniac intensity while he was writing *A Moon for the Misbegotten,* and his mood of black despair was, in itself, enough to give both him and Carlotta a retrospective hatred of the play.

One night during the time O'Neill was working on the script, Carlotta was in her room listening to a Hitler speech on the radio. She was lying on her Chinese bed, the twin of O'Neill's converted opium couch.

"Gene came in and asked if he could lie down beside me and listen to the speech," Carlotta recalled. "It was horrible, guttural—and Gene was terribly distressed by it."

When the speech was over, Carlotta tried to soothe her husband. Suddenly he sprang from the bed.

"Goddam whore!" he shouted, and ran from the room.

A few seconds later Carlotta heard him weeping in his own room. Controlling her mortification, she went to comfort him, and found him lying, face down, on the floor.

"He implored me to forgive him," Carlotta said. "He told me he hadn't known what he was saying, and explained that he had been reliving his days with Jamie—the days they had spent in whorehouses together. He was completely shattered. We talked and talked for the rest of the night.

"Gene was such a peculiar mixture. Sometimes he was so soft-spoken, and he had the smile of a child of five; you would forgive him anything. But then he could turn around and—like that—I don't think the word 'savage' exaggerates when he was in those moods. He was very much a sadist at times, terribly so; but if he did anything, when the mood changed and he realized it, he suffered terribly from guilt. And his guilt—to watch his guilt hurt me much more than when he was a sadist. I couldn't stand to see my child so miserable."

Years later, inscribing a copy of the published version of *A Moon for the Misbegotten* to Carlotta, O'Neill wrote:

"To darling Carlotta . . . This token of my gratitude . . . a poor thing—a play she dislikes, and which I have come to loathe—dating back to 1944—my last."

Yet despite his expressed loathing, the play is among O'Neill's greatest, rich in Irish humor and enormously moving in its brutal tragedy—a powerful expression of individualism from a dramatist who wrote to the sound of strange harmonies within his own soul and with disregard for the conventions of Broadway. Even as he wrote it he was aware that he was imposing conditions which would render it virtually unproducible. His Josie Hogan, for example, is a woman "so oversize . . . that she is almost a freak—five feet eleven in her stockings and weighs around one hundred and eighty. . . . She is more powerful than any but an exceptionally strong man. . . . But there is no mannish quality about her. She is all woman."

While O'Neill created Josie as though she were a character in a novel and he knew it would be impossible to reproduce her on a stage with physical accuracy, he felt that his description would at least make potential producers think twice before deciding to cast a typical ingénue in the role.

When he was finishing *A Moon for the Misbegotten* in the spring of 1943, O'Neill's already taut nerves received another onslaught. On June 17 he read the news that Oona, recently turned eighteen, had married Charlie Chaplin.

Oona had arrived in San Francisco some months earlier with her friend Carol Grace. Carol, also seventeen, was engaged to William Saroyan who, at thirty-five, was an established playwright. Saroyan, about to be inducted into the army in California, where he lived, had asked Carol to come west to meet his family, and Oona had decided to join her. After being inducted, Saroyan was sent to Sacramento for his basic training, and Carol and Oona followed him there, staying at a motel. From Sacramento Oona telephoned to her father, asking if she could visit, but she was put off with an excuse. Her own plans still unformed, Oona marked time in Sacramento, where she lightheartedly collaborated with Carol in a plot to advance her tempestuous romance with Saroyan.

Saroyan had made Carol promise that she would send him a letter every day during his two-week period of training, and Carol, who had never written to him before, was afraid that her letters would disappoint him.

"Oona was receiving a letter almost every day from a boy named Jerry in New York," Carol recalled. "Some of the letters were fifteen pages long, and they were very witty, with comments about all kinds of things. I told Oona I was afraid that if I wrote to Bill, he'd find out what an idiot I was, and decide not to marry me, so she marked the clever passages in her letters from Jerry and let me copy them, as my own, in my letters to Bill.

"When Bill's two-week training period was up and I went to see him at camp, he was terribly surly. I asked him what was the matter, and he told me he'd changed his mind about marrying me. He said he had thought I was a sweet girl, but that 'those lousy, glib letters' I'd been sending him had made him wonder. I was very upset, and told Oona about it, and she said we'd have to tell Bill the truth about the letters.

But I knew that Bill hated liars more than anything else, so I didn't tell him.

"We left Sacramento for Hollywood, where Oona was met by her mother, and after a while I went back to New York. Later, Bill looked me up in New York and we were married, after all."

(Carol did not confess her subterfuge. But, about eight years later, when she and Saroyan were spending a weekend with Oona and Chaplin, Saroyan began talking about a book he was reading. It was J. D. Salinger's recently published first novel, *The Catcher in the Rye*, and Saroyan was full of enthusiasm for it. "This kid is great," he told Oona and Chaplin. "He's got it!" Oona threw Saroyan a wicked glance. "You didn't think much of his style eight years ago," she said. And Saroyan finally heard the story of the borrowed phrases—for the "Jerry" from whose letters Carol had cribbed was, of course, J. D. Salinger.)

After Carol had left, Oona joined her mother in Hollywood. Agnes, now fifty, was in love with a married man named Morris Kaufman, many years her junior. (About two years later, Kaufman's wife sued him for divorce in New York; the divorce was uncontested. At that time, newspaper stories quoted Mrs. Kaufman's accusation that her husband had committed adultery with Agnes in New York and Hollywood. "My husband," she said, "first met Mrs. O'Neill at a writers' club. At that time, he was manager of a wholesale tobacco shop, and had no literary ambitions. Shortly thereafter he got his first tuxedo and began eating steaks at the Stork Club and other places." Mrs. Kaufman added that she had gone to Agnes to protest against her friendship with Kaufman, and Agnes had told her that she and Kaufman were in love.)

Kaufman, who was known as "Mack," was offered a writing job in Hollywood by Charlie Chaplin, whom Agnes had known from Greenwich Village days. Oona met Chaplin soon after arriving to stay with her mother and before long he offered her dramatic lessons and coached her for a screen career. Within a few months Oona and Chaplin fell in love. They decided to marry as soon as Oona reached her eighteenth birthday.

At West Point Pleasant, when reporters brought Agnes the news of the imminent marriage, she said: "I am very happy about it and the only reason I will not be present at the ceremony is that it is necessary for me to be in New York."

Oona and Chaplin were married by a justice of the peace in Santa Barbara and the newspapers made much of the event. Chaplin had been married three times before. He was fifty-four, the father of two boys— one the same age as Oona and one a year younger—and he was in the midst of a paternity suit instituted by a young actress named Joan Berry.

O'Neill, already estranged from Oona, received the news of her marriage to a man his own age in grim silence; he could not muster, for his daughter, any trace of the warmth, compassion or understanding he displayed toward the characters born of his imagination.

Friends of O'Neill, shocked by his absolute rejection of Oona, speculated that one of the reasons for his anger over the marriage was a strong (and purely egotistical) prejudice against Chaplin as an intimate friend of Carlotta's ex-husband, Ralph Barton. Chaplin had been one of the last people to spend time with Barton before his suicide. Carl Van Vechten, for one, was convinced that this was the real reason for O'Neill's disapproval of the marriage.

When reporters tried to reach O'Neill, they were denied access to him—and the fact that he would not comment was noted in the newspapers. According to Carlotta, O'Neill would not comment privately either.

"Oona broke Gene's heart," Carlotta said. "He never mentioned her name after her marriage. Friends would ask him about her, and he simply wouldn't answer. Finally, people had enough sense to realize that he didn't want to talk about her."

Oona never saw her father again, though she made several attempts at a reconciliation. She once urged Waldo Frank to intercede for her with O'Neill. Frank wrote to O'Neill on the basis of their old friendship and received a curt reply from Carlotta, precluding any other attempts on Oona's behalf.

As for O'Neill's two sons, Eugene Jr. continued, for the moment, to be in the good graces of both his father and Carlotta, while Shane was proving a disappointment. Eugene, following the O'Neill tradition, had been divorced and remarried. At thirty-three he was an authority on Greek drama, an assistant professor at Yale, and highly distinguished in academic circles. He was always welcome at Tao House and, though he did not visit often, he and his father remained warm friends.

Though Shane also had been made welcome periodically at Tao House during the late thirties, he had upset his father by failing to find a direction for his life. He had worked at odd jobs in New York, taken a trip to Mexico, and in 1941 joined the Merchant Marine. He was discharged in 1943, after having been hospitalized for shock.

Meeting a girl he liked, he tried to make some sort of life with her in New York and again worked at odd jobs. But at twenty-four he was still drifting. He began drinking excessively and tried on more than one occasion to commit suicide. His father knew as little about the sordid details of his life in New York as James O'Neill had known about *his* son's sordid life at Jimmy-the-Priest's; O'Neill only heard about Shane when he applied to O'Neill's lawyer for a loan—which was as often refused as it was granted. In Shane's case, at least, the "sins of the father" seemed to have been visited—with a vengeance—on the son. O'Neill was too ill—or too uninterested—to attempt to wrestle with what he regarded as the workings of fate.

A month after Oona's marriage, on his own fourteenth wedding anniversary, O'Neill wrote to the only person who had any real importance to him:

"Darling One: Every day, in every way, you are more and more beautiful and I love you more!"

But beauty and love were not enough to keep life going at Tao House; once more a carefully-planned sanctuary was crumbling. O'Neill became ill again early that fall, and the servant problem was starting to wear Carlotta down. O'Neill's siege of illness lasted six weeks and was severe enough to require the attendance of a trained nurse. Commencing with an abscessed tooth, it went on to a case of bronchitis and then intensified his chronic ailments.

"The old Parkinson's went wild and woolly," O'Neill informed Nathan on September 25, when he was convalescing.

He told Nathan that his doctors had discovered he had an adrenal deficiency and that he had to drink large tumblers of salt water "with a bit of lemon juice to take the curse off." The beverage, he added, would "never, never become a favorite tipple at Lüchow's."

By the end of the fall of 1943 the O'Neills decided they would have to leave Tao House. O'Neill needed to be within easier access of medical treatment, and Carlotta needed a respite from bedmaking, cooking, cleaning and gardening; secretarial work and nursing were about as much as her own frayed nerves could sustain.

"We stayed at Tao House for six whole years, longer than we lived anywhere else," Carlotta said. "Of course, there were many hardships, but it was a beautiful place and I hated to leave."

They put the house on the market, planning to move to a hotel in San Francisco as soon as they found a buyer. That Christmas was the last they spent at Tao House.

By January, 1944, a buyer had been found. With deep regret Carlotta arranged to sell most of her precious Chinese furnishings back to Gump's. She packed her own and O'Neill's thousands of books, together with a few of their most cherished ornaments, for shipment to their new quarters —a suite of rooms in the Huntington Hotel on San Francisco's Nob Hill.

They were to leave Tao House the last week in February. On February

21, 1944, O'Neill destroyed the manuscripts of the first two double-length plays of his cycle—the two plays which, before he had decided to divide them into four, he had called *The Greed of the Meek* and *And Give Me Death*. He kept the overlong manuscript of what was still the projected sixth play of the cycle, *More Stately Mansions*, and, of course, the completed fifth play, *A Touch of the Poet*.

He also kept drafts or scenarios of the seventh, eighth, ninth, tenth and eleventh plays (*The Calms of Capricorn*, *The Earth's the Limit*, *Nothing is Lost Save Honor*, *The Man on Iron Horseback* and *The Hair of the Dog*), and he preserved most of his notes for the over-all cycle scheme, for he still hoped to finish the cycle, though in a greatly revised form.

O'Neill also destroyed the scenarios of all the one-act plays he had outlined for the *By Way of Obit* series, preserving only the completed *Hughie*. To Carlotta the process of destruction was shocking and painful, but, she said, she did not presume to question it, knowing that O'Neill had often before indulged in this sort of ruthless editing.

The O'Neills lived in even greater seclusion in San Francisco than they had at Danville. Only a handful of people knew their whereabouts, for most of O'Neill's mail was routed through the Random House office in New York. One of their visitors on Nob Hill was Kenneth Macgowan, who was then living on the West Coast.

"When I saw him in San Francisco," Macgowan recalled, "Gene showed me some poetry he had just written. It was free verse, and I liked it. He inscribed two poems to me and gave them to me. His hands were so unsteady that he wrote the inscriptions with one hand helping the other to hold the pen."

O'Neill was too ill to work in San Francisco, but he supervised the final typing of the manuscripts of the plays he had written at Tao House and continued to emphasize to inquirers that he had not been creatively idle in the decade since Broadway had had its last O'Neill production.

Though still adamant about not having anything produced until after the war, he was aware that his abstention, as far as the world was concerned, indicated that he had ceased to exist as a force in the American theatre. He steadfastly declined to change the situation, but he did think about it, as an exchange of letters with Mark Van Doren in the spring of 1944 indicates.

Van Doren was working on a War Bond drive at the time and applied to O'Neill for an original manuscript that could be auctioned to raise funds. O'Neill carefully cross-examined Van Doren about the current market value of the O'Neill name. Telling Van Doren he had certain scripts that might serve the purpose (he had recently come across the original longhand scripts of the first three one-act plays he had written, he said), he questioned whether they would bring in enough money to justify his parting with them.

He would gladly contribute them, he said, "*if* you think the contribution can be important enough to the drive to justify the gift."

"You can imagine how much these scripts mean to me," he added, and explained that Yale, Princeton or the Museum of the City of New York would all be glad to add them to their O'Neill collections, in the event that the War Bond auction could not fetch a really high price for them.

"So what I want to know is," said O'Neill, "have they any such value for a War Bond auction?"

Van Doren replied that the O'Neill manuscripts were unquestionably of great value. The information boosted O'Neill's morale. He said he was "greatly pleased" and that it salved all his "sentimental pangs."

In reply to a gracious remark of Van Doren's about Eugene Jr., whom he had recently met, O'Neill said—not without a tinge of bitterness about his other children: "I am so glad you liked Eugene. I am damned proud of him. And I'm selfishly grateful for his learning because I can always learn so much from him. It is grand to have a son who is an education instead of one who makes you doubt the value of education."

Early in the summer of 1944 Lawrence Langner and his wife visited the O'Neills in San Francisco.

"We found Gene and Carlotta considerably healthier and happier," Langner recorded. "We discussed what plays were in shape for production and were being typed in final draft in San Francisco."

O'Neill told Langner that he could produce *The Iceman Cometh* a little while after the war was over.

"He felt," according to Langner, "that the timing for the play's opening was very important, and that if it were to be produced immediately after the war was over, the pessimism of the play would run counter to public optimism, and would result in a bad reception by the audience. He thought a year or so after the peace, there would be considerable disillusionment, and that the public would then be more inclined to listen to what he had to say in this play."

O'Neill also gave Langner the manuscripts of *A Moon for the Misbegotten* and *A Touch of the Poet,* and they discussed long-range casting and production plans for all three plays. They agreed that *A Touch of the Poet* should be done last but were undecided about whether to do *The*

Iceman Cometh or *A Moon for the Misbegotten* first. The latter, of course, presented an almost insuperable problem in the casting of the Irish giantess, Josie; as Langner later pointed out, it called for "exactly the kind of woman who, when she comes to see you and asks you to advise her whether she should attempt a career in the theatre—you look embarrassed and reply, "Well, I'm afraid you're rather a big girl—how are we to find a man tall enough to play opposite you?"

The Iceman seemed easier to cast; Nathan, after having read the script, had suggested Eddie Dowling for the role of Hickey and O'Neill had gone to see Dowling's performance in Saroyan's *The Time of Your Life* in San Francisco in 1940.

"Carlotta called for me in her car and took me out to Tao House," Dowling recalled. "She left me alone with Gene and we talked for three hours; he felt me out about *The Iceman*, which I'd already read. He told me he wouldn't have it produced until after the war, but said he wanted me to play Hickey when it was done.

"There were other visits and discussions after that, and I heard often from Carlotta by mail. I remember that during one visit O'Neill said to me, 'If the Holy Father would just tell Hitler off, I'd go back to the Church.'"

Dowling, a practicing Catholic, pointed out to O'Neill that he was not eligible to return to the Church. "I don't mean I'd go back formally," O'Neill said. "I mean my heart would go back."

"What would be accomplished if the Pope told Hitler off?" Dowling persisted.

"Well," O'Neill replied, "I'd just like to turn on the radio and hear the Pope call Hitler a son of a bitch."

Regarding the production of *A Touch of the Poet,* no casting was discussed during the Langners' visit with O'Neill. But O'Neill told Carlotta, half seriously, that he would like *her* to play the role of Deborah Harford.

"I will, if you'll play one of the drunks in the barroom," Carlotta retorted.

The Langners left San Francisco in a state of high optimism over O'Neill's willingness to discuss future productions—but their optimism dimmed soon after, when O'Neill's health again took a turn for the worse and his outlook became gloomier than ever.

He celebrated his fifty-sixth birthday by visiting what he referred to as "a really swell Columbarium."

Describing the trip to a friend, he declared:

"California, as is well known, leads the world in the swellness of its columbariums designed, apparently, to keep the dead lively, cheerful and constantly amused." He had intended, he said, "to price a few snappy urns," just by way of safeguarding his future; but neither the "curator of the dump" nor he could make themselves heard above "the roaring of ten thousand savage canary birds and horrid gush of fancy fountains," so it all came to nothing. He had left the place, he said, swearing he would live forever "to spite those damned canaries" and vowing that his next pet bird would be a buzzard.

At the year's end O'Neill was still too ill to work. He could not even think of an adequate sentiment to inscribe to Carlotta in the copy of Grimm's Fairy Tales he gave her that year for her birthday.

". . . the mind and heart are too heavy and creation fails," he wrote on the flyleaf of the book. "So I have to fall back on . . . My love and your love . . . With that love we can grow old together without fear, even in this kind of world."

Sometime in 1944 Theresa Helburn, suspecting that O'Neill was beginning to be hard up for cash, wrote to ask him if he wanted her to renew her efforts to sell *Mourning Becomes Electra* to the movies. (She reminded him that in 1935 she had interested Katharine Hepburn in playing Lavinia, but that when Miss Hepburn had tried to sell the project to Louis B. Mayer, Mayer had said, "over my dead body.") O'Neill was not interested in Miss Helburn's proposition, because the badly mangled version of *The Hairy Ape* had been released that year, and he was feeling bitter about the movies.

"I've never liked having distorted pictures made of my plays," he advised Miss Helburn, and, forgetting his earlier enthusiasm for the talkies, added:

"The picture medium has never interested me. . . . Talking pictures seem to me a bastard which has inherited the lowest traits of both parents. It was the talkless part of *The Long Voyage Home*—the best picture ever made from my stuff—that impressed me the most. . . .

"So you may understand what my feeling is about a film sale of a favorite play I know Hollywood will distort. Let's consider *The Hairy Ape*. It remains one of my favorites. . . . I sold it [to films] because, with Tao House and ranch overhead on my neck, I had to sell it or sell some of my securities whose income pays the alimony! . . . I didn't really want to sell because I knew no one in Hollywood had the guts to film *my play*, do it as symbolic expressionism as it should be done, and not censor it into imbecility, or make it a common realistic stoker story. . . . So when I tell you I am not going to see the film—nor read one word written about it—nor even admit that it exists, I sure mean it! But all the same, I will always feel guilty. The memory of what *The Hairy Ape* is, was and should be, will, in a sense, be spoiled for me. The picture, even if financially a hit [it wasn't] will soon be forgotten, and the play will remain as if no picture had ever touched it. But still, I will always regret."

As for *Mourning Becomes Electra,* he said, he was sure Katharine Hepburn would be "splendid" as Lavinia, but the screenplay would end as "a dreadful hash of attempted condensation and idiotic censorship, as the *Strange Interlude* film was." He was almost convinced, he added, that he should not sell *Mourning Becomes Electra* to the movies "at any price."

A little later, O'Neill publicly affirmed his antipathy to the motion-picture industry. "Plays should never be written with actors or Hollywood in mind," he declared. "This is a terrific handicap to an author, although few of them seem to realize it.

"The theatre should be their sole thought. If this were only true, you would find sound development underneath the plays of today. Unfortunately, just the opposite is occurring." (Some years earlier, while in Europe, O'Neill had received a cable on behalf of Jean Harlow, explaining that Miss Harlow wanted the best available American dramatist to write a screen-play for her. Would O'Neill please cable back, collect, confining his answer to twenty words. O'Neill cabled: "No No No No No No No No No No No No No No No No No No No O'Neill.")

When the European war ended in May, 1945, the O'Neills immediately began planning their return east, but the state of O'Neill's health and nerves made it difficult to set a date for the trip. Civilian travel was still restricted. Carlotta would pull strings, wait, clear away red tape and, finally, get space on a train. With the hard-won tickets in her pocket, she would find that O'Neill could not make the effort to move.

"I once had everything packed and on the train," Carlotta recalled, "and just at the last moment Gene said 'No, I don't think I want to go.' So I had to return to the public relations man at the railroad, thank him for his courtesy, and tell him I was very sorry, but Mr. O'Neill had changed his mind. He told me I needn't be sorry, he had a hundred people waiting for the canceled space. But then we had to start all over again, waiting; we weren't able to get space on a train until almost the end of 1945."

By that time the war with Japan was over and there was no longer any obstacle to O'Neill's return to Broadway.

LX

THE O'NEILLS MOVED INTO AN EIGHTH-FLOOR SUITE
of the Barclay Hotel, in the East Forties, on their return to New York.
Langner and his wife, among the first to greet O'Neill, were taken aback
by the change in his appearance since they had last seen him in San
Francisco.

"He seemed to have lost a great deal of weight," Langner recalled.

But, oddly enough, the life of activity on which O'Neill now embarked
—for him it was the equivalent of a wild social whirl—appeared to
soothe his nerves.

"After a few weeks in New York," Langner said, "Gene's health
improved, especially after he began to work on *The Iceman Cometh.*
He enjoyed his visits to the Guild every afternoon and he began to put
his manuscript into final shape. We all felt the fact that he was at
work again in the theatre was doing wonders in bringing him back
to health."

O'Neill did not confine his new gregariousness to Guild personnel.
He resumed his friendship with a number of people he had not seen
in years, made new friends, went out to bicycle races, ball games, race
tracks, prizefights and Fifty-second Street jazz places, and granted
interviews and entertained visitors. He bought a television set and went
to movies. On a few occasions he dined out and attended the theatre.
He also sat through a fellow playwright's dress rehearsal, sipped champagne
at a party, flirted with young actresses, and even made a speech at a
semi-formal banquet. He spoke of settling down permanently somewhere
near New York and expressed regret at having stayed away from Broadway
so long. In fact, he totally reversed his ivory tower attitude, and to many
of his friends he seemed to have acquired a new vitality.

The pattern that had followed his return from France and precipitated
his flight to Georgia and subsequent breakdown and immolation in
California was beginning to repeat itself. This time, though, the state
of social euphoria was far more pronounced and lasted for over a year.

One of O'Neill's earliest visitors at the Barclay was the theatrical
producer Max Gordon, who had co-sponsored the vaudeville production
of *In the Zone* in 1917. Gordon entertained O'Neill for three hours one

afternoon, telling him George M. Cohan jokes and singing him Cohan songs, among them some unpublished ones that Gordon had committed to memory.

"O'Neill loved the songs," Gordon recalled. "They almost lifted him out of his seat. He particularly enjoyed my telling him what Cohan had said to me when I once expressed the fear that the success of radio would hurt theatre business. 'Max, don't worry about radio,' said Cohan. 'The only thing that will keep an American in a room is a dame.'"

Other visitors to the Barclay included Richard Weeks, O'Neill's Princeton classmate and fellow culprit in the affair of the stationmaster. "Gene remembered every detail of the jam we got ourselves into at Princeton," Weeks said. "He loved to reminisce about those days. Mrs. O'Neill told me my visit had done Gene a lot of good and she asked me to come again. I saw Gene several times after that."

Walter Casey, a boyhood friend from New London, also was warmly welcomed by O'Neill. Casey, several years O'Neill's junior, had worked on the New London *Telegraph* with O'Neill, and hero-worshiped him. Now living in New York and doing free-lance writing, he maintained his ties with New London, which was one of the reasons O'Neill enjoyed seeing him. (When Casey's sister, Anne, who lived in New London, attended a dress rehearsal of *The Iceman Cometh*, she told O'Neill, "Every time I go past your house, I think of you." O'Neill answered, "Every time you go past, give it my love.")

Among O'Neill's companions when he went out on the town were Joe Heidt, the Guild's press agent, and Winfield Aronberg, his attorney, who had "inherited" O'Neill as a client in 1944 after Harry Weinberger's death.

"I took O'Neill and sometimes Carlotta, too, to hockey games and bike races," Heidt said. "There were fistfights at a couple of the hockey games, and O'Neill got a big kick out of that."

O'Neill's strong point of contact with Aronberg, a man with wild eyebrows and an ebullient manner, was their common love of jazz.

"Gene would phone me, and we'd hit the jazz joints along Fifty-second Street," Aronberg recalled. "Once in a while, he'd take a sip of a drink, just for appearances. Gene would applaud and thank the musicians when he liked a number. He once inscribed a book to me: 'To my office hound lawyer and jazz around pal.'

"He liked going to the races, too. We'd hire a limousine to drive us out to the track. He was a $10 bettor."

One of the first services Aronberg performed for O'Neill was settling his alimony problems with Agnes.

"Gene had been paying alimony for years," Aronberg said. "I wrote Agnes saying I thought it would be to her benefit to make a settlement. I meant to imply that a settlement would leave her free to remarry. She agreed to the settlement."

Aronberg did not hit it off well with Carlotta. "She was too much of the grande dame for me," he said. "She fancied herself an old-line aristocrat." He made no effort to disguise his feelings for Carlotta, and she did not put herself out to be cordial to him. "She hates my guts," he once told O'Neill. O'Neill did not contradict him.

During the early winter and spring of 1946 O'Neill also saw a good deal of Saxe Commins, who was working with him on the book version of *The Iceman Cometh,* and of Robert Edmond Jones, who was to design the sets for the play. In addition, he spent some time with Charles O'Brien Kennedy and resumed his personal contact with George Jean Nathan. Barrett Clark also came to see him. Clark, who had not seen O'Neill in ten years, was shocked by his altered appearance when he visited him in March. Clark found him to be "painfully thin and shrunken," looking "as though he should be in a hospital."

Clark also discovered that O'Neill's "interest in the world about him seemed deeper and broader than before."

"He seemed no longer to object to being a part of the practical theatre; he made no complaints about publicity, casting, having to meet strangers," Clark recorded. "I thought I could detect in him, even, a little pleasure and excitement in the prospect of casting his new play, being on hand at rehearsals."

O'Neill also renewed his acquaintance with S. N. Behrman and attended a rehearsal of Behrman's play, *Dunnigan's Daughter,* which the Theatre Guild was producing. Behrman was puzzled when O'Neill told Langner afterward that the play was "much too optimistic."

"That's an odd thing to say," Behrman remarked, and Langner explained that O'Neill was deeply pessimistic about the state of the world; he had recently observed, said Langner, that the atomic bomb was a wonderful invention because it might annihilate the whole human race.

As a safeguard, in the event that the human race survived, O'Neill, on his arrival in New York, made a careful disposition of *Long Day's Journey Into Night.* On November 29, 1945, he carried the manuscript of the play to the offices of Random House, where Bennett Cerf and Saxe Commins were waiting for him. He told them, as he had told a number of other people, that the play must not be published until twenty-five years after his death.

"When O'Neill gave us the script of *Long Day's Journey*, he wanted to seal it up," Cerf recalled. "He insisted it be done with red sealing wax. We sent out for some, but when it arrived, none of us knew how to use it. We used up two boxes of matches and got wax all over our hands before we finally managed to seal the envelope that held the script. After the ceremony, we put it in our downstairs safe."

Before leaving, O'Neill dictated and signed a covering document, asking Cerf to countersign it:

"I am this day depositing with you, on condition that it not be opened by you until twenty-five years after my death, a sealed copy of the manuscript of an original play which I have written, entitled *Long Day's Journey Into Night*." The document went on to stipulate that when the play was published twenty-five years after his death, an advance of $5,000 should be paid to his "Executors or Administrators."

Cerf accepted the terms on behalf of Random House.

(When, about two years after O'Neill's death, Carlotta asked Random House to break the seal and publish the play, Cerf refused to do so, believing himself honor-bound to respect the stipulation of the document. Carlotta, who, under the terms of O'Neill's will, possessed the legal right to dispose as she saw fit of O'Neill's literary estate, thereupon withdrew the manuscript from Random House. She presented it to the Yale University Press, which published the play in February, 1956, and found itself with a best seller. Carlotta's explanation for disregarding her husband's recorded wishes was that O'Neill had agreed to withhold publication of the play only because his son, Eugene Jr., had asked him to, and that Eugene's subsequent death had removed the restriction. O'Neill himself had changed his mind frequently and radically about how he wanted his plays handled, and he had, in a sense, bequeathed to Carlotta the right to be inconsistent for him. Around the time that she gave the manuscript to Yale, Carlotta also sent a copy to Dr. Karl Ragnar Gierow, director of the Royal Dramatic Theatre in Stockholm, and a Nobel Prize judge. Dag Hammarskjöld had approached Carlotta at the request of Dr. Gierow, who knew of O'Neill's admiration for the Royal Dramatic Theatre, particularly for its successful production, in 1953, of *A Moon for the Misbegotten*. The Secretary-General persuaded Carlotta to allow *Long Day's Journey Into Night* to be done in Stockholm. The Royal Dramatic Theatre produced it with stunning success on February 2, 1956, and the play received world-wide attention. Almost every prominent American producer and director asked for permission to stage the play on Broadway, but Carlotta at first refused to release it. On April 7, 1956, for instance, she wrote to the Broadway producer Alexander H. Cohen, informing him that she was carrying out her husband's wishes in withholding the play from production in the United States. O'Neill, she said, had wished her to publish the play, but had instructed her not to allow it to be produced. However, a few months later she decided to give the script to the young producers, José Quintero, Theodore Mann and Leigh Connell, who had won acclaim for their revival of *The Iceman Cometh* at their off-Broadway theatre, the Circle in the Square. With Quintero as director, the Broadway production of *Long Day's Journey* was a huge success and won for O'Neill a posthumous, fourth Pulitzer Prize.)

In the spring of 1946 the O'Neills moved from their hotel to a penthouse apartment at 35 East Eighty-fourth Street, which had been occupied, until his death that April, by Edward Sheldon. Always at home with his own "ghosts of the past," O'Neill was spiritually attuned to the ghost of his tragic fellow dramatist. Sheldon had been blind and partially paralyzed for twenty years when he collapsed in his apartment of a coronary thrombosis. Possibly Carlotta found the atmosphere less congenial, though she labored, as usual, to make a comfortable and gracious home for her husband. She decorated the six large rooms in bright colors, moved in some favorite Chinese furniture, and bought a canary (not, as O'Neill had threatened, a buzzard), which she named Jeremiah.

But the strain of an urban existence soon began to fray Carlotta's nerves. A conciliatory note written to Carlotta by O'Neill on their fifteenth wedding anniversary in a shaky, almost illegible hand, indicated that all had not been perfectly serene between them:

". . . I wish you could . . . forgive all the mistakes and injuries done one to another through thoughtlessness or lack of understanding.

"In justice, as everyone but ourselves seems to know, our marriage has been the most successful and happy of any we know—until late years.

"Here's for a new beginning! . . ."

O'Neill was now at work preparing *The Iceman Cometh* for production. It had been decided that Eddie Dowling would direct the play, and that it would be too much for him to take on the role of Hickey as well. James Barton, who had been scheduled to play Harry Hope, was assigned the part of Hickey, and Dudley Digges was cast as Hope.

O'Neill incorporated a few songs into the play, and he paid careful attention to their rendering. One of them was a rowdy ballad, "The Sailor Lad," which O'Neill wanted sung drunkenly in Act One by Willie

Oban. He asked Saxe Commins' wife, Dorothy, who was a concert pianist, to help put the music on paper.

"Gene sat beside me at the piano," Dorothy Commins recalled, "and croaked the words slowly—'Jack, oh, Jack, was a sailor lad,' and so on, with all the 'rap, rap, raps,' and I played the notes and finally got it all down."

In his inscription to her copy of *The Iceman Cometh* O'Neill later wrote: "With much love and devotion and gratitude for your collaboration with me with your 'The Sailor Lad' music."

As was usual with an O'Neill play, there was the problem of script length.

"I marked lots of places for possible cuts," Langner said. "O'Neill then went over my suggestions and wrote 'Yes' or 'No' in the margin next to the places I'd marked. There were mostly 'No's,' and the 'No's' were written in a firm hand. The 'Yes's' were written in a trembling hand—obviously with reluctance."

O'Neill ultimately consented to considerable cutting, but not enough to satisfy Langner.

"On one occasion," according to Langner, "I told Gene that at my request my assistant, Paul Crabtree, who played the part of Don Parritt, had counted the number of times a certain point was repeated, and this, in actual fact, was eighteen times. Gene looked at me and replied in a particularly quiet voice, 'I *intended* it to be repeated eighteen times!' "

The Guild had assigned one of its production assistants, Shirlee Weingarten, then in her early twenties, to provide O'Neill with secretarial assistance. Shirlee, a slender, dark-haired girl with enormous blue eyes and a pretty, sensitive face, quickly endeared herself to O'Neill.

"At our first meeting I was scared," she later recalled. "O'Neill had been an institution to me. The day after we were introduced, he was given a little office at the Guild, where he arranged to come every afternoon at two o'clock. He was in his office ahead of me the first day he came in to work, and when I arrived he stood up."

"Please don't stand up, you don't have to do that sort of thing in an office," Shirlee murmured.

"But offices would be so much more pleasant if men would observe the rules," O'Neill replied.

Shirlee offered O'Neill a cup of tea, which he accepted. But his hands trembled so that he could not get the cup to his mouth. Embarrassed for his sake, Shirlee remarked that the day was too warm for tea and asked if O'Neill wouldn't prefer Coca-Cola.

O'Neill, embarrassed by Shirlee's embarrassment, agreed to the Coca-

Cola, and she gratefully hurried to a nearby store and returned with a bottle and two straws, which O'Neill had no trouble managing.

Shirlee worked with O'Neill almost daily, typing not only the edited version of *The Iceman,* but also the revised versions of *A Moon for the Misbegotten* and *A Touch of the Poet.* She had to use a magnifying glass to read O'Neill's small writing.

"He would go over the typed pages very carefully," Shirlee said. "He knew exactly where every comma should be, without referring to the original script."

O'Neill grew so dependent on Shirlee's assistance that he asked her to be present at all rehearsals when the play was ready for production in September.

"I became a cigarette fiend at rehearsals," she said. "O'Neill smoked a lot and it was difficult for him to light a cigarette because of his trembling hands. I thought it would embarrass him if I lit his cigarette for him, so every time he reached for a cigarette, I took one, too; that way I could light his without making a production of it."

In her copy of *The Iceman,* O'Neill later wrote: "With affection and gratitude for all she has done since the first typing job—all the kindnesses in the many small things that only the sensitive do, or the sensitive appreciate. I have a guilty feeling I have not been sufficiently appreciative at times, or have even been downright rude, taking it for granted you should light cigarettes for playwrights!"

Carlotta also became fond of Shirlee, and Shirlee warmly returned her affection. She dined at the O'Neills' penthouse on several occasions and confided in Carlotta about her impending marriage to Steve Alexander, the production assistant on *The Iceman.*

Shirlee gradually acquired a cozy knowledge of O'Neill's and his wife's points of view on various subjects. They told her, for instance, of their battle with their newly acquired television set. They bought it mainly because O'Neill wanted to watch the fights, but apparently they mistrusted it from the beginning. One night they were watching a particularly exciting bout when the picture suddenly faded away.

"O'Neill was fit to be tied," Shirlee said. "He made a series of phone calls, until he got the home telephone number of the salesman who had sold him the set. He was terribly insulted, and he demanded that the set be removed the next day. It was."

O'Neill also told Shirlee that he loved French prizefights, because the spectators took such an active part in them.

"He talked about a fight he saw in France when the spectators beat up the referee because they thought he had given an unfair decision,"

Shirlee said. "I asked him if he approved of that, and he said, of course he did—the referee's decision *had* been unfair."

The Iceman Cometh was scheduled for a Broadway opening on October 9, 1946, and extra rehearsals had been allotted because O'Neill, once again, declined to submit to a pre-Broadway tryout. He was never absent from rehearsals, however, and he managed to find time to flirt quietly with the actresses in the play. The cast called for only three women—the status-conscious prostitutes who insist on being called tarts, not whores. Marcella Markham, a young actress with flaming red hair, had been personally cast by O'Neill as Cora.

"I was eager to do well in the part," she later recalled, "and one day at rehearsals, with the Stanislavsky idea in mind, I asked O'Neill if he'd really known a Cora."

"Now, Marcella," O'Neill chided her, "do you want to know, did I know a Cora, or how well did I know a Cora?" Marcella blushed, and O'Neill smiled at her confusion.

"He loved to tease the girls in the play," she said, "not only me, but Ruth Gilbert, whom he knew from *Ah, Wilderness!* Once during a rehearsal he happened to overhear a kidding conversation I had with one of the actors. The actor was propositioning me, and I told him he was marvelous, but he didn't have the right smell. O'Neill told the actor, 'Too bad, boy.' When the actor walked away, O'Neill asked me, 'Do I have the right smell?' I told him, 'Positively.' Even though he was obviously ill, he had a remarkable vitality. And he was the most gentlemanly man I've ever known."

During a later rehearsal Marcella told him she had heard a rumor that he had once been an anarchist. "Did you ever blow anything up?" she asked him. O'Neill replied: "The only thing I ever blew up was the foam off a schooner of beer."

O'Neill's vitality was also apparent to his director, Eddie Dowling.

One day during the dress-rehearsal period Dowling arranged for O'Neill, himself and the whole cast of nineteen to have lunch at Gilhuly's, a well-known Eighth Avenue saloon. They began walking from the theatre, the actors still in the *Iceman* costumes and make-up that made them look like bums. On the way along Eighth Avenue they picked up half a dozen real bums, who followed the actors, thinking they were fellow derelicts. When they arrived at Gilhuly's, the owner started throwing the bums out—including some of the actors. O'Neill asked Gilhuly to let them all stay. The real bums lunched there, along with the actors, as O'Neill's guests.

[866]

Another time, when O'Neill and Dowling were about to enter Gilhuly's for lunch, a tall man wearing a black beard came up to them and, to Dowling's amazement, addressed O'Neill as "Dad." It was Eugene Jr. He asked if he could look in on a dress rehearsal. O'Neill said he could if it was all right with Dowling, and Dowling told him to come that afternoon. After the rehearsal Eugene told his father the play was wonderful.

That evening, though a light rain was falling, O'Neill decided to walk all the way home from the theatre to his apartment. Dowling was afraid the walk would be too much for him, but O'Neill insisted that he would enjoy it. Dowling decided to accompany him and as they walked O'Neill talked about Eugene Jr., with warmth and admiration for his accomplishments as a scholar.

Eugene Jr. attended several other rehearsals, and his father was always glad to see him. It had become uncomfortable for father and son to meet in O'Neill's home because Carlotta's affection for Eugene Jr. had cooled. Eugene Jr. knew that Carlotta disapproved of his leftist political affiliations and he enjoyed teasing her about it. "How's the old Tory?" became his habitual greeting when he and Carlotta met.

"He changed suddenly," Carlotta said years later. "He grew a beard, got a fat belly from drinking and became a Communist."

The beard was grown as payment for an election bet and was considered rather attractive by Eugene's friends. The fat belly was barely noticeable, for Eugene's large frame could carry considerable weight; it was true that he was a consistent drinker, but none of his friends considered him an alcoholic; at his worst, he never matched his father's youthful excesses. It was also true that he had been a Communist for six months, before the war.

"Gene's politics were mixed up," his friend Frank Meyer, a radically reformed ex-Communist himself, once said. "His general tendency was anarchistic. He was anti-war [as his father had been in 1914]. But he tried to enlist, only to be turned down because of the injury to his skull as a result of his boyhood bicycle accident. He tried to get into the OSS but was rejected. Politically, I was moving to the right much faster than he, and we had a lot of arguments."

Eugene, at thirty-six, was teaching classics at Yale and had co-edited a two-volume edition of the Greek drama, which was acknowledged as a major contribution to scholarship. But his political and personal life were becoming increasingly unstable, and Yale was beginning to have misgivings about him. He had been divorced from his second wife and was living with a woman named Ruth Lander, who was separated from her husband.

"Gene was running away from his real gifts," Meyer said. "He was diverting his real talent. By 1946 he had half a dozen things on his mind other than his teaching career at Yale. He was interested—foolishly, I thought—in mass education, and was beginning to think in terms of radio and television commentary. He also had an idea he could act—he did have a wonderful voice."

Carlotta was much more disturbed by Eugene's activities than his father was.

"I used to argue with Eugene Jr.," she said. "I told him my first husband was a Tory, and a brilliant man, known all over Europe. Eugene's father would just sit there and never interfere. After Eugene left, I would say: I make a home for you. How can you sit there and let him talk to me that way? Gene would say, Why don't you leave the room when he comes? Why don't you go into the bedroom?"

Carlotta was more kindly disposed toward Shane—for a time. When the O'Neills arrived in New York at the end of 1945, Shane was working as a mechanic and living in lower Manhattan, on King Street, with Catherine Givens, to whom he had been married in 1944. At the instigation of Eugene Jr., who was trying to keep a big brother's eye on Shane, O'Neill saw Shane and his wife.

"I liked Gene," Catherine once said of her father-in-law. "He was fun to be with. But he wasn't a man you could turn to when you needed help. I think he felt, somehow, that his children had betrayed him."

Catherine gave birth to a son on November 16, 1945, and she and Shane named him Eugene for his grandfather. O'Neill never saw the child, but Carlotta visited Catherine at the hospital and later called at their cold-water flat on King Street, bringing a layette.

A few weeks later Catherine and Shane were invited to dinner by Carlotta and spent a pleasant evening with her and O'Neill. The older O'Neills continued to see both Shane and Catherine at intervals until the end of the year. Their cordial relationship was abruptly broken off early in 1946.

On February 10, at 2:03 P.M., Eugene O'Neill III, aged two months, twenty-four days, was brought to St. Vincent's Hospital by ambulance. The examining doctor pronounced him dead on arrival. According to the records of the Chief Medical Examiner's Office at Bellevue Hospital, where an autopsy was performed the following day, Shane had told the examining doctor, Peter Castiglia, that Catherine had last seen the infant alive and well at 4 A.M. on February 10. At noon, she awoke and found him in his crib, not breathing. "The infant showed evidence of neglect,"

[868]

Dr. Castiglia's report continued, "with maceration of scrotal tissue and lower abdomen, probably the result of unchanged diapers."

The death certificate listed the probable cause of death as "postural asphyxia from bed-clothes, accidental."

Carlotta was appalled when she heard the news, and later said that O'Neill was no less so.

Neither Shane nor his wife ever saw O'Neill again, but months later, O'Neill received a phone call saying Shane was ill and needed help. O'Neill agreed to send Winfield Aronberg, his friend and attorney, to visit Shane.

"Gene called me," Aronberg said, "and told me to see what I could do for Shane, who was then living in a little hotel in Greenwich Village. I took a friend who was a doctor along with me and we went up to Shane's room. I'd never met Shane, and we assumed the young man in the room was O'Neill's son. The doctor asked him to strip, examined him, and said there was nothing wrong with him."

Finally realizing the mistake in identities, the young man told Aronberg and the doctor that he was not Shane. He said he was a friend who had dropped in and been offered the use of the room by Shane, who had gone out to dinner.

"I called Gene and told him what had happened," Aronberg said. "He thought it was very funny."

The impending Broadway opening of the first new O'Neill play in more than twelve years and O'Neill's personal re-emergence from isolation did not go unmarked by the press. He was interviewed by a rash of newspaper and magazine reporters and within the next few months became the subject of a number of full-length studies, including a three-part Profile in *The New Yorker*.

Most of the reporters found him genial and expansive, if physically frail. Early that August he sat on the terrace of his penthouse and told the columnist Earl Wilson, among other things, that Carlotta could not join them because she was busy in the kitchen killing cockroaches. (The immaculate Carlotta was annoyed when Wilson printed this.)

A few weeks later O'Neill permitted Nathan to interview him for his column; for the benefit of Nathan's readers, O'Neill discussed not only his new plays but also, among other things, a scheme to open a saloon in partnership with Nathan.

He had tried to cut *The Iceman Cometh* by about three quarters of an hour, he told Nathan, but had been unable to cut it more than fifteen minutes. "If there are repetitions," he added, "they'll have to remain in, because I feel they are absolutely necessary to what I am trying to get over."

As for *A Moon for the Misbegotten,* he said, it would go into rehearsal immediately after *The Iceman Cometh* had opened and needed no cutting, "which gives me just that much extra time to eat spaghetti and lie in the sun and worry about the third play, *A Touch of the Poet.*"

As for the saloon, it was to be the realization of a boyhood ambition. "When these three plays of mine are on, why don't we open up one together?" Nathan quoted O'Neill. "Not in town, but somewhere out on Long Island near the ocean, because I still don't want to miss my swimming. You once said you had a good name for such a dump, 'High Dive.' It wouldn't cost us much to start it, and I'll throw in my old barroom piano that you drop nickels into. . . . It's in storage now and I'm getting lonesome for it. We might not make any money, considering that most of our friends would open charge accounts and lovably forget them, but it would be a great sensation again to eat up the free lunch."

On September 2 O'Neill held a press interview at the Theatre Guild, as he had done shortly before the production of *Mourning Becomes Electra.* As always, he was outspoken, taking little cognizance of whatever may have been the fashionable attitudes of the times. In an era of postwar optimism, and a surge of elation over his country's victorious emergence as the leading world power, O'Neill calmly expressed his view that the victory was a hollow one and that America was a flop.

"I had a French friend, one of the delegates at the San Franscisco Conference, who came to see me," O'Neill said. "I asked him, 'If it's not betraying any great secrets, what's really happening at the Conference?' He shrugged his shoulders and said, 'It's the League of Nations, only not so good.' And I believe it. Of course, I may be wrong. I nearly always am."

Reiterating the philosophy underlying his eleven-play cycle, he declared:

"I'm going on the theory that the United States, instead of being the most successful country in the world, is the greatest failure. It's the greatest failure because it was given everything, more than any other country. Through moving as rapidly as it has, it hasn't acquired any real roots. Its main idea is that everlasting game of trying to possess your own soul by the possession of something outside it, thereby losing your own soul and the thing outside of it, too.

"America is the prime example of this because it happened so quickly and with such immense resources. This was really said in the Bible much better. We are the greatest example of 'For what shall it profit a man, if he shall gain the whole world and lose his own soul?' We had so much and could have gone either way.

"If the human race is so damned stupid that in two thousand years it hasn't had brains enough to appreciate that the secret of happiness is contained in that one simple sentence, which you'd think any grammar school kid could understand and apply, then it's time we dumped it down the nearest drain and let the ants take over."

After allowing this statement to sink in, O'Neill shifted to a lighter vein, complaining half-jokingly of the fact that during his absence from New York "they tore down the old Cadillac Hotel where I was born." He added, "That was a dirty trick."

He then answered questions about *The Iceman Cometh* and his other unproduced plays, and said he hoped to resume writing soon.

"But the war has thrown me completely off base," he explained, "and I have to get back to a sense of writing being worthwhile.

"There is a feeling around, or I'm mistaken, of fate. Kismet, the negative fate; not in the Greek sense . . . It's struck me as time goes on, how something funny, even farcical, can suddenly without any apparent reason, break up into something gloomy and tragic. . . . A sort of unfair *non sequitur*, as though events, as though life, were being manipulated just to confuse us. I think I'm aware of comedy more than I ever was before; a big kind of comedy that doesn't stay funny very long. I've made some use of it in *The Iceman*. The first act is hilarious comedy, *I think*, but then some people may not even laugh. At any rate, the comedy breaks up and the tragedy comes on . . ."

When most of the members of the press had departed, an out-of-town reporter, Herbert Stoeckel, broached O'Neill about his plan to open a saloon in Long Island.

"I haven't forgotten about it," O'Neill told Stoeckel. "Nathan can handle the bar, but I want to be at the cash register." He added that living in a New York apartment was not his idea of living. "Our next and permanent home," he said, "will likely be on Long Island."

In a separate interview for *The New York Times Magazine* a few days later O'Neill once again sat for the writer-artist S. J. Woolf, who drew him with sunken cheeks and fiercely burning eyes. "Like Poe . . . he looks as if he were surrounded by an aura of mysterious sorrow," Woolf noted in his text.

O'Neill talked to Woolf of James O'Neill. "Almost the first words I remember my father saying," O'Neill remarked, are, 'the theatre is dying.'

[871]

And those words seem to me as true today as when he said them. But the theatre must be a hardy wench, for although she is still ailing, she will never die as long as she offers an escape."

Analyzing his father's era, he added:

"It was a prudish age which has left its impress in the form of present-day censorship. This to me is one of the biggest obstacles to the artistic development of the theatre. Now, before a play can be safely produced, somebody has to say it will not corrupt the morals of six-year-olds."

Switching to the topic of movies, O'Neill, who had finally decided to sell *Mourning Becomes Electra* to the films, remarked that, though he deplored the inroads of Hollywood into the Broadway theatre, it did not mean that he was opposed to motion pictures. "I enjoy many of them," he declared. "I recently saw a new picture based on the life of Nurse Kenny that I liked tremendously."

Rosalind Russell's performance in the role of Sister Kenny had helped influence O'Neill's decision to sell *Mourning Becomes Electra* to RKO, for it was Miss Russell who was to play Lavinia. But the most important factor in his decision was that Dudley Nichols would write, direct and produce the film. Having made up his mind to sell *Electra,* O'Neill set about being as picky as possible about the details.

After studying the contract, which covered something like fifty pages, O'Neill said to Shirlee Weingarten, "I think there's going to be trouble here."

Assuming he was serious, Shirlee asked, "What trouble?"

O'Neill told her that there was some small print that gave the movie company the jukebox rights. With a smile he added that he didn't know whether he should hand over those rights, as they might amount to something in the future.

Then O'Neill advised RKO that he would sign the contract only under condition that they buy a jukebox for him. It was his idea of a joke about all the financial mistakes he had made in the past with regard to his works. When RKO was unsuccessful in unearthing a jukebox, O'Neill signed the contract anyway. (The film was released in the winter of 1947. Despite a cast that included, in addition to Miss Russell, Katina Paxinou, Raymond Massey, Michael Redgrave, Leo Genn and Kirk Douglas, the picture was both an artistic and a commercial failure.)

Around this time O'Neill was also the subject of a long article for *Life* by Tom Prideaux. O'Neill gave Prideaux permission to print a passage from the sealed *Long Day's Journey Into Night,* telling him it was the best play he had ever written but otherwise maintaining what Prideaux called his "mysterious silence" about the work. The passage was Edmund

Tyrone's monologue about the sea's mystic influence on his soul.

To obtain illustrations for the article, *Life* sent the photographer Arnold Newman to O'Neill's apartment. The magazine acceded to O'Neill's request that Newman spend only thirty minutes with his subject.

"Thirty minutes was just about the time it usually took me to put my equipment away," Newman later said. "But I went up with Tom and rushed through the assignment. We had to move some furniture, and when the shooting was over we tried to put a Chinese cabinet back in place. O'Neill insisted on helping. I grabbed the legs of the cabinet and some delicate, carved wood came apart in my hands. I was horrified and offered to pay for the damage. O'Neill wouldn't hear of it, said it was nobody's fault. He was charming.

"Then he took me to the door to say good-by, and we got into a conversation about painters and art that lasted a half hour; this, after being warned not to stay more than thirty minutes.

"He invited me to a rehearsal of *The Iceman Cometh,* and several *Life* editors asked if I'd take along some pictures of O'Neill and ask him to sign them. I took a dozen prints with me, and, after the rehearsal, I started giving them to him one at a time. Because of his tremor, it took him almost ten minutes to sign just two pictures. He would have signed them all, but I told him that was all I needed. I didn't have the heart to ask him to sign any more. He then asked me to photograph his wife, but somehow we never got around to making the arrangements."

Three days before the opening of *The Iceman Cometh,* O'Neill was interviewed for *The Times* Sunday drama section. Recovering from a bad cold and dressed in slacks, sport jacket and red carpet slippers, he received his interviewer, Karl Schriftgiesser. He said he was confident that the play could hold the interest of the audience throughout its four-hour running time, and added: "I do not think that you can write anything of value or understanding about the present. You can only write about life if it is far enough in the past. The present is too much mixed up with superficial values; you can't know which thing is important and which is not. The past which I have chosen is one I knew. . . .

"You ask, what is the significance, what do these people [of *The Iceman*] mean to us today? Well, all I can say is that it is a play about pipe dreams. And the philosophy is that there is always one dream left, one final dream, no matter how low you have fallen, down there at the bottom of the bottle. I know, because I saw it."

Before the play's opening O'Neill took the trouble to autograph advance copies of the published version of *The Iceman,* scheduled to be released on the same day as the Broadway première, for every member of the cast and production staff.

"Carlotta called me to get the list of names," Shirlee Weingarten said. "It must have taken O'Neill days to write all the inscriptions, because of the difficulty he had using a pen."

The last O'Neill play to be produced on Broadway during his lifetime opened at 4:30 on October 9, 1946, a Thursday afternoon.

O'Neill gave his opening-night tickets to Aronberg and spent the evening at home. In theatre circles the opening was considered a momentous event and more than the usual number of celebrities crowded into the Martin Beck Theatre, gulped down an intermission dinner at the theatrical restaurant, Sardi's, and hurried back to their seats. Although many members of the audience were fascinated, a good number were puzzled and bored—a fact that must, in retrospect, be blamed to some extent on the production. (Ten years later, when the play was revived at off-Broadway's Circle in the Square under José Quintero's direction, and with Jason Robards, Jr., in the role of Hickey, it was far more successful than the original; it made a star of Robards, established Quintero's reputation, and led to a complete re-evaluation of both the play and O'Neill's stature.)

Lawrence Langner, though unwilling to shoulder the blame for the inadequacies of the Guild production (he has justifiably pointed out that O'Neill had considerable supervisory power at all stages), later conceded that James Barton's performance in the pivotal role of Hickey was a disappointment:

"During the opening night dinner intermission," Langner wrote, "unfortunately for us all, James Barton . . . was forced to entertain a crowd of friends . . . in his dressing room, instead of resting, so that by the time he came to make the famous speech which lasted nearly twenty minutes in the fifth act, he had little or no voice left with which to deliver it. As a result, the last act, which should have been the strongest of all, fell apart in the center. . . . As it was, *The Iceman Cometh* had a considerable run, and one which I think would have been much longer had not James Barton developed a case of laryngitis, so that it became increasingly difficult to hear him during the latter part of the play."

Langner telephoned a report to O'Neill during the dinner intermission, and when the last-act curtain fell he went to the O'Neills' apartment, accompanied by other members of the Guild.

"I could not help remarking to Gene that, in my opinion, *The Iceman Cometh*, like *Saint Joan*, would never be properly presented until after the

[874]

expiration of the copyright, when it might be possible to cut it," Langner said. "Gene smiled at me in his usual disarming way and said it would have to wait for just that." Later O'Neill gave Langner a copy of the manuscript, on whose first page he had written: "To Lawrence Langner, The hell with your cuts!"

Most of the daily newspaper critics applauded the Guild production. As for the play itself, the critics were divided among those who considered it a masterpiece, those who praised it with reservation, and those who found it a great disappointment. Most of the reviewers, even those favorably disposed, complained that the play was unnecessarily long and repetitious.

Richard Watts, Jr., led off the praise in the New York *Post,* writing that *The Iceman* was "a superb drama of splendid and imposing stature, which is at once powerful, moving, beautiful, eloquent and compassionate.

"There is a wild, cascading power in O'Neill dramas, which, if tamed, would destroy the freedom and scope of his fierce and brooding imagination, and the excessive length, the sometimes unnecessary verbiage and the deceptively leisured interludes of an O'Neill play are a small price to pay for keeping his essential quality intact. Editing might make 'The Iceman' seem more efficient, but it would endanger the magnitude of its spirit. . . ."

John Chapman, of the *Daily News,* found it "a magnificent drama—magnificent in plan, in size, in scope, in depth.

"It is a frightening play, too—" Chapman went on, "terrifying and shocking . . . a powerful and moving thing, a part of life itself. A great dramatist has cut the ordinary commercial stage down to its tiny real size."

Brooks Atkinson, on *The Times,* felt that O'Neill had written "one of his best plays" and saluted him as "a man who writes with the wonder and heart of a poet." Murmuring gently about its great length, Atkinson wrote:

"But if that is the way Mr. O'Neill wants to afflict harmless playgoers, let us accept our fate with nothing more than a polite demurrer. For the only thing that matters is that he has plunged again into the black quag·mire of man's illusions and composed a rigadoon of death as strange and elemental as his first works."

Ward Morehouse of the *Sun* said "for all its long-windedness" the play "has power and intensity," and Robert Coleman of the *Mirror* predicted it would be "a terrific hit."

Howard Barnes, critic for the *Herald Tribune,* was among those who found the play unsatisfactory. He said O'Neill had "peopled the stage of the Martin Beck with fascinating characters," had "involved them in a magnificent riddle of life and death," and then "left them and an audience singularly untouched."

Writing for the newspaper *PM,* Louis Kronenberger echoed Barnes's disappointment.

". . . to say that I do not find 'The Iceman' very impressive is not to imply that a great deal of it is not interesting, is not individual, is not expert, is not finely theatrical—or that in a theatre where mere slickness is too quickly applauded and real seriousness is too seldom apparent, 'The Iceman' is not worth having or seeing. It should be seen . . .

"But 'The Iceman' leaves me dissatisfied . . . it is much too long for what it says . . . [O'Neill's] play is more longwindedly explicit than it is in any way profound."

John Mason Brown, discussing the play in the *Saturday Review of Literature* some days later, found more merit in it than Kronenberger, but felt there was "no excuse for his having said at least twice everything that could have been better stated by being suggested," and added that if anyone but O'Neill had written the play it would have been drastically, and properly, cut.

Most severe in his criticism was Robert Garland, of the *Journal American,* who said the play was "neither first-rate Broadway, first-rate Theatre Guild, nor first-rate Eugene O'Neill." (A few days later in the same newspaper, however, George Jean Nathan said, in his feature column, that the play had his total endorsement. "Hallelujah, Hosanna, hail, heil, hurrah, huzza banzai and gesundheit!" said Nathan quietly. "With the appearance of Eugene O'Neill's 'The Iceman Cometh,' our theatre becomes dramatically alive again.")

O'Neill was disappointed by the play's reception but unshaken in his own high opinion of it and far from despondent. An interview in *Time* twelve days after *The Iceman* had opened and five days after he had reached his fifty-eighth birthday, quoted him as saying, "I'm happier now than I've ever been—I couldn't ever be negative about life. On that score, you've got to decide Yes or No. And I'll always say Yes. Yes, I'm happy."

Time followed this ebullient—for O'Neill—comment with its appraisal of O'Neill as "a master craftsman of the theatre," but not "a great dramatist." "O'Neill does not seem to be a man of great, searching or original intelligence," said *Time,* adding, however: "But as a playwright, O'Neill remains the greatest master of theatre the U.S. has ever produced."

Many other publications, both in the United States and abroad, chose this period to review the body of O'Neill's work and a surprising number of them took a far less flattering viewpoint—both of *The Iceman* and his other plays—than *Time.* During the next few years O'Neill's stature underwent a steady decline, and the consistent sniping of small but shrill voices did much to undermine his already ragged health.

"Curiously, *The Iceman Cometh*, like any great play, reveals its reviewers more than they reveal the play," Dudley Nichols remarked, on the occasion of the play's successful off-Broadway revival. "All of them complain of its length. Yet they are held by it to the end. What is really at fault is ourselves. We have lost the faculty of sustained attention.

"I use the phrase which Gene used in telling me, years ago, why he was reluctant to have the play produced even the first time. He said we have been conditioned by radio, TV, the movies, advertising, capsule news and a nervous brevity in everything we do, to a point where we have lost the power of sustained attention, which full-bodied works of art demand.

"Unless something moves and jerks, we soon turn away from it. If it doesn't chatter or talk like a machine gun, we don't listen for long. [Walter] Winchell knows this perfectly—he adopted a style which can hold anyone's attention for fifteen minutes and make what he says sound important no matter how trivial it may be. Winchell is a master of the modern style. He is its arch-creator. Joshua Logan catches this style in the theatre; he makes things happen for the eye all the time, no matter whether the play is saying anything or not. Now, a trivial play can be all movement, but a great play cannot. . . .

"The truth is, about *The Iceman Cometh*, all kinds of things are happening all the time, but you have to listen and watch, and you hear repetition because that is the way O'Neill planned it, so that you cannot miss his meaning, and the emotions generated by his drama."

Late in 1946 O'Neill answered a letter from Tennessee Williams, who had written to him in praise of *The Iceman*. He said Williams' note had been particularly welcome because it came at a time when he was "down in the dumps." ("O'Neill," Williams said, years later, in recalling the exchange of correspondence, "gave birth to the American theatre and died for it.")

It was another year before the accumulated tension of public-under-evaluation, continued inability to write, and the pressure of a new production caught up with O'Neill. During the next few months his geniality and social expansiveness reached an unprecedented high.

At the end of November he accepted an invitation to dine with Russel Crouse and his wife at their home and to meet the Irving Berlins.

Carlotta called Crouse before the evening of their date to say she and O'Neill had decided to come after dinner, because O'Neill was having too much difficulty with his tremor to be comfortable dining with strangers.

She explained that she had to cut his food for him. Crouse said he would ask the Berlins to come after dinner, instead.

"Gene and Carlotta came for dinner," Crouse said, "and at nine the Berlins arrived, wary of the meeting themselves. I found out later they'd told their chauffeur to wait, thinking they'd stay for a short time. They stayed until two o'clock.

"Berlin started to play some of his songs on the piano, and before long O'Neill was standing next to him, croaking along with the tunes. Berlin went on to other popular songs after he'd exhausted his own.

At 11:30, the Howard Lindsays and the Bennett Cerfs arrived, having been summoned by Crouse when he saw how well things were going.

"Carlotta, who had been a little stiff at first, had fun too, after a while," Crouse recalled. "And Gene had the time of his life. Carlotta told me later that Gene had been so stimulated he had not been able to sleep for hours after he got home."

She wrote Crouse a note thanking him for "making Gene so happy."

Inspired by the success of Crouse's Irving Berlin evening, Cerf, soon after, invited O'Neill to his home for a Burl Ives evening.

Ives sang after dinner and later O'Neill joined him in some sea chanties, Ives picking up the accompaniment.

"The songs got dirtier and dirtier," said Cerf, "and Carlotta finally went home by herself. I took Gene home at 3 A.M."

Cerf did not receive a "thank you" note from Carlotta.

On December 5, Crouse invited the O'Neills to accompany him to a performance of the Berlin musical *Annie Get Your Gun,* starring Ethel Merman, and after some hesitation they accepted.

"Carlotta made me promise not to let anyone know they were going," Crouse said. "She was afraid Gene would be swamped by acquaintances and autograph hunters. They both enjoyed the show, and, afterwards, I took them backstage to meet Merman. They spent about an hour in her dressing room. She and Gene got on very well. Chorus kids kept coming in for autographs and Gene had a wonderful time."

Carlotta, however, was not enjoying her husband's social blossoming as much as he seemed to be. O'Neill was dispelling in only a few months the aura of unapproachability which she had helped him nurture for years; he appeared to be responding too readily to the admiration of attractive young actresses; and Carlotta, at fifty-eight, though still lovely, could no longer compete on the level of glamour that had been her mainstay for so many years. In addition, she was concerned about O'Neill's health and was worried, justifiably as it turned out, that too much social exposure would wear him down. It was on her that the burden fell when

O'Neill was in ill-health, and he had several bouts of flu and nerves during this period.

In November, for example, Carlotta wrote for O'Neill to Mrs. Clayton Hamilton, who had sent word of her husband's death (Mrs. Hamilton subsequently published the letter in an article for *Theatre Arts Magazine*): "I am writing to you because it is so terribly difficult for [Gene] to write. You no doubt know he has paralysis agitans, which is heart breaking to us who love him." And on the same date Carlotta typed a letter dictated by O'Neill to Charles O'Brien Kennedy, in which he wrote, "I've been laid up not from punches [a reference to the criticism of *Iceman*] but from just plain fatigue and flu."

A reflection of the state of stress that existed between O'Neill and Carlotta was manifested in a note he wrote to her at the end of the year and which, together with a number of other love letters, notes and dedications, has been reproduced in a volume called *Inscriptions*, privately printed by the Yale University Library, under Carlotta's supervision):

". . . I am sorry for the unhappiness I have caused you. How unhappy it has made me, you have seen and know.

"Let us forget and forgive, Darling . . . We have love still, Sweetheart. We have the chance of a new life!"

LXI

A Moon for the Misbegotten, WHICH THE THEATRE GUILD decided to put into rehearsal early in 1947, was a quick disaster—a playwright's and producer's nightmare: O'Neill was displeased from the start with some of the casting (though, of course, he had a hand in it); he became ill during rehearsals with one of his habitual respiratory infections; in spite of his antipathy to tryouts, the production was sent out of town and was met with the same sort of puerile censorship that had beset *All God's Chillun Got Wings, Desire Under the Elms* and *Strange Interlude*.

The production never reached New York and it wasn't until ten years later that the play was presented posthumously on Broadway. Since then it has had several productions, but it has not yet come into its own in America. Its power and beauty may not be fully appreciated until it is offered, some ideal day, in repertory with *Long Day's Journey Into Night* and with the same actor alternating in the role of the 1912 Jamie Tyrone and the 1926 Jamie Tyrone.

The major casting problem, of course, is the twenty-eight-year-old Josie Hogan, who not only has to be huge, but must possess the range and experience of an enormously seasoned actress.

When the Theatre Guild began casting, O'Neill insisted that all three major roles—Josie, her father, Hogan, and Tyrone—be filled by actors of Irish descent. Langner and his associates interviewed countless women for the role of Josie. Marcella Markham was among those who felt she had a chance of getting the part, but she was abruptly disqualified when it became known she was Jewish.

"We just killed ourselves trying to find Irish actors," Langner said. "Judy Holliday has never forgiven me for not letting her read for the part; I had to tell her she couldn't because Gene wanted only Irish."

The actress who finally won the role was Mary Welch. (Miss Welch kept voluminous notes about her experiences with the play, and later based an article on them, which appeared in *Theatre Arts Magazine*.) Having read in a newspaper drama column of the search for a Josie, she presented herself at the Theatre Guild.

"I had just returned from playing a leading part on tour with Ethel

Barrymore and was full of youthful arrogance," she recalled. "I announced that I was ready to play Josie for them."

Miss Welch was told that she was the right age, temperament and origin but that she looked too "normal." They wanted someone who weighed at least fifty pounds more than she did, and also someone with much more acting experience. Since Miss Welch was persistent, she was finally advised that she could meet O'Neill the following week, when he would be interviewing other actresses.

"I arrived for my appointment about eight pounds heavier (also padded)," Miss Welch said, "and dressed in Kelly green."

When O'Neill was confronted by Miss Welch, he nodded pleasantly but remained silent as he was informed of her qualifications.

"It wasn't until we were left alone that he seemed to relax and then try to put me at ease," said Miss Welch. "His searching eyes focused constantly right on my face, but instead of their arousing a self-conscious behavior in me, they seemed to put me on my absolute honor to express myself as clearly and as simply as I could."

O'Neill's first questions were, "Are you Irish with that pug nose? What per cent? From what part of Ireland are your people?" He said he wanted as many people as possible connected with the play to be Irish, explaining that, although the setting was New England, "the dry wit, the mercurial changes of mood, and the mystic quality of the three main characters are so definitely Irish."

"Of course, I'm Irish, one hundred per cent, County Cork," replied Miss Welch.

O'Neill's smile emboldened Miss Welch to slip into a brogue and tell him about her grandmother, who used to say, "I'll never eat a plate of stew—those dishes of mystery!" After discussing Ireland at some length, O'Neill gave Miss Welch a script of the play and asked her to come back and read for him in two weeks, which she did.

"O'Neill's previous warmth and my own overwhelming love and desire for the part had given me courage to memorize large sections of the play and to boldly use Josie's main prop, an old broom," Miss Welch said. "The Guild seemed impressed with at least the long preparations I had made but they were still worried."

Dismissing the Guild's reservations about Miss Welch's size, O'Neill said:

"She can gain some more weight. I think the emotional quality is just right."

Within the next few months Miss Welch added five more pounds, by stuffing herself with potatoes, bananas and desserts, and gave three more readings of the role. On the day the final decision was to be made between her and several other contenders for the part, she was invited to O'Neill's apartment an hour before the audition. He had simply wanted to put her at ease before the ordeal, and he assured her that she was his choice.

"That day I signed the contract to play Josie," she said, "with the added, unusual clause, 'The artist agrees to gain the necessary weight required for the role.'"

James Dunn had previously been selected to play James Tyrone. J. M. Kerrigan was engaged to play Hogan, after unsuccessful efforts were made to induce Barry Fitzgerald to take on the role. And Fitzgerald's brother, Arthur Shields, was assigned to direct.

During the first rehearsal the actors were so moved by the play that they dissolved, one by one, into tears. O'Neill, who wept along with them, told the cast of his agony when writing the play.

At the end of the reading O'Neill expressed some misgivings to Langner.

"We were not at all certain of our cast," Langner said, "but while we were worried about Mary Welch, Gene was worried about James Dunn. I had taken him to see a screening of the movie, 'A Tree Grows in Brooklyn,' and he had liked Dunn enormously in it and said he was just right for James Tyrone. But during rehearsals he kept complaining that Dunn wasn't playing the role with enough gentlemanliness; he kept telling me that his brother was a gentleman. I told him that his brother may very well have been a gentleman, but the way he'd written James Tyrone, that quality didn't exactly come across, and that Dunn was playing the role as written. O'Neill couldn't accept this. I felt that he had idealized his brother, and would never be able to accept any actor in the part."

Since no one was at all confident about the production that had been assembled, it was decided to have an out-of-town tour in a series of midwestern cities, a decision in which O'Neill concurred reluctantly.

Because of his ill-health O'Neill did not attend rehearsals regularly, but he turned up as often as he could, to complain to Langner and to offer suggestions to the actors.

"He gave us some notes that really helped us," Mary Welch recalled. "One of them was that we were playing the tragedy of the play too soon. He felt it should be played almost for farce in the first act, and develop into tragic stature in the fourth. During breaks in the rehearsal, he often told us jokes about his early days. He seemed to look for humor everywhere."

Once, during the rehearsal of a drinking scene, he provided the male members of his cast with some Method instruction. "You don't get drunk that way on bonded whiskey—you get drunk that way on bootlegger stuff," he told them.

Arthur Shields, who was not called in until after the cast had already been engaged, met O'Neill shortly before the first rehearsal.

"We agreed," said Shields, "that the play should be staged with as little movement as possible—that is, with very little bouncing around. He asked me if I wanted to cut the play, and I said no. I explained that I had been brought up in the Irish theatre, where the author was considered more sacred than in this country.

"Three days before we left New York, he asked me again if I thought there were portions that should be cut, and I told him no, that I felt there was a flow and rhythm to the play, as in a poem, and that the flow would be hurt by cutting."

O'Neill did not plan to go out of town with the play, but he attended the final dress rehearsal in New York with Carlotta.

"I know you will play Josie the way I want it," he told Mary Welch, as he embraced her.

At the play's opening night on February 20, 1947, in Columbus, Ohio, Miss Welch received a dozen red roses from O'Neill, with a card that read: "Again my absolute confidence."

At the end of the second act, Langner noticed a group of people leave the theatre. He wondered whether they had been upset by some of the language in the play, and he asked the doorman whether they left on this account. The doorman replied, "No, they just said they were Irish."

The play received uneven notices in Columbus and in several other midwestern cities. When it reached Pittsburgh early in March it was scored by the local press and greeted with indignation by the chamber of commerce, whose secretary declared himself shocked by reports of "the smut in it."

The play's reputation had preceded it to Detroit, and when the production opened there on March 10 the city was aroused. On the second night the play was closed by the police, and the Detroit *Times* announced the news on its front page in inch-high red letters.

"Whole Theme Too Smutty, Snyder Says," read a smaller headline over the story.

"It isn't just a matter of profanity," declared Police Censor Charles Snyder. "The whole theme is obscene. It is a slander on American motherhood. The play will have to be rewritten before I will let it go on."

Langner's wife, Armina Marshall, and Theresa Helburn, who were touring with the play, were summoned to meet with a member of the censor's staff.

"One of the objections he made," recalled Miss Marshall (as Langner later recorded in his autobiography, *The Magic Curtain*), "was that the word 'mother' was used in the same sentence with the word 'prostitute.' He mentioned other words which, he said, should not be used on the stage."

"Now, mind you," the censor warned, "the actor can go ahead and say the sentence right up to the obscene word, and then he can make a gesture. But he cannot use the word."

"You've allowed *The Maid of the Ozarks* to play here in Detroit," retorted Miss Marshall, "and yet you will not allow a play written by Eugene O'Neill, the greatest playwright in America, who won the Nobel Prize?"

"Lady," said the censor, "I don't care what kind of prize he's won, he can't put on a dirty show in *my* town."

"This is not a dirty show," protested Miss Marshall. "This is a great play—which *The Maid of the Ozarks* is not."

"Lady," he replied, "when *The Maid of the Ozarks* came here, it was a very different play. I helped rewrite *that* play, and we finally let it stay here."

"Well, I'm afraid you'd have your problems cut out for you to rewrite a play by Mr. O'Neill," said Miss Marshall.

The remark upset him considerably. "Listen, lady," he shouted. "I don't have to sit here and take that from a woman."

James Dunn then entered and pacified him. The official agreed to talk over the matter with Dunn but stipulated that he did not want a woman present. After a lengthy conference, an agreement was reached to delete eight words.

Joe Heidt, who was still handling publicity for the Theatre Guild, telephoned O'Neill in New York about the deletions. O'Neill laughingly agreed to them.

St. Louis was the last stop on the line for *A Moon for the Misbegotten*. O'Neill had never seen it performed, having been too ill and too disgusted to travel to one of its out-of-town stands. The Guild wanted to recast the play and have another try at it but, according to Langner, "Gene asked us to defer this until he was feeling better, and he also asked us to postpone the production of *A Touch of the Poet* for the same reason."

The Guild reluctantly acceded to O'Neill's wishes about delaying *A Touch of the Poet,* even though Robert Edmond Jones had already drawn preliminary sketches for the sets and plans had been formulated to have either Spencer Tracy or Laurence Olivier portray Cornelius Melody. O'Neill himself had told Nathan not long before that there was no contemporary actor who could do justice to the role.

"What that needs is an actor like Maurice Barrymore or my old man," said O'Neill. "One of those big-chested, chiseled-mug, romantic old boys who could walk onto a stage with all the aplomb and regal splendor with which they walked into the old Hoffman House bar, drunk or sober. Most actors in these times lack an air. If a playwright doesn't work up entrances fifteen minutes long for them and have all the other characters describe them in advance as something pretty elegant, noble, chivalrous and handsome, the audiences won't be able to accept them for much more than third assistant barkeeps, if that."

(*A Touch of the Poet,* like *Long Day's Journey Into Night,* was published posthumously. It was finally produced on Broadway on October 2, 1958, with Eric Portman as Melody, Helen Hayes as his wife, and Kim Stanley as their daughter. But, like *A Moon for the Misbegotten,* it was not an overwhelming success. While it is not so fine a play as *A Moon for the Misbegotten,* it does belong in the top rank of O'Neill works—a fact that has been recognized in Sweden, where the play, as well as *Long Day's Journey Into Night* and *A Moon for the Misbegotten* had its world première.)

Shortly before *A Moon for the Misbegotten* left for its tryout, O'Neill had run into censorship problems with *The Iceman Cometh,* which had concluded its Broadway run of 136 performances and was being readied for a road tour. In this instance it was the Boston censor who took umbrage at some of the "unclean" O'Neill dialogue. O'Neill flatly refused to make any of the requested changes, characterizing them as "idiotic."

"Boston audiences, I am sure, want plays as written by their authors and as produced originally in New York," O'Neill declared to the newspapers. "They do not want plays weakened and made silly by an ignorant and stupid censorship which knows and cares nothing about drama. This is the sort of censorship I experienced years ago with *Strange Interlude,* which was barred from Boston and forced to play in Quincy so Bostonians could see it."

The Guild rerouted the play to Baltimore. The National Theatre in Washington, D.C., also was on the *Iceman* itinerary at a time when public feeling was aroused over the theatre's policy of barring Negroes from the audience. A group calling itself the Washington Committee for Racial Democracy had been picketing the theatre for several months. Presumably the theatre's contract with the *Iceman* company was legally unbreakable and the show went on there, but O'Neill indicated that he would not have permitted his play to appear had he been aware of the National's policy. In reply to a wire from a committee member, the Rev. Wilfred Parsons, O'Neill stated:

"I am and always have been opposed to racial discrimination of any kind. I assure you I will insert a nondiscrimination clause in all future contracts."

With the burden of production a constant annoyance, O'Neill's health continued shaky during the winter and early spring of 1947, but his thirst for social contacts remained unslaked. He even managed to have several brief, platonic, but decidedly clandestine meetings with a young actress, Patricia Neal. She had been among those who had read for the role of Josie, and O'Neill had considered her for Sara Melody in *A Touch of the Poet*. In November of 1946 she had gone into the Broadway production of Lillian Hellman's *Another Part of the Forest*. Between then and the period of rehearsals and out-of-town run of *A Moon for the Misbegotten*—about three and a half months—she and O'Neill met four or five times. She had written O'Neill to tell him she liked *The Iceman Cometh,* and O'Neill had replied, thanking her and congratulating her on her success in *Another Part of the Forest*. Soon after, he decided to pursue the relationship.

"The Theatre Guild would call me," she said, "and ask me to come to their offices to see O'Neill. We would sit and talk in Miss Marshall's office, usually for about two hours. He'd insist on lighting my cigarettes, even though it might take as much as two minutes. We talked about everything. Once we talked about my name. I had some Irish blood, and my grandmother's name was Fitzgerald. He said he was sure that the name, Neal, was actually O'Neill, gone north.

"After one of our meetings, he decided to take me to Hick's for a soda. He held his glass in both hands, close to his chin, and kept it there, drinking his soda through a straw. He was pleased he did so well. He had the kind of face I loved—craggy.

"That day at Hick's I told him, 'I'm twenty-one today.' He said, 'I wish I'd known someone like you when I was twenty-one.'

"During one of our meetings, he told me that I could do any of his plays I wanted to. A little later that year I went to Hollywood, and he wrote me several times. In one letter he told me he was convinced I'd be a great actress." (Miss Neal never saw O'Neill again after she left for Hollywood, but her brief friendship with him had repercussions. In 1952, when a revival of *Desire Under the Elms* was being planned, she was asked by the producer, Robert Whitehead, to play the role of Abbie Putnam. "I began arranging my Hollywood schedule so I could come east to do the play; suddenly I got word from Robert Whitehead that I couldn't have the role, after all. He told me he had received a wire instructing him to stop negotiations with me. He said that the O'Neills felt I hadn't developed enough as an actress to play Abbie.")

By the spring of 1947 Carlotta was generally, if not specifically, aware that O'Neill was overextending himself. On June 8 she wrote to Charles O'Brien Kennedy, complaining (in a restrained and ladylike way) of her husband's activities.

"Carlotta said that Gene had been confined to bed, with temperature, as a result of over-fatigue," Kennedy later recalled. "She mentioned that his doctor had warned him against doing too much, and that she had done her best to see that he followed instructions, but that Gene was a stubborn Irishman."

During this period O'Neill was being interviewed by Hamilton Basso for *The New Yorker* Profile, published the following winter. O'Neill advised Basso to see Doc Ganey in New London for background on his youth. Increasingly preoccupied with nostalgic memories of his past, O'Neill was, nevertheless, still hopeful about his future creativity. He told Basso:

"It's very hard right now, not being able to work. I want to get going again. Once I get over this thing—these shakes I have—I feel I can keep rolling right along."

O'Neill also told Shirlee Weingarten, around this time, that he had an idea for a comedy he hoped to be able to write soon, but when Shirlee offered to give up her job with the Guild and devote herself to taking his dictation, he declined the offer, saying he could not possibly dictate. "My pencil has become a part of my brain," he explained.

Shirlee married Steve Alexander on November 7 and invited the O'Neills to a small wedding party. Carlotta declined, saying that she and O'Neill never went to parties, but that she would like to arrange a wedding dinner at her apartment.

To Shirlee's surprise, O'Neill did come to her party—but without Carlotta.

"He was gracious to everyone, and wonderfully alive," Shirlee said. "He drank two glasses of champagne. One of the guests, a drama reporter, asked him if he would sign his collection of O'Neill plays, and O'Neill promised he would. When I asked him if he didn't think that would be a big chore for him, he said, 'If someone takes the trouble to read all my plays, I have to sign them.'

"Another guest, a pretty actress, gave him a lecture for being too reserved and for not having a political conscience. She shook a finger at him. He adored it."

Two other guests at the party were Lewis Nichols and his wife. Nichols, who had served as *The Times* drama critic while Brooks Atkinson was a war correspondent, took the newlyweds and O'Neill home in his station wagon. O'Neill was dropped at his apartment house, and as he left the car, he remarked, "I'm going to catch hell for this."

O'Neill apparently relished his little fling and was rather pleased to have piqued Carlotta, for soon after that he gleefully told his Princeton classmate, Richard Weeks, of his escapade and of Carlotta's disapproval.

Carlotta gave the dinner party for Shirlee and her husband a week later. But Carlotta's affection for Shirlee evidently had begun to wane. The O'Neills' wedding present to the Alexanders was a check for $170—the royalties for the Czechoslovakian production of *The Iceman Cometh*.

Years later, Shirlee attributed Carlotta's coolness in part to an incident that had taken place before her wedding. Shirlee had read the somewhat ribald novel, *Nightwood*, by Djuna Barnes, and knowing that O'Neill had been interested in Miss Barnes's work during his Greenwich Village days, had discussed it with him. O'Neill had asked Shirlee to get him a copy of the book and she had done so. The next time she saw the O'Neills, according to Shirlee, Carlotta expressed her disapproval of the book, and of Shirlee's interest in it.

To such transgressions as his meetings with Patricia Neal and his attendance at Shirlee's party, O'Neill added another social engagement. On December 18 he attended a stag dinner at a West Forty-fifth Street restaurant to celebrate the sixtieth birthday of Robert Edmond Jones. O'Neill arrived after the meal and apologized for being late, explaining that it was embarrassing for him to dine in public because of his tremor. He did, however, speak in tribute to Jones, painstakingly signed the souvenir programs of all the other twenty-two guests, among whom were Arthur Hopkins, Jo Mielziner, Lee Simonson, Walter Huston and John Mason Brown, and sat for a group photograph, in which he smiled happily.

O'Neill, soon after, became remorseful about upsetting his wife. His birthday message to her on the 28th was abject.

Asking Carlotta please not to "sneer," he assured her, once again, of his love for and need of her—a truth, he said, which could support them in their old age against "the sneers of the world."

"I do not offer you anything but my love, my heartbreak, my need of your love—and my apology that I should have forgotten your card at Christmas. I paid for that in tears," he wrote.

[888]

"I love you, Carlotta, as I have loved you, as I always will!"

Carlotta apparently chose to disbelieve him. It was not long after that she felt herself sufficiently put upon to leave her husband.

During the second week in January, 1948, O'Neill learned through friends that Eleanor Fitzgerald, with whom he had had no communication in many years, was seriously ill and had been ordered to the hospital for an operation.

Fitzi telephoned O'Neill and, according to Saxe Commins, who was present at the O'Neill apartment during the telephone conversation, Fitzi told O'Neill she needed money for the hospital.

"Gene was very sympathetic and said he would send a check for $100," Commins recalled. "Gene and I started reminiscing about the Greenwich Village days, and Carlotta seemed annoyed. The next day, Gene called me and said, 'My frau has flown the coop.'"

Carlotta had, indeed, walked out.

Since O'Neill apparently had no idea where Carlotta had gone or how long she would stay away, and since he was too ill to be left alone, Walter Casey moved into the apartment to take care of him. O'Neill must either have discovered Carlotta's whereabouts within a few days (she had moved into a midtown hotel) or else found a friend in common who knew where she was, for he sent her an anguished note on January 19:

"Darling: For the love of God, forgive and come back. You are all I have in life. I am sick and I will surely die without you. You do not want to murder me, I know, and a curse will be on you for your remaining days.

"I love you and I will! Please, Darling!"

But Carlotta did not return. Nine days later O'Neill, as though determined to make good his threat, slipped and fell in his apartment, fracturing his left shoulder.

At about one in the morning of the day of the accident—January 28—Saxe Commins, who had spent the evening at O'Neill's apartment, left O'Neill and Casey together and went home. They had been drinking coffee all evening, but when Commins left they switched to whiskey. At three they both went to bed, Casey taking several sleeping pills. About an hour later O'Neill tripped on his way to the bathroom. He felt sharp pain in his arm but did not know how badly he had injured it, and he tried to get up.

"You don't realize," he later told Shirlee, "that when you lose the use of an arm, you lose your equilibrium. I couldn't co-ordinate—couldn't get to my feet."

He shouted for Casey, but Casey, in a deep sleep, did not hear him. He kicked his feet against the floor, hoping to arouse the tenants below, but that brought no response. "It was a terrifying experience," he told Shirlee, "I lost all track of time. I felt as though I was alone, in a nightmare."

Finally, at about five in the morning, Casey awoke and found O'Neill lying on the floor. He was terribly distressed at not having heard him and remorseful over the drinking and the sleeping pills. He immediately telephoned to O'Neill's doctor, George Draper, who called a younger associate, Dr. Shirley Fisk, and asked him to take the case.

When Dr. Fisk reached the apartment he decided that O'Neill should be hospitalized. Since Casey was unwilling to assume responsibility for the move, and since O'Neill apparently did not wish Carlotta called or did not know where to reach her, Casey asked that Commins be notified.

"I got to Gene's apartment quickly," Commins said. "I called a private ambulance, and Dr. Fisk put Gene on a stretcher and we rode with him to Doctors Hospital. Casey stayed in the apartment to take care of things there."

Dr. Fisk, an engaging, lanky, blond, blue-eyed man in his thirties, was aware that O'Neill had been drinking before the accident. Like practically every doctor who ever treated O'Neill, he was immediately attracted to him, and so was his orthopedist, Dr. Robert Lee Patterson, whom Dr. Fisk called in on the case. Dr. Patterson, also in his thirties, was congenial and dapper, with more than a trace of the southern drawl his name warranted.

"O'Neill was a damn good patient," Dr. Patterson recalled. "He would always greet me with a little smile, and say, 'Nice to see you, Doctor.' He never complained. It was very difficult to estimate whether to write orders for sedatives because of this. But the X rays showed that the fracture was severe, and he must have had considerable pain.

'We didn't have his arm in a cast. It was in a sling with a circular bandage around the chest wall. I always saw him when he was propped up in a semi-sitting position—we kept him cranked up like that because it made it easier for the fracture to heal. He always managed a smile at the end of our meeting. even when he was uncomfortable."

O'Neill had a corner room on the tenth floor, overlooking the East River.

"He could see the boats passing by," said Dr. Patterson. "During our first meeting, we talked about John Masefield. O'Neill had mentioned a passing boat, and I told him I didn't know anything about the sea. He said he'd just love to get near it, and that brought up the subject of Masefield. He quoted a few lines from 'Sea-Fever,' and I told him I'd met Masefield during the war, when I'd been with an Army Hospital Unit in England."

O'Neill also talked to Dr. Patterson about Carlotta.

"He didn't know where she was," Dr. Patterson said, "and told me he had detectives out looking for her. As it happened, Carlotta was also my patient during this time. While O'Neill was in the hospital, she came to me for treatment of an acute back pain. I put her into the hospital, without telling her that her husband was there. As a matter of fact, I think *she* had detectives out looking for *him*, too. She was in a room on the ninth floor of the hospital for a time, and neither of them knew the other was there. I'd listen to her side of the story, and then take the stairs up to the tenth floor and listen to O'Neill's side. I talked to both of them about being understanding."

During this time other friends of both O'Neill and Carlotta also were attempting to reunite them. Lillian Gish, who visited O'Neill and was in touch with Carlotta, told him, "Carlotta loves you, Gene. I believe you need her and she needs you."

There is no doubt that O'Neill wanted a reconciliation. He and Carlotta eventually learned of each other's whereabouts, and less than two weeks after O'Neill had been hospitalized—which happened to be the twentieth anniversary of his and Carlotta's elopement to Europe—he wrote to her reminding her of the occasion, and imploring her not to regard the date as the commemoration of a "flop."

"Please, Sweetheart," he said, "I have been through hell and you have. I could never act again as I have acted.

"I love you, Darling, Darling! . . . Don't leave me!"

Carlotta was not quite ready for a reconciliation. But she kept track of her husband from a distance. She telephoned Dr. Fisk about him, and talked to him at length about her domestic difficulties.

"She talked about what a difficult man O'Neill was to live with," Dr. Fisk recalled. "I was young then, and felt emotionally involved in the life of a great playwright. My sympathies were all with him. He was such a benign man, such a warm, understanding human being.

"One day Mrs. O'Neill came to see me in my office at Ninetieth Street. She again spoke of her problems with O'Neill and implied that I was incapable of understanding her difficulties. She found out, once, that an actress had been to visit him and she called me and gave me hell about it."

O'Neill received a good many visitors, and Dr. Fisk was unable to recall which actress it was to whom Carlotta objected. It may have been Claire Luce, who had not seen O'Neill in many years, and who hurried to his bedside when she heard of his accident.

"I was shocked at how changed he was," she said, "and shocked by the sadness in his eyes. He spoke to me haltingly and painfully about his tremor, and I suggested that he try Yoga, which I had once tried, and he seemed interested. I thought it would help him relax while he had to be in bed.

"He reminded me of the time we'd gone to a nightclub together. He remembered every detail, and said it was the only time he'd ever been inside one. He enjoyed talking about it."

O'Neill seemed in good spirits to many of his other visitors. Shirlee spent some time with him, offering her services as secretary, and he dictated cheerful notes to friends and answered business letters. He signed some of the letters himself.

"I'd love to see you anytime in the evening beginning next week," he wrote to Russel Crouse on February 3. "By then I ought to be able to cook up a smile of welcome or sing to you faintly, 'Oh, Come and Be Sweet to Me, Kid.' " He also wrote to the Van Vechtens, thanking them for a gift of flowers and asking them to visit.

"One day he was signing papers and laughing," Shirlee said. "I asked him what he was amused about, and he said, 'Well, Agnes is finally getting married.' " (Agnes married Mack Kaufman and settled down with him in her old house in New Jersey. Though later separated, they were not divorced, and she was still Mrs. Kaufman when she died in 1968.)

O'Neill was in a good enough mood to talk about the screening of the movie *Odd Man Out* that Shirlee had arranged for him some months before.

"He loved the picture," Shirlee said. "He was very moved by the woman's sacrifice at the end. He said that was the role a woman should play—the role of sacrifice for her man.

"He talked a great deal about the old days. He spoke of the old chorus girls and of New York and Chicago gangsters."

The Langners visited him, as did Nathan. Some of his friends thought that his cheerful frame of mind indicated he was resigned to a permanent break with Carlotta, and several, who believed that she had been holding too tight a rein on him, were ready to congratulate themselves on what they regarded as his escape. But others were convinced from the start that the separation was only temporary.

"It was Tristan and Isolde, all the time," Crouse said, adding that whenever Carlotta got angry with O'Neill she would buy a hat, and that sometime during this period she showed Mrs. Crouse her wardrobe of headgear, which ran to about thirty or forty hats.

"We knew Gene couldn't live without Carlotta," Fania Marinoff said. "A great many people thought he could, but Carl and I knew they needed each other, and would always go back together."

Carlotta believed that efforts were being made in some quarters to turn O'Neill permanently against her; as impetuous in her dislikes as she was in her friendships, she could grow wrathful in the face of what she regarded as betrayal. Shirlee Weingarten was among those who were affected by the situation.

"One day, while O'Neill was still in the hospital," Shirlee said, "I was at the Guild and a secretary said there was a 'Miss Monterey' on the telephone, asking for Armina Marshall. The secretary was puzzled by the use of the name, 'Monterey,' but she was sure she recognized Mrs. O'Neill's voice, and since Armina wasn't in, and she knew all O'Neill matters were routed through me, she called me to the phone. I said, 'Is It you, Carlotta?' She answered, in an icy voice, 'I am calling to speak with Miss Marshall. Get off the phone.'

"I was stunned. It was the last time I ever spoke to her."

According to Dr. Patterson, Carlotta eventually came to see her husband at Doctors Hospital. Dr. Patterson looked in on O'Neill after she left and found him in an emotional state. "He couldn't sleep after her visit," he said.

By mid-April O'Neill's shoulder was healed. He and Carlotta had reached an agreement, stipulating that they would leave New York City and return to seclusion. They decided to go to Boston, and then look for a house not too far from that city, so that O'Neill could be near the specialists he required and yet reside in isolation with Carlotta.

When O'Neill left the hospital on April 19 and said good-by, Dr. Patterson told him he wanted to receive a letter from him in his own hand.

"I can't do it," O'Neill said.

"You go to your desk and sit down," said Dr. Patterson, "and you'll hear a voice. It will be Robert Lee, and he'll say, 'Quit shaking and write me.'"

A few weeks later Dr. Patterson received the letter; it came from the Ritz-Carlton in Boston, and was written shakily in O'Neill's own hand:

"Just a few inadequate words of gratitude: that my arm was saved, that I had for a while the privilege of knowing as fine a man as you—and lastly that through your influence Mrs. O'Neill and I are together again with hope and love and a future!"

Dr. Patterson was touched by the letter. He wrote back that he was pleased O'Neill had settled in Boston, "which, in orthopedic circles, is considered to be the home and the tops in our profession." That August he heard from Carlotta, also on Ritz-Carlton stationery.

"She wrote that she and O'Neill were very happy," Dr. Patterson said. "She complained that O'Neill was doing too much smoking and coughing. She said that both she and O'Neill realized 'it takes two people to make a marriage go,' that you must help each other in the end, that she and her husband had 'always been happy when living alone in the country and working;' and that they were looking for a small house, 'which we can take care of.' She said she was tired of building big houses. New York, she added, was a horrible place."

LXII

LIFE FOR THE O'NEILLS WAS RELATIVELY CALM DUR-
ing the next year or so and for a time it seemed as though Carlotta had
been right in persuading her husband to return with her to seclusion. Early
in July of 1948 O'Neill wrote to Carlotta, in her copy of *The Iceman
Cometh,* that out of their sorrow, pain and misunderstanding had come a
"new vision of deeper love and security and above all, serenity, to bind
us ever closer in our old age." And several days later, on their nineteenth
wedding anniversary, he presented her with a two-volume edition of the
poetry of Christina G. Rossetti, which he inscribed:

". . . Now, with our sixtieth birthdays looming close upon us . . . I
want to say to you—'You are my love—forever my love, Sweetheart!' And
I want to promise you that I will do my utmost to cast out whatever
remains in me of selfishness or thoughtlessness that could possibly hurt
you, wishing with all my heart only for that which will make you happy;
for your happiness is my happiness! . . ."

He was feeling chipper enough, soon after, to compose a rhyme to
Russel Crouse's newly arrived daughter, which he dispatched from the
Ritz-Carlton:

Welcome Lindsay Ann!
I wish I'd just been born, too,
Cause then in sixteen years, or moo
I'd be saying I love oo!"

At the end of July Carlotta found "the small house by the sea" she had
been looking for. She later described it as "a dinky summer cottage," but
added that she turned it into "a beautiful little house" with a total expenditure of about $85,000 of her own money. The house was a six-room,
fifty-year-old frame structure perched on a cliff overlooking the Atlantic
in Marblehead Neck, about twenty-five miles from Boston. The neck,
separated from Marblehead proper by a long causeway, was an exclusive,
affluent summer resort and a haven for yachtsmen. The house Carlotta
bought was set on a small, hilly plot on the outermost curve of land, a
stretch called Point O'Rocks Lane.

Of all the houses O'Neill had occupied, it resembled most closely his former home at Peaked Hill Bar, for, though considerably more elegant, it too was as close to being seaborne as any building based on land could be. Carlotta added a glass-enclosed porch facing out to sea, from which it was possible to imagine oneself afloat. Gazing ahead, the view was unbroken. Europe lay in a straight line over the horizon; Cape Cod was to the south, Cape Ann to the north, and the treacherous waters of Marblehead Harbor were guarded by a favorite bit of O'Neill scenery, an offshore lighthouse.

"The house was so much on the water," Carlotta said, "that it was tied to rocks by steel cables and when the storms came up they came right up over our heads—we expected to go out to sea at any moment."

It took nearly three months to complete the renovations, which included the installation of an elevator between the first and second floors, thorough insulation such as double-layered windows, and, of course, the carefully selected furnishings which were Carlotta's trademark.

While waiting in Boston for the house to be ready, O'Neill received word from New York that confirmed his belief in the utter hopelessness of his younger son. On August 20 Shane, having been arrested ten days earlier with three capsules of heroin in his possession, pleaded guilty to a charge of narcotics addiction and received a two-year suspended sentence on condition that he enter the Federal hospital at Lexington, Kentucky, for treatment. O'Neill offered no assistance and had no further contact with Shane.

"His children hurt him," Carlotta said, "and when he was hurt, he never said a word. He just sat there and died. He knew I'd stick, and he'd take it out on me."

Though O'Neill rarely mentioned Shane and Oona, and though he chose to regard himself as the injured party, it is impossible to doubt that he felt some measure of guilt and failure toward them both. (Shane's life, as it happened, became an example of how much more grotesquely tragic truth could be than even O'Neill's fiction. Shane and his wife had several more children; but Shane could not hold a job long enough to support his family, which was able to get along for a while on some money his wife had inherited. Even that small boon, however, came to them tainted by the sort of horror O'Neill was fond of visiting on the characters in his plays. The inheritance was from Catherine's mother, who had been murdered by her stepfather.)

O'Neill, just past his sixtieth birthday, moved into his new house in October, 1948. Although he had done no work for many months, he still harbored a shred of hope that he could take up his writing again. For while the tremor had spread to other parts of his body, notably his legs, he thought that the shaking of his hands had lessened somewhat. It must have been this hope that sustained, for a time, the illusion of serenity he had envisioned a few months earlier in his note to Carlotta. At the end of 1948 he still seemed to be in relatively good spirits. On December 6 he wrote a long and cheerful letter, in his own hand and in writing that was tiny and shaky, to Charles O'Brien Kennedy, apologizing for not having acknowledged sooner some nostalgic photographs Kennedy had sent him. His only excuse, he said, was that he had been busy getting settled in his new house "just big enough for us two."

But O'Neill could not work and as the months went by he was gradually forced to realize that he would never be able to finish his cycle or even attempt one of the lesser plays he had outlined. His tremor grew worse and worse, and though he received constant medical treatment from the best doctors in Boston, it could not be alleviated. The sustained physical effort of writing pages of manuscript was beyond his strength.

He sat in his study or on the porch and brooded, staring for hours out to sea through a pair of powerful binoculars. He read desultorily, dipping, most often, into Spengler's *The Decline of the West*. Few people visited, for the list of those who were welcome had dwindled and those who were still personae gratae—Crouse, the Langners, Charles Kennedy, Robert Jones, Dudley Nichols and Mai-mai Sze were among them—now trod warily, conscious that Carlotta was on her guard against a repetition of the recent New York debacle.

With work no longer filling his life, and love—much as he tried to persuade himself to the contrary—no longer the spontaneous passion it had been, O'Neill seemed pathetically happy when one of his few remaining friends made an appearance during the long, idle months at Marblehead.

Charles Kennedy recalled O'Neill's tremulous welcome when he visited. On one occasion Kennedy brought O'Neill some tomatoes picked from his sister's garden in the nearby Massachusetts town of Waltham. Kennedy's sister had wrapped each of the large, ripe, tomatoes separately in cellophane and put them into a paper bag. As the two men sat on the porch in companionable silence, O'Neill, with the bag on his lap, peeled the paper from each tomato with trembling hands and stared at it in silent appreciation. Kennedy was touched by O'Neill's pleasure and saddened by his isolation.

"Another time, I remember sitting on the porch and looking out at the boats in the harbor," Kennedy said. "It was a beautiful scene, and I knew, in his heart, Gene would have liked to be on one of those boats. He said very little, but once in a while he'd drop a word, and the longing was evident. I would never want to repeat those heartbreaking visits."

Another person who was warmly welcomed by O'Neill and upset by his barren existence was a local doctor who was called in frequently to treat his patient for colds and other minor ailments. (The doctor eventually became much involved in O'Neill's personal life and, because of his request for privacy, will be called by a fictitious name.)

Dr. Dana was a tall, crisp New Englander, with a hesitant, boyish smile, and a long-legged stride. His initial reaction to O'Neill's situation in Marblehead was shock at the famous writer's lack of contact with the outside world. He knew little of O'Neill's personal background but fell quickly under the spell of his charm.

The doctor responded to O'Neill's seeming need to be rescued from himself and made several efforts to rouse his patient from the apparent apathy in which he was immersed; for he could not, at first, bring himself to accept O'Neill's sedentary resignation to his illness. But his well-meant attempts to get his patient out of the house for a change of scene were abortive. For instance, O'Neill vetoed Dr. Dana's suggestion of an outing or a quiet boat ride. The doctor resigned himself to supplying O'Neill with the companionship he seemed to crave. He would often extend his professional visits, at his patient's invitation, to include an hour or more of talk or a session of listening to jazz records. Once he brought his patient a newly issued Louis Armstrong record and O'Neill, after listening appreciatively but not uncritically, said, "Louis can't hit that high C any more."

One day Dr. Dana suggested that a drink now and then might relax him, but O'Neill said that even the mildest apéritif intensified his palsy. According to Dr. Dana, when, around Christmastime, he asked if any of O'Neill's children would be coming to spend the holidays, inquiring particularly for Oona, Carlotta quickly interposed with, "Please don't ever mention her name here." O'Neill was silent.

Carlotta had become more necessary to O'Neill than ever. She seldom left his side now, for his food had to be cut for him, his cigarettes lighted, and many other homely chores managed for him, all of which she attended to. She nursed him tenaciously, and although she sometimes complained to friends of the grueling job, she refused to engage anyone at that time to help care for her husband.

Toward the end of 1949 Carlotta made a statement to the press about her husband's health. "He hasn't worked for three years—and God only knows if he ever will be able to," she was quoted as saying by *The New*

York Times. "It's terrible. It gets worse. The hands tremble and then the feet." Explaining that O'Neill was obliged to live in seclusion, rarely seeing anyone but herself and a servant, she added, "It makes him nervous to have someone in the house."

The house on Point O'Rocks Lane, while it was picturesque and gay during the summer, was something less than cheerful during the fall and winter. Most of the residents abandoned their houses then, and if O'Neill ventured outdoors, which he seldom did except to visit medical specialists in Boston, he was greeted by the gloomy aspect of shuttered windows, frozen brown earth, wind-torn, naked trees, and a hostile, gray sea. Little by little the snug, love-filled, new home became a prison haunted, like Lavinia Mannon's mansion, by ghosts of the past.

Added to his frustration over not being able to finish the work he had planned was the knowledge that the reputation based on work he had completed was either being attacked or ignored. Eric Bentley and Mary McCarthy were among the leading anti-O'Neillians in the United States.

"Among the untragic tragedians the most spectacular is Eugene O'Neill," wrote Bentley. "At everything in the theatre except being tragic and being comic he is a success." He added that the "good clean fun of a Hitchcock movie is better." Miss McCarthy found O'Neill's work "maudlin," "crude," and, of course, repetitious.

In April, 1948, when *The Iceman Cometh* had been published in England, the *Times* of London Literary Supplement carried such a scathing attack on O'Neill that the New York newspapers reported it. The anonymous critic for the most important of Britain's literary publications had a good word to say for only a couple of the twenty-nine O'Neill plays that had been published in England up to that time.

"Mr. O'Neill is as puritanical as Mr. Shaw, but his puritanism, unlike Mr. Shaw's, unlike Milton's, unlike Andrew Marvell's, has no grace or geniality," said the London *Times,* adding that O'Neill's characters were "ineffectual egoists" and that his stage tricks were the "sort of stuff that might be written by an earnest sophomore."

In the United States, Brooks Atkinson vigorously took up O'Neill's defense, and a revival of the S. S. *Glencairn* plays at New York's City Center helped somewhat to reaffirm O'Neill's stature, but in many literary quarters he was a dismissed or forgotten man.

Langner thought a production of *A Touch of the Poet* or a new attempt to present *A Moon for the Misbegotten* would be a healthy thing both for the theatre and for O'Neill. O'Neill, however, could not make the effort. "I don't believe I could live through a production," he told Langner.

With his Christmas gift to Carlotta in 1949 O'Neill wrote, in a painfully shaky hand:

"To 'Mama'—and still as over all the years, 'Sweetheart' and 'Darling' and 'Beloved Wife' and 'Friend,' too!—in these days of sickness and despair . . ."

Carlotta's health was poor too. She occasionally suffered from arthritis, and the constant strain of caring for O'Neill was sapping her strength.

O'Neill's boyhood friend, Joseph McCarthy, recalled hearing from her in the spring of 1950.

"Mrs. O'Neill wrote that she and O'Neill were both ill and in very low spirits," McCarthy said.

And in June O'Neill wrote to Dr. Lyman, from whom he had just heard for the first time in many years:

"My own health has been extremely poor. . . . All the drugs tried have made me feel worse instead of better. I wish I were back at Gaylord Farm lolling on one of the rest chairs!"

O'Neill had become so depressed over his illness, which he now understood could never be alleviated, that he had begun once again to think about taking the long swim into the moon's wake that had tempted him several times before. He spoke often of suicide and, sometime in 1949, formally joined the Euthanasia Society of America and permitted his name to be used on its letterhead. A pamphlet issued by the society about that time, and bearing O'Neill's name as a member of the American Advisory Council along with, among others, those of Max Eastman, Robert Frost, Somerset Maugham and Robert Sherwood, listed a group of "Typical Tragedies" in which a wife or husband gave or attempted to give the gift of annihilation to a suffering spouse. Mercy killing was one of the few methods of death-dealing O'Neill had never got around to in a play.

An added source of distress for O'Neill during this period was his almost total estrangement from Eugene Jr. Under the new regime of exclusivity, O'Neill had been out of touch with his elder son, for Eugene had suggested to his father, during the O'Neills' separation in New York, that he leave Carlotta permanently and move in with him. Eugene had recently become a member of a bohemian colony in Woodstock, New York, where he had rented a small house and bought some acreage adjoining the property of his friend, Frank Meyer. He no longer was on Yale University's teaching staff but held part-time jobs at other institutions, including lecturing at Princeton; he made some radio appearances and joined Meyer on lecture platforms, debating such topics as current best sellers, the modern guilt complex, and the American educational system.

Meyer was Eugene's frequent companion and confidant from the summer of 1947, when Eugene arrived in Woodstock. Meyer lived there permanently, supporting himself and his family by writing and editing, and Eugene spent several days a week there, occupying his Greenwich Village apartment during the days his teaching or his radio work called him to New York.

"He moved into his rented house with Ruth Lander, and soon after paid $4,000 for a twenty-eight-acre tract of land, which he began clearing for the site of a house," Meyer recalled. "He loved the outdoors, and enjoyed chopping wood. He told me his father had co-signed a bank loan for the payment on the property. He also told me, soon after his father left New York for Boston, that he didn't think he'd be seeing him any more. His relationship with Carlotta had deteriorated, he said. During one of his visits to the hospital his father had told him, 'I have to go back to her; I can't live without her.' Eugene had interpreted this as a farewell speech; he had the impression his father was telling him he had been given a choice between him and Carlotta, and that his choosing Carlotta meant Eugene's exclusion in the future."

While the elder O'Neill took refuge with Carlotta, the younger tried to console himself with Ruth. But it was not a tranquil relationship. Eugene was unfaithful to her and occasionally beat her. Ruth, however, continued to keep house for him over a period of several years.

"We would both cook meals," she later said in discussing their domestic arrangement. "Eugene was a good cook and had his favorite recipes—one of them was eels in a sauce. We usually had two Martinis before dinner and he had sherry with his coffee every morning.

"His hands often trembled, especially when he was shaving the side of his face and trimming his beard and mustache. He kept three or four straight razors for this job. His tremor was worst in the morning. He thought he was getting Parkinson's like his father.

"He told me that he knew he needed a psychiatrist, but that, as he put it, the daddy of them all—the only one who could have understood him—was dead.

"One morning, he said to me, 'As of today, I can commit suicide any time.' He explained he had just gotten a special clause written into his life insurance policy. He told me he had tried to kill himself once, in New Haven."

In the summer of 1949 Ruth walked out on Eugene. According to Meyer, the incident set Eugene off on a year-long orgy. "He had eighteen girls during that period," Meyer recalled. "He also started drinking heavily, more than I realized at first— although I never saw him really drunk."

By the summer of 1950 Eugene, who was now forty, persuaded himself he really loved Ruth and decided to try to get her back by asking her to be his third wife. After leaving Eugene, Ruth had formed a friendship with a man in the garment business who lived near Woodstock, and she occasionally encountered Eugene in local saloons. Some time in September Ruth agreed to return to Eugene. "He told me we'd have a baby, and I could leave my hair blond, although he preferred me as a brunette," Ruth said.

Eugene conveyed the good news to Meyer. "I told Gene to stop worrying about women and get back to serious work," Meyer recalled. "Gene said he had to have someone to work *for*. I told him he had himself to work for and asked him if he couldn't make the effort to get back on the right track."

Eugene answered: "I've slipped too far. I can't get back."

The reconciliation with Ruth did not last long.

"I had told Gene I'd marry him, after he'd pounded me about it for three hours," Ruth said. "I was slightly hysterical by the time I said yes. But when I went back to his house with him, later, I told him I couldn't go through with it. I felt sorry for him. He had been rejected by everyone —first by his father, then his mother, then Yale, then his father again, then me—but I couldn't stay with him. There was insanity in his eyes."

Late on Saturday night, September 23, a common friend of Eugene's and Meyer's telephoned Meyer that Eugene had been seen in various bars around town talking of Ruth's desertion and declaring he was going to commit suicide.

"I didn't think Gene would kill himself over Ruth," Meyer said, "but I knew he was capable of suicide. We'd discussed the subject many times and we were thoroughly agreed that in a case where things became intolerable for a person he should kill himself. Both of us were against the Christian viewpoint of suicide being sinful."

Meyer and his wife, Elsie, went in search of Eugene, but failed to find him in any of the bars or in his home. "I even searched his land, to see if he'd tried to hang himself from a tree," Meyer said. Finally, early on Sunday morning, the Meyers gave up their search and went to sleep.

Eugene telephoned them late Sunday morning. Meyer and his wife drove down the road a quarter of a mile to visit him at his house.

"He looked beat," Meyer said. "I didn't want him to be alone and asked him to come to us for dinner. He didn't want to, at first, but he finally said he'd drive over in a little while.

"At dinner we talked about our worry of the night before. Elsie told

Gene he shouldn't speak of suicide, and added, 'Of course, you'll never kill yourself.'

"I said I realized now I had been foolish to worry, that I should have known he would never commit suicide impulsively, but would take time to plan it properly."

Then Eugene, in perfect seriousness, told the Meyers that he had been thinking, the night before, of using the chain that hung across a private lane adjoining his and Meyer's property to hang himself with.

"I thought you'd plan something more thorough than that," said Meyer uneasily.

Eugene left Meyer's house at eleven. He had had a few drinks before dinner and some beer after. He seemed relaxed, but he was unusually quiet and his face was gray.

"I went to bed at three but couldn't sleep," said Meyer. "Around 3:30, Gene came back. He said he'd slept, but was wide awake now and wanted a drink; he had no liquor in his house. I had half a bottle of bourbon, and each of us had two stiff drinks. We sat talking for about two hours, mostly reminiscing. He mentioned at one point that perhaps he had been wrong about suicide, that maybe the Christian viewpoint was the right one, after all. Elsie was in bed in the adjoining room and she didn't get up, but she and Gene exchanged a few words through the door. He told her, 'I'm a man of iron if I come through this.'

"He had a teaching engagement in New York later that day—it was now 5 A.M. Monday—so he decided to get a few hours of sleep on my couch. He asked me to leave the bottle where he could find it, and I did. There wasn't enough left in it to make him drunk.

"I went to sleep, and when I got up at eleven, Gene was gone and so was the bottle. I guessed he had followed his usual routine of driving to Poughkeepsie, from where he would take the train to New York."

An hour later Ruth telephoned Elsie Meyer.

"She said Gene had given her permission, before she left, to go back to his house and pick up her clothes," Elsie recalled, "but she claimed she was afraid to go alone, because she couldn't be certain Gene had gone to New York, and if he was home he might hit her. I was positive Gene *was* in New York, but I said I'd pick her up and go with her to the house."

Elsie put her five-year-old son, John, into the car, and started out. She had to pass Eugene's house to fetch Ruth and was startled to see his jeep parked in the driveway. He must have felt ill and canceled his teaching appointment, she thought. She parked, told her child to wait in the car, and knocked at the front door. There was no answer, but the door was open, and Elsie, fearing that Eugene might be really ill, walked into the living room. She saw Eugene lying at the foot of the stairs.

"Intellectually I knew he was dead," Elsie said. "But emotionally I couldn't accept it."

Eugene's telephone had been disconnected because he had carelessly neglected to pay the bill, so Elsie ran to the nearest neighbor's house and phoned for a doctor. Then she called her husband and told him, "He's done it."

"When I got back to my house," Elsie added, "Ruth telephoned, wanting to know what had happened to me. I'd forgotten about meeting her. I told her Gene had killed himself."

Eugene had apparently left Meyer's house around seven or eight that morning, possibly intending to bathe, shave and change for his trip to New York—for Monday, according to Ruth, was the day he always went through the ritual of trimming his beard and mustache. But sometime during his preparations he decided to put his razor to a different use. He drank off the last of Frank Meyer's bourbon, sat down at the driftwood desk on which his father had written plays in Provincetown, and scribbled on a scrap of paper: "Never let it be said of O'Neill that he failed to finish a bottle. Ave atque vale."

Then he climbed the stairs, filled the bathtub, stepped into it and slashed his wrists and left ankle. According to the coroner's report, he had apparently stumbled downstairs about twenty minutes later, in a kind of animal-panic attempt to save himself.

Neither the Meyers nor Ruth attributed Eugene's death (as gossip subsequently did) to straitened finances; he had back salary coming to him and was due to earn a minimum of $10,000 during the coming year, from lectures and various other free-lance activities to which he was committed. Nor did the Meyers consider the possibility that Ruth's rejection caused the suicide, although Ruth herself had a hysterical tendency, at first, to take the blame.

"I went to pieces after Gene died," she said. "I went to a psychiatrist for help, and he finally convinced me that the most I could have done was postpone his suicide, but that I couldn't have prevented it."

It devolved on Elsie Meyer to break the news of Eugene's death to his mother, early that evening. Kathleen Pitt-Smith, now widowed and still living in Douglaston, had a standing dinner date with her son in New York for either Monday or Tuesday of each week. If Kathleen did not hear from Eugene on Monday, she knew he would call her Tuesday to confirm the time and place of their meeting.

At 5:50 P.M. that Monday, the 25th, a newspaper reporter telephoned her and asked if she expected to hear from her son that day.

"I thought Gene had gotten married suddenly," Kathleen later said. "He had told me he was planning to marry Ruth. I told the reporter I didn't expect to hear from Gene any more that day, but that I'd be seeing him the next day."

The reporter, with a tact Kathleen later acknowledged gratefully, informed Kathleen her son had been involved in an accident in Woodstock that morning, and urged her to telephone the Meyers at once. Not until then did she learn, from Elsie, that Eugene had killed himself.

It was Aronberg on whom fell the burden of notifying O'Neill. But he did not reach O'Neill personally. He telephoned Marblehead, and Carlotta came to the phone.

"Gene was sitting in a chair right across from me," Carlotta recalled. "The lawyer told me, 'Eugene has killed himself.' I said, 'Are you sure?' and he said, 'Yes,' and I said, 'I don't believe it,' but he repeated that he was sure. I hung up the phone and sat down, Gene watching me with those black eyes of his.

" 'Well, come out with it, what is it?' Gene said. And I told him, 'Eugene is ill, very ill.' "

" 'When did he die?' Gene said.

"I told him what the lawyer had told me, and after that he never mentioned Eugene again—except that one time, when he said we could publish *Long Day's Journey* now that Eugene was dead."

O'Neill did not attend his son's funeral but, according to Kathleen Pitt-Smith, he paid all the expenses. He and Carlotta each sent separate flower pieces for the coffin.

Not long after Eugene's death a former Yale associate of his visited O'Neill in Marblehead. When he was alone in the room with his visitor, O'Neill asked: "Why did he do it?" The visitor was unable to enlighten him.

O'Neill did not put the question to Frank Meyer, but Meyer nevertheless volunteered a partial answer and received a warm acknowledgment from O'Neill.

Two and a half weeks after the suicide Meyer wrote to O'Neill that Eugene had always wanted his father to have his Ph.D. diploma, in case of his death, and asked if he could forward it to him in Marblehead.

"I should have written you much sooner had there been anything I could presume to say," Meyer went on. "You are probably the only person to whom I can say nothing of significance about him which you do not already know. But if you would like me to write—or care at any time to talk to me—please say so.

"The bite was deep. The woman had little to do with it—and whiskey nothing. Dispossession. Othello's occupation gone."

O'Neill answered from Point O'Rocks Lane a week later that Meyer's letter had been a great pleasure to him. "To learn that Eugene had wanted me to have his Ph.D. diploma warmed my heart," he said, and asked that it be sent to him in Marblehead.

Meyer was one of the very few people who heard from O'Neill in the weeks following Eugene's death; the blow caused O'Neill to insulate himself more than ever from the world outside Marblehead. But at least one other person—and, surprisingly, a member of the long since rejected Provincetown Playhouse group—did hear from him. She was Edna St. Vincent Millay's sister, Norma. When O'Neill heard of Edna St. Vincent Millay's death, on October 19, he sent a floral wreath to her home in Austerlitz, New York.

"I was very impressed," Norma Millay recalled. "I suppose it was just by chance, but the flowers were fall colors—all Vincent's favorite colors."

O'Neill's health, both mental and physical, declined steadily during the next three months. He dwelt more and more on suicide as a possible solution for his own problems and deplored the vestiges of Catholic indoctrination which held him back from this step.

He told Langner, with whom he discussed the subject more than once, that he had decided he couldn't commit suicide by jumping into the water. With bleak humor he explained that he was too good a swimmer and would instinctively try to save himself.

One of the few outsiders who had an occasional glimpse of O'Neill during the bitter months immediately following Eugene's death was a local foot patrolman named John Snow. Snow, a fair-haired man of medium height in his early forties, was a familiar figure to residents of the area. He had been assigned to the same beat, which included Point O'Rocks Lane, during five consecutive winters, and he made it a part of his routine to drop in on the isolated winter residents in his area two or three times a year, as a gesture of reassurance.

On several occasions he was invited into the O'Neill house by Carlotta, who brought him into the dining room for a five- or ten-minute chat with O'Neill. Seated at the long, wooden dining table, O'Neill would exchange brief pleasantries with the patrolman. Although he found it difficult to follow O'Neill's halting speech during his first visit, Snow gradually grew accustomed to it, and he listened attentively when O'Neill explained that he had come to Marblehead both for seclusion and for the pleasure it gave him to listen to the pounding surf, especially during stormy weather.

Snow found Carlotta pleasant and gracious, and he commiserated with her about her arthritis. The last time Snow visited the house O'Neill did not speak at all; Snow assumed that speech was now too much of an effort.

By the end of 1950 the little house on Point O'Rocks Lane had become a trap of smoldering emotions. Carlotta's arthritis caused her severe pain. Both Carlotta and O'Neill were taking pain-killing and sedative drugs. O'Neill was at the end of his rope—forced to live a life of idleness, in which he could do nothing but brood about past failures, present futility, and a future in which he would grow increasingly helpless and dependent upon Carlotta.

As a friend later put it, "With two towering personalities like Gene and Carlotta, ill, cooped up and cut off from the world that way, the lid was bound to blow off sooner or later."

That Christmas there was no written greeting of love from O'Neill to Carlotta, no birthday salutation, and no message of hope for the new year. The O'Neills, now both past their sixty-third birthdays, managed—but only just—to get through the first month of the year 1951 with no outward sign of the storm that was gathering momentum within.

LXIII

SOMETIME AFTER NIGHTFALL ON FEBRUARY 5, 1951, O'Neill walked out the front door of his house. Where he thought he was going—whether it was just as far as his legs could carry him, or whether it was for a final swim in the ocean—will probably never be known. But it is plain that he was not going for a turn about his garden, for he could walk only with great difficulty. Even with the aid of a cane his legs were unreliable; he would sometimes try to take a step forward and crumple backward instead. Yet, when he left his house that night, he was in such haste that he forgot his cane. Moreover, eight inches of snow had fallen the day before and lay in a frozen crust over the ground; the temperature was in the low thirties, but O'Neill wore no overshoes, coat or hat. He was dressed in slacks and a wool shirt.

O'Neill took a half dozen faltering steps, then stumbled and fell heavily to the ground. He lost consciousness from the pain; his right leg was broken at the knee. For some time, perhaps as long as an hour, he lay in the snow.

Carlotta was wrestling with her own demons inside the house. She had been taking a medicine containing bromide for nervous tension, not knowing she was allergic to the drug; the bromide was beginning to have a toxic effect. Although unaware of it at the time, Carlotta had gradually been giving herself a galloping case of what was later diagnosed as "bromide intoxication"—an illness that arises in some people when the bromide, instead of being excreted, is absorbed by the blood and affects cerebral centers. This condition is often characterized by periods of confusion, dizziness and disorientation.

Carlotta later said she waited for O'Neill to return from his walk. But her memory of that night, and of the events following, was clouded by drug-induced psychosis and must be evaluated accordingly. "When he didn't come back, I became very much worried," she added. "And I heard a noise, like an animal caught in something. Walking to the balcony, I saw it was O'Neill, who had fallen on the rocks and could not get up. I went to him and tried to lift him." At that moment, she said, Dr. Dana arrived.

"I thought it was very strange he should arrive, when neither of us had telephoned for him to come," Carlotta recalled.

Dr. Dana, however, said he had received a message at about nine o'clock that night, summoning him to Point O'Rocks Lane. He had been making house calls and had been notified by his office that someone had telephoned from the O'Neill house. Since the message had not stipulated an emergency, Dr. Dana had assumed he was being summoned, as he had been on other occasions, to treat one of the O'Neills for a sore throat or some other minor ailment, and he completed his round of house calls before heading for Point O'Rocks Lane.

According to his account, it was about ten o'clock when he turned his car into the driveway of the O'Neill house. He climbed the front steps and rang the doorbell. As he waited in the dark, he thought he heard a faint cry from somewhere in the yard, but wasn't sure of its source. The door opened, spilling light from the house, when Dr. Dana heard the cry again. This time he recognized it as a call for help.

He sprang down the steps and across the yard, almost tripping over O'Neill. Dr. Dana helped him up, noticing his injured leg. Half dragging him, Dr. Dana said, he got O'Neill to the house.

According to Carlotta's recollection, she helped the doctor carry O'Neill into the house.

"The doctor took O'Neill's arms and shoulders, and I took his legs very carefully, and we carried him inside," she said.

As Dr. Dana later recalled, both of the O'Neills were overwrought. He said that O'Neill lay silently in the room, while Carlotta uttered phrases of dismay, wringing and twisting her hands. Preoccupied as he was with O'Neill's broken leg and chilled condition, it did not occur to him that Carlotta was herself in need of medical attention. He was concerned with getting O'Neill quickly into a hospital, and he telephoned for an ambulance—a private one, so that the call would not be registered in the local police office and there would be no publicity in the newspapers. He wondered fleetingly what had led up to O'Neill's fall, but he did not ask for an explanation, and neither Carlotta nor O'Neill offered one.

Carlotta said she asked the doctor what should be done about O'Neill's injured leg. "He said," Carlotta reported, "that O'Neill had better go to the hospital; the next thing I knew, an ambulance drove up. The Japanese boy [who was the O'Neill's house servant] went to the door and said, 'Madam, ambulance for the Master.'" Carlotta added that she thought the ambulance's arrival was "very strange," because, as far as she knew, nobody had rung for one.

"But I didn't say anything, because I didn't think it was my place to say it," she observed, adding that she realized it was necessary for her husband to get proper medical care. "So we helped him into the ambulance," she said, "and off he went to the hospital."

Dr. Dana, who referred to his records for confirmation of the episode, followed the ambulance in his car to the hospital in the nearby town of Salem. He saw O'Neill comfortably installed in the modern red-brick hospital at eleven-thirty o'clock and made arrangements for a bone surgeon to attend to the broken leg. Then he drove home, haunted by the look of desperation on O'Neill's ashen face. Dr. Dana felt a deep sense of dismay. He thought of the mental torment O'Neill had endured in recent months and he wondered whether it was at all possible that O'Neill might have been on his way to commit suicide when he fell.

Carlotta said that she became terribly nervous and worried after her husband left, and that she took a large dose of her medicine to calm her nerves. She had been instructed, she said, to take the medicine whenever she was "very nervous and felt really on the edge of things."

"After a bit," she continued, "I began to feel very dizzy. And I began to get more worried." She recalled that she put on her street clothes and then told her houseboy: "Saki, I'm going over to the hospital to see Mr. O'Neill.

"He said, 'Shall I take you in my car?' and I said, 'No, you better stay here and take messages if anything happens.'

"I walked out to the main road and stood there, thinking maybe a taxi would come along and I could take it, and if not, I'd start to walk. Well, I was walking along, quietly, and an automobile stopped; it was an automobile the Marblehead Neck police officers used for going over all the roads in the area once or twice a day."

Carlotta remembered getting into the car at the suggestion of one of its occupants, and asking him to take her to see her husband at Salem Hospital.

"While we drove, things began to get a bit fuzzy," she said. The last she remembered, she was taken to the patients' entrance of Salem Hospital. Then she "went out like a light."

O'Neill had departed for Salem on Monday night; police and medical records show it was late Tuesday evening when Carlotta was admitted to the hospital.

On Tuesday, February 6, the Langners arrived at their home in Westport, Connecticut, from a trip to Nassau and were given a message by their caretaker to the effect that Mr. O'Neill had broken his leg and Mrs. O'Neill would like Mrs. Langner to please come to Marblehead.

Mrs. Langner immediately put through a call to the house at Point O'Rocks Lane, but was told by the servant who answered the telephone that Mrs. O'Neill had gone out. Puzzled, Mrs. Langner said she would call again later. She kept trying, unsuccessfully, to reach Carlotta, and then made a series of calls which eventually elicited the information that O'Neill was at Salem Hospital.

Toward nightfall of that day, Patrolman John Snow, making his rounds on foot, recognized Carlotta as she walked down the street not far from her house. He noticed with surprise that she was inadequately dressed against the biting cold. He greeted her and immediately saw there was something wrong. He tried to persuade her to return to her house, but she said she would not go back. Shifting his tactics, he fell into step with her. She seemed tired, and when they turned the corner she told Snow she would walk no farther.

After trying vainly to induce her to come into the neighbor's house before which they had stopped, Snow left her outside and entered the house alone. From the front hall he kept a watchful eye on the forlorn figure standing in the cold night, and telephoned the police station. He explained the situation and asked for a police car.

In a few moments the car arrived. In it were Patrolmen John Tucker and Norman Powers; they spent some time trying to induce Carlotta to enter the car, and she finally did.

Tucker, recalling the incident some years later, said that she seemed, immediately after entering the car, to recover her self-possession. She confided to him that she wished to visit her husband in Salem and indicated that she would like them to drive her there. But seconds later she became hysterical.

The policemen, realizing that their passenger needed medical attention, headed the car back toward the O'Neill house, from where they could call a doctor.

Dr. Dana arrived, calmed Carlotta with sedatives and made an official request to the station house for the use of Car Number 1 to convey her to Salem Hospital; the request was granted by the officer on duty, George E. Girard. The doctor followed the police vehicle to Salem in his own car and saw to Carlotta's formal admission into the hospital at 9:45. It was the third time in their marriage that O'Neill and Carlotta were patients simultaneously under the same hospital roof.

Dr. Dana was troubled about Carlotta's condition. Salem had no facilities for the care of mental patients, and, unaware that she was suffering from bromide poisoning, he was convinced that she needed psychiatric care. Although it was within his power—and was he believed, his duty—to have her transferred as quickly as possible to a mental institution, he hesitated to assume the responsibility. This, he said, was not because he was unfamiliar with the procedure; in his years of practice he had frequently been obliged to fill in and sign a "pink slip," which is the order for temporary (ten-day) care required in such cases by the Commonwealth of Massachusetts. But the patient was Mrs. Eugene O'Neill and there was sure to be widespread concern and publicity over her transfer to a mental institution. He therefore took the precaution of telephoning Dr. Melvin Goodman, who was a psychiatrist on the staff of Salem Hospital, and asking him to examine his patient early the next morning.

(Carlotta, though she remembered nothing about the hours she spent in Salem Hospital, said she was later told that she had kept repeating, "My husband is sick, my husband is sick, please take me to my husband, I want to see how he is.")

On the morning of February 7, O'Neill's second day in Salem Hospital, Dr. Dana, making his daily call, found O'Neill despondent. His leg had been put in a cast and everything that could be done for his physical comfort had been attended to. Dr. Dana told him that Carlotta had been brought to the hospital the night before, that a psychiatrist had examined her this morning and found her, in the official words of the "Temporary Care" request issued by the Commonwealth of Massachusetts, to be "in need of immediate care and treatment."

O'Neill listened, but said nothing. Dr. Dana told him as gently as he could that it was thought best by him and other hospital personnel that Carlotta be removed, within the next few hours, to McLean Hospital, a private psychiatric facility in the nearby town of Belmont. O'Neill was still silent. At noon Carlotta was taken away. She remembered nothing until she woke up "just a little bit" in an ambulance. She also remembered that her feet hurt her because they had been tied. She was brought into McLean Hospital and then lost consciousness again.

A few hours after Carlotta left Salem O'Neill received a telephone call from New York. It was Mrs. Langner.

"He told me, 'It was just like the last time,'" Mrs. Langner said. She assumed he was referring to his previous fall in New York.

After assuring herself that O'Neill was getting all necessary care, Mrs. Langner said she would visit him soon at Salem.

O'Neill had private nurses and a pleasant room with a private bath on the third floor of the hospital. His day nurse, Mrs. Claire Bird, was tall and pretty with blond hair, light-brown eyes, and a mild, gentle manner. When she first came on the case, the morning after O'Neill's arrival, she found him difficult to understand. His speech was so thick it was almost incomprehensible and his hands shook pitifully. He seemed disoriented and the words he mumbled made little sense. His mind was cloudy at times, particularly during the night, when he sometimes had hallucinations. During the day he had been taking, for his tremor, something called "831," a mixture of chloral and bromide that was a standard sedative of the time. Although no one realized it then, O'Neill, like Carlotta, was suffering from bromide poisoning.

An experienced nurse and an intuitive woman, Mrs. Bird imposed as little routine as possible on her patient, while at the same time tactfully rendering him such help and sympathy as she sensed he wanted and could accept. Although he ate poorly—sometimes he took an hour to finish his breakfast—she realized it embarrassed him to be fed, and upset him even more to be watched while he fed himself. So she saw to it that his food was cut, and then left the room. She did light his cigarettes for him and always stayed while he smoked, for fear he would burn himself. He talked to her of his wife, one minute in an objective, oriented way, and the next minute, weeping, he would ask to see her.

"At first, he didn't seem to know what he wanted," Mrs. Bird recalled. "He just lay there, looking so helpless. Sometimes he'd talk to me about his older son's suicide. He never mentioned his daughter directly, but he gave the impression, in his ramblings, that his entire family had gone wrong. He seemed to want to be alone most of the time, but every once in a while he wanted to talk and then he would ramble on about what a mess everything was."

Since O'Neill's leg, which had turned out to have a fracture into the knee joint, was in a cast, he had to lie in bed during the early part of his stay. But after a while he was helped to get out of bed and into an armchair, and then he was taught how to get about on crutches. Mrs. Bird would walk him down the corridor.

"He appreciated everything I did for him," she said.

O'Neill felt guilty when his nurse had to spend Easter Sunday at the hospital.

"You should have been in the Easter parade," he told her, giving her a check for $35 with which to "buy an Easter bonnet." Mrs. Bird was touched. She was particularly appreciative of the gift because she knew how painful it was for O'Neill to write a check.

"I used to make out his checks for him at Salem," she said. "He barely had enough stamina to sign his name. I felt guilty every time I had to get my salary, it seemed so painful for him just to scribble his signature."

While O'Neill appreciated Mrs. Bird's brand of solicitude, he objected to the less tactful pampering of others. "Get rid of my night nurse," he once admonished Mrs. Bird. "Every time I turn over she throws a wet washcloth at me."

O'Neill's pitiful craving in the hospital to be physically independent resulted one day in a near disaster that set the whole staff by the ears. Mrs. Bird had left briefly to have her dinner, enjoining O'Neill to ring for the floor nurse if he needed anything. He was not supposed to get out of bed unassisted, for his leg was still in a cast and the crutches were troublesome to manage. As she returned from her dinner Mrs. Bird was greeted by a breathless floor nurse, who told her she had just looked into O'Neill's room, and he wasn't there. Mrs. Bird was flabbergasted. She hurried into the room, saw it was empty, and dashed for the bathroom.

"He had fallen backwards into the bathtub," she said. "There he was, with his feet up in the air. When he saw me, he started laughing, and I couldn't help but laugh too."

The cast had not broken, and O'Neill was unhurt, but it took the combined efforts of Mrs. Bird, an intern and a male nurse to pry him out of the tub. When he was mildly rebuked for jeopardizing his safety, O'Neill explained that he hadn't wanted to bother anyone.

As the weeks went by and O'Neill's leg began to mend, he seemed to settle down with some measure of resignation at Salem. He accepted the routine of heat lamp treatments and exercises for his leg and appeared, according to his doctor, to be in better spirits than he had been during recent months at home. A bout with flu set him back briefly but he made a good recovery with the help of aureomycin. Although he showed little interest in reading or in any other occupation except meditation, broken by occasional, desultory conversation, both Mrs. Bird and the doctor felt that O'Neill was relatively at peace. Certainly he never complained to either of them or expressed any desire for change. He seemed reluctant to face a decision regarding his future—and Carlotta's. On the other hand, he recognized that he could not stay at Salem indefinitely; some gesture toward Carlotta, who was still at McLean, would soon be mandatory. And while his doctor and nurse felt that O'Neill had arrived at a state of utter pliability, with little will to live or fight, there were others who thought he could and would rally.

Since arriving at Salem O'Neill had resumed contact with the world—or, rather, the world had resumed contact with him. A small group of friends, informed of O'Neill's condition by the Langners, began flying up from New York to visit him. Among them were a few who had not been welcome at Marblehead. Saxe Commins, Shirlee Weingarten, and a handful of others visited fairly regularly. To some of his friends it seemed that O'Neill, with his air of helplessness, needed their assistance in re-assembling his life. And he impulsively and dramatically responded to their sympathy; he listened, not without a certain amount of pleasurable self-pity, to their advice, and indicated that he was open to their suggestions.

Some time in March, believing that O'Neill required professional therapeutic support in addition to the ministrations of his friends, Lawrence Langner called in the Boston psychiatrist Merrill Moore. Dr. Moore, who had been recommended to Langner by the Broadway director, Joshua Logan, was a prominent man in his field. As a sideline he wrote pornographic poetry.

Dr. Moore's entrance into the case complicated rather than solved it, however. His diagnosis of O'Neill's condition was summed up by him on March 19, 1951, for O'Neill's physician. In it he stated flatly (and, as it turned out, erroneously) that O'Neill was not suffering from what he called "bromide intoxication." He said O'Neill was mentally ill and could not take care of himself. He suggested two alternatives: a mental hospital or a legal guardian. O'Neill's mental condition, said Dr. Moore, was due to his son's recent death and worry over his wife's illness. Dr. Moore felt that O'Neill needed protection from his "difficult domestic situation" and recommended temporary separation from Carlotta. He added that O'Neill was unable to plan and incapable of making decisions, that he could not stay indefinitely at Salem and that it would be unsuitable for him to return to Marblehead.

Dr. Moore also looked into the situation regarding Carlotta, whose ten-day stay at McLean had been extended. He went to visit her at the hospital.

"I have never felt so frightened of a human being in my life," Carlotta later said. She added that she had not wanted to see him, and that her doctors at McLean had not been happy about Dr. Moore's visit, either; in fact, one of them said he would stay in the room with her while Dr. Moore interviewed her.

"He took my hand and kissed it and said, 'Beautiful Carlotta Monterey. Oh, this is such a pleasure,'" Carlotta recalled with a shudder.

She told Dr. Moore that the only reason she was seeing him was that she wanted to know about her husband. Dr. Moore told her O'Neill was ill and needed quiet.

"I noticed there was a sort of accentuation on the word, 'quiet,'" Carlotta recalled, "and I said, well, I've lived with him a good many years and we've never had anything *but* quiet. I said if there was ever any noise or disturbance, it was through him, not through me."

After talking for some time, Dr. Moore finally said, according to Carlotta:

"I have something to suggest to you. I think it would be better if you made up your mind to live in one place and take up writing, or whatever you like, and allow your husband to have quiet in some sanitarium we can find for him. You know, dear Carlotta Monterey, you wouldn't want to see the leaf wither on the vine."

Carlotta said she was so nervous after Dr. Moore left that she was unable to sleep. "I walked the floor all night," she added.

Dr. Moore, on his part, made a singular and, in light of subsequent developments, unwarranted recommendation. He suggested that Carlotta's condition necessitated prolonged treatment. This recommendation was met by some of O'Neill's friends with considerably more enthusiasm than the suggestion regarding O'Neill (which was virtually ignored and was later modified by Dr. Moore himself). It was at this confused point in the proceedings that lawyers entered.

James E. Farley, a portly man with shrewd eyes and a shy smile, was called upon by O'Neill's New York attorney to represent him in Massachusetts. A self-styled country lawyer, Farley conducted a practice in and around Salem that consisted largely of estate settlements. He had had some experience with marital difficulty cases, which was what he was given to understand he was now being asked to handle.

When Farley visited O'Neill at Salem Hospital, he could not have been more surprised by his client's appearance and manner. Having read his plays and found them "lusty," he was startled, as many people had been before him, to meet a gentle, considerate, polite man who seemed to bear no resemblance whatever to the violent characters of his creation.

"He was so darn nice—he wouldn't have done wrong to a sparrow. If he were hurt, he didn't want to say anyone had hurt him," the lawyer later recalled, admitting that he himself felt personally pained that O'Neill should be reduced to the cheerless existence he was leading. Farley took particular care, of course, to observe O'Neill's mental condition from a legal point of view. Unlike Dr. Moore, Farley came away from his visits convinced that O'Neill was under no mental confusion whatever; he talked clearly, if haltingly, and appeared perfectly aware of what he was doing.

Toward the end of March, after more than six weeks at Salem, O'Neill made a decision that pleased some of his friends, drew the attention of the press and public, and undoubtedly satisfied his own abeyant sense of dramatics.

On March 23 he filed a petition in the Probate Court of the County of Essex, in Salem, stating that Carlotta, who was still a patient at McLean, was "an insane person and incapable of taking care of herself." His petition went on to request that "James E. Farley . . . or some other suitable person, be appointed guardian of said Carlotta Monterey O'Neill." The petition, signed in O'Neill's shaky and barely legible hand, and signed also by Dr. Moore, was returnable in one month's time—on April 23.

It is difficult to determine whether O'Neill really wanted to sign the petition or whether he had been talked into it. He later told several people that he hadn't known what he was doing when he signed.

What the authorities of McLean Hospital thought of Carlotta's mental condition was demonstrated six days after the filing of the petition. They released her.

"McLean was the most decent hospital I've ever known," Carlotta said. "I'd been in hospitals in different parts of the world, but I'd never met doctors who were so understanding or gentlemanly."

Carlotta recalled that on her first day at McLean she had been "scared to death." Awaking in a strange bed, she saw bars on the windows and doors.

"I didn't know whether I was in jail, or *where* I was—or what O'Neill had done to me—a little drama being practiced in the home."

But finally, she said, a nurse came in and soothed her, explaining where she was and assuring her that everything would be all right.

Soon Carlotta was moved to a building in which the patients could come and go as they pleased. The doctors, she said, told her, "You shouldn't be here. You should never have been sent here."

In a paper prepared just prior to her release, analyzing the bromide poisoning, Dr. William H. Horwitz, a McLean Hospital psychiatrist, stated, in part, that Carlotta's illness had had a very gradual onset some time before admission to McLean, when "she became more nervous and began taking several teaspoonsful of liquid sleeping medicine every night that she thought was chloral hydrate. . . ."

The report said that examination on admission to the hospital had revealed a disoriented woman, at times calm and at other times very excited, with periods of confusion and poor memory. After outlining her treatment, which, beyond eliminating the bromide, had been mainly supportive, the report added that eventually "it was possible for her to be moved to an open ward, where she had friendly relations with many of the other patients and was able to go to the library, to the coffee shop and out of the hospital for walks or drives."

On at least one of these occasions, accompanied by a nurse, Carlotta visited her husband at Salem. Mrs. Bird, who had left the room during the half-hour reunion, found O'Neill listless after the visit. But she had found him to be equally cheerless after the visits of his friends.

"He never got excited when they came to see him and when they left he would sometimes shrug, as though to say he was glad they were gone," she recalled. "He just let anyone do what they wanted with him."

When on March 29, a Thursday, Carlotta was discharged from McLean Hospital, the prognosis on her discharge summary read "Good." A recommendation added that she should return home to the care of a doctor, and arrangements were made for her to see "an outside psychiatrist." Since McLean was thoroughly convinced of Carlotta's sanity and was aware of the guardianship petition pending against her, the hospital was anxious to see her rights protected and called in Dr. Harry Kozol, a young, dynamic and highly regarded Boston psychiatrist on the Harvard staff, who was an expert in legal medicine.

The O'Neills' situation was taking on the earmarks of a public, last-ditch battle. Newspapers all over the country were publishing accounts of the insanity proceedings and many people felt that the O'Neill marriage, whatever strains it had managed to withstand in the past, could not possibly survive this round of hostilities.

Lawrence Langner had been trying for some time to induce O'Neill to come to New York. He was convinced that O'Neill would be better off where his friends could more easily be in touch with him and attend to his wants. Langner said he felt that O'Neill truly wanted to get away from the Boston area. According to Langner, O'Neill had expressed anxiety over the possibility of political pressure being exerted to have him confined to an institution; O'Neill, added Langner, seemed hypersensitive about the fact that Boston political authorities had frequently been hostile to his plays, and that if any question of his sanity arose, he might have a hard time eliciting sympathy.

"I loved and respected Gene," Langner said, in justification of the manipulations that went on in Salem. "I felt the transfer would be in his best interests."

Mrs. Bird recalled that O'Neill betrayed considerable doubt about leaving Salem.

"He finally agreed to go, with a reluctant 'Yes,'" she said. "But even on the day he was supposed to leave, I thought he might change his mind."

O'Neill, in the end, did not change his mind. Significantly, it was on the morning after Carlotta's discharge from McLean—a Friday—that his friends arranged for him to be taken by ambulance to Boston's South Station.

O'Neill's leg was still in a cast, although it was healing nicely, and he was carried by stretcher to a compartment on the New York-bound train.

Carlotta lost no time in retaliating for the past weeks of humiliation and frustration. That same day, through her lawyers, Nutter, McLennan and Fish, of Boston, she filed a petition in the Salem Court; in it she asked for separate maintenance, charging her husband with cruelty.

The petition stated that O'Neill had failed, "without just cause, to furnish suitable support for her," that she was living apart from her husband "for justifiable cause," and that on or about the 1st day of February, 1951, and "at divers other times prior thereto," O'Neill had been guilty of "cruel and abusive treatment" of her. The petition was signed by Carlotta in a firm hand. It was returnable on the same date as O'Neill's insanity petition against her.

O'Neill's train ride to New York was a dreary one. Mrs. Bird accompanied him, at his request. She recalled that it rained all the way and that O'Neill napped during a good part of the trip.

It was still drizzling when the train pulled into Grand Central, four hours later. An ambulance waited to take O'Neill to a small private hospital in the East Seventies, where a room had been reserved for him. When they arrived at the hospital, which was more like a convalescent home, O'Neill was exhausted, and Mrs. Bird got him into his bed.

He looked around at the dreary, hotel-like atmosphere of the room and said, "Get me out of this place." Mrs. Bird telephoned to several of O'Neill's friends, including Winfield Aronberg, and they promised to have him transferred the next morning. It was still raining when O'Neill, with Mrs. Bird seated by his side, sank into troubled sleep.

LXIV

ON SATURDAY, MARCH 31, 1951, O'NEILL WAS TRANS-
ferred by ambulance to Doctors Hospital. Gratefully he found himself
once more in the hands of Drs. Fisk and Patterson; and once again, too,
he had a cheerful room with a river view.

Mrs. Bird stayed with him that day, seeing him settled into his new
hospital routine, and in the evening she joined her husband at a hotel.
O'Neill was paying Mr. Bird's, as well as his wife's, weekend expenses
in Manhattan. On Sunday Mrs. Bird, accompanied by her husband, came
to say good-by to O'Neill, and she handed him $400 in cash that she had
been holding for him.

O'Neill asked her plaintively why she couldn't stay and nurse him
in New York, and Mrs. Bird smilingly gestured toward her husband,
whose job, O'Neill knew, was in Massachusetts. Resignedly, O'Neill
shook her hand, and then kissed her cheek.

'I don't care whether your husband is here or not," he said, in a
feeble attempt at jocularity. But there were tears in his eyes.

Dr. Fisk and Dr. Patterson both greeted O'Neill warmly. Dr. Fisk had
already received a report from Dr. Dana and was prepared to find O'Neill's
nervous disorder worse than it had been three years before; Dr. Dana
had also cautioned that O'Neill was still subject, intermittently, to hallucinations. But Dr. Fisk found O'Neill fairly well oriented for the most part.
Dr. Patterson recalled, however, that O'Neill had periods of deep depression, that he occasionally had what he called a "frozen face," and that
for a time he was practically unable to get out of bed; there were bars
at the side of his bed to deter him from trying.

One of the first things Dr. Fisk did was to try straight chloral instead
of the chloral-bromide mixture O'Neill had been taking. With the new
medicine the hallucinations gradually disappeared. But Dr. Fisk found
O'Neill to be in a generally "frail and unsteady" condition. He weighed
something under a hundred pounds.

Dr. Patterson, who had received a briefing from the Salem Hospital
orthopedic specialist, was less concerned over O'Neill's broken knee than
he was over the palsy. He angrily refused to believe that O'Neill had to
tremble.

"I would give him heck for shaking," Dr. Patterson recalled. "I'd get furious. I'd see he'd be ready for a cigarette and start to shake. I'd scold him for it—with a smile, of course. And when he thought about it he *could* control it."

Dr. Patterson also tried to persuade O'Neill to do some writing because he felt it would have a therapeutic effect. "I offered to bring him my dictaphone or get a secretary for him to take his dictation," Dr. Patterson said. But of course O'Neill declined the offer, explaining, for perhaps the hundredth time, that he could only write by himself with a pencil.

Dr. Patterson arranged his schedule of rounds so that his last call at night would be made on O'Neill—"because then I could talk to him, relax and have a cigarette."

During the two and a half months O'Neill spent at Doctors Hospital he seemed to take a savage, if quiet, delight in putting on what can only be described as a multiple-faceted and theatrical performance. He told a variety of conflicting stories about his relationship with and feelings for Carlotta, and conveyed—one can only assume deliberately—a number of highly contradictory impressions. To some friends he indicated that he could not face a return to Carlotta; to other friends he gave every sign that a reconciliation was the one thing he longed for.

Probably he was releasing the pent-up dramatics that should have gone into writing—testing the various psychological effects on the people with whom he found himself surrounded during the last-act denouement. Carlotta's response was the only one he was ultimately interested in, but apparently he had to have a dramatic outlet while he was waiting to see which way the climactic scene would be played. He knew that he hadn't much longer to live. "I'm done for," he told Russel Crouse early in his hospital stay. Possibly he recalled, and decided to abide by, some Nietzschean advice that was still an integral part of his philosophy:

"To many men life is a failure; a poison-worm gnawing at their heart. Then let them see to it that their dying is all the more a success."

O'Neill had, to a remarkable degree, adhered to the pattern of Nietzsche's life during much of his own. The final years of the lives of both men present a striking parallel. Like O'Neill's collapse in Marblehead, Nietzsche's final breakdown was brought on, in part, by prolonged physical suffering, heightened by his mental isolation, and increased by the excessive use of the very drug O'Neill had taken—chloral. And, as was the case with Nietzsche, whose friends thought he had gone insane, O'Neill's sanity was questioned at this period, not only by Dr. Moore but by a number of other acquaintances.

For O'Neill a success meant a dramatic success, and he managed to wring the last ounce of dramatics out of the weeks at Doctors Hospital. A few days after his arrival in New York, and unknown to at least half the friends who were visiting and solacing him, he was in touch with Carlotta and making overtures for a reunion.

In Boston, Carlotta told a correspondent for *Time*, Francis (Jeff) Wylie, that O'Neill had been writing her love letters and sending her red roses.

"She says that she loves him and feels that he needs her more than anything else," Wylie reported to his New York office on April 6, trying to interest *Time* in doing a story about the O'Neills' difficulties. He went on to say that Dr. Kozol, who was seeing Carlotta regularly, was "confident there will be a reconciliation in three weeks." *Time*'s home office considered the story "too sad" and Wylie ultimately agreed, but he continued to keep his editors posted, so that they would have the background if and when the O'Neills became reconciled.

On April 7, having had a long talk with Carlotta, Wylie reported that, according to her, O'Neill had been "completely broken by Parkinson's disease."

"Carlotta thinks that O'Neill would have committed suicide long ago if it weren't for his Catholic training," he went on. "Carlotta feels that his action in trying to have a guardian appointed for her was partly in response to his own instinct for drama. He could no longer arouse her romantic interest in him (she is sixty-two), so he had to do something else to get some sort of a passionate response."

Carlotta complained to Wylie that Langner was angry with her because she was firmly behind O'Neill in withholding permission to produce *A Touch of the Poet* and a new presentation of *A Moon for the Misbegotten,* and she was also indignant about "the meddling of Dr. Merrill Moore."

"Although her psychiatrist, Dr. Harry Kozol . . . said the O'Neills would be reconciled in three weeks," Wylie continued, "Carlotta thinks not. She loves the man and wants to be with him, she says, but is doubtful that he has the capacity to appreciate her devotion any more."

A day later—April 8—another document in the Guardianship Petition was received and placed on record in the Essex Probate Court; if Carlotta was aware of its arrival, it must have strengthened her in her doubts about O'Neill's capacity to appreciate her, for the document was part of the machinery O'Neill had set in motion. It was a letter from Carlotta's daughter, Cynthia, now Mrs. Stram, of Sausalito, California. It read, in part:

"I have received notification that a petition has been presented in your Court . . . asking that a suitable person be appointed as [my mother's] guardian. If . . . there is sufficient evidence . . . for you in your judgment to consider her incapable of caring for herself, I have no objection to the appointment of . . . some . . . suitable person to act as her guardian. My paramount consideration . . . is her welfare and proper treatment. Living at such a great distance and working at a job that pays $48.00 per week which goes for the support of my crippled husband, twelve year old son, home and myself, I am in no position to actively participate in the care of my mother."

At least two of O'Neill's frequent visitors at Doctors Hospital were also in touch with Carlotta in Boston and had a pretty good idea that the O'Neills would eventually resolve their problems. One of them was Russel Crouse. He recalled that Carlotta was bitter, but he had the impression that she would take O'Neill back; she even suggested to Crouse that he relay messages to O'Neill, and O'Neill, who knew Crouse was having conversations with Carlotta, also asked him to relay messages. But Crouse insisted on maintaining his neutrality. He told each of them that he could not intercede without clearance from the lawyers, as the case was a legal matter and would only become more complicated if he involved himself.

Armina Marshall Langner also was in contact with Carlotta by telephone during this period. Carlotta would no longer speak to Langner, but his wife had maintained friendship with her and had, in fact, paid her several visits while she was confined at McLean. Once, according to Mrs. Langner, Carlotta, telephoning from Boston, said that O'Neill had asked her to take him back. Mrs. Langner said that, of course, Carlotta must take O'Neill back, that she knew O'Neill loved her and needed her.

While the battle of wills between O'Neill and Carlotta was being waged long-distance and under the eyes of one faction of friends—which included Charles O'Brien Kennedy and George Jean Nathan, both of whom were sure from the start that the O'Neills would patch up their differences—another faction hadn't the faintest idea that O'Neill was in touch with Carlotta. Significantly, this faction consisted in the main of people who had been rebuffed by Carlotta—people who, O'Neill knew, felt they had been wounded by her and would obviously not be sympathetic to his real feelings about her.

One exception, however, was Kenneth Macgowan. Macgowan, among the earliest and staunchest supporters of the O'Neill–Carlotta alliance, had visited O'Neill once or twice in Marblehead and still got on tolerably well with Carlotta. For some reason, though, he had the impression that O'Neill was now through with her.

"When I saw Gene in the hospital, he took my hand in both of his, and said, 'It's nice to see you this way.' I thought he meant without Carlotta around. When I saw him the next day, he spoke very little, but I felt very strongly that he was not going back to Carlotta."

The most misled, and ultimately the most grievously wounded, among his friends was Saxe Commins. Commins, whose devotion to O'Neill seemed at times possessive, was almost tearfully grateful to be able to re-establish his interrupted friendship with him. Snubbed by Carlotta since O'Neill's previous hospitalization in New York, Commins was convinced that Carlotta was now completely and permanently out of the picture; he made every effort to persuade O'Neill that a future without Carlotta would not be black and assured O'Neill that he would take care of him. An emotional man, Commins had suffered a good deal since being cut off from O'Neill. He had remained unflaggingly loyal and would willingly have sacrificed much personal comfort for his friend. But Commins' strong devotion to O'Neill prevented his seeing that no amount of sacrifice or loyalty would cut any ice when and if Carlotta chose to re-enter the picture.

One of Commins' plans to cheer up O'Neill and compensate him for his loss of Carlotta was to notify a number of the old Provincetown crowd of O'Neill's presence in (and Carlotta's absence from) New York. Joyfully they flocked to see him—and with each he played a touching scene of reunion. O'Neill's visiting hours were limited to two a day, and only two visitors were allowed into his room at a time. The anteroom outside his door was almost always thronged, and sometimes people had to wait as many as three days before they could see him. (As often as not, the pair of visitors spent their allotted time talking to each other, for O'Neill's silences had become heavier and more frequent.)

James Light was one of those who patiently waited his turn.

"Hello, Jimmy. How about a cig?" was O'Neill's greeting, accompanied by a feeble smile which, in Light's opinion, easily spanned the two dozen years during which the two had not seen each other. Light proffered the cigarette, which O'Neill took with violently trembling hands. Light began to strike a match, but O'Neill snatched the book of matches from him and with a painful effort lighted his own cigarette. He leaned back and relaxed. He seemed, to Light, genuinely happy with the visit.

Aside from Commins, who arranged the flow of visitors, the person who spent the most time with O'Neill was Shirlee Weingarten. Shirlee had been divorced and remarried and she brought her new husband, Robert Lantz, a literary agent, to the hospital to meet O'Neill.

Early in his hospital stay O'Neill told Shirlee that he did not want to read any of his mail. He refused even to be told who had written to him. He asked Shirlee to deal with the letters in any way she saw fit—imposing a rather frightening responsibility on her. Shirlee had no way of knowing in what relationship many of O'Neill's correspondents stood to him; she was obliged to trust to her instinct, and the sheaf of correspondence she conducted on O'Neill's behalf during that time is a remarkable testament to the art of tactful evasion.

Despite her best efforts, she was rebuffed once or twice by return mail. A letter arrived during the first week in April, for example, from O'Neill's second cousin, Agnes Brennan. Miss Brennan, by then a spinster of advanced age, wrote to "Eugene dear" that she could not conceive of him without Carlotta nor of Carlotta without him. "I always think of you as the little dark-eyed youngster that all we Brennans loved so much," the letter ended. As Shirlee dared not even ask O'Neill whether Miss Brennan and he were actually acquainted—she knew he would tell her he didn't care if she tore up every letter that arrived—she composed a model of noncommittal graciousness. For her trouble she shortly thereafter received a brief, outraged note—this time addressed directly to her— scoring O'Neill's coldness. Shirlee patiently filed the letter, along with all the others, and O'Neill never knew or cared about the ire he was arousing.

"He was interested in hardly anything," Shirley remembered. "He was barely articulate most of the time."

There was only one thing that seemed to give him momentary pleasure, according to Shirley, and that was listening to classical music over radio station WQXR. "It was one of his nurses who interested him in that," Shirlee said.

Shirlee was among those with whom O'Neill discussed his future more or less honestly. Within the first week or two of his arrival she asked him if he would write to Oona, hoping that a renewal of his relationship with his daughter would give him something to live for. O'Neill was firm in his refusal.

Shirlee was aware that several plans had been presented to O'Neill as alternatives to his going back to Carlotta. But she interpreted O'Neill's remarks to her to mean that O'Neill, in spite of the pending insanity and separate maintenance proceedings, was "never anything but enroute to his wife—even while he appeared to be traveling away from her." Shirlee added that in her opinion the return to Carlotta "was never weighed against any other possibility."

"Where can I go?" O'Neill asked her. "*You* can't take care of me."
And Shirlee wept silently over his predicament.

"I held him in my arms once, and he cried," Shirlee recalled, some
years after his death. "He didn't seem to have any flesh left. I don't think
he weighed more than ninety pounds. The neurologist at the hospital
told me one day that in the type of disease O'Neill was suffering from
the heart goes on, but little else. The doctor said, too, that shortly he
would become a vegetable. When he told me that I was so upset I felt
like slapping him."

O'Neill explained to Shirlee what she already instinctively knew—
that he was terribly sensitive about the loss of dignity involved in his
disease. He could not bear the thought of letting his friends take care of
him nor could he face the dreary prospect of spending his last days alone
in an apartment with a male nurse.

That, however, was one of the plans that had been advanced for his
consideration.

Dr. Moore, for some reason, was still active in the case and was summoned to New York to help O'Neill get straightened out. This time he
recommended that O'Neill take an apartment in New York and hire a
male nurse, while Carlotta was to take an apartment in Boston. The two
were to be on friendly terms, although they were to agree not to live
together. Dr. Moore had some misgivings about the reception of his plan
and called on Russel Crouse for help. He suggested that Crouse present
the apartment-with-male-nurse idea to O'Neill as "The Crouse Plan."

"*You* present it to him as 'The Moore Plan,'" said Crouse.

A few days later, on April 26, Crouse dryly noted in his diary: "Gene
wants none of the Moore Separation Plan."

Crouse, a conscientious diarist, also recorded that O'Neill was suicidal
during the early part of his hospital stay and that the windows of his
room were kept locked. One diary entry quoted O'Neill as having said,
"I dreamt I was in Japan two thousand years from now; they showed
me their scientific inventions, but wouldn't say how they were done."

At the end of April O'Neill was recuperating from a severe case of
pneumonia, which had lasted for six days. He was conscious during his
illness, but ran a high fever.

"We had a bad scare," Dr. Fisk later recalled. "But after the pneumonia he improved quickly. He was up and about most of the day. His
tremor improved too."

His visitors, from that point on, were likely to find O'Neill standing
to greet them, for the cast had been removed from his leg. One of the

visitors he received during this semiconvalescent period was Eugene Jr.'s Ruth. It was a strange and poignant meeting for both.

Ruth had met Winfield Aronberg before Eugene's death, and when she came to New York to look for a job she renewed her acquaintance with him. On one occasion Aronberg took Ruth to a restaurant to meet Dr. Moore—possibly with the idea that the psychiatrist might have a soothing effect on Ruth's jangled nerves. After Dr. Moore had questioned her extensively about Eugene Jr.'s death, Aronberg was suddenly struck with the idea of taking Ruth to visit O'Neill and, receiving an affirmation from Dr. Moore, ushered her to the hospital. Aronberg took Ruth through the waiting room full of people and presented her to O'Neill.

"I want you to meet someone, Gene," he said. Ruth and O'Neill shook hands and Ruth understood that she was to go back to the anteroom and wait. She did so, trembling with anxiety. She had met O'Neill only once before, with Eugene, at a dress rehearsal of *The Iceman Cometh,* and she wondered if O'Neill had recognized her.

Aronberg appeared in the waiting room. "Gene amazes me," he said to Ruth. "He told me, 'I know who she is. Bring her back.'"

When Ruth re-entered the room, O'Neill was standing, shaking.

"He embraced me," Ruth recalled, "and buried his head on my shoulder."

In early May Dr. Fisk found O'Neill so much improved that he felt justified in recommending an outing. Illustrative of the esteem in which he held O'Neill, Dr. Fisk proffered his own services as chauffeur on the expedition. At O'Neill's request, Dr. Fisk headed downtown.

"We drove along the waterfront and O'Neill pointed out to me many of the places where he had spent his early days—here had stood Jimmy-the-Priest's, there a brothel."

O'Neill talked about the dockworkers and the men of the sea. They led a rough life, he told Dr. Fisk, and they had been his friends.

Dr. Fisk and O'Neill looked at ships for a while and then they drove through Greenwich Village. O'Neill began to talk about whores, comparing them with Mother Earth, endowing them, as he had done in so many of his plays, with what he called "real souls" and the capacity to "solace man and give him comfort."

"Once I said something to O'Neill about what my colonel, during the war, used to refer to as a 'two-bit whore,'" Dr. Fisk recalled. "O'Neill was upset by that."

Several times O'Neill brought up the subject of the mythological giant Antaeus, whose mother was Earth. Antaeus was indestructible as long as he stood on the earth, but Hercules, who knew the secret of

Antaeus' strength, defeated him by lifting him away from his strength-giving source.

Dr. Fisk interpreted O'Neill's comments as an indication that O'Neill felt he had been separated from the lives of the whores and laborers and all those who live closest to the earth. O'Neill, however, may have been thinking of the often acknowledged strength he derived from Carlotta.

O'Neill was urged by Dr. Fisk to take several walks in the mild spring air with his nurse. O'Neill was rapidly mending—at least in so far as his broken bone and respiratory condition were concerned—and the time was approaching when he could no longer lay claim to the strained facilities of an acute-disease hospital.

Dr. Fisk, who also had received one or two telephone calls from Carlotta, was among those most firmly convinced that O'Neill would go back to her. He, too, believed that a sense of drama had contributed to the separation.

Carlotta had returned to Marblehead by the end of April, to dismantle her house. She was in temporary financial difficulties, as the legal proceedings against her had made it difficult for her to get at her bank account. Mai-mai Sze received a letter from her soon after, asking her to come up to Marblehead and bring some cash. Mai-mai Sze was stunned, upon her arrival at Marblehead, to find Carlotta looking ill and gray—and behaving more nervously than she had ever seen her act before. But she was impressed by Carlotta's conviction, at this point, that O'Neill would soon be back with her.

Carlotta was also visited at Marblehead by Francis Wylie, who wanted to check on some further details for his magazine. On a Sunday afternoon in early May, Wylie, accompanied by his wife, found Carlotta in the last stages of packing up the house. He and his wife sipped sherry while Carlotta told them how much she loved O'Neill and how cruelly she had been treated by him. She was planning to move to Boston and sell the Marblehead house, she said. Wylie recalled the start it gave him to see the stacks of cardboard packing cartons piled up in the house, with "Eugene O'Neill" written on them.

Although it was known only to some of his friends, O'Neill's petition for guardianship over Carlotta had been legally dropped by a paper filed in the Essex County Probate Court on April 23, the date for which the hearing had been originally set. Carlotta's countersuit for separate maintenance had previously been blocked on O'Neill's behalf by Farley, who claimed that it could not be heard in Massachusetts, as O'Neill's legal residence was in New York. By the tacit consent of all concerned, no further action was ever taken in the matter.

On May 2 O'Neill told Crouse during a hospital visit that he definitely wanted Carlotta back. He asked Crouse to relay the message and Crouse, after being apprised by O'Neill's attorney that legal actions were no longer pending, telephoned Dr. Kozol in Boston the following day and was then able to assure O'Neill that a reconciliation was imminent.

On May 9 Dr. Kozol arrived in New York to have a talk with O'Neill. Later that day Dr. Kozol met Crouse at the Waldorf Astoria Hotel and informed him of his conference with O'Neill. On May 13, after seeing O'Neill, Crouse wrote in his diary: "Gene very gay and reports he and Carlotta will live in a hotel opposite Dr. Kozol's office [in Boston] which is good."

Two days later Dr. Kozol wrote to Dr. Fisk that he had acted as a friendly go-between, an emissary at the request of both O'Neills. The O'Neills, he continued, had decided to come together and live at the Shelton Hotel, a family establishment on Bay State Road in Boston. The reconciliation was scheduled for May 17.

O'Neill had been reasonably sure for several weeks that he was going back to Carlotta—on her terms—but in this case, again, he gave completely different impressions of his feelings and plans. To Joe Heidt, for instance, he confided early in May that he was anxious to get "home."

"He was all smiles," Heidt recalled. "He had just talked to Carlotta on the telephone, and he said he was just waiting to get a little stronger. He also told me that he didn't want most of his friends to know he was going back."

O'Neill was particularly reluctant to mention his imminent return to Carlotta to those people who, he knew, would never see him again. There was, consequently, a group to whom his departure was a staggering surprise. Some of these friends came, or were summoned, for a farewell; others did not know he had left the hospital until he was already on his way to Boston.

Among those who saw him on the eve of his departure or the morning of the next day were Heidt, Aronberg, Kennedy, Crouse, Shirlee Lantz, Dorothy and Saxe Commins, Armina Marshall Langner, Bennett Cerf and Brooks Atkinson.

Heidt visited on May 16, and O'Neill told him he was leaving the following day. Heidt offered to take him to the train, but O'Neill declined, saying, "No, there'll be a nurse with me and I'll be all right."

Crouse and Atkinson visited the same day. Crouse thought O'Neill in relatively "fine shape." Atkinson also observed that he was in good spirits. "O'Neill said he was happy about going back," Atkinson recalled, "but I was shocked at how thin he was; and his hands shook so. He was in a humorous mood. I told him I had just seen the movie version of *The Long Voyage Home* and he said he had had the opportunity of taking a flat sum or a royalty on the deal; he'd chosen the flat sum and lost a lot of money. He said he always made the wrong decision when it came to money." (The surprising fact is that O'Neill's enormous output during his lifetime brought him a net profit of less than a million dollars.)

Charles Kennedy also found O'Neill in a humorous frame of mind. Like Russel Crouse, Kennedy learned that O'Neill had been having Oriental dreams. "He related a strange dream laid in China and lasting a thousand years," Kennedy recalled. "We joked over the possibility that perhaps he was rewriting *Marco Millions* in his sleep." Kennedy ventured to offer O'Neill some mild advice—something he rarely took it upon himself to do.

"If I were you, Gene, I'd get out more often when you're back in Boston," Kennedy said.

"Yes," O'Neill agreed. "When you come to Boston we'll go to a lot of ball games together."

The most emotional leave-taking occurred between O'Neill and Commins. Commins, who had been among the last to be told that O'Neill was going back, was convinced he would never see O'Neill again. He went with his wife to say good-by.

"Saxe brought a letter he had gotten from Oona," Dorothy Commins said. "Oona had asked Saxe to give the letter to her father. Gene said he'd like to have it, and he put it under his pillow." (The gesture was probably less to gratify himself than to avoid offending the Comminses, who, being devoted parents themselves, were terribly distressed about his estrangement from his children.)

"Saxe and I had offered Gene a home with us in Princeton," Dorothy added. "I would have nursed him. But Gene said, 'I'm absolutely helpless. I can't even hold a cup of water. I can't burden you with this.'

"Gene put his arms around Saxe; his whole frame shook. He said, 'Good-by, my brother!' I went out of the room, weeping."

Commins was shattered, though he tried to understand O'Neill's motives in preferring to return to Carlotta rather than live with him and Dorothy. He was wounded to such a degree that, sometime later, he confided his distress to Professor Albert Einstein, a fellow resident at Princeton and a close friend. Dr. Einstein was very much interested in O'Neill's character and in his relationship with Carlotta. Indeed, he tried to comfort Commins, but he was not able to give him a satisfactory answer; the paradoxes and complexities of the Black Irish temperament were out of his sphere.

Bennett Cerf also saw O'Neill on May 16 but, far from bidding him good-by, Cerf discussed his own offer of moving O'Neill into a suite at the Carlyle Hotel with a male nurse. Cerf had apparently not been informed of O'Neill's reaction to the Merrill Moore plan, and O'Neill, for reasons of his own, chose not to enlighten him.

"The nurse was supposed to call for him the next day," Cerf said. "He was all set to go to the Carlyle. The next day he left for Carlotta, instead."

Shirlee came to say good-by on the morning of May 17. She was touched when O'Neill, forming the words painfully, commented on the new hat she was wearing. "That is very natty!" he said. Shirlee herself was all but inarticulate with grief.

"You can't look at someone you love and just say good-by, when you know it's the last time you'll see him," she later said.

She finally thought of a way to save both herself and O'Neill the pain of an emotional farewell.

"I'd like to take you to your train," she told him, knowing that arrangements had already been made for a nurse to take him, and that neither she nor O'Neill would have wished to say good-by at the station. O'Neill understood. Gratefully he answered, "I'd like you to do that." Shirlee, throwing him a kiss, said, "I'll phone you later," and hurried from the room, fighting back her tears.

Later she called the hospital and was told by a nurse that O'Neill had left a message for her, just as Shirlee had known he would. O'Neill had said good-by and asked Shirlee not to come to the train because he did not want a dramatic farewell scene. He had already played too many.

Taking his leave of Armina Langner the same day, O'Neill told her:

"I know you and Lawrence and Saxe would do everything to help me, but I just can't live on your doorstep—or on anyone else's." According to Mrs. Langner, O'Neill thought he and Carlotta might be short of cash when he got to Boston and asked her for a loan of $5,000.

"Of course, I wrote him a check at once," Mrs. Langner recalled, "and I asked him to sign a slip of paper with 'I.O.U. $5,000' written on it—no date, no strings or anything—just a note for the Theatre Guild's records."

A few days after O'Neill's departure, Carlotta sent Mrs. Langner a check for the $5,000 and asked for the I.O.U. Mrs. Langner put the I.O.U. in the mail. She never heard from either of the O'Neills again.)

Aronberg, though he lent O'Neill no money and did not offer him a home, knew he was in line for amputation because of his part in the legal proceedings against Carlotta. With cynical foresight he told O'Neill the day he left the hospital, "Good-by, Gene. I'll be fired in a week or so." O'Neill protested. But within a few days Aronberg received a notice that he was dismissed.

A little before noon on May 17 O'Neill left Doctors Hospital with a nurse. The nurse, a middle-aged woman named Sally Coughlin, settled him in a roomette on the Yankee Clipper for the four-hour ride to Boston's Back Bay Station. O'Neill, though he had gained a little, still weighed only a hundred seventeen pounds. He sat huddled in an overcoat that emphasized his fragility. Miss Coughlin sat on a bench opposite him. That was the way Dr. Patterson found them when, taking time off from his busy schedule, he came down to the train to say good-by to O'Neill.

'I don't think I would have done this for any other patient," Dr. Patterson later said. "I wanted to make his trip easier for him. I felt that he loved Carlotta and wanted to go back to her. But he was suffering from hospitalitis. Everything had been secure for him at the hospital. We took care of all his thinking, and he hated to make a break."

Dr. Patterson stepped up to O'Neill and patted his shoulder. "He looked small for all the clothes he was in," Dr. Patterson recalled. "I was used to seeing him in his bathrobe."

"You're going to a good place," the doctor told his patient. "Everything is going to be all right."

O'Neill at first could not bring out his words, although he was not shaking. Finally he managed a broken "Thank you." The two men shook hands and Dr. Patterson, with a cheery wave, left the cramped roomette.

LXV

"WHEN O'NEILL CAME BACK TO ME IN BOSTON, I didn't go to the train to meet him," Carlotta said. "I couldn't do it. He had done something to me that never could be erased. I didn't know how he would act. The nurse brought him to the Shelton Hotel and when he came in he looked like a dead man. And as he walked by me he said, 'I'm sorry, forgive me, I love you.' He didn't even *stop* to say it. He walked right on and into his room. And that was that."

Shortly after O'Neill's arrival, Carlotta told Boston reporters, "We haven't decided yet about where we're going to live," and added that the Marblehead house was up for sale. On the same day, in New York, Winfield Aronberg issued a press statement announcing that O'Neill and his wife had withdrawn all legal actions and were completely reconciled and that O'Neill was "well again and in good spirits."

Elliot Norton, a leading Boston drama critic, reached Mrs. O'Neill by telephone that afternoon and was told by her, "I'm very glad to have him home."

O'Neill, who was now very much on the defensive with Carlotta, felt that she was making a sacrifice in taking him back, for he was now not only an invalid but insolvent. His helplessness and Carlotta's sacrifice were subjects both of them dwelt on with masochistic pleasure.

"When Gene came back, he had no money and his friends had deserted him," according to Carlotta. "Some time after his return he threatened to go away again. I said, 'No one is keeping you—but let's not have another scandal.' He said, 'Oh, shut up!' and he never brought it up again. But another time, he said, 'Why do you stick with me?' I said that I wanted to help him, that he was no ordinary man. He would say, 'I love you! I hate you!'

"He was $17,000 in debt when he came back. I'd been able to get only $40,000 for the Marblehead house, and I had to pay off a $20,000 mortgage out of that. With the rest of the money I paid Gene's debts."

Immediately on O'Neill's return Carlotta went on twenty-four-hour-a-day nursing duty. On many days O'Neill was totally incapacitated, though there were periods when he could hobble about, feed himself, and even write with a pencil. On bad days, however, Carlotta had to do everything for him. Since illness had reduced her husband to fragility, she was able to lift him and carry him about.

"My back still aches from lifting him," she complained to a number of acquaintances several years after O'Neill's death.

O'Neill fully appreciated Carlotta's sacrifice. He had been home only ten days when he took steps to let her know of his gratitude.

On May 28, 1951, he wrote a will, in which he made his wife his sole heir and executrix. The will, which began by stating, "I . . . do . . . expressly revoke all other wills or testamentary instruments heretofore made by me," may have replaced one in which he had named his children among his heirs. (Friends heard rumors that he had made such a will during his stay at Salem Hospital.)

In his new will O'Neill specifically and explicitly cut off Shane and Oona, as well as "their issue now or hereafter born."

An attorney, Albert B. Carey, drew up the will for O'Neill, and was one of the witnesses to O'Neill's signature. He found his client mentally alert. Another witness was Dr. Kozol.

A day or two before the will was signed Dr. Kozol wrote to Dr. Fisk, reporting that the O'Neills "had a happy reunion" and that he hoped "it will continue." He was keeping a professional eye on them both, at their request.

A few days after signing the will—on June 3—O'Neill inscribed for Carlotta a set of uncorrected proofs of *A Moon for the Misbegotten* (which Random House was preparing for publication):

". . . in a spirit of the humblest gratitude for her love which has forgiven my recent shameful conduct toward her . . ."

The suite in the Shelton Hotel became O'Neill's permanent home; his precarious health and Carlotta's unwillingness to struggle with the servant problem were among the principal reasons why a hotel residence was now the most practical form of housekeeping for them. In addition to bedrooms and living room, there was a small room whose windows overlooked the Charles River. O'Neill spent most of his waking hours there, seated in an armchair, thumbing through old copies of *Theatre Magazine*. He saw practically no one but Carlotta, his doctors, his lawyers, and the hotel manager, Philip McBride, who, being a notary public, was summoned occasionally to put his official seal on legal documents.

"Mr. O'Neill hardly ever left his room," McBride recalled. "He would just sit there and look out at the Charles."

O'Neill did occasionally receive Russel Crouse as a visitor. "I called on him whenever I happened to be in Boston," Crouse said. "Carlotta was always in the room with him. He seemed comfortable."

On July 12 Dr. W. Richard Ohler, a Boston internist, was asked by Dr. Kozol to visit O'Neill. There was nothing specifically wrong, but Dr. Kozol thought O'Neill should have on call a doctor who was familiar with his condition. Dr. Ohler, like all his predecessors, was immediately taken with O'Neill.

"He was a pliable, lovable patient," Dr. Ohler said. "But he struck me as a man in whom the flame had died. His wife would complain to me about him, and I had the feeling that they argued a lot.

"When I visited, I would usually find him sitting by the window, watching the sailboats on the river or the cars on the road along the river-bank. He was usually fully dressed—when he couldn't dress himself, his wife dressed him.

"One of my big problems was trying to get him to eat. I thought if I could interest him in something, his appetite might improve. I was a detective story fan, and I urged him to read some. He did, and we used to discuss them. At one point he told me he could write a better detective story than any he'd read, and he said he was planning to write one. I don't think he ever did, but his appetite eventually picked up and he began to look better.

"O'Neill spoke slowly and was slow in his movements, but his mind was alert. What he lacked was spirit. We kept him on barbiturates to ease his tremor, but none of the drugs we had could help him fundamentally."

At the urging of Dr. Ohler, Carlotta engaged a professional nurse to relieve her for eight hours a day.

"Gene didn't want a nurse," she said. "He wanted no one else around. But his doctors told him that if he didn't get a nurse, *I* would end up needing one, because my spine wouldn't hold out, and he'd end up having to have *two* nurses around. So he agreed, and we hired Miss [Jean] Welton, a charming Canadian woman."

After seven months of isolated, sedentary life at the Shelton, O'Neill suffered a gastrointestinal attack that was serious enough to warrant his removal to Falkner Hospital. Dr. Ohler was out of town attending a medical conference, but he followed the case by telephone.

"O'Neill had always suffered from gallstone inflammation," Dr. Ohler said. "The newspapers thought he was dying, and they called me in San Francisco." On December 6, about a week later, the hospital disclosed that O'Neill was no longer on the danger list. All the newspapers, however, reported that Carlotta was "constantly at his side." On December 11 he was discharged.

On Carlotta's sixty-third birthday, a little over two weeks later, O'Neill gave her a typescript (the third) of *Long Day's Journey Into Night*, inscribing it, with many crossings-out, "To Carlotta, again, wife, friend, helper and lover. . . . I have loved you for twenty-three years now, Darling, and now that I am old and can work no more, I love you more than ever!"

The new year saw two revivals of O'Neill plays in New York—*Anna Christie* at the City Center and *Desire Under the Elms* at the ANTA Playhouse. Far from being a sign that O'Neill was at last being recognized as a theatre staple, this double revival simply served to emphasize how much in neglect he was in his own country. Harold Clurman, who directed the revival of *Desire Under the Elms*, called attention to this fact in an interview.

"*Desire* has been played all over the world and it makes ninety-five per cent of the plays written sound like pretty weak sisters," said Clurman. "If O'Neill had written in Germany or France his plays would be done in the national theatre. Here we neglect them."

On March 3, 1952, O'Neill presented Carlotta with a new token of his love by drawing up, with the help of his lawyers, a detailed literary trust that transferred to her absolute ownership and control of all his plays after his death; this document, in fact, went so far as to stipulate that if Carlotta should predecease him, ownership and control should pass, on his death, to "her estate or to such persons as she may have designated by will or otherwise by instrument executed during her lifetime."

"I make these provisions," explained O'Neill, "in recognition of the loyalty and care afforded me by my said wife as well as the expenditure by her of her own substantial funds as well as funds I provided her with and which were prematurely disbursed because of compelling needs."

He pointed out that he was making no provision for his children, since he had "otherwise provided for them heretofore"—an obvious reference to the fact that he had turned over the Bermuda estate to them years before.

That summer attention was again briefly focused on O'Neill when *A Moon for the Misbegotten* was published by Random House. The magazine *Time*, which had scheduled a review of the book for the week of July 20, 1952, assigned Francis Wylie to ask O'Neill a few specific questions. Wylie was unable to reach O'Neill, but Carlotta, after scolding Wylie for trying to bother her husband, told him (in answer to one of the stipulated questions) that there was no particular reason for the decision to publish the play at this particular time.

In a brief foreword to the published text dated the previous April O'Neill had written: "It has never been presented on the New York stage nor are there outstanding rights or plans for its production. Since I cannot presently give it the attention required for appropriate presentation, I have decided to make it available in book form."

Wylie, however, advised his office, off the record, that he had it "on good authority" that the play "was published at this time because the O'Neills are very hard up." Carlotta later confirmed this. "In 1952 we were terribly hard up," she said. "My income was getting low, Gene's was getting low, and I was very worried."

It was also at this point, according to Carlotta, that O'Neill told her the publication restrictions on *Long Day's Journey Into Night* no longer applied.

"He said, 'What are you worried about?' and I said, 'Money,'" Carlotta reported. "He said, 'But you don't have to worry, we've got a nest egg.' I said, 'Where is it?' 'Why,' he said, '*Long Day's Journey.*' Well, I thought he had completely gone out of his mind."

It was then, Carlotta continued, that O'Neill disclosed for the first time that Eugene Jr. had asked him to withhold the play because of its personal nature, and that Eugene's death now made it possible to release it. "If things get worse," Carlotta later quoted O'Neill as having said, "We will publish it."

A Moon for the Misbegotten did not receive much critical acclaim, but its sales apparently alleviated O'Neill's financial straits sufficiently so that the nest egg did not have to be tapped.

Later in July, on his wedding anniversary, O'Neill gave Carlotta a copy of the newly published play. On the flyleaf he wrote, in a surprisingly steady hand, what are probably the last consecutive sentences he ever set down in his own writing.

"To darling Carlotta, my wife, who for twenty-three years has endured with love and understanding my rotten nerves, my lack of stability, my cussedness in general . . ." he wrote.

"I am old and would be sick of life, were it not that you, Sweetheart, are here, as deep and understanding in your love as ever—and I as deep in my love for you as when we stood in Paris, Premier Arrondissement, on July 22, 1929, and both said faintly 'Oui'!"

That Christmas Carlotta reported to George Jean Nathan that she was still on sixteen hours a day nursing duty, though O'Neill was better, physically, than he had been for years. She added that she hoped Nathan knew she was doing the best she could.

❖

On a dark winter afternoon in the early part of 1953 O'Neill and Carlotta sat quietly in their living room. A while before O'Neill had been talking, as he did almost every day, of his own death. In spite of what he had written to Carlotta in July, he was sick of life. He spoke to Carlotta longingly of death by euthanasia and of death by suicide—but he was waiting for death by atrophy. Suddenly he said:

"Nobody must be allowed to finish my plays."

He was speaking of the six cycle plays. which still existed in scenario or rough draft. He asked Carlotta to fetch all the manuscripts so that he could destroy them.

("Didn't you try to dissuade him?" Carlotta was asked by an interviewer some years later. "Certainly not," she replied. "I'd not be so presumptuous. No one could get very far trying to persuade him to do anything.")

"It isn't that I don't trust you, Carlotta," she later reported O'Neill's saying, as she brought him the manuscripts, "but you might drop dead or get run over and I don't want anybody else working on these plays."

O'Neill began tearing the manuscript pages into pieces.

"He could only tear a few pages at a time, because of his tremor," Carlotta said. "So I helped him. We tore up all the manuscripts together, bit by bit. It took hours. After a pile of torn pages had collected, I'd set a match to them. It was awful. It was like tearing up children."

O'Neill did not ask for, or destroy, the sheaf of notes he had made, outlining the cycle families' genealogy and planned changes in the various plays; and, somehow, a typed, unedited draft of the sixth play in the series, *More Stately Mansions*, was overlooked—probably because another version of the play was on hand to be torn up. This manuscript, five times the length of a conventional play, was later sent to Yale, along with other papers and documents.

With the destruction of the cycle, O'Neill gave up his last feeble pretense of a hold on life. Nietzsche's "poison-worm" gnawed more fiercely at his heart every day. Often he wept with despair that death would not come.

"There was nothing Gene wanted to do, no one he wanted to see," Carlotta said. "I'd ask him if there were any of his old friends he wanted me to write to for him, or ask to come for a visit, and he always said, "No."

One day Carlotta tried to feel him out about his wishes regarding a funeral. She decided to approach the subject obliquely.

"If I should die, I want a simple burial and no man of God," she began.

"I'll go long before you," O'Neill predicted dryly and accurately.

"Well, what do you want if you do?" asked Carlotta.

"Get me quietly and simply buried," he said. "And don't bring a priest. If there is a God and I meet Him, we'll talk things over personally, man to man." He added that he wanted no one at his funeral except Carlotta and his nurse, Miss Welton.

On October 16, 1953, O'Neill reached his sixty-fifth birthday. He was determined it would be his last. He found he could no longer smoke a cigarette without burning himself. He lost his appetite and barely ate at all. One day in mid-November he tried to get out of bed and, with the aid of a cane, walk by himself.

"He asked me very quietly to please not help him," Carlotta said. "I handed him his cane, and he started forward, then fell back and hit his head. He lay on the floor, and wouldn't let me help him up. Finally, he turned himself over on his stomach and pulled himself up. But that was when he gave up.

"Later he told me he had tried to walk to see 'if this was the end,' and he'd found that it was. After that he didn't get off the bed again. I nursed him and stayed with him constantly, except for the eight-hour shift when Miss Welton took over.

"He would have night sweats, and I'd have to change his clothes. I'd have to lift and turn him all by myself. He tried to help, but he just couldn't. He had great trouble moving, and even talking."

On November 21 Carlotta opened a letter from the American Academy, which requested O'Neill to sign his ballot for the election of new members; she took the time to write a desperate little note at the bottom of the letter: "My husband is too ill to sign anything. Would you kindly sign for him— if this is legal—I thank you!"

On November 24, a Tuesday, O'Neill stopped eating entirely.

"An infection had set in," Dr. Ohler recalled. "What he had was the rapidly fulminating type of pneumonia. It spread quickly because he was at a low level. He had shortness of breath, a cough, and a high fever. He was given antibiotics, but the heart was too weak to rally, and there seemed to be no will to live."

The fever raged for three days, rising to 104 degrees. Once during this time O'Neill clenched his fists, raised himself slightly in his bed and gasped: "Born in a hotel room—and God damn it—died in a hotel room!"

"Very early one morning I had to climb onto the bed and sort of straddle Gene to get him changed into fresh pajamas," Carlotta said. "He stared into my eyes. He seemed to be looking right through me. Then he tried to say something. 'Gene,' I said, 'speak very slowly; try to tell me what you want to say very, very slowly, and maybe I'll be able to understand.' He strained terribly, but the words wouldn't come.

"Then his head fell back. He never said another word. He'd gone into a coma. I called the doctor, of course, but there was nothing more to be done. He had simply worn himself out.

"He was in a coma for thirty-six hours. He never opened his eyes or moved all that time. There was no suffering. I don't know whether I could have stood it if I'd had to watch him suffer. I never left him during the whole time. I held his hand and stayed at his side. He had beautiful hands."

O'Neill died at 4:39 o'clock on Friday afternoon, November 27, 1953.

LXVI

"WHEN GENE DIED I HAD AN AUTOPSY PERFORMED BE-cause I wanted to know what in the name of God was the matter with this man I had nursed so long," Carlotta told an interviewer nearly three years after O'Neill's death. "He never had Parkinson's disease. Never."

The autopsy revealed that O'Neill had suffered from a rare disease, only superficially resembling Parkinson's, in which the cells of the cerebellum were subject to a slow, degenerative process. Drawing no conclusions about whether, in O'Neill's case, the disease had been inherited, the autopsy did point out that the initial symptoms were generally trembling hands and speech impairments, and that both O'Neill's mother and brother had been known to have tremors of the hands.

"The sickness destroys only the motory system of the organism," Dr. Karl Ragnar Gierow once wrote, in an interpretation of the report, after Carlotta had shown it to him. "Thus the horror of it is that the cerebrum remains unharmed. O'Neill's mind was completely clear the entire time, able to comprehend his misery."

Dr. Gierow pointed out that as a result of the affliction, "from top to toe the body loses all control; a helpless wreck, a foundering ship, a hull without a helm."

O'Neill's body was placed in the J. S. Waterman Funeral Parlor, but plans for his burial were kept secret. Local newspapermen and representatives of the wire services tried for four days to find out when and where O'Neill would be buried. O'Neill's friends in New York, where a newspaper strike was in effect, also tried, vainly, to discover when the funeral would take place. But Carlotta, maintaining that she was following O'Neill's instructions, secluded herself and issued no comment.

"I carried out every wish of his to the letter," she said, "and it was very difficult. He wished to keep everything from the papers; he wished no publicity; he wished nobody to be at his funeral; he wished no religious representative of any creed or kind.

"Well, what I went through! But the employees of the hotel, and particularly two men who were strong of arm and determined, good Bostonians, were throwing people downstairs and I don't know what.

"And the nurse and I would have to go out of our way and change taxis to get to the undertaker's, which was only two blocks from where we lived. We'd ride miles to keep the place a secret.

"And then my lawyer and I went out and bought the lot. Gene wished a simple lot, big enough for two people. He wished me to be buried beside him and he wished a stone with his name and date of birth and death, and my name and date of birth and a line left open for my death." Apparently he did not even consider burial in his family's plot in New London; without re-embracing the Catholic faith, he could not, in any case, have gained access to St. Mary's Cemetery.

O'Neill had written in his will: "I desire to be buried in a burial lot with my wife and I authorize my Executrix to purchase such a lot and erect a simple stone thereon."

A little before ten o'clock on the morning of December 2, a hearse and one car moved quietly away from the Waterman undertaking parlor and took its place unobtrusively in the stream of Boston traffic. In the car were Carlotta, Miss Welton and Dr. Kozol. In the hearse was the body of Eugene O'Neill. No one would have guessed, not even the reporters who had been waiting and watching for the sign of a funeral, that this inconspicuous procession was O'Neill's funeral cortege.

The two vehicles drove to a remote corner of Forest Hills Cemetery, on the outskirts of Boston. There, under a pale sun that gave no warmth, Carlotta, Miss Welton and Dr. Kozol watched O'Neill's coffin being lowered into its grave.

Only one story describing the burial appeared in the newspapers; it was written by Warren Carberg, of the Boston *Post*, and he was given his information after being sworn to secrecy about his source.

"There were no formal prayers," wrote Carberg. "A funeral director's assistant stepped forward and placed a single spray of white chrysanthemums on the casket, and then the three mourners turned and walked to the automobile.

"Not a word was spoken. No hymns were sung. Mrs. O'Neill wore simple black clothing, with no mourning veil. She was pale and appeared without make-up. There seemed to be tiny lines of grief about her eyes and mouth. No tears showed in her eyes."

Carlotta eventually provided the stone—cut from Italian marble, rough around the edges but highly polished in front, where the lettering is engraved. It is four feet high and six feet wide, and is inscribed as O'Neill wished.

"It's a very lovely cemetery," Carlotta said. "It's got beautiful trees, enormous rhododendrons, and in the spring and summer, with the dogwood, it's quite, quite lovely. I planted laurel around the headstone, like the laurel wreaths of the Greek heroes. . . ."

CHRONOLOGICAL TABLE OF O'NEILL'S PUBLISHED PLAYS

(See individual titles in Index for additional data)

TITLE	YEAR WRITTEN	DATE AND PLACE OF FIRST NEW YORK PRODUCTION
A Wife for a Life	1913–1914	Unproduced
Thirst	1913–1914	(Wharf Theatre, Provincetown, Mass., summer, 1916)
The Web	1913–1914	Unproduced
Warnings	1913–1914	Unproduced
Fog	1913–1914	The Playwrights' Theatre, Jan. 5, 1917
Recklessness	1913–1914	Unproduced
Bound East for Cardiff	1913–1914	The Playwrights' Theatre, Nov. 3, 1916
Servitude	1913–1914	Unproduced
Abortion	1913–1914	Unproduced
The Sniper	1915	The Playwrights' Theatre, Feb. 16, 1917
Before Breakfast	1916–1917	The Playwrights' Theatre, Dec. 1, 1916
The Movie Man	1916–1917	Unproduced
'Ile	1916–1917	The Playwrights' Theatre, Nov. 30, 1917
In the Zone	1916–1917	Comedy Theatre, Oct. 31, 1917
The Long Voyage Home	1916–1917	The Playwrights' Theatre, Nov. 2, 1917
The Moon of the Caribbees	1916–1917	The Playwrights' Theatre, Dec. 20, 1918
The Rope	1918	The Playwrights' Theatre, April 26, 1918
The Dreamy Kid	1918	The Playwrights' Theatre, Oct. 31, 1919
Beyond the Horizon	1918	Morosco Theatre, Feb. 2, 1920
Where the Cross is Made	1918	The Playwrights' Theatre, Nov. 22, 1918
Chris Christopherson	1919	(Atlantic City, March 8, 1920)
The Straw	1918–1919	Greenwich Village Theatre, Nov. 10, 1921
Gold	1920	Frazee Theatre, June 1, 1921
Anna Christie	1920	Vanderbilt Theatre, Nov. 10, 1921
The Emperor Jones	1920	The Playwrights' Theatre, Nov. 3, 1920
Diff'rent	1920	The Playwrights' Theatre, Dec. 27, 1920
The First Man	1921	Neighborhood Playhouse, March, 4, 1922
The Hairy Ape	1921	The Playwrights' Theatre, March 9, 1922
The Fountain	1921–1922	Greenwich Village Theatre, Dec. 10, 1925
Welded	1922–1923	39th Street Theatre, March 17, 1924
All God's Chillun Got Wings	1923	Provincetown Playhouse, May 15, 1924
Desire Under the Elms	1924	Greenwich Village Theatre, Nov. 11, 1924
Marco Millions	1923–1925	Guild Theatre, Jan. 9, 1928
The Great God Brown	1925	Greenwich Village Theatre, Jan. 23, 1926
Lazarus Laughed	1925–1926	(Pasadena, Cal., April 9, 1928)
Strange Interlude	1926–1927	John Golden Theatre, Jan. 30, 1928
Dynamo	1928	Martin Beck Theatre, Feb. 11, 1929
Mourning Becomes Electra	1929–1931	Guild Theatre, Oct. 26, 1931
Ah, Wilderness!	1932	Guild Theatre, Oct. 2, 1933
Days Without End	1932–1933	Guild Theatre, Jan. 8, 1934
A Touch of the Poet	1935–1942	Helen Hayes Theatre, Oct. 2, 1958
The Iceman Cometh	1939	Martin Beck Theatre, Sept. 2, 1946
Long Day's Journey Into Night	1939–1941	Helen Hayes Theatre, Nov. 7, 1956
Hughie	1941–1942	Royale Theatre, Dec. 22, 1964
A Moon for the Misbegotten	1943	Bijou Theatre, May 2, 1957
More Stately Mansions	Unfinished	Broadhurst Theatre, Oct. 31, 1967

EPILOGUE

CARLOTTA MONTEREY O'NEILL SURVIVED HER HUSBAND by seventeen years. Far from being released by his death from the role of tragic heroine in which O'Neill had cast her, she continued to follow his script. O'Neill had chosen her to be his antagonist in a passionate personal drama of love and fury. She had fulfilled his expectations of her. She had helped him to live and she had helped him to die.

Carlotta assumed with gusto her new role as widow and literary heir of the great dramatist. Her methods, particularly with regard to the disposition of some of the O'Neill plays, were sometimes viciously disparaged by O'Neill's friends and associates, but O'Neill himself would probably have viewed her actions with ironic detachment. He knew her character thoroughly and, knowing it, had left her the absolute right to dispose as she pleased of his literary estate.

Her final years of loneliness and desperation and her eventual mental collapse were part of the O'Neill scenario. She became, like Mary Tyrone of *Long Day's Journey Into Night*, a ghost haunting the past. There were no happy endings for O'Neill heroines, and Carlotta was the ultimate O'Neill heroine.

For a while after O'Neill's death, Carlotta continued to live in semi-isolation at the Shelton Hotel. She saw her lawyers and doctors, and corresponded with a handful of people, mostly with regard to one or another aspect of O'Neill's plays and papers.

Gradually, and uncannily, she began assuming O'Neill's character, in much the same way that Lavinia Mannon, in *Mourning Becomes Electra*, assumed the character of her dead mother, Christine. Carlotta played a dual role—that of the dramatically mourning widow, who dressed exclusively in black, down to her carefully chosen jewelry of jet, and that of O'Neill's alter-ego, managing his literary property in a manner that was, she believed, dictated to her in vaguely mystical terms by O'Neill's spirit.

Six months after O'Neill's death, Carlotta wrote to Brooks Atkinson, from the Shelton:

"Have been working *hours* a day—up to eleven or twelve at night—Good, in a way. I sleep at least four solid hours a night! A heart-breaking job—beginning February 10, 1928 until Gene's death. But, this *must* be done—I found the diaries were fading! And it *must* be done *right* and *honestly*." (There were murmurs among some of O'Neill's friends that Carlotta was editing and re-writing the diaries to present herself in a flattering light. It is doubtful, however, that she would have attempted any re-writing; she would have to have been an extremely skillful forger to simulate O'Neill's distinctive, crabbed penmanship. But it is quite possible that she did do some editing. She told at least one friend, in a burst of candor, that she was deleting certain diary entries of O'Neill's later years "to avoid scandal.")

"I must stick to the diaries—which will take me all summer!" she wrote to Atkinson. "All I do is work and talk to Mr. [Robert W.] Meserve —my lawyer here."

Three months later, she wrote again to Atkinson, this time complaining, with mixed anger and humor, that the Random House set of O'Neill's plays had been allowed to go out of print. If the books were not to be had in the stores, she wrote, "the would-be purchaser gives up his effort of owning O'Neill's works—and *Mrs.* O'Neill eats less— so to speak! All this disturbs me more than I care to say. *Not* for me! Gene isn't dead nine months and this is how they behave! It *sickens* me!"

Late in 1955 Carlotta moved from Boston to the Lowell Hotel in New York. She and O'Neill had stayed there briefly years earlier, and now his ghost moved in with her. On November 27, she wrote to Atkinson:

"Two years ago today—at this hour—Gene was dying! Will I ever be able to free myself from this man—and the love I felt for him!"

For the next twelve months Carlotta engaged in a tug of war about *Long Day's Journey Into Night*. The war took place on several levels. There was the initial struggle with Random House, which was trying to honor O'Neill's written wishes with regard to withholding the play for twenty-five years after his death. Carlotta, of course, triumphed, and gave the play to the Yale University Press, which published it in February of 1956. In the same month it was produced in Stockholm with great success. And now Carlotta, not entirely convinced that she was really carrying out O'Neill's wishes, began struggling with her conscience.

In April of 1956 she wrote to the Broadway producer, Alexander H. Cohen:

"I regret to have to tell you *Long Day's Journey Into Night* is *not* available for production in this country. I am carrying out O'Neill's wishes to the letter. He wished me to *publish* this play but *not* to allow it to be *produced* by *anyone* under *any* conditions! I hope you understand." The letter mystified Cohen, who, of course, knew the play *had* been produced in Sweden.

A month later, Carlotta did a turnabout (as O'Neill had often done) and gave the play for production on Broadway to the young producing-directing team of Theodore Mann and José Quintero. Her reason was that she admired their off-Broadway revival, that May, of *The Iceman Cometh*—a superb production that featured an unknown actor named Jason Robards in the role of Hickey. The revival was enormously successful, and critics began re-evaluating O'Neill's gift; Carlotta was shrewd enough to realize that a production of *Long Day's Journey* could revitalize O'Neill's reputation—and that *Mrs.* O'Neill could eat more— "so to speak!"

Carlotta liked to eat well. She had been accustomed all of her adult life to luxurious and elegant surroundings. At sixty-eight, she was still a handsome, vital woman. After her many years of seclusion with O'Neill and following his death, she was enjoying her re-emergence into the world. Not that she became a social butterfly. Her social and business contacts were strictly limited, and she carefully maintained an air of semi-seclusion and noblesse oblige, inviting a select group of acquaintances to lunch—or, more rarely, dinner—from time to time. The meals—sometimes served in her hotel suite, sometimes at the Quo Vadis restaurant, sometimes at Passy, sometimes in the dining room of the Carlton House, where she moved from the Lowell—were always lavish, prolonged, and festive, and quite often very gay. While Carlotta was exceedingly erratic and volatile and could strike like a serpent when she fancied herself crossed, she could also be warm, funny, loquacious and entertaining.

But to all those to whom she drew close during the next dozen years, it was apparent that she was a haunted soul, still embattled with O'Neill, reliving and questioning her relationship with him. The emotional whirlpool in which she spun was exhausting. Every decision she made regarding the production of an O'Neill play seemed to intensify the deadly struggle in which she was locked with O'Neill's ghost.

Carmen Capalbo and Stanley Chase were two in the series of young producers and directors who caught Carlotta's fancy and were, for a time, captivated by her. In May of 1957 they produced on Broadway *A Moon for the Misbegotten* (which had been published but never produced in New York after its disastrous road tour six years before O'Neill's death).

One day, in the fall of 1956, Capalbo and Chase were invited to the Lowell for dinner. They sent ahead a huge bouquet of yellow pompons and brought with them a bottle of wine.

"Mrs. O'Neill was appreciative, but acted very coy," Capalbo recalled. "She said, 'So charming, so European.'"

Carlotta's suite was sparingly dotted with memorabilia—framed inscriptions of plays from O'Neill to his wife, photographs of both O'Neills, including a particularly charming one taken in the woods in France, showing them leaning against a thick, ivy-covered tree trunk, smiling tenderly. A small ceramic Dalmatian, symbolizing the O'Neills' beloved Blemie, stood on the mantelpiece of the living room. And, of course, there was Estaban on the couch.

"That monkey had the silliest grin you ever saw," Capalbo said. "Mrs. O'Neill would jokingly address wisecracks to it, every so often."

There were bookcases filled with volumes of O'Neill's plays. Capalbo was surprised at the lack of sentimental clutter, and ventured to ask where all of O'Neill's scrapbooks and other effects were kept.

"I sent everything to Yale," Carlotta said. "When I need something they send it here for me."

Carlotta asked Capalbo and Chase what they wanted to drink. They hesitated, not knowing whether she approved of drinking, and finally took a chance on asking for cocktails.

"Good," Carlotta said. "I like people who take a drink. There are three important things in this world: Eating, drinking and making love."

The meal was sent up from Passy.

"It was sumptuous," Capalbo recalled. "Steak, broccoli Hollandaise, French peas, wine, etc. The waiter who served us was an old man whom Mrs. O'Neill had known for years. They reminisced a little about the old days at the restaurant. She treated him in the manner of a great lady to an old retainer—warmly, but aware of the distinction."

After dinner, Carlotta insisted on serving brandy. The apartment was uncomfortably hot, and Capalbo, slightly stupefied from the meal, the liquor and the heat, suggested opening a window. Carlotta said she kept the windows closed, because the cold affected her arthritic hands, but she allowed him to open a window for a few minutes.

"We'd open it and close it every so often till around 12:30 A.M., when we finally left," Capalbo said. "Stanley and I were reeling. We went to Reuben's and sat up all night talking about the evening. It was an extraordinary experience.

"There had been no sequence to her conversation—it was as though she were on a psychiatrist's couch. Within a half-hour after we arrived, she started telling us the most intimate things about her relationship with O'Neill. We were stunned, not so much by the information she gave us, but because she talked so freely. She would say things like, 'Gene was such a horror, crazy.' Then she'd cast her eyes heavenward and say, 'Oh, Gene, he was my darling baby. I was his mother. He never had a mother. She was a dope fiend.'"

Most of the people Carlotta saw were men. She throve on being courted, and had little use for women, with one or two exceptions. Most women, particularly on short acquaintance, made her nervous.

A woman writer who was asked to lunch by Carlotta at Quo Vadis in the spring of 1957 found her personality almost painfully forceful, but her looks surprisingly drab. Her face was bloodless and she wore no trace of makeup. The white skin was unlined, but there were purple shadows under her eyes. She wore tinted glasses, and explained that she had ruined her eyesight deciphering O'Neill's handwriting. Her hair was iron gray, thick, silky, short, and brushed straight back in a boyish style. She was, as always, dressed in black—black stockings, a black wool suit, a black silk blouse, a black satin pill box hat.

Her hands were remarkable—square, puffy, with thick fingers and heavily mottled skin. During the luncheon, they were never still for a moment. While she spoke, her hands were busy playing out a private, almost frantic pattern of their own, unrelated to what she was saying. She moved the silverware about, arranging and rearranging the knives and forks into vertical and horizontal patterns. She smoothed her napkin along the edge of the table, pleated it, crumpled it, then smoothed it again. After lunch, in her suite, she pulled and twisted the wire of a table lamp with such unconscious abandon that she nearly toppled the lamp.

By contrast with this near-hysterical manipulation, her voice was deep, vibrant, theatrical and beautifully controlled, often conveying the effect of rehearsed speeches. In speaking of O'Neill's and her own friends and acquaintances, she showed a marked preference for the men they had known; she slandered every woman whose name was mentioned, with the exception of the nurse who had attended O'Neill in his final months of illness.

In parting from her bemused guest, Carlotta suddenly confided that she was "terribly shy."

"Even the butcher or baker can terrify me," she said. "You wouldn't think it, with all my English training, but I really am shy." It might very possibly have been the truth.

Carlotta was established at the Carlton House, an elegant residential hotel on Madison Avenue, when Theodore Mann began seeing her regularly. (In 1963 he produced a revival of *Desire Under the Elms*, and he would discuss with Carlotta his ideas for casting and other details of the production. By the time the production was mounted, he had fallen into the habit of calling on her once or twice a week.)

Her flat on the eleventh floor, 11C—"C for Carlotta," she would gaily tell visitors—was painted a bright, pumpkin yellow and was tastefully and comfortably furnished.

"I got to feel very responsible for her," Mann said. "I had moved into an apartment not far from the Carlton House and I would drop in very often to see her. To spend lunch with her was to practically spend the day."

While Carlotta's appetite was undiminished, she was, by this time, feeling her age.

"When we walked to a restaurant," Mann said, "she used to walk very, very slowly. She was afraid of falling down. But she enjoyed the exercise. Sometimes we'd walk to the Central Park Zoo. She always went to the monkey house. She loved the monkey house." Mann was amused but not surprised by Carlotta's evident affinity for monkeys. He had heard that Carlotta had met O'Neill for the first time during the Broadway production of *The Hairy Ape*, and he had been introduced to Estaban and told that the stuffed monkey had been O'Neill's first gift to her. But he *was* startled to see that the monkeys in the zoo seemed to return Carlotta's affection.

"Even when there was a whole crowd of people looking at the monkeys, they would pick her out," he said. "They would look right at her. She really had a very close thing with them."

Mann felt that if he did not regularly accompany Carlotta on walks, she would not go out at all.

"I'm sure that, like every other woman, she was seeing other people and had a whole other life," he recalled. "But the man always likes to think he's the only one."

During the next few years, Carlotta would often complain of being short of money, of being harassed by business responsibilities—and of being haunted by O'Neill. She tended, at times, out of loneliness and depression, to drink too much. But she had lapses that were due to more than overdrinking. She would give things away impulsively—jewelry, clothing, bric-a-brac, even the rights to plays. Once, during the summer, her behavior became so erratic that her doctor put her into Regent Hospital, a small, private facility on East Sixty-first Street.

"She just clicked out," Mann recalled. "She was there about four weeks. I visited her, but I'm not sure she knew who I was. She made a remarkable recovery, though. Later on, I saw her at the Carlton House and she was fine. She was never quite the same as she had been. But she would have periods of tremendous lucidity. And then there would be times when she would kind of drift off. Her whole life at this time was totally centered on O'Neill. Everything was a recalling of her various experiences with O'Neill. And she would interweave episodes and characters from the plays into her conversation, without making any distinction between them and the actual episodes and people in her and O'Neill's lives.

"She would also say, often, that she wanted to die. She wasn't bitter about it, she just said she was tired."

The three persons who were most closely in touch with Carlotta throughout the time she lived in New York, following O'Neill's death, were O'Neill's literary agent, the lawyer handling O'Neill's estate, and the curator of the O'Neill collection at Yale. Of the three, O'Neill's agent, Jane Rubin, was perhaps the most long-suffering. Miss Rubin had been handling the O'Neill plays since the death of Richard Madden. After O'Neill's death, she found herself assuming a number of duties for Carlotta, out of old friendship, above and beyond those of a literary representative. When Carlotta was in failing health, physically or emotionally, Miss Rubin helped to look after her. There were times when Carlotta was completely helpless. She had no relatives on whom she could call. Her daughter, Cynthia, lived in California and had serious difficulties of her own. Over the years, Carlotta's close friends had either been cut off, or died, or moved far away. Miss Rubin seems to have been the only woman friend Carlotta had within calling distance.

It was Miss Rubin who, in consultation with Carlotta's doctor, oversaw her stays in the hospital, visited her regularly, brought her the things she needed, and acted as a buffer between Carlotta and her social and business obligations.

Richard Crockett, of the law firm Cadwalader, Wickersham & Taft, paid Carlotta's bills and also made it a point to visit her regularly.

Carlotta probably felt the closest, however, to Dr. Donald Gallup, because of his guardianship of, and intimacy with, the O'Neill papers at Yale. In a sense, he and Carlotta now shared O'Neill's life. Carlotta lived with her memories of O'Neill, and Dr. Gallup lived with the tangible evidence of O'Neill's life work. He spent the major part of almost every day at the Beinecke Rare Book and Manuscript Library, collating the material in the vast O'Neill collection.

Dr. Gallup's involvement with both O'Neill and Carlotta led him, in 1962, to undertake a somewhat quixotic project. He edited a version of *More Stately Mansions*—with, of course, Carlotta's blessing—and this, in turn, eventually led to a Broadway production.

In the Prefatory Note to the published version of *More Stately Mansions*, Dr. Gallup has described the circumstances that inspired the project:

"In the spring of 1957, Mrs. O'Neill informed Karl Ragnar Gierow, then Director of the Swedish Royal Dramatic Theatre, of the existence of *More Stately Mansions* and eventually gave him permission to attempt to shorten the script for possible production in Swedish translation [in Stockholm]. There was at that time no question of its publication, either in Swedish or in English. . . . After five years Mr. Gierow succeeded in making an acting version, guided in part by the author's own notes, but following Mrs. O'Neill's stipulation that only O'Neill's words could be used. . . .

"Mrs. O'Neill now [in 1964] feels that this play should be produced in future only in the repertory of the Swedish Royal Dramatic Theatre, but she has agreed that its text may be made available for students of O'Neill's work. . . .

"Had he lived . . . O'Neill would certainly have revised and rewritten extensively, as he always did. . . . But shortened by a friend, [Gierow] in whose judgment he had confidence, the text is one which O'Neill himself might well have authorized for publication."

Dr. Gallup was aware—he referred to it in his preface—that on a flyleaf laid into the unfinished manuscript of *More Stately Mansions*, O'Neill had written, "Unfinished work. This script to be destroyed in case of my death!"

That Carlotta, in her highly volatile state, should have disregarded O'Neill's enjoinder to her ("I don't want anybody else working on these plays") is understandable, if dismaying. On April 26, 1961, she told a drama reporter, who had heard about Dr. Gierow's attempt to shorten *More Stately Mansions*:

"I can't stand it when people question what I'm doing with O'Neill's plays. I am carrying out his wishes. He gave me the plays and said I could do anything I wanted with them—burn them, destroy them. O'Neill held the Swedish Royal Dramatic Theatre in very high esteem. Giving them this play to do is a tribute from my husband to that theatre. The play is not to be produced by any other theatre and not to be published ever."

That O'Neill's *written* instructions were ignored, and that the published version of *More Stately Mansions* was proclaimed as "a new play by Eugene O'Neill" is more difficult to accept. The play, as published, is clumsy and unconvincing. It might have been clumsy and unconvincing had O'Neill completed it himself. But he did not, and, in fairness, the record should show that *More Stately Mansions* is, quite simply, *not* an O'Neill play.

More Stately Mansions was produced on Broadway in October, 1967—again in the guise of "a new play" by O'Neill. It was not well received by the critics, but had a run of several months, largely because Ingrid Bergman, making a Broadway comeback, looked beautiful and youthful and glamorous in the leading role. The production was directed by José Quintero, whose perceptive interpretations of *Long Day's Journey Into Night* and *The Iceman Cometh* had been largely responsible for America's resurgence of interest in O'Neill during the 1950's and 1960's.

Quintero, since 1956, had had a very close relationship with Carlotta. Their friendship had its ups and downs.

"She would drive me, sometimes, to the point where I wanted to choke her," he said. "She had a tongue that could cut."

The qualities that enabled Quintero to interpret O'Neill brilliantly and intuitively were also those that recommended him to Carlotta, and that caused their quarrels. Quintero was sensitive, mercurial and often passionately theatrical. In his early thirties at the time, he was handsome, slim and dark, with piercing eyes that resembled O'Neill's. In a number of ways (and quite evidently in Carlotta's eyes) he might have been a Latin incarnation of the Black Irish O'Neill.

Quintero was dazzled by Carlotta. Having long been an ardent admirer of O'Neill's work, he found it easy to be swept into the aura of O'Neill's widow. And, of course, he was flattered by her interest in him.

Quite early in their friendship, Carlotta gave Quintero O'Neill's wedding ring and insisted that he wear it. Later, during her lapses, Carlotta would often address him as "Gene." During these times she grew very defensive, shouting at "Gene" to stop tormenting her, stop accusing her.

At other times she would tell Quintero, "He comes and stares at me in the night."

On these occasions Quintero did his best to defend Carlotta to her husband's ghost. Carlotta was grateful, as she was to anyone who seemed sympathetic and understanding about her relationship with O'Neill. She knew there were some who believed O'Neill had hated her and had been imprisoned by her, and accused her of inventing the ardent inscriptions to her in the published versions of his later plays. This infuriated her by its injustice.

Primarily to dispel this myth, Carlotta collected about a hundred letters, poems and inscriptions that O'Neill had written to her between

1926 and 1952, and arranged to have them photographed and privately printed by the Yale University Library.

In May of 1960, she sent the book to O'Neill's biographers, with a triumphant note:

"Now that you have *Inscriptions* there can be no question as to *who* wrote them!" Indeed there cannot.

Shortly before the breakdown that sent her to Regent Hospital (surely caused, in part, by overwhelming frustration) Quintero became aware, on his visits, that Carlotta was beginning what he later came to regard as "a certain kind of pattern."

"She gave away a ruby bracelet to the elevator operator," he said. "She would give me jewelry for my sister and my mother. I'd leave it on the table when I went. One time she began talking to an empty chair, as though O'Neill were sitting on it.

"But when she was at her best, she was the most charming conversationalist. She had a very broad, all-encompassing kind of humor. She was enormously pleasant to look at. She hadn't just shared a life with O'Neill. She had embraced his life and lived it with him. She really had a right to be Mrs. Eugene O'Neill. And she was tremendously loyal to him as an artist."

Early in 1968 Quintero left for Mexico. (He had not planned a long stay, but for various reasons his visit there was extended to a year.) Not long before he left, Carlotta asked him if he knew of a lawyer who might represent her personally.

"She said she wanted someone for herself—not a lawyer for the O'Neill estate," Quintero said, "someone who would look after her personal interests, since she had no family to do this for her.

"I went to see a lawyer, and I took him to Mrs. O'Neill. He called Jane Rubin, and I don't know what happened, but the lawyer called me and said he didn't think he could handle it. Jane Rubin was cool to me after that."

By October of 1968, Carlotta again seemed to be verging on a breakdown. Her behavior had become irrational. Some members of the Carlton House staff attributed it to drinking, but it was actually due to a psychiatric disorder. Carlotta was now nearly eighty.

Dr. Gallup, who saw her in October, said that it was he who persuaded her to enter a nursing home. "It was very plain that she needed care," he said.

But it was Miss Rubin who accompanied her, once again, to Regent Hospital toward the end of October. Among the personal effects that Miss Rubin took along for Carlotta was Estaban. Miss Rubin said it was shortly after this that she became convinced, after consulting with Carlotta's doctor, Gilbert R. Cherrick, that Carlotta would never again be able to live by herself.

Confirming this, Dr. Cherrick said that it was "clearly hopeless" for Carlotta to remain at the Carlton House.

"The management was becoming exercised about Mrs. O'Neill's behavior," he added. "She would wander in the halls, and go down to the desk and complain that people were spying on her."

Carlotta became Dr. Cherrick's patient in 1967, when the older doctor who had attended her for many years during her stays in New York retired and left his practice to Dr. Cherrick. Though quite young, Dr. Cherrick had excellent credentials. He became quickly convinced that Regent Hospital could not give Carlotta the care she needed. In November, 1968, he arranged for her to be admitted to the psychiatric ward at St. Luke's Hospital on Amsterdam Avenue at 114th Street.

The apartment at the Carlton House was given up, and Miss Rubin packed up all of Carlotta's possessions and sent them to storage. Among them were several wardrobe trunks of clothes, her jewelry, books, papers and a few items of furniture. (Much of the furniture in her apartment belonged to the hotel.)

There was one item, of little intrinsic value, but of major significance to all those who knew Carlotta in her final years, that Miss Rubin could not account for. It was the stuffed monkey, Estaban. Miss Rubin could not recall ever seeing it again after she deposited it with Carlotta at Regent Hospital. (Estaban's disappearance became a source of distress, after Carlotta's death, to a number of her friends, who keenly felt its sentimental value. Rightfully, it should have taken its place in the O'Neill collection at Yale, among other memorabilia. "I went through Carlotta's effects at the warehouse after her death," Dr. Gallup recalled, "to see if there was anything that belonged with the collection. I did not find Estaban." Richard Crockett could not account for the monkey's disappearance, either.)

Miss Rubin's explanation of why Carlotta, with her ample financial means and access to the best medical care, was transferred to St. Luke's and not to one of the better known psychiatric facilities, such as Payne Whitney, was that "we wanted to avoid publicity, we wanted Carlotta somewhere she would not be known."

Dr. Gallup's recollection was that St. Luke's was chosen simply because Dr. Cherrick was an attending physician there, and Dr. Cherrick himself said he believed St. Luke's psychiatric facilities were much the same as those of any other reputable hospital.

"The only thing better would have been round-the-clock nursing care in her own home," he said, "and that kind of arrangement for Mrs. O'Neill, or for almost anyone, would have been prohibitively expensive.

"At St. Luke's Mrs. O'Neill was very attentively looked after by the staff, and she could not have had better treatment in any other hospital."

Carlotta, according to Dr. Cherrick, was suffering from senile psychosis in one of its more aggravated forms.

"Her behavior was, at times, violent," he said. "She was somewhat paranoid and believed that certain people were out to molest her. She had delusions." At St. Luke's she was given custodial care and treated with Thorazine, a strong tranquilizer.

Dr. Gallup saw Carlotta for the first time at St. Luke's in late December, 1968.

"She was on the violent ward, and a visitor had to be passed through locked doors. Off the corridor there were four rooms, and Mrs. O'Neill was in one of them. It was a large, bare room, with a barred window. She seemed quite rational."

On Dr. Gallup's second visit, about a month later, he felt that Carlotta's condition had worsened. He attributed this to her grim surroundings.

"At one point," he said, "a woman wandered into Mrs. O'Neill's room and began talking to me about something that was obviously very important to her, but didn't make much sense. Mrs. O'Neill said, 'Pay no attention, she's a loony.'"

Dr. Gallup spoke to Dr. Cherrick about the possibility of moving Carlotta into a more felicitous atmosphere. Dr. Cherrick had to agree that Carlotta was deteriorating rapidly, but believed, as he put it, that "she would not have reacted well to any institutional setting," and her disorder was such that an institutional setting was mandatory.

But he was concerned.

"At one time, I really feared for her life," he said. "She stopped eating, and lost a shocking amount of weight." But Carlotta made a sudden and surprising recovery.

"In a sense, you could say it was a complete recovery," Dr. Cherrick said. "She got back to the state she had been in before coming to St. Luke's. She still had senile trends."

On his final visit to St. Luke's, shortly before Carlotta was discharged, Dr. Gallup found she had been moved out of the psychiatric ward into a private room in the general medical section.

Quintero returned to New York at the end of January, 1969. He had brought back a few small gifts for Carlotta, and he telephoned her at the

Carlton House the day he arrived. He met what he regarded as "very mysterious" resistance.

The manager told him Carlotta had left, but would not say when or where she had gone. "He was very courteous," Quintero said, "but told me he was under strict orders not to let anyone know where Mrs. O'Neill was." Quintero, aware that Jane Rubin was not likely to receive him with much warmth, nevertheless telephoned her.

"I could tell by her voice that she was sorry she had answered the phone," Quintero said. "But I told her that the hotel would not tell me anything about Mrs. O'Neill, and that I wanted to know where she was. She said she was very sorry, but she couldn't tell me that. I said I had to find her, I was going to find her some way, even if I had to put an ad in the newspapers. Finally she said that the best she could do was to give me the name of Mrs. O'Neill's doctor."

Quintero telephoned Dr. Cherrick, who, after some hesitation, conceded that Carlotta was "very ill" and was at St. Luke's. (This was the period when Carlotta was at her worst.) According to Quintero, Dr. Cherrick suggested they meet in the hospital lobby at seven that evening. The visiting hour was from seven to eight, he said. They would have coffee in the cafeteria, and he would "explain certain things."

"I went, and it got to be 7:15—no doctor; 7:30—no doctor." At 7:40, fearful of missing the visiting hour completely, Quintero, armed with the doctor's name, talked his way onto the floor where Carlotta was a patient. There, he told the nurse that he was a relative of Carlotta's "on the Spanish side, the Monterey side, we're first cousins." He was let into the ward.

"It was not a private room. It was not even a room for two," Quintero said, recalling his initial shock. "Three women were in this room. There was a small window with bars in it. Part of the room was in gloom. Mrs. O'Neill's lamp was off and she was sitting at the very edge of the bed, looking out through the barred window. I didn't recognize her from the back at first, because her hair was down to her shoulders.

"I said, 'Mrs. O'Neill.' No response. I said, 'Carlotta.' No response. Finally, she looked at me and said, 'There you *are*—bothering me again, Gene. Haven't I expiated enough? Not even Lavinia had to go through what I've gone through.'

"Finally," said Quintero, "she recognized me, and we had a chat." He was horrified at the way Carlotta looked. She was wearing a once-elegant black street dress, now stained and soiled all over.

"Her hair was a mess, and her nails, which she always wore very short and polished, were so long and ragged . . . I couldn't believe that the widow of America's greatest playwright was in this kind of situation. Not only the madness, because I know that was inherent in Carlotta, but to see the conditions in which that madness was surrounded.

"And she told me she had only that one dress she was wearing, and a white hospital gown that she could change into while the black dress was being cleaned. She said she didn't need much."

During the course of the conversation, Carlotta would switch back and forth between recognition of Quintero and addressing him as "José," and accusing him of being Gene, come to upset her. At one point she began talking about "those beautiful kimonos we bought in Shanghai."

"Don't you remember, Gene?" she said. "Or were you too drunk to remember?"

Knowing something of the O'Neills' background and the China episode, Quintero could follow Carlotta's conversation.

"The conversation did not seem mad at all to me," he said. Carlotta had moments in which she was oriented enough to ask Quintero quite rational questions about his mother and sister. She also told him that she wanted to leave the hospital, and asked if he would come back.

At one point Quintero asked her why she had let her hair grow so long. She replied that she would not let "that butcher" (the hospital barber) touch her hair.

Quintero, like Dr. Gallup, felt that Carlotta's surroundings might be a contributing factor in her mental condition.

"I could understand how she felt," he said. "You couldn't ask Carlotta Monterey O'Neill to submit to that. She had grown accustomed to a certain way of being handled. It was impossible for her, really impossible. She was a vain woman—with cause.

"When I left, I promised her I would come back."

Quintero did the one thing he could do for Carlotta, to mitigate somewhat the squalor of her existence. He made an appointment with her hairdresser from the Carlton House, to accompany him to St. Luke's and give her hair a proper trim.

"He cut her hair, and she was perfectly willing to let him trim her nails, too," Quintero said. "People came to the door to watch. I chatted with her, and she was quite lucid. We talked about the theatre, and about O'Neill. She was wearing a clean dress. Jane had brought it."

Shortly after this visit, Quintero's father died, and he returned to his native Panama for a long stay. He never saw Carlotta again.

In March of 1968, Carlotta was transferred to the DeWitt Nursing Home on East Seventy-ninth Street, where she spent the next fifteen months—until July of 1970. There, again, she was visited regularly by Crockett, Dr. Gallup and Miss Rubin. Dr. Cherrick continued to attend her.

"She was no longer on Thorazine," he said. "That had gradually been tapered off before she left St. Luke's." With Dr. Cherrick, Carlotta would "ruminate about her past, about O'Neill, and often about her own early life."

In the winter of 1970, Miss Rubin was seriously injured in a car accident and was confined for some time to a hospital. When she recovered, she decided to retire and move with her husband to Sarasota, Florida.

"Carlotta didn't know me," Miss Rubin said, recalling her last visits before she left New York. "There was really nothing I could do for her anymore."

To fill the gap left by Miss Rubin, Richard Crockett engaged an English woman, Marjorie Miller, to act as a kind of companion to Carlotta.

"She looked after her clothes, bought her underwear, did the kind of things Carlotta needed a woman for," Crockett said. "She visited Carlotta twice a week."

Carlotta grew unhappy with DeWitt.

"It was as good a nursing home as any," Crockett said, "but it was a big institution, with all the drawbacks of that sort of place. One of the things Carlotta complained about was that an attendant was always at her side. Carlotta still had a tendency to wander. She would wander into other patients' rooms and disturb them. And DeWitt insisted on keeping someone with her to prevent this. She didn't like the way she was handled."

It was felt that Carlotta would be happier in the country. In June of 1970, Crockett and Miss Miller drove Carlotta to Westwood, New Jersey, to look at the Valley Nursing Home. It seemed to please her, and she was, accordingly, transferred there in July.

Only eight years in existence at the time Carlotta became a patient, the Valley Nursing Home was pleasantly situated in a country atmosphere.

"It was not a place you'd choose to give a party," Crockett said, "but for a nursing home, it was pleasant." Both Crockett and Dr. Gallup, who visited her there, felt that Carlotta was reasonably contented.

Crockett, who saw her for the last time in October of 1970, said that she was aware of her surroundings and seemed to relate to the staff and other patients. Dr. Gallup saw her at the beginning of November. Both

[959]

men spoke with her attending physician, Dr. H. Richard Hoff, and were assured that for a woman of her age—she was now nearly eighty-two—she was in good health and might live to be one hundred.

Carlotta's death, on November 18, 1970, was a shock to both men. Evidently it was sudden, for neither had had any word from the nursing home that she was failing. "Arteriosclerotic coronary thrombosis" was given as the cause of death. More simply, her heart had worn out.

Carlotta had instructed in her will that her remains be cremated, and her ashes interred in the lot she had bought for O'Neill and herself. She had left no other instructions in her will regarding the disposition of her remains, but Crockett said she had written him memoranda asking that there be no religious rites at her burial. Only a handful of people were notified.

Crockett sent a paid announcement of Carlotta's death to *The New York Times*, and it appeared in the agate-type, alphabetical listing on the obituary page. He reasoned that someone on the *Times* would recognize Carlotta's name, know that his law firm represented her, and call him for details. That is what happened. An alert editor spotted it, and ordered a full-length obituary, which appeared in the *Times* on November 21. The date of the burial was not given.

On November 28, within four days of the date that O'Neill, seventeen years earlier, had been secretly buried in the Forest Hills Cemetery in Boston, Carlotta's ashes were placed beside her husband's grave, under the Italian marble headstone Carlotta had bought. Several of the mourners who attended the interment—which, like O'Neill's, was accompanied by no ceremony—were the same as those who had looked on when O'Neill was buried. Dr. Kozol was there, and O'Neill's nurse, Jean Welton. Also present were Crockett, Dr. Gallup and Carlotta's Boston lawyer, Robert Meserve.

No one planted laurel for Carlotta.

Carlotta Monterey O'Neill wrote a will, on October 23, 1964 ("revoking all former wills made by me"), bequeathing all of O'Neill's papers not yet at Yale to the O'Neill collection, and making Yale the beneficiary of all royalties from the O'Neill plays. (Yale now shares the interest in some of these royalties with Oona Chaplin and Shane O'Neill, under a complicated copyright arrangement.) Carlotta stipulated that a portion of the royalties be used for the establishment of "Eugene O'Neill Scholarships," to be awarded to "worthy students of playwrighting." (In 1954, she had written to Brooks Atkinson that she was "working with Mr. Meserve on a will that will be unbreakable," and asking if she could designate Atkinson as a consultant "if any *problem* appears, relative to Gene's work." Atkinson said she could. His name did not appear in her final will.)

Richard Crockett and another member of his law firm, Jacqelin Swords, were named Carlotta's trustees. Swords was personally acquainted with Carlotta, and was chosen as the second trustee because of his experience with copyright litigation.

"Carlotta would sign over the rights to things she didn't own," Crockett said, "things she had already signed over to someone else. That was when we needed someone experienced in litigation to act for her."

Carlotta left all of her jewelry, wearing apparel and personal household effects to her daughter, Cynthia (who survived her by only eight months). And in a codicil to the will, made on March 3, 1967, Carlotta left bequests of $25,000 each to Cynthia and to her grandson, Jerry Eugene Stram, directing that these sums be paid "as soon as possible after my death."

This was done to sidestep an intricate tax problem. The codicil made it possible, according to Crockett, for the estate to dispense the cash bequest quickly. Carlotta's signature on the will, while not as flamboyantly aggressive as it once had been, still had the large capital C and flowing connectives of former years. On the codicil, signed two and a half years later, her signature is that of a feeble old woman—not minuscule, like O'Neill's, but every bit as shaky. The two signatures symbolize Carlotta's decline from the assertive, still forceful woman she was at seventy-five to the distraught wraith she had become at seventy-nine.

"Carlotta had been in poor health for some time," Crockett recalled. "Her eyesight was bad. She was almost blind." In order for her to be able to see to sign the codicil, Crockett arranged a chair for her under the brightest lamp in her apartment, and handed her the magnifying glass she had used to decipher O'Neill's writing.

Carlotta's jewelry was sold at auction, at Cynthia's request, by the Parke Bernet Gallery in May of 1971. The most expensive piece was a platinum, diamond and sapphire ring that brought $4,000; the whole lot brought only $6,980. (It is impossible to estimate the value of the jewelry Carlotta had erratically given away.)

Another auction was held to dispose of furniture, bric-a-brac and clothing, also at Cynthia's request. This sale netted $2,690.

"Cynthia had asked that a few of her mother's things be sent to her," Crockett said. "We packed them up and shipped them to California in two of Carlotta's old and very expensive Vuitton trunks. And certain things Cynthia asked us to give away. She wanted Marjorie Miller to have her mother's television set, for example."

Carlotta's most priceless possession, her memories of O'Neill, she could bequeath to no one. They were painfully, preciously, her own.

She tried to share some of them with O'Neill's biographers in a taped interview, at the end of 1961, when her mind was still clear, her voice dramatically self-assured, and her collapse into a haunted past still some years off.

These memories—random, rambling, but throbbing with the wonder and exultation of having captivated and been held captive by the extraordinary man who was her husband—are Carlotta Monterey O'Neill's most fitting epitaph:

"He asked me [in the fall of 1926] if he could come to tea. He came, and he drank four cups. And he sat there, looking like Hamlet in distress.

"And he started talking, and began with his birth, almost, with his earliest memories of babyhood. And he talked and he talked and he talked, the whole time looking as if he were *tortured*. Then suddenly he looked at the clock, and said, 'Oh, my God, I've got to go,' and off he flew.

"Then he rang up again, asking if he could come up to tea again. I thought, what is this, that poor man. So I said, 'Certainly.' He came to tea and he began right where he'd left off the last time. He looked so *tortured*. He looked so *unhappy*. And he was dressed—almost shabby. He didn't have the right things on.

"And then I didn't see him for months. And then he asked me if I'd have lunch with him. And he was staying at a funny, rat trap hotel. And I said, 'Why, yes, I'd be delighted.' And I became interested in him— what was he like, this man who had this talent? But he was not the kind of man you fall in love with. I don't think any woman could fall in love with him, because they were all frightened. Even after I married him I was frightened.

"I went to this frowzy hotel, with rubber plants sitting around, and I went to the desk and said 'I have an appointment for lunch with Mr. O'Neill,' and they phoned up and said for me to go upstairs. I said, 'Has he a sitting room?' They said, 'Yes, he has a sitting room,' so I went up. I wish you'd seen the sitting room. It had a table and a frowzy couch and a couple of chairs.

"I broke my nail and I said to him, 'Have you a nail file, please?' And he went in to his frowzy little bedroom and he was fussing, fussing, fussing, and I said, 'Do you want me to look?'

"I wish you'd seen his suitcase. It had nothing in it but a couple of frowzy, torn pajamas—no dressing gown, no bedroom slippers, no *anything*. That's what got old, maternal Monterey, you see.

"We went downstairs and had a not-too-good luncheon. And I said, 'Thank you so much, what size is your neck?' And I went over to Abercrombie and Fitch and I bought him a fitted case, and pajamas and socks and a dressing gown and God knows what else, and sent them to him. Why, he nearly had fits when he got them. He'd never *seen* such things.

"I don't know what his life was like, but he didn't have anything to wear. And he was working all the time, making money, and I don't know where the money went. I didn't see him for months after that.

"I think O'Neill looked upon me at that time very much as a savior and a mother. I really do.

"If you live with a man, you're either his wife or his mistress, whichever he wishes you to be. The wife tends to the house, and the mistress wants to love him."

Speaking of *Mourning Becomes Electra*:

"We wrote that play—he wrote that play six times. And then he'd tear it up at the end of the year and write it all over again. He wrote it six times and I typed it six times. I said to him, 'Why do I have to re-type the whole damn thing six times?' He would write it from a different angle. Some men, when they rewrite plays, they keep this page and they keep that page, to put in here, and this scene can be used over again. Not him. The whole thing—and he would think, think, think, and start from a new point of view. And that's the way it went."

Speaking of her husband's entry into the world:

"There she [Ella O'Neill] was, in a hotel room again. She felt pains, and what not, and she rang for the maid and told her to go down to the bar and see if her husband was there, and tell him to come quick. So he came up quick. He was in the bar. And she said, 'Get me a doctor, quick.' And this is what angers me, and upsets me. They had no nurse arranged. They had no layette. They had *nothing*. And he goes downstairs, asking for the hotel doctor. Now you can imagine what the hotel doctor is like. He comes upstairs smoking a cigar, and he doesn't even wash his hands. Well, she's delivered of Eugene O'Neill. I'm surprised that he lived. . . .

"I asked him once how he had the guts to quit drinking. And he said, 'Carlotta, I came to the place where I had to decide whether I was going to be a drunk or a writer. And I preferred to go through the hell of never drinking, and being a writer.' He had three or four lapses. But he had them cold-bloodedly. This is what I think is wonderful. . . .

"And he had Mama there to help him. And Mama was *pleased* to help him. I didn't do him any favor. It was a joy to help him in his work. I married him because I was proud of his work. And that is a much deeper feeling than having a wild flame for a man and marrying him. I really wanted to marry that man and stick to him and help him. And I think I did. This may sound boastful, but I do think I did help him. . . ."

INDEX

[968]

[974]

Roosevelt, Theodore, 198-199, 200, 201, 262-263
Rope, The, 157, 372, 375, 377, 378, 379-380, 395, 539
Rosenthal, Herman "Beansy," 173
Ross, Harold, 737
Ross, Ishbel, 731
Rossetti, Christina G., 895
Rothschild, Baron, 717
Rousseau, J. J., 84
Royal Box, The, 103, 104
Royal Dramatic Theatre (Stockholm), 862
Royalton Hotel (N.Y.), 787-788
Royle, Selena (Mrs. Earle Larimore), 777-778, 783
Rubáiyát, 85
Rubin, Jane, 951 ff.
Rumsey, John, 391
Runyon, Damon, 644
Russell, Bertrand, 283
Russell, Lillian, 94, 103-104
Russell, Rosalind, 872
Ryskind, Morrie, 756

"Sailor Lad, The," 863-864
Sailor's Opera saloon, 152-153
Saint, The, 563, 567
St. Aloysius Academy, 65
St. Ann's Church (N.Y.), 38
Saint-Gaudens, Augustus, 406
Saint-Gaudens, Homer S., 406, 470-471
"St. James Infirmary," 708
Saint Joan, 647, 874-875
St. John's College and Preparatory School, 65, 71
St. Louis *Post-Dispatch,* 426
St. Mary's Academy (Notre Dame, Ind.), 13, 26
Salem (Mass.) Hospital, 910, 911 ff.
Salinger, J. D., 843, 850, 851
Salomé, 109
Salvation Nell, 140, 264
Salvini, Tommaso, 27
Sammy (dog), 747-748, 751
Samovar cafe (N.Y.), 324

Samson and Delilah, 449, 476
San Francisco, 31-32, 43, 44, 46-47
San Francisco *News Letter,* 50
Sandburg, Carl, 283
Sandy, Sarah, 61, 64
Saratoga, 43
Sardi's restaurant, 874
Sardou, Victorien, 391
Saroyan, William, 850-851, 856
Saturday Evening Post, 398, 488
Saturday Review of Literature, 811-812, 876
Saturday's Children, 654
Sayler, Oliver, 476, 480, 488, 489, 507, 508, 544, 560
Schenley Hotel (Pittsburgh), 773
Schnitzler, Arthur, 421, 567
Schopenhauer, Arthur, 88, 210, 353
Schriftgiesser, Karl, 873
Schwartz, Sam, 459, 554-555
Scott, Adam, 202-203, 439
Scott, Arlene (Mrs. Byram Fones), 206, 207, 208-209, 741
Scott, Maibelle, 205 ff., 237, 240, 248, 249, 265, 266, 741, 771
Scott, Thomas A., 206
Scott, Walter, 88
"Sea-Fever," 890
Sea Gull, The, 352
Sea Island, Ga., 756, 759 ff.
Sea Island Inn, 760
Sea-Mother's Son, 146, 671, 675, 679, 687
Seaman, Alfred, 42
Seattle, Wash., 806 ff.
Seattle *Times,* 806, 808
Second Man, The, 654
Second Story Club (New London), 89, 98, 124, 203, 204
"Second Thoughts on First Nights," 410, 662
Selwyn Theatre (N.Y.), 448
Sergeant, Elizabeth Shepley, 64, 75, 477, 488-489, 599, 605, 611-

Sergeant, Elizabeth Shepley (*Cont.*) 612, 626, 627, 629, 632, 633, 655, 656, 708-709
Servitude, 140, 250, 261
Seven Arts, The (magazine), 328-329, 331, 356
Seymour, May Davenport, 786-787
Shakespeare, William, 5, 24, 27-31, 100, 112, 353, 381, 530, 571-572, 647, 754, 813
Shanghai, 680-685
Shaw, George Bernard, 5, 104, 118, 119, 262, 318, 428-429, 463, 474-475, 522, 647, 652, 654, 750, 754, 791, 798, 810, 899
Shay, Frank, 319-320, 395, 472, 567, 710, 730
Shay, Jim, 96
Shearer, Norma, 662, 761
Sheffield, Mrs. E. Chappell, 95
Sheldon, Edward, 140, 264, 273, 863
Shell-Shock, 381
Shelton Hotel (Boston), 929, 933 ff.
"Shenandoah," 150, 724, 749
Sheridan, Bessie, 93, 99, 434
Sheridan, Irene, 99
Sheridan, Phil, 99, 239, 532, 796
Sheridan, Richard Brinsley, 24
Sheridan family, 92-93, 432, 434, 500-501
Sherwin, Louis, 341
Sherwood, Robert, 155, 654, 785, 900
Shields, Arthur, 882, 883
Shipman, Sam, 315
Shubert, Lee, 674
"Silence," 314
Sill's Oyster Restaurant (N.Y.), 731
Silver Cord, The, 653
Simon, Bernard, 540, 541, 557-559
Simonson, Lee, 633, 645, 677, 687, 777, 781, 888

[986]

74 75 76 77 10 9 8 7 6 5 4 3 2 1